Understanding Abnormal Behavior

Understanding Abnormal Behavior

Second Edition

David Sue
Western Washington University

Derald Sue
California State University, Hayward

Stanley Sue
University of California, Los Angeles

HOUGHTON MIFFLIN COMPANY   BOSTON
Dallas   Geneva, Illinois   Lawrenceville, New Jersey   Palo Alto

Credits

Part-opener art by Omnigraphics, Inc. (photographed by James Scherer)

Cover photography by Ann McQueen

Chapter-opener photographs by Ann McQueen

Photo Credits

Page 9: © Michael Weisbrot and Family. *Page 11 left:* Courtesy Franklin D. Roosevelt Library. *Page 11 right:* Courtesy of The New York Historical Society. *Page 16:* © Richard Stack/ Black Star. *Page 21 left:* © Yada Claassen/Jeroboam, Inc.

(Photo and text credits continue following subject index)

Printed in the U.S.A.

Library of Congress Catalog Card Number: 85-60475

ISBN: 0-395-36947-9

ABCDEFGHIJ-VHP-898765

Contents

vii

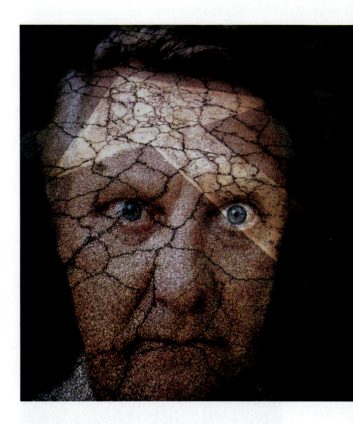

PART 3 DISORDERS INVOLVING CONDUCT

PART 4 SEVERE DISORDERS OF MOOD AND THOUGHT

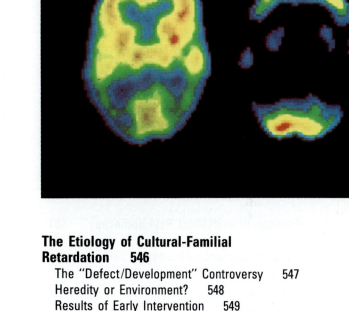

Preface

This second edition of *Understanding Abnormal Behavior* is intended for undergraduates enrolled in an abnormal psychology course. Our goal is to help students to understand the symptoms, causes, and treatment of deviant behaviors, and the contemporary issues facing mental health researchers and practitioners. We believe that presenting abnormal psychology as both a scientific and a clinical endeavor will give students the clearest understanding of the field. To reach this goal, we have presented and critically examined current research findings and different theoretical approaches. We have supplemented these with clinical case examples and analyses of contemporary issues.

The text covers the major categories of disorders listed in the third edition of the *Diagnostic and Statistical Manual of Mental Disorders* (DSM-III). As a context for understanding the disorders, we have presented historical perspectives on abnormal behavior, different theoretical approaches, and research methods and results. The field of abnormal psychology must also address various issues related to assessment and diagnosis, mental health and the law, the relative value of individual and community interventions, and results from cross-cultural research. We discuss and critically examine these issues. Even the DSM-III nosological system itself has been the center of much controversy, and we indicate the strengths and weaknesses of the system.

Our Approach

Authors make a variety of decisions about what to include in a text and how to present the material. These decisions account in part for the diversity of books on the market today. For example, abnormal psychology texts can be classified according to the type of theory espoused, and whether a single theoretical approach or an eclectic approach is taken. Texts can also differ on whether more coverage is devoted to research and theory or to clinical concerns. The text's scope can vary from narrow to encyclopedic. The authors can offer critiques of research, theory, and practice or can take an uncritical view. Texts can emphasize etiology or intervention, and the orientation of a text can lean toward theory or can focus on applied concerns.

Perhaps the best way to convey the approach we take in this text is to explain the factors that we considered when writing it. First, we adopt an eclectic approach and use important contributions from various disciplines, areas within psychology, and theoretical stances. Our view is that different combinations of life experiences, constitutional factors, and circumstances influence behavioral disorders. For example, an analysis of schizophrenia would be incomplete if both psychosocial and psychophysiological factors were not discussed. We also believe that an examination of abnormal behavior and treatment in different cultures can greatly enhance our understanding of behavioral disorders. One of the best ways to test the adequacy of theories and practices is to make cross-cultural comparisons, and we have paid special attention to cross-cultural phenomena.

Second, we want students to think critically about the knowledge they acquire. We want students to develop an appreciation of the study of abnormal behavior rather than to assimilate a collection of facts and theories. On the one hand, there have been many methodological, conceptual, and substantive advances made in the field; on the other hand, there are issues, controversies, and inconsistent findings that are currently unresolved. In order to understand these recent advances and unresolved issues, the student must be able to analyze and evaluate them. We hope that students can learn to critically examine the work in the field by using our discussions of these important issues.

Third, as psychologists we know that learning is enhanced whenever material is presented in an engaging and stimulating manner. We purposely wrote the text so that it is highly readable and meaningful. For example, given several cases that illustrate a particular concept or disorder, we chose the most interesting one. Further, we have tried something unique. We present an extended case study of a hypothetical client—Steven V.—and discuss it in various chapters of the book. His symptoms, personality structure, personality test findings, and treatment are examined from different theoretical perspectives. When students follow one case example throughout the text they can develop a sense of how assessment, etiology, and treatment are interrelated.

Finally, we offer a balance between research and clinical work. There is no question that the textbook is based on research and theory on behavioral disturbances. But behavioral disturbances occur, of course, in people. Therefore, we quote clients' descriptions of their experiences to illustrate various disorders and treatments and to highlight the experiences of clients and therapists.

Changes in the Second Edition

Writing this second edition gave us the opportunity to make several improvements on the first edition. The comments of students and colleagues on the first edition and the feedback from reviewers of this edition were most helpful. While the basic emphasis of the book remains the same—it still presents a comprehensive and eclectic view of abnormal behavior—several facets have changed. For example, we expanded the sections on the problems associated with the elderly, family therapy, and personality disorders. Therapy and intervention are discussed both in the final two chapters and in each of the chapters that examine particular behavioral disorders. This dual presentation allows us to discuss what can be done to treat specific

disorders as well as to contrast different intervention approaches.

We included exciting and contemporary developments in the field. Recently the results of some interesting large-scale epidemiological studies have become available. Sophisticated diagnostic tools have been developed and are now being used. Computer technology is having a major impact in many areas of the field including assessment, diagnosis, and research. Finally, since we wrote the first edition researchers and clinicians have had more experience with DSM-III.

The second edition has several new features. Each chapter opens with a chapter outline indicating the major topics to be discussed. Key terms and other important terms appear in boldface throughout the text. In addition, the key terms and their definitions appear at the end of each chapter. All important terms and key terms appear in a full glossary at the end of the book. Instructors as well as students should find the book attractive and appealing because many of the illustrations, photographs, and drawings are in full color. Chapters 15 and 16 include the work of artists who have been diagnosed as schizophrenic.

In addition to these new features, we have attempted to improve on pedagogical devices that appeared in the first edition, including the Focus boxes that isolate important issues, applications of concepts, or controversies; interesting clinical case vignettes of disorders; quoted extracts that present issues in a cogent and forceful manner; and summaries that provide point-by-point abstracts of the chapters.

Organization of the Text

The textbook is organized into six major sections. Part 1 (Chapters 1 through 5) provides a context for viewing abnormal behavior and treatment by introducing students to historical contributions (Chapter 1) and to the diverse theoretical perspectives that are currently used to explain deviant behaviors. These theoretical perspectives are categorized into biogenic and psychogenic models, which are presented in Chapter 2, and behavioral and family systems models, which are presented in Chapter 3. The section ends with chapters on classification and assessment (Chapter 4) and scientific methods (Chapter 5). These last two chapters provide the conceptual tools for analyzing psychopathology, namely the strategies used to classify disorders and the methods used to advance our knowledge of abnormal behavior.

The bulk of the textbook (the fourteen chapters in Parts 2 through 5) presents the major disorders covered in DSM-III. These chapters are organized so that the symptoms are presented first, followed by diagnosis, theoretical perspectives, etiology, and treatment.

Part 2 contains four chapters that deal with anxiety and stress. Anxiety is discussed in Chapter 6, somatoform and dissociative disorders in Chapter 7, stress and reactive disorders in Chapter 8, and psychophysiological disorders in Chapter 9. Current contributions from health psychology and behavioral medicine are featured as well as the transactional model of stress reactions.

Part 3 covers deviations from societal codes of conduct. Included are three chapters dealing with personality disorders and crime (Chapter 10), substance abuse (Chapter 11), and psychosexual disorders and dysfunctions (Chapter 12). We have grouped these topics together because they pose not only clinical issues but also societal dilemmas. For example, Chapter 10 includes the "Hillside Strangler" case, which involves an apparent sexual psychopath. The case raises dilemmas concerning mental health and the law, the insanity plea, and treatment versus punishment, in addition to the issues of diagnosis and etiology. Crime and delinquency, substance use disorders, and certain sexual practices (such as sexual sadism and rape) also raise such dilemmas.

Part 4 contains four chapters that deal with affective disorders, suicide, and schizophrenia. We have placed these disorders together because of their relative severity. This grouping, however, is a loose one since it is not based on any conceptual similarity between the disorders. Although affective disturbances can be arranged on a continuum from less to more severe, we chose to devote a substantial part of the material in the chapter on affective disorders (Chapter 13) to the more severe range of the continuum. Suicide (Chapter 14) is included in Part 4 because of the close relationship between depression and suicide. Two chapters (15 and 16) are devoted to schizophrenia because of its debilitating nature and the sheer amount of research that has been conducted. Part 4 devotes particular attention to contemporary research on the possible interplay between genetic factors, physiological factors, and environmental conditions in schizophrenia and certain affective disorders.

Part 5 encompasses organic and developmental problems. One chapter is devoted to each of the following topics: organic brain dysfunctions (Chapter 17), disorders of childhood and adolescence (Chapter 18), and mental retardation (Chapter 19). Although organic brain dysfunctions can occur at any age, we have paid particular attention to those associated with the aging process.

Part 6, the final part, has two chapters that examine treatment and community intervention. As noted previously, the therapies used to treat specific disorders are discussed following each disorder. Moreover, the treatment chapter (Chapter 20) indicates the full range of therapies used with clients and an overall analysis of their effectiveness. The final chapter on community psychology (Chapter 21) presents the argument that community and institutional forces have a major impact on emotional well-being and that community interventions can be used to promote mental health.

Study Guide

The text is accompanied by a separate study guide prepared by Alan Glaros of the University of Florida. The study guide consists of twenty-one chapters that complement those in the text. Each chapter begins with a schematic drawing that visually summarizes the content of the text chapter. Next is a list of learning objectives provided to guide the student's reading. Each chapter also includes a programmed chapter review and multiple-choice review questions that will help the student assess his or her comprehension and retention of the text material.

Acknowledgments

The publication of a textbook results from the efforts of many people. We are especially indebted to Professor Richard Leavy of Ohio Wesleyan University, who contributed detailed suggestions for improving each chapter of the manuscript, to Professor Jane Smith of the University of New Mexico for contributing a wealth of material on current practices in the treatment of disorders, and to Steven Fisher for providing suggestions from a student's point of view. We are grateful for the assistance provided by the following colleagues and reviewers, who guided us on the project:

Edward Abramson, California State University, Chico
Paul Abramson, University of California, Los Angeles
George Albee, University of Vermont
Deborah Anderson, Saint Olaf College
Susan Andrews, University of Wisconsin, Waukesha
Ira Bernstein, University of Texas, Arlington
Thomas Boll, University of Alabama
Frank Calabrese, Community College of Philadelphia
David Celani, private practice, South Burlington, Vermont
Lee Anna Clark, Southern Methodist University
Robert W. Collins, Grand Valley State College
Michael Connor, California State University, Long Beach
Winifred Curtis, Community College of Rhode Island
Ajit K. Das, University of Minnesota, Duluth
Anthony Davids, Brown University
Kenneth France, Shippensburg University
John Garske, Ohio University
Alan Glaros, University of Florida
Charles Golden, University of Nebraska Medical Center

Sol Gordon, Syracuse University
John Greaves, Jefferson State Jr. College
Nancy Gulanick, University of Notre Dame
Richard Halgin, University of Massachusetts
Raymond H. Holden, Rhode Island College
James Hollandsworth, University of Southern Mississippi
Philip Holzman, Harvard University
William L. Hoover, Suffolk County Community College, New York
Gerard Jacobs, Ohio University
Eldon E. Jacobsen, Central Washington University
Robert W. Kapche, California State University, Long Beach
Jeffrey Kern, Texas A & M University
Daniel Klein, University of Illinois
Richard Kolotkin, Moorhead State University
Maria Krasnec, University of Idaho
Edward Lichtenstein, University of Oregon
Robert Lueger, Marquette University
Irwin Mahler, Occidental College
Henry Marcucella, Boston University
Michael Nash, North Texas State University
Esther Rothblum, University of Vermont
Joseph Rychlak, Loyola University of Chicago
Theodore Sarbin, Professor Emeritus, University of California, Santa Cruz
Kay Schaffer, University of Toledo
Jonathan Stone, Dutchess Community College
Paul Thetford, Texas Woman's University
David Van Nuys, Sonoma State University
Cathy Spatz Widom, Indiana University

Finally, it has been our pleasure to work with the highly competent professional staff at Houghton Mifflin.

D. S.

D. S.

S. S.

Understanding Abnormal Behavior

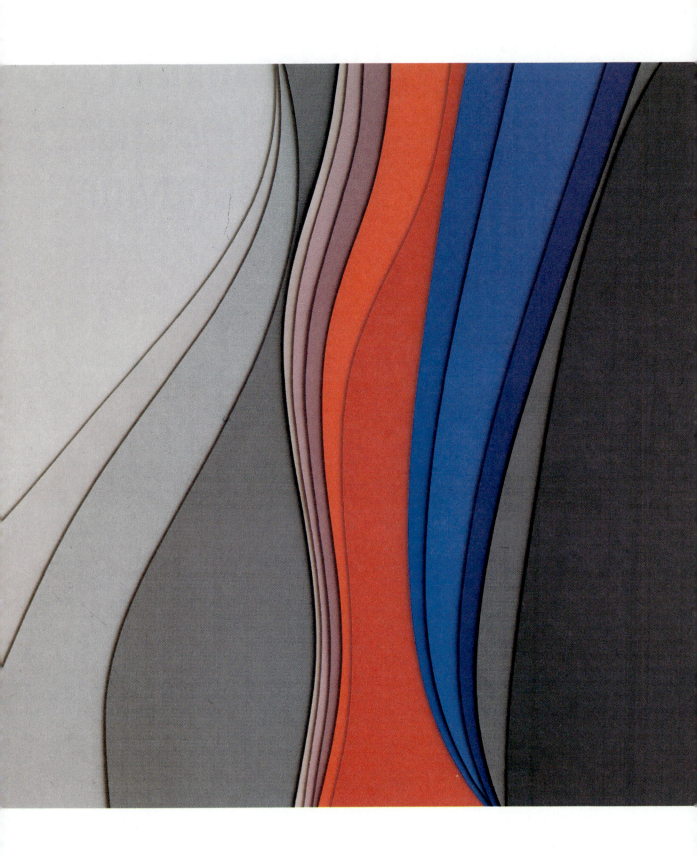

PART 1

The Study of Abnormal Psychology

1
Abnormal Behavior

The study of abnormal psychology is a journey into the known and unknown territories of the mind. To help you understand the scope and dynamics of this field, we would like to start our journey by introducing you to Steven V. Steve is a twenty-one year old college student who exemplifies many of the issues to be discussed in this text. We begin his story in the office of his therapist.

The therapist could feel himself becoming tense, apprehensive, uncertain: How should he interpret the threat? How should he act on it? One wheel of his swivel chair squealed sharply, breaking the silence, as he backed it away from his client, Steven V.

Eighteen months earlier, Steve's woman friend, Linda, had broken off her relationship with Steve. Steve had fallen into a crippling depression. During the past few weeks, however, with the encouragement of the therapist, Steve had begun to open up—to express his innermost feelings. His depression had lifted, but it was replaced by a deep anger and hostility toward Linda. In today's session, Steve had become increasingly loud and agitated as he recounted his complaints against Linda. Minutes ago, with his hands clenched into fists, his knuckles white, he had abruptly lowered his voice and looked his therapist in the eye.

"She doesn't deserve to live," Steve had said. "I swear, I'm going to kill her."

Until this session, the therapist had not believed Steve was dangerous. Now he wondered whether Steve could be the one client in ten thousand to act out such a threat. Should Linda, or the police, be told of what Steve had said?

Steven V. had a long psychiatric history, beginning well before he first sought help from the therapist at the University Psychological Services Center. (In fact, his parents wanted their son to continue seeing a private therapist, but Steve terminated his therapy during his junior year at the University.) Steve had actually been in and out of psychotherapy since kindergarten; while in high school, he was hospitalized twice for depression. His case records, nearly two inches thick, contained a number of diagnoses, including *schizoid personality, paranoid schizophrenia,* and *manic–depressive psychosis.* Although his present therapist did not find these labels particularly helpful, Steve's history provided clues to the causes of his problems.

Steven V. was born in a suburb of San Francisco, California, the only child of an extremely wealthy couple. His father was a prominent businessman whose responsibilities entailed long workdays and frequent travel. On those rare occasions when he was at home, Mr. V. was often preoccupied with business matters and was quite aloof from his son. The few interactions they had were characterized by his constant ridicule and criticism of Steve. Mr. V. was greatly disappointed that his son seemed so timid, weak, and withdrawn. Steve was extremely bright and did well in school, but Mr. V. felt he lacked the "toughness" needed to survive and prosper in today's world. Once, when Steve was about ten years old, he came home from school with a bloody nose and bruised face, crying and complaining of being picked on by his schoolmates. His father showed no sympathy but instead berated Steve for losing the fight. In his father's presence, Steve usually felt worthless, humiliated, and fearful of doing or saying the wrong thing.

Mrs. V. was very active in civic and social affairs, and she too spent relatively little time with her son. Although she treated Steve more warmly and lovingly than his father did, she seldom came to Steve's defense when Mr. V. bullied him. She generally allowed her husband to make family decisions.

When Steve was a young child, his mother had been quite affectionate at times. She had often allowed Steve to sleep with her, in her bed, when her husband was away on business trips. She usually dressed minimally on these occasions and was very demonstrative—holding, stroking, and kissing Steve. This behavior had continued until Steve was twelve, when his mother abruptly refused to let Steve into her bed. The sudden withdrawal of this privilege had confused and angered Steve, who was not certain what he had done wrong. He knew, though, that his mother had been quite upset when she awoke one night to find him masturbating next to her.

Most of the time, however, Steve's parents seemed to live separately from one another and from their son. Steve was raised, in effect, by a full-time maid. He rarely had playmates of his own age. His birthdays were celebrated with a cake and candles, but the only celebrants were Steve and his mother. By the age of ten, Steve had learned to keep himself occupied by playing "mind games," letting his imagination carry him off on flights of fantasy. He frequently imagined himself as a powerful figure—Superman, Batman, or Zorro. His fantasies were often extremely violent, and his foes were vanquished only after much blood had been spilled.

As Steve grew older, his fantasies and heroes became increasingly menacing and evil. When he was fifteen, he obtained a pornographic videotape that he viewed repeatedly on a video player in his room. Often, Steve would masturbate as he watched scenes of women being sexually violated. The more violent the acts against the women, the more aroused he became. Steve now recalls that he spent much of his spare time between the ages of fifteen and seventeen watching X-rated videotapes or violent movies like *The Texas Chainsaw Massacre,* in which a madman saws and hacks women to pieces. Steve always identified with the character perpetrating the outrage; at times, he imagined his parents as the victims.

At about the age of sixteen Steve became convinced that external forces were controlling his mind and behavior and were drawing him into his fantasies. He was often filled with guilt and anxiety after one of his "mind games." Although he was strongly attracted to his fantasy world, he also felt that something was wrong with it and with him. After seeing the movie *The Exorcist,* he became convinced that he was possessed by the devil.

Until this time, Steve had been a quiet, withdrawn person. In kindergarten the school psychologist had diagnosed his condition as *autisticlike,* because Steve seldom spoke, seemed unresponsive to the environment, and was socially isolated. His parents had immediately hired a prominent child psychiatrist to work with Steve. The psychiatrist had assured them that Steve was not autistic but would need intensive treatment for several years. And throughout these years of treatment, Steve never acted out any of his fantasies. But with the development of his interest in the occult and in demonic possession, he became outgoing, flamboyant, and even exhibitionistic. He read extensively about Satanism, joined a "Church of Satan" in San Francisco, and took to wearing a black cape on weekend journeys into that city. Against his will, he was hospitalized twice by his parents with diagnoses of, respectively, manic–depressive disorder and schizophrenia in remission.

Steve was twenty-one years old when he met Linda at an orientation session for university freshmen. Linda struck him as different from the other female students: unpretentious, open, and friendly. He quickly became obsessed with their relationship. But although Linda dated Steve frequently over the next few months, she did not seem to reciprocate his intense feelings. She took part in several extracurricular activities, including the student newspaper and student government, and her willingness to be apart from him confused and frustrated Steve. When her friends were around, Linda seemed almost oblivious to Steve's existence. In private, however, she was warm, affectionate, and intimate. She would not allow sexual intercourse, but she would engage in heavy petting.

Even while he and Linda were dating, Steve grew increasingly insecure about their relationship. He felt slighted by Linda's friends and began to believe she disliked him. Several times he accused her of plotting against him and deliberately making him feel inadequate. Linda continually denied these allegations. Finally on one occasion, feeling frightened and intimidated by Steve, she acquiesced to having sex with him. Unfortunately, in that instance Steve could not maintain an erection. When he blamed her for this "failure" and became verbally and physically abusive, Linda put an end to their relationship and refused to see him again.

During the next year and a half, Steve suffered from severe bouts of depression and twice attempted suicide by drug overdose. For the past six months, up to the time of his threat, he was seen on a regular basis at the University Psychological Services Center.

What do you make of Steven V.? His behavior is certainly beyond almost anyone's definition of normal. But is he a dangerous person from whom society must be protected? Is he a pathetic figure, doomed to fail in relationships with others as he did with Linda? Or is his major problem simply a lack of social skills that, once learned, will enable him to interact comfortably and confidently with other people?

In a sense, the purpose of *Understanding Abnormal Behavior* is to help you formulate enlightened responses to such questions. But these questions are premature at this point. Let us first examine some of the more basic aspects of the study of abnormal behavior, including a bit of its history. Then, at the end of this chapter, we shall again discuss the case of Steven V. and its place in this book.

THE CONCERNS OF ABNORMAL PSYCHOLOGY

Abnormal psychology is the scientific study whose objectives are to describe, explain, predict, and control behaviors that are considered strange or unusual. Its subject matter ranges from the bizarre and spectacular to the much more commonplace—from the violent homicides and ''perverted'' sexual acts that are widely reported by the news media to such unsensational (but more prevalent) behaviors as stuttering, depression, ulcers, and anxiety concerning examinations.

Describing abnormal behavior

The description of a particular case of abnormal behavior must be based on systematic observations by an attentive professional. These observations, usually paired with the results of psychological tests and with the individual's psychological history, become the raw material for a **psychodiagnosis,** an attempt to describe, assess, and systematically draw inferences about an individual's psychological disorder.

Diagnosis is obviously an important early step in the treatment process. But a diagnosis that is not developed with great care can end up as nothing more than a label that tends to impede rather than facilitate treatment. There are two major problems with such labels. First, a term such as *manic–depressive* (which was used to describe Steven V.) can cover a wide range of behaviors. Unfortunately, this label may convey different things to different psychologists. Hence, a label may be too general; it may describe something other than a client's specific behaviors. Second, a person's (and especially a young person's) psychological problems are likely to change over time. A previous diagnosis can quickly become a label that is no longer descriptive of that person. To guard against these problems, the sensitive therapist ensures that labels, either old or new, are not used as substitutes for careful investigation of a client's condition.

Explaining abnormal behavior

To explain abnormal behavior, the psychologist must identify its causes and determine how they led to the described behavior. This information, in turn, bears heavily on the choice of a program of treatment.

As you will see in later chapters, explanations of abnormal behavior do vary, depending on the theoretical orientation of the psychologist. For example, Steve's therapist might stress his client's loneliness, lack of self-esteem, and feelings of worthlessness brought about by his parents' actions—primarily his father's—and his lack of companions of his own age. To make up for what was missing from his life (the therapist might contend), Steve created a fantasy world in which he could feel powerful, freely express his anger toward his parents, and experience a sense of self-worth. But when Steve became disturbed by his own anger and hatred toward his parents, he protected himself by adopting

During a therapy session, the therapist not only hears about the client's problems, but also carefully observes the client's behavior and emotional reactions. These observations can help to form the basis of a psychodiagnosis.

the belief that these feelings were implanted by a demon and beyond his (Steve's) control.

The explanations of other psychologists might be more biological in nature, emphasizing genetics or a biochemical imbalance. Still other psychologists might stress Steve's inadequate interpersonal skills: He cannot make friends or develop meaningful relationships because he has never learned how to act around others. And still others might see Steve's behavior as resulting from a combination of these causes and then attempt to treat it as such.

Predicting abnormal behavior

If a therapist can correctly identify the source of a client's difficulty, he or she should be able to predict the kinds of problems the client will face during therapy and the symptoms the client will display. And the therapist should attempt to do so, in order to prepare the client for potential problems. The truth is, though, that therapists have difficulty predicting the future course of many disorders. Even an experienced professional finds it hard to foretell how a particular client will behave.

Consider, as an example, Steve's threat to kill Linda. Was it an empty threat—just Steve's way of venting his anger—or was it serious? Research shows that mental health professionals do a poor job of answering such questions; they tend to greatly overpredict violence.

Steve's threat raises another significant issue—that of the legal, moral, and ethical responsibilities of the therapist. Psychologists almost routinely grapple with questions of social responsibility. In particular, should

Steve's therapist make the threat known, and, if he does, how will his doing so affect the therapeutic process?

In a landmark legal case, the California Supreme Court has ruled that, if a therapist hears a client threaten someone and does not inform the threatened person, and if the threat is carried out, then the injured person has the right to sue the therapist. Naturally, no therapist wants a client to hurt or kill anyone. But the ruling has unpleasant implications for the confidentiality of the client–therapist relationship. One therapist summed it up this way: "No one wants a shrink who's a fink."

Controlling abnormal behavior

Abnormal behavior may be controlled through **therapy,** a program of systematic intervention whose purpose is to modify a client's behavioral, affective (emotional), or cognitive state. For example, many therapists would believe that allowing Steve to vent his anger at Linda would reduce the chances of his harming her. Other therapists might also recommend family therapy, or social-skills training, or medication. As we have noted, the treatment for abnormal behavior generally follows from its explanation. Just as there are many ways to explain abnormal behaviors, many ways have been proposed to control them.

DEFINING ABNORMAL BEHAVIOR

Implicit in our discussion so far is the one overriding concern of abnormal psychology: abnormal behavior itself. But what exactly is abnormal behavior, and how does the psychologist recognize it?

We shall examine three types of criteria that may be used to define or characterize behaviors as abnormal. Two of them—statistical criteria and ideal mental health criteria—define abnormal behavior as, essentially, deviations

from what is considered normal. The third type—consisting of the practical criteria—takes account of the effect of the behavior on the person exhibiting it or on others.

Statistical criteria

Statistical criteria equate normality with those behaviors that occur most frequently in the population. Then abnormality is defined in terms of those behaviors that occur least frequently. For example, data on IQs may be accumulated and an average calculated. Then IQ scores near that average are considered normal, and relatively large deviations from the norm (in either direction) are considered abnormal. In spite of the word *statistical,* however, these criteria need not be quantitative in nature: Individuals who talk to themselves, disrobe in public, or laugh uncontrollably for no apparent reason are considered abnormal according to these criteria simply because most people do not behave in that way.

Statistical criteria may seem adequate in specific instances, but they are fraught with problems. For one thing, they fail to take into account differences in place, community standards, and cultural values. For example, some lifestyles that are acceptable in San Francisco and New York may be judged abnormal by community standards in other parts of the country. Likewise, if deviations from the majority are considered abnormal, then many ethnic and racial minorities that exhibit strong subcultural differences from the majority have to be so classified. When we resort to a statistical definition, the dominant or most powerful group generally determines what constitutes normality and abnormality.

In addition, the statistical criteria do not provide any basis for distinguishing between desirable and undesirable deviations from the norm. An IQ of 100 is considered normal or average. But what constitutes an abnormal deviation from this average? More important,

Eleanor Roosevelt and Thomas Jefferson were two self-actualized people, according to Abraham Maslow. Both made extensive commitments and contributions to society, and both led rich personal lives as well.

is abnormality defined in only one direction or in both? An IQ of 55 would be considered abnormal by most people; but should people with IQ scores of 145 or higher also be considered abnormal? How does one evaluate personality traits like assertiveness and dependence in terms of statistical criteria?

Two other central problems also arise. First, people who strike out in new directions— artistically, politically, or intellectually— may be seen as candidates for psychotherapy simply because they do not conform to normative behavior. Second, statistical criteria may "define" quite widely distributed but undesirable characteristics, such as anxiety, as normal.

In spite of these weaknesses, the statistical criteria remain among the most widely used determinants of normality and abnormality. Not only do they underlie the lay person's evaluation of behaviors, but they are the most frequently used criteria in psychology. Many

psychological tests and much of the diagnosis and classification of behavior disorders are based in part on statistical criteria.

Ideal mental health criteria

The concept of ideal mental health has been proposed as a criterion of normality by psychologists Carl Rogers and Abraham Maslow. Deviations from the ideal are then taken to indicate varying degrees of abnormality.

Such criteria stress the importance of attaining some positive goal. Maslow and his followers suggest *self-actualization* or *creativeness*. Psychoanalytically oriented psychologists have used the concept *consciousness* (awareness of motivations and behaviors) and *balance of psychic forces* as criteria for normality. Aspects of maturity such as *competence, autonomy,* and *resistance to stress* have also been proposed. But using any of these constructs as the sole criterion for defining normality leads to a number of problems.

First, which particular goal or ideal should be used? The answer depends largely on the particular theoretical frame of reference or values embraced by those proposing the criterion. Second, most of these goals are vague; they lack clarity and precision. If resistance to stress is the goal, is a healthy person only someone who can always adapt? Recent experiences with prisoners of war indicate that, under repeated stress, many eventually break down. Should we label them as unhealthy? Third, ideal criteria exclude too many people: Most individuals would be considered mentally unhealthy by these definitions.

Practical criteria

Practical, or clinical, criteria are subject to many of the same criticisms as other criteria. Nonetheless, according to Buss (1966), they are often the basis on which people who are labeled abnormal or unhealthy come to the attention of psychologists or other mental health specialists. Moreover, clinicians often must act primarily on the basis of pragmatic manifestations. The practical criteria for abnormality include subjective discomfort, bizarreness, and inefficiency.

Discomfort   Most people who see clinicians are suffering physical or psychological discomfort. Many *physical* reactions stem from a strong psychological component; among them are such disorders as asthma, hypertension, and ulcers, as well as such physical symptoms as fatigue, nausea, pain, and heart palpitations. Discomfort can also be manifested in extreme or prolonged *emotional* reactions, of which *anxiety* and *depression* are the most significant. Of course, it is normal for a person to feel depressed after suffering a loss or a disappointment. But if the reaction is so intense,

exaggerated, and prolonged that it interferes with the capacity of the individual to function adequately, it is likely to be considered abnormal.

Bizarreness   As a practical criterion for abnormality, bizarreness is closely related to the statistical criteria. Bizarreness, or unusual behavior, is an abnormal deviation from an accepted standard of behavior (such as an antisocial act) or a false perception of reality (such as a *hallucination*). This criterion is very subjective; it depends on the individual and the particular culture.

Certain sexual behaviors, delinquency, and homicide are examples of acts that our society considers abnormal. But social norms are far from static, and behavioral standards cannot be considered absolute. Changes in our attitudes toward human sexuality provide a prime example. During the Victorian era, women wore six to eight layers of underclothing to make sure every part of the body, from the neck down, was covered. Exposing an ankle was roughly equivalent to wearing a topless bathing suit today (Kirkpatrick 1975). Taboos against public recognition of sexuality dictated the careful choice of words to avoid any sexual connotation. Victorians said ''limb'' instead of ''leg,'' because the word *leg* was thought to possess erotic reverberations. (Even pianos and tables were said to have limbs.) Those who did not adhere to these strict codes of conduct were considered immoral or perverted.

Nowadays, however, magazines and films openly exhibit the naked human body, and topless *and* bottomless nightclub entertainment is hardly newsworthy. Various sex acts are explicitly portrayed in X-rated movies. More and more, homosexuals ''come out'' publicly, professing their sexual orientation without shame, guilt, or much fear of public reaction. In fact, homosexuality is no longer classed as a mental disorder by the American Psychiatric Association. Women are freer to

When the "Abnormal" is Healthy: An Unhappy Consequence of Racism

In response to their slave heritage and a history of white discrimination against them, blacks have adopted various behaviors (in particular, behaviors toward whites) that have proved important for survival in a racist society (Sue 1981). "Playing it cool" has been identified as one means by which blacks, as well as members of other minority groups, may conceal their true thoughts and feelings. A black person who is experiencing conflict, anger, or even rage may be skillful at appearing serene and composed. This tactic is a survival mechanism aimed at reducing one's vulnerability to harm and exploitation in a hostile environment.

Suppose a personality test were given to a group of black Americans, and it was found that they were more suspicious than their white counterparts. What would this mean? Some psychologists have used such findings to label black subjects as *paranoid*. But members of minority groups who have consistently been victims of discrimination and even oppression in a culture that is not yet free of racism have good reason to be suspicious and distrustful of white society. In their book *Black Rage,* psychiatrists William Grier and Price Cobbs point out that, to survive in a white racist society, blacks have had to be suspicious and distrustful of whites. So the "paranoid" orientation is actually a functional mechanism used by blacks to protect themselves from physical and psychological injury. As such, this "cultural paranoia" is both adaptive and healthy (Grier and Cobbs 1968).

---

question traditional sex roles and to act more assertively in initiating sex. Such changes in behavioral standards make it difficult to subscribe to absolute standards of normality. (Another example, pointing up a different type of danger inherent in applying absolute standards of normality, appears in Focus 1.1.)

Nevertheless, some behaviors can usually be judged abnormal without hesitation. Among these are hallucinations, delusions, and severe disorientation. **Hallucinations** are false impressions that involve the senses. Those suffering hallucinations may hear, feel, or see things that are not really there: voices accusing them of vile deeds, insects crawling on their bodies, or monstrous apparitions. **Delusions** are false beliefs steadfastly held by the individual despite contradictory objective evidence. A delusion of *grandeur* is a belief

that one is an exalted personage, such as Jesus Christ or Joan of Arc; a delusion of *persecution* is a belief that one is controlled by others or is the victim of a conspiracy. An example of a delusionary system involving both grandiosity and persecution is reported by Schroth and Sue (1975).

> A young schizophrenic believed that there was an elaborate plot to kill him because he was, in truth, Jesus Christ. The plotters had discovered his true identity and were themselves agents of Israel. He believed he was sent to earth to save humanity from Communist and Jewish foolishness. He said God had told him personally of his role but requested him to maintain secrecy while saving the world. Somehow the word got out, even to his relatives, who had been corrupted by his enemies, and they were trying to keep him in the hospital (p. 291).

Disorientation is confusion with regard to identity, place, or time. Persons suffering disorientation may not know who they are, where they are, or what historical era they are living in.

Inefficiency In everyday life, people are expected to fulfill various roles—as students or teachers, as workers, as parents, lovers, and marital partners. Emotional problems sometimes interfere with the performance of these roles, and the resulting role *inefficiency* may be used as an indicator of abnormality.

One way to assess efficiency (or inefficiency) is to compare an individual's performance with the *requirements* of the role. Another, related means is to compare the individual's *performance* to his or her *potential*. An individual with an IQ of 150 who is failing in school can be labeled inefficient. (The label *underachiever* is often hung on students who possess high intelligence but obtain poor grades in school.) Similarly, a productive worker who suddenly becomes unproductive may be experiencing emotional stress. The major weakness of this approach is that it is difficult to assess potential accurately. How do we know whether a person is performing at his or her peak? Psychologists, educators, and the business sector have relied heavily on testing. Tests of specific abilities and of intelligence are attempts to assess potential and to predict performance in schools or jobs.

The concept of multiple perspectives

Different definitions of abnormality carry different implications, and there is no easy consensus on a best definition. All the criteria we have discussed have shortcomings. Some are more precise than others in specifying what behaviors are or are not to be considered abnormal; some seem to fit our beliefs about abnormality better than others; all of these criteria are sensitive to such variables as psychological orientation and societal and individual value systems.

Perhaps, then, abnormality should not be viewed from a single perspective or measured in accordance with a single criterion. Two researchers, working together, have proposed a three-part means of defining normality and abnormality. They identify three vantage points from which a person's mental health can be judged: that of society, that of the individual, and that of the mental health professional. Each operates from a different perspective, perhaps using different criteria. At times, the three parties would agree that a person is either mentally disturbed or mentally healthy. At other times, they might disagree. Nonetheless, the problems inherent in imposing a single criterion would be alleviated (Strupp and Hadley 1977).

We must give two important points careful consideration as we assess the value of the concept of multiple perspectives. First, a person who feels subjectively contented—mentally sound—may be perceived as unhealthy from a societal perspective. For example, people who commit antisocial acts such as rape, murder, or robbery may not feel remorseful but may be quite contented with their acts. Likewise, an artist living a very unconventional lifestyle may be judged maladapted from society's perspective; but from the individual's perspective and that of many mental health professionals, he or she is intact and sound.

Second, judgments made from any of the three vantage points must be recognized as stemming from that specific origin; otherwise, greater confusion may result.

A truly adequate understanding of mental illness and health could come about through comprehensive evaluation from all points of view. It may not be enough to rely solely on the judgments of mental health professionals, for they are not immune to biases and shortcomings.

A definition of abnormal behavior

In light of the foregoing, we may define **abnormal behavior** as behavior that departs from some norm and is detrimental to the affected individual or to others. This definition encompasses—or at least allows room for—the various criteria and perspectives on behavior. It also accurately implies that there is no precise, universally acknowledged line of demarcation between normal and abnormal behavior.

Somewhat more loosely, we shall speak of the *mentally disturbed* as those individuals who display abnormal behavior. And, by a *mental disorder* or *mental disturbance* we shall mean some recognizable pattern of abnormal behavior.

THE INCIDENCE OF ABNORMAL BEHAVIOR

A student once asked one of the authors, "How crazy is this nation?" Couched in somewhat more scientific terms, this question has occupied psychologists for some time. A number of studies have been conducted in an attempt to answer it.

Current research into the epidemiology of mental disorders

An early but highly regarded and frequently cited study, the Midtown Manhattan Study, was performed in 1950 (Srole et al. 1962). Fifteen hundred New Yorkers were interviewed and rated as to psychological health impairment. The results were startling: Approximately 25 percent of the subjects exhibited severe impairment. About 55 percent were mildly impaired. And only 20 percent (one in five) were rated unimpaired.

Some social commentators contend that our mental health has deteriorated since the Midtown Manhattan Study was conducted. They point to such "evidence" as the mushrooming of cults, a revival of belief in the supernatural, the incidence of mass and serial murders, and attempts at political assassination. To ascertain whether the population's mental health was deteriorating, a similar study was carried out in the 1970s (Srole and Fisher 1980). The investigators found no support for this contention. But neither did they find any evidence that the mental health of Americans had improved in the intervening decades!

Perhaps the most thorough and comprehensive study ever conducted on the incidence of mental disorders in the U.S. adult population indicates that almost one adult in five (29.4 million) suffers from a mental disorder (*Archives of General Psychiatry,* October 1984). The study, sponsored by the National Institute of Mental Health, is still in progress and will eventually include about 20,000 subjects. Some of the preliminary results are fascinating. For example, researchers found that men and women are equally likely to suffer from mental disorders but that they differ in the kinds of disorders they experience: Women are more likely to suffer anxieties, depression, and phobias. Men are more likely to exhibit substance abuse and antisocial personality.

With regard to incidence, anxiety disorders are the most common (8.3 percent or 13.1 million Americans), followed by drug and alcohol abuse (6.4 percent or 10 million Americans). Schizophrenia, often one of the most severe mental disturbances, afflicts 1 percent of the population, or about 1.4 million Americans.

In the National Institute study, an individual who is not in need of professional help is considered not to be afflicted by a mental disorder. A number of other studies applied less stringent criteria (Dohrenwend and Dohrenwend 1982; Dohrenwend et al. 1980; Regier, Goldberg, and Taube 1978; and Mechanic 1978). These studies estimate that

According to research done in 1984, almost one out of every five Americans suffers from some kind of mental disorder. This incidence rate was about the same in 1950.

some 25 to 40 million Americans, or approximately 15 percent of the population, suffer from emotional disorders that could be considered serious. Counting both severe and milder disturbances, estimates are that 44 million Americans suffer from symptoms of depression, 20 million have drug-related problems, 4 to 9 million suffer from some form of phobic or anxiety disturbance, 6 million are mentally retarded, and 2 million suffer from schizophrenia. In addition, some 25,000 to 60,000 people commit suicide each year, and another 200,000 attempt it. These estimates do not include such disorders as child abuse, sexual dysfunctions, and pathological expressions of violence, which could increase the total substantially. For example, crime statistics show that 456,000 acts of family violence are committed yearly in the United States, and that

figure is probably a gross underestimate because many such acts go unreported.

The psychologically oriented society

Afflicted individuals and their families and friends pay a huge price in human suffering. In addition, the American public spends increasing amounts each year in either direct or indirect expenses for mental health care. In 1974 we spent $40 billion, of which nearly 40 percent went for direct care, including therapy and hospitalization (Levine and Willver 1976). And as Americans have become more "psychological minded," the demand for various forms of mental health treatment has increased. This demand is evident in the following statistics:

☐ The proportion of Americans seeking mental health consultation increased from 4 to 14 percent between 1957 and 1976. Among the college-educated, the increase has been even greater—from 9 to 21 percent.

☐ Mental health professionals seem to believe in what they do, as they are the heaviest consumers of therapy. Seventy-four percent have been in treatment, one-third have been treated more than once, and the average time spent in treatment was 4½ years.

☐ More than 5 million people have taken part in encounter or sensitivity groups in the past 15 years; over a million have been taught Transcendental Meditation; over a million have participated in marriage enrichment programs; and countless millions have entered nonprofessional therapeutic programs for drug, alcohol, smoking, and weight control (Zilbergeld 1983).

Focus 1.2 (p. 18) examines the beliefs that underlie this enthusiasm for psychological therapy and self-enhancement.

Stereotypes of the mentally disturbed

Despite our "psychological mindedness" and our belief in the efficacy of various therapies, we tend to regard the mentally disturbed with suspicion. Are most of them really maniacs who, at any moment, may be seized by uncontrollable urges to murder, rape, or maim? Such portrayals seem to emerge from the news media and the entertainment industry, but they are rarely accurate. Like other minority groups in America, the mentally disturbed are the subject of rampant stereotyping and popular misconceptions. It would be worthwhile, at this point, to dispel the most common of these misconceptions, or myths.

Myth: Mentally disturbed people can always be recognized by their consistently deviant abnormal behavior.

Reality: Mentally disturbed people are not always distinguishable from others on the basis of consistently unusual behaviors. Even in an outpatient clinic or a psychiatric ward, it is often difficult to identify the patients on the basis of behavior alone. There are two main reasons for this. First, as we have noted, no sharp dividing line usually exists between "normal" and "abnormal" behaviors. Rather, there is a continuous spectrum of behaviors, ranging from abnormal to normal. Depending on the situational context and the perspective of the person judging the behavior, many behaviors could be considered either normal or deviant. Second, even when people are suffering from some form of emotional disturbance, it may not always be detectable in their behavior.

Myth: The mentally disturbed have inherited their disorders. If one member of a family has an emotional breakdown, other members will probably suffer a similar fate.

Reality: The belief that insanity runs in certain families has caused misery and undue anxiety for many persons. Except for *certain forms* of mental retardation, schizophrenia, and depression, heredity does not seem to play a significant role in most mental disorders, although the data are far from conclusive. Evidence suggests that, even though heredity may predispose an individual to certain disorders, environmental factors are extremely important. In families where many members suffer from mental disorders, there is usually a stress-producing environment acting on this predisposition. If the environment is benign, however, or if the individual takes steps to modify a stressful environment, psychopathology may never occur.

Myth: The mentally disturbed can never be cured and will never be able to function "normally."

Reality: This erroneous belief has caused great distress to many persons who have been labeled mentally ill. Former mental patients have endured social discrimination and have been denied employment because of the public perception that "once insane, always insane." Unfortunately, this myth may keep former mental patients or those currently experiencing emotional problems from seeking help. Although most people do not hesitate to consult a doctor, dentist, or lawyer for help, many who need mental health services feel fearful and anxious about the social stigma attached to the "mentally ill." However, according to a World Health Organization study of schizophrenia (1973), more than 70 percent of those hospitalized for mental illness improve and go on to lead productive lives.

Myth: Persons become mentally disturbed because they are weak-willed. To avoid emotional disorders or cure oneself of them, one need only exercise will power.

Reality: These statements reveal a lack of understanding of the nature of mental dis-

FOCUS 1.2

The Psychologizing of America

In his book *The Shrinking of America* (1983), psychologist Bernie Zilbergeld contends that Americans seem to have set out to psychologize almost every aspect of their lives. A main theme of Zilbergeld's is that our national history and cultural values have prepared us for this "psychological minded" orientation. He notes that our culture is strongly committed to the following propositions:

□ We are endowed with an unalienable right to the pursuit of happiness.
□ We have a duty to better ourselves.
□ Individual freedom is important.
□ There are no limits to what we can do in life.
□ We are highly malleable.
□ Solutions to an individual's problems do exist, and finding a cure is possible.

Acceptance of these basic tenets leads thousands of people each year to try to banish all conceivable forms of failure and misfortune from their lives. Millions of dollars and countless hours of effort are spent in attempts to improve behavior, attitudes, personality, and moods. Zilbergeld argues that the following beliefs underlie what he calls our "therapeutic sensibility."

1. *The world is best understood in psychological terms.* It appears that psychology has become the most important way of understanding our internal and external world. When we think of ourselves or others, we often think of psychological characteristics—anxiety, insecurity, passivity, depression, paranoia, hostility, and unconscious processes. When some important person is assassinated or a bizarre killing is reported, the media call on mental health experts to analyze the slayer's state of mind. On radio and television programs and in newspaper columns, mental health professionals dispense advice to callers or readers. High on the best-seller lists are self-help psychology books with titles such as *Your Erroneous Zones, Looking Out for Number One,* and *When I Say No I Feel Guilty.*

2. *There is much more than meets the eye.* Unconscious processes and hidden meanings have become important in our

orders. Needing help to resolve difficulties does not indicate a lack of will power. In fact, recognition of the need for help may be seen as a sign of strength rather than weakness. Many problems in living stem from situations that are not under the individual's immediate control, such as the death of a loved one or the loss of a job. Other problems stem from life-long patterns of faulty learning, and it is naive to expect a simple exercise of will to override years of experience.

Myth: The mentally disturbed person is unstable and potentially dangerous.

Reality: This misconception has been perpetuated by the mass media. Many murderers on television are labeled "psychopathic," and the news media concentrate on the occasional mental patient who kills. But the thousands of mental patients who do not commit crimes, do not harm others, and do not get into trouble with the law are not news. An important study of the issue does not support the notion that

belief system. Such thinking was popularized through the writings of Sigmund Freud, who claimed that hidden purposes lay behind nearly all human behavior: A desire for bananas, hot dogs, or carrots may represent unfulfilled sexual cravings. A person's charity work may be an expression of repressed hostility. Illness may be a result of the need to be loved and cared for. As a result of this emphasis, insight into one's own motives and behaviors has become highly valued.

3. *People are not okay.* In general, mental health professionals tend to focus on pathology rather than on healthy characteristics. People are often described in terms of their inadequacies or deficiencies. A large portion of the public seems to have accepted a fantasy model of well-being and mental health that none of us can attain.

4. *Individuals need to be liberated.* People are basically good, creative, and aspiring, but their nature has been blocked, inhibited, distorted, or repressed by the traditions and institutions of society. Excessive guilt may be caused by religious teachings, confining family ties, or rigid sex

roles. We need to liberate ourselves in order to be whole, free, and well.

5. *Everyone needs and can benefit from therapy.* The number of people who sought some form of counseling or therapy increased threefold between 1957 and 1976, and the trend seems to be continuing. When other forms of treatment such as encounter groups, Weight Watchers, Synanon, EST, and TM are included, it becomes obvious that this belief has been widely taken to heart.

6. *The therapist is an expert and knows best.* Ours is a highly credentialed society, and the title "therapist" evokes the image of a person with much wisdom and knowledge. However, even though therapy is supposed to free the client and allow him or her to advance and grow, therapists may inadvertently foster reliance on their "expert" judgment.

Zilbergeld may be correct in asserting that "psychological man reigns supreme." To the question, "Whatever became of sin?" he answers, "It was psychologized away."

mental patients are seriously dangerous (Rabkin 1979). Unfortunately, the myth persists.

THE MENTAL HEALTH PROFESSIONS

The traditional therapy fields have grown along with our demand for mental health treatment. In 1968 there were 12,000 clinical psychologists in America; today there are 40,000. We now have some 280,000 professional therapists (primarily in clinical psychology, counseling psychology, psychiatry, psychoanalysis, social work, and marriage and family counseling). As one writer observed, there are more professional therapists than librarians, firefighters, or mail carriers, and twice as many therapists as dentists and pharmacists (Zilbergeld 1983). Let us turn our attention briefly to the qualifications, training, and functions of the people who work within these specialties and, in the process, clarify the distinctions among them.

Clinical psychology

Clinical psychology is the professional field concerned with the study, assessment, treatment, and prevention of abnormal behavior in disturbed individuals. ("Abnormal psychology" is the name, not of a professional field, but of a course of study.) Clinical psychologists must hold the Ph.D. degree from a university or the Psy.D. (Doctor of Psychology) degree, a more practitioner-oriented degree granted by several institutions. Their training includes coursework in psychopathology, personality, diagnosis, psychological testing, psychotherapy, and human physiology. Apart from these and other course requirements, there are two additional requisites for the Ph.D. degree. First, the candidate must complete a doctoral dissertation, which is an original research study on some aspect of the can-

didate's area of specialization—therapy, diagnosis, or test interpretation, for example. This requirement is imposed to familiarize clinical psychologists with research design and methods so that they can critically analyze published reports of current research. Second, a practicum experience or internship, usually one year at a psychiatric hospital or mental health center, is required. This allows Ph.D. candidates to gain practical experience and sharpen their clinical skills. Furthermore, those desiring to enter private practice must obtain a psychology license, which requires additional post-doctoral clinical practice.

Clinical psychologists work in a variety of settings, but most commonly they provide therapy to clients in hospitals and clinics and in private practice. Some choose to work in an academic setting, where they can concentrate on teaching and research. (Your course instructor has probably chosen this option.) Other clinical psychologists are hired by government or private organizations to do research. It is not unusual, however, for clinical psychologists to assume a number of different roles. For example, many professors not only teach and do research but engage in part-time clinical work as well.

Counseling psychology

To a great extent, our description of clinical psychology applies to counseling psychology as well. The academic and internship requirements are similar, but there are some differences in emphasis. Whereas clinical psychologists are trained to work specifically with a disturbed client population, counseling psychologists are usually more immediately concerned with the study of life problems in relatively normal people. Furthermore, counseling psychologists are more likely to be found in educational settings than in hospitals and clinics. These are not rigid distinctions, however, because counseling psychologists can choose to practice in the clinical setting.

Mental health professionals differ in their training, the settings where they work, the techniques they use, and the kinds of clients they treat. On the left, a consulting psychiatrist meets with day care workers. The psychologist on the right is conducting a group therapy session.

Psychiatry

Psychiatrists hold the M.D. degree. Their education includes the four years of medical school required for that degree, along with an additional three or four years of training in psychiatry. Of all the specialists involved in mental health care, only psychiatrists can prescribe drugs in the treatment of mental disorders.

Psychoanalysis

Psychoanalysis has been associated with medicine and psychiatry because its founder, Sigmund Freud, and his major disciples were physicians. But Freud was quite adamant in stating that one need not be medically trained to be good psychoanalyst. Nevertheless, most psychoanalysts hold either the M.D. or the Ph.D. degree. In addition, psychoanalysts receive intensive training in the theory and practice of psychoanalysis at an institute devoted to the field. This training includes the individual's own analysis by an experienced analyst.

Psychiatric social work

Those entering psychiatric social work are trained in a school of social work, usually in a two-year graduate program leading to a master's degree. Included in this program is a one-year internship in a social-service agency, sometimes a mental health center. Some social workers go on to earn the D.S.W. (doctor of social work) degree, which requires additional training and dissertation. Traditionally, psychiatric social workers have worked in family counseling services or community agencies, where they specialize in intake (assessment and screening of clients), take psychiatric histories, and deal with other agencies. However, many engage in private practice as well.

Marriage and family counseling

In the past, the counseling of married couples was usually performed by the clergy or social workers in churches, public welfare agencies, and family-service organizations. Counseling and clinical psychologists may also work with couples and families. However, a specialty in marriage and family counseling has recently emerged, with its own professional organizations, journals, and state licensing requirements. Marriage and family counselors have varied professional backgrounds, but their training usually includes a master's degree in counseling and many hours of supervised clinical experience.

This wide variety of specialties has created some problems. There are occasional disputes about the overlapping of specialties, limitations that should or should not be placed on each specialty, and licensing standards. Nevertheless, the development of new specialties is inevitable, if only to satisfy the various preferences of a psychologically aware public. Moreover, the range of psychological problems may be too vast for just a few kinds of specialists. What has begun to evolve is a multidisciplinary perspective on the treatment of mental disorders, a team approach in which psychologists, social workers, psychiatrists, and other professionals work together to prescribe and provide therapy.

EARLY EXPLANATIONS OF ABNORMAL BEHAVIOR

In this section and the next we shall briefly review the historical development of Western thought concerning abnormality. Many current attitudes toward abnormal behavior, as well as modern ideas about its causes and treatment, have been influenced by early beliefs. In fact, some psychologists contend that modern societies have, in essence, adopted more sophisticated versions of earlier concepts. For example, the use of electroconvulsive therapy to treat depression is in some ways similar to ancient practices of exorcism, in which the body was physically assaulted. The Greek physician Hippocrates believed

2500 years ago that many abnormal behaviors were caused by imbalances and disorders in the brain and the body, a belief shared by many contemporary psychologists.

Early ideas about abnormal behavior were firmly rooted in the system of beliefs that was operative in a given society at a given time. Perhaps for that reason, advances—especially in the form of new ideas—did not come quickly or easily. Individuals who dared to voice ideas that differed from the prevalent beliefs of their time were often made outcasts in their profession; some were even executed. Yet in spite of the difficulties, we have evolved a humanistic and scientific explanation of abnormal behavior. It remains to be seen whether such an explanation will still be thought valid in decades to come.*

Demonology and ancient explanations

Primitive societies some half a million years ago failed to distinguish sharply between mental and physical disorders. Abnormal behaviors, from simple headaches to convulsive attacks, were attributed to evil spirits that inhabited or controlled the afflicted person's body. According to historians, these ancient peoples attributed all forms of illness to the loss of the soul—by demonic possession, by sorcery, or at the behest of an offended ancestral spirit. Within this system of belief, called **demonology,** the victim was usually held at least partly responsible for the misfortune.

Stone Age cave dwellers may have treated behavior disorders with a surgical method called *trephining,* in which part of the skull was chipped away to provide an opening through which the evil spirit could escape. It

*Much of this history section is based on discussions of deviant behavior by Zilboorg and Henry (1941), Hunter and Macalpine (1963), Alexander and Selesnick (1966), and Neugebauer (1979).

was believed that, when the evil spirit left, the victim would return to his or her normal state. Surprisingly, some trephined skulls have been found to have healed over, indicating that some patients survived this extremely crude operation.

Another treatment method, used by the early Greeks, Chinese, Hebrews, and Egyptians, is called *exorcism*. In an exorcism, elaborate prayers, noise-making, emetics (drugs that induce vomiting), and such extreme measures as flogging and starvation were marshaled to cast the evil spirit out of the afflicted person's body.

Naturalistic explanations

In the ancient world, then, illness both physical and mental was thought to be the work of demons. But with the flowering of Greek civilization (about 500 B.C.) and its continuation into the era of Roman rule (100 B.C.–A.D. 600), naturalistic explanations gradually became distinct from supernatural ones. Early thinkers such as Hippocrates (460–370 B.C.), a physician who is often called the father of medicine, actively questioned prevailing superstitious beliefs, proposing much more rational and scientific explanations for mental disorders.

The beliefs of many thinkers of this era were based on incorrect assumptions. However, they all relied heavily on observations and explanations, which form the foundation of the scientific method. And they denied the intervention of demons in the development of abnormality and instead stressed organic causes, so the treatment they prescribed for mental disorders tended to be more humane than previous treatments.

Hippocrates believed that, because the brain was the central organ of intellectual activity, deviant behavior was caused by **brain pathology**—that is, a dysfunction or disease of the brain. He also considered heredity and environment important factors in psychopathology. He classified mental illnesses into three categories—mania, melancholia, and phrenitis (brain fever)—and for each category gave detailed clinical descriptions of such disorders as paranoia, alcoholic delirium, and epilepsy. Many of his descriptions of symptoms are still used today, eloquent testimony to his keen powers of observation.

To treat melancholia, Hippocrates recommended tranquility, moderate exercise, a careful diet, abstinence from sexual activity, and bloodletting if necessary. His belief in environmental influences on behavior sometimes led him to separate disturbed patients from their families. He seems to have gained insight into a theory popular among psychologists today, the theory that the family constellation often fosters deviant behavior in its own members.

Other thinkers who contributed to the organic explanation of behavior were the philosopher Plato and Galen, a Greek physician who practiced in Rome. Plato (429–347 B.C.) carried on the thinking of Hippocrates; he insisted that the mentally disturbed be the responsibility of the family and not be punished for their behavior. Galen (A.D. 129–199) made major contributions through his scientific examination of the nervous system and his explanation of the role of the brain and central nervous system in mental functioning.

Reversion to superstition

With the collapse of the Greco–Roman Empire, rationalism and naturalism gave way to the ancient, superstitious beliefs.

Early Christianity did little to promote science and in many ways actively discouraged it. The Church demanded uncompromising adherence to its tenets. Christian fervor brought with it the concepts of heresy and punishment; certain truths were deemed sacred, and those who challenged them were

Hippocrates and Galen, two early physicians, defied popular thinking and proposed organic explanations for abnormal behavior and illness. They are depicted together in this thirteenth-century fresco even though they lived centuries apart.

denounced as heretics. Scientific thought that was in conflict with Church doctrine was not tolerated.

Rationalism and the scholarly scientific works went underground for many years, preserved mainly by Arab scholars and European monks. Natural and supernatural explanations of illness became fused.

People came to believe that illnesses, although they had natural causes, were the result of God's wrath. Relief could come only through atonement or repentance. With illness perceived as punishment, the sick person was assumed to be guilty of wrongdoing.

Treatment of the mentally ill during this period consisted of torturous exorcistic procedures seen as appropriate to combat Satan and eject him from the possessed person's body. Prayers, curses, obscene epithets, and the sprinkling of holy water—as well as such drastic and painful "therapy" as flogging, starving, and immersion in hot water—were utilized to drive out the devil. The humane treatments that Hippocrates had advocated centuries earlier were nowhere to be found. A time of trouble for everyone, the Dark Ages (A.D. 400–900) were especially bleak for the mentally ill.

Mass madness

Belief in the power of the supernatural became so prevalent and intense that it frequently affected whole populations. Early in the thirteenth century, large numbers of people were affected by various forms of group hysteria, or **mass madness.** Among the better known of these mental disorders was *tarantism,* a dance mania characterized by wild raving, jumping, dancing, and convulsions. The "disease" was most prevalent during the height of the summer and was attributed to the sting of a tarantula. A victim would leap up and run out into the street or marketplace, jumping and raving, to be joined by others who believed they had also been bitten. The mania, which started in Italy, soon spread throughout the rest of Europe, where it became known as *St. Vitus's Dance.*

Another form of mass madness during the late Middle Ages (to about 1500) was *lycanthropy,* a mental disorder in which the victim imagines himself or herself to be a wolf and imitates a wolf's actions. (Motion pictures about *werewolves*—people who assume the physical characteristics of wolves during the full moon—are modern reflections of this delusion.) Yet another form of mass madness was *flagellantism,* the practice of self-inflicted whipping. People who achieved a state of ecstacy by scourging themselves often traveled about in bands through cities and towns, where they were joined by others seeking cures or public penance for real or imagined wrongdoing. Focus 1.3 (p. 26) describes what may have been a much more recent case of mass madness.

Witchcraft

Several factors contributed to a growing belief in witches at this time. The bubonic plague had killed off half the population of Europe, and the feudal social order was crumbling. Misery and suffering—social oppression, war, famine, and pestilence—were everywhere. People turned desperately to the Church for guidance. At the same time, however, reformers were beginning to attack corruption and abuses by the clergy, foreshadowing the Protestant Reformation of the sixteenth century. The Church believed Satan himself fostered these attacks. By doing battle with Satan and with persons supposedly influenced or possessed by Satan, the Church actively endorsed an already popular belief in demonic possession and witches.

To counter the climate of demoralization, fear, and helplessness, Pope Innocent VIII issued a papal decree in 1484 calling on the clergy to identify and exterminate witches. Means of detecting witches were publicized. For example, red spots on the skin (birthmarks) were supposedly made by the claw of the devil in sealing a blood pact and were thus damning evidence of a contract with Satan. Such birth defects as the club foot and the cleft palate also aroused suspicion.

The church initially recognized two forms of demonic possession: unwilling and willing. God let the devil seize an unwilling victim as punishment for a sinful life. A willing person, who made a blood pact with the devil in exchange for supernatural powers, was able to assume animal form and to cause such disasters as floods, pestilence, storms, crop failures, and sexual impotence. Although an unwilling victim of possession was at first treated with more sympathy than one who willingly conspired with the devil, this distinction soon evaporated.

Persons whose actions were interpreted as peculiar were often suspected of witchcraft. Mentally or emotionally disturbed persons were particularly vulnerable. It was acceptable to use torture to obtain confessions from suspected witches, and many victims confessed because they preferred death to prolonged agony. Thousands of innocent men, women, and even children were beheaded, burned alive, or mutilated.

FOCUS 1.3

Mass Hysteria: Did an Age-Old "Illness" Crop Up Again?

Berry is a quiet town of about 1,000 people in the soybean and cotton growing areas of northwestern Alabama. Its one-story, 15-room elementary school draws the children of farmers and factory workers from 20 miles around. Not much exciting about that.

Rather commonplace, that is, except for one week that Berry Elementary School went berserk. For seven days in May, a frightening "epidemic" sent a third of its 400 pupils, even a few teachers, into a frenzy of scratching, fainting, vomiting, numbness, crying, and screaming.

Ambulances carried more than 70 children, 20 of them unconscious, to the county hospital in nearby Fayette on Friday, May 11, when the strange malady first struck. Frantic parents arrived to take home their children, some of whom had scratched themselves bloody. They were convinced along with school and local authorities that some disease or toxic substance or perhaps a swarm of biting insects was to blame.

It began, they say, when a fifth-grader who had had a skin rash began scratching so vigorously that the teacher asked her to sit in the hall. During the 10:30 A.M. class break, the girl's classmates gathered around her in the hall, and they began scratching furiously. They ran to a room to wash off whatever was causing the itch, where they "infected" others.

The epidemic spread rapidly, class by class. Teachers vainly tried to ease the itching, applying alcohol, but many children scratched their skin raw and the alcohol stung them more, adding to the panic. . . .

Bit by bit, medical sleuths ruled out one after another of the possible causes for the epidemic, until they were left with one conclusion: hysteria. The outbreak had begun before lunch—ruling out a toxic substance in the food; water was out because not all children with symptoms had used the school fountains that morning. Except for a few pupils with slightly elevated temperature, no fever was present, and blood studies showed nothing abnormal—making it unlikely that a bacterial or viral infection was at work; what's more, no known infectious agent could spread that fast. Whereas most students were well an hour after the attack, an infection would last longer.

An allergy perhaps? Allergies that make you itch cause you to itch all over. Dr. _____ notes that the affected children only scratched where it was easy to reach. Since no one in the immediate neighborhood of the school was affected, toxic substances in the air were ruled out (not to mention the fact that investigators could not find any possible source in the area). . . .

What happened at Berry is, in fact, an old human afflication that has popped up in various forms over the centuries, including dancing manias of the Middle Ages, biting and mewing nuns in European convents, and the "phantom anesthetist" of Mattoon, Illinois. In all cases, groups of people suffer bizarre symptoms of mental or bodily illness, for which there is no physical cause and only excess fear of some imagined danger.

SOURCE: Barry Kramer, "Mass Hysteria: An Age-Old 'Illness' Still Crops Up in Modern Times," *Wall Street Journal*, November 16, 1973, p. 36b. Reprinted by permission of *The Wall Street Journal*, copyright © Dow Jones & Company, Inc. 1983. All rights reserved.

This painting depicts the examination of a young woman during the Salem witchcraft trials in colonial Massachusetts. New historical evidence suggests these trials were a case of socio-political persecution rather than persecution of the mentally ill. Other evidence implicates ergot poisoning as the culprit.

Witch hunts also occurred in colonial America. The witchcraft trials of 1692 in Salem, Massachusetts, were the most infamous. Authorities there acted on statements taken from children who may have been influenced by the sensational stories told by an old West Indian servant. Several hundred persons were accused, many were imprisoned and tortured, and twenty were killed.

The rise of humanism

Those who questioned the practice of demonology were in danger of being branded as heretics—or witches. Yet dissenting voices were raised, and a swing from supernatural to natural explanations and human concerns marked the end of the Middle Ages. A resurgence of rationalism and scientific inquiry after the Renaissance (fifteenth and sixteenth centuries) led to great advances in science and to **humanism,** with its emphasis on human welfare. Until this time, most asylums were at best custodial centers where the mentally disturbed were chained, caged, starved, whipped, and even exhibited to the public for a small fee, much like animals in a zoo. But if people were ''mentally ill,'' not possessed, they should be treated as though they were

As skeptics look on, Philippe Pinel orders the chains removed from the inmates of La Bicêtre. Jean-Baptiste Pussin, an untrained ward superintendent, actually abolished the chaining of inmates. Pinel introduced even more radical changes, such as talking with the patients to give them comfort and advice.

sick. A number of new methods for treating the mentally ill reflected this humanistic spirit.

In 1563 Johann Weyer (1515–1588), a German physician, published a revolutionary book that challenged the validity of demonology. Weyer asserted that many people who were tortured, imprisoned, and burned as witches were mentally disturbed, not possessed by demons. The emotional agonies he was made to endure for committing this heresy are well documented. His book was severely criticized and banned by both church and state, but it proved to be a forerunner of the humanitarian perspective. Others eventually followed his lead.

In France Philippe Pinel (1745–1826), a physician, was put in charge of La Bicêtre, a hospital for insane males in Paris. Pinel instituted what came to be known as the **moral treatment movement.** He ordered that inmates' chains be removed, replaced dungeons with sunny rooms, encouraged exercise out of doors on hospital grounds, and treated patients with

kindness and reason. Surprising many disbelievers, the freed patients did not become violent; instead this humane treatment seemed to foster recovery and improved behavior. Pinel later instituted similar equally successful reforms at La Salpêtrière, a large mental hospital for women in Paris.

In England William Tuke (1732–1822), a prominent Quaker tea merchant, established a retreat at York for the "moral treatment" of mental patients. At this pleasant country estate, the patients worked, prayed, rested, and talked out their problems—all in an atmosphere of kindness quite unlike that of the lunatic asylums of the time.

In the United States, three individuals were important contributors to the moral treatment movement: Benjamin Rush, Dorothea Dix, and Clifford Beers. Benjamin Rush (1745–1813), widely acclaimed as the father of American psychiatry, attempted to train physicians to treat mental patients and to introduce more humane treatment policies into mental hospitals. He insisted that patients be accorded respect and dignity and that they be gainfully employed while hospitalized, an idea that anticipated the modern concept of work therapy. Yet Rush was not unaffected by the established practices and beliefs of his times; his theories were influenced by astrology, and his remedies included bloodletting and purgatives.

Dorothea Dix (1802–1887), a New England schoolteacher, was the pre-eminent American social reformer of the nineteenth century. While teaching Sunday school to female prisoners, she became familiar with the deplorable conditions in which jailed mental patients were forced to live. (Prisons and poorhouses were commonly used to incarcerate these patients.) For the next forty years, Dix worked tirelessly for the mentally ill. She campaigned for reform legislation and funds to establish suitable mental hospitals and asylums. She raised millions of dollars, established more than thirty modern mental hospitals, and greatly improved conditions in countless others. But the struggle for reform was far from over. The large hospitals that replaced jails and poorhouses had better physical facilities, but the humanistic, personal concern of the moral treatment movement was lacking.

That movement was given further impetus in 1908 with the publication of *A Mind That Found Itself,* a book by Clifford Beers (1876–1943) about his own mental collapse. His book describes the terrible treatment he and other patients experienced in three mental institutions, where they were beaten, choked, spat upon, and strait-jacketed. His vivid account aroused great public sympathy and attracted the interest and support of the psychiatric establishment, including such eminent figures as psychologist–philosopher William James. Beers founded the National Committee for Mental Hygiene, an organization dedicated to educating the public about mental illness and about the need to treat the mentally ill rather than punish them for their unusual behaviors.

Dorothea Dix was an exceptional contributor to the social reform movements of the nineteenth century—an era when women were discouraged from political participation.

It would be naive to believe that these reforms have totally eliminated inhumane treatment of the mentally disturbed. Books like Mary Jane Ward's *The Snake Pit* (1946) and films like Frederick Wiseman's *Titicut Follies* continue to document harsh treatment of mental patients. Even the severest critic of the mental health system, however, would have to admit that conditions and treatment for the mentally ill have improved in this century.

CAUSES: TWO VIEWPOINTS

Paralleling the rise of humanism in the treatment of mental illness was an expanding inquiry into its causes. Two main schools of thought emerged. The organic viewpoint holds that mental disorders are the result of physiological damage or disease, whereas the psychological viewpoint stresses an emotional basis for mental illness.

The organic viewpoint

Hippocrates' suggestion of an organic explanation for abnormal behavior was ignored during the Middle Ages but was revived after the Renaissance. However, it was not until the nineteenth Century that the organic or **biogenic view** attained prominence. The ideas of Wilhelm Griesinger (1817–1868), a German psychiatrist who believed that all mental disorders had physiological causes, received considerable attention. Emil Kraepelin (1856–1926), a follower of Griesinger, observed that certain symptoms tend to occur regularly in clusters, called **syndromes;** he believed that each cluster of symptoms represented a mental disorder with its own unique—and clearly specifiable—cause, course, and outcome. He attributed all disorders to one of four organic causes: metabolic disturbance, endocrine difficulty, brain disease, or heredity. In his *Textbook of Psychiatry* (1883), Kraepelin outlined a system for classifying mental illnesses on the basis of their organic causes. That system is still the basis for the diagnostic categories in the *Diagnostic and Statistical Manual of Mental Disorders* (DSM), the classification system of the American Psychiatric Association.

The acceptance of organic causation for mental disorders was accelerated by breakthroughs in the study of the nervous system. The relationship of brain pathology to cerebral arteriosclerosis, mental retardation, senile psychoses, and certain other psychoses led many scientists to suspect or advocate organic factors as the sole cause of all mental illness.

The organic point of view gained even greater strength with the discovery of the organic basis of general *paresis,* a progressively degenerative and irreversible physical and mental disorder. Several breakthroughs had led scientists to suspect that the deterioration of mental and physical abilities exhibited by certain mental patients might actually be caused by an organic disease. The work of Louis Pasteur (1822–1895) established the germ theory of disease (invasion of the body by parasites). Then in 1897 Richard von Krafft-Ebing (1840–1902), a German neurologist, inoculated paretic patients with pus from syphilitic sores; when they failed to develop the secondary symptoms of syphilis, he concluded that the subjects had been previously infected by that disease. Finally, in 1905 a German zoologist, Fritz Schaudinn (1871–1906), isolated the microorganism that causes syphilis and thus paresis. These discoveries convinced many scientists that every mental disorder might eventually be linked to an organic cause.

The psychological viewpoint

Some scientists noted, however, that certain types of emotional disorders failed to be associated with any organic pathology in the patient. Such observations led to another view, stressing psychological factors rather than organic factors as the cause of many disorders. For example, the inability to attain personal goals and resolve interpersonal conflicts could lead to intense feelings of frustration, depression, failure, anger, and consequent disturbed behavior.

Mesmerism   The unique and exotic techniques of Friedrich Anton Mesmer (1734–1815), an Austrian physician who practiced in Paris, presented an early challenge to the organic point of view. It is important to note, however, that Mesmer was really an anomaly and not part of mainstream scientific thinking. Mesmer developed a highly controversial treatment that came to be called *mesmerism* and was the forerunner of the modern practice of hypnotism. He subscribed to the idea that the planets controlled the distribution of a universal magnetic fluid and that the shiftings of this fluid in the body determined a person's mental and physical health. Mesmer believed that every person possessed magnetic forces (animal magnetism) that could influence the distribution of this fluid in others, thereby curing them of both mental and physical illnesses.

Mesmer performed his most miraculous cures in the treatment of *hysteria*—the appearance of symptoms such as blindness, deafness, loss of bodily feeling, and paralysis that seem to have no organic basis. According to Mesmer, hysteria was a manifestation of the body's need for a redistribution of the magnetic fluid. His techniques for curing this illness involved inducing a sleeplike state, during which his patients became highly susceptible to suggestion. As Mesmer, clad in flowing robes, performed a ritual designed to redistribute their magnetic fluids, many of his patients went into convulsions, after which their symptoms disappeared. Their exclamations of joy at being cured led other patients to expect the same results, paving the way for still more cures.

Mesmer's dramatic and theatrical techniques earned him censure as well as fame. A committee of prominent thinkers, including American ambassador Benjamin Franklin, investigated Mesmer and declared him a fraud. He was finally forced to leave Paris.

Although Mesmer's basic assumptions were discredited, the power of suggestion proved to be a strong therapeutic technique in the treatment of hysteria. The cures he effected stimulated scientific interest in, and much bitter debate about, the view that mental disorders are **psychogenic** in nature—that is, caused by psychological and emotional rather than organic factors.

Hypnotism An English physician, James Braid (1795–1860), renamed mesmerism *neurohypnotism* (later shortened to **hypnotism**) because he believed the technique induced sleep by producing paralysis of the eyelid muscles. (The Latin word *hypnos* means sleep.) Braid's trance-induction technique of having a subject gaze steadily at an object has now become almost a standard procedure in hypnosis.

Later a number of researchers began to experiment with hyponosis. Jean-Martin Charcot (1825–1893), a neurosurgeon at La Salpêtrière Hospital in Paris and the leading neurologist of his time, was among them. His initial experiments with hypnosis led him to abandon it in favor of more traditional methods of treating hysteria, which he claimed was caused by organic damage to the nervous system. However, he was eventually won over by the results of other experimenters, and his own subsequent use of hypnosis in the study of hysteria did much to legitimize the application of hypnosis in medicine.

The experimenters most instrumental in Charcot's conversion were two physicians practicing in Nancy, in eastern France. First working separately, Ambroise-Auguste Liébeault (1823–1904) and Hippolyte-Marie Bernheim (1840–1919) later came together to work as a team. As a result of their experiments, they hypothesized that hysteria was a form of self-hypnosis. The results they obtained in treating patients attracted other scientists, who collectively became known as the "Nancy school." In treating hysterical patients under hypnosis, they were often able to *remove* symptoms of paralysis, deafness, blindness, and anesthesia. Likewise, they were able to *produce* these symptoms in normal subjects through hypnosis. Their work demonstrated impressively that suggestion could cause certain forms of mental illness; that is, symptoms of mental and physical disorders could have a psychological rather than an organic explanation.

This conclusion represented a major breakthrough, and the idea that psychological processes could produce mental and physical disturbances began to gain credence among several physicians who were using hypnosis. Among them was the Viennese doctor Josef Breuer (1842–1925). He discovered accidentally that, after one of his female patients spoke quite freely about her past traumatic experiences while in a trance, many of her symptoms abated or disappeared. He achieved even greater success when the patient recalled previously forgotten memories and relived their emotional aspects. This latter technique became known as the **cathartic method.** It foreshadowed psychoanalysis, one of the major theories of psychopathology, whose founder, Sigmund Freud (1856–1939), was influenced by Charcot and was a colleague of Breuer. Freud's theories have had a great and lasting influence in the field of abnormal psychology.

WHAT LIES AHEAD IN THIS TEXT

The first part of this text is intended to acquaint you with the study of abnormal psychology. In this first chapter, we have marked out the boundaries of our subject and surveyed its historical antecedents. In Chapters 2 and 3 we discuss several explanations of abnormal behavior, including those that have their roots in the organic and psychological views of mental disorder. Chapter 4 is a discussion of the contemporary means by which abnormal behavior is classified and individual problems are assessed. Then, to help you understand and evaluate the psychological research cited and described in this text, Chapter 5 explains the use of scientific methods in abnormal psychology.

The next four parts cover specific disorders. Part 2 contains four chapters on disorders that are characterized predominantly by anxiety and stress. In Part 3 we examine disorders commonly associated with social problems: crime, alcohol and drug abuse, and psychosexual problems. Part 4 covers disorders that often have an exceptional impact on individual

functioning, those that used to be labeled psychotic disorders—schizophrenia and the affective disorders. Suicide, too, is discussed in Part 4. Part 5 is devoted primarily to organic brain dysfunction and mental retardation.

Finally, in Part 6, we discuss and evaluate the major approaches to therapy, as well as an exciting and relatively new field—community psychology—that seeks to identify and implement ways to prevent disorders from occurring.

In Chapters 2 and 3, we shall discuss the case of Steven V. Gradually, we will uncover more and more of his past. You will be able to take part in a search through the details of Steve's life for clues to his current condition. Then, in Chapter 20, we shall discuss a therapeutic approach to Steve's problems. There you will also see how Steve's therapist solved the dilemma brought about by Steve's threat against Linda.

Steve's behaviors are, by any definition, abnormal. But Steve does not suffer from every mental disorder known to psychology. His problems are different from those faced, for example, by the mentally retarded child, by the eighty-pound teenager suffering from anorexia nervosa, or by the older person deteriorating from Alzheimer's disease. Why spend so much time with Steven V.?

There are two good reasons to dwell on Steve. The first is to emphasize the fact that abnormal behavior is nonetheless human behavior. We hope that Steve will become, for you, an animate human being rather than some specimen exhibiting strange behavior. (Steve is actually a composite character based on various clients whom the authors have treated.)

Second, through Steve's psychological history we can examine a variety of concerns and issues that arise in virtually every case of abnormal behavior. What are the most important features of the behavior? Would all psychologists diagnose a given condition similarly? What kind of treatment, in what setting, would promise the best results? And so on. Steve's case provides a format for discussing such questions more explicitly and concretely than we could in the more conventional textbook discourse.

We would like to close this chapter with a word of caution. To be human is to encounter difficulties and problems in life. A course in

abnormal psychology dwells on human problems, and many of these problems are familiar to us all. As a result, we may be prone to the "medical student syndrome" (see Focus 1.4): Reading about a disorder may lead us to suspect we *have* the disorder or that a friend or relative has it. This is a common reaction to

FOCUS 1.4

"I Have It Too": The Medical Student Syndrome

Medical students probably caught it first. As they read about physical disorders and listened to lecturers describe illnesses, some students began to imagine that they themselves had one disorder or another. *Diarrhea? Fatigue? Trouble sleeping? That's me!* Thus could a cluster of symptoms—no matter how mild or how briefly experienced—lead some people to suspect that they were very sick.

Students who take a course that examines psychopathology may be equally prone to believe they have a mental disorder that is described in their text. It is possible, of course, that some of these students do suffer from a disorder and would benefit from counseling or therapy. Most, however, are merely experiencing an exaggerated sense of their susceptibility to disorders. In one study, it was found that one of every five individuals responded *yes* to the question "Have you ever felt that you were going to have a nervous breakdown?" Of course, most of those people never suffered an actual breakdown (U.S. Department of Health, Education and Welfare 1971).

Two influences in particular may make us susceptible to these imagined disorders. One is the universality of the human experience. All of us have experienced misfortunes in life. We can all remember and relate to feelings of anxiety, unhappiness,

guilt, lack of self-confidence, and even thoughts of suicide. In most cases, however, these feelings are normal reactions to stressful situations, not symptoms of pathology. Depression that follows the loss of a loved one, or anxiety prior to giving a speech to a large audience, may be perfectly normal and appropriate. The second influence is our tendency to compare our own functioning with our *perceptions* of how other people are functioning. The outward behaviors of fellow students may lead us to conclude that they experience few difficulties in life, are self-assured and confident, and are invulnerable to mental disturbance. If we were privy to their inner thoughts and feelings, however, we might be surprised to find that they share our apprehension and insecurities.

If you see yourself anywhere in the pages of this book, we hope you will take the time to discuss the matter with a friend or your professor. You may be responding to pressures that you have not encountered before—a heavy course load, for example—and to which you have not yet adjusted. These are things that other people can help point out to you. On the other hand, if your discussion *supports* your suspicion that you have a problem, then by all means consider getting a professional evaluation.

the study of abnormal behavior, but one that it pays to guard against.

SUMMARY

1. The objectives of abnormal psychology are to describe, explain, predict, and control behaviors that are strange or unusual. Various criteria may be used to define such behaviors. Statistical criteria define abnormality in terms of those behaviors that occur least frequently in the population. Ideal mental health criteria characterize abnormality as an inability to attain some positive goal. The various practical criteria define abnormality on the basis of discomfort, either physical or psychological, suffered by the affected individual; the bizarreness of the individual's actions; or the inefficiency of the individual in filling his or her life roles. It may be that a single criterion or viewpoint is not sufficient but that abnormality should be defined from the combined vantage points of society, the individual, and the mental health professional.

2. Mental health problems are widespread in the United States, and more and more Americans are seeking professional help. The result has been a gigantic growth in the number of mental health professionals practicing in the United States. These professionals include clinical psychologists, counseling psychologists, psychiatrists, psychoanalysts, psychiatric social workers, and marriage and family counselors.

3. Many of our current concepts of mental illness have their roots in past beliefs and practices. Ancient people believed in demonology and attributed abnormal behaviors to evil spirits that inhabited the victim's body. Treatment consisted of trephining or exorcism. Rational and scientific explanations of abnormality emerged during the Greco–Roman era. Especially influential was the thinking of Hippocrates, who believed that abnormal behavior was due to brain pathology. However, the collapse of the Roman Empire ushered in a revival of demonology. During the Middle Ages, famine, pestilence, and dynastic wars caused much social and personal disorganization. Group disorders known as mass madness drove people increasingly to the Church for guidance. The Church's response, the endorsement of witch hunts, reinforced a belief in evil, supernatural powers. Among the numerous men, women, and children who were tortured and killed as witches were some whom we would today call mentally ill. A return to rationalism and scientific inquiry after the Renaissance was followed by heightened interest in humanitarian methods of treating the mentally ill.

4. In the nineteenth and twentieth centuries major medical breakthroughs fostered a belief in the organic roots of mental illness. The discovery of the microorganism that caused general paresis was especially important in this regard. Scientists were heartened by the belief that they would eventually find organic causes for all mental disorders. The successful practice of mesmerism (hypnosis) supported another view, however. The uncovering of a relationship between hypnosis and hysteria corroborated the belief that psychological processes could produce many emotional disturbances.

KEY TERMS

abnormal behavior Behavior that departs from some norm and is detrimental to the affected individual or to others

abnormal psychology The scientific study whose objectives are to describe, explain, predict, and control behaviors that are considered strange or unusual

biogenic view The belief or theory that mental disorders have a physical or physiological basis

brain pathology A dysfunction or disease of the brain

cathartic method The therapeutic use of verbal expression to release pent-up unconscious conflicts

humanism An emphasis on human welfare and on the worth and uniqueness of the individual

moral treatment movement A shift to more humane treatment of the mentally disturbed, generally attributed to Philippe Pinel

psychodiagnosis An attempt to describe, assess, and systematically draw inferences about an individual's psychological disorder

psychogenic view The belief or theory that mental disorders are caused by psychological and emotional factors

syndrome A cluster of symptoms that tend to occur together and are believed to be indicative of a particular disorder

therapy A program of systematic intervention whose purpose is to modify a client's behavioral, affective, or cognitive state

2
Biogenic and Psychogenic Models of Abnormal Behavior

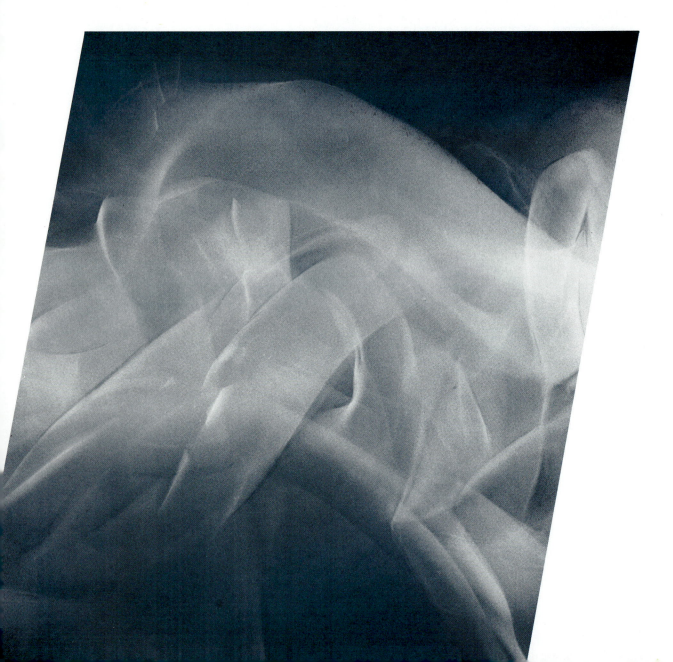

In Chapter 1 we described the rise of humanism in society's attitude toward mental disorders. As enlightenment conquered superstition in the eighteenth and nineteenth centuries, the mentally disturbed were increasingly regarded as unfortunate human beings who deserved respectful and humane treatment, not as monsters inhabited by the devil.

This humanistic view gave rise, in the late nineteenth and early twentieth centuries, to two differing schools of thought about the causes of mental disorders. According to one group of thinkers, mental disorders were *biogenic*—that is, caused by biological problems. The disturbed individual, this group contended, was displaying symptoms of physical disease or damage. A second group of theorists found organic explanations inadequate. These thinkers believed that abnormal behavior was essentially *psychogenic*, rooted not in cells and tissues but in the invisible complexities of the human mind.

In this chapter we trace the evolution of these two schools of thought and bring them up to date. We begin with the biogenic perspective and then examine three psychogenic perspectives: the psychoanalytic theory first articulated by Sigmund Freud and the more recent humanistic and existential perspectives. Later, in Chapter 3, we shall discuss two additional perspectives on abnormal behavior, the behavioral and family systems theories.

The five theories that we shall examine are by no means the only possible explanations of abnormal behavior. One survey identified more than 130 such theories in the United States alone (National Institute of Mental Health 1975). However, many of these are variants of the more basic theories to be discussed here; others have never gained widespread acceptance.

To help bring the major theories to life, and to show how they may be applied to individual problems, we continue in Chapters 2 and 3 to explore the case of Steven V. Immediately after our discussion of each major approach, we shall examine Steve's problems through the eyes and insights of a hypothetical adherent to that approach.

Let us begin our discussion by clarifying two terms that we shall use frequently. The first is **psychopathology,** which clinical psychologists use as a synonym for abnormal behavior. The second is **model,** a term that requires a more elaborate explanation.

MODELS IN THE STUDY OF PSYCHOPATHOLOGY

When they need to discuss a phenomenon that is difficult to describe or explain, scientists often make use of an analogy, in which they liken the phenomenon to something more concrete. A **model** is such an analogy, and it is most often used to describe something that cannot be observed directly. In an analogy, terms, concepts, or principles are borrowed from one field and applied to another. The person who likens the heart to a pump or the eye to a camera is making use of a model.

When psychologists speak of deviant behavior as "mental illness" or refer to their "patients," they are borrowing the terminology of medicine and, in essence, applying a *medical model* of abnormal behavior. They may also describe certain external symptoms as being visible signs of deep underlying conflict. Again, the medical analogy is clear: Just as fevers, rashes, perspiration, or infections may be symptoms of a bacterial or viral invasion of the body, bizarre behavior may be a symptom of a mind "invaded" by unresolved conflicts.

Psychologists have used models extensively to help them conceptualize the causes of abnormal behavior, ask questions, determine what information or data are relevant, and interpret data. Each model is a means of viewing abnormal behavior, and it generally embodies a particular theoretical approach. Hence we tend to use the terms *model, theory, viewpoint,* and *perspective* somewhat interchangeably.

Every model, however apt, is limited in its usefulness. None provides all the answers. The complexity of human behavior and our relatively shallow understanding of it prevent psychologists from developing *the* definitive model.

But, as one prominent student of theories has pointed out, "Few theorists expect the models they adopt to represent accurately all of the features of psychopathology. Rather, the model is used merely as a way to visualize psychopathology 'as if it worked like this'" (Millon 1973).

In reality, most practicing clinicians do not adhere rigidly to any one model. In a survey of clinical psychologists, 64 percent identified their position as **eclectic** (Garfield and Kurtz 1975, 1976). These therapists remain open to all perspectives; they borrow diagnostic techniques and treatment strategies from all approaches and use them selectively with clients. To the eclectic therapist, the important question is always "What theories will work best with this particular client, in what setting, and with what expected therapeutic outcome?"

To be sure, there are disadvantages to the eclectic approach (Brammer and Shostrom 1984). Because it often is not rooted in a carefully constructed system of concepts and assumptions, the eclectic approach may result in uncritical picking and choosing: one therapeutic technique from column A, another from column B, and so on down the menu of theories. Furthermore, any novel mixture of concepts and techniques necessarily lacks a substantial base of research to show how effective it has proved to be; it is almost educated guess work. And finally, therapists who do not associate themselves with a traditional theory of psychopathology may be especially prone to embrace the fad therapy of the moment.

Despite these potential shortcomings, eclecticism is inevitable in the absence of a single "true" model of abnormal behavior. In fact, most psychologists see considerable value in an eclectic approach. They recognize that different models of psychopathology do not utterly contradict each other on every point. Rather, the elements of various models can complement each other to produce a broad and detailed explanation of an individual's condition.

THE BIOGENIC MODEL

The idea that mental disorders are caused by organic problems was proposed by Hippocrates around 400 B.C., but this organic viewpoint was not generally accepted until the late eighteenth and early nineteenth centuries. The contributions of Wilhelm Griesinger, Emil Kraepelin, and other pioneers; Pasteur's formulation of the germ theory of disease; and Fritz Schaudinn's discovery of the microorganism that caused general paresis all reinforced the belief that abnormal behavior is symptomatic of organic disease. And, if every mental disorder has a physiological source, it should also have an organic cure. This is the essence of the **biogenic model** of psychopathology.

Support for the biogenic model

In the first half of the twentieth century, researchers and physicians, in their rush to find cures for abnormal behavior, made several other apparent advances that lent credibility to the biogenic model.

☐ In 1927 Julius Wagner von Jauregg was honored with the Nobel Prize in medicine for his discovery of so-called fever treatments. By infecting paretic patients with malaria and thus inducing high fevers, he was able to kill the syphilitic organism responsible for general paresis.

☐ In Germany, a treatment called insulin shock therapy seemed to have a positive effect on severely disordered patients. The patients were given high doses of insulin, which caused coma or convulsions. When the patients awoke, they appeared to be more rational and were easier to manage. Unfortunately, the possibility of irreversible coma, respiratory collapse, and other medical risks made insulin shock treatment quite dangerous.

☐ In 1933 Laszlo von Meduna acted on the mistaken belief that schizophrenia and epilepsy rarely occur in the same person and are thus incompatible disorders. (Evidence does not support this idea.) Meduna reported positive results with his *metrazol shock therapy,* in which metrazol, a chemical that produces seizures like those of grand mal epilepsy, was used to produce convulsive seizures in schizophrenic patients.

☐ In 1938 Ugo Cerletti and Lucio Bini, two Italian psychiatrists, administered the first electroshock treatment to a schizophrenic patient. Cerletti shared Meduna's belief that schizophrenia and epilepsy could not coexist in the same patient. Cerletti decided to use electric currents to induce seizures after discovering that agitated pigs in a slaughterhouse could be stupefied by electric shocks before slaughter. [This treatment was the forerunner of the electroconvulsive therapy (ECT) discussed in Chapter 20. Although ECT is still used today—with depressed patients rather than schizophrenics—it is a controversial treatment whose use has declined drastically in recent years (Fink 1979).]

☐ Another controversial physical treatment, a surgical procedure known as *lobotomy,* was introduced in the 1930s by Egas Moniz. In the procedure, the surgeon deliberately destroyed selected brain tissues. The result

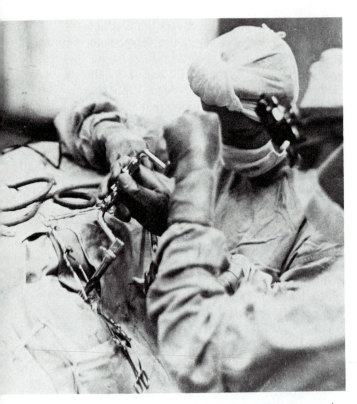

During a prefrontal lobotomy, surgeons used a drill to open the skull. Because of severe side-effects, lobotomies have rarely been used since the 1950's.

was a more docile patient—and, in many cases, sharply impaired memory and reduced cognitive skills. Although it was originally used only as a last resort, lobotomy soon became a fairly common treatment for severely disturbed patients. Between 1935 and 1950, at least 40,000 lobotomies were performed in the United States.

Note that nearly all these early organic treatments were based on mistaken notions or false assumptions. Even their creators did not know exactly why they worked to the extent that they did. Note too that most of the treatments harmed many patients. Nevertheless, because they were *physiological* treatments that had seemingly appropriate *behavioral* effects, they reinforced the belief that some or-

ganic function or mechanism had gone askew in the psychiatric patient.

There are, of course, many biological causes for psychological disorders. Damage to the nervous system is one: As Schaudinn demonstrated, general paresis results from brain damage caused by parasitic microorganisms. Tumors, strokes, excessive intake of alcohol or drugs, and external trauma (such as a blow to the head) have also been linked to cognitive, emotional, and behavioral pathology. However, two specific biological sources deserve special attention here, for they have given rise to important modern biogenic theories of psychopathology. These causes are body chemistry and heredity.

Biochemical theories

Most physiological and mental processes, from sleeping and digestion to reading and thinking, involve chemical actions within the body. Thus it seems likely that body chemistry has at least some effect on behavior. The basic premise of the biochemical theories is that chemical imbalances underlie mental disorders. Support for these theories has been provided by research into anxiety disorders, affective disorders (both depression and bipolar disorder, or manic depression), and schizophrenia (McGeer and McGeer 1980).

Differential effects of drugs   The search for chemical causes and cures for mental disorders accelerated tremendously in the early 1950s with the discovery that different tranquilizers have different effects on mental disorders (NIMH 1970). These drugs (chemicals) can play the role of "bloodhounds" in leading us to specific problem areas in an individual's biochemical system (Sahakian 1979). For example, some drugs, such as diazepam (Valium) and chlordiazepoxide (Librium), dramatically decrease anxiety in milder disorders but do nothing for schizophrenia—even though schizophrenics commonly exhibit anxiety. Certain other drugs (the phenothiazines) affect schizophrenics but not individuals with phobias or panic disorder.

Such findings also seem to indicate that the milder (neurotic) disturbances are totally different from the more severe (psychotic) disorders (Snyder et al. 1974). They cast doubt on the assumption that mental disorders exist on a continuum from the mildest to the most severe.

Nevertheless, the fact is that a number of different sorts of mental disturbances are responsive to specific medications. According to some psychologists, a sophisticated understanding of drug therapy should be part of every clinician's repertoire of treatment strategies (Wender and Klein 1981). The success of drug treatments, they say points to the effectiveness of medication in normalizing deep abnormality and relieving symptoms. If drugs do not provide a permanent cure, then neither (in most cases) does the traditional psychotherapy. The discoveries that antipsychotic drugs have beneficial effects on schizophrenics, that lithium is useful in controlling affective disorders, and that tricyclic and monoamine oxidase inhibitors alleviate symptoms of severely depressed patients have led some psychologists to seek "the right drug for the right patient."

The dopamine hypothesis Much research into the biochemistry of mental disorders has focused on the **neuroregulators,** chemicals that transmit information from nerve cell to nerve cell and control the level of nerve cell activity. Increasing numbers of neuroregulators have been implicated in abnormal behaviors in the past few decades.

Various researchers have studied particular neuroregulators in detail, seeking to identify the specific moods and behaviors that these chemicals influence. This research has yielded a number of hypotheses about how certain disorders develop. One particularly popular explanation is the *dopamine hypothesis*.

Dopamine is a neuroregulator that has been implicated in the development of schizophrenia. The **dopamine hypothesis** proposes that schizophrenia may be the result of an excess of dopamine at certain synaptic sites in the brain (Snyder 1976; Langer, Brown, and Docherty 1981). Researchers have speculated that schizophrenics may possess too many postsynaptic dopamine receptors or that their receptors are supersensitive to dopamine. Evidence in support of the dopamine hypothesis comes from two primary sources. First, antipsychotic drugs like the phenothiazines, which control the hallucinations and delusions that many schizophrenics experience, reduce or block dopamine transmission. Second, drugs like amphetamines, which increase such activity, often exaggerate psychotic symptoms in active and partially remitted schizophrenics (Langer, Brown, and Docherty 1981).

The dopamine hypothesis remains the most compelling biochemical explanation of how a severe disorder develops. But evidence has accumulated that challenges the credibility of the hypothesis (Lake et al. 1980). For example, dopamine-blocking drugs accomplish their blocking effect within hours. This relatively quick reaction contrasts with the clinical picture of *gradual* improvement in schizophrenics. Furthermore, the bizarre behaviors associated with some schizophrenic conditions are not reduced by phenothiazine treatment.

Of course, no single hypothesis can provide a completely satisfactory explanation of all abnormal behavior. Researchers seeking a single neuroregulator as the cause of all mental disorders should instead be looking for the hundreds—or perhaps thousands—of pieces in the biochemical puzzle.

Genetic explanations

It seems evident that genetics also plays an important part in the development of certain abnormal conditions. For instance, it has been shown that "nervousness" can be inherited in animals by breeding generations of dogs that were either fearful or friendly (Murphree and

Dykman 1965). There is evidence that autonomic nervous system (ANS) reactivity may be inherited in humans as well; that is, some people may be born with an ANS that makes an unusually strong response to stimuli. But to show that anxiety is inherited, researchers must show that anxiety is caused by biological rather than environmental factors, that closer genetic relationships produce greater similarity of ANS reactivity in human beings, and that people with marked anxiety have similar ANS patterns (Gottesman and Shields 1976).

Biological inheritance is transmitted by the genes. A person's genetic makeup is called his or her **genotype;** interaction between the genotype and the environment results in the person's **phenotype,** or physical and behavioral characteristics. However, at times it is difficult to determine which influence predominates. For example, characteristics such as eye color are determined solely by the coding of the genes (genotype). But other physical characteristics, such as height, are determined partly by the genetic code and partly by environmental factors. Undernourished children can grow up shorter than the height they are genetically capable of reaching. On the other hand, even the most effective nutrition cannot spur people to grow taller than their "programmed" height limit.

As is detailed more fully in Chapter 16, one of the most useful procedures for studying the contributions of heredity is to compare the degree of similarity between identical twins and same-sex twins who are not identical. Identical or **monozygotic** (MZ) twins are twins derived from a single egg; they have the same genetic makeup. It can be assumed that differences between MZ twins are due to their environment. **Dizygotic** (DZ) twins, derived from two eggs, do not share the same genes.

Numerous studies of human twins indicate that MZ twins tend to be more alike on autonomic measures than DZ twins (Kringlen 1964; Cohen et al. 1972; Vandenberg, Clark, and Samuels 1965; Lader and Wing 1966). A study of anxiety reactions among 17 pairs of MZ twins and 28 pairs of DZ twins also found strong evidence that there is an inherited component to anxiety reactions (Slater and Shields 1969). In 65 percent of the cases where one MZ twin received a diagnosis of marked anxiety, the other twin received the same diagnosis. By contrast, both DZ twins received a diagnosis of marked anxiety in only 13 percent of the cases.

These results do not explain why, in 35 percent of the MZ cases, one identical twin became disordered and the other did not. It seems, however, that interactions between heredity and environment can either facilitate or retard the manifestation of disorders (Thomas, Chess, and Birch 1968). For example, a person with an inherited predisposition to anxiety may be born into a benign environment, peopled with supportive parents and friends, that retards anxiety development.

Overall, it is clear that heredity influences autonomic reactions, that heredity contributes to the development of anxiety reactions, and that individual exposure to the environment can moderate the effects of an inherited predisposition.

There also appears to be a strong correlation between genetic inheritance and the development of bipolar affective disorder, some forms of schizophrenia, and certain kinds of mental retardation. Down's syndrome, for example, is a result of chromosomal aberrations. Except in some specific cases, however, the exact influence of the genes is difficult to ascertain. Because law and basic morality prohibit selective breeding of humans, we rely on correlational studies in seeking the relationship between heredity and mental disorders. But such studies are really just comparisons of existing frequencies of mental disorders in various populations; no matter how strong the correlations they reveal, they do not demonstrate a cause-and-effect relationship. For that reason, they must be interpreted with caution.

Criticisms of the biogenic model

The biogenic model of abnormal behavior, which drifted out of favor when psychoanalysis was at the peak of its influence in the 1940s has recently enjoyed a resurgence of popularity. But the biogenic model of mental disorders has some major shortcomings.

First, one of its basic tenets is that abnormal behavior results from an underlying physical condition, such as damage to the brain or malfunction of neural processes. It implies that treatment should be aimed at controlling the underlying disease by changing the individual's biochemistry or removing toxic substances. This approach ignores the many empirical findings that emphasize the importance of environmental factors. It does not acknowledge the interpersonal and social causes of abnormal behavior. Nor does it adequately account for more complex abnormal behavior for which no organic etiology, or cause, can be found. For example, the American Psychiatric Association recognizes five categories of schizophrenia. One of the categories, the "undifferentiated" type, is a grab-bag classification that includes schizophrenics who exhibit atypical as well as traditional symptoms. Biochemical treatment has mixed and uneven effects on these patients.

Second, the biogenic model implicitly assumes a correspondence between organic dysfunction and mental dysfunction. Environmental or cultural influences are thought to have minimal impact. But rarely are the equations of human behavior so uncomplicated. More often there are a multitude of causes behind any human behavior, and environmental factors seem to play as important a role as any other. Increasingly, mental health research has focused on the **diathesis–stress theory,** originally proposed by Meehl (1962) and developed further by Rosenthal (1970). The diathesis–stress theory holds that it is not a particular abnormality that is inherited but rather a predisposition to develop illness. Cer-

Members of all four generations shown in this family portrait bear a striking resemblance to each other. Clearly, some characteristics are determined in large part by the genetic code.

tain environmental forces, called *stressors,* may activate the predisposition, resulting in a disorder. Alternatively, in a benign and supportive environment, the abnormality may never materialize.

A third shortcoming, related to the preceding one, is revealed by our accumulating knowledge that biochemical changes often occur *because of* environmental forces. We know, for example, that stress-produced fear and anger cause the secretion of adrenalin and noradrenalin. Similarly, it could be that excess amounts of chemicals such as dopamine in schizophrenics tend to *result from the disorder* rather than to cause it.

Last, wholesale adoption of the biogenic model could foster helplessness in the patient by eliminating patient responsibility. The patient might be seen—both by the therapist and by himself or herself—as a passive participant to be treated only with appropriate drugs and medical interventions. For patients who are already suffering from feelings of helplessness or loss of control, such an approach could be devastating.

A BIOGENIC VIEW OF STEVEN V.

How would a biogenically oriented psychologist view the case of Steven V.? If Steve's therapist were so oriented, we believe he would discuss Steve's behavior in the following terms.

Before I interpret the symptoms displayed by Steven V. and speculate on what they mean, I must stress my belief that many "mental disorders" have a strong biological basis. I do accept the importance of environmental influences; but, in my view, the biological bases of abnormality are too often overlooked by psychologists. This seems clearly to be the case with Steven V.

Much of Steve's medical history is missing from his case records, along with important information about his biological and developmental milestones. We do not have the data necessary to chart a family tree, which would illustrate whether other members of his family have suffered from a similar disorder. This lack of information about possible inherited tendencies in Steve's current behavior pattern is a serious shortcoming.

At age 15, Steve was given a diagnosis of manic–depressive psychosis (now called bipolar affective disorder). Pharmacological treatment was moderately effective in controlling his symptoms. After Steve's condition became stabilized, lithium carbonate treatment was instituted for a period of time, and Steve was free of symptoms during that period. Unfortunately, Steve apparently disliked taking medication and did so only sporadically.

In any case, there is evidence to document and support a diagnosis of bipolar affective disorder. Steve displays the behaviors associated with this disorder, ranging from manic episodes (elevated mood characterized by expansiveness, hyperactivity, flight of ideas, and inflated self-esteem) to depressive episodes (depressed mood characterized by loss of interest, feelings of worthlessness, and thoughts of death or suicide). These symptoms are not of recent origin but probably were evident very early in his life. Steve's first contact with a mental health professional was with the school psychologist in kindergarten, who described him as "autistic-like." I believe the child psychiatrist whom Steve subsequently visited was correct in saying Steve was not autistic. The chief symptoms described in his early years and used to indicate autism (social isolation and unresponsiveness) are similar to those of depression. I suspect Steve was experiencing a major depressive episode, and it may not have been his first. Unfortunately, we do not have access to Steve's pediatrician, who may have observed even earlier signs of bipolar disorder. What we do have, however, are several statements from his parents indicating that "even at birth, Steve did not respond in a normal way."

Thus the following conclusions can be drawn: Steve's disorder was evident early in his life. In spite of a shortage of information, there is some indication that other relatives may have suffered from a similar disorder. The most defensible diagnosis is bipolar affective disorder. The most effective treatment in the past was drug treatment.

These conclusions strongly support a biological interpretation of the patient's psychopathology. Heredity seems to have played a part; we have some evidence that relatives may have suffered a similar disorder. The precise biological mechanism that triggered the disorder is probably within one of the two major classes of neurotransmitters (catechol-amines and indoleamines). If this diagnosis is accurate, the patient should resume taking medication. Of course, stressful life events may also be contributing to Steve's emotional problems, and I intend to continue psychotherapy with him. But I believe that many of Steve's depressive episodes would have occurred regardless of *psychological* intervention. And they will probably continue to occur unless Steve controls his biological problem with medication. I am not an M.D. and therefore cannot prescribe drugs, so I have arranged for Steve to visit a physician at the college medical center. Only when Steve's organic problem is under control can I or any other therapist begin to make headway with Steve's problems in relating to other people.

THE PSYCHOANALYTIC MODEL

The **psychoanalytic model** of abnormal behavior has two main distinguishing features. First, this approach places strong emphasis on childhood experiences in explaining adult behavior. Psychoanalysts view disorders in adults as the result of traumas or anxieties experienced in childhood. Second, the psychoanalytic model holds that many of these childhood-based anxieties operate unconsciously; because they are too threatening for the adult individual to face, they are repressed through mental defense mechanisms. As a result, individuals exhibit symptoms they are unable to understand. To eliminate the symptoms, the therapist must make the patient aware of these unconscious anxieties or conflicts.

The early development of psychoanalytic theory is generally credited to Sigmund Freud (1938, 1949), a Viennese neurologist. Before he developed the technique of psychoanalysis, Freud had already made significant contributions in neurology. He was acquainted with the methods of the "Nancy school" (see Chapter 1) and had worked with Josef Breuer, a colleague who was successfully using hypnosis to treat hysterical patients (those who exhibited physical symptoms for which no organic cause could be found). This background led his creative and tenacious mind into the field of psychiatry. During his clinical work, Freud became convinced that powerful mental processes could remain hidden from consciousness and could cause abnormal behaviors. He believed the therapist's role was to help the patient achieve insight into these unconscious processes. Although he originally relied on hypnosis for this purpose, Freud soon dropped it in favor of other techniques. He felt that cures were more likely to be permanent if patients became aware of their problems without the aid of hypnosis. This led Freud to his formulation of psychoanalysis.

An elderly Sigmund Freud (1856–1939), at work in his study, with his dog Jo-fi, a chow.

Although critics have vehemently attacked the psychoanalytic view on the grounds that it is not a scientific theory, there is no doubt of its profound impact on Western thought. Not only is it an extremely popular explanation of abnormal behavior among the lay public, but many other theories of psychopathology are derivatives of, or reactions to, its basic tenets. "Slips of the tongue" or pen, the dynamic workings of the unconscious, the importance of childhood experiences, "defense mechanisms," and countless other concepts and terms that permeate our thinking and language have their roots in the work of Sigmund Freud.

Personality structure

Freud believed that the personality is composed of three major components and that all behavior is a product of their interaction. He called these mental structures the id, the ego, and the superego.

Id The **id** is the only component of the personality present at birth, and it includes the instinctual drives. Both the ego and the superego develop from the id. The id is subjective, impulsive, and pleasure-seeking; it is completely selfish. It seeks the immediate gratification of instinctual needs and the reduction of tension (this is Freud's *pleasure principle*). If persons operated totally under the influence of id impulses, they would be wild and unsocialized animals. According to Freud, the most dangerous impulses, which need to be controlled, are those that derive from the sexual and aggressive instincts. Psychopathology inevitably involves one or both of these instincts.

Ego   The **ego** comes into existence because the human personality must be able to cope with the external world if it is to survive. Unlike the id, which operates in accordance with the pleasure principle, the ego is influenced by a *reality principle;* it is the realistic part of the mind. For that reason, it is often in conflict with the id. The ego's principal role is to act as mediator between our instinctual urges and the surrounding environment. Although the ego may delay immediate gratification, its basic purpose is not to prevent it but rather to ensure that it is obtained at a socially appropriate time and place.

Let us say a young woman has just come back from a long cruise without any male companionship. As she disembarks she feels strong sexual impulses. An attractive male appears. His approach heightens her sexual desire. If she were to obey her id demands for release of energy, she could conceivably approach this young man and seek immediate gratification of her sex drive. However, her ego prevents this ill-advised and perhaps dangerous behavior by delaying her sexual activity until she finds an appropriate consenting sex partner. Note that the ego decision is dictated by *realistic* considerations (the possibility of embarrassment or punishment for unrestrained sexual advances) rather than by moral judgment.

Superego   Moral judgments and moralistic considerations are the domain of the **superego.** The superego is the internal representation of society's traditional values and ideals, as taught by parents or significant others. It is composed of the *conscience,* which inculcates guilt feelings about engaging in immoral or unethical behavior, and the *ego ideal,* which rewards altruistic or moral behavior with feelings of pride. The superego is the moral arm of the personality, so it strives for perfection instead of pleasure; its goals are idealistic rather than realistic. Thus the superego is at odds not only with the id's sexual and aggressive impulses but also with the ego; it attempts to substitute moralistic goals for realistic ones.

Take the case of a young soldier who has been raised to respect and value human life. He may find the act of killing abhorrent even in a war. However, witnessing the death of several of his closest friends in bloody hand-to-hand combat may cause the soldier to feel severe conflict. Filled with anger and a desire to avenge the death of his friends (id impulses), he may also feel guilty about having these thoughts (superego versus id). Now suppose he suddenly encounters a new situation: He spots an enemy soldier aiming a rifle at him from behind a tree. Here the soldier experiences a conflict between superego and ego. His superego tells him not to kill because it is "bad" (a moralistic consideration), whereas his ego tells him to defend himself (a realistic consideration).

Instincts

According to Freud, **instincts** are the energy system from which the personality operates. Instincts give rise to our thoughts and actions and fuel their expression. They have four major features: a source, a driving force or energy, an aim, and an object.

The *source* of an instinct is the biological process itself. The *energy* of an instinct is a state of biological deprivation; for example, hunger is the result of being deprived of food. Tension builds up and causes discomfort. The *aim* of the instinct, therefore, is to reduce or remove this tension. The *object* or objects of the instinct are those external things or events that satisfy or ease the tension (for example, food for hunger and water for thirst).

Freud postulated two large classes of instincts: the life instincts and the death instincts.

Life instincts   The *life instincts,* also referred to by the Greek term *Eros,* consist of self-preservation (the need for food, air, water, and warmth) and the sexual drive. Because Freud felt that most bodily instincts relating to survival are fufilled, he did not deal much with self-preservation in his theory. Instead he focused on the sexual drive as the most important human motivation. The manifestation of sexual instincts, called the *libido,* plays a central role in Freud's theory of abnormal behavior. Freud's concept of *sex,* however, was much broader than that which is common today and might better be conceived of as "sensual pleasure."

Death instincts   During his later years Freud became convinced that there is a second large class of instincts. He termed these the *death instincts* (they are now popularly called *Thanatos*). The death instincts function antithetically to the life instincts, and their ultimate goal is the biological death of the organism. Freud saw aggression and hostility as manifestations of the death instincts. He interpreted suicide as aggression against the self and saw war as the mass expression of the death instincts. It is interesting that Freud formulated his notion of the death instincts when he found himself facing old age and the ravages of jaw cancer.

Freud emphasized sex and aggression as the dominant human instincts because he recognized that society places strong prohibitions on these drives and that, as a result, people are taught to inhibit them. A profound need to express one's instincts is often frightening and can lead one to deny their existence. Indeed,

Freud felt that most impulses are hidden from consciousness but that, more often than not, they determine human actions.

Psychosexual stages

According to psychoanalytic theory, all human beings develop through a sequence of five stages. Each of these five **psychosexual stages** brings with it a unique challenge. If unfavorable circumstances prevail, the personality may be drastically affected. Because Freud stressed the importance of early childhood experiences, he saw the human personality as largely determined in the first five years of life—during the **oral, anal,** and **phallic stages.** The last two psychosexual stages are the **latency** and **genital stages.**

Oral stage   The first year of life is characterized by a focus of instincts on the oral cavity. For infants the mouth is not only the primary source of pleasurable sensations, as in sucking and feeding, but also the mechanism with which they can respond to and deal with the outside world. Infants place almost everything in their mouths; they explore objects through oral activities.

The importance of the oral stage for later development lies in how much *fixation* occurs during that stage. (**Fixation** is the arresting of emotional development at a particular psychosexual stage.) If the infant is traumatized in some way during this period, much fixation can occur; that is, some of the instinctual energy becomes trapped and does not move on to more mature stages. Consequently, the adult personality exhibits strong features of this stage. Passivity, helplessness, obesity, chronic smoking, and alcoholism may all be characteristics of an oral personality. The symbolism of these traits is readily apparent. An individual who as a baby was denied the oral gratification that results from a loving relationship with his or her mother may overeat

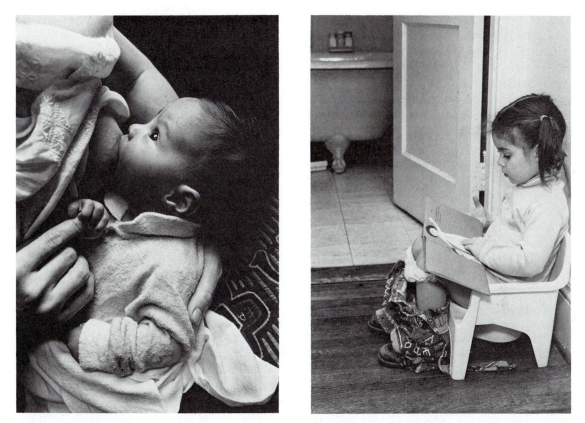

During the oral stage, the first stage of psychosexual development, the infant not only receives nourishment but also derives pleasure from sucking and being close to its mother. Later, during the anal (second) stage, toilet training can be a time of intense emotional conflict between parent and child—or it can be a time of cooperation, as evidenced by this toddler.

or drink excessively as a means of compensation. Freud believed that food can come to represent love.

Anal stage   Toward the end of the first year of life, the anal region becomes the zone of pleasurable sensations, and the second psychosexual stage begins. During the anal stage, parents demand that the child control what is a normal biological and innate urge—evacuation of feces. Toilet training is rarely achieved smoothly, and the child may react in one of two ways. First, the child may defy this early attempt to regulate his or her anal gratification and refuse to defecate. The child who

takes this tack often becomes locked into battle with the parents. A parent may insist that the child stay in the bathroom until he or she has had a bowel movement. Because the child is afraid to defy the parent in a direct way, he or she may simply refuse to comply. Children have been known to remain constipated for days until parents finally call a truce. A child who gets involved in this struggle may exhibit an *anal–retentive* character as an adult. This type of personality is stubborn, stingy, and constantly procrastinating. The *passive–aggressive* individual is one who is said to be fixated in the anal stage. Such a person finds it difficult to express anger or hostility in a direct manner. For example, some clients may arrive late at a therapy session, or may not come at all, as a way of indirectly expressing resistance.

Alternatively, a child may comply but anxiously. Fear of parents coupled with rage at interference with the id's demand for gratification leads to exaggerated compliance as a means of expressing anger. Symbolically, the expulsion of feces or gas from the bowels at inappropriate times may represent a revolt against authority. This kind of revolt is referred to as the *anal–sadistic* phase and is most characteristic of the *obsessive–compulsive* individual (one who is frugal, orderly, punctual, and cruel). Doing things "by the book," following rules and regulations, and keeping things in order may be seen as attempts to control rage and anger.

Again, symbolism plays a major role in this particular stage. To many children, feces represent objects of considerable interest, and the process of defecation may be fascinating. Freud felt that the feces came to represent material possessions, such as money. Children often feel that their feces are part of them, that they have created something of value. A proper resolution of this stage is believed to result in a creative and productive person.

Phallic stage   During the third and fourth years of life, the genitals (the boy's penis and the girl's clitoris) become the focus of pleasurable sensations. In both sexes, incestuous feelings for the opposite-sex parent become very strong. The **Oedipus complex** and its female counterpart, the **Electra complex,** appear at this phallic stage. The terms defining these complexes are taken from ancient Greek myths: Oedipus killed his father and married his mother; Electra conspired to kill her mother to avenge the death of her beloved father.

In essence, the Oedipus complex is a *conflict*: a *wish* for a form of sexual possession of the mother (for her warmth, nurturance, and so on) countered by a *fear* of reprisal from a powerful rival for the mother's affection, the father. (**Castration anxiety** is the young boy's fear that the father will punish him for his forbidden desires by cutting off the guilty organ, his penis.) The conflict is resolved through the mechanism of **identification** with the parent of the same sex, which is motivated by reduction of fear ("If I am my father, then he can no longer hurt me") and attainment of the wish ("If I am my father, I possess my mother"). Through such identification the child takes on the values, sexual orientation, and mannerisms characteristic of adults of the same sex.

The Electra complex is characterized by **penis envy,** a desire by the female child to possess a penis. Because she lacks the valued organ, the female child believes castration has already taken place as a punishment by the mother. The child sees her mother as a hostile rival in competition for the father's penis. Like the Oedipus complex, the Electra conflict becomes very intense. The female child resolves it in the same way and for the same reasons as the male—by identifying with the same-sex parent. Consequently, according to Freud, the female accepts her "classic" feminine traits: passivity, dependency, and emotionalism. (See the discussion of Karen Horney's view rejecting the theory of penis envy farther on in this chapter.)

The phallic stage of development is crucial to sexual identity in later adult life. According to psychoanalytic theory, if incomplete resolution occurs, impotence, frigidity, promiscuity, and homosexuality may result. Because this stage is characterized by development of the superego, anxiety disorders and personality disorders have their roots in this stage. According to Freud, *hysteria* more than any other psychopathological disorder is the result of fixation at the phallic stage. (A "textbook" case is described in Focus 2.1, p. 52.) Freud saw hysteric symptoms as concealed sexual excitement. Moreover, the hysteric's sexual-

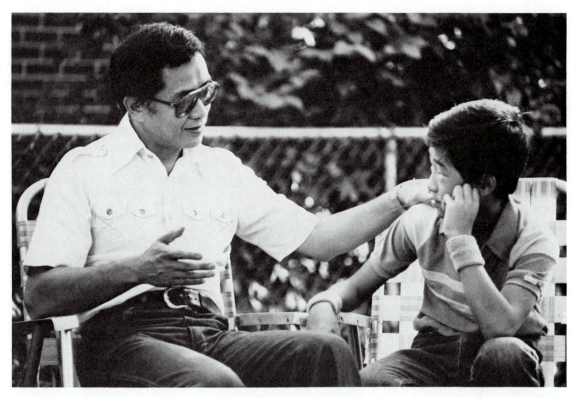

According to Freud, a young boy's identification with his father resolves the Oedipus conflict. As shown by this young man, boys will take on the values, sexual characteristics, and even the mannerisms of their fathers.

ity is infantile in character. He or she is unable to distinguish between incestuous love, based on genital gratification, and an orientation toward others in interpersonal relationships. The hysteric experiences conflicts relating to masturbation and masturbatory equivalents, manifested in hysterical symptoms such as tics, spasms, and uncontrollable muscular contractions.

Latency stage Freud believed that the years from six to twelve were generally devoid of sexual motivations. Developmental skills, activities, and interests are the primary concern during this latency stage. Sexuality is repressed because of strong social taboos against its expression. Children may become upset upon encountering overt sexual displays.

Genital stage The reawakening of sexual urges during puberty and adolescence ushers in the genital stage. Physiological and physical changes occur that drastically affect heterosexual relationships. The first relationship is generally *narcissistic* in nature: Affection is directed toward one's own body. True heterosexual love does not develop until the emotional investment can be transferred to a member of the opposite sex. That is, intense interest in one's own body and concern with its health indicate a ''self'' orientation rather than the ''other'' orientation needed for interpersonal relationships.

The Case of Lorna M.

Lorna was what Freud might consider a classic case of phallic sexuality, disguised in hysterical symptoms. Since the age of eight, her emotional attachment to her father had been highly visible. She would frequently cling to him, sit on his lap, or hug and kiss him. Her father seemed to encourage her behavior and would reciprocate the affectionate gestures, which bordered on the erotic. Lorna's mother had died in an automobile accident when Lorna was five years of age, so she enjoyed her father's total attention and jealously guarded her time with him. Lorna first began to develop muscular spasms in her abdomen and thighs at the age of fourteen. Her hysterical attacks seemed strongly correlated with her father's romantic interest in an attractive divorcée. The attacks generally occurred

only in the father's presence when he was about to see the woman.

Concerned about his daughter's condition, the father soon took her to a nearby clinic, where she was diagnosed as a *conversion hysteric*. Her attacks seemed suggestive of a woman having sexual intercourse; she would fall to the floor on her back and begin to undulate her hips and experience muscular spasms in her right thigh. She also reported nightmares of having sexual relations with an elderly man whose description sounded very much like her father's. Therapy did not seem to help her until the age of nineteen when, upon her father's marriage, she moved out of the home. At that time she became involved with an older man very similar to her father in temperament and physique.

Freud believed that a person who was able to transcend the various fixations would develop into a normal, healthy individual. Heterosexual interests, stability, vocational planning, marriage, and other social activities would become a person's prime concern during this stage.

Anxiety and psychopathology

Anxiety is at the root of Freud's theory of psychopathology. The three-part personality structure that Freud postulated can produce a number of conflict situations. Freud identified three types of anxiety (shown diagrammatically in Figure 2.1). *Realistic anxiety* occurs when there is potential danger from the external environment. When one smells smoke in a building, the ego warns one to take action to protect oneself from physical harm. *Moralistic*

anxiety results when an individual does not live up to his or her own moral standards or engages in unethical conduct. In this case, the ego warns of possible retaliation from the superego. *Neurotic anxiety* often results when id impulses seem to be getting out of hand, bursting through ego controls. In all these cases anxiety is a signal that something bad is about to happen and that appropriate steps should be taken to reduce the anxiety.

Although Freud dealt with all three types of anxiety, he concentrated mainly on neurotic anxiety. We shall do the same, although much of our discussion applies to the other two types as well. Current changes in the *Diagnostic and Statistical Manual* (DSM-III) of the American Psychiatric Association have replaced the traditional subcategories of neurotic behavior with other, more refined concepts, but we shall use the term *neurotic* because of its importance to Freud's theory.

Figure 2.1 *Three Types of Anxiety*

Freud believed that people suffer from three types of anxiety, arising from conflicts involving the id, ego, and superego. Each type is, in essence, a signal of impending danger.

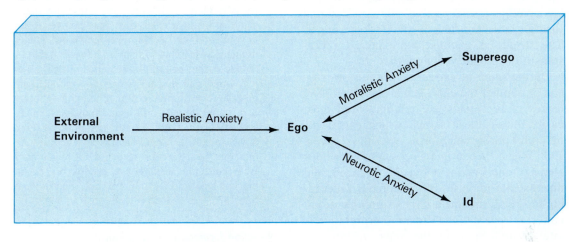

Defense mechanisms

Neurotic behavior develops from the threat of overwhelming anxiety, which may lead to full-scale panic. To forestall this panic, the ego often resorts to **defense mechanisms** to reduce anxiety. These mechanisms are ways of preventing awareness of anxiety-arousing impulses and thoughts. Defense mechanisms have three characteristics in common: They protect the individual from anxiety, they operate unconsciously, and they distort reality (Hall and Lindzey 1970).

All individuals make use of strategies to reduce anxiety. The defense mechanisms discussed here are considered maladaptive, however, when they become the predominant means of coping with stress and when they interfere with one's ability to handle life's everyday demands.

Repression Repression is the blocking of forbidden or dangerous desires and thoughts to keep them from entering one's consciousness. According to Freud, it is the most basic defense mechanism and is generally the first used. However, simply forcing this material into what Freud called the *unconscious* does not solve the problem. Unconscious material continually seeks consciousness, which means the ego must constantly expend energy to keep it hidden. This draining of psychic energy leaves the person less energy to use for more adaptive functions. Moreover, unconscious material often tends to increase in energy and strength. The simple analogy of a soup kettle can illustrate this process.

Picture a kettle full of soup, on the verge of boiling over. The kettle's contents represent the id's unconscious impulses, wishes, and desires. The lid on the pot, which is keeping the soup from boiling over, represents the ego defenses. As the pot's contents heat up, the steam pressure increases. "Keeping the lid on" may require increased repressive force.

The steam pressure can become so great, however, that it blows the lid off the pot (overpowering the forces of repression). If this happens, a full-scale panic ensues, and a *psychotic episode* (a break with reality) results. Ego functions have been crippled, and the ability to cope with reality diminishes. In other cases, instead of blowing the lid off the pot, the steam may also seep out through cracks and crevices in the lid (circumventing the forces of repression). However, just as the escaping steam looks very different from the soup in the pot, the unconscious material that escapes is disguised. This is because the ego has acted as a safety valve, allowing material to attain consciousness only after disguising it. The disguised unconscious material represents a deep underlying conflict.

During states of *ego-weakness,* for one reason or another the ego's guard is relaxed. The forces of repression are circumvented most easily during these states, which can occur naturally during sleep or as a result of excessive fatigue. When one sleeps, the conscious guard of one's ego is noticeably reduced, and unconscious impulses often seep out. According to Freud, dreams are thus symbolic of unconscious events, and dream interpretation is vital to understanding the inner workings of the mind. Likewise, slips of the tongue or pen ("Freudian slips") occur when people are tired or off guard. Nothing, according to Freud, occurs accidentally in human behavior.

As well as preventing dangerous and unacceptable desires from reaching consciousness, repression expels painful or traumatic memories from consciousness. During World War II many soldiers were treated for so-called *combat neuroses* in which they were amnesiac to (lost memory about) life-threatening battle experiences. Because these soldiers found their combat experiences too painful to recall, they repressed them. Here is an example of this pain-denying function of repression.

> Mr. X was a 35-year-old veteran who complained of listlessness, occasional anxiety, and inability to taste the flavor of foods. In addition, he complained of numbness throughout his body and a ringing in his ear that correlated with certain mood states. For example, a high pitch meant he was angry, and a low pitch meant he would become elated. A thorough neurological exam revealed no significant organic problem, so he was referred to the psychology service for further evaluation. Subsequent interviews revealed a strange obsession on the part of Mr. X.

> For the past two months he had found himself drawn to reading the obituary column of the local newspaper, although he found such activity extremely frightening. He could not make sense of his obsession, nor could he ever recall anything related to this preoccupation. Under hypnosis, Mr. X was finally able to recall that as an adolescent he had broken into several cemeteries and had dug up graves as a prank. One night he broke into a coffin containing the body of a young female and found himself sexually aroused by the body. The thought of being sexually attracted to a corpse was so abhorrent to him that he . . . repressed the entire memory from consciousness. However, his repressive mechanisms were beginning to fail. (Schroth and Sue 1975, pp. 253–254)

Reaction formation   In **reaction formation** dangerous impulses are repressed and then converted to their direct opposite. Feelings of hate may be converted to superficial love, sexual desires to rigid morality, and pessimism to optimism. The extremely overprotective mother, who is afraid to let her seven-year-old child play anywhere but in the back yard, may be masking unconscious resentment and hostility toward an unwanted child who has tied her down for years. Because mothers are supposed to love their children, she cannot admit these feelings and converts them to their opposite by showering the child with superficial attention.

Projection   The defensive reaction in which individuals rid themselves of threatening desires or thoughts by attributing them to others is called **projection.** Projection can be manifested in two ways. First, a person may blame his or her mistakes or shortcomings on some external source. A worker may mask unpleasant feelings of inadequacy by blaming his poor performance on the incompetence of fellow workers. Second, in extreme cases a person may form a *delusional system,* in which the person believes that enemies are disrupting his or her life.

Rationalization **Rationalization** is a common defense in which a person gives well-thought-out and socially acceptable reasons for certain behavior—but these reasons do not happen to be the real ones. For example, a student may explain flunking a test as follows: "I'm not interested in the course and don't really need it to graduate. Besides, I find the teacher extremely dull." These may be plausible and rational statements. However, the student has failed to mention the fact that she did not try hard because she was afraid the course was too difficult for her to pass. In essence, rationalization helps people justify their behavior and softens disappointments connected with unattainable goals.

It can be very difficult for rationalizer and listener alike to tell the difference between objective truths and rationalizations. People who rationalize fequently become upset when their reasons are questioned. They never tire of dredging up justifications. A common example of rationalization is the myriad of reasons that smokers can generate to justify their habit.

Displacement **Displacement** is the directing of an emotion such as hostility or anxiety toward a substitute target. For example, a meek clerk who is constantly belittled by his boss may build up tremendous resentment. If he were to express this anger openly at work, he might be fired. Instead, he snaps at family members or teases the dog at home. Commonly referred to as *scapegoating,* displacement occurs when the expression of feelings toward their real source is too threatening. Displacement is generally directed toward a less powerful object (human or pet). Prejudice and discrimination against certain identifiable groups may be partly explained as displacement.

Displacement can also be self-directed; that is, people may unconsciously turn their anger in on themselves. In most cases, such people have inhibited personalities and can be described as passive. They allow others to take

Lady Macbeth, a tragic Shakespearean character, tried to undo her traitorous act by obsessively making handwashing motions (as if to rinse her hands of blood) after she had goaded her husband to kill the king.

advantage of them and then build up a great deal of resentment. On the subconscious level these people castigate themselves for not being able to stand up to others. A poor self-image begins to form, accompanied by self-hatred that is manifested in self-recriminations and strong guilt feelings. Some clinicians feel that people who are depressed harbor much hostility that needs to be expressed.

Undoing In most cases, **undoing** can be viewed as a symbolic attempt to right a wrong or negate some disapproved thought, impulse, or act. It tends to be ritualistic and repetitive. Lady Macbeth, who in Shakespeare's play goaded her husband into slaying the king, tried to cleanse herself of sin by constantly going through the motions of washing her hands. More commonplace examples of this defense mechanism may be seen in the superstitious behaviors people engage in to ward off bad luck and to maximize good luck—for example, knocking on wood.

Regression **Regression** is a retreat to an earlier developmental level that demands less mature responses and aspirations. Freud believed that a person using this defense generally moves back to his or her most fixated psychosexual stage. Whether this interpretation is true or not, many people, when faced with severe stress, often resort to immature or infantile behavior. They seem to want to remove themselves from the threatening situation by regressing to a stage in which they were allowed to be dependent, helpless, and irresponsible.

Examples of regression may be found everywhere, from the child who reverts to infantile behavior, such as thumb sucking or bed wetting, when a sibling is born, to the dignified college president who whoops it up at a reunion with college classmates. However, regression becomes extremely pathological when the person begins to live in the era to which he or she has regressed and cannot function as a mature individual. In severe forms, the individual loses contact with reality. Certain forms of schizophrenia, such as *catatonia,* represent the ultimate in regression from the psychoanalytic perspective. Here the person withdraws completely into his or her own world and becomes mute and deaf. The catatonic frequently assumes rigid postures—often the fetal position—for long periods of time.

As we noted earlier, all people use defense mechanisms to some extent. However, persons with emotional disorders are likely to overutilize them. The difference is one of degree, not of kind.

Psychoanalytic therapy

Besides occurring in the natural states of sleep and excessive fatigue, ego-weakness can be externally induced. To rid people of maladaptive behaviors, **psychoanalytic therapy,** better known as **psychoanalysis,** induces ego-weakness through such techniques as hypnosis and *projective tests,* in which such ambiguous stimuli as ink blots, word associations, or pictures provoke revealing verbal responses. These techniques allow the therapist (called a *psychoanalyst* or just an *analyst*) to gain access to unconscious material. This material is used to help patients achieve insight into their own inner motivations and desires. The basic premise of psychoanalysis is that a cure can be effected only in this way; psychoanalytic methods will be discussed in Chapter 20.

Neo-Freudian perspectives

Freud's psychoanalytic movement attracted many followers. Some of Freud's disciples, however, came to disagree with his insistence that the sex instinct is the major determinant of behavior. Many of his most gifted and capable adherents broke with him and formulated coherent psychological models of their own. These thinkers have since become known as the **neo-Freudians** (or post-Freudians) because, despite their new ideas, they remained strongly influenced by Freud's constructs. For example, nearly all of them continued to believe in the power of the unconscious, in the use of ''talking'' methods of psychotherapy that rely heavily on the patient's introspection, in the three-part structure of personality, and in the one-to-one analyst–patient approach to therapy.

The major differences between the various neo-Freudian theories and psychoanalytic theory lie in the emphasis that the neo-Freudians placed on four areas:

1. Freedom of choice and the importance of future goals
2. Consciousness and ego autonomy
3. The influence of social forces on psychological functioning
4. The need to treat the seriously disturbed individual

Let us look at each of these areas in greater detail.

Choice and future goals   Two of the first pupils to break with Freud were Alfred Adler (1870–1937) and Carl Jung (1875–1961). Adler developed his own approach, called *individual psychology*. He contended that human beings are much less at the mercy of instinctual unconscious motivations than Freud had indicated. Adler de-emphasized biological drives and stressed social drives instead. Psychologically healthy individuals, Adler believed, have some freedom of choice in their actions; their behavior is directed toward goals they value and is guided in part by their vision of what they want their future to become. Adler thought psychopathology to be the result of inappropriate child-rearing practices, and he thought therapists should focus on the social context of their patients' lives.

Like Adler, Carl Jung believed human beings are goal-directed and future-oriented and that these characteristics help to guide behavior. Although he shared Freud's premise that the unconscious is a powerful force, Jung was more optimistic in outlook. He asserted that the unconscious is composed of two parts: the individual unconscious, as in the Freudian theory, and the collective unconscious. The **collective unconscious** contains positive attributes and life-giving elements; it is a kind of storehouse of religious and aesthetic values derived from the cumulative experience of the human species.

More than any other prominent psychologist, Jung was a student of history. His writings on mythology, religion, folklore, ancient symbols and rituals, dreams, and visions have had a great impact on art, literature, and sociology. In addition, his concepts of introversion and extroversion have permeated psychological thinking.

Ego autonomy   Whereas Adler and Jung moved contemporary psychoanalytic theory toward a more optimistic, less deterministic, and less biological orientation, others, such as Freud's daughter Anna Freud (1895–1982) and Erik Erikson (1902–1982), emphasized the

Carl Jung (1875–1961) proposed the collective unconscious to represent the cumulative experience that all humans share. Unlike Freud's psychoanalysis, Jung's theory took an optimistic view of human beings.

role, operation, and importance of the ego. Thus they and their followers are often called *ego psychologists*. Ego psychologists accept Freud's three-part division of the personality, but they believe the ego is an autonomous component. The ego is not at the mercy of the id; it is able to be creative while remaining independent of the sexual and aggressive drives.

Erik Erikson is perhaps the most influential of the ego theorists. His outstanding contribution was formulation of the stages of ego development from infancy to late adulthood—one of the first truly developmental examinations of personality structures and

Erik Erikson (1902–1982) studied with Anna Freud (Freud's daughter). He formulated an important theory of psychosocial ego development from infancy to late adulthood.

processes. His analyses of identity crises in youth are held in especially high regard. Unlike Freud, Erikson considered personality to be flexible and capable of growth and change throughout the adult years. He believed, in other words, that we do not have to be prisoners of our past.

Social forces A third major influence in contemporary psychoanalytic theory came from thinkers such as Erich Fromm (1900–1980),

Karen Horney (1885–1952), and Harry Stack Sullivan (1892–1949). Despite considerable differences among their ideas, all three agreed on the primary role of interpersonal relationships in the development of the personality.

Although Erich Fromm drew heavily on psychoanalytic concepts, his major themes emphasize the social and interpersonal aspects of psychological development. According to Fromm, people have become separated from nature and have lost a sense of community with other persons. In his book *Escape from Freedom* (1941), Fromm points out that the price of greater freedom and individuation is loneliness. Thus people attempt to *escape* freedom, which has become a negative condition (see Focus 2.2, p. 60). To find meaning in their lonely lives, they have two choices: unite in a spirit of love and shared work or seek security through submission and conformity. The former leads to the development of a better society; the latter may lead to behavior disorders.

Karen Horney argued that the cause of behavior pathology is *basic anxiety,* a disturbance of the child's security resulting from parental rejection or overprotection. This interpersonal childhood disturbance may lead to the development of a need to move *closer to* people, a need to move *away from* people, or a need to move *against* people. Neurotic behavior then results from this need.

Horney is also considered by many to be the first feminist psychologist. She rejected Freud's concept of penis envy, denying that feminine psychology had anything to do with either male or female anatomy. She also rejected the concept of psychopathology as a sexual-aggressive conflict resulting from an Oedipus or Electra complex.

Harry Stack Sullivan's major contribution was his interpersonal theory of psychological disorders. Sullivan believed that the individual's psychological functions could be understood only in the context of his or her social relationships. We shall have considerably more to say about Sullivan and his interpersonal theory in Chapter 3.

Treatment of the seriously disturbed During the 1950s and 1960s, a number of psychoanalysts admitted that there were weaknesses inherent in classical psychoanalysis. For example, Freud disqualified from psychoanalysis a large percentage of the population that he considered "analytically unfit." Very seriously disturbed individuals, particularly schizophrenics, were viewed as unfit because they did not respond to the "verbal interpretive" techniques advocated by Freud. In addition, certain narcissistic neurotic patients were too isolated (not psychologically minded) to respond to verbal therapy.

Under the rubric of *modern psychoanalysis,* Hyman Spotnitz (1963, 1968, 1976) and his colleagues have introduced new treatment techniques that do not require the patient to be emotionally or intellectually capable of understanding interpretations. These are, in essence, reflective and mirroring techniques, in which the analyst actively provides feedback to the patient. The patient is then helped to resolve conflicts by experiencing the conflicts rather than understanding them. Although Spotnitz's work is not well known outside the psychoanalytic movement, it has become an important contribution to contemporary psychoanalysis.

Criticisms of the psychoanalytic model

Psychoanalytic theory has had a tremendous impact on the field of psychology. Psychoanalysis and its variations are very widely employed. Nonetheless, the usefulness of the psychoanalytic view in explaining and treating behavior disorders has been challenged. Two major criticisms are often leveled at psychoanalysis (Hall and Lindzey 1970).

First, there are grave shortcomings in the empirical procedures by which Freud validated his hypotheses. His observations about human behavior were often made under uncontrolled conditions. For example, he relied heavily on case studies and his own self-analy-

Karen Horney (1885–1952), one of the first feminist psychologists, developed a theory of personality development and pathology based on the social relationship between the parent and child.

sis as a basis for the formulation of psychoanalytic theory. His patients, from whom he drew conclusions about universal aspects of personality dynamics and behavior, tended to represent a narrow spectrum of people. Although case studies are often a rich source of clinical data, the fact that Freud did not keep verbatim notes means his recollections were subject to distortions and omissions. Furthermore, he seldom checked the accuracy of the material related by his patients through any form of external corroboration (relatives, friends, test data, documents, or medical records). Such private and uncontrolled methods of inquiry are fraught with hazards.

Freud failed to make explicit the line of reasoning by which he drew inferences and conclusions. In his numerous writings he presented the end results of his thinking without giving the original data on which they were based, his method of analysis, or any systematic presentation of his empirical findings. It is difficult, if not impossible, to replicate many of Freud's investigations. Thus the reliability of his observations is impossible to evaluate. Did he really find a relationship between alcoholism and orality, between obsessive–compulsive behavior and anality, and between hysteria and phallic fixation? Did he read into his cases only what he wanted to find? How much was he influenced by his own personal biases and needs? Freud's reluctance to follow the conventions of full scientific reporting leads many to view his concepts and explanations with skepticism.

Much of psychoanalytic theory, then, cannot be empirically validated. A "good" theory should clearly and precisely explain phenomena, specifying the relationship between events and forces. It should also be capable of predicting what will happen, given certain conditions. Psychoanalysis falls short on both scores. The vagueness with which certain re-

Cults: Escape from Freedom?

What do the followers of Bhagwan Shree Rajneesh and Rev. Sun Myung Moon, the Hare Krishnas, and the members of an estimated 2500 additional cults in the United States have in common? If Erich Fromm were alive today, he might well view young people's joining of cults as an "escape from freedom." Confronted with the many choices of life and the need to establish greater independence and individual identity, some young people have found only unbearable insecurity and loneliness. Cult membership has often been their answer.

A recent analysis of cult followers that reiterates Fromm's escape-from-freedom theme is Saul V. Levine's *Radical Departures: Desperate Detours to Growing Up* (1984). Levine's study of cults began in the 1960s. He studied more than 1000 individuals belonging to 15 different groups—drug groups, religious cults, political organizations, and therapy groups. To augment this broad perspective, Levine concentrated on 9 young men and women as they journeyed into and out of communal groups.

Levine did not find the typical group member to be a loner, a failure, a substance abuser, or a misfit. Nor did he find that members were controlled, duped, or held captive. Group members by and large showed no serious signs of pathology, came from pleasant homes, were raised by concerned parents, were well-off financially, and had much to look forward to. These "radical departers," as Levine prefers to call the group members, are generally between 18 and 26 years of age, unmarried, affluent, well-educated, white, and from intact families.

Levine's findings seem to make the radical departer's sudden leave-taking from the family strange and puzzling. He believes that joining a cult may represent a desperate attempt to avoid choice and responsibility. To understand the framework of his analysis, we need to recognize the pressures that adolescents experience as they enter adulthood.

In our middle-class culture, we stress the importance of children growing up, separat-

lationships are presented makes them virtually useless. What exactly is the relationship between the superego and the Oedipus complex? How intense must an experience be to become traumatic? Exactly how strong must instinctual forces be to overcome the ego? Not only does psychoanalytic theory lack specificity, but it cannot adequately predict what will happen. For example, the concept of a death instinct can be used to explain certain events, such as suicides and wars, after the fact. Yet such a vague concept helps us little in understanding or predicting such events.

A second criticism of psychoanalysis is that it cannot be applied to a wide range of disturbed people. Individuals who have speech disturbances or are inarticulate (talking is important in therapy), people who have urgent, immediate problems (classical psychoanalysis requires much time), and people who are too young or too old may not profit from psychoanalysis (Fenichel 1945). Research studies have shown that psychoanalytic therapy is best suited to well-educated people of the middle and upper socioeconomic classes who exhibit neurotic rather than psychotic behavior. It is more limited in therapeutic value with people of lower socioeconomic levels and with those who are less verbal, less intelligent, and more severely disturbed (Sloane et al. 1975).

ing from their parents, and establishing their own independence and identity. As children become teenagers, their parents begin to relinquish control, allowing them greater freedom and decision-making power. Parents make it clear that adult responsibilities loom ahead. Young adults must think about college, make career choices, leave home. Not only do adolescents feel a sense of loss and loneliness as this occurs; they also grope with identity issues. In the normal course of growing up, they seek intimacy with friends and lovers. But radical departers seem to have been unable to form satisfactory relationships with others or to commit themselves to a value system. Separation from parents then involves pain, and cults seem to offer a magical solution: separation without accompanying pain. Submission and conformity to a group bring temporary security. For as long as this commitment lasts, the struggle to form an independent self is given up in favor of a flawless "group self." Radical departers, then, are escaping from freedom—making a temporary retreat from growing up.

Levine does not believe, however, that joining a cult is wholly negative. He observes, for example, that more than 90 percent of radical departers return home within 2 years and that virtually all eventually abandon their groups. A radical departure thus may represent a rehearsal for separation from the parents. Levine also argues that joining a cult and voluntarily separating can be a therapeutic process. He warns against "deprogramming," which involves kidnaping the member and then systematically assailing the values and beliefs the group has instilled. Deprogramming, that is, interferes with the natural and normal departure process.

A PSYCHOANALYTIC VIEW OF STEVEN V.

Let us hypothesize again. Suppose Steven V.'s therapist had a psychoanalytic orientation. Here is what we believe he might have to say about his patient.

In Steve's case records I see many possible explanations for his continuing problems. I will focus on four areas that I find particularly important: Steve's early childhood experiences; his repression of conflicts, intense feelings, and other impulses; the Oedipal dynamics that seem to be at work; and the unconscious symbolism behind his relationship with Linda.

Steve did not receive the love and care, at critical psychosexual stages, that a child needs in order to develop into a healthy adult. He was neglected, understimulated, and left on his own. The result was that he felt unloved and rejected. We have evidence that he was prone to "accidents"—being hit on the head by a swing, burning himself severely on an electric range, numerous falls. I believe these were not really accidents. They represented Steve's unconscious attempts to gain attention and to test his parents' love for him. Further, I believe his proneness to accidents was the forerunner of his attempts at suicide, a reflection of the death instinct and a desire to punish himself. Although Steve may not have been conscious of his feelings or able to verbalize them, it is obvious that he was deeply affected by his parents' negative attitudes. It must be an awful experience for a young child to believe he is unloved. For many of us, it is easier to deny or repress this belief than to face up to it.

Steve may have been the victim of marital unhappiness between his mother and father. The records indicate that they lived rather separate lives and that Mr. V. kept several mistresses whom he saw on his frequent "business trips." In one therapy session, when Mrs. V. was seen alone, she stated that she knew of her husband's extramarital affairs but never confronted him about them. Apparently she was fearful of his dominating and abusive manner at home, and she avoided potential conflicts by playing a passive role. When Mr. V. belittled Steve, she chose not to intervene; but secretly she identified with her son's predicament. Unable to form an intimate relationship with her husband, she became physically seductive toward Steve. As you recall, Mrs. V. frequently caressed and kissed her son and even had him sleep with her. To a youngster still groping his way through Oedipal conflicts, nothing could have been more damaging. Steve's sexual feelings toward the mother were no doubt intensified by her actions.

Mr. V.'s verbal abuse of Steve also aggravated Steve's problems. One of his father's common remarks to Steve was "You've got no balls." Abuse such as this deepened and prolonged Steve's Oedipal feelings of rivalry with and fear of his father. Steve's Oedipal conflict was never adequately resolved. His continued feelings of inadequacy and anger, and his sexual drives as well, have remained repressed and are expressed symbolically.

Repressed anger is certainly present in both Steve's fantasies and his behavior. His violent "mind games" and his preference for sadistic pornographic films is an indirect expression of anger at his father, whom he continues to see as a powerful feared rival (he has failed to identify with his father in resolution of the Oedipal conflict), and at his mother, who never came to his defense and suddenly withdrew his "bed privileges" when she became aware of Steve's sexual excitement. There also appears to be a strong relationship between anger and depression. Steve's periodic bouts of depression are probably anger turned inward. His frequent accidents, his depression, and his attempts at suicide are classic manifestations of the death instinct.

Steve's early childhood experiences continue to affect his behavior with women. Note the similarities between his woman friend, Linda, and his mother. Linda is described as being active in student affairs; the mother was always involved with civic activities. Linda seemed oblivious to Steve's existence in the presence of others, and he felt slighted by her friends; his mother seems never to have introduced Steve to her friends and relatives. Linda was "warm, affectionate, and intimate" in private; the mother, when "alone with Steve," was quite affectionate. Linda would consent to "heavy petting" but drew the line short of intercourse; the mother suddenly withdrew "bed privileges" when Steve showed incestuous sexual interest. It is clear that Steve continues to search for a "mother figure" and unconsciously selects women who are most like his mother. His impotence with Linda is additional evidence that Steve unconsciously views her as his mother. (In our society, incest is an unthinkable act.)

If Steve is to become a healthier individual, he must commit himself to intensive, long-term therapy aimed at helping him gain insight into his deep conflicts and repressed experiences. Resolving past traumas, overcoming resistance, and working through a transference relationship with the therapist will be crucial components of his therapy.

HUMANISTIC AND EXISTENTIAL APPROACHES

The humanistic and existential approaches evolved as a reaction to the determinism of other behavioral models. For example, many proponents of these approaches were disturbed that Freudian psychology did not focus on the inner world of the client but rather categorized the client according to a set of preconceived diagnoses (May 1967). Psychoanalysts, these critics said, described clients in terms of blocked instinctual forces and psychic complexes that made them victims of some mechanistic and deterministic personality structure.

It is important to note that the humanistic and existential perspectives cannot be classified as a single school of thought. But they do share a set of assumptions that distinguish them from other approaches.

First, both view an individual's reality as a product of that person's unique perceptions of the world. How the individual experiences the world determines his or her behavior. Hence, to understand why an individual behaves as he or she does, the psychologist must reconstruct the world from that individual's vantage point. Moreover, the subjective universe of this person—how he or she construes events—is more important than the events themselves. Second, both humanistic and existential theorists stress the ability of individuals to make free choices and to be responsible for their own decisions. Third, these theorists believe in the "wholeness" or integrity of the individual. Attempts to reduce human beings to a set of formulas, to explain us simply by measuring our responses to certain stimuli, are viewed as pointless. And last, according to the humanistic and existential perspectives, people have the ability to become what they want, to fulfill their capacities, and to lead the lives best suited to themselves.

Humanistic perspectives

The psychoanalytic view of personality places strong emphasis on unconscious determinants of behavior. And, if unconscious forces determine behavior, then free choice is not really available. As we have noted, a number of theorists take issue with these concepts, placing greater emphasis on people's conscious experiences and their ability to choose among alternatives.

Carl Rogers is perhaps the best-known humanistic psychologist. Rogers's theory of personality (1959) reflects his concern with human welfare and his deep conviction that humanity is basically "good," forward-moving, and trustworthy. One of the major contributions of the **humanistic perspectives** has been this positive view of the individual.

Besides being concerned with treating the mentally ill, psychologists such as Rogers (1961) and Abraham Maslow (1954) have focused on improving the mental health of the person who is considered normal. This focus has led humanistic psychologists and others to explore the characteristics of the healthy personality (see Focus 2.3).

The actualizing tendency Instead of concentrating exclusively on behavior disorders, the humanistic approach is concerned with help-

FOCUS 2.3

The Healthy Personality

One of the major contributions of humanistic psychologists has been their optimistic perception of people. Rather than focusing on pathology, they have stressed our assets and strengths. Psychologist Abraham Maslow has identified characteristics of mental health in well-known figures, including Thomas Jefferson, Albert Einstein, and Eleanor Roosevelt. Other studies have provided additional information about healthy individuals. Here are some of the traits that are most prominent in the healthy personality—traits that, according to humanists, distinguish human beings from other species.

1. *An ability to accept oneself, others, and nature.* Self-actualizers accept their shortcomings and are not ashamed of being what they are. They have a positive self-concept and feel they are making contributions to the world. They are also receptive to others—even others who are different.

2. *An adequate perception of and comfortable attitude toward reality.* Self-actualizers prefer to cope with unpleasant realities rather than to avoid or deny them. They waste little time in feeling sorry for themselves. They base decisions on how things really are rather than on how they wish they were.

3. *Spontaneity.* Healthy individuals are relatively spontaneous in their behavior, thoughts, and inner impulses. They tend to behave naturally.

4. *Focus on external problems.* Most healthy people tend to focus on external problems rather than worrying about themselves. For example, Maslow's subjects were concerned with the major world issues of the day and were also interested in developing a philosophy of life. Not overly self-conscious, they could devote their attention to a task that seemed particularly appropriate for them.

5. *A need for privacy.* Self-actualizers

ing people *actualize* their potential and with bettering the state of humanity. The quintessence of humanistic psychological theory is the concept of **self-actualization.** This term, popularized by Maslow, implies that people are motivated not only to fill their biological needs (for food, warmth, and sex) but also to cultivate, maintain, and enhance the **self.** The self is one's image of oneself, the part one refers to as ''I'' or ''me.''

The humanistic psychologist believes that all people are born with an inherent tendency to become actualized or fulfilled. This tendency can be defined as the impetus to achieve one's inherent potential as a fully functioning person. As one psychologist has pointed out, the actualizing tendency can be viewed as fulfilling a grand design or a genetic blueprint (Maddi 1972). This thrust of life that pushes people forward is manifested in such qualities as curiosity, creativity, and joy of discovery. According to Rogers (1961), this inherent force is common to all living organisms; its psychological manifestation is *self-actualization* (Maslow 1954; Rogers 1959). How one views the self, how others relate to the self, and what values are attached to the self constitute one's **self-concept.**

During the course of their development, children increase their awareness of the world and gain experience in it. From various encounters they learn of two needs that affect the self-concept: the need for *positive regard* (how they think others perceive them) and the need for *positive self-regard* (how they perceive themselves). All people are sensitive to

seem to enjoy solitude and privacy more than others. Other people may perceive them as being somewhat aloof, reserved, and unruffled by events that disturb most people. But although they do need time to be by themselves, they also appreciate other people and enjoy being around them.

6. *Independence from the environment.* Mentally healthy people remain relatively stable and secure in spite of harsh environmental conditions. They can maintain happiness in circumstances that might upset others. In other words, they are able to withstand severe forms of stress such as economic deprivation, the loss of a loved one, or physical hardships.

7. *A continued freshness of appreciation.* Self-actualizers have the capacity to appreciate again and again the basic joys of nature. They have an ability to see uniqueness and wonder in many apparently commonplace experiences. In essence, the mentally healthy person is creative, open, and possesses a strong feeling of ''belongingness'' with all humanity.

In evaluating these traits, however, we must bear two cautions in mind. First, in almost all cases where criteria are used (as here), the issue of values and subjectivism arises. The fact that the researchers and their subjects do not represent a cross section of socioeconomic classes or subcultures in our society may result in overgeneralizations. Second, as was noted in Chapter 1, mental health can be viewed from several perspectives. For example, one healthy trait is spontaneity—the uninhibited expression of thoughts and feelings. Yet various cultural groups value restraint with regard to feelings and discourage direct expression.

SOURCES: Maslow (1954), Rogers (1961), Jahoda (1958), Sibler et al. (1961), Coelho, Hamburg, and Murphy (1963), Wild (1965), Barron (1963), Korchin and Ruff (1964), and Ruff and Korchin (1964).

Abraham Maslow (1908–1970) proposed that people are motivated toward self-actualization once more basic needs are met. He based his ideas on his study of self-actualized, healthy people such as Einstein, Spinoza, and Eleanor Roosevelt.

and influenced by others' opinions and reactions; group or peer pressure can be extremely powerful. People need positive feedback from others and feel frustration when they are looked on with disapproval. Each person also needs to approve of his or her self and feels distress when that need goes unmet. Both needs define how the actualizing tendency will be expressed.

Development of abnormal behavior Rogers believes that, if people were left unencumbered by societal restrictions and allowed to grow and develop freely, the result would be self-actualized, fully functioning persons. In such a case, the self-concept and the actualizing tendency would be congruent.

However, society frequently imposes *conditions of worth* on its members. These conditions are standards by which people determine whether they have worth. They are transmitted via *conditional positive regard*. That is, significant others (parents, peers, friends, spouse, and so forth) in a person's life accept some but not all of that person's actions, feelings, and attitudes. The person's self-concept

becomes defined as having worth only when others approve. But this forces the individual to develop a distorted self-concept that is inconsistent with his or her self- actualizing potential, inhibiting that person from being self-actualized. A state of disharmony or *incongruence* is said to exist between the person's inherent potential and his or her self-concept (as determined by significant others).

According to Rogers, behavior disorders are a result of this state of incongruence. The developing child who attempts to become what others wish is at odds with what he or she wants or was meant to be (see Focus 2.4). This conflict forms the basis of abnormal behavior.

Rogers believed that fully functioning people have been *allowed to grow* toward their potential. The environmental condition most suitable for this growth is called **unconditional positive regard** (Rogers 1951). In essence, people who are significant figures in someone's life value and respect that person *as a person*. Giving unconditional positive regard is valuing and loving regardless of behavior. People may disapprove of someone's actions, but they still respect, love, and care for that someone.

The assumption that humans need unconditional positive regard has many implications for child rearing and psychotherapy. For parents it means creating an open and accepting environment for the child. For the therapist it means fostering conditions that will allow clients to grow and fulfill their potential; this approach has become known as *nondirective* or *person-centered* therapy.

Person-centered therapy Carl Rogers emphasized that therapist attitudes are more important than specific counseling techniques. The therapist needs a strong positive regard for the client's ability to deal constructively with all aspects of life. The more willing the therapist is to rely on the client's strengths and potential, the more likely the client is to discover such strengths and potential. The therapist cannot help the client by explaining the client's behavior or by prescribing actions. Ther-

The Case of Bill M.

Bill M. was a nineteen-year-old college sophomore. All through high school and in his freshman year at college, his grades were straight A's. Many students would have been elated to have his fine record, but Bill was depressed and unhappy; he felt life had no meaning.

Bill's parents had always praised his intellectual accomplishments, and they presented him with gifts whenever he excelled in school. To some degree of awareness, Bill felt his worth as a person was dependent on earning good grades. Attempting to please his parents, who unwittingly imposed these conditions of worth, Bill denied his own hopes, aspirations, and feelings. His prime objective was to remain a straight-A student. Although he had originally loved the excitement of learning, achieving, and mastering new knowledge, he now became cautious and obsessed with "safety." As his string of perfect grades became longer and longer, safety (not risking a B grade) became more and more important. He began to choose safe and easy topics for essays, to enroll in very easy courses, and to take "incompletes" or withdraw when courses appeared tough. Bill's fear of receiving any grade less than an A prompted defensive maneuvers that denied and blocked his actualizing tendency.

apy techniques involve expressing and communicating respect, understanding, and acceptance. The therapist tries to understand the client's internal frame of reference by thinking, feeling, and exploring with him or her. Indeed, Rogers shuns the term *patient* because it denotes a helpless and disabled person in need of help to "cure" the disorder. The therapist needs to avoid seeing the person as "sick," which is why Rogers prefers the term *client*.

Reflection of feelings is the way the person-centered therapist most commonly communicates understanding of the client's subjective world. In "saying back" to the client what he or she understood the client to say, the therapist provides a "mirror" for the client. The client can then actively evaluate thoughts and feelings with less distortion. Even in very strained situations, the person-centered therapist relies on reflection of feelings and on acceptance in working with the client. The following dialogue between client (S) and counselor (C), transcribed by Rogers, illustrates the technique.

S: [Silent for two minutes. Then begins to talk in hard, flat voice, quite unlike her usual tone. Does not look at counselor. There was much repetition but the following excerpts give the major thoughts.] You feel I want to come, but I don't! I'm not coming anymore. It doesn't do any good. I don't like you. I hate you! I wish you never were born.
C: You just hate me very bitterly.
S: I think I'll throw you in the lake. I'll cut you up! You think people like you, but they don't . . . I wish you were dead.
C: You detest me and you'd really like to get rid of me.
S: You think my father did bad things to me, but he didn't! You think he wasn't a good man, but he was. You think I want intercourse, but I don't.
C: You feel I absolutely misrepresent all your thoughts. (Rogers 1951, pp. 211–213)

You might well sense a lack of direction here and wonder where this conversation is leading. The therapist, as you can see, is not steering this exchange but is using a standard technique of humanistic therapy, the understated reflection of the client's feelings. It is

Carl Rogers (b. 1902) believes people need both positive regard from others and positive self-regard. When positive regard is given unconditionally, a person can develop freely and become self-actualized.

the client who will ultimately move on his or her own in the direction of health; the client, that is, wants to be healthy.

The existential perspective

The **existential approach** is really not a systematized school of thought but a set of attitudes. It shares with humanistic psychology an emphasis on individual uniqueness, a quest for meaning in life and for freedom and responsibility, a phenomenological approach to understanding the person, and a belief that the individual possesses positive attributes that will eventually be expressed unless they are distorted by the environment. But the existential perspective is suffused with considerably less optimism than the humanistic; it emphasizes the irrationality, difficulties, and suffering encountered in life.

Existential psychology is an outgrowth of the European existential philosophy of Kierkegaard, Heidegger, and Sartre. Psychologist Rollo May was especially influential in developing an existential perspective in the United States (May, Angel, and Ellenberger 1958; May 1958, 1961). He and other existen-

tial psychologists stress that rapidly accelerating technology, a reliance on science to solve pressing human problems, increasing urbanization, and emphasis on naturalistic rather than religious or spiritual explanations of human nature have led to great personal confusion and strain. Alvin Toffler's popular book *Future Shock* (1970) explores this theme. Technology and all the accoutrements of a modern society have reduced people to "cogs in the machine." Such rapid and dehumanizing change has led to a questioning of old values, of the meaning of life, and of basic human nature.

Indeed, many therapists *have* observed an increase in the number of patients complaining about the meaninglessness of life and reporting a sense of emptiness. Such symptoms as loneliness, alienation, isolation, detachment, and depersonalization have increased. Many psychotherapists find American psychology's naturalistic view of people inadequate in helping others. They feel that essential human characteristics—awareness of self (existence) and self-directed, goal-oriented striving (becoming)—have been ignored. Many find that the concepts underlying existential analysis fill this void.

Existential concepts   Three concepts are essential to existential thought: being, nonbeing, and being-in-the-world.

☐ *Being.* The distinctive character of human existence is that human beings are aware of themselves and their experience of being (existence) at a particular point in time and space. Because people are *conscious* of their existence, existentialists say, they are *responsible* for it and are capable of *choosing* their direction. They are *free,* and such factors as heredity, environment, and culture are merely excuses for not experiencing the process of "becoming"—attaining their potential.

☐ *Nonbeing.* People also know that at some future time they will cease to exist (not be). Awareness of eventual nonbeing or nonexistence is necessary to fully understand and experience being. Death gives life reality because it is an absolute fact that must be confronted. Impending nonbeing is the source of anxiety, aggression, and hostility. Because the threat is always present, the anxiety it produces is considered normal. This anxiety is frequently called *existential anxiety* because it represents a conflict between being and nonbeing. When one cannot accept this condition without repression, choices become restricted and the actualization of potentials is thwarted.

☐ *Being-in-the-world*. We are all beings-in-the-world. The "world" can be described as the structure of meaningful relationships in which all people must function. One of the major problems caused by the complexity of contemporary society is that many people have lost their world. This loss is reflected in alienation—estrangement from other human beings or from the natural world. The French writer Albert Camus brilliantly portrays this predicament of modern people in his novel *The Stranger* (1946):

> . . . a man who is a stranger in his world, a stranger to other people to whom he speaks or pretends to love; he moves about in a state of homelessness, vagueness, and haze as though he has no direct connection with his world but were in a foreign country where he does not know the language and has no hope of learning it, and is always doomed to wander in quiet despair, incommunicado, homeless, a stranger. (p. 85)

Development of abnormal behavior Abnormal behavior results from conflicts between people's essential nature and the demands they make on themselves or others make on them. The more alienated a person becomes from his or her total being, the fewer alternatives are available: Behavior becomes increasingly stereotyped, inhibited, conforming, and morally rigid. The potential for disturbance is ever present.

Loneliness, alienation, isolation, and depersonalization can lead to abnormal behavior, according to existential psychology. In existential therapy the client's major task is to become responsible for his or her world, life, and future.

Anxiety stems from two main sources: the threat of imminent nonbeing, of losing oneself to nothingness, and the inability to relate to all the ways of our world. When these two conflicts (nonbeing and being-in-the-world) are not confronted and adequately resolved, crippling anxiety results. This anxiety leaves one with a sense of living a meaningless life; ultimately, it causes despair.

Existential therapy The goal of the existential approach to therapy is to help the individual become aware of his or her own potential for growth, for choice, and for finding meaning in life. The existential approach is not a fixed system of therapy or a set of techniques; it is a means of understanding and illuminating the patient's being-in-the-world through exploration by therapist and patient together. People who are being helped are not placed in theoretical categories, because categories are inconsistent with the existential situation. Therapy techniques are de-emphasized in favor of the therapist's ability to see the patient's "reality" from the patient's perspective. In fact, because techniques must evolve from an understanding of the patient, the approach used may be derived from almost any school of therapy.

May (1961)* lists six characteristics of existential therapy:

1. Techniques vary from patient to patient; the goal is to illuminate the person's being-in-the-world.
2. Although therapists use concepts such as *transference, repression,* and *resistance,* they always relate these psychoanalytic terms to the existential situation of the patient's immediate life.
3. Therapists emphasize that the patient is not a subject but an "existential partner" with the therapist in a genuine encounter.
4. The therapist attempts to avoid behavior that would impede or terminate the genuine quality of the relationship. A full encounter with a person can create anxiety even within the therapist. Overreliance on therapy techniques permits a therapist to avoid the full encounter and is undesirable.
5. Therapy is aimed at having the patient experience and become aware of the fact that his or her existence is redefined at each moment.
6. For the patient, increased awareness of potentialities and the possibility of commitment will enable the patient to make decisions and to implement actions.

These characteristics of existential psychotherapy may seem excessively vague and insubstantial. Nowhere is there any systematic

*From May, Rollo, *Existential Psychology.* Copyright © 1961 by Rollo May. Used by permission of Random House, Inc.

explication of existential therapy and its procedures and techniques. Indeed, there *is* no single existential therapy. Instead, the therapy springs from a collaborative and shared venture between therapist and patient. Both are open to experience, are honest with each other, and act as authentically as possible. It is what the therapist *is* rather than what he or she does that matters. The therapist's task is to understand the private meaning of the patient's existence (being-in-the-world), and the patient's task is to be responsible for accepting his or her existential being. Each client is the author of his or her world and is responsible for his or her life and future.

Criticisms of the humanistic and existential approaches

Many psychologists have criticized the formulations of the humanistic and existential perspectives (Holt 1962; Millon 1973; Smith 1950). Although these phenomenological approaches have been extremely creative in describing the human condition, they have been less successful in constructing theory. Moreover, they are not suited to scientific or experimental investigation. Emphasis on subjective understanding rather than prediction and control, on intuition and empathy rather than objective investigation, and on the individual rather than the more general case tend to hinder empirical study.

Carl Rogers has certainly expressed many of his ideas as researchable propositions, but it is difficult to verify scientifically the humanistic concept of people as rational, inherently good, and moving toward self-fulfillment. The existential perspective can be similarly criticized for its lack of scientific grounding and for its reliance on the unique experiences of individuals to describe the inner world. Nevertheless, the existential concepts of freedom, choice, responsibility, being, and nonbeing have had a profound influence on contemporary thought beyond the field of psychology.

Another major criticism leveled at the humanistic and existential approaches is that they do not work well with severely disturbed clients. They seem to be most effective with intelligent, well-educated, and relatively "normal" individuals who may be suffering adjustment difficulties. In fact, Carl Rogers's person-centered counseling originated from his work with college students who were bright, articulate, and psychological-minded—what some psychologists described as the "worried well." This limitation, along with the occasional vagueness of humanistic and existential thought, has made it difficult to apply these ideas broadly to abnormal psychology.

A HUMANISTIC–EXISTENTIAL VIEW OF STEVEN V.

A therapist who strongly endorses the humanistic or existential approach would see Steven V. quite differently from a psychoanalyst or a proponent of the biogenic model. If Steve's therapist were so oriented, we believe he would consider the case of Steven V. very much as follows.

I must begin by stressing a point that is likely to be underemphasized by many other psychologists. Steven V. is not merely the sum of the voluminous case records I have before me. Steve is a flesh-and-blood person, alive, organic, and moving, with thoughts, feelings, and emotions. How could anyone hope to understand Steve by reading a pile of material that is static and inorganic and occasionally seeks to pigeonhole him into diagnostic categories? To classify Steve as schizophrenic, manic–depressive, or suicidal does not help me understand him. Indeed, such labels might serve as barriers to the development of a therapeutic relationship with him.

I intend to develop such a relationship with Steve, to engage him in a dialogue that will require no pretenses or self-justifications, and to travel with him on a journey whose destination neither of us will know until we get there. What makes me so sure that such a journey will be worthwhile? Almost everything I know of

Steve, I learned from Steve himself. Here, for example, is an entry from Steve's diary, written when he was in his junior year in high school.

> Seems like I can't do anything right. Why does he always pick on me? Came home with top scores on my SAT. Mother was impressed. Showed Dad. Wouldn't even look up from his newspaper. All he's interested in is the *Wall Street Journal*. Make money, that's the goal!!
>
> Tried to tell him at dinner again. Got top score, Dad!! Don't you care?? Of course not! Said he expected it from the family. Said he wanted me to do better next time. Said I should sit up and not slurp my soup . . . Said I should learn better table manners . . . Said I was an *asshole!!!* I am an asshole, I am, I am, who am I? Who cares?

There are strong feelings and emotions in this passage. Steve is deeply hurt by his father, he is angry at his father, and he seems to be seeking approval and validation from his father; he is also grappling with identity issues. These themes, but especially that of seeking approval from his father, are sounded throughout Steve's diary. His self-image and self-esteem seem to depend on his father's reaction to him. He clings to this perception of himself because he is afraid that, without it, he would not know who he is. This is illustrated in his questions: "Who am I? Who cares?" Until Steve knows who he is, he cannot understand what he might become.

Now here is another diary entry, this one during his senior year in high school:

Hello diary! Another do-nothing day! Parents won't let me do anything. Maybe I should jackoff . . . Got another good porno tape. This room's like a prison. Hello walls . . . hello desk . . . hello fly . . . hello hell! Ha, that's a good one . . .

Every day's the same.
When you're in the well!
Every day's a game.
When you're in hell!

This passage reveals another aspect of what is happening with Steve. He feels trapped, immobilized, lonely, and unable to change his life. He has never recognized or accepted the responsibility of making choices. He externalizes his problems and views himself as a passive victim. In this way Steve evades responsibility for choosing and protects himself by staying in the safe, known environment of his room.

Steve needs to realize that he is responsible for his own actions, that he cannot find his identity in others. He needs to get in touch with, and express directly, his feelings of anxiety, guilt, shame, and anger. And he needs to be open to new experiences. All this can be accomplished through a free, open, and unstructured relationship.

SUMMARY

1. Psychologists use theories, or models, to explain behavior. Each model is built around its own set of assumptions. The model one adopts determines not only how one explains abnormal behavior but also what treatment methods one is likely to consider using. Most clinicians, however, take an eclectic approach, blending and using components of various models.

2. Biogenic models cite various organic causes of psychopathology. Damage to the nervous system is one such cause. Another is biochemical imbalances; several types of disturbances have been found to respond to drugs. In addition, a good deal of biochemical research has focused on identifying the role of neuroregulators in abnormal behavior. Still another biogenic theory cites heredity in mental disorders: Correlations have been found between genetic inheritance and certain psychopathologies.

3. Psychoanalytic theory emphasizes past experiences and the role of the unconscious in

determining present behavior. Sigmund Freud, the founder of psychoanalysis, believed personality has three components: the id, which represents the impulsive, selfish, pleasure-seeking part of the person; the ego, which represents the rational part; and the superego, which represents society's values and ideals. Each component checks and balances the others. The life instincts and the death instincts are the energy system from which the personality operates. These instincts manifest themselves in various ways during the five different periods of life, or psychosexual stages, through which people pass: the oral, anal, phallic, latency, and genital stages. Each stage poses unique challenges that, if not adequately resolved, can result in maladaptive adult behaviors.

4. According to Freud, neurotic behavior results from the threat that unconscious thoughts will attain consciousness. To repress forbidden thoughts and impulses, the ego uses defense mechanisms: repression, reaction formation, projection, rationalization, displacement, undoing, and regression. Psychoana-

lytic techniques induce an ego-weakness that allows access to unconscious material, which the therapist uses to help the patient achieve insight into his or her unconscious.

5. Advocates of the humanistic approaches see people as capable of making free choices and fulfilling their potential. This viewpoint emphasizes conscious rather than unconscious processes. Perhaps the best-known humanistic formulation is Carl Rogers's person-centered approach. Rogers believes that people are motivated not only to meet their biological needs but also to grow and to enhance the self, to become actualized or fulfilled. Behavior disorders result when a person is forced to develop a self-concept that is at odds with his or her actualizing tendency. In person-centered therapy, the therapist projects a strong belief in the ability of the client to deal with life, to grow, and to reach his or her potential.

6. Existentialists believe that rapidly accelerating technology and an emphasis on naturalistic rather than spiritual explanations of the world have led to much personal trauma. Loneliness, alienation, isolation, and depersonalization have all been increased in contemporary times, as a direct result of society's treating persons like objects. Existentialists see behavior disorders as a product of the conflict between people's essential natures and the demands made on them by themselves and others. Three concepts essential to existentialism are: being (human awareness of existence), nonbeing (human awareness of death), and being-in-the-world (existing in a social context). Existential therapy is an unstructured collaborative venture between therapist and patient; its objective is to illuminate the patient's being-in-the-world.

KEY TERMS

biogenic model The theory or expectation that every mental disorder has an organic basis and cure

defense mechanism In psychoanalytic theory, the unconscious and automatic means by which the ego is protected from anxiety-provoking conflicts

diathesis–stress theory The theory that a predisposition to develop mental illness is inherited and that this predisposition may or may not be activated by environmental factors

eclectic approach An openness to all models of abnormal behavior, along with a willingness to borrow techniques from all approaches and to use them selectively with clients

existential approach The belief that contemporary society has a dehumanizing effect and that mental disorders result from a conflict between the essential human nature and the demands made on people by themselves and others

humanistic perspective The optimistic viewpoint that people are born with the ability to fulfill their potential and that abnormal behavior results from disharmony between the person's potential and his or her self-concept

model An analogy, most often used to describe or explain something that cannot be directly observed

neo-Freudians Psychologists whose ideas are strongly influenced by Freud's psychoanalytic model but who have modified that model in various ways

psychoanalysis Therapy based on the Freudian view that unconscious conflicts must be aired and understood by the patient if abnormal behavior is to be eliminated

psychoanalytic model The view that adult disorders arise from the unconscious operation of repressed anxieties originally experienced during childhood

psychopathology Abnormal behavior

3

Behavioral and Family Systems Models of Psychopathology

*T*his is the second of two chapters concerned with models of abnormal behavior. Recall that such models are idealized constructs or analogies; their purpose is to provide insight into the causes of abnormal behavior and thus to suggest methods of treatment. In the previous chapter we discussed the biogenic model and three psychogenic models. The biogenic model of abnormal behavior emphasizes an organic basis for mental disorders and, therefore, medical therapies. The psychogenic models look to the mind, or psyche, for both causes and treatment.

The models discussed in this chapter focus more on the environment than on the inner life of the individual. The *behavioral models* hold that all behavior—normal and abnormal—is learned through interaction between the person and the environment. The mentally disturbed person either has learned the wrong behaviors or has not learned the right ones. Therapy should be directed toward helping the client replace inappropriate behaviors or learn appropriate ones.

The *family systems model* of abnormal behavior concentrates on a particular part of the total environment. According to its proponents, individual identity and the quality of our relationships with others are largely the result of our family experiences. When psychopathology occurs, the therapist must look to the family for causes and for possible approaches to treatment.

BEHAVIORAL MODELS OF PSYCHOPATHOLOGY

Behaviorism was suggested as a unique approach to psychology in 1913 by John B. Watson (1878–1958) in a lecture delivered at Columbia University. Watson contended that, if

Ivan Pavlov (1849–1936), a Russian physiologist, discovered the associative learning process we know as classical conditioning while he was studying salivation in dogs. Pavlov won the Nobel Prize in physiology and medicine in 1904 for his work on the principal digestive glands.

psychology were ever to become a science, it must be limited to the study of directly observable and measurable events. Further, he declared that there was no place in psychology for the subjective study of mind, emotions, and thought processes. (In this, Watson's view stood in contrast to the intrapsychic approach of Freud.) The single goal of the science of psychology, Watson said, should be the prediction and control of human behavior.

At the time, several scientists were performing laboratory experiments on *conditioning,* or basic learning processes. Watson saw such experimentation as a proper part of the science of psychology, and he viewed these investigators' results as closely related to the study of behavior. Watson himself began to experiment with conditioning, and learning became the primary focus of behaviorism.

The **behavioral models** of psychopathology are thus concerned with the role of learning in abnormal behavior. The differences among them lie mainly in their explanations of how learning occurs. Although there are disagreements among some models, they generally tend to complement each other. That is, each of the four models discussed here is, for the most part, applied to a different type of behavior.

The classical conditioning model

Principles of classical conditioning Early in the twentieth century, Ivan Pavlov (1849–1936), a Russian physiologist, discovered an associative learning process that is known as **respondent** or **classical conditioning.** This process is involved with the involuntary responses (such as reflexes, emotional reactions, and sexual arousal), which are controlled by the autonomic nervous system.

Pavlov's discovery was accidental. He was measuring dogs' salivation as part of a study of their digestive processes when he discovered that the dogs would begin to salivate at the sight of an assistant carrying food powder. The dogs' salivation in response to a stimulus other than food placed in their mouths puzzled Pavlov and led to his discovery of classical conditioning. He reasoned that food is an **unconditioned stimulus** (UCS) that, in the mouth, automatically produces salivation; this salivation is an unlearned or **unconditioned response** (UCR) to the food. Pavlov then presented a previously *neutral* stimulus (one that does not initially produce salivation), such as the sound of a bell, to the dogs just before presenting the food. He found that, after a number of repetitions, the sound of the bell alone elicited salivation. This learning process is based on *association:* The neutral stimulus acquires some of the properties of the unconditioned stimulus when they are repeatedly paired together. When the bell alone can provoke this response, it is called a **conditioned stimulus** (CS),

Figure 3.1 *A Basic Classical Conditioning Process*
Dogs normally salivate when food is provided (left drawing). With his laboratory dogs, Ivan Pavlov paired the ringing of a bell with the presentation of food powder (middle drawing). Eventually, the dogs would salivate to the ringing of the bell alone, when no food was near (right drawing).

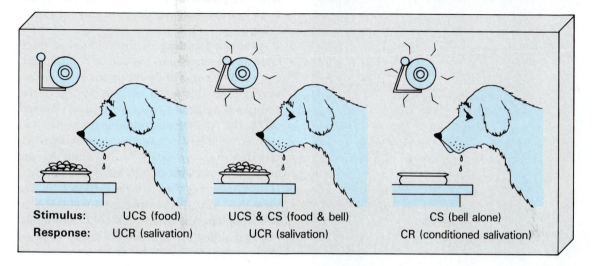

| Stimulus: | UCS (food) | UCS & CS (food & bell) | CS (bell alone) |
| Response: | UCR (salivation) | UCR (salivation) | CR (conditioned salivation) |

and the salivation it elicits is termed a **conditioned response** (CR). Each time the conditioned stimulus is paired with the unconditioned stimulus, the conditioned response is said to be reinforced, or strengthened. Pavlov's conditioning process is illustrated in Figure 3.1.

Pavlov discovered other principles governing classical conditioning. If he presented the bell many times without following it with the meat powder, the animals would gradually salivate less and less in response to the bell. This process, by which a response is eliminated when it is not reinforced, is called **extinction.** Pavlov also observed that the dogs salivated when he presented stimuli that were similar to the original conditioned stimulus. For example, a bell with a somewhat different tone might elicit salivation. This process is called **generalization.** The reverse of generalization, **stimulus discrimination,** is learning *not* to respond to a stimulus that is different from the conditioned stimulus. For example, most people have learned to respond favorably to a smile, even on a face that they have never

seen before; however, they do not respond so favorably to a frown. When the occurrence or nonoccurrence of a particular behavior is controlled by a preceding stimulus, that behavior is said to be under **stimulus control.**

Classical conditioning in psychopathology A **phobia** is an exaggerated, seemingly illogical fear of a particular object or class of objects. In an important study, John B. Watson and his associate Rosalie Rayner (1920) used classical conditioning to induce a phobia in a child. Watson had theorized that infants are born with only a few emotional response patterns (fear, rage, and love), and he hypothesized that there must be some "simple method" by which other stimuli also elicit these emotions. This method could, he thought, be association. Watson and Rayner decided to test the hypothesis on an eight-month-old infant named Albert.

They observed the child for any signs of fear when they confronted him suddenly with a series of different stimuli, including a white rat. "At no time did this infant ever show fear

Phobias are often produced by a traumatic event. A young child who has been frightened by a ferocious dog may subsequently react with fear to a friendly, curious dog.

in any situation. . . . The infant practically never cried'' (p. 66). They did, however, elicit a fear response in Albert by striking a suspended steel bar with a hammer. They then attempted to generate a fear response toward a previously neutral stimulus (the white rat) by coupling it with the fear-producing stimulus (the loud sound). They presented the white rat to Albert and, as he began to reach for it, made the frightening sound. Albert soon displayed fear whenever they presented the white rat. This fear also *generalized* to other stimuli with furry characteristics—a rabbit, a sealskin coat, a Santa Claus mask, cotton wool, and Watson's hair—items that Albert had not feared before.

Watson and Rayner considered their experiment a demonstration of a process by which conditioned fears can be produced. (We must note, however, that conditioning fear in humans would be considered highly unethical today.)

Although the case of little Albert is often cited as evidence that fear can be conditioned, one scholar has cast doubt on the conclusions drawn from this study (Harris 1979). Harris compared several articles written by Watson on ''Little Albert'' and found that misinterpretations could be made on the basis of the separate reports, especially with regard to the number of pairings of the UCS and the CS. Harris believes there is little evidence for the view that Albert developed a phobia. He also believes that Watson's work contained methodological flaws that make it difficult to draw *any* conclusions from the study. However, it must also be noted that Albert did display an emotional reaction to the white rat approximately one month after the conditioning trials.

Other studies and observations provide some support for the contention that fears and sexual attractions may be acquired through classical conditioning. In studies of phobic patients, approximately 50 percent were able to recall frightening experiences in the development of their excessive fears (Ost and Hugdahl 1981; Rimm et al. 1977). The relationship between the development of a phobia and a traumatic event is illustrated in the case of a seventy-year-old woman who developed an extreme fear of dogs after being attacked by a Saint Bernard. She was bitten repeatedly on the head, stomach, and buttocks. After this event, she experienced terror when she saw any dog and she went so far as to curtail her shopping because of this fear (Thyer 1981).

Sexual deviations and preferences may also be learned through an association process. A mild sexual response to women's shoes was produced in male graduate students by pairing the shoes with slides of nude females. Through association, the shoes acquired some of the properties of the sexual stimuli (Rachman 1966).

Therapy based on classical conditioning The various processes involved in classical conditioning can be used to treat behavior problems. For example, two researchers used conditioning to design an electrical device for treating **enuresis,** or bedwetting (Mowrer and Mowrer 1938). The device is a special pad, placed under the child's bed sheet, which causes a bell to ring when it is wet. The bell is an unconditioned stimulus that causes the child to awaken (the unconditioned response). After it is paired with the ringing of the bell a number of times, the distended bladder (the urge to urinate) serves as a conditioned stimulus. This CS becomes a signal to wake up or tighten the sphincter muscle to prevent urination: a conditioned response. This conditioning apparatus has been used quite successfully for a number of years.

Fears and sexual response patterns acquired through classical conditioning can be removed through extinction—that is, by repeatedly presenting the conditioned stimulus *without* the unconditioned stimulus. Because it is no longer paired with the UCS, the CS gradually loses its acquired properties. The seventy-year-old woman with the fear of dogs was gradually and systematically exposed to dogs under safe conditions over a period of time until her fear had completely faded away. The male students' sexual response to women's shoes gradually disappeared when the shoes were no longer paired with slides showing nude women.

Just as it is possible to create a phobia by repeatedly pairing a neutral stimulus with an unpleasant stimulus, it is also possible to eliminate a phobia through a slightly different procedure, called **counterconditioning.** In this case, the negative stimulus for the undesirable response is paired with a pleasant stimulus until its negative aspects are lost. A three-year-old boy, Peter, who had a fear of rabbits, was treated for his phobia with this method. Peter was given his favorite food to eat while the therapist gradually introduced a rabbit at distances that were not unduly disturbing. The positive aspects of the food eventually overcame the negative (fear-arousing) aspects of the rabbit (Jones 1924). In the case of a $5\frac{1}{2}$-year-old boy with an extreme fear of the dark, the positive effects of a fictional character were employed. The child was especially interested in the cartoon character Batman, so he was asked to imagine that he and his hero were working together on a secret project. While imagining scenes involving himself and Batman, the child was able to tolerate more and more time alone in the dark, until his fear was entirely lost (Jackson and King 1981).

In a process called *systematic desensitization,* Joseph Wolpe (1958, 1973) has used relaxation, assertion, and sexual arousal as anxiety-inhibiting responses to fearful situations. In time, these positive responses reduced or completely eliminated clients' anxieties in such situations.

In the foregoing cases, the capacity of a conditioned stimulus to elicit anxiety was eliminated by associating the CS with a positive response. A reverse process can be employed to reduce the *attractiveness* of a conditioned stimulus. This procedure might be useful in treating problems such as the consumption of alcohol, cigarette smoking, and deviant sexual patterns. To reduce the attractiveness of these behaviors, the therapist associates them with negative responses. For example, an individual who wants to quit smoking might be asked to imagine feeling sick when picking up a cigarette. The therapist might say,

> As you pick up the cigarette, you feel your stomach churning. When you place the cigarette to your lips, you feel vomit entering your throat. You swallow it back down. Lighting the cigarette causes vomit to stream into your mouth. You swallow it back down and take a puff. Vomit ejects from your mouth and nose. It soils your clothes. The smell is terrible. You put out the cigarette, take a shower, and feel relieved.

This use of the imagination to associate a negative quality with a bad habit, called *covert sensitization,* was developed by Joseph Cautela (1966).

The principles of classical conditioning can also be used to produce or strengthen a nondeviant sexual pattern. In *orgasmic reconditioning,* a weak sexual response to an appropriate stimulus is made stronger by pairing it consistently with sexual arousal and orgasm. For people who are sexually excited by inappropriate stimuli, such as children, sexually arousing procedures can be used to increase the sexual attractiveness of adult partners (Leonard and Hayes 1983).

The operant conditioning model

An **operant behavior** is a voluntary and controllable behavior, such as walking or think-

ing, that "operates" on an individual's environment. Suppose you are in an extremely warm room. It would be very difficult for you to consciously control your sweating—to "will" your body not to perspire. You could, however, decide to change your environment by simply walking out of the uncomfortably warm room.

Most human behavior is operant in nature. The concept of **operant conditioning** was formulated by Edward Thorndike (1874–1949) and developed by B. F. Skinner (b. 1904). This type of learning differs from classical conditioning primarily in two ways. First, classical conditioning is involved in the development of involuntary behaviors such as fear, whereas operant conditioning is related to voluntary

FOCUS 3.1

Biofeedback and Involuntary Responses

There has been considerable controversy over the distinction between operant and classical conditioning. At one time some psychologists thought operant procedures were effective only on voluntary behaviors (walking, talking, and so on), which are controlled by the central nervous system, and that only classical conditioning procedures were capable of modifying "involuntary" processes, which are controlled by the autonomic nervous system. In the past, the autonomic nervous system, which controls skin temperature, heart rate, and blood pressure, has been considered beyond conscious control and not amenable to change through reinforcement. Recent studies, however, indicate that operant procedures using **biofeedback** (giving people information about minute changes in their bodily processes) can influence such involuntary processes as irregular heartbeats (Bleeker and Engel 1973), blood pressure

(Miller 1974), skin temperature (Green, Green, and Walters 1970), and cephalic blood volume pulse (Bild and Adams 1980). The results of these studies may lead to a redefinition of the distinction between operant and classical conditioning. Because certain autonomic processes can be controlled through reinforcement, it is possible that many psychophysiological reactions are learned through this procedure. This research also suggests that disorders such as diarrhea, asthma, and hypertension may be treatable with operant principles.

Biofeedback procedures are not a panacea for all problems involving the autonomic nervous system. This form of treatment has clearly helped with migraine headaches and certain forms of seizures, but results with cardiovascular and other conditions have been mixed (Rimm and Masters 1979).

behaviors. (However, as Focus 3.1 notes, this distinction may not be an absolute one.)

Second, as we discussed earlier, behaviors based in *classical* conditioning are controlled by stimuli, or events *preceding* the response: Salivation occurs only when it is preceded by a UCS (food in the mouth) or a CS (the thought of a sizzling, juicy steak covered with mushrooms). In *operant* conditioning, on the other hand, behaviors are controlled by events that *follow* them. Positive consequences increase the likelihood and frequency of a response. But when the consequences are negative, the behavior is less likely to be repeated. For example, a student is likely to raise his or her hand in class often if the teacher recognizes the student, smiles, and seems genuinely interested in the student's comments. However, if the instructor frowns, looks disgusted, or yawns, the student's hand-raising behavior will probably become less frequent.

Principles of operant conditioning   The principles of operant conditioning are statments about the relationships between behavior and consequences (also called *contingencies*). Let us look at some of the most basic of these principles.

☐ *Reinforcement.* Anything that increases the frequency or magnitude of the behavior it follows is called a **reinforcer.** A **positive reinforcer** does so by providing a positive or wanted or pleasant consequence; it may be tangible (money, food, sexual activity) or social (attention, praise, a smile).

Whether a consequence is a reinforcer depends only on its effect. Certain consequences that are aversive to most people can function as reinforcement to others. One study recorded the number of times school children left their seats, and the number of teacher reprimands, in a classroom (Madsen et al. 1970). To assess the relationship between these two variables, teachers were asked to triple the frequency of reprimands. Amazingly, the out-of-seat

The attention, praise, and smiles (positive social reinforcement) this child is getting as he graduates from nursery school should serve as strong inducement for future academic involvement.

behaviors increased. The greater the number of commands to sit down, the more often children stood up! In this situation, reprimands functioned as a reinforcer because they increased the frequency of the response.

A **negative reinforcer** increases the frequency of a behavior by removing an aversive (noxious or punishing) event. A student can alleviate anxiety over a forthcoming exam (which is aversive) by studying lecture notes and the text. The activity of studying increases in frequency because it reduces test anxiety.

☐ *Punishment.* A **punishment** is either the removal of a positive reinforcer or the presentation of an aversive stimulus. Both reduce the probability of the response. In the first kind of punishment, privileges such as use of the car, television viewing, or access to games may be withdrawn after an inap-

Table 3.1 *Increasing and Decreasing the Frequency of Behavior Through Operant Conditioning*

These *increase* the frequency of a behavior	These *decrease* the frequency of a behavior
Positive Reinforcement: Presentation of a positive reinforcer	Punishment: Presentation of an aversive stimulus or removal of a positive reinforcer
Negative Reinforcement: Removal of an aversive event	Extinction: Removal of a positive reinforcer

propriate action is performed. This is often referred to as *response cost*. The second kind of punishment involves the presentation of an aversive consequence such as a reprimand or a spanking.

☐ *Extinction.* You have already seen how extinction works in classical conditioning: After the conditioned stimulus is presented repeatedly without the unconditioned stimulus, the conditioned response disappears. In operant conditioning, **extinction** is the process of eliminating a behavior through nonreinforcement. When the reinforcement for a behavior is discontinued, the behavior usually disappears.

These four basic components of operant conditioning are listed and distinguished in Table 3.1. In addition, you should be aware of two more concepts that are important in the operant conditioning model.

☐ *Discriminative stimulus.* A cue that is usually present when reinforcement occurs is known as a *discriminative stimulus*. For example, through experience people learn that success is more likely when they address a request to a person who is smiling than when they approach one who looks angry. Most people are more likely to cross a street when the light is green than when it is red because of the consequences associ-

ated with the color of the light. In other words, the smile and the green light indicate that reinforcement is likely to follow.

☐ *Shaping.* **Shaping** is the process of developing a new or complex behavior by reinforcing successive behaviors that increasingly approximate the final goal desired by the experimenter. Many responses are very complex and do not usually occur spontaneously. In these cases, the experimenter can break down a response into a series of small steps and can reinforce each step.

Operant conditioning in psychopathology Studies of various types have demonstrated a relationship between environmental reinforcers and certain abnormal behaviors. For example, self-injurious behavior, such as head banging, is a dramatic form of psychopathology that is often reported in psychotic and mentally retarded children. It has been hypothesized that some forms of head banging may be linked to reinforcing features in the environment (Schaefer 1970). To test this hypothesis, a self-injurious behavior (head hitting) was shaped in two monkeys through successive approximations. First the raising of the animal's paw was reinforced, then holding the paw over the head, and finally bringing the paw down on the head. This sequence of behaviors was shaped in about sixteen minutes in both monkeys. The discriminative stimulus for reinforcement was the words, "Poor boy! Don't do that! You'll hurt yourself." Head hitting occurred whenever these words were spoken by the experimenter, because they had been associated with reinforcement (bananas). It seems clear from these findings that self-injurious behaviors can be developed and maintained through reinforcement.

In another instance, an unusually large number of mentally retarded children were engaging in head banging at one institution—a hospital. The superintendent of the hospital became alarmed at the number of children displaying self-injurious behavior and discovered the following sequence of events. As soon as the children began to hit their heads against the wall, the nurses rushed over to comfort them and provided candy. In other words, the nurses were offering rewards contingent on head banging; the candy and attention were serving as positive reinforcers for that behavior! Furthermore, the mere sight of candy functioned as a discriminative stimulus: Children immediately began their head-banging behavior whenever a nurse appeared with candy (Schaefer and Martin 1969).

Although positive reinforcement can account for some forms of self-injurious behaviors, there are instances in which other variables appear to be more important (Carr 1977). Negative reinforcement, for example, can also strengthen and maintain unhealthy behaviors. Consider a student who has enrolled in a class in which the instructor requires oral reports. The thought of doing an oral presentation in front of a class produces feelings of anxiety, sweating, an upset stomach, and trembling in the student. Having these feelings is aversive. To terminate the unpleasant reaction, the student switches to another section whose instructor does not require oral presentations. The student's behavior is reinforced by escape from aversive feelings, and such avoidance responses to situations involving "stage-fright" will increase in frequency.

A type of research that lends itself to study of the relationship between environmental contingencies and problem behaviors is called the single-subject experiment. This research strategy is discussed in Chapter 5, but the steps involved can be demonstrated with the case of Mary, a nine-year-old who had received diagnoses of mental deficiency, autism, and childhood psychosis. Her problem behaviors involved hitting, slapping, pulling hair, tantrums, and spitting. During the *baseline period,* the frequency of these behaviors was recorded. Next, during the *intervention phase,* Mary received praise and a favorite food if she displayed none of the aggressive behaviors during a specified period, as measured by a timer. If any of the target behaviors

occurred during the period, the timer was reset. During this phase, there was a 60 percent drop in the problem behaviors. To make certain that the experimental manipulation was responsible for this reduction, the baseline conditions were reinstated, and Mary was treated as in the baseline period. During this *reversal phase,* her aggressive behaviors returned to preintervention levels. When the experimental procedures were again employed, her problem behaviors plummeted to very low levels (Luiselli and Slocumb 1983). Behaviorists believe that such results clearly indicate the influence of environmental factors in producing and maintaining problem behaviors.

Therapy based on operant conditioning In later chapters on specific psychological disorders, and in Chapter 20 on treatment approaches, we shall discuss a variety of ways in which operant conditioning has been applied to the treatment of abnormal behaviors. Here, we intend only to illustrate the use of the basic principles in treatment procedures.

☐ An eleven-year-old child was suffering delusions (recall from Chapter 1 that delusions are false beliefs held in spite of contrary evidence). The child's delusional statements were reduced when experimenters ignored any statements that stemmed from delusions and fantasies. Appropriate statements increased when *positive reinforcement* was given every time they were made. Overall, the percentage of appropriate verbalizations in the child was increased significantly (Varni et al. 1978).

☐ *Negative reinforcement* in the form of nagging was used to increase the duration of speech in a withdrawn psychotic patient. When the patient spoke only briefly, he was told to speak for longer periods of time. If he did not comply within three seconds, nagging would begin. To avoid this aversive consequence, the patient spoke for longer periods (Fichter et al. 1976).

☐ A fourteen-year-old retarded boy was subject to severe tantrums that caused substantial damage in his home. As operant *punishment,* the boy was required to perform approximately one hour of clean-up work, repairing any damage he had done, after every tantrum. The frequency of tantrums dropped from an average of one per week to none during the final three months of treatment (Altman and Krupsaw 1983).

☐ Two psychologists used *extinction* to eliminate a case of operant vomiting. An eleven-year-old boy was vomiting from two to ten times a day. Physical examinations and tests revealed no organic problem. However, sympathetic attention by family members and assistance in cleaning up consistently followed the vomiting episodes. The psychologists felt that the behavior was being maintained by this social attention. Family members were trained to ignore the vomiting and told not to help the child clean up. Eventually the vomiting ceased (Munford and Pally 1979).

☐ Autistic children are profoundly disturbed; they generally give few vocal responses and show little or no social interaction with peers. Two experimenters (Hingtgen and Trost 1966) were able to *shape* vocal and physical responses in two pairs of autistic children. The experimenters initially rewarded the children for any sound—even a cough, sneeze, or yell. After this, they gave reinforcement only for recognizable syllables. To shape physical contact, they first rewarded the children for physical closeness, then for accidental physical contact, and finally for actual hand-to-body contact. To pair physical contact with vocalizations, they gave reinforcement after one child had touched the other and had made a vocal response. They obtained the final goal of vocal response and physical interaction by reinforcing the children only after *both* had touched each other with their hands and *both* had made vocal responses.

The observational learning model

The traditional behavioral theories of learning—classical conditioning and operant conditioning—require that the individual actually perform behaviors in order to learn them. **Observational learning** theory suggests that an individual can acquire new behaviors by simply watching them performed (Bandura 1969; Bandura and Walters 1963). The process of learning by observing models (and later imitating them) is called vicarious conditioning or **modeling.** Direct reinforcement for imitation of the model is not necessary, although reinforcers are necessary to *maintain* behaviors learned in this manner. Observational learning can involve both respondent and operant behaviors, and its discovery has had such an impact in psychology that it has been propounded as a third form of learning.

Vicarious classical conditioning You would probably not be surprised to hear that an eight-year-old boy who has never left his hometown of Seattle is afraid of snakes, elephants, and monsters, none of which he has ever met. Some of these fears can be explained by the phenomenon of *generalization:* The boy perhaps generalized fears of animals he had encountered, or had been warned about, to creatures he had never seen. However, persons may also acquire fears by seeing others exhibit fear or arousal (through vicarious classical conditioning).

In one study, subjects watched a person go through a classical conditioning procedure in which a neutral stimulus was presented and followed by an electric shock (Berger 1962). The model displayed pain cues (grimaces and jerks) in response to the shock (UCS). The observers, whose emotional reactions were monitored, also developed responses to the conditioned stimulus, although they never received a shock.

In another study, four individuals experienced such symptoms as anxiety reactions,

Young children often learn to play "war" or "shoot-out" by observing adults on television and then imitating what they see. Children's favorite heroes serve as models when the children pretend to be like them and act out their roles.

an inability to sleep, and disturbed physiological functioning after watching the movie *The Exorcist* (Bozzuto 1975). These symptoms were experienced within 24 hours of viewing the film, and all 4 individuals sought psychiatric therapy. One, a 22-year-old female, reported obsessions about whether or not the young priest had gone to hell and about the existence of evil. Problems with insomnia and the inability to eradicate her obsessional thoughts resulted in thoughts of suicide. All 4 patients were restored to their prior level of functioning after 3 to 7 sessions of therapy.

Vicarious operant conditioning   Operant behavior can also be learned through modeling. Some of the most compelling research in this area has examined the acquisition of aggressive behaviors in children.

The finding that symbolic representations of aggressive action in films and television can increase aggression in children has alarmed parents, educators, and researchers. Heavy viewing of aggressive programs, including cartoon shows, on television appears to be related to overt aggression in preschool children (Singer and Singer 1983). The National Institute of Mental Health also found a relationship between the viewing of violent fare on television and aggressive behavior in children (Pearl et al. 1982). In a long-term study, L. D. Eron (1963) surveyed hundreds of third-grade students to assess their television viewing habits and found that children who preferred violent programs were more likely than children who preferred nonviolent fare to be rated aggressive by peers. A follow-up study of this same sample of children ten years later (when the subjects were approximately nineteen years old) again found a correlation between preference for violent programs and aggressiveness ratings (Eron et al. 1972).

Although these studies were correlational, the link between modeled television violence and aggressive behavior has also been demonstrated experimentally. In one study, children were exposed to either a violent television program or a sports show involving track events. When the researchers later observed both groups of children during play activities, they saw significantly more aggression among the children who had watched the violent scenes (Liebert and Baron 1972).

Observational learning does not, however, have to be negative. Prosocial behaviors such as cooperation, empathy, friendliness, and delay of gratification can be increased through appropriate modeling (Rubinstein 1983).

Observational learning in psychopathology and therapy Observational learning approaches, like those emphasizing classical and operant conditioning, assume that abnormal behaviors are learned in the same manner as normal behaviors; exposure to disturbed models is likely to produce disturbed behaviors. Observational learning can have four possible effects on the observers (Spiegler 1983): New behaviors can be acquired by watching a model. A model may serve to elicit particular behaviors by providing observers with cues to engage in those behaviors. Behaviors that are inhibited because of anxiety or other negative reactions may be performed after they are observed. And a behavior may become inhibited in the observer if the model's similar behavior resulted in aversive consequences.

Observational learning has also been applied to the elimination of problem behaviors. For example, a 48-year-old man had been claustrophobic for over 30 years. His extreme fear of confinement probably originated when, as a child, he suffered a severe asthmatic attack while playing underneath his home (which was built on stilts). Being in elevators, sleeping bags, boats, or shower stalls provoked strong anxiety reactions. The client's fear had generalized to the point where he was afraid of being under bed covers or of enduring any kind of oral or nasal constriction, such as wearing a scarf over his mouth. He was also unable to work beneath his automobile, and he had resigned from membership in a volunteer fire department, an activity he valued highly, because he could not tolerate wearing an oxygen mask. Two psychologists treated this client using *participant modeling,* in which the therapist demonstrates the behaviors that the client is to perform. The thirteen-week treatment program involved the therapists' demonstrating tasks such as wearing a handkerchief over the mouth and then having the client perform the same task. At the end of the program, the client had progressed to the point where he could wear a surgical mask and lie in a zipped-up sleeping bag (Speltz and Bernstein 1979).

The cognitive behavioral model

Cognitive behaviorism was developed partly in reaction to the criticism that the traditional behavioral approaches ignore the influence of thought processes (cognition) on behavior. A number of behavior therapists have argued that strict behaviorist approaches overemphasize the importance of external influences at the expense of *mediating processes*— thoughts, perceptions, and self-evaluations— that also determine behavior (Mahoney 1977; Ellis 1962). Because the traditional behaviorists exclude events that are not subject to observation, they do not consider internal mediating processes significant in modifying behavior.

Cognitive behaviorists, on the other hand, feel that the way an individual perceives, anticipates, or evaluates an event—rather than the event itself—often has the greatest impact on his or her behavior. They argue further that the modification of thoughts and feelings is essential to changing behavior. In this respect, the cognitive behavioral model resembles the psychogenic models examined in Chapter 2. However, this approach shares many characteristics with the traditional behavior models. It places great stress on altering behavior, de-emphasizes the importance of childhood experiences, and does not consider that it is necessary to have insight into a problem in order to alleviate it (Beck 1970; Rimm and Masters 1979). Other similarities include a strong emphasis on changes in overt behaviors as the criterion for successful treatment and a heavy reliance on experimental methodology to validate techniques.

Do mediating processes affect an individual's behaviors? Velten (1968) asked subjects to read statements to themselves. Some statements were positive ("I really feel good"); others were negative ("I have too many bad things in my life"). Velten found that subjects' moods varied directly with the type of statement they had read. In a similar experiment, it was found that college students who read negative sentences ("My grades may not be good enough this semester" or "I might flunk out of school") experienced more emotional arousal than subjects who read neutral statements (Rimm and Litvak 1969). In addition, test-anxious individuals and some persons suffering phobic anxieties report having disruptive thoughts in the fear-producing situation (Meichenbaum 1972; Rimm et al. 1977). These studies all support the view that internal processes—at least in the form of verbal self statements—contribute to one's emotional state and thus to one's pattern of behavior.

Cognitive therapy is generally aimed at modifying the client's perception or evaluation of events and situations. To give some indication of the direction taken by therapists, we shall examine two types of cognitive behavioral therapy that are in current use.

Rational–emotive therapy The therapeutic system called **rational–emotive therapy (RET),** identified with Albert Ellis (1962, 1971), strongly emphasizes cognitive variables. Ac-

Albert Ellis (b. 1913) believes that psychological problems occur because of irrational thought processes. In his rational-emotive therapy, the therapist disputes the client's irrational beliefs and helps the client to replace them with more reasonable ideas.

cording to Ellis, psychological problems are produced by irrational thought patterns that stem from the individual's belief system. Unpleasant emotional responses that lead to anger, unhappiness, depression, fear, and anxiety result from one's thoughts about an event rather than from the event itself (see Focus 3.2, p. 88). A student who becomes depressed when he or she fails in a dating situation develops the depression not because of the failure but because of an irrational belief regarding the failure. An appropriate emotional response in such an unsuccessful dating situation might be frustration and temporary disappointment, but a more severe depression develops only if the student adds irrational

Some Common Irrational Assumptions

Rational–emotive therapy (RET) is based on the principle that psychological problems are produced by irrational assumptions like those listed below. Making such irrational assumptions, RET advocates contend, results in anger, fear, anxiety, or depression.

1. It is necessary to be loved or approved by virtually every significant other.
2. One should be thoroughly competent, adequate, and achieving in all possible respects if one is to consider oneself worthwhile.
3. Certain people are bad, wicked, or villainous, and they should be severely blamed and punished for their villainy.
4. It is awful and catastrophic when things are not the way one would like them to be.
5. Human unhappiness is externally caused, and people have little or no ability to control their sorrows and disturbed behavior.

6. If something is or may be dangerous or fearsome, a person should be terribly concerned about it and should constantly dwell on the possibility of its occurring.
7. It is easier to avoid than to face certain responsibilities and difficulties in your life.
8. Each person should be dependent on others; people need someone stronger than themselves to rely on.
9. A person's past history is the all-important determinant of his or her present behavior. Because something once strongly affected a person's life, it should have a similar effect indefinitely in the future.
10. People ought to become quite upset over other people's problems and disturbances.

SOURCE: Adapted from Ellis, A. (1962). *Reason and emotion in psychotherapy* (pp. 61–80). New York: Lyle Stuart. Reprinted with permission of Lyle Stuart, Inc.

---

thoughts, such as "Because this person turned me down, I am worthless . . . I will never succeed with anyone of the opposite sex . . . I am a total failure."

These thoughts continually sustain and regenerate the negative emotions. If the student were to eradicate the irrational self-statements, the negative emotional reaction would also fade away. The rational–emotive therapist asks the student to discriminate between the real event and the untenable assumptions. "Not succeeding with the opposite sex is frustrating," the therapist might point out, "but the conclusion that you are a worthless failure and will never succeed does not follow. The

idea that you will always fail in future encounters is an irrational belief that is producing your depression."

Once the student understands and accepts this interpretation, he or she is trained to eliminate such thoughts and to replace them with more reasonable notions. The student is also assigned "homework" tasks, such as asking others out on dates. It is emphasized that failure is possible until the student develops more social skills or meets more compatible dating partners. However, he or she is to consider these unsuccessful ventures as part of the learning experience—perhaps unpleasant, but necessary.

Ellis (1957) claims a 90 percent success rate using RET, with an average of 27 therapy sessions. Other studies (Meichenbaum et al. 1971) have also reported success. However, most of the experimental support for RET has involved treatment of mild fears in college students; there are few controlled studies involving clinical populations.

Coping strategies   One prominent cognitive theorist, Donald H. Meichenbaum (1976), suggests that therapists not only should deal with clients' specific problems but also should teach them cognitive and behavioral skills—**coping strategies**—that can be applied in a variety of stressful situations. He has developed a training program that can be useful in "inoculating" clients against future problems and in facilitating the development of self-control. His program involves determining his clients' thought patterns and strategies in stressful situations and teaching them more productive self-statements. Table 3.2 (p. 90) gives some examples of coping self-statements designed to be used in a variety of situations.

Learning to replace irrational self-statements with more productive ones allows the client both to adopt problem-solving strategies when faced with a problem and to self-reinforce the appropriate use of these strategies. The program has been used successfully with schizophrenics, who were trained to monitor their own behavior and thinking and to be sensitive to cues from others that they were emitting psychotic symptoms. With this internal approach, the schizophrenics were able to improve their performance in reducing "sick talk," in proverb abstraction, and in inkblot tests. The self-statements included comments such as "be relevant," "be coherent," "make oneself understood," and "give healthy talk" (Meichenbaum 1977).

Although more evaluative research must be conducted before the cognitive learning approach can be evaluated, this approach, with its emphasis on the powerful influence of internal mediating processes, seems to offer an

Donald H. Meichenbaum (b. 1940) suggests that problematic behavior, especially stress-related behavior, can be changed for the better if the person learns new behavior strategies and uses more productive self-statements. Meichenbaum was recently named by his peers as one of the ten most influential clinical psychologists of this century.

exciting new direction for behaviorists. One proponent goes so far as to speculate that psychology is undergoing a "revolution" in that cognitive and behavioral approaches are being integrated—and with the acceptance of many psychologists (Mahoney 1977).

Criticisms of the behavioral models

Behavioral approaches to psychopathology are a strong force in psychology today. The behaviorist perspectives have had tremendous impact in the area of etiology and therapy. Some of these contributions have been

☐ To question the adequacy of the organic model of psychological disorders

Table 3.2 *Examples of Coping Self-Statements*

Preparing for a Stressful Situation

What is it you have to do?
You can develop a plan to deal with it.
Just think about what you can do about it. That's better than getting anxious.
No negative self-statements; just think rationally.
Don't worry; worry won't help anything.
Maybe what you think is anxiety is eagerness to confront it.

Confronting and Handling a Stressful Situation

Just "psych" yourself up—you can meet this challenge.
One step at a time; you can handle the situation.
Don't think about fear; just think about what you have to do. Stay relevant.
This anxiety is what the therapist said you would feel. It's a reminder to use your coping exercises.
This tenseness can be an ally, a cue to cope.
Relax; you're in control. Take a slow deep breath. Ah, good.

Coping with the Feeling of Being Overwhelmed

When fear comes, just pause.
Keep the focus on the present; what is it you have to do?
Label your fear from 0 to 10 and watch it change.
You should expect your fear to rise.
Don't try to eliminate fear totally; just keep it manageable.
You can convince yourself to do it. You can reason your fear away.
It will be over shortly.
It's not the worst thing that can happen.
Just think about something else.
Do something that will prevent you from thinking about fear.
Describe what is around you. That way you won't think about worrying.

Reinforcing Self-Statements

It worked; you did it.
Wait until you tell your therapist about this.
It wasn't as bad as you expected.
You made more out of the fear than it was worth.
Your damn ideas—that's the problem. When you control them, you control your fear.
It's getting better each time you use the procedures.
You can be pleased with the progress you're making.
You did it!

SOURCE: Meichenbaum, D. H. (1976). Cognitive behavior modification. In J. T. Spence, R. C. Carson, and J. W. Thibaut (Eds.), *Behavioral approaches to therapy.* Reprinted by permission of Donald Meichenbaum.

☐ To stress the importance of external influences on behavior
☐ To require strict adherence to scientific methodology
☐ To encourage continuing evaluation of the techniques employed by psychologists

These features endow behaviorism with a degree of effectiveness and accountability that is lacking in the insight-oriented perspectives.

However, a strict behaviorist orientation excludes from consideration the inner determinants of behavior. (This does not, of course, apply to the cognitive learning approaches.) This exclusion has been criticized, as has the behaviorists' extension to human beings of results obtained from animal studies. A lack of attention to human values in relation to behavior has also led to the charge that the behaviorist perspective is mechanistic, viewing people as "empty organisms" (Hayes and Zettle 1979, p. 5). Some critics complain that behaviorists are not open-minded and tend to dismiss out of hand the advances and data accumulated by other approaches to therapy (Hayes and Zettle 1979; Lazarus 1977).

There is, in fact, a movement among some therapists of different schools of thought to seek the best ideas and techniques from all the psychotherapies. They feel that both psychoanalysts and behavior therapists could offer a more complete form of psychotherapy if they listened more carefully to each other and borrowed useful ideas from one another (Wachtel 1977). Cognitive learning theorists are now stressing the importance of internal mediating processes (the individual's perception of events), which has always been emphasized by humanistic psychologists.

It is clear from recent writings and research publications that a major evolution, or revolution, is occurring in behaviorism. This movement may lead to an integration of some of the currently contrasting views on treatment and psychopathology, in line with the eclectic approach discussed in Chapter 2. However, such integration is a long way off, and there are still strong fundamental differences among the major schools of psychotherapy.

A BEHAVIORAL VIEW OF STEVEN V.

In the previous chapter we included three possible treatment approaches to the case of Steven V., as his therapist might apply them. Now suppose that Steve's therapist is strongly oriented toward the behavioral models. He would then discuss Steve's problems, we believe, in terms very much like the following. (Before going on, you may find it useful to refresh your memory by rereading the discussion of Steve's case at the beginning of Chapter 1.)

Let me start by drawing an analogy between behavior and music. In music, all the songs a performer has learned to sing or play are said to make up the performer's *repertoire.* Quite similarly, all the behaviors an individual knows—all the responses the person has learned to make in each given situation—constitute the person's *behavioral repertoire.*

The roots of Steve's problems can be traced to his behavioral repertoire. Many of the behaviors he has learned are inappropriate (much like songs that nobody wants to hear), and his repertoire is deficient in useful, productive behaviors.

Many of Steve's troubles stem from his deficiency in, or lack of, social skills. He has had little practice in social relationships and, as a result, has difficulty distinguishing between appropriate behavior and inappropriate behavior. You can see evidence of these problems in his withdrawn behavior when he is in the company of relatives or his parents' friends and when Linda's friends are around. Steve himself reports that he feels apprehensive and anxious in the company of others (for example, Linda's friends) and finds himself with no idea what to do or say. While others seem to have no difficulty making "small talk,"

Steve remains silent. When he does speak, his statements are ususaly perfunctory, brief, and inappropriate. I think this deficiency stems from Steve's early social isolation, which prevented him from developing interpersonal skills, and from his lack of good role models. His parents seldom interacted with one another or with Steve. Recall that Mr. V.'s manner of relating to his son was generally antagonistic; he did not model effective and appropriate skills.

I am also interested in exploring Steve's bouts of depression, but I need to know several things: First, through what specific behaviors is Steve's depression made manifest? Does he withdraw from social contact? Lose his appetite? Weep? Make negative statements? If we are to help Steve change his behavior, we must know what behavior we are talking about. Too often terms like *depression, passivity,* and *anxiety* are used without a common referent. For example, when a client calls himself "shy," we must be sure that both therapist and client understand the term in the same way.

Second, what situations tend to elicit his depression? If the events share common characteristics, then we may be able to control or alter them to Steve's advantage. Again, it appears that Steve experiences depression when he believes himself to be worthless: when rejected by his lady friend, when belittled by his father, and on becoming impotent in his first sexual encounter. Steve may be able to master such situations by developing more effective behaviors. He might benefit, for example, from learning to respond to his father's bullying by telling his father how hurt and angry he feels when antagonized. A behavioral program designed to enhance Steve's sexual functioning could also prove helpful in combatting his depression. And Steve must learn to challenge his own irrational beliefs—for example, the belief that his father's failure to acknowledge Steve's academic achievements is somehow Steve's fault.

Heterosexual anxiety and impotence also need to be addressed. I believe Steve has a conditioned or learned anxiety toward females and especially toward sexual intercourse. This anxiety not only blocks his ability to relate to members of the opposite sex; it also directly affects his autonomic nervous system, so that sexual arousal is impaired. We must teach Steve through classical conditioning how to subtract anxiety from the sexual encounter. Counterconditioning techniques seem to offer promise in treating Steve's impotence; relaxation could be used as a response that is antagonistic to his anxiety about sexual intercourse.

I have purposely saved the discussion of Steve's delusional system for last. Perhaps you find it difficult to imagine a behavioral analysis of delusions. But I am not concerned with the phenomena of Steve's imagination; my concern is with the behaviors that are alleged to express a delusional system. Many people display inappropriate behaviors that are considered aversive, odd, or unusual but that may be somehow reinforced. Steve's repeated assertion that he is controlled by demonic forces and his continual thinking about Satanism disturb many people. But the people who call him crazy and are occasionally frightened by him may actually be reinforcing these behaviors. When Steve behaves in this way, he garners much attention from his parents, peers, and onlookers. Fully seven pages of a ten-page psychological report, prepared by a therapist two years ago, are devoted to Steve's delusional system. I submit that the therapist found the topic fascinating and spent a lot of time talking with Steve about his delusions. He thus *reinforced* the client's verbal behavior! I am not the only behaviorist who contends that psychoanalytically oriented therapists make this mistake. Many behavioral therapists believe, for example, that psychoanalysts elicit so much sexual material from their clients precisely because they unwittingly reinforce this concentration on sex. Is it possible that Steve's verbal and other behavioral evocations of Satanism would diminish if people ignored them? It is more than possible.

In sum, modeling, role playing, and assertiveness training could be used to enhance Steve's social skills. I would use cognitive strategies and teach him behaviors through which he may more adequately control his environment in order to combat his depression. His heterosexual anxiety and impotence would be treated via counterconditioning methods and relaxation training. Finally, the use of extinction strategies might reduce his excessive concern with Satanism.

THE FAMILY SYSTEMS MODEL OF PSYCHOPATHOLOGY

The biogenic and psychogenic approaches to psychopathology focus on the individual. Even the behavioral schools of thought, though they are concerned with external determinants of behavior, are mainly involved with assessing and altering individual behavior. Given the American emphasis on individual achievement and responsibility—our "rugged individualism"—it is not surprising that these approaches have been very popular in the United States.

The family systems model of psychopathology does not isolate the individual as other theories do. As the term *family systems* indicates, this viewpoint holds that all members of a family are enmeshed in a network of interdependent roles, statuses, values, and norms. What one member does directly affects the entire family system. Correspondingly, individuals typically behave in ways that reflect family influences. Thus the **family systems model** concentrates on the influence of the family on individual behavior.

We can identify three distinct characteristics of the family systems approach (Robinson 1975). First, personality development is ruled largely by the attributes of the family, especially the way our parents behave toward us and around us. Second, abnormal behavior in the individual is usually a reflection or "symptom" of unhealthy family dynamics and, more specifically, of poor communication among family members. Third, the therapist must focus on the family system, not solely on the individual, and must strive to involve the entire family in therapy (see Focus 3.3, pp. 94–95).

Development of personality and identity within the family

One of the earliest and most important proponents of the family systems model was American psychiatrist Harry Stack Sullivan (1892–1949). Sullivan started out with a strong psychoanalytic orientation but eventually broadened his focus to include interpersonal relations. He proposed that our concepts of self, identity, and self-esteem are formed through our interactions with "significant others," typically parents, siblings, and peers (Sullivan 1953). Parents, of course, have the major share of responsibility for socializing the child. If parents behave toward the child as though he or she is worthwhile, the child is likely to develop a positive self-image and sense of self-worth. This sense of self, in turn, provides the emotional resiliency that all people need if they are to persevere through defeats, conflicts, and the many other stressors that day-to-day life serves up. Those parents who do not see their child as a worthwhile person, and who belittle or antagonize the child, may cause the child to develop a negative self-image: "I am worthless." "If I try I'll only fail."

Another neo-Freudian, Erik Erikson, also stressed child-parent relationships. He pointed out that parental love and attention are important in the child's development of a sense of trust (Erikson 1968). We all need a few people whom we can rely on and confide in with confidence. Without this trust we are likely to see the world as dangerous, hostile, and threatening. As a result, we may shun close personal relationships and avoid even casual social interactions. How trust develops in a child depends very much on the parents, as is illustrated in the following case.

Jonathan R. first came to the attention of juvenile authorities at the age of thirteen, when he was picked up for vandalism and repeated truancy from school. At age fifteen he was arrested again, this time for shoplifting and assaulting a clerk. At first Jonathan refused to give his name or cooperate with the police in any way. Finally, when the prospect of incarceration was raised, he relented, giving his name and the names of his parents. He was referred to a child welfare agency.

The social worker assigned to the case found Jonathan guarded, openly hostile, and suspicious of her. He responded noncommittally, disclosed a minimum of information about himself, and would not submit to any diagnostic tests until told their purpose. When a psychiatric evaluation was ordered by the court, he refused to say anything to the examining psychiatrist. During the administration of psychological tests, Jonathan appeared apprehensive and frequently

FOCUS 3.3

Can Psychopathology Serve a Family Function?

Family systems practitioners commonly observe that when two siblings are raised under the same pathological influences, one may be normal but the other quite disturbed. Common sense would lead us to expect that all the siblings should be affected equally by pathological family dynamics. Why aren't they? Could it be that the family systems approach is misguided and that influences outside the family are more powerful shapers of behavior?

Actually, family systems theorists can account for this perplexing situation. According to family systems theory, each family has a wholeness or unity greater than the sum of its parts. An individual child may develop pathological symptoms not from internal conflict, but from the unhealthy values and pressures of family life. Some theorists assert that this pathological behavior may actually serve a family function. Scottish psychiatrist R. D. Laing (1965) has applied the term *mystification* to this phenomenon. Deviances in a family, Laing contends, have meaning and purpose in the context of family interactions. A family member's "madness" may actually preserve the fragile equilibrium of the family. For example, a husband and wife who are experiencing marital discord may avoid potentially damaging conflicts in their marriage by "forcing" one of their children to play the "sick role." In this way, attention is diverted from the parents' unhappiness

stated that he knew "what you're trying to do."

A work-up of Jonathan's family revealed an unemployed father who himself had had numerous run-ins with the law, a mother who worked as a clerk, and two younger brothers who also attended school sporadically. The family atmosphere appeared to be extremely "paranoid" in that all members perceived the outside world as hostile. This was demonstrated during the social worker's first visit to Jonathan's home. When she rang the doorbell, the social worker heard noises behind the door—and the sounds of people scurrying around. After a few moments, she rang the bell again. This time she noticed curtains moving slightly as though someone were peeking at her. When she called out, asking whether anyone was home, a male voice from behind the door asked her what she wanted. She said she was the social worker *who had called earlier*. The voice asked if she had identification. She pushed her business card through the mail slot, and the man asked for further identification. At this point, the social worker became angry and threatened to leave, informing the man that he and his family would then have to visit the agency. At that point she was allowed into the home.

As the social worker became familiar with the family, it became increasingly clear to her that many of Jonathan's problems stemmed from his pathological family identity and upbringing. The father in particular raised his children to trust no one. The parents had no identifiable friends, kept primarily to themselves, and seldom ventured out of their home.

Jonathan manifested many of the behavioral characteristics of the family. His mistrust of people, tendency to be a loner, and inability to form close relationships with others were clearly evident during the time he spent at juvenile hall. When other boys made efforts to include him in their activities, he rebuffed them. In group therapy, Jonathan usually contributed only statements indicating that "You've got to look out for number one!" and "You can't trust no one."

As the case of Jonathan R. illustrates, personality and identity are highly dependent on the attitudes of parents toward their children, and unfulfilled needs. Identifying one member of the family as the problem seems to relieve the entire family system. Parents can avoid their marital conflicts, and siblings can pursue their own development.

Some family systems theorists also assert that if the identified patient is treated *individually* and gets better, another family member may show stronger signs of pathology. This tendency to regain a kind of family equilibrium has been called *family homeostasis*. Many families exist in a closed system: An accepted state of equilibrium or balance has been attained, and change is unwelcome. When a child is treated outside the system and improvement occurs, it unbalances the system. The husband and wife described above can no longer use their "sick" child as an excuse to avoid marital conflicts. To restore balance to the system, the child may be forced to play the sick role again; the family may go to great lengths to undermine the child's treatment and consequent improvement! If this approach does not work, another sibling may begin to exhibit symptoms that represent family pathology. Or the husband and wife may begin to express their conflicts with each other in unhealthy ways, creating an atmosphere of strife and discord.

If such analyses are accurate, an individual's pathological behavior can serve a function in the family. This phenomenon certainly dramatizes the assertion of family therapists that treating one individual in an unhealthy family system is unproductive. The entire family should be the focus of treatment.

Family interaction patterns can exert tremendous influence on a child's personality development, determining the child's sense of self-worth and acquisition of appropriate social skills. A chaotic family life can foster psychological problems in a child.

the values they instill, and the models they provide.

Family dynamics

By **family dynamics** we mean the day-to-day "operation" of the family system, including communication among its members. Inconsistent communication or distorted patterns of operation can cause children to develop a misconception of reality.

Inconsistent messages   A number of theorists have proposed that psychopathology may be the result of inconsistency in family communi-

cations (Bateson et al. 1956; Weakland 1960). Most communications occur at two levels—verbal and nonverbal. The verbal content of a message can be enhanced or negated by its nonverbal content. For example, a father who insists "I am not angry!" but raises his voice, clenches his fists, and pounds the table is physically contradicting his verbal message. Inconsistency may also result when family members continually disqualify one another's messages. For example, a mother who tells her child one thing may have her message negated by the father: "Your mother doesn't know what she's talking about." Such contradictions create a *double bind* within the child, which may result in an inability to communicate, social withdrawal, and eventually schizophrenia (Smith 1972; Abels 1975, 1976; Bateson 1978; Nichols 1984). The process is discussed in greater detail in Chapter 16.

Pathological family patterns A number of studies have suggested that psychopathology may be the result of disturbed relationships within families (Lidz et al. 1957; Hoffman 1981; Framo 1982; Trotzer 1982). Two patterns of family interaction have been implicated in the development of serious personality problems: marital schism and marital skew.

In *marital schism,* the husband and wife have an antagonistic relationship and openly derogate one another. Threats of separation and divorce, mutual defiance and mistrust, and attempts to coerce the children to side with one parent or the other are recurrent if not constant. The child is often expected to fulfill the needs of both parents, a role in which the child is almost certainly doomed to fail. Often the child becomes the parents' scapegoat, taking the blame for the parents' hostility toward each other.

In *marital skew,* the serious pathology of one parent dominates the home. Interactions within the family system are structured such that family members support the pathological behavior. The following case illustrates this pattern.

> Mario C., a former marine sergeant, ran his family like a military unit. His wife catered to his every wish and forced her four children (two boys, ages twelve and sixteen; two girls, ages thirteen and fifteen) to be equally obedient. All had to rise at 6 A.M. The girls would help their mother cook breakfast while Mr. C. and his sons went through a 45-minute exercise routine. He inspected each child's bed, making sure it was properly made. When a bed did not meet his standards, Mr. C. ripped off all the bedding and forced the offending child to remake the bed completely.
>
> On one occasion the oldest son became angry and said other children did not live the way they did. Mr. C. struck his son, knocking him to the floor. For nearly half an hour, Mr. C. gave the boy a stern lecture about other families that had lost the values of love and respect for one another; divorce and juvenile delinquency were the result. He, however, ran a good family and was teaching his children to respect their parents. At the end of the lecture, Mr. C. ordered his son to do fifty pushups and one hundred situps as punishment.
>
> On the rare occasions when the children complained to their mother, Mrs. C. staunchly defended her husband. She pointed out that Mr. C. worked hard for a living, that he was teaching them good survival skills, that he knew how the world worked, and that there was nothing wrong with him. It would benefit them, she said, to be more like their father.

The dynamics of the C. family are typical of marital skew. Here the husband exhibits a serious pathology that dominates the family, and the wife supports the husband's interpretation of reality. Suggestions that something may be wrong within the family are flatly denied. As a result, the children are daily subjected to a deviant picture of reality. Among children from such a background, the risk of psychopathology is relatively high.

Family therapy

In family systems therapy, the therapist's objective is to help clients understand the alliances and relationships among family members, try new patterns of interactions, and develop new ways to communicate with one another.

Two theorists and practitioners who have contributed valuable ideas to the practice of family therapy are Virginia Satir (1967) and Salvador Minuchin (1974, 1981). They share many assumptions concerning the development of pathology and its treatment, but their focal points differ. Satir emphasizes communication in her *conjoint family therapy;* family members are taught message-sending and message-receiving skills and are encouraged to use them. Minuchin concentrates on changing the roles and relationships within the family system in his *structural family therapy.* Restructuring a pathogenic family system, Minuchin contends, and having members alter their relationships with one another can result in a healthier family.

Criticisms of the family systems model

The family systems approach has added an important social dimension to our understanding of abnormal behavior, and there is no denying that we are social creatures. There is, in fact, much evidence that unhealthy family relationships can contribute to the development of disorders. But the family systems model is subject to a number of criticisms. For one thing, both its basic tenets and its specific applications are difficult to study and quantify. As you will see in Chapter 16, the double-bind hypothesis is very controversial, and the controversy intensifies when the hypothesis is applied to the acquisition of severe disorders like schizophrenia. For example, it is often difficult to obtain agreement among psychologists on whether a double bind actually exists within a given family. Then there is the fact that not all siblings raised in a pathological family environment become disturbed. It seems that factors beyond family life may be equally influential in mental health.

As we have stated frequently, a psychologist who places too much emphasis on any one model may overlook the influence of factors that are not included in that model. But exclusive emphasis on the family systems model may have particularly unpleasant consequences. Too often, psychologists have pointed an accusing finger at the parents of children who suffer from certain disorders, despite an abundance of evidence that parental influence may not be a factor in those disorders. The parents are then burdened with guilt over a situation they could not have controlled. (We shall discuss this problem in greater detail when we examine childhood disorders in Chapter 18.)

A FAMILY SYSTEMS VIEW OF STEVEN V.

What if Steven V.'s therapist was a proponent of the family systems model? We believe he would view Steve and his family very much as follows.

Officially, only Steve is my client. In reality, however, Steve's father and mother are also suffering, and their pathological symptoms are reflected in Steve. My attempts to help Steve must therefore focus on the entire family. It is obvious that the relationship between Steve and his father, that between Steve and his mother, and that between his father and mother are unhealthy. Let me comment briefly on each of these relationships.

Relationship between Steve and his father If we accept that a person's identity, self-concept, and feelings of self-worth are based on how significant others treat the person, it is not hard to see why Steve has very low self-esteem. It appears that he could do nothing right in his father's eyes. Mr. V. constantly derogated his son, seldom praised him, and always focused on Steve's inadequacies and mistakes. Steve's case records are filled with examples of this negative interaction:

☐ Steve had many medical problems as a young child. He was prone to ear infections and colds, had multiple allergies, and seemed to contract an unusual number of childhood illnesses. He also seemed accident-prone and one time suffered a near-fatal injury when he walked into a playground swing. Instead of expressing concern and sympathy when his son was ill or got hurt, Mr. V. became irritated and angry at Steve. He teased him, called him a "weakling," and blamed him for the illness or injury.

☐ At school Steve was frequently the butt of his classmates' pranks and was constantly teased and beaten by them. His father's reaction to these incidents was to call his son a "sissy," someone who was unmasculine and "didn't have the guts to defend himself."

☐ Even when Steve had successes (academically he was outstanding), Mr. V. did not praise him but instead emphasized that Steve could do better still. Early in his life his father labeled him a "bookworm," a social isolate who would "never amount to anything."

As a result of this consistently negative interaction, Steve's self-concept is negative. He sees himself as inadequate and ineffectual. For this reason he withdraws from social interactions, neglects to learn new behaviors, and has a fatalistic outlook on life.

Relationship between Steve and his mother   This relationship is more complicated than that between father and son. On the surface it appears that his mother was affectionate, warm, and loving toward Steve. But much of this behavior seems to have been simulated by, or to have arisen out of, the mother's unfulfilled needs. We have considerable evidence that the mother continually gave inconsistent messages to Steve. I submit that Mrs. V. actually had a deep-seated hostility toward her son but masked it in socially appropriate ways. For example, Steve's childhood illnesses seemed to upset Mrs. V. quite a bit—not out of concern for her child, but because these illnesses interfered with her own social plans. She sent double messages to Steve: "I'm worried about you. Are you okay?" on the one hand, and "Why did you have to get sick? Now I can't go to the theatre this evening" on the other. One message is "I love and care about you," and the other is "I don't love you." Consider the confusing double bind Steve experiences. If he responds to the first message, he must deceive himself into believing his mother loves him—a distortion of reality. If he responds to the second and more accurate message, he must asknowledge that he is unloved. He's damned if he does and damned if he doesn't. Other examples of double messages can be seen in the mother's alternately seductive and withdrawing behavior toward Steve. Mrs. V. was physically sexual in having him sleep with her when she was scantily clothed, but she withdrew and punished him when he became sexually aroused.

Relationship between husband and wife   Mr. and Mrs. V. had a relationship that we can characterize as isolative. Each seemed to live a separate life, even when they were together in the same house. Both had unfulfilled needs, and both denied and avoided interactions and conflicts with one another. Publicly they maintained the façade of the ideal family, but privately they seemed to care little for one another. Neither wanted to confront their unfulfilling relationship: The wife knew of the husband's extramarital affairs but pretended she didn't, and the husband knew of his wife's unhappiness but never mentioned it. To avoid dealing with their marital disappointments, the parents made Steve their scapegoat. As long as Steve was the "identified patient" and was seen as "the problem," Mr. and Mrs. V. could continue in their mutual self-deception that all was well between them.

Even though Steve does not live at home while college is in session, his psychological roots remain there, and his parents are still enormously influential in his life. It would therefore be most desirable to include the entire family in a program of therapy.

Table 3.3 *A Comparison of the Most Influential Models of Psychopathology*

	Biogenic	Psychoanalytic	Humanistic
Motivation for Behavior	State of biological integrity and health	Unconscious influences	Self-actualization
Basis for Assessment	Medical tests, self-reports, and observable behaviors	Indirect data, oral self-reports	Subjective data, oral self-reports
Theoretical Foundation	Animal and human research, case studies, and other research methods	Case studies, correlational methods	Case studies, correlational and experimental methods
Source of Abnormal Behavior	Biological trauma, heredity, biochemical imbalances	Internal: early childhood experiences	Internal: incongruence between self and experiences
Treatment	Biological interventions (drugs, ECT, surgery, diet)	Dream analysis, free association, transference; locating unconscious conflict from early childhood; resolving the problem and reintegrating the personality	Nondirective reflection, no interpretation; providing unconditional positive regard; increasing congruence between self and experience

A FINAL NOTE ABOUT THE MODELS OF PSYCHOPATHOLOGY

Table 3.3 compares the models of psychopathology that we have discussed in Chapter 2 and this chapter. Each model has devout supporters who, in turn, are influenced by the model they support. But even though theory building and the testing of hypotheses are critical to psychology as a science, it seems evident that we can best understand abnormal behavior only by integrating the various approaches. We are all biological, psychological, *and* social beings. To neglect any one of these aspects of human life would be to deny an important part of our existence.

SUMMARY

1. Behaviorism evolved in the early twentieth century, at a time when the existing theories of psychology emphasized the subjective

Table 3.3 (continued)

Existential	Traditional Behavioral	Cognitive Behavioral	Family Systems
Capacity for self-awareness; freedom to decide one's fate; search for meaning in a meaningless world	External influences	Interaction of external and cognitive influences	Interaction with significant others
Subjective data, oral self-reports, experiential encounter	Observable, objective data, overt behaviors	Self-statements, alterations in overt behaviors	Observation of family dynamics
An approach to understanding the human condition rather than a firm theoretical model	Animal research, case studies, experimental methods	Human research, case studies, experimental methods	Case studies, social psychological studies, experimental methods
Failure to actualize human potential; avoidance of choice and responsibility	External: learning maladaptive responses or not acquiring appropriate responses	Internal: learned pattern of irrational or negative self-statements	External: faulty family interactions (family pathology and inconsistent communication patterns)
Provide conditions for maximizing self-awareness and growth, to enable clients to be free and responsible	Direct modification of the problem behavior; analysis of the environmental factors controlling the behavior and alteration of the contingencies	Understanding relationship between self-statements and problem behavior; modification of internal dialogue	Family therapy involving strategies aimed at treating the entire family, not just the identified patient

analysis of the inner—and unobservable—workings of the mind. John B. Watson proposed that psychology's goal should be the prediction and control of human behavior and that, as a science, psychology should be limited to the study of observable and measurable events. Traditional behaviorists are concerned primarily with the influence of environmental factors on behavior through the processes of learning.

2. The traditional behavioral models of psychopathology hold that abnormal behaviors are acquired through association (classical conditioning) or reinforcement (operant conditioning). Negative emotional responses such as anxiety can be learned through classical conditioning: A formerly neutral stimulus evokes a negative response after it has been presented along with a stimulus that already evokes that response. Negative voluntary behaviors may be learned through operant conditioning if those behaviors are reinforced (rewarded) when they occur.

3. Some psychologists assert that the acquisition of many complex behaviors cannot be explained solely by classical or operant conditioning. These behaviors may, however, be acquired through observational learning, in which an individual learns behaviors by observing them in other people, who act as models, and then imitating them. Pathological behavior results when inappropriate behavior is imitated or when normal behavior is inappropriately applied.

4. Cognitive behaviorism developed partly as a reaction to the criticism that traditional behaviorists ignore the influence of thought processes on behavior. According to the cognitive behavioral model, perceptions of events are mediated by thoughts and feelings, and the perception may have a greater influence on behavior than the event itself. Despite this emphasis on cognition, the model shares many characteristics with the traditional behavioral models. Cognitive therapeutic approaches, such as rational–emotive therapy and coping strategies, are generally aimed at normalization of the client's perception of events.

5. The family systems model asserts that family interactions guide the individual's development of personal identity and a sense of reality. Abnormal behavior is viewed as the result of distortion or faulty communication within the family. Children who receive inconsistent messages from parents, or who are subjected to skewed family patterns, may develop behavioral and emotional problems. Therapeutic techniques generally focus on the family as a whole, rather than on one disturbed individual.

KEY TERMS

behavioral models Models that are based on the idea that all behavior, normal and abnormal, is learned through interaction between the person and the environment

classical conditioning An associative learning process through which neutral stimuli become able to evoke involuntary responses

cognitive behaviorism A theory of learning which holds that conscious thought mediates, or modifies, an individual's behavior in response to a stimulus

counterconditioning A therapeutic means of eliminating anxiety by gradually pairing the fear-producing stimulus with an opposing response, such as relaxation

extinction In classical and operant conditioning, the process by which a response is gradually eliminated by not being reinforced

family systems model A model of psychopathology that emphasizes the influence of the family on individual behavior

observational learning theory A theory of learning which holds that individuals can learn new behaviors by watching other people perform those behaviors and then imitating them

operant conditioning A theory of learning, applying primarily to voluntary behaviors, which holds that these behaviors are controlled by the consequences that follow them

reinforcer In operant conditioning, a consequence that increases the frequency or magnitude of the behavior it follows; may be positive or negative

stimulus control In classical and operant conditioning, the situation in which the occurrence or nonoccurrence of a particular behavior is influenced by a preceding stimulus

4

Classification and Assessment of Abnormal Behavior

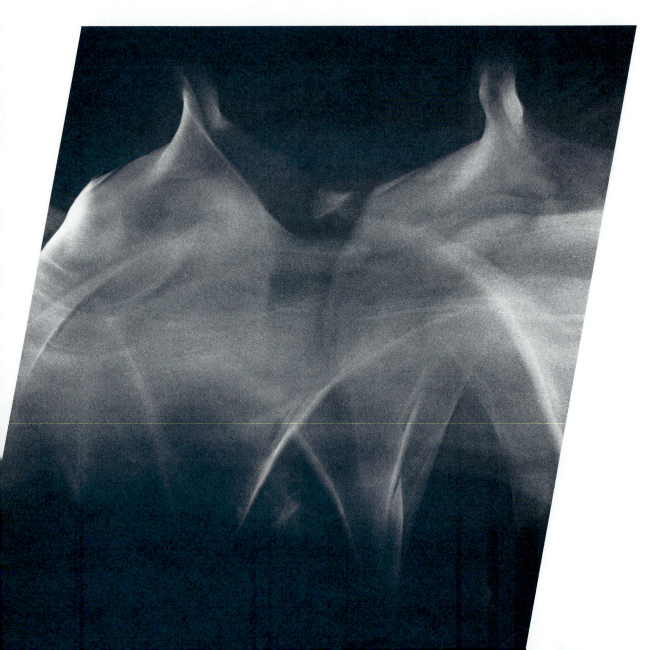

We noted in Chapter 1 that a psychodiagnosis, which involves describing and drawing inferences about an individual's psychological state, is often an early step in the treatment process. It is for many psychotherapists the basis on which a program of therapy is first formulated. This diagnosis is developed by *assessing* the patient's condition—that is, by obtaining and evaluating as much information as possible about the patient. Among the assessment tools available to the clinician are observation, conversations and interviews, a variety of psychological tests, and the reports of the patient and his or her relatives and friends. When the data gathered from all sources are combined and analyzed, the therapist can have a good picture of the patient's behavior and mental state.

In most cases, the information-gathering process results in a rather bulky file on the patient. The information needs to be sorted and integrated—boiled down to its essentials and categorized on the basis of similarities or relatedness.

This *classification* of behaviors or of information about behaviors offers several advantages. First, it helps to clarify the therapist's "picture" of the client's mental state; once the data are organized, they are easier to analyze. Second, if the classification scheme is an effective one, it can lead the therapist to possible treatment programs. Third, the names of the categories within a classification scheme provide concise descriptions of or referents to symptoms and disorders; these are useful in communications among psychologists, including the reporting of research findings, to the extent that each name means the same thing to all those who use the scheme. Finally, the use of a classification scheme has the effect of standardizing psychological assessment procedures. That is, if particular information is required for classification, therapists tend to use the assessment techniques that provide that information. Thus classification may affect the entire psychodiagnostic process, as well as the treatment program that follows it.

In this chapter we examine the most-used diagnostic classification system and assessment methods and discuss some of the issues involved in their use.

THE CLASSIFICATION OF ABNORMAL BEHAVIOR

The goal of having a **classification system** for abnormal behaviors is to provide distinct categories, indicators, and nomenclature for different patterns of behavior, thought processes, and emotional disturbances. Thus the pattern that is classified as, say, *paranoid schizophrenic* should be clearly different from the pattern named *borderline personality*. At the same time, the categories should be constructed in such a way as to accommodate the wide range of possible variation in these patterns. That is, the clinician should be able to readily categorize paranoid schizophrenic behavior as such, even when the patient does not exhibit the "perfect" or "textbook" paranoid schizophrenic pattern.

Problems with early diagnostic classification systems

As indicated in our brief history in Chapter 1, the first effective classification scheme for mental disorders was devised by Emil Kraepelin toward the end of the nineteenth century. Kraepelin was a proponent of the organic view of psychopathology, and his system had a distinctly biogenic slant. Classification was based on symptoms exhibited by the patient, as is the case in medicine. It was hoped that disorders evidenced by similar

groups of symptoms would possess a common **etiology** (the causes or origins of the disorders); would require similar treatments and would respond to those treatments similarly; and would progress similarly if left untreated.

Many of these same expectations were held for the *Diagnostic and Statistical Manual of Mental Disorders* (DSM-I) published by the American Psychiatric Association in 1952 and based on Kraepelin's system. However, these expectations were not realized in DSM-I or in DSM-II, a revised version of DSM-I that was published in 1968. The major criticism of these two classification manuals was that they were not sufficiently reliable or valid for general diagnostic purposes (Rosenhan 1973). Reliability and validity are fundamental to any diagnostic scheme and, in fact, to any scientific construct.

Reliability The **reliability** of a procedure or test is the degree to which it yields the same result repeatedly, under the same circumstances. The greater the difference between repeated trials, the lower the reliability.

A variety of techniques may be used to test the reliability of a diagnostic classification system (Anastasi 1982). One that is of particular interest to psychologists is the extent to which different clinicians using the system agree on the diagnosis for a particular patient. We should expect a certain amount of disagreement among different clinicians using any classification system. However, the amount of disagreement between professionals using DSM-I and DSM-II was so pronounced that the reliability of these systems of classification was seriously questioned.

Early studies that compared the diagnoses of pairs of clinicians found poor agreement between the members of each pair (Ash 1949; Schmidt and Fonda 1956). The greatest disagreement was found in *specific* categories, even though, in about 80 percent of the pairs, both clinicians agreed on which *general* category (organic, psychotic, or personality disturbance) a particular disorder belonged in.

The fact that agreement was high in the larger, more inclusive classes indicates that these categories are not totally arbitrary. Nonetheless, reliability in pinpointing broad categories is not very helpful in rendering a specific diagnosis.

Other reliability studies, in which the same information was presented to clinicians on two occasions or at different times, revealed that their diagnoses did not usually agree (Beck 1962; Wilson and Meyer 1962). Personal bias, too, seems to have affected the particular diagnosis given. Relationships have been found between the characteristics of psychiatrists who diagnosed the patients and the particular diagnoses that the patients received (Mehlman 1952; Raines and Rohrer 1955).

Much of the unreliability of DSM-I and DSM-II can be attributed to the diagnostic categories themselves. Three sources of diagnostic error have been identified: Five percent of the errors were attributable to the patients, who gave different material to different interviewers. Nearly one-third (32.5 percent) of the errors were due to inconsistencies among diagnosticians in interview techniques, in interpretation of similar data, and in judging the importance of symptoms. Most significantly, however, 62.5 percent of the errors derived from inadequacies of the diagnostic system (Ward et al. 1962). It was simply not clear which behavior patterns belonged in which categories.

Validity The **validity** of a procedure or test is the degree to which it actually performs the function it was designed to perform. With respect to diagnosis, a classification scheme that is supposed to distinguish, say, depression from anxiety should not misclassify an anxiety disorder as depression.

Many critics questioned the validity and usefulness of psychiatric classification (Kanfer and Phillips 1970; Ferster 1965; Ullmann and Krasner 1965; Jones, Kahn, and Langsley 1965). They claimed that DSM did not adequately convey information about underlying

In an 1883 publication, the psychiatrist Emil Kraepelin (1856–1926) proposed that mental disorders could be directly linked to organic brain disorders, and further proposed a diagnostic classification system for disorders. Kraepelin is also noted for being a pioneer in experimental abnormal psychology. He established his own laboratory where he conducted research on mental illness.

causes, processes, treatment, and prognosis. (A **prognosis** is a prediction of the future course of an untreated disorder.) In a study conducted on 793 psychiatric patients, one group of researchers found that "the problem of validity lies at the heart of the confusion which surrounds psychiatric diagnosis. . . . Beyond the gross symptomology of the patient, . . . the criticism that *class membership does not predict important aspects of a disorder* appears to be a legitimate one" (Zigler and Phillips 1961, p. 612, emphasis added). In other words, knowledge of which particular diagnostic category the patient had been placed in (such as paranoid schizophrenic) revealed relatively little about the actual behavior of the patient, the cause of such behavior, or the type of treatment most likely to help the patient.

The problem arose because DSM-I and DSM-II were strongly influenced by the biogenic model of mental illness, in which etiology is supposed to be a basis of classification. With the exception of the categories of organic mental disorders (brain damage), which may parallel diseases, most of the other DSM categories were purely descriptive. Kraepelin's attempt to develop a classification system that would identify causes and differential treatment was not realized, especially in the case of functional disorders where the physical causes are unknown.

The current system: DSM-III

The problems inherent in the 1952 and 1968 editions of the DSM led to the 1980 version, DSM-III. Although Kraepelin's concepts still underlie some of its categories, DSM-III is innovative and substantially revised from the previous manuals. For example, to improve reliability, the exact criteria to be used in rendering a diagnosis are specified. Clinical usefulness and suitability for research studies were considered. DSM-III is intended to be atheoretical and descriptive, making it more useful to clinicians of varying orientations. Although the newest version is still undergoing extensive field testing, preliminary studies suggest that reliability of diagnosis is higher in DSM-III than in DSM-I or DSM-II (Millon 1983; Spitzer and Forman 1979; Spitzer, Forman, and Nee 1979).

DSM-III recommends that the individual's mental state be examined and evaluated with regard to five factors or dimensions (called *axes* in the manual). The five-dimensional evaluation is intended to provide more comprehensive and useful information than previous systems (Millon 1983). Axes I, II, and III deal with the individual's present condition.

- □ *Axis I—Chief clinical syndrome.* The patient's most serious problem is classified in one or more of the diagnostic categories listed in the manual.
- □ *Axis II—Personality or specific developmental disorders.* Along with the chief problem, patients may also have personality or, in the case of children, developmental disorders; these are specified, also from a list.
- □ *Axis III—Physical disorders.* Listed here are any physical or medical problems that accompany the mental disorder. This axis was included because physical disorders are potentially relevant to the understanding and treatment of the individual.

Axes IV and V provide additional information about the person's life situation and probable degree of success in coping.

- □ *Axis IV—Psychosocial stressors.* The severity of stressors contributing to the disorder is rated on a seven-point scale from *none* to *catastrophic.* This information can provide insight into the causes or prognosis of the disorder.
- □ *Axis V—Highest level of adaptive functioning.* The patient's highest level of functioning during the past year is rated on a seven-point scale from *superior* to *grossly impaired.* This information, too, may be of significance in prognosis, because the disturbed individual may return to the previous level of adaptive functioning after an episode of the disorder (American Psychiatric Association 1980).

Table 4.1 (pp. 110–111) lists the disorders (categories) that are included in DSM-III. Specific criteria for applying each of these categories are given in the manual, in a form that is expected to add both reliability and validity.

A Classification According to DSM-III

The Client: Mark is a 56-year-old machine operator who was referred for treatment by his supervisor. The supervisor noted that Mark's performance at work had deteriorated during the past 9 months. Mark was frequently absent from work, had difficulty getting along with others, and often had a strong odor of liquor on his breath after his lunch break. The supervisor knew Mark was a heavy drinker and suspected that Mark's performance was affected by alcohol consumption. In truth, Mark could not stay away from drinking. He consumed alcohol every day; during weekends, he averaged about 16 ounces of scotch per day. Although he had been a heavy drinker for 30 years, his consumption had increased after his wife divorced him a year ago. She claimed she could no longer tolerate his drinking, extreme jealousy, and unwarranted suspicions concerning her marital fidelity. Co-workers avoided Mark because he was a cold, unemotional person who distrusted others.

During interviews with the therapist, Mark revealed very little about himself. He blamed others for his drinking problems: If his wife had been faithful or if others were not out to get him, he would drink less.

Mark appeared to overreact to any perceived criticisms of himself. A medical examination revealed that Mark was developing cirrhosis of the liver as a result of his chronic and heavy drinking.

The Evaluation: Mark's heavy use of alcohol, which interfered with his functioning, resulted in an *alcohol abuse* diagnosis on Axis I. Mark also exhibited a personality disorder, which was diagnosed as *paranoid personality* on Axis II because of his suspiciousness, hypervigilance, and other behaviors. Cirrhosis of the liver was noted on Axis III. Primarily because of Mark's divorce, a rating of 5 (severe) was given him on Axis IV to indicate the level of psychosocial stressors. Finally, on Axis V, Mark was rated 4 (fair) for his highest level of functioning, mainly because, until about 9 months ago, he seemed to be able to function reasonably.

Mark's diagnosis, then, was as follows:
Axis I—Syndrome: alcohol abuse
Axis II—Personality disorder: paranoid personality
Axis III—Physical disorder: cirrhosis
Axis IV—Stressors: divorce, 5 (severe)
Axis V—Highest level of functioning: 4 (fair)

Focus 4.1 provides an example of the diagnoses that result from the five-axis evaluation.

Evaluation of DSM-III

It is too soon to provide a comprehensive evaluation of DSM-III. Clinicians need time to become accustomed to this diagnostic system; extensive research needs to be conducted on its reliability and validity with different populations; and the social and research consequences of its use need to be studied.

Nevertheless, objections have been raised by a number of psychologists who feel that DSM-III has a strong medical orientation, even though more than half the disorders listed are not attributable to known or presumed organic causes and should not be considered biogenic in nature (Schacht and

Table 4.1 *DSM-III Classification: Categories for Axes I and II*

DISORDERS USUALLY FIRST EVIDENT IN INFANCY, CHILDHOOD OR ADOLESCENCE

Mental retardation

Mild mental retardation
Moderate mental
    retardation
Severe mental retardation
Profound mental
    retardation
Unspecified mental
    retardation

Attention deficit disorder

    with hyperactivity
    without hyperactivity
    residual type

Conduct disorder

Undersocialized,
    aggressive
Undersocialized,
    nonaggressive
Socialized, aggressive
Socialized, nonaggressive
Atypical

Anxiety disorders of childhood or adolescence

Separation anxiety
    disorder
Avoidant disorder of
    childhood or adolescence
Overanxious disorder

Other disorders of infancy, childhood or adolescence

Reactive attachment
    disorder of infancy
Schizoid disorder of
    childhood or adolescence
Elective mutism
Oppositional disorder
Identity disorder

Eating disorders

Anorexia nervosa
Bulimia
Pica
Rumination disorder of
    infancy
Atypical eating disorder

Stereotyped movement disorders

Transient tic disorder
Chronic motor tic disorder
Tourette's disorder
Atypical tic disorder
Atypical stereotyped
    movement disorder

Other disorders with physical manifestations

Stuttering
Functional enuresis
Functional encopresis
Sleepwalking disorder
Sleep terror disorder

Pervasive developmental disorders

Infantile autism
Childhood onset pervasive
    developmental disorder
Atypical

Specific developmental disorders
Note: These are coded
on Axis II.

Developmental reading
    disorder
Developmental arithmetic
    disorder
Developmental language
    disorder
Developmental
    articulation disorder
Mixed specific
    developmental disorder
Atypical specific
    developmental disorder

ORGANIC MENTAL DISORDERS

Section 1. Organic mental disorders whose etiology or pathophysiological process is listed below

Dementias arising in the senium and presenium

Primary degenerative
    dementia, senile onset,
    with delirium
    with delusions
    with depression
    uncomplicated
Primary degenerative
    dementia, presenile onset
Multi-infarct dementia

Substance-induced

Alcohol
    intoxication
    idiosyncratic intoxication
    withdrawal
    withdrawal delirium
    hallucinosis
    amnestic disorder
    dementia associated
    with alcoholism
Barbiturate or similarly
    acting sedative or
    hypnotic
    intoxication
    withdrawal
    withdrawal delirium
    amnestic disorder
Opioid
    intoxication
    withdrawal
Cocaine
    intoxication
Amphetamine or similarly
    acting sympathomimetic
    intoxication
    delirium
    delusional disorder
    withdrawal
Phencyclidine (PCP) or
    similarly acting
    arylcyclohexylamine
    intoxication
    delirium
    mixed organic mental
    disorder
Hallucinogen
    hallucinosis
    delusional disorder
    affective disorder
Cannabis
    intoxication
    delusional disorder
Tobacco
    withdrawal
Caffeine
    intoxication
Other or unspecified
substance
    intoxication
    withdrawal
    delirium
    dementia
    amnestic disorder
    delusional disorder
    hallucinosis
    affective disorder
    personality disorder
    atypical or mixed
    organic
    mental disorder

Section 2. Organic brain syndromes whose etiology or pathophysiological process is either noted as an additional diagnosis or is unknown.

Delirium
Dementia
Amnestic syndrome
Organic delusional
    syndrome
Organic hallucinosis
Organic affective
    syndrome
Organic personality
    syndrome
Atypical or mixed organic
    brain syndrome

SUBSTANCE USE DISORDERS

Alcohol abuse
Alcohol dependence
    (Alcoholism)
Barbiturate or similarly
    acting sedative or
    hypnotic abuse
Barbiturate or similarly
    acting sedative or
    hypnotic dependence
Opioid abuse
Opioid dependence
Cocaine abuse
Amphetamine or similarly
    acting sympathomimetic
    abuse
Amphetamine or similarly
    acting sympathomimetic
    dependence
Phencyclidine (PCP) or
    similarly acting
    arylcyclohexylamine abuse
Hallucinogen abuse
Cannabis abuse
Cannabis dependence
Tobacco dependence
Other, mixed or
    unspecified substance
    abuse
Other specified substance
    dependence
Unspecified substance
    dependence
Dependence on
    combination of opioid and
    other nonalcoholic
    substance
Dependence on
    combination of
    substances, excluding
    opioids and alcohol

Table 4.1 *(continued)*

SCHIZOPHRENIC DISORDERS

Schizophrenia,
  disorganized
  catatonic
  paranoid
  undifferentiated
  residual

PARANOID DISORDERS

Paranoia
Shared paranoid disorder
Acute paranoid disorder
Atypical paranoid disorder

PSYCHOTIC DISORDERS NOT ELSEWHERE CLASSIFIED

Schizophreniform disorder
Brief reactive pyschosis
Schizoaffective disorder
Atypical pyschosis

AFFECTIVE DISORDERS

Major affective disorders

Bipolar disorder,
  mixed
  manic
  depressed
Major depression,
  single episode
  recurrent

Other specific affective disorders

Cyclothymic disorder
Dysthymic disorder
  (or Depressive neurosis)

Atypical affective disorders

Atypical bipolar disorder
Atypical depression

ANXIETY DISORDERS

Phobic disorders (or
Phobic neuroses)
  Agoraphobia with panic
    attacks
  Agoraphobia without
    panic attacks
  Social phobia
  Simple phobia

Anxiety states (or Anxiety
neuroses)
  Panic disorder
  Generalized anxiety
    disorder
  Obsessive compulsive
    disorder (or
    Obsessive
    compulsive neurosis)
Post-traumatic stress
  disorder
  acute
  chronic or delayed
Atypical anxiety disorder

SOMATOFORM DISORDERS

Somatization disorder
Conversion disorder (or
  Hysterical neurosis,
  conversion type)
Psychogenic pain disorder
Hypochondriasis
  (or Hypochondriacal
  neurosis)
Atypical somatoform
  disorder

DISSOCIATIVE DISORDERS (OR HYSTERICAL NEUROSES, DISSOCIATIVE TYPE)

Psychogenic amnesia
Psychogenic fugue
Multiple personality
Depersonalization
  disorder
  (or Depersonalization
  neurosis)
Atypical dissociative
  disorder

PSYCHOSEXUAL DISORDERS

Gender identity disorders

Transsexualism
Gender identity disorder
  of childhood
Atypical gender identity
  disorder

Paraphilias

Fetishism
Transvestism
Zoophilia
Pedophilia
Exhibitionism
Voyeurism
Sexual masochism
Sexual sadism
Atypical paraphilia

Psychosexual dysfunctions

Inhibited sexual desire
Inhibited sexual
  excitement
Inhibited female orgasm
Inhibited male orgasm
Premature ejaculation
Functional dyspareunia
Functional vaginismus
Atypical psychosexual
  dysfunction

Other psychosexual disorders

Ego-dystonic
  homosexuality
Psychosexual disorder not
  elsewhere classified

FACTITIOUS DISORDERS

Factitious disorder with
  psychological symptoms
Chronic factitious disorder
  with physical symptoms
Atypical factitious disorder
  with physical symptoms

DISORDERS OF IMPULSE CONTROL NOT ELSEWHERE CLASSIFIED

Pathological gambling
Kleptomania
Pyromania
Intermittent explosive
  disorder
Isolated explosive disorder
Atypical impulse control
  disorder

ADJUSTMENT DISORDER

  with depressed mood
  with anxious mood
  with mixed emotional
    features
  with disturbance of
    conduct
  with mixed disturbance of
    emotions and conduct
  with work (or academic)
    inhibition
  with withdrawal
  with atypical features

PSYCHOLOGICAL FACTORS AFFECTING PHYSICAL CONDITION

Note: Specify physical condition on Axis III.

PERSONALITY DISORDERS

Note: These are coded on Axis II.

Paranoid
Schizoid
Schizotypal
Histrionic
Narcissistic
Antisocial
Borderline
Avoidant
Dependent
Compulsive
Passive–Aggressive
Atypical, Mixed or other
  personality disorder

CONDITIONS NOT ATTRIBUTABLE TO A MENTAL DISORDER THAT ARE A FOCUS OF ATTENTION OR TREATMENT

Malingering
Borderline intellectual
  functioning
Adult antisocial behavior
Childhood or adolescent
  antisocial behavior
Academic problem
Occupational problem
Uncomplicated
  bereavement
Noncompliance with
  medical treatment
Phase of life problem or
  other life circumstance
  problem
Marital problem
Parent–child problem
Other specified family
  circumstances
Other interpersonal
  problem

Note: The categories that in DSM-II were grouped together as Neuroses are included in Affective, Anxiety, Somatoform, Dissociative, and Psychosexual Disorders.

There is a fine line between mental disorders and extreme but normal behavior. Shy children could easily be diagnosed as disordered, when instead their social development may simply be delayed.

Nathan 1977). Many psychologists believe that the medical emphasis of DSM-III is due in part to the need of psychiatrists to define abnormality more strongly within their profession. A survey of psychotherapists who are psychologists indicated that there was little enthusiasm for DSM-III (Smith and Kraft 1983). Most of the respondents rejected the notion that mental disorders form a subset of medical disorders. They preferred a social–interpersonal, rather than a medical, approach to mental disorders. However, no such alternative to DSM-III enjoys widespread use at present.

Other psychologists question the utility of the DSM-III classification scheme for research purposes. Some of the categories were created out of compromises between conflicting views or were rooted in practical considerations such as ease of application and acceptability to practitioners. For these reasons, DSM-III may be difficult to use for scientific purposes (Zubin 1977/1978).

While agreeing that DSM-III is an improvement over previous versions, Garmezy (1978) feels that too many behaviors of children are considered as deficits and mental disorders. For example, *avoidant disorder of childhood* is defined as "persistent and excessive shrinking from contact with strangers." Under this rubric, millions of shy children might be considered to be suffering from a mental disorder when it might be more appropriate to characterize their behaviors as delayed social development.

Millon (1983) has tried to clarify the intent of DSM-III and to respond to critics. He noted that the classification system was not intended to imply that all mental disorders have an organic basis. To Millon the important question is whether DSM-III is a substantial improvement over past systems. He believes it is. Millon also points out that the construction of a diagnostic classification system is an ongoing process, requiring continual revision and improvement. Criticisms of DSM-III will, no doubt, be considered in the development of DSM-IV.

As noted earlier, preliminary research suggests that DSM-III yields greater reliability in diagnosis than previous versions. In fact, one would expect better reliability on logical grounds alone. DSM-III specifies the criteria for rendering a diagnosis much more clearly than DSM-II, and in much greater detail. (As an example, Table 4.2 compares the DSM-II and DSM-III definitions of paranoid personality disorder.) Through the specific nature of its criteria, and through the inclusion of such measures as age of onset of the disorder and the number of symptoms required for each diagnosis, DSM-III eliminates much of the guesswork and ambiguity that plague DSM-II. Whether such criteria are better able to distinguish disorders—to provide greater validity—remains to be determined. We should note, however, that improved reliability may be one means of improving validity.

An alternative approach: behavioral classification

Some alternatives to the traditional (DSM) classification and diagnostic procedures have gained support; those that have been developed furthest are behavioral in outlook. Goldfried and Davison (1976), in their classification scheme, categorize deviant behaviors according to the variables that are maintaining these behaviors (see Table 4.3, p. 114). They use five categories to classify disorders. The first involves *stimulus control:* Either different stimuli do not produce different (and appropriate) behaviors, or particular stimuli produce inappropriate behaviors. For example, a child may learn to be physically aggressive playing

Table 4.2 *Comparison of the DSM-II and DSM-III Definitons of Paranoid Personality Disorder.*

The vague prose of DSM-II has been replaced with lists of precise, readily applicable criteria in DSM-III.

Paranoid Personality (DSM-II)
This behavioral pattern is characterized by hypersensitivity, rigidity, unwarranted suspicion, jealousy, envy, excessive self-importance, and a tendency to blame others and ascribe evil motives to them. These characteristics often interfere with the patient's ability to maintain satisfactory interpersonal relations. Of course, the presence of suspicion of itself does not justify this diagnosis, since the suspicion may be warranted in some instances.

Diagnostic criteria for Paranoid Personality Disorder (DSM-III)

A. Pervasive, unwarranted suspiciousness and mistrust of people as indicated by at least three of the following:
(1) expectation of trickery or harm; (2) hypervigilance, manifested by continual scanning of the environment for signs of threat, or taking unneeded precautions; (3) guardedness or secretiveness; (4) avoidance of accepting blame when warranted; (5) questioning the loyalty of others; (6) intense, narrowly focused searching for confirmation of bias, with loss of appreciation of total context; (7) overconcern with hidden motives and special meanings; (8) pathological jealousy.

B. Hypersensitivity as indicated by at least two of the following:
(1) tendency to be easily slighted and quick to take offense; (2) exaggeration of difficulties, e.g., "making mountains out of molehills"; (3) readiness to counterattack when any threat is perceived; (4) inability to relax.

C. Restricted affectivity as indicated by at least two of the following:
(1) appearance of being "cold" and unemotional; (2) pride taken in always being objective, rational, and unemotional; (3) lack of a true sense of humor; (4) absence of passive, soft, tender, and sentimental feelings.

D. Not due to another mental disorder such as Schizophrenia or a Paranoid Disorder.

SOURCE: DSM-II, p. 42, DSM-III, p. 309.

Table 4.3   *A Behavioral Approach to Classification*

I. Difficulties in Stimulus Control of Behavior
   Environmental stimuli may fail to control maladaptive instrumental behavior or
   some stimuli may elicit maladaptive emotional reactions.
   A. Defective stimulus control. The individual possesses an adequate behavioral
      repertoire but is unable to respond to socially appropriate discriminative
      stimuli.
   B. Inappropriate stimulus control. The individual has intensive aversive emo-
      tional reactions that are elicited by objectively innocuous cues.

II. Deficient Behavioral Repertoires
    The individual lacks social skills needed to effectively cope with situational de-
    mands.

III. Aversive Behavioral Repertoires
     Maladaptive behavior patterns that are aversive to other people are included here.

IV. Difficulties with Incentive Systems (Reinforcers)
    Deviant behaviors that are functionally tied to reinforcing consequences would be
    placed in this category.
    A. Defective incentive system in individual. The person's behavior is not under
       the control of social stimuli that are reinforcing to most people.
    B. Inappropriate incentive system in the individual. This category includes indi-
       viduals for whom the incentive system itself is maladaptive. Those things
       reinforcing are harmful and/or culturally disapproved.
    C. Absence of incentives in environment. The person's environment is lacking in
       reinforcement.
    D. Conflicting incentives in environment. In this category are maladaptive be-
       havior patterns stemming from conflicting environmental consequences.

V. Aversive Self-Reinforcing Systems
   It is assumed that cognitive processes can maintain behavior so that the presence
   or absence of self-reinforcement influences behaviors and emotions.

SOURCE: Goldfried, M. R. & Davison, G. C. (1976). *Clinical Behavior Therapy.* New
York: Holt, Rinehart and Winston. Copyright © 1976 by Holt, Rinehart and Winston, Inc.
Reprinted by permission of CBS College Publishing.

football and then bring such behavior into the classroom. The change of stimuli (playing field to classroom) fails to change the child's behavior. Or a stimulus or situation, such as the classroom, may elicit a strong and inappropriate emotional response, such as fear.

The second category comprises deficiencies in the range of skills required for day-to-day living. When one or more of these skills are lacking in an individual, he or she is said to exhibit a *deficient behavioral repertoire.*

The third category involves *aversive behaviors*—those that are unpleasant, irritating, or harmful to others.

Difficulties with *incentive systems,* or reinforcers for appropriate behavior, are included in the fourth category. As indicated in Table 4.3, these difficulties are of four types: the reinforcers may be defective or weak, they may themselves be inappropriate, some reinforcers may be missing, or various reinforcers may conflict with each other.

Finally, the fifth category involves *aversive self-reinforcement* or the absence of positive self-reinforcement. Persons who have unrealistically high standards of behavior, for instance, may be very critical of their own performance. As a result, they may fail to appreciate their accomplishments and become depressed or feel inadequate.

Obviously, an individual may manifest problems that can be classified in several of these categories. Nevertheless, because this system emphasizes the variables that maintain behavioral patterns, it enables the therapist to isolate those variables for treatment purposes (Goldfried and Davison 1976).

There is evidence that the reliability and validity of the behavioral classification approach is superior to those of DSM (Bellack and Hersen 1980). However, many clinicians and therapists prefer a psychodynamic (rather than a purely behavioral) approach to disorders and thus to assessment and classification as well.

Objections to classification

Diagnostic classification has been criticized on the grounds that it fosters belief in an erroneous all-or-nothing quality of psychopathology. As we noted in Chapter 1, behaviors lie on a spectrum from normality to abnormality. To place a diagnostic label on someone categorizes that person as "abnormal" and implies that he or she is qualitatively different from normal. Many psychologists now perceive that, for many disorders, the differences between normal and abnormal are differences of degree, not of kind.

In Chapter 1 we also touched on two problems that can arise when a diagnosis becomes a label. Here are three more.

1. *A label can cause people to interpret all activities of the affected individual as pathological.* A young psychology intern, who was training in the psychiatric ward of a VA hospital, was extremely open in talking about his feelings of inadequacy. Most people have such feelings, but his openness gave him the reputation of being anxious. On the basis of this prejudgment and label, his supervisor became concerned about the young intern's competence and watched him very closely. One of the supervisor's chief complaints about the intern was that his anxiety prevented him from acquiring sufficient information during interviews with patients. Frustrated by his inability to shake this impression from the supervisor's mind, the intern took copious notes on all his patients. When he was next scheduled to present a case to his supervisor, the young intern prepared thoroughly and memorized details of the patient's life. He displayed a remarkable knowledge of the patient's life history to his supervisor that day, but the supervisor's response was not at all what he expected. The supervisor felt that the intern's *anxiety* had caused him to become so compulsive in obtaining information from patients that he was not listening to their feelings! Thus a label can predispose one to distort even contradictory evidence to fit into the frame of reference dictated by the label.

2. *A label may cause others to treat an individual differently even when he or she is perfectly normal.* A study by Rosenthal and Jacobson (1968) has shown how a label can cause differential treatment. They randomly assigned school children to either of two groups. Teachers were told that tests of one group indicated that they were potential intellectual "bloomers" (gaining in competence and maturity); the other group was not given this label. After a one-year interval, children from both groups were retested (they had also been tested the year before). The experimenters found that those identified as bloomers showed dramatic gains in IQ. How did this occur? Many have speculated that the label led teachers to have higher intellectual expectations for the "bloomers" and thus to treat them differently. Even though there was no significant difference in IQ between the two groups to begin with, differences *were* present by the end of the year. (The Rosenthal and Jacobson study has been criticized on the basis of its methodology and statistical analy-

Sanity or Insanity: The Consequences of Labeling?

Can sane people be diagnosed as disturbed? To find out, psychologist D. L. Rosenhan (1973) sent eight experimenters as *pseudopatients* to different psychiatric hospitals. Their assignment was first to simulate psychiatric symptoms so as to gain admission into psychiatric wards and, once there, to behave in a normal manner. Rosenhan wanted the pseudopatients to record their experiences as patients without hospital staff members becoming aware of the experiment.

Several interesting and provocative findings emerged. First, no one on the ward staff in the hospitals ever detected the fact that the pseudopatients were normal—despite the fact that many *patients* suspected the pseudopatients were not crazy but were merely "checking up on the hospital." In fact, the pseudopatients' length of hospitalization ranged from 7 to 52 days. Second, nearly all the pseudopatients were initially diagnosed as schizophrenic. And

many of their normal behaviors on the ward were subsequently interpreted as manifestations of schizophrenia; one example was "excessive note-taking." Third, the staff failed to interact much with patients, who were treated as powerless, irresponsible individuals.

Rosenhan concludes that it is difficult to distinguish the sane from the insane in mental hospitals, that the labels applied to patients often outlive their usefulness, and that the hospital environment is harsh and frequently maintains maladaptive behaviors. His study has generated a great deal of controversy (Millon 1975; Weiner 1975). One critic argues that, because patients did report abnormal symptoms at the time of hospital admission, it is understandable that they were hospitalized (Spitzer (1975). And, although the pseudopatients were not detected by the staff, they were all released within 60 days. All were said to be "in remission."

sis. Nevertheless, other studies have yielded similar results) (Rappaport and Cleary 1980).

3. *A label may cause those who are labeled to believe that they do indeed possess such characteristics. In these cases, the label becomes a self-fulfilling prophecy.* In the Rosenthal and Jacobson study cited above, the label not only caused teachers to behave differently but also affected the children. It is possible that, when people are constantly told by others that they are stupid or smart, they may come to believe such labels. For example, if people ascribe certain stereotypical traits to a racial minority or an ethnic group, then it is reasonable to believe that they will behave differently toward that group and cause cognitive and behavioral changes among members of

that group. Rosenhan (1973) has shown how people labeled mentally ill can become trapped by this label. Rosenhan's most renowned research study is discussed in Focus 4.2.

THE ASSESSMENT OF ABNORMAL BEHAVIOR

Assessment is the process of gathering information and drawing conclusions about the traits, skills, abilities, emotional functioning, and psychological problems of the individual, generally for use in developing a diagnosis. Three principal means of assessment are available to clinicians: observations, interviews, and psychological tests.

Observations

Observations of overt behavior provide the most basic method of assessing abnormal behavior; indeed, observation is the most basic tool in all of science. Because research methods are examined in Chapter 5, we shall concentrate here on clinical observations. These can be either controlled or naturalistic. *Controlled* observations are made in a laboratory, clinic, or other contrived setting. *Naturalistic* observations, which are much more characteristic of the clinician's work, are those made in a natural setting—a schoolroom, an office, a hospital ward, or a home—rather than in a laboratory.

Observations of behavior are usually made in conjunction with an interview, although verbal interaction is not necessary. A trained clinical psychologist watches for external signs or cues and expressive behaviors that may have diagnostic significance (Kleinmuntz 1967). The client's general mode of dress (neat, conventional, sloppy, flashy), significant scars or tattoos, and even the type of jewelry worn may be correlated with personality traits or perhaps with pathology. Likewise, people's expressive behaviors, such as body posture, facial expression, body type, language and verbal patterns, handwriting, and self-expression through graphic art, may all reveal certain characteristics of their lives. Here is an example:

> It was obvious from even a casual glance that Margaret had not taken care of herself for weeks. Her face and hands were dirty. Her long hair, which had originally been done up in a bun, had shaken partially loose on one side of her head and now hung down her left shoulder. Her blouse hung out of her skirt, and her sweater was worn inside out. Her beat-up tennis shoes were only halfway on her stockingless feet. She wore no makeup; her unkempt and disheveled

appearance and her stooped body posture would lead one to believe she was much older than her actual age.

> When first interviewed, she sat as though she did not have the strength to straighten her body. She avoided eye contact with the interviewer and stared at the floor. When asked questions, she usually responded in short phrases: "Yes," "No," "I don't know," "I don't care." There were long pauses between the questions and her answers. Each response seemingly took great effort on her part.

> Margaret is a 37-year-old depressive patient who was seen by one of the authors in a hospital psychiatric ward. She had recently been admitted for treatment.

Some psychologists rely on trained raters, or on parents, teachers, or other third parties, to make the observations and gather information for assessment and evaluation. Others prefer their own observations to those of a third party.

Interviews

The clinical interview is a time-honored tradition as a means of psychological assessment. It provides the opportunity for observation of the subject as well as for collection of data about the person's life situation and personality. But, although mental health practitioners tend to rely heavily on the interview, they differ in the importance they place on the data obtained.

Depending on the particular disciplinary training of the interviewer, the frame of reference for the interview and its emphasis may vary considerably. (This has been a source of inconsistency and error in the assessment of clients.) Psychiatrists, being trained in medicine, may be much more interested in biological or physical variables. Social workers may be more concerned with life-history data and the socioeconomic environment of the client. Clinical psychologists may be most interested in establishing rapport with clients as a form of therapy.

During the clinical interview the therapist can observe and gather information about the client. Moreover, the client can use the interview to gather important information about the therapist, such as his or her training, theoretical orientation, licensure status, and overall manner and style.

Likewise, variations within the discipline of psychology affect the interview. Because of their strong belief in the unconscious origin of behavior, psychoanalysts may be more interested in psychodynamic processes than in the surface content of the client's words. They are also more likely to pay particular attention to life-history variables and dreams. Behaviorists are more likely to concentrate on current environmental conditions as related to the client's behavior. However, it should be noted that, in practice, different mental health practitioners can also exhibit a great deal of similarity in style.

Standardization   Interviews vary in the degree to which they are structured and consistently conducted in the same manner. In some, the patient is given considerable freedom about what to say and when to say it. The clinician does little to interfere with conversation or direct its flow. Psychoanalysts, who use free association, and Rogerians, who carry on non-directive therapy, tend to conduct highly unstructured interviews. Behaviorists tend to use more structured interviews.

The most highly structured interview is the formal standardized interview. The questions are usually arranged as a checklist, complete with scales for rating answers. The interviewer uses the checklist to ask the same set of questions of each interviewee, so that errors are minimized.

Samples of questions and rating scales from Spitzer's psychiatric evaluation form are shown in Table 4.4. The left-hand column contains specific questions to be asked by the interviewer and comments for the interviewer. The right-hand column provides scales and instructions for rating the patient's answers. Although this type of assessment instrument usually has high reliability, it does not allow the kind of free-flowing (and generally useful) interaction that occurs in less structured interviews.

Errors   In the field of mental health, straightforward questions do not always yield usable or accurate information. Believing personal information to be private, patients may refuse to reveal it, may distort it, or may lie about themselves. Furthermore, many patients may not be able to articulate their inner thoughts and feelings. The interview should therefore be considered a measurement device that is fallible and subject to error (Wiens 1983).

Three sources of interviewing errors were summarized by Kleinmuntz (1967). One is the interview process itself and the relationship between the interviewer and interviewee. If either the client or the clinician does not respect the other, or if one or the other is not feeling well, information exchange may be blocked. A second source of error may be intense anxiety or preoccupation on the part of the interviewee; his or her revelations may be inconsistent or inaccurate. Third, the interviewer may be a source of error. A clinician's unique style, degree of experience, and theoretical orientation definitely will affect the

Table 4.4 *Sample Structured Interview Questions from Spitzer's Psychiatric Evaluation Form*

Interview Guide	Scales

Original Complaint

If a psychiatric patient: Now I would like to hear about your problems or difficulties and how they led to your coming to the (hospital, clinic).

General Condition

Tell me how you have been feeling recently. (Anything else been bothering you?)

Physical Health

How is your physical condition?

Does any part of your body give you trouble?

Do you worry much about your health?

            Physical Health

    Somatic Concerns

Excessive concern with bodily function, preoccupation with one or more real or imagined physical complaints of disabilities; bizarre or unrealistic feelings or beliefs about his body or parts of body.

Do not include mere dissatisfaction with appearance.
  ? 1 2 3 4 5 6

If necessary, inquire for doctor's opinion about symptoms or illnesses.

When you are upset do you react physically . . . like (stomach trouble, diarrhea, headaches, sick feelings, dizziness)?

Appetite-Sleep-Fatigue

Disturbances in these areas are often associated with Depression, Anxiety, or Somatic Concerns.

What about your appetite for food?

Do you have any trouble sleeping or getting to sleep? (Why is that?)

How easily do you get tired?

              Mood

This section covers several methods. The interviewer must determine to what extent the symptoms are associated with either one or the other or several of the dimensions.

What kinds of moods have you been in recently?

              Mood

Elated Mood

Exhibits or speaks of an elevated mood, exaggerated sense of well being or optimism, of feelings of elation. Examples: Says "everything is great," jokes, witticisms, silly remarks, singing, laughing or trying to get others to laugh or smile.
  ? 1 2 3 4 5 6

What kinds of things do you worry about? (How much do you worry?)

What kinds of fears do you have? (Any situation . . . activities . . . things?)

How often do you feel anxious or tense? When you are this way, do you react physically . . . like sweating, dizziness, cramps?)

Anxiety

Remarks indicate feelings of apprehension, worry, anxiety, nervousness, tension, fearfulness, or panic. When clearly associated with any of these feelings, consider insomnia, restlessness, physical symptoms (e.g., palpitations, sweating, dizziness, cramps), or difficulty concentrating, etc.
  ? 1 2 3 4 5 6

SOURCE: Spitzer, R. L., Endicott, J., Mesnikoff, A. and Cohen, G. (1967–1968) *Psychiatric evaluation form: Diagnostic version.* New York: Biometric Research, New York State Psychiatric Institute.

Table 4.5 *Interview Errors and Their Possible Resolutions*

Error Source	Description	Resolution
Interview process	Error results from the complex interaction of interviewer, interviewee, and the setting; usually results in random, rather than directional, error.	Conduct as many interviews as feasible with the same respondents.
Interviewee	Error results from fears and anxieties, misinformation, role expectations.	Carefully structure the interview situation and anticipate expectations.
Interviewer	Error results from idiosyncrasies of various interviewers, recording errors, making inferences beyond obtained data, poor training, theoretical biases, inexperience.	Standardize interviewer strategies and intensive training; establish a uniform system for collecting data.

SOURCE: Kleimuntz, B. (1982). *Personality and psychological assessment.* New York: St. Martin's Press, p. 195.

interview. Table 4.5 summarizes these three sources of interviewing errors and suggests potential resolutions.

Psychological tests

Psychological tests have been used to assess maladaptive behavior, development of social skills, intellectual abilities, vocational interests, and brain damage. Tests have also been constructed for the purpose of understanding personality dynamics and conflicts. They vary in form (that is, they may be oral or written and may be administered to groups or to individuals), structure, degree of objectivity, and content. Most do, however, share two characteristics: First, they provide a standard situation in which certain kinds of responses are elicited. The same instructions are given to all who take the same test, the same scoring is applied, and similar environmental conditions are maintained to ensure that the responses of each test taker are due to his or her unique attributes rather than due to differences in situations. Second, by comparing them with norms, the therapist uses these responses to

make inferences about the underlying traits of the person. For instance, a person who answers "yes" to questions like "Is someone trying to control your mind?" more frequently than most other persons might be assumed to be responding in a manner similar to diagnosed paranoids.

In the remainder of this section we examine two different types of personality tests (projective and objective) and tests of intelligence and brain damage.

Projective personality tests A **projective personality test** is one in which the test taker is presented with ambiguous stimuli, such as inkblots, pictures, or incomplete sentences, and is asked to respond to them. The stimuli are generally novel, and the test is relatively unstructured. Conventional or stereotyped patterns of response usually do not fit the stimuli. The person must "project" his or her attitudes, motives, and other personality characteristics into the situation. The nature of the appraisal is generally well disguised: Subjects are often unaware of the true nature or purpose of the test and usually do not recognize the significance of their responses.

No matter which form of test is used, the goal of projective testing is to obtain a multi-faceted view of the total functioning person, rather than a view of a single facet or dimension of personality. We shall concentrate on inkblot descriptions and storytelling because they are both popular and typical of projective tests.

The **Rorschach technique** was devised by Swiss psychiatrist Hermann Rorschach in 1921 for personality appraisal. A Rorschach test consists of a series of cards displaying symmetrical inkblot designs. The cards are presented one at a time to subjects, who are asked (1) what they see in the blots and (2) what characteristics of the blots make them see what they say they see. Inkblots are thought to be appropriate stimuli because they are ambiguous, are nonthreatening, and do not elicit learned responses.

What people see in the blots, whether they focus on large areas or details, whether they respond to color, and whether their perceptions suggest movement are assumed to be symbolic of inner promptings, motivations, and conflicts. Subjects must react in a personal and "unlearned" fashion, because there are no right or wrong answers. These reactions are interpreted by the psychologist. Both the basic premise of the Rorschach test and the psychologist's interpretation of the symbolism within the patient's responses are strongly psychoanalytic. Seeing eyes or buttocks may imply paranoid tendencies; fierce animals imply aggressive tendencies; blood, strong uncontrolled emotions; food, dependency needs; and masks, avoidance of personal exposure (Klopfer and Davidson 1962).

There are actually a variety of approaches to the interpretation and scoring of Rorschach responses. The most extensive and recent is that of Exner (1983), whose scoring system is based on reviews of research findings and studies of the Rorschach technique. Exner thinks of the Rorschach as a problem-solving task; test takers are presented with ambiguous stimuli that they interpret according to their

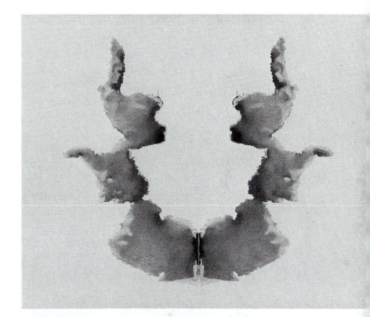

The Rorschach technique uses a number of cards that each show a symmetrical inkblot design. The earlier cards in the set are black and white, while the later cards are more colorful. A client's responses to the inkblots are interpreted according to assessment guidelines and can be compared by the therapist to the responses that other clients have made.

preferred mode of perceptual–cognitive processing. His ideas have generated a great deal of excitement among clinicians who have been dissatisfied with the many approaches that were not strongly based in research findings.

The **Thematic Apperception Test** (TAT) was first developed by Henry Murray in 1935 (Murray and Morgan 1938). Like the Rorschach, the TAT taps underlying motives, drives, and personality processes through projection. However, most clinicians agree that the TAT is best at uncovering aspects of interpersonal relationships. It consists of thirty picture cards, each typically depicting two human figures. Their poses and actions are vague and ambiguous enough to be open to different interpretations. Some cards are designated for specific age levels or for a single sex, and some are appropriate for all groups.

In the Thematic Apperception Test, clients tell a story about each of a series of pictures they are shown. These pictures—often depicting one, two, or three people doing something—are less ambiguous than Rorschach inkblots.

Generally, twenty TAT cards are shown to the subject, one at a time, with instructions to tell a story about each picture. Typically, the tester says, "I am going to show you some pictures. Tell me a story about what is going on in each one, what led up to it, and what its outcome will be." The entire story is recorded verbatim. There is usually no limit on time or the length of the stories.

The subject's responses are interpreted by a trained clinician, either subjectively or by using a formal scoring system. Both usually take into account the style of the story (length, organization, and so on); recurring themes, such as retribution, failure, parental domination, aggression, and sexual concerns; the outcome of the story in relationship to the plot; primary and secondary identification (the choice of hero or secondary person of importance); and the handling of authority figures and sex relationships. The purpose is to gain insight into the subject's conflicts and worries as well as clues about his or her core personality structure.

Other types of projective tests are briefly described in Focus 4.3.

The analysis and interpretation of responses to projective tests are subject to wide variation. Clinicians given the same data frequently disagree with one another about scoring. Much of this disparity is due to the fact that clinicians differ in orientation and personal style. But, as noted earlier, the demonstrably low reliability and validity of these instruments means that they should be used with caution. And even when projective tests exhibit reliability, they may still have low validity. For example, many clinicians may agree that certain specific responses to the Rorschach inkblots indicate repressed anger. The fact that many clinicians agree makes the test reliable, but those specific responses could be indicators of something other than repressed anger. Some have warned that illusory correlations may exist and that clinicians may erroneously link a patient's response to the existence of a syndrome (Chapman and Chapman 1967).

Objective personality inventories   Unlike projective tests, **objective personality tests** supply the test taker with a list of alternatives from which an answer is selected. The "questions" are usually self-descriptive statements with which subjects are asked to either agree or disagree. Because a predetermined score is assigned to each possible answer, human judg-

Two Additional Projective Techniques

In the *sentence-completion* test, the subject is given a list of partial sentences and is asked to complete each of them. Typical examples:

My ambition _____.
My mother was always _____.
I can remember _____.

One popular sentence-completion instrument is the *Incomplete Sentences Blank* (ISB) developed by Rotter (Rotter and Rafferty 1950). Although the ISB is considered a projective technique, it actually falls somewhere between the purely objective and the purely projective extremes. It is direct, it lacks disguise, can be objectively scored on an adjustment–maladjustment scale, and scoring does not require the degree of training that is necessary to score the Rorschach and TAT tests (Phares 1984).

In *draw-a-person* tests such as the Machover D-A-P (Machover 1949), the subject is actually asked to draw a person. Then he or she may be asked to draw a person of the opposite sex. Finally, the subject may be instructed to make up a story about the characters that were drawn or to describe the first character's background. Many clinicians analyze these drawings for size, position, detail, and so on, under the assumption that the drawings provide diagnostic clues. For example, disproportionately large heads may be drawn by persons suffering from organic brain disorders. The validity of such assumptions is open to question, and well-controlled studies cast some doubt on diagnostic interpretations (Anastasi 1982).

mental factors in scoring and interpretation are minimized. In addition, subjects' responses and scores can be compared readily.

Perhaps the most widely used personality inventory is the **Minnesota Multiphasic Personality Inventory** (MMPI) (Hathaway and McKinley 1943). This test consists of 566 statements and subjects are asked to indicate whether each statement is true or false as it applies to them. There is also a "cannot say" alternative, but using this category is strongly discouraged because too many such responses can invalidate the test.

The test taker's MMPI results are rated on ten clinical scales and three validity scales. The clinical scales were constructed by analyzing the responses of different types of diagnosed psychiatric patients (and the responses of normal subjects) to the 566 test items to determine the kinds of responses each of the various types of psychiatric patients usually made. Table 4.6 (p. 124) shows the possible responses to ten sample items and the kinds of responses that contribute to a high rating on each scale. The validity scales assess the degree of candor, confusion, and falsification. They help the clinician detect potential faking or special circumstances that may affect the outcome of other scales.

A basic assumption of the MMPI is that people whose MMPI answers are similar to those of diagnosed patients are likely to behave similarly to those patients. However, single-scale interpretations are fraught with hazards. Although a person with a high rating on Scale 6 may be labeled paranoid, many "paranoids" are not detected by this scale. Interpretation of the MMPI scales can be quite complicated and requires special training. Generally, multiple-scale interpretations (pattern analysis) and characteristics associated with the patterns are examined.

Table 4.6   *The Ten MMPI Clinical Scales and Sample MMPI Test Items.* The answers shown on the grid contribute to high ratings on the related clinical scales.

Ten MMPI Clinical Scales with Simplified Descriptions	I like mechanics magazines.	I have a good appetite.	I wake up fresh and rested most mornings.	I think I would like the work of a librarian.	I am easily awakened by noise.	I like to read newspaper articles on crime.	My hands and feet are usually warm.	My daily life is full of things that keep me interested.	I am about as able to work as I ever was.	There seems to be a lump in my throat much of the time.
1. Hypochondriasis (Hs)—Individuals showing excessive worry about health with reports of obscure pains.		NO	NO				NO		NO	
2. Depression (D)—Individuals suffering from chronic depression, feelings of uselessness and inability to face the future.			NO		YES			NO	NO	
3. Hysteria (Hy)—Individuals who react to stress by developing physical symptoms (paralysis, cramps, headaches, etc.)		NO	NO			NO	NO	NO	NO	YES
4. Psychopathic Deviate (Pd)—Persons who show irresponsibility, disregard social conventions, and lack deep emotional responses.								NO		
5. Paranoia (Pa)—Persons who are suspicious, sensitive, and feel persecuted.										
6. Psychasthenia (Pt)—People troubled with fears (phobias) and compulsive tendencies.			NO					NO		YES
7. Schizophrenia (Sc)—People with bizarre and unusual thoughts or behavior.								NO		
8. Hypomania (Ma)—Persons who physically and mentally are overactive and who shift rapidly in ideas and actions.										
9. Masculinity–Feminity (Mf)—Persons tending to identify with the opposite sex rather than their own.	NO			YES						
10. Social Introversion (Si)—People who tend to withdraw from social contacts and responsibilities.										

SOURCE: Summarized from Dahlstrom, W. G., and Welsh, G. S. (1965). *An MMPI handbook.* Minneapolis: University of Minnesota Press.

A number of criticisms have been leveled against personality inventories.

1. The fixed number of alternatives offered to subjects can limit them in presenting a true picture of themselves. Being asked to answer true or false to the statement "I am suspicious of people" does not permit an individual to qualify the item in any way.
2. Though some personality tests are devised to measure "normal" psychological traits, most clinicians tend to be most alert to responses in these instruments that may signal pathology. Thus the best the subject can do is avoid a "bad" score.
3. Many individuals are able to fake their scores in a direction they see as desirable (for example, to secure a psychiatric discharge from the army or to get a job). Even the MMPI, which has controls to detect faking, can sometimes be "psyched out."
4. A subject's unique response style may distort the results. For example, many people have a pressing need to present themselves in a favorable light, and this may cause them to give socially acceptable answers that are inaccurate.
5. Interpretations of responses of individuals from different cultural groups may not be accurate if norms for these groups have not been developed.

Despite these objections, personality inventories are used widely. Some, like the MMPI, have been extensively researched and their validity in many cases has been established. In general, inventories are easier to administer than projective tests, are inexpensive, and can be scored without much difficulty. (In fact, some inventories are now scored and interpreted by computer.) These features make the use of objective personality inventories desirable, especially in the busy clinic or hospital environment.

Moreover, although progress has been agonizingly slow, the predictive ability and validity of personality assessment tools have been improved. **Psychometric techniques**—the techniques used in making mental measurements—are becoming increasingly sophisticated. Further refinement will be achieved when situational variables that help determine behaviors can be taken into account and when fluctuations in mood and other more stable personality processes can be measured.

Intelligence tests Intelligence testing has two primary diagnostic functions and one secondary function. First, it is used to obtain an estimate of a person's current level of cognitive functioning, called the **intelligence quotient** (IQ). An IQ indicates an individual's level of performance relative to others of the same age. As such, it is significant in the prediction of school performance and the detection of mental retardation. (Through statistical procedures, IQ test results are converted into numbers such that 100 is the mean, or average, score. An IQ score of about 130 indicates performance exceeding that of 95 percent of all same-aged peers.) Second, intelligence testing is used to assess intellectual deterioration in organic or functional psychotic disorders. Third, an individually administered intelligence test may yield additional useful data for the clinician. Observations of how the subject approached the task (systematic versus disorganized), handled failure (depression, frustration, or anger), and persisted (or gave up) in the task may also prove important.

The two most widely used intelligence tests are the Wechsler scales (Wechsler 1981) and the Stanford–Binet scales (Terman and Merrill 1960). The **Wechsler Adult Intelligence Scale** (the WAIS and its revised version WAIS-R) is limited to ages 16 and older, though two other forms are appropriate for ages 6 to 16 (WISC-R) and 4 to 6 (WPPSI). The WAIS-R consists of 6 verbal and 5 performance scales, which yield verbal and performance IQ scores. These scores are combined to present a total IQ score. (Table 4.7, p. 127, shows subtest items similar to those used in the WAIS-R.)

The **Stanford–Binet Scale** is used for ages 2

Intelligence tests provide valuable information about intellectual functioning and can help psychologists to assess mental retardation and intellectual deterioration. Although these tests have been severely criticized with regard to racial discrimination, they can be a beneficial tool.

and older. Much more complicated in administration and scoring, and not standardized on an adult population, the Stanford–Binet requires considerable skill in its use. The test procedure is designed to establish a basal age (the subject passes all subtests for that age) and a ceiling age (the subject fails all subtests for that age), from which an IQ is calculated.

IQ testing (and some other standardized testing) has come under attack by many ethnic groups. There are three major issues. First, some investigators believe that IQ tests have been popularized as a means of measuring innate intelligence, when in truth the tests largely reflect cultural and social factors (Garcia 1981; Williams 1974). In that case, the tests may bestow an unfair advantage on members of the groups whose culture they reflect. Second, and related to the first point, is the issue of the predictive validity of IQ tests. That is,

do IQ test scores accurately predict the future behaviors or achievements of different cultural groups? Proponents and critics disagree on this point (Anastasi 1982). Third, there has been disagreement over criterion variables (in essence, what is actually being predicted by IQ tests). For example, two investigators may be interested in the ability of IQ tests to predict future success. The first may try to find a correlation between test scores and grades subsequently received in school. The second investigator may argue that grades are a poor indicator of success—that leadership skills and ability to work with people are better indicators of success.

One finding is clear: Reliance on IQ scores has resulted in discriminatory actions. In California, for example, black children were disproportionately assigned to classes for the educable mentally retarded on the basis of IQ results. Mercer (1979) has argued that all cultural groups have the same average intellectual potential. On a given IQ test, members of a cultural minority may score low, not because of mental retardation, but because they are less familiar with the tasks required on such tests. She has developed the *System of Multicultural Pluralistic Assessment* through which performance on the WISC-R is assessed in relation to that of groups with similar social and cultural backgrounds. In other words, an individual is compared with others who have similar backgrounds, rather than with others from different backgrounds. This assessment procedure results in fewer children who represent ethnic minorities being assigned to classes for the mentally retarded.

A different approach to the removal of cultural bias from intelligence tests is described in Focus 4.4 (p. 130).

Tests for brain damage   Clinical psychologists, and especially those who work in a hospital setting, are concerned with the detection and assessment of damage to the central nervous system (**organicity**). Identification of organic brain damage can sometimes be aided by the

Table 4.7 *Simulated Items for the Wechsler Adult Intelligence Scale*

Information

1. How many nickels make a dime?
2. What is steam made of?
3. What is pepper?

Comprehension

1. Why do some people save sales receipts?
2. Why is copper often used in electrical wire?

Arithmetic (all calculated "in the head")

1. Sue had 2 pieces of candy and Joe gave her 4 more. How many pieces of candy did Sue have altogether?
2. If 2 pencils cost 15¢, how much will a dozen pencils cost?

Similarities

In what way are the following alike?

1. lion/tiger
2. saw/hammer
3. circle/square

Vocabulary

What is the meaning of the following words?

1. chair
2. mountain
3. guilt
4. building
5. foreboding
6. prevaricate
7. plethora

SOURCE: Modeled on Wechsler, D. (1981). *Wechsler Adult Intelligence Scale* New York:– Revised Harcourt.

use of individual intelligence tests like the WAIS. Discrepancy between an individual's verbal and performance scores or the pattern of scores on the individual subtests often suggests possible organicity. For example, a difference of twenty points between verbal and performance scores indicates the possibility of brain damage. Subtests that measure verbal concept formation or abstracting ability (comparison and comprehension) can also reveal brain damage. Because impairment of abstract thinking may be characteristic of organicity, a lower score on this scale (when accompanied by other signs) must be investigated.

One of the routine means of assessing organicity is the **Bender–Gestalt Visual–Motor Test,** shown in Figure 4.1 on pages 128–129 (Bender 1938). Nine geometric designs, each drawn in black on a piece of white cardboard, are presented one at a time to the subject, who is asked to copy them on a piece of paper. Certain errors in the copies are characteristic of neurological impairment. Among these are

rotation of figures, perseveration (continuation to an exceptional degree), fragmentation, oversimplification, inability to copy angles, and reversals.

The **Halstead–Reitan Neuropsychological Test Battery,** developed by Reitan from the earlier work of Halstead, has been used successfully in differentiating patients with brain damage from those without brain damage and in providing valuable information about the type and location of the damage (Boll 1983). The full battery consists of eleven tests, though several are often omitted. Patients are presented with a series of tasks that assess sensorimotor, cognitive, and perceptual functioning, including abstract concept formation, memory and attention, and auditory perception. The full battery takes over six hours to administer, so it is a relatively expensive and time-consuming assessment tool.

A less costly test for organicity is the **Luria–Nebraska Neuropsychological Battery,** which requires about $2\frac{1}{2}$ hours to administer and is

Figure 4.1 *The Nine Bender Designs*
The figures presented to subjects are shown below. The distorted figures drawn by subjects are possibly indicative of organicity. They are shown at the right.

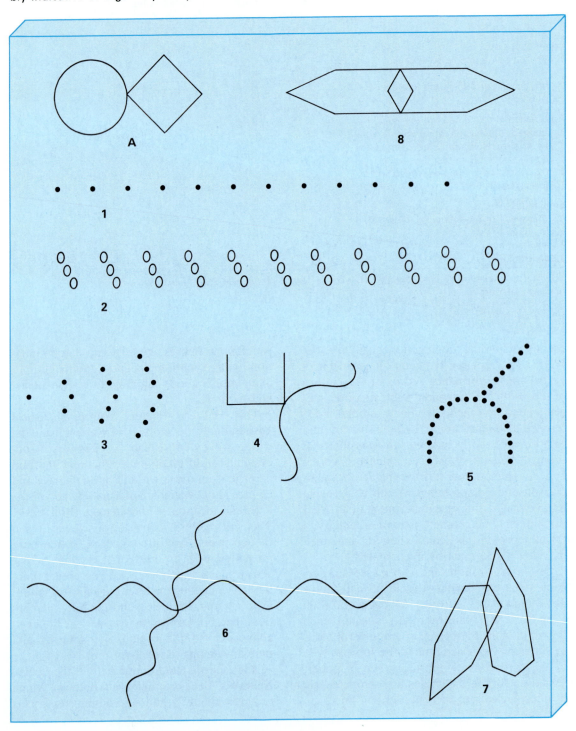

Figure 4.1 *(continued)*

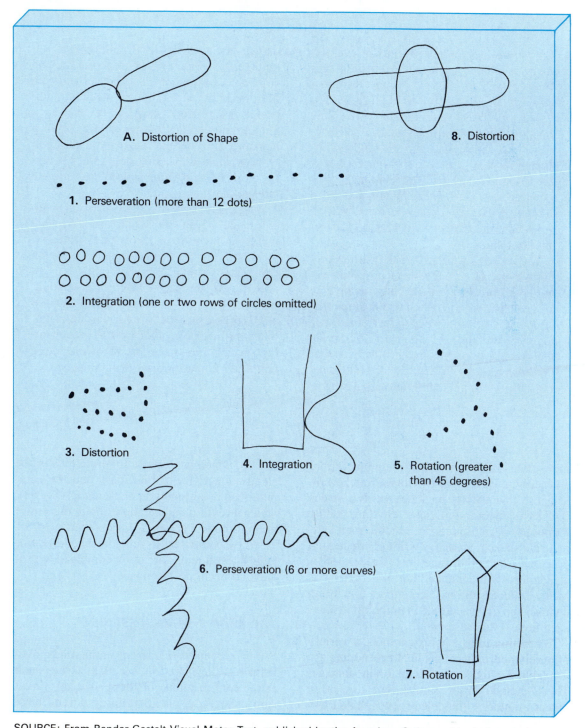

A. Distortion of Shape

8. Distortion

1. Perseveration (more than 12 dots)

2. Integration (one or two rows of circles omitted)

3. Distortion

4. Integration

5. Rotation (greater than 45 degrees)

6. Perseveration (6 or more curves)

7. Rotation

SOURCE: From Bender-Gestalt Visual Motor Test, published by the American Orthopsychiatric Association.

The K-ABC

An increasingly popular means of evaluating the intelligence and achievement of children aged 2½ to 12½-years is the Kaufman Assessment Battery for children (K-ABC). Based on theories of mental processing developed by neuropsychologists and cognitive psychologists, the K-ABC is intended for use with both the general population and special populations. For example, the assessment battery has been employed with children who have hearing or speech impairments and who have learning disabilities.

The K-ABC can also be used with exceptional children and members of ethnic minority groups. Its applicability to diverse groups has been attributed to measures that (1) are less culturally dependent than those found on traditional tests and (2) focus on the process used to solve problems rather than on the specific content of test items. Verbal performance and nonverbal performance are assessed, and children are administered a wide variety of tasks, such as copying a sequence of hand movements performed by the examiner, recalling numbers, assembling triangles to match a model, and demonstrating reading comprehension. For certain language-disordered or non-English-speaking children, nonverbal performance can be used to estimate intellectual functioning.

A Spanish version of the K-ABC is available, and norms for black and Hispanic children have been developed. Interestingly, differences in performance between white and ethnic minority children are much lower on the K-ABC than on traditional IQ tests. Kaufman and Kaufman (1983) report that the K-ABC has high reliability and validity. This new approach offers promise in the effort to devise more culturally unbiased tests of intelligence.

more standardized in content, administration, and scoring. Developed by Golden and his colleagues, this battery includes twelve scales that assess motor functions, rhythm, tactile functions, visual functions, receptive and expressive speech, memory, writing, intellectual processes, and other functions (Golden 1981). Validation data indicate that the battery is highly successful in screening for brain damage and quite accurate in pinpointing damaged areas (Anastasi 1982).

In addition to psychological tests, a variety of purely neurological medical procedures are available for the diagnosis of brain damage. These include brain X-rays that can often detect tumors; the electroencephalograph (EEG), which can detect abnormalities in the electrical activity of the brain; and the computerized axial tomographic scan (CAT scan), which provides information about the entire brain through a series of X-rays that are processed by computer. Psychological and neurological test findings are often combined to produce an accurate diagnosis.

The ethics of assessment

Within recent years a strong antitesting movement has developed in America. Issues such as the confidentiality of client's records, invasion of privacy, client welfare, cultural bias, and unethical practices have increasingly been raised (Bersoff 1981). In assessing and treating emotionally disturbed people, the clinical psychologist must often ask embarrassing questions or use tests that may be construed as invasions of privacy. In many cases, the clinician may not know beforehand whether the results of the tests will prove beneficial to the client. Yet to exclude testing because it may offend the client or place him or her in an uncomfortable position could ultimately deprive the client of its long-range benefits.

Some have strongly criticized tests on the grounds that they can have undesirable social consequences. Who will use the test results, and for what purpose is the test employed? Test results may be used to the client's detriment in some rare instances. Such was the intent, during President Nixon's administration, of the so-called plumbers unit that broke into the office of a psychiatrist, hoping to find psychological evidence with which to discredit a political enemy.

The use of psychological tests has ethical, legal, and societal implications that go beyond the field of psychology. Certainly, psychologists should be aware of these implications and should guard against the misuse of test results. But they should carefully weigh the consequences of permitting such considerations to interfere with their task of devising, improving, and applying tests that will benefit their patients.

THE NEED FOR CLASSIFICATION AND ASSESSMENT

Classification schemes and assessment tools are necessary to the study and practice of mental health. Without them, data could not be collected, and psychologists could not conduct meaningful research, develop theories, or engage in psychotherapy. Data collection necessarily involves the use of tools to systemati-

cally record the observations, behaviors, or self-reports of individuals. For example, if a researcher believes that a certain mental disorder (such as schizophrenia) is caused by faulty communication patterns in the family, some means must be found to measure and record the communication styles of families. Means must also be available to distinguish the concept of "schizophrenia" from normal behavior and other abnormal behaviors. In other words, there must be some means of assessing and classifying behaviors. Although researchers may disagree about which assessment measures or classification schemes are the most useful, few would object to their existence.

As we have mentioned, considerable controversy exists over classification and assessment in clinical practice. Some critics point to problems of reliability and validity; others challenge the ability of classification schemes to provide insight into the etiology, prognosis, and treatment of disorders; still others point to undesirable consequences, such as labeling, and to the cultural biases that particular psychological tests betray. The effect of the controversy has, however, been positive. The mental health professions and the general public are increasingly aware of the need to guard against possible abuses and to continually refine and improve classification systems and assessment procedures.

Changes are already taking place. Some psychologists now make use of computer-assisted diagnostic systems. Information gleaned from patient interviews, ratings of the clinician, and psychological test results is fed into a computer that has been programmed to yield a diagnosis and assessment. Such a procedure can reduce the subjective biases of clinicians in making a diagnosis and can shorten the time required for the diagnostic process (Greist, Klein, and Erdman 1976). Obviously, the accuracy of the computer diagnosis is highly dependent on the validity of the diagnostic software, the type of problem being diagnosed, and the accuracy and completeness of the information that has been gathered and submitted to the computer.

There is speculation that more sophisticated use of computers in mental health is likely in the near future (Sundberg, Taplin, and Tyler 1983). At least one clinician has predicted that assessment and psychological testing will be applied more and more broadly as that occurs (Cummings 1984).

SUMMARY

1. The traditional psychiatric classification manuals (DSM-I and DSM-II) were based to a large extent on the biogenic model of mental illness. They assumed that people classified in a psychodiagnostic category exhibit similar symptoms, possess a common etiology, should be treated in a certain manner, and have similar prognoses. Criticisms specifically leveled at DSM-I and DSM-II dealt with their questionable reliability and validity. In the current version, DSM-III, detailed diagnostic criteria are given; as a result, its reliability appears to be higher than that of the previous manuals. Furthermore, data are collected on five axes so that much more information about the patient is systematically examined. General objections to classification are primarily based on the problems involved in labeling.

2. Clinicians primarily use three methods of assessment: observations, interviews, and psychological tests. Observations of external signs and expressive behaviors are often made during an interview and can have diagnostic significance. Interviews, the oldest form of psychological assessment, involve a face-to-face conversation after which the interviewer differentially weighs and interprets verbal information obtained from the interviewee. Psychological tests provide a more formalized means of obtaining information. Most testing situations have two characteristics in com-

mon. They provide a standard situation in which certain responses are elicited. And responses from subjects are measured and used to make inferences about underlying traits. In personality testing, projective techniques or personality inventories may be used. In the former, the stimuli are ambiguous; in the latter, the stimuli are much more structured. Two of the most widely used projective techniques are the Rorschach inkblot technique and the Thematic Apperception Test (TAT). Unlike projective tests, objective personality inventories, such as the Minnesota Multiphasic Personality Inventory (MMPI), supply the test taker with a list of alternatives from which to select an answer. Intelligence testing can be used to obtain an estimate of a person's current level of cognitive functioning and to assess intellectual deterioration. Behavioral observations of how a person takes the test are additional sources of information about personality attributes. The WAIS, Stanford–Binet, and Bender–Gestalt tests can be used to assess brain damage, as can various strictly neurological tests.

3. In addition to issues involving their reliability and validity, a number of ethical questions have been raised with regard to classification and assessment. These include confidentiality, privacy, and cultural bias. Concerned with these issues, psychologists have attempted to improve classification and assessment procedures and to define the appropriate conditions for testing and diagnosis. For, in spite of the problems and criticisms, classification and assessment are necessary to psychological research and practice.

KEY TERMS

assessment With regard to psychopathology, the process of gathering information and drawing conclusions about the traits, skills, abilities, emotional functioning, and psychological problems of an individual

classification system With regard to psychopathology, a system of distinct categories, indicators, and nomenclature for different patterns of behavior, thought processes, and emotional disturbances

etiology The causes or origins of a disorder

objective personality test An inventory of personality attributes in which the test taker either agrees or disagrees with specific self descriptive statements; administration, scoring, and interpretation are largely independent of the test giver's subjectivity

prognosis A prediction of the future course of a disorder

projective personality test A personality assessment technique in which the test taker is presented with ambiguous stimuli and is asked to respond to them in some way

psychological test Any test instrument used to assess personality, maladaptive behavior, development of social skills, intellectual abilities, vocational interests, or brain damage

psychometrics Mental measurement, including its study and techniques

reliability The degree to which a procedure or test yields the same result repeatedly, under the same circumstances

validity The degree to which a procedure or test actually performs the function that it was designed to perform

5

The Scientific Method in Abnormal Psychology

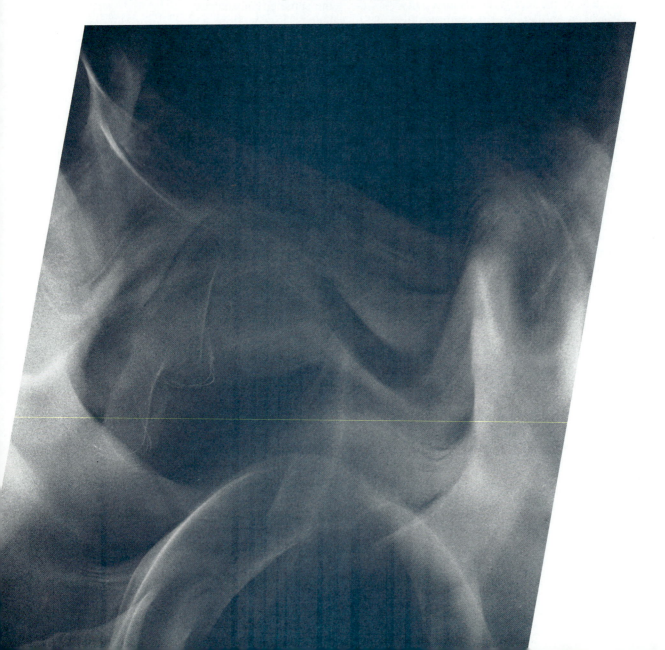

Those who work in the field of abnormal psychology have, as their primary goal, the understanding of abnormal behavior and the use of that understanding to describe, explain, predict, and control such behavior. In this chapter, we are concerned with the means scientists use to add to their knowledge of psychopathology.

Historically, two approaches have been used. The first (and earliest) is called the "armchair approach." It consists of the personal observation of behavior and events, followed by the drawing of conclusions from these observations, on the basis of the observer's speculations.

The problem with this approach stems from the multitude of variables that are at work in any situation involving human behavior. The armchair researcher does not control any of these variables. Instead, he or she must decide, after the fact, which of them is primarily responsible for the observed behavior: which is cause and which is effect. That decision is much influenced by the researcher's own experience, attitudes, and convictions; another researcher might well choose some other variable (or variables) as being paramount. Furthermore, it is extremely difficult—often impossible—to duplicate the observed situation and behavior exactly, with the result that the original observer's conclusions cannot easily be tested and either verified or shown to be erroneous.

Despite these problems, armchair speculation has been a useful means of generating hypotheses about abnormal behavior. (A **hypothesis** is a conjectural statement, usually describing a relationship between variables.) However, as we noted, armchair speculation does not provide a way of testing hypotheses.

The second approach has come to be called the **scientific method;** it is a method of inquiry that provides for the systematic collection of data through controlled observation and for

135

This now-classic still photo was taken at the moment Lee Harvey Oswald, the accused assassin of President Kennedy, was shot by Jack Ruby. It reveals the startled responses of the onlookers. Were it not for an objective recording of the event by cameras, many of these spectators would have been unable to describe exactly what happened.

the testing of hypotheses based on those data. The *systematic* and *controlled* collection of data ensures that situations and events (including experiments) are open to **replication**—that is, to repeated demonstration. The *testing* of hypotheses insures against conclusions that are biased or subjective.

We believe that the scientific approach is the better method for discovering the facts and relationships of abnormal psychology. In fact, the remainder of this chapter is a discussion of the characteristics of the scientific method and its techniques, as they are applied to the study of psychopathology. However, two points need to be emphasized before we move on to these topics.

The first concerns the "purity" of the scientific method as we know it. This approach has been developed and refined over the years, by people who were—and people who are—influenced by the beliefs, values, and cultural forces of their times. In other words, the concept that has been accepted as "*the* scientific method" in each time and place has been determined in part by the values prevalent in that time and place (Sarason 1984). Thus neither the scientific method as we now know it nor the results we achieve with that method should be viewed as perfect or ultimate (Bergin 1980; Kilbourne and Richardson 1984). As our values change, so will our constructs. What is more important is that we remain open to differing views and alternative realities and that we continue to improve our methodology.

Our second point concerns the substantial "nonscientific" component in the work of most practicing counselors and clinicians. Ideally, psychotherapy should be based on empirical knowledge, and its practitioners should be able to consult and make use of a full body of literature that reports scientifically conducted research. This state of affairs would allow the clinician to move beyond armchair speculation and the trial-and-error application of techniques, to the integrated and rational application of principles. Unfortunately, the results provided by researchers have not yet caught up with the needs of clinicians; moreover, much of psychological research is not easily put into practice in the clinic. For these reasons, the therapist must often rely on his or her own personal experiences, creativity, and convictions in treating clients—must, in fact, become an armchair researcher.

CHARACTERISTICS OF THE SCIENTIFIC METHOD

Perhaps the unique and most general characteristic of scientific inquiry is its capacity for self-correction. Data and conclusions are freely exchanged and experiments are replicable, so that all are subject to discussion, testing, verification, and modification. As a result, the knowledge that is developed is as free as possible from the scientist's personal beliefs, perceptions, biases, values, attitudes, and emotions.

Four additional, and more specific, characteristics of the scientific method have been identified: the use of conceptual schemes and theoretical structures, the testing of hypotheses and theories, the control of extraneous variables, and the avoidance of metaphysical explanations (Kerlinger 1971). Let us examine

each of these and, in the process, describe the scientific method.

Use of conceptual schemes and theoretical structures

At any given time, there is an existing body of knowledge (and beliefs) about each area of science. The bits of information that compose this knowledge are very much like the individual pieces of a newly purchased jigsaw puzzle. Each bit or piece must be scrutinized to determine where it fits into the overall picture. In the case of a science, the "overall picture" is a *conceptual* scheme or framework—a broad, general explanation that serves as a means of organizing known facts and relationships. There may be more than one such conceptual scheme at any one time; an example is the several viewpoints on the origins of abnormal behavior.

The conceptual scheme itself is sometimes called a theory. But more often a **theory** is a substructure consisting of a group of principles and hypotheses that together explain a particular aspect of the area of inquiry. Like the conceptual scheme, the theory is a means of organizing available information (generally, more detailed information). It also provides a framework for speculating on (and then verifying) the nature of yet-undiscovered facts and principles through the formulation (and then testing) of hypotheses. And theory serves to provide direction for scientific research by pointing up gaps in current knowledge.

Testing of theories and hypotheses

Theories, then, are explanations, and hypotheses are specific conjectures that form part of those explanations. Examples of hypotheses include statements like "Frustration leads to aggression," "Anxiety causes increased

Researchers use observation and measurement to test hypotheses. In studying the effect of watching television on aggression, for instance, researchers might observe a child's overt behavior while measuring physiological arousal and responses.

affiliation behavior (seeking the company of others)," and "Electroconvulsive shock therapy reduces the symptoms of depression." A theory is tested when any of its hypotheses is tested; a theory is confirmed only when *all* of its hypotheses have been verified.

Scientific testing can proceed only when the relationship expressed in a hypothesis is clearly and systematically stated and when the variables of concern are measurable. Suppose scientists are interested in testing the hypothesis that frustration leads to aggression. How can they measure the variables *frustration* and *aggression*, when each scientist may define these terms differently? In such cases, psychologists often resort to **operational definitions,** which describe concepts in terms of the operations used to measure them. For example, *aggression* may be operationalized as "the number of times the subject strikes a large inflated doll," and *frustration* may be defined as "physically preventing the person from reaching a desirable goal."

Control of extraneous variables

The scientific method requires the systematic investigation of relationships, and that includes elimination of the possible effects of variables that are *not* under investigation. If scientists were interested in studying the relationship between alcoholism and hallucination, for example, they would certainly avoid including psychotic subjects, who might be hallucinating for reasons that have nothing to do with their alcoholic condition. Psychosis in subjects would introduce an *extraneous variable,* one that is not going to be tested or observed but that may affect the outcome of the study.

In psychological studies, an extraneous variable can be controlled in three ways. If possible, the variable is *eliminated* from the study (for example, by excluding psychotic subjects). Or, the extraneous variable may be *randomized* (included randomly in all groups studied, so that its effects are canceled out). Finally, the variable may be *included* in the study for investigation as another *variable.* The important point is that such control provides reliability and enhances confidence in the results of a scientific investigation.

Avoidance of metaphysical explanations

Science does not involve itself with metaphysical (supernatural) explanations because they cannot be tested. To say that we have become ill because of bad luck, that God is punishing poor people for their past sins, or that all human beings are evil is to make a metaphysical statement. Such explanations have been labeled **parascientific** (apart from, or outside, the realm of science). Belief in the occult, for example, rests on currently untestable private convictions. For parascientists, reality is based on a kind of evidence that is alien to science (McNeil 1974).

Let us now examine the major techniques of scientific research.

EXPERIMENTS

The **experiment** is perhaps the best tool for testing cause–effect relationships. In its simplest form the experiment involves

1. An *experimental hypothesis,* which is the relationship to be tested
2. An *independent variable* (the possible cause), which the experimenter manipulates so as to determine its effect on a dependent variable
3. A *dependent variable* that, according to the hypothesis, is somehow controlled by the independent variable

As we noted, the experimenter is also concerned with controlling extraneous variables.

Let us clarify these concepts with a short example:

> A young boy is filled with dread and apprehension whenever he has to visit the dentist. His anxiety is strongest as he waits in the dentist's office. He feels a desperate urge to go to the bathroom and an equally desperate need to keep up a brave facade. He is nearly at the breaking point when his turn comes. However, on those occasions when his mother or even other patients wait with him, their presence dissipates much of his anxiety. It seems that his misery is alleviated when he has the company of others.

Can we test the hypothesis that anxiety motivates persons to seek the company of others (increases affiliation behavior)?

The experimental group

An experiment designed to confirm or disconfirm our hypothesis was reported by Schachter (1959). The plan was to create an anxiety-provoking situation to which subjects could respond either by seeking the company of others or by remaining alone. Schachter advertised for student volunteers to participate in a psychology experiment. He also obtained, as a collaborator, an elderly, distinguished-looking psychologist from another university, who was to address the subjects in a solemn manner designed to induce anxiety.

On the day of the experiment he assembled all volunteers in a room where an awesome-looking electrical apparatus was prominently displayed. His colleague then entered, wearing a white lab coat, with a stethoscope dangling from his neck. Introducing himself as a physician from the neuropsychiatric department of the university medical school, the colleague explained the need for researching the effects of electric shock, owing to the increasing use of electricity in medical therapy. He told the student volunteers that they were about to participate in an experiment on the effects of strong, painful electric shocks but added that the shocks to be administered would cause no permanent tissue damage. The students were then told that they could choose to await their turn alone or in the company of others.

The collaborator's comments, his manner, and the displayed apparatus were calculated to induce a high level of anxiety in the subjects. In psychological research, subjects exposed to such manipulation are said to be members of the **experimental group,** the group that is subjected to the independent variable—in this case, anxiety. The dependent variable was affiliation behavior, operationally defined in terms of the preference for waiting either alone or with others. Schachter recorded the number of volunteers who chose each category, and he found that 63 percent of the subjects preferred to wait in the company of others. Did this result confirm the hypothesis that anxiety motivates people to seek the company of others?

The control group

The mere fact that 63 percent of the subjects in the experimental group preferred the company of others does not tell us very much. We cannot conclude that the induced anxiety caused these subjects to choose the company of others, because it is possible that they would have made the same choice without the anxiety. Results for the experimental group need to be compared with results for a group that is similar in every way *except for* the manipulation of the independent variable. Such a group of subjects is called a **control group.**

To establish a control group in his experiment, Schachter selected another assemblage of volunteers, whom the collaborator addressed in an informal, matter-of-fact manner. The subjects were reassured frequently that the shocks would not be unpleasant, and the "mad scientist" trappings and electrical apparatus were absent. Such conditions were calculated to induce a much lower level of anxiety than that induced in the experimental group.

Schachter found that 33 percent of the control group preferred the company of others. Now, on the basis of a comparison of the results for the two groups, it is reasonable to conclude that anxious people tend, more than people who are not anxious, to desire the company of others. However, these findings should be replicated before more definitive cause–effect statements are made.

Extraneous variables and validity

In an experiment, the control group and the experimental group must be as similar as possible. If males were used in Schachter's experimental group and females in the control group, the experimenter would not know whether the results were due to differences in anxiety or differences between males and females. Or, if experimental-group members were significantly younger than control-group members, how would the experimenter know whether the results were due to the effects of age? These questions deal with the **internal validity** of the experiment, or the extent to which changes in the dependent variable are actually brought about by the independent variable. Internal validity is essentially a problem of controlling extraneous variables.

One way to control extraneous variables in Schachter's experiment would be to select only college-age females for the entire study. Age and sex variables would be easily controlled. However, the experimental findings would be applicable only to this specific population, and the experimenter may want more generality. The **external validity** of an experiment is the generalizability or representativeness of the results it yields. To the extent that the results can be generalized to different populations, the experiment has external validity.

Probably the best way to control extraneous variables in an experiment is to assign volunteers *randomly* to each group. Random assignment ensures that differences due to age, sex, and personal attributes are probably balanced out and do not affect the study.

CORRELATIONS

A **correlation** is a measure of the extent to which variations in one variable are accompanied by variations in a second variable. It is expressed as a statistically derived *correlation coefficient,* symbolized by r, which has a numerical value between -1 and $+1$.

The greater the value of r, positive *or* negative, the stronger the relationship. Thus the correlation expressed by $r = .88$ is much stronger than that expressed by $r = .15$. (The correlation expressed by $r = -.88$ is also much stronger than that expressed by $r = .15$.) A correlation coefficient of $r = +1.00$ indicates a *perfect positive correlation* between two variables. We all know, for instance, that the taller people are, the more they are likely to weigh. If there were a perfect positive correlation between height and weight, then one of these variables could be predicted on the basis of the other, and the relationship between them would be expressed as $r = +1.00$. This does not happen to be the case, however; perfect correlations are rare in the field of abnormal psychology.

The absence of a relationship (or correlation) between two variables is signified by $r = 0$. For example, no relationship whatsoever has been found between the number of lumps on a person's head and that person's character traits; thus these two variables have a correlation coefficient of 0.

A negative correlation coefficient indicates an *inverse* relationship, meaning that an increase in one of the two variables is generally accompanied by a decrease in the other. For example, depression and activity level are often inversely related—the *more* depressed a person is, the *lower* his or her activity level. A correlation coefficient of -1.00 indicates a *perfect negative correlation* between two variables.

The correlation coefficient r is computed with a statistical formula. The data for the computation are obtained by measuring the values of the two variables in a sample of the population of interest. Note that there is no manipulation of a variable, as there is in experimentation; existing values of the variables are simply measured. However, as in experimentation, researchers try to reduce the effect of extraneous variables, primarily by randomization and the use of large samples. They may also calculate a *level of significance* α (alpha) for the computed value of r, to determine how likely it is that the relationship it indicates is due to chance. When $\alpha = .01$, for example, the result (the correlation) could have occurred by chance in only 1 of 100 studies.

Depression is often inversely related to activity level. The more depressed a person is, the less likely he is to engage in any activities, particularly physical ones. It is not surprising that recent research shows jogging or other aerobic activity may help to reduce depression.

Figure 5.1 (p. 142) shows various possible results of correlation studies and the correlation coefficients they would produce. Each plotted point represents a measurement of variable X and of variable Y in a single individual.

Correlational techniques are extremely useful research tools, especially when experimentation would be difficult or inadvisable, or when past events are being investigated. But extreme care must be taken in interpreting a

Figure 5.1 *Possible Correlation between Two Variables.*
The more closely the data points approximate a straight line, the greater the magnitude of the correlation coefficient *r.* The slope of the regression line rising from left to right in example (a) indicates a positive perfect correlation between depression and poor self-esteem, whereas example (b) reveals a negative correlation. Example (c) shows a lower positive correlation. Example (d) shows no relationship whatsoever.

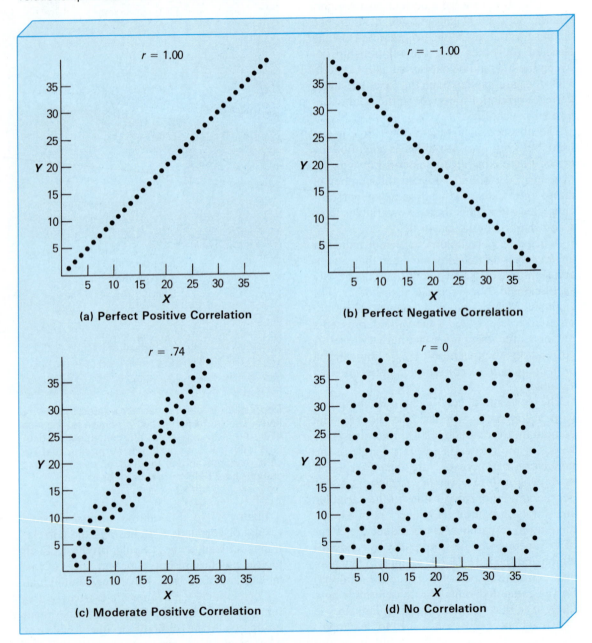

(a) Perfect Positive Correlation

(b) Perfect Negative Correlation

(c) Moderate Positive Correlation

(d) No Correlation

correlation, because *correlation does not necessarily imply a cause–effect relationship.* Here is an example that illustrates the problems that can arise in inferring a cause–effect relationship from a correlation. Several years ago, a newspaper story announced a significant negative correlation between smoking and academic grades. How should such a relationship be interpreted? One might conclude that *smoking causes poor grades;* however, a case can also be made that *poor grades cause increased smoking.* In other words, we cannot determine the *direction* of causality, if there is any causality at all. For it is entirely possible that some third variable is causing both poor grades and smoking. Perhaps, if teachers prefer that students do not smoke, they may unconsciously assign lower grades to those who do. Or high-strung students may tend both to smoke more and to have poor study habits that adversely affect their grades (Ruch and Zimbardo 1971).

Such third-variable possibilities in correlations are endless. Consider the following actual observations. What third-variable explanations can you suggest?

1. The number of storks nesting on rooftops in certain New England communities is positively correlated with the human birth rate.
2. The number of violent crimes committed in a community is positively correlated with the number of churches in the community.
3. The number of traffic fatalities and indices of progress in Third World countries are negatively correlated.

SIMULATION TECHNIQUES

In **simulation,** the investigator attempts to create, under controlled conditions, a situation as close as possible to real life. Besides replicating a real-life situation for experimen-

tal investigation, as in Schachter's anxiety-provoking experiment, researchers in abnormal behavior may also use simulation to create an artificial "abnormal" state in order to study a particular condition more carefully or to determine the effectiveness of therapist–client interaction.

As we noted earlier, evidence that mental disorders can be caused by psychological factors is provided by the fact that a hypnotist can induce hysterical symptoms—an abnormal state—in normal subjects. Hypnosis has been widely used to confirm the existence of unconscious motivations and, in extreme cases, **amnesia** (the partial or total inability to recall one's own life experiences).

One of the authors once implanted the posthypnotic suggestion in a subject's mind that, upon awakening from her hypnotic state, she would experience a powerful urge to smoke, even though she was a nonsmoker. She was instructed to have no memory of this suggestion or her motivation. When awakened, the subject began to converse with the experimenter as he lit a cigarette. She leaned forward, asked what brand he smoked, and began to describe the many cigarette advertisements she had seen that day. Offered a cigarette, she politely declined, saying she considered smoking hazardous to one's health. The experimenter placed his pack of cigarettes on the table. In the course of her monologue, the subject drew a cigarette from the pack and placed it between her lips. When the experimenter commented on her action, she showed complete bewilderment at her behavior and could not explain her apparent desire to smoke.

Hypnosis was used in an especially interesting series of studies to examine the hypothesis that an individual's emotional state in conflict situations affects his or her psychophysiological reactions (Grace and Graham 1952; Graham, Stern, and Winokur 1958; Graham, Kabler, and Graham 1962). Through posthypnotic suggestion subjects came to exhibit attitudes and emotions similar to those of hard-driving executives, angry individuals, or resentful and sexually unresponsive marriage partners. The subjects showed the same physiological reactions and symptoms as individuals who had developed these emotional patterns "naturally."

Other examples of this technique include the inducing of artificial abnormal states via sensory deprivation (restriction of external stimulation) and the use of psychoactive drugs to study so-called schizophrenic processes (hallucinations and delusions). Simulation is also used in the training of therapists (through role-playing) and in such therapeutic techniques as psychodrama (Moreno 1959).

One problem in simulation studies is that the investigators can never be sure that the analog they have created reproduces the essential characteristics of the natural event. For example, researchers once thought that certain drugs (such as LSD) could engender a psychotic experience similar to those suffered by mental patients. Although there are similarities between hallucinogenic states and psychotic states, the analogy has proved weak. Furthermore, most simulation techniques do not allow the control that is possible in an experiment; as a result, it is difficult to make statements about causality on the basis of a simulation study.

FIELD STUDIES

In some cases, a simulation would be too contrived to accurately represent the real-life situation. Investigators may then resort to the **field study,** in which behaviors and events are observed and recorded in the natural environment. The subjects of a field study are most often the members of a given social unit—a group, institution, or community. However, the investigation may also be limited to a single individual; single-subject studies are discussed in the next section.

Such data-collection techniques as questionnaires, interviews, and the analysis of existing records may be used in field studies, but the primary technique is observation. The observers must be highly trained individuals with enough self-discipline to avoid disrupting or modifying the behavior processes that they are observing and recording. The observers in one study also had to be careful not to disclose the fact that they were indeed observers:

In 1954 several psychologists became intrigued by the beliefs of a certain Ms. Kreech, who claimed she received messages from superior beings inhabiting a planet called Clarion. These beings, who had visited Earth in flying saucers, noticed fault lines in Earth's crust that indicated a forthcoming catastrophe. They claimed that a cataclysmic flood would strike Earth in December 1954. Kreech gathered about her a group of dedicated believers, and together they went into seclusion to prepare for the terrible event. Their preparation included group indoctrination meetings, during which members explored the meanings of their mystical experiences and dreams. When no flood appeared by December 21, many of the followers left. The most dedicated followers, however, persisted in their beliefs and even recruited new members.

Several psychologists and their students, pretending to be believers, joined the group and diligently observed the believers and their attitudes. The results of their study were published in the book *When Prophecy Fails* (Festinger, Riecken, and Schachter 1957). Their work proved invaluable to our understanding of conformity and attitude change.

The field study may be used to examine mass behavior after events of major consequence, such as wars, floods, and earthquakes (see Focus 5.1, pp. 146–147). It may also be applied to the study of personal crises, as in military combat, major surgery, terminal disease, or the loss of loved ones.

Although field studies offer a more realistic investigative environment than other types of research, they suffer from certain limitations. First, as with other nonexperimental research,

People react to natural disasters in many ways, and until recently psychologists relied largely on historical reports and laboratory experiments to study these reactions. When Mt. St. Helens erupted in 1980, psychologists were able to use field study techniques in a natural setting to evaluate stress responses to a cataclysmic event.

it is difficult to determine the direction of causality because the data are correlational in nature. Second, in real-life situations so many variables are at work that it is impossible to control—and sometimes even to distinguish—them all. As a result, the uncontrolled variables may contaminate the findings. Third, observers can never be absolutely sure that their presence did not influence the interactions they observed.

SINGLE-SUBJECT STUDIES

Most scientists advocate the study of large groups of people in order to uncover the basic principles governing behavior. This approach, called the **nomothetic orientation,** is concerned with generating general laws while ignoring individual variations or differences. Experiments and correlational studies are nomothetic in nature. Other scientists advocate the in-depth study of one individual. This approach, exemplified by the single-subject study, has been called the **idiographic orientation.** Ever since Allport (1937) argued for making a distinction between these two study methods, there has been much heated debate over which method is more fruitful in the study of psychopathology (Beck 1953; Eysenck 1954).

Although the idiographic method has many limitations, especially the lack of generality, it has proved very valuable in applied clinical work (Maher 1966). Furthermore, the argument over which method is more fruitful is not productive, because both approaches are needed in the study of abnormal behavior. The nomothetic approach seems appropriate for laboratory scientists, whereas the idiographic approach seems appropriate for their clinical counterparts, the psychotherapists, who daily face the pressures of treating disturbed individuals.

There are two types of single-subject studies: the *case study* and the *single-subject experiment.* Both techniques may be used to examine a rare or unusual phenomenon, to demonstrate a novel diagnostic or treatment

Field Study of a Natural Disaster: The Mt. St. Helens Eruption and Ashfall

Mount St. Helens, a volcanic peak located near Seattle, Washington, erupted on Sunday morning, May 18, 1980. Several local residents were killed, and the force of the explosion and the subsequent lava flow caused miles of destruction to vegetation and wildlife. In addition, the disaster sent tons and tons of ashes throughout Washington, Oregon, and Idaho. In many communities, the ashfall was so heavy that it blotted out the sun, leaving residents in total darkness.

The Mt. St. Helens ashfall provided a natural setting for the study of stress reactions to catastrophic events. Two researchers conducted a field study of the disaster to evaluate what DSM-III now calls "post-traumatic stress disorder" (Adams and Adams 1984). Studies generally support the belief that severe stress can result in psychological disturbances, but the Mt. St. Helens disaster provided a unique opportunity to address two questions: Does such stress cause long-term psychological disturbances in relatively normal people? Do

the symptoms disappear as quickly as the environmental stressor? To answer these questions, the investigators used the following procedure.

1. They selected for study a single social unit—Othello, Washington, a town of approximately 5000 people. They identified the characteristics of its population and its community help-giving networks, from which data were collected.

2. They developed a conceptual model in which, according to theory, a stressor (here, the Mt. St. Helens disaster) is seen as creating a two-part stress reaction. One part is associated with physiological responses, and the second with psychoemotional responses; both are believed to be manifested in overt behavior.

3. They divided the observable behaviors and/or consequences into five categories and selected operational definitions for each, as shown in the table.

4. They established postdisaster (experimental) and predisaster (control) time peri-

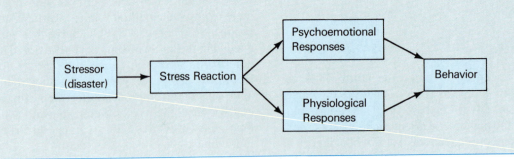

Behaviors/Consequences	Operational Definitions
Increased susceptibility to illness and a greater frequency of psychosomatic illnesses and illnesses aggravated by stress	Total patient contacts at medical clinic; hospital emergency room visits; psychosomatic problems diagnosed; employee sick leave and vacation time used; average patient census at hospital; death rate; absenteeism; welfare caseloads; diagnoses of illness aggravated by stress; mental illness diagnoses
Marital and family problems	Divorces filed; child-abuse investigations; police calls for domestic violence; juvenile court referrals
Alcohol abuse	Clients served in community alcohol program; citations issued for driving while intoxicated; other alcohol-related tickets or arrests; rate of auto accidents; police "breathalyzer" tests for intoxication
Aggression and violence	Police calls; criminal bookings; criminal cases opened in Superior Court
Adjustment problems	Psychiatric commitment investigations; District and Superior Court caseloads; mental health appointments; crisis-line calls

ods in which they could measure and compare behaviors. First, the researchers took the postdisaster period as the seven-month period following the disaster. Then, to eliminate (control) the effect of seasonal fluctuations on the measured behaviors, they took, as the predisaster period, the identical seven-month period of the *preceding year.*

5. The results revealed that cases of mental illness increased by nearly 236 percent, psychosomatic illness by 219 percent, and stress-aggravated illness by 198 percent. The researchers concluded that a disaster of this sort is likely to increase physical and psychosomatic illness, alcohol-related problems, aggression and violence, and family stress. They cautioned, however, that although they were able to control for seasonal variations, such variables as economic factors also need to be considered.

In any case, this particular field study is a prime example of the application of the scientific method: the formulation of hypotheses (here, as questions), identification of the unit of study, development of a conceptual scheme to guide the research, control of variables to the greatest extent possible, provision of an objective measurement scheme, reporting of the results, and critical analysis of the findings.

In *The Three Faces of Eve,* Joanne Woodward played Eve White, who suffered from multiple personality disorder. More recent cases of this disorder—those of Sybil and Billy Milligan—have also been highly publicized. Through case study techniques, psychologists have been able to gain considerable insight into this disorder.

procedure, to disconfirm an assumption, to generate future hypotheses for controlled research, and to collect comprehensive information for a better understanding of the individual (Garfield 1974).

The case study

Physicians have used the case study extensively in their description and treatment of medical disease. In psychology, the **case study** is based on clinical data (observations, psychological tests, and historical and biographical information on the subject) and thus lacks

the control and objectivity of many other methods. It serves as the primary source of data where systematic experimental and naturalistic procedures are not feasible (Millon and Diesenhaus 1972). It is especially valuable for studying phenomena that occur only rarely.

An interesting case study is that of Thigpen and Cleckley (1957), who describe in detail an exceedingly rare but classic multiple personality disorder. Eve White was a 25-year-old woman who sought therapy because of severe headaches and blackouts. Many of her symptoms seemed related to her marital conflicts and forced separation from her four-year-old daughter. Eve seemed to be a demure, reserved, and retiring person until one day, during an interview, she was seized by a sudden pain.

> After a tense moment of silence, her hands dropped. There was a quick, restless smile, and in a bright voice that sparkled, she said, "Hi there, Doc." . . . There was in the newcomer a childishly daredevil, erotically mischievous glance, a face marvelously free from the habitual signs of care, seriousness, and underlying distress, so long familiar in her predecessor. This new and apparently carefree girl spoke casually of Eve White and her problems, always using *she* or *her* in every reference, always respecting the strict boundaries of a separate identity. When asked her own name she immediately replied, "Oh, I'm Eve Black." (Thigpen and Cleckley 1957, p. 137)

After months of therapy two more personalities emerged, making a total of four. This rare case study provided valuable insights into the causes and treatment of multiple personalities.

The single-subject experiment

The **single-subject experiment** differs from the case study in that the former is actually an experiment in which some aspect of the person's own behavior is taken as the control. An interesting type of single-subject experiment is the **multiple-baseline design,** which involves measuring changes (or the lack of change) in several related behaviors over a given period of time. The experimenter first makes a careful record of each behavior to establish multiple baselines (Risley and Baer 1970). Once this task is completed, the experimenter applies a modification to one of the behaviors until a change occurs. Then the experimenter applies the same modification to the second behavior, to the third, and successively to all the others being measured. If in all cases the behavior changes when the experimenter applies the modification, a strong inference of causal relationship can be made.

Schmidt (1974) used the multiple-baseline design to gauge his success in treating an eighteen-year-old client who wished to increase her verbal skills. After determining that three types of behavior were related to verbal skills (frequency of verbal statements, loudness of voice, and number of times conversations are initiated), Schmidt had the client count the frequencies of all three behaviors for one week. During that week, the mean baselines were found to be 1.0 times per day for the number of times she spoke at work, .8 times per day for speaking loudly, and .4 times per day for initiating conversations. These figures reveal an extremely withdrawn individual.

At the beginning of the second week, Schmidt told the client that, any time she spoke with someone at work that day (behavior A), she would be allowed two minutes with Schmidt to discuss anything she wanted. Her mean frequency for speaking at work increased to 8.2, whereas speaking loudly increased slightly and initiating conversations remained the same (see Figure 5.2, p. 150). At the beginning of the third week, he told her she could have one minute per day with him for each time she engaged in either speaking at work or speaking loudly (behaviors A and B). The frequencies of these behaviors increased to 15.8 and 5.2 times per day, respectively; the third behavior remained the same. The fourth week, Schmidt told his client she could have one minute per day for each time she engaged in any of the three verbal behaviors. The mean frequencies for speaking at work, speaking loudly, and initiating conversations became 14.6 (down an insignificant amount), 12.2, and 7.4 times per day, respectively.

Because each behavior changed successively with the introduction of the same technique, we can be fairly certain that "talking to the counselor" caused the behavior changes. Of course, such a technique worked because the client obviously found talking to the counselor highly desirable or reinforcing. If that had not been the case, another change-inducing reward would have had to be identified.

Figure 5.2 *A Single-Subject Experiment with Three Baseline Variables.*
The first week was the baseline period. Behavior A was treated during the second week, behaviors A and B during the third week, and all three behaviors during the fourth week.

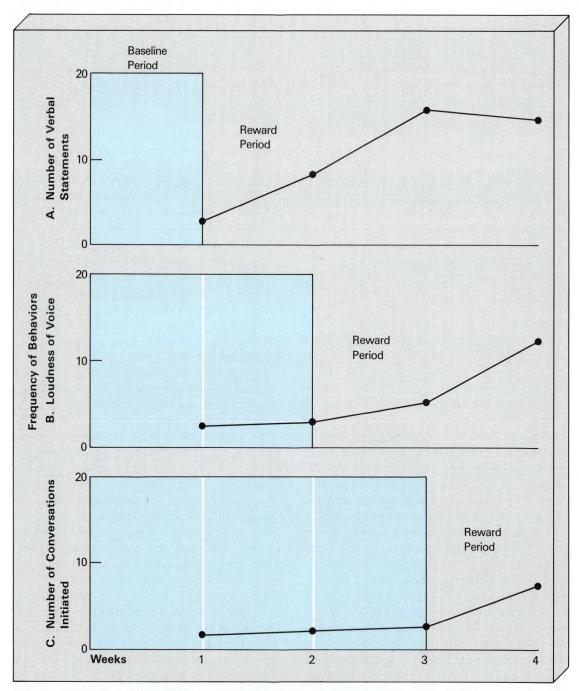

HISTORICAL RESEARCH

Historical research is the least understood method of inquiry—one that many consider something less than a "legitimate" means of study in science. Although it has been used extensively by historians and other scholars involved with human events, it has been criticized as being unsystematic and susceptible to researcher bias. But, to the extent that such criticisms are accurate, they are criticisms of techniques rather than of historical research itself. The fact is that most of our understanding of past conceptions of abnormal behavior, and of their effect on present conceptions, has been obtained through careful historical research.

The purpose of **historical research** is to reconstruct some aspect of the past systematically and objectively by collecting, verifying, evaluating, and synthesizing the evidence available in historical documents and, from that reconstruction, to establish facts and reach defensible conclusions. These conclusions are often formulated in relation to a particular hypothesis.

Five important characteristics of historical research were described by Isaac and Michael (1977).

1. Historical research depends upon data observed by others rather than by the investigator. Good data result from painstaking detective work which analyzes the authenticity, accuracy, and significance of source material.

2. Contrary to popular notions, historical research must be rigorous, systematic, and exhaustive; much "research" claiming to be historical is an undisciplined collection of inappropriate, unreliable, or biased information.

3. Historical research depends upon two kinds of data: primary sources where the author [of a document being researched] was a direct observer of the recorded event, and secondary sources where the author is reporting the observations of others and is one or more times removed from the original event. Of the two, primary sources carry the authority of firsthand

evidence and have priority in data collection.

4. Two basic forms of criticism weight the value of the data: external criticism which asks, "Is the document or relic authentic?" and internal criticism which asks, "If authentic, are the data accurate and relevant?" Internal criticism must examine the motives, biases, and limitations of the author which might cause him to exaggerate, distort, or overlook information. This critical evaluation of the data is what makes true historical research so rigorous—in many ways, more demanding than experimental methods.

5. While historical research is similar to the "review of the literature" which precedes other forms of research, the historical approach is more exhaustive, seeking out information from a larger array of sources. It also tracks down information that is much older than required by most reviews and hunts for unpublished material not cited in the standard references. (p. 17)

As an example, Focus 5.2 (pp. 152–153) contains excerpts from a report of historical research into the portrayal of members of minority groups in the mental health literature. The researcher concludes that social scientists are not immune to the biases and stereotypes of their society and that, as a result, the charactristics and lifestyles of minority group members have often been unjustifiably equated with pathology. These conclusions, which are shared by many mental health researchers and practitioners, challenge the traditional mental health criteria used to determine normality and abnormality. They have also led to concern about the control of biases and stereotypes in the conduct of research.

ETHICAL ISSUES IN RESEARCH

Earlier in this chapter, we discussed Schachter's anxiety experiment, in which subjects were not informed of the true nature of the study. And in Chapter 4 we described the Rosenhan study in which researchers falsely gained admission to a psychiatric hospital as patients. Are such deceptions unethical, or are they justified by the potential benefits of psychological research?

Questions concerning the ethics and morality of research—and, in particular, experimentation—take on greater import when subjects are not only deceived but also exposed to potential physical harm.

☐ It has come to light that the U.S. Army conducted mind-altering experiments on unsuspecting soldiers by administering LSD to them. Army researchers justified their actions by noting that the experiments were in the interest of national security (LSD could be used against us by our enemies, so we need to know how to counteract its effects).

FOCUS 5.2

Historical Research: Minority Groups and Pathology

When we seriously study the "scientific" literature of the past relating to the culturally different, we are immediately impressed with how an implicit equation of minority groups and pathology is a common theme. The historical use of science in the investigation of racial differences seems to be linked with white supremacist notions. A. Thomas and Sillen (1972) refer to this as "scientific racism" and cite several historical examples to support their contention: (1) In 1840 fabricated census figures were used to support the notion that blacks living under "unnatural" conditions of freedom were prone to anxiety. (2) Mental health for blacks was taken to consist of contentment with subservience. (3) It was assumed that psychologically normal blacks were faithful and happy-go-lucky. (4) Influential medical journals presented as facts fantasies supporting the belief that the anatomical, neurological, or endocrinological attributes of blacks were always inferior to those of whites. (5) The black person's brain was assumed to be smaller and less developed. (6) Blacks were thought less prone to mental illness because their minds were so simple. (7) The dreams of blacks were judged juvenile in character and not so complex as those of whites.

Furthermore, the belief that various human groups exist at different stages of biological evolution was accepted by G. Stanley Hall (1904). He stated explicitly that Africans, Indians, and Chinese were members of adolescent races and in a stage of incomplete development. In most cases, the evidence used to support these conclusions was fabricated, extremely flimsy, or distorted to fit the belief in nonwhite inferiority (A. Thomas and Sillen, 1972). For example, Gossett (1963) reports how, when one particular study in 1895 revealed that the sensory perception of Native Americans was superior to that of blacks, and that of blacks to that of whites, the results were used to support a belief in the mental superiority of whites. "Their reactions were slower because they belonged to a more deliberate and reflective race than did the members of the other two groups" (p. 364). The belief that blacks are "born athletes" as opposed to scientists or statesmen derives from this tradition. The fact that Hall was a well-respected psychologist often referred to as "the father of child study" and first president of the APA did not prevent him from inheriting the racial biases of his times.

The portrayal of the culturally different in the literature has generally taken the form of stereotyping them as "deficient" in certain "desirable" attributes. For example, de Gobineu's (1915) *Essay on the Ine-*

Informing the soldiers that they had been administered the drug would have invalidated the findings. Nevertheless, some soldiers have experienced flashbacks (recurring hallucinations) and lifelong psychiatric problems that they claim are results of their participation in the study.

☐ Many studies are aimed at understanding the effects of alcohol on the mental, emotional, and physical functioning of both alcoholics and nonalcoholics. But by providing alcohol to subjects, the researchers can harm these individuals in several ways: (1) Alcoholics may be led to drink excessively after participating in the study. (2) Giving alcohol to alcoholics may violate the estab-

---

quality of the Human Races and Darwin's (1859) *On The Origin of the Species by Means of Natural Selection* were used to support the genetic intellectual superiority of whites and the genetic inferiority of the "lower races." Galton (1869) wrote explicitly that African "Negros" were "half-witted men" who made "childish, stupid and simpleton like mistakes," whereas Jews were deemed inferior physically and mentally and fit only for a parasitical existence on other nations. Using the Binet scales to test Spanish Indian, Mexican American, and black families, Terman (1916) concluded that they were uneducable.

That the genetic deficiency model still exists can be seen in the writing of Shuey (1966), Jensen (1969), Herrnstein (1971), and Shockley (1972). These writers have adopted the position that genes play a predominant role in the determination of intelligence. Shockley (1972) has expressed fears that the accumulation of genes for weak or low intelligence in the black population will seriously affect overall intelligence. Thus he advocates that people with a low IQ should not be allowed to bear children; they should be sterilized.

Even more disturbing have been recent allegations that the late Cyril Burt, eminent British psychologist, fabricated data to support his contention that intelligence is inherited and that blacks have inherited infe-

rior brains. Such an accusation is immensely important when one considers that Burt is a major influence in American and British psychology, is regarded as the father of educational psychology, was the first psychologist to be knighted, and was awarded the APA's Thorndike Prize. Furthermore, his research findings are the foundation of the belief that intelligence is inherited. The charges, leveled by several people (Dorfman, 1978; Kamin, 1974; Gillie, 1977), can be summarized in four assertions: (1) Burt guessed at the intelligence of parents he interviewed and later treated his guesses as scientific facts. (2) Two of Burt's collaborators never existed, and Burt wrote the articles himself while using their names. (3) Burt produced identical figures to three decimal places from different sets of data (a statistical impossibility). (4) Burt fabricated data to fit his theories. In a thorough review of one of Burt's most influential publications, Dorfman (1978) concludes as follows:

Cyril Burt presented data in his classic paper "Intelligence and Social Class" that were in perfect agreement with a genetic theory of IQ and social class. A detailed analysis of these data reveals, beyond reasonable doubt, that they were fabricated from a theoretical normal curve, from a genetic regressions equation, and from figures published more than 30 years before Burt completed his surveys. (p. 1177)

SOURCE: Adapted from Sue 1981, pp. 12–14.

lished treatment principle of abstinence. (3) Alcohol may be harmful to certain people with specific medical conditions, including ulcers and liver damage.

Furthermore, in many behavioral studies, psychological (rather than physical) stress is induced in subjects. Guilt, fear, and shame are aroused in individuals; they are tempted to lie, cheat, or steal; or they are presented with unpleasant stimuli so that the effects may be studied. Here is an example, one that raised "ethical questions of the most serious type" according to the individual who reported it.

> The work . . . occurred in a military setting. It involved taking untrained soldiers, disorienting them, placing them in an isolated situation, giving them false instructions and leading them, as individuals, to believe that they had caused artillery to fire on their own troops and that heavy casualties had occurred. The subjects ran, cried, and behaved in what they could only consider an unsoldierly way, and no amount of debriefing could remove the knowledge that they had done so. (American Psychological Association 1973, p. 74)

Objections to research on moral and ethical grounds can be summarized as follows: Many experimental procedures require deception, which, of itself, violates the subject's trust in the experimenter. Then, after being deceived, many subjects may feel betrayed and need some form of corrective emotional experience to vent their feelings. Moreover, some experimental procedures may induce permanent psychological damage. In particular, because it is impossible for researchers to know each subject thoroughly, potentially unstable personalities are especially at risk in stressful experiments. A number of critics feel that the potential generality and importance of research findings often do not warrant drastic experimental procedures (Kennedy 1975; Smith 1976). In other words, the ends do not necessarily justify the means, even in scientific research.

The APA "principles of conduct"

Concern with the ethics of research has led most educational institutions and government agencies to establish review boards whose purpose is to survey all research being conducted or proposed by investigators. The American Psychological Association (APA) adopted a set of guidelines, Ethical Principles of Psychologists (1981), part of which is intended to endorse and promote ethical principles in psychological research. The APA has also established a Committee on Scientific and Professional Ethics and Conduct, which has the power to levy sanctions on members for violations of varying seriousness. The sanctions range from the purely educative and advisory to expulsion (Hall and Hare-Mustin 1983).

Here are the ten principles of conduct as set forth in the American Psychologist (1981).

1. In planning a study, the investigator has the responsibility to make a careful evaluation of its ethical acceptability. To the extent that the weighing of scientific and human values suggests a compromise of any principle, the investigator incurs a correspondingly serious obligation to seek ethical advice and to observe stringent safeguards to protect the rights of human participants.

2. Considering whether a participant in a planned study will be a "subject at risk" or a "subject at minimal risk," according to recognized standards, is of primary ethical concern to the investigator.

3. The investigator always retains the responsibility for ensuring ethical practice in research. The investigator is also responsible for the ethical treatment of research participants by collaborators, assistants, students, and employees, all of whom, however, incur similar obligations.

4. Except in minimal-risk research, the investigator establishes a clear and fair agreement with research participants, prior to their participation, that clarifies the obligations and responsibilities of each. The investigator informs the participants of all aspects of the research that might reasonably be expected to influence will-

If research is to be conducted ethically, then certain guidelines must be agreed upon by the scientific community and must be followed. To ensure respectful treatment of research subjects, an investigator must carefully explain all features of the research to a prospective participant, especially those features that might influence willingness to participate.

ingness to participate and explains all other aspects of the research about which the participants inquire. Failure to make full disclosure prior to obtaining informed consent requires additional safeguards to protect the welfare and dignity of the research participants. Research with children or with participants who have impairments that would limit understanding and/or communication requires special safeguarding procedures.

5. Methodological requirements of a study may make the use of concealment or deception necessary. Before conducting such a study, the investigator has a special responsibility to (i) determine whether the use of such techniques is justified by the study's prospective scientific, educational, or applied value; (ii) determine whether alternative procedures are available that do not use concealment or deception; and (iii) ensure that the participants are provided with sufficient explanation as soon as possible.

6. The investigator respects the individual's freedom to decline to participate in or to with-

draw from the research at any time. The obligation to protect this freedom requires careful thought and consideration when the investigator is in a position of authority or influence over the participant. Such positions of authority include, but are not limited to, situations in which research participation is required as part of employment or in which the participant is a student, client, or employee of the investigator.

7. The investigator protects the participant from physical and mental discomfort, harm, and danger that may arise from research procedures. If risks of such consequences exist, the investigator informs the participant of that fact. Research procedures likely to cause serious or lasting harm to a participant are not used unless the failure to use these procedures might expose the participant to risk of greater harm, or unless the research has great potential benefit and fully informed and voluntary consent is obtained from each participant. The participant should be informed of procedures for contacting the investigator within a reasonable time period following

participation should stress, potential harm, or related questions or concerns arise.

8. After the data are collected, the investigator provides the participant with information about the nature of the study and attempts to remove any misconceptions that may have arisen. Where scientific or humane values justify delaying or withholding this information, the investigator incurs a special responsibility to monitor the research and to ensure that there are no damaging consequences for the participant.

9. Where research procedures result in undesirable consequences for the individual participant, the investigator has the responsibility to detect and remove or correct these consequences, including long-term effects.

10. Information obtained about a research participant during the course of an investigation is confidential unless otherwise agreed upon in advance. When the possibility exists that others may obtain access to such information, this possibility, together with the plans for protecting confidentiality, is explained to the participant as part of the procedure for obtaining informed consent.

Implications for research, theory, and practice

It is clear from the foregoing discussion that contemporary science, along with its goals, assumptions, and methods, represents only one way of viewing the world. We must never forget that other, non-science-oriented groups may not share this view. As psychologists, the authors are strongly committed to the scientific method as the most beneficial way of asking and answering questions about the human condition. But we live in a real world, not an ideal one. As a result, our research strategies must be adapted to fit not only the objective world of science but the social, cultural, political, and clinical realities as well. Even within this broad framework, many research tools are available to us. Unfortunately, we tend to lose sight of this fact, and often become embroiled in debates about whether one technique (usually the experiment) is better than

others. These arguments are fruitless. All approaches have contributed to our understanding of abnormal psychology and will continue to do so.

SUMMARY

1. The scientific method provides for the systematic and controlled collection of data and the formulation of objective hypotheses based on those data. Its characteristics include self-correction, the use of conceptual schemes and theoretical structures, the testing of theories and hypotheses, the control of variables, and the avoidance of metaphysical explanations.

2. The experiment is the most powerful research tool for determining and testing cause–effect relationships. In its simplest form, the experiment involves an experimental hypothesis, an independent variable, and a dependent variable. The experimental group of subjects consists of those for whom the independent variable is manipulated. Extraneous variables are controlled through the use of control groups (of subjects).

3. A correlation is a measure of the degree to which two variables are related. It is expressed as a correlation coefficient, a numerical value between -1 and $+1$, symbolized by r. Correlational techniques provide less precision, control, and generality than experiments, and they cannot be taken to imply cause–effect relationships.

4. In the study of abnormal behavior, simulation is used to create, under controlled conditions, a situation as close to real life as possible. One use for simulation is in creating an artificial ''abnormal'' state.

5. The field study relies primarily on naturalistic observations. In this technique the psychologist enters a situation as unobtrusively as possible in order to observe and record behavior as it occurs naturally.

6. Rather than studying large groups of peo-

ple, many scientists advocate the in-depth study of one individual. Two types of single-subject techniques are the case study and the single-subject experiment. The case study is especially appropriate when a phenomenon is so rare that it is impractical to try to study more than one instance of it. Single-subject experiments differ from case studies in that they rely on experimental procedures; some aspect of the person's own behavior is taken as the control.

7. A seldom discussed but frequently used scientific strategy is historical research, an attempt to reconstruct the past objectively and accurately from existing documents. Like other research techniques, it is most often undertaken to test a hypothesis.

8. The scientific method is not without its weaknesses and limitations. Like other tools it is subject to misuse and misunderstanding, both of which can give rise to moral and ethical concerns. Such concerns have led to the development of guidelines for ethical conduct and the means of dealing with violations within the mental health professions.

KEY TERMS

correlation The degree to which two variables covary or are associated with each other in a population

experiment A technique of scientific inquiry in which an independent variable is manipulated, the changes in a dependent variable are measured, and extraneous variables are controlled to the extent possible

external validity The degree to which the results of an experiment may be generalized

field study An investigative technique in which behaviors are observed and recorded in the natural environment

historical research The systematic and objective reconstruction of some aspect of the past by use of the evidence available in historical documents

hypothesis A conjectural statement that describes a relationship between variables

internal validity In an experiment, the extent to which changes in the dependent variable are actually brought about by the independent variable (rather than extraneously)

scientific method A method of inquiry that provides for the systematic collection of data through controlled observation and for the testing of hypotheses based on those data

simulation An investigative technique in which a real-life situation is recreated under controlled conditions

theory A group of principles and hypotheses that together explain some aspect of a particular area of inquiry

PART 2

Anxiety and Stress

6

Anxiety Disorders

The disorders discussed in this chapter are all characterized by **anxiety,** or feelings of fear and apprehension. These disorders can produce seemingly illogical—and often restrictive—patterns of behavior.

☐ A college instructor is continually "nervous"; several times each week he suffers anxiety attacks during which he develops an intense fear of dying or becoming insane *(panic disorder)*.
☐ A thirty-year-old woman is afraid of enclosed places, such as elevators and very small rooms, and of being surrounded by people *(simple phobia)*.
☐ A fifteen-year-old boy is compelled to touch a glass exactly sixteen times before he can drink from it without anxiety *(obsessive–compulsive disorder)*.

The anxiety may itself be the major disturbance, as in the *panic disorders* and *generalized anxiety disorders;* it may be manifested only when the affected individual encounters particular situations, as in the *phobias;* or the anxiety may result from an attempt to master other symptoms, as in *obsessive–compulsive disorders*. We shall discuss all four of these major groups of **anxiety disorders.** Still another, called *posttraumatic stress disorders,* is discussed in Chapter 8 with other problems stemming from stressful events.

The anxiety disorders do not involve a loss of contact with reality: People suffering from them can usually go about most of the day-to-day business of living. Although these people are aware of the illogical and self-defeating nature of certain of their behaviors, they seem incapable of controlling them. In severe cases, the disturbed individuals may spend great amounts of time dealing with their debilitating fears—but to little effect. This preoccupation may, in turn, lead to emotional stress and turmoil, maladaptive behaviors, and disruptions in interpersonal relationships.

Until recently the anxiety disorders were classified as *neuroses*, along with the dissociative and somatoform disorders that are described in Chapter 7. The term **neurosis** had been associated with anxiety by Sigmund Freud, and it was applied to these three diverse classes of disorders because they were all believed to be based in, or characterized by, anxiety. But when the authors of DSM-III examined these disorders, they encountered two problems. First, anxiety is present in many mental illnesses that had *not* been classified as neuroses; and, although anxiety was assumed to underlie certain neurotic disorders, it was not always a visible symptom of those disorders. As a result, anxiety was not an effective indicator of the very disorders it was supposed to characterize. Second, the disorders that were classified as neuroses seemed too disparate to be placed in a single category; they included such problems as *multiple personality, amnesias,* and *hypochondriasis,* as well as the phobias and other specific anxiety disorders.

After much discussion among mental health professionals, the former neuroses were reclassified as anxiety disorders, dissociative disorders, or somatoform disorders. A diagnosis of anxiety disorder is not made if anxiety is found to accompany some other disorder (American Psychiatric Association 1980). Thus the word *neuroses* no longer signifies a particular category of disorders. However, it is still used in a general sense to refer to the less severe mental illnesses.

ANXIETY

Anxiety is a fundamental human emotion that was recognized as long as 5000 years ago (Cohen 1969; May 1958). Everyone has experienced it, and all of us will continue to experience it throughout our lives. Many observers regard anxiety as a basic condition of modern existence. The British poet W. H. Auden, for instance, called the twentieth century "the age of anxiety."

Some theorists see anxiety as a *response* to threatening situations; others explain it as a *drive* that leads to coping responses. But whatever the mechanism, most agree that "reasonable doses" of anxiety act as a safeguard to keep us from ignoring danger (see Focus 6.1). It is only when overwhelming anxiety disrupts social functioning or produces significant distress that an anxiety disorder is indicated.

> Joanne W. was known by her college friends as a worrier. She worried about anything and everything: failing in school, making friends, eating the right foods, maintaining her health, and being liked. Joanne also had difficulty making decisions. Her insecurity was so great that even the most common decisions—what clothes to wear, what to order at a restaurant, which movies to see—became major problems. At night Joanne reviewed and re-reviewed every real and imaginary mistake she had made or might make. This added yet another problem, not being able to sleep.

Manifestations of anxiety

Anxiety is manifested in four ways: *cognitively* (in a person's thoughts), *motorically* (in a person's actions), *somatically* (in physical or biological reactions), and *affectively* (in a person's emotions).

Cognitive manifestations may vary from mild worry to panic. Severe attacks can bring a conviction of impending doom (the end of the world or death), a preoccupation with unknown dangers, an inability to concentrate or make decisions, and difficulty in sleeping. In one study, patients suffering from *panic disorder* had such terrifying cognitions as dying of suffocation and physical catastrophe befalling a family member. Patients with *generalized anxiety disorders* tended to have milder anxiety-evoking thoughts dealing with, for

FOCUS 6.1

Anxiety and Fear: Do We Need Them?

Fear and anxiety have unpleasant effects, can lead to psychomotor and intellectual errors, can impair psychological functioning, and can disturb concentration and memory. Yet some psychologists point to evidence that anxiety may serve an adaptive or stimulating purpose (Antonovsky 1979; Epstein 1972; Lazarus 1966; Rachman 1974). To survive organisms must be able to assess a dangerous situation rapidly and take immediate action. When a dangerous threat appears, the organism becomes aroused (via fear or anger) in preparation for flight or attack. If too much time elapses between assessing a threat and taking action, the organism's survival is jeopardized.

Thus fear and anxiety can serve to arouse a person in preparation for constructive action. Indeed, the absence of appropriate fear can foster careless behavior in dangerous situations. Smith (1949) found that inexperienced combat soldiers displayed little fear and often engaged in careless behavior that placed their lives in jeopardy. After exposure to combat, they were more fearful but also more vigilant and careful. Janis (1971) found that moderate anticipatory fear about realistic threats is necessary

for the development of coping behavior. He divided patients about to undergo major surgery into three groups on the basis of the degree of fear they expressed. After the operation the highly fearful group displayed considerable pain and discomfort; the moderately fearful group coped better and displayed less pain; and the fearless patients suffered excessive postoperative anger, resentment, discomfort, and pain. Janis believes the moderately fearful patients were able to rehearse mentally what was about to happen and what was to follow and thus reduced both novelty and surprise. The highly fearful group tended to become defensive and preoccupied with their problem. The fearless group did not have realistic expectations about what was to occur and responded negatively.

Thus moderate fear levels can enhance vigilance and aid in a realistic appraisal of what is to come, both of which help the individual develop the coping responses necessary for survival. Functional fear appeals have been used in advertising campaigns to encourage people to stop smoking cigarettes, to use seat belts, and to have regular health checkups.

example, criticism from others, appearing foolish, and rejection (Beck et al. 1974).

Motor behaviors are often affected; anxious persons exhibit random movements that range from fine trembling to more pronounced skeletal shaking. A whole assortment of behaviors such as general restlessness, pacing, squirming, tics, lip biting, fingernail biting, knuckle cracking, and jumpiness may be exhibited. One can almost imagine that the body is pre-

paring for flight from some threat that is expected to appear at any moment.

Somatic changes may show up as shallow breathing, mouth dryness, cold hands and feet, diarrhea, frequent urination, fainting, heart palpitations, elevated blood pressure, increased perspiration, muscular tenseness (especially in the head, neck, shoulders, and chest), and indigestion.

Most individuals with anxiety disorders

The Scream, by Edvard Munch, depicts some of the symptoms that accompany anxiety. The swirling colors of the background evoke a feeling of uncontrollable disorder that cannot be escaped. The subject, clutching his head, seems terrorized by something, which must be in his own mind, for the scene is otherwise peaceful.

exhibit increased heart rate, respiration, muscle tension, and blood pressure. However, individuals with *hematophobia* (fear of blood) appear to show a different pattern of physiological reactions. Patients with this disorder were found to first display the usual anxiety reactions, and then a sudden slowing of the heart rate and a decrease in blood pressure. This sudden change often led to fainting, and it may be the process that causes some people to faint when confronted with a fearful situation (Ost, Sterner, and Lindahl 1984).

The most pronounced manifestation of anxiety is in the affective domain: Feelings of tense excitement may border on terror in chronic anxiety. In this state the person is continually uneasy and worried about imminent danger, no matter how well things are going. This "baseline" of fear may be punctuated by acute panic attacks, as it was for the following patient.

> While driving across the San Francisco Bay Bridge, John M., a fifty-year-old business executive, was suddenly seized by a tightening of the muscles around his neck and shoulders. He had been mildly apprehensive, but this was anything but mild. Was it a heart attack? Soon his heart was pounding so rapidly and loudly that the beats echoed in his ears. John became terrified, sure that death was imminent. He could not breathe; he broke out in a profuse sweat and felt he was about to faint.

The assessment of anxiety

The degree of anxiety within a patient cannot be measured precisely. However, the psychologist has a number of tools that can be used to generally assess the various symptoms. We shall discuss three of these: *self-reports,* which provide information about cognitive and affective manifestations; *observations* of motoric manifestations; and *physiological measures* of somatic processes.

Self-reports One obvious means of assessing anxiety is simply to ask the client what he or she is thinking and feeling, and a convenient time to do so is during an interview. Here is an edited and condensed transcript of a self-report in which a young woman describes her chronic state of anxiety and panic attacks.

> I've always been tense from as far back as I can remember. . . . but lately . . . it's getting worse. Sometimes I think I'm going crazy—especially at . . . at nights. . . . I can't sleep for fear of what has to be done the next day. . . . Should I go to my psych class tomorrow or skip it and study for my stat exam? If I skip it, maybe the prof will throw a pop quiz . . . he's known for that, you know. . . . These attacks are frightful. I had another one last week. It was horrible . . . I thought I would die. My roommate didn't know what to do. . . . By the time it was over my blouse was completely drenched. My room-

mate was so scared she called you. I was so embarrassed afterward . . . I think she [the roommate] wants to move out . . . I don't blame her.

Such reports are extremely valuable in diagnosing and treating emotional disorders, but they don't tell us everything we need to know. No doubt the client *believes* she has always been tense and suffers from insomnia, indecisiveness, and periodic panic attacks. But it is impossible to quantify such a report. Because the degree of anxiety and the factors associated with it are not always clear to the client, they are rarely clear to the therapist. More formalized or objective measures would be extremely helpful, and a number have been developed. These are also self-reports in essence, but they require clients to respond to specific questions or statements rather than to describe their condition in their own words. Among the most frequently used are the Taylor Manifest Anxiety Scale (Taylor 1953), the Test Anxiety Scale (Sarason 1958), the Willoughby Schedule (Wolpe 1958), and the Fear Survey Schedule (Wolpe and Lang 1964).

In the Taylor Manifest Anxiety Scale, the patient answers true or false to statements such as "I work under a great deal of strain," "I sweat very easily even on cool days," "I always have enough energy when faced with difficulties," and "My sleep is restless and disturbed." The higher the person's "anxious" responses, the more anxiety is assumed. The Taylor Scale consists of 225 items of which 50 contribute to the anxiety score.

In contrast to the Taylor Scale, which attempts to measure *general* anxiety, the three other anxiety instruments are aimed at assessing more *specific* anxieties. The Willoughby Schedule consists of 25 questions that the subject answers on a five-point scale ranging from "no, never, or not at all" to "almost always." Typical questions are "Do you get anxious if you have to speak or perform in any way in front of a group of strangers?" and "Do you lack confidence in your general ability to do things and to cope with situations?" The Fear Survey Schedule attempts to isolate fears related to objects, places, or events.

Motoric observations Many psychologists prefer direct observation of motoric behavior to self-reports. As we noted in Chapter 4, observational data may be obtained in naturalistic settings (home visits or interviews) or in the more structured environment of the laboratory. But the data obtained are valuable only if the observed behaviors are representative of the client's general reactions and are indicative of anxiety.

Physiological measures The **autonomic nervous system** (ANS) is directly involved in the physiology of anxiety. Its main function is to regulate the organism's internal environment (through digestion, elimination, blood pressure, and so on). There are two main parts to the ANS: the **sympathetic division** and the **parasympathetic division.** Because the sympathetic division tends to help the person expend energy, and the parasympathetic division tends to help conserve energy, they may work against one another as well as facilitate each other's functions.

The sympathetic division expends unusual effort to help the individual cope with emergency situations (the "fight or flight" response): The body exhibits increased heart rate, constricted blood vessels to the digestive tract and skin, inhibited salivation, muscular contraction of the stomach and intestines, and gastric secretion. In addition, the bronchial passages of the lungs become dilated to allow greater oxygen intake, and the pupils of the eyes dilate to increase visual acuity. The palmar surfaces of the hands and the plantar surfaces of the feet perspire. Increased blood flow to the heart, brain, and muscles is a direct result of these sympathetic division activities, which seem to have one common goal—to prepare for emergency action.

On the other hand, the parasympathetic division of the ANS functions to conserve energy by decreasing heart rate, dilating skin and visceral blood vessels, promoting digestive

Anxiety generated by modern life can set off the flight or fight response. The body becomes physically aroused when a person is confronted with a real, physical threat or with an imagined threat. Consequently, some anxious people could find themselves in a continual state of arousal.

processes, constricting the pupils, and facilitating elimination processes. The sympathetic and parasympathetic systems thus operate in "opposite directions" to provide equilibrium of the person's internal environment. When anxiety is experienced, the ANS is activated such that both sympathetic and parasympathetic responses occur. Although sympathetic responses usually dominate, chronic or acute anxiety may result in a mixed effect (Gelhorn 1967). Thus people who are overly anxious may feel a need to urinate or defecate frequently (parasympathetic function).

Information concerning the activities of the ANS has proved to be valuable in diagnosing, understanding, and treating anxiety. ANS re-

activity can be measured chemically, via the amount of epinephrine or norepinephrine in the blood. It may also be measured in terms of palmar skin resistance (electrical resistance to a very small current), which drops for several seconds after an anxiety-arousing stimulus is presented. Measurements of blood pressure (via sphygmomanometer) and heart rate (via stethoscope or electrocardiograph) are also used in assessing ANS activity and anxiety.

The fact that such physiological differences are correlated with anxiety responses has led to speculation that there are physiological differences between individuals who experience marked anxiety and those who don't. If this is so, further study may reveal important facts about the functioning of pathological anxiety and the major types of anxiety disorders, which are discussed in the remainder of this chapter.

PANIC DISORDERS AND GENERALIZED ANXIETY DISORDERS

The predominant characteristic of these disorders is unfocused, or *free-floating*, anxiety. That is, the affected individual is fearful and apprehensive but does not know what he or she is afraid of.

Generalized anxiety disorders are characterized by persistent high levels of anxiety and hypervigilance and their physiological symptoms, even in situations where no realistic danger is present. Afflicted individuals may have difficulty sleeping, are easily startled, and are continually "on edge." The inability to discover the source of their fears acts to maintain the level of anxiety and occasionally to cause more acute attacks of anxiety.

In **panic disorders** there are severe and frightening episodes of apprehension and feelings of impending doom. These attacks usually last a few minutes but can go on for several hours. They often occur unpredictably and are accompanied by physical sensations of fainting, choking, sweating, and heart palpitations (Martin 1971). In a substantial number of cases, afflicted individuals become frightened about leaving the home, for fear that an attack will occur in a public place. Such cases are diagnosed as agoraphobia with panic attacks. The following case seems typical:

> Lois R. was 16 when she had her first panic attack. "Suddenly I felt that I was going to die," she says. "My heart was beating so fast that I thought I was having a heart attack, my mouth was very dry, I couldn't think. . . ."
>
> That was only the start. At school she began running to the nurse's office several times a week, in terror and asking for help. She lived in fear of attacks and of being where she could not cope with them. She stopped riding in elevators. She was afraid to go anywhere in a car. Open spaces seemed threatening, especially if she was alone.
>
> For the next 39 years fear plagued her. It sometimes waned but never left her. She saw many doctors: a family physician who thought she was having a nervous breakdown and tried to cure her by making her sleep for a week; a psychiatrist who prescribed Valium and other tranquilizers, plus sleeping pills, over a 10-year period; a psychologist who hypnotized her to bring her back to her childhood. "It was expensive," she says, "and it didn't help." (*Novato* (Calif.) *Independent Journal,* July 6, 1984, p. C3)

Individuals with panic disorders report periods of relatively low anxiety alternating with intense panic attacks, whereas those with generalized anxiety disorders are likely to show a continually high anxiety level. The majority of panic-attack patients report a disturbed childhood environment; most indicate that they first experienced panic attacks after some form of separation, such as leaving home or the loss or threatened loss of a loved one (Raskin et al. 1982).

Most clinicians believe that an external source of anxiety cannot be identified in panic disorders and generalized anxiety disorders. However, a study of 32 anxious patients indicated some relationship between the patient's cognitions (thoughts) and fluctuations in his or her anxiety level (Beck, Laude, and Bohnert 1974). In this sense, generalized anxiety is similar to a *phobia,* in which a particular thing or situation gives rise to the anxiety. The thoughts that were associated with increased anxiety were fears of physical attacks, accident, illness, social rejection, or humiliation. Most of these cognitions involved an unrealistically high expectation of harm.

A majority of the patients exhibited threatening cognitions prior to the onset of acute anxiety attacks. (See Table 6.1, p. 168 for examples of these fantasies.) But the researchers who reported the study argue that these patients are not suffering from phobias. Phobic individuals can avoid the situations that produce their anxiety, but these patients cannot avoid the fear of having a heart attack, of suffocation, or of social disapproval.

Etiology of panic disorders and generalized anxiety disorders

In our discussions of the causes and origins of mental disorders in this chapter and ensuing chapters, we must distinguish among the viewpoints that derive from the various models of psychopathology. Here we shall examine the etiology of unfocused anxiety disorders from the learning, psychoanalytic, and biological perspectives.

Learning perspective   The behaviorists believe that anxiety is a learned response to external stimuli. Wolpe (1958) argues that so-called free-floating anxiety stems from classical conditioning to an omnipresent stimulus, such as light or shade contrasts, size, or the passage of time. Wolpe also prefers the term *pervasive* to *free-floating,* because the latter implies the lack of an external source for the anxiety.

Wolpe suggests that two factors may be involved in producing pervasive anxiety. One is the intensity of the unconditioned stimulus; an intense UCS may produce conditioning to more of the stimulus elements that are present

Table 6.1

Patient	Stimuli Producing Acute Anxiety	Content of Cognitions
25-year-old teacher	Anticipation of giving lectures	Fears inability to function as a teacher and ending up on skid row
30-year-old homemaker	Sirens, news of deaths, accidents, fires	Fears physical catastrophe to family members
19-year-old student	Being alone with a boy, social situations where there is a potential for kissing	Fears sexual activity and consequently being seen as "cheap"
28-year-old clerk	Any physical symptom, crowds, buses	Fears suffocation, heart attacks, going insane, public faintings, humiliation
35-year-old teacher	Any contact with other people or anticipation of contact with other people	Fears people will openly criticize him

SOURCE: Adapted from Beck, A. T., Laude, R., and Bohnert, M. (1974). Ideational components of anxiety neurosis. *Archives of General Psychiatry, 31,* 319–325. Copyright © 1974, American Medical Association. Reprinted with permission.

at the time of conditioning. The second factor is the lack of a distinct environmental stimulus during conditioning. Wolpe presents a case study involving a patient whose pervasive anxiety developed after a guilt-ridden sexual experience that took place in the dark and evoked a great deal of emotional turmoil. This individual developed anxiety in many situations in which sexual cues and darkness were present.

Although classical conditioning to an omnipresent stimulus may account for some cases of panic and generalized anxiety disorder, it is difficult to believe that all cases develop in this manner.

Psychoanalytic perspective The psychoanalytic view stresses the importance of internal conflicts (rather than external stimuli) in the origin of panic disorders and generalized anxiety disorders. Because the problem originates in sexual and aggressive impulses that are seeking expression, anxiety is always present. When a forbidden impulse threatens to disturb the ego's integrity, an intense anxiety reaction

occurs. Because this conflict is unconscious, the individual does not know the source of the anxiety.

The defense against this unfocused anxiety is generally considered to be poorly organized and less effective than those mounted against other anxiety disorders. In a phobia, for example, the conflict between id impulses and ego is displaced onto a specific external stimulus that can be controlled simply through avoidance. But the individual with generalized anxiety disorder has only one defense—to try to repress the impulses. When that defense weakens, panic attacks may occur.

Biological perspective Generalized anxiety disorder has received some attention from biological and genetic researchers. Slater and Shields (1969), for example, hypothesize that individuals with this disorder may inherit a tendency to be autonomically unstable and that this tendency may predispose them to develop generalized anxiety disorder. In a sample of pairs of twins, the researchers found **concordance rates** (or percentages sharing the same disorder) of 41 percent for identical twins and 4 percent for fraternal twins—findings that could be consistent with their genetic hypothesis. Their sample size was small, however, and in the studies they analyzed, environmental influences may not have been sufficiently controlled.

Other researchers have compared patients with chronic generalized anxiety to other outpatient groups. For example, a number of groups were compared on such measures of anxiety as forearm blood flow, heart rate, and self-ratings of anxiety (Kelly and Walters 1968). Physiological measurements were obtained during a basal or resting period and during a stress period in which the patients were required to do rapid numerical calculations while exposed to criticisms and harassment. The measurements revealed that the chronically anxious patients exhibited higher anxiety than any other group. These patients also had a higher anxiety level during basal periods than patients in the normal control group (Lader 1967; Lader and Wing 1964). Such studies support the suggestion that individuals with generalized anxiety disorder may be predisposed to developing this condition.

Treatment of panic disorders and generalized anxiety disorders

The anxiety disorders have received increasing attention from researchers over the past few years. An issue of particular concern is whether or not some types of anxiety disorders (in particular, panic disorders and generalized anxiety disorders) are really distinct disorders, each requiring special treatment. Because this question has not been resolved, we shall discuss their treatments separately here.

Panic disorders Treatments for panic disorders can generally be divided into two approaches: biological (via medication) and psychotherapeutic. With regard to medication, both antidepressant drugs and tranquilizer

drugs have been used. Although there is considerable controversy about how antidepressants work against panic attacks, it appears that these drugs reduce not only depression but extreme fears as well (Mavissakalian et al. 1983). Success has been reported in the treatment of panic disorders with a particular antidepressant, imipramine (Garakani, Zitrin, and Klein 1984; Pohl, Rainey, and Gershon 1984).

In a study of ten patients with panic disorders, Garakani and his colleagues found that nearly all of them improved. However, four of the patients discontinued the medication because of its side effects, and the researchers' report of success was based on the self-reports of the patients. Moreover, it is possible that altered patterns of exposure to anxiety-producing situations had an affect on the results. (This is true of most studies of the effect of medication that do not control for exposure.) The reported success of antidepressants may be due to the ability of those drugs to help patients expose themselves to fearful stimuli more easily, which decreases the occurrence of subsequent panic attacks (Telch et al., in press).

Similar results with minor tranquilizers have been reported, and some have been refuted. It is still too early to tell which drugs, if any, will be successful—and to what extent—in treating panic disorders.

A basic conclusion of many researchers is that a panic-disorder patient's cognitions specifically require treatment (Butler and Mathews 1983). One approach to such treatment is *cognitive restructuring* (Hibbert 1984). In this psychotherapeutic approach, the therapist helps the patient to identify his or her anxiety-arousing thoughts, to examine the basis for these thoughts, and to change them into more realistic thoughts. Cognitive restructuring has been suggested for use in combination with muscle relaxation or biofeedback training to help reduce anxiety levels (Barlow et al. 1984). There are, however, few controlled studies on the effectiveness of this procedure.

In another approach, researchers concentrated on the similarities between panic attacks and hyperventilation sensations, rather than on cognitions (Clark, Salkovskis, and Chalkley, in press). Their goal was to prove the effectiveness of *respiration training* in treating the disorder. This training consisted of teaching patients a slow method of breathing to use whenever they were threatened by hyperventilation, which is a common complication of panic attacks. The respiration training did result in a reduction of symptoms, but that result must be interpreted with caution because the study did not include a control group. A second study replicated and supported this result, but again without a control group; more study is obviously required (Salkovskis, Jones, and Clark, in press).

Generalized anxiety disorders Biological, psychodynamic, and behavioral approaches have been used in the treatment of general anxiety. However, the behavioral (or cognitive behavioral) techniques collectively known as *stress management* have received the most attention. Although stress management has not routinely and specifically been tested with patients suffering from generalized anxiety disorder, it seems to hold much promise for such individuals.

Today's stress-management programs employ a variety of behavioral strategies for reducing anxiety (Greenberg 1983; Curtis and Detert 1981).

□ *Cognitive preparation,* which involves learning to reconceptualize anxiety-producing situations in such a way as to reduce emotional arousal
□ *Skills development,* in which the skills necessary to reduce anxiety (such as in initiating conversations) are learned and practiced
□ *Deep muscle relaxation,* which is a coping response to anxiety-arousing situations

These strategies reduce anxiety by reducing the stress produced in fearful situations.

Another behavioral technique that has been used to combat anxiety is *countercondition-*

ing. Wolpe (1973) attempted a unique version of this technique when he instructed subjects to inhale air enriched with CO_2. The enriched air served to stimulate respiration, which Wolpe believed was incompatible with anxiety. Unfortunately, Wolpe came up against the major stumbling block in such studies—a lack of generalization from the clinic to nontreatment settings. In other words, the subjects learned to decrease their anxiety during training sessions, but they were much less successful in doing so on their own.

One cognitive behavioral treatment that has specifically been tested with patients suffering from generalized anxiety disorder is the thought-stopping technique of Butler and Shaw (1977). This treatment involves training the client to scream "Stop!" loudly whenever an undesired thought or feeling intrudes. Probably the most important aspect of this experiment was the demonstration, once again, that cognitions need to be addressed in the treatment of anxiety disorders.

PHOBIAS

The word *phobia* comes from the Greek word meaning *fear.* A **phobia** is a strong, persistent, and unwarranted fear of some specific object or situation. Nearly anything can become the source of this intense fear. In fact there is even a fear of phobias, called *phobophobia* (see Table 6.2).

DSM-III includes three subcategories of phobias: agoraphobia, which is a single irrational fear that may be manifested in different ways; the social phobias, which generally involve social situations; and the simple phobias, which include most of the fears listed in Table 6.2.

Agoraphobia

Agoraphobia is an intense fear of open spaces; it may also manifest itself as a fear of being alone, of being in public places where escape or help may not be readily available, of being in crowds, or, in extreme cases, of leaving one's home. Many individuals with this disorder have frequent panic attacks. The phobia has its onset during early adulthood and tends to lead to a severe restriction of activity and to social isolation (Rohs and Noyes 1978). It occurs more frequently in women than in men and is the most common form of phobic disturbance seen by therapists (DSM-III 1980).

The following report illustrates some of the characteristics associated with agoraphobia.

> The patient was a 28-year-old woman whose attacks of anxiety were triggered by the terrifying sensation of impending death. This feeling was so horrifying that she would clutch passers-by and beg them for help. These episodes were acutely embarrassing to her, because no physical illness could be found. She was at first diagnosed as suffering from a panic disorder. In a later interview, it was discovered that her anxiety attacks occurred in situations where she felt trapped, such as in a crowded restaurant. Finally, her discomfort reached the point where she became unwilling to leave her home unless she was accompanied by her husband. At this point, a diagnosis of agoraphobia with panic attacks was given.

A nationwide survey of over 900 agoraphobics revealed that nearly 75 percent of those surveyed could recall an event that

Agoraphobics may suffer extreme anxiety or panic attacks when they are outside, alone, or in a crowd. Many agoraphobics can recall the situation that instigated the disorder, which was often a conditioning experience.

Table 6.2 *Phobias and Their Objects*

Acrophobia—fear of heights	Microphobia—fear of germs
Agoraphobia—fear of open spaces	Monophobia—fear of being alone
Ailurophobia—fear of cats	Mysophobia—fear of contamination or germs
Algophobia—fear of pain	
Arachnophobia—fear of spiders	
Astraphobia—fear of storms, thunder, and lightning	Nyctophobia—fear of the dark
	Ocholophobia—fear of crowds
Aviophobia—fear of airplanes	Pathophobia—fear of disease
Brontophobia—fear of thunder	Phobophobia—fear of phobias
Claustrophobia—fear of closed spaces	Pyrophobia—fear of fire
Dementophobia—fear of insanity	Syphilophobia—fear of syphilis
Gentophobia—fear of genitals	Trichophobia—fear of hair
Hematophobia—fear of blood	Xenophobia—fear of strangers
	Zoophobia—fear of animals or some particular animal

precipitated the disorder. In 38 percent of the cases, this event was a conditioning experience; in 23 percent it was the death of a family member or friend; in 13 percent, a personal illness; in 8 percent, giving birth; and in 4 percent, marital difficulties. The situations most likely to produce anxiety involve being trapped, having to wait in line, being far away from home, and having domestic arguments. But most of those surveyed feel less anxious when they are accompanied by a spouse or friend or when they have easy access to an exit. The fears most commonly displayed by agoraphobics involve physical harm or illness, such as fainting, heart attacks, and dying (Thorpe and Burns 1983).

Reports of such physical reactions as heart palpitations, weakness, and lightheadedness are not uncommon among agoraphobics (Tearnan et al. 1984). However, a diagnosis of agoraphobia can be given whether or not the individual suffers from panic attacks.

There is some question about whether agoraphobia actually is a phobia. Hallam (1978) feels that the anxiety displayed in agoraphobia is not aroused by an object or situation but is due to the absence of familiarity and safety. He views the disorder as a variant of an anxiety state rather than a phobia. A possible connection between anxiety states and agoraphobia is implied in the DSM-III discussion of panic disorders:

> A common complication of this disorder is the development of an anticipatory fear of helplessness or loss of control during a panic attack so that the individual becomes reluctant to be alone or in public places away from home. (DSM-III 1980, p. 230)

If this "complication" does occur, a diagnosis of agoraphobia with panic attacks is more appropriate.

Rachman (1984) also feels that the puzzling symptoms of agoraphobia are best interpreted from a safety perspective, not as a phobic reaction: In agoraphobics, an internal balance between danger signals and safety signals is upset in situations where a speedy return to safety is limited or impossible. Such an interpretation would explain why agoraphobic individuals prefer to sit near exits and feel less anxious when they do so. This view would also explain the onset of the disorder after the loss of a friend or relative; here again, the balance between safety and danger would be upset. To explain why some individuals develop agoraphobia and others do not under the same set of conditions, Rachman suggests that the former tend to be overanxious and dependent, which makes them more vulnerable.

The safety perspective of Hallam and Rachman can thus account for much of what is known about agoraphobia. However, many agoraphobics do not perceive their problems as involving safety.

Social phobias

A **social phobia** is an irrational fear of social situations. The most common forms include extreme fear of public speaking, of eating in restaurants, of using public restrooms, or of performing in public. There is no fear when the individual engages in any of these activities in private. The fear stems from anxiety that, in the company of others, one of these activities will be performed in a manner that is embarrassing or humiliating: A 21-year-old man was so anxious when using public toilet facilities that he would search for an isolated restroom when he needed to urinate. Even when he was alone in the restroom, urination was difficult; it became impossible when another individual entered the facility. His anticipatory anxiety eventually became so great that he severely restricted his intake of liquids during the day.

As is true of other phobics, socially phobic individuals usually realize that their behavior and fears are irrational, but this understanding does not reduce the distress they feel. Nor does it help them to reason their fears away.

One common type of social phobia is an irrational fear of public speaking. For some people, the anxiety felt before a public speaking engagement is so overwhelming that they are unable to deliver their prepared talk.

Unlike agoraphobia, however, social phobias are rarely incapacitating, because it is usually possible to avoid the anxiety-producing situations.

Social *phobias* are relatively rare according to DSM-III, but *anxiety* in social situations is fairly common. Focus 6.2 (p. 174) explores the difference between the two.

Socially phobic (and anxious) individuals are concerned that their nervousness and anxiety will be detected by others. However, it has been found that other people do not detect many behavioral signs of anxiety in highly socially anxious subjects (McEwan and Devins 1983). Thus it seems that socially anxious individuals are more aware of their anxiety than other people. Most likely, negative self-evaluation and cognitions play a much greater role in the social phobias than in agoraphobia and simple phobias.

Simple phobias

A **simple phobia** is an extreme fear of a specific object (such as snakes) or situation (such as being in an enclosed place). In a sense, the simple phobias provide a catch-all category for those irrational fears that are neither agoraphobia nor social phobias. The only similarity among the various simple phobias is the existence of an irrational fear. The most common of these fears involve small animals, heights, the dark, and lightning; others involve death, exams, deep water, and being mentally ill (Kirkpatrick 1984). Unusual and uncommon simple phobias have involved bathwater running down the drain (after pulling out the plug, the affected individual would dash out of the bathroom with great anxiety); snow (the fear developed after the individual got stuck in a snowstorm and arrived too late to talk to his

When Is a Fear a Phobia?

Social fears are common. In one study, only 26 percent of the women in the sample reported no fears at all (Costello 1982). In another study, 40 percent of college and high school students were found to suffer from social fears (Zimbardo 1977). These students displayed excessive self-consciousness and concern about what others thought, along with such physiological reactions as increased pulse rate, blushing, and perspiration.

Social phobias, however, are considered to be relatively uncommon. But when is a fear extreme enough to be considered a phobia? According to DSM-III, two elements must be present for the diagnosis of phobia: (1) a persistent and irrational fear with a compelling desire to avoid the situation, and (2) significant distress because of realization of the excessive nature of the fear.

Are these criteria fulfilled in the case of a student with public speaking anxiety who drops out of classes where oral participation is required, or in the case of a student with heterosexual anxiety who will not talk to individuals of the opposite sex even when there is a strong desire to do so? The subjective nature of the criteria makes that question a difficult one to answer. Exactly how "compelling" must the fear be, and how much distress is "significant"? Even the usually very specific DSM-III is less than clear on this issue. Public speaking anxiety is presented in the manual as an example of a social phobia. But later on, DSM-III also states that "avoidance of certain social situations that are normally a source of some distress, which is common in many individuals with 'normal' fear of public speaking, does not justify a diagnosis of social phobia" (p. 228).

So the question still remains: When does a "normal" fear become "abnormal"?

dying father); and a woman who was terrified of three-legged stools (Adler, Hager, Zabarsky, Jackson, Friendly, and Abramson 1984).

The following report of a fairly common simple phobia demonstrates one treatment method as well.

Ms. B, a 23-year-old woman, complained of a phobia of spiders that had not changed for as long as she could remember. She had no history of any other psychiatric symptoms. In treatment, when initially approached with a closed glass jar containing spiders, she breathed heavily, wept tears, and rated her subjective distress as 70 to 80. She suddenly began scratching the back of her hand, stating she felt as though spiders were crawling under her skin, although she knew this was not the case. The sensation lasted only a few seconds and did not recur. Her total treatment consisted of four 1-hour sessions distributed over the span of a month. At completion she had lost all fear of spiders and became able to let them crawl freely about her arms, legs, and face as well as inside her clothing with no distress whatever. She remained free of fear at 1-year follow-up, expressing disbelief that she had allowed such a "silly fear" to dominate her life for so long. (Curtis 1981, p. 1095)

Simple phobias are more prevalent in women than in men and are rarely incapacitating. The degree to which they interfere with daily life depends on how easy it is to avoid the feared object or situation.

The simple phobias often begin during childhood. In a study of 139 phobic patients, retrospective data revealed that animal phobias

Simple phobias, unlike agoraphobia or social phobia, do not interfere greatly with daily life. Some people have an irrational fear of tunnels—they cannot drive or walk through a tunnel because of an overwhelming belief that it will collapse when they are halfway through. Other people have a similar irrational fear of heights.

tend to start by the age of 5, whereas specific situational phobias involving things such as heights, darkness, and thunderstorms show a wide range of onset—from age 5 to adulthood (Marks and Gelder 1966).

Fears are quite common in children. In interviews of 398 children between the ages of 5 and 12, the greatest number of fears reported were of supernatural agents (such as ghosts and witches), finding oneself in the dark, animals, bodily injury, and traffic accidents (Jersild, Markey, and Jersild 1960). These fears very seldom remain to become phobias; most are lost as the child gets older. Even in phobic children, the majority of disorders dissipated within one year without treatment (Hampe et al. 1973). However, phobias that begin during later adolescence or adulthood tend to persist without treatment.

Etiology of phobias

Psychoanalytic perspective   According to this viewpoint, phobias are symptomatic of unconscious sexual or aggressive conflicts that are displaced (or shifted) from their original internal source to an external object or situation. The phobia is less threatening to the individual than recognition of the actual unconscious impulse underlying the fear. A fear of knives, for example, may represent castration fears produced by an unresolved Oedipus complex or aggressive conflicts. Agoraphobics may develop their fear of leaving the home because of an unconscious fear of acting out unacceptable sexual desires. The presence of a friend or spouse lowers anxiety because it provides some protection against the agoraphobic's impulses.

In this sense, phobias represent a compromise between the ego and the impulses seeking gratification. The individual blocks from consciousness the real source of anxiety and is able to avoid the dangerous impulse that the phobia represents.

Psychoanalysts believe the level of phobic fear indicates the strength of the underlying conflict. This formulation, presented by Freud in 1909, was based on his analysis of a fear of horses displayed by a five-year-old boy named Hans (Freud 1959). Freud believed that the phobia represented a symptomatic or displaced fear arising from the Oedipus complex. The factors involved were incestuous attraction of the mother, hostility toward the father because of his sexual privileges, and castration fear (fear of retribution by the father). Freud became convinced that all these elements were present in the phobic boy.

At the age of three, Hans had displayed an interest in his penis, which he called his "widdler"; he would examine animate and inanimate objects for the presence of a penis. One day as he was fondling himself, his mother threatened to have a physician cut off his penis. "And then what will you widdle with?" (p. 151). Hans enjoyed having his mother bathe him and especially wanted her to touch his penis. Freud interpreted these events to indicate that Hans was aware of pleasurable sensations in his penis and that he knew it could be "cut off" if he did not behave. Wanting his mother to handle his genitals indicated Hans's increasing sexual interest in her.

Hans's fear that horses would bite him developed after he saw a horse-drawn van overturn. According to Freud, little Hans's sexual jealousy of his father and the hostility it aroused in Hans produced anxiety because his father could retaliate by castrating him. This unconscious threat was so unbearable that the fear was displaced to the idea that horses "will bite me." Freud concluded that phobias were adaptive because they prevent the surfacing of more traumatic unconscious conflicts.

Although Freud's formulation has clinical appeal, it is not without problems. According to the psychoanalytic perspective, if the phobia is only a symptom of an underlying unconscious conflict, treatment directed to that symptom—the feared object or situation—should be ineffective, or leave the patient defenseless and subject to overwhelming anxiety, or lead to the development of a new symptom. But the evidence does not support the view that eliminating the symptom is ineffective (Yates 1958).

Classical conditioning perspective The behavioral position regarding the origin of phobias—that they are conditioned responses—is based primarily on Watson's conditioning experiment with little Albert (see Chapter 3). However, the use of classical conditioning principles to produce intense fears in humans was demonstrated more recently (Campbell et al. 1964). This experiment, however, has been *severely* criticized on several ethical grounds. In the experiment, a traumatic conditioning procedure was used to establish fear of a sound tone in five alcoholic patients. The unconditioned stimulus was a drug (scoline) that paralyzes the skeletal musculature. The drug makes breathing very difficult, although the patient is still conscious and aware of what is happening. The experimenters sounded a tone at the first signs of paralysis. The paralysis produced an inability to breathe for 90 to 130 seconds, which resulted in feelings of utter terror on the part of the subjects. All the subjects thought they were going to die.

This conditioned emotional reaction was highly resistant to extinction; in three of the patients, 100 extinction trials led to no reduction in the fear response. Two patients, whose fear was extinguished after the first 10 trials, displayed spontaneous recovery of the emotional reaction, and it was not extinguished again after another 100 extinction trials. One patient generalized the fear to the building where he was conditioned and had to take several deep breaths before he could enter.

Although some phobias may result from a

Table 6.3 Means of Acquiring Phobias, as Reported by Patients (in percentages)

Means of Acquisition	Study	
	Ost and Hugdahl (1981)	Rimm et al. (1977)
Direct conditioning	57.5	44.4
Indirect conditioning	17	8.3
Information/instruction	10.4	11.1
No recall	15.1	36.1

traumatic event or from classical conditioning, the experimental data do not entirely support this view. English (1929) was unable to replicate the results of Watson and Rayner's experiment when he tried to establish a conditioned fear in a 14-month-old girl by presenting a painted wooden duck while banging a steel bar behind her. Conditioning did not take place (although the noise upset teachers and students throughout the building). Bregman (1934) was also unable to condition 15 infants aged 8 to 16 months to fear wooden blocks and triangles by using a loud electric bell as the unconditioned stimulus. It is possible, however, that these experiments failed to replicate that of Watson and Rayner because it is more difficult to establish a fear response to inanimate objects than to animate stimuli, or because the experimenters did not use an unconditioned stimulus that was sufficiently potent.

In two studies on the acquisition of phobias, more patients attributed their disorders to direct (classical) conditioning experiences than to any other factor (Table 6.3). Ost and Hugdahl (1981) found that animal phobics were more likely to attribute their disorders to direct conditioning experiences than were other groups of phobic patients. In addition, the reported indirect (or vicarious) conditioning experiences involved cognitive and subjective factors more than physiological factors. These findings suggest that the cognitive, behavioral, and physiological elements of anxiety are not always correlated with one another and that certain types of phobias may differ both in the acquisition of the fear and in its expression.

There is some clinical and survey support for the classical conditioning perspective on phobias. However, a substantial percentage of surveyed patients report something other than a direct conditioning experience as the "key" to their phobias. And, in the Rimm et al. (1977) study, 36 percent could not recall how their fear was acquired. Moreover, the classical conditioning perspective does not explain why only a small percentage of those exposed to potential conditioning experiences actually develop phobias.

Observational learning and operant conditioning perspectives Emotional conditioning can be developed through modeling, or observational learning. An observer who watched while a model exhibited pain cues in response to an auditory stimulus (a buzzer) gradually developed an emotional reaction to the sound (Bandura and Rosenthal 1966). The buzzer, formerly a neutral stimulus, became a conditioned stimulus for the observer. In a clinical (rather than an experimental) example involving modeling, several people who had seen the horror film *The Exorcist* had to be treated for a variety of anxiety reactions.

Table 6.3 shows that only a small proportion of surveyed patients indicated that they acquired phobias through vicarious (indirect) conditioning, or modeling. If information or instruction received is also considered as leading to observational learning, this means of acquisition would account for about 20 to 25 percent of the phobias. (One interpretation of the high incidence of anxiety reactions among close relatives of phobics involves modeling as a cause, rather than genetics.) However, the data in Table 6.3 are based on patients' recollections of past events, and such data are subject to a variety of errors.

The observational learning perspective seems to suffer from the same problem as classical conditioning with regard to the etiology of phobias. It is insufficient, in and of itself, to explain why only some individuals develop phobias after exposure to a vicarious experience.

It has been suggested that phobias may be learned through reinforcement (operant conditioning). For example, a child who is reinforced—perhaps by being held and comforted—after making statements about fears tends to increase such verbalizations of fears. However, in light of the aversive nature of phobias and the distress they produce, reinforcement is not likely to be a major factor in their development.

Biological perspective   If a higher-than-average incidence of a disorder is found in close relatives, or if identical twins (who share the same genetic makeup) show a higher concordance rate for the disorder than fraternal twins (who have different genetic makeups), a case can be made for the role of genetic factors in the disorder. In a pilot study, Harris and her colleagues (1983) found that the incidence of reported anxiety disorders for *first-degree relatives* (parents and siblings) of agoraphobic patients was more than twice that for first-degree relatives of a control group (32 percent versus 15 percent). The authors interpret these findings as supporting the view that agoraphobia is a familial disorder. However, as we noted earlier, an alternative explanation for such results is that they are due to modeling.

Strong evidence for the direct genetic transmission of specific anxiety disorders is lacking. More support exists for the view that constitutional or physiological factors may *predispose* individuals to develop fear reactions. It is possible that a certain level of auto-nomic nervous system (ANS) reactivity is inherited; then people born with high ANS reactivity respond more strongly to stimuli, and their chances of developing an anxiety disorder are increased. In support of this possibility, researchers found that individuals with high arousal levels showed easier conditioning to certain stimuli than individuals with low arousal levels (Hugdahl, Frederickson, and Ohman 1971).

Numerous studies of human twins show that identical twins tend to be more alike autonomically than fraternal twins (Jost and Sontag 1944; Vandenberg, Clark, and Samuels 1965; Lader and Wing 1966). However, even among identical twins, the concordance rate is less than 100 percent. Why does one identical twin develop an anxiety disorder while the other does not? The answer appears to lie in the interaction between heredity and the environment. Heredity can influence the individual's ANS reactivity and, in that way, can contribute to the development of anxiety disorders, but the environment either facilitates or retards manifestation of the disorders (Thomas, Chess and Birch 1968).

A different biological approach to the development of fear reactions is that of **preparedness** (Seligman 1971). Proponents of this position argue that fears develop nonrandomly. In particular, it is easier for humans to learn fears to which we are physiologically predisposed. Such quickly aroused (or "prepared") fears may have been necessary to the survival of pretechnological humanity in the natural environment. One proponent notes that it is rare to encounter phobias involving automobiles or electrical appliances, which are of very recent origin: "It seems likely that the majority of specific phobias result from activation in childhood of an inbuilt potential phobic response, such activation at least at times being due to a conditioning process" (McConaghy 1983, p. 171).

The preparedness hypothesis could explain why it is easier to condition fear of some objects or situations than fear of others. It could also account for some of the puzzling aspects of phobias, such as their persistence and the fact that phobics recognize them as irrational. In addition, prepared fears should be easy to acquire but difficult to lose, and they should be relatively free of cognitive control.

Some predictions of the preparedness hypothesis have received experimental support (Ohman et al. 1975, 1976), but more study is necessary. The combination of classical conditioning and prepared learning is also a promising area for further research. But it is difficult to believe that many (or even most) phobias stem from prepared fears, simply because they just do not fit into that model. It would be difficult, for example, to explain the survival value of such social phobias as the fear of public restrooms and of eating in public, of agoraphobia, and of many simple phobias.

Treatment of phobias

We begin our discussion of the treatment of phobias with agoraphobia, the disorder on which most treatment effort has been focused.

Agoraphobia   The primary treatment approaches for agoraphobia are medical, behavioral, and a combination of the two. A number of studies have shown that antidepressants such as imipramine are useful not only in reducing depression but also in treating the extreme fear and anxiety that is displayed by agoraphobics (Garakani, Zitrin, and Klein 1984; Mavissakalian et al. 1983). But less positive results with imipramine were reported when the antidepressant was compared with a placebo and exposure to the feared object; these researchers concluded that the effective component was exposure (Mark et al. 1983).

Methodological flaws tend to hamper the evaluation of drugs in treating agoraphobia, because most studies rely only on self-reports as measures of success, because control groups are generally not employed, and be-

cause patients are often encouraged to expose themselves to the fear-producing situation while they are receiving medication. One study was designed specifically to separate and compare the contributions of drugs and exposure in the treatment of agoraphobics. The patients were randomly assigned to treatment with imipramine alone, imipramine plus exposure, or placebo plus exposure. An important element in the study was control of the possible effects of exposure on the drug-only group: Patients in this group were told not to enter fear-arousing situations until the medication had a chance to build up (some six or eight weeks). Results were measured via self-reports and behavioral and physiological scales. Both exposure groups showed significant improvement according to all three measures. The imipramine-only patients showed no improvement on any of the measures, although they did show a significant reduction of depressed mood. Imipramine plus exposure showed a slight advantage over placebo plus exposure in reducing phobic anxiety (Telch 1982).

Agoraphobics treated with imipramine seem to require behavioral treatment as well, to reduce anxiety and avoidance of the feared situation. "The fact that 60–70% of agoraphobics are successfully treated by exposure methods [alone] . . . indicates that pharmacological suppression of panic attacks is not necessary in the majority of patients" (Mavissakalian et al. 1983). Thus there seems to be some question whether antidepressants alone provide adequate treatment for agoraphobics.

The behavioral treatment of agoraphobia (and other phobias) has centered on the method of **exposure.** In this technique, the patient is gradually introduced to increasingly difficult encounters with the feared situation (Biran and Wilson 1981). An agoraphobic might, for example, be asked to take longer and longer walks outside the home with the therapist. The earliest of these encounters may often be only imagined or visualized by the patient at the request of the therapist.

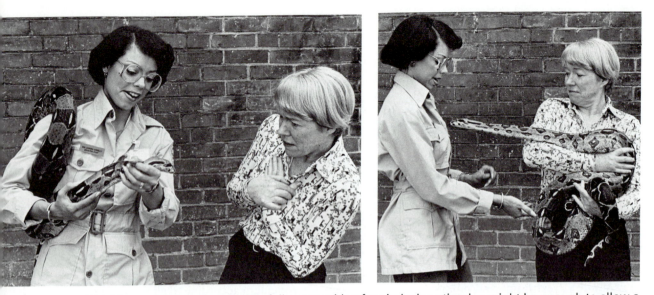

Watching another person successfully cope with a fear-inducing stimulus might be enough to allow a person with snake phobia to do the same. The phobic person learns vicariously that responding fearlessly and appropriately is rewarding.

Over the past decade, **flooding,** or continued exposure to the fearful situation, has emerged as the most promising purely behavioral treatment for agoraphobia (Goldstein and Chambless 1978). Unfortunately, this technique causes some clients to drop out of therapy due to "unmanageable anxiety" resulting from the flooding (Hafner 1983). One group of researchers discovered that *breathing retraining* (in which subjects were taught to use the diaphragm rather than the upper chest in breathing) added significantly to the already encouraging results of flooding (Bonn, Readhead, and Timmons 1984). But another group concluded that relaxation training was generally as effective as flooding (Ost, Jerremalm, and Jansson 1984).

Another version of exposure therapy includes the spouses of agoraphobics in the therapy. Some clinicians feel that agoraphobia itself signals marital discord. Others feel that spouses of agoraphobics needed to be actively involved in the therapeutic process so that they can gradually adjust to more independent husbands or wives (Chambless and Goldstein 1980). In an attempt to clarify this issue, two

groups of female agoraphobics were treated with cognitive restructuring and self-initiated exposure; only one of the two groups was accompanied by their husbands. The results generally supported the inclusion of spouses, but they were not particularly conclusive (Barlow, O'Brien, and Last 1984).

Social and simple phobias One treatment promising for the social and simple phobias is also behavioral, but a number of different behavioral techniques appear to be beneficial. For example, **systematic desensitization** has been used as a treatment for phobias. Wolpe (1958, 1973), who introduced the treatment, taught phobics a response (relaxation) that is incompatible with fear by repeatedly pairing relaxation with visualizations of the feared stimulus. Systematic desensitization has been shown to be effective with snake phobics and public speaking phobics (Lang and Lazovik 1963; Paul 1966; Hekmat, Lubitz, and Deal 1984).

Flooding is used to treat social and simple phobias as well as agoraphobia, but results are mixed. Studies of flooding indicate that extinction of the phobia is ensured only with a sufficient number of exposures to the anxiety-provoking stimulus. Comparisons of exposure and various other behavioral techniques are somewhat confused, probably because some exposure is subtly built into most other techniques. For example, a coping-skills training program was reported to be superior to flooding, but it was not pointed out that such programs typically include some sort of repeated exposure to the feared stimulus (Hayes and Marshall 1984). Similarly, a group of researchers showed that exposure plus anxiety management was more effective than exposure alone in decreasing social anxiety (Butler et al. 1984). But, because most anxiety-management programs include exposure in some format, they may have proved only that more exposure is better than less exposure.

Modeling therapy procedures have also been highly effective in treating certain phobias. When modeling is used as therapy, the phobic individual observes a fearless model in the act of coping with, or responding appropriately in, the fear-producing situation. Some researchers feel that modeling is a unique therapeutic approach in its own right, whereas others feel that it is one more variation of exposure.

There is some controversy as to which of these approaches—systematic desensitization, flooding, or modeling—is the most effective. But they all provide reasonably good results with a variety of phobias, so future research efforts will probably concentrate on enhancing their effectiveness, rather than on trying to prove the superiority of one behavioral technique over another.

OBSESSIVE–COMPULSIVE DISORDERS

Obsessive–compulsive disorders are anxiety disorders that are characterized by intrusive and uncontrollable thoughts or the need to perform specific acts repeatedly, or both. Obsessive–compulsive disorders are highly

distressing because they involve a lack of voluntary control over one's own thoughts and actions. The inability to rid oneself of uncontrollable, alien, and often unacceptable thoughts, or to keep from performing ritualistic acts over and over again, arouses intense anxiety. In one study of obsessive–compulsives, 70 percent indicated that their rituals were distressing to themselves and their families; 78 percent considered their rituals absurd; and over 50 percent attempted to resist carrying out the rituals (Stern and Cobb 1978). But failure to engage in ritual acts often results in mounting anxiety and tension.

Some features of obsessive–compulsive disorders are obvious in the following case.

> A 24-year-old single man felt compelled to ruminate practically all his waking hours. He had a 7-year history of obsessional ruminations, had been out of work for 3 years and was living with his parents. Ruminations usually involved worrying in case he had made a mistake in the course of performing some quite trivial action. Anxiety and doubt would be evoked by mundane activities, such as turning a light switch, changing direction when walking or going from one room to another. For example, when driving his car and taking a right turn at a traffic light, he would start thinking. "What would happen if I had turned left?" His ruminations would only come to an end once he had gone through all the possible alternative routes in his head. The degree of doubt felt by this patient was so strong that at times, when switching on a light, he would not trust his perception, and wondering if he had made a mistake, he would attempt to trace the wiring behind the wall in order to try to follow where the current went back to the switch, thus convincing himself that the bulb was actually illuminated.
>
> If necessary, his ruminations could be postponed for some hours but as long as they remained "unresolved" he would feel subjectively anxious. As a child, he remembered checking his schoolbooks and homework excessively. Later, mental checks replaced physical ones because they were quicker and unobtrusive. He reached university, but his obsessions had greatly multiplied by then. Yet he qualified as an engineer and started work. The necessity to take

responsibility and make decisions caused a significant deterioration and eventually forced him to abandon the job. His basic fear was that of making a mistake and appearing foolish in front of others. At the time of his admission to hospital, he was thinking of hypothetical solutions to hypothetical errors following almost every activity he did. (Robertson et al. 1983, p. 352)

The disturbed individual may be plagued by either obsessions (which involve thoughts) or compulsions (which involve acts) or by both. Or, as in this case, one may be replaced by the other at different stages of the disorder. Obsessive–compulsive individuals are highly secretive about their disorders and seldom become totally disabled. The majority develop the disorder before the age of fifteen; they tend to have high IQs and high social status (Pollitt 1960; Adams 1972). Obsessive children are often characterized by an active fantasy life and verbalized guilt feelings (Judd 1965).

Obsessions

An **obsession** is an intrusive, uncontrollable, and persistent thought. The individual may realize that the thought is irrational, but he or she is incapable of keeping it from occurring repeatedly. Obsessions may take a number of forms (Goodwin, Guze, and Robins 1969).

1. Obsessional *ideas, words,* or *phrases,* often dealing with obscene or nonsensical themes
2. Obsessional *images* of anxiety-evoking scenes like the death of a loved one, accidents, or sexual behavior
3. Obsessional *beliefs* that a thought will produce an effect—for example, that a wish for someone's death will cause it to occur
4. Obsessional *ruminations* or lengthy inconclusive attempts to make a decision
5. Obsessional *impulses,* such as desires for self-injury (driving off a cliff) or embarrassment (shouting obscenities in inappropriate places such as a classroom or church)

6. Obsessional *fears* of potentially dangerous objects or situations, such as a fear of scissors or a knife on a table

Although most of us have experienced persistent thoughts—for instance, a song or tune that keeps running through one's mind—clinical forms are stronger and more intrusive. Many individuals who suffer from this disorder become partially incapacitated. Howard Hughes, a spectacularly successful businessman, a pilot, and a movie producer withdrew so completely from the public that his only communication with the outside world was through telephones and intermediaries. His penchant for seclusiveness was connected to his obsessional fear of germ contamination.

He took to refusing to shake hands with people and covering his hands with the ubiquitous sheets of Kleenex when he had to hold a glass or open a door. He forbade aides to eat onions, garlic, Rocquefort dressing or other "breath destroyers." He considered air conditioners deadly germ collectors; he is said to have taken to sitting naked in darkened, sweltering hotel rooms, surrounded by crinkled Kleenex and covered only with a few sheets over his privates. (*Newsweek,* April 19, 1976, p. 31)

Covering his hands with Kleenex as a defense against germs indicates that Hughes had also developed compulsions. In addition, he was preoccupied with the care of women's breasts. If women were passengers in his car, he would instruct his chauffeur to slow down when going over bumps in the road. Otherwise, he felt, the stress on the breasts would cause tissue breakdown and sagging; he was very concerned about preventing this.

Compulsions

A **compulsion** is an involuntary impulse to perform a particular act repeatedly. Compulsions are usually, but not always, associated with obsessions. Mild forms include such behaviors as refusing to walk under a ladder or to step on cracks in sidewalks, throwing salt over your shoulder, and knocking on wood. In the severe compulsive state, the behaviors become stereotyped and rigid; if they are not performed in a certain manner or a specific number of times, the compulsive individual is flooded with anxiety. To the compulsive, these behaviors often seem to have magical qualities, as though their correct performance warded off danger. The following case, known to the authors and touched on at the beginning of this chapter, is fairly typical:

> A fifteen-year-old boy had a two-year history of compulsive behaviors, involving sixteen repetitions of the following behaviors: opening and closing a door, touching glasses before drinking from them, walking around each tree in front of his house before going to school. These compulsive acts produced a great deal of discomfort in the boy. His schoolmates ridiculed him, and his parents were upset because his rituals prevented him from reaching school at the appropriate time. An interview with the boy revealed that his compulsive behaviors were associated with the onset of masturbation, an act that the boy considered "dirty," although he was unable to refrain from it. It was when he began to masturbate that the first of his compulsive behaviors (touching a glass sixteen times before drinking from it) developed.

Table 6.4 (p. 184) contains additional examples of obsessions and compulsions.

Etiology of obsessive–compulsive disorders

The causal factors involved in obsessive–compulsive disorders remain unclear. There is, in fact, still argument about whether obsessions elevate or reduce anxiety. We shall examine three theories that have been advanced to explain obsessive–compulsive behavior: the substitution, anxiety-reduction, and superstition hypotheses.

Howard Hughes (1905–1976), a phenomenally successful businessman, pilot, and movie producer, is probably one of the more famous cases of a person suffering from obsessions and compulsions. He had an obsessional fear of germs and compulsively tried to protect himself from them. Eventually Hughes became a recluse with eccentric behaviors.

Substitution hypothesis The *substitution hypothesis* is psychoanalytic in nature. Freud (1949) believed that obsessions represent the substitution or replacement of an original conflict (usually sexual in nature) with an associated idea that is less threatening. He found support for his notion in the case histories of some of his patients. One, a girl, had disturbing obsessions about stealing or counterfeiting money, thoughts that were absurd and untrue. During analysis, Freud discovered that these obsessions reflected anxiety that stemmed from guilt about masturbation. When the patient was kept under constant observation,

Table 6.4   *Clinical Examples of Obsessions and Compulsions*

Patient		Duration of Obsession in Years	Content of Obsession
Age	Sex		
21	M	6	Teeth are decaying, particles between teeth.
42	M	16	Women's buttocks, own eye movements.
55	F	35	Fetuses lying in the street, killing babies, people buried alive.
24	M	16	Worry about whether he has touched vomit.
21	F	9	Strangling people.
52	F	18	Contracting venereal disease.

Patient		Duration of Compulsions in Years	Compulsive Rituals
Age	Sex		
47	F	23	Handwashing and housecleaning. Contact with dirt, toilet, or floor triggers about 100 hand-washings per day.
20	F	13	Severe checking ritual; checks 160 times to see if window is closed. Also compelled to read the license number of cars and the numbers on manhole covers.
21	M	2	Intense fear of contamination after touching library books, money. Washes hands 25 times a day and ruminates about how many people had handled the objects before him.

SOURCE: From Boersma et al. (1976), Rachman, Marks, and Hodgson (1973), Roper, Rachman, and Marks (1975), Stern, Lipsedge, and Marks (1973), Shahar and Marks (1980).

which prevented her from masturbating, the obsessional thoughts ceased.

The dynamics of obsession have been described as involving "the intrusion of the unwelcome thought [that] 'seeks' to prevent anxiety by serving as a more tolerable substitute for a subjectively less welcome thought or impulse" (Laughlin 1967, p. 311). Freud's patient found thoughts involving stealing less disturbing than masturbation. Her displacement of that feeling to a substitute action prevented her ego defenses from being completely overwhelmed.

Several other psychoanalytic defense mechanisms are considered prominent in obsessive–compulsive behaviors. For example, *undoing* is canceling or atoning for forbidden impulses by engaging in repetitive, ritualistic activities. Washing one's hands may symbolically represent cleansing oneself of uncon-

scious wishes. However, because the original conflict remains, one is compelled to perform the act of atonement over and over again. *Reaction formation* provides a degree of comfort because it counterbalances forbidden desires with diametrically opposed behaviors. To negate problems stemming from the anal psychosexual stage (characteristic of obsessive–compulsives), such as the impulse to be messy, patients tend toward excessive cleanliness and orderliness. Obsessive–compulsives may also employ the defense of *isolation*, which allows the separation of a thought or action from its effect. Aloofness, intellectualization, and detachment allow a reduction in the anxiety produced by patently aggressive or sexual thoughts.

Rosen (1975) has developed a view of obsessive–compulsive disorders that is similar to the psychoanalytic concept of thought substitution. In Rosen's formulation, however, unconscious conflicts do not directly motivate the behavior. Instead, they motivate an intervening variable—guilt—which in turn motivates the behavior. He believes that obsessive thoughts associated with guilt ("What if I have a deformed baby?") and self-punitive compulsive behaviors (such as pulling hair from one's head) are aversive in nature and do not have the purpose of reducing anxiety. His hypothesis incorporates the following sequence: (1) the external instigation of anger or sexual arousal; (2) an angry or erotic thought; (3) the production of guilt; (4) an obsessive thought ("I am losing my mind") or compulsive behavior; and (5) a reduction of guilt. In this framework, obsessions and compulsions serve to punish the individual for thoughts and feelings that deviate from childhood standards and thus reduce guilt.

Rosen believes that the backgrounds of obsessive–compulsive individuals would probably reveal a highly moralistic upbringing with emphasis on the evils of sin and the necessity of retribution. Although both Freud's position and that espoused by Rosen have intuitive appeal, there is little supportive data for either.

Anxiety-reduction hypothesis Proponents of the *anxiety-reduction hypothesis* tend to be behaviorists. They maintain that obsessive–compulsive disorders develop because they reduce anxiety. A distracting thought or action recurs more often if it reduces anxiety. For example, mild forms of compulsive behavior may occur during exam periods for many college students. During this stressful and anxiety-filled time, students may find themselves engaging in escape activities, such as daydreaming, straightening up their rooms, or eating five or more times a day, all of which serve to shield them from thoughts of the upcoming tests. If the stress lasts a long time, a compulsive behavior may develop.

Although the anxiety-reduction hypothesis is popular among learning theorists, it has not been very helpful in explaining how a behav-

ior, such as handwashing for hours, can originate. Maher (1966) suggests that a compulsion is acquired through operant conditioning. For example, an individual who has developed a compulsion for handwashing might have been reinforced in the past by parents for cleanliness, and therefore he or she considers such behavior desirable. When a transgression occurs, performing a socially learned anxiety-reducing response reduces the transgressor's guilt. Because this response is reinforcing, the person uses it in any situation where anxiety or some other negative emotion occurs. Unfortunately, this formulation does not explain why childhood anxiety-reducing behaviors are displayed by some adults and not by others. Neither does it explain why some compulsives perform acts that certainly were not endorsed by parents or otherwise socially reinforced—for example, walking around every tree in the back yard before performing a task.

Researchers have attempted to obtain support for the anxiety-reduction hypothesis with a specific sample of patients: obsessive washers and checkers. If the hypothesis is correct, touching a contaminated item should increase anxiety, and performing the compulsive act should reduce anxiety (Carr 1974; Hodgson and Rachman 1972; Roper and Rachman 1976). Carr found that compulsive acts were performed when there were high levels of autonomic activity and that their performance reduced the individual's arousal levels to those of a resting state. A more direct test of the anxiety-reduction hypothesis is discussed in Focus 6.3 (p. 186).

Superstition hypothesis According to the *superstition hypothesis*, a chance association of a behavior with a reinforcer is responsible for continuation of the behavior. According to some theorists, this is the mechanism by which superstitions are formed. Skinner's (1948) classic example of the causation of superstitious behavior involved reinforcing pigeons (with food) at regular intervals, regardless of their behavior. Each pigeon began to display unique head or body movements,

FOCUS 6.3

Experimental Evidence for the Anxiety-Reduction Hypothesis

The anxiety-reduction hypothesis is a *behavioral* explanation for the maintenance of compulsive disorders. Yet support for this hypothesis has come primarily through the evaluation of case studies rather than by direct experiment. To correct this shortcoming, Hodgson and Rachman (1972) conducted an experiment on a group of twelve obsessional patients who had contamination fears and washing rituals. These patients were randomly assigned to one of the following groups or subgroups: (1) a control group whose members touched a neutral object, and (2) groups whose members touched a contaminated object and then (a) washed immediately, (b) washed later, or (c) were interrupted in their washing. Pretest and posttest anxiety measures included fluctuations in pulse-rate and subjective ratings of anxiety and discomfort.

The results were consistent with the anxiety-reduction hypothesis. Touching a "contaminated" object increased subjective anxiety, which was reduced when patients were allowed to complete their washing rituals. Differences in pulse rate were not significant, although increases were related to the contaminating event, and reductions were related to the compulsive act. Similar results were obtained with a group of twelve compulsive checkers: The provoking act increased subjective discomfort, which the checking ritual then reduced (Roper and Rachman 1976).

The anxiety-reduction hypothesis does have some value in explaining the *continuation* of compulsive acts (the acts are reinforcing because they reduce anxiety). However, the hypothesis does not make clear how these behaviors *originate*. The experimental results must be interpreted cautiously because they may apply only to the types of patients tested.

Another difficulty with the anxiety-reduction hypothesis lies in the apparent anxiety-elevating properties of some obsessive-compulsive disorders (Walker and Beech 1969; Rosen 1975; Wolpe 1958). Walker and Beech report the case of a woman with two compulsions: a hair-combing ritual that lasted approximately eight hours a day and impaired her mood, and a handwashing ritual that lasted an hour and a half and improved her mood. Many forms of obsessional rumination involve disease, insanity, mutilation, murder, and other negative events that one would expect to elevate anxiety. As yet we can only speculate about the reinforcements associated with them.

presumably because these happened to be behaviors the birds were engaged in when they were given food.

Many obsessive–compulsive rituals may be reinforced by chance when a positive outcome is obtained following performance of a certain behavior (O'Leary and Wilson 1975). A student may take exams with only one special pencil or pen because this item has been associated with past success. Sports figures have been reported to continue wearing the same dirty uniform as long as a winning streak is in progress. Even though there is no actual relationship between these behaviors and a favorable or unfavorable outcome, the obsessive–compulsive may behave as though such a relationship exists. Anxiety develops if these rituals are not observed, because the individual feels they are necessary to produce a positive outcome.

Although the hypothesis that obsessive–compulsive disorders are produced by the chance association of a behavior with a reinforcer is plausible, the proponents of the hypothesis have not specified the conditions under which "superstitious" behavior develops. Further, the hypothesis does not explain the development of powerful and intrusive thoughts or rituals.

Treatment of obsessive–compulsive disorders

The primary modes of treatment for obsessive–compulsive disorders are either biological or behavioral in nature. Behavioral therapies have been used successfully for a number of years, but treatment via medication has recently enjoyed increased attention.

Biological treatments One of the earliest biological treatments for obsessive–compulsive disorders was a psychosurgical procedure called *leukotomy*. The procedure initially reduced anxiety in most patients, but anxiety remained low in only 50 percent of the cases (Sykes and Tredgold 1964). Moreover, the obsessive–compulsive symptoms were not generally alleviated. Psychosurgery is an extreme and irreversible procedure and should be used only as a last resort.

Medication, rather than psychosurgery, is always the first choice for the biological treatment of mental disorders. Because obsessive–compulsive disorders are classified as anxiety disorders, it would seem that minor tranquilizers would be helpful. However, these drugs have not proved capable of decreasing—to any extent—the incidence of obsessive thoughts or compulsive rituals in patients. They are occasionally used to reduce tension in patients who are about to participate in psychotherapy (Ananth 1976).

Antidepressant drugs have also been tried, with mixed results. Some researchers report that these drugs are successful only in alleviating an obsessive–compulsive patient's depression (Annesley 1969). Others report that particular antidepressants (MAO inhibitors) decreased obsessive–compulsive symptoms only in patients who also experienced phobic anxiety or panic attacks (Jenike et al. 1983). Still others report results ranging from negative to favorable. A review of nineteen studies led to the conclusion that antidepressants were a beneficial part of the treatment for obsessive–compulsive disorders if the patient exhibited signs of depression. In these cases, the drugs not only alleviated depression but also decreased ritualistic behavior (Marks 1983).

One final medication should be mentioned here. Some obsessive–compulsive patients appear to improve when treated with *lithium,* a drug that is typically used to treat bipolar disorders (Rasmussen 1984). In all probability, the effectiveness of lithium treatment will be investigated further. At present, however, a combination of medical and behavioral techniques seems to offer the most hope.

Behavioral treatments One of the earliest behavioral treatments for obsessive–compulsive patients was systematic desensitization. The purpose of this relaxation treatment was to break the bond that had formed between the conditioned stimulus (for example, germs or dirt) and anxiety. It was believed that, if anxiety was no longer generated by contact with the conditioned stimulus, the compulsive rituals would disappear.

Wolpe (1973) successfully used the method to treat an 18-year-old male with a severe hand-washing compulsion. The disorder involved a fear of contaminating others with urine. After urinating, the patient felt compelled to spend 45 minutes cleaning his genitalia, 2 hours washing his hands, and 4 hours showering. If other "contamination" occurred, he would spend additional time on these rituals. These behaviors presumably developed as a result of his having shared a bed with his sister until he was 15 years old and his sister was 17. He reported having had erotic responses and feeling guilty and ashamed. This developed into a revulsion toward his own urine. Treatment involved placing the young man in a state of relaxation and then asking him to imagine low-anxiety scenes (such as an unknown man touching a trough of water containing one drop of urine). As the patient's anxiety gradually dissipated, Wolpe gradually increased the imaginary concentration of urine. In addition, a real bottle of urine was presented at a distance and moved closer to the patient in gradual steps. Finally Wolpe could apply drops of diluted urine to the back of the patient's hand without evoking anxiety. A follow-up four years later revealed complete remission of the compulsive behaviors.

Even though impressive results may be obtained in specific cases, systematic desensitization is successful in only about 50 percent of its uses with obsessive–compulsives. In general, systematic desensitization is viewed as more promising in patients with circumscribed problems (Leitenberg et al. 1970) and when symptoms are of recent onset (Foa and Tillmanns 1980).

A promising treatment for obsessive–compulsive disorders is the combination of flooding and *response prevention*. This approach typically requires fewer therapy sessions than systematic desensitization, and the results have been consistently impressive. Meyer, Levy, and Schnurer (1974) were the first to treat obsessive–compulsives with this two-stage program. In the flooding segment they repeatedly exposed patients to the anxiety-producing stimulus; in the response-prevention stage they blocked patients' performance of rituals. As an example, consider a patient who fears that he will develop a fatal infection from contact with germs. The flooding stage could involve exposing the patient to something he perceives as containing deadly germs (perhaps dirt, a newspaper, or leftover food). The client would be required to touch the items at first, and later to smear them over his body. Once he was properly "contaminated," the client would not be allowed to cleanse himself by engaging in his compulsive ritual (such as repeated handwashing). Instead, in

this response-prevention stage, he would be required to remain "contaminated" until his anxiety had extinguished.

In this approach, the flooding is used to extinguish anxiety as a response to the conditioned stimulus, and the response prevention serves to further extinguish anxiety and to aid in elimination of the avoidance behavior (the ritual). The treatment is more effective if the exposure occurs *in vivo* (that is, in actuality) rather than in the imagination (Marks 1976). And *in vivo* exposure plus imagined exposure is significantly better than *in vivo* exposure alone (Foa et al. 1980).

SUMMARY

1. The anxiety disorders are all characterized by anxiety—by feelings of fear and apprehension. The anxiety may be the major disturbance (as it is in panic disorders and generalized anxiety disorders), it may arise when the individual confronts a feared object or situation (as in the phobias), or it may result from an attempt to master the symptoms (as in obsessive–compulsive disorders).

2. Anxiety is an emotion that is experienced by all individuals. It is manifested in cognitions or thoughts, in motoric behaviors, in physical reactions, and in affective or emotional reactions. The means of assessing anxiety include self-reports, observations of motoric or behavioral reactions, and physiological measures.

3. Panic disorders and generalized anxiety disorders are characterized by direct and unfocused anxiety. In panic disorders there are episodes of extreme anxiety and feelings of impending doom. In generalized anxiety disorders there are chronically high levels of anxiety, hypervigilance, and apprehension. Psychoanalysts feel that these disorders are unfocused because they stem from conflicts that remain in the unconscious. Behaviorists believe they are the result of conditioning to

an omnipresent stimulus. Drug therapy and behavioral therapies have been used to treat these disorders.

4. Phobias are strong fears that are considered beyond the demands of the situation. Agoraphobia is an intense fear of open spaces; it can keep afflicted individuals from leaving the home, because attempts to do so may produce panic attacks. Social phobias are irrational fears involving situations in which the individual can be observed by others. The anxiety generally stems from the possibility of appearing foolish or making mistakes in public. Simple phobias include all the irrational fears that are not classed as social phobias or agoraphobia. Common objects of fear in simple phobias include small animals, heights, and the dark. In the psychoanalytic view, phobias represent unconscious conflicts that are displaced to an external object. In the classical conditioning view, phobias are based on an association between some aversive event and a conditioned stimulus. Biological explanations are based on genetic influences or on the concept of preparedness to develop certain fears. The most effective treatments for phobics seem to be medicinal (via antidepressants) and behavioral (via exposure and flooding, systematic desensitization, and modeling).

5. Obsessive–compulsive disorders involve involuntary, intrusive, and uncontrollable thoughts or actions. Most obsessive–compulsives are aware that their distressing behaviors are irrational. Obsessions (which involve thoughts) and compulsions (which involve actions) may occur together or separately. Freud believed that these disorders represent the substitution of a threatening conflict with a behavior or thought that is less threatening. According to the anxiety-reduction hypothesis, obsessions and compulsions develop because they reduce anxiety. The superstition hypothesis holds that the disorders stem from the chance association of a behavior with a reinforcer. The most commonly used treatments are behavioral: systematic desensitization or flooding plus response prevention.

KEY TERMS

agoraphobia An intense fear of open spaces or of being alone where help may not be available; in extreme cases, a fear of leaving one's home

anxiety Feelings of fear and apprehension

anxiety disorders Disorders (panic disorders, generalized anxiety disorders, phobias, and obsessive–compulsive disorders) whose major characteristic irrational feelings of fear and apprehension

compulsion An involuntary impulse to perform a particular act repeatedly

flooding A therapeutic technique that involves continued *in vivo* or imagined exposure to a fear-arousing situation

generalized anxiety disorders Disorders characterized by persistent high levels of anxiety in situations where no real danger is present

neurosis Formerly a category of mental disorders including what are presently called the anxiety, dissociative, and somatoform disorders; now generally used to denote any less severe mental disorder

obsession An intrusive, uncontrollable, and persistent thought

obsessive–compulsive disorders Anxiety disorders characterized by intrusive and uncontrollable thoughts, or the need to perform specific acts repeatedly, or both

panic disorders Anxiety disorders characterized by severe and frightening episodes of apprehension and feelings of impending doom

phobia A strong, persistent, and unwarranted fear of a specific object or situation

simple phobia An extreme fear of a specific object or situation; a phobia that is not classed as either agoraphobia or a social phobia

social phobia An irrational and strong fear of social situations

7

Dissociative Disorders and Somatoform Disorders

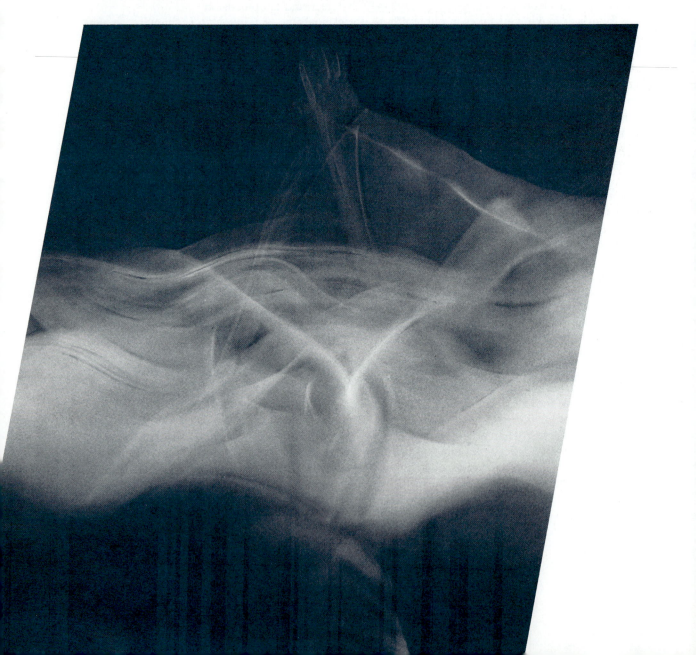

*I*n 1978, at the age of 23, Billy Milligan became the first person in the United States to be acquitted of a major crime because of having a *multiple personality* disorder. He was tried for rape, was found not guilty by reason of insanity, and was sent to a psychiatric hospital for therapy (Footlick and Lowell 1978). Milligan had raped several women near the Ohio State University campus. He first claimed not to remember these attacks, then later suggested that it was his lesbian personality, Adelena, who had committed the acts.

The Milligan case raises several issues concerning the diagnosis of mental disorders and the appropriateness of the insanity plea. The prosecution and some mental health professionals felt that Milligan was deceiving the court about having different personalities; a number of inconsistencies were found in his testimony. The defense, however, with the help of psychiatrist Cornelia Wilbur, a specialist in multiple personality, convinced the judge that Milligan actually suffered from the disorder and that his present personality was not responsible for the rapes. Milligan also showed some of the childhood background typically found in cases of multiple personality. His stepfather had abused him sexually and had once buried him in the ground with only a length of pipe left open to the air. Incidents like these were thought to have precipitated the disorder. But even if Milligan did have multiple personality, questions remain about the appropriate treatment or punishment for individuals who are found "not guilty by reason of insanity." When and how can the public be reasonably certain that such an individual will not be involved in a major crime in the future? (This issue is discussed in Chapter 10.) Milligan, for instance, was released on probation after receiving psychotherapy for multiple personality.

Multiple personality is one of four **dissociative disorders**—mental disorders in which the individual's identity and consciousness are altered or disrupted. These disorders and the **somatoform disorders,** which involve physical symptoms or complaints that have no physiological basis, are the subjects of this chapter. Both the dissociative disorders and the somatoform disorders, like the anxiety disorders discussed in Chapter 6, were classified as neuroses in DSM-II but are accorded separate diagnostic categories in DSM-III. Both occur as a result of some psychological conflict or need.

The symptoms of the dissociative disorders and the somatoform disorders, such as loss of memory or hysterical blindness, generally become known through self-reports. There is, then, the possibility of faking, as was suspected in the case of Billy Milligan's multiple personality. However, the fact remains that such symptoms can be and are produced "involuntarily" or unconsciously; and testing shows them to be so produced. But that fact leads to a paradox: A person *does* suffer loss of memory in amnesia, yet that memory must exist somewhere in the neurons and synapses of the brain. An individual *does* lose his or her sight in hysterical blindness, yet physiologically the eyes are perfectly capable of seeing. What exactly has happened? The dissociative disorders and the somatoform disorders are among the most puzzling disorders discussed in this text.

DISSOCIATIVE DISORDERS

The dissociative disorders are *psychogenic amnesia, psychogenic fugue, depersonalization disorder,* and *multiple personality.* Each involves some sort of dissociation, or breaking away, of a part of the individual's consciousness or identity. They are highly publicized and sensationalized disorders, though all except depersonalization seem to be relatively uncommon. Only 200 documented cases of dissociative disorder were found in a 1966 re-

view of the psychological literature (Abse 1966).

Psychogenic amnesia

Amnesia is the partial or total loss of memory, due to either organic or psychological causes. **Psychogenic amnesia,** however, is the psychologically based inability to recall information that is of personal significance. This disorder usually occurs suddenly after a traumatic event. The disturbed individual may forget his or her name, address, friends, relatives, and so on, but he or she remembers the necessities of daily life—how to read, write, and drive, for example.

There are four types of psychogenic amnesia. The most common, *localized amnesia,* involves the loss of all memory of a particular short period of time. Most often, this "lost" period includes an event which was highly painful or disturbing to the afflicted individual.

☐ An eighteen-year-old woman who survived a dramatic fire claimed not to remember it or the death of her child and husband in the fire. She claimed that her relatives were lying about there having been a fire. She became extremely agitated and emotional several hours later, when her memory abruptly returned.
☐ A four-year-old boy whose mother was murdered in his presence was found mopping up her blood. During interviews with a psychiatrist, however, he denied any memory of the incident.

Selective amnesia involves the failure to remember only some details of an incident. For example, a man remembered having an automobile accident but could not recall the fact that his child had died in the crash.

In *generalized amnesia* there is a total loss of memory of the individual's past life. This is illustrated by the case of a woman who was discovered partly clothed, poorly fed, and dis-

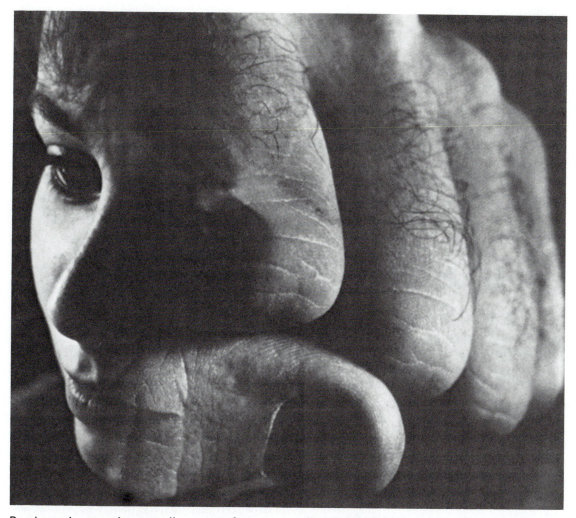

Psychogenic amnesia generally occurs after a traumatic event, either physical or psychological. Jerry Uelsmann's print *Symbolic Mutation* (1961) seems to reflect the trauma and confusion that someone who cannot remember his or her name, friends, family, and work might feel.

oriented, wandering through a Florida park in 1980. She claimed to have no knowledge of her past. Her parents identified her when she appeared on the "Good Morning America" television news program. She seemed perplexed and confused while being interviewed on the program, and she could not remember her parents when they arrived to get her. Psychologists theorized that an extremely traumatic incident was responsible for this massive memory blockage.

Finally, *continuous amnesia*, which is the least common form of psychogenic amnesia, is the inability to recall any events that have occurred from a specific time in the past, up to the present time.

Psychologists are uncertain about the processes involved in psychogenic amnesia, but they believe it results from the repression of a traumatic event or from some process closely related to repression. Posthypnotic amnesia, in which the subject cannot recall certain events, is somewhat similar to this disorder. In both cases, the lost material can be retrieved with help or in certain circumstances. However, there is one important difference. In posthypnotic amnesia the hypnotist suggests what is to be forgotten, whereas in psychogenic amnesia both the source and the content of the amnesia are unknown (Sarbin and Cole 1979). Because the disorder involves a lack of knowledge, no experiment can be designed by which to study it. Instead, information on psychogenic amnesia has been gathered primarily through case studies.

Psychogenic fugue

Psychogenic fugue (also called *fugue state*) is psychogenic amnesia accompanied by flight. The affected individual leaves the area in which he or she lives and works and establishes a new identity. Most cases involve only short periods away from home and less than a complete change of identity. However, there are exceptions:

A 38-year-old man who had been missing for a year was found to be living in another state when relatives saw his photograph printed in a newspaper. The man had established a new identity and was spearheading a charitable drive in his new home state; the newspaper article praised him for his energy and leadership. When confronted by his relatives, the man initially denied knowing them. The relatives were certain of their identification but also puzzled by his outgoing personality. The person they knew had always been shy and retiring.

As with psychogenic amnesia, recovery from fugue state is usually abrupt and complete.

Depersonalization disorder

Depersonalization disorder is perhaps the most common dissociative disorder. It is characterized by feelings of unreality concerning the self and the environment. At one time or another, most young adults have experienced some of the symptoms typical of depersonalization disorder: perceptions that the body is distorted or the environment has somehow changed, feelings of living out a dream, or minor losses of control. But episodes of depersonalization can be fairly intense, and they can produce great anxiety because the individuals who suffer from them consider them unnatural.

A 20-year-old college student became alarmed when she suddenly perceived subtle changes in her appearance. The reflections she saw in mirrors did not seem to be hers. She became even more disturbed when her room, her friends, and the campus also seemed to take on a slightly distorted appearance. The world around her felt unreal and was no longer predictable.

During the day prior to the sudden appearance of the symptoms, the woman had been greatly distressed by the low grades she received on several important exams. When she finally sought help at the university clinic, her major concern was that she was going insane.

Like other dissociative disorders, depersonalization can be precipitated by physical or psychological stress. Individuals with the disorder are generally able to function with minimal impairment of work or social activities. However, the anxiety that is generated and the fear of losing one's mind can be terribly disruptive.

Multiple personality

Multiple personality is a dramatic disorder in which two or more relatively independent personalities exist in one individual. "Each ego state has its characteristic attitudes, perceptions, memories, associations, and behavior" (Jeans 1976, p. 250). The relationship between the personalities is often complex. Only one personality is evident at any one time, and the alternation of personalities usually produces periods of amnesia in the personality that has been displaced. However, one or several personalities may be aware of the existence of the others. The personalities involved are usually quite different from one another and, in some cases, are direct opposites.

Most known cases of multiple personality have involved women. Around the turn of the century, Prince (1906) described a woman with three personalities, whom he designated "the saint" (reserved, overly conscientious, idealistic), "the devil" (impulsive, seductive, fun-oriented), and "the woman" (future-oriented, ambitious). "The devil" enjoyed playing tricks on the others, such as getting drunk and allowing "the saint" to suffer the effects of the hangover.

In the best-known case of multiple personality, Eve White, described as sad, conservative, dignified, and passive, alternated with Eve Black, who was flirtatious, light-hearted, and sexy (Thigpen and Cleckley 1957). During therapy a third personality, Jane, emerged. And Jane was subsequently replaced by an even more mature personality, Evelyn.

Although it is widely reported that Eve was successfully treated, she recently wrote a book indicating that during therapy she actually had more than the four personalities reported by her therapists, and that an additional nine personalities emerged after she completed psychotherapy. With further treatment and the support of her family, she feels that she became an integrated personality at the age of 48 (Sizemore and Pitillo 1977).

A large number of personalities were reported in the case of the "sixteen selves of Sybil," although three personalities were generally dominant (Schreiber 1973). Each of the sixteen personalities had its own distinctive style, mannerisms, facial expressions, and skills. Two of the personalities were male; both were carpenters and were handy with tools.

Objective personality tests have been used to confirm the existence of distinct personalities in multiple personality disorders (Jeans

Under great stress our environment and even our own selves can seem unreal, unnatural, or distorted. The anxiety produced by these feelings of depersonalization can be extremely disruptive.

1976; Osgood, Luria, and Smith 1976). A fairly involved attempt to validate the existence of multiple personalities is discussed in Focus 7.1 (pp. 196–197).

We noted earlier that multiple personality is among the less common dissociative disorders, but there is some question about how rare it really is. The sudden increase in reports of multiple personality in the 1970s may mean it is a relatively common disorder that is frequently misdiagnosed (Greaves 1980). Hundreds of cases of multiple personality have been reported in recent years (Fagan and McMahon 1984); one clinician alone reported over 130 cases (Kluft 1982). The identification of multiple personality in children has also increased. Fagan and McMahon (1984) diagnosed 11 childhood cases in 18 months and noted that:

> It we extrapolate 11 children seen in 18 months multiplied by the number of child care workers and other professionals who work with abused, neglected, institutionalized or delinquent children, then we are looking at an epidemic infecting thousands of children. (p. 32)

Fagan and McMahon feel that parents, teachers, and mental health professionals should be aware of the signs of multiple personality in children, including trance states and confusion about time, place, or person; responding to more than one name; marked and rapid shifts in personality; forgetting recent events; extreme or odd variation in skills such as handwriting, in food preferences, and in artistic abilities; varying responses to discipline; self-injurious behavior; multiple physical complaints and hysteric symptoms such as sleepwalking, sudden blindness, or loss of

FOCUS 7.1

A Study of Multiple Personality

A. M. Ludwig and his colleagues (1972) performed an elaborate study to clarify the processes underlying multiple personalities. The specific questions that the study addressed were as follows: (1) What functions do the alternating personalities perform for the individual, and under what conditions do they emerge? (2) In what areas is each personality dependent or independent from the others? (3) If one personality is amnesiac from the behavior of another, is this amnesia total or does some transfer of learning occur?

The patient involved in the study was a 27-year-old man who complained of headaches and lapses of memory. During these episodes, the patient referred to himself as Usoffa Abdulla or Son of Omega and became highly violent toward others. Hypnosis was used to elicit each of his four different personalities for interviewing and testing.

Jonah ("The Square") was regarded as the primary personality. Jonah was unaware of the existence of the others and was described as shy, retiring, sensitive, polite, and passive. His demeanor during interviews was anxious and frightened.

Sammy ("The Lawyer"), who represented the intellectual and rational side, enjoyed gaining knowledge and debating; he emerged every time Jonah ended up in jail. The existence of the other personalities was known to him, and he could coexist in consciousness with Jonah.

King Young ("The Lover") was only indirectly aware of the other personalities and appeared whenever shy Jonah was encountering difficulties interacting with a woman. He was pleasure-seeking, a ladies' man, and a glib talker. During interviews, he radiated charm and smiled frequently, especially if women were present. (Jonah's mother used to dress him in girl's clothes, which created confusion in Jonah about his sexual identity. King Young had appeared to set Jonah straight.)

Usoffa Abdulla ("The Warrior") was aware of Jonah but only indirectly aware of the others. His role was to protect and watch over "defenseless" Jonah. He appeared at the first sign of physical danger and left after the problem was (often violently) resolved. He was a cold, angry, and belligerent person whom Ludwig and his associates described as "a formidable and scary person to interview." Usoffa first appeared at age 10 when a group of boys

sensation; and reports of hearing voices, losing track of time, or being innocent when punished. The more such symptoms the child displays, the more likely that the diagnosis of incipient multiple personality is appropriate.

It is entirely possible that multiple personality has been underreported because some cases have been misdiagnosed. The disorder shares many symptoms with psychoses, so it might very well be diagnosed as such. Table 7.1 (pp. 198–199) compares the frequencies

with which psychotic-like symptoms were reported by multiple personality patients and by normal subjects. (The list can also give you an idea of the number and variety of symptoms that may be reported by individuals with these disorders.)

Of course, misdiagnosis works both ways, and it may be that cases of other disorders are now being misdiagnosed as multiple personality. The increased number of reported cases of multiple personality may also reflect better

were beating Jonah. When Jonah lost consciousness, Usoffa emerged and was so violent that he nearly killed several of the boys.

Clinical tests were conducted, and physiological and neurological measures were obtained on each of the personalities.

Clinical tests: Objective psychological tests, including the MMPI, the Adjective Check List, and the McDougall Scale of Emotions, revealed consistent differences in personality among the four entities. An IQ was determined for each personality (all four scored in the low normal range), and they responded with similar answers to test questions.

Learning and memory tasks: Paired learning tasks were used to assess the transfer of learning among the personalities, and different paired associations were administered to each personality. When mistakes were corrected by the experimenter, material learned by one personality facilitated learning by the following personalities. However, when corrective feedback by the experimenter was eliminated, there was no transfer effect.

Two standard forms of the logical memory task were presented to the personalities in two different orders. The experimenter read stories of paragraph length and asked

each personality to recall as many details as possible. Again, transfer of learning occurred from one personality to another.

Physiological measures: Each personality was asked to supply words of personal emotional significance. Two words were selected for each personality and interspersed with 12 neutral words to make a standard list of 20 words. Each personality's galvanic skin response (GSR) was measured after he heard each of the 20 words. Jonah responded to the emotional words of all his alternating personalities, although they responded only to their own words and exhibited little response to the words supplied by the other personalities. It is interesting to note that Jonah's response to emotional words supplied by his alternative personalities was greater than his response to his own.

Neurological examinations: Electroencephalograms (measures of brain wave activity), obtained for each personality, revealed significant differences. In addition, meticulous neurological examinations were performed on each of the personalities. Unlike the other personalities, "The Warrior" had a markedly reduced sense of pain. He displayed a hysterical conversion reaction (*hypalgesia*) indicating that portions of his body were immune to pain.

Table 7.1 *Incidence of Psychiatric Symptoms as Reported by 26 Normal and 11 Multiple Personalities (in percents).*

Symptoms	Controls	Patients
Anxiety Symptoms		
Severe anxiety attacks	27	100
Severe dyspnea (breathlessness)	19	73
Palpitations	31	100
Chest pains	12	55
Choking, smothering	4	64
Dizziness	46	91
Numbness, tingling	12	82
Trembling, shaking	31	91
Stomach upset	38	91
Fear of dying	12	55
Excessive worrying	8	91
Hysterical Symptoms		
Severe headaches	4	91
Muscle weakness	4	36
Severe nausea	23	73
Abdominal pains	42	91
Burning pain in sex organs	12	55
Fainting spells	4	45
Sick much of the time	8	64
Severe constipation	19	73
Paralysis, limbs	4	36
Numbness	0	55
Aphonia (loss of voice)	4	36
Loss of consciousness	4	36
Amnesia	4	91
Ataxia (difficulty coordinating voluntary movements)	8	45
Globus (choking)	0	64
Irregular menstruation	23	64
Phobias		
Multiple fears	0	64

SOURCE: Adapted from Bliss (1980). Copyright 1980, American Medical Association.

and more accurate diagnosis or an increased incidence of the disorder. Another possibility is that multiple personality is a fad—a cultural event, just as hysteria was a "fad" in Freud's time—that has been given impetus by sensational media coverage.

Etiology of dissociative disorders

The diagnosis and etiology of dissociative disorders are subject to a great deal of conjecture. Diagnosis is difficult because it is highly dependent on patients' self-reports. Of a group of military personnel who claimed to be amnesiac, two-thirds finally admitted under hypnosis or amytal (truth serum) that they were feigning the condition (Kiersch 1962). It is possible that objective measures such as electroencephalogram (EEG) readings can indicate the presence of multiple personality (Ludwig et al. 1972). However, in a study of two multiple personalities, the researchers concluded that EEG differences among the different personalities reflect differences in concentration, mood changes, and degree of muscle tension rather than some inherent difference between the brains of persons with

Table 7.1 *(continued)*

Symptoms	Controls	Patients
Depression		
Depression	12	100
Suicide attempts	8	91
Schizophrenic Symptoms		
Hears voices	0	64
Visions	0	36
Someone trying to influence mind	0	73
Being followed	0	45
Someone controls mind	0	73
Thoughts being broadcast	0	27
Someone trying to kill me	0	27
Smell foul odors	0	27
Body undergoing transformation	4	36
Borderline or Possible Psychotic Symptoms		
Feel confused, in a daze	12	82
Mind blocks, goes empty	8	64
Go into trance, like hypnosis	8	82
Visual Problems		
Things unclear	4	55
Things become larger or smaller	0	36
Things look strange	4	36
Miscellaneous		
Can't control thoughts	0	91
Limbs move on their own	4	36
Mind goes dead	4	64
Sometimes don't know who or where I am	4	82
When I speak, words don't come out right	0	73
Problem understanding others' speech	0	64
People look strange, unusual	0	36
Suddenly feel hot	4	64
Feel like someone else	4	55

multiple personality and those of normal persons (Coons et al. 1982).

We shall examine the etiology of dissociative disorders from the psychoanalytic perspective and from the learning perspectives, but it is important to realize that neither provides a completely satisfactory explanation of their causes.

Psychoanalytic perspective In the psychoanalytic view, the dissociative disorders involve the use of repression to block from consciousness certain impulses that are seeking expression. When complete repression of these impulses is not possible because of the strength of the impulses or the weakness of the ego state, dissociation or separation may occur. In psychogenic amnesia and fugue, the ego is threatened; its defense is the massive repression of a large part of the individual's identity. Several subjects in one study exhibited self-induced amnesia after facing a traumatic situation that they lacked the resources to deal with directly (Keirsch 1962). These psychogenic amnesiacs displayed poor ego strength and exhibited a large number of immature reactions on personality tests.

The dissociation process is carried out to an

Multiple personality, once thought to be quite rare, may actually be a relatively common but misdiagnosed disorder. Stress or extreme trauma during childhood seems to be at the root of the disorder.

extreme in multiple personality. Equally strong and opposing personality components (stemming from the superego and the id) render the ego incapable of controlling all incompatible elements. A compromise solution is then reached in which the different parts of the personality are alternately allowed expression and repressed. Because intense anxiety and disorganization would occur if these personality factions were allowed to coexist, each is sealed off from the other. In most cases of multiple personality, a character desiring immediate gratification (id) coexists with a moralistic personification (superego) and a personality representing the ego.

The split in personality may develop as a result of traumatic early experiences com-

bined with an inability to escape them. From case histories, we have learned about some of the conditions that may produce a dissociative reaction. In the case of Sybil, for example, Sybil's mother perpetrated appalling atrocities on her child. Dr. Wilbur, Sybil's psychiatrist, speculated that "by dividing into different selves [which were] defenses against an intolerable and dangerous reality, Sybil had found a [design] for survival" (Schreiber 1973, p. 158). The majority of individuals with multiple personalities do report a history of physical or sexual abuse during childhood (Fagan and McMahon 1984; Rosenbaum and Weaver 1980).

In a related view, Bliss (1980) feels that multiple personalities are produced through self-hypnosis—that they involve the individual's attempt to escape unpleasant experiences by entering into a hypnotic state. Many of his patients did, in fact, report that they had experienced trance-like states.

Learning perspective   Learning theorists suggest that the avoidance of stress by indirect means is the main factor to consider in explaining dissociative disorders. For example, psychogenic amnesia and fugue patients are often people who are ill-equipped to handle emotional conficts. Their way of fleeing stressful situations is to forget or block out disturbing thoughts. These individuals typically have much to gain and little to lose from their dissociative symptoms.

Behavioral explanations of multiple personality include the additional factors of role-playing and selective attention. Each of us exhibits a variety of behaviors that are appropriate to particular situations but that may be quite different from one another. For example, an individual wears different clothes and displays different styles or mannerisms depending on whether he or she is scrubbing a floor, going shopping, working, or socializing. In multiple personality, role-playing may be combined with selective attention to certain cues. The individual responds to only certain environmental stimuli and then behaves in a manner that would be appropriate if only those stimuli were present.

Treatment of dissociative disorders

Psychogenic amnesia and psychogenic fugue The symptoms of these disorders tend to remit, or abate, spontaneously. Moreover, patients typically complain of psychological symptoms other than the amnesia, perhaps because the amnesia interferes only minimally with their day-to-day functioning. As a result there is usually little therapeutic intervention. Instead, therapists provide supportive counseling for clients with amnesia.

It has been noted, however, that depression is often associated with fugue state and that stress is often associated with both fugue and psychogenic amnesia (Sackheim and Vingiano 1984). A reasonable therapeutic approach is then to treat these dissociative disorders indirectly by alleviating the depression (with antidepressants or cognitive behavior therapy) and the stress (via stress-management techniques).

Depersonalization disorder This disorder is also subject to spontaneous remission, but at a much slower rate than psychogenic amnesia and fugue. Treatment generally concentrates on the feelings of anxiety or depression, or the fear of going insane.

Occasionally a behavioral approach has been tried. For example, behavior therapy was successfully used to treat depersonalization disorder in a fifteen-year-old female who had blackouts that she described as "floating in and out." These episodes were associated with headaches and feelings of detachment, but neurological and physical examinations revealed no organic cause. The treatment involved increased attention from her family and reinforcement from them when the frequency of blackouts was reduced, training in

the appropriate responses to stressful situations, and self-reinforcement (Dollinger 1983).

Episodes of depersonalization disorder often occur at times when the individual is fatigued or has been deprived of sleep (Bliss, Clark, and West 1959). Relaxation training could be instrumental in alleviating such symptoms.

Multiple personality The mental health literature contains more information on the treatment of *multiple personality* than on the other three dissociative disorders combined. The most widely reported approaches combine *psychotherapy* and *hypnosis*. One suggested procedure begins with hypnosis. With the patient in a hypnotic state, the different personalities are asked to emerge and introduce themselves to the patient, in order to make the patient aware of their existence. Then they are asked to help the patient recall the traumatic experiences or memories that originally triggered the development of new personalities as a repression mechanism. An important part of this recalling step is to experience the emotions associated with the traumatic memories. The therapist then explains to the patient that these additional personalities did serve a purpose when the patient was a child, but that alternative coping strategies are available now. The final step involves (1) selecting those characteristics of each personality that the client wishes to retain, and (2) discarding the remaining characteristics (Bliss 1980).

Behavioral therapy has also been used successfully in some cases of multiple personality. Here is an example:

A 51-year-old male who was diagnosed as a schizophrenic with multiple personalities was treated through selective reinforcement. The reinforcement consisted of material and social rewards; the patient received reinforcement only when he displayed his "healthiest" personality. Eventually his other two personalities were completely eliminated, and the patient was discharged. (Kohlenberg 1973)

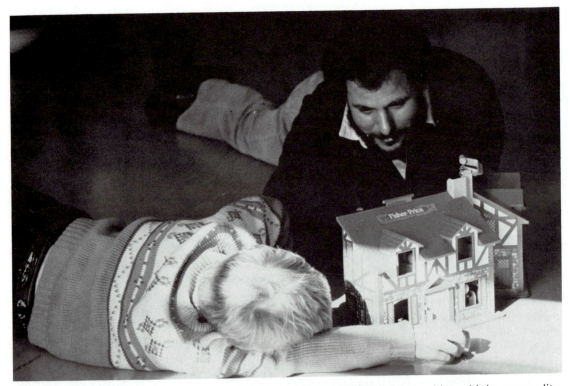

Family therapy and play therapy are two treatments advocated for children with multiple personality. The most important aspect of play therapy seems to be a supportive, nonthreatening environment in which the child can explore all the personalities.

An interesting aspect of this case is the finding that reinforcement can dramatically increase the frequency with which each personality appears.

A number of clinicians advocate the use of family therapy in treating multiple personalities. In one case, the therapist regarded a female client's symptoms as signifying an imbalanced family situation; he found an unusually strong, dependent, and emotional attachment between the client and her mother. He viewed the girl as being part of an emotional triangle between her mother and father, and he interpreted her transformations to different personalities as an attempt to include the father in her family life. As the client gradually became somewhat detached from her mother, her relationship with her father improved and the family system became more balanced. The multiple personalities appeared less frequently as the client accepted more responsibility for her actions (Beal 1978).

Fagan and McMahon (1984) recommend family therapy for children displaying multiple personalities. In addition, for the child client they suggest play therapy, in which games and fantasy are used to explore the child's other personalities in a nonthreatening manner. Particularly intriguing is their method of fusing the child's different personalities by having them hug each other repeatedly, a little harder each time, until they become one.

SOMATOFORM DISORDERS

The **somatoform disorders** involve complaints of physical symptoms that closely mimic authentic medical conditions. Although there is

Table 7.2 DSM-III Diagnostic Criteria for the Somatoform Disorders

Somatization Disorder (Briquet's syndrome)	Conversion Disorder	Psychogenic Pain Disorder (Psychalgia)	Hypochondriasis
1. History of dramatic, vague, and multiple physical complaints before the age of 25. 2. At least twelve specific symptoms in men or fourteen in women, from the general areas below: a. The individuals claim to have been sick most of their lives. b. Conversion symptoms (loss or disturbance of physical function) c. Gastrointestinal symptoms d. Female reproductive problems e. Psychosexual problems f. Pain g. Cardiopulmonary symptoms	1. Loss or disturbance of physical functioning resembling a physical disorder. 2. Psychological factors involved in either: a. Initiating or exacerbating the symptoms. b. Allowing individual to avoid aversive activity. c. Receiving reinforcement for sick behaviors. 3. Symptom is not under voluntary control. 4. No underlying physical conditions are found.	1. Pain is main symptom. 2. Complaint does not fit neurological patterns. No organic basis. 3. Psychological factors involved in either: a. Initiating or exacerbating the symptoms. b. Allowing individual to avoid aversive activity. c. Receiving reinforcement for sick behaviors.	1. Preoccupations with bodily function and disease. 2. Fewer symptoms reported than in Briquet's syndrome. 3. No organic basis for complaint. 4. Belief in physical problems persists despite medical results and reassurance.

SOURCE: DSM-III, pp. 243–251. Used by permission of the American Psychiatric Association.

no actual physiological basis for the complaints, the symptoms are not considered voluntary or under conscious control. The patient believes that the symptoms are real and that they indicate an organic problem.

The somatoform disorders are as follows:

☐ *Somatization disorder*, characterized by multiple physical complaints and an early onset of the condition
☐ *Conversion disorder*, characterized by the loss or alteration of physical functioning
☐ *Psychogenic pain disorder*, in which pain is the main complaint
☐ *Hypochondriasis*, characterized by fear and complaints of bodily disease

The major differences among these disorders are given in Table 7.2. Before we discuss the somatoform disorders individually, we should note that they are wholly different from the **factitious disorders.** The latter are mental disorders in which the symptoms of physical or mental illnesses are deliberately induced or simulated (see Focus 7.2, p. 204).

Somatization disorder

In **somatization disorder,** also known as *Briquet's syndrome,* the individual chronically complains of a number of physical symptoms that have no physical basis.

Factitious Disorders

A most remarkable type of mental disorder is illustrated in the following quotation.

The woman had an FUO (a fever of unknown origin) and nothing seemed to help. For two-and-a-half months, specialists at two hospitals studied her X-rays and blood tests, prescribed penicillin and a variety of other antibiotics, and had no success at all—until doctors at Massachusetts General tried a massive dose of skepticism. She was whisked off for X-rays and her belongings searched, and in her purse was found the source or her baffling sickness: three used syringes and a cup with traces of spittle. She had been injecting herself with traces of spittle. . . .

A recent survey by the National Institute of Health suggests that the problem deserves more attention. Of 343 FUOs recorded over 16 years, 32 patients (nearly 10 percent) were found to be faking their fevers. Among them was a 25-year-old practical nurse who underwent exploratory surgery 4 times before it was discovered she was injecting herself with fecal matter. Others have used actual disease cultures and given themselves tuberculosis or gonorrhea; some have dosed their bodies with lighter fluid, milk, or deadly tetanus toxin. (Adler and Gosnell 1979, p. 65)

These cases illustrate a group of mental disorders, termed **factitious disorders** in DSM-III, in which individuals voluntarily simulate physical or mental conditions or voluntarily induce an actual physical condition. (This differs from **malingering**, which involves the simulation of a disorder so as to achieve some goal—such as feigning sickness to collect insurance.) In factitious disorders, the purpose of the simulated or induced illness is much less apparent, and complex psychological variables are assumed to be involved (Spitzer, Williams, and Skodol 1980). According to DSM-III, "... a diagnosis of a factitious disorder always implies a psychopathology, most often a severe personality disturbance." Because this is a relatively new diagnostic category, little information is available on prevalence, age at onset, or familial pattern.

A 29-year-old married mother, admitted via the emergency room complaining of acute right flank pain, revealed only right flank tenderness on examination. Because of [her] history of a very brief admission to another hospital for a "kinked right ureter" around the time of her first child's birth, she was hospitalized on a medical floor with a provisional diagnosis of ureteral colic. In 16 days of hospitalization, all diagnostic tests were normal, and despite complaints of poor appetite, nausea, severe pain, and insomnia, no definitive organic diagnosis could be supported, even with consultations with a surgeon, a gynecologist, a gastroenterologist, and an internist. Her medical intern began to doubt her stories of pain although he could elicit tenderness on examination; she did not look distressed or depressed. . . .

In subsequent post-discharge interviews, she spent most of the time complaining about pain and discouragement about her unaltered condition. She later returned to see the surgeon, who thought she had a retrocecal appendix and scheduled her for surgery three days hence. . . . Following surgery, she called to say she had immediately developed joint pains. . . . After a few psychiatric interviews . . . she recalled how, in her childhood, her parents used to argue but would be harmonious and caring when she was sick or hurt. She remembered how she always had to take care of everyone: mother who got sick; father who was partially disabled; husband who was moody; children who needed mothering. Now she was working in a nursery school. She began to recognize resentment of the demands upon her. . . . She saw that being sick might have been the only acceptable way for her to express her feelings. . . . She saw similarities in the ways both she and her mother "used" illness to achieve their aims. (Lipsitt 1974, pp. 134–136)

This case illustrates several characteristics of somatization disorder. There are complaints about a number of concurrent physical symptoms (somatization disorder differs from hypochondriasis primarily in the number of physical symptoms involved). There are a constant "shopping around" for doctors, numerous negative medical findings, and often unnecessary operations. Psychiatric interviews typically reveal psychological conflicts that may be involved in the disorder. Anxiety and depression are common complications of somatization disorder.

Historically, somatization disorder (or *hysteria,* as it was called) has been reported primarily in women; estimates are that 1 percent of all females suffer from the disorder (DSM-III 1980). However, accurate data on its incidence are difficult to obtain because, until DSM-III was published, somatization disorder and conversion disorder were grouped together in prevalence studies. The frequency of hysteria seems to have decreased by half, from 6 percent of all outpatients in the period 1948–1950 to only 3.1 percent in 1969–1971. However, it is uncertain whether this finding represents an actual decrease in the incidence of the disorder or simply the unwillingness of clinicians to employ the "humiliating" diagnostic label *hysteric* (Stetanis et al. 1976).

Kroll, Chamberlain, and Halpern (1979) tried to discover whether Briquet's syndrome was present in a male population that is at risk for developing this disorder. Using the DSM-III diagnostic criteria for somatization disorder, they examined a group of fifty psychiatric inpatients. No men were found to have the disorder. Of the necessary diagnostic criteria,

the researchers seldom encountered "dramatic" presentation of the symptoms, sexual complaints, or conversion reactions (discussed in the next subsection).

Conversion disorder

In **conversion disorder,** also known as *conversion reaction,* there is significant organ impairment without an underlying physical cause. Such impairment may take the form of partial paralysis, blindness, deafness, or loss of speech or feeling. It is often difficult to distinguish between actual physical disorders and conversion reactions. However, conversion disorder usually involves either the senses or motor functions that are controlled by the voluntary (rather than the autonomic) nervous system, and there is seldom any actual organic damage. For example, a person with hysterical paralysis of the legs rarely shows the atrophy of the lower limbs that occurs when there is an underlying organic pathology (though in some persistent cases, disuse can result in atrophy).

Some symptoms, such as glove anesthesia (the loss of feeling in the hand, ending in a straight line at the wrist) are easily diagnosed as conversion disorder because the area of sensory loss does not correspond to the distribution of nerves in the body. Others may require extensive neurological and physical examinations to rule out a true medical disorder before a diagnosis of conversion disorder can be made. However, the art of medical diagnosis is limited, and the possibility that a condition is actually a physical illness should always be considered (Hyler and Spitzer 1978). In fact, in a follow-up of patients originally diagnosed as suffering from conversion disorders, about half had actual physical conditions, such as multiple sclerosis or colitis (Slater 1975).

The impairment itself is not considered to be under voluntary control. However, psychological factors are considered important with regard to either the timing of a conflict or the immediate function that episodes may serve. Both are illustrated in the following case.

> The patient, a 42-year-old white, married male, was admitted in a wheelchair to the Psychiatry Service of the Veterans Administration Center, Jackson, Mississippi. When admitted, he was bent forward at the waist (45-degree angle) and unable to straighten his body or move his legs. For the past 15 years, he had consistently complained of lumbosacral [lower back] pain. On two occasions (12 and 5 years prior to admission) he underwent orthopedic surgery; however, complaints of pain persisted. In the last 5 years the patient had numerous episodes of being totally unable to walk. These episodes, referred to by the patient as "drawing over," typically lasted 10–14 days and occurred every 4–6 weeks. The patient was frequently hospitalized and treated with heat applications and muscle relaxants. Five years prior to this admission the patient had retired on Social Security benefits and assumed all household duties, as his wife was compelled to support the family.
>
> Orthopedic and neurological examinations failed to reveal contributory causes. An assessment of the patient's family life revealed that there were numerous stresses coinciding with the onset of "drawing over" episodes. Included were the patient's recent discharge from the National Guard after 20 years of service, difficulties with his son and youngest daughter, and "guilt" feelings about the role reversal he and his wife had assumed. Moreover, it was clear that the patient received considerable social reinforcement from family members when he presented symptoms of "illness" (e.g., receiving breakfast in bed, being relieved of household chores . . .). (Kallman, Hersen, and O'Toole 1975, pp. 411–412)

In a study of the prevalence and type of conversion symptoms in forty male patients at a Veterans Administration hospital, it was found that the most common were *paresis* (muscle paralysis), *anesthesia* (loss of bodily sensation), *paresthesia* (prickling or tingling sensations), and dizziness (Watson and Buranen 1979). Conversion reactions were also diagnosed in fifteen children, of whom nine were female. Their most common problems involved the function of the legs (paralysis, and flexing or walking difficulties), whereas problems involving vision and speech accounted for only three cases. Twelve of the fifteen children had had psychiatric problems in the past.

There seems to be a contradiction between the belief that conversion disorders are involuntary rather than faked and some of the physical evidence. For example, sophisticated visual tests on a sixteen-year-old girl who reported tunnel vision showed that she made significantly more "seeing" errors than would be predicted by chance. To explain this result, the researchers hypothesized that the girl could indeed see peripherally but chose, either consciously or unconsciously, to deny it. A review of experimental studies on psychogenic blindness led to the conclusion that patients with this symptom are "considerably under the control of visual stimuli" (Sackeim, Nordlie, and Gur 1979). The reviewers feel that hypnotically induced blindness may shed light on the processes involved.

Psychogenic pain disorder

Psychogenic pain disorder (or *psychalgia*) is characterized by severe pain that has a psychological rather than a physical basis. The reported pain may have no physiological or neurological basis, it may be greatly in excess of that expected with an existing physical condition, or it may linger long after a physical injury has healed. Psychalgia occurs more frequently in women than in men; as with the other somatoform disorders, psychological conflicts or "gains" are involved. Because the pain is real, individuals with psychogenic pain disorder make frequent visits to physicians and may end up as drug or medication abusers.

Psychogenic pain was considered a conversion disorder in the past, but it was differentiated from that disorder in DSM-III. However, this distinction may be difficult to maintain. A recent study, based on a number of clinical and demographic variables, indicated no significant difference between patients classified as having conversion disorder and those having psychalgia (Bishop and Torch 1979). The two disorders *do* differ in form. Conversion reactions involve actual organ impairment, whereas psychalgia involves pain. In psychalgia, the onset or worsening of pain is often related to psychological and emotional factors.

Hypochondriasis

The primary characteristic of **hypochondriasis** is a persistent preoccupation with one's health and physical condition, even in the face of physical evaluations that reveal no organic problems. Individuals with this disorder are hypersensitive to bodily functioning and processes. A twinge in the arm might be interpreted as a sure sign of a heart condition, or a stomachache as an indication of an ulcer.

Hypochondriacs seem to enjoy discussing their symptoms, make eager use of technical medical jargon, and display satisfaction when actual ailments are found (McCranie 1979). However, in a study of 45 hypochondriacs (28 females and 17 males), one researcher found that fear, anxiety, and depression were common. Each patient feared that he or she had an undetected physical illness; anxiety was increased by the expectation that the disorder was progressive and terminal. As a group, the subjects also felt that previous physical examinations had been inaccurate (Kellner 1982).

An analysis of the factors involved in hypochondriasis revealed a syndrome comprised of a great deal of *family illness* coupled with *unnecessary operations, low pain threshold,* and *life defeats* (Bianchi 1973).

Neurasthenia, a condition that is related to hypochondriasis, is characterized by com-

Both neurasthenia and hypochondriasis involve a preoccupation with physical symptoms and frequent visits to the doctor. Either diagnosis, however, may be applied inappropriately if a physician can find no readily discernible cause for a physical complaint.

plaints of extreme mental and physical weariness. Chronic fatigue and lack of enthusiasm are often found, together with an inability to concentrate, feelings of inferiority, and dependency behavior (McCranie 1980). In one reported case of neurasthenia, a 36-year-old research chemist complained of fatigue, headaches, weakness, sexual problems, and other bodily ailments. To conserve his energy, the chemist worked only 4 hours a day; he was considering giving up work entirely. At home, each half-hour of activity necessitated another half-hour of rest. These symptoms so severely restricted the patient's life that he contemplated suicide (Laughlin 1967).

Like hypochondriacs, neurasthenic individuals exhibit an extreme awareness of symptoms and may visit doctors quite often. Their exhaustion is frequently selective; that is, they often regain their energy when given the opportunity to engage in activities that really interest them. It has been suggested that neurasthenia is a *stress-intolerance syndrome,* a condition characterized by a lowered tolerance to stress (Berger 1973).

Individuals who suffer from hypochondriasis or neurasthenia display behaviors that may represent displaced anxiety, modeling, or early conditioning. Many children learn that they can avoid their responsibilities when they are ill. Thus they are rewarded through hypochondriasis or neurasthenia by gaining attention, sympathy, and concern from their loved ones and by being allowed to escape responsibility.

Both neurasthenics and hypochondriacs seem to find it less threatening to believe themselves to be suffering from medical disorders than to acknowledge the presence of psychological problems. It has also been suggested, however, that these diagnostic categories are both ambiguous and extensively misused. In other words, a physician or psychiatrist who is unable to discover the cause of a patient's complaint may label the condition either neurasthenia or hypochondriasis because it is a convenient and available diagnosis (Berger 1973; Lipsitt 1974).

Etiology of somatoform disorders

Psychoanalytic perspective Sigmund Freud believed that hysterical reactions (psychogenic complaints of pain, illness, or loss of physical function) were caused by the repression of some type of conflict, usually sexual in nature. To protect the individual from intense anxiety, this conflict is *converted* into some physical symptom (Breuer and Freud 1957). For example, in the case of a 31-year-old female who developed visual problems with no physical basis, therapy revealed the woman had, as a child, witnessed her parents engaging in sexual intercourse. The severe anxiety associated with this traumatic scene was later converted into visual difficulties (Grinker and Robbins 1954).

The psychoanalytic view suggests that there are two mechanisms that produce and then sustain somatoform symptoms. The first provides a *primary gain* to the individual by protecting him or her from the anxiety associated with the unacceptable desire or impulse; it is the need for protection that gives rise to the conversion. Then a *secondary gain* accrues when the individual's dependency needs are fulfilled through attention and sympathy. Consider the case of an 82-year-old man who reported the sudden onset of diffuse right-abdominal pain in March 1977. No abnormal signs were found at that time. In August 1977 he was rehospitalized for the same complaint. Again nothing physical was found. In an analysis of the case, Weddington (1979) noted that the patient's symptom first developed in the month of his wife's death but 12 years after her death. His second hospitalization occurred in the month of his mother's death, which had occurred 12 years after the patient's birth. Weddington hypothesized that the painful memories were converted to a physical symptom and that the care and attention bestowed by the hospital staff fulfilled the patient's dependency needs.

Learning perspective Learning theorists generally contend that individuals with somatoform disorders assume the "sick role" because it is reinforcing and because it allows them to escape unpleasant circumstances or avoid responsibilities. Ullman and Krasner (1975) feel that the two most important elements involved in somatoform disorders are observing an individual with a physical ailment and seeing that individual receive reinforcement for playing the sick role. These elements seemed to be present in the conversion reactions of 56 student naval pilots seen by psychiatrists at a naval hospital (Mucha and Reinhart 1970). The patients were described as achievement-oriented individuals who could not admit failure. An investigation of their backgrounds revealed that the majority of these students had previously had physical injuries and that more than 70 percent of their parents had histories of recurrent illnesses or hospitalizations. In accordance with the view of Ullman and Krasner, modeling of parents and possible early conditioning through personal experience with injuries provided the cadets with an "honorable" means of escaping the stressful training situation.

Fordyce (1982) analyzes psychogenic pain from the operant perspective. He points out that the only available data concerning the pain (or any other somatoform symptoms) are the subjective reports of the afflicted individuals and that the medical profession is highly sensitive to pain cues. Physicians and nurses are trained to be attentive to reports of pain. Medication is given quickly to patients suffering pain. Exercise and physical therapy programs are set up so that exertion continues until pain or fatigue is felt. All of these practices serve to reinforce the expression of pain.

Fordyce contends that psychogenic pain is under the influence of these and other external (or environmental) variables rather than being controlled from within. He cites several studies that support his contention. For example, when chronic pain patients were asked to perform physical therapy exercises until "the pain becomes too great," approximately half of the time they stopped after multiples of five exercises! This leads to the suspicion that something other than pain was controlling their behavior. When pain patients exercised on bicycles arranged so that they received no feedback as to their performance, their tolerance for exercise was no different from that of nonpain patients. But when performance feedback was available, the pain patients performed significantly worse. It was clear that the "tolerance" of the pain patients depended on more than their internal bodily sensations.

The importance of reinforcement was indicated in a study of male pain patients. Individuals who had supportive wives (wives who were attentive to pain cues) reported significantly greater pain when their wives were present than when they were absent. The reverse was true of patients with wives who were nonsupportive. In this case, reports of pain were greater when the spouse was absent.

Sociocultural perspective   Hysteria was originally perceived as a problem that afflicted only women. Hippocrates felt that a shift or movement of the uterus resulted in complaints involving breathing difficulties, anesthesia, and seizures. The movement was presumed to be due to the uterus "wanting a child." Although Freud was among the first to indicate that hysteria could also occur in males, the majority of his patients were women. Satow (1979) has argued that hysteria was more prevalent in women when social mores did not provide them with appropriate channels for the expression of aggression or sexuality. Hollender (1980) stresses the importance of societal restrictions in producing hysterical symptoms in women and suggests the case of Anna O. as an example.

> Anna O., a patient of Freud and Breuer, was a 20-year-old woman who developed a variety of symptoms including dissociation, muscle rigidity, and insensitivity to feeling. Freud and Breuer both felt that these symptoms were the result of intrapsychic conflicts. They did not consider the impact of social roles on abnormal behavior.
>
> According to Hollender, Anna O. was highly intelligent, but her educational and intellectual opportunities were severely restricted because she was female. She was described as "bubbling over with intellectual vitality" by Breuer. As Hollender points out, "Not only was Anna O., as a female, relegated to an inferior position in her family with future prospects limited to that of becoming a wife and mother, but at the age of 21 she was suddenly called on to assume the onerous chore of nursing her father" (p. 798). He suggests that many of her symptoms were produced to relieve the guilt she felt because of her resentment of this duty—as well as to maintain her intellectually stimulating contact with

Breuer. After treatment via Breuer's cathartic method was terminated, Anna found an outlet for her intellectual talents: She headed a home for orphans, was involved in social work, and became recognized as a feminist leader. [Interestingly, Ellenberger (1972) found that the cathartic treatment was unsuccessful and that Anna O. remained severely disturbed and required further treatment.]

Satow feels that, as societal restrictions on women are loosened, the incidence of somatoform disorders among females should be reduced. However, the diagnostic criteria involved in some of these disorders tends to ensure the overrepresentation of women.

Biological perspective   Some physical complaints may have more than a merely imaginary basis. Researchers have found that hypochondriacal patients were more alert to internal processes than phobic individuals; they were better at estimating their own heart rates when exposed to short films (Tyrer, Lee, and Alexander 1980). It has been hypothesized that ". . . people who continually report being bothered by pain and bodily sensations [hypochondriacs] may have a higher-than-normal arousal level, which results in increased perception of internal stimuli" (Hanback and Revelle 1978, p. 523). Innate factors may account for greater sensitivity to pain and bodily functions.

However, the role of biological factors in the etiology of somatoform disorders is less evident than their role in the more severe disorders (psychoses). A direct link between genetic influences and specific forms of somatoform disorders has not been found. But much research has been directed toward examining differences in concordance rates between identical twins and fraternal twins, in an effort to estimate the heritability of somatoform disorders.

In a study involving 15,909 pairs of twins, researchers analyzed the concordance rate for anxiety, somatoform disorders, and dissociative disorders. The concordance rate of identical twins was one and one-half times as high as

that for fraternal twins. But the researchers concluded that environmental factors could account for this difference and that heredity plays a minimal role in the development of these disorders (Pollin et al. 1969).

A more profitable approach might be to examine personality traits that interact with environmental factors to produce psychopathology, or to examine such inherited *predispositions* as an unstable autonomic nervous system. These predispositions may not be evident under normal circumstances but might surface when an individual is subjected to stress. And certain personality traits may be associated with specific symptomatology (Slater and Cowie 1971).

In one study of the influence of predisposition, investigations found that certain identifiable characteristics of infants—irregular eating or bowel habits, excessive crying, and negative response to new stimuli—increased the probability of an infant's having emotional problems later in life (Chess, Thomas, and Birch 1965). However, the evidence supporting the role of heredity in the development of somatoform disorders is still inconclusive.

Treatment of somatoform disorders

Psychoanalytic treatment   The earliest treatment for somatoform disorders was *psychoanalysis*. Over the years Freud (1905) and Freud and Breuer (1895) reported numerous cases of "hysterical" patients who, like Anna O., would probably now be classified as exhibiting conversion reaction or somatization disorder. Freud believed that the crucial element in treating hysterical patients via psychoanalysis was to help them *relive* the actual feelings associated with the repressed traumatic event—and not simply to help them remember the details of the experience. Once the emotions connected with the traumatic situation were experienced, the symptoms would disappear.

Although Freud eventually dropped hypnosis from his psychoanalytic repertoire, many of his disciples continued to find it beneficial, and variations of it became known as hypnotherapy. Bliss (1984) was a modern advocate of hypnotherapy as treatment for somatization disorder and conversion symptoms. In essence, Bliss argued that individuals afflicted with a somatoform disorder engage in involuntary self-hypnosis as a defense, much as multiple personality patients do. Hypnotherapy involves the bringing to consciousness of repressed conflicts, the mastering of these traumas, and the learning of defenses that are more adaptive than self-hypnosis.

Behavioral treatment Although psychoanalytic treatments are most often associated with certain somatoform disorders, several behavioral methods appear worth investigating.

> A 43-year-old man exhibited a motor disturbance in which he was sometimes unable to keep his eyes open or to pry up the lids when asked to do so. Although the initial diagnosis was *myasthenia gravis* (a neuromuscular disorder characterized by weakness of the voluntary muscles), no organic pathology could be found. The problem occurred mainly at home, where a great deal of strain between the patient's mother and the patient's wife was evident. The patient was tense during familial disagreements but handled the tension by passively withdrawing from the conflicts. He had complained about headaches and various eye problems two years before the eyelid impairment occurred.
>
> Because interpersonal stress seemed to be the precipitating factor, the patient was taught direct means of resolving conflicts. After a three-month assertiveness training program, the problem was eliminated (Meichenbaum 1966).

On the basis of his contention that psychogenic pain is reinforced in patients by the attention and nurturance of their families, Fordyce (1976) explained how this pain could easily be placed under operant control. The control would be in direct response to the patient's secondary gain (fulfillment of dependency needs). Treatment would involve teach-

Freud dropped hypnosis as a treatment for hysteria because he believed the patient must reexperience the traumatic event; hypnosis actually prevented this reliving. Some modern treatments for somatization and conversion disorders are beginning to rely on hypnosis once again, based upon the belief that these disorders are induced by self-hypnosis.

ing the family to reinforce only "healthy" behavior and helping the patient to discover alternative ways of obtaining reinforcement.

Family systems treatment   The role of the family in maintaining somatoform symptoms has also been recognized by promoters of family therapy for the disorder. Chronic pain is often used to gain rewards (such as attention) and to disclaim responsibility for certain behaviors (such as anger) within the family system. Thus family therapy is recommended as an essential part of the treatment for somatoform disorders (Hudgens 1979).

Research has indicated that, in families of somatization disorder patients, a disproportionately high number of female relatives also have somatization disorder, and a large number of male relatives are labeled either antisocial personalities or alcoholics (Arkonac and Guze 1963; Bohman et al. 1984). It is certainly not necessary to have multiple cases of psychiatric disorders in a family before considering family therapy, but these research findings strongly suggest that the entire family be drawn into the treatment process. The therapy could then be used to place the identified patient's disorder in proper perspective, to teach the family adaptive ways of supporting each other, and to prepare family members to deal with anticipated (and predicted) problems.

SUMMARY

1. The dissociative disorders involve an alteration or disruption of the individual's identity or consciousness; they are considered relatively rare. Psychogenic amnesia and psychogenic fugue involve a selective form of forgetting in which the individual loses memory of information that is of personal significance. Depersonalization disorder is characterized by feelings of unreality—distorted perceptions of one's self and one's environment. Multiple personality involves the alter-

nation of two or more relatively independent personalities in one individual.

2. Psychoanalytic perspectives on the etiology of dissociative disorders attribute them to the repression of certain impulses that are seeking expression. Learning explanations suggest that the avoidance of stress by indirect means is the main causal factor. Psychogenic amnesia and psychogenic fugue tend to be short-lived to remit spontaneously; behavioral therapy has also been used successfully. Multiple personality has most often been treated with a combination of psychotherapy and hypnosis, as well as with behavioral and family therapies. In most cases, the therapist attempts to fuse the several personalities.

3. Somatoform disorders involve complaints about physical symptoms that mimic actual medical conditions but for which no organic basis can be found. Instead, psychological factors are directly involved in the initiation and exacerbation of the problem. Somatization disorder, or Briquet's syndrome, is characterized by chronic multiple complaints, dramatic presentation of the symptoms, and early onset. Conversion disorder involves such problems as the loss of sight, paralysis, or some other physical impairment with no organic cause. Psychogenic pain disorder, or psychalgia, is a condition in which reported severe pain has a psychological rather than a physical basis. Hypochondriasis involves a persistent preoccupation with bodily functioning and disease, and neurasthenia involves chronic complaints of extreme fatigue.

4. The psychoanalytic perspective holds that somatoform disorders are caused by the repression of sexual conflicts and their conversion into physical symptoms. Learning theorists contend that the role of "being sick" is reinforcing and allows the individual to escape from unpleasant circumstances or avoid responsibilities. Further, psychogenic pain is often reinforced by the external environment. From the sociocultural perspective, the somatoform disorders are seen to result from

the societal restrictions placed on women, who are affected to a much greater degree than men by these disorders. Psychoanalytic treatment emphasizes the reliving of emotions associated with the repressed traumatic event. Other treatment approaches involve the reinforcement of only "healthy" behaviors rather than the pain or disability. If possible, treatment is administered within the family system.

KEY TERMS

conversion disorder A somatoform disorder in which there is significant impairment of organic function without an underlying physical cause

depersonalization disorder A dissociative disorder in which there are feelings of unreality or distortion concerning the self or the environment

dissociative disorders Mental disorders characterized by alteration or disruption of the individual's identity or consciousness; include psychogenic amnesia, psychogenic fugue, depersonalization disorder, and multiple personality disorder

hypochondriasis A somatoform disorder characterized by a persistent and strong preoccupation with one's health and physical condition

multiple personality A dissociative disorder in which two or more relatively distinct personalities exist in one individual

psychogenic amnesia A dissociative disorder characterized by the inability to recall information of personal significance, usually after a traumatic event

psychogenic fugue A dissociative disorder in which psychogenic amnesia is accompanied by flight from familiar surroundings

psychogenic pain disorder A somatoform disorder characterized by pain that has a psychological, rather than a physical basis; also called *psychalgia*

somatization disorder A somatoform disorder in which the individual chronically complains of a number of physical symptoms for which no physiological basis can be found; also called *Briquet's syndrome*

somatoform disorders Mental disorders that involve complaints of physical symptoms that closely mimic authentic medical conditions, but that have no physical basis; they include somatization disorder, conversion disorder, psychogenic pain disorder, and hypochondriasis

8

Stress and the Reactive Disorders

All three of the individuals quoted below are victims of stress, which is the topic of this chapter.

The next one's going to be a big one. I know it is. All the experts predict California will be hit by a 7.0 earthquake soon. . . . What will I do? . . . I've never been so scared in my life. When our trailer—mobile home—fell off its foundation, I couldn't stop screaming. My daughter kept crying and yelling for me, but all I could do was hide under the kitchen table. . . . What kind of mother is that? . . . I can't sleep, or eat, or take care of the house anymore. I'm a nervous wreck. Every time a plane passes over . . . or a loud noise . . . I get panicky. I keep seeing all our dishes falling off the shelves, hitting the floor, and the glass breaking. (1980 earthquake victim, Livermore, California)

It was the pressure that got to me. I started drinking every day after work . . . first one or two, then more. My blood pressure was already too high, I had a high cholesterol count, I couldn't sleep and I didn't eat right. Little things irritated me all out of proportion, so when I got home after work I wouldn't even talk to my wife or kids. . . . I knew I had to leave the job after I blanked out at work. It was right at the end of a twelve-hour shift. One of the planes I was guiding in asked for landing instructions. Simple— I've done it a thousand times . . . more. Only that time I couldn't move, or say anything. I was numb; I just stared at the screen. We were all lucky that my relief controller was there to take over. (Air traffic controller, San Francisco)

Do you know what it's like to live with constant pain? Since my accident I haven't been able to sleep one night through. I can't even do the simplest things, like tie my shoelaces. My strength is gone; I can't hold a job; I can't even be a husband to my wife . . . even in bed. Sometimes the pain is so bad, all I can do is cry. Medicine doesn't help either. It dulls the pain, but it makes you a walking zombie. . . . It's been nearly a year now, with two operations. I'm just

215

Both natural catastrophes and high-pressure occupations are likely to be stressors and produce physical and psychological symptoms. Stress induced by a disastrous flood can lead to posttraumatic stress disorder, while the stress felt by an air traffic controller can lead to adjustment disorder.

afraid it will be like this for as long as I live. If it is, maybe it won't be worth going on. (Chronic pain sufferer—spinal injury, Duluth)

In conversational English we use the word *stress* in two ways. It can mean a sort of mental pressure placed on an individual by a demanding situation, or it can mean the individual's internal reaction to that pressure. Until recently, psychologists used the term in these same two ways. Now, however, we distinguish between "cause" and "effect" by using two separate terms. A **stressor** is a physical or psychological demand that is placed on an individual by some external event or situation. **Stress** is the individual's internal reaction to a stressor—that is, to a physical or psychological demand. We can then loosely view the stressor as an *external cause* and the stress as an *internal effect*. The stress, in turn, gives rise to action (behaviors) on the part of the individual.

In DSM-III, unusual or even bizarre behaviors exhibited under stress-producing conditions are categorized as "**reactive disorders** not elsewhere classified." These disorders are divided into two groups, according to the stressors involved. The **posttraumatic stress disorders** result from stressors that are so severe and outside the range of common experience that they produce significant distress in most people. Reactive disorders resulting from large-scale catastrophes, natural disasters such as earthquakes, and military combat are included in this group. The *adjustment disorders* result from the more common situations of everyday life, including illness, financial difficulties, bereavement, and marital conflicts. The air traffic controller and the chronic pain victim quoted above obviously find their situations stressful; their stress is a reaction to the type of stressors involved in adjustment disorders.

In this chapter we first examine three models or theories that provide insight into the mechanism of stress. Next we look at the major stressors that can lead to adjustment disorders and posttraumatic stress disorders. Finally, we discuss some of the factors that seem to determine how much stress an individual feels and some methods that anyone can use to prepare for, reduce, or alleviate stress.

MODELS FOR UNDERSTANDING STRESS

As we have noted, stress is an internal response to an external stimulus or situation. But something that is a source of disturbance to one individual is not necessarily disturbing to another individual. Moreover, different people react differently to the same stressors. For example, most of the people who experienced the 1980 Livermore earthquake were eventually able to get on with their lives. Others, like the woman we quoted, exhibited intense and relatively long-lasting psychological symptoms. Why did she react in such an extreme manner? Is her tolerance for stress lower than that of other people?

The three stress models discussed in this section are attempts to explain the development and differential effects of stress; the apparent ability of relatively weak stressors to result in strong stress reactions; and the ability of some individuals to cope more "easily" with stress. The models purport to answer a number of questions regarding stress, including those posed above.

The general adaptation model

To be alive is to be constantly exposed to stressors: illness, marriage, divorce, the death of a loved one, hunting for and keeping a job, aging, retiring, even schoolwork. Most people can cope with most of the stressors they encounter, provided those stressors are not excessively severe and do not "gang up" on the individual. But when an individual is confronted with excessive external demands—stressors—coping behaviors may fail and the individual may resort to immature means of dealing with them. The result may be psychosomatic symptoms, apathy, anxiety, panic, stupor, depression, violence, and even death.

There are, in general, three kinds of stressors:

☐ **Biological stressors** such as infection, physical trauma, disease, malnutrition, and fatigue
☐ **Psychological stressors** such as threats of physical harm, attacks on self-esteem, and guilt-inducing attacks on one's belief system
☐ **Social stressors** such as crowding, excessive noise, economic pressures, and war

A helpful model for understanding the body's physical reaction to biological stressors was proposed by Hans Selye (1956, 1982). He identified three stages in the **general adaptation syndrome** (GAS): (1) the alarm stage, (2) the stage of resistance, and (3) the stage of exhaustion.

Selye describes the first stage as a "call to arms" of the body's defenses when it is invaded or assaulted biologically. During this *alarm stage* there is an immediate reaction to the noxious agent (rapid heartbeat, loss of muscle tone, decreased temperature and blood pressure) followed by a rebound reaction in which the adrenal cortex is enlarged and corticoid hormones are secreted by the adrenals. With continued exposure to the stressor, the *adaptation or resistance stage* ensues. Now the body mobilizes itself to defend, destroy, or coexist with the injury or disease. Either there is an improvement or the symptoms of illness disappear. At the same time, however, there is a decrease in the body's resistance to most other assaults on the body. That is, the affected person may become susceptible to other infections or illnesses. If the stressor continues to act and further taxes the body's finite resistive resources, the symptoms may reappear as the organism becomes exhausted (hence the name *exhaustion stage*). If stress continues unabated, death may result.

Biological consequences of stress Although Selye developed his model as a means of describing physical responses to biological stressors, continuing research now indicates that psychological and social stressors have similar effects. In fact, sustained stress—resulting from psychological or social stressors—may not only make the individual more susceptible to illness, but may actually alter the course of a disease. For example, it has been documented that recently bereaved widows are three to twelve times more likely to die than married women; that tax accountants are most susceptible to heart attacks around April 15; that individuals living in high-noise areas near airports have more hypertension and medical complaints than other people; and that air traffic controllers suffer four times as much hypertension as the general population (Wilding 1984). The common factor in all these high-physical-risk groups is *stress.*

For years scientists were skeptical about the supposed effects of stress on the body and dismissed any relationship between the two as folklore. However, we now know that stress affects the immune system, heart function, hormone levels, the nervous system, and metabolic rates. Bodily "wear and tear" due to stress can contribute to diseases like hypertension, ulcers, heart attacks, cancer, and the common cold. (Stress-induced physical disorders are discussed in Chapter 9.)

The discovery of a relationship between stress and physical illness has spawned a new field of study called *behavioral medicine,* which is concerned with health, illness, and the lifestyles that affect them (Matarazzo 1980). Already behavioral medicine has given us a better understanding of how diet and exercise affect our ability to tolerate stress (see Focus 8.1, pp. 220–221).

Psychological consequences of stress Most of us maintain certain levels of psychological adjustment that vary little over time. When we encounter a crisis situation that cannot be resolved through our customary method of coping, our behaviors can become disorganized and ineffective in solving problems. Brady (1975) has described stages in crisis decompensation that parallel the three stages of Selye's general adaptation syndrome. (**Decompensation** is loss of the ability to deal successfully with stress, resulting in a more primitive means of coping.)

During the impact of a crisis (the first stage), the person experiences a sense of confusion and upset. He or she is bewildered and wonders what is happening, why it is happening, and how a situation so far beyond his or her experience can be resolved. Feelings of panic are not unusual. This disequilibrium is followed by a period of attempted resolution (the second stage) during which all resources are mobilized to deal with the situation. In the case of a divorce, the person may seek out friends for emotional support or validation. In the case of a disaster, the person may selectively perceive the situation in a more favorable light ("We've lost our home and all our possessions, but we're lucky to be alive. We can always rebuild.") When individuals are successful in their coping, they are likely to resume functioning once more at the precrisis level and, in some cases, move into a growth adjustment phase. There are some indications that the experience of coping with and mastering a personal crisis or disaster may even enhance a person's psychological well-being (Taylor 1983). If coping is ineffective, however, the person is likely to move into a decompensated adjustment phase (the third stage). This phase may be characterized by withdrawal, depression, guilt, apathy, anxiety, anger, or any number of extreme psychological consequences. The precise symptomology depends on both personal and emotional variables.

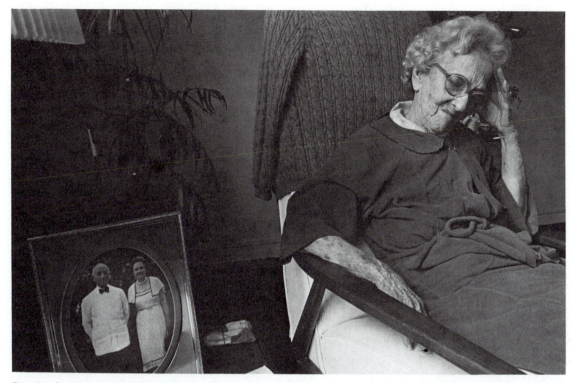

Death of a spouse is a life-change event that requires considerable readjustment. Loss of a husband or wife can lead to many changes in lifestyle—financial, social, and physical changes. These changes occur at a time when an individual is already profoundly bereaved, and the resulting stress can be overwhelming.

The life-change model

Thomas H. Holmes and his associates accepted the GAS model for the physical and psychological reactions to stressors. They noted, though, that the events that led to stress reactions need not be of crisis proportions; seemingly small, everyday events could also create stress. Their work led to the formulation of the **life-change model,** which assumes that all changes in a person's life—large or small, desirable or undesirable—can act as stressors. And the accumulation of small changes is thought to be as powerful as a major stressor.

In their study, they interviewed more than 5000 medical patients about the life events that had preceded their illnesses (Holmes et al. 1950). In this retrospective study, the investigators found that many life events may help cause diseases such as colds, tuberculosis, and skin disorders. They then asked patients who had either colds or nasal infections to return when they recovered. Each patient who returned was measured for blood flow, breathing ease, secretions, and swelling of the nose. He or she was then asked to talk about the situation that existed just prior to the onset of the illness. It was found that simply talking about the situation—a mother-in-law's visit, a divorce, or being fired from a job—brought back the cold symptoms! And biopsies of nasal tissues confirmed the fact that merely discussing these psychologically charged life events caused tissue damage.

Similar results were found for tubercular patients who were caught up in dramatic life changes. However, listing the most frequently cited events revealed that the majority were not negative in nature (as are jail terms, being fired from a job, or sexual difficulties). Rather, they represented everyday life occurrences: getting a mortgage, marriage, beginning or ending school, the birth of a child, or a son or daughter leaving home.

Intrigued with the possibility of identifying

FOCUS 8.1

Behavioral Medicine: Reducing Stress by Changing Lifestyles

Behavioral medicine is the interdisciplinary field concerned with the integration of behavioral and biomedical science, knowledge, and techniques relevant to health and illness. Many of the techniques of behavioral medicine are aimed at changing the person's lifestyle to prevent or treat physical illness or to enhance the quality of life.

For example, Meyer Friedman and his colleagues in 1984 reported a study of 591 coronary patients in which they found that those patients who changed their lifestyles experienced a drastic decline in the recurrence of heart attacks. They discovered that 95 percent of patients who suffer heart attacks exhibit what is called "Type A" behavior, which is characterized by time urgency (the compulsion to finish tasks early, be early for appointments, and always race against the clock), attempts to perform several tasks at once, the propensity to anger quickly when others don't perform as expected, and rapid speech and body movements (Friedman and Rosenman 1974).

The patients in Friedman's Recurrent Coronary Prevention Project learned to control and change their Type A behaviors through such practice drills as the following:

☐ Keep track of what makes you angry, and set it down in writing.

☐ Sometimes play sports to lose, so as to improve your skills or to provide joy for your less-accomplished opponents.
☐ Walk, talk, and eat more slowly.
☐ Buy a small but thoughtfully chosen gift for your spouse or a family member.
☐ Leave your watch off.
☐ Stop trying to think or do more than one thing at a time.
☐ Start smiling at other people and laughing at yourself.
☐ If you see someone doing a job more slowly than you know you would do it yourself, do not interfere.
☐ Deliberately say "Maybe I'm wrong" to someone at least twice today, even when you are not at all certain that you are in error.
☐ Try to hear out at least two persons on separate occasions without interrupting even once.

Here are some other suggestions, techniques, and activities that may be helpful:

1. *Establish priorities*. It is important for each of us to determine where to put our time and energies. When we deal with situations and stresses as they occur, we become the victims of our surroundings. Instead, establish a daily or weekly priority list, including everything that is to be done. Those tasks with the highest priority should be accomplished first. If time is limited,

these *life-change events* and determining which had more or less effect on illness, the researchers asked a number of people to rate each of 43 events in terms of the amount of readjustment required (Holmes and Rahe 1967). From these ratings they developed the Social Readjustment Rating Scale (SRRS), on which the events were ranked from those requiring the most readjustment to those requiring the least. The ratings and rankings were found to be highly reliable, regardless of sex, race, or income. As shown in the left-hand column of Table 8.1 (p. 222), the death of a spouse was rated as requiring the greatest ad-

learn to postpone those of less importance without feeling guilty.

2. *Avoid stressful situations.* Do not place yourself in situations that involve unnecessary stress. For example, if you find that a particular traffic route involves constant tie-ups, consider another time for your commuting or take another route. If your study room has inadequate lighting, consider purchasing an inexpensive reading lamp. If you are distracted and irritated by inconsiderate or noisy roommates, take action to leave them. Remember, we can and do have control over "hassles." It's amazing how many of us accept situations as they are without considering constructive actions.

3. *Take time out for you.* We all need to engage in activities that bring pleasure and gratification. Whether they involve going fishing, playing cards, talking to friends, or taking a vacation, they are necessary for physical and mental health. And they give the body time to recover from the stresses of everyday life.

4. *Exercise regularly.* Exercise is effective in reducing anxiety and increasing our tolerance for stress. Furthermore, a healthy body gives us greater energy to cope with stress and greater ability to recover from a stressful situation. There is evidence that modest exercise prolongs life, lowers high blood pressure, lowers cholesterol, and releases endorphins, our body's natural opi-

ates, which are useful in combatting stress-related depression.

5. *Eat right.* You've heard this advice before, but it happens to be excellent advice: Eat well-balanced meals that are high in fiber and protein but low in fat and cholesterol. Nutritional deficiencies can lower our resistance to stress. Stress may alter your normal body chemistry, resulting in a change in your nutritional requirements. But if you feel physically fit and are at your normal weight, you will be better able to cope with stress.

6. *Make friends.* Research shows that married people are more likely to live longer than people who are single, divorced, or widowed. Evidence also indicates that loners are three times more likely to die prematurely and are at significantly greater risk of physical and mental disease. So friendship may be a valuable prescription against stress. Good friends share our problems, accept us as we are, and laugh and cry with us. Their very presence enables us to reduce or eliminate much of the stress we may be experiencing.

7. *Learn to relax.* A major finding in stress management is that tense and "uptight" individuals are more likely to react negatively to stress than relaxed individuals. Relaxation can do much to combat the autonomic effects of anxiety and stress; thus the various relaxation techniques are helpful in eliminating stress.

Table 8.1 *Life Events Ranked in Order of Stress Potential.* Ranks are based on ratings of readjustment requirements. LCU values are derived from hospital reports.

Rank	Social Readjustment Rating Scale Life Event	LCU, Mean Value
1	Death of spouse	100
2	Divorce	73
3	Marital separation	65
4	Jail term	63
5	Death of close family member	63
6	Personal injury or illness	53
7	Marriage	50
8	Fired at work	47
9	Marital reconciliation	45
10	Retirement	45
11	Change in health of family member	44
12	Pregnancy	40
13	Sex difficulties	39
14	Gain of new family member	39
15	Business readjustment	39
16	Change in financial state	38
17	Death of close friend	37
18	Change to different line of work	36
19	Change in number of arguments with spouse	35
20	Mortgage over $10,000	31
21	Foreclosure of mortgage or loan	30
22	Change in responsibilities at work	29
23	Son or daughter leaving home	29
24	Trouble with in-laws	29
25	Outstanding personal achievement	28
26	Wife begins or stops work	26
27	Begin or end school	26
28	Change in living conditions	25
29	Revision of personal habits	24
30	Trouble with boss	23
31	Change in work hours or conditions	20
32	Change in residence	20
33	Change in schools	20
34	Change in recreation	19
35	Change in church activities	19
36	Change in social activities	18
37	Mortgage or loan less than $10,000	17
38	Change in sleeping habits	16
39	Change in number of family get-togethers	15
40	Change in eating habits	15
41	Vacation	13
42	Christmas	12
43	Minor violations of the law	11

SOURCE: Holmes, T.H., and Rahe, R.H. (1967). The Social Readjustment Rating Scale. *Journal of Psychosomatic Research,* II 213–218. Reprinted with permission. Copyright © 1967, Pergamon Press, Ltd.

justment. Divorce, marital separation, and a jail term followed in that order. The least stressful event was a minor law violation.

Next, from hospital data collected over a 10-year period, each of the life events was given a numerical value that corresponds to its strength as a stressor (Wyler, Masuda, and Holmes 1971). These "stress potential" values are referred to as *life-change units* (LCUs). As shown in the rightmost column of Table 8.1, the death of a spouse was assigned 100 LCUs, divorce 73, and so on.

The investigators found that 93 percent of health problems (infections, allergies, bone and muscle injuries, and psychosomatic illness) occurred in patients who, during the previous year, had been exposed to events whose LCU values totaled 150 or more. Although a minor life change was not sufficient to constitute a serious stressor, the cumulative impact of many events could be considered a crisis. Particularly revealing was the finding that exposure to a greater number of LCUs increased the chances of illness. Of those exposed to mild crises (150 to 199 LCUs), 37 percent reported illness; to moderate crises (200 to 299 LCUs), 51 percent; and to major crises (more than 300 LCUs), 79 percent.

Other studies not only support these findings but indicate that, when the life crisis is more severe, more serious illnesses also result: A high life-change score was likely to be associated with the more severe chronic diseases (leukemia, cancer, and cardiac attack). Constant stress and the activity of coping may lower a person's resistance to disease; when that happens, illness may result (Masuda and Holmes 1976; Rahe 1968).

> Janet M., a college freshman, had always been a top-notch student in her small-town high school and had been valedictorian of her graduating class. Her SAT test scores placed her in the ninety-fifth percentile of all students taking the exam. Her social life was in high gear from the moment she arrived on the Berkeley campus. Yet Janet was suffering. It started with a cold that she seemed unable to shake. During her first quarter, she was hospitalized once with the "flu" and then three weeks later for "exhaustion." In high school Janet had appeared vivacious, outgoing, and relaxed; at Berkeley she became increasingly tense, anxious, and depressed.

What was happening to Janet is often seen, to various degrees, among entering college students. Going to college is a major life change for students and may result in stress. Most students are able to cope with the demands, but others need direct help. In Janet's case, all the classic symptoms of stress were present. No single stressor was responsible, but rather a series of life changes had had a cumulative impact. An examination of Janet's intake interview notes at the Counseling Center revealed the following stressors:

1. Change from a relatively conservative small-town environment to a more permissive atmosphere on a liberal campus
2. Change from being the top student in her high school class to being a slightly-above-average one at Berkeley
3. Change in living accommodations from a home with a private room to a dormitory with a roommate
4. Change from being completely dependent on family finances to having to work part-time for her education
5. Change from having a steady boyfriend in her home town to being unpaired
6. Change in family stability (her father recently lost his job, and her parents seem headed for divorce)
7. Change in food intake from home-cooked meals to dormitory food and quick snacks

Though each of these changes may seem small and relatively insignificant by itself, their cumulative impact can be anything but insignificant. You might want to use Table 8.1 to approximate Janet's LCU "score."

How about psychological disorders? Are they correlated with life changes, as biological disorders are? The answer seems to be that certain psychological disorders, such as acute schizophrenia, depression, anxiety, and suicidal behavior, also follow the occurrence of stressful life events (Holmes and Masuda 1974; Hudgens 1974; Paykel 1974; Brown 1974). And the numbers of events experienced seem to be correlated with different disorders (Paykel 1974). Suicide attempters report the highest numbers of stressful events, then depressives, and then schizophrenics. With regard to anxiety disorders, a linear relationship exists between the number of stressors experienced and the severity of the symptoms; the greater the number of stressors, the more severe the symptoms.

Clearly, stressful life events *do* play some part in the occurrence of physical and psychological illnesses in many people. Yet it is too soon to say that one is caused by the other. Most of the studies that have been cited are retrospective and correlational in nature, so no cause–effect relationship can be inferred. In addition, the data used in the studies depend on (1) people's perceptions of health and illness, (2) their recollections and reports of illness (both psychological and physical), and (3) their health histories over a defined period of time (Mechanic 1974). Furthermore, the illnesses of many individuals do not appear to be preceded by identifiable stressors, and some people who experience stressful life events do not seem to become ill. Finally, there is now evidence that positive and negative life events do not have equal effects and that personal interpretations or characteristics modify the impact of life changes (Lazarus 1983; Kobasa, Hilker, and Maddi 1979; Sarason, Johnson, and Seigel 1978). Obviously, further investigation of the relationship between life changes and illness is necessary. We need to know *what events* influence *what illnesses* under *what conditions* and through *what processes* (Mechanic 1974).

The transaction model

The GAS model is concerned with the process by which the body reacts to stressors, and the life-change model is concerned with external events that cause stress as a response. But neither of these models takes into consideration the person's subjective definition or interpretation of stressful events or life changes. R. S. Lazarus (1966) argued that a number of processes intervene between the stressor and the development of stress. In particular, the thoughts we have about impending threats (stressors), the emotions we attach to them, and the actions we take to avoid them can either increase or decrease the impact of stressors. In his classic book *Psychological Stress and the Coping Process* (1969, 1983), Lazarus formulated a **transaction model** of stress. He noted that stress resides neither in the person alone nor in the situation alone, but is a transaction between the two. Let us use an example to illustrate this point:

> On the morning of August 16, 1984, Mrs. Marva B. discovered a small lump near the left side of her right breast. She immediately contacted her doctor and made an appointment to see him. After examining her, the physician stated that the lump could be a cyst or a tumor. He recommended a biopsy, which revealed that the tumor was malignant.
>
> Mrs. B. accepted the news with some trepidation but went about her life with minimal disruption. When she was questioned about the way in which she was handling the situation, she replied, in essence, that there is no denying that this is a serious illness, and there is great ambiguity in the prognosis; but people are successfully treated for cancer, she planned to undergo treatment, and she would not give up.

Unlike Mrs. B., many patients would have been horrified at even the thought of having cancer. The news that the tumor was malignant would have been viewed as a catastrophe. Thoughts of dying would have arisen; all hope might have been abandoned. This sort of reaction differs from Mrs. B.'s in how the individual *perceives and copes with* the stressor via internal processes.

Support for the transaction model has come from several quarters. We shall examine three supporting lines of research, which deal with the effect of the desirability of life changes, with "hardiness," and with cognitive adaptation.

Desirable versus undesirable life changes   Recall that one of the primary assumptions in the life-change studies was that change alone, not its desirability or undesirability, is the important determinant of stress. To test this assumption, one group of researchers developed a Life Experience Survey in which they assessed the impact of desirable and undesirable changes. What they found did not confirm this hypothesis (Sarason, Johnson, and Siegal 1978). Undesirable life changes *were* correlated with various measures of anxiety, depression, and psychosomatic symptoms, but the positive changes appeared unrelated to them. Thus it would appear that, in most cases, negative life changes are more detrimental than positive life changes.

The "hardiness" factor   In support of the transaction model, Kobasa, Hilker, and Maddi (1979) formulated a concept that they call the *hardiness factor*. They were particularly upset with the advice, based on life-change studies, that people avoid stress in order to stay healthy. Kobasa and Maddi believe that whether novelty (change) is good or bad depends on how it is experienced. Even Hans Selye, who developed the GAS model, has stated that certain kinds of stress, which he calls *eustress,* are good for people (Selye 1956).

Kobasa, Hilker, and Maddi conducted large-scale research on highly stressed executives in various occupations, in an attempt to identify the traits that distinguish those who

Even desirable, positive events can change our lives dramatically. Depending on the individual, these changes may or may not produce stress. Stress produced by negative life changes, however, is far more detrimental than that produced by positive life changes.

handle stress well from those who do not. They found that high-stress executives who reported few illnesses exhibited three kinds of hardiness. In their attitudes toward life, these stress-resistant individuals showed an *openness to change,* a feeling of *involvement* or *commitment,* and a *sense of control* over their lives (Kobasa, Hilker, and Maddi 1979).

The most important protective factor correlated with health was one's attitude toward change (or *challenge*). Those who are open to change are more likely to interpret events to their advantage and to reduce their level of stress. For example, suppose two people lose their jobs. The person who is open to change may view this situation as an opportunity to find a new career better suited to his or her abilities. The individual who is not open to change, however, is likely to see it as a devastating event.

The stress-resistant group's high rating on commitment means that they engage in life rather than "hanging back." They are active in their work and in their family lives, and they see their roles as interesting and important. Members of the stress-resistant group also believe they have an impact on their environment (as sense of control). What they do matters and affects the outcome of their lives.

Cognitive adaptation   Taylor (1983) has proposed a theory of *cognitive adaptation* to threatening events that again supports the transaction model of stress. In work with women suffering from breast cancer, Taylor observed adjustment processes revolving around three themes: a search for *meaning* in the experience, an attempt to regain *mastery* over the event, and efforts to *enhance one's self-esteem.*

The search for meaning involves the need to understand why the crisis occurred and its implication for life. For example, 95 percent of the cancer patients studied had explanations about why they developed cancer (stress, carcinogenic agents, heredity, diet, and so on). Many tended to reappraise their lives to add meaning to the event. Positive meaning might be construed as follows:

"You take a long look at your life and realize that many things you thought were important before are totally insignificant. That's probably the major change in my life. What you do is put things into perspective. You find that things like relationships are really the most important things you have—the people you know and your family—everything else is just way down the line." (Taylor 1983, p. 1163)

Negative meaning might be voiced in terms such as these:

"I thought I was a well-cared-for, middle-class woman who chose her doctors carefully and who was doing everything right. I was rather pleased with myself. I had thought I could handle pretty much what came my way. And I was completely shattered. My confidence in myself was completely undermined." (Taylor 1983, p. 1163)

It appears that no particular construed meaning was more functional than any other, but positive meaning produced better psychological adjustment.

Gaining a sense of mastery or control over one's body and life was also a predominant cognitive process in the cancer patients. Two-thirds of the patients believed they could control the course, outcome, and recurrence of the cancer. Most of the efforts at control were mental.

"I believe that if you're a positive person, your attitude has a lot to do with it. I definitely feel I will never get it again."

"I think that if you feel you are in control of it, you can control it up to a point. I absolutely refuse to have any more cancer." (Taylor 1983, p. 1163)

Control was also manifested as changes in lifestyle.

Studies have consistently indicated that threatening events or crises can reduce self-esteem. Taylor found that most cancer patients tended to employ self-enhancement methods to boost their self-esteem. In most cases, they did this by making comparisons with less fortunate others, or with those in worse situations, so as to indicate to themselves that they were relatively well off.

"I think I did extremely well under the circumstances. I know that there are just some women who aren't strong enough, who fall apart and become psychologically disturbed and what have you. It's a big adjustment for them" (Taylor 1983, p. 1165).

"The people I really feel sorry for are those young gals. To lose a breast when you're so young must be awful. I'm 73; what do I need a breast for?" (Taylor 1983, p. 1166)

When no comparison group was easily available, the patients manufactured a less-well-off norm.

Taylor's theory and research strongly support the contention that internal (cognitive) mediating forces enable victims of stress to cope more adequately. In a fascinating description of his own fight with cancer, *The*

Road Back to Health (1984), Neil Fiore notes that he used such cognitive strategies to cope with his illness. Meaning, mastery, and self-enhancement have been consistently observed in cancer patients, rape victims, and victims of other life-threatening events. Additionally, Taylor believes that *illusion* may be essential to normal cognitive functioning (Focus 8.2).

FOCUS 8.2

Healthy Denial: A Means of Coping with Stress

According to Lazarus (1983) and Lazarus and Launier (1979), denial and illusions may not always be pathological. This line of thought runs counter to the belief that a healthy person accurately recognizes what is real in the world. Lazarus (1979) points out that collective illusions ("Government always deals fairly with citizens") and individual illusions ("I am superior to most people in intelligence") add richness and meaning to our lives. This does not negate the fact that *denial* is often pathological. A woman who finds a lump on her breast and denies that it can be cancer may put off seeing a doctor until too late.

Lazarus distinguishes between two different coping responses to stress: problem-solving responses and emotion-focused responses. A *problem-solving response* is an attempt to change the troublesome situation. For example, a person trapped in a house that has just collapsed during an earthquake may handle the anxiety by sizing up the situation and deciding to systematically shout at the top of his or her voice while trying to crawl out. A woman who finds a lump on her breast may become anxious but seek additional clarification through medical examination and advice. In these cases, the circumstances may be changed by means of problem-solving re-

sponses. Some realities, however, cannot be changed. In such cases, emotion-focused modes may be used.

Emotion-focused responses do not alter the relationship between the person and the environment, but they make the person feel better. The most common of these are thinking of something else, distancing, minimizing, and making light of the situation. These defenses are frequently referred to as *intrapsychic* or *cognitive* means of coping.

Traditionally, psychologists have contended that "healthy" people use problem-solving modes, whereas "sick" people use emotion-focused responses. The proponents of "healthy denial" believe that serious sources of stress in life—circumstances for which very little can be done to alleviate the stress—require emotion-focused modes of coping. The healthy person in this case is one who handles his or her feelings through denial. For example, a patient with a terminal illness may choose to deny his or her ultimate fate and sustain hope. According to Lazarus, the competent coper is one who can use problem-solving strategies when something can be done to change the environmental factors that brought on stress, and one who can use denial to soothe feelings when nothing can be done.

STRESSORS IN EVERYDAY LIFE

In our discussions of stressors, we shall follow the lead of DSM-III by distinguishing between common and extraordinary stress-producing events and situations. In this section we discuss the common, everyday, "garden-variety" stressors that we are exposed to simply by living our lives—those that can lead to the adjustment disorders. Then, in the next section, we examine the less common but much more severe stressors that may give rise to the posttraumatic stress disorders.

Social and economic change

In his highly popular book *Future Shock* (1970), Alvin Toffler expounds the thesis that contemporary human beings are exposed to too much change in too short a time. Every day, people are bombarded with a multitude of choices that require instant decisions: from consumer choices to choices of school or job to interpersonal decisions. Coupled with this multitude of choices is the impermanence of people's lifestyles: movable modular architecture, computers that create new information so fast we cannot absorb it, telephone directories that need daily updates to keep pace with the mobility of our society. Our bodies can be renewed with organ and tissue transplants, prosthetics, and facial rejuvenation. Research on human reproduction leads one to imagine a baby marketplace where parents will be able to specify the sex, color, and IQ potential of the children they will have. Human relationships have also become caught up in the rapidity of change; modern marriage in particular reflects the impermanence of "traditional" values. Confronted with computerization, genetic planning, and biotechnology, people find it harder and harder to escape from change. And in the wake of change come stress and tension.

Although human beings have shown themselves to be very adaptive organisms, they have become estranged from their natural biological rhythms and inclinations (Dubos 1965, 1971). Uncontrolled social changes have led to crowding, pollution, ecological imbalance, and economic and energy crises. These—along with higher and higher levels of technology and the competitive, educational, marital, and occupational pressures of modern life—have pushed human beings to their limits. Unless people are able to control change and technology in such a way that the process of biological, mental, and social adaptation can keep pace, they will suffer a breakdown in their ability to relate to their environment and themselves. The result, according to theorists Toffler and Dubos, will be an increase in the incidence of psychopathology.

Psychiatric epidemiology, the study of relationships between immediate environmental stressors and psychopathological reactions, lends credence to this line of thought. For example, Brenner (1969, 1973) has studied the impact of economic change on the rates of mental disturbance and hospitalization among lower socioeconomic groups. His studies show that, from 1922 to 1968, mental hospital admissions rose when the economic situation worsened and decreased when the economy improved. According to Brenner, economic downturns give rise to stress because the people involved have no sense of control over the economy. In a special feature called "Unemployment and Mental Health," the *APA Monitor* (1983) interviewed a number of researchers and practitioners about the human toll of unemployment. Most agreed that an economic recession is highly correlated with increased suicide, homicide, family violence, child abuse, and other mental health problems.

Marital and family difficulties

For many of us, the most significant and intimate human relationships we shall ever experience are our relationships with our spouses and families. Yet marrying, adjusting to marriage, becoming parents, and raising children are fraught with adjustive demands that may be quite stressful.

In a new marriage, even when the couple has known each other or lived together for some time, the partners are often unaware of how different each other's values, beliefs, and lifestyles really are. Differences seem to come out most strongly during child rearing. Most parents want their children to do well, to be happy in life, and to be successful. Yet when they try to be more specific (How does a child become succesful? What is success? When is a child doing well? What will make the child happy?), parents often disagree with one another. The results are conflict and stress. The following case exemplifies some of these conflicts and differences.

Marriage, at its best, can be an enriching and fulfilling experience. At its worst, marriage can be disappointing and tormenting. Either way, the experience requires continual adjustment and readjustment, which can lead to stress.

Mr. and Mrs. T. were seen for marital counseling because of increasing difficulties over how they should raise their eight-year-old son Michael. Prior to the birth of their son, they described their marriage as "happy and fulfilling," but when Michael was born, their relationship suddenly changed. They became increasingly isolated from one another because their discussions turned into disagreements and their disagreements frequently became conflicts. Arguments generally focused on how to raise Michael. Mrs. T., who was raised an Episcopalian, wanted their son to be baptized. She had not attended church regularly during their early marriage, but Mrs. T. now felt it important to expose Michael to a more traditional and systematic moral upbringing. Mr. T., an avowed atheist, felt uncomfortable about his wife's insistence on a religious upbringing for their son. He was especially put off by her request that he too attend services because "we've got to be consistent in how we raise Michael."

They argued about other facets of Michael's upbringing as well. For example, Mr. T. had been quite athletic when he was younger. He was on the all-star basketball team in high school and was a starting guard for his college team. During his junior and senior years he won All-America honors and would probably have played professional ball if not for a knee injury

he sustained in an automobile accident. Sports, athletic prowess, and a competitive spirit were important to him. Mr. T. enrolled his son in the city soccer league at age six, and then volunteered to be the assistant coach of his son's team. He spent long hours of practice with his son, often stressing the importance of winning. When Michael did well, he was praised loudly by his father. When Michael did "poorly," Mr. T. would admonish him for letting another player "beat him." This "winning isn't everything, it's the only thing" attitude greatly upset Mrs. T. She felt that her son and husband were too preoccupied with sports and too concerned about Michael becoming "a man." She was fearful that Michael would develop into a person who was insensitive to the needs of others. When she raised these concerns with the husband, Mr. T. only laughed and stated that it was important for Michael to become independent, to grow up a man and not a sissy.

During counseling, it became apparent that

Mr. and Mrs. T. had never thoroughly explored the effect that their differences might have on their relationship. The things that disturbed them now were things that had attracted them to one another in the beginning. Before the birth of their son, these differences were acknowledged and even viewed as a novelty; they could be compartmentalized as long as Mr. and Mrs. T. were the only ones involved. With the birth of their son, the value differences became real and imposing, and their forced interactions with one another created conflicts and subsequent stress.

Another major source of stress in marriage arises when one partner changes and the other doesn't, or when they change in different ways. For example, when college students marry, it is often not possible for both to continue their education. Even in our somewhat sexually liberated society, it is usually the wife who drops out of school to accept a low-paying job in order to help the husband attain his educational goal. The husband, perhaps a medical student, may then outgrow his wife intellectually and find his campus acquaintances more stimulating. Their circle of friends may change, and the wife may become insecure and jealous, or she may feel that she has been taken advantage of. On the other hand, the husband may have difficulty reconciling the traditional male role with his financial dependence on his wife. He may feel she is blackmailing him, restricting his freedom, and holding him back.

Other major changes in the marital relationship, or in the business–domestic career conflict faced by the wife, can result in stress in a marriage. The following case illustrates some of the dynamics of these situations.

Wendy H. is a 34-year-old stockbroker who works for a large well-known brokerage house in San Francisco. She was married 4 years ago to a highly successful industrial psychologist with a thriving consulting practice. This was her first marriage; it was her husband's third. Wendy recently gave birth to a boy and had to take time off from work because of the pregnancy. Her husband, Fred, had wanted a child badly (he did not have children from his two previous marriages). Although Wendy had also wanted a child, her pregnancy could not have come at a worse time. When she became pregnant, she was being considered for a promotion that she wanted very much. The promotion was given to a male co-worker because, as a fellow female worker sarcastically said to her, "Women aren't reliable. They take time off to have babies and call in sick when their period begins."

In addition to the loss of her promotion, Wendy was becoming increasingly resentful toward Fred, who seemed never to be around when she needed him most. His practice required long hours at the office and frequent trips—a fact he had explained carefully before their marriage. But, although Wendy had accepted this condition at the beginning (she had had her own career), she now felt deserted. After their child was born, her husband had insisted that she take responsibility for finding a full-time housekeeper and making arrangements for child care if she decided to return to work—which she did.

It was in this context that Wendy sought therapy for her feelings of depression, guilt, and anger. The therapist, a well-established psychiatrist, tried to clarify the issues for her: First, her boss promoted a man rather than her for what seemed to be logical reasons. She couldn't blame him for the decision. If she were a client, wouldn't she prefer someone who was always available when major financial decisions had to be made? Second, although her anger toward Fred was understandable, it was not justified; he had made his work demands clear to her before their marriage. Furthermore, wasn't Fred's income nearly five times what Wendy made? Wouldn't it be logical for Wendy to take a more active role in managing the household chores while cutting down on the time she spent at the brokerage firm?

The therapy seemed to help initially, but then Wendy became increasingly depressed and guilt-ridden. Her depression became especially acute several months after she returned to work. Friends and co-workers would make such comments as "Who's taking care of the kid?" or

''You really don't need to work with your husband's income'' or ''If I didn't have to work, I'd quit right now.''

The case of Wendy H. illustrates some of the gender-role conflicts that husbands and wives need to be aware of, as well as the societal pressures that often seem stacked against women who desire careers. Unfortunately, this case also shows how easily an unenlightened therapist can make matters worse.

When a marriage deteriorates to such a painful and unhappy level, divorce or separation may be the result. An estimated 10 million divorces occurred between 1970 and 1980. In most cases, the divorce was a result of continuing conflicts and stress within the marriage and family. Yet the decision to divorce, the process of divorcing, and the postdivorce adjustment are also stressful (Moreland and Schwebel 1981). It is not uncommon for the divorced partner to experience hurt, resentment, and anger. To many people, divorce signifies failure in an extremely important relationship. Lowered self-esteem and feelings of worthlessness and rejection are also common and stress-producing results. If children are involved, the stress can be even greater. Parent–child interactions may become difficult, because the children of divorced families tend to exhibit more inappropriate behavior than those in intact homes (Wallerstein and Kelly 1980). And, when a divorce is contested, our adversarial legal system seems to add to its negative impact and prolong the time needed to adjust (Kressel and Deutsch 1977).

In an effort to eliminate some of the stress-producing elements of the divorce process and its outcome, many couples have chosen an alternative—*divorce mediation.* In mediation, an impartial third party helps to negotiate the conditions of the separation. The mediator deals with all aspects of the divorce, from interpersonal conflicts to the details of the divorce settlement, alimony, and child custody and support (Schwebel et al. 1982).

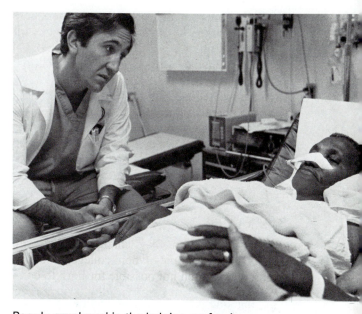

People employed in the helping professions are very susceptible to occupational stress or burnout. A dedicated doctor may feel helpless in the face of terminal or incurable diseases. He may eventually experience a variety of stress reactions.

Occupational demands

Occupational stress, or ''burnout'' as it is often called, may affect people in any occupation. However, it seems to occur most frequently in those service professions wherein workers have continuing contact with others who are in trouble or who have problems (Savicki and Cooley 1982). The symptoms of burnout are like those of other stress reactions; they may involve physical, cognitive, emotional, and behavioral manifestations. Here are some of the major findings concerning burnout:

1. The greater the job intensity, as measured by such factors as length of contact with clients and size of caseload, the greater the probability of burnout (Maslach and Pines 1977). Increasing job intensity often means

less time to spend with fellow workers, less free time, and more stress. Techniques for combatting or alleviating work-related stress include work breaks, work sharing, and job rotation.

2. Burnout also tends to occur when individuals perceive that they have very little control over their work environment. Many organizations routinely exclude workers from partaking in policy decisions that affect those workers' job satisfaction and activities. Burnout can be reduced by involving workers in decisions that affect their work life.

3. The availability of socially supporting co-workers reduces burnout. Fellow workers can be a valuable resource; isolation and the resulting stress can be reduced by sharing one's thoughts and feelings with co-workers.

4. Those in the helping professions who tend to overidentify with, or become overinvolved with, clients may experience greater job stress and burnout. A confusion of boundaries between helper and client can allow the client's problems to become those of the counselor. Strangely, when such burnout occurs, it is not uncommon for the helping professional to shift to the opposite extreme: The client is now seen as depersonalized—a thing rather than an individual—and there is a loss of concern for clients. This depersonalization can become generalized to all aspects of life, including one's family and friends. As a New York City police officer put it,

"You change when you become a cop—you become tough and hard and cynical. You have to condition yourself to be that way in order to survive this job. And sometimes, without realizing it, you act that way all the time, even with your wife and kids. But it's something you have to do, because if you start getting emotionally involved with what happens at work, you'll wind up in Bellevue [psychiatric hospital]. (Maslach and Jackson 1979, p. 59)

Job burnout and its prevention have received increased attention in recent years. Among the responses to this phenomenon are the teaching of stress-reduction techniques to workers, job-enrichment programs, in-plant exercise facilities, and fundamental organizational and policy-making changes based on an awareness of the workplace as a potential stress producer.

Adjustment to middle age

The term *middle-age crisis* usually calls up the image of a middle-aged man who gives up his job and family to run off with a much younger woman in hopes of recapturing his youth. Unfortunately, although it touches on the conflicts involved in the middle-adulthood transition stage, this image masks the stressors that all of us—male and female—will face or have faced already.

At some point between the ages of thirty and fifty, each and every individual recognizes that he or she is beginning to age. This realization does not occur suddenly but rather develops from a series of events within the vocational, marital, civic, physical, social, and economic spheres.

Most people reach their peak occupational status in their forties. Then their morale may begin to decline when they realize that advancement will no longer be forthcoming and that at least some of their vocational goals and hopes will not be realized. Their physical and mental abilities may begin to decline, and they see younger, more vigorous co-workers promoted to better jobs. At the same time, it becomes more difficult to make progress in leisure pursuits, and familiar recreational activities seem less satisfying.

A gradual reduction of physical energy is noticed during middle age. Eyesight and hearing may fail, weight gains are the rule, strength and psychomotor speed decrease, and recovery from physical exertion is slower than it has been. Sexual arousal also occurs less readily in the middle-aged adult, and sexual activity may decrease.

For people whose hopes and aspirations now seem unattainable, and whose identities and self-concept seem very much linked to their early adulthood period, the recognition that one is barely holding on or is losing ground can be quite painful. Middle age can be an extremely stressful period, during which people react with disillusionment, anxiety, and concern. Some may suddenly return—with a vengeance—to the activities of their youth. They may become interested in body building and physical fitness, change their life-styles by dressing in youthful clothing or buying a sports car, change jobs abruptly, or take up with a younger man or woman. Such actions and activities seem to be strategies for avoiding the inevitable realization that we are all aging.

EXTRAORDINARY STRESSORS

Here we discuss two relatively uncommon, but nonetheless too common, stress-producing conditions—catastrophe and war. There are many others, the most notable nowadays being violence and the threat of violence. They all have in common the capability of producing, through a single event or situation, a posttraumatic stress disorder.

Catastrophes

Devastating earthquakes, tidal waves, hurricanes, fires, ship and train wrecks, plane crashes, and wartime bombing raids—each of these situations imposes severe stress on survivors. It is no little wonder that most people who are exposed to such situations exhibit some form of temporary personality disintegration.

Two seafaring examples that illustrate the effects of stress on the individual were the 1912 sinking of the "unsinkable" *Titanic* and the 1956 collision of the luxury liner *Andrea Doria* with the Swedish liner *Stockholm,* which caused the *Andrea Doria* to sink. In a vivid description of the *Titanic* disaster, which took the lives of 1503 persons, Lord (1955) reported that terror-stricken survivors who were lucky enough to make it to lifeboats refused to let swimmers aboard, even though their boats were only half full. Boat occupants beat off the struggling swimmers with oars, and only 1 of 18 lifeboats returned to the scene to help others. Taking advantage of the traditional law of the sea ("women and children first"), at least one man donned a dress in an attempt to save himself. Another man changed into evening dress and sat in the lounge listening to the ship's orchestra, which continued to play until the end.

An insightful account of the psychological reactions of the *Andrea Doria* survivors was published by two psychiatrists who were on a rescue ship (Friedman and Linn 1957). The survivors appeared sedated; they moved extremely slowly, were passive, compliant, and suggestible, and showed signs of memory loss concerning the event. After some time had passed, many exhibited a preoccupation with the tragedy and a compulsive need to tell the story of the collision over and over.

Similarly, the trauma of a natural disaster may cause long-standing psychological scars. Adams and Adams (1984) reported that residents of a small town near the Mt. St. Helens eruption and ashfall of 1980 showed long-term mental disturbance (see Focus 5.1). In 1953 a tornado struck San Angelo, Texas, taking 11 lives, injuring more than 150 people, and destroying or damaging 500 homes. A year later another tornado struck the same town. Among residents interviewed after the first tornado, 73 percent reported that some family member was suffering emotionally. After the second storm, 50 percent of those interviewed said

A skywalk bridge collapsed, killing 114 people and injuring 200 others in the Kansas City Hyatt Regency hotel on July 17, 1981. Victims, observers, and rescuers all exhibited psychological symptoms of stress in response to the disaster.

they had had emotional problems during the entire time between the two storms (Moore 1958). A later study indicated that the family social system is critical in determining reactions to a tornado experience (Perry 1956). Mothers who "went to pieces," wept, and became hysterical made the experience worse for their children. (See, for example, the self-reported behavior of the earthquake victim at the beginning of this chapter.) Furthermore, supportive mothers who cuddled and reassured their children came through the experience in much better shape themselves.

It appears that one does not have to be a direct victim of a catastrophe to exhibit psychological problems. An observer or a person involved in a rescue attempt can also be affected by the horror of the event. Such a case was reported by Wilkinson (1983), who studied the aftermath of the collapse of the Hyatt

Regency Hotel skywalks. The event occurred on Friday, July 17, 1981, in Kansas City during a dance. It was estimated that some 2000 people were present. Many were on the dance floor, and others were dining and watching the dancers. At approximately 7:05 P.M., two of the three skywalk bridges at the second and fourth levels collapsed, cascading an estimated 65 tons of steel and concrete onto the crowded lobby floor. The result was utterly gruesome; 114 people were killed and 200 persons were injured. Wilkinson surveyed victims, observers, and rescuers in a follow-up study some 5 months later. Virtually all the subjects exhibited psychological symptoms, and only slight differences were observed among the three groups.

Panic Immediate reactions to a disaster vary among individuals. About 10 to 20 percent of those involved remain calm and collected; 70 percent are likely to become confused and stunned; and another 20 percent may show extreme anxiety and panic (Moore 1958). Panic, however, is less common among victims of a disaster than might be expected.

Observations and studies of panic behavior indicate that panic arises in certain specific conditions (Lazarus 1966, 1983; Lazarus and Launier 1979). What a person does in a dangerous situation depends on (1) his or her assessment of the extent of the danger, (2) the availability of coping alternatives, and (3) the existence of, and practice in, prearranged plans for dealing with the threat. In holocausts like the 1903 Iroquois Theatre fire in Chicago, the 1942 Coconut Grove fire in Boston, and the 1977 Beverly Hills Supper Club fire in Southgate, Kentucky, hundreds of people were trampled to death or asphyxiated rather than burned. In the rush to get out, panic-stricken people jammed all the exits. In each case, people's assessment of the situation indicated great danger, the only available means of coping was flight toward the exits, and there were no prearranged plans for escape.

Mintz's (1951) classic study of panic indicates that an additional factor should be considered. Mintz was able to show that cooperation among individuals reduced traffic jams at an entrance and that competition increased it. If people perceive that they have no hope of escaping by behaving in a civilized way, panic is likely. Other investigators have found that the chance of panic is greater when the threat is greater or when the threatened group is larger (because then, individuals perceive their chances of escape as being poor). However, if people see others willing to wait and behave rationally, the likelihood of panic is reduced (Kelley et al. 1965).

The disaster syndrome   The typical response to a catastrophe has been called the **disaster syndrome** (Wallace 1956; Raher, Wallace, and Raymer 1956). It consists of three succeeding stages, or reactions.

☐ *Shock reaction.* During the initial stage, survivors exhibit a type of mental paralysis and confusion about what has actually happened. Disorientation, stupor, and amnesia may be characteristic of these people. They may wander about silently, like automatons, or they may recount losses of family members without apparent concern. In the shock stage, lamentations or tears are seldom seen unless physical injury is present. Even with injuries, some may be unaware of the extent and seriousness of their physical condition. Psychologists speculate that, under extreme stress, psychological forces are set in operation that protect the person from the full impact of the experience. He or she appears to be in a daze.

☐ *Recoil reaction.* During the recoil stage, the survivor emerges from the state of shock and discovers that the danger is over but that life must be faced. Facing life often means coping with severe losses—close family members gone or property destroyed. Emotionality, ranging from sobbing and giggling to anger, hostility, irritability, and feelings of hopelessness, frequently results. People in this stage begin to exhibit outward concern for themselves and others and will generally follow directions. Psychological help at this point has maximum effect. There is a strong need to vent feelings about the tragic event.

☐ *Recall reaction.* In this stage survivors are filled with memories of the horrifying experience and are likely to be tense and restless. Sleeplessness, nightmares, and a compulsion to recount the disaster in detail, over and over again, are common. It is as though the person needs to relive the entire event in order to control and desensitize the experience of the trauma. Intense emotional upsets, anxiety, and hypersensitivity are frequently seen.

Fortunately, long-term psychological catastrophes are more the exception than the rule. For example, trauma after the saturation bombings in Great Britain and Germany during World War II did not lead to an increase in mental hospitalization rates, suicides, or alcoholism (U.S. Strategic Bombing Survey 1945). Some of the reactive disorders that resulted might have been alleviated by prompt psychotherapy. In other cases, it is believed that those who were most acutely affected were probably people who had previously made less-than-satisfactory adjustments to life.

Military combat

The anxiety-provoking conditions of war make heavy demands on a soldier's emotional adjustment. The entire military experience involves stress, from induction through training camp to being shipped overseas and the prospect of battle. For many the trauma of combat is added, with its constant physical and psychological threat.

Some soldiers who enter combat may not be fearful at first. However, they soon learn to anticipate harm when they see the damage that can be done by firepower. Under such pressure, some soldiers may exhibit what has been called "shell shock," "war neurosis," "combat fatigue," or "combat exhaustion." In World War II, 50 percent or more of air crews who flew repeated combat missions eventually developed severe symptoms of combat neuroses (Grinker and Spiegel 1945). Similar statistics were found to apply to ground forces (Lewis and Engle 1954), leading to the conclusion that combat exhaustion caused the greatest single loss of troops during World War II (Bloch 1969). On the basis of World War II experience, military psychiatrists were able to institute procedural changes that diminished the number of psychological casualties in the Korean and Vietnam conflicts (Horowitz and Solomon 1975). These changes will be disucssed shortly.

Combat symptoms   Symptoms of the *precombat syndrome* were most typically found in troops on the eve of a battle (Johnson 1969). Men would report to medical officers with imaginary hypochondriacal complaints (which they believed to be real) of headache, toothache, indigestion, fatigue, and worry over past wounds. In most cases, the precombat syndrome can be attributed to the soldier's unconscious or consicous desire to avoid the impending combat.

Of the nonmedically caused disorders reported during a 6-month period in Vietnam, only 5 percent were well-defined psychoses (Bowman 1967). The majority of cases represented behaviors or symptoms that would temporarily remove the soldier from combat. Among these were *somnambulism* (sleepwalking), anxiety dreams, *syncope* (loss of consciousness) and vertigo, narcolepsy-like complaints and seizures, blurred vision, and *aphonia* (loss of speech). Disabling psychological symptoms usually developed after hospitalization if they were not present on admission; these symptoms tended to persist and increase in severity. Again, the implication is that the presence of these symptoms prevented the soldier from returning to combat.

In rare instances, self-inflicted wounds were reported among soldiers. While often minor, the injury served to remove the soldier from the feared situation. That the wound was self-inflicted is supported by observations that soldiers so wounded were less likely than others to show anxiety and combat exhaustion symptoms (Tuohy 1967). A wound provided an "honorable way out" of the stressful combat situation.

Menninger (1948) identified a constellation of physical symptoms, which he calls the *normal battle reaction,* among infantry soldiers. Approximately 50 percent experienced a pounding heart, 45 percent a sinking stomach, 30 percent cold sweat, 25 percent nausea, 25 percent shakiness and tremulousness, 25 percent stiff muscles, 20 percent vomiting, 20 percent general weakness, 10 percent involuntary bowel movement, and 6 percent involuntary urination.

A triad of psychological symptoms seen in World War II (Bartemeier et al. 1946) were also seen in Korea and Vietnam:

1. Extreme signs of *irritability* are common among soldiers who experience combat exhaustion. They may overreact to minor vexations by becoming snappish or angry, by uttering a stream of profane language, or even by becoming tearful. Bartemeier and co-workers report the incident of a soldier becoming angry when one of his comrades unwrapped a piece of candy and crumpled up the cellophane; the noise sounded to him like a forest fire. Hypersensitivity to minor external disturbances may produce jumpiness, involuntary twitches of the body, and sudden leaping.
2. The *startle reaction* to noise, sudden movement, and light flashes is indicative of overvigilance in preparation for fight or flight.
3. *Sleep disturbances*—insomnia, recurrent dreams, or nightmares—almost always are associated with hypersensitivity.

In many instances, combat experiences and the stress of military life may promote uncontrollable anger, which is manifested in acts of violence and aggression that are ordinarily considered atrocities. The looting, torture, and outright murder seen during warfare may be due to the purposeful dehumanization of the enemy; the fear that anyone, of any age or sex, civilian or not, can be responsible for the soldier's death; the feelings of hatred and anger that are aroused by battle; and the promotion of aggression in combat training.

Military psychology The Vietnam war had the lowest incidence ever (12 cases per 1000 troops per year) of combat psychiatric casualties. Much of the improvement is attributed to preventive treatment policies developed from experience in previous wars and instituted in Vietnam. These policies are based on the concepts of immediacy, expectancy, simplicity, and centrality (Jones and Johnson 1975).

The term *immediacy* refers to the early treatment of combat fatigue, in its initial stages. Immediate intervention is aimed at preserving the soldier's identification with the interests of the group and submerging his feelings of self-preservation. These latter feelings tend to result in symptoms that take the soldier out of action. Because the patient is quite suggestible at this level, immediate intervention tends to be quite effective.

Expectancy, simply stated, is the attitude that all patients *will return to duty* and that the importance of the symptoms is minimal. The idea of illness and the temptation to avoid combat are thus neutralized. Behind this principle is the belief that patients respond with symptoms according to their image of what is expected of them.

On practical grounds, lengthy and complicated forms of treatment are not often possible in a combat area. Beyond that, however, (Freidman and Rosenman 1959) *simplicity* in treatment also conveys to the soldier an impression of normalcy and of the minor nature of the illness, and it encourages the expectation of recovery. Treatment consists of rest, food, drink, mild sedation, verbal reassurance, and the encouragement of open expression. The rationale for this approach is that the soldier's condition is due to immediate external circumstances, so attempts to uncover lifelong patterns of maladjustment are unproductive.

The term *centrality* refers to the placement of psychiatric facilities close to the battlefront and close to medical treatment facilities. Seeing a psychiatrist delivering the same type of therapeutic effort as other physicians, and in the same place, provides the soldier with the best expectation of successful treatment. In most cases, soldiers were treated as near to the combat unit as possible. It was found that soldiers removed from the combat zone for treatment had a more difficult time returning to battle. In fact, removal seemed to encourage the maintenance of symptoms (Menninger 1948).

Long-term psychological effects The majority of combat fatigue cases show rapid recovery after a period of mild supportive psychotherapy, a warm bed, food, and rest. In a minority of cases, however, the residual effects of combat stress tend to persist. A follow-up study revealed that veterans of World War II and the Korean war were more likely than nonveterans to show symptoms of depression, irritability, fatigue, difficulty concentrating, pounding heart, combat dreams, and diarrhea (Archibald and Tuddenham 1965). Findings are similar for Vietnam war veterans (Strange and Brown 1970); however, certain mitigating features of that war may have added to their difficulties in readjusting to civilian life. Popu-

lar movies like *Coming Home* and *The Deerhunter* have dealt with some of these themes.

In addition to experiencing the residual effects of combat stress, the Vietnam veteran returned to a society that rejected his war as well as his sacrifices. There was an unnerving absence of cheering crowds and employers offering jobs. Suicides, drug overdoses, and unemployment among Vietnam veterans were well above national averages (Strayer and Ellenhorn 1975). Many such veterans did not take advantage of the educational opportunities of the GI Bill because they felt alienated from the college scene, which they associated with war protesters. Other students, they sensed, looked at them with disdain for their

FOCUS 8.3

Posttraumatic Stress Disorder in a Vietnam Veteran

Many cases of delayed posttraumatic stress reaction in Vietnam veterans have been documented. The diagnosis is usually reserved for disorders that arise some time after the combat experience. In many instances, the soldiers appear to have performed quite well while in the service. Upon their return home, however, they begin to experience such symptoms as excessive alcohol consumption, irritability, and recurrent nightmares, which may or may not be triggered by some external event. Often the stress response is intimately related to how the person interprets the meaning of combat and war in relationship to his own unique characteristics.

Mr. B was 21 years old and single when he was drafted. He was a model soldier, rated highest in his outfit in basic training. On search-and-destroy missions in Vietnam he was exposed to every imaginable combat

stress, had a confirmed "kill count" of 15, and received many decorations and medals. He dealt with combat by hypervigilance and by a protective reaction toward the men in his squad. He was proud that none of his men were killed while he was in Vietnam.

During the year after he returned home Mr. B developed a severe delayed stress reaction, spent his time drinking, and did not work until his money ran out. His intrusive disturbing thoughts of combat centered first on a Viet Cong soldier whom he had taken prisoner. This prisoner was later transferred to the charge of other troops, who transported him in a helicopter for further interrogation. During this trip the prisoner was pushed out of the helicopter. Mr. B, who was on the ground below, saw him fall. Because Mr. B had captured this prisoner, he felt some responsibility for the prisoner's death and believed that he could have prevented the incident had he been in the helicopter.

Mr. B was even more disturbed by an event that occurred after he had returned

participation in the war (Strayer and Ellenhorn 1975).

Horowitz and Solomon (1975) believe that, over the next few years, mental health professionals will see *posttraumatic stress disorders* in Vietnam veterans (see Focus 8.3). Such delayed stress reactions have frequently been reported in the clinical literature (Christensen et al. 1981; Lacoursiere, Godrey, and Ruby 1980; Hendin et al. 1981). Some studies, however, seem to support the belief that delayed stress reactions are more frequent in Vietnam veterans than in other veterans (Thienes-Hontos, Watson, and Kucala 1982). The reasoning is based on the manner in which severe stress reactions are sometimes manifested over time, combined with the unique aspects of the Vietnam war. Instead of the combat symptoms discussed previously, some persons who are exposed to severe stress exhibit an emotional numbness and denial that interrupt the working-through of the experience to completion (Krystal 1968; Lifton 1970). (This response is similar to the shock reaction seen in civilian disasters; it protects the person from intolerable ideas and emotions.) The denial and numbing may go unobserved.

The shorter periods of combat, the rotation policy, and the wide availability of drugs in Vietnam made it possible for a soldier to enter into and remain in this denial and numbing phase. Thus, according to Horowitz and

home. One of his squad members was sent into a well on a search for Viet Cong firearms and was killed by a booby trap. Mr. B knew he would have grenaded the well instead of ordering it searched. Thus Mr. B felt that, had he remained in Vietnam as squad commander, this particular squad member would not have died.

Mr. B had learned self-sufficiency and protectiveness toward others from his family experience. His parents paid little attention to their children: Mr. B and his older brother and sister raised themselves and tried to support one another. When Mr. B was 4 years old, his mother was hospitalized for a "nervous breakdown."

As Mr. B grew up, he learned to deal with his feelings by himself. Consequently, he found it difficult to express what he felt in his work or in his marriage. His resentment of his enforced self-sufficiency was reflected by his irritation with irresponsible co-workers and perhaps in his own frequently mentioned fantasies of not having to work.

Although he had experienced overpowering frustration of his early needs for care and attention, he managed a successful adaptation by becoming self-sufficient and responsible and not sharing his feelings with others. While he was in Vietnam, Mr. B's sense of responsibility widened into the protective role he adopted toward his men, permitting him to repress the fears generated by combat. Yet combat threatened this lifelong adaptation, making him vulnerable in a particular way to the death of his squad member and of the prisoner he had captured.

The meaning of combat for Mr. B is illuminated by the adaptation which he continues in civilian life. For instance, he joined the Veterans of Foreign Wars to help raise money for better services for veterans. It is significant that Mr. B's becoming a father coincided with a marked lessening of his stress symptoms and the end of his excessive drinking. He still suffered from some stress symptoms, such as his need to hide his emotions and the particular irritability he felt toward others who were not as responsible as he was. (Hendin et al. 1981, p. 1491)

Many veterans of the Vietnam war are still experiencing the emotional and psychological after-effects of combat or even posttraumatic stress disorder. The combination of combat stress and the national ambivalence toward the war may be partial causes of the problems. These soldiers are in a foxhole during the battle to recapture Khe Sanh in 1968.

Soloman (1975), some veterans in whom symptoms have not appeared may still harbor great rage that could erupt in violence or depression.

FACTORS THAT DETERMINE THE SEVERITY OF STRESS

In our discussions of stress models and stress-producing situations, we have identified a number of factors that determine the degree to which the individual experiences stress. We can summarize the effects of those factors as follows:

1. *When people anticipate or experience physical or psychological pain, they are likely to experience stress.* Victims of natural disasters, people who have been taken hostage, and those in concentration camps often describe their ordeal as one of "constant fear for their lives." When torture is part of a person's incarceration, there is not only the anticipation of physical harm but also actual bodily injury. However, the sources of psychological pain are not limited to the fear and anxiety that arise in such situations. Even a threat to one's self-esteem, as in a divorce or illness, can produce pain and stress.

2. *The more life changes a person experiences during a given period of time, the greater the probability of stress.* A person who has recently seen a loved one die, has been involved in a bitter divorce, and has recently lost his or her job experiences greater stress than the person who has only had the misfortune of losing a parent. These are obviously stressful events, but, as we have noted, life changes need not be massive disruptions to be stressful. A series of minor events may have a cumulative effect that is strong enough to warrant being termed a "life crisis." For example, research now reveals that such seemingly minor changes as moving to a new

home or going on a vacation can add stress to one's life. We are almost forced to conclude that stress is inevitable, because life requires continual change.

3. *As the level of stress increases, the more likely it is that personality decompensation will occur.* This statement is supported by life-change studies and clinical observations of victims of catastrophes, panic, and war. For example, a study of personnel assigned to wartime bombing missions indicated that greater danger causes more severe reactive stress (Thompkins 1959). However, there often is a difference between the actual severity of danger and one's appraisal of that danger. In addition, individuals vary in their ability to tolerate perceived stress.

4. *The fewer social supports a person has (friends, peers, family, and interpersonal communications), the greater the stress he or she feels in a potentially dangerous situation.* In a disaster, friends and relatives may be missing or killed. In less dramatic situations such as divorce, job loss, and the death of a loved one, the individual may become separated from his or her friends or family members. In such cases, stress may be increased. On the other hand, reassurance and support from others tend to reduce fear and panic. We have already seen that mothers who cuddled their children and talked to them calmly during a tornado minimized the trauma for their children and for themselves. And we noted that panic is noticeably reduced when individuals are able to observe others cooperating and acting calmly.

5. *The more limited the number of available coping responses in a threatening situation, the greater the stress experienced.* When numerous options are perceived to be available for dealing with a stressful situation, people are likely to feel that the probability of eliminating the threat is high. When options are limited, however, people may see that probability as being low. There is then a sense of helplessness and loss of control of the situa-

tion. Thus, for example, panic is more likely when a burning building has only one exit than when it has many. But people who see no options at all may experience a sense of hopelessness, rather than panic, and give up. Prisoners of war who could find no way to escape or otherwise deal with their internment sank into apathy and depression (and in some cases, death). The band members on the *Titanic,* who sat together and played "Nearer My God to Thee" as their ship sank, were also experiencing this sense of hopelessness.

6. *The greater the ambiguity or suddenness of the situation, the greater the potential for stress.* Major catastrophes are overwhelming because people's previously learned means of coping become inadequate. There is no time to prepare for the problem or to practice new skills to deal with it. Not knowing what is about to happen evokes considerable anxiety. This anxiety is especially acute in cases of kidnapping and hostage-taking.

7. *The amount of stress that an individual experiences depends very much on the emotional characteristics of the individual.* Studies have revealed that some people are more emotionally immune to stress than others. This "immunity factor" has been called *hardiness, ego strength,* and *ability to cope.* It appears to help buffer life events, reducing their stressfulness and ensuring continued good psychological and physical health.

RESISTING STRESS

What can people do to resist the build-up of stress or to reduce the severity of stressful situations and events? Focus 8.1 provides some suggestions that can be implemented in everyday life. In addition, our summary of the effects of stress-determining factors suggests four more techniques: practice, preparation, the reduction of ambiguity, and reliance on social support and reassurance.

Practice

Victims of civilian disasters, combat, and imprisonment are thrown into situations that most have never encountered before. They are often at a complete loss about how to deal with them. Old patterns of behavior are not effective, and effective modes of coping have not been learned. Furthermore, considerable confusion and disorientation may occur in a disaster. Unless a coping behavior has been well learned and rehearsed, the victim is likely to be in such a state of shock that he or she can become immobilized.

One revealing experiment involving the role of practice or experience in combating stress was reported by Epstein (1962). A group of experienced parachutists (each with 100 or more jumps) and inexperienced parachutists (with fewer than 5 jumps each) were asked to rate the amount of anxiety they felt at different times: one week before a jump, the morning of the jump, when boarding, at the ready signal, during the fall, and on landing. The results indicated that the inexperienced jumpers' anxiety steadily increased until they jumped, whereas the experienced jumpers reached the high point of anxiety on the morning of the jump, and their anxiety declined quickly from that point.

Practice tends to increase coping skills, to reduce uncertainty, and to enhance one's confidence that one can deal with a situation successfully. Fire drills in public schools reflect the importance of practice in reducing panic and stress. The armed forces have also instituted programs that prepare personnel for survival as prisoners of war. Simulated capture and interrogation prepare the soldier for what to expect and *what to do* if captured.

Preparation against harm

When people know the type of threat they are likely to encounter and the probability of its occurrence, they can take specific actions to reduce or eliminate the danger. For example, storm shelters can be built against tornadoes, dams can be used against floods, increased studying can guard against the possibility of failing an exam, and so on. About one-third of the residents of San Angelo, Texas, built storm shelters after the first tornado struck. Interviews indicated that these families exhibited less fear during the subsequent storm.

Reduction of ambiguity

Before one can prepare against harm, one needs to know what to expect. Human beings (and animals) prefer predictable aversive events (Seligman 1975); high anxiety is likely to result when the situation is ambiguous.

People placed in a confused or disoriented situation have a strong need to clarify the situation by actively seeking information. Sometimes the unknown is much more frightening than a known threat. For example, a young boy well known to one of the authors found going to the dentist an anxiety-provoking event. The dentist would hide the instruments behind his back (so as not to frighten the child) and then slowly approach the boy, instructing him to open his mouth. The author can recall vividly how the boy entreated the dentist to tell him what was going to happen. An evasive answer only served to heighten the fear. Later the same boy, now a young man, went to another dentist who explained—step by step—what he was going to do. Even after he told the young man that there would be some pain involved in the process, the patient's anxiety was never so great as it had been when he did not know what was about to happen.

Preparatory information tends to give the individual a feeling of cognitive control by allowing him or her to classify events and situations into expectations: Researchers tested the value of providing surgical patients with preparatory explanations about the expected type and duration of postoperative pain. About half of a large group of patients were given this type of preparatory information, while the other half received only minimal information. The fully prepared patients recovered more quickly and experienced less pain and discomfort. Their mental rehearsal of the after effects of surgery acted to reduce novelty and surprise (Egbert et al. 1964).

As noted in Focus 8.2, several investigators have begun to argue that, under certain conditions of stress, it may be healthier *not* to face all of the facts, but rather to use denial as a coping mechanism (Lazarus 1979; Lazarus and Launier 1979). In simple terms, ignorance may indeed be bliss. Denial often buys preparation time, preserves hope, and reduces intrapsychic anxiety that would otherwise take a physiological as well as a psychological toll on the body. This seems especially true in situations where the person has limited resources with which to change the environment. When the situation *can* be changed, however, denial becomes pathological.

Social reassurance and support

To a large extent, people depend on others for social support, reassurance, and confirmation. One's resources against a threat are drawn largely from those people on whom one has learned to depend. Reactions to the death of a loved one, for example, vary from culture to culture, depending on the supports provided by each culture (Lindemann 1960). In Italy, severe mourning reactions are less likely than in the United States because of Italy's extended kinship system. Social reassurance also tends to let the person know that others have experienced similar difficulties and survived—and thus reduces the perceived magnitude of the crisis.

In short, the easiest way for a person to withstand or reduce the stress he or she feels is to prepare for it. Together, the techniques

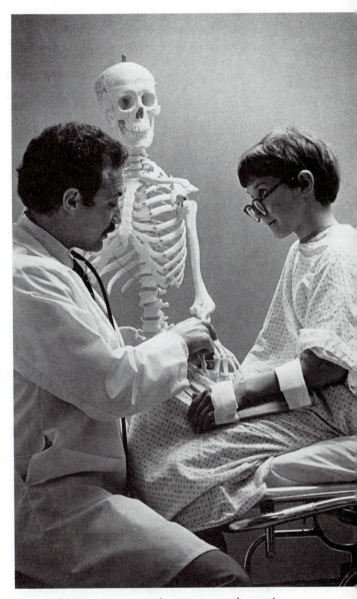

One of the best ways to reduce preoperative and postoperative stress is to fully explain medical procedures and aftereffects. With children, it is important to carefully and calmly inform them of what will happen next without arousing their natural fears.

we have discussed can inoculate people against the potentially damaging consequences of excessive stress. They represent preventive, rather than remedial, mental health measures.

SUMMARY

1. A stressor is a demand that is placed on the individual by the environment; stress is the individual's internal reaction to that demand. According to DSM-III, unusual or bizarre behaviors exhibited under stressful conditions are adjustment disorders if they result from the more common stressors of everyday life, such as illness, marital conflicts, and unemployment. They are posttraumatic stress disorders if they result from stressors that are severe and are outside the range of common experience, such as natural disasters and military combat.

2. Three models are helpful in understanding stress. The general adaptation syndrome (GAS) model identifies three stages in the individual's biological and psychological reactions to stressors: the alarm stage, the stage of resistance, and the stage of exhaustion. According to the life-change model, almost any change in an individual's life can act as a stressor. Different types of changes produce different amounts of stress, but the effects of these changes can accumulate over time. The transaction model of stress emphasizes that stress resides neither in the person alone nor in the stressor alone. Rather, a stressor's impact is mediated by such internal processes as thoughts, emotions, and perceptions.

3. The commonly encountered stressors—those that can lead to adjustment disorders—include social and economic change, marital and family problems (especially divorce), occupational situations that may lead to "burnout," and difficulty in adjusting to middle age.

4. Extraordinary stressors such as civilian catastrophes and military combat typically produce a disaster syndrome consisting of three stages. In the shock stage, the victim is confused, disoriented, and stunned. In the recoil stage, he or she begins to face reality and experience emotionality. In the recall stage, memories of the experience cause the victim to be tense and restless. Soldiers exposed to combat may develop a group of symptoms referred to as the normal battle reactions. Military psychiatric casualities have been successfully controlled through a treatment policy that stresses immediacy, expectancy, simplicity, and centrality.

5. A number of factors seem to affect the degree to which a person experiences stress: the anticipation or experience of physical or psychological pain, the number of life changes experienced, the level of stress itself, the number of available social supports, the number of coping responses available, the ambiguity or suddenness of the stressful situation, and the emotional characteristics of the person. Methods of resisting or reducing the buildup of stress include practicing what to do, preparing against harm, gathering information to reduce the ambiguity of unfamiliar situations, and relying on social support and reassurance.

KEY TERMS

adjustment disorders Reactive disorders resulting from the more common stressors of everyday life, such as illness and marital conflicts

general adaptation syndrome A model for understanding the body's physical and psychological reaction to biological stressors

life-change model A model for understanding the cumulative effects of changes in an individual's life, which act as stressors on the individual

posttraumatic stress disorders Reactive disorders resulting from extraordinary stressors that are severe and are outside the range of common experience

reactive disorders Unusual or bizarre behaviors exhibited under stress-producing conditions

stress An individual's internal reaction to a physical or psychological demand placed on the individual by the environment

stressor A physical or psychological demand placed on an individual by some external event or situation

transaction model A model in which stress is considered a transaction between the person and the stressful situation; that is, the person's internal processes and makeup intervene between the stressor and the development of stress

9

Psychological Factors in Physical Disorders

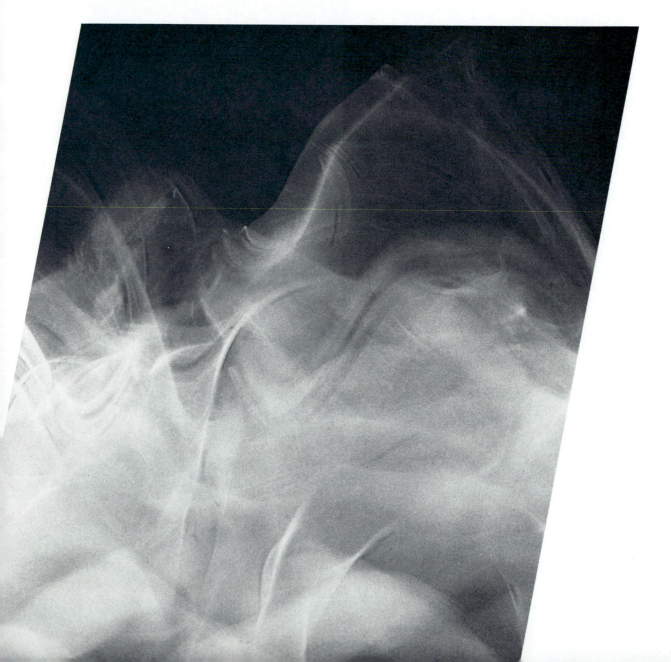

Can people "worry themselves to death"? Medical evidence seems to indicate that they can. Stress and anxiety appear to have at least some role in what is called the "sudden death syndrome"—deaths that have no specific physical basis.

A study of 170 cases of sudden death reported in newspaper articles indicated that most were related to the loss of significant others in victims' lives (Engel 1971). One article reported the case of a 61-year-old woman who had taken her ailing 71-year-old sister to the hospital. After hearing that her sister had died, the 61-year-old woman developed an irregular heartbeat and also died. The death of the sister appears to have created severe emotional distress which, in turn, produced the physical symptoms.

Emotional factors are also implicated in the case of a 22-year-old woman who pleaded to be admitted to a hospital. She reported that she and her two sisters had been cursed by a midwife, who said that one of them would die before her sixteenth birthday (one sister did die in an automobile accident before her sixteenth birthday); another would die before becoming 21 (the second sister died on the evening of her twenty-first birthday); and the last would die before her twenty-third birthday. The surviving sister was only a few days away from her birthday and was obviously frightened. She was admitted into the hospital but was found dead the next morning.

Such sudden deaths are believed to be caused by specific physiological responses to extreme stress. These responses may take the form of **bradycardia** (slowing of the heart), **tachycardia** (speeding up of the heart), or **arrhythmia** (irregular heartbeat, as in the case of the 61-year-old woman). Sudden death is probably most likely in individuals who have a susceptible coronary condition (Lown et al. 1980).

Death from bradycardia, in particular, may

result from feelings of helplessness or from the victim's giving up on life. Seligman (1974) reports the case of a prisoner of war named Ronald who collaborated with his Viet Cong captors because they indicated he would be released in return for his cooperation. When he discovered that he would not be set free, he became depressed and did nothing but lie in bed in the fetal position, sucking his thumb. He died shortly afterward.

Bradycardia—the slowing down of the heart—has also been reported in humans undergoing stress.

> The patient was lying very stiffly in bed, staring at the ceiling. He was a 56-year-old man who had suffered an anterior myocardial infarction some 2½ days ago. He lay there with bloodshot eyes, unshaven, and as we walked into the room, he made eye contact first with me and then with the intern who had just left his side. The terror in his eyes was reflected in those of the intern. The patient had a heart rate of 48 that was clearly a sinus bradycardia. I put my hands on his wrist, which had the effect of both confirming the pulse and making some physical contact with him, and I asked what was wrong. "I am very tired," he said. "I haven't slept in 2½ days, because I'm sure that if I fall asleep, I won't wake up."
>
> I discussed with him the fact that we had been at fault for not making it clear that he was being very carefully monitored, so that we would be aware of any problem that might develop. I informed him further that his prognosis was improving rapidly. As I spoke, his pulse became fuller. (Shine 1984, p. 27)

In this case, the patient's physiological response was counteracted by the physician's assurance that his situation was not hopeless— in essence, by removal of the source of stress. Richter (1957) was able to induce sudden death in rats by producing a feeling of helplessness in the rats; he was also able to eliminate the syndrome by eliminating the helplessness. But in most cases the source of the stress is not so apparent (see Focus 9.1).

Certainly, the sudden death syndrome is an extreme example of the power of anxiety and stress to affect physiological processes. But the examples cited here and those discussed in the last chapter should have convinced you that feelings and emotional states can have an impact on physical well-being. Traditionally, physical disorders that stem from psychological problems, such as asthma, ulcers, hypertension, and headaches, were called *psychosomatic disorders,* partly to distinguish them from conditions that were considered strictly organic in nature. However, mental health professionals now recognize that almost any physical disorder can have a strong psychological component or basis.

Previously, the psychosomatic disorders were considered a separate class of disorders. However, DSM-III does not categorize them as such. Instead, it contains a new category called **psychological factors affecting physical condition.** Because these are psychological factors, they are listed on Axis I; the physical disorders themselves are listed on Axis III. This new classification method acknowledges the belief that both physical and psychological factors—both body and mind—are involved in all human processes. And the term *psychosomatic disorder* has been replaced with **psychophysiological disorder,** meaning *any* physical disorder that has a strong psychological basis.

The psychophysiological disorders should not be confused with the conversion disorders discussed in Chapter 7. The conversion disorders do involve physical symptoms, such as loss of feeling, blindness, and paralysis, but they do not involve any physical pathology or process; they are considered essentially psychological in nature. By contrast, most of the psychophysiological disorders involve actual tissue damage (such as an ulcer) or physiological dysfunction (as in asthma or migraine headaches). Medical treatment is usually required in conjunction with psychotherapy.

The relative contributions of physical and

The Hmong Sudden Death Syndrome

Vang Xiong is a former Hmong (Laotian) soldier who, with his wife and child, was resettled in Chicago in 1980. The change from his familiar rural surroundings and farm life to an unfamiliar urban area must have produced a severe "culture shock." In addition, Vang vividly remembered the people he saw killed during his escape from Laos, and he expressed feelings of guilt about having to leave his brothers and sisters behind in that country. He reported problems almost immediately.

[He] could not sleep the first night in the apartment, nor the second, nor the third. After three nights of sleeping very little, Vang came to see his resettlement worker, a young bilingual Hmong man named Moua Lee. Vang told Moua that the first night he woke suddenly, short of breath, from a dream in which a cat was sitting on his chest. The second night, the room suddenly grew darker, and a figure, like a large black dog, came to his bed and sat on his chest. He could not push the dog off and he grew quickly and dangerously short of breath. The third night, a tall, white-skinned female spirit came into his bedroom from the kitchen and lay on top of him. Her weight made it increasingly difficult for him to breathe, and as he grew frantic and tried to call out he could manage but a whisper. He attempted to turn onto his side, but found he was pinned down. After 15 minutes, the spirit left him, and he awoke, screaming. (Tobin and Friedman 1983, p. 440)

About forty of the Laotion refugees who settled in the United States have died from the "Hmong sudden death syndrome." All the reports were the same: An individual in apparently good health went to sleep and died in his or her sleep. In many cases, the victim displayed labored breathing, screams, and frantic movements before death occurred. The Center for Disease Control conducted an investigation of these mysterious deaths, but no medical cause has yet been found (Center for Disease Control, 1981). Some consider the deaths to represent an extreme and very specific example of the impact of psychological stress on physical health.

Vang was one of the lucky victims of the syndrome—he survived it. He went for treatment to a Hmong woman, a Mrs. Thor, who is highly respected in Chicago's Hmong community as a shaman. She interpreted his problem as being caused by unhappy spirits and performed the ceremonies that are required to release them. After that, Vang reported that he had no more problems with nightmares or with his breathing during sleep.

psychological factors in a physical disorder may vary greatly. DSM-III suggests that psychological factors be suspected of involvement when there is evidence that environmental stressors preceded the onset or worsening of the disorder. Although the presence of stressors is often difficult to detect, repeated association between stressors and the disorder or its symptoms should increase the belief that a psychological component is involved.

In this chapter, we discuss several of the more prevalent psychophysiological disorders: coronary heart disease, hypertension (high blood pressure), ulcers, headaches, and asthma. Then we examine two eating disorders—anorexia and bulimia—that are increasing in reported incidence and have a strong basis in psychological stress.

Before we turn to these disorders, however, we should emphasize that the change from the "psychosomatic" to the "psychophysiological" view is more than a change in terminology. It is representative of an enlarging and redirecting of efforts to control disease. The new field of *behavioral medicine,* which was mentioned in Chapter 8, is an important product of this redirection. The field of behavioral medicine, which includes a number of disciplines that are concerned with illness, encompasses the following (Gentry 1984):

1. *Etiology,* involving the study of how stress, lifestyle, and personality characteristics interact to affect one's susceptibility to illness
2. *Host resistance,* the study of the effects of such factors as social and economic support, cognitive style, and personality in reducing the impact of stress
3. *Disease mechanisms,* in particular, determining how stress changes the physiology in such a way as to produce such problems as gastrointestinal disorders and cardiovascular disease
4. *Patient decision making,* the study of the process by which patients make decisions about their health practices
5. *Compliance,* the development of programs to increase patient cooperation in taking medications, exercising, and participating in other therapies and preventive measures
6. *Intervention,* through educational and behavioral therapies aimed at altering unhealthy lifestyles and indirectly reducing illnesses or illness-inducing behavior

PSYCHOPHYSIOLOGICAL DISORDERS

Most Americans are affected to some degree by psychophysiological disorders. A majority of the people interviewed in a five-year epide-

miological study reported some type of psychophysiological complaint (Schwab, Fennell, and Warheit 1974). Almost 50 percent had suffered from headaches during the previous year, and 60 percent reported indigestion or constipation. The most prevalent psychophysiological *condition* (as distinguished from *symptom*) among those interviewed was hypertension; approximately 14 percent of those interviewed reported high blood pressure. Table 9.1 lists the rates (in percents) at which these and other symptoms and conditions were reported.

Although Table 9.1 shows that more than 50 percent of the population suffered from at least one symptom or condition regularly, it does not present the complete picture. The study did not include one of the major psychophysiological disorders, coronary heart disease.

Coronary heart disease

It is estimated that over 600,000 people die of coronary heart disease each year in the United States; of these, more than one third are individuals under 65 years of age (Fishman 1982). **Coronary heart disease** (CHD) is a narrowing of the arteries in or to the heart, which results in the restriction or partial blockage of the flow of blood and oxygen to the heart. Its symptoms may range from chest pain *(angina pectoris)* to heart attack or, in severe cases, cardiac arrest. Cigarette smoking, physical inactivity, obesity, hypertension, and elevated serum cholesterol have been found to increase the risk of coronary heart disease. However, these factors alone do not seem to be sufficient to cause the disease; studies suggest that other variables are involved as well.

Social factors   In a study of Japanese living in Japan, Hawaii, and California, it was found that those residing in California had the highest CHD mortality rate and that those living in Japan had the lowest. This difference was not accounted for by differences in the risk factors listed above. In trying to determine what was responsible for the variation in mortality rates, the researchers compared Japanese immigrants who had maintained a traditional orientation with those who had acculturated (adopted the habits and attitudes prevalent in their new home). The CHD rate for acculturated Japanese turned out to be five times greater than that for Japanese who had retained the traditional values (Marmot and Syme 1976). It is possible that breaking close social and community ties, which is part of the acculturation process, caused the acculturated individuals to become more vulnerable to the disease.

In another study of social relationships and CHD, it was found that mortality rates were higher for individuals with fewer friends and social contacts (Berkman and Syme 1979). As we noted in Chapter 8, social supports tend to reduce the impact of stressors, and CHD is a stress-related disorder.

Table 9.1 Reported Psychophysiological Symptoms and Conditions

	Percent Reporting Symptoms or Conditions	
	Regularly	*Occasionally*
Symptoms:		
Headache	8.7	38.0
Indigestion	6.4	27.5
Constipation	6.9	19.6
Nervous Stomach	5.2	17.5
Stomachache	3.7	18.8
Diarrhea	0.9	14.4
Conditions:		
Hypertension	6.2	8.0
Asthma	1.9	2.9
Ulcers	0.9	1.4
Colitis	0.4	0.9
Weight trouble	39.3	
(Overweight 28.0)		
(Underweight 7.6)		
(Weight fluctuation 3.7)		

SOURCE: Schwab, Fennell, and Warheit (1974).

Social factors can influence vulnerability to coronary heart disease. Japanese immigrants who maintain traditional values and close social and community ties are less likely to die from coronary heart disease than are assimilated Japanese immigrants.

Personality and lifestyle In Focus 8.1 we noted that Friedman and Rosenman (1974) identified a behavior pattern, called Type A behavior, that they believe is associated with increased risk of heart attack. The pattern involves aggressiveness, competitiveness, hostility, time pressure, and constant striving for achievement. In self-reports, Type A individuals indicate that they are easily aroused to anger and that they experience this emotion intensely and frequently (Levenkron et al. 1983; Stevens et al. 1984). A second behavior pattern, Type B, is characterized as relaxed and not subject to time pressure. Coronary heart disease is more likely in Type A individuals than in Type B (Suinn 1977).

Because of their sense of time urgency, Type A individuals perceive time as passing more quickly, and they work more rapidly than Type B individuals. On tasks, they try to accomplish as much as possible in the shortest amount of time (Yarnold and Grimm 1982). Type A individuals also push themselves to the limit physically. The responses of Type A and Type B subjects on a treadmill task were compared by Glass (1976). The Type A subjects performed more vigorously and denied feeling tired. Their performance reflected a need to obtain superior scores on the task. Stress has been found to increase blood pressure, and hypertension is a major factor in heart attacks and strokes, so the constant pressure under which Type A individuals perform presumably increases the risk of heart attacks. It has been suggested that cholesterol and serum triglycerides also increase with stress and are thus higher in Type A individuals (Suinn 1982). These substances tend to be deposited on the arterial walls, narrowing or blocking the arteries and causing CHD.

Recently Freidman and his co-workers (1984) refined their characterization of behavior patterns. They now feel that some individuals are misidentified as coronary-prone when they are actually "healthy expressives"— individuals who are confident, dominant, and active in expression. They also feel that a distinction should be made between Type B (healthy and relaxed) individuals and unhealthy individuals who are quiet, slow to speak, and unaggressive but who harbor repressed hostility and may be disease-prone. In other words, they now propose four behavior classifications or types, rather than two:

☐ Healthy and charismatic individuals who display expressiveness, dominance, and an orientation toward achievement but who have good coping skills and feel they are in control

☐ Competitive individuals who are also expressive and dominant but are easily threatened and are hostile (true Type A)
☐ Tense and overcontrolled individuals who are unexpressive and inhibited but may explode under certain conditions
☐ Relaxed and quiet individuals who are content and unassertive (true Type B)

Friedman feels that some conflicting findings on the Type A personality may be due to confusion among these four behavior patterns.

Essential hypertension

High blood pressure with no known organic cause, or **essential hypertension,** is a common disorder that can lead to heart attacks or serious circulatory problems. Between 10 and 15 percent of the population of the United States suffers from this condition (Surwitt et al. 1982). However, in only about 10 percent of all hypertension cases is there an identifiable physical cause (Shapiro and Goldstein 1982). For this and other reasons, stress and personality characteristics have been suggested as contributing to the disorder.

Thirteen undergraduates who scored high on a life-stress measure (these could be called "stressful" individuals) were compared with thirteen who scored low (Pardine and Napoli 1983). Their heart rate, systolic blood pressure, and diastolic blood pressure were monitored before, while, and after they were subjected to a stressor in the laboratory. The heart rate and blood pressure of individuals who had high life-stress scores remained elevated for a long time after stress was eliminated, whereas those of low-stress individuals quickly returned to their prestress levels. In another study, significant increases in blood pressure were obtained by requiring subjects to work on stress-producing ambiguous and unsolvable discrimination tasks (Tasto and Huebner 1976). On the other hand, the reduction of stress through relaxation, both at home

Does expressing anger lead to hypertension? The evidence is mixed. Some studies show that expressing anger can elevate blood pressure. Other studies show that expressing anger and irritation when provoked can lower blood pressure.

and at work, has been found to produce significantly *lower* blood pressure (Pickering et al. 1982). Such studies indicate that stress has a definite impact on blood pressure and support the contention that individuals who suffer from chronic stress may be at risk of developing hypertension.

Emotions, and the way in which one deals with them, have also been suggested as being involved with hypertension. In a study of blacks living in Detroit, suppressed hostility, unexpressed anger, and low socioeconomic class were associated with high blood pressure. However, blood pressure could also be elevated by expressing anger: The investigators asked individuals whether they would respond to an angry boss by (1) keeping anger in (''just walk away from the situation''); (2) letting anger out (''protest to someone higher up''); or (3) reflection (''talk to the boss about it after he or she has cooled down''). Those

who indicated they would choose the reflective response had lower blood pressure than those who responded with anger. But reflective coping was more characteristic of female than of male respondents (Harburg et al. 1979).

In spite of such studies, the relationship between anger and hypertension is less than clear. Keane and his co-workers (1982) examined the hypothesis that hypertension is associated with the individual's inability to express assertive emotions (such as anger) when encountering conflict. They compared the performance of hypertensive patients on behavioral, physiological, and subjective tests with that of another (nonhypertensive) patient group and a nonpatient group. The hypertensive individuals responded with less assertion than the nonpatient group, but their responses did not differ significantly from those of the other patient group. Keane and his colleagues suggest that the inability to express anger or assertiveness may be a response to chronic disorders and part of the illness syndrome, rather than a cause of hypertension. Complicating the matter still further is the finding that individuals who regularly expressed anger and irritation when provoked had lower blood pressure than individuals who habitually suppressed such feelings (Gentry et al. 1982).

The role of other factors in hypertension is much clearer. For example, it is known that high sodium consumption, obesity, and heavy use of caffeine and alcohol all contribute to high blood pressure.

Peptic ulcers

Tony L. is a hard-working and competitive student. For a period of about a year, he has felt a burning sensation in his stomach. On the day before he is to take his graduate record examinations, he feels an overwhelming pain in his abdomen. He collapses and is taken to a hospital, where examination reveals that he has a duodenal ulcer.

Peptic ulcers, which are essentially open sores within the digestive system, cause 10,000 deaths each year in the United States. One of every ten persons will be afflicted by this disorder at some point in their lives (Whitehead et al. 1982). The most common site for ulcers is the small intestine; ulcers located there are called *duodenal ulcers.* A somewhat less common site is the stomach, where they are called *gastric ulcers.* As is shown in Table 9.2, location is only one of several differences between the two types.

Ulcers are thought to result from excessive secretion of stomach acid, insufficient secretion of the mucus that coats and protects the walls of the stomach, or both. In conjunction with psychological stress, these conditions seem to produce a predisposition to peptic ulcers.

Much of the research on genetic predisposition in psychophysiological disorders has involved peptic ulcers. Dragstedt (1956) reported that ulcer patients secrete four to twenty times as much stomach acid as normal individuals. However, because Dragstedt's patients already had ulcers, it is possible that the condition produces the increase in stomach acid, rather than the other way around.

The proposition that a high level of *pepsinogen* (a digestive system chemical), along with stress, predisposes an individual to the formation of ulcers was examined by Weiner et al. (1957). From 2073 newly inducted soldiers, a group of 63 oversecretors of pepsinogen and a group of 57 undersecretors were selected. None of the soldiers in these groups had ulcers at the beginning of their training period. After 16 weeks of basic training, however, 9 of the oversecretors had developed ulcers, whereas none of the undersecretors displayed this disorder.

It is clear from these studies that the level of stomach acid is related to the development of ulcers (and possibly other gastrointestinal disorders). The level of stomach acid certainly cannot be the only factor involved, however, because 86 percent of the oversecretors did not develop ulcers in the Weiner et al. study.

Migraine and tension headaches

Headaches are among the most common psychophysiological complaints. Nearly 50 percent of the general population suffers from this problem, either regularly or occasionally (Schwab et al. 1974), and more than half of all college students report having headaches once or twice a week (Andrasik et al. 1979). We shall discuss migraine headaches and tension headaches separately, but the same individual can be susceptible to both. Furthermore, in spite of some apparent differences that we shall examine, Blanchard and Andrasik (1982), who analyzed well-designed research studies comparing the two forms of headaches, concluded that there is little support for the view that they can be easily distinguished from one another.

Table 9.2   *Some Differences between Duodenal and Gastric Ulcers*

Duodenal Ulcer	Gastric Ulcer
1. More frequent in young people	More frequent in older people
2. Associated with oversecretion of stomach acid	Associated with normal amounts of stomach acid
3. Occurs in members of higher social classes	Usually occurs in members of lower social classes
4. Associated with intellectually demanding jobs	Associated with jobs involving heavy manual labor
5. Eating relieves symptoms	Eating causes discomfort
6. Occurs mainly in males	Somewhat more common in males than in females

SOURCE: Adapted from Eisenberg (1978). Copyright © 1968 by Michael M. Eisenberg, M. D. Reprinted by permission of Random House, Inc.

Migraine headaches   Dilation of the cerebral blood vessels and spasms in the cranial arteries, resulting in moderate to severe pain, are the distinguishing features of **migraine headache.** Anything that affects the size of these blood vessels, which are connected to sensitive nerves, can produce a headache. Thus certain chemicals, such as sodium nitrate (found in hot dogs), monosodium glutamate (used generously in Oriental restaurants), and tyramine (found in red wines), can produce headaches by distending blood vessels in sensitive individuals (Goleman 1976). Migraine headaches, however, are usually severe, may last from a few hours to several days, and are often accompanied by nausea and vomiting. Women report twice as many migraine episodes as men (Henryk-Gutt and Rees 1973).

Migraine headaches are of two general types: classic and common. The *classic* type begins with an intense constriction of the blood vessels in the brain, which dramatically diminishes the supply of blood to certain areas. Depending on which part of the brain is affected most, the individual may show various neurological symptoms, such as distortion of vision, numbness of parts of the body, or speech and coordination problems. When the blood vessels then become distended to compensate for the diminished blood supply, severe pain occurs. The nerves become so sensitive that the blood, as it courses through the vessels with each heartbeat, produces a characteristic pulsating or throbbing pain (Goleman 1976; Walen, Hauserman, and Lavin 1977).

With *common* migraine headaches, the first phase is less severe and neurological symptoms may not be evident. The pain also appears to be less intense than in classic migraine headaches.

Migraine sufferers have typically been described as being ethical, ambitious, and perfectionistic and as having above-average intelligence and a tendency to repress emotions (Marussen and Wolff 1949). But in a well-controlled study, migraine sufferers were not found to be especially ambitious or highly desirous of perfection (Henryk-Gutt and Rees 1973). Although their headaches were precipitated by emotional stress, the sufferers were not generally exposed to more stressors than the controls. It was concluded that migraine patients are congenitally (rather then environmentally) predisposed to headaches.

Prolonged contraction of the scalp and neck muscles can produce tension headaches. Relaxation training or biofeedback training may be effective treatments for these headaches, and can even be used to teach people to prevent them.

An extensive review of the migraine headache literature also indicated that this problem probably has a hereditary basis, which is responsible for excessive cranial vascular reponsiveness (Bakal 1975).

Tension headaches **Tension headaches** are produced by prolonged contraction of the scalp and neck muscles, resulting in vascular constriction and steady pain. As many as 40 percent of American adults may be afflicted with tension headaches (Kashiwagi, McClure, and Wetzel 1972). In some cases, stress may produce a chronic contraction of the scalp muscles, without any awareness on the part of the affected individual.

Friedman (1979) listed some of the complaints of 1420 individuals who experienced tension headaches:

☐ "Feeling as if my head is being squeezed in a vise"
☐ "A tight headband that keeps getting tighter"
☐ "Top of the head is blown off"

Psychological factors were the precipitants in 77 percent of the cases, and most of the patients (78 percent) were women.

Tension headaches are generally not so severe as migraine headaches, and they can usually be relieved with aspirin or other analgesics.

Asthma

Asthma is a respiratory disorder that is thought to result from constriction of the airways in the lungs, due to spasms of the muscles or to excessive secretion of mucus (Creer 1982). During asthmatic attacks, breathing becomes very difficult and produces a wheezing sound. The individual struggles for breath and may develop acute anxiety, which worsens the situation.

Pollens or other substances to which an asthmatic individual is allergic can produce such attacks; but in some cases psychological factors seem more important. In a detailed study of the causes of asthma, it was found that psychological factors were the main causes in 37 percent of the cases; infections were most important in 38 percent; and allergies were the dominant factors in 23 percent (Rees 1964). In most cases there is an interaction between physical and psychological causes.

Many results tend to support the contention that psychological factors are important in asthma. For example, when asthmatic children were exposed to tape recordings of emotional incidents from their earlier life, they displayed a decrease in forced expiratory rates—a response that is related to respiratory attacks (Tal and Miklich 1976).

Straker and Tamerin (1974) hypothesized that there is a relationship between suppressed aggression and asthmatic attacks. They noted that when children with chronic asthma were separated from their parents and placed in a camp setting, a number of them exhibited marked increases in aggressive behavior, while at the same time they displayed very little asthmatic symptomology. The researchers suggest that the fear of parental punishment resulted in an inhibition of aggression, which in turn produced the asthmatic symptoms. The expression-of-aggression hypothesis was also examined by Mathe and Knapp (1971), who compared the reactions of six male college asthmatics under conditions of stress with the reactions of six matched controls. Both groups were asked to mentally complete timed arithmetic problems during which they were subjected to criticism. It was found that the control subjects exhibited a significantly greater number of direct hostile reactions to the stress, whereas the asthmatic subjects manifested more anxiety and depressed reactions. Although these two studies on aggression inhibition are suggestive, the results should be viewed with caution because both studies involve correlational data.

As you will see in our discussion of etiology, according to learning theorists, both operant and classical conditioning may aggravate asthmatic attacks or increase their number. Through association with bronchial irritation, stressors or other stimuli may be conditioned to produce the respiratory attacks (classical conditioning). It is also possible that getting special attention reinforces asthmatic responses, especially because many asthmatics are children (operant conditioning).

Perspectives on etiology

Why does stress produce a physical disorder in some individuals but not in others? If a disorder does develop under emotional duress, what determines which of the psychophysiological illnesses it will be? There is certainly an interaction of innate, developmental, and acquired characteristics, but the nature and contribution of each are far from well understood. In this section we discuss the different etiological positions, but none of them adequately accounts for all the factors involved.

Psychodynamic perspective Psychoanalysts have developed several formulations to explain physical disorders associated with psychological factors. According to these formulations, each type of psychophysiological disorder is produced by a specific form of unconscious conflict. Fenichel (1945) proposed that the choice of a particular body part or function as the one to discharge id impulses (resulting from the conflict) was determined by the following:

1. *The psychosexual stage in which fixation occurred.* For example, conflicts during the oral stage could produce disorders centering on the mouth and digestive processes (ulcers, colitis); disturbances at the phallic stage might develop into impotence, orgasmic dysfunctions, or other sexual problems.
2. *The person's area of somatic weakness.* Conflicts tend to be symbolized in the organ of the body that offers the least resistance to the symptom. For example, a respiratory system that has been weakened as a result of congenital factors, trauma, or illness may predispose an individual to asthma as the disorder through which conflicts are discharged.

A more specific hypothesis, which is consistent with the psychoanalytic position but has more of a physiological base, was suggested by Alexander (1950). According to Alexander, an early unresolved childhood conflict produces a visceral response that is reactivated in adulthood. For example, the inhibition of aggressive feelings may produce hypertension or other cardiovascular disorders.

According to this hypothesis, aggression and dependency needs are the basis for most of the psychophysiological disorders. The expression of dependency needs leads to an increase in the activity of the parasympathetic division of the autonomic nervous system. (Recall that the parasympathetic division tends to help a person conserve energy.) Chronic activation of this system leads to the development of such disorders as peptic ulcers, diarrhea, and colitis. If feelings of anger predominate, the energy-expending sympa-

thetic nervous system is activated, which may result in hypertension, migraine headaches, or arthritis.

A list of the unconscious complexes associated with certain disorders is given in Table 9.3. Although Alexander's theory is impressive in its breadth and specificity, his propositions have not been supported experimentally.

The psychoanalytic hypothesis that subjects who inhibit the expression of hostility have higher levels of physical complaints than those who express hostility verbally was tested in a study by Robbins, Tanck, and Meyersburg (1972). No relationship between inhibition (or expression) of hostility and physical symptoms was found. Cochrane (1973) also found no support for the proposition that hypertensives show more "repressed" aggression than subjects with normal blood pressure readings.

Table 9.3 *A Psychodynamic Etiology: The Unconscious Correlates to Certain Physical Disorders*

Disorder	Unconscious correlates
Peptic ulcer	A conflict over dependency needs produces guilt and hostility. The person unsuccessfully attempts to sublimate these aggressive tendencies through achievement. Unsatisfied oral needs produce overactivity of gastrointestinal function, which produces an ulcer.
Asthma	The person has an unresolved dependency on his or her mother, who is perceived as cold; a fear of separation; or a need to be protected. The person feels guilty about the dependency needs. Instead of crying, he or she develops a wheeze that can develop into respiratory disorder.
Hypertension	The person experiences a struggle against unconscious hostile impulses and fluctuates from excessive control to outbursts of aggression. Repression of these hostile feelings leads to chronic blood pressure elevation.
Arthritis	The person experiences an inhibition of hostile impulses or has experienced parental restrictions of freedom of movement. Developing arthritis allows the individual to escape from the physical expression of aggression.

SOURCE: Adapted from Alexander, F. (1950). *Psychosomatic medicine.* New York: Norton.

Biological perspective There is some evidence of genetic factors in some of the psychophysiological disorders. For example, ulcers are twice as common in siblings of ulcer victims as in siblings of nonvictims. And people with Type O blood are more likely to develop duodenal ulcers than those with Type A, B, or AB blood (Eisenberg 1978). In addition, three other biological explanations for psychophysiological disorders have been suggested.

The *somatic weakness hypothesis* is a common-sense explanation for the development of particular psychophysiological disorders. This view suggests that congenital factors or a vulnerability acquired through physical trauma or illness may predispose a particular organ to develop irregularities or become weakened structurally by stressors. Therefore, which particular physiological disorder develops is determined by which system is the "weakest link" in the body. For example, 80 percent of the asthmatics in one study had had previous respiratory infections, compared to only 30 percent of the nonasthmatic controls (Rees 1964). The infection may have weakened the respiratory system and made it more vulnerable to the development of asthma. Logical as it seems, the somatic weakness hypothesis is difficult to validate, because it is not yet possible to measure the relative strengths of the different physical systems in the human body before an organ weakness appears.

Closely related to the somatic weakness hypothesis is the concept of *autonomic response specificity:* Each individual has a unique physiological reaction to all types of stressful situations (Wolff 1950). This specific response is largely inherited, but it can be affected by a previously acquired vulnerability. Moreover, it has been demonstrated experimentally: College students subjected to a variety of stressors (from cold water to tough mathematics problems) tended to show stable and consistent idiosyncratic patterns of autonomic activity in the different stress-producing conditions. That is, an individual who displayed a rise in blood pressure when reacting to one type of stressor showed this same reaction to other types of stressors (Lacey, Bateman, and Van Lehn 1953). Similar consistency was found in individuals who suffered migraine headaches, but not in a control group who did not experience migraines (Cohen, Rickles, and McArthur 1978). The suggestion that these physiological responses are innate is supported by researchers who observed that distinctive autonomic behavior patterns in infants tended to persist throughout early childhood (Thomas, Chess, and Birch 1968).

The *general adaptation syndrome,* consisting of an alarm stage, a resistance stage, and an exhaustion stage in response to a stressor, was discussed in Chapter 8. According to Selye (1956), continued stress after the final stage may result in *diseases of adaptation* such as ulcers or hypertension. Unfortunately, this formulation is very general, and it does not explain why these diseases do not occur in all individuals undergoing long-term stress. Nor does it specify which of the psychophysiological disorders will develop.

Classical conditioning perspective We have noted that classical conditioning may be involved in the psychophysiological disorders. The conditioning of neutral stimuli can elicit or activate a physiological response through generalization, as discussed in Chapter 4. For example, when egg white was administered to guinea pigs as an aerosol spray, an allergic breathing pattern (asthma) was produced (Ottenberg et al. 1958). This same allergic reaction was generalized to the aerosol spray container itself and even to the pen used by the experimenter. It seems probable that, the greater the number of stimuli that can produce a physical reaction, the more likely a chronic condition is to develop.

Psychophysiological reactions can occur in response even to words or thoughts. The bronchial reactions of forty asthmatic subjects were compared with those of a normal control

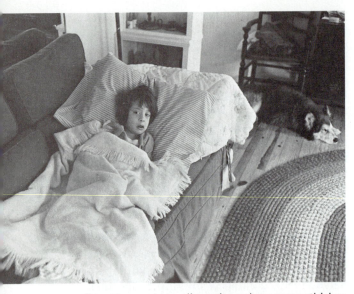

Parents must use discretion when sympathizing with their child's physical complaints. Staying home from school and getting attention from parents serves to reinforce the child's physical symptoms. Thus, parents can unwittingly foster ailments such as gastrointestinal disorders in their children.

group. The subjects were informed that they were being exposed to different concentrations of substances to which they were allergic, when in fact they were exposed only to neutral saline solution. Nearly 50 percent (nineteen) of the asthmatic subjects displayed bronchial constriction (a symptom of asthmatic attacks), and twelve developed full-blown asthmatic attacks. None of the controls showed any of these symptoms (Luparello et al. 1968). The experimenters hypothesized that principles of classical conditioning could account for their finding. The thought of inhaling an allergic substance had become a conditioned stimulus capable of inducing asthmatic symptoms or attacks.

The hypersensitivity of asthmatic children to nonallergic stimuli may be caused by its association with bronchial irritation or allergens (Kahn, Staerk, and Bonk 1974). Any cue or stimulus present during an asthmatic attack

may acquire the power to elicit attacks. An important stimulus precipitating asthmatic attacks in one female patient was meeting her mother at home. But meeting her mother outside the home produced few allergic reactions (Metcalf 1956). It is possible that the asthmatic attacks had occurred so often at home with her mother present that her home environment had become a conditioned stimulus.

The classical conditioning position alone cannot, however, account for the etiology of the disorders discussed in this section. Physiological reactions must occur before other stimuli can be conditioned to them, or before generalization can occur. Hence classical conditioning may explain the continuation or increased severity of a disorder, but not its origin.

Operant conditioning perspective   Although it was first believed that the autonomic nervous system is not amenable to operant control, recent research has indicated that involuntary processes such as heart rate, blood pressure, and a variety of other functions can be influenced through reinforcement principles. These findings have important implications for the origin and the treatment of psychophysiological disorders.

Evidence that operant learning influences visceral (digestive tract) responses supports the possibility that disorders involving the autonomic nervous system can be learned (Miller 1974). A child who is fearful of school, for example, may exhibit a variety of physiological responses (increase in heart rate, changes in blood pressure, constriction of the bronchioles, and increased gastrointestinal activity). Attention shown by the parents to a particular physical symptom can reinforce the appearance of that symptom. Thus expressing sympathy or allowing a child to stay home to recover from a stomachache might contribute to the development of gastrointestinal disorders such as ulcers, colitis, or diarrhea.

The precise role of operant conditioning in the etiology of the disorders discussed here is still not clear. There is support for the contention that autonomic processes can be altered through reinforcement. But there is also controversy about the magnitude of the changes that are possible and about whether the disorders develop through shaping or through other operant processes.

Treatment of psychophysiological disorders

Treatment programs for psychophysiological disorders generally consist of both medical treatment for the physical symptoms and conditions and psychological therapy to eliminate stress and anxiety. Behavioral medicine has provided an array of psychological approaches to these disorders, with mainly positive results. Among these are the stress-management and anxiety-management programs, which usually include either relaxation training or biofeedback. The concept of combined therapies is illustrated in the following case.

Jerry R. is a 33-year-old male who has always taken pride in the vigor with which he attacks everything he does, whether it involves work or social activities. He worries about keeping slim, so he exercises at a health spa three nights a week. He is shocked to discover, during a routine physical examination, that he has borderline high blood pressure. His physician explains that exercise is not enough, particularly when he uses a lot of salt, drinks coffee throughout the day, and overdoes the "drinking with the boys."

Jerry is told that antihypertensive medication is not indicated, primarily because his blood pressure is only mildly elevated at this point. However, he must take steps to reduce his blood pressure, and he is advised to reduce his intake of salt, caffeine, and alcohol. Upon learning that coronary heart disease runs in Jerry's family, the physician also strongly suggests that Jerry decrease his cholesterol intake by reducing the amounts of eggs, saturated fats (red meat, butter), and whole milk in his diet. He commends Jerry for having given up smoking five months ago.

Finally, Jerry is urged to become active in a stress management program geared toward lowering his blood pressure and preventing coronary heart disease. Although the effectiveness of these programs is somewhat controversial, Jerry's physician feels that Jerry has more to gain than he has to lose by participating in a course of biofeedback and relaxation training.

The success of such combined treatment programs suggests that the psychological approach to the treatment of certain physical disorders is much more than a passing fad (Rees 1983; Ford et al. 1982; Miller 1983; Barber 1984). Focus 9.2 (p. 262) describes one difficulty that is still to be overcome.

In the remainder of this section, we shall discuss relaxation training and biofeedback, which are emerging as the primary stress-management techniques of behavioral medicine. They are used in the treatment of all the psychophysiological disorders described in this chapter.

Relaxation training Present **relaxation training** programs are typically modeled after Jacobson's (1938, 1967) progressive relaxation training. A patient who is beginning the training is instructed to concentrate on one set of muscles at a time—first tensing them and then relaxing them. The client first clenches the fists as tight as possible, for approximately ten seconds, and then releases them. As the tightened muscles are released, the patient is asked to focus on the sensation of warmth and looseness in the hands. This tightening and relaxing cycle is practiced several times before the patient proceeds to the next muscle group, in the lower arms. After each muscle group has received individual attention in the form of tensing and relaxing, the client is asked to first tighten and then to relax the entire body. The emphasis throughout the procedure is on the contrast between the feelings produced during tensing and those produced during relaxing. For a novice, the entire exercise lasts about 30 minutes.

FOCUS 9.2

Are You Saying It's All in My Head?

Physicians and psychologists have encountered an unexpected problem in the treatment of psychophysiological disorders: the extreme resistance of many patients to accept psychological treatment for their physical disorders (Holt and LeCann 1984). When a physician suggests that they see a psychologist for their migraines or ulcers, most patients respond by assuming that the physician does not believe they even have a physical problem. In their minds, seeing a psychologist implies that they have somehow imagined the whole thing. They fail to realize that the psychologist and physician do not dispute the fact that the patient *has* a physical problem. They are simply offering a new way of treating it.

Psychologists face a number of obstacles in attempting to treat these reluctant individuals. Many patients feel the need to exaggerate their symptoms in order to convince the therapist that they really have a serious physical disorder. Others refuse to take an active role in the treatment program and instead wait for the therapist to "cure" them. And some demonstrate their resistance to the entire notion of seeing a non-

medical professional for a medical condition by canceling appointments, arriving late for sessions, or excusing themselves from completing home assignments.

A number of strategies have been proposed for dealing with the client who exhibits a psychophysiological disorder. Above all, therapists should not argue about the etiology of the symptoms. Second, the selected treatment strategy should be presented as the *treatment of choice* for the physical disorder rather than as a last resort. Third, a realistic course of treatment should be outlined, so that the patient knows what type of progress to expect, the rate at which progress will occur, and the importance of the patient's own active involvement in the program. Fourth, the therapist should be familiar with the various medical treatments the patient is receiving. And finally, the therapist should elicit the support of the patient's spouse or family. This will ensure that they serve as a therapeutic resource for the patient, and it will provide the psychologist with information about their relationship to the patient's symptoms (DeGood 1983).

With practice, an individual eventually learns to relax the muscles without first having to tense them. He or she can then use the technique to relax at almost any time during the day, even when only a few moments are available for the exercise.

Biofeedback In **biofeedback training,** the client is taught to control a particular physiological function voluntarily. During training, the client is provided with second-by-second in-

formation (feedback) regarding the activity of the organ or function of interest. For an individual suffering from high blood pressure, for example, the biofeedback training would focus on giving the patient the ability to lower his or her blood pressure. The feedback might be actual blood pressure readings presented visually on a screen or some auditory representation of blood pressure presented over a set of headphones. The biofeedback device enables the patient to learn his or her own idi-

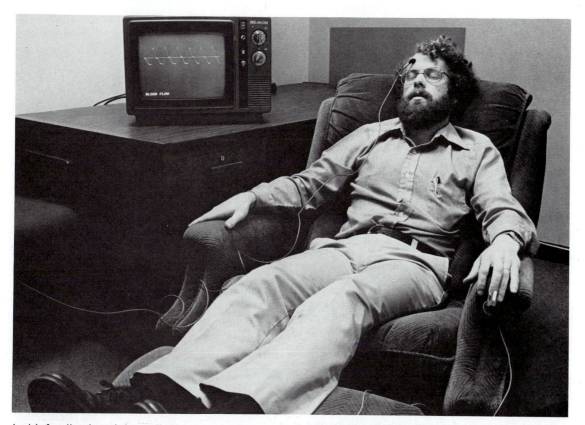

In biofeedback training, clients can get instant-by-instant information about their heart rate, blood pressure, gastrointestinal activity, muscle tension, or other physical functions. Through operant conditioning techniques, they learn to control their physiological functions.

osyncratic method for controlling the particular physiological function. Eventually the patient learns to use that method without benefit of the feedback device.

A 23-year-old male patient was found to have a resting heart rate that varied between 95 and 120 beats per minute. He reported that his symptoms first appeared during his last year in high school, when his episodes of tachycardia were associated with apprehension over exams. The patient came into treatment concerned that his high heart rate might lead to a serious cardiac condition.

The treatment consisted of eight sessions of biofeedback training. The patient's heart rate was monitored, and he was provided with both a visual and an auditory feedback signal. At the end of the treatment period, his heart rate had stabilized and was within normal limits. One year later, his heart rate averaged 73 beats per minute. The patient reported that he had learned to control his heart rate during stressful situations such as going for a job interview, by both relaxing and concentrating on reducing the heart rate. (Janssen 1983)

Biofeedback is essentially an operant conditioning technique in which the feedback serves as reinforcement. It has been used to help individuals to lower the heart rate (Engel and Bleecker 1974), decrease the blood pressure (Glasgow, Gaarder, and Engel 1982), reduce muscle tension (Gamble and Elder 1983), and redirect blood flow (Reading and Mohr 1976). Patients with duodenal ulcers have been taught to decrease the level of gastric acid secretion by providing feedback on stomach acidity (Welgan 1974). Biofeedback and verbal reinforcement were used to help asthmatic children control their respiratory functioning (Kahn, Staerk, and Bonk 1974). In an interesting marriage of operant and classical conditioning techniques, the children were also trained to control constriction of the bronchi by producing bronchodilation when exposed to previously conditioned stimuli.

EATING DISORDERS

Cherry O'Neil, the daughter of singer Pat Boone, went from a body weight of 140 pounds to only 80 pounds. She exercised up to 6 hours a day and wore heavy clothing to hide her condition. To keep her weight down she took diet pills, as well as large amounts of laxatives when she thought she had overeaten *(anorexia nervosa)*. (Seligman et al, March 7, 1983)

A 20-year-old female university student followed a strict diet, consuming between 800 and 1200 calories during the day. But between 7 P.M. and 11 P.M. she would lose control and eat huge portions of high-calorie foods; twenty slices of toast with peanut butter and jelly or eight chocolate bars was not unusual for her. After overeating, she would walk to the bathroom and induce vomiting *(bulimia)*. (Linden 1980)

Eating problems are becoming more prevalent in the United States, especially among younger people. In a recent survey of over 2000 high school students, 20 percent indicated that they overeat at least once a week to the extent that their stomachs hurt, 20 percent felt completely out of control over food at least once a week, and 11 percent of the females ate in response to emotional distress (Kagan and Squires 1984). Eating problems may be a result of both the availability of a wide variety of attractive high-calorie foods and the American pursuit of thinness. A pre-

occupation with weight and body dimensions may become so extreme that it develops into one of the eating disorders—anorexia nervosa or bulimia.

Anorexia nervosa

Although **anorexia nervosa** has been known for over a hundred years, it has received increased attention recently, owing to both the death of singer Karen Carpenter from anorexia at the age of 32 and the apparent increase in its incidence.

Anorexia is a bizarre and puzzling disorder. An individual with the disorder literally engages in self-starvation. Even when they are skeletal in appearance, patients claim to be overweight. As Bruch (1978) notes, anorexics will "vigorously defend their often gruesome emaciation as not being too thin . . . they identify with the skeleton-like appearance, actively maintain it, and deny its abnormality" (p. 209). The inability to assess one's physical condition objectively is characteristic of this disorder. Because of their belief that they are overweight, anorexic patients deny that their weight loss is a problem. The DSM-III criteria for anorexia nervosa include:

1. An intense fear of becoming obese, which does not diminish even with weight loss
2. Body-image distortion (not recognizing one's thinness)
3. A weight loss of 25 percent of the original body weight
4. Refusal to maintain a body weight that is above the minimum normal weight for one's age and height

The disorder occurs primarily in adolescent girls and young women, and only rarely in males. Estimates of its incidence range from .4 to .7 percent of the female population (Pope et al. 1984; Hertzog 1982).

Self-starvation produces a variety of physical complications along with weight loss. Anorexic patients often exhibit cardiac arrhythmias as a result of electrolyte imbalance; nine out of ten display bradycardia and *hypotension* (low blood pressure). One female patient had a pulse rate of 28 beats per minute and no measurable diastolic blood pressure (Brotman and Stern 1983). In addition, the heart muscle is often weakened, because the body may use it as a source of protein during starvation. One result of such complications is a mortality rate of approximately 6 percent (Schwartz and Thompson 1981).

There appear to be subgroups of patients with anorexia. Of 105 patients hospitalized with this disorder, 53 percent had achieved their weight loss through constant fasting; the remainder had periodically resorted to bulimia (purging or vomiting). Although both groups displayed a vigorous pursuit of thinness, some differences were found. The anorexics who fasted were more introverted and tended to deny that they suffered hunger and psychological distress. The bulimic anorexics were more extroverted; reported more anxiety, depression, and guilt; admitted more frequently to having a strong appetite; and tended to be older. The bulimic anorexics also showed a strong attraction for food, but they did not like to cook because of the temptations involved. On the other hand, the fasting anorexics enjoyed cooking (Casper et al. 1980).

Bulimia was also discovered among a group of diagnosed anorexics (Garfinkel et al. 1980). These researchers found that bulimic anorexics were more likely to have histories of alcohol and drug abuse, to have engaged in stealing, and to have tried to commit suicide. A small percentage of anorexics may also have a concurrent affective disorder (Katz et al. 1984).

Etiology of anorexia nervosa

Bruch (1976) has hypothesized the existence of three factors in the development of anorexia nervosa. The first is poor self esteem. Anorexics do not think highly of themselves, and they exhibit significant psychopathology (Katz et al. 1984).

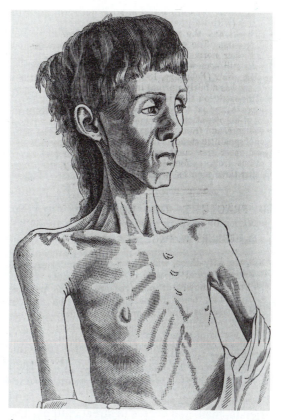

Anorexia nervosa is a devastating eating disorder that involves self-starvation. Although the incidence of the disorder has been increasing, it existed during the 1800's, as evidenced by this 1888 engraving from the *Lancet*. The disorder is most prevalent in adolescent and young adult women.

They are significantly more introverted, anxious, and dependent than normal subjects and tend to have marked obsessional tendencies (Smart, Beumont, and George 1976).

The second factor is a feeling of ineffectiveness in achieving and attaining goals. Anorexic women are perfectionists who often feel that they have failed in life. To counterbalance this sense of failure, they exert control in an area (body weight) that promises some success.

The ability to use severe weight loss as a form of control over others is the third factor in the development of anorexia. One recovered anorexic, whose weight had gone down to 70 pounds, put it this way: "It's such a manipulative disease. . . . You get people wrapped around your little finger. Any time I wanted my father to visit me in the hospital, I knew he'd be there in a second" (Seligman, Zabarsky, Witherspoon, Rotenberk, and Schmidt 1983, p. 59).

Treatment of anorexia nervosa The first step in the treatment of anorexia is to have the patient gain weight; the goal is to ensure that the body is not endangered by the electrolyte imbalance and weakened muscles caused by starvation (Brotman and Stern 1983). Either a medical or a behavioral inpatient weight-gain program can be implemented. The medical approach generally involves complete bed rest and either intravenous or nasogastric (tube through the nose) feeding. The behavioral approach is designed to positively reinforce weight gain. Among the reinforcers that may be earned through weight gain are television or telephone privileges, visits from family and friends, mail, and access to street clothes. The particular reinforcers that are used, of course, depend on the likes and dislikes of the patient. Weight-gain plans are generally aimed at increases of up to 1 pound per day.

Once the patient has gained sufficient weight to become an outpatient, family therapy sessions may be implemented. Experience with anorexics has shown that this approach helps to maintain the treatment gains achieved in the hospital (Minuchin, Rossman, and Baker 1978; White 1983). The patient also continues with a weight-gain program and may receive additional psychotherapy.

About 50 percent of treated anorexics recover completely (remain within the normal weight range), and another 30 to 40 pecent show some weight gain but remain underweight (Schwartz and Thompson 1981; Anderson, Hedblom, and Hubbard 1983). For the most part, these percentages do not include cases in which the family therapy approach

was used; expectations are that it will improve overall therapeutic results. There are still two major concerns about recovering anorexics, however. First, although many gain some weight, the majority remain obsessed with the fear of getting fat (Anderson et al. 1983; Mintz 1983). Second, 14 to 50 percent become bulimics upon recovering from anorexia (Hsu 1980).

Bulimia

Bulimia is an eating disorder characterized by binge eating (the rapid consumption of large quantities of food). Eating episodes may be terminated when abdominal pain develops or by self-induced vomiting. Bulimics may attempt to repeatedly lose weight through severe dieting, self-induced vomiting, or the use of laxatives, and frequent weight fluctuations of more than 10 pounds often result from alternating binges and fasts.

> Sandy, a singer–actress who appeared in Broadway musicals such as "Grease" and "Nine," would secretly gorge herself with enormous amounts of food and then stick her fingers down her throat to induce vomiting. She describes a typical dinner as composed of one large pizza, spaghetti and meat sauce, two veal parmesan sandwiches, two pecan pies, and one cherry pie. Her late night "snack" included a club sandwich, two grilled cheese sandwiches with bacon, an order of onion rings and french fries, three cartons of milk, two root beers and one glazed donut. (Bartlett 1984)

Bulimic individuals realize that their eating patterns are not normal and are frustrated by that fact. They become disgusted and ashamed of their eating and attempt to hide it from others. Some will not eat during the day but lose control and binge in late afternoon or evening. As in Sandy's case, weight is controlled through vomiting or the use of laxatives (Johnson and Berndt 1983). The vomiting, or purging, produces feelings of relief and, often, a commitment to a severely restrictive diet—one that ultimately fails (Stevens and Salisbury 1984).

Bulimia is much more prevalent than anorexia, although prevalence estimates depend on the sample being described. These estimates range from 2 to 10 percent of the general population (Fairburn and Cooper 1983; Pope et al. 1984). Only a small number of males exhibit the disorder, presumably because there is less cultural pressure for them to remain thin.

Pope and his colleagues estimate that approximately 7.6 million women and girls in the United States will have bulimia at some point in their lives. Females who are attending college seem to be at a much higher than average risk: In a study of this population, it was found that 19 percent of college women suffered from bulimia (Halmi et al. 1981).

The individual's weight seems to have little to do with bulimia. Of a sample of 40 females with the disorder, 25 were of normal weight, 2 were overweight, 1 was obese, and 12 were underweight. The average number of binging episodes for these women was 12 per week, and the estimated number of calories consumed in a binge ranged from 1200 to 11,500. Typical binge foods included ice cream, candy, bread or toast, and donuts (Mitchell et al. 1981).

Side effects and complications occur in bulimics as a result of self-induced vomiting or the excessive use of laxatives. The effects of vomiting include swollen parotid glands, which produces a puffy facial appearance. Vomited stomach acid can erode the enamel of the teeth. Possible gastrointestinal disturbances include esophagitis and gastric and rectal irritation. Vomiting also results in a loss of potassium, which can weaken the heart and cause arrhythmia and cardiac arrest (Stevens and Salisbury 1984).

Etiology of bulimia Bulimia can be a result of several factors. One is our society's emphasis on thinness in women. This, coupled with a suspected body-image distortion that leads

women to perceive themselves as heavier and more overweight than they actually are, provides a motivation to be thin (Collins et al. 1983; Gray 1977). In conflict with this motivation is the availability of attractive high-calorie foods.

There is some evidence that bulimics eat not only out of hunger but also as an emotionally soothing response to distressing thoughts or stress (Casper et al. 1980). Women with this disorder have been found to have a negative self-image, feelings of inadequacy, dissatisfaction with their bodies, and a tendency to perceive events as more stressful than most people would (Kagan and Squires 1984; Wolf and Crowther 1983; Gray 1977). Stress and emotional difficulties may lead them to consume food for gratification. Sandy, the bulimic actress–singer, reported that ''I would stuff down my feelings with the food. . . . I used the food as a catalyst to flush my feelings down the toilet and watch them go away. It was numbing'' (Bartlett 1984, p. 1). However, we should note that these characteristics of diagnosed bulimics may be a *result* of their loss of control over eating patterns, rather than causes of the disorder.

Treatment of bulimia Bulimia has been successfully treated through psychotherapy and biologically, by use of antidepressant medication (Bruch 1982; Pope et al. 1983). One behavioral treatment for bulimia consists of exposure and response prevention. Patients are taught to consume enjoyable foods (exposure) without vomiting afterward (response prevention). An important aspect of this approach is that it proves to bulimics that they can control their eating patterns (Rosen and Leitenberg 1982; Leitenberg et al. 1984).

A somewhat novel treatment method is the *psychoeducational group approach,* in which a number of behavioral and educational techniques are combined. In this approach, clients are told that they must eat regularly to eliminate binges. They are taught how to anticipate the urge to binge and how to either prevent or delay binges. Clients also learn to delay purging for as long as possible after an eating binge (in which case they may not require purging at all) and then to go back to eating regularly. Each binge is considered an isolated incident, rather than part of a pattern. Additional aspects of this generally successful approach include training in assertiveness and relaxation (Johnson, Connors, and Stuckey 1983).

SUMMARY

1. The sudden death syndrome is an extreme example of the effect of psychological factors on physical health. In sudden death, stress is thought to produce bradycardia, tachycardia, or arrhythmia, leading to the death of susceptible individuals.

2. Traditionally, the term *psychosomatic* was used to categorize a number of specific physical disorders that are produced or aggravated by emotional stress. Unfortunately, this usage fostered the view that only certain physical conditions have significant psychological components. Instead, DSM-III contains the category "psychological factors affecting physical condition" in recognition of the belief that both physical and psychological factors may be involved in any illness. The field of behavioral medicine represents this new direction in controlling disease.

3. Coronary heart disease (CHD) and essential hypertension are the most pervasive cardiovascular disorders. The incidence of CHD appears to be influenced by social factors, personality, and lifestyle, as well as such risk factors as smoking and inactivity. Hypertension appears to be related to the emotions and how they are expressed, especially anger.

4. Peptic ulcers—duodenal or gastric—will afflict 10 percent of all individuals at some point in their lives. Along with stress, oversecretion of stomach acid and insufficient secretion of protective mucus are thought to create a predisposition to ulcers.

5. Headaches are among the most common psychophysiological complaints. Migraine headaches involve the constriction and then the dilation of blood vessels in the brain. Tension headaches are caused by contraction of the neck and scalp muscles, which results in vascular constriction.

6. Asthma attacks result from constriction of the airways in the lungs. Breathing is extremely difficult during the attacks, and acute anxiety may worsen the situation. Suppressed aggression and conditioning have been suggested as causes.

7. Etiological theories must be able to explain why some individuals develop a physical disorder under stress, whereas others do not, and what determines which psychophysiological illness develops. According to psychodynamic formulations, the particular illness that is manifested depends on the stage of psychosexual development and the type of unresolved unconscious conflict involved. Biological explanations focus on somatic weakness and response specificity. Learning theorists emphasize the importance of classical and operant conditioning in acquiring or maintaining these disorders.

8. Psychophysiological disorders are generally treated through stress-management or anxiety-management programs, combined with medical treatment for physical symptoms or conditions. Relaxation training and biofeedback training, which help the client learn to control muscular or organic functioning, are usually a part of such programs.

9. The eating disorders, anorexia nervosa and bulimia, are becoming more prevalent in the United States. In anorexia there are a loss of body weight through self-starvation, body-image distortion, and an intense fear of becoming obese that does not diminish with weight loss. Anorexics have poor self-esteem and may use their bizarre behavior as a form of control. Bulimia is characterized by episodes of binge eating followed by self-induced vomiting or purging. The excessive weight-consciousness of bulimics may be a result of

societal emphasis on thinness, especially for women. The disorders are treated primarily through reinforcement of desirable behaviors.

KEY TERMS

anorexia nervosa An eating disorder in which the affected individual is intensely fearful of becoming obese and engages in self-starvation

asthma A respiratory disorder characterized by attacks in which breathing becomes extremely difficult due to constriction of the airways in the lungs

biofeedback training A therapeutic technique in which the individual is taught to control a particular physiological function such as heart rate or blood pressure

bulimia An eating disorder characterized by the rapid consumption of large quantities of food, usually followed by self-induced vomiting

coronary heart disease A cardiovascular disease in which the flow of blood and oxygen to the heart is restricted by a narrowing of the arteries in or near the heart

essential hypertension High blood pressure with no known organic cause

migraine headache Severe headache resulting from dilation of the cerebral blood vessels after an initial constriction

peptic ulcer An open sore within the digestive system

psychophysiological disorder A physical disorder that has a strong psychological basis or component

relaxation training A therapeutic technique in which the individual acquires the ability to relax the muscles of the body in almost any circumstances

tension headache A headache that is produced by prolonged contraction of the scalp and neck muscles

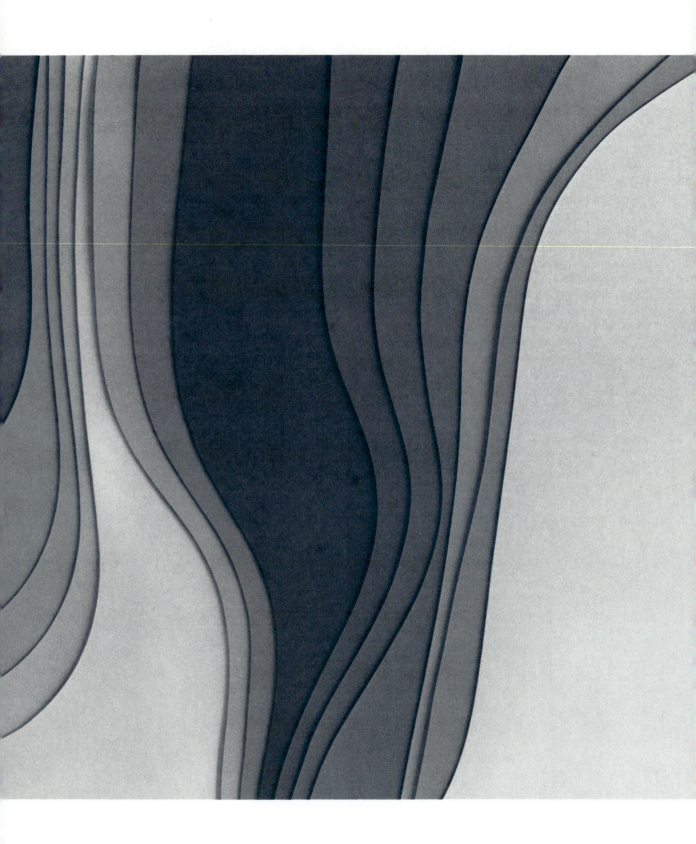

PART 3

Disorders Involving Conduct

10
Personality Disorders And Crime

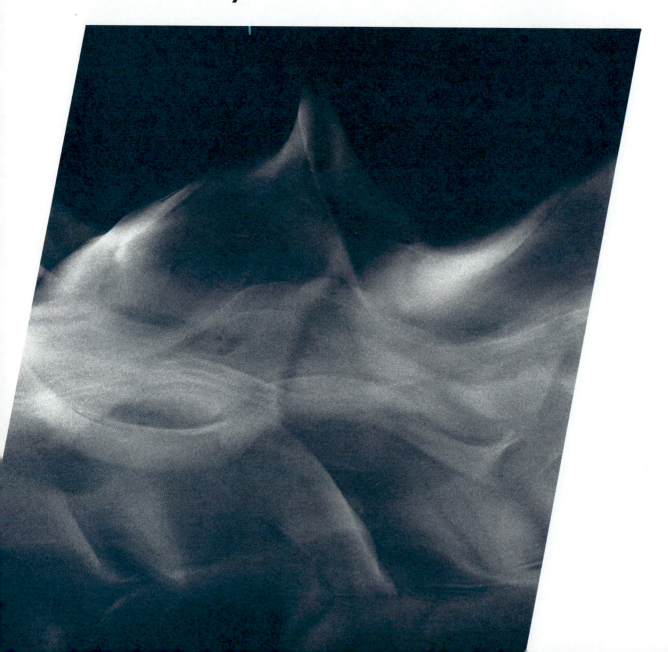

A **personality disorder** is a maladaptive behavior pattern that stems from an immature or distorted personality structure. Individuals with these disorders consistently exhibit personality traits that cause personal difficulties or affect their ability to function in society. These persons are also characterized by temperamental deficiencies or aberrations, rigidity in dealing with life problems, and defective perceptions of the self and others.

In spite of all this, people with personality disorders can often function well enough to get along without aid from others. For this reason, and because these individuals rarely seek help from mental health professionals, the incidence of personality disorders has been difficult to ascertain. Available statistics indicate that the personality disorders account for about 5 to 15 percent of admissions to hospitals and outpatient clinics. It should be noted that many individuals exhibit certain traits that characterize personality disorders—for example, suspiciousness, sensitivity to rejection, or compulsiveness. In fact, we all exhibit some of these traits, to varying degrees and at various times. However, to be diagnosed as having a personality disorder, the individual *must* exhibit a specific minimum number of traits as detailed in DSM-III. Those traits must be characteristic of the person's current and long-term functioning, and their effect must be detrimental to the person or to his or her social or occupational functioning. (Table 4.2, pp. 110–111 includes the DSM-III criteria for diagnosing paranoid personality disorder. You might want to turn back to that table now, to see just how elaborate and specific the diagnostic criteria are.)

The signs of a personality disorder usually become evident during adolescence. In some cases, a person with a personality disorder may have had a similar childhood disorder. For example, it is not uncommon to find that a person who is diagnosed as having *schizoid*

273

personality disorder has previously received a diagnosis of *schizoid disorder of childhood*. When the features of certain childhood disorders persist into adulthood (that is, beyond the age of 18), the diagnosis may be changed to that of a personality disorder.

In the diagnostic scheme of DSM-III, personality disorders are recorded on Axis II. This means that an individual may receive diagnoses on both Axis I and Axis II. For example, a person with a personality disorder may also be diagnosed as schizophrenic or alcohol dependent. Usually, individuals with personality disorders are hospitalized only when a second, superimposed disorder so impairs social functioning that they require inpatient care.

DSM-III lists eleven specific personality disorders and groups them into three clusters, depending on whether they may be characterized by (1) odd or eccentric behaviors; (2) dramatic, emotional, or erratic behaviors; or (3) anxious or fearful behaviors. We shall first discuss each of the eleven personality disorders rather briefly. Then we shall discuss two of them—the *paranoid* and the *antisocial* personality disorders—in more detail, primarily because there is more information available regarding these disorders. Finally, we shall examine some of the causes and consequences of crime. This is not to imply that personality disorders necessarily result in criminal behavior or that all criminals have personality disorders. Rather, some of the topics discussed in relation to personality disorders, and particularly antisocial personality, are relevant to the field of criminology.

THE PERSONALITY DISORDERS

Disorders characterized by odd or eccentric behaviors

Three personality disorders are included in this cluster: paranoid personality, schizoid personality, and schizotypal personality.

Paranoid personality disorder Individuals with **paranoid personality disorder** exhibit unwarranted suspiciousness, hypersensitivity, and restricted affect (that is, aloofness and lack of emotion). They tend to be rigid and to be preoccupied with unfounded beliefs that stem from their suspicions and sensitivity. These beliefs are extremely resistant to change.

The paranoid personality will be described at more length later in this chapter, in our extensive discussion of the disorder. We should note here, however, that the paranoid personality pattern can be distinguished from the occasional unwarranted suspiciousness or feelings of persecution seen in normal persons by the intensity and degree of inappropriateness of these feelings, the individual's preoccupation with the beliefs, and the long-term, deeply rooted nature of the problem. To an extent, these distinctions are applicable to all the personality disorders. Thus, although relatively normal persons may have unjustified beliefs that they are being laughed at (persecution) or that they are extremely important and influential (grandiosity), these beliefs are not as intense, unjustified, preoccupying, or deeply rooted as those observed in paranoid personalities.

Schizoid personality disorder The **schizoid personality disorder** is marked primarily by social isolation. Individuals with this disorder have a long history of impairment of social functioning. They are often described as being reclusive and withdrawn (Siever 1981). Many live alone in apartments or furnished rooms and engage in solitary recreational activities such as watching television, reading, or taking walks. Because of a lack of capacity or desire to form social relationships, schizoid individuals are perceived by others as peculiar and aloof and therefore inadequate as dating or marital partners.

Schizoid individuals may have to relate to others in certain situations—for example, at work. But then their relationships are superficial and frequently awkward. They tend to comply with the requests or feelings of others, perhaps in an attempt to avoid extensive involvements and conflicts.

Social isolation can be found even in their marital relationships. Spitzer and co-workers (1981) describe the case of a man who had married primarily to please his parents. After a while, his wife literally forced him to see a therapist because he lacked affection, interest in sex, and willingness to participate in family activities. He was as emotionally unresponsive to members of his family as he was to his colleagues at work.

The relationship between this disorder and schizophrenia (which is described in Chapter 15) is unclear. One view is that schizoid personality is a beginning stage of schizophrenia. Another is that schizophrenia may develop as a complication of the schizoid personality disorder.

Schizotypal personality disorder Individuals with **schizotypal personality disorder** exhibit oddities in various aspects of their thinking and behavior. Many victims believe they possess magical thinking abilities or special powers ("I can predict what people will say before they say it"). Some are subject to recurrent illusions ("I feel as if my dead father is watching me"). Speech oddities, such as frequent digression or vagueness in conversation, are often apparent.

The peculiarities seen in schizotypal personality disorder stem from distortions or difficulties in cognition (Siever 1981). That is, there appear to be problems in thinking and perceiving. Persons with this disorder often show social isolation, hypersensitivity, and inappropriate affect (emotions). However, it is believed that the disorder is defined primarily by cognitive distortions and that affective and interpersonal problems are secondary.

The woman described in the following paragraph was diagnosed as having schizotypal personality disorder.

> The patient is a 32-year-old unmarried, unemployed woman on welfare who complains that she feels "spacey." Her feelings of detachment have gradually become stronger and more uncomfortable. For many hours each day she feels as if she seems unreal. She feels especially strange when she looks into a mirror. For many years she has felt able to read people's minds by a "kind of clairvoyance I don't understand." According to her, several people in her family apparently also have this ability. She is preoccupied by the thought that she has some special mission in life, but is not sure what it is; she is not particularly religious. She is very self-conscious in public, often feels that people are paying special attention to her, and sometimes thinks that strangers cross the street to avoid her. She is lonely and isolated and spends much of each day lost in fantasies or watching TV soap operas. She speaks in a vague, abstract, digressive manner, generally just missing the point, but she is never incoherent. She seems shy, suspicious, and afraid she will be criticized. She has no gross loss of reality testing, such as hallucinations or delusions. She has never had treatment for emotional problems. She has had occasional jobs, but drifts away from them because of lack of interest. (Spitzer et al. 1981, pp. 95–96)

As peculiar as the patient's behaviors may seem, they are not serious enough to warrant a diagnosis of schizophrenia. Her belief that she is clairvoyant does not appear to be delusional; it is not firmly held (she admits to being confused about it), and there is no gross loss of contact with reality. Moreover, no previous history of psychosis was found. All these factors point to a personality disorder.

As is true of schizoid personality, many characteristics of schizotypal personality disorder resemble those of schizophrenia (although in less serious form). Again, the relationship between the two disorders is unclear.

Disorders characterized by dramatic, emotional, or erratic behaviors

This group includes four personality disorders: histrionic, narcissistic, antisocial, and borderline.

The symptoms of histrionic personality disorder include exaggerated emotional expression, attention-seeking or manipulative behavior, self-dramatization, egocentrism, and a lack of genuineness. A person must exhibit a combination of these characteristics along with subjective distress in order to be diagnosed as histrionic.

Histrionic personality disorder The person who has **histrionic personality disorder** engages in self-dramatization, the exaggerated expression of emotions, and attention-seeking behaviors. Despite superficial warmth and charm, the histrionic individual is typically shallow and egocentric. These behaviors were evident in a female client seen by one of the authors:

The woman was a 33-year-old real estate agent who entered treatment for problems involving severe depression. She had recently been told by her boyfriend that she was a self-centered and phony person. He found out that she had been dating other men, despite their understanding that neither would go out with others. The woman claimed that she never considered her ''going out with other men'' as actual dating. Once their relationship was broken, her boyfriend refused to communicate with her. The woman then angrily called the boyfriend's employer and told him that unless the boyfriend contacted her, she would commit suicide. He never did call, but instead of attempting suicide she decided to seek psychotherapy.

The woman was attractively dressed for her first therapy session. She wore a tight and clinging sweater. Several times during the session she raised her arms, supposedly to fix her hair, in a very seductive manner. Her conversation was animated and intense: When she was describing the breakup with her boyfriend, she was tearful; later, she raged over the boyfriend's failure to call her and, at one point, called him a ''son of a bitch.'' Near the end of the session, she seemed to be upbeat and cheerful, commenting that the best therapy might be for the therapist to arrange a date for her.

None of the behaviors exhibited by this client would, by itself, warrant a diagnosis of histrionic personality disorder. However, the combination of her subjective distress (or depression), self-dramatization, incessant drawing of attention to herself via seductive movements, angry outbursts, manipulative suicide gesture, and lack of genuineness points to this disorder (which, in fact, is diagnosed far more frequently among women than among men).

Narcissistic personality disorder The clinical characteristics of **narcissistic personality disorder** involve an exaggerated sense of self-importance. Persons with this disorder require attention and admiration and have difficulty in accepting personal criticism. In conversations, they talk about themselves and show a lack of interest in others. Many have fantasies about power or influence, and they constantly overestimate their talents and importance. Owing to their sense of self-importance, narcissistic individuals expect to be the superior participant in all relationships. For example, they may be impatient and irate if others arrive late for a meeting, but they may frequently be late themselves and think nothing of it.

One narcissistic client reported, "I was denied promotion to chief executive by my board of directors, although my work was good, because they felt I had poor relations with my employees. When I complained to my wife, she agreed with the board, saying my relations with her and the children were equally bad. I don't understand. I know I'm more competent than all these people" (Masterson 1981, p. ix). The client was depressed and angry about not being promoted and about the suggestion that he had difficulty in forming social relationships. His wife's confirmation of his problems further enraged him. During therapy, he was competitive and sought to devalue the observations of the therapist.

Narcissistic persons may often use denial and devaluation of others to maintain an inflated self-concept (Kernberg 1975). These are then the tools with which they take the offensive in response to criticism.

Antisocial personality disorder   Chronic antisocial behavioral patterns such as irresponsibility, lying, using other people, and aggressive sexual behavior are indicative of **antisocial personality disorder.** Persons with this disorder fail to conform to social norms or legal prescriptions but exhibit little guilt for their wrongdoing. Relationships with others are superficial and fleeting, and little loyalty is involved.

Antisocial personality, which is far more prevalent among men than among women, is the second of the two disorders that we shall deal with in greater detail later.

Borderline personality disorder   Contrary to popular belief, **borderline personality disorder** is not a condition that is midway between, or that fluctuates between, neurotic and psychotic disturbances (Gallahorn 1981). It is a disorder in and of itself, manifested by intense fluctuations in mood, self-image, and interpersonal relationships. Here is an example:

> Joan D. is an attractive 27-year-old woman who is employed as a sales representative. She recently sought psychotherapy because her employer indicated that, unless she became less moody and intense, he would have to find another person for the job. Joan has had a history of emotional instability. She frequently finds herself falling in love and having affairs with men, but these relationships last only briefly. Within a short period of time, she changes her mind about each man and angrily asks herself what she ever saw in him.
>
> Joan hates to be alone, yet others never enjoy her company for very long because of her quick temper and chronic feelings of boredom and meaninglessness. Her co-workers feel that she is unpredictable, moody, self-centered, and highly manipulative.
>
> Joan's intense but brief relationships with men, the marked and continual shifts in her feelings and moods, and her boredom with others in spite of her need for social contact all point to borderline personality.

Masterson (1981) believes many clients with borderline personality disorder lack purposiveness. One of his clients reported, "I have such a poor self-image and so little confidence in myself that I can't decide what I want, and when I do decide, I have even more difficulty doing it" (p. ix). This is seen by Masterson as a deficiency in the borderline personality's emotional investment in the self—a lack of directedness in long-term goals.

Persons with borderline personality may exhibit psychotic symptoms, such as auditory hallucinations (for example, hearing imaginary voices that tell them to commit suicide), but the symptoms are usually transient. Borderline individuals also usually have an *ego-dystonic* reaction to their hallucinations (Spitzer et al. 1981). That is, they recognize the imaginary voices or other hallucinations as being unacceptable, alien, and distressful. By contrast, in a psychotic disorder the individual may not realize that the hallucinations are of a pathological nature.

People with avoidant personality disorder fear and avoid social contacts because they are hypersensitive to potential rejection. At the same time, they want affection and an active social life.

Disorders characterized by anxious or fearful behaviors

This last cluster of personality disorders includes the avoidant, dependent, compulsive, and passive–aggressive personalities.

Avoidant personality disorder   The essential feature of **avoidant personality disorder** is a hypersensitivity to potential rejection, humiliation, and shame. Avoidant personalities are reluctant to enter into social relationships without a guarantee of uncritical acceptance by others. This reluctance is not derived from a desire to be alone. On the contrary, people with this disorder crave affection and an active social life. They want—but fear—social contacts. Their ambivalence may be reflected in different ways: For example, many avoidants engage in intellectual pursuits, wear fine clothes, or are active in the artistic community (Millon 1981). Their need for contact and relationships is often woven into their activities. Thus an avoidant individual may write poems expressing the plight of the lonely or the need for human intimacy.

People who have avoidant personality disorder are caught in a vicious cycle: Because of their concern with rejection, they are constantly alert to signs of derogation or ridicule. This concern, along with many perceived instances of rejection, causes them to avoid others. Their social skills may then become deficient and invite criticism from others. In other words, their very fear of criticism may lead to criticism. Avoidants often feel depressed, anxious, angry at themselves, and inadequate.

Jenny L., an unmarried 27-year-old bank teller, shows several of the features of avoidant personality disorder. Although she functions adequately at work, Jenny is extremely shy, sensitive, and quiet with fellow employees. She perceives others as being insensitive and gross. If the bank manager jokes with other tellers, she feels that the manager prefers them to her.

Jenny has very few hobbies. A great deal of her time is spent watching television and eating chocolates (as a result, she is about 40 pounds overweight). Television romances are her favorite programs; after watching one, she tends to daydream about having an intense romantic relationship.

Jenny L. eventually sought treatment for her depression and loneliness.

Dependent personality disorder   People who are unwilling to assume responsibility because of an inability to function independently exhibit **dependent personality disorder.** These individuals lack self-confidence, and they subordinate their needs to those of the people on whom they depend. However, their dependency may go unrecognized or may be misinterpreted by casual observers. For example, a dependent personality may allow his or her spouse to be dominant or abusive for fear that the spouse will otherwise leave.

Friends may perceive dependent personalities as understanding and tolerant, without realizing that they are fearful of taking the initiative because they are afraid of disrupting their relationships. Depression, helplessness, and suppressed anger are often a part of dependent personality disorder. All are evident in the following case.

> Jim is 56, a single man who was living with his 78-year-old widowed mother. When his mother recently was hospitalized for cancer, Jim decided to see a therapist. He was distraught and depressed over his mother's condition. Jim indicated that he did not know what to do. His mother had always taken care of him, and, in his view, she always knew best. Even when he was young, his mother had "worn the pants" in the family. The only time he was away from the family was during his 6 years of military service. He was wounded in the Korean War, was returned to the United States, and spent a few months in a Veterans Administration hospital. He then went to live with his mother. Because of his service-connected injury, Jim was unable to work full time. His mother welcomed him home, and she structured all of his activities.
>
> At one point, Jim met and fell in love with a woman, but his mother disapproved of her. During a confrontation between the mother and Jim's woman friend, each demanded that Jim make a commitment to her. This was quite traumatic for Jim. His mother finally grabbed him and yelled that he must tell the other woman to go. Jim tearfully told the woman that he was sorry but she must go, and the woman angrily left.

While Jim was relating his story, it was clear to the therapist that Jim harbored some anger toward his mother, though he overtly denied any feelings of hostility. Also clear were his dependency and his inability to take responsibility. His life had always been structured, first by his mother and then by the military. His mother's illness meant that his structured world might crumble.

Compulsive personality disorder The individual with **compulsive personality disorder** exhibits an inability to express warmth or warm feelings, coupled with excessive perfectionism, stubbornness, indecision, and devotion to details. Many of these traits are found in normal persons. Unlike normals, however, compulsive personalities show significant impairment in occupational or social functioning. Furthermore, the extent of the character rigidity is greater among persons with this disorder (Weintraub 1981).

Coworkers may find the compulsive individual too demanding and perfectionistic. Compulsives may actually be ineffective on the job, despite long hours of devotion. Their preoccupation with details, rules, and possible errors leads to indecision and an inability to see "the big picture."

> Cecil, a third-year medical student, was referred for therapy by his graduate advisor. The advisor told the therapist that Cecil was in danger of being expelled from medical school because of his inability to get along with patients and with other students. He often berated patients for failing to follow his advice. In one instance, Cecil told a patient with a lung condition to stop smoking. When the patient indicated that he was unable to stop, Cecil angrily told the patient to go for medical treatment elsewhere; the medical center had no place for such a "weak-willed fool."
>
> Cecil's relationships with others were similarly strained. He considered many members of the faculty to be "incompetent old deadwood," and he characterized fellow graduate students as party-goers.
>
> The graduate advisor told the therapist that Cecil had not been expelled only because several faculty members thought that he was brilliant. Cecil studied and worked sixteen hours a

day. He was extremely well read and had an extensive knowledge of medical disorders. Although he was always able to provide a careful and detailed analysis of a patient's condition, it took him a great deal of time to do so. His diagnoses tended to cover every disorder that each patient could conceivably have, on the basis of all possible combinations of symptoms.

Passive–aggressive personality disorder Individuals with **passive–aggressive personality disorder** are extremely resistant to demands for adequate performance. Their resistance may be exhibited in procrastination, stubbornness, and intentional inefficiency, which are all means of passively or indirectly expressing aggression.

> Ryan O. is a 21-year-old college student who visited his university's counseling center at the strong suggestion of his parents. Arriving about 15 minutes late for his first appointment with the counselor, Ryan indicated that his parents felt he should receive help because his grades were so low. The reason for his poor academic performance, he said, was the noisiness of his dormitory; he could not study elsewhere because the "conditions" were not right. For example, studying in the library made him sleepy.
>
> During his interview with the counselor, Ryan said very little. When asked whether he felt he could be helped in counseling, Ryan responded, "Oh, I've heard that therapy can be very effective—for some people." In later visits, Ryan indicated a long-term pattern of resistance: He would procrastinate, dawdle, or rationalize his failure to meet demands or requests from others.

Ryan's tardiness, his blaming others for his poor grades, and his reluctance to provide information to the therapist are indicative of a passive–aggressive pesonality.

Normal individuals may resort to passive–aggressive behaviors in situations where direct and assertive responses are punished. However, passive–aggressive personalities compulsively repeat such behaviors in a variety of inappropriate situations. Their behaviors are neither flexible nor adaptable (Malinow 1981).

The lack of information on the personality disorders

These brief descriptions may have led you to ask a number of general questions about the personality disorders; Focus 10.1 is included here in an attempt to answer them. Questions about the specific disorders are more difficult to answer. Although investigators have offered some hypotheses about their causes, not much empirical research has been conducted on most of them. Two exceptions are the paranoid and the antisocial personality disorders, which have received quite a lot of attention. In the next two sections we shall focus on these disorders in much more detail.

PARANOID PERSONALITY DISORDER

> Ralph and Ann married after knowing each other for two months. The first year of their marriage was relatively happy, although Ralph tended to be domineering and very protective of his wife. Ann had always known that Ralph was a jealous individual who demanded a great deal of attention. She was initially pleased that her husband was concerned about how other men looked at her; she felt that it showed Ralph really cared for her. It soon became clear, however, that his jealousy was excessive. One day when she came home from shopping later than usual, Ralph exploded. He demanded an explanation but did not accept Ann's, which was that she stopped to talk with a neighbor. Ralph told her he wanted her to be home when he returned from work—always. Believing him to be in a bad mood, Ann said nothing. Later, she found out that Ralph had called the neighbor to confirm her story.
>
> The situation progressively worsened. Ralph began to leave work early in order to be with his wife. He said that business was slow and they could spend more time together. Whenever the phone rang, Ralph insisted on answering it himself. Wrong numbers and male callers took on special significance for him; he felt they must be trying to call Ann. Ann found it difficult to dis-

Personality Traits: Normal or Abnormal?

There are three questions that students often raise concerning personality disorders: Isn't it true that all human beings show many of the traits that are found in the personality disorders? If normals also exhibit these traits, how do we know whether or not a disorder exists? And, in view of the fact that some symptoms of one personality disorder are also symptoms of other disorders, how do clinicians decide which personality disorder a client has? These are excellent questions. Although they were briefly addressed in the text, we should elaborate on them.

Individuals vary in the degree to which they possess any particular trait. Consider dependency, for example. At one extreme, some people may show very severe dependency; at the opposite extreme, others may demonstrate total independence; and most individuals would fall somewhere between the two extremes.

DSM-III asserts that a number of traits, not just one, must be considered in determining whether a disorder exists. For a diagnosis of dependent personality to be made, a constellation of characteristics (such as lack of self-confidence and subordination of one's own needs) must be present. But, if all people possess traits to different degrees, how do we know the point at which a particular constellation of traits becomes a personality disorder? This is a question of reliability and validity, as discussed in Chapter 5. The mere possession of a certain set of traits is insufficient to warrant a diagnosis of personality disorder; other criteria or factors must also be considered. The personality patterns must be characteristic of the individual's current and long-term functioning, must not be limited to episodes of illness, and must cause either significant impairment in social and occupational functioning or subjective distress. Thus a person who is temporarily dependent because of an illness would not receive a diagnosis of dependent personality disorder.

Finally, although it is true that some traits exhibited in one disorder may also be indicators of another disorder, there is never a complete overlapping of traits. To make a differential diagnosis (that is, to distinguish one disorder from another), clinicians look to the presence or absence of other symptoms that define each of the disorders. There is also the possibility that, if the client's symptoms meet the respective diagnostic criteria, more than one personality disorder may be diagnosed. In addition, the client may also be given a diagnosis on Axis I of DSM-III.

cuss the matter with Ralph. He was always quick to take the offensive, and he expressed very little sympathy or understanding toward her.

Arguments between the two increased. Ann could not convince him that she had no interest in other men. At one point, she threatened to leave him; Ralph told her he would never let her go and warned her of physical harm. He then produced a diary, which detailed his account of her behaviors. Ann was shocked to find out how many of her behaviors and the behaviors of others Ralph had interpreted as signs of infidelity. Her smiles or remarks to other men on the telephone or in stores were seen as secret messages inviting sexual contact; her neighbor was perceived as acting as a go-between for Ann and other men; dressing in a particularly attractive manner meant that she was going to see another man or that she was flirting with others. After reading the diary, which went back to the day they met, Ann realized that Ralph was disturbed, something she had not been willing to admit to herself before. Failing to convince her husband that he needed help, Ann went alone to a psychologist.

Ralph's suspicions regarding his wife's fidelity were obviously unjustified. Nothing that Ann did implicated her with other men. Yet Ralph persisted in his pathological jealousy and suspiciousness, and he took the offensive when she suggested that he was wrong in distrusting her. This behavior pattern, along with Ralph's absence of warmth and tenderness, is indicative of paranoid personality disorder.

This disorder is on the "benign" end of a spectrum of disorders that also includes *paranoid states, paranoid schizophrenia,* and *paranoia* (Weintraub 1981). Unlike these other disorders, paranoid personality does not involve delusions (false beliefs that are maintained despite obvious evidence to the contrary). In Ralph's case, it was later determined that his suspiciousness was not delusional. (He finally came to the conclusion that Ann was not seeking relationships with other men, although he remained suspicious that she might do so in the future.) Ralph was, however, generally distrustful of others, and he externalized blame for his shortcomings.

All of us have experienced transient feelings of jealousy, suspiciousness, and hypersensitivity. The central question is how such characteristics persist and become intense in some individuals. Occasionally the use of drugs such as amphetamines, LSD, and even marijuana may produce distrust or paranoid delusions. However, it is not known whether these responses result directly from the action of the drugs on the body or the drugs tend to promote the expression of pre-existing paranoid tendencies.

Various hypotheses have been advanced, and much research has been performed, in an attempt to explain the development of paranoid patterns. A good deal of this work is relevant to the understanding of paranoid personality disorder.

Explanations for paranoid personality

The psychodynamic explanation   Freud thought that paranoid individuals have latent homosexual tendencies and use the defense mechanism of projection to shield themselves from awareness of their homosexual desires. He believed paranoid persons repress and deny their homosexuality because it is threatening to their self-concept. The feeling of "I love him" is thus replaced with "I hate him." But hating others is also threatening to the person's self-concept, so the defense mechanism of projection is employed. Instead of feeling "I hate him," the individual feels that "he hates me."

Freud thought that this sequence in the development of paranoid disorders held particularly for males. There is, however, general agreement today that no linkage exists between homosexuality and paranoia (Colby 1977). Just as heterosexuals may or may not be paranoid, one can be homosexual without being paranoid and paranoid without being homosexual. Some clinicians do, however, feel that projection plays a role in paranoid ideation (Meyer and Osborne 1982).

The paranoid pseudocommunity   An interesting view of the development of paranoid tendencies has been suggested by Cameron (1959). Central to this view is the process of *sharing*. When individuals are anxious or insecure, they ordinarily share their problems with friends, colleagues, family members, or others. Through sharing, they can obtain feedback on how realistic their feelings are and can receive assistance in confronting the situations that give rise to those feelings.

But paranoid individuals fail to adequately

share or discuss their problems with others, which reduces their opportunities to receive feedback regarding the accuracy of their perceptions. They do not know how others might interpret their problems, so they are left with only their own highly restricted, idiosyncratic, and subjective interpretations.

Cameron believes that these individuals develop a **paranoid pseudocommunity,** a fantasy community constructed of their own subjective interpretations. Their view of the world is filled with paranoid and delusional elements. For example, a person may be quite concerned over his or her unpopularity at school. Being unable to share this concern with others, the person is unable to discover the reason for the unpopularity. So he or she constructs a subjective interpretation of the situation, perhaps something on the order of "others don't like me because they are jealous of my intelligence." This interpretation typically does not reflect reality; for example, the unpopularity may actually be due to the person's sarcastic verbal responses to others. In this way the person develops a paranoid pseudocommunity and becomes convinced that a community of jealous individuals is united in a conspiracy. All events and all reactions from others are then perceived as emanating from the pseudocommunity. To this person, a smile from another student might, for example, be interpreted as a sneer rather than a friendly overture.

Pathological jealousy, suspiciousness, an absence of warmth, and an inability to trust others are hallmarks of paranoid personality disorder. People with this disorder rarely seek treatment, and when they do therapy is very difficult. They believe that others, rather than themselves, have created their problems.

Social-learning and cultural explanations Several studies have supported Cameron's contention that paranoid tendencies are characterized by a lack of interaction with others. As children, many paranoid persons do not show normal patterns of play and socialization with other children (Swanson, Bohnert, and Smith 1970). Paranoid patients are more likely than other patients to lead secluded lives (Kay and Roth 1961). Thus early isolation from the usual social activities is associated with paranoid tendencies. It seems reasonable that such isolation prevents individuals from understanding the motives and behaviors of others. And, once they start to act out their idiosyncratic beliefs, others often react in a way that confirms those beliefs. For example, individuals who are extremely mistrustful of others may behave so inappropriately that others begin to react with ridicule and laughter, which helps to maintain the paranoid belief.

Family or cultural perspectives that encourage suspiciousness and feelings of persecution may influence the development of paranoid beliefs. **Folie à deux** (called shared paranoid disorder in DSM-III) refers to paranoid beliefs that are shared by two or more persons. For example, suppose a mother believes that all men want to exploit females for sex. Her suggestible or submissive daughter may also become distrusting of male–female relationships, to the point where mother and daughter are unable to interpret correctly any situations involving men or their motives. Certain "paranoid" cultures also exist, in which members freely develop delusions of persecution, suspiciousness, or grandiosity. For example, the Kwakiutl Indians of Canada often demonstrate well-accepted beliefs in persecution by spirits or witches.

The paranoid personality may learn to blame others in order to avoid the unpleasantness of shame or humiliation (Colby 1977). Thus, paranoid tendencies may be especially strong in cultures where shaming is an important part of child rearing.

Although individuals in certain subcultures may be socialized to attitudes of suspiciousness, however, the subcultural explanation is inadequate to explain paranoid personality. Grier and Cobbs (1968) have argued that, in the case of American blacks, what may appear to be paranoid tendencies—suspiciousness, distrust, and hostility toward whites—may actually be appropriate and mentally healthy reactions to years of oppression (see Focus 1.1). The explanation for these reactions lies more within the dominant sector of the society than in black subcultural values. And, as we pointed out in Chapter 1, definitions of abnormality differ, and societal variations in defining abnormal behavior must be considered.

Treatment of paranoid personality

Individuals with paranoid personality seldom seek treatment. They do not believe that they have a problem; rather, they feel that others have created their problems. Those that do find their way to therapy may be quite resistant to change. It is often difficult for therapists to establish trust and rapport with para-

noid personalities, primarily because therapy necessitates some degree of openness and self-disclosure.

Some therapists try to "crash through" the defenses of paranoid patients very early in the therapeutic process by directly interpreting their paranoid conflicts in gut-level language (Meyer and Osborne 1982). Other therapists approach treatment in a less confrontational style. Their focus is more on the development of trust and rapport, and sensitive issues are discussed only when the patient has become comfortable with those issues. For example, Weintraub (1981) suggests that therapists be firm and rigorously honest, in light of the suspiciousness of paranoid clients. The therapeutic contract between therapist and client should be spelled out in detail so that misunderstandings are kept to a minimum. Therapists should avoid taking sides when paranoid individuals make accusations against others, so as not to strengthen their clients' defenses of denial and projection. Weintraub also believes that the paranoid client will change only slowly over time.

Behavioral techniques that can alter delusional beliefs include withdrawing reinforcement when the person displays socially disturbing behaviors and shaping alternative reactions to social situations (Ullmann and Krasner 1975). Behavior therapists feel that beliefs can be changed by changing behaviors first. For example, in one case, a woman often refused to feed herself because she believed the food was poisoned. Rather than providing attention (a potential positive reinforcer) when the patient refused to feed herself, the nurse gave her attention only when self-feeding occurred. Moreover, if the patient had to be spoon-fed by others, food was spilled on the patient's clothes intentionally. Because she seemed to value neatness, the spilling of food was aversive; it could be avoided by self-feeding. The experimenters noted that after several weeks the patient began to eat on her own, gained weight, and ceased to talk about poison in her food (Ayllon and Michael 1959).

ANTISOCIAL PERSONALITY DISORDER

Roy W. is a seventeen-year-old high school senior who was referred by juvenile court for diagnosis and evaluation. He was arrested for stealing an automobile, something he had done on several other occasions. The court agreed with Roy's mother that he was in need of evaluation and perhaps psychotherapy.

During his interview with the psychologist, Roy was articulate, relaxed, and even witty. He stated that stealing was wrong but that none of the cars he stole was ever damaged. The last theft occurred because he needed transportation to a beer party (which was located only a mile from his home) and his leg was sore from playing basketball.

When Roy was asked how he got along with girls, he grinned and said that he was very outgoing and could easily "hustle" girls. He then related the following incident: "Let me tell you what happened about three months ago. I was pulling out of the school parking lot real fast and accidentally sideswiped this other car. The girl who was driving it started to scream at me. God, there was only a small dent on her fender! Anyway, we exchanged names and addresses and I apologized for the accident. When I filled out the accident report later, I said that it was *her* car that pulled out from the other side and hit *my* car. How do you like that? Anyway, when she heard about my claim that it was her fault, she had her old man call me. He said that his daughter had witnesses to the accident and that I could be arrested. Bull, he was just trying to bluff me. But I gave him a sob story—about how my parents were ready to get a divorce, how poor we were, and the trouble I would get into if they found out about the accident. I apologized for lying and told him I could fix the dent. Luckily he never checked with my folks for the real story. Anyway, I went over to look at the girl's car. I really didn't have any idea of how to fix that old heap so I said I had to wait a couple of weeks to get some tools for the repair job. Meanwhile, I started to talk to the girl. Gave her my sob story, told her how nice I thought her folks and home were. We started to date and I took her out three times. Then one night I laid her. The crummy thing was that she told her folks about it. Can you imagine that? Anyway, her old man called and told me never to get near his precious little thing again. She's actually a slut. At least I didn't have to fix her old heap. I know I shouldn't lie but can you blame me? People make such a big thing out of nothing."

The irresponsibility, disregard for others, and disregard for societal rules and morals evident in this interview indicated to the psychologist that Roy exhibits antisocial personality disorder. Historically, the terms *moral insanity, moral imbecility, moral defect,* and *psychopathic inferiority* have been attached to this condition. An early nineteenth-century British psychiatrist, J. C. Prichard (1835), described it as one in which

> the moral and active principles of the mind are strongly perverted or depraved; the power of self-government is lost or greatly impaired and the individual is found to be incapable, not of talking or reasoning upon any subject proposed to him, but of conducting himself with decency and propriety in the business of life.

Prichard believed that the disorder was not reflected in a loss of intellectual skills but in gross violations of moral and ethical standards.

The antisocial personality diagnosis (also referred to as *sociopathic* or *psychopathic* personality) has now lost some of its original moral overtones. Nevertheless, persons with antisocial personalities do show a disregard for conventional societal rules and morals. They seem to be incapable of loyalty to others and to demonstrate little guilt or remorse for their transgressions. Selfishness, irresponsibility, low frustration tolerance, pathological lying, and impulsivity are other characteristics of this disorder.

On first acquaintance, antisocial individuals often appear quite charming and sociable. Many are adept at manipulating others in sexual encounters or in gaining favors. However, the charm and friendliness are superficial. Relationships tend to be short-lived and devoid of stability and meaning. Work habits are often unstable. Friends, who are initially impressed, soon become disappointed over the unreliable and immature behaviors of these **psychopaths** (individuals with antisocial personalities). Despite the loss of friends and the punishment often received for their behaviors, psychopaths seem unable to learn from experience. Hostile, impulsive, or even criminal actions are repeated again and again.

Roy W., for example, felt no guilt for his actions or for manipulating the girl and her family. In fact, he was quite proud of his skill in obtaining sex from the girl and avoiding responsibility for the automobile repair. The ease with which Roy related his story to the psychologist demonstrated his lack of concern for those who were hurt by his behaviors. Roy exhibited no anxiety during the interview. Cleckley (1964) and Karpman (1941) have argued that "real" psychopaths lack anxiety and guilt and should be designated as *primary* psychopaths. *Secondary* psychopaths are those who show conduct problems but also exhibit tendencies toward anxiety and guilt. This distinction between primary and secondary psychopathic personalities seems appropriate, and our discussion emphasizes the former type, as represented by Roy.

The incidence of antisocial personality disorder is estimated to be 3 percent for American men and less than 1 percent for American women (DSM-III, 1980). However, estimates vary from study to study. The differences may be due to differences in the sampling, diagnostic, and methodological procedures used. Goodwin and Guze (1984) conclude that antisocial personality is fairly common, and probably increasingly so. It is much more frequent in urban than in rural environments, and in lower socioeconomic groups.

A distinction should be made between the behavior patterns associated with antisocial personality disorder and behaviors involving social protest or criminal lifestyles. Individuals who engage in civil disobedience or violate the conventions of society or its laws as a form of protest are not as a rule psychopathic. These persons may be quite capable of forming meaningful interpersonal relationships and of experiencing guilt. Their violations of rules and norms may be perceived as an act performed for the greater good. Similarly, engaging in delinquent or adult criminal behavior is not a necessary or sufficient condition for the diagnosis of antisocial personality. Although many convicted criminals have been found to be psychopathic, many others are not. They may come from a subculture that encourages and reinforces criminal activity; hence, in perpetrating such acts they are adhering to group mores and codes of conduct.

Psychopaths are a difficult population to study because they do not voluntarily seek treatment. Consequently, researchers often seek psychopathic subjects in prison populations, where there is presumably a relatively large proportion of psychopaths. But now a different problem arises: Researchers cannot know whether or not the psychopaths in prison are representative of the nonprison psychopathic population as well.

Using an ingenious research approach, Widom (1977) tried to find a number of nonprison psychopaths in order to discover whether their characteristics matched those typically found in prison groups. She placed the following advertisement in a major Boston counterculture newspaper:

Are you Adventurous? Psychologist studying adventurous carefree people who've led exciting impulsive lives. If you're the kind of person who'd do almost anything for a dare and want to participate in a paid experiment, send name, address, phone, and short biography proving how interesting you are.

Widom reasoned that such an ad might appeal to psychopaths. Of the 73 people who responded, 28 met her criteria for antisocial personality and were studied further. On the basis of psychological tests and interviews, Widom concluded that the individuals she studied did

Social protestors may exhibit behaviors similar to some antisocial acts, but are not psychopathic. They are capable of feeling guilt and of forming meaningful interpersonal relationships. People who have antisocial personality disorder neither feel guilt nor form meaningful relationships.

have characteristics similar to those frequently associated with psychopathy. However, her respondents tended to have a higher level of education and, although they were often arrested, they were convicted of crimes infrequently.

Explanations for antisocial personality

Antisocial individuals have an apparent inability to learn from past experience. They continue to engage in antisocial behaviors despite criticism and scorn from others, the disruption of close personal relationships, and their frequent encounters with legal authorities. They often sincerely promise to change their lives and make amends, only to return to antisocial behavior soon after.

Theories of the etiology of antisocial personality vary with theoretical orientation and with the theorist's definition of psychopathy. We shall examine a number of the most frequently cited constructs from the psychoanalytic, behavioral, and biological perspectives.

Psychoanalytic theory According to one psychoanalytic approach, the absence of guilt and the frequent violation of moral and ethical standards in psychopaths are the result of faulty superego development (Fenichel 1945). Id impulses are more likely to be expressed when the weakened superego cannot exert very much influence. Individuals exhibiting antisocial behavior patterns presumably had inadequate identification with their parents. Frustration, rejection, or inconsistent treatment resulted in fixation at an early stage of development.

Learning theories: Temperament   Some learning theorists view the person with an antisocial personality as an individual who lacks adequate socialization to the rules and norms of society (Eysenck 1957; Eysenck and Rachman 1965). Eysenck focused on two personality dimensions, or temperamental characteristics. **Neuroticism** is autonomic instability or emotionality. Individuals high in neuroticism have an easily aroused and overactive autonomic nervous system. Those low on neuroticism show the opposite characteristics—little anxiety or emotionality. The second personality dimension is **introversion–extraversion.** Introverts are inhibited, less sociable, and quick to learn. Extraverts tend to be impulsive, sociable, uninhibited, and slow to learn.

Eysenck hypothesized that temperamental characteristics are inherited and that primary psychopaths are low on neuroticism and extraverted. They exhibit little anxiety and emotionality, and they are impulsive and uninhibited. They are slow to learn, quick to develop reactive inhibition (fatigue in learning), and slow to dissipate that reactive inhibition. The low anxiety and the difficulty in learning become a handicap in developing normal social patterns.

Eysenck argues that psychopaths can learn but that they require more trials or repetitious experiences than others. Hence antisocial patterns are seen primarily in youths or young adults who have not yet been exposed to enough experiences to learn to control their behaviors. Eysenck's theory does account for the low anxiety and the undersocialization often seen in psychopaths, but the notion of inherited temperament for this disorder has yet to be confirmed by research.

Learning theories: Social   Psychopaths can learn and use skills very effectively (Ullmann and Krasner 1975), as shown in their adeptness at manipulation and at being charming and sociable. The difficulty is that, in many areas of learning, these individuals do not pay attention to social stimuli and have different schedules of reinforcement from most other people. Perhaps because they received inconsistent reinforcement from parents or inadequate feedback for behaviors, psychopaths find little reason to attend to social stimuli. Consequently, they feel no concern for others and easily use lying, cheating, and manipulation to their own advantage.

Learning theories: Family dynamics   A variety of other theories have also emphasized the inability of psychopaths to learn appropriate social and ethical behaviors. The reasons given for this defect, however, are quite diverse. Some theorists feel that relationships within the family, the primary agent of socialization, are paramount in the development of antisocial patterns (McCord and McCord 1964). Rejection or deprivation by one or both parents may provide little opportunity to learn socially appropriate behaviors or may diminish the value of people as socially reinforcing agents. Hence psychopaths may find little satisfaction in close or meaningful relationships with others. Psychopaths do show a significant amount of misperception about people in general (Widom 1976). The inability to perceive another's viewpoint would be likely to create problems in personal interactions.

Another explanation is that the child may have modeled the behaviors of a parent who had antisocial tendencies. In one study, researchers examined the past records and statuses of nearly 500 adults who had been seen about 30 years earlier as children in a child-guidance clinic. More than 90 of the adults exhibited antisocial tendencies. These subjects were compared with a control group of 100 adults who, as children, had lived in the same geographic area but had never been referred to the clinic. Results indicated that (1) there was little relationship between having antisocial personality as an adult and participation in gangs as a youth; (2) antisocial be-

Psychopathy is more prevalent among men than among women. One reason might be that aggressive behavior is encouraged and is more acceptable in males than in females. As traditional sex roles change, psychopathy may become more prevalent among women.

havior (theft, aggression, juvenile delinquency, lying) in childhood was a predictor of psychopathy in adults; (3) the adjustment level of fathers, but not that of mothers, was significant—having a father who was antisocial was related to adult psychopathy; and (4) growing up in a single-parent home was not related to psychopathy (Robins 1966).

The study seems to indicate that antisocial behavior is probably influenced by the presence of an antisocial father who either serves as a model for such behavior or provides inadequate supervision, inconsistent discipline, or family conflict. The father's influence on antisocial behaviors in children may be a result of traditional sex role training. Males have traditionally received more encouragement to engage in aggressive behaviors than females, and psychopathy is more prevalent among men than among women. If traditional sex roles change, one might reasonably expect psychopathy to increase among females and expect mothers to play a greater role in the development of antisocial behaviors in children.

A disturbed family background or disturbed parental model is neither a necessary nor a sufficient condition for the development of antisocial personality. Indeed, there are probably multiple causes of psychopathy.

Genetic factors Throughout history, many people have speculated that some individuals are "born to raise hell." These speculations are difficult to test because of the problems involved in distinguishing between the influences of environment and those of heredity on behavior. Within the last decade, however, some interesting research has been conducted on genetic influences in psychopathy.

One strategy has been to compare concordance rates for identical, or monozygotic (MZ), twins with those for fraternal, or dizygotic (DZ), twins. Recall from Chapter 2 that MZ twins share exactly the same genes. On the other hand, DZ twins share about 50 percent of the same genes; they are genetically no more alike than any two siblings. Most studies show that MZ twins do tend to have a higher concordance rate than DZ twins for psychopathy, delinquency, and criminality (Mednick and Christiansen 1977); this finding tends to support a genetic basis for these behavior patterns.

Another strategy for studying genetic influence is to note the rate of psychopathy among adopted persons with psychopathic biological parents. Because these adoptees were separated from their biological parents early in life, it would have been difficult for them to learn antisocial behaviors from their parents. Results generally show that adoptees whose biological parents were psychopathic have a higher rate of psychopathy than adoptees whose biological parents were nonpsychopathic (Cadoret and Cain 1981).

How about the influence of the adoptive parents of psychopathic adoptees? (This would be an environmental influence.) Results show that the rate of criminality or psychopathy is higher among the biological parents than among the adoptive parents (Hutchings and Mednick 1977; Schulsinger 1972). Again the evidence suggests that antisocial personality patterns are influenced by heredity (Goodwin and Guze 1984).

However, this evidence should be examined carefully, for several reasons. First, many of the studies do not clearly distinguish between psychopaths and criminals; or, as we noted earlier, they may draw subjects only from criminal populations. Truly representative samples of individuals with antisocial personality disorder should be investigated. Second, evidence that supports a genetic basis for antisocial tendencies does not preclude the environment as a factor. Psychopathy is undoubtedly caused by environmental as well as genetic influences, and the interaction between heredity and environment should be investigated. Third, studies indicating that genetic factors are significant do not provide much insight into *how* antisocial personality is inherited (into what exactly is transmitted genetically). We need to understand more thoroughly the process that leads to the disorder.

Central nervous system abnormality Some early investigators suggested that psychopaths tend to have abnormal brain wave activity (Hill and Watterson 1942; Knott et al. 1953). In these studies, the brain waves, or electroencephalograms (EEGs), of psychopaths were sometimes found to be similar to those of normal young children. According to one survey, most studies revealed that between 31 and 58 percent of psychopathic individuals showed some EEG abnormality, frequently in the form of slow-wave *(theta)* activity (Ellingson 1954). It is possible that brain pathology may inhibit the capacity of psychopaths to learn how to avoid punishment and that, accordingly, they seem unable to learn from experience (Hare 1970). This explanation is plausible, but there is simply not enough evidence to merit its acceptance. Many diagnosed psychopaths do not show EEG abnormalities, and nonpsychopathic individuals may also exhibit theta-wave activity. In addition, the EEG is an imprecise diagnostic device, and abnormal brain wave activity in psychopaths may be simply correlated with, rather than a cause of, disturbed behavior.

Autonomic nervous system defects The inability to learn from experience and the absence of anxiety or regret for antisocial behaviors were major characteristics of Cleckley's (1964) classic description of primary psychopaths. Pioneering and extremely promising research into the apparent absence of anxiety and guilt among psychopaths has been conducted by Lykken (1957) and Hare (1975).

Lykken (1957) studied the behaviors of prisoners judged to be primary psychopaths, of prisoners judged to be nonpsychopathic, and of students matched with the prisoners in socioeconomic background, age, and intelligence. He hypothesized that the psychopathic group would show less anxiety and greater deficiencies in avoidance learning. His results generally confirmed the hypotheses. In a classical conditioning procedure, wherein a buzzer (CS) was paired with a shock (US), psychopaths showed less galvanic skin response (GSR) reactivity than the nonpsychopathic prisoners and the students. (GSR measures sweating, which is presumed to be an indicator of emotional reaction or anxiety.) On the Activities Preference Questionnaire devised by Lykken, the psychopaths exhibited less aversion to unpleasant social situations, perhaps reflecting their low anxiety in such situations. In an avoidance-learning task, there was evidence that psychopaths were poorer in learning. Given a task in which errors could produce an electric shock, psychopaths made more errors than nonpsychopathic prisoners, who in turn made more errors than the students. Lykken's work suggests that, because psychopaths do not become conditioned so readily as nonpsychopaths, they fail to acquire avoidance

behaviors, experience little anticipatory anxiety, and consequently have fewer inhibitions about engaging in antisocial behavior.

Hare's (1968) findings support Lykken's. In Hare's experiment, the resting-state reactivity and the stress-produced reactivity of primary psychopaths, secondary psychopaths, and nonpsychopaths were determined through cardiac, electrodermal (GSR), and respiratory measures. Hare found that psychopaths demonstrated less autonomic reactivity in both the resting state and in response to stressors than did nonpsychopaths. In other words, it takes a more intense stimulus to elicit a reaction in psychopaths than in nonpsychopaths. It has been suggested that their lowered levels of reactivity cause psychopaths to show impulsive, stimulus-seeking behaviors in order to avoid boredom (Quay 1965). In one study, antisocial preadolescent children were found to exhibit stimulus-seeking behaviors (Whitehill, DeMeyer-Gapin, and Scott 1976).

If psychopathic learning deficiencies are due to the absence of anxiety and to lowered autonomic reactivity, is it possible to improve learning by increasing the anxiety or arousal ability of these individuals? The ability of psychopaths and nonpsychopaths to perform an avoidance learning task with electric shock as the US was tested under two conditions: Subjects were administered at different times an injection of adrenaline, which presumably increases arousal, and an injection of a placebo. In the placebo condition, psychopaths made more errors in avoiding the shocks than nonpsychopaths; in the adrenaline condition, however, psychopaths tended to perform better than nonpsychopaths (see Figure 10.1, p. 292). These findings imply that psychopaths do not react to the same amount of anxiety as nonpsychopaths and that their learning improves when their anxiety is increased (Schachter and Latané 1964).

The *kind* of punishment used in avoidance learning is also an important consideration in the evaluation of learning deficiencies in

Figure 10.1 *Anxiety and Avoidance Learning among Psychopaths and Others*
Effects of anxiety-increasing (adrenalin) and placebo injections on the avoidance learning of psychopaths, of a group with mixed characteristics, and a control group.

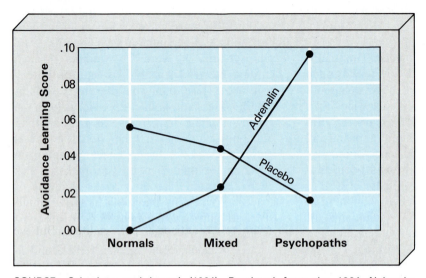

SOURCE: Schachter and Latané (1964). Reprinted from the 1964 *Nebraska Symposium on Motivation,* edited by David Levine, by permission of the University of Nebraska Press. Copyright © 1964 by the University of Nebraska Press.

Figure 10.2 *Effect of Type of Punishment on Psychopaths and Others*
Mean avoidance-learning scores plotted for three types of punishment among three subject groups.

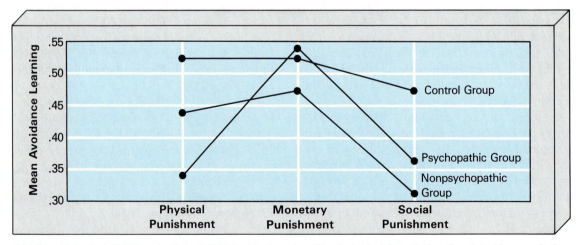

SOURCE: Schmauk (1970). Copyright © 1970 by the American Psychological Association. Reprinted by permission of the author.

psychopaths (Schmauk 1970). Whereas psychopaths may show learning deficits when faced with physical (electric shock) or social (verbal feedback) punishments, they learn as well as nonpsychopaths when the punishment is material (losing money for an incorrect response). Figure 10.2 charts the results of Schmauk's study of convicted psychopaths.

The *certainty* of punishment may also influence the responsiveness of psychopaths to punishment. Psychopaths and nonpsychopaths do not seem to differ in responding when punishment is a near certainty (Siegel 1978). When the probability of punishment is highly uncertain, however, psychopaths do not suppress their behaviors. Threats of punishment alone do not seem to be sufficient to discourage psychopaths.

Normals respond to physical, social, or material punishment, and they are influenced by uncertain as well as certain punishment. The work of Schmauk and Siegel suggests that psychopaths do not respond to the same range of aversive conditions. Hare (1975) has proposed a psychophysiological model for this lack of responsiveness. He believes that psychopaths tend to lack anxiety, which makes learning difficult for them, and speculates that this lack of anxiety results from a defensive mechanism which reduces the aversiveness of painful stimuli. In other words, psychopaths may develop a psychophysiological ability to reduce the emotional impact (or anxiety-producing effect) of situations—a defense against anxiety and pain.

Hare's hypothesis is interesting but highly speculative. It, along with other hypotheses regarding anxiety, is based on a number of measures that do not always produce the same results. That is, a person may exhibit anxiety according to one measure but not according to another. Furthermore, some measures indicate not only anxiety but also other states, such as general arousal. Obviously, an important goal in research on antisocial personality disorder is to develop a clearer concept of

anxiety (and arousal) and a "pure" measure of this reaction.

Reid (1981) agrees that psychophysiological factors may be involved in the disorder. However, he views antisocial personality as a heterogeneous condition, caused by many factors. Diverse groups of factors (or correlates)—familial, biological, social, and developmental—may converge and provide a coherent picture in explaining the disorder.

Treatment of antisocial personality

As you have seen, there is growing evidence that low anxiety and low autonomic reactivity characterize antisocial personalities. But we still do not know whether the low anxiety and autonomic underreactivity are due to inherited temperament, an acquired congenital defect, or social–environmental experiences that occur during childhood. The theory that psychopaths have developed a defense against anxiety is intriguing, but the factors behind the development of such a defense have not been pinpointed.

Because individuals with antisocial personalities exhibit little anxiety, they are poorly motivated to change themselves; they are also unlikely to see their behaviors as "bad." Thus traditional treatment approaches, which require the cooperation of the client, have not been very effective with psychopaths. For the same reason, relatively little research has been conducted on the efficacy of various treatment approaches. In some cases, tranquilizers (phenothiazines and dilantin) have been helpful in reducing antisocial behavior (Meyer and Osborne 1982). However, psychopaths are not likely to follow through with the ritual of taking drugs; moreover, drug treatment is effective in only a few cases, and it can result in such side effects as blurred vision, lethargy, and neurological disorders.

It may be that successful treatment can

occur only in a setting in which behavior can be controlled (Vaillant 1975). That is, treatment programs need to provide enough control so that psychopaths cannot avoid confronting their inability to form close and intimate relationships and the effect of their behaviors on others. Such control is sometimes possible in the case of psychopaths who are imprisoned for crimes or who, for one reason or another, are hospitalized. Intensive group therapy may then be initiated to help psychopaths in the required confrontation.

Some behavior modification programs have been tried, especially with delinquents who exhibit antisocial behavior. Money and tokens that can be used to purchase items have been used as rewards for youths who show appropriate behaviors (discussion of personal problems, good study habits, punctuality, and prosocial and nondisruptive behaviors). This use of material rewards has been fairly effective in changing antisocial behaviors (Van Evra 1983). However, once the youths leave the treatment programs, they are likely to revert to antisocial behavior unless their families and peers help them to maintain the appropriate behaviors.

Working with youths is very important, because antisocial behavior patterns can often be identified early in life. Then early intervention also serves as a beneficial preventive strategy.

CRIME AND VIOLENCE

Americans are much concerned about crime and violence—and with good reason: Our crime rate is higher than those of most other countries. In 1982 over 12 million serious crimes were reported in the United States; the serious crimes, as categorized by the FBI, include homicide, forcible rape, aggravated assault, robbery, burglary, larceny, and auto theft (*Uniform Crime Reports* 1983).

Crime statistics tend to vary from year to year, and the variation may represent real changes in crime rates. However, it may also result from changes in record-keeping systems or in the willingness of victims to report crimes. In any event, the statistics do indicate that demographic factors such as age, sex, race, and social class are highly related to the commission of crime.

At least half of all reported murders, violent street crimes, and thefts are committed by persons under twenty-six years of age. One of every ten children will probably appear in juvenile court before the age of eighteen. [We should note, however, no sharp line of demarcation separates delinquent individuals, on the one hand, from nondelinquent individuals on the other (Van Erva 1983). Among all juveniles, one may find almost every degree of delinquent behavior, as measured by frequency and seriousness.] Because age is related to the commission of certain crimes, a change in the age composition of a population may alter the frequency of these crimes. The United States population is now growing older (that is, we have a higher proportion of older persons than ever before). Individuals born during the post-World-War II baby boom are now nearing 40 years of age. This demographic shift may signal lower rates for those crimes that are associated with youth.

The vast majority of crimes among both adults and juveniles are committed by males, although females are committing a greater proportion of total crimes each year. In terms of race and socioeconomic status, statistics indicate that blacks and individuals from the lower socioeconomic classes are overrepresented among those arrested for and convicted of crimes—especially violent crimes. Victims tend to be of the same race or socioeconomic class as the perpetrator of the crime. A word of caution: There is often a tendency to use such statistics in a way that exaggerates the amount of crime among members of certain ethnic or socioeconomic groups, or even to attribute most crime to those groups. But a variety of factors combine to result in the published crime figures, and the figures alone cannot indicate what those factors are.

Theories of crime

What type of individual commits crimes? According to Megargee and Bohn (1977, 1979), criminals are a heterogeneous group. On the basis of psychological tests, personal histories, and observations of inmates in prison, they were able to categorize prisoners into no fewer than ten classes.

1. *Items* are friendly and nonaggressive individuals who have been convicted of such crimes as drug dealing. Comprising a large subgroup of prisoners, they come from stable family backgrounds and are good candidates for probation.
2. *Easy* inmates come from good family backgrounds and are underachievers. They have low recidivism rates and are good candidates for probation.
3. *Bakers* are anxious, socially isolated, and frequently alcoholic. They appear to be neurotic delinquents who would benefit from treatment.
4. *Ables* are somewhat psychopathic, immature, and amoral. They would function well in a controlled living situation in the community.
5. *Georges* are criminals whose crimes are economically motivated. They are loners and are somewhat psychopathic. Treatment should initially be targeted toward their motives for committing crime.
6. *Deltas* are psychopathic and bright. They are impulsive, show little anxiety, and are easily provoked to violence. Their antisocial nature should be addressed in any treatment program.
7. *Jupiters* come from severely deprived family backgrounds. They are motivated to

adjust, but they lack the necessary skills, abilities, and education. Educational and academic training, along with supportive group psychotherapy, may be beneficial.
8. *Foxtrots* are emotionally disturbed and antisocial. They rebel against authority, and treatment is often ineffective.
9. *Charlies* are probably the most disturbed of any subgroup. They are violent, bitter, and paranoid. Treatment is difficult because of their strong paranoid tendencies.
10. *Hows* come from deprived backgrounds. They are anxious and are isolated because their social behaviors result in rejection from others. They need almost all forms of treatment.

Megargee and Bohn thus found that prison inmates vary considerably with regard to a number of characteristics: emotional disturbance, family background, skills and abilities, propensity for violence, motivation for crime, type of treatment needed, and response to treatment. Given the diversity of individuals who exhibit delinquent or criminal behavior, it is not surprising that there are a number of theories about the causes of crime and aggression. Many of these theories are variations of the explanations for antisocial personality. However, it is important to realize that, even in prison populations, fewer than 30 percent of the inmates are considered psychopathic (Hare 1981). Indeed, most criminals are not disturbed in the clinical sense, and criminality cannot be attributed to a single specific personality type.

Genetic and physiological research Early investigators were interested in determining whether there are physiological differences between criminals and noncriminals. Some researchers felt that criminals were more likely to show EEG or genetic abnormalities. As in the case of antisocial personality, however, there is little evidence that such abnormalities can explain criminal behavior.

More recently, researchers have sought to establish whether criminal behavior patterns can be influenced by heredity. The research strategies used and the results obtained are very similar to those discussed with respect to antisocial personality. For example, MZ twins show a higher concordance rate than DZ twins for criminality; and, among criminals adopted early in life, their biological parents show a higher rate of criminality than their adoptive parents (Hutchings and Mednick 1977; Mednick and Christiansen 1977). Such findings show at most a hereditary *tendency* toward criminality, thus suggesting that environmental factors are also important. In fact, in the "adopted criminal" study, the highest rate of crime among offspring occurred when both the biological *and* the adoptive fathers had committed crimes.

These heredity studies suffer from two major limitations: First, they do not include individuals who commit crimes but have escaped detection or conviction. Second, they do not indicate *how* hereditary factors might predispose one toward criminality—how one's genetic makeup leads to criminality or interacts with environmental factors to produce criminality.

Family factors Megargee and Bohn (1977, 1979) also noted that many criminals are reared in unstable or detrimental family environments. Criminals often come from families where parents are separated or divorced. Some are subjected to inconsistent or harsh forms of punishment as children. Others have parents who were themselves antisocial or criminal. Presumably, children may learn delinquency and criminal behavior through the modeling of parents who use physical punishment or engage in antisocial behavior.

Criminals frequently described their home environments as frustrating and as lacking affectionate relationships. Such conditions may not allow youngsters the opportunity to learn to internalize the values associated with prosocial or appropriate behaviors (Hetherington

and Martin 1979). In a study of correlates of serious and repeated crime among adolescents, Hanson et al. (1984) found that low levels of mother–son affection and cold and conflicting father–son relations were predictors of criminal activity in the sons. There is general agreement that family environment plays a role in delinquency and criminality (Van Evra 1983).

Sociocultural factors Merton (1968) has suggested that certain conditions in American society combine to encourage crime. These are the common goals of wealth, power, and status; the existence of "haves" and "have-nots"; and the limited availability of legitimate means for achieving goals. The "American dream" is that these goals are attainable by all in this, the land of opportunity. Yet inequities exist and the have-nots are unable to succeed. For example, the children of wealthy and well-educated parents find it easier to obtain good educations and pursue professional careers than the children of poor families or members of ethnic minority groups. The have-nots may resort to illegitimate means (that is, crime) as a strategy for surviving or getting ahead.

Whereas Merton stresses motivation and opportunities as factors in crime, Sutherland and Cressey (1966) have argued that individuals may be *socialized* into a life of professional crime through exposure to the value systems of criminals. A powerful predictor of serious and repeated crime among male adolescents is their loyalty to and strong participation in *delinquent peer groups*. These peer groups provide adolescents with a sense of belongingness, support, and the behavioral norms of delinquency (Hanson et al. 1984). Sutherland and Cressey's hypothesis and that of Merton may also explain white-collar crime (such as illegal financial dealings, price fixing, and bribery) and organized crime, in which "families" or hierarchies of criminals engage in extortion, gambling, prostitution, drug dealing, and loan-sharking.

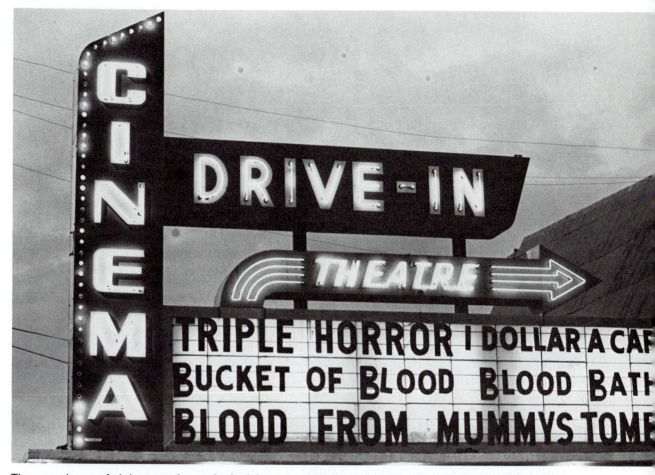

The prevalence of violent movies and television programs may contribute to increased violent behavior. The mass media reflect the concerns and interests of society, but they also can influence society through socialization.

The role of television and other mass media in American society has come under increasing scrutiny. Although it can be argued that television programming merely reflects the preferences and practices of society, television programs can also be a powerful force in socialization. Many investigators believe that the frequent displays of criminal behavior and violence on television shows can increase the tendency of viewers to engage in such behaviors (see Focus 10.2, pp. 298–299 for a discussion of violence on television). Because the content of media presentations is both influenced by the preferences of society and capable of influencing vast numbers of people, it is viewed as a sociocultural force.

Treatment and punishment

In our society, the treatment of crime and criminals has generated divergent opinions and emotional arguments. One segment of society is primarily concerned with the treatment and rehabilitation of criminals. From its perspective, society is best served by efforts

Symptoms of Social Pathology: Violence and the Mass Media

Despite almost two decades of research on the display of violence in the mass media, controversy still rages over its effect on aggressive behavior. Does portrayal of violence encourage the viewer to respond violently, or does it channel off healthy aggressive impulses? Even if violence in the media does not cause normal people to become aggressive, does not repeated exposure to violence brutalize people and make them insensitive to suffering?

Media representatives claim that "television has no influence on aggression." These same groups, however, believe that values and behaviors *can* be changed by commercials. Then why not by programs? Some argue that observing violence actually reduces rather than increases aggressive tendencies. Through catharsis, they claim, the viewer is able to dissipate his or her aggressive impulses by vicarious participation in aggression. The theories of Freud and Lorenz on aggression are consistent with this notion, but the evidence for this position is not convincing (Johnson 1972). There is some evidence that watching aggression on television may channel hostile feelings in highly aggressive boys (Feshbach and Singer 1971). But, in the majority of cases, the overall pattern of laboratory and field studies indicates that normal adults and children can become more aggressive after watching aggression (Walters, Thomas, and Acker 1962; Berkowitz and LePage 1967).

Whether aggression increases or decreases after an individual watches media violence depends on a number of variables: (1) the amount of violence observed; (2) the quality of violence observed; (3) the dramatic context; (4) the personal qualities of the aggressor; (5) the justifiability of the aggression; (6) the results of the violence; (7) the rewards or punishments accompanying the aggressive acts; (8) how the violence observed is related to previously witnessed aggression; (9) the emotional state of the beholder; (10) the personality of the beholder; and (11) the age, sex, and intelligence of the beholder (Feshbach and Singer 1971). Singer (1971) argues that the majority of studies that show a relationship between media violence and increased aggression are *laboratory* studies and are *correlational* in nature. Actual viewing experiences may show different results from laboratory studies; correlational studies, as we observed in Chapter 5, do not prove a causal link.

Nevertheless, the bulk of scientific studies and a review of the research clearly warn of the potential detrimental effects of media violence (Berkowitz 1962; Baker and Ball 1969; Goranson 1969; 1970; Johnson 1972; Kaufmann 1970; Siegel 1970; Bryan and Schwartz 1971).

The data suggest consistently that children are exposed to a heavy dose of violence on television. It is also clear that they can and do retain some of the aggressive behaviors, which they see and are often able to reproduce. . . . Punishment [of] an aggressive model leads children to avoid reproduction of the exemplary behavior but does not prevent learning or subsequent performance under more favorable circumstances. . . . It is important to note that the correlational results, while generally consistent, point to a moderate (rather than a strong) relationship between watching television and subsequent aggressive attitudes and behavior. (Liebert 1972, pp. 27–28)

The following statistics about television-watching habits and the content of programs are extremely revealing.

1. Children begin watching TV at age 2 or 3 and by age 5 are watching 2 to 3 hours a day (Siegel 1970). In lower-income families, 10-and 11-year-olds watch from 5 to 6 hours of TV per day (NCCPV 1969). By the age of 16, a child has spent more time watching TV than in school classrooms (Siegel 1970).

2. A child who watches TV during prime time witnesses a violent incident every 16 minutes and a murder every 31 minutes (Schramm, Lyle, and Parker 1961).

3. In an analysis of prime-time TV programs, Baker and Ball (1969) found that violence occurred in 8 out of 10 programs; that 93.5 percent of all children-oriented cartoons included violence; that more than half of all major characters committed violence, with the "good guys" committing as much as the "bad guys"; that the pain and suffering accompanying violence was rarely shown; and that nearly half the killers suffered no consequences for their acts.

Under these circumstances, children cannot help but learn from this powerful socializing agent that aggression, torture, and murder are acceptable; that war is commonplace and unavoidable; that good guys often resort to violence; that violence is a successful means to an end; and that violence often goes unpunished. The National Commission on the Causes and Prevention of Violence (NCCPV 1969) reported that:

It is reasonable to conclude that a constant diet of violent behavior on television has an adverse effect on human character and attitudes. Violence on television encourages violent forms of behavior and fosters moral and social values about violence in early life which are unacceptable in a civilized society. (p. 202)

Interestingly, Eron (1980) speculates that there may be a critical developmental period when a child is very susceptible to violent television. In a longitudinal study, he found that the amount of violent television viewed by 8-year-old children is positively correlated with aggressive behavior at 19. His correlation is, in fact, higher than the correlation betweeen watching violent television at age 8 and aggressive behavior at age 8. In other words, watching violent programs at a young age may establish a pattern that results in aggressive behaviors later on in life. Eron (1982) also notes that aggressive children prefer violent television, which promotes even more aggressive behavior.

to find a means of reforming criminals and preventing recidivism. Rather than punish criminals, society should work to change the lifestyles, personality patterns, and behaviors of criminals.

In opposition to this view, another segment of society believes that criminals should be punished. Its members advocate certain, immediate, and severe punishment for crime, with fixed rather than indeterminate sentences. Punishment is viewed as a form of retribution through which criminals pay for their crimes. It may also serve to deter others from crime or to isolate criminals in prison, away from law-abiding citizens and the opportunity to commit more crimes.

Still another segment of society is primarily concerned with the conditions that give rise to crime. Its emphasis is on the prevention of crime through modification of the social and economic conditions that breed crime. The elimination of poverty, racial inequities, and motives for committing crime is its objective.

Obviously, it is possible to hold all three views. One may advocate treatment for those who commit first-time, minor offenses; swift and severe punishment for "hardened" criminals who engage in heinous crimes; and the alteration of social conditions that encourage criminal behavior. However, we should note that attempts to find a way to reduce crime and prevent recidivism among criminals have been largely unsuccessful (Rappaport 1977). What is needed is a continuing effort to test alternative programs, including reform within the criminal justice system.

MENTAL HEALTH AND THE LAW

Mental health issues often become legal issues. The public is most aware of this fact when criminal defendants plead "not guilty by reason of insanity" (see Focus 10.3, pp. 302–303). But there are actually four situations in which mental health issues become legal ones: when decisions have to be made on the involuntary commitment of individuals to mental hospitals; when the competence of persons to stand trial is in doubt; when an accused person bases his or her criminal defense on insanity or diminished mental responsibility; and when the rights of mental patients are legally tested.

Involuntary commitment is the hospitalization for treatment without their consent, of persons who are judged to be mentally disturbed and a danger to themselves or to others. Friends, relatives, the police, or mental health professionals may initiate commitment procedures. In many states an individual cannot be committed without a legal hearing where evidence is presented before a judge, and legal counsel is available to the person who is to be committed. The criteria used to determine whether a person should be committed vary among the states. In addition to a determination that because of *mental disturbance* a person is dangerous to others or to self, general criteria usually involve an inability to take care of oneself or an inability to manage one's financial affairs. (The term *mental disturbance* is used to distinguish these persons from dangerous individuals who are sent to prisons rather than to hospitals.) When committed, they can usually be held for only a few days. After this period, their mental status must be reexamined to ensure that continued detainment is justified.

Competence to stand trial must be ruled on when a defendant appears unable to understand the charges against him or her, the facts relevant to the case, or the legal issues involved. In our legal system, defendants must be able to participate fully in defending themselves against the charges at the time of their trial. If they are ruled incompetent to stand trial, defendants cannot be held in indefinite confinement. Once the judgment is made that a defendant is unlikely to be competent to stand trial in the near future, either he or she must be released or involuntary commitment proceedings must be undertaken. If the accused is ruled competent the trial can begin.

Criminal insanity or **diminished mental responsibility** may be offered as a defense in a criminal case. A number of court rulings serve as the basis for such a defense: The McNaghten Rule (established in England in 1843) held that an accused person could be acquitted of a crime if it could be shown that, at the time of the act, the defendant had such defective reasoning that he or she was unaware of the action or, if aware, was unable to comprehend that the act was wrong. Of course, it was never easy to evaluate the defendant's "awareness" or "comprehension." At about the same time (1834), an Ohio court handed down the "irresistible impulse" ruling whereby individuals could be found not guilty if, because of mental illness, they could not resist committing the criminal act. Here, again, though, it was difficult for the courts to determine what were resistible or irresistible impulses. The 1954 ruling in *Durham v. United States* brought criminal insanity deeper into the domain of mental health professionals. This ruling stated that a defendant could be found not guilty if the unlawful act was a product of a mental disease or defect. Under the more recent Brawner Rule *(United States v. Brawner,* 1972), persons are not responsible for criminal conduct if, at the time of such conduct, there is substantial incapacity to appreciate the wrongfulness of the conduct or to conform to the requirements of the law because of mental disease or defect.

These rulings make obvious the fact that legal definitions of mental disorder or abnormality differ markedly from the definitions used by mental health professionals. Furthermore, when psychiatrists or psychologists testify at trials involving insanity, they often disagree about the mental status of the defendant at the time of the crime or about the proper interpretation of the legal definitions. Some mental health professionals advocate the elimination of insanity pleas in criminal trials.

Among these critics are Szasz (1977), who argues against any role for the psychiatrist or psychologist in the courtroom. Szasz contends that people should be held legally responsible for their behavior.

In many cases where individuals are found not guilty by reason of insanity, they end up worse off than if they had been convicted. Confinement in a mental institution may be longer than the time a convicted criminal has to spend in prison. Furthermore, mental hospitals are often not equipped to handle potentially dangerous persons.

The **rights of mental patients** constitute both a legal and a moral issue. Whether individuals are confined voluntarily or involuntarily, they have the right to receive adequate treatment and therapy. But what constitutes *adequate* treatment? In 1972, in *Wyatt v. Stickney,* the Alabama State Court specified that adequate food, exercise, bathing facilities, and privacy must be provided for patients. Furthermore, patients must be treated with dignity and respect and must be provided with individualized therapy programs.

Although nearly everyone would endorse these minimal requirements, they raise some very important issues. For example, in behavior modification programs, aversive forms of treatment may be involved: Electric shock may be used to modify children's self-destructive behaviors; comforts may be withheld from patients as negative reinforcement for inappropriate behaviors; and electroconvulsive shock may be administered to severely depressed patients. Here we have a conflict between what may be therapeutically beneficial for patients and the patients' legal right to refuse aversive forms of treatment. Those charged with resolving this conflict must weigh the effectiveness of the treatment procedures and the seriousness of the disorder against the availability of alternative forms of treatment for the problem and against the moral and legal rights of patients to reject even those alternative forms of therapy.

Guilty or Not Guilty of Murder: The Case of the Hillside Strangler

For five months between 1977 and 1978, Los Angeles was terrorized by a series of murders of young women whose bodies were left on hillsides. All the women had been raped and strangled; some were brutally tortured. Why would someone commit such crimes? Was this the act of an insane person? These questions were addressed in a *Frontline* (1984) Public Broadcasting System program.

About a year after the Los Angeles murders, two university students were found strangled to death in Bellingham, Washington. Police arrested 27-year-old Kenneth Bianchi for the murders. Then Los Angeles police found that Bianchi had been in Los Angeles during the hillside stranglings. The key link, however, was Bianchi's fingerprints, which matched those found during the investigation of the hillside murders. From this and other evidence, police were certain that Bianchi was the murderer (later, his cousin Angelo Bono was also charged with the stranglings).

Bianchi was an unlikely murder suspect. Those who knew him said that they could not believe he had committed the crimes, that he was a dependable and conscientious person, that he was like the "boy next door." Furthermore, despite the strong evidence against Bianchi, he insisted that he was innocent. Police also noticed that Bianchi was unable to remember much of his past life. Attorneys for Bianchi wanted to focus on his state of mind and asked a psychologist to interview and hypnotize Bianchi to restore his memory.

During one of a series of interviews, there was a startling development: Bianchi exhibited another "personality." Steve, the other personality, stated that Ken was a "turkey" and didn't know anything about the murders. On the other hand, Steve freely admitted killing the women with the help of Angelo Bono. When Bianchi was shown a videotape of the interview in which Steve appeared, Bianchi indicated he was shocked by what he had seen.

Was Bianchi a true multiple personality, or was he feigning insanity? Several psychiatrists were convinced that he was indeed a multiple personality. This might explain why so many of his friends described him as being sincere, "all American," and a proud father. When he was Ken, he was a good citizen; as Steve, he was a sadistic murderer. On the other hand, police were convinced Bianchi was a calculating, cold-blooded murderer who was pretending to be a multiple personality. Which view was valid?

Psychologist Martin Orne, an internationally recognized expert on hypnosis, was asked by the prosecution to examine Bianchi. Orne knew that Bianchi could be a multiple personality or a clever liar. He reasoned that, if Bianchi was pretending, he would be highly motivated to convince others that he was a multiple personality. Orne thought that, if he told Bianchi that multiple personalities rarely show just two distinct personalities, Bianchi might show still another personality to convince Orne his was a true case of multiple personality. After hinting to Bianchi in the waking state that two personalities are rare, Orne placed Bianchi under hypnosis. Bianchi took the bait. Another personality—Billy—emerged. (Other experts were unable to draw out more than two personalities.)

Orne also noticed that Bianchi's behaviors were unusual for someone under hypnosis. For example, during one session Orne wanted Bianchi to hallucinate the presence of his attorney, so he suggested to Bianchi that his attorney was sitting in the room. Bianchi immediately got up and shook hands with his (imaginary) attorney. Orne then asked whether his attorney was shaven. Bianchi responded, ''Oh, no. Beard. God, you can see him. You must be able to see him.'' (*Frontline*, part II, 1984, p. 11). These behaviors of Bianchi were unusual for deeply hypnotized subjects. First, they almost never shake hands spontaneously, because that requires a tactile hallucination. Bianchi would have to image not only seeing his attorney but also feeling the touch of his hand. Second, the statement ''You can see him. You must be able to see him'' seemed to be excessive and to be aimed at convincing Orne that he (Bianchi) really saw his attorney.

Orne believed Bianchi was faking. His work, coupled with other evidence, forced a change in Bianchi's plea from not guilty by reason of insanity to guilty. In exchange for testifying against Bono, Bianchi would not be sentenced to death. Interestingly, at the time of sentencing, Bianchi was tearful and expressed regret and sorrow. Within minutes of leaving the courtroom, however, he was sitting with his feet up on a table, laughing and smoking a cigarette. Orne felt that Bianchi was a sexual psychopath, seeking sexual violence and yet able to exhibit superficial charm and sincerity in order to manipulate others.

The hillside strangling case raises a number of issues. First, defendants in criminal trials may try to fake insanity in order to escape guilty verdicts. The number of individuals who deceptively use the insanity plea for this reason is not known. However, a defense based on insanity is quite rare, and the judge or jury must ultimately render a decision based on the convincingness of the defense and prosecution cases. Second, mental health experts can differ in their opinions about a defendant's sanity, as was dramatically illustrated in Bianchi's case. Third, the mere fact that a defendant has a mental disorder is not sufficient for an insanity plea. Insanity is a legal ruling, and the legal criteria for insanity must be fulfilled. Finally, those with mental disorders are not more likely than normal individuals to commit crimes. Certain disorders (such as psychopathy) *are* overrepresented among criminals, but this is not the case for mental disorders in general.

SUMMARY

1. The personality disorders include a diversity of behavioral patterns in persons who are typically perceived as being odd, overly sensitive and emotional, hot-tempered, suspicious, moody, or impulsive. DSM-III lists eleven specific personality disorders; each of them causes significant impairment in social or occupational functioning or subjective distress for the individual. They are usually manifested in adolescence and continue into adulthood.

2. Paranoid personality disorder is characterized by hypersensitivity, suspiciousness, and restricted affect. The paranoid personality seems to begin in early social isolation, in which children have little opportunity to share beliefs and ideas with others. This lack of feedback may give rise to idiosyncratic beliefs and deficient role-taking skills, resulting in the creation of a paranoid pseudocommunity or fantasy world. Once paranoid tendencies develop, they are maintained by the reactions of others.

3. The main characteristics of antisocial (or psychopathic) personality are selfishness, irresponsibility, lack of guilt and anxiety, failure to learn from experience, superficiality, and impulsivity. Psychopaths frequently violate the rules, conventions, or laws of society. Most explanations of antisocial personality attribute its development to temperamental predisposition, modeling and socialization, heredity, or neurological defects. Traditional treatment approaches are not particularly effective with psychopaths.

4. The United States has extremely high rates of crime and violence. Those who commit crimes vary in their personality characteristics, family backgrounds, and motives for engaging in crime. Researchers have focused on genetic and social factors in the development of criminal behavior patterns. With regard to treatment, one segment of society advocates punishment for those convicted of crimes, a second segment advocates rehabilitation, and a third prevention.

5. Mental health issues become legal issues when the involuntary commitment of an individual to a mental hospital is proposed; in questions regarding the competence of accused persons to stand trial; when insanity is used as the defense in a criminal trial; and when the rights of mental patients are tested. Legal precedents tend to be applied to these situations on a case-by-case basis.

KEY TERMS

antisocial personality disorder A personality disorder characterized by failure to conform to social and legal norms, superficial relationships with others, and lack of guilt feelings for wrongdoing

avoidant personality disorder A personality disorder characterized by a fear of rejection and humiliation and, as a result, reluctance to enter into social relationships

borderline personality disorder A personality disorder characterized by intense fluctuations in mood, self-image, and interpersonal relationships

compulsive personality disorder A personality disorder characterized by perfectionism, indecision, devotion to details, and a lack of personal warmth

dependent personality disorder A personality disorder characterized by extreme reliance on others and an unwillingness to assume responsibility

histrionic personality disorder A personality disorder characterized by self-dramatization, the exaggerated expression of emotions, and attention-seeking behaviors

narcissistic personality disorder A personality disorder characterized by an exaggerated sense of self-importance

paranoid personality disorder A personality disorder characterized by unwarranted suspiciousness, hypersensitivity, a lack of emotion, and preoccupation with unfounded beliefs

passive–aggressive personality disorder A personality disorder characterized by the passive expression of aggression through stubbornness, inefficiency, procrastination, and, generally, resistance to reasonable demands

personality disorder A maladaptive behavior pattern that stems from an immature or distorted personality structure

schizoid personality disorder A personality disorder characterized by social isolation and emotional coldness

schizotypal personality disorder A personality disorder characterized by such oddities of thinking and behavior as recurrent illusions, belief in the possession of magical powers, and digression or vagueness of speech

11
Substance Use Disorders

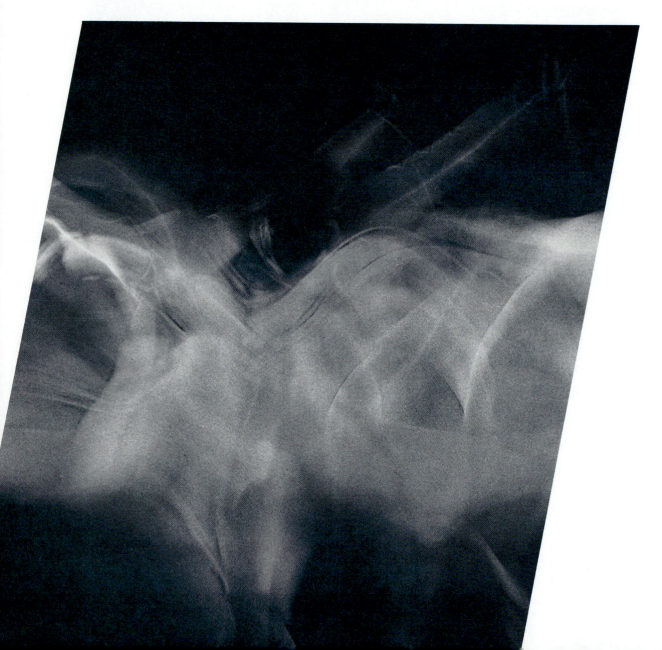

*T*hroughout history, individuals have swallowed, sniffed, smoked, or otherwise taken into their bodies a variety of chemical substances for the purpose of altering their moods, levels of consciousness, or behaviors. The widespread use of drugs in our society today is readily apparent in our vast consumption of alcohol, cigarettes, coffee, medically prescribed tranquilizers, and such illegal drugs as cocaine, marijuana, and heroin. Society is generally permissive with regard to the use of such substances. But individuals and public institutions become concerned when the ingestion of drugs results in (1) the impairment of a person's social or occupational functioning; (2) an inability to abstain from use of the drug despite its harmful effects on the body; (3) the user becoming a danger to others; or (4) criminal activities, such as the sale of illegal drugs or robbery to support a drug habit. The first two of these problems are directly involved in **substance use disorders,** or maladaptive behavior associated with the pathological use of a substance over a period of at least one month. The others arise as concomitants of such use.

In DSM-III, the substance use disorders are distinguished from each other with regard to the actual substance used, as well as in terms of two levels of severity—substance abuse and substance dependence. **Substance abuse** is a pathological pattern of excessive use in which the person is unable to cease or reduce the intake of a substance, even though it may be causing physical damage or impairing social relationships and occupational functioning. Need for the substance may lead to a preoccupation with its acquisition and use.

Substance dependence is the more severe of the two levels of substance-use disorders. It implies a physical dependence on the substance (addiction), resulting in tolerance and/or withdrawal symptoms. **Tolerance** is a condition in which the body needs increasing doses of the substance to obtain the desired effect (such as a "high"). In other words, after regular and repeated consumption of a certain dosage, that dosage becomes insufficient. **Withdrawal symptoms** are physical or emotional symptoms (such as shaking, irritability, or the inability to concentrate) that appear when the intake of a regularly used substance is reduced or halted.

In this chapter, we shall first examine the effects, possible causes, and treatment approaches for alcohol use disorders. Then we shall do the same for disorders involving the use of various other substances.

ALCOHOL USE DISORDERS

Frank is a 42-year-old alcoholic. Before he turned 16, he had already tried some liquor, but he did not like the taste at all. Soon after his sixteenth birthday, however, he and some friends "threw" a drinking party. Frank forced himself to drink, and the liquor lost its aversive quality; Frank became drunk and then quite ill. The next day he swore that he would never "touch the stuff again." But over the next 3 years, he developed a taste for alcohol. Drinking relieved his anxieties and made him feel uninhibited. In college he was proud of the fact that he could drink others "under the table" and then act "normal," even though other students who drank the same amount would either act immaturely or become intoxicated.

Initially, his drinking did not interfere with his school work or social life. Frank was an average student, but he became quite dependent on alcohol to relieve tensions. Before making a presentation in a speech class one day, Frank had a few drinks. He carefully controlled the amount he drank so that he would feel confident but would be able to speak without any telltale signs. He even used a mouthwash so that others would not suspect he had been drinking. After he was successful with the speech, Frank started to drink in the daytime. Social drinking was no longer sufficient; he now had to drink to the point of intoxication. He was careful to ensure that others did not become aware of his drinking, and he believed that he was not an alcoholic.

Frank's preoccupation with alcohol grew; his subsequent inability to control his drinking and his frequent binges made it difficult to continue his education. So Frank did not graduate from college. For years he was unable to hold a steady job because of his frequent absences and ineffectiveness on the job.

On the day after he was arrested for public drunkenness, Frank entered his first treatment program. Depressed over his inability to lead a stable life, he finally admitted he was an alcoholic. For the next 5 years, he experienced alternating periods of sobriety and drunkenness and was in and out of different treatment programs, including Alcoholics Anonymous. At the age of 41, he was brought to a mental hospital for a treatment program aimed at changing his entire lifestyle. The program seems to have been helpful; Frank has currently not had a drink for 11 months.

Problem drinking can develop in many different ways and can begin at almost any age. However, Frank's history is typical in several respects. First, as is true of most individuals, he initially found the taste of alcohol unpleasant, and, after his first bout of drunkenness, he swore he would never drink again. However, he did return to drinking. Second, heavy drinking served a purpose: It reduced his anxiety, particularly in social settings. Third, Frank took great pains to hide from others the fact that he had been consuming alcohol, although such tactics often fail. Friends and colleagues usually smell liquor on the breath or notice the unsteady gait of the problem drinker. Finally, heavy daytime drinking, a preoccupation with alcohol consumption, and the deterioration of social and occupational functioning are also characteristic of the problem drinker.

Alcohol consumption in the United States

Considerable amounts of alcohol are consumed in the United States. Two surveys sponsored by the National Institute on Alco-

Alcohol is the most widely used drug among high school students. Nearly 75 percent of high school students drink alcohol, and about 14 percent drink heavily at least once a week.

hol Abuse and Alcoholism (1981) revealed that adult consumption has slowly increased over the past ten years. At present, about one-tenth of the adult population are considered heavy drinkers, and one-fourth consume alcohol in moderate amounts. Approximately one-third are considered light drinkers, and only one-third abstain from alcohol. Although the proportion of female imbibers has increased dramatically, men continue to be more likely to drink. Alcohol is the most widely used drug among tenth- to twelfth-grade adolescents. Only about one-fourth of these teen-agers are abstinent, and approximately one out of seven typically drinks large amounts of alcohol at least once a week. Problem drinking is particularly high among young adults (Mulford 1982).

Add to these statistics the estimates of the Office of Technical Assessment (1983) on the social, medical, and physical costs of drinking, and you can see how immense the problem really is.

1. An estimated 10 million to 15 million Americans have serious problems directly related to alcohol consumption, and about 35 million individuals are indirectly affected.
2. Alcoholism may be responsible for up to 15 percent of the nation's health care costs and for significantly lowering the productivity of workers in all economic strata. It is estimated that alcoholism costs our society almost $50 billion per year.
3. The life expectancy of an alcoholic is 10 to 12 years shorter than average, and alcohol-

ism is related to such health problems as organ damage, brain dysfunction, cardiovascular disease, and mental disorders.

4. Alcoholics have a significantly higher suicide rate than nonalcoholics (up to 58 percent greater in some groups of alcoholics). In addition, alcohol is associated with nearly 55 percent of all automobile accidents (see Focus 11.1), with home and industrial accidents, and with crimes such as assault, rape, and spouse abuse.

5. Alcoholism is estimated to be a factor in up to 40 percent of all problems brought to family courts, is known to be a major factor in divorce, and has been associated with family destabilization.

6. Despite the high cost of alcoholism and the wide range of problems associated with alcoholism, an estimated 85 percent of alcoholics never receive any treatment.

With such grim results, why do individuals continue to create serious problems for themselves, their families, their employers, and

FOCUS 11.1

MADD

On May 3, 1980, a thirteen-year-old girl was walking to a church carnival in Fair Oaks, California. A car suddenly swerved out of control and killed her. The vehicle's driver, who was intoxicated, was arrested by police. A check of the driver's record revealed that he had a long history of arrests for drunk driving. And only one week before, he had been bailed out of jail after being charged with hit-and-run drunk driving.

Candy Lightner, the mother of the girl, was furious over the death of her daughter and concerned that the driver might not be sent to prison for the crime. At that time the penalties for drunk driving were frequently light, even when injury or death resulted. Lightner wanted to find ways to keep intoxicated persons from driving and to help the victims of drunk drivers and victims' families. She decided to form an organization called Mothers Against Drunk Drivers (MADD).

Initially Lightner was unsuccessful. She wanted to meet with California Governor Jerry Brown to find a means of dealing with drunk drivers, but the governor declined to see her. Finally, after Lightner began to show up at his office day after day and succeeded in obtaining newspaper publicity for her crusade, Brown took action. He appointed a task force to deal with drunk driving and named her a member.

As a result of the efforts of Lightner and the task force, California eventually passed tough new laws against drunk driving. Lightner's organization has grown as well; MADD now has 320 chapters nationwide and 600,000 volunteers and donors. They have succeeded in convincing most states to enact more severe penalties for drunk driving. In addition, MADD was the most aggressive group lobbying Congress for a law that would compel every state to set its minimum drinking age at twenty-one or higher. Such a law was passed by Congress—and signed by President Reagan—in the summer of 1984. Now, any state that does not comply by a certain fixed date can lose millions of dollars in federal highway funds.

Incidentally, the driver responsible for the death of Lightner's daughter did eventually serve twenty-one months in jail (Friedrich 1985).

strangers on the highways through problem drinking? Before we can explore this question, we need to examine the effects of alcohol.

The effects of alcohol

Alcohol abuse and alcohol dependence are, of course, substance abuse and dependence in which the substance is alcohol. Individuals who have alcohol dependence are referred to as **alcoholics,** and their disorder is **alcoholism.** According to DSM-III, alcohol abuse can be exhibited in two ways. First, the person may need to use alcohol daily in order to function; that is, he or she may be unable to abstain from alcohol. Second, the person may be able to abstain from consuming alcohol for certain periods of time but is then unable to control or moderate the intake of alcohol once drinking resumes. This person is a "binge" drinker. Both patterns of drinking can result in deteriorating relationships, loss of job, family conflicts, and violence while intoxicated.

Alcohol dependence is the more serious drinking problem. Like other dependence disorders, it is characterized by tolerance and/or withdrawal symptoms, as well as impairment of functioning.

Alcohol produces short-term and long-term physiological and psychological effects. Once swallowed, it is absorbed into the blood without digestion. When it reaches the brain, its *short-term physiological effect* is to depress functioning of the central nervous system. When the alcohol content in the blood stream (the blood alcohol level) is about 0.1 percent (the equivalent of drinking 5 ounces of whiskey), muscular coordination is impaired. The drinker may have trouble walking a straight line or pronouncing certain words. At the 0.5 percent blood alcohol level, the individual may lose consciousness or even die.

The short-term physiological effects of alcohol on a specific individual are determined by body weight, the amount of food present in the stomach, the drinking rate over time, prior drinking experience, heredity, and the personality and culture of the drinker. Table 11.1 shows the effect of alcohol intake on blood alcohol level as a function of body weight.

The *short-term psychological* effects of alcohol include feelings of happiness, loss of inhibitions (due to alcohol's depressive effects on inhibitory brain centers), poor judgment, and reduced concentration. Heavy drinking often causes a *hangover* (disagreeable aftereffects ranging from headache to upset stomach) the following morning.

The *long-term psychological* effects of

Table 11.1 *Blood Alcohol Level as a Function of Number of Drinks Consumed and Body Weight*

Body Weight, pounds	Number of Drinks Consumed*						
	1	*2*	*3*	*4*	*5*	*6*	*7*
100	.020	.055	.095	.130	.165	.200	.245
120	.015	.045	.075	.105	.135	.165	.195
140	.010	.035	.060	.085	.115	.140	.165
160	.005	.030	.050	.075	.095	.120	.145
180	.0	.025	.045	.065	.085	.105	.125
200	.0	.020	.040	.055	.075	.095	.110
220	.0	.020	.035	.050	.065	.085	.100
240	.0	.015	.035	.045	.060	.075	.090

*The given blood alcohol levels are those that would exist 1 hour after the start of drinking. Because alcohol is metabolized over time, subtract .015 from the given level for each additional hour. For example, a 100-pound person consuming 2 drinks would, after 2 hours, have a blood alcohol level of .055 − .015 = .040. One drink equals 12 ounces of beer, 4 ounces of wine, or 1.25 ounces of liquor.

SOURCE: Adapted from Vogler, R. E., and Bartz, W. R. (1983). *A better way to drink.* New York: Simon & Schuster. Copyright © 1983 by Robert E. Vogler and Wayne R. Bartz. Reprinted by permission of Simon & Schuster, Inc.

Alcohol reduces inhibitions and tension because it is a central nervous system depressant. In social situations, which can be anxiety provoking, a person may drink for its relaxing effect. Eventually, over a period of months or years, a person's tolerance level may increase, and alcoholism may develop.

heavy drinking are more serious. In particular, alcoholics are thought to progress through four stages (Jellinek 1971). In the *prealcoholic symptomatic phase,* individuals begin to drink in social situations. Because the alcohol relieves tension, the drinkers tend to drink more and to drink more frequently. Tolerance levels may increase over a period of months or years.

During the *prodromal phase,* the individuals are preoccupied with thoughts of alcohol. They may worry about whether there will be enough alcohol at a party; they may try to drink inconspicuously, or even furtively. They begin to consume large amounts and may "gulp" their drinks. Such drinkers frequently feel guilty; they are somewhat aware that their drinking is excessive. This phase is also characterized by *blackouts,* periods of time for which drinkers have no memory of their activities.

The *crucial phase* occurs when drinking individuals lose control of their alcohol intake. Once drinking starts, they must continue (or cannot stop) until they become intoxicated. Although it is possible for them to abstain from drinking, they have lost the ability to regulate their drinking after the first drink. They may go on drinking binges that last for days.

The *chronic stage* is the final one in alcohol addiction. Alcohol is consumed frequently, to the point of total intoxication. The alcoholic is now openly drunk in the daytime and constantly concerned with obtaining alcohol. Deterioration in his or her social, familial, and occupational functions is now evident. The affected individual is essentially living only to drink.

This perspective is largely a biological one in that it suggests that alcoholics cannot control their drinking because of their physical need and craving for alcohol. As is discussed later, this "loss of control" notion has come under attack.

The *long-term physiological effects* of alcohol consumption include an increase in tolerance as the body becomes used to alcohol, physical discomfort, anxiety, and hallucinations. Chronic alcoholism destroys brain cells and is often accompanied by poor nutritional habits and physical deterioration. Thus, the left brain hemispheres of alcoholics have been found to show less density than those of a control group of nonalcoholics (Golden et al. 1981). Other direct or indirect consequences generally attributed to chronic alcoholism are such liver diseases as *cirrhosis,* in which an excessive amount of fibrous tissue develops and impedes the circulation of blood; heart failure; and hemorrhages of capillaries, particularly those on the sides of the nose. Heavy alcohol consumption among pregnant women may affect their unborn children: Children who suffer *fetal alcohol syndrome* are born mentally retarded or physically deformed.

Interestingly, the *moderate* use of alcohol (one or two drinks a day) in adults has been associated in some studies with lowered risk of heart disease. The precise reasons for this effect are unknown. What is clear, though, is that chronic heavy consumption has serious negative consequences.

DSM-III lists a variety of organic mental disorders attributed to the ingestion of alcohol. Included are alcohol idiosyncratic intoxication, alcohol hallucinosis, alcohol withdrawal, and alcohol amnestic disorder. In these disorders, a psychological or behavioral abnormality is associated with transient or permanent dysfunction of the brain.

The essential feature of **alcohol idiosyncratic intoxication** is an acute behavior change. After the ingestion of a relatively small amount of alcohol, the person may become hostile, assaultive, depressed, confused, or disoriented, in marked contrast to the behavior shown by the person when not drinking. It seems that small amounts of alcohol trigger atypical behaviors in the drinker until the blood alcohol level decreases. Some researchers have speculated that the individual with this disorder may have brain damage that, combined with alcohol consumption, results in unusual behavior.

In **alcohol hallucinosis,** the cessation or reduction of alcohol intake leads to vivid auditory hallucinations. Often the hallucinations involve voices that accuse the alcoholic individual of sins or misdeeds. The individual may respond to the voices—that is, talk to himself or herself—or may try to ignore them and hide the problem from others.

In **alcohol withdrawal,** the cessation or reduction of alcohol ingestion by an individual who has been drinking for several days results in tremors of the hands and other parts of the body, nausea and vomiting, weakness, tachycardia, sweating, anxiety, or depression. Hallucinations and sleep disturbances may also occur. If delirium (confusion, difficulty in maintaining attention and concentration, and delusions) is also involved, the disorder is called **alcohol-withdrawal delirium.**

Alcohol amnestic disorder, or **Korsakoff's disease,** is sometimes found in chronic alcoholics who ignore proper nutrition and diet. The precise etiology of Korsakoff's disease is unknown, but the prevailing belief now is that nutritional deficiencies, particularly the lack of B-complex vitamins result in a serious disruption of brain function and in brain damage (Redlich and Freedman 1966). The classic symptoms of Korsakoff's psychosis are the loss of memory for very recent or immediately preceding events (*anterograde amnesia*) and the filling in of memory gaps with false or fanciful accounts (*confabulation*). For example, a patient may be asked what she just saw on television. Rather than report on the football game that was just shown and which she has forgotten, the patient may say that she saw a great adventure movie and then proceed to describe the imaginary movie in detail. When confronted with the fact that she actually saw a football game, the patient may insist she is correct, even if her story is illogical or clearly inaccurate. She may even forget the confabulated story and give another response entirely. Other symptoms of Korsakoff's disease include general confusion, disorientation, and hallucinations.

Etiology of alcohol use disorders

Why do individuals become dependent on alcohol? Is alcoholism a disease, or is it learned? A number of theories have been propounded in the attempt to answer such questions. Of these, the major types are either biological–physical in perspective (involving genetic or congenital factors) or psychological–cultural in perspective (involving personality or learning factors). Both perspectives may have some validity in explaining alcoholism. The biological–physical theories focus on dependence, or the bodily need for alcohol. The psychological–cultural theories help to explain how drinking patterns develop before actual addiction and why alcoholics who have stopped drinking and no longer have physical cravings may return to drinking.

Investigators have often assumed that the *acquisition* of drinking behavior is the result of psychological factors, whereas the *maintenance* of heavy drinking results from physical dependence on alcohol. That is, one first drinks because of curiosity; exposure to drinking models such as parents, peers, or television characters; and the tension-reducing properties of alcohol. After prolonged consumption, however, the person becomes physically dependent and drinks heavily to satisfy bodily needs. This assumption is overly simplistic. As you will see shortly, the acquisition and maintenance of drinking behavior are both influenced by the complex interaction of psychological and physical factors.

Biological–physical explanations Because alcohol affects metabolic processes and the central nervous system, investigators have explored the possibility that heredity or congenital factors increase susceptibility to addiction. The Research Task Force (1975) suggested that alcoholism "runs in families" and that 20 to 30 percent of the children of alcoholics eventually develop alcoholism. The challenge in these observations is to separate the contributions of genetic and environmental factors, because children share both genetic and environmental influences with their parents.

Several studies have indicated that children whose parents were alcoholics but who were adopted and reared by nonrelatives are more likely to develop drinking problems than adopted children whose biological parents were not alcoholics (Research Task Force 1975; Goodwin et al. 1973; Goodwin et al. 1977; Goodwin 1979). Research comparing the concordance rates for alcoholism among identical (MZ) and fraternal (DZ) twins indicates that, although MZ twins have higher concordance rates, DZ twins also have high rates (Rosenthal 1971). These findings suggest that both heredity and environmental factors are important.

The work of Sue and Nakamura (1984) suggests that alcohol *consumption* is influenced by both genetic and environmental factors. They found that Chinese and Japanese in the United States have traditionally exhibited low rates of alcohol consumption; these low rates have been attributed to genetic racial differences. For example, there is evidence that Chinese and Japanese are more likely than Caucasians to exhibit fast metabolism of alcohol following its ingestion. Presumably, this faster metabolism of alcohol leads to an accumulation of acetaldehyde in the body. Acetaldehyde causes adverse reactions and dysphoria (a general sick feeling), so Chinese and Japanese may keep their consumption levels low to avoid these reactions. However, as noted by Sue and Nakamura, a strictly genetic interpretation is significantly weakened when two facts are considered. First, assimilated Asians in the United States tend to consume more alcohol than unassimilated Asians, perhaps pointing to environmental factors in drinking. Second, some Japanese in Japan now show heavy rates of alcohol consumption as part of the accepted practice of drinking while entertaining business clients.

Finally, there have been attempts to implicate nutritional or vitamin-use deficiencies, hormonal imbalances, or abnormal bodily processes as causes of alcoholism. No clear-cut evidence has been found to indicate that these congenital factors are important in human alcoholism.

Psychological–cultural explanations The psychological–cultural perspective on alcoholism includes two basic assumptions: Alcoholism is learned, and alcohol temporarily serves to reduce tension. Some researchers believe that certain *personality characteristics* make individuals vulnerable to alcoholism. These characteristics may predispose individuals to use alcohol, rather than some other coping strategy, to deal with stressors. Low frustration tolerance, emotional immaturity, feelings of inadequacy, a need for power, and dependent personality characteristics have all been associated with alcoholism or heavy drinking (Jones 1968, 1971; McClelland et al. 1972; Winokur et al. 1970).

Findings regarding a predisposition to drinking are mixed. In one long-term study, researchers found that adolescents reported increased drunkenness when they had (1) lower personal regard for academic achievement, (2) higher tolerance for deviance, (3) more positive reasons, in relation to perceived drawbacks, for drinking, and (4) more positive reasons, for drug use (Jessor and Jessor 1977). Although these four personality characteristics were significantly correlated with being drunk, the correlations were not strong. In another long-term study (of male drinkers only) evidence was found that an unhappy childhood does not cause alcohol abuse, as is

popularly believed. Rather, the abuser is unhappy because of heavy drinking (Vaillant and Milofsky 1982).

Obviously, a direct linkage between personality traits and alcoholism has not been proved. Such a linkage would have to include explanations of why some persons with the "right" personality characteristics do not use alcohol and of why some alcoholics do not possess these characteristics. Furthermore, it is difficult to determine whether certain personality patterns actually cause alcoholism, or whether alcoholism causes the personality patterns. Alcoholism may very well influence personality; for example, some alcoholics may develop feelings of inadequacy because of their dependency on alcohol.

Cultural factors, however, appear to be highly important. For example, ethnicity and social class have been related to rates of alcoholism (McCord, McCord, and Gudeman 1960). Native Americans and Americans of Irish extraction were more likely to become alcoholics than Americans of Italian and Hispanic backgrounds. Furthermore, a direct relationship was found between incidence of alcoholism, level of education, and socioeconomic class. Religious affiliation can also be a factor in alcohol consumption. For example, a high proportion of heavy drinkers are Catholic.

These various cultural factors can combine to influence the extent and nature of drinking. Italy, for instance, has a high rate of alcohol *consumption* but a low incidence of *alcoholism*. Drinking wine at mealtime is customary in Italy, but drinking to become intoxicated is discouraged. France has high rates of both consumption and alcoholism. Drinking patterns in France are characterized by moderate alcoholic intake throughout the day, and drunkenness is more permissible there than in Italy.

One usually learns cultural values and behaviors in one's family and community. A review of the literature on adolescent drinking led researchers to conclude that teen-aged problem drinkers are exposed first to parents who are themselves heavy drinkers and then to peers who act as models for heavy consumption (Braucht 1982). The parents were found to not only consume a great deal of alcohol but also to exhibit inappropriate behaviors such as antisocial tendencies and rejection of their children. When those children loosen their parental ties, they tend to be strongly influenced by peers who are also heavy drinkers.

Some interesting research has been conducted on the anxiety-reducing properties of alcohol. In a classic experiment, an "experimental neurosis" was induced in cats. After the cats were trained to approach and eat food at a food box, they were given an aversive stimulus (an air blast to the face or an electric shock) whenever they approached the food. The cats stopped eating and exhibited "neurotic" symptoms—anxiety, psychophysiological disturbances, and peculiar behaviors. When the cats were given alcohol, however, their symptoms disappeared and they started to eat. As the effects of the alcohol wore off, the symptoms began to reappear (Masserman et al. 1944).

The experimenters also found that these cats now preferred "spiked" milk (milk mixed with alcohol) to milk alone. Once the stressful shocks were terminated and the fear responses extinguished, however, the cats no longer preferred spiked milk. Alcohol apparently reduced the cats' anxieties and was used as long as the anxieties were present. (Note that the cats were placed in an *approach–avoidance* conflict. That is, their desire to approach the food box and eat was in conflict with their desire to avoid the air blast or shock.)

An experimenter wanted to test the hypothesis that alcohol reduces the anxiety of conflict—that it resolves conflicts by increasing approach behaviors or by decreasing avoidance behaviors. He placed rats in a conflict situation and measured the strengths of approach behaviors and avoidance behaviors

before and after the use of alcohol (Conger 1951). He found that the main effect of alcohol was to reduce avoidance behaviors, and concluded that alcohol helps resolve conflicts by reducing fear of the noxious or aversive element. Many theorists believe that the anxiety-reducing properties of alcohol are reinforcing and are therefore largely responsible for maintaining the drinking behavior of the alcoholic.

A group of researchers have challenged the disease concept of alcoholism—the notion that drinking small amounts of alcohol leads, in an alcoholic, to involuntary consumption to the point of intoxication. In their study, alcoholics and social drinkers were recruited to participate in what was described as a tasting experiment. Both the alcoholics and the social drinkers were divided into four groups:

1. Members of the *told alcohol–given alcohol group* were told that they would be given a drink of alcohol and tonic, and they were actually given such a drink.
2. Members of the *told alcohol–given tonic group* were told that they would receive a drink of alcohol and tonic, but they were actually given only tonic.
3. Members of the *told tonic–given alcohol group* were told that they would receive a drink of tonic, but they were actually given an alcohol-and-tonic drink.
4. Members of the *told tonic–given tonic group* were told that they would be given tonic, and they were actually given tonic.

The experimenters used a mixture of five parts tonic and one part vodka for their alcohol-and-tonic drink; these proportions made it difficult to tell whether or not the drink contained alcohol. Subjects were asked to rinse their mouths with a mouthwash that, unknown to the subjects, was used to dull their sense of taste. At the beginning of the experiment, the subjects were "primed" with an initial drink—either alcohol and tonic or tonic only, depending on which group they were in. (That is, the *given alcohol* groups were primed with alco-

Table 11.2 The Role of Expectancy in Drinking Behavior

Group	Average Number of Ounces Consumed				Combined Average of Alcoholics and Social Drinkers
	Alcoholics		*Social Drinkers*		
	Told Tonic	*Told Alcohol*	*Told Tonic*	*Told Alcohol*	
Given tonic	10.9	23.9	9.3	14.6	14.7
Given alcohol	10.2	22.1	5.9	14.4	13.2
Combined average of given tonic and given alcohol	10.6	23.0	7.6	14.5	13.9

SOURCE: Adapted from Marlatt, G. A., Demming, B., and Reid, J. (1973). Loss-of-control drinking in alcoholics: An experimental analogue. *Journal of Abnormal Psychology, 81,* 233–241. Copyright by the American Psychological Association. Reprinted with permission.

hol, and the *given tonic* groups were primed with tonic.) After the primer drink, subjects were given instructions on the kind of drink they would receive. They were free to sample as much of the drink as they wished, alone and uninterrupted.

If alcoholism is a *condition* in which alcoholics lose control of drinking, then those *given* an alcohol primer should drink more alcohol. Alternatively, if alcoholics *learn* that alcohol reduces anxiety or enhances feelings of well-being, then those *told* that they would receive alcohol (whether or not alcohol was actually given) would drink more because they *expected* alcohol. Table 11.2 shows the results of the experiment. Note that alcoholics drank more tonic or alcohol than social drinkers; subjects who were told they would receive alcohol drank more than those who were told they would receive tonic; and those who actually consumed alcohol did not drink more than those who consumed tonic (Marlatt, Demming, and Reid 1973).

These results suggest that alcoholism is *not* simply a disease in which a person loses control over drinking. The subjects' *expectancy* had a stronger effect than the actual content of their drinks on how much they consumed. In fact, several subjects who were given tonic when they believed they were imbibing alcohol acted as though they were "tipsy" from the drinks!

These experiments on drinking behavior suggest that *psychological factors,* such as tension reduction and expectancy, are important in maintaining drinking behavior. The tension-reduction model, which assumes that alcohol reduces tension and anxiety and that the relief of tension reinforces the drinking response, is difficult to test, and research with alcoholics has produced conflicting findings. In fact, prolonged drinking is often associated with *increased* anxiety and depression (McNamee, Mello, and Mendelson 1968). Although alcoholics who have high blood alcohol levels after drinking may show low muscular tension, they tend to report a high degree of distress (Steffen, Nathan, and Taylor 1974). Although alcohol is a sedative that can reduce anxiety, is is possible that the knowledge that one is drinking alcohol can increase one's level of anxiety (Polivy, Schueneman, and Carlson 1976).

There is some evidence that the tension-reduction model is too simplistic. For example, when a group of subjects expected to receive a painful shock, they did not consume any more alcohol than subjects who expected to receive a nonpainful shock. However, when a social, rather than a physical, source of tension or anxiety was anticipated (for example, when male subjects were told that they would be rated on their personal attractiveness by a group of females), subjects tended to consume more alcohol than a control group that did not expect to be evaluated by others. Thus different types of tension (electric shock versus social evaluation) produced different results (Marlatt 1975). Marlatt suggests that the type of stressor, the loss of a sense of personal control over situations, and the lack of alternative coping responses influence drinking as indicated in his analysis of relapse.

Relapse is the resumption of drinking after a period of voluntary abstinence. Many alcoholics who try to stop drinking return to alcohol within a matter of weeks. Reviewing the circumstances leading to the relapse, Marlatt (1978) concluded that feelings of frustration or anger, social pressure to drink, or temptations (such as walking by a bar) are important preconditions for the resumption of drinking. Such "high-risk" situations make the person vulnerable. If the person has a coping response (a means of resisting social pressure—for instance, by insisting on a soft drink), that response provides an alternative to drinking. Coping responses include assertion (such as saying "no" when pressured by others to drink), avoidance (such as not walking near a favorite bar), and more satisfactory means of dealing with anger or anxiety. This, in turn, enables the person to feel control over drinking and to continue abstinence. If a person does not have a coping response to the high-risk situation, however, he or she takes that first drink.

A person can obviously stop drinking after one drink. To explain the full-blown resumption of drinking that occurs with the alcoholic's first drink, Marlatt proposes the notion of an *abstinence violation effect*. That is, once drinking begins, the person senses a loss of personal control. He or she feels weak-willed and guilty and gives up trying to abstain. The abstinence violation effect can also be applied to other relapse behaviors, such as overeating, masturbating, and smoking. Treatment to overcome the abstinence violation effect would focus on giving persons coping responses for high-risk situations.

Treatment for alcohol use disorders

Although alcoholism and its treatment have been studied for decades, no consensus exists on the most effective of the various treatment approaches (Nathan and Wiens 1983). Many of these approaches include **detoxification,** in which the alcoholic is allowed no alcohol at all. If withdrawal symptoms occur, the patient may receive tranquilizers as medication. Individual or group psychotherapy is often initiated after detoxification begins. The alcoholic may also be sent from the hospital to a halfway house, where support and guidance are available in a community setting.

In this section, we shall discuss several approaches to the treatment of alcoholism and then review their effectiveness.

Alcoholics Anonymous Alcoholics Anonymous (AA) is a self-help organization composed of alcoholics who want to stop drinking. Perhaps a million or more alcoholics worldwide participate in the AA program, which is completely voluntary. There are no fees; the only membership requirement is the desire to stop drinking. Members must recognize that they can never drink again and must concentrate on abstinence, one day at a time. As a means of helping members to abstain, each is often assigned a sponsor who provides individual support, attention, and help. Fellowship, spiritual awareness, and public self-revelations about past wrongdoings due to alcohol are encouraged during group meetings.

Some individuals believe that membership in AA is one of the most effective treatments for alcoholism. However, objective outcome studies are difficult to find. Furthermore, it appears that the success rate of AA is not so high as AA members claim it is (Brandsma 1979). About half the alcoholics who stay in the organization are abstinent after 2 years (Alford 1980). But many drop out of the program and are not counted as failures (when, perhaps, they should be). Thus, although many persons are helped by AA, its success rate has not been established.

Antabuse Some alcohol treatment programs have made use of the chemical *antabuse* (disulfiram) to produce an aversion to alcohol. If an individual consumes alcohol within one to two days after taking antabuse, he or she suffers a severe reaction, including nausea, vomiting, and discomfort. Antabuse has the effect of blocking the progressive breakdown of alcohol so that excessive acetaldehyde accumulates in the body; and, as we noted earlier, acetaldehyde causes dysphoria. Most alcoholics will not consume alcohol after ingesting antabuse. Those who do risk not only discomfort but in some cases death.

While patients are taking antabuse and are abstinent, psychotherapy and other forms of treatment may be used to help them develop coping skills or alternative life patterns. The families of patients may also be encouraged to try again to work at solving the problems created by the drinking. Knowing that alcohol consumption is unlikely during antabuse treatment, the families do not have to rely solely on the victims promise to stop drinking—a promise that alcoholics often make but rarely can keep.

The problem with antabuse treatment is that alcoholic patients may stop taking the drug once they leave the hospital or are no longer being monitored. And some may drink anyway, because they believe the effects of antabuse have dissipated, because they have forgotten when they last took it, or because they are tempted to drink in spite of the antabuse.

Cognitive and behavioral approaches Cognitive and behavioral therapists have devised several strategies for treating alcoholics. **Aversion therapy,** which is based on classical conditioning principles, has been used for many years. Aversion therapy is a process by which the sight, smell, or taste of alcohol is paired with a noxious stimulus. For example, alcoholics may be given painful electric shocks while drinking alcohol. Or they may be given emetics (agents that induce vomiting) when they get the urge to drink or after smelling or tasting alcohol. After several sessions in which the emetic is used, alcoholics may vomit or feel nauseated whenever they smell, taste, or think about alcohol.

Imagery has been used as part of aversion conditioning in a technique that is also known as **covert sensitization:** Alcoholic patients are trained to imagine nausea and vomiting in the presence of alcoholic beverages (Cautela 1966). In addition, relaxation and systematic desensitization may be used to reduce anxiety. Almost any aversive-conditioning procedure may be effective in the treatment of alcoholism if there is also a focus on enhanced social functioning, resistance to stress, and reduction of anxiety (Nathan 1976).

Recently, a great deal of controversy has been generated by the suggestion that it is possible for alcoholics to control their intake and learn to become social drinkers. Proponents of **controlled drinking** assume that, under the right conditions, alcoholics can learn to limit their drinking to appropriate levels. The finding that alcoholics tend to gulp drinks rather than sip them (as social or moderate drinkers do), to consume straight rather than mixed drinks, and to drink many rather than a few drinks gave investigators clues to the behaviors that require modification. Alcoholics were then trained to drink appropriately. In a setting resembling a bar, they were permitted to order and drink alcohol; but they were administered an aversive stimulus for each inappropriate behavior. For example, if the alcoholics gulped drinks or ordered too many, they would be given painful electric shocks.

One problem with this technique is that patients need to receive periodic retraining or to learn alternative responses to drinking. Otherwise, they tend to revert to their old patterns of consumption upon leaving the treatment program (Marlatt 1983).

Opponents of controlled drinking generally believe that total abstinence should be the goal

The Controlled-Drinking Controversy

In the 1970s, Sobell and Sobell (1978) conducted an experiment to determine whether alcoholics could learn to control their drinking. Up to this time, the goal of most treatment programs was total abstinence. The Sobells worked with forty hospitalized male alcoholics. (Other alcoholics in different treatment programs were studied by the Sobells, but they were not part of the controlled-drinking controversy.) Half of the subjects (the control group) received conventional treatment designed to promote abstinence. The other half (the experimental group) received behavior therapy designed to train them to control, rather than abstain from, drinking. These subjects participated in therapy sessions in which they saw themselves drinking on videotapes, received electric shocks for inappropriate drinking behaviors (such as ordering drinks too frequently), and learned how to use alternative responses in drinking situations. After treatment and for about two additional years, the outcomes for the experimental and control groups were compared. In general, this comparison revealed that the controlled drinkers were functioning better and spent less time in hospitals than the abstainers.

The controversy started when another group of investigators decided to assess the long-term effects of the treatment and to conduct a follow-up investigation of the patients in the Sobells' experimental group. In addition to raising questions about some of the methods used by the Sobells, the later investigators came to very different conclusions about the success of the controlled-drinking subjects. Using hospital and arrest records and interviews of the subjects, they found that the majority of the controlled drinkers had been hospitalized within one year of the experiment. Only one subject had maintained a pattern of controlled drinking. The majority showed drinking problems (Pendery, Maltzman, and West 1982).

Debates over the effectiveness of various treatment approaches are expected, and they serve to stimulate research. However, when researchers dispute the facts (that is, the outcomes) of a particular study, the situation becomes quite serious and confusing. Some accused the Sobells of fraudulent and sloppy work; others defended their research. The controversy over this particular experiment has not yet ended, and it may never be resolved.

of treatment, that controlled drinking cannot be maintained over a period of time, and that alcoholism is a genetic–physiological problem. Furthermore, by trying to teach alcoholics that they can resume and control drinking, proponents are unwittingly contributing to the alcoholics' problems. There have even been questions about the validity of the findings in controlled-drinking programs (see Focus 11.2).

Multimodal treatment In view of the many factors that maintain alcohol consumption, some treatment programs make systematic use of combinations of approaches. For example, alcoholics may be detoxified through antabuse treatment and simultaneously receive behavioral training (via aversion therapy, biofeedback, or stress management) as well as other forms of therapy.

Other therapies may include combinations

of Alcoholics Anonymous, educational training, family therapy, group therapy, and individual psychotherapy. Proponents of multimodal approaches recognize that no single kind of treatment is likely to be totally effective and that successful outcomes often require major changes in the lives of alcoholics. The combination of therapies that works best for a particular individual in his or her particular circumstances is obviously the most effective treatment.

Effectiveness of treatment With respect to the general effectiveness of the various treatment efforts, Moos and Finney (1983) note that they have indeed helped a number of alcoholics to function normally. Estimates of the proportion of treated alcohol abusers who improve range from 32 to 53 percent, depending on the criteria that are used to measure improvement. In addition, 10 to 20 percent of alcohol abusers recover ''spontaneously,'' without formal treatment. Moos and Finney note further that ''treatment apparently facilitates the recovery process in that treated individuals show higher rates of improvement in many studies than do minimally treated or untreated comparison groups'' (p. 1036).

But Moos and Finney also note that

Relapse rates during the year after the completion of treatment may be as high as 60% or more. . . . Moreover, researchers have not been very successful in identifying superior treatment methods or in finding treatment approaches that are particularly effective for specific types of patients. Even the idea that more treatment (longer treatment of greater intensity) is better than less treatment has not received much support. . . . Finally, a large number of persons do not recover ''spontaneously,'' but continue to drink heavily and to incur substantial personal and social costs by doing so.

Such apparently divergent findings indicate that intervention programs and life-context factors can have a powerful impact on the course of alcoholism. By suggesting that this impact can

Alcoholism generally affects more than just an individual. In families of alcoholics the spouse and children are also affected. Alateen is a group founded to help adolescents cope with the stress and problems produced by having an alcoholic parent.

be for better or for worse, they highlight a set of important issues: Why do some alcohol abusers respond positively to an intervention while others show little or no response and quickly resume problem drinking? In what ways do the characteristics of an individual's life context foster or inhibit the recovery process? How do patient, intervention, and life-context factors interrelate to affect recovery and relapse? (p. 1037)

Such issues obviously need to be resolved as part of the effort to improve the effectiveness of alcohol treatment programs.

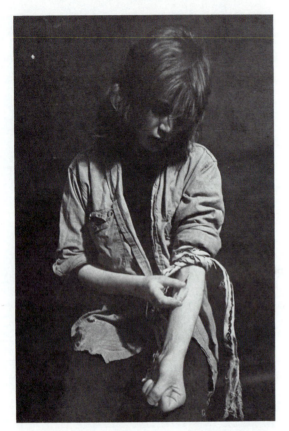

Heroin is a highly physiologically addictive narcotic that is generally taken through hypodermic injection. It acts as a sedative that relieves pain, tension, and anxiety and produces feelings of euphoria and well-being. The dependency is so strong that addicts are unable to maintain normal social relationships or a legitimate career.

DRUG USE DISORDERS

Miriam K. was a 44-year-old divorced pharmacist. She had been married for over 20 years, but, during the last few years of the marriage, Miriam and her husband had talked about divorce. They had lost interest in each other and pretty much lived their own lives. After their son and daughter left home to attend college, they obtained a divorce.

Although the divorce was relatively amicable, Miriam felt lonesome. With her children at college and her divorce completed, she was very much alone at home. Several of her friends took her along to ''singles club'' activities to establish some new social relationships. However, Miriam had mixed feelings about men. She was excited about meeting them, but she also felt anxious and inadequate. In addition, Miriam was facing additional responsibilities and demands at work, where a promotion now required that she supervise the operation of three pharmacies.

Although Miriam had occasionally used drugs to calm her nervousness, she now began taking Valium regularly to reduce tension and bring on sleep. Because she worked at pharmacies, she had no trouble in obtaining the drug secretly. Gradually she took more and more. Over the course of several years, her tolerance and intake increased to the point where she was consuming about 75 milligrams a day. This heavy consumption of Valium resulted in a general lethargy, and Miriam was absent from work a great deal. Her employer finally told her that she had to perform better or he would find someone else for her job. Immediately thereafter, Miriam sought help for her dependency on Valium.

In the remainder of this chapter, we discuss a number of additional substance-use disorders. The substances used include both prescription drugs like Valium, and also cigarettes, narcotics, and LSD. To differentiate them easily from alcohol, we have lumped them together as ''drugs.'' However, you should realize that alcohol too is a drug—and, in fact, the most widely used drug with potentially harmful effects.

The drugs that we shall discuss can all cause psychological or physical problems; and many can cause legal problems as well. The use of certain substances, except under strict medical supervision, is expressly prohibited by law. Hence the user must obtain them illegally. We shall specifically discuss three classes of drug: depressants (or sedatives), stimulants, and hallucinogens. Each of the drugs within these classes can be the object of an abuse disorder or a (more severe) dependence disorder. Table 11.3 lists some of these drugs and their effects.

Table 11.3 *Drugs and Their Effects*

Drugs	Short-Term Effects*	Potential Pattern	
		Abuse	*Dependence*
Sedatives			
Narcotics (codeine, morphine, heroin, opium, methadone)	Central nervous system (CNS) depressant, pain relief	Yes	Yes
Barbiturates (amytal, nembutal, seconal)	CNS depressant, sleep inducer	Yes	Yes
Benzodiazepines (Valium)	CNS depressant, anxiety relief	Yes	Yes
Stimulants			
Amphetamines (Benzedrine, Dexedrine, Methedrine)	CNS energizer, euphoria	Yes	Yes
Caffeine	CNS energizer, alertness	Yes	†
Nicotine	CNS energizer	Yes	†
Cocaine	CNS energizer, euphoria	Yes	Transitory
Hallucinogens			
Marijuana, Hashish	Relaxant, euphoria	Yes	Tolerance
LSD	Hallucinatory agent	Yes	No
Mescaline	Hallucinatory agent	Yes	No
Psilocybin	Hallucinatory agent	Yes	No
PCP	Hallucinatory agent	Yes	No

*Specific effects often depend on the quality and dosage of the drug as well as on the experience, expectancy, personality, and situation of the person using the drug.
†Although physical dependence may develop, its clinical significance is considered minor.

Depressants or sedatives

Narcotics The organic **narcotics**—opium and its derivatives morphine, heroin, and codeine—are drugs that depress the central nervous system. They act as a sedative to provide relief from pain, anxiety, and tension. Feelings of euphoria and well-being (and sometimes negative reactions such as nausea) often accompany narcotics use. However, opium and its derivatives (especially heroin) are physiologically addictive. One's tolerance for narcotics builds rapidly, and withdrawal symptoms are severe.

Because of their strong psychological and physical dependency, narcotics addicts are usually unable to maintain normal relationships with family and friends or to pursue legitimate careers. They live to obtain the drug through any possible means. The nonmedical use of these narcotics is illegal, and many addicts have little choice but to turn to criminal activities to obtain the drug and to support their expensive habits.

Barbiturates Synthetic **barbiturates,** or "downers," are powerful depressants of the central nervous system that are commonly used to induce relaxation and sleep. Next to the narcotics, they represent the largest category of illegal drugs, and they are quite dangerous for several reasons. First, psychological and physical dependence can develop. Second, although their legal use is severely restricted, their widespread availability makes it difficult to control misuse or abuse. Over 1 million persons are now estimated to be barbiturate addicts. Third, users often experience harmful physical effects. Excessive use of either barbiturates or heroin can be fatal, but the former are the more lethal. Constant heroin use increases the amount of the drug required for a lethal dosage. The lethal dosage of barbiturates *does not* increase with prolonged use, so accidental overdose and death can easily occur. And combining alcohol with barbiturates can be especially dangerous, because alcohol compounds the depressant effects of the barbiturates.

> Kelly M., a seventeen-year-old girl from an upper-middle-class background, lived with her divorced mother. Kelly was hospitalized after her mother found her unconscious from an overdose of barbiturates consumed together with alcohol. She survived the overdose and later told the therapist that she had regularly used barbiturates for the past year and a half. The overdose was apparently accidental and not suicidal.
>
> For several weeks following the overdose, Kelly openly discussed her use of barbiturates with the therapist. She had been introduced to the drugs by a boy in school who told her they would help her to relax. Kelly was apparently unhappy over her parents' divorce. She felt her mother did not want her, especially in view of the fact that her mother spent a lot of time away from home building a real estate agency. And, although she enjoyed her occasional visits with her father, Kelly felt extremely uncomfortable in the presence of the woman who lived with him. The barbiturates helped her to relax and relieve her tensions. Arguments with her mother would precipitate heavy use of the drugs. Eventually she became dependent on barbiturates and always spent her allowance to buy them. Her mother reported that she had no knowledge of her daughter's drug use. She did notice, though, that Kelly was increasingly isolated and sleepy.
>
> The therapist informed Kelly of the dangers of barbiturates and of combining them with alcohol. Kelly agreed to undergo treatment, which included the gradual reduction of barbiturate use and psychotherapy with her mother.

A hazardous practice illustrated in the case of Kelly M. is *polydrug use,* or the use of more than one chemical substance at the same time. This practice can be extremely dangerous. For example, heavy smokers who consume a great deal of alcohol run an increased risk of esophageal cancer. Chemicals may also exhibit a synergistic effect, in which drugs that are taken simultaneously interact to multiply each other's effects. For example, when a large dose of a barbiturate is taken along with alcohol, death may occur because of a synergistic effect that depresses the central nervous system. Furthermore, one of the substances (such as alcohol) may reduce the person's judgment, resulting in excessive (or lethal) use of the other drug. Equally dangerous is the use of one drug to counteract the effect of another. For instance, a person who has taken a stimulant to feel euphoric may later take an excessive amount of a depressant (such as a barbiturate) in an attempt to get some sleep. The result can be an exceedingly harmful physiological reaction.

Benzodiazepines One member of this category of drugs is Valium, which is one of the most widely prescribed drugs in the United States today. As in the case of Miriam K. (described at the beginning of this section), Valium is often used to reduce anxiety and muscle tension. Individuals who take the drug seem less concerned with, and less affected by, their problems. Some side effects may occur, such as drowsiness, skin rash, nausea, and depression, but the greatest danger in using Valium is its abuse. Because life stressors are unavoidable, many persons use Valium as their sole means of dealing with stress; then, as tolerance develops, dependence on the drug may also grow.

Stimulants

Amphetamines The **amphetamines**, also known as "uppers" or "pep pills," speed up activity of the central nervous system and bestow on users increased alertness, energy, and sometimes feelings of euphoria and confidence. Amphetamines inhibit appetite and sleep. These stimulants may be physically addictive and become habit-forming with a rapid increase in tolerance. "Speed freaks" are those who inject amphetamine into their blood vessels and become extremely hyperactive and euphoric for days. Assaultive, homicidal, and suicidal behaviors can occur during this period of time. Overdoses are fatal, and brain damage has been observed among chronic abusers. Some persons may use amphetamines to achieve "highs" and then use barbiturates to "come down"—an extremely dangerous practice, as we have noted.

Caffeine and nicotine   Two widely used and legal stimulants are caffeine and nicotine. **Caffeine** is ingested primarily in coffee, tea, and cola drinks. It is considered intoxicating to an individual when, after the recent ingestion of 250 milligrams or more of caffeine, the person shows several of the following symptoms: restlessness, nervousness, excitement, insomnia, flushed face, and cardiac arrhythmia. The consequences of caffeine intoxication are usually transitory and relatively minor. In some cases, however, the intoxication is chronic and seriously affects the gastrointestinal or circulatory system.

The major source of **nicotine** is cigarette smoking. DSM-III lists tobacco addiction as a mental disorder if at least one of the following three criteria is met.

☐ Attempts to stop or reduce tobacco use on a permanent basis are unsuccessful.
☐ Attempts to stop smoking have led to withdrawal symptoms such as a craving for tobacco, irritability, difficulty in concentrating, and restlessness.
☐ The individual continues to use tobacco despite a serious physical disorder, such as emphysema, that he or she knows is exacerbated by tobacco use.

Ironically, a heavy smoker who has never tried to stop smoking, who has never developed withdrawal symptoms, and who has no major tobacco-related physical problem would not be considered to have the disorder, even though he or she would in all probability be dependent on tobacco.

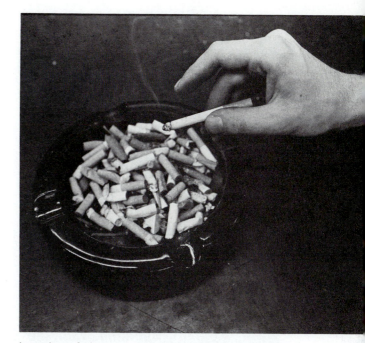

In spite of the strong evidence linking smoking to cancer, lung disease, and heart disease, millions of people continue to smoke, and are probably dependent on tobacco. Nicotine addiction is especially difficult to overcome because it has both physiological and psychological components.

Focus 11.3 (pp. 326–327) discusses two views on the development and maintenance of smoking behaviors.

Cocaine   Lately, a great deal of publicity and concern have been devoted to the use of **cocaine.** A number of major-league baseball players, film stars, political figures, and other notable individuals have been found to use this drug regularly. Indeed, its use is rapidly expanding, particularly among the young and the upwardly mobile. Because of its high cost and euphoria-inducing properties, cocaine is considered a fashionable drug, especially among middle-class and upper-class professionals.

In the late 1800s, cocaine was heralded as a wonder drug for remedying depression, indigestion, headaches, pain, and other ailments. It was often included in medicines, tonics, and wines; it was even used in cola drinks such as Coca-Cola. However, in the early 1900s, its use was controlled, and the possession of cocaine is now illegal.

Cocaine can be eaten, injected intravenously, or smoked, but it is usually "snorted" (inhaled). Eating does not produce rapid effects, and intravenous use requires injection with a needle that leaves needle marks and introduces the possibility of infection. When cocaine is inhaled into the nasal cavity, however, the individual quickly begins to feel euphoric, stimulated, and confident. The heart rate and blood pressure increase, and (according to users) fatigue and appetite are reduced.

Users do not seem to become physiologically dependent on cocaine, but psychological dependence can result from its use. That is, the individual who has used it regularly can develop a craving for the drug and be unable to stop using it. Then the constant desire for cocaine can impair social and occupational functioning, and the high cost of the substance can cause users to resort to crime to feed their habit. In addition, side effects can occur. Feelings of depression and gloom may be produced when a cocaine high wears off. And heavy users sometimes report weight loss, paranoia, nervousness, fatigue, and hallucinations.

FOCUS 11.3

Smoking: Can the Body "Kick the Habit"?

Cigarette smoking is harmful to the body. Many people assume that sufficient will power and motivation on the part of smokers, or legal and social sanctions from nonsmokers (such as prohibiting smoking in public facilities), can reduce or eliminate the smoking habit. Judging from current statistics, however, efforts to motivate smokers to quit, to prohibit smoking in certain areas, and to regulate advertising by the tobacco industry have not been very successful in achieving that goal. Why do smokers continue to smoke? The answer may lie in the physiological effects of smoking. Even though smokers report feeling more relaxed during smoking, cigarettes act as a stimulant. Heart rate, for instance, increases during smoking.

Stanley Schachter, a noted psychologist, argues that people smoke because they are physically addicted to nicotine. In a series of experiments, Schachter (1977) drew two conclusions: First, chronic smokers need their "normal" constant intake of nicotine.

When heavy smokers are given low-nicotine cigarettes, they smoke more cigarettes and puff more frequently. Withdrawal symptoms, such as irritability and increased eating, appear when smokers do not receive their "dose" of nicotine. Second, smoking does not reduce anxiety or calm the nerves. But *not smoking* increases anxiety and produces withdrawal reactions. Smokers can tolerate less stress when they are deprived of cigarettes than when they are able to smoke. However, even with cigarettes, smokers do *not* perform better under stress than nonsmokers. Stress seems to deplete body nicotine, so that smoking is necessary to maintain the nicotine level.

Without denying the role of nicotine in physical dependence, Lichtenstein (1982) sees the development and maintenance of smoking as a complex process involving a variety of factors. For example, such factors as the availability of cigarettes, curiosity, and smoking models influence the ini-

Hallucinogens

Hallucinogens are not considered physiologically addictive. There is no physical dependence (that is, no increased tolerance or withdrawal reaction), although psychological dependency may occur. Hallucinogens such as marijuana, LSD, and phencyclidine (PCP) are used by many individuals to experience certain illusions, such as more vivid sensory awareness, heightened alertness, or increased insight.

Marijuana   The mildest and most commonly used hallucinogen is **marijuana,** also known as

"pot." This substance is generally smoked in a cigarette, or "joint." About 20 percent of the U.S. population (including youngsters) have used marijuana, although it is considered an illegal substance. In a large-scale survey, Mills and Noyes (1984) found that marijuana use by school-age children had declined from 1978 to 1980, but it was still one of the most widely used substances, along with alcohol (see Table 11.4, p. 328).

The subjective effects of marijuana use include feelings of euphoria, tranquility, and passivity. Once the drug has taken effect, time passes slowly, and some users report increased sensory experiences as well as mild

---

tial use of cigarettes. Then physiological and psychosocial factors such as nicotine addiction and positive consequences maintain smoking. For psychosocial reasons including health and the expense of smoking materials, the person may try to stop smoking. However, withdrawal symptoms, social pressure, and alcohol consumption (former smokers who drink are often tempted to smoke while consuming alcohol) are powerful factors in the resumption of smoking.

Lichtenstein's analysis emphasizes the value of multicomponent programs for the treatment and prevention of smoking. His factors are listed in the table below.

Factors Involved in Smoking Behaviors

Starting (psychosocial factors)	Continuing (physiological and psychosocial factors)	Stopping (psychosocial factors)	Resuming (psychosocial and physiological factors)
Availability	Nicotine	Health	Withdrawal symptoms
Curiosity	Immediate positive	Expense	
Rebelliousness	consequences	Social support	Stress and frustration
Anticipation of	Signals (cues) in	Self-mastery	Social pressure
adulthood	environs		Alcohol consumption
Social confidence	Avoiding negative	Aesthetics	
	effects (withdrawal)		Abstinence violation
Social pressure/		Example to others	effect
modeling: peers,			
siblings, parents,			
media			

SOURCE: Lichtenstein (1982). Copyright 1982 by the American Psychological Association. Adapted by permission of the author.

Table 11.4 *Percentages of Eighth-, Tenth-, and Twelfth-Grade Students Reporting the Use of Selected Substances*

		Substance						
Grade	Year	Alcohol	Marijuana	Tranquilizers	Amphetamines	Cocaine	Hallucinogens	Heroin
8	1978	67.2	21.1	4.2	4.8	3.6	2.8	3.6
	1980		15.1	3.8	5.7	4.7	3.6	2.7
10	1978	81.6	42.3	7.7	8.3	9.2	7.6	3.1
	1980		32.4	7.9	10.2	8.1	7.6	3.3
12	1978	87.4	46.6	8.4	8.4	9.0	5.6	1.0
	1980		37.6	7.2	10.0	11.1	7.4	2.4

SOURCE: Mills and Noyes (1984). Copyright 1984 by the American Psychological Association. Adapted by permission of the authors.

perceptual distortions. One's prior experience with the drug, one's expectancy of its effects, and the setting in which one uses marijuana influence the precise reactions.

In one experiment, marijuana smokers were given either a marijuana or a placebo cigarette to smoke. Some subjects were told to overcome the drug's effects in performing tasks; others were not given this instruction. The researchers wanted to find out whether subjects could control their performance even after marijuana intoxication—that is, whether they could "come down" from a "high" at will. Their results indicated that marijuana intoxication influences the ability to estimate time and to remember lists of words. Moreover, by motivating subjects to overcome the effects of marijuana, they could improve the subjects' performance at estimating time but not their ability to remember lists of words (Cappell and Pliner 1973).

Although there has been much controversy over the effects of marijuana, many states have now decriminalized the possession of small quantities of this substance. Focus 11.4 is a brief report on some of the risks of marijuana smoking.

Lysergic acid diethylamide (LSD) LSD gained notoriety as a hallucinogen in the mid-l960s. Praised by users as a potent psychedelic, consciousness-expanding, "turning on" drug, LSD produces distortions of reality and hallucinations. "Good trips" are experiences of sharpened visual and auditory perception,

heightened sensation, convictions that one has achieved profound philosophical insights, and feelings of ecstasy. "Bad trips" include fear and panic from distortions of sensory experiences, severe depression, marked confusion and disorientation, and delusions. Some users report "flashbacks" or the recurrence of hallucinations or other sensations days or weeks after ingesting LSD. Fatigue, stress, or the use of another drug may trigger a flashback.

LSD is considered a *psychotomimetic* drug because, in some cases, it produces reactions that mimic those seen in acute psychotic reactions. It does not produce physical dependence, even in users who have taken the drug hundreds of times. Aside from its psychological effects, there is no substantial evidence that LSD is dangerous in and of itself. Overdoses do not lead to death, although there are reports of individuals who have unwittingly committed suicide while under the influence of LSD. It was initially believed that LSD caused chromosomal damage and spontaneous abortions, but such negative consequences are probably attributable to impurities in the drug, the use of other drugs, or the unhealthy lifestyles of many users.

Phencyclidine (PCP) Phencyclidine, also known as PCP, "angel dust," "crystal," "superweed," and "rocket fuel," has emerged as one of the most dangerous of the widely distributed drugs. Originally developed for its pain-killing properties, PCP is a hallucinatory drug that causes perceptual distortions, eu-

FOCUS 11.4

Marijuana Smoking: Are There Harmful Effects?

There is now growing concern over the potentially harmful physical effects of marijuana (Coates 1980). A new report to be issued by the National Institute of Drug Abuse indicates that smoking marijuana may cause more serious lung damage than smoking cigarettes. Indeed, smoking four joints a week may be as bad as smoking sixteen cigarettes a day. There is also some evidence that marijuana smoking may affect the reproductive systems of males and females: Heavy marijuana use reduced sperm concentration and sperm motility in males and was associated with failure to ovulate in females. Because these findings are correlational in nature, it cannot be concluded that marijuana smoking *causes* problems in the reproductive system. The results do suggest, however, that much more caution should be exercised in the use of marijuana, in view of the possible consequences.

In the past, the physiological effects of marijuana smoking were greatly exaggerated. More recently it was believed that these effects were insignificant. Now researchers are reexamining *that* belief.

The National Academy of Science (1982) has taken a dim view of marijuana use. Marijuana smoke can cause serious lung and respiratory problems and can increase the risk of cancer. Furthermore, because the drug affects memory and causes intoxication, individuals who have recently smoked marijuana may pose a danger while driving a car, operating machinery, or working in occupations that require judgment and decision making (such as air traffic control).

On the other hand, Coates (1980) points out the benefits of marijuana in treating certain physical ailments. For example, open-angle glaucoma, an eye disorder that can lead to blindness, temporarily responds to the drug; patients nauseated by chemotherapy for cancer often find relief with marijuana treatment. Researchers are now experimenting with the use of marijuana for victims of multiple sclerosis and for persons afflicted by seizures.

Such findings—and there seem to be new ones almost every week—show how little we know about marijuana and how much we still have to learn.

phoria, nausea, confusion, delusions, and violent psychotic behavior. Reactions to the drug are influenced by dosage, the individual user, and the circumstances in which it is taken. One thing is clear: PCP has in many cases produced aggressive behaviors, violence, or deaths due to recklessness or delusions of invincibility. The drug is illegal, but it is showing up in significant quantities "on the street."

Spitzer and co-workers (1981) described the effects of PCP on a chronic user. As you will see, one long-term effect may have been a personality change.

The patient is a 20-year-old male who was brought to the hospital, trussed in ropes, by his four brothers. This is his seventh hospitalization in the last two years, each for similar behavior. One of his brothers reports that he "came home crazy" late one night, threw a chair through a window, tore a gas heater off the wall, and ran into the street. The family called the police, who apprehended him shortly thereafter as he stood, naked, directing traffic at a busy intersection. He assaulted the arresting officers, escaped them, and ran home screaming threats at his family. There his brothers were able to subdue him.

On admission the patient was observed to be agitated, his mood fluctuating between anger and fear. He had slurred speech and staggered when he walked. He remained extremely violent and disorganized for the first several days of his hospitalization, then began having longer and longer lucid intervals, still interspersed with sudden, unpredictable periods in which he displayed great suspiciousness, a fierce expression, slurred speech, and clenched fists.

After calming down, the patient denied ever having been violent or acting in an unusual way (''I'm a peaceable man'') and said he could not remember how he got to the hospital. He admitted to using alcohol and marijuana socially, but denied phencyclidine (PCP) use except for once, experimentally, three years previously. Nevertheless, blood and urine tests were positive for phencyclidine, and his brother believes ''he gets dusted every day.''

According to his family, he was perfectly normal until about three years before. He made above-average grades in school, had a part-time job and a girlfriend, and was of a sunny and outgoing disposition. Then, at age 17, he had his first episode of emotional disturbance. This was of very sudden onset, with symptoms similar to the present episode. He quickly recovered entirely from that first episode, went back to school, and graduated from high school. From subsequent episodes, however, his improvement was less and less encouraging.

After three weeks of the current hospitalization he is sullen and watchful, quick to remark sarcastically on the smallest infringement of the respect due him. He is mostly quiet and isolated from others, but is easily provoked to fury. His family reports that ''This is as good as he gets now.'' He lives and eats most of his meals at home, and keeps himself physically clean, but mostly lies around the house, will do no housework, and has not held a job for nearly two years. The family does not know how he gets his spending money, or how he spends his time outside the hospital. (pp. 229–230)

Etiology of drug use disorders

Why are drugs overused? The answer to this question is complicated by the number of different kinds of drugs that are used and the number of factors that interact to account for the use of any one drug. An explanation of drug abuse must take into account several general observations. First, we do not know whether personality characteristics are related to drug dependence. For example, one researcher tried—but failed—to find a specific personality pattern for heroin addicts (Platt 1975). However, in a comparison of heroin addicts, amphetamine users, and barbiturate users, personality differences were noted between heroin addicts and the other two groups. Heroin users tended to be less disturbed, depressed, anxious, and rebellious (Penk, Fridge, and Robinowitz 1979). Compounding the problem is the finding that users tend to take many different drugs (Kohn, Barnes, and Hoffman 1979).

Second, physical addiction and the attempt to avoid withdrawal symptoms are insufficient to explain continued narcotics use. Withdrawal reactions have been characterized as being no more agonizing than a bad case of the flu (Ausubel 1961). We know that heroin addicts who enter the hospital and who do not receive heroin while hospitalized cease to have withdrawal symptoms in a week or two. Yet the vast majority who have lost their bodily need for the drug usually return to heroin after hospitalization. Can situational factors explain why they resume heroin use after physical dependence is overcome? Many Vietnam servicemen who were addicted to heroin when they returned to the United States *did* discontinue its use upon their return because of such situational factors as the easier access to alcohol and the difficulty of procuring heroin (Pilisuk 1975).

Third, the conditions that cause a person to try a drug have not been identified (Solomon 1977). The best predictor of drug sampling is drug availability, but drug use is too widespread and drug addiction too rare for the mere sampling of a drug to be a major cause of subsequent addiction. Solomon suggests that the initial reasons for using drugs are complex, varied, and obscure. Most drug usage is probably reinforcing at the outset—an attempt to solve some social problem, to respond to peer-group influences, to relieve unpleasant emotional states, or to become "high." Then, after continued use, the motivation for drug use changes. The user now must cope with drug craving, a fear of withdrawal, and other *acquired* motivations. The addict's desire to maintain social relationships and a certain lifestyle may also be a motivating factor.

In other words, Solomon believes that attempts to find a simple, single-cause explanation for drug addiction are fruitless; addiction is an acquired motivation, much like other acquired motivations such as love or attachment. To explain the process, Solomon (1980) has proposed the *opponent-process theory of acquired motivation,* which is summarized in Table 11.5. Consider first the individual who has used a drug only a few times. Before taking the drug again, that person, who is not yet addicted, is in a resting state. Then, during ingestion of the drug, a peak state (the rush) and euphoria are experienced; in other words, the psychopharmacological properties of the drug cause the user to feel "high." After the effects subside, there may be mild discomfort ("coming down" from the drug). The individual may start to crave the drug in order to combat the discomfort, but the discomfort soon subsides and the individual returns to a resting state. The motivation for use is to achieve the high and to avoid the aversiveness of the craving.

For the chronic user, however, the process is somewhat different. During the period before the drug is consumed, this individual experiences a craving for the drug. Then, during ingestion of the drug, the experienced user feels only contentment rather than a rush and intense euphoria. And once the effects of the drug wear off, he or she experiences withdrawal reactions and intense physiological and/or psychological craving, which do not subside without further drug use. In essence, the motivation for drug use has changed with experience, from positive to aversive control. A new motivation for drug use has been acquired.

Table 11.5 *Changes in Affect Before, During, and After Self-Dosing with Opiates, for the First Few Experiences and After Many Experiences*

Period	Affect	
	First Few Experiences	*After Many Experiences*
Before use	Resting state	Craving
During use	Rush, euphoria	Contentment
After use	Craving; then resting state	Abstinence-agony and craving

SOURCE: Solomon (1980). Copyright 1980 by the American Psychological Association. Reprinted by permission of the author.

Treatment for drug use disorders

During the 1970s, a great deal of effort was directed toward the treatment of drug-use disorders. An extensive range of therapeutic approaches was studied, including psychoanalytic, behavioral, family, and educational therapy and the residential or therapeutic-community approach, in which a number of addicts live together in a drug-free environment and work together to change their attitudes and lifestyles. Treatment concentrated primarily on users of heroin, LSD, and marijuana. Disappointing results with educational "scare tactics" programs and the difficulties involved in measuring progress in the psychoanalytic approach have largely removed these two strategies from general use in the 1980s (Braucht et al. 1973; Bratter 1973). And, although heroin remains the most popular drug to study for treatment purposes, LSD and marijuana have been replaced by cocaine and nicotine.

But how does one even begin to treat a drug user? For the most part, the answer depends on both the individual user and the type of drug being used. However, the typical treatment program consists of two phases: the immediate removal of the abusive substance and long-term maintenance without it. The immediate removal of the drug usually triggers withdrawal symptoms that are *opposite* in effect to the reactions produced by the drug. For instance, if a person is physically addicted to a

A popular treatment for drug addiction during the 1970's was the residential approach. Addicts would live together in a drug-free environment. Through group meetings, support, and encouragement they hoped to help each other effect a permanent change in their attitudes and lifestyles.

CNS depressant such as a barbiturate, he or she experiences drowsiness, decreased respiration, and reduced anxiety upon taking the drug. When the depressant is withdrawn, the user experiences symptoms that resemble the effects of a stimulant—agitation, restlessness, increased respiration, and insomnia. Helping an individual successfully cope during withdrawal has been a concern of many treatment strategies dealing with various drugs, but it has been of particular interest in the treatment of heroin addicts.

Methadone treatment for heroin addiction During heroin detoxification (withdrawal), the drug *methadone* is prescribed to decrease the intensity of the withdrawal symptoms. Methadone is a synthetic chemical that eliminates the craving for heroin without producing eu-

phoria (the "high"). It was originally felt that reformed heroin addicts could then quite easily discontinue the methadone at a later date. Methadone initially seemed to be a simple solution to a major problem, but it has an important drawback: It can become addicting. The following case illustrates this problem, as well as other facets of the typical two-phase heroin addiction treatment program.

After several months of denying the seriousness of his heroin habit, Gary B. finally enrolled in a residential treatment program that featured methadone maintenance, peer support, confrontational therapy, and job retraining. At first Gary responded well to the residential program. However, he soon began to notice signs of depression. He was reassured by the staff that recovering heroin addicts frequently experience depression and that several treatment options existed. A fairly low dose of tricyclic antidepressant medication was prescribed, and Gary also began supportive–expressive (psychodynamic) therapy.

Psychotherapy helped Gary identify the difficult relationships in his life. His dependence on these relationships and his dependence on drugs were examined for parallels. His tendency to deny problems, and to turn to drugs as an escape, was pointed out. The therapy then focused on the generation of suitable alternatives to drugs. He worked hard during his therapy sessions and made commendable progress.

For the next three months Gary enjoyed his life in a way that previously had been foreign to him. He was hired by a small restaurant to train as a cook. He was entirely satisfied with the direction in which his life had turned, until the day he realized that he was eagerly looking forward to his daily methadone dose. Gary knew of individuals who had become addicted to methadone, but it was still a shock when it happened to him. He decided almost immediately to terminate his methadone maintenance program. The withdrawal process was physically and mentally painful, and Gary often doubted his ability to function without methadone. But by joining a support group composed of others who were trying to discontinue methadone, he was eventually able to complete methadone withdrawal. Gary had never imagined that the most difficult part of his heroin treatment would be giving up methadone.

Other drug use disorders Treatment for the use of most other substances follows a much different course from that for the heroin addict, and it seems to be constantly undergoing modification. One technique that was used more in the past than it is now is covert sensitization, which, as we noted, is often used with alcoholics. One difficulty with this technique is the inability of some patients to generalize the treatment—that is, to pair the learned aversive reaction (nausea and vomiting) with the stimulus (taking a particular drug) once they are outside the clinic or hospital.

The generalization problem has led to criticisms of most behavioral approaches to drug use therapy. Nowadays most treatment programs are multimodal in nature. For example, an amphetamine abuser might initially be admitted to an inpatient facility for approximately 30 days. There he or she would receive individual and group therapy, take part in occupational and recreational therapy, stress-management counseling, and perhaps be introduced to a support group modeled after Alcoholics Anonymous. The patient's spouse might also be asked to participate in the group sessions.

Once the patient had successfully completed this inpatient phase, he or she would be scheduled for outpatient treatment. As part of this treatment, the patient would be asked to agree to unannounced urine screenings to test for the presence of drugs. The patient would be encouraged to continue attending the support group, along with his or her spouse, and to become involved in individual outpatient therapy. Family therapy would be the treatment of choice for adolescent substance users at this point (Reilly 1984; Rueger and Liberman 1984; Haley 1980), and it is highly recommended for adults. The outpatient program typically continues for about two years.

Cigarette smoking Behavioral techniques have been used almost exclusively by individuals who wish to end their addiction to cigarette smoking. Most aversive procedures (such as covert sensitization and shock) have yielded rather disappointing results, but "rapid smoking" appears promising. This technique requires that the client puff a cigarette once every six seconds, until he or she absolutely cannot continue any longer. Its purpose is to pair a highly aversive situation (the feeling of illness that results from extremely rapid smoking) with the act of smoking. It is expected that this will eliminate or reduce the person's desire to smoke. Although the method has been reasonably effective over both the short and the long term, it is somewhat controversial: The rapid smoking introduces such health hazards as increased heart rate and blood pressure (Lichtenstein and Rodriguez 1977; Lichtenstein and Glasgow 1977). It can also aggravate existing cardiovascular problems.

Another noteworthy treatment for cigarette smoking is *nicotine fading* (Foxx and Brown 1979). In this method, the client attempts to gradually withdraw from nicotine by progressively changing to cigarette brands that contain less and less nicotine. When clients reach the stage where they are smoking cigarettes that contain only 0.1 milligram of nicotine, their reduced dependence should enable them to stop altogether (Lichtenstein and Danaher 1976).

SUMMARY

1. Substance abuse and dependence are widespread problems that can result in wasted lives, personal misery, crime, the inability to function socially or occupationally, and danger to the substance user and to others. Substance abuse is a pathological pattern of excessive use in which the person is unable to reduce or cease intake. Substance dependence is physical addiction in which tolerance and/or withdrawal symptoms occur.

2. Alcoholism is a major social problem in the United States. The consumption of alcohol results in both long-term and short-term psychological and physiological effects. Chronic consumption can cause a number of organic mental disorders. There is no clear-cut evidence that alcoholism is caused by congenital factors, although some research suggests that heredity may be important, along with environmental factors. Recent experiments have indicated the importance of cognitive factors in drinking behavior. The tension-reduction hypothesis alone is inadequate to account for alcoholism, because alcohol consumption sometimes results in *increased* feelings of depression or anxiety. Rather, drinking and alcoholism may be closely related to the type of stress anticipated, the perceived benefits of alcohol, the availability of alternative coping responses in a particular situation, and the drinker's genetic or physiological makeup. A variety of treatment approaches have been used, including detoxification, drug therapies, psychotherapy, and behavior modification. Multimodal approaches (the use of several treatment techniques) are probably the most effective. There is evidence that many alcoholics are helped by treatment and that some achieve abstinence by themselves.

3. The use of drugs—depressants, stimulants, and hallucinogens—can result in psychological or physiological problems. There is no single explanation for drug abuse or dependence. In the case of narcotics, both physical and psychological factors are important. According to one theory, drug usage is reinforcing at first because it reduces tension, allows conformance to peer-group pressures, and provides feelings of euphoria. After continued use, the motivation for using the drug changes. Then the desire to avoid withdrawal symptoms or to maintain social relationships and a particular lifestyle may motivate drug use. The treatment prescribed for drug users depends on the type of drug and on the user. Heroin addicts usually undergo detoxification followed by methadone maintenance and such forms of treatment as residential treatment programs, psychotherapy, behavior therapy, and group therapy. Detoxification and occupational, recreational, and family therapies may be suggested for users of other drugs. For addiction to cigarette smoking, aversive procedures, including "rapid smoking" and nicotine fading (the use of brands containing less and less nicotine), have been successful.

KEY TERMS

alcoholism Substance dependence in which the substance that is used is alcohol
aversion therapy A conditioning procedure in which the response to a stimulus is de-

creased by pairing the stimulus with an aversive stimulus

detoxification A treatment aimed at removing all alcohol (or other substance) from a user's body and ensuring that none is ingested

substance abuse A pathological pattern of excessive use of a substance, resulting in physical harm or impaired social and occupational functioning

substance dependence A pathological pattern of excessive use of a substance, resulting in tolerance and/or withdrawal symptoms

substance use disorder Maladaptive behavior associated with the pathological use of a substance over a period of at least one month

tolerance A condition in which the body requires increasing doses of a substance in order to achieve the effect desired of the substance or a markedly diminished effect is experienced with regular use of the same dose

withdrawal symptoms Physical or emotional symptoms such as shaking or irritability that appear when the intake of a regularly used substance is reduced or halted

12

Psychosexual Disorders and Dysfunctions

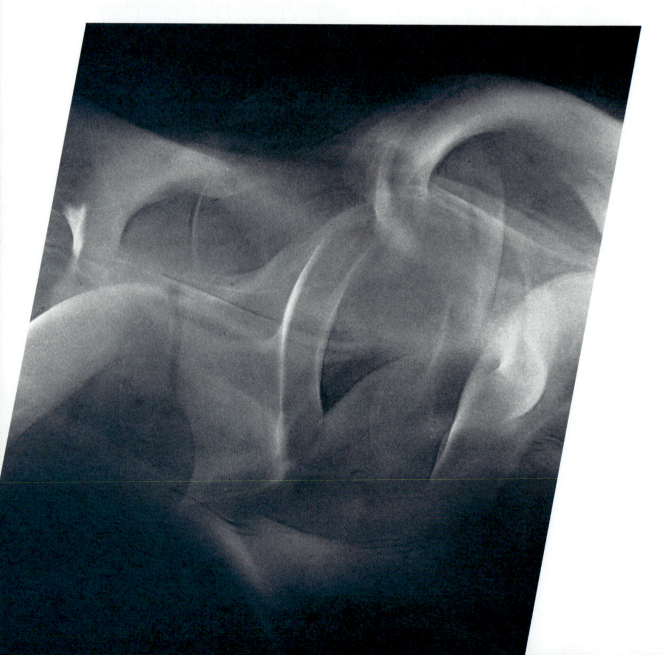

*T*he four brief descriptions below illustrate the major groups of psychosexual disorders that appear in DSM-III.

☐ As a child [although born with male genitalia], Murray/Mary had dressed like a girl, played like a girl, and fantasized about "really" being a girl. . . . Her childhood playmates were girls, and she had no interest in boys' games like "ball or bat or dumb marbles." She always went to the ladies' restroom and never learned to urinate while standing. . . . She regrets that, despite sex-reassignment surgery, she will be unable to bear a child by the man she loves (Sabalis et al. 1974, p. 907).

☐ Mr. A, a 47-year-old man, complained of being unable to obtain sexual satisfaction unless he hurt his wife. His preoccupation with sadistic fantasies made it difficult for him to concentrate, even at work. . . . Every few weeks his cravings would build up to a point where he could not control them. During 25 years of marriage, he had frequently handcuffed his wife, shaved her head, stuck pins in her back and struck her. . . . Ejaculation could not be achieved unless he hurt her (Berlin and Meinecke 1981, p. 605).

☐ I haven't had an orgasm during my marriage (twenty-seven years) or with the two other men with whom I had sex besides my husband. I remember an experience when I was fourteen or fifteen . . . I believe I had a mild orgasm. . . . That's the closest I've come to it. I have masturbated occasionally, but nothing happens. I have no idea what would cause me to respond (Hite 1976, p. 207).

☐ An unemployed 39-year-old single white male sought treatment to decrease homosexual behavior and to increase heterosexual arousal. . . . Since the age of 12, his masturbatory images had been exclusively

337

homosexual. . . . He claimed his homosexual contacts were not emotionally satisfying, and condemned himself for having ''hundreds of partners.'' He had very strong religious beliefs that homosexuality was wrong. He was steadfast in his desire to decrease homosexual behavior and to develop conventional relationships with women, although he had received extensive therapy over several years aimed primarily at greater ''acceptance of himself'' (Hayes, Brownell, and Barlow 1983, p. 385).

The psychosexual disorders are considered to be produced by psychological factors. The four DSM-III categories are:

□ The *gender-identity disorders* involve an incongruity or conflict between one's anatomical sex and one's own feeling of being male or female. Included in this class is the transsexualism illustrated by Murray/Mary.

□ The *paraphilias* involve sexual arousal due to situations, objects, or persons that are not part of the usual arousal pattern that leads to reciprocal and affectionate sexual activity. Included in this category is the sexual sadism exhibited by Mr. A.

□ The *psychosexual dysfunctions* involve problems of inhibited sexual desire, arousal, and response, such as the inhibited-orgasm disorder of the married woman in the third description.

□ *Ego-dystonic homosexuality* is an unwanted and distressful homosexuality, such as that experienced by the 39-year-old male. This category does not include homosexuality in which the individual is comfortable with his or her sexual orientation.

All four groups of disorders are considered to be produced by psychological factors.

A number of the psychosexual disorders discussed in this chapter present us with a problem of distinguishing between ''abnormal'' (maladaptive) behavior and variant behavior that is not harmful but rather reflects personal values or tastes that depart signifi-

cantly from societal norms. In this regard, there would be no objection to our considering rape as deviant behavior; it includes the elements of nonconsent, force, and victimization. But sexual arousal due to an inanimate object (fetishism) or low sexual drive is not a threat to society. Moreover, these problems may not cause distress to individuals who experience them, and they may not result in impaired social or occupational functioning. They are deviant simply because they are not ''normative arousal-activity patterns.'' And they are considered deviant even though what constitutes a ''normative'' sexual pattern is a subject of controversy.

Such controversies will become more obvious as we discuss the four groups of psychosexual disorders in the remainder of this chapter.

GENDER-IDENTITY DISORDERS

The **gender-identity disorders** are characterized by conflict between the individual's anatomical sex and his or her sexual identity, or self-identification as male or female. These disorders are relatively rare, and they may be manifested in adults (as transsexualism) or in children (as gender-identity disorder of childhood).

Transsexualism

In **transsexualism,** the individual identifies with the opposite sex. There is thus a conflict between the individual's own gender identity and his or her biological sex. It is the lifelong conviction of the transsexual that nature has perpetrated a perverse hoax by placing him or her in a body of the wrong sex. Transsexualism is more common in males than in females. According to various estimates, there may be as many as 30,000 transsexuals worldwide (Lothstein 1982).

Transsexuals tend to exhibit sex-role conflicts at an early age. Males display early interests and characteristics that are considered feminine, and they are frequently labeled "sissies" by their male peers. They prefer playing with girls and generally avoid the rough-and-tumble activities in which boys are traditionally encouraged to participate (Green 1968; Sabalis et al. 1974). In one sample, adult transsexual males were given masculine–feminine pattern tests; they scored lower on masculinity than 90 percent of the normal male population. In addition, they scored higher on femininity than most females (Money and Primrose 1968).

Female transsexuals report being labeled "tomboys" during their childhood. As adults, they score low on tests of femininity and high on an inventory of masculine characteristics (Money and Brennan 1968). Although they are attracted to members of the same sex, transsexuals do not consider themselves to be homosexuals.

Etiology The etiology of transsexualism is unclear. The major etiological theories have focused on either environmental or biological variables. In a study of 110 *pseudohermaphrodites* (individuals whose gonads and genetic sex are consistent but whose external genitalia resemble those of the opposite sex), researchers concluded that gender identity is highly malleable (Money, Hampson and Hampson 1957). The subjects had adopted the gender identity of their upbringing, even though it was opposite to their genetic and constitutional makeup. However, a later study of 25 subjects—biological and genetic females who were exposed to an excess of male hormones during their fetal development—seemed to indicate that biological factors are also important. The subjects were raised as girls and accepted this gender identity, but they displayed interest in rough-and-tumble play and were not interested in traditional feminine activities (Money and Ehrhardt 1972).

The conditions of early childhood seem to have much to do with the development of male transsexualism (Green 1974; Bernstein et al.

1981). The factors that contribute to male transsexualism include parental encouragement of feminine behavior and dependency, excessive attention and overprotection by the mother, the absence of an older male as a model, a relatively powerless or absent father figure, a lack of exposure to male playmates, and the encouragement of crossdressing. A childhood background that results in other-sex behavior often leads to ostracism and rejection by one's peers; in that case, the only course available to the male child is complete adoption of the already familiar feminine role. However, not all male transsexuals describe their fathers as weak or passive, nor do they all have excessively attentive mothers (Sabalis, Staton, and Appenzeller 1977).

Treatment There is, at present, a controversy regarding the appropriate treatment for transsexuals. Some professionals advocate sex reassignment through surgery, and others believe that a suitable psychotherapy can and should be found instead.

In the 1960s and early 1970s, there was considerable enthusiasm for sex-conversion surgery. This enthusiasm was partially a response to the extreme resistance of patients to psychotherapy. Most transsexuals regarded therapeutic exploration of their gender conflicts as an obstacle blocking the path to a sex-change operation (Lothstein 1977; Weitz 1977). Since that time, however, successful behaviorally oriented therapy programs may have reduced the demand for sex-change surgery. These behavioral programs consist of strategies for modifying effeminate behavior through modeling and behavioral rehearsal. The therapist demonstrates appropriate masculine behavior and mannerisms (modeling) in a number of different situations, and then patients practice their own versions of these behaviors. This is followed by a behavioral procedure that reinforces heterosexual fantasies; electric shock is applied whenever transsexual fantasies are reported. Positive results are apparent for as long as six years after treatment (Barlow, Abel, and Blanchard 1979).

One of the treatments advocated for transexuals is sex reassignment through surgery. Some research reports that the outcome of such surgery is often positive. British author James Morris (left) became Jan Morris (right) and wrote about the change in the book *Conundrum.*

In spite of gains with psychotherapy and behavioral procedures, sex-change operations are indicated for some transsexuals. But even for these patients, a five-stage program is recommended:

1. Preliminary evaluation to determine the appropriateness of the patient for sex-reassignment surgery
2. Exploratory psychotherapy to detect whether there is severe psychopathology, to investigate the patient's motives, and to clarify his or her misconceptions about the surgery
3. Modification of the patient's secondary sex characteristics through hormone administration
4. A one-year trial as a member of the opposite sex, which includes wearing the clothes of the desired sex, continuing hormone treatment, and working and socializing as the opposite sex (Shore 1984)
5. Sex-reassignment surgery (Kaplan 1983; Roberto 1983)

For males desiring a sex change, the sex-conversion operation begins with removal of the penis and testes. This is followed by plastic surgery to construct female genitalia, including an artificial vagina. The skin of the penis is used in this construction, because the sensory nerve endings that are preserved enable many transsexuals to experience orgasm (Benjamin 1967). Females wishing to be males generally request operations to remove their breasts, uterus, and ovaries, and some ask for an artificial penis to be constructed (Fleming et al. 1982).

Society often has difficulty in accepting and understanding individuals who undergo such extreme operations: Renée Richards was denied entry into female tennis tournaments for a long time, because she was not considered to be ''really a woman.'' A 21-year-old male transsexual who was charged with carrying a concealed weapon was placed in a maximum security prison with several thousand men. This individual had already had breast implants and was taking hormones (Blank 1981).

A number of postoperative studies of transsexuals have indicated positive outcomes (Pauly 1968; Fleming et al. 1982). However, there are also many reports of transsexuals who remain depressed and suicidal after surgery (Meyer and Peter 1979; Hershkowitz and Dickes 1978). Psychotherapy is typically recommended for patients who discover that their problems have not disappeared as a result of the operation (McCauly and Ehrhardt 1984).

Childhood gender-identity disorder

The **gender-identity disorder of childhood** entails many of the same characteristics as transsexualism, though only a small percentage of children with the disorder become transsexuals as adults. According to DSM-III, this disorder is indicated by a strong and persistent desire to be a member of the opposite sex or claims to be a member of the opposite sex. For female children, the gender identity disorder may involve the insistent claim of having a penis and an avid interest in rough-and-tumble play. A male child with this disorder may claim that he will grow up to be a woman, may demonstrate disgust with his penis, and may be exclusively preoccupied with activities considered ''feminine.'' The disorder is much more common in males than in females.

The play behavior of boys diagnosed as having gender-identity disturbances was compared with that of boys and girls who constituted a control group. It was found that the former were more likely than normal boys to play with ''feminine'' toys and that they did not differ from girls in this respect. These results were observed in boys as young as three years of age (Rekers and Yates 1976; Bates, Bentler, and Thompson 1979). Boys with the gender-identity disorder also scored very low on an extroversion scale and scored significantly higher than boys in the control group on a behavior-disturbance scale. Moreover, gender-disorder boys show a general personality problem, in addition to their adoption of deviant gender attitudes and behaviors (Bates, Bentler, and Thompson 1979).

Gender disorders in children lead to a variety of complications. Boys with this problem are often subject to rejection and ridicule from peers; these reactions may spur the development of transsexualism, transvestism, or homosexuality (Rekers and Lovaas 1974; Rekers and Varni 1977). Retrospective reports of their childhood by transsexuals and transvestites include many of the atypical patterns of childhood gender-identity disorders (Ehrhardt, Grisanti, and McCauley 1979; Green 1974; Lambley 1974; Sabalis et al. 1974).

Table 12.1 (p. 342) lists the most frequently reported symptoms of 55 boys who displayed effeminate behavior. In a long-term follow-up, it was found that 35 of these boys (64 percent) became homosexuals (included in this group were one transvestite and one transsexual); only 3 (5 percent) were heterosexual. For 10 of the subjects the outcome was uncertain, and 7 (13 percent) were not included in the follow-up (Zuger 1984).

Etiology   The etiology of gender-identity disorders in children is assumed to include some of the same variables involved in transsexualism, such as the physical absence of an opposite-sex parent or the presence of a nonnurturing one, the encouragement of opposite-sex behaviors and crossdressing, and a lack of exposure to same-sex peers (Green 1974; Rekers and Varni 1977; Stoller 1969). However, not all studies report this type of family pattern (Erhardt et al. 1979; Sabalis, Staton, and Appenseller 1977).

Table 12.1 *Frequency of Symptoms in 55 Effeminate Boys (Elicited as part of a structured interview)*

Symptom	Number of Boys			
	Present	*Absent*	*Uncertain*	*No data*
Feminine dressing	50	2	2	1
Aversion to boys' games	50	1	3	1
Desire to be female	43	6	2	4
Girl playmate preference	42	5	3	5
Doll playing	41	5	4	5
Feminine gestures	40	5	5	5
Wearing lipstick	34	12	3	6

SOURCE: Zuger (1984), p. 93. © 1984 The Williams & Wilkins Co., Baltimore. Used by permission.

Treatment Most treatment programs for children identified as having a gender-identity disorder include separate components for the child and for his or her parents. For the child, treatment begins with sex education. The favorable aspects of the child's physical gender are highlighted, and his or her reasons for avidly pursuing opposite-sex activities are discussed. An attempt is made to correct stereotypes regarding certain roles that are "accepted" for one gender and not for the other. Young boys are always assigned to male therapists, so that positive male identification is facilitated. Meanwhile, the child's parents receive instruction in the behavior modification practice of reinforcing appropriate gender behavior and extinguishing "inappropriate" behavior (Roberto 1983).

Some programs have successfully utilized an "economy" system of reinforcement in which the children are awarded tokens (poker chips or play money) for engaging in gender-appropriate behavior. These tokens can be used to purchase reinforcers such as television time or candy (Rekers and Lovaas 1974).

It appears that such programs do lead to more gender-appropriate behavior (Rekers and Varni 1977). Nevertheless, there is concern that reinforcement programs merely teach children to suppress "undesirable" opposite-sex behaviors, without addressing the associated emotional and cognitive factors.

PARAPHILIAS

Paraphilias are sexual disorders in which unusual or bizarre acts, images, or objects are necessary for sexual arousal. They may involve the preference for a nonhuman object for sexual arousal, as in fetishism and transvestism; sexual activity involving real or simulated suffering, as in sadism and masochism; or repetitive sexual activity with nonconsenting others, as in exhibitionism, voyeurism, and pedophilia. All of these disorders are much more prevalent in males than in females.

Fetishism

Fetishism is an extremely strong sexual attraction for a particular nongenital part of the anatomy (such as hair, feet, or fingers) or for an inanimate object (such as panties, bras, or shoes) to the exclusion of all other sexually arousing stimuli. It is certainly not unusual for males and females to display erotic interest in the bodily attributes of members of the opposite sex. For example, the preferences of undergraduate males for specific body parts of females (breasts, legs, buttocks) were found to be correlated with personality traits (Wiggins, Wiggins, and Conger 1968). These choices simply reflect ordinary male and female preferences. Fetishism exists when the part of the body or the inanimate object assumes such importance that it becomes the sole focus of sexual interest. An individual with a foot fetish, for example, may be able to achieve sexual arousal only by observing and manipulating feet.

Likewise, most males find the sight of female undergarments sexually interesting and stimulating; again, this does not constitute a fetish. (On the other hand, most women show little erotic interest in male underwear.) An interest in such inanimate objects as panties, stockings, bras, and shoes becomes a sexual deviation when sexual arousal to the point of erection occurs frequently in the presence of the fetish item, when this item becomes necessary for sexual arousal during intercourse, when sexual partners are chosen on the basis of possession of the item, or when these items are collected (Jones, Shainberg, and Byer 1977). In many cases the fetish item is sufficient in and of itself for complete sexual satisfaction through masturbation, and contact with a partner is not sought.

Fetishism is rare in comparison with *voyeurism* (observing nude bodies or couples engaged in intercourse) and *exhibitionism* (indecent exposure), and it occurs almost exclusively in males. Kinsey et al. (1953) found only two or three females in their sample who were aroused by inanimate objects not directly associated with sexual activity. Because their behavior occurs in private, fetishists do not usually come to public attention. Many of them become statistics only when they are caught in the act of stealing an item of fetish interest. (Few fetishists *buy* these articles, because they possess greater erotic properties when they have been worn by a woman.) As a group, fetishists are not dangerous nor do they tend to commit more serious crimes, although they may be involved in other indirect forms of sexual offense, such as voyeurism and exhibitionism (Gebhard et al. 1965).

Etiology In psychodynamic terms, sexual deviations of all kinds are symbolic represen-

Female undergarments such as bras, panties, or stockings, particularly those designed to display female sexual characteristics, can be erotically stimulating to most males. But when such inanimate objects become the focal point of sexual arousal and become necessary for sexual satisfaction, they are fetish items.

tations of unconscious conflicts involving aggression, castration anxiety, and dependency. As is the case with many psychodynamic formulations, however, no sound experimental study has validated the existence of castration anxiety. Also, because psychoanalysts believed that sexual deviations involve castration themes to some degree, the factors that dictate the appearance of a particular form of sexual deviance are not clearly defined.

Learning theorists stress the importance of early conditioning experiences with the fetish item. One case involved a male with a fetish of twenty-one years' duration. The behavior began at the age of twelve, when the subject became sexually excited by watching girls come down a slide with their panties exposed. After a period of time, he masturbated while fantasizing girls with their panties showing. When he entered treatment, his behavior involved masturbating while wearing women's panties he had stolen (Kushner 1965).

To establish a fetish after the initial conditioning experience, continued masturbation in association with the object itself or with fantasies of the object is necessary. The continued masturbation maintains and strengthens the importance of the object in sexual arousal and orgasm, especially when there is no heterosexual experience. Masturbation to deviant fantasies also increases the habit strength of the behavior (Evans 1968). Most convicted fetishists report few female companions or friends (Gebhard et al. 1965); this may increase their need for indirect forms of sexual expression.

Support for the possible role of conditioning in the development of a fetish was demonstrated by Rachman (1966). Three male subjects were exposed to slides of nude females, which produced sexual arousal (as measured by penile volume). Preceding these slides, they were shown a picture of a pair of women's black boots. Initially, this picture did not elicit any increases in penile volume. But after slides of boots and nude females were paired a number of times (classical conditioning), all three subjects developed conditioned sexual arousal at the sight of the boots alone. Although the conditioned responses were weak, they might have been strengthened through masturbation during the presentation of the boots.

Treatment The current treatment strategy for paraphilias often involves two stages. The first stage concentrates on elimination of the sexually inappropriate behavior, and the second emphasizes the acquisition of sexually appropriate behaviors. It is of utmost importance to have a satisfying replacement for the deviant sexual behavior that has been removed from the client's repertoire (Brownell and Barlow 1980).

Such a twofold procedure was used to treat a male with a fetish for female clothing (Cooper 1963). Chemical aversive conditioning was used first, to pair an aversive physical state (nausea) with items of clothing. The noxious physical state was triggered by a chemical agent, and the patient was asked to handle the clothing at precisely the time when the nausea began. Several repetitions of this procedure effectively reduced the patient's fetish for female clothes.

It was still necessary to increase the patient's use of appropriate sexual behavior. As is the case with many fetishists, this patient did not engage in appropriate sexual behavior, largely because of his anxiety involving intimate heterosexual contact. *In vivo* (real-life) desensitization was chosen to treat his fear. First the client was asked to construct a hierarchy of anxiety-provoking scenes that were associated with heterosexual contact. Then he was instructed to engage in the least anxiety-producing scene with his partner (in this case, lying in bed next to his wife) and to stop whenever he began feeling anxious. He was then to use relaxation procedures until he could again attempt to lie next to his wife. Once he felt sufficiently relaxed while engaging in this first anxiety-producing scene, he was to proceed to the second item on his list. Each new item was addressed in turn, after the anxiety involved with the previous item had been totally extinguished. This *in vivo* desensitization effectively increased the client's appropriate heterosexual behavior (Cooper 1963).

A number of similar treatments have also had positive outcomes with fetishists. But the fact that they were all applied in case studies, without control groups, indicates that we must interpret the results with caution (Kilmann et al. 1982).

Transvestism

Transvestism is a disorder in which sexual gratification is obtained through crossdressing, or the wearing of attire appropriate to members of the opposite sex. This sexual deviation is more common among males than females; its incidence is estimated at 1 percent of the population (Brown 1961). Several aspects of transvestism are illustrated in the following case study.

> A 26-year-old graduate student referred himself for treatment following an examination failure. He had been crossdressing since the age of 10 and attributed his exam failure to the excessive amount of time that he spent doing so (four times a week). When he was younger, his crossdressing had taken the form of masturbating while wearing his mother's high-heeled shoes, but it had gradually expanded to the present stage in which he dressed completely as a woman, masturbating in front of a mirror. At no time had he experienced a desire to obtain a sex-change operation. He had neither homosexual experiences nor homosexual fantasies. Heterosexual contact had been restricted to heavy petting with occasional girlfriends. (Lambley 1974, p. 101)

Not all individuals who crossdress are transvestites; some homosexuals and transsexuals also engage in this activity. By contrast to these latter two groups, however, the majority of transvestites are exclusively heterosexual, 74 percent are married, and 69 percent have fathered or borne children (Benjamin 1967).

Because transvestites are secretive about their behavior and usually crossdress in private, data on their characteristics are scarce. In one national survey, a sample of 181 transvestites was obtained from the files of a magazine published for transvestites; their responses were compared with those of a control group on personality tests. The transvestites presented themselves as more controlled in impulse expression, more inhibited in interpersonal relations, less involved with others,

and more dependent (Bentler and Prince 1969); they showed no major psychiatric symptomatology. Another study found that transvestites scored higher on neuroticism and reported greater stress than a control group (Buhrich 1981).

Transvestites crossdress to facilitate sexual arousal, often wearing female undergarments during sexual intercourse with their wives:

> He continued to have sexual intercourse (while clad in a woman's nightgown) with his wife, while imagining that they were no longer man and wife, but rather two women engaged in a lesbian relationship. He especially enjoyed it when she cooperated with his idea and referred to him by his chosen feminine name. (Newman and Stoller 1974, p. 438)

Many transvestites feel that they possess masculine and feminine personalities that alternate with one another. In a feminine role, they can play out such behavior patterns as buying nightgowns and trying on fashionable clothes. Many transvestites introduce their wives to their female personalities, and urge them to go on shopping trips together as women (Buckner 1970). Other transvestites crossdress only for the purposes of sexual arousal and masturbation and do not fantasize themselves as members of the opposite sex.

Etiology In the traditional psychoanalytic interpretation, transvestism results from castration anxiety. Acknowledging that women lack the male phallus raises the fear that a danger of castration does exist. To refute this possibility, the male transvestite "restores" the penis to women through fantasy and identifies himself with the phallic woman. Through this unconscious process, he is able to reduce his castration anxiety (Shave 1976). Along this same line, female transvestites are thought to suffer from penis envy and, therefore, to crossdress as a means of compensating for the lack of male genitals. There is little empirical support for these psychoanalytic hypotheses.

The learning perspective is represented by the view of Buckner (1970), who enumerates the following steps in the development of transvestism:

1. The association of some item of feminine apparel with sexual gratification, usually between the ages of 5 and 14. Masturbation using these items is not unusual, and some transvestites do show an early orgasmic experience with female clothing (Gershman 1970; Lambley 1974).
2. Sociosexual deprivation. A youth who lacks heterosexual social skills, who is shy and inhibited, may have difficulty forming relationships with women.
3. Continued conditioning through masturbatory activity with female clothing and through the development of fantasies involving a female self.

Treatment   Treatment strategies for transvestism are generally behavioral in nature and quite similar in form to those used with fetishism. The following composite case illustrates some of the elements of the two-stage program in which inappropriate behaviors are eliminated and appropriate behaviors are taught and reinforced.

> William J., a 24-year-old male, had tried to hide his crossdressing behavior for years. Eventually he grew tired of dealing with the guilt and shame he experienced whenever he donned women's clothing. He made an appointment to see a psychologist at a local mental health clinic. William was amazed to learn that a wide variety of techniques had been tested with transvestites, and that several produced encouraging results. The twofold approach of eliminating his deviant behavior and reinforcing his sexually appropriate behavior made ultimate sense to him.
>
> William investigated the various aversive techniques that had been studied with transvestites in the past. Because of the potential health hazards, expense, and length of time associated with the chemical aversion approach (via nausea-stimulating drugs), he requested a program utilizing electrical shock as the aversive stimulus. During sessions, William received shocks both when he was demonstrating his crossdressing and when he was imagining that he was crossdressing (Gelder and Marks 1969).
>
> Shortly after the start of the aversive conditioning phase, William was asked whether he had any preference regarding the segment of the treatment designed to increase appropriate sexual behavior. He considered his social-skills adequate and, instead of a behavioral social skills training program, chose analytic insight-oriented therapy.

At this point, it would be difficult to develop a prognosis for William. The immediate results of such therapy are positive (Feldman et al. 1966; Gershman 1970); however, long-term follow-up reports have been less favorable (Rosen and Rehm 1977).

Exhibitionism

Exhibitionism is the exposure of one's genitals to strangers for the purpose of attaining sexual arousal. Often there is a wish to shock the victim. Exhibitionism is relatively common, and it accounts for approximately one-third of all reports of sex crimes (Rooth 1973). The exhibitionist is almost always male and the victim female. Surveys of selected groups of young women in the United States indicate that between one-third and one-half have been victims of exhibitionists (Cox and McMahon 1978; Rhoads and Borjes 1981):

> A 19-year-old single white college male reported that he had daily fantasies of exposing and had exposed himself on three occasions. The first occurred when he masturbated in front of the window of his dormitory room, when females would be passing by. The other two acts occurred in his car; in each case he asked young females for directions, and then exposed his penis and masturbated when they approached. He felt a great deal of anxiety in the presence of females and dated infrequently. (Hayes et al. 1983)

The sexual arousal obtained through exposure seems to be the main goal of the exhibitionist; the majority of exhibitionists have no desire for further contact. In a study of thirty convicted exhibitionists who had a history of exposing, only five out of several hundred offenses committed by these men were for indecent assault, and these five cases were restricted to attempts to touch the breast or genitals (Rooth 1973). Although a small number of exhibitionists may be aggressive and assaultive, "it is reasonably safe to generalize that nine out of ten exhibitionists are less apt to make a pass or sexual advance than is the boy next door" (Hackett 1975, p. 140). But there may be two types of exhibitionists—those who have been involved with crime and those who have not. The former tend to be sociopathic and impulsive, and may be more likely to exhibit aggression (Forgac and Michaels 1982; Forgac, Cassels, and Michaels 1984).

Exhibitionists may expect to produce surprise, fear, sexual arousal, or disgust in the victim (Katchadourian and Lunde 1975). The act may involve the exposure of a flaccid penis or the masturbation of an erect penis, culminating in ejaculation. In a study of 96 exhibitionists, however, only 50 percent reported erections "almost always" or "always" when exposing, although a large percentage of the men wanted the female victim to be impressed with the size of their penis. Fantasies about being watched and admired by female observers were common among exhibitionists. Over two-thirds reported that they would not have sex with the victim even if she were receptive (Hackett 1975; Langevin et al. 1979).

The majority of exhibitionists are in their twenties—far from being the "dirty old men" of popular myth. Most are married. Their exhibiting has a compulsive quality to it, and they report that a great deal of anxiety accompanies the act. One exhibitionist would feel the urge to exhibit whenever he was confronted by a shapely young female wearing nylons and high-heeled shoes. The patient would first become sexually aroused and anxious, and would fantasize about exposing. He would then compulsively expose himself even when his wife was present (she described him as looking "paralyzed, with glazed eyes"). The only effective way for the wife to prevent him from exposing was to forcefully drag him away (Bond and Hutchinson 1965).

A typical exposure sequence involves first entertaining sexually arousing memories of previous exposures; then returning to the area where previous exposures took place; next, locating a suitable victim and rehearsing the exposure mentally; and finally, exposing. As the individual progresses through this sequence, his self-control weakens and disappears (Abel, Levis, and Clancy 1970). Exposure usually takes place out-of-doors in parks and other public areas or while the exhibitionist is seated in his car (Hackett 1975).

The onset of exhibitionism appears to be associated with interpersonal stressors. Compared to control groups, exhibitionists reported less heterosexual petting as adolescents, poorer marital adjustment, lower assertiveness, and deficits in social skills (Blair and Lanyon 1981).

Etiology Psychoanalytic theory contends that exhibitionism is a reaction to incomplete resolution of the Oedipus complex. Because the boy's incestuous desires are only partially repressed, and because he observes that his penis is the locus of sexual desire for his mother, he becomes fearful of retribution from his father in the form of castration. To alleviate his anxiety regarding castration and to reassure himself that castration has not occurred, he exhibits. The shock that registers on the faces of others assures him that he still has a penis. Because castration anxiety stems from an unconscious source, however, the fear is never completely allayed, and the individual is propelled into a pattern of repetitive exposures.

Kinsey et al. (1953) found that 56 percent of males have been sexually aroused by observing their own genitals as they masturbated.

These researchers hypothesized that exhibitionism may be performed by males to arouse females in the belief that the latter are similarly aroused.

Some learning theorists support the notion of one-trial learning, through an accidental association between sexual arousal and exposure. In one such case, two young men became sexually aroused after they were surprised by women passersby while urinating in a semiprivate area. Episodes of exhibitionism followed (McGuire, Carlisle, and Young 1965). Fantasies of exhibiting while masturbating may strengthen the response. Indeed, the etiology of exhibitionism may involve a combination of all of these processes: social and heterosexual deprivation, conditioning, and continued masturbation to fantasies of exhibiting.

Treatment More than twenty treatment studies with exhibitionists have been recorded within the last fifteen to twenty years. The results have been generally positive, but the majority of the studies involved single-subject designs. Few control groups were included. Another problem in interpreting the results of these studies becomes apparent when we examine the approaches that were employed. For the most part, several different behavioral techniques were used within each study, so evaluation of a particular technique is impossible (Wickramasekera 1976). Among the few promising outcomes reported with nonbehavioral approaches was that of an insight-oriented therapy group conducted with males arrested for indecent exposure (Mathis and Collins 1970). The study claimed a complete absence of second arrests for those participants who remained in treatment. However, over one-third of the original participants dropped out of treatment prematurely, and those that continued were still receiving treatment three years later.

One of the more unique treatments for exhibitionism is the *aversive behavior rehearsal* (ABR) program developed by Wickramasekera

(1976). This "shame aversion" technique utilizes shame or humiliation as the aversive stimulus. The program is based on the assumption that exhibitionism is reinforcing only if the exhibitor is able to remain anonymous to his observer. The technique requires that the patient exhibit himself in his usual manner to a preselected audience of females. These observers resemble the exhibitionist's typical victim as much as possible. During the exhibiting act, the patient must verbalize a conversation between himself and his penis. He must speak about what he is feeling emotionally and physically and must explain his fantasies regarding what he supposes the female observers are thinking about him. The observers are trained to stare expressionless at the exhibitor and to interrupt his demonstration with brief questions about what he is doing. The session is also videotaped, so that the patient can later see how his deviant behavior looks to others.

It is interesting to note that the developer of ABR feels that exhibition often occurs when the person is in a hypnotic-like state. At that time, the exhibitionist's fantasies are extremely active and his judgment is impaired. The ABR method forces him to experience and examine his act while fully aware of what he is doing (Kilmann et al. 1982).

Voyeurism

Voyeurism is (1) sexual gratification obtained through the observation of the genitals and other body parts of unsuspecting members of the opposite sex or (2) the observation of couples engaging in sexual intercourse, for the purpose of obtaining sexual gratification. It is not surprising that males are aroused by uncovered female bodies. The proliferation of topless bars, explicit sexual magazines, and X-rated movies all point to the voyeuristic nature of our society. Of interest in this regard is the recent increase in the number of "night clubs" featuring male exotic dancers and attended by women. This may be indicative of women's increasing interest in male bodies, although it is uncertain whether this behavior is engaged in for the purpose of sexual arousal.

"Peeping," as voyeurism is sometimes termed, is considered deviant when it includes serious risk, is done in socially unacceptable circumstances, or is preferred to coitus. The typical voyeur is not interested in looking at his wife or girlfriend (95 percent of the cases of voyeurism involve strangers). Observation alone produces sexual arousal and excitement, and the voyeur often masturbates during this surreptitious activity (Katchadourian and Lunde 1975).

The voyeur is similar to the exhibitionist in that sexual contact is not the goal; viewing an undressed body is the primary motive. However, a voyeur may also be involved in exhibiting or in other indirect forms of sexual expression (Abel, Levis, and Clancy 1970). The average voyeur is a male in his mid-twenties and is unmarried when first arrested. Approximately 90 percent of the offenses are premeditated. The peeper walks through alleys, climbs ledges, and trespasses to engage in voyeurism (Gebhard et al. 1965). He or she is secretive and patient while awaiting an opportunity. Gebhard describes the voyeur as a "persevering optimist" who is undaunted by failure and always hopes that a rewarding event will occur. Because of the repetitive nature of the act, arrest is predictable. Usually an accidental witness or the victim notifies the police. It is not uncommon, however, for a potential rapist or burglar who is behaving suspiciously to be arrested as a voyeur.

Etiology   The causal factors involved in voyeurism are similar to those involved in exhibitionism. Voyeurs report that they did not socialize well with their peers and had no heterosexual friendships during their late childhood period. A large number report little sexual activity during adolescence and adulthood. They are characterized as being socially inad-

Many features of our society, such as topless bars, X-rated movies, or explicitly sexual magazines, are voyeuristic in nature and are accepted, if not approved of, by many people. When voyeurism includes serious risk, is done in socially unacceptable circumstances, or is preferred to coitus, the behavior is abnormal or deviant.

equate and shy, which makes indirect forms of sexual expression the only avenue open to them (Gebhard et al. 1965).

Treatment   The treatment for voyeurism is also similar to that for exhibitionism. Therapy may include aversive conditioning, perhaps through the shame aversion used with exhibitionists (Serber 1970). It usually involves training to develop adequate social skills or systematic desensitization to decrease the anxiety that the peeper associates with appropriate heterosexual acts.

Voyeurism has also been shown to decrease after behavioral marital therapy. A voyeur and his wife were taught to keep behavioral records of their interactions with each other, including their sexual activity. They were also asked to try to increase the frequency of intercourse. The effect of the increased intercourse on the husband's subsequent urges to peep was monitored, and the outcome was positive (Stoudenmire 1973).

It seems reasonable to use *couples therapy* as an adjunct to behavioral techniques aimed at eliminating peeping. Such therapy is, in fact, a means of indirectly improving and reinforcing the voyeur's appropriate heterosexual behavior by first enhancing his general relationship with his wife.

A somewhat novel technique for reducing voyeurism was introduced in Denmark. An 80 percent decrease in the frequency of arrests for peeping was reported from 1959 to 1969, after easy access to pornography was permitted by law (Kutchinsky 1973). It may be that sexually explicit material provides a sufficient outlet for the voyeur.

Rape

It is important that we distinguish between **statutory rape** (the seduction of a girl who has not yet reached the legal age of consent) and forcible rape. The first category—a legal one—is based on the assumption that a girl who is under a certain age (12 to 17 years, depending on the state statute) does not have sufficient maturity and understanding to consent to coitus. Thus, any adult male having sexual intercourse with a minor has broken a law, even if the girl was a willing participant.

The second category, forcible rape, is the focus of our discussion here. In most states, **forcible rape** is defined as an act of intercourse accomplished by a male with a female other than his wife, through the use of force or the threat of force. Twenty-four states have now revised their rape laws so that a husband can be charged with rape. In sixteen other states, a woman can charge her husband with rape if the couple is living apart or has filed divorce or separation papers. In the ten remaining states, a husband cannot be charged with raping his wife.

According to FBI statistics, approximately 77,000 cases of rape were reported in 1982. However, only about 16 percent of reported cases result in a conviction for this crime. Another 4 percent of those charged with rape are convicted of lesser offenses (Rabkin 1979). The low conviction rate and the humiliation and shame involved in a rape trial keep many women from reporting rapes, so the actual incidence of the crime is probably much higher than reported. Estimates based on surveys indicate that as many as one of every four women will be a rape victim at some time during her life (Resick 1983). Rape is not usually an impulsive act; in nearly 75 percent of the cases, it is premeditated (Amir 1971).

One form of rape that is being reported with increasing frequency is "acquaintance" or "date" rape:

> Colleen, twenty-seven, a San Francisco office manager, had been involved with her boyfriend for about a year when it happened. After a cozy dinner at her apartment, he suggested that she go to bed while he did the dishes. But a few moments later he stalked into Colleen's bedroom with a peculiar look on his face, brandishing a butcher knife and strips of cloth. After tying her, spread-eagled, to the bed, the formerly tender lover raped her brutally for three hours, using his fist, the knife, a shampoo bottle and other household objects. When it was all over, he fell soundly asleep. (Seligman, Huck, Joseph, Namuth, Prout, Robinson, and McDaniel 1984, p. 91)

It is possible that "date" rapes account for the majority of all rapes. However, the victim may be reluctant to report such an attack; she feels responsible—at least in part—because she made a date with her attacker.

Are most rapes perpetrated by strangers or by acquaintances? One police official, in reacting to the high number of rapes reported in his community, noted that "We definitely do not have a serious rape problem in this city. The problem is in the classification. If you took all our rapes one by one, you'd see that nine out of ten are a girlfriend–boyfriend thing. These people are known to each other" (Girard, August 5, 1984, p. 12). The assumption made here is that forced intercourse between acquaintances should not be considered rape. Unfortunately, sexual aggression by males is quite common. Fifteen percent of a sample of college males reported that they did force intercourse at least once or twice (Rapaport and Burkhart 1984). Other forms of coercive sex were reported by 28 percent of the sample. Individuals who reported being directly coercive were more likely to score low on responsibility and to view women as adversaries. Only 39 percent of the males admitted to no coerced sex.

It is difficult to establish a composite description of the typical rapist, because there appear to be different motivations for rape. Several studies have found that most rapists are young men between the ages of sixteen and twenty-five, from lower socioeconomic classes, who have had prior conflicts with the law (Gebhard et al. 1965; Rabkin 1979). In Gebhard's sample, these offenders exhibited more aggression and conflict with society than other offenders; they used unnecessary violence to obtain either money or sex. A minority of rapists do not fit this description but seem to be ordinary and rather constrained citizens. (These characteristics are based on a population of convicted rapists, however, and they may not apply to all individuals who have committed rape.)

Victims of rape Most rape victims are young women in their teens or twenties (Amir 1971; Gebhard et al. 1965), although victims as young as five and as old as seventy-three have been reported (Burgess and Holmstrom 1979a). In about half of all rape cases, the victim is at least acquainted with the rapist and is attacked in the home or in an automobile (Kilpatrick, Veronen, and Resick 1979). One-fourth of the women attacked by strangers in Denver in a three-year period were responding to the offender's request for help (Selkin 1975).

Based on personality test scores, a comparison of twenty rape victims and sixteen women who successfully resisted attack showed that successful resisters scored higher on dominance, sociability, and social presence. The successful resisters felt more socially competent than the victims and could express themselves better both physically and verbally (Selkin 1975).

Needless to say, rape is a highly traumatic event. Victims may experience psychological distress, phobic reactions, and sexual dysfunction. A one-year follow-up of rape victims found that they were significantly more fearful than control groups. The fears were selective and involved such things as darkness and enclosed places—conditions that are likely to be associated with rape (Calhoun, Atkeson, and Resick 1982). Duration and intensity of fear were also found to be related to perceptions of dangerousness. Attacks in circumstances that were defined as "safe" had a greater emotional impact than those in places that were felt to be dangerous. Many of the women drastically changed their perception of the safety of the environment (Scheppele and Bakt 1983).

In one survey, about two-thirds of rape victims reported that they were unable to resume sexual activity for at least six months (Burgess and Holmstrom 1979a). Sexual enjoyment was strongly affected. One victim described her attitude toward sex after the rape as follows:

> It depends how I relate to the man. If I'm in a position to enjoy it—a 50-50 thing—then I'm ok. But if I'm feeling that I'm only doing this for him and not for my own enjoyment, then I feel like the incident again . . . then sex is bad. (p. 648)

Flashbacks were reported by 50 percent of the sexually active victims. These ranged from fleeting thoughts of the rape that could not be repressed, through reliving of the experience, to association of the present sex partner with the rapist. Sympathetic understanding, nondemanding affection, and a positive attitude

Women have made two general responses to the recent increased incidence of rape: support and care for the victims and prevention. Crisis lines and rape assistance programs are widely publicized in communities (top). Women's groups have held anti-rape protests, such as this Take Back the Night rally (bottom). Martial arts and self-defense have been particularly emphasized.

from the partner have been found to be beneficial. Hugging and gentle caressing are generally satisfying to the victim even if sexual approaches are aversive (Feldman-Summers, Gordon, and Meagher 1979).

In light of the severe sexual and psychological problems that a rape victim may experience, the availability of multiple support systems and counseling becomes very important. Most large cities now have rape crisis centers that provide counseling, as well as medical and legal information, to victims. Trained volunteers often accompany the victim to the hospital and to the police station (Kollias and Tucker 1974). Through the efforts of women's organizations, many hospital personnel and police officers have become more aware of the trauma of rape and are more sensitive in their interactions with victims.

Motivation to rape   Rape is not specifically listed in DSM-III as a maladaptive behavior, because the act can have a variety of motivations. In an analysis of 133 rapists, Groth, Burgess, and Holstrom (1977) distinguished three different motivational types.

1. *Power Rapist.* This type of rapist (comprising 55 percent of those studied) is primarily attempting to compensate for feelings of personal or sexual inadequacy by trying to intimidate his victims.
2. *Anger Rapist.* The individual in this category (40 percent of those studied) is angry at women in general; the victim is merely a convenient target.
3. *Sadistic Rapist.* This type (5 percent of those studied) derives satisfaction from inflicting pain on the rape victim and may torture or mutilate her.

These findings tend to support the contention that rape has more to do with power, aggression, and violence than with sex. In fact, a study of over 100 rapists indicated that 58 percent exhibited some form of sexual dysfunction during the attack (Groth and Burgess 1977).

Although these distinctions are of interest, there was little empirical research on the importance of aggressive cues in the sexual arousal of rapists until a study performed by Abel and colleagues (1977). These investigators recorded the degree of penile erection of rapists and nonrapists in response to two-minute audio tapes describing violent and nonviolent sexual scenes. The nonviolent tape described an incidence of mutually enjoyable sexual intercourse. The violent tape described a rape in which the male forced himself on an unwilling victim. The rapists were aroused by both tape descriptions, whereas the nonrapists displayed a significantly lesser degree of erection in response to the portrayal of violent sex, preferring the scene involving mutually enjoyable sex. Some rapists also showed strong sexual arousal in response to another tape that was entirely aggressive in content.

It appears that aggressive cues do play a larger role in the sexual arousal of rapists than in that of nonrapists and that some rapists do respond sexually to cues that are primarily aggressive. The difference between rapists and nonrapists may be the failure of rapists to inhibit sexual arousal when cues of force, violence, and nonconsent are present (Barbaree, Marshall, and Lanthier 1979). Focus 12.1 (p. 359) examines the relationship between pornography and rape.

Sadism and masochism

Sadism and **masochism** are deviations that involve the association of pain with sexual gratification. In particular, the sadist obtains sexual gratification by inflicting pain on others; the masochist, by receiving pain or punishment. The word *sadism* was coined from the name of the Marquis de Sade (1740–1814), a French nobleman who wrote extensively about the sexual pleasure of inflicting pain on helpless female victims. The marquis himself exhibited such cruelty to his sexual victims that he was declared insane and incarcerated

for twenty-seven years of his life. The word *masochism* is derived from the name of Leopold von Sacher-Masoch, a nineteenth-century Austrian novelist whose fictional characters obtained sexual satisfaction only when pain was inflicted on them.

Sadists usually direct their activities toward prostitutes or masochistic consenting partners. Sadistic behavior may range from the pretended or fantasized infliction of pain, through mild to severe cruelty toward partners, to an extremely dangerous pathological form of sadism that may involve mutilation or murder. Because of their passive roles, masochists are not considered dangerous. For some sadists and masochists, coitus becomes unnecessary; pain alone is sufficient to produce sexual pleasure.

Sadomasochistic tendencies exist to some extent in many individuals. For instance, Kinsey et al. (1953) found that 54 percent of females and 50 percent of males report some or frequent erotic response to being bitten during sexual intercourse. And, in a national survey, 10.3 percent of single males reported having obtained sexual pleasure from inflicting or receiving pain (Hunt 1974). In the same survey, single women were much more likely to report sexual pleasure when receiving pain (10.0 percent) than when inflicting pain (5.2 percent). In addition, fantasies involving sexual abuse, rejection, and forced sex are not uncommon among college students of both sexes (Sue 1979).

Most of these reports involve very mild forms of pain (such as in biting or pinching) that are accepted in our society. Sadomasochistic behavior is considered deviant when pain, either inflicted or received, is necessary for sexual arousal and orgasm. Sadists and masochists often find each other through advertisements aimed at individuals interested in S&M (sadomasochistic) or B&D (bondage and discipline) activities.

Etiology Psychoanalysts explain sadomasochistic behavior using several hypotheses: Ac-

Pornography and Rape

In December 1983, the City Council of Minneapolis passed an ordinance declaring pornographic literature and movies a violation of women's rights. The mayor vetoed the ordinance on the grounds that it violated the freedom-of-speech provisions of the First Amendment.

The Indianapolis City Council also recently passed an ordinance against pornographic material as a violation of the civil rights of women. It, in particular, outlawed material presenting "the sexually explicit subordination of women, graphically depicted, whether in pictures or in words."

Efforts are being initiated to pass similar ordinances in other cities, in the belief that exposure to pornography increases sex crimes.

There is much controversy about the relationship betwen pornography and sexual violence. The Presidential Commission on Obscenity and Pornography (1970), after extensive research and analysis, concluded that there was no relationship between exposure to erotic material and sex crimes; the commission recommended the repeal of laws regulating adults' access to pornography. However, its conclusion should probably be reexamined in light of recent research on sexual arousal and currently available means of measuring arousal precisely. Such a reexamination is also important because of the proliferation of violent sex in movies, television programs, and books.

Viewing films with sadomasochistic themes may desensitize people to these practices. Modeling, or observational learning, has been shown to have a powerful effect in reducing inhibitions against antisocial behaviors. Male subjects who were exposed to rape stimuli reported more fantasies dealing with violent or forced sex than those exposed to consenting sexual themes (Malamuth 1981). Males exposed to violent sex films were subsequently more aggressive toward women than those who watched consensual sex (Donnerstein and Berkowitz 1981). It is also possible that aggression is eroticized by a recurring theme in pornography—that women eventually begin to enjoy sexual abuse. In any event, recent research findings are making it clear that violent sexual themes are not harmless and that they do not serve as a safety valve for aggressive sexual tendencies.

cording to one of these, the child may have witnessed his or her parents engaged in sexual intercourse (the "primal scene") and may have misinterpreted it as a brutal relationship that exists between males and females. Thus the child now sees aggression as a part of sexuality. Interestingly, however, no evidence of any links between primal scene experiences and psychosocial development were found in a recent mixed-sex study of adults who reported witnessing their parents engaged in sexual intercourse (Hoyt 1979).

According to another psychoanalytic hypothesis (one that applies only to male sadists) the ability to inflict pain assures the sadist that he is not castrated, thus protecting him from castration anxiety. In psychodynamic terms, masochism also represents an attempt by the male to reduce castration anxiety. The masochist accepts pain as a form of self-castration, which limits the power of others to castrate him.

Social learning theory proposes that sado-masochistic behaviors develop through the association of sexual arousal with pain. For example, a child who is placed across his mother's lap and spanked may experience both erotic sensations and pain. This early conditioning experience may lead to the development of masochistic behaviors.

Aggression is often displayed during sexual *arousal,* and it may become sufficiently associated with arousal to produce sadomasochistic behavior. For example, Kanin (1969) analyzed the dating behavior of 341 undergraduate, unmarried male university students; 87 of them reported at least one sexually aggressive episode with a female. In a more recent study, very little change was found in the incidence and frequency of sexual aggression toward university women (Kanin and Parcell 1977). More than 50 percent of the women surveyed reported being a victim of aggression that involved attempts at kissing (35.8 percent), breast fondling (34.1 percent), genital fondling (17.2 percent), or intercourse (12.3 percent). As is the case with psychodynamic explanations, however, this learning perspective explanation is inadequate: Most individuals who have experienced pain with sexual arousal do not become sadists or masochists.

Treatment For some reason, the treatment of sadism and masochism is rarely reported in the psychological literature. In one approach that was reported, deviant masochistic behavior was reduced by shocking the subject during the presentation of taped sequences describing masochistic behavior and by rewarding the verbalization of normal sexual behavior (Abel, Levis, and Clancy 1970).

One treatment that has produced positive results the few times it has been used with sadomasochists is *orgasmic reconditioning* (Davison 1968; Marquis 1970). This behavioral technique is aimed at increasing appropriate heterosexual arousal. The sadomasochist is first instructed to masturbate to sexually arousing deviant imagery, until he is on the verge of ejaculating. At this point the client is directed to substitute nondeviant sexual images for the deviant images, while continuing to masturbate. It is not unusual for the client to lose his erection the first few times he switches images in this way. If so, he is simply told to begin masturbating to the deviant imagery again, and again to change his imagery to nondeviant material just prior to ejaculating. When the client is able to maintain an erection while imagining appropriate sexual acts, he is asked to introduce the nondeviant images earlier in the process of masturbating. Eventually, the deviant sexual imagery is completely replaced by the nondeviant images.

Orgasmic reconditioning has also been used to treat other forms of deviant sexual behavior, such as voyeurism (Jackson 1969) and pedophilia (Annon 1971).

Pedophilia

Pedophilia is a disorder in which an adult obtains erotic gratification through sexual contact with children. The majority of pedophiles prefer female children, although a few choose prepubertal boys. Child sexual abuse is far from rare. In one study, between 20 and 25 percent of women reported having had a childhood sexual encounter with an adult male (Herman and Hirschman 1981). And, contrary to the popular view of the pedophile (or child molester) as a stranger, pedophiles were found to be mainly relatives (14 percent), friends (37 percent), or casual acquaintances (31 percent) of their victims (Mohr, Turner, and Jury 1964).

In most cases of abuse, only one adult and one child are involved, but cases involving several adults or groups of children have recently been reported. For example, a 54-year-old man, a person who had won a community award for his work with youth, was arrested for child molestation involving boys as young as ten years old. The man would encourage and photograph sexual acts between the boys, including mutual masturbation and oral and anal sex. He then would have sex with one of them (Burgess et al. 1984).

The sexual molestation of even younger children has recently been reported. Early in 1984, Virginia McMartin and six other adults (three family members and three teachers) who operated a prestigious preschool in Manhattan Beach, California, were charged with 115 counts of sexually molesting eighteen children. It was reported that more than one hundred children may have been involved over a ten-year period. In New York, three employees of a city-funded day care center were arrested for the rape and sodomy of children aged four to eight. The children reportedly had been threatened and beaten, to keep them from talking about the abuse they suffered. The center was investigated after one of its clients, a four-year-old girl, complained of pain in her groin and the examining physician discovered that she had been raped.

Such cases represent extreme examples of pedophilia. In most instances, the pedophile's sexual interest is demonstrated by touching, fondling, caressing, sucking, and smelling the child. Only a minority of molesters attempt to penetrate the child with the penis (Cohen, Seghorn, and Calmas 1969).

Victims of sexual abuse show a variety of physical symptoms such as urinary tract infections, poor appetite, and headaches. The psychological symptoms that have been reported include nightmares, difficulty in sleeping, a decline in school performance, acting-out behaviors, and sexually focused behavior. One boy was overheard asking another to take down his pants, which was the request made by the person who had molested him (Burgess, Groth, and McCausland 1981). Some child victims show the symptoms of posttraumatic stress disorder. In a sample of sixty-six victims, forty-five reported experiencing flashbacks of the molestation. They also demonstrated diminished responsiveness to their environment, hyperalertness, and jumpiness (Burgess et al. 1984).

Etiology   Little information is now available on the characteristics of individuals who sexually abuse children. The data that are available apply only to convicted pedophiles. Individuals in this group tend to have experienced a conservative attitude toward sex at home. They report that there was little discussion of sex in their families, and that their families frowned on premarital sex. Pedophiles were the least comfortable of any group of sex offenders in talking about sex (Goldstein 1973).

Several types of pedophiles were found in one survey (Gebhard et al. 1965). The largest group (one-third) had adequate sexual relationships at the time of their offenses; they did not prefer children as sexual partners but found them acceptable. Mentally retarded individuals (17 percent) formed the next largest group of offenders. These individuals acted like overgrown children engaging in prepubertal play; they were seeking attention and affection from the molestation as much as sexual gratification. About 10 percent of the offenders were socio-sexually deprived. These individuals had little heterosexual experience and felt inferior and shy with women. Children provided their only outlet. The molesters who did not fall into one of these categories were either reacting to stress or were intoxicated when the episodes occurred.

Treatment   It is only in the last ten years that pedophiles have received any treatment other than imprisonment for their deviant behavior. Many of the current programs of therapy for pedophiles involve both treatment to eliminate deviant sexual behavior and treatment to enhance appropriate behavior. The following case, reported by Brownell and Barlow (1980), illustrates a typical combination of techniques: covert sensitization and orgasmic reconditioning.

The client was a 46-year-old married executive with three children. He had recently been reported to the police for having sexual contact with a ten-year-old girl. The client recalled first feeling aroused in the presence of young girls about fifteen years before. Since then he had exposed himself to several girls and had engaged in sexual contact (touching) with three of his daughters' friends. He began experiencing impotency problems with his wife at age forty, and since that time their frequency of sexual contact had decreased markedly.

During the initial stages of therapy, the client was asked to keep a written record of his appropriate and inappropriate sexual fantasies and urges. (This pretreatment information could later be compared with the posttreatment frequency of urges and fantasies, to determine whether any progress had been made.) His record also provided the content for scenes to be used in the covert sensitization part of the treatment.

Orgasmic reconditioning was the first technique introduced. Its goal was to increase the frequency of appropriate sexual urges and to develop a series of heterosexual images suitable for use during masturbation. It was considered extremely important to offer a pleasurable replacement for the deviant sexual arousal before decreasing it. The following excerpt from a therapy session demonstrates the manner in which the therapist explained orgasmic reconditioning to the client.

> THERAPIST: In essence, orgasmic reconditioning consists of gradually modifying the images you have during masturbation. At present you are easily aroused by sexual fantasies of young girls. We want to replace these with images of your wife. I would like you to achieve an erection by the images of young girls. Use the images you are accustomed to and make sure you are highly aroused. Just prior to ejaculation, secure an image of your wife in a sexual position. If you lose the erection, regain the image of the young girl until the erection returns. At the point of ejaculatory inevitability, switch to the image of your wife.
>
> CLIENT: What is ejaculatory inevitability?
>
> THERAPIST: For all males, there is a period of time just before they ejaculate in which they know they can't avoid ejaculation. This period of time can range from 3 to 6 seconds and is called ejaculatory inevitability. It is at this point that you should bring in the images of your wife.

Young children who have been sexually abused often find it difficult to talk about the incident. They may not know the words to communicate their distress, or they may have been threatened with violence to prevent them from talking. In a recent technique, a therapist gives the child a puppet and has the child *show* what the abuser did.

We want to completely replace the young girl images with images of your wife. The most effective way to accomplish this is by a process we call shaping. This refers to taking small and gradual steps towards your final goal with no step being undertaken until you are comfortable with the last. Therefore, if you can comfortably insert the image of your wife 3 seconds prior to ejaculation, try to increase the time span to 10 seconds. (Brownell and Barlow 1980, p. 646)

As the client became more proficient at masturbating to the images of his wife, she was able to arouse him more and more in real life. A decline in arousal by young girls was also noted.

Although the client reported substantial improvement in terms of decreased sexual urges and fantasies about young girls, he did not totally trust his ability to remain in control of himself at all times. Consequently, covert sensitization was introduced to treat the deviant sexual arousal directly. Its aim was to train the client to experience automatically an aversive reaction to any arousing situations with young girls. This was to be accomplished by repeatedly pairing an aversive image with the image that aroused deviant behavior. Here is an example of the pairing of the arousing scene with an aversive scene:

> THERAPIST: Sit back in the chair and get as relaxed as possible. Close your eyes and concentrate on what I'm saying. Imagine yourself in the playroom of your home. Notice the furniture . . . the walls . . . and the feelings of being in the room. The door opens and the 10-year-old girl walks in. As she comes toward you, you notice the color of her hair . . . the clothes she is wearing . . . and the way she is walking. She comes over and sits by you. She is being flirtatious and very cute. You touch her playfully and begin to get aroused. She is asking you questions about sex education, and you begin to touch her. You can feel your hands on her smooth skin . . . on her dress . . . and touching her hair.
>
> As you become more and more aroused, you begin taking off her clothes. You can feel your fingers on her dress as you slip it off. You begin touching her arms . . . and her back. . . . Feel your hands on her thighs and buttocks. As you get more excited, you take her hand and place it on your penis. She begins rubbing your penis. You're noticing how good it feels. You are stroking her thighs and getting very aroused. As you both get more aroused. she begins using her mouth on your penis. You can feel how warm and wet it is, and how very good it feels.
>
> You hear a scream! As you turn around you see your daughter! She sees you there—naked and molesting that little girl. She begins to cry. She is sobbing hysterically. She falls to her

knees and holds her head in her hands. She is saying "I hate you, I hate you!" You start to go over to hold her, but she is afraid of you and runs away. You start to panic and lose control. You want to kill yourself and end it all. You can see what you have done to yourself. (Brownell and Barlow 1980, p. 653)

The treatment ended when the client was not reporting arousal or showing physiological signs of arousal in response to scenes with the young girl. His sexual contact with his wife remained frequent and positive.

Incest

Incest is sexual relations between close relatives. The most commonly reported incidents of incest involve a father and his daughter. However, in a survey in which 15 percent of the respondents reported sexual contacts with relatives, the most common incestuous relationship involved *siblings* (Hunt 1974). Less than 0.5 percent of the women reported sexual contact with their fathers. In another study, sexual activities between siblings were again found to be relatively frequent: 15 percent of the females and 10 percent of the males reported sexual involvement with their siblings. In 75 percent of these cases, mutual consent was involved. Approximately 50 percent considered the experience to be positive; the other half, negative (Finkelhor 1980). Mother–son incest appears to be rare.

Estimates of the incidence of incest range from 48,000 to 250,000 cases per year (Stark 1984). Yet the television program "Something about Amelia," which portrayed father–daughter incest, elicited over 5000 telephone calls to hot-line numbers.

Most research has focused on father–daughter incest. This type of incestuous relationship generally begins when the daughter is between six and eleven years old, and it continues for at least two years (Stark 1984). Unlike sex between siblings, father–daughter incest is always exploitive. The child is especially vulnerable because she depends on her father for emotional support. As a result, the victims of father–daughter incest often experience feelings of guilt and powerlessness. Their problems continue into adulthood and are reflected in high rates of drug abuse, sexual dysfunction, and psychiatric problems later in life (Emslie and Rosenfeld 1983; McGuire and Wagner 1978). Incest victims often have difficulty establishing a trusting relationship with other males.

Etiology Three types of incestuous fathers have been described (Rist 1979). The first is a socially isolated individual who is highly dependent on his family for interpersonal relationships. His emotional dependency gradually evolves (and expands) into a sexual relationship with his daughter. The second type of incestuous father is an individual with a psychopathic personality who is completely indiscriminate in his choice of partners for sexual gratification. The third type has pedophilic tendencies and is sexually involved with several children, including his daughter. In addition, family patterns in which the father is violent and the mother is unusually powerless have been reported by incest victims (Herman and Hirschman 1981).

Treatment As with pedophilia, prison has been the main form of treatment for incest offenders, although an effort is usually made to keep the family intact for the benefit of the child. Public revulsion and outrage against incest offenders, pedophiles, and rapists have resulted in a call for severe punishment. A recent trial involved an heir to a large pharmaceutical company, a man who had had an incestuous relationship with his step-daughter for seven years. As part of his sentence, he was ordered to be chemically "castrated." This judicial ruling caused an uproar. Some groups felt that the punishment was inadequate, some felt that it would not work, and others indicated that it was "cruel and unusual."

Surgical castration has been employed to treat sexual offenders in many European countries, but there have been few studies of its effectiveness. An investigation of sex offenders (rapists, heterosexual pedophiles, homosexual pedophiles, bisexual pedophiles, and a sexual murderer) who were surgically castrated did demonstrate decreases in reported sexual intercourse, masturbation, and frequency of sexual fantasies. However, 12 of the 39 were still able to engage in sexual intercourse several years after being castrated. The rapists constituted the group whose members were most likely to remain sexually active (Heim 1981).

Obviously, there is continuing controversy over the appropriate treatment and/or punishment for sexual offenders such as incest offenders, pedophiles, and rapists.

PSYCHOSEXUAL DYSFUNCTIONS

In contrast to the paraphilias, which are characterized by sexual arousal as a response to unusual situations, acts, or objects, a **psychosexual dysfunction** is a disruption of any part of the *normal* sexual response cycle. This normal cycle consists of four stages:

1. The *appetitive* phase, characterized by the desire for sexual activity. The dysfunction in which there is a lack of sexual desire is called *inhibited sexual desire*.
2. The *excitement* phase, during which the normal male attains erection and the normal female attains vaginal lubrication. Psychologically based difficulties with these physiological changes are termed *inhibited sexual excitement*.
3. The *orgasm* phase, characterized by the release of sexual tension. The inability to achieve an orgasm after entering the excitement phase and receiving "adequate" sexual stimulation is termed *inhibited orgasm*.

4. The *resolution* phase, characterized by relaxation of the body after orgasm. Problems with this last stage are rare.

Other problems that may be involved with the sexual response cycle include *functional dyspareunia,* or pain associated with sexual intercourse but not due to a physical condition; *premature ejaculation* in males; and *functional vaginismus* in females.

Most of these psychosexual dysfunctions are considered fairly common. However, to be diagnosed as a dysfunction, the problem must be "recurrent and persistent." DSM-III also requires that such factors as "frequency, chronicity, subjective distress, and effect on other areas of functioning" be considered in the diagnosis.

Inhibited sexual desire in males and females

Inhibited sexual desire involves a lack of sexual interest, as reflected in low levels of sexual activity and sexual fantasizing. This dysfunction is more common in females than in males. Some clinicians estimate that 40 percent of all sexual dysfunctions involve deficits in desire (Southern and Gayle 1982). In a population of clients who had no identified sexual dysfunction, 35 percent of the women and 16 percent of the men complained of lack of interest in sex (Frank, Anderson, and Rubenstein 1978). Complaints of low sexual desire were also reported in a substantial number of male and female patients being treated for other sexual dysfunctions (LoPiccolo 1980).

Individuals with inhibited sexual desire are capable of experiencing orgasm. However, they claim to have little interest in, or to derive no pleasure from, sexual activity.

Problems with etiology and treatment It is difficult to discuss either the etiology or the treatment of inhibited sexual desire because of a lack of information about what constitutes

normal sexual desire. Some individuals may simply have an innate low motivation for sexual activities; these people would *normally* report few sexual thoughts or fantasies and little sexual desire.

A lack of sexual desire may be physiological. One group of women reported no feelings of anxiety about, or aversion to, sexual intercourse; but they showed significantly lower levels of vaginal blood volume (a physiological measure of sexual arousal) than sexually active women during exposure to erotic stimuli. Moreover, sexual arousal treatment did not increase their responsiveness (Wincze, Hoon, and Hoon 1978). The researchers concluded that the absence of sexual arousal in these women is "primary," and the appropriate treatment for this condition is unknown.

Other individuals may report low sexual desire because of "inexperience." A large percentage of individuals of this type may not have learned to label or identify their own arousal levels, may not know how to increase their arousal, and may have a limited expectation for their ability to be aroused (LoPiccolo 1980).

Again, low sexual desire could be the result of a traumatic sexual experience, an overly moralistic background, or an unfulfilling or frustrating relationship. Such an event or situation could cause an individual to become neutral about sex or actually to have an aversion to it. In one group of men and women who complained about lack of interest in sex, 28 percent of the women and 10 percent of the men reported an aversion to sex (Frank, Anderson, and Rubenstein 1978). In another group, composed of 120 women who were sexually dysfunctional, 22 percent complained of sexual aversion (Hoch et al. 1981).

Just as we do not really know what constitutes "normal" sexual desire, we know little about what frequency of sexual fantasies or activities is "normal." Kinsey (1948) found tremendous variation in reported total sexual outlet, or release. One male reported that he had ejaculated only once in 30 years; another claimed to have averaged 30 orgasms per week for 30 years. After analyzing mean frequencies of orgasm from sex surveys, a group of researchers noted that ''A total orgasmic outlet of less than once every two weeks is considered one marker of low desire . . . unless extenuating circumstances such as a lack of privacy occur'' (Schover et al. 1982, p. 616). However, the use of some average frequency of sexual activity does not seem to be appropriate for categorizing other individuals as having inhibited sexual desire. The sexually unresponsive women studied by Wincze, Hoon, and Hoon reported that their marriages were quite satisfactory with regard to communication, respect, and positive regard. It may be that some individuals are just not so interested in sex as others. And until we can decide on a normal range of sexual desire, we can make little progress in discovering the causes of or developing treatments for inhibited sexual desire.

Inhibited sexual excitement in males

In males, inhibited sexual excitement takes the form of **erectile dysfunction,** the inability of a man to attain or maintain a penile erection that is sufficient for sexual intercourse. The man may feel fully aroused but is unable to consummate the sex act. *Primary* erectile dysfunction is a total inability—the man has never been able to successfully complete an act of sexual intercourse. That this difficulty often has a psychological origin is evident, because many males with this dysfunction are able to achieve penile erection and orgasm during masturbation and to exhibit erection during the REM (rapid eye movement) phase of sleep, which is associated with dreaming. *Secondary* erectile dysfunction refers to a situation in which the man has had at least one successful coital experience but is currently having erectile difficulty. Failure to achieve an erection and vaginal intromission in 25 percent

of sexual attempts is sufficient for this diagnosis (Masters and Johnson 1970).

> A twenty-year-old college student was suffering from secondary erectile dysfunction. His first episode of erectile difficulty occurred when he attempted sexual intercourse after drinking heavily. Although to a certain extent he attributed the failure to alcohol, he also began to have doubts about his sexual ability. During a subsequent sexual encounter, his anxiety and worry increased. When he failed in this next coital encounter, even though he had not been drinking, his anxiety level rose even more. The client sought therapy after the discovery that he was unable to achieve an erection even during petting.

The incidence of erectile dysfunction is difficult to determine because it often goes unreported. Clinicians estimate that approximately 50 percent of males have experienced transient impotence (Kaplan 1974). In a representative sample of 58 married men, however, only 7 percent reported this problem (Nettelbladt and Uddenberg 1979). Of 448 male sexual dysfunctions treated at the Masters and Johnson sex clinic, 32 were suffering from primary erectile dysfunction and 213 from secondary erectile dysfunction. The number of cases reported may be increasing now, as individuals feel freer to talk about this problem and as it becomes more acceptable for women to expect greater satisfaction in sexual relationships.

Unfortunately, in the American cultural perspective, the male is still viewed as the expert in sexual matters. In fact, the woman who accepts this cultural perspective may blame the male if she is unresponsive (Zussman and Zussman 1976). Sexually normal males and females who had sexually dysfunctional partners were assessed by Derogatis, Meyer, and Gallant (1977). They found that the nondysfunctional male partners were less relaxed and had a disproportionately higher level of psychological symptoms than their female counterparts. This finding indicates that many adults consider the male to be the partner responsible for sexual satisfaction.

Etiology Traditional psychotherapists have stressed the role of unconscious conflicts, such as fear of or hostility toward women, in the development of psychogenic erectile dysfunction. Cooper (1969), however, found that in most cases, situational or coital *anxiety* was the culprit. In his study, forty-nine patients with psychogenic erectile dysfunction were asked to describe their anxiety during sexual overtures (actual or imagined). Marked increases in subjective anxiety as well as somatic symptoms (sweating, trembling, muscle tension, headaches, and heart palpitations) were reported. The specific fears associated with these reactions are presented in Table 12.2; note that "fear of failure" is the most frequently mentioned. The males in this sample were not well informed on human sexuality and had only limited premarital sexual experience. Their sexual problem was often exacerbated by a partner who was similarly inexperienced. Even though they were impotent, the males reported spontaneous erections to erotic stimuli, such as sexually attractive females or sexually explicit films and

literature. These findings support situational anxiety as the cause of the dysfunction. Situational anxiety is also implicated in the finding that males tend to become secondarily dysfunctional after their partners have been treated for orgasmic difficulties and begin to place sexual demands on them (Schneidman and McGuire 1976).

Masters and Johnson (1970) feel that the performance anxiety produced by constant and critical self-focus during sexual interaction is a major etiological factor in erectile dysfunction. Self-observation has been assumed to interfere with normal sexual processes, and some experimental support has been found for this view. When male subjects were directed to focus on their own erectile responses to erotic videotapes, their sexual arousal was reduced—but only when the arousal level was low or moderate (Sakheim et al. 1984). It is possible that, during low arousal, self-focus acts as a distraction or increases performance anxiety, which reduces sexual arousal. During high arousal, however, focusing on erectile responses appeared to facilitate further arousal.

Beck, Barlow, and Sakheim (1984) studied the impact of self-focus and partner focus on

Table 12.2 *Specific Coital Anxieties* Most Frequently Associated with Male Potency Disorders*

Specific Anxiety	Number of Times Mentioned	% (n = 46)
Fear of failure	26	56.3
Fear of being seen by wife as sexually inferior	20	43.5
Fear of ridicule (from wife)	19	40.0
Fear of pregnancy	11	24.0
Anxiety over size of genitals	7	15.2
Fear of physical disease	7	15.2
Pervasive anxiety (no specific cause)	5	11.0
Fear of detection	3	6.7

*Refers to manifest anxieties experienced by the patient during coital attempts. Only anxieties specifically and spontaneously (sometimes with a minimum of prompting) mentioned by the patient were included. No attempt was made either to "interpret" the statements, or to unearth fears that may have been "unconscious." The majority of the patients complained of three or more specific anxieties.

SOURCE: Cooper, A. J. (1969). A clinical study of coital anxiety in male potency disorders. *Journal of Psychosomatic Research, 13,* 143–147. Copyright © 1969, Pergamon Press, Ltd.

William Masters and Virginia Johnson are pioneers in sex research and sex therapy. Their research has contributed much to our current understanding of normal sexual functioning. Many individuals suffering from various sexual dysfunctions have been successfully treated with therapy techniques developed at Masters' and Johnson's clinic.

sexual responding, in sexually functional and dysfunctional men. They also took into account the impact of the partner's arousal level. The results indicated that observation of oneself or one's partner during intercourse does affect arousal for both functional and dysfunctional men. However, the type of cognition, whether the focus is on the partner or the self, and the level of arousal seem to interact in a manner that is more complex than that stated by Masters and Johnson.

Alcohol consumption may also play a role in erectile dysfunction. Increasing levels of alcohol consumption have been associated with a decrease in sexual arousal in males (Malatesta et al. 1979).

Treatment Behavioral therapy for erectile dysfunction has yielded a cure rate of approximately 70 percent (Wolpe 1973; Kaplan 1974; Masters and Johnson 1970). The various systematic desensitization techniques that are used all have in common a deemphasis on sexual performance, a graded and gradual approach to sexual arousal and intercourse, and the elimination of anxiety associated with coitus. These techniques can be modified when no one sexual partner is involved. Imagination was successfully used to treat a 24-year-old single male who became dysfunctional with every new sexual partner. The patient was taught to fantasize erotic scenes to the point of sexual arousal, in order to overcome the anxiety of imagining sexual intercourse with a new female (Bass 1974). In addition, sexual enhancement procedures have successfully used masturbation and fantasizing to reduce coital anxiety (Sue 1978).

Inhibited sexual excitement and orgasm in females

Inhibited sexual excitement in females involves an inability to attain arousal or to sustain it until the completion of sexual intercourse. **Orgasm** is the release of tension that occurs after erotic arousal has reached a peak. In **inhibited orgasm,** the person is unable to achieve an orgasm during coitus with ''adequate and appropriate'' stimulation after entering the excitement phase. However, an exception regarding female orgasm in included in DSM-III: ''Some women are able to experience orgasm during noncoital clitoral stimulation, but are unable to experience it during coitus in the absence of manual clitoral stimulation. There is evidence to suggest that in some instances this represents a pathological inhibition that justified this diagnosis whereas in other instances it represents a normal variation of the female sexual response'' (p. 279). Whether the lack of orgasm is categorized as a dysfunction or as a ''normal variant'' is left to the judgment of the clinician. As is noted in Focus 12.2, the criteria that define adequate functioning during sexual intercourse are quite controversial.

Inhibited female orgasm may be termed *primary,* to indicate that orgasm has never been experienced—or *secondary,* to show that orgasm has occurred in the past. Primary orgasmic dysfunction is relatively common in females. Perhaps 8 to 10 percent of all women have never achieved an orgasm by any means (Hite 1976; Kaplan 1974; Kinsey et al., 1953). This disorder is not equivalent to primary orgasmic dysfunction in males, who often can achieve orgasm through masturbation or by some other means.

Etiology Several causal factors are involved in female orgasmic dysfunction. One contributing factor is faulty learning based on parental or societal injunctions such as ''Premarital sex is wrong, but it's 'wronger' for women,'' or ''Good girls save it for marriage.'' Kaats and

Davis (1975) discovered that the double standard still exists among college students. Whereas males felt that their families would disapprove slightly of their having sexual intercourse with a casual date, they perceived that they would receive support and approval from their peers and close friends. By contrast, college women perceived that all groups (including peers and friends) would disapprove of their having sexual intercourse, even if they were in love with their partner. Such attitudes can make any coital opportunity highly anxiety-provoking for females.

The experience of rape is also implicated in orgasmic dysfunctions and aversion to sex (Burgess and Holmstrom 1979a, 1979b; Feldman-Summers, Gordon, and Meagher 1979).

Other contributing factors may include the frustration of having a sexually inexperienced or dysfunctional partner; the crippling fear of performance failure, of never being able to attain orgasm, of pregnancy, or of venereal disease; an inability to accept the partner, either emotionally or physically; and misinformation or ignorance about sexuality or sexual techniques. Often, neither partner is aware of the importance of precoital stimulation of sensitive areas (the *erogenous zones*). Lovemaking may consist of vaginal penetration as soon as the male has an erection and split-second ejaculation, without consideration of the partner's readiness. ''Such couples genuinely wonder why the wife does not reach orgasm'' (Kaplan 1974).

Treatment Extensive reviews of the literature have yielded a number of promising treatments for female orgasmic dysfunction (Sotile and Kilmann 1977; Andersen 1983). For example, Wolpe (1973) removes misconceptions about sex by reeducating and systematically desensitizing the patient, using gradated exercises with the male partner. Kaplan (1974) and Masters and Johnson (1970) utilize similar procedures but treat both partners as a unit, assuming both are responsible for the dysfunc-

FOCUS 12.2

Sexual Dysfunction or Normal Variant?

Should women who do not regularly have orgasms during coitus be labeled ''sexually dysfunctional''? This question is being debated more frequently as researchers and clinicians alike are discovering that infrequent coital orgasm is a common occurrence in women. Hite (1976) reports that only 30 percent of the women in her study could experience orgasm regularly during sexual intercourse. Similar findings have been reported by Hoch et al. (1981). Hite argues that the prevailing view of orgasm, that it ''counts'' only during sexual intercourse, is a reflection of our male-dominated society. Kaplan (1974) also indicates her resistance to the belief that women who are otherwise sexually responsive are nonetheless ''sick'' because they do not have coital orgasms. She feels that ''a woman who is otherwise orgasmic, but does not reach orgasm during coitus, is neither frigid nor sick. This pattern seems to be a normal variant of female sexuality for some women'' (p. 83). Hoch goes even further and suggests that the inability to achieve an orgasm without additional stimulation is ''not a normal variation of female sexuality but rather normal sexuality for the majority of females'' (p. 82).

This controversy has had an impact on sexual therapy. Some sex therapists believe that orgasm during coitus is a justifiable goal for ''normal'' sexual functioning (Zeiss, Rosen, and Zeiss 1977). Others are satisfied when patients are able to achieve orgasm through manual stimulation (Schneidman and McGuire 1976). Regardless of the controversy, however, a reexamination of the ''necessity'' for coital orgasm in women (and men?) would seem to be in order. To require that women be able to achieve orgasm during sexual intercourse may be to do a disservice to women and to their sex partners.

Male sexual dysfunction is also defined in terms of coital success. Does this mean that men who ejaculate rapidly or not at all during coitus, but who show the normal sexual cycle during masturbation and oral sex, are suffering from sexual problems? Perhaps. But many questions remain concerning the appropriate criteria for sexual dysfunction.

tion. Their method of treating orgasmic dysfunction involves the examination and mutual expression of sexual attitudes, sensate-focus exercises (fondling of the body and genital regions without demands for sexual arousal or orgasm), and a gradated approach to sexual intercourse. Masters and Johnson claim an 83 percent success rate in a group of 193 women with primary orgasmic dysfunction and 87 percent success with secondary dysfunction.

Procedures that incorporate masturbation have also been effective (Kohlenberg 1974a; LoPiccolo and Lobitz 1971). Even though some psychoanalysts are beginning to successfully treat the symptoms directly, they consider analysis necessary if the dysfunction is part of an underlying problem (Gershman 1978; Holt 1978).

Inhibited male orgasm

In males, orgasm is usually followed by ejaculation. **Inhibited male orgasm** is the inability to ejaculate intravaginally, even with full arousal and penile erection. As we have noted, males who exhibit this dysfunction can usually ejaculate through masturbation (Masters and Johnson 1970). Inhibited orgasm is estimated to occur in approximately 1 of every 700 males (Kinsey, Pomeroy, and Martin 1948). Treatment is often urged by the wife, who may want to conceive or who may feel (because of the husband's lack of orgasm) that she is not an exciting sexual partner (McCary 1973). However, because coitus may last 30 to 60 minutes without ejaculation, some wives of inhibited-orgasm males report that they are multiorgasmic.

Etiology An examination of the background of men with this dysfunction reveals either the occurrence of some traumatic event or a severely restrictive religious background in which sex is considered evil. Masters and Johnson (1970) give an example of a man who discovered his wife engaged in sexual intercourse with another man. Although they remained married, he could no longer ejaculate during intercourse.

Treatment Treatment involves stimulating the penile area until the male is about to ejaculate (to the point of ejaculatory inevitability) and inserting the penis immediately thereafter. If ejaculation occurs once, the psychological block is generally eliminated (Masters and Johnson 1970; Kaplan 1974).

Premature ejaculation

Premature ejaculation is a relatively common sexual dysfunction in males, but sex researchers and therapists offer different definitions of it. Kaplan (1974) defines prematurity as the inability of a man to tolerate high (plateau) levels of sexual excitement without ejaculating reflexively; Kilmann and Auerbach (1979) suggest that less than five minutes from coital entry is a suitable criterion of premature ejaculation; Masters and Johnson (1970) contend

that a male who is unable to delay ejaculation long enough during sexual intercourse to produce an orgasm in the female 50 percent of the time is a premature ejaculator. The difficulty with the last definition is the possibility that a man may be "premature" with one partner but entirely adequate for another.

Some support has been found for Kaplan's definition. The sexual responsiveness of ten premature ejaculators was compared with that of fourteen normally functioning men, and no differences were found in rate of arousal, degree of arousal, or amount of arousal, either subjectively or physiologically. However, the premature ejaculators did ejaculate at lower levels of arousal. In addition, speed of ejaculation was found to be inversely related to the period of abstinence, or the time between sexual episodes (Spiess, Geer, and O'Donohue 1984).

The inability to satisfy a sexual partner is a source of anguish for many males. In a campus newspaper column at a midwestern college, premature ejaculation was the largest single source of concern in the realm of male sexual dysfunctions (Werner 1975). In one sample of married men, 38 percent reported problems of too-rapid ejaculation (Nettlebladt and Uddenberg 1979). And, of the sexually dysfunctional males seeking treatment at a clinic, 29 percent were diagnosed as having premature ejaculation (Hoch et al. 1981).

Three-fourths of the males in one study reported they reach an orgasm within two minutes of the beginning of sexual intercourse, and a large number may reach orgasm less than one minute after coital entry (Kinsey, Pomeroy, and Martin 1948). In a survey of white, married females, information on the duration of penile intromission revealed that most husbands could delay ejaculation for two minutes, but few could delay more than seven. This finding has bearing on other sexual dysfunctions as well, because the female orgasmic rate has been directly related to the duration of penile intromission (Gebhard 1966).

In another study, 300 middle-class wives

were asked to estimate the amount of time needed to achieve an orgasm (Fisher 1973). They reported that, on the average, their husbands required 40 to 80 percent less time than they did. This difference in duration contributes to the high premature ejaculation rate.

Etiology   Premature ejaculation may have a biological basis. In most species of mammals, the male ejaculates almost instantly upon intromission (Kinsey, Pomeroy, and Martin 1948). Masters and Johnson (1970), however, suggest that the dysfunction is due to early conditioning experiences, when rapid ejaculation was necessary (such as intercourse in the parents' home, in a dorm room, or at drive-in movies). Heavy and sustained petting may also induce premature ejaculation, although masturbatory patterns do not seem to contribute to this dysfunction (Masters and Johnson 1970).

Treatment   In the past, treatments for premature ejaculation ranged from physical means and mechanical aids (such as applying local anesthetics to the glans of the penis, wearing condoms, biting the tongue, or pinching oneself) to mental distractions during arousal (adding numbers or imagining anxiety-provoking situations such as failing in school). None of these procedures is very effective, and they all tend to reduce sexual pleasure and satisfaction.

Psychoanalysts consider premature ejaculation a reflection of unconscious hostility toward women, and psychodynamic treatment is directed toward uncovering and resolving the underlying hostility. The results of this type of therapy have, however, been disappointing (Kaplan 1974; Kilmann and Auerbach 1979).

The most successful types of therapy are those that recondition the ejaculatory process. In one technique, the partner stimulates the penis extravaginally until the sensation of impending ejaculation occurs. At this point, stimulation is stopped for a short period of time, and then it is continued again. The pattern is repeated until the man can tolerate increasingly greater periods of stimulation before ejaculation (Semans 1956). Masters and Johnson (1970) and Kaplan (1974) used essentially the same procedure, called "the squeeze technique," and they reported a success rate of nearly 100 percent. The treatment is easily learned. Zeiss (1977) implemented a successful training program using a standardized instruction manual and only minimal therapist contact.

Functional vaginismus

Vaginismus is the involuntary muscular constriction of the outer part of the vagina, severely restricting or preventing penile penetration. The incidence of this dysfunction is not known, but it is considered very rare.

Etiology   Several causal factors have been identified in vaginismus. Masters and Johnson (1970) found one or more of the following conditions among many women with this dysfunction: (1) a husband or partner who was impotent; (2) rigid religious beliefs about sex; (3) prior sexual trauma, such as rape; (4) prior homosexual identification; and (5) *dyspareunia,* or painful intercourse.

Kaplan (1974) stresses the importance of similar variables. She suggests that vaginismus results when a woman associates penile penetration with pain and fear. The precipitating event may be either physical pain (perhaps due to rigid hymen, inflammated pelvic tissue, or lack of lubrication) or psychological stress (misinformation or guilt about sex). Fuchs (1975) sees vaginismus occurring in a manner similar to a phobia. The phobia is the fear of penetration of a private part of the body.

Treatment   The results of treatment for vaginismus have been uniformly positive (Kaplan 1974; Wolpe 1973; Masters and Johnson 1970). The involuntary spasms or closure of the

Homosexuality is controversial in both the mental health community and the community at large. According to DSM-III homosexuality is not a mental disorder. But DSM-III does have a compromise category called ego-dystonic homosexuality. Many therapists, however, question whether ego-dystonic homosexuality is truly a psychological disorder.

vaginal muscle can be deconditioned by first training the woman to relax so as to reduce anxiety, and then inserting successively larger dilators while she is relaxed until insertion of the penis can occur. A success rate of 100 percent was reported by Masters and Johnson in 29 cases of vaginismus.

EGO-DYSTONIC HOMOSEXUALITY

Homosexuality is sexual desire that is directed toward members of one's own sex. **Ego-dystonic homosexuality** is homosexuality that is "unacceptable to the ego" and is thus a source of personal anxiety and conflict. The inclusion of this category in DSM-III seems to be a compromise resulting from the continuing controversy between those who consider homosexuality a maladaptive behavior and the many clinicians (supported by members of the gay community) who see homosexuality as a normal variant of sexual expression. This controversy was aired at a special session of the American Psychiatric Association, held to determine whether the classification of homosexuality as a mental disorder should be retained in the then-existing DSM-II (Stoller et al. 1973).

At that meeting, two well-known psychiatrists, Irving Bieber and Charles Socarides, supported the traditional view of homosexuality as a psychosexual disorder resulting from disturbed relationships between parents and their children; they recommended that the classification be retained in DSM-II. When that proposal encountered opposition, Bieber suggested that homosexual behavior be reclassified as a category of sexual dysfunction, because "most homosexuals (especially those who are exclusively homosexual) cannot function heterosexually" (Stoller et al. 1973). This too was considered inappropriate by many clinicians and practitioners, who see the issue as one of preference rather than function.

Stoller, Marmor, and Spitzer supported the removal of homosexuality from the DSM-II nomenclature, preferring to consider it a normal variant of human sexual behavior (Stoller et al. 1973). Marmor was critical of generalizing from studies of samples of homosexuals seeking treatment: "If our judgment about mental health was based only on those whom we see in our clinical practices, we would have to conclude that all heterosexuals are also mentally ill" (p. 1209). From various nonclinical samples of homosexuals it can be concluded that many are well-adjusted (Siegelman 1972; Strassberg et al. 1979; Thompson, McCandless, and Strickland 1971).

After considering the issues, the trustees of the American Psychiatric Association voted, on December 15, 1973, to remove homosexuality from DSM-II. A new category, "sexual orientation disturbance," was created and applied to those individuals who desired to change from a homosexual to a heterosexual orientation. DSM-III retained this compromise category, which is now called *ego-dystonic homosexuality*. Members of the gay community object to this category, however, because it means that some homosexuals may be viewed as "sick."

Although DSM-III states explicitly that "homosexuality itself is not considered a mental disorder," it adds that "factors that predispose an individual to ego-dystonic homosexuality are those negative societal attitudes towards homosexuality that have been internalized" (p. 282). In other words, pressures to conform to societal standards and the desire to have children and a "socially sanctioned family life" may be incompatible with homosexuality. (See Focus 12.3 for discussion of this issue.) The diagnostic criteria for this disorder

FOCUS 12.3

Are Children Raised by Homosexuals Confused about Gender Identity?

In the face of strong objections, a growing number of homosexuals and transsexuals are asserting their right to raise children. The objectors argue that homosexuals and transsexuals follow deviant lifestyles and that children living with such parents will adopt their maladaptive orientation. In fact, both social learning and psychoanalytic theorists might predict that such children would be likely to have some form of gender-identity problem or other serious confusion.

The development of 21 children (average age, 8 years) living with homosexual parents was investigated by Green (1978). The children had lived in these households for an average of $4\frac{1}{2}$ years. In nearly all cases, the children were aware of their parents' atypical sexual orientation. For example, four of the girls living in a transsexual household saw their mother undergo androgen hormone treatment and sex conversion surgery. This individual became their "father," who then married their "stepmother."

Measures of sexual identity (toy and game preference, peer-group composition preference, clothing preference, roles in fantasy games, vocational aspirations, reported romantic crushes, and fantasies) were obtained on all the children. *All of them* displayed heterosexual preferences that were appropriate for their sex. Green cautions that this is a preliminary report and that no control group was present, nor are longer-term effects known. Given these limitations, Green tentatively suggests that "children being raised by transsexual or homosexual parents do not differ appreciably from children raised in more conventional family settings on macroscopic measures of sexual identity" (pp. 696–697).

In another study, ten boys and ten girls between the ages of 5 and 12 who were living with their lesbian mothers were compared with children raised by heterosexual mothers. The two groups of children did not differ with respect to the sex of the first figure they drew, play and sexual preferences, and playroom behavior (Kirkpatrick et al. 1981). However, Green's comments regarding better control and longer-term studies apply to these results as well as to his own. Additional research is required if we are to determine whether gender identity and sex-role development are influenced by homosexual or transsexual parentage.

include "a persistent pattern of absent or weak heterosexual arousal" that interferes with establishing *desired* heterosexual relationships and a "sustained pattern of homosexual arousal" that is *unwanted* and distressing to the individual.

This diagnosis becomes inappropriate if an individual adjusts to his or her sexual orientation. There is some evidence that, in time, many individuals with homosexual inclinations give up the yearning to become heterosexual. In addition, DSM-III points out that without intervention the development of heterosexual adjustment in these individuals is "rare" and that even with therapy the outcome is "disputed."

The question of choice

In the most comprehensive study of homosexuals to date, researchers analyzed data obtained from 4-hour interviews with 979 male and female homosexuals and 477 matched controls (Bell and Weinberg 1978; Bell, Weinberg, and Hammersmith 1981). The majority of both male and female homosexuals indicated no regrets at being homosexual and were accepting of their sexual orientation. Those who expressed regret regarding their homosexuality cited, as major problems, the lack of acceptance by society, not being able to have children, and loneliness:

> My regret is not [in] being a homosexual but [in] being a homosexual in this society. . . . I'd like to be a teacher right now. I really would. But I won't go where I have to live a lie and where homosexuals are not accepted or welcome. (Bell and Weinberg, p. 123)

> The person I love and live with might someday want a child, and I could never give it to her, nor could she to me. This is often important to women. (Bell and Weinberg, p. 126)

With regard to psychological adjustment, few differences were found between homosexual and heterosexual females. However, homosexual males were more likely than heterosexual males to report feelings of loneliness, depression, and low self-esteem. This difference was accounted for by those relatively few male homosexuals who were dissatisfied with their orientation. Homosexuals who accepted themselves as such did not differ from heterosexuals on psychological adjustment measures.

Like their heterosexual neighbors, the homosexual individuals experienced some problems with sexual functioning: 23 percent of the males reported problems in attaining or maintaining erection (of these problems, about one-fifth were reportedly severe, and the remainder mild); and 28 percent complained of "coming too fast" (again, in about one-fifth this problem was severe). Lack of orgasm was reported by 14 percent of the males and 20 percent of the females.

The researchers found that homosexual individuals did not differ from heterosexuals in frequency of dating during high school. Most had their first homosexual experience with a friend or acquaintance of about their own age.

A major criticism of ego-dystonic homosexuality as a diagnostic category is its acceptance of heterosexual functioning as the norm. There is no parallel category for a heterosexual who shows a "persistent pattern of absent or weak homosexual arousal" that interferes with "establishing desired homosexual relationships." Spitzer (1981) acknowledges this criticism and counters that "there is not a single case in the scientific literature that describes an individual with a sustained pattern of heterosexual arousal who was distressed by being heterosexually aroused and wished to acquire homosexual arousal to initiate or to maintain homosexual relationships." This statement, however, does not take into consideration the tremendous amount of prejudice and discrimination faced by homosexuals. Heterosexuals who would prefer to be homosexuals may be intimidated by this societal pressure and simply not identify themselves. Or, in accordance with this bias, a male or female complaining of weak heterosexual arousal may be labeled as suffering from inhibited sexual desire or arousal.

Treatment of ego-dystonic homosexuality

A great deal of controversy surrounds the treatment of homosexuality. Some clinicians feel that a homosexual's request for treatment merely reflects societal pressure (Silverstein 1972; Davison 1974).

> To grow up in a family where the word "homosexual" was whispered, to play in a playground and hear the words "faggot" and "queer," to go to church and hear of "sin" and then to college and hear of "illness," and finally to the counseling center that promises to "cure" is hardly an environment of freedom and voluntary choice. (Silverstein 1972, p. 4)

Treatment is thus seen as an effort to produce conformity.

Other clinicians disagree and feel that both homosexuals and heterosexuals should have a choice of sexual orientation. In support of this philosophy, Masters and Johnson (1979) established a program to treat sexually dysfunctional homosexuals without changing their sexual orientation. Their program is similar to those developed for heterosexuals, and its failure rate is quite low.

When ego-dystonic homosexuals present themselves for treatment, therapists must decide whether to treat them or refer them. If a therapist chooses to treat a client, the client must first specify whether he or she wants the treatment to focus on eliminating the distress associated with the homosexuality, or on eliminating the homosexual behavior. A homosexual patient seeking to be rid of the ego-dystonicity (the distress) would probably receive either supportive counseling, insight-oriented psychotherapy, cognitive-behavioral therapy (examining the irrational beliefs that foster distress), or relaxation training.

If the individual is interested in a change of sexual orientation, one available technique is aversion relief. Prior to the start of the procedure, varying levels of electric shock are tested on the patient until he or she designates one as "very unpleasant." Then the aversion-relief procedure begins with the presentation of a series of slides depicting (for a male homosexual client) nude or seminude males. The patient is instructed to press a button when he no longer finds the current slide sexually arousing, and pressing the button automatically removes the slide. Approximately eight seconds after a slide is first presented, the "very unpleasant" shock is introduced. It remains on and increases in intensity until the patient presses the button to terminate the slide. The patient quickly learns the association between slide termination and shock termination. The sense of relief accompanying the removal of the slide serves to reinforce the event (Feldman and MacCulloch 1965).

Aversion relief has occasionally appeared to be a beneficial treatment for homosexuality, as well as some types of sexual deviation. However, some researchers question its effectiveness (Barlow 1974).

AGING AND SEXUAL ACTIVITY

We should not leave this chapter on sexual functioning without at least briefly considering the effect of aging on sexual activity. Sexuality during old age has been the subject of many myths and jokes. In our youth-oriented society, sexual activity is simply not associated with aging. However, it is clear that a large percentage of older Americans have active sex lives.

In a study of sexual functioning in 60- to 79-year-old married males, a clear relationship was found between the reported frequency of intercourse at younger ages and at present. The most active respondents reported a present frequency that was 61 percent of their frequency between ages 40 and 59, whereas the least active reported a present frequency of only 6 percent of that between ages 40 and 59. The most active also indicated that they became aroused on seeing women in public situations and in response to visual stimuli. The vast majority (69 percent) felt that sex was important for good health, and most (63 percent) accepted masturbation as an acceptable outlet. Sexual dysfunctions were also more prevalent in this population than in younger groups, and their prevalence was affected by the prior and present sexual activity levels of the individuals. Of the least active, 21 percent suffered from premature ejaculation, and 75 percent were either impotent or had erectile difficulties. For the most active group, the corresponding percentages were 8 and 19 percent (Martin 1981).

Physiologically based changes in patterns of sexual arousal and orgasm have been found in people over age 65 (Masters and Johnson 1966). For both males and females, sexual arousal takes longer. Erection and vaginal lubrication are slower to occur, and the urgency for orgasm is reduced. However, both males and females are fully capable of attaining sexual satisfaction if no organic conditions interfere.

Sexual activity does, however, appear to play a less important part in the lives of the elderly. They feel that a decline in sexual interest is a natural part of aging, and only 35 percent would seek treatment to obtain greater sexual vigor if this were possible. With or without sex, the elderly men in the Martin (1981) study regarded their marriages as highly successful and their wives as physically attractive; and they themselves were free of performance anxiety.

SUMMARY

1. The gender-identity disorders include transsexualism and childhood gender-identity disorder. Transsexuals feel a severe psychological conflict between their sexual self-concept on the one hand and their physical gender on the other. Many transsexuals seek sex-conversion surgery, although behavioral therapies are being used increasingly. Gender-identity disorders can also occur in childhood. Children with this problem identify with members of the opposite sex, deny their own physical attributes, and often crossdress. Treatment generally includes the parents and is behavioral in nature.

2. The paraphilias are of three types, characterized by a preference for nonhuman objects for sexual arousal, the association of real or simulated suffering with sexual activity, or repetitive sexual activity with nonconsenting partners. Suggested causes of the paraphilias are unconscious conflicts (the psychodynamic perspective) and conditioning, generally during childhood. Treatments are usually behavioral and are aimed at eliminating the deviant behavior while teaching more appropriate behaviors.

3. Psychosexual dysfunctions are disruptions of the normal sexual response cycle. They are fairly common in the general population and may affect the person's ability to become sexually aroused or to engage in intercourse. Many result from fear or anxiety regarding sexual activities; the various treatment programs are generally successful.

4. Ego-dystonic homosexuality (homosexuality that is unacceptable to the person) is the most controversial of the subcategories of psychosexual disorders. This diagnosis applies only to those who experience homosexual arousal but desire to initiate and maintain heterosexual relationships. It is in the area of psychosexual disorders that distinctions between what is deviant and what is normal are most affected by moral and legal standards. In particular, this category of disorder is a compromise between those who consider homosexuality a normal variant of sexual expression and those who believe it is maladaptive. The most effective treatment for ego-dystonic (distressful) homosexuality is behaviorally oriented.

5. Despite myths to the contrary, sexuality extends into old age. However, sexual dysfunction becomes increasingly prevalent with aging, and the frequency of sexual activity typically declines.

KEY TERMS

ego-dystonic homosexuality Homosexuality that is unacceptable to the ego and is thus a source of distress

erectile dysfunction The inability of a male to attain or maintain a penile erection that is sufficient for sexual intercourse

exhibitionism A disorder in which sexual gratifiction is obtained through exposing the genitals to strangers

fetishism A disorder characterized by an extremely strong sexual attraction for a particular nongenital part of the anatomy or for an inanimate object

forcible rape An act of sexual intercourse that is accomplished through force or the threat of force

gender-identity disorder A psychological disorder characterized by conflict between an individual's anatomical sex and his or her sexual identity

incest Sexual relations between close relatives

inhibited orgasm A sexual dysfunction in which the individual is unable to achieve orgasm during coitus with adequate stimulation after entering the excitement phase of the sexual response cycle

inhibited sexual desire A sexual dysfunction involving a lack of sexual interest as reflected in low levels of both sexual activity and fantasizing

inhibited sexual excitement A sexual dysfunction characterized by erectile dysfunction in males or by an inability to attain or sustain arousal in females

masochism A sexual disorder in which erotic or sexual gratification is obtained by receiving pain or punishment

paraphilias Sexual disorders in which unusual or bizarre acts, images, or objects are required for sexual arousal

pedophilia A disorder in which an adult obtains erotic gratification through sexual contact with children

premature ejaculation Ejaculation before penile entry into the vagina or so soon after entry that an unsatisfactory sexual experience results

psychosexual dysfunction A disruption of any part of the normal sexual-response cycle, in a male or female

sadism A sexual disorder in which erotic or sexual gratification is obtained by inflicting pain or punishment on others

transsexualism The self-identification of an individual with the opposite sex

transvestism A disorder in which sexual gratification is obtained by wearing clothing that is appropriate to the opposite sex

vaginismus Involuntary contraction of the outer part of the vagina, which restricts or prevents penile insertion

voyeurism A disorder in which sexual gratification is obtained through the surreptitious observation of disrobing individuals or couples engaged in coitus

PART 4

Severe Disorders of Mood and Thought

13

The Affective Disorders

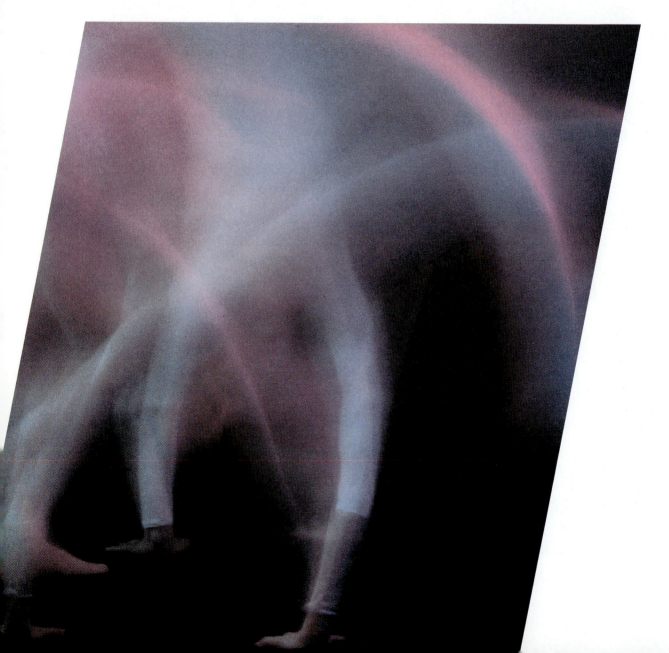

Depression is an emotional state characterized by intense sadness, feelings of futility and worthlessness, and withdrawal from others. It is one of the most commonly diagnosed conditions among patients hospitalized for mental disorders (National Center for Health Statistics 1980). It is also quite prevalent among the general population: In one large-scale survey, researchers found that approximately one-fifth of all individuals residing in Los Angeles County exhibited significant clinical symptoms of depression (Frerichs, Aneshensel, and Clark 1981). Severe depression does not respect socioeconomic status, educational attainment, or personal qualities; it may afflict rich or poor, successful or unsuccessful, highly educated or uneducated.

Amanda J. is a 39-year-old homemaker with three children, ages 9, 11, and 14. Her husband is the sales manager for an auto agency. The family does well financially and lives comfortably, but Mr. J. began to notice that his wife was becoming more and more unhappy and depressed. She reiterated constantly that she lacked any goals in life. Mr. J. would try to reassure her, pointing out that they had a nice home and that she had no reason to be unhappy. He suggested that she find some hobbies or socialize more with their neighbors. But Mrs. J. became progressively more absorbed in her belief that she had no goals in life.

After a while, Amanda no longer bothered to keep the house clean, to cook, or to take care of the children. At first Mr. J. had thought she was merely in a "bad mood" and that it would pass, but now he was becoming worried. Either she was sick or she no longer loved him and the children. Mr. J. was quite puzzled about her behavior and could not imagine why she was so unhappy; he decided to try to talk out the problem with her. Mrs. J. told him that she no longer had any motivation, that simple household chores took too much energy. She believed that she still loved Mr. J. and the children, but she indicated that she no longer had strong feelings for anything. Mrs. J. did display some guilt about her inability to take care of the children and to be a wife, but everything was simply too depressing. Life was no longer important, and she just wanted to be left alone. At that point she began to cry uncontrollably. Nothing Mr. J. said could bring her out of the depression or stop her from crying. He decided that she had to see a physician, and he made an appointment for the following afternoon.

The next day Mr. J. worked only until noon so that he could accompany his wife to the physician's office. On arriving home, he found Mrs. J. nearly unconscious; she had taken a number of sleeping pills in an apparent suicide attempt. She was rushed to a hospital where her life was saved. Mrs. J. is currently receiving medication and psychotherapy to treat her depression.

Even among individuals who do not exhibit the severe clinical signs of depression, most have experienced some depressive symptoms at one time or another. In such cases the symptoms are generally within the normal range of emotional reactions and are attributable to some specific situation—the loss of a job, perhaps, or the death of a loved one. But severe depression that colors one's whole life, that persists over a long period of time, or that occurs for no apparent reason indicates a mental disorder.

Depression is the major element in the **affective disorders,** which are severe disturbances of mood. In these disorders, severe depression may be accompanied by and alternate with **mania,** an emotional state characterized by great elation, seemingly boundless energy, and irritability.

The affective disorders get their name from the extremes of *affect* (that is, emotion or mood) that are displayed. In this chapter we shall first describe the clinical symptoms of depression and mania, the two components of the affective disorders. Then we shall discuss the various affective disorders, their causes, and their treatment. In the next chapter we shall examine the very serious problem of suicide—a phenomenon that has been strongly linked to depression.

THE SYMPTOMS OF DEPRESSION AND MANIA

Depression and mania, the two extremes of mood, can be considered the opposite ends of a continuum that extends from deep sadness to wild elation. Of the two, depression is by far the more prevalent. It is exhibited in 90 percent of all diagnosed cases of affective disorders, and it would be expected to show up in the other 10 percent if they remained untreated.

Clinical symptoms of depression

Among the variety of symptoms that may be exhibited by depressives is a core group of characteristics that tend to identify this disturbance. These may be organized within the four psychological domains used to describe anxiety: the affective domain, the cognitive domain, the behavioral domain, and the physiological domain. Table 13.1 shows this organization and the core group of symptoms.

Affective symptoms   Mood is the most striking symptom of depression. Depressives experience feelings of sadness, dejection, and an excessive and prolonged mourning. Feelings of worthlessness and loss of the joy of living are common. Wild weeping may occur as a general reaction to frustration or anger. Such crying spells do not seem to be directly correlated with a specific situation.

To illustrate these affective characteristics, here is a condensed transcript of the words of a patient who has been excessively depressed for nearly six months over the death of her husband in an automobile accident:

> I don't know what to do anymore (weeps) . . . ever since my husband died . . . life . . . It isn't worth (weeping) . . . worth it. My life is empty . . . why should I go on . . . all I do is cry like a baby . . . why can't you help me. . . . All I do now is (weeps) . . . lay in bed and feel miserable.

We should note here that severe depressive symptoms often occur as a normal reaction to the death of a loved one. This intensive mourning is thought to have a positive psychological function. However, an excessively long period of bereavement (and cultures vary in the normal duration of mourning), accompanied by a preoccupation with one's worthlessness, marked functional impairment, and serious psychomotor retardation, can be indicative of a major affective disorder.

Cognitive symptoms   Besides general feelings of futility, emptiness, and a sense of "giving up," certain thoughts and ideas are clearly related to depressive reactions. Self-depreciation and a profound pessimism about the future can be identified. Loss of interest, a decrease in energy, difficulty in concentration, and loss of motivation make it difficult for the depressive to cope with everyday situations. Work responsibilities become monumental tasks and are avoided. Thoughts of one's own incompetence and general self-denigration are common. Suicidal ideation frequently accompanies these other thoughts.

Depression may be considered to be reflected in a *cognitive triad*, which consists of negative views of the self, of the outside world, and of the future (Beck 1974). The person has a pessimistic belief about what he or she can do, about what others can do to help, and about his or her prospects for the future. Some of this triad can be seen in the following

The single most striking symptom of depression is mood. Feelings of sadness, dejection, and excessive mourning are the predominant moods during depression. Also common are feelings of worthlessness and loss of the joy of living.

description of the thoughts and feelings of a severe depressive.

> The gradual progression to this state of semicognizance and quiescence was steady; it is hard to trace. People and things counted less. I ceased to wonder. I asked a member of my family where I was and, having received an answer, accepted it. And usually I remembered it, when

Table 13.1   *Symptoms of Depression*

Domain	Symptoms
Affective	Sadness, unhappiness, "blue" moods, apathy
Cognitive	Pessimism, ideas of guilt, self-denigration, loss of interest and motivation, decrease in efficiency and concentration, suicidal ideation
Behavioral	Neglect of personal appearance, psychomotor retardation, agitation, suicidal gestures
Physiological	Loss of appetite, loss of weight, constipation, poor sleep, aches and pain, diminished sex drive

SOURCE: Adapted from Mendels, J. (1970). *Concepts of depression.* New York: Wiley.

I was in a state to remember anything objective. The days dragged; there was no "motive," no drive of any kind. A dull acceptance settled upon me. Nothing interested me. I was very tired and heavy. I refused to do most of the things that were asked of me, and to avoid further disturbance I was put to bed again. (Hillyer 1964, pp. 158–59)

Ezra Pound, one of the most original American poets of the twentieth century, suffered a severe depression when he was in his seventies. He told an interviewer bitterly, "I have lived all my life believing that I knew something. And then a strange day came and I realized that I knew nothing, nothing at all. And so words have become empty of meaning. Everything that I touch, I spoil. I have blundered always" (Darrach 1976, p. 81). Pound stopped writing for years; for days on end, he ceased to speak. For both Hillyer and Pound, motivation, activity, vitality, and optimism had declined drastically.

Behavioral symptoms   The appearance and outward demeanor of a person is often a telltale sign of depression. The person's clothing may be sloppy or dirty; hair may be unkempt and personal cleanliness neglected. A dull, mask-like facial expression may become characteristic. Body movements are slow, and new activities are not initiated. Speech is reduced and slow, and the person may respond with short phrases. This apparent slowing down of all bodily movements, expressive gestures, and spontaneous responses is described as *psychomotor retardation.*

By contrast to this typical retarded condition of depressives, however, some may manifest an agitated state and symptoms of restlessness.

Physiological symptoms   Six somatic symptoms are frequently found in depressives (Mendels 1970).

1. Depressed people often experience a *loss of appetite and weight,* although a very few

may actually experience an increase. The loss of appetite *(anorexia)* is often attributed to the depressive's lack of interest in eating; food seems to have become tasteless. In severe cases, the accompanying weight loss can be so extreme as to be life-threatening.

2. Depressives may experience *constipation* and may fail to have bowel movements for days at a time.

3. *Sleep disturbance* is a common complaint. Difficulty in falling asleep, waking up early, waking up erratically during the night, insomnia, and nightmares leave the depressive exhausted and tired during the day. Many depressives dread the arrival of night because it represents a major fatigue-producing battle to fall asleep.

4. Some depressives complain about a vague assortment of *aches and pains.* Every system of the body may be involved: headaches, upset stomachs, gastrointestinal pain, back pains, chest pains, and just plain fatigue may be evident.

5. Depression may *disrupt the normal menstrual cycle.* Usually, the length of the cycle is prolonged, with possible skipping of one or several periods. The volume of menstrual flow may decrease.

6. Many depressives report an *aversion to sexual activity.* Sexual arousal may be dramatically reduced.

Clinical symptoms of mania

Alan C. was a 43-year-old unmarried computer programmer who had led a relatively quiet life until two weeks before, when he returned to work after a short absence for illness. Alan seemed to be in a particularly good mood. Others in the office noticed that he was unusually happy and energetic, greeting everyone at work. A few days later, during the lunch hour, Alan bought a huge cake and insisted that his fellow workers eat some of it. At first everyone was surprised and amused by his antics. But two colleagues working with him on a special project became increasingly irritated, because Alan failed to devote any time to the project. He merely insisted that he would finish his part in a few days.

On the day the manager had decided to inform Alan of his colleagues' concern, Alan exhibited delirious manic behaviors. When he came to work, he immediately jumped on top of a desk and yelled, "Listen, listen! We are not working on the most important aspects of our data! I know since I've debugged my mind. Erase, reprogram, you know what I mean. We've got to examine the total picture based on the input!" Alan then proceeded to spout profanities and address obscene remarks to several of the secretaries. Onlookers thought that he must have taken drugs. Attempts to calm him down brought angry and vicious denunciations. The manager, who had been summoned, was also unable to calm him. Finally the manager threatened to fire Alan. At this point, Alan called the manager an incompetent fool and stated that he could not be fired. His speech was so rapid and disjointed that it was difficult to understand him. Alan then picked up a chair and said he was going to smash the computers. Several co-workers grabbed him and held him on the floor. Alan was yelling so loud that his voice was quite hoarse, but he continued to shout and struggle. Two police officers were called, and they had to handcuff him to restrain his movements. Within hours, he was taken to a psychiatric hospital for observation.

Manic individuals like Alan C. show boundless energy, enthusiasm, and self-assertion. Their mood is one of elation or irritability, grandiosity, and exaggeration. Manic patients are often uninhibited, engaging impulsively in sexual activity or abusive discourse. The energy and excitement exhibited by these patients may cause them to lose weight or to go without sleep for long periods. If frustrated, they may become profane and quite belligerent.

Cognitive symptoms are generally reflected in the verbal processes of manic patients. For example, their speech is usually quite accelerated and pressured. They may change topics in mid-sentence or utter irrelevant and idio-

syncratic phrases. Although much of what they say is understandable to others, the accelerated and disjointed nature of their speech makes it difficult to follow their train of thought. They seem incapable of controlling their attention, as though they are being constantly distracted by new and more exciting thoughts and ideas.

Three levels of manic intensity have been recognized. In the mildest form, *hypomania*, affected individuals appear to be "high" in mood and overactive in behaviors. Judgment is usually poor, although delusions are rare. Many projects are started, but few if any are completed. When they interact with co-workers, hypomanics dominate the conversation and are often grandiose.

Behaviors are more intense in persons suffering from *acute mania*. Overactivity, grandiosity, and irritability are more pronounced; speech may be incoherent; persons with acute mania do not tolerate criticisms or restraints imposed by others. The acute manic reaction may develop out of the hypomanic state or may appear suddenly with little warning.

In the most severe form, *delirious mania*, the individual is wildly excited, rants, raves (the stereotype of a wild "maniac"), and is constantly agitated and on the move. Hallucinations and delusions often appear, and the individual is uncontrollable and frequently dangerous to self or others. This disturbance is so severe that physical restraint and medication are frequently necessary.

CLASSIFICATION OF AFFECTIVE DISORDERS

In DSM-III, the affective disorders are categorized primarily according to (1) severity and (2) whether or not depression is accompanied by mania. The more severe disturbances are called *major affective* disorders (these are the disorders in the first group in Table 13.2, p. 382). In addition, a major affective disorder may be classified as having *psychotic features* if the symptoms include delusions or hallucinations, or if the patient exhibits stupor (is unresponsive and unable or unwilling to speak). A **psychosis** is a severe disorder in which there is a loss of contact with reality or a significant distortion of reality.

The less serious, but still significant, affective disorders are referred to as *other specific affective disorders* (those in the second group in Table 13.2). The essential feature of these disorders is long-standing mood disturbance, either sustained or intermittent. The symptoms are less severe than in the major disorders, and no psychotic features are exhibited.

The third category in Table 13.2 provides for those affective disorders that cannot be classed in either of the first two groups.

Table 13.2 *Affective Disorders According to DSM-III*

1. Major affective disorders
   a. Bipolar disorder, mixed—intermixed or rapidly alternating manic and major depressive episodes
   b. Bipolar disorder, manic—currently in a manic episode
   c. Bipolar disorder, depressed—currently in a major depressive episode with one or more previous manic episodes
   d. Major depression, single episode—a single depressive episode with no history of mania
   e. Major depression, recurrent—more than one depressive episode with no history of mania

2. Other specific affective disorders
   a. Cyclothymic disorder—numerous periods of depression and mania during the past two years, but not of sufficient severity and duration to be included in major affective disorders
   b. Dysthymic disorder—frequent experiences of depression during the past two years, but not of sufficient severity and duration to be included in major affective disorders

3. Atypical affective disorders—a category for affective disorders that cannot be classed under 1 or 2 above
   a. Atypical bipolar disorder
   b. Atypical depression

SOURCE: DSM-III. Used by permission of the American Psychiatric Association.

Within the category of major affective disorders, a disturbance is classified as a *bipolar disorder* if mania is or has been exhibited; whereas it is classed as *major depression* if there is no history of mania. (The major-depression disorders are also occasionally referred to as *unipolar disorders*.) The milder specific affective disorders are similarly classified as either *cyclothymic* or *dysthymic*, depending on whether or not mania is exhibited.

Exogenous and endogenous depression

Traditionally, many clinicians and researchers have distinguished between what were presumed to be psychologically caused (or *exogenous*) depression and biologically caused (or *endogenous*) depression. Many psychologists believed that the former was precipitated by external events, such life stressors as the loss of a job, the death of a loved one, or divorce, whereas the latter was not. The evidence does not seem to support that particular distinction, because in many cases endogenous depression may also be triggered by life stressors (Leff, Roatch, and Bunney 1970).

However, there does seem to be some difference between the two. What was called endogenous depression (and is now called **melancholia** in DSM-III) appears to be a more severe disturbance involving a loss of pleasure in all activities, significant weight loss, and excessive guilt. Persons with this form of depression may also respond better to some types of biological treatment, such as antidepressant drugs and electroconvulsive therapy.

Bipolar disorders

As we have noted, the **bipolar disorders** are affective disorders in which manic episodes are or have been experienced. (These disorders were formerly called *manic–depressive dis-*

orders.) In most cases of bipolar disorders, patients exhibit both manic and depressive episodes; cases in which one or more manic episodes are exhibited without a depressive episode are extremely rare (Winokur 1974; DSM-III 1980). Thus, if a depressive episode has not yet occurred, one presumably will occur.

In bipolar disorders, the manic and depressive phases may alternate regularly with only brief intervening "normal" periods, or the two phases may appear irregularly with long periods of relative normality in between. In some cases, there may be no intervening normal mood at all. One manic–depressive patient was reported to demonstrate manic behaviors for almost exactly 24 hours, immediately followed by depressive behaviors for 24 hours. At the manic extreme, the patient was agitated, demanding, and constantly shouting; the next day, he was almost mute and inactive. The alternating nature of the disorder lasted 11 years (Jenner et al. 1967). Typical manic episodes appear suddenly and last from a few days to months. Depressive episodes tend to last longer.

Several types of evidence seem to support the distinction between unipolar and bipolar disorders (Goodwin and Guze 1984; Research Task Force of the National Institute of Mental Health 1975): First, genetic studies reveal that blood relatives of patients with bipolar disorders have a higher incidence of manic disturbances than relatives of unipolar patients. In addition, there is stronger evidence of genetic influences in bipolar disorders than in unipolar disorders. Second, the age of onset is typically earlier for bipolar disorders (the late twenties) than for unipolar disorders (the midthirties). Third, bipolars have retarded depressions (involving a slowing down of movements and speech) and a greater tendency to attempt suicide than unipolars, whose depressive symptoms often include anxiety. And fourth, as you will see, bipolars respond to lithium, whereas the drug has little effect on unipolars.

This etching by Georges Rouault, from *Miserere et Guerre,* suggests the extreme melancholy that can characterize the depressive side of manic–depressive disorders.

Only about 1 percent of the adult population have experienced bipolar disorder, whereas about 15 percent have at some time experienced a major depressive episode (DSM-III). Major depression seems to be more common in females than in males (see Focus 13.1, p. 384), but no apparent sex differential exists in the frequency of bipolar disorders (Weissman and Klerman 1977).

THE ETIOLOGY OF AFFECTIVE DISORDERS

Despite the increasing evidence for a unipolar–bipolar distinction, little is known about the cause of the extreme mood changes displayed

Are Women More Likely than Men to Be Depressed?

Worldwide, the incidence of depression is far higher among women than among men. According to DSM-III, 18 to 23 percent of females and 8 to 11 percent of males have at some time experienced a major depressive episode. Is this sex difference in depression a real one and, if so, what can account for the difference?

Although women are more likely than men to be seen in treatment and to be diagnosed as depressed, this may not mean that women *are* more depressed, for several reasons: First, women may simply be more likely than men to seek treatment when depressed; this would make the depression rate for women higher, even if the male and female rates were actually equal. Second, women may be more willing to report depression to others. That is, there may be sex differences in self-report behaviors, rather than in actual depression rates. And third, diagnosticians or the diagnostic system may be biased toward finding depression among women.

Some clinicians feel that these three possibilities account for only part of the sex difference in depression, and that women do have higher rates of depression (Radloff and Rae 1981). The reasons for these differ-

ences are, unclear, however. Speculation has involved physiological or social–psychological factors.

Genetic or hormonal differences between the sexes were once thought to influence depression. However, the failure to find consistent relationships between hormonal changes and depression has led researchers to propose social or psychological factors. One of these is the woman's traditional sex role. Subservience to men and a lack of occupational opportunities, for example, may cause women to exhibit more depression (Bernard 1976). For the same reason, women may be more likely than men to experience lack of control in life situations. They may then attribute their "helplessness" to an imagined lack of personal worth. Finally, the traditional feminine sex-role behaviors (gentleness, emotionality, and self-subordination) may not be so successful in eliciting reinforcement from others as the assertive and more forceful responses typically imputed to males.

As you will see later in the chapter, this lack of reinforcement, like learned helplessness, may contribute to depression (Kaplan 1983).

in the bipolar disorders. Perhaps the regulatory process for maintaining *homeostasis,* or stability of mood, is dysfunctional. Another possibility is that mania is a defensive means of trying to deal with depression. Or the apparent euphoria, irritability, and overactivity seen in mania may be attempts to deny or ward off depression. In any event, much more is known about the causes of depression than about the etiology of the bipolar disorders.

The causes of depression

Psychoanalytic explanations   In explaining depression, the psychoanalytic perspective focuses mainly on two concepts: separation and anger. Separation may occur when a spouse, lover, child, parent, or significant other person dies or departs for one reason or another. But the loss (separation) need not be physical; it can also be symbolic. For example, the withdrawal of affection or support, or a rejection (a symbolic loss), can induce depression.

In their early attempts to distinguish normal grief from depression, Abraham (1948) and Freud (1924) postulated several differences between the two. In normal mourning, the loss of a significant other is a *conscious* concern of mourners. They are aware of their own feelings, of what the lost person means to them, and of how the loss may change their lives. This is in marked contrast to what Freud labeled "neurotic depression," which operates on an *unconscious* level because mourners are not aware of the true loss. The loss is generally symbolic and strikes at their ego. The most common reaction to a loss for depressives is a loss of self-esteem.

Freud believed that depressives are excessively dependent individuals because they are fixated in the oral stage. As we discussed in Chapter 2, he viewed the oral cavity as the primary mechanism by which infants relate to the world, so being fixated at this stage fosters dependency. Being passive and having others fill one's needs (being fed, bathed, clothed, cuddled, and so forth) results in emotional dependency that continues into adult life. Thus, for those fixated in the oral stage, self-esteem is dependent on other important people in the environment. When a significant loss occurs, the self-esteem of the mourner plummets.

Freud also believed that the depressive exhibits a failure to follow through in the normal mourning process, which he called "mourning work." In the normal course of mourning, there is conscious recall and expression of memories about the lost person in an attempt to undo the loss. In addition, the mourners are flooded with two strong sets of feelings: anger and guilt. The anger, which arises from their sense of being deserted, can be quite strong:

> A young female depressive finally was able to express her feelings of anger toward her deceased husband after nearly six months of treatment. She seemed to blame her husband for his death, even though the circumstances under which he died were not of his making. Yet she expressed feelings of being deserted, left to make it on her own in a cruel world, left to raise her four children alone, left with only minimal life insurance, and left to clean up her husband's business affairs. She made statements in therapy that reflected a high degree of bitterness and blame: "He shouldn't have made me so dependent on him! Why didn't he take out more life insurance? Did he think he was indestructible? He should have planned for something like this!"

Mourners may also be flooded with guilt feelings about real or imagined sins committed against the lost person. For example, a father who has just lost a child may think, "My daughter always wanted to go to Disneyland. Why didn't I take her? Now it's too late." These feelings must be resolved through grief, or Freud's "mourning work." In the attempt to free himself or herself from the lost person, the mourner's emotions become redirected toward new tasks and the formation of new relationships.

In the severely depressed, however, the loss is not only conscious but may also be symbolic of an earlier traumatic event (such as the loss of a parent or desertion), one that predisposes the person to depression. When the mourning work does not progress through its normal course, the depressive person heaps blame and belittlement upon himself or herself, unconsciously expressing his or her feelings toward the lost person. Instead of directing anger toward the lost person for desertion, the depressive assumes the lost person's perceived anger-arousing attributes. The depression becomes self-centered and inner-directed rather than an outer-directed grief.

Because depression cannot always be correlated with the immediate loss of a loved one, Freud used the construct of "symbolic loss" to account for depression that did not result directly from a loss. That is to say, any form of rejection or reproach may be perceived by the depressive as *symbolic* of an earlier loss.

For example, suppose a woman terminates a long-term romance with a potentially depressive male. Although she has not died, her withdrawal of affection has two effects on her partner: (1) Fixation at an oral stage has predisposed him to perceive the withdrawal as indicative of his own worthlessness. Thus his self-esteem takes a nose dive. (2) The withdrawal may symbolize an earlier traumatic loss that was not properly resolved. It may symbolize his early loss of a parent, spouse, or friend.

Psychoanalysis has placed much emphasis on the dynamics of anger in explaining depression. Many depressed patients have strong hostile or angry feelings, and some clinicians believe that getting clients to express their anger reduces their depression. Such a belief has led some to speculate that depression is really *anger turned against the self*. This hypothesis was formulated by Freud (1924), who believed that depression becomes a narcissistic inner-directed process because depressives turn their anger inward.

Freud suggested that, when a person experiences a loss (symbolic or otherwise), he or she may harbor feelings of resentment and hostility toward the lost person in addition to feelings of love and affection. The lost person could easily have possessed deficiencies, quirks, or inadequacies that may have been bothersome, irritating, or, at times, anger-provoking. Thus the anger need not arise solely from a feeling of being deserted. And again, in the course of normal grief or mourning, the anger would ordinarily be directed outward toward the lost person and eventually resolved as one "lets go" of the lost object. But a mourner who has been too emotionally dependent on the lost person does not loosen emotional bonds easily. Instead the bonds may become strengthened through the process of *introjection*. That is, the depressed person identifies with those faults and shortcomings that were perceived in the loved person. The mourner's anger toward the lost one becomes directed inward against the self. Exaggerated

accounts of sin and inadequacies are often expressed by depressives, even though these accounts may have no objective reality. Self-abuse and self-deprecation are symbolic of anger turned inward.

The belief that depression is anger turned inward can be explained in other than psychoanalytic terms, and it may have broad application. For instance, when a person is repeatedly prevented from expressing normal aggression and hostility in response to frustrating situations, depression may result. The expression of anger may be blocked due to social conditioning or to external constraints. Thus, if individuals have been repeatedly punished since childhood for the expression of anger, they may find it difficult as adults to express it. In situations that would ordinarily elicit anger, such persons keep theirs under tight rein. Likewise, in certain situations, hostility might not be expressed because of the possible consequences. For example, POWs may feel great hatred toward their captors, but the overt expression of such feelings could bring torture or death. It is this repressed anger that may lead to depression.

The hypothesis that the blocking of anger results in depression has been tested, and a correlation was found between the two. Especially significant is the fact that the relationship held not only for individuals but for cultures as well: The fewer outlets that are allowed by a given culture for the expression of anger in reaction to frustrating situations, the greater the incidence of depression (Kendell 1970).

The following case exemplifies the concept of anger turned inward.

> Ralph S. was a 20-year-old college junior who first came to the counseling center suffering from depression. A detailed history revealed that Ralph was raised by parents who punished any outward expression of anger or hostility. His mother often reminded him that "nobody likes a mischievous brat" and that "to keep friends you must behave yourself." As a result he became extremely compliant and conform-

ing, fearful of losing the goodwill of friends and family. In high school and college, Ralph found himself the continual victim of his dormitory peers. He found it difficult to say *no* to them when they asked to borrow his car or to copy his homework. Unable to assert himself, he was often exploited and even mistreated.

Each time such an incident occurred, Ralph denied his anger. Yet he could not completely deny his realization that he was a "doormat" for the rest of the world. Rather than expressing his anger toward others, however, he became angry at himself. Seeing himself as weak-willed and spineless, he developed a negative self-image that resulted in depression. Only when the counselor was able to get Ralph to redirect his anger outward did the depression finally lift.

Learning explanations Behaviorists also view the separation or loss of a significant other as important in depression. However, behaviorists tend to see the cause as a reduction in reinforcement rather than as the untestable concept of fixation or symbolic grief. When a loved one is lost, an accustomed level of reinforcement (whether affection, companionship, pleasure, material goods, or services) is immediately withdrawn. No longer can one obtain the support or encouragement of the lost person. When this happens, one's level of activity (talking, expressing ideas, working, joking, engaging in sports, going out on the town, or whatever) is significantly diminished because an important source of reinforcement has disappeared. Thus many behaviorists view depression as a product of inadequate or insufficient reinforcers in a person's life, leading to a reduced frequency of behavior that previously was positively reinforced (Ferster 1965; Lazarus 1968; Lewinsohn 1974b).

As the period of reduced activity (resulting from reduced reinforcement) continues, the person labels himself or herself "depressed." If the new lower level of activity causes others to show sympathy, the depressed person may remain inactive and chronically "depressed." By being sympathetic about the incident (loss), friends, relatives, and even strangers

may be reinforcing the depressive's current state of inactivity. (This reinforcement for a lower activity level is known as *secondary gain*.) The depression tends to deepen, and, as it does, the person disengages still further from the environment and reduces further the chance of obtaining positive reinforcement from normal activity. The result may be a continual deepening of the depression.

Depression has been associated with both low levels of self-reinforcement and reductions in environmental reinforcements (Heiby 1983). In other words, when individuals experience a reduction in the reinforcement available from the environment and do not provide themselves with reinforcement, they are prone to depression. So it may be that depressives lack the skills required to provide replacements for missing environmental reinforcements.

This behavioral concept of depression can be elaborated to cover many situations that may elicit depression (such as failure, loss, change in job status, rejection, and desertion). Lewinsohn's model of depression is perhaps the most comprehensive of the behavioral explanations (Lewinsohn 1974a, 1974b; Lewinsohn and Graf 1973; Lewinsohn and Libet 1972; Lewinsohn, Weinstein, and Alper 1970). Along with the reinforcement view of depression, Lewinsohn postulates three sets of variables that may enhance or inhibit a person's access to positive reinforcement.

First, *the number of events and activities that are potentially reinforcing* to the person is important. This depends very much on individual differences and varies with the biological traits and experiential history of the person. For example, age, sex, or physical attributes may determine the availability of reinforcers. Handsome people are more likely to receive positive attention than those with nondescript looks. Young people are likely to have more social interaction than retirees. A task-oriented individual who values intellectual pursuits may not be so responsive as other people to interpersonal or affiliative

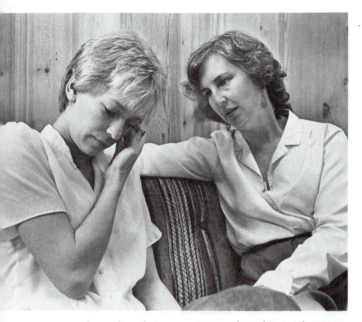

Learning theory suggests that depression may be a product of reduced reinforcement in a person's life. The reduced reinforcement leads to reduced activity levels. Unfortunately, consolation and sympathy from others may sometimes serve to reinforce the depressed person's low activity level.

forms of reinforcement. To such a person, a compliment such as "I like you" may be less effective than "I see you as an extremely competent person."

Second, *the availability of reinforcements in the environment* can also affect the person. Harsh environments, such as regimented institutions or remote isolated places, reduce reinforcements.

Third, *the instrumental behavior of the person*—the number of social skills that can be exercised to bring about reinforcement—is important. Depressed patients are lacking in social behaviors that can elicit positive reinforcements (Lewinsohn, Weinstein, and Alper 1970). They interact with fewer people, respond less, emit very few positive reactions, and initiate less conversation. Depressed persons also feel more uncomfortable in social situations (Youngren and Lewinsohn 1978), and they elicit depression in others (Hammen

and Peters 1978). Further, depressed persons seem to be preoccupied with themselves; they tend to talk about themselves (more so than nondepressed individuals) without being asked to do so (Jacobson and Anderson 1982). For this reason or others, nondepressed individuals may not enjoy talking to those who are depressed and may provide little positive reinforcement to depressives during social interactions. Depressives may even drive others away and thus lose any social reinforcement that others could provide (Coyne 1976).

A low rate of positive reinforcement in any of these three situations can lead to depression. A beautiful person who begins to age may notice a reduction in interest from possible lovers. A person who has recently lost a loved one through divorce or death and has no other friends or family will receive little or no support. And a young student who lacks social skills in heterosexual relationships may be denied the pleasures of such interactions. Behavioral approaches to treating depression might attempt to intervene under any of these conditions.

Cognitive explanations Some psychologists believe that low self-esteem is the key to depressive reactions. All of us have both negative and positive feelings about what we see as our "self." There are certain things we like or value about ourselves and other things we dislike. Some individuals, especially depressed ones, have a generally negative self-concept. Such people perceive themselves as inept, unworthy, and incompetent, regardless of reality. If they do succeed at anything, they are likely to dismiss it as pure luck or to forecast eventual failure. Hence a cognitive interpretation of one's self-concept as being unworthy may lead to a host of thinking patterns that reflect self-blame, self-criticism, and exaggerated ideas of duty and responsiblity.

One major cognitive theory regards thought processes as causes of depression (Beck 1976). According to this theory, depression is a primary disturbance in *thinking* rather than a basic disturbance in *mood*. How people structure and interpret their experiences determines their affective states. If one conceptualizes a situation as having an unpleasant content, one will experience an unpleasant affect. Depressed patients are said to have *schemas* that predispose them to depression. (A **schema** is a pattern of thinking or a cognitive set that determines an individual's reactions and responses. In other words, one's schema tends to modify, or color, one's interpretation of incoming information.)

According to this theory, depressives operate from a "primary triad," which consists of negative views toward oneself, one's present experiences, and the future. Four logical errors typify this negative schema, which leads to depression and is characteristic of depressives.

1. *Arbitrary inference.* The depressive has a tendency to draw conclusions that are not supported by the evidence. For example, a woman may conclude that "people dislike me" because no one speaks to her on the bus or in the elevator. Or a man who invites a woman out to dinner and finds the restaurant closed that evening may see this as evidence of his own unworthiness. In both cases, these people draw erroneous conclusions from the available evidence. Depressives are apparently unwilling or unable to see other, more probable, explanations.

2. *Selected abstraction.* The depressive takes a minor incident or detail out of context, and the incidents on which the depressive focuses tend to be trivial. The depressive who is corrected for a minor aspect of his or her work takes the correction as a sign of his or her incompetence or inadequacy—even when the supervisor's overall feedback is highly positive.

3. *Overgeneralization.* A depressive tends to draw a sweeping conclusion about his or her ability, performance, or worth from one single experience or incident. A person who is laid off the job because of budgetary cuts may conclude that he or she is worthless. The comments of a student seen by one of the authors

at a university psychology clinic provide another illustration of overgeneralization: When he missed breakfast at the dormitory because his alarm clock didn't ring, he concluded, "I don't deserve my own body because I don't take care of it." Later, when he showed up late for class through no fault of his own, he thought, "What a miserable excuse for a student I am." When a former classmate passed by and smiled, he thought, "I must look awful today or she wouldn't be laughing at me."

4. *Magnification and minimization.* The depressive tends to exaggerate (magnify) limitations and difficulties, while playing down (minimizing) accomplishments, achievements, and capabilities. The depressed patient who is asked to evaluate his or her strengths and weaknesses, catalogues shortcomings or unsuccessful attempts endlessly but finds it almost impossible to enumerate achievements.

All four of these cognitive processes can be seen as results or causes of low self-esteem, which makes the individual expect failure and engage in self-criticism that is unrelated to reality. People with low self-esteem must have experienced much disapproval in the past from significant others, such as parents. Their parents or significant others may have responded to them by punishing failures and not rewarding successes or by holding unrealistically high expectations or standards. The following case is an example.

> Paul R. was a 20-year-old college senior majoring in chemistry. He first came to the student psychiatric clinic complaining of headaches and a vague assortment of somatic problems. Throughout the interview, Paul seemed severely depressed and unable to mobilize enough energy to talk with the therapist. Even though he had maintained a B+ average, he felt like a failure and was uncertain about his future.
>
> His parents had always had high expectations for Paul, their eldest son, and had transmitted these feelings to him from his earliest childhood. His father, a successful thoracic surgeon, had his heart set on Paul's becoming a doctor. Academic success was seen as very important, and

Paul did exceptionally well in school. While his teachers would praise him for being an outstanding student, his parents seemed to take his successes for granted. In fact, they would often make such statements as "You can do better." When he failed at something, his parents would make it obvious to him that they not only were disappointed but felt disgraced as well. This pattern of punishment for failures without recognition of successes, combined with his parents' high expectations, led to the development in Paul of an extremely negative self-concept.

As a refinement of his cognitive theory of depression, Beck recently raised the possibility that personality patterns may also be important (Beck 1982): These patterns may influence the kinds of situations or stressors that lead to negative cognitions and, ultimately, to depression.

Although the cognitive explanation of depression has merit, it appears to be oversimplified. At times, negative cognitions may be the result of, rather than the cause of, depressed moods, as noted by Hammen (1985). That is, one may first feel depressed and then, as a result, have negative or pessimistic thoughts about the world. Hammen has also found that one's schema tends to mediate the relationship between stress and depression. Stress can lead to depression if one has developed the "right" schema.

Learned helplessness   A unique and interesting view of depression is the *learned helplessness theory* of Seligman (1975). Its basic assumption is that cognitions and feelings of helplessness are learned. When one sees that one's responses continually have only minimal effects on the environment, one develops an expectation of helplessness. When this expectation is borne out in settings that may not be controllable, passivity and finally depression may result.

Susceptibility to depression, then, depends on one's experience with controlling the environment. In his study of helplessness, Seligman discovered strong parallels between the symptoms, etiology, and means of preventing helplessness and those for depression (see Table 13.3). He also noticed similarities in cure. One could say the depression is cured when the person believes he or she is not helpless.

To understand this intriguing theory, it is necessary to reconstruct certain laboratory findings about learned helplessness. The first evidence of the phenomenon was obtained accidentally. Dogs that were given inescapable shocks while strapped in a Pavlovian harness showed major differences in their later behavior from dogs who had not received inescapable shocks (Seligman and Maier 1967; Overmier and Seligman 1967). When the dogs were placed in a two-compartment shuttlebox, they were supposed to learn to escape shock by jumping over a barrier separating the compartments. When placed in the electrified compartment, dogs that had not been given inescapable shocks would howl, urinate, defecate, thrash, and run about until they accidentally scrambled over the barrier, terminating the shock. They soon learned that to avoid the shock they simply had to jump the barrier.

The dogs that had received inescapable shocks earlier, however, reacted quite differently. Although at first they behaved in much the same manner as the dogs that had not received inescapable shocks (howling and running about), most of them soon stopped their attempts to escape and lay down whimpering, apparently having given up! Regardless of the experimenters' coaxing, pleading, prodding, and offerings of food, these dogs made virtually no attempt to escape on the first or subsequent trials (Seligman 1975). In addition, these dogs exhibited another difference. Some that did occasionally jump the barrier in training failed to *learn* or *profit* from this experience.

As research later showed, the helplessness of the dogs did not result from the trauma *per se* (the electric shock) but from the experience of *having no control* over shock. The dogs that had been strapped into the harness and given the inescapable shocks could do nothing to

Table 13.3 *Similarities between Helplessness and Depression*

	Learned Helplessness	Depression
Symptoms:	Passivity	Passivity
	Difficulty learning that response produces relief	Negative cognitive set
	Dissipates in time	Time course
	Lack of aggression	Introjected hostility
	Weight loss, appetite loss	Weight loss, appetite loss
	Social and sexual deficits	Social and sexual deficits
Cause:	Learning that responding and reinforcement are independent	Feelings of helplessness Belief that responding is useless

SOURCE: Adapted from Seligman, Martin E. P. (1975). *Helplessness: On depression, development, and death.* San Francisco: W. H. Freeman, p. 106. Used by permission of the publisher.

prevent them. They had learned that their actions did not matter—and that they were *helpless*. Dogs that had not received inescapable shocks, on the other hand, continued their attempts to escape. The key ingredient that prevented the occurrence of learned helplessness appeared to be the perception of having control in an aversive situation. On the other hand, the experience of lack of control appears to predispose one to later passivity (Seligman 1975).

This phenomenon is not unique to animals; studies have documented it in human subjects as well. Loud noise, rather than electric shock, was used with college student subjects in one study (Hiroto 1974). Uncontrollable noise in one situation resulted in passive acceptance of similar aversive stimuli in later situations: Subjects failed to move their hands back and forth in a shuttle box, which would have turned off the noise. Other subjects, who had no previous experience with uncontrollable noise, learned to control the noise through their own activities.

The learned helplessness phenomenon in human beings does, however, seem to be more complicated than in animals. How a situation is perceived, what is expected, and what is believed are important determinants of human helplessness. Merely believing that one has the option of terminating an aversive noise (regardless of whether one actually has

the option) is enough to prevent the helplessness phenomenon (Glass and Singer 1972).

What does all this have to do with depression? Seligman describes depression as a *belief in one's own helplessness*. Many other investigators have described depression in terms of hopelessness, powerlessness, and helplessness. For example, "The severely depressed patient believes that his skills and plans of action are no longer effective for reaching the goals he has set" (Melges and Bowlby 1969, p. 693). And, according to Seligman (1975), "the expectation that an outcome is independent of responding: (1) reduces the motivation to control the outcome; (2) interferes with learning that responding controls the outcome; (3) produces fear for as long as the subject is uncertain of the uncontrollability of the outcome, and then produces depression" (pp. 55–56).

When a trauma occurs, Seligman argues, the initial reaction is anxiety. The uncertainty of the situation and its unpredictability keep one constantly guessing about whether it is controllable. The person searches for ways to control or predict what will happen. If he or she succeeds, much of the anxiety may be alleviated. However, if one learns that responding is independent of the trauma and that nothing one does matters, anxiety is replaced by depression. Almost all the recognized situations that elicit depression (failure, loss of

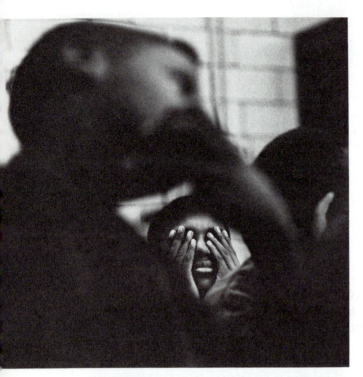

Learned helplessness is the belief that outcomes are independent of responding, that one's skills and actions have no influence on one's environment. Learned helplessness first produces fear, so long as outcomes are seen as uncertain or uncontrollable, and then produces depression.

loved ones, loss of job, aging, and terminal illness) are events characterized by the absence of control. (See Focus 13.2 for a seemingly different and unusual source of depression.)

Seligman's theory of learned helplessness was first published in 1975. Three years later, he and his co-workers revised the model to include more cognitive elements (Abramson, Seligman, and Teasdale 1978). Essentially, they believe that human beings who encounter helplessness make causal attributions (that is, they speculate on why they are helpless). These attributions can be internal or external, stable or unstable, and global or specific. For instance, suppose a student in a math course receives the same low grades regardless of how much he or she has studied. The student may attribute the low grades to internal or personal factors ("I do not do well in math

courses because I am afraid of math") or to external factors ("The teacher does not like me, so I can't get a good grade"). The attribution can also be stable ("I'm the type of person who can never do well in math") or unstable ("My poor performance is due to the heavy work load that I have at this time"). And the attribution can be global or specific. A global attribution ("I am a poor student") has broader implications for performance than a specific one ("I am poor at math but good in other subjects"). Abramson and co-workers believe that an individual whose attributions for helplessness are internal, stable, and global is likely to have more pervasive feelings of depression than one whose attributions are external, unstable, and specific.

The learned helplessness model has generated a great deal of research. There is evidence that depressed persons show the "depressive" attributional tendencies and feel that their lives are less controllable than do nondepressives (Raps et al. 1982). However, as in the case of the cognitive theory, there are questions about whether this model, even with its attributional components, can adequately explain depression and about whether attributions are the result or the cause of depression. Cognitions and attributions may be important factors in depression, but the disorder is a complex one; current models tend to include or explain only particular facets of depression (Hammen 1985).

Biological perspectives on affective disorders

Biological approaches to the etiology of affective disorders generally focus on genetic predisposition, physiological dysfunction, or combinations of the two.

Genetic factors   Affective disorders tend to run in families, and the same type of disorder is generally found among members of the same family (Perris 1966; Winokur, Clayton, and Reich 1969). One way to assess the role of

The Paradox of "Success Depression"

After years of hard work and perseverance, a scholar is awarded the Ph.D. Instead of elation and joy, he or she experiences unhappiness and depression. It doesn't seem to make sense. So-called success depression, in which a person devotes considerable time and energy to achieving a goal only to become depressed when he or she succeeds, is an apparent paradox. How does such a thing happen?

Mendels (1970) examines a number of possible reasons. First, achievement of the goal may bring new demands, requiring greater responsibility and competence. Because the person feels fearful of shouldering new demands, he or she may become depressed. Second, the person may be predisposed to dependency. When success is achieved the person may no longer be able to play dependent roles. Third, the person with low self-esteem may have a negative cognitive set ("I am not good enough to deserve this.") Fourth, the success of the individual may unconsciously symbolize a competitive feeling toward a love object (mother, father, or sibling). A victory at a conscious level produces guilt feelings and may result in depression. Fifth, after achieving a long-sought-after goal, the person may experience an emotional and physical slackening that may be guilt-producing and consequently depressing.

Another explanation is related to the learned helplessness model (Seligman 1975). Apparently successful people, such as the beautiful woman who is appreciated for physical attributes beyond her control or the famous writer whose reputation and laurels were gained long ago, may be prone to depression. From a learned helplessness viewpoint, success depression may occur because reinforcers are no longer contingent on present responding. In the case of the new Ph.D., recognition and respect are now a function of the title rather than of the individual's actions. Seligman postulates that much of the increase in depression that clinicians see in today's youth results from a perceived lack of connection between their own efforts and their affluence.

heredity is to compare the incidence of affective disorders among the biological and adoptive families of individuals who were adopted early in life and who had the disorders. If heredity is important, the biological families (which contributed the genetic makeup) should exhibit a high incidence of the disorders. If environment is more important, the adoptive families (which provided the early environment) should show a high incidence. The results of such a comparison indicated that the incidence of affective disorders was higher among the biological families than among the adoptive families; the latter exhibited an incidence similar to that of the general population (Kety 1979).

Another way to study the possible genetic transmission of affective disorders is to compare identical (MZ) and fraternal (DZ) twins. Nine such studies of twins have been reported. The concordance rate for bipolar affective disorders was 72 percent for MZ twins and 14 percent for DZ twins. By contrast, the concordance rate for unipolar affective disorders was 40 percent for MZ twins and 11 percent for DZ twins (Goodwin and Guze 1984).

Both of these research approaches (and others as well), consistently turn up evidence that genetic influences are involved in affective disorders. Moreover, the bulk of the research suggests that heredity is a stronger factor in bipolar affective disorders than in unipolar disorders.

Biochemical factors   But how is heredity involved in the major affective disorders? A growing number of researchers feel that genetic factors influence the amounts of certain substances (the *catecholamines*) that are found at specific sites in the brain. These substances contribute to the transmission of nerve impulses from one neuron to another. They are often termed **neurotransmitters,** and it has been suggested that they mediate between active motor behavior and emotions (Weiss, Glazer, and Pohorecky 1975; Becker 1974).

Nerve impulses are transmitted from neuron to neuron across *synapses,* which are junctions where the axon (or transmitting end) of one neuron is adjacent to the dendrites (or receiving end) of another neuron. According to the *catecholamine hypothesis,* or *biogenic amine theory* of affective disorders, depression is caused by a deficit of specific neurotransmitters (*norepinephrine, dopamine,* or *serotonin*) at brain synapses, whereas mania is caused by an oversupply of these substances (Bunney et al. 1979; Schildkraut 1965).

Two lines of research have implicated neurotransmitters in affective disorders: findings that have established a relationship between levels of biogenic amines and motor activity, and studies of the effects of medication on these neurotransmitters and on mood changes. As noted earlier, depression is characterized by lower motor activity, and mania by overactivity. When rats are placed in certain stressful situations—for example, when they are subjected to a series of inescapable shocks—the level of norepinephrine in their brains is reduced. The animals then exhibit ''depressive'' behaviors such as motor passivity and an inability to learn avoidance-escape responses. Giving rats *tetrabenazine,* which depletes brain norepinephrine also results in motor passivity and an inability to learn. But the drug *paragyline* protects against the deple-

tion of norepinephrine. If this drug is administered to rats prior to an experience with inescapable shock, they become immunized against passivity and poor learning (Weiss, Glazer, and Pohorecky 1975).

These findings do not only suggest the importance of norepinephrine in depressive behaviors. They also demonstrate that environmental stressors result in biochemical and behavioral changes and, conversely, that biochemical changes can produce behavioral effects similar to those of environmental stressors. Even so, no matter how similar they may be in various respects, animal behavior is not human behavior. Investigators obviously need a more direct link between the role of neurotransmitters and depressive behaviors in human beings.

Some evidence implicating neurotransmitters in human depression and mania was obtained accidentally (Goodwin 1974). For example, it was discovered that, when the drug *reserpine* was used in the treatment of hypertension, many patients exhibited depression. (Reserpine depletes the level of neurotransmitters in the brain.) Similarly, when the drug *iproniazid* was given to tubercular patients, it elevated the mood of depressed patients. (Iproniazid inhibits the destruction of brain amines.) Thus mood levels in human beings were found to vary with the level of neurotransmitters in the brain. These variations are consistent with the catecholamine hypothesis.

Some researchers have suggested that the level, or amount, of neurotransmitters present is not the primary factor. They note that, to travel from one neuron to another, an electrical impulse must cause the release of neurotransmitters that stimulate the receiving neuron. The problem may not be the amount of neurotransmitter produced or available, but rather a dysfunction in *reception* of the neurotransmitter by the receiving neuron (Sulser 1979).

Other findings, of a different sort, have also stimulated interest in biological or physiological processes in depression. Depressed adults have been found to differ from nondepressed persons in their sleep patterns, particularly in rapid eye movement (REM) sleep. (There are several stages of sleep, and during REM sleep the eyes move rapidly about.) Depression is associated with a relatively rapid onset of, and an increase in, REM sleep (Goodwin and Guze 1984). Moreover, a reduction in the REM sleep of depressives seems to be beneficial (Vogel et al. 1980). The reason for this association between sleep patterns and depression is unclear.

Evaluation of the causation theories

The theories of depression presented in this chapter explain certain aspects of the disturbance, but all have weaknesses. From the psychoanalytic perspective, loss and separation precipitate a depressive reaction. But what determines the extent and severity of depression? Fixation at the oral stage, dependency, and symbolic loss are psychoanalytic concepts that are difficult to test. The psychoanalytic assumption that depression may simply be hostility turned inward to the self seems open to question. When some depressed patients experienced success on experimental tasks, their self-esteem and optimism increased (Beck 1974). If depression is hostility turned inward, why would success alleviate some of its symptoms?

As we have noted, Beck's construct, which stresses a negative cognitive set as a causal factor in depression, suffers from an inability to demonstrate that a cognitive disturbance *precedes* depression. It is possible that a depressed mood or affect *causes* a negative cognitive set.

Lewinsohn's behavioral theory and Seligman's learned helplessness theory have great appeal because they are well grounded in research findings. Lewinsohn's work has mainly demonstrated the relationship between depression and low rates of positive reinforce-

ment. More investigation is needed to demonstrate that these low rates actually cause depression. Seligman has shown that learned helplessness can lead to depressive behaviors. However, this model explains only certain kinds of depression—those that are reactions to environmental stresses of a noncontrollable nature.

All three of these theories have strengths and weaknesses; in terms of their adequacy in explaining depression, it is not possible to select one theory over the others.

Endogenous (congenital) factors appear to play a critical role in major affective disorders. Although genetic studies have not been extensive, there is support for the position that heredity is involved. The precise genetic mechanisms in depression are not known, but research into biochemical factors or neurotransmitters seems quite promising.

One fruitful way to conceptualize affective disorders is to view them as the result of an interaction between environmental and biological factors (Kraemer and McKinney 1979). Consider a spectrum that ranges from mild sadness through normal grief and the specific affective disorders to the major affective disorders. Milder instances of depression (or, for that matter, mania) may be more exogenous (externally caused) in nature. In the case of affective disorders in the middle of the continuum, both exogenous and endogenous factors may be important. When the disorders are severe, including psychotic forms of the major affective disorders, endogenous factors may become more prominent (Goodwin 1977).

THE TREATMENT OF AFFECTIVE DISORDERS

Biological approaches to the treatment of affective disorders are generally based on the catecholamine hypothesis. That is, treatment consists primarily of a means of controlling

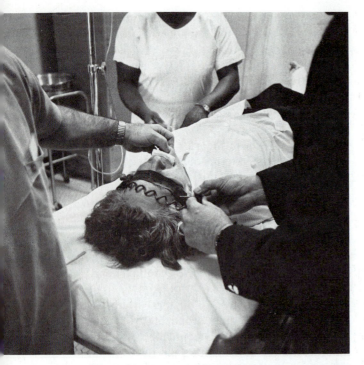

Severely depressed individuals whose depression cannot be relieved by tricyclics or MAO inhibitors are treated with electroconvulsive therapy. Although most seriously depressed patients show some improvement after about four treatments, there can be detrimental side effects.

the level of neurotransmitters at brain synapses. In addition, at least one psychological treatment seems to offer promise for use with depressives.

Biomedical treatments for unipolar disorders

Medication   The drugs that are used to treat unipolar depression are of two general types; both were introduced in the mid-1950s. The tricyclic antidepressants, which make up the first group, are still considered the most effective; approximately 65 percent of moderately to severely depressed individuals improve on tricyclics (Klein et al. 1980). These drugs seem to act by blocking the re-uptake of norepinephrine. (*Re-uptake* is the process in which a neurotransmitter is taken back into the nerve cells.) When re-uptake is inhibited, an increased amount of norepinephrine is left at the synapses. The resulting higher levels of norepinephrine appear to be correlated with a reduction in depressive symptoms.

The monoamine oxidase (MAO) inhibitors, which make up the second group of antidepressants, also work by increasing the level of norepinephrine at the brain synapses. However, rather than blocking re-uptake like the tricyclics, the MAO inhibitors act by preventing the body's MAO enzyme from breaking down norepinephrine that is already available at the synapse.

Currently, MAO inhibitors are prescribed only for depressed patients who have not responded favorably to treatment with tricyclics. The problem is the variety of side effects that are associated with the use of MAO inhibitors. These include insomnia, irritability, dizziness, constipation, and impotence, but the most serious incompatibility response is the "tyramine-cheese" reaction. One of the normal functions of the MAO enzyme is to break down tyramine, a substance found in many cheeses, as well as in some beers, wines, pickled products, and chocolate. The MAO inhibitors interfere with this function, of course, so an individual who is using one of these drugs must severely restrict his or her intake of tyramine. Failure to do so triggers the tyramine-cheese reaction, which begins with increased blood pressure, vomiting, and muscle twitching and can, if untreated, result in intracranial bleeding followed by death.

Such side effects are a major drawback of the antidepressant drugs. (The tricyclics, too, may cause such reactions as drowsiness, insomnia, agitation, fine tremors, blurred vision, dry mouth, and reduced sexual ability.) Careful monitoring of the patient's reactions is thus an absolute necessity. Another drawback is the fact that, for some unknown reason, the antidepressant drugs are essentially ineffective during the first two weeks of use. This is a serious concern, particularly in cases where suicide is a threat.

Electroconvulsive therapy   Electroconvulsive therapy (ECT) is generally reserved for severely depressed unipolars who have not responded to tricyclics or MAO inhibitors. The procedure is described in Chapter 20; in essence, it consists of applying a moderate electrical voltage to the brain, for up to half a second. The patient's response to the electrical voltage is a convulsion (seizure) lasting for 30 to 40 seconds, followed by a 5- to 30-minute coma.

Most seriously depressed patients show at least a temporary improvement after about four ECT treatments (Campbell 1981). The mechanism of ECT is not fully understood, but it is thought to operate on the neurotransmitters at the synapses, similarly to the antidepressants. Part of the decrease in depressive symptoms may also be due to the amnesia developed by the patient for a short time after the treatment. One major advantage of ECT is that the response to treatment is relatively fast (Gangadhar, Kapur, and Kalyanasundaram 1982).

Focus 13.3 (pp. 398–399) describes a case in which medication was used in combination with ECT to treat a bipolar affective disorder.

Cognitive–behavioral treatment for unipolar disorders

Because the use of antidepressant medication or ECT involves a number of disadvantages, clinicians have sought a therapeutic approach to depression that would either supplement or replace medical treatment. The most promising replacement is cognitive–behavioral therapy (Kovacs et al. 1981; Williams 1984a).

As its name implies, cognitive–behavioral therapy is a combination of cognitive and behavioral strategies. The cognitive component involves teaching the patient (1) to identify negative, self-critical thoughts (cognitions) that occur automatically; (2) to note the connection between negative thoughts and the resulting depression; (3) to carefully examine each negative thought, deciding whether there is any support for it; and (4) to try to replace distorted negative thoughts with more realistic interpretations of each situation (Beck et al. 1979). Cognitive therapists believe that distorted thoughts cause such psychological problems as depression and that changing the former can eliminate the latter.

PATIENT: Not being loved leads automatically to unhappiness.
THERAPIST: Not being loved is a "nonevent." How can a nonevent lead automatically to something?
PATIENT: I just don't believe anyone could be happy without being loved.
THERAPIST: This is your belief. If you believe something, this belief will dictate your emotional reactions.
PATIENT: I don't understand that.
THERAPIST: If you believe something, you're going to act and feel as though it were true, whether it is or not.
PATIENT: You mean if I believe I'll be unhappy without love, it's only my belief causing my unhappiness?
THERAPIST: And when you feel unhappy, you probably say to yourself, "See, I was right. If I don't have love, I am bound to be unhappy."
PATIENT: How can I get out of this trap?
THERAPIST: You could experiment with your belief about having to be loved. Force yourself to suspend this belief and see what happens. Pay attention to the natural consequences of not being loved, not to the consequences created by your belief. For example, can you picture yourself on a tropical island with all the delicious fruits and other food available?
PATIENT: Yes, it looks pretty good.
THERAPIST: Now imagine that there are primitive people on the island. They are friendly and helpful, but they do not love you. None of them loves you.
PATIENT: I can picture that.
THERAPIST: How do you feel in your fantasy?
PATIENT: Relaxed and comfortable.
THERAPIST: So you can see that it does not necessarily follow that if you aren't loved, you will be unhappy. (Beck et al. 1979, p. 260)

At the outset of the cognitive therapy, the client is usually asked to begin monitoring his or her negative thoughts and listing them on a chart. It is important for the client to include *all* the thoughts and emotions that are associated with each distressing event that takes place each day (see Figure 13.1, p. 400).

The client brings the chart to the session each week, and the therapist uses it to demonstrate that the client's distress is being caused by his or her own unnecessarily negative thoughts. The client's own rational alternatives to these thoughts are discussed, and the client makes a conscious effort to adopt those alternatives that seem plausible. The goal of the cognitive part of the therapy is to train the client to automatically substitute logical interpretations for self-denigrating thoughts. Cognitive therapists maintain that, when a patient's thoughts about himself or herself become more consistently positive, the emotions follow suit.

The second part of the cognitive–behavioral approach is behavior therapy. This is usually indicated in cases of severe depression in which the patient is virtually inactive. One of the primary assumptions underlying this approach is that a depressed person is not engag-

FOCUS 13.3

I Am Suffering from Depression

I honestly felt subhuman, lower than the lowest vermin. Furthermore, I was self-deprecatory and could not understand why anyone would want to associate with me, let alone love me. . . . I was also positive that I was going to be fired from the university because of incompetence and that we could become destitute—that we would go broke. . . . I was positive that I was a fraud and phoney and that I didn't deserve my Ph.D. I didn't deserve to have tenure; I didn't deserve to be a Full Professor; I didn't deserve to be Chairman of the Psychology Department. . . . I couldn't understand how I had written the books and journal articles that I had and how they had been accepted for publication. (Endler 1982, pp. 45–48)

So wrote Dr. Norman Endler, a prominent clinical psychologist, stable family man, and chairman of the psychology department at York University. In a poignant and very explicit book, Endler described his experiences with a bipolar disorder and his reactions to treatment.

Until the spring of 1977 Endler felt fine. He was at the height of his successful career. He was active in sports and was constantly on the move. In retrospect, Endler has realized that he was hypomanic in the fall of 1976, but it was not until the following April that he became aware that something was wrong. He had difficulty sleeping and had lost his sex drive. "I had gone from being a winner to feeling like a loser. Depression had turned it around for me. From being on top of the world in the fall, I suddenly felt useless, inept, sad, and anxious in the spring." (p. 11)

Endler sought treatment and was administered several drugs that did not prove effective. He was then given electroconvulsive therapy (ECT). Endler describes his experience with ECT as follows:

I was asked to lie down on a cot and was wheeled into the ECT room proper. It was about eight o'clock. A needle was injected into my arm and I was told to count back from 100. I got about as far as 91. The next thing I knew I was in the recovery room and it was about eight-fifteen. I was slightly groggy and tired but not confused. (p. 81)

ing in a sufficient number of pleasant, rewarding activities. Depressed people tend to withdraw from others at the times when they are belittling themselves; then they interpret their self-imposed social isolation as a sign of their being unpopular and inadequate (Lewinsohn 1977).

To address this problem, depressed patients are asked to keep a daily activity schedule on which they list life events hour by hour and rate the "pleasantness" of each event. When a person is asked to monitor and rate events or activities, those activities generally increase in frequency. This, by itself, is a worthwhile objective for severely depressed patients; simply getting depressed individuals to engage in more activities increases the chance that they will become involved in some pleasant, reinforcing events. The patient's chart of this information also enables the therapist to spot specific patterns. For instance, a client who insists that he or she does not enjoy anything may actually rate as "slightly pleasant" any hour of the day that is spent outdoors. The therapist would point out this pattern and encourage the client to spend more time outdoors (Beck et al. 1979).

Once the severely depressed client becomes

After about seven ECT sessions, his depression lifted dramatically: "My holiday of darkness was over and fall arrived with a bang!" (p. 83).

The next few months were free of depression, and Endler enjoyed everything he did. Later, he realized that he was actually hypomanic during *this* period also. He was a bit euphoric, energetic, and active; he talked incessantly. Then depression struck again. He recognized that he was experiencing the initial signs of depression and again underwent drug treatment and ECT. This time the treatments were ineffective. Slowly, over the course of about 2 years, his depression was dissipated with the aid of medication.

Endler concludes by offering some advice. First, when individuals think they are depressed, they should seek treatment immediately. Second, some combinations of such treatments as psychotherapy, antidepressant drugs, and ECT may be effective. Third, the depressive's family can have an important effect on recovery: When a family member becomes severely depressed, existing family conflicts may become exacerbated. A supportive and understanding family can help the depressive to survive.

Depression is a common pervasive illness affecting all social classes, but it is eminently treatable. A great deal of heartbreak can be avoided by early detection and treatment. There is nothing to be ashamed of. There is no stigma attached to having an affective disorder. It is unwise to try to hide it and not seek help. I lived to tell and to write about it.

As of this writing . . . I have been symptom-free for almost three years. . . . I am not experiencing an emotional crisis and I hope I never do again. . . . I am reminded of a telephone conversation I had with my wife. . . . I mentioned that I had to do a lot of work to finish the first draft of Chapter 12, the last chapter in this book, before I left Stanford at the end of the month. Beatty said to me, "What's so terrible if you don't finish?" That put it all in perspective for me. I intend to live life to the fullest, but carefully. The sun will rise and shine whether or not I finish things today. But it's nice knowing that I did finish the first draft of this book before I left Stanford! (pp. 167–169)

Figure 13.1   Daily Cognition Chart for a Typical Depressive Client

Date	Situation	Automatic Thoughts	Emotions	Rational Alternative	Emotion
2/9	I sat home all alone on a Fri. night.	Nobody likes me or I would have been asked out.	Depressed	Most people know that I usually work Fri. nights. Maybe nobody knew I had the night off.	Relief, contentment
2/10	I had trouble understanding my reading assignment.	I must be an idiot. This should be an easy subject.	Depressed, anxious.	If I don't understand the material, I bet a number of others don't either.	Calm, determined

SOURCE: After Beck, A. T., Rush, A., Shaw, B., and Emery, G. (1979). *Cognitive therapy of depression.* New York: Guilford Press, p. 403.

more active, he or she may be asked to attend a social-skills training program. Improvements in social skills generally prompt and encourage clients to become more socially involved and can make that involvement a rewarding experience (Hersen, Bellack, and Himmelhoch 1980).

Cognitive–behavioral therapy seems to offer great promise as a plausible treatment for depression, although some methodological problems still need to be investigated (Kovacs 1980; Williams 1984b). Also of very much interest at present is the combination of cognitive–behavioral therapy and antidepressant medication. Preliminary findings on such a treatment package have been positive (Roth et al. 1982; Wilson 1982; Goodwin and Guze 1984).

Biomedical treatment for bipolar disorders

Since it was introduced to the United States in 1969, lithium (in the form of lithium carbonate)

has been the treatment of choice for bipolar and manic disorders (Fieve et al. 1976). As we have noted, the manic phase of bipolar disorder seems to be caused by an excess of neurotransmitters (primarily norepinephrine) at brain synapses. Lithium decreases the total level of neurotransmitters in the synaptic areas by *increasing* the re-uptake of norepinephrine into the nerve cells (Barchas et al. 1977).

The generally positive results achieved with lithium are currently being overshadowed somewhat by reports of distressing side effects (Dubovsky et al. 1982). The earliest danger signals are gastrointestinal complications (such as vomiting and diarrhea), fine tremors, muscular weakness, and frequent urination. The more serious side effects, which are associated with excessively high levels of lithium in the blood, are a lack of bladder control, slurred speech, blurred vision, seizures, and abnormal heart rate. Fortunately, accurate measurements of the amount of lithium present in the blood are easily obtained, and dosages can be adjusted accordingly.

Another problem associated with lithium is lack of compliance with the treatment program. For some reason, this is consistently more of a problem with bipolar patients taking lithium than with any other group of patients taking any other drug. Bipolar patients often report that they have tried to adjust their lithium dosage, by themselves, so that they will experience the mania but not the depression of bipolar disorder. Unfortunately, lithium levels cannot be manipulated in this manner. When the dosage is decreased, the initial slightly manic state quickly develops into either a severe manic state or depression.

SUMMARY

1. Severe depression is a major component of the affective disorders; it is evidenced in affective, cognitive, behavioral, and physiological symptoms. Mania, which may accompany depression in these disorders, is characterized by elation, grandiosity, irritability, and almost boundless energy.

2. The bipolar affective disorders are those in which manic episodes occur, or alternate with depressive episodes. In the unipolar disorders (major depression and dysthymic disorder), only depression is exhibited. Psychotic symptoms may also be displayed in the more severe affective disorders. The depressive disorders are the most common mood disorders; there is some evidence that they are distinct from the bipolar disorders.

3. Psychological theories of depression have been proposed by adherents of the psychoanalytic, cognitive, and behavioral viewpoints, but each has certain weaknesses. According to the ''learned helplessness'' theory of depression, one's susceptibility to depression depends on one's experience with controlling the environment. Genetic and bio-

chemical research has demonstrated that heredity plays a role in depression and mania, probably by affecting neurotransmitter levels within the brain.

4. Biological approaches to the treatment of depression focus on increasing the amounts of neurotransmitters available at brain synapses, through either medication or electroconvulsive therapy. A cognitive–behavioral treatment for depression includes the replacement of negative thoughts with more realistic (and positive) cognitions. The most effective treatment for bipolar disorders is lithium, a drug that decreases the level of synaptic neurotransmitters.

KEY TERMS

affective disorders Severe disturbances of mood involving depression or mania, or both

bipolar disorder An affective disorder in which both depression and mania are exhibited, or one in which only mania has been exhibited

depression An emotional state characterized by intense dysphoria, sadness, feelings of futility and worthlessness, and withdrawal from others

mania An emotional state characterized by great elation, seemingly boundless energy, and irritability

neurotransmitters Substances that contribute to the transmission of nerve impulses from one neuron to another

psychosis A severe mental disorder in which there is a loss of contact with reality or a significant distortion of reality

schema A pattern of thinking or a cognitive set that determines (or colors) an individual's reactions and responses

14
Suicide

*O*ur society views **suicide,** the taking of one's own life, with repugnance, and there are strong religious sanctions against it as well (Redestam 1977). Suicide is both a sin in canonical law and an illegal act according to the laws of most countries. Yet, in the United States, we are witnessing increased openness in discussing death and dying, the meaning of suicide, and the right to take one's own life. Nonetheless, most suicide is a tragic and baffling act.

☐ Late one evening Carl Johnson, M.D., left his downtown office, got into his Mercedes 500 SL, and drove toward his $400,000 suburban home. He was in no particular hurry because the house would be empty anyway; the year before, his wife had divorced him and with their two children had moved back east to her parents' home. Carl was deeply affected. For the past several months his private practice had declined dramatically. He used to find his work rewarding, but now he found people boring and irritating. Carl knew he had all the classic symptoms of depression. He was, after all, a psychiatrist. The garage door opened automatically as he rolled up the driveway. Carl parked hurriedly, not even bothering to press the switch that closed the door. Once in the house, he headed directly for the bar in his den; there he got out a bottle of bourbon and three glasses, filled the glasses, and lined them up along the bar. He drank them down, one after the other, in rapid succession. Then Carl sat down at his mahogany desk and unlocked one of the drawers. Taking a loaded .38 calibre revolver from the desk drawer, Dr. Carl Johnson held it to his temple and fired.

☐ In December 1983, Jenny Williams, a 62-year-old housewife, suffered a severe stroke that resulted in crippling paralysis, loss of speech, and an inability to attend to

403

her basic eliminative functions. Although she had the total support of her husband, two sons, and a daughter, Mrs. Williams was distressed at having to rely on basic life-support machinery. She could not speak, but it was clear to her family that she did not want to live in this manner and did not want to be a burden to others. Over several weeks Mrs. Williams's condition improved moderately, until she was able to move about with great effort. But she still could not speak or attend to her own needs. She was discharged from the hospital and was then cared for at home by a part-time nurse and her devoted husband. Two weeks after her discharge, Mrs. Williams took her own life by swallowing a bottle of sleeping pills. Mr. Williams had known of his wife's intention, but he did nothing to prevent her suicide. He did not have the heart to go against her wishes.

☐ Ten-year-old Tammy Jimenez was the youngest of three children—a loner who had attempted suicide at least twice in the past two years. Tammy's parents seemed always to be bickering about one thing or another and threatening divorce. She and her sisters were constantly abused by their alcoholic father. Finally, in February 1980, Tammy was struck by a truck when she darted out into the highway that passed by her home. The incident was listed as an accident, but her older sister said Tammy purposely killed herself. On the morning of her death, an argument with her father had upset and angered her. Her sister said that, seconds before Tammy ran out onto the highway, she had said she was unwanted and would end her own life.

☐ On October 23, 1983, a lone man in a truck containing six tons of explosives drove up to the U.S. Marine barracks in Beirut, Lebanon. The individual, believed to be a Shi'ite Muslim terrorist, did not pause when Marine guards signaled him to stop. Instead he drove on through the entrance barricades and set off a blast that killed himself and 240 American soldiers.

Why do people attempt suicide? Are persons who commit suicide always mentally disturbed? These questions are difficult to answer, for two important reasons.

First, those who commit suicide—who complete their suicide attempts—can no longer be asked about their motives, frame of mind, and emotional state. At best we have only indirect information, in the form of case records and reports of significant others, to help us understand what led them to their tragic act. The systematic examination of such information, for the purpose of understanding and explaining the behavior exhibited by an individual prior to his or her death, is called a **psychological autopsy** (Shneidman, Farberow, and Litman 1970). A *medical autopsy* is an examination of a body after death, to determine the cause or nature of the biological death. The *psychological autopsy* is patterned after the medical autopsy; it is an attempt to make psychological sense of an individual's suicide or homicide. Its intended use is obvious: If psychologists are able to isolate the events and circumstances that lead to suicide and to outline the characteristics of potential suicide victims, they may be able to prevent other people from performing this irreversible act.

Although psychological autopsy is a modern technique, it is similar in concept to the development of case studies or biographies of famous (or infamous) people. Among the better-known of these psychohistories are analyses of Martin Luther (Erikson 1962) and Adolph Hitler (Langer 1973). Although popular writers often attempt psychological explanations, they are generally not so systematic as a mental health professional would be in making a psychological autopsy. The writer Norman Mailer, for example, who is not a psychologist, wrote a psychological analysis of Marilyn Monroe (1973). Perhaps the most grisly and

Over 400 members of the People's Temple, a cult led by James Jones, committed suicide in 1978. Jones died of gunshot wounds, while most of the cult members died of poisoning. Many explanations for the mass suicide have been offered, including collective hysteria, forced compliance, mass insanity, and hypnosis.

dramatic example of incomprehensible suicidal behavior was the mass suicide of over 400 followers of cult leader James Jones in Guyana in 1978. A number of individuals, with a variety of backgrounds, have tried to determine what made so many people end their lives as suicides. Explanations ranged from collective hysteria and forced compliance to mass insanity and hypnosis.

The second reason why we lack a clear understanding of suicide is that no single explanation seems to account for all forms of suicide. The examples given at the beginning of this chapter reveal the diversity of life situations that may result in suicide. Common

sense alone should lead you to the conclusion that Jenny Williams's reasons for taking her own life are different from those of the terrorist or of Tammy Jimenez. In their attempts to understand suicide, researchers have focused on events, characteristics, and demographic variables that recur in psychological autopsies and are highly correlated with the act. Our first example, the case of Dr. Carl Johnson, includes some of their findings. For example, higher suicide rates are associated with divorce and with certain professions (psychiatry in particular), and men are more likely to kill themselves using firearms than by other means. (See Focus 14.1, pp. 406–407 for other research results.) But the factor that is most closely associated with suicide is *depression*.

SUICIDE AND DEPRESSION

Although it is dangerous to assume a causal relationship between suicide and depression, a number of studies indicate that there is a very high correlation between the two. For example, it was found that *suicide wishes* occurred in 74 percent of a group of severely depressed individuals, compared to only 12 percent in a nondepressed group (Beck 1967). Of course, a suicide wish is far different from a suicide attempt; yet in another study, 80 percent of the patients admitted to a general hospital because of a *suicide attempt* were found to be depressed at the time of initial observation

FOCUS 14.1

Some Facts about Suicide

1. Every 20 to 30 minutes, someone in the United States takes his or her own life. More than 25,000 people kill themselves each year. Suicide is among the top 10 causes of death in the industrialized parts of the world; it is the second or third leading cause of death among youths. There is some evidence that the number of actual suicides is probably 25 to 30 percent higher than that recorded. Many deaths that are officially recorded as accidental, such as single-auto crashes, drownings, or falls from great heights, are actually suicides. According to some estimates, for every person who completes a suicide, 8 to 10 persons make the attempt.

2. Recent reports suggest that about 12,000 children aged 5 to 14 are admitted to psychiatric hospitals for suicidal behavior every year, and it is believed that 20 times as many actually try. Suicides among young people aged 15 to 24 have increased by more than 40 percent in the past decade (50 percent for males and 12 percent for females); suicide is now the second leading cause of death for this group.

3. Suicide is the second or third leading cause of death among college students. The suicide rate for college students is twice as high as that for persons not in college.

4. The suicide rate for men is about 3 times that for women; among the elderly, the rate for men is 10 times that for women. However, women *attempt* suicide 3 times as often as men. The suicide rate for black men between the ages of 20 and 35 is twice that for white men in the same age group.

5. In terms of marital status, the lowest incidence of suicide is found among the married, and the highest among the divorced. The suicide rates for single and widowed or divorced men are about twice those for females with similar marital status.

6. Physicians, lawyers, and dentists have higher than average rates of suicide. Among medical professionals, psychiatrists have the highest rate and pediatricians the lowest. Marked differences among medical specialties raise the question of whether the specialty influences susceptibility or suicide-prone persons choose the specialty.

7. Suicide is represented proportionately among all socioeconomic levels. Level of wealth does not seem to affect the suicide rate as much as changes in that level. In the Great Depression of the 1930s, suicide was highest among the suddenly impoverished rather than among those who had always been poor.

(Silver et al. 1971). And, again, a study of successful suicides by mental patients in Massachusetts showed that the suicide rate for depressives was 36 times higher than that for the general population (Temoche, Pugh, and MacMahon 1964). Retrospective studies have also revealed that 80 percent of patients who committed suicide were depressed prior to the fatal act (Barraclough et al. 1969). Among children and adolescents as well, depression seems to be highly correlated with suicidal behavior (Kosky 1983; Rosenthal and Rosenthal 1984).

Such data must lead one to the conclusion that depression plays an important role in suicide. Yet other studies indicate that this role is far from simple. For example, there is evidence that severely depressed patients *seldom* commit suicide (Mendels 1970). Such patients generally exhibit motor retardation and low

8. Men most frequently choose firearms as the means of suicide; poisoning and asphyxiation via barbiturates are the preferred means for women. The violent means (which men are more likely to choose) are more certain to complete the act; this partially explains the disproportionately greater number of incomplete attempts by females. Among children below the age of 15, the most common suicide method tends to be jumping from buildings and running into traffic. Older children try hanging or drug overdoses. It appears that younger children attempt suicide impulsively and thus use more readily available means.

9. Religious affiliation is correlated with suicide rates. In countries where Catholic Church influences are strong—Latin America, Ireland, Spain, Italy—the suicide rate is relatively low. Islam, too, condemns suicide, and the suicide rates in Arab countries are correspondingly low. In the Scandinavian countries, Czechoslovakia, and Hungary—where church authority is weaker—higher rates are observed.

10. Suicide rates tend to decline during wars and natural disasters but to increase during periods of shifting norms and values or social unrest, when traditional expectations no longer apply. Sociologists speculate that during wars, people "pull together" and are less concerned with their own difficulties.

11. More than two-thirds of the people who commit suicide communicate their intent to do so within three months of the fatal act. (The belief that people who threaten suicide are not serious about it, or will not actually make such an attempt, is ill-founded.) Most people who attempt suicide appear to have been ambivalent about death until the suicide. It has been estimated that fewer than 5 percent unequivocally wish to end their lives.

SOURCES: Shneidman, E. S. et al. (Eds.). (1970). *The psychology of suicide*. New York: Jason Aronson.
Dublin, L. I. (1963). *Suicide: A sociological and statistical study*. New York: Ronald Press.
Shneidman, E. S. (1976). Introduction: Contemporary overview of suicide. In *Suicidology: Contemporary developments*. New York: Grune & Stratton.
Wexler, L. et al. (1978). Suicide attempts 1970–1975: Updating a U.S. study and comparison with international trend. *British Journal of Psychiatry*, 132, 180–185.
Kosky, R. (1983). Childhood suicidal behavior. *Journal of Child Psychology and Psychiatry*, 24, 457–468.
Rosenthal, P. and Rosenthal, S. (1984). Suicidal behavior by preschool children. *American Journal of Psychiatry*, 141, 520–525.

energy, which keep them from attaining the level of activity required for suicide. The danger period often comes after some treatment, when the depression begins to lift. Patients then begin to redevelop the energy and motivation needed to carry out the act. Most suicide attempts occur during weekend furloughs from hospitals or soon after discharge, a fact that supports this contention (Wheat 1960). The risk of suicide seems to be only about 1 percent during the year in which a depressive episode occurs, but it is about 15 percent after that (Klerman 1982).

THE DYNAMICS OF SUICIDE

Some clinicians believe that everyone, at one time or another, has wished to end his or her life. Fortunately, most of us do not act on such wishes, even during extreme distress. But why do some individuals do so? Because suicide is closely linked to depression, many of the theories of depression apply to suicide as well, but still the question is not easy to answer. We have already noted the variety of motivations for suicide and the difficulty of studying this phenomenon. We can never know for certain what causes a person to take his or her life. Yet on a very general level there does appear to be one common motive: to gain relief from a life situation that the person finds unbearable.

Sociocultural explanations

Early explanations of suicide emphasized its relationship to various social factors. Rates of suicide have been found to vary with occupation, the size of one's city of residence, socioeconomic status, age, sex, marital status, and race. Higher rates are associated with high- and low-status (as opposed to middle-status) occupations, urban living, middle-aged men, single or divorced persons, and the upper and lower socioeconomic classes (Weile 1960). In a pioneering work, the French sociologist Emile Durkheim related differences in suicide rates to the interplay of social forces on the individual (Durkheim 1897). His conclusions led him to propose three categories of suicide: egoistic, altruistic, and anomic.

Egoistic suicide results from an inability to integrate oneself with society. A failure to keep close ties with the community deprives the individual of the support systems that are necessary for adaptive functioning. Without such support, and unable to function adaptively, the individual becomes isolated and alienated from other people.

Altruistic suicide is motivated by the need to further group goals or to achieve some greater good. One's life is given up for a higher cause (in a religious sacrifice or the ultimate political protest, for example). Group pressures make such an act highly acceptable and honored. During World War II, Japanese *kamikaze* pilots voluntarily dove their airplanes into enemy warships "for the Emperor and the glory of Japan." The self-immolation of Buddhist monks during the Vietnam war and the terrorist truck bombing of the Marine barracks in Lebanon are in this category.

Anomic suicide results when a person's relationship to society is unbalanced in some dramatic fashion. When an individual's horizons are suddenly broadened or constricted by unstable conditions, he or she may not be able to handle the change or cope with the new status and may choose suicide as an "out." The suicides of individuals who lost their personal wealth during the Great Depression are of this type. Similarly, a person who suddenly and unexpectedly acquires great wealth may be prone to suicide.

Psychosocial explanations may be valid to an extent, but attributing suicide to a single sociological factor (economic depression, residence, occupation) is too simplistic and mechanistic. As we have noted several times, correlations do not imply cause-and-effect relationships. Thus, Durkheim's three catego-

As an act of political protest, a Palestinian terrorist drove his truck loaded with explosives into a U.S. Marines headquarters building in Beirut, Lebanon. His act of suicide killed almost 200 American and French soldiers stationed in Lebanon as part of a Peace Task Force.

ries are more descriptive than explanatory. Moreover, purely sociological explanations that take into account only one psychosocial factor—group cohesion, for example—omit the intrapsychic dimension of the struggles of the individual. They fail to explain why only *certain* members of any of the aforementioned groups commit suicide whereas others do not.

Intrapsychic explanations

Early psychological explanations of suicide tended to ignore social factors in favor of intrapsychic ones. In the classical Freudian approach, for example, self-destruction was seen as the result of hostility that was directed inward against the *introjected love object* (the loved one with whom the person has identified). That is, individuals who kill themselves are really directing anger and the suicidal act against others whom they have incorporated within themselves. If the angry feelings (death instinct) attain murderous proportions, a suicide attempt is the result.

Unfortunately, such a conceptualization is not supported by evidence. Carefully analyzed psychological autopsies indicate that hate and revenge are not the only reasons for suicide; people kill themselves for a number of other psychological reasons—shame, guilt, hopelessness, pain. An analysis of 165 suicide notes over a 25-year period revealed that only 24 percent of the suicides expressed hostile or negative feelings toward themselves, whereas

51 percent expressed positive attitudes and another 25 percent were neutral. The investigators concluded that there is insufficient support for a hypothesis in which hostility is the sole precipitant of suicide (Tuckman, Kleiner, and Lavell 1959).

Other factors in suicide

It seems, then, that neither a purely sociological nor a purely psychological perspective is adequate to explain the causes of suicide. It is most likely that both sociological and psychological factors are involved; Focus 14.2 discusses a classification scheme that includes both.

It is also likely that other factors are involved as well. For example, consistent with the strong evidence that chemical neurotransmitters are associated with depression and mania, there is similar evidence that suicide is influenced by biochemistry. This evidence was discovered in the mid-1970s, when researchers identified a chemical called *5-hydroxyindoleacetic acid* (5HIAA). The spinal fluid of some depressed patients had been found to contain abnormally small amounts of 5HIAA, which is produced when serotonin, a neurotransmitter that affects mood and emotions, is broken down in the body. Preliminary statistics on low-5HIAA patients indicate that they are more likely than others to commit suicide, more likely to select violent methods of killing themselves, and more likely to have a history of violence, aggression, and impulsiveness. Researchers believe that the tendency toward suicide may develop from a combination of aggression and depression.

This discovery may lead to a chemical means of detecting individuals who are at high risk to attempt suicide. However, researchers in this area caution that social and psychological factors also play a role in suicide. Low 5HIAA levels do not cause suicide, but it may make people more vulnerable to environ-mental stressors (Pines 1983). And still another caution is in order: This evidence is correlational in nature; it does not indicate whether low 5HIAA is a cause of or a result of particular moods and emotions—or even whether there is a direct relation between the two.

THE VICTIMS OF SUICIDE

Here we shall briefly discuss four groups of individuals who are especially victimized by suicide: the very young, college students, the elderly, and those who are left behind by suicides.

Suicide among children and adolescents

Suicide among the young is an unspoken tragedy within our society. We have traditionally avoided the idea that some of our precious youths find life so painful that they consciously and deliberately take their own lives. As in the case of Tammy Jimenez, it may be easier to categorize a suicide by calling it an accident. Yet, as is indicated in Focus 14.1, as many as 250,000 children aged 5 to 14 may attempt suicide each year (Rosenthal and Rosenthal 1984). The suicide rate for children under 14 is increasing at an alarming rate, and the rate for adolescents is rising even faster (Kosky 1983; Cosand, Bourque, and Kraus 1982). Suicide is now second only to automobile accidents as the leading cause of death among teenagers, and some automobile accidents may also be suicides.

A lack of research in the field of childhood suicides has generally kept psychologists from understanding why such acts occur. However, two recent studies have helped identify the characteristics of the suicidal child.

In a retrospective study of admissions to a

Suicide Notes

Suicide victims often leave notes that can provide clues to their mental state and motivation. One suggested classification scheme for suicides is based in part on information from these suicide notes (Shneidman 1957, 1961).

The *egoistic* suicide is the result of an intrapsychic debate, a struggle within the victim's mind. The victim's inner torment may be philosophical or religious in nature.

> Mr. Brown:
> . . . It seems unnecessary to present a lengthy defense for my suicide, for if I have to be judged, it will not be on this earth. However, in brief, I find myself a misfit. To me, life is too painful for the meager occasional pleasure to compensate. It all seems so pointless, the daily struggle leading *where?* Several times I have done what, in retrospect, is seen to amount to running away from circumstances. I could do so now—travel, find a new job, even change vocation, but why? It is *Myself* that I have been trying to escape, and this I can do only as I am about to do! Goodbye!
>
> Bill Smith
>
> (Shneidman 1968, p. 5)

The *dyadic* suicide is interpersonal in nature and is influenced primarily by unfulfilled wishes or needs involving a significant other. Frustration, rage, manipulation, and attempts to elicit guilt are common.

> Bill,
> You have killed me. I hope you are happy in your heart, if you have one which I doubt.

Please leave Rover with Mike. Also leave my baby alone. If you don't I'll haunt you the rest of your life and I mean it and I'll do it.

> You have been mean and also cruel. God doesn't forget those things and don't forget that. And please no flowers; it won't mean anything. Also keep your money. I want to be buried in Potter's Field in the same casket with Betty. You can do that for me. That's the way we want it. . . . (Shneidman 1968, p. 6)

The *ageneratic* suicide is characteristic of the person who has lost the sense of participating in the transgenerational flow of human life—of belonging to "the scheme of things." Alienation, disengagement, and isolation are involved; the feeling and sense are existential.

> To the authorities:
> Excuse my inability to express myself in English and the trouble caused. I beg you not to lose time in an inquest upon by body. Just simply record and file it because the name and address given on the register are fictious and I wanted to disappear anonymously. No one expects me here nor will be looking for me. I have informed my relatives in America. *Please do not bury me!* I wish to be *cremated* and the ashes tossed to the winds. In that way I shall return to the nothingness from which I have come into this sad world. This is all I ask of the Americans for all that I have intended to give them with my coming into this country.
> Many thanks.
>
> Jose Marcia
>
> (Shneidman 1968, p. 8)

pediatric hospital emergency room over a 7-year period, researchers identified 505 children and adolescents who had attempted suicide (Garfinkel, Froese, and Hood 1982). This group was compared with a control group of children who were similar in age, sex, and date of admission. The suicidal group was found to exhibit the following characteristics:

1. There were three times as many girls as boys, and the boys who attempted suicide were significantly younger than the girls. The gender rates are consistent with adult rates, but the younger age of the boys is not.
2. The psychiatric symptoms most often exhibited by both children and adolescents were fluctuating affect and aggressiveness and/or hostility.
3. Most of the suicide attempts (73 percent) occurred at home; 12 percent occurred in public areas, 7 percent at school, and 5 percent at a friend's house. In 87 percent of the attempts, someone else was nearby—generally parents. The fact that most suicide attempts occur at home implies that parents are in the best position to recognize and prevent suicidal behavior.
4. Most of the attempts occurred during the winter months, in the evening or afternoon.
5. Drug overdose was the primary means of attempted suicide, accounting for 88 percent of the attempts. Next, in order, were wrist laceration, hanging, and jumping from heights or in front of moving vehicles.
6. Over 77 percent of the attempts were judged to be of low lethality; 21 percent were moderately lethal; and slightly more than 1 percent were highly lethal. Most attempts were judged to have been made in a way that ensured a high likelihood of rescue. These figures lend credence to the belief that most children who attempt suicide do not really want to end their lives.

The researchers found that the families of the suicidal group were under greater eco-nomic stress than the families of the control group. The former had twice the rate of paternal unemployment. It may be that parents who are preoccupied with economic concerns are less readily available to support their children in time of need. Further, fewer than half the families of those who attempted suicide were two-parent families. The families of suicide attempters also had higher rates of medical problems, psychiatric illness, and suicide than control-group families. The dominant psychiatric problem was alcohol or drug abuse.

In the second study as well, family instability and stress and a chaotic family atmosphere were correlated with suicide attempts (Cosand, Bourque, and Kraus 1982). Suicidal children seemed to have experienced unpredictable traumatic events and to have suffered the loss of a significant parenting figure before the age of 12. Parents tended to be alcohol or drug abusers who provided poor role models for coping with stress. As in the first study, the child's self-destructive behavior seemed to be a last-ditch attempt to affect or coerce those who threatened his or her psychological well-being. Considerable anger was observed in the suicidal children.

When they remain unrecognized and untreated, such children are at great risk to commit suicide. Thus the early detection of their distress signals is vital. Intensive family therapy, including the education of parents with regard to parenting roles, can help. Parents can be taught to recognize the signs of depression, to become aware of their children's after-school activities, and to be cognizant of the role and accessibility of drugs. Finally, in some cases, the solution to the problem of childhood suicide may be removal of the child from the family (Berman et al. 1982).

College-student suicides

When one considers how well endowed college students as a group are—with youth, intelligence, and boundless opportunity—one wonders whether there is something about the college situation that fosters self-destructive acts among college students. Most of the studies that attempt to answer this question have described the characteristics of suicidal students without controlling for the possibility that nonsuicidal students may share the same traits. What is needed is a clear understanding of the characteristics that differentiate suicidal from nonsuicidal students. These characteristics seem to have been pinpointed in the study discussed next—one in which a comparison group *was* included for control (Seiden 1966). Although we should not generalize its results without exercising caution, other later studies have provided similar findings (Klagsbrun 1976; Rule 1969).

Characteristics of student suicides   At the University of California at Berkeley, suicide ranked second only to accidents as the major cause of student deaths. Several characteristics of student suicides were distilled from a ten-year study of suicide on the Berkeley campus (Seiden 1966). Compared to nonsuicidal students, students who committed suicide:

☐ Tended to be older than the average student by almost four years
☐ Were significantly overrepresented with postgraduate students
☐ Were more likely to be males, although the proportion of female suicides was higher than among the general population
☐ Were more likely to be foreign students and language or literature majors
☐ As undergraduates tended to have better academic records, but as postgraduate students were below the graduate grade-point average

In addition, more suicides occurred in February and October (near the beginning of a semester) than in the other months of the year. Thus the notion that suicides occur in response to anxiety over final examinations was

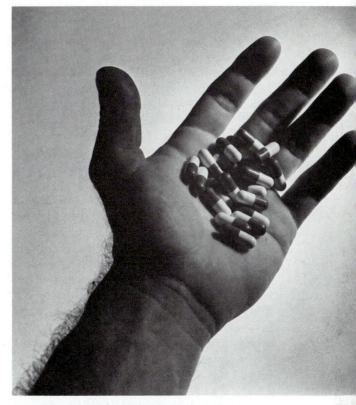

College students most frequently commit suicide through drug overdose. Most of the deaths occur at the beginning of the school semester in campus residences. Firearms are another frequently used method.

not supported by the results. In fact, the danger period appeared to be the start, not the finish, of the school semester. Most of the students committed suicide at their campus residence. Firearms were the most common means of committing suicide; ingestion of drugs was next. In later studies on other campuses, however, drug overdose was found to be more frequently used than firearms (Klagsbrun 1976).

Reasons for student suicides   These findings suggest several lines of explanation for student suicides. First, whereas the ratio of male suicides to female suicides in the general population is 3:1, for college students it is 1.5:1.

The greater risk of suicide among female college students may result from the increase in conflicting social pressures that accompanies a rapid shift in sex roles among women entering college (Gibbs and Martin 1964).

Second, the fact that undergraduates who commit suicide have better scholastic records than the general college population reveals an interesting paradox. By objective standards, suicidal students had done well. In almost all cases, however, friends and relatives report that these students were dissatisfied with their academic performance. They were filled with doubts about their own ability to succeed. One explanation for such a feeling is that these students were highly motivated to achieve and had unrealistically high expectations. For example, at a large eastern university several years ago, an outstanding young female student, who had consistently made the Dean's List and had obtained nearly straight-A grades, leaped to her death from her dormitory room late one winter night. It seemed inconceivable that a student with so much intellectual promise could commit such an act. Interviews with her friends, family, and fiancé indicated that she had been despondent over receiving a B in one of her courses, which spoiled her unbroken string of A's. Seiden (1966) describes the psychological dynamics of this situation as follows:

> The internal standards these students applied to themselves were so Olympian, the demands they imposed upon themselves so exacting, that they were destined to suffer frustration and disappointments no matter how well they fared. . . . Whereas they had previously been crackerjack students in high school or junior college, excelling without much difficulty, the precipitous drop in grade points . . . threatened their feelings of self-esteem. Faced with a sudden loss of status, they may have suicided as a response to their egoistic conflict. (p. 391)

Third, and related to the previous explanation, many suicidal students feel overwhelming shame and disgrace because of their sense of failing others. On a particularly lovely June day, Patrick C. Do of Hong Kong, a graduate student at Florida State University, committed suicide after shooting his adviser, Professor James R. Fisher. Observers noted that Do had recently failed to pass a Ph.D. examination in chemistry (*East-West,* June 16, 1976). We might speculate that Patrick Do could no longer tolerate the experience of failure. He had indeed failed, and he partially blamed his adviser for the outcome. Death seemed the only alternative left.

Foreign students, especially, are under considerable pressure from families and friends to excel and achieve in this country. Their greatest fear is that they may not fulfill the expectations of their families, who may have sacrificed much to finance their educations. The pressures become even stronger for students who come from cultures in which it is important to bring honor to the family name (Sue 1975). Academic achievement or occupational success reflects creditably on the whole family, not just on the individual; and conversely, unsatisfactory behaviors such as juvenile delinquency, mental illness, and failure in school are sources of shame to the family. Faced with such pressures, some foreign students may report only successes to their families and cover up their failures. Needing to constantly reinforce the precariously fabricated image of continuous achievement, and knowing that a day of reckoning will eventually arrive, some students, like Patrick Do, choose suicide. Interestingly, Seiden's study revealed that 17 percent of the Berkeley suicides were Chinese students.

Finally, it is quite possible that the common denominator among suicidal students may simply be *emotional disturbance.* The other factors may all play a part, but it may be psychopathology that predisposes students to overreact to them. In fact, some believe that suicide—any suicide—is not the act of a rational person. That is, some deviation within the individual's personality causes or predisposes him or her to break with reality. Even the Japanese *kamikaze* pilots and the Shi'ite Muslim terrorist, who sacrificed their lives for a cause, are perceived in Western theories as mentally disturbed. Neverthless, some psychologists hold firmly to the belief that some suicides may be culturally sanctioned and may represent rational responses to intolerable situations.

Suicide among the elderly

Aging inevitably results in generally unwelcome physical changes, such as wrinkling and thickening skin, graying hair, and diminishing physical strength. In addition, the elderly encounter a succession of life changes, stressors, and status changes as the years roll on. Friends and relatives die, social isolation may increase, and the prospect of death becomes more real (Goodstein 1981). Mandatory retirement rules may lead to the need for financial assistance and the difficulties of living on a fixed and inadequate income. Among the elderly, nearly 30 percent have an annual income of less than $3,200 (Baum and Boxley 1983). Such conditions make depression one of the most common psychiatric complaints of the elderly. And their depression seems to be involved more with "feeling old" than with their actual age or poor physical health (Baum and Boxley 1983).

Suicide seems to be a concomitant of depression for older adults. Their suicide rates (especially for elderly white males) are higher than those for the general population (Pfeffer 1977; McIntosh and Santos 1981). In one study comparing rates of suicide among different racial groups, it was found that the white elderly committed almost 18 percent of all suicides but formed only about 11 percent of the population; however, the suicide rate for elderly white Americans has been declining over the past 20 years (McIntosh and Santos 1981). Suicide rates for Chinese–Americans, Japanese–Americans, and Filipino–Americans were found to be even higher than that

for the elderly white. Native Americans and blacks show the lowest rates of suicide among older adults (although both groups are at high risk for suicide during young adulthood).

Of the Asian–American groups, the greatest risk of suicide was among first-generation immigrants. One possible explanation for this finding is that the newly arrived Asian–Americans had intended to earn money and then return to their native countries. When they found that they were unable to earn enough either to return home or to bring their families here, they developed feelings of isolation and an increased risk of suicide. Subsequent generations of Asian–Americans (and, probably, other immigrant groups as well) have acculturated and now have family ties that reduce the potential for suicide.

Still another facet of suicide among older individuals is discussed in the final section of this chapter.

The "other" victims of suicide

When a suicide occurs, our thoughts immediately turn to the person who has taken his or her own life. What unbearable pain was he or she suffering to justify such an end? Yet the true victims of this tragedy are often the family, relatives, and friends who are left behind to face the *meaning* of this act.

Elisabeth Kübler-Ross, a psychiatrist who has researched and written extensively about death and dying, has outlined a series of reactions experienced by individuals when a family member commits suicide. The first of three stages is characterized by shock, denial, and numbness. The act is often incomprehensible to loved ones, who find it difficult to talk about. They tend to avoid using the word *suicide*, and they go through the motions of arranging the funeral as though it had no personal meaning. The depths of pain are too great to be confronted, and family members close themselves off from their feelings. In this state the bereaved individual appears to be detached and out of contact with others. Kübler-Ross suggests that, at this stage, friends of the family can help most by making themselves available day and night.

In the second stage, family members begin to experience grief. For the spouse especially, anguish is mixed with feelings of anger. There is an attempt to blame someone for something—oneself, for example: "Why didn't I see what was happening?" However, such self-blame for the death of one's spouse or child is often only symptomatic of one's true anger, which is directed toward the suicide. And eventually that anger and rage toward the deceased is expressed: "How could you desert me and our children? How could you do this to us? Why didn't you have the courage to face life? Damn you, why didn't you tell me you were hurting?"

Kübler-Ross feels that this stage is a difficult one for family and friends to handle. Most people stay away from the parents or spouse of a suicide, whose rage can often make them quite abusive to everyone. It is important, however, that someone be there to listen, to act as a sounding board, and to be "fuel for the fire," because the expression of anger is necessary and is preferable to denial. The family must be helped to experience the pain, rather than postpone or deny it. They need empathic and understanding people, not sedation. Kübler-Ross states that, in suicide, extreme and prolonged grief can be avoided by not fostering denial. The words *suicide*, *death*, and *dead* should be used directly, without attempts to soften or disguise them (as in "passed away"). Moreover, it is important for the family to see the corpse, to identify it, and to touch it, so that they face the reality of death.

The third and last stage is letting go, or completing "unfinished business." In cases of suicide, there is usually much unfinished business to take care of. A husband may think, "I never told her I loved her," or "There's so much we haven't talked about or shared." It is often helpful for the family to say these "un-finished" things to the suicide victim, either at the funeral or in a role-played situation. Letting go, saying goodbye, and accepting the feelings one has are important therapeutic events for the survivor.

PREVENTING SUICIDE

In almost every case of suicide, there are hints that the act is about to occur. Suicide is irreversible, of course, so preventing it depends very much on early detection and successful intervention. Mental health professionals involved in suicide prevention operate under the assumption that potential victims are ambivalent about the act. That is, the wish to die is strong, but there is also a wish to live. Potential rescuers are trained to exert their efforts on the side of life.

Clues to suicide

The prevention of suicide depends very much on the ability to recognize its signs, both demographic and specific. We have already discussed a number of demographic factors, such as the fact that men are three times more likely to kill themselves than are women and the fact that increased age increases the probability of suicide. And, although the popular notion is that frequent suicidal gestures are associated with less serious intent, most suicides do have a history of suicide threats; to ignore them is extremely dangerous.

General characteristics are often helpful in the detection of potential suicides, but individual cases vary from statistical norms. What does one look for in specific instances? Danto (1971) points out that the seriousness of the intent is indicated by the amount of detail involved in a suicide threat. A person who provides specific details, such as method, time, and place, is more dangerous than one who is vague in describing these factors. Suicidal potential increases if the person has direct access to the means of suicide, such as a loaded pistol. Also, on occasion, a suicide may be preceded by a precipitating event. The loss of a loved one, family discord, or chronic or terminal illness may contribute to a person's decision to end his or her life.

A person contemplating suicide may *verbally* communicate the intent. Oral cues can vary from a very direct statement ("I'm going to kill myself," "I want to die," or "If such and such happens, I'll kill myself") to indirect threats. Examples of the latter are "Goodbye," "I've had it," "You'd be better off without me," and "It's too much to put up with." These cues are frequently very subtle:

> A patient says to Nurse Jones, who is leaving on vacation, "Goodbye, Miss Jones, I won't be here when you come back." If some time afterward Nurse Jones, knowing that the patient is not scheduled to be transferred or discharged prior to her return, thinks about that conversation, she may do well to telephone her hospital. (Danto 1971, p. 20)

Behavioral clues can be communicated directly or indirectly. The most direct clue is a "practice run," an actual suicide attempt. Regardless of the failure to complete the act, such gestures should be taken seriously; they often communicate deep suicidal intentions that may be carried out in the future. Indirect behavioral communications can include actions such as putting one's affairs in order, taking a lengthy trip, giving away prized possessions, buying a casket, or making out a will, depending on the circumstances. In other words, the more unusual or peculiar the situation, the more likely it is that the action is a cue to suicide.

Suicide prevention centers

The first suicide prevention center (SPC) was established in Los Angeles in 1958 by psychologists Norman L. Farberow and Edwin S.

There are about two hundred suicide prevention centers throughout the United States. They operate twenty-four hours a day, seven days a week, and have well-publicized telephone numbers. The mental health profession continues to support these centers even though there is little evidence that they actually help prevent suicide.

Shneidman. The center first sought patients from the wards of hospitals, but now, owing to its reputation, 99 percent of its contacts are by phone (Farberow 1970). In the last 25 years, hundreds of similar suicide prevention centers have sprung up throughout the United States. These centers are generally adapted to the particular needs of the communities they serve, but they all share certain operational procedures and goals (see Focus 14.3, p. 418).

Suicide prevention centers typically operate 24 hours a day, 7 days a week. Because most suicide contacts are by phone, a well-publicized telephone number is made available for calls at any time of the day or night. Furthermore, many of the centers provide inpatient or outpatient crisis treatment. In cases where

Goals of Suicide Prevention Centers (SPCs)

In general, suicide prevention centers try:

1. *To increase the ability of lay people and professionals to recognize the signs of and clues to potential suicides.* Workers try to inform physicians, members of the clergy, police, educators, spouses, parents, neighbors, and friends about the early signs of suicide.

2. *To make it easier for each person to utter a "cry for help" against suicide.* Suicide continues to be considered a sign of weakness, insanity, sin, and lack of courage. The potential suicide's guilt about the act often gives rise to the feeling that he or she does not deserve treatment or help.

These taboos must be overcome so that the person in distress will see that he or she has a legitimate reason for requesting treatment and assistance.

3. *To provide resources for managing suicidal crises.* Before the establishment of suicide prevention centers, very few facilities were available to the suicidal person. Now special units staffed by specially trained personnel may be found almost everywhere.

4. *To disseminate the facts about suicide.* SPCs engage in public education by providing facts to combat the many ill-founded beliefs and superstitions concerning suicide.

---

they lack such resources, the centers develop cooperative programs with other mental health facilities in the community. All workers are trained in crisis intervention techniques and have been exposed to crisis situations under supervision. Among these techniques are the following (Heilig 1970):

1. *Maintaining contact and establishing a relationship.* The skilled worker who establishes a good relationship with the suicidal caller not only increases his or her chances of working out an alternative solution but also can exert more influence. Thus it is important for the worker to show interest, concern, and self-assuredness.

2. *Obtaining necessary information.* Besides demographic data, the caller's name and address are elicited. This information is very valuable if there arises an urgent need to locate the caller.

3. *Evaluating suicidal potential.* The staff

person must determine quickly the seriousness of the caller's self-destructive intent. Most centers use lethality rating scales to help the worker determine suicide potential. These usually contain questions on age, sex, onset of symptoms, situational plight, prior suicidal behavior, and the communication qualities of the caller. Staffers also elicit other demographic and specific information that might provide clues to lethality, such as the information discussed in the section entitled "Clues to Suicide."

4. *Clarifying the nature of the stress and focal problem.* The worker must help the caller clarify the exact nature of the stress, recognize that he or she may be under so much duress that thinking may be confused and impaired, and realize that there are other solutions besides suicide. The caller is often disoriented, so it is important that the worker be specific in attempting to bring the caller back to reality.

5. *Assessing strengths and resources.* In working out a therapeutic plan, the worker can often mobilize the caller's strengths or available resources. In their agitated state, suicidal people tend to forget the strengths they possess. Their feelings of helplessness are so overwhelming that helping them recognize *what they can do* about a situation is important. The worker explores the caller's personal resources (family, friends, co-workers), professional resources (doctors, members of the clergy, therapists, lawyers), and community resources (clinics, hospitals, social agencies).

6. *Recommending and initiating an action plan.* Besides being supportive, the worker is highly directive in recommending a course of action. Whether the recommendation entails immediately seeing the person, calling the person's family, or referring the person to a social agency the next day, it is presented as a plan of action and outlined step by step.

This list implies a rigid sequence, but in fact the approach (as well as the order of the steps) is adjusted to fit the needs of the individual caller.

The effectiveness of suicide prevention centers

As of this writing, there are approximately 200 SPCs in the United States, as well as numerous "suicide hotlines" in mental health clinics. However, there has been little research concerning their effectiveness, owing to both the difficulty of researching suicide and the fact that many clients of SPCs wish to remain anonymous.

Some data are available, however. For example, it is known that 95 percent of callers to SPCs never use the service again (Speer 1971). This finding may be interpreted to indicate that the service was so helpful that no further treatment was needed. An equally viable in-

terpretation is that callers do not find SPCs helpful and feel it is useless to call again. Worse yet, they may have killed themselves after the contact. Another study has shown that potential suicides do not perceive contact with an SPC as more helpful than discussion with friends (Speer 1972). Furthermore, cities with hotline services did not have lower suicide rates than those without such services (Werner 1969).

Before you jump to the conclusion that SPCs are ineffective, it is important to note that the studies we have cited could have been affected by several factors. For example, cities with and cities without SPCs might differ so much that they are incomparable. Or clients may contact SPCs only when they are in such great distress that they despair of asking friends for help. They may then perceive their contacts with friends as being more beneficial relative to the distress they feel. Finally, despite the fact that convincing evidence is lacking, there is always the possibility that SPCs do help. Because life is precious, the mental health profession continues to support them.

THE RIGHT TO SUICIDE: MORAL, ETHICAL, AND LEGAL IMPLICATIONS

The choice of suicide is ours to make. It is our life we are giving up, and our death we are arranging. The choice does not infringe on the rights of others. We do not need to explain and excuse. (Portwood 1978, p. 68)

These words were written by Doris Portwood, who believes that elderly people have the right to end their own lives if their continued existence would result in psychological and physical deterioration. Portwood contends that these individuals should be allowed the choice of dying in a dignified man-

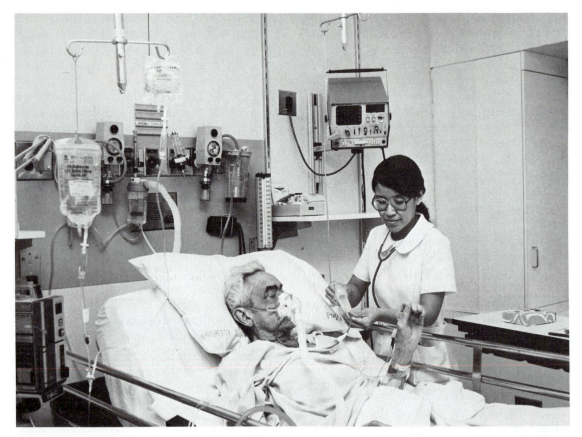

While modern medicine has made incredible advances in prolonging life, many of the procedures simply sustain life without regard to its quality. Many terminally ill or elderly patients, wishing to die with dignity, feel that they have a basic right to refuse treatment and end their own lives. The ethical and legal considerations are complex.

ner, particularly if they suffer from a terminal illness or a severely incapacitating illness that would cause misery for their families and friends. Such was the case with Mrs. Jenny Williams (described at the beginning of this chapter), who chose death over life.

As a part of our remarkably successful efforts to prolong life, we have begun also to prolong dying. And this has caused many elderly people to fear the medical decision maker who is intent only on keeping them alive, giving no thought to their desires or dignity. They, and many others, find it abhorrent to impose on a dying patient a horrifying array

of respirators, breathing tubes, feeding tubes, and repeated violent cardiopulmonary resuscitations—procedures that are often futile *and* counter to the wishes of the patient and his or her family. Humane and sensitive physicians, who believe that the resulting quality of life does not merit such heroic measures, but whose training impels them to sustain life, are caught in the middle of this conflict. There is also the danger of a civil or criminal lawsuit being brought against the physician who agrees to allow a patient to die.

More and more people now hold the view that individuals ought to have the right to end their own lives, at least in certain circumstances. In cases of obvious terminal illness, when the patient has a short time to live and is suffering unbearable pain, the right-to-die argument seems to make sense. In 1976 the California State Assembly became one of the first state legislatures to provide that right to individuals in such situations. Since then, fifteen states have passed "living will" laws that offer protection against dehumanized dying and confer immunity on physicians and hospital personnel who comply with a patient's wishes.

Advocates of such laws frequently use the terms *quality of life* and *quality of humanness* as the criteria for deciding between life and death. The meanings of these phrases are, however, somewhat indistinct and subjective. At what point do we consider the quality of life sufficiently poor to justify terminating it? Should people who have been severely injured or scarred (through, say, the loss of limbs, paralysis, blindness, or brain injury) be allowed to end their own lives? What about mentally retarded or emotionally disturbed individuals? It can be argued that their quality of life is equally poor. Moreover, who is to decide that a person is or is not terminally ill? There are many recorded cases of "incurable" patients who recovered when new medical techniques arrested, remitted, or cured their illnesses. Such questions cannot be answered easily because they deal with ethics and human values.

Yet the mental health practitioner cannot avoid these questions. Like their medical counterparts, clinicians are trained to save people's lives. They have accepted the philosophical assumption that life is better than death, and that no one has a right to take his or her own life. Strong social, religious, and legal sanctions support this belief. Therapists work not only with terminally ill clients who wish to take their own lives but also with disturbed clients who may have suicidal tendencies. These clients are not terminally ill but may be

suffering severe emotional or physical pain; their deaths would bring immense pain and suffering to their loved ones. Moreover, most individuals who attempt suicide do not want to die, are ambivalent about the act, or find that their suicidal urge passes when their life situation improves (Murphy 1973).

In working with clients who express suicidal wishes, the practicing therapist must confront the following questions (Corey et al. 1984).

1. Do therapists have a right and responsibility to forcefully protect people from the potential harm that their own decisions may bring?
2. Do therapists have an ethical right to prevent clients from carrying out a suicide when they have clearly chosen death over life?
3. What ethical and legal considerations are involved in right-to-die decisions?
4. Once a therapist determines that a significant risk exists, must some course of action be taken? What are the consequences when a therapist fails to take steps to prevent a suicide?

Of course, these questions would be answered differently by different individuals. We can, however, directly address one of the issues they raise—the legal implications. According to one observer, there is no clear constitutional or legal statement that gives a person the right to choose death. But the Constitution does appear to provide a basis for the right to refuse treatment, even life-saving treatment (Powell 1982). Therapists, however, have a responsibility to prevent suicide if they can reasonably anticipate the possibility of self-destruction. Failure to do so can result in legal liability (Shultz 1982).

Clearly, suicide and suicide prevention involve a number of important social and legal issues, as well as the personal value systems of clients and their families, mental health professionals, and those who devise and enforce our laws. And just as clearly, we need to know much more about the causes of suicide and the detection of high-suicide-risk individuals, as well as the most effective means of intervention. Life is precious, and we need to do everything possible, within reason, to protect it.

SUMMARY

1. Strong social, legal, and religious sanctions against suicide are evidence that this tragic and puzzling act is abhorrent to our society. Although depression is highly correlated with suicidal acts, the complex relationship between depression and suicide is not simply one of cause and effect.

2. Early explanations of suicide were based on either a sociological or an intrapsychic view. Durkheim identified three categories of suicide on the basis of the nature of the individual's relationship to a group: Egoistic suicide results from an inability to integrate oneself with society; altruistic suicide is motivated by the need to further the goals of the group or to achieve a "higher good"; and anomic suicide results when a person's relationship to the group becomes unbalanced in some dramatic fashion. In the psychoanalytic view, self-destruction results when hostility toward another person turns inward. More recent evidence indicates that biochemistry may be involved, but no single explanation seems sufficient to clarify the many facets of suicide.

3. In recent years, childhood and adolescent suicides have increased at an alarming rate. A lack of research has limited our understanding of why children take their own lives. However, the available studies indicate that those who attempt suicide come from families characterized by psychiatric illness (primarily drug and alcohol abuse), suicide, paternal unemployment, and the absence of one parent. Most childhood suicide attempts occur in the home, and drug overdose is the primary means.

4. Suicide among college students is particularly perplexing. Studies indicate that students who commit suicide can be distinguished from their nonsuicidal classmates: They are older and more likely to be postgraduate students, male, language or literature majors, and foreign students. As undergraduates, they have better academic records than their peers. Most college-student suicides occur at the beginning of a semester. They may be related to unrealistically high internal expectations, excessive pressures to excel from family and friends, or simply emotional disturbance.

5. Many individuals tend to become depressed about "feeling old" as they age. And with depression there are often thoughts of suicide among the elderly. Suicide rates seem to be highest among first-generation elderly Americans.

6. Suicide affects not only the person who commits the act but the survivors as well. Loved ones who are left behind frequently respond with denial and shock, followed by grief and anger. The anger may be directed toward the self, but it is usually meant for the person who commits the act. The survivor's grief is resolved if and when he or she is able to "let go" of the deceased.

7. Perhaps the best way to prevent suicide is to recognize its signs and intervene before it occurs. People are more likely to commit suicide if they are older, male, have a history of attempts, describe in detail how the act will be accomplished, and give verbal hints about self-destruction. Suicide prevention centers operate 24 hours a day to provide intervention services to all potential suicides. Telephone hotlines are staffed by well-trained professionals who will work with anyone contemplating suicide. In addition, these centers provide preventive education to the public. There is no evidence, however, that they are effective in lowering suicide rates.

8. The act of suicide raises moral, ethical, and legal concerns. Do people have a right to take their own lives? This is a difficult question to answer in the case of the elderly or of people who are terminally ill and wish to end their suffering. Nevertheless therapists, like physicians, have been trained to preserve life, and they have a legal obligation to do so.

anomic suicide Suicide that results from a maladaptive relation to society

egoistic suicide Suicide that results from an inability to integrate oneself with society

psychological autopsy A systematic examination of existing information in order to understand and explain the behavior exhibited by an individual prior to his or her death

KEY TERMS

altruistic suicide Suicide that is motivated by the need to further group goals or to achieve some greater good

15
Schizophrenia: Symptoms and Diagnosis

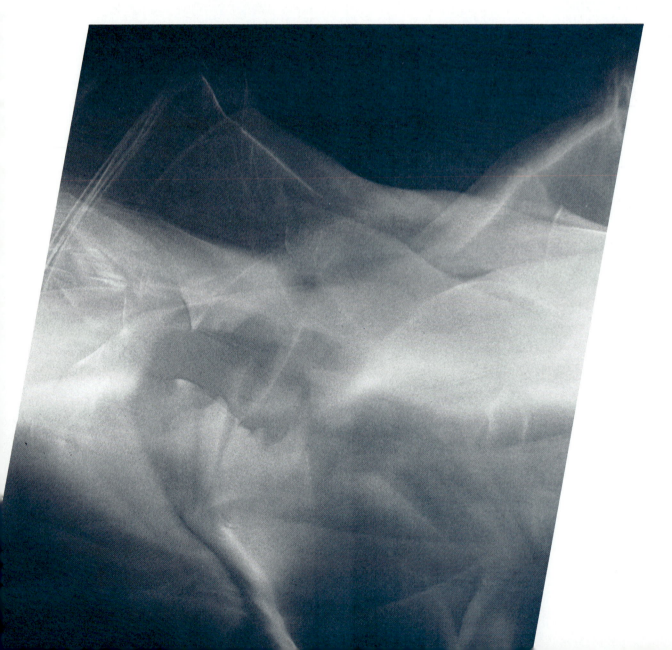

David Zelt is the pseudonym of a scientist who suffered a schizophrenic episode following three traumatic events—the death of a parent, the end of an important personal relationship, and a change of career. Zelt wrote an account of his "growing retreat from mundane reality" in the third person, to "convey a sense of my psychological distance from the experience" (Zelt 1981). His account began immediately after he had presented a scientific paper at a conference on human psychology.

Each speaker focused on David. By using allusions and nonverbal communication that included pointing and glancing, each illustrated different aspects of David's contribution. . . . Extraordinary powers of perception, a gift for telepathy, and the intellectual prowess of an Einstein were mentioned. . . . He was compared to a lion—courageous, regal, and wholesome; or a bird that could soar high like an eagle—extremely intuitive. He felt glorified.

David's sensitivity to nonverbal communication was extreme; he was adept at reading people's minds. His perceptual powers were so developed that he could not discriminate between telepathic reception and spoken language by others. He was distracted by others in a way that he had never been before. It was as if the nonverbal behavior of people interacting with him was a kind of code. Facial expressions, gestures, and postures of others often determined what he felt and thought.

During the next few weeks, David came to believe that he was the reborn figure of Jesus Christ. . . .

David began to suspect and then perceive that a federal agency was observing him. . . . Wondering whether the Federal Bureau of Investigation was observing him, David decided to employ his telepathic powers to find out. An agent at a local agency told him there was no investigation. David read the agent's mind, however, and determined that the Central Intelligence Agency was conducting an investigation.

It dawned upon David that the CIA was listening to most of his thoughts wherever he went,

425

even sometimes during sleep. . . . His thoughts in words gave rise to subvocal movements that produced specific patterns of sounds during breathing; the patterns were immediately picked up and deciphered by hidden CIA electronic equipment. . . . The CIA tormented David by playing his thoughts aloud and also by making comments and criticisms about his thoughts. . . . Because his thoughts were broadcast around him, David often felt that his consciousness was controlled from outside himself and that he had merged with the external environment. . . .

The television and radio stations used electrical signals and verbal messages to convey their attitudes about David. The electrical signals, such as a flicker on the television set or a burst of static on the radio, meant that the immediately preceding remarks referred to David. . . . [NBC] often designated David as Jesus Christ. CBS usually described David as having schizophrenia. ABC expressed mixed feelings; either David was divine or ill. . . . The degree of attention was so painful that David tried to avoid contact with any media. (Zelt 1981, pp. 528–529)

Even these few excerpts from Zelt's account illustrate many features of the schizophrenic disorders, which have been called disorders of thought or cognition. More specifically, **cognition** consists of the processes of thinking, perceiving, judging, and recognizing. And **schizophrenia** is a group of disorders that are characterized by severe impairment of cognitive processes, personality disintegration, and social withdrawal. The schizophrenic disorders are severe disturbances (psychoses) that always involve some disruption of thought processes. Affected individuals may lose contact with reality, may see or hear things that are not actually occurring, or may develop false beliefs about themselves or others.

Schizophrenia has received—and continues to receive—a great deal of attention, for several reasons. First, because the disorders are severely disabling, they frequently necessitate hospitalization. The financial costs of hospitalization and the psychological costs to patients, families, and friends can become enormous. Second, the lifetime prevalence rate of

schizophrenia in the United States is nearly 1 percent, so it affects millions of people directly (it occurs equally among males and females). And third, the causes of the disorders are not well known, and it has been difficult to find effective treatments. In fact, the various schizophrenic disorders may have different etiologies (Bleuler 1984; DSM-III). This possibility may account for the fact that research results concerning these disorders are often in conflict. At any rate, after a period during which more and more was learned about the disorders, our understanding of schizophrenia has now "reached a plateau" (Zubin and Ludwig 1983).

In this chapter we discuss the symptoms of schizophrenia, the different types of schizophrenic disorders, and some of the problems involved in diagnosing them. Then, in Chapter 16, we shall be concerned with the etiology and treatment of these disorders.

THE SYMPTOMS OF SCHIZOPHRENIA

Schizophrenic disorders are characterized primarily by impaired or disordered thinking. This may be accompanied by disturbances of perception, psychomotor behavior, and affect (mood and emotion). Each of these general categories of symptoms may be represented in a variety of specific symptoms. The most common of these are listed in Focus 15.1 (p. 428), where some related diagnostic problems are also discussed.

Thought disturbances

According to the World Health Organization study cited in Focus 15.1, the most common symptom of schizophrenia is *lack of insight;* during the active phase of their disorder, schizophrenics are unable to recognize that their thinking is disturbed. In the case of David Zelt, for instance, one of his therapists

Untitled (pencil, watercolor, and crayon), August Klett (pseudonym, Klotz)

The paintings, etchings, sketches, and sculpture pictured in this chapter are from the Prinzhorn Collection. Hans Prinzhorn (1886-1933) was a German psychiatrist who also had a degree in art history. During his career he collected about 5,000 pieces of art produced by inmates of psychiatric institutions in Germany, Austria, Switzerland, Italy, and Holland. Although trained in psychoanalysis, Prinzhorn refrained from interpreting the symbolism in the artwork. Instead, he focused on the shape and form of the art.

The artists were mentally ill patients, with no formal artistic training, who lived during the late 1800s to early 1900s. They were most often diagnosed as schizophrenic and did not express themselves artistically until after the onset of their illness. A remarkable aspect of this art is that it was produced spontaneously, not as part of a therapy program, by people who were living in socially isolated, unstimulating environments (von Baeyer 1972).

noted that "it was impressive to me to find someone with an exhaustive intellectual knowledge about psychosis and still unable to bring his critical faculties to bear upon the onslaught of ideation" (Zelt 1981, p. 531).

The disordered thinking of schizophrenics may be exhibited in delusions and in the inappropriate and bizarre use of language. A

delusion is a false belief that is firmly and consistently held despite disconfirming evidence or logic. Zelt, for example, believed that he was Jesus Christ and that the CIA was involved in an elaborate plot to discredit him. (Before his breakdown, he had never been deeply religious, nor had he ever felt harassed by the CIA.) Although there is almost no limit

Symptoms of Schizophrenia

The World Health Organization conducted a large-scale diagnostic study of schizophrenia to determine its characteristics. Patients from the United States, England, the Soviet Union, China, India, Denmark, Czechoslovakia, Colombia, and Nigeria were included in this *International Pilot Study of Schizophrenia* (WHO 1973, 1981). The following symptoms were reported in 50 percent or more of schizophrenic individuals:

Symptom	Percentage of schizophrenics
Lack of insight	97
Auditory hallucinations	74
Verbal hallucinations	70
Ideas of reference	70
Suspiciousness	66
Flat affect	66
Voices speaking to patient	65
Delusional mood	64
Delusions of persecution	64
Inadequate description of problem	64
Thought alienation	52
Thoughts spoken aloud	50

These are the symptoms most frequently seen in schizophrenics. For two reasons, however, they are not sufficient to ensure the accurate diagnosis of schizophrenia. First, many of these symptoms also occur in other disorders. Delusions, hallucinations, and lack of insight, for example, may be exhibited by patients with major affective disorders (Harrow et al. 1982; Carpenter et al. 1973). Second, some of the most frequently observed symptoms, including lack of insight and flat affect, are defined in different ways by different clinicians, so that the symptoms themselves have low reliability in pinpointing schizophrenia.

What is needed for accurate diagnosis is a set of symptoms that are specific to schizophrenia. Unfortunately, these might not be the most common symptoms. An example is neologisms, or made-up words; their appearance in the speech of a patient almost guarantees a diagnosis of schizophrenia in any country in the world (Kaplan and Sadock 1981). However, they are a fairly rare symptom. Of the common symptoms, those that are the most discriminant—and therefore the most helpful in diagnosing schizophrenia—are auditory hallucinations, voices speaking to the patient, thought alienation, thoughts spoken aloud, and delusions of control.

---

to the subject matter of delusions, they tend to be of several types:

☐ *Delusions of grandeur*. A belief that one is a famous or powerful person. Schizophrenics may assume the identities of these other persons, living or dead.

☐ *Delusions of bodily disintegration*. A belief that one's body is rotting away—for example, that one's vital organs are dissolving and turning to water.

☐ *Delusions of control*. A belief that other persons, animals, or objects are trying to influence or take control of one.

☐ *Delusions of nothingness*. A belief that nothing really exists. Everything is unreal.

☐ *Delusions of persecution*. A belief that others are plotting against, mistreating, or even trying to kill one.

☐ *Delusions of reference*. A belief that one is always the center of attention, or that all happenings revolve about oneself. Others are always whispering behind one's back, for example.

☐ *Delusions of sin.* A belief that one has committed some great wrong or sin that can never be forgiven.

Delusions may be centered on the schizophrenic's own thoughts. For example, *thought broadcasting* is the belief that one's thoughts are being disseminated to the entire world—a belief that was held by David Zelt. *Thought insertion* is the belief that thoughts are being placed in one's head by others. And, conversely, *thought withdrawal* is the belief that one's thoughts are being removed from one's mind by others.

The strength with which delusions are held varies from individual to individual and within a single individual. In a study of fifty-two delusional patients, researchers identified four dimensions of delusions (Kendler, Lager, and Morgenstern 1983).

The *conviction* of a delusion is the degree to which the individual is convinced of the delusion. In the study, a 48-year-old woman who was concerned about infecting others with a disease sometimes indicated that her concern could be due to her imagination. At the other extreme, a man who claimed to be in communication with aliens responded "Absolutely not!" to the suggestion that his imagination was involved.

The *extension* of a delusion is the degree to which it involves other individuals. One 42-year-old woman complained about being poisoned by her boss, who was using radioactivity near her desk at work; this delusion involved only her boss and had effect only while she was at work. In another case, a 22-year-old man felt persecuted by friends and strangers alike.

Disorganization involves the degree of internal consistency of the delusional system. One 48-year-old man indicated that a committee made up of members of his law school class persecuted him "because they are jealous of my great legal mind." The persecution involved the hiring of actors by the committee to jeer and insult him. Cameras and monitors were placed in his apartment so that the com-

Universe Inversion (crayon), Joseph Schneller (pseudonym, Joseph Sell)

mittee could alert the actors whenever he left his home. In a case exhibiting high disorganization, a 24-year-old woman claimed that her parents had leukemia, that people were being killed, and that she was being poisoned and turned into a lesbian. She made no attempt to relate these delusional concepts.

The *pressure* of a delusion is the degree to which the individual is preoccupied with the belief. A 28-year-old woman was convinced she was the Virgin Mary; when asked how often she thought of herself in that way, she replied, "Oh, it comes to me now and then." On the other hand, great preoccupation was demonstrated by a 56-year-old man who was convinced that he was a government double agent. He spent all his waking hours trying to recall how and when he first became involved.

Thought disturbances are also exhibited in unusual patterns of speech or writing. The **loosening of associations,** or *cognitive slippage,* is the continual shifting of thoughts from topic to topic without any apparent logical or meaningful connection among topics. It may be evidenced in incoherent speech and bizarre and idiosyncratic responses. In addition, communication may show overgeneralization or vagueness, or may be overly concrete (as opposed to abstract). Some of these characteristics are illustrated in the following patient responses to test questions:

> Q: Why does a train have an engine?
> A. To give it a fantasy of imagination that requires it useless until you produce it.
> Q: [What is meant by] "One swallow doesn't make a summer"?
> A: That's oriental. When the first bird in the summer swallows the first worm, then she can start to produce eggs. Which do you think came first, the chicken or the egg? I think the egg, definitely. And it was fertilized with the sperm, so the sperm came first, too. Which came first, though, the egg or the sperm? (Harrow et al. 1982, p. 666)

As noted in Focus 15.1, the speech of some schizophrenics contains **neologisms,** which are new words that are typically formed by combining words in common usage. One psychologist asked a patient, "How do you feel today?" The patient responded,

> Yes, sir, it's a good day. Full of rainbows you know. They go along on their merry way without concern for asphyxiation or impurities. Yes sir, like unconcerned flappers of the cosmoblue.

The patient's "cosmoblue" is a neologism, a combination of "cosmos" and "blue," the color of the sky. The response is also *tangential;* rather than answering the question directly, it seems to ramble through a series of asides.

Problems with attention

Schizophrenics experience difficulty in directing their attention to a particular aspect of their environment and in keeping their attention focused on a particular thing. In other words, they find it difficult to concentrate, even for short periods of time: "My mind was so confused I couldn't focus on one thing . . . a hard time concentrating . . . an external stimulus would take my attention off the book" (Freedman and Chapman 1973, p. 50).

Schizophrenics are easily distracted (Wahba et al. 1981). Perhaps as a result of their continual shifting of attention to various distractions, they are unable to organize incoming information. However, antipsychotic medication has been found to increase their ability to screen out distracting stimuli while attending to a task (Oltmanns, Ohayon, and Neale 1978).

Perceptual distortion

Schizophrenics often report **hallucinations,** which are sensory perceptions that are not directly attributable to environmental stimuli. They may claim to see persons or objects, to hear voices, or to smell peculiar odors that are not really present. (Note the distinction between hallucinations and delusions: hallucinations are false sensory experiences, whereas delusions are false intellectual experiences.)

Hallucinations may involve any of the sensory modalities: hearing (*auditory* hallucinations), seeing (*visual* hallucinations), smelling (*olfactory* hallucinations), feeling (*tactile* hallucinations), and tasting (*gustatory* hallucinations). They may sometimes accompany and be related to delusional beliefs. For example, a patient who believes that he or she has committed an unforgivable sin (delusion of sin) may hear imaginary voices (auditory hallucinations) saying that he or she is evil and worthless. Such an individual may become extremely guilt-ridden, distraught, and even suicidal in the attempt to atone for the imagined sin.

Here is a transcript of a telephone call to a crisis clinic. The caller, who was extremely agitated, had obviously experienced an auditory hallucination:

> CALLER: (almost yelling) I can't stand it anymore! I'm going insane! Everywhere I go, people are looking at me and laughing! They pretend not to laugh, but I can hear them. They know what's going on but won't do anything. I tried to call the Soviet Union to tell the Premier, but the operator who answered just laughed at me.
> COUNSELOR: I'm not sure what's going on.
> CALLER: You know what's going on. I have evidence that the country is rotten to the core. They—they have bugged my phone and are watching me with binoculars because I've criticized the government. The police, FBI, and the courts refuse to listen to me. They just laugh. Goddamn rotten government! Goddamn it, Goddamn it (sobbing)! No one wants to do anything about it!
> COUNSELOR: You feel no one is willing to help.
> CALLER: I don't feel; I know, I know. The laughs are always in a high-pitched voice. It's always the same.
> COUNSELOR: I would like to help you.
> CALLER: Then get them to stop laughing at me. It's driving me insane! What was that?
> COUNSELOR: What do you mean?
> CALLER: You laughed! I heard you, you laughed! (Hangs up the phone.)

The caller appears to be suffering a delusion of persecution. Ironically, his belief that other people are laughing at him may have had some basis in reality. It is easy to imagine the caller's eliciting laughter from others because of his agitated condition and claims of persecution.

Untitled sculpture (wood) (top) and *The Church* (painted wood) (bottom), Carl Genzel (pseudonym, Karl Brendel)

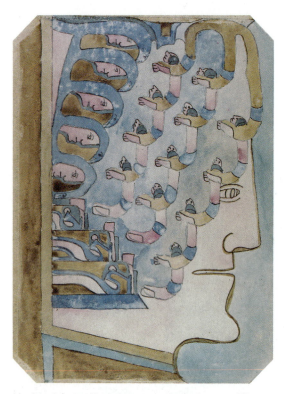

Untitled (pencil and watercolor), August Klett

able from reality (Larkin 1979). This may be true with regard to delusions as well (Sacks, Carpenter, and Strauss 1974). However, as Focus 15.2 suggests, some schizophrenic individuals may be able to break into the process by which hallucinations or delusions are developed and to actually ward them off.

Motoric disturbances

The symptoms of schizophrenia that involve motor functions can be quite bizarre. They may be exhibited as extreme activity levels (either unusually high or unusually low), peculiar body movements or postures, strange gestures and grimaces, or a combination of these. Like hallucinations, a patient's motoric behaviors may be related to his or her delusions. For example, during a clinical interview one schizophrenic patient kept lowering his chin to his chest at periodic intervals and then raising his head again. When asked why he lowered his head in that way, the patient replied that the atmospheric pressure often became too great to bear, and it forced his head down.

Individuals displaying extremely high levels of motor activity may move about quickly, swing their arms wildly, talk rapidly and unendingly, or walk constantly. At the other extreme, some patients may hardly move at all, staring out into space (or perhaps into themselves) for prolonged periods of time. The patients who exhibit low activity levels also tend to show little interest in others, to respond only minimally, and to have few friends. During periods of withdrawal they are frequently preoccupied with personal fantasies and daydreams.

The assumption and maintenance of an unusual (and often awkward) body position is characteristic of the *catatonic* type of schizophrenia (to be discussed shortly). A catatonic patient may stand for hours at a time, perhaps with one arm stretched out to the side. Or the patient may lie on the floor or sit awkwardly on a chair, staring, aware of what is going on all around, but not responding or moving. If a

However, his belief that the laughs are all in the same high-pitched voice and his unjustified accusation of the counselor indicate that at least some of the laughter he heard was hallucinatory.

As this case illustrates, delusions and hallucinations can be extremely distressing to schizophrenics as they respond to their internal realities. But are these disturbances recognized as such by the patients themselves? One college student who suffered auditory hallucinations involving messages from radio and television programs asked, "How can I tell when the radio is really on and when it is my imagination?" This question obviously reflects an attempt to discriminate between reality and hallucinations.

During acute stages (when the symptoms are most prominent), the individual may be so involved in hallucinations that he or she cannot do anything but respond as though they were real, whether or not they are distinguish-

Can Schizophrenics Control Their Symptoms?

A 24-year-old male, diagnosed as paranoid schizophrenic, reported that he could sometimes stop or diminish both auditory hallucinations and the belief that he was being persecuted. Two researchers became intrigued by his report and began a study of twenty psychiatric patients, to determine whether and how patients could control their symptoms (Breier and Strauss 1983). Specifically, they attempted to find out whether self-control methods are used by patients, the types of methods employed, and why some patients are unsuccessful in utilizing these methods. They found that the majority of the patients (seventeen) did try to control their symptoms. The most important factor for these patients seemed to be to identify the feelings and thoughts that occurred prior to a psychotic episode. One man, for example, learned to be alert to a ''high'' sensation. If he took no action in response to that feeling, it evolved into psychotic symptoms.

Three general approaches were used by the patients to control their hallucinations or delusions. The first involved self-instruction. One woman would tell herself to ''act like an adult'' and to ''be responsible.'' Others would actively compare their behavior with that of people nearby or get feedback from such people about their perceptions. The second approach involved a reduction of activity when the symptoms began to appear. One woman found that she could reduce the severity of her symptoms by isolating herself in the bathroom. Others would stop what they were doing and take a walk or simply relax. The third approach involved an increase in activity. For example, one patient found that her symptoms would worsen if she remained unoccupied, but she could reduce their severity by keeping busy.

Interestingly, the three patients who did not use self-control or were unsuccessful with it had failed to identify the thoughts or feelings that preceded their symptoms.

The study illustrates that many psychotic patients are aware of the negative nature of their symptoms and take active steps to regulate their psychopathology. It also appears to be easier for patients to break the chain leading to a psychotic episode earlier rather than later in its development—and that the key may be identification of the antecedents to psychotic behavior. These findings have obvious implications for the treatment of schizophrenia and other thought disorders.

hospital attendant attempts to change the patient's position, the patient may either resist stubbornly or simply assume and maintain the new position.

Affective symptoms

The affective symptoms of schizophrenia are usually manifested as either inappropriate emotions or a lack of emotion. Schizophrenic patients may exhibit wild laughter or uncontrollable weeping that bears little relationship to current circumstances; they may display an ambivalence of feelings and rapid changes of mood that seem to occur for no reason at all. Some are extremely suspicious of everyone and react with anger or rage to all personal encounters, including those that are obviously beneficial in nature.

Schizophrenics may express the wrong emotions or may express them inappropri-

Untitled (crayon), Franz Karl Bühler

ately. For example, one patient was severely depressed about the death of her father. While describing the rather gory automobile accident in which her father was killed, however, the patient frequently smiled and giggled about the fact that her father would no longer have to worry about the family's economic situation.

At the opposite end of the emotional spectrum, some schizophrenics may show little or no emotion in situations where one would expect strong reactions. A delusional patient, for instance, might be explaining in precise detail how portions of his or her body are rotting

away but would show absolutely no concern or worry through either intonation or facial expression. This abnormal lack of emotional response, in which no emotion is expressed by any means, is called **flat affect.**

DSM-III AND THE DIAGNOSIS OF SCHIZOPHRENIA

Peter was quiet and shy from early childhood. On entering kindergarten, he exhibited *separation anxiety:* He would cry and throw a temper tantrum when his mother left him at school. Separation anxiety is quite common among children, but an inordinately long time was required for Peter to interact even minimally with other children. His teacher commented that Peter was compliant but withdrawn.

As the school years went by, some of Peter's teachers indicated that his work was barely adequate, but they noted that at times he was creative and original. This led Peter's mother to tell friends and relatives that he was very bright and that his only problem was shyness. Peter seemed to avoid other children, and he spent a great deal of time daydreaming. When other children teased him, he would become enraged and would scream and cry.

Peter's parents were divorced when he was about nine years old. They had quarreled frequently, and Peter's mother had constantly derogated her husband, accusing him of laziness and of "not making much of himself." Peter adopted his mother's view of his father.

When Peter was ten, his mother began to notice unusual behaviors on his part. For example, he would often walk to a neighbor's house when no one was home and abuse the neighbor's dog, which was chained outside the house. Another neighbor, who saw Peter harassing the dog, complained to his mother. Peter admitted to teasing the dog on several occasions and agreed to stop; his mother thought this was simply a case of a very sensitive and unusual child playing "childhood pranks."

By the time he got to high school, Peter was becoming increasingly isolated. He did not like school, and his grades were barely passing. Telling his mother that other students were "stupid,'' Peter would often avoid going to school with the excuse that he felt sick. Although his mother was concerned, she was spending less and less time at home with Peter because of her job and her social life. Peter seemed content to stay in his room.

One day his mother was contacted by a teacher who indicated that Peter was not adjusting well in class. He said that, whenever Peter became frustrated or felt that he was under pressure, he would speak in a way no one could understand. This unusual behavior was becoming more frequent, and the teacher believed that Peter should receive some treatment. As a result of the discussion, his mother took Peter to a psychiatric clinic, where a psychiatrist recommended long-term psychotherapy. Two months later, however, therapy was discontinued because Peter's mother took a more lucrative job in another city. Peter did manage to graduate from high school but was unable to find steady employment because of his inclination to stay away from people.

At age twenty-three, Peter tried to join the army but was rejected for ''psychiatric reasons.'' He told his mother that some of his former schoolmates had secretly written to the army and had sabotaged his efforts to enlist. He knew this was the case because the army recruitment officers were aware of some information that only his schoolmates had known. Peter then contacted the FBI and the CIA to alert them to this ''plot.'' When his mother expressed the opinion that he was probably mistaken, Peter became extremely upset. He revealed that he had known for many months that others were out to get him, that he heard a real voice from within his head warning him of these dangers, and that his enemies would be destroyed. Alarmed, his mother persuaded Peter to go with her to a community mental health center. There he was diagnosed as paranoid schizophrenic.

According to the DSM-III criteria, a diagnosis of schizophrenic disorder should be given only if delusions, auditory hallucinations, or marked disturbances in thinking or speech are exhibited. Furthermore, the patient must have displayed a deterioration from a previous level of functioning with regard to work, interpersonal relationships, self-care, or the like.

Church Light (watercolor), Konrad Zeuner

There should be evidence that the disorder has lasted at least six months at some time in the patient's history and has currently been present for at least two weeks. Organic mental disorders and affective disorders must have been ruled out as causes of the patient's symptoms, and the major symptoms must have appeared before age forty-five.

The actual DSM-III criteria are somewhat more precise and much more extensive than our brief summary, so that the diagnosis of schizophrenia would appear to be rather straightforward. Yet there is disagreement over the effectiveness of the criteria and the inclusion of some symptoms among them. Recall from Chapter 4 the Rosenhan (1973) study in which eight pseudopatients gained admission to psychiatric hospitals. The eight experimenters all reported auditory hallucinations (a voice saying "empty," "hollow," or "thud") that had occurred for a period of three weeks. Except for their names, vocations, and occupations, all the other information they provided to the hospital staff was true. All but one received a diagnosis of schizophrenia, and that one was labeled manic–depressive; all were admitted for treatment.

DSM-III had not been published at the time of the Rosenhan study, so the pseudopatients were diagnosed according to DSM-II or some other classification scheme. The obvious question is "Would these individuals have been diagnosed as schizophrenic under the DSM-III criteria?" The answer is "No," provided that the criteria were followed strictly. Among the requirements that would not have been fulfilled are those calling for deterioration from a previous level of functioning and symptoms with a duration of six months or more. In addition, DSM-III requires that auditory hallucinations involve "more than one or two words." Actually, it appears that the symptoms reported by Rosenhan's pseudopatients do not fully meet the criteria for any of the psychotic disorders. (However, it would have been the duty of any clinician to admit the pseudopatients, for further observation, on the basis of their claims that they heard voices.)

The DSM-III criteria for diagnosing schizophrenia are more restrictive than those of DSM-II and will probably lead to greater diagnostic reliability and validity. One clinician who is wholeheartedly in support of the change wrote, "Thanks to DSM-III, we no longer approach schizophrenia as blind men to one huge elephant. . . . It has dissected the monster into one medium-sized animal, i.e., schizophrenia proper, and a pack of pigmy pachyderms" (McGlashon 1982, p. 752). Other investigators (Fenton, Mosher, and Matthews 1981; Morey and Blashfield 1981) note that there are problems in the DSM-III definition of schizophrenia and feel that DSM-III has not been shown to be superior to other

diagnostic systems (Fenton, Mosher, and Matthews 1981; Morey and Blashfield 1981). The new criteria will most assuredly result in fewer diagnoses of schizophrenic disorders. When they were applied to a group of sixty-eight patients who had previously been diagnosed as schizophrenic, approximately half did not meet the new requirements; these patients were instead suffering from affective disorders (Winter, Weintraub, and Neale 1981).

The value of a diagnostic system such as DSM-III stems from its consistent and appropriate use—and it seems that this has yet to come about. In one survey, 301 psychiatrists were asked to "Describe the clinical findings that would lead you to a diagnosis of schizophrenia" (Lipkowitz and Idupuganti 1983). Only 1 respondent listed all 6 findings necessary for such a diagnosis (symptoms, deterioration, onset before age 45, 6 months' duration, and absence of major organic or affective disorder). Of further interest is the fact that 49 percent said they used only *one* of the diagnostic criteria, and some used idiosyncratic criteria that are obviously not listed in DSM-III:

The "smell of schizophrenia"
Patient "doesn't add up"
"Poor ego functions or boundaries"
"Poor eye contact"
"Rapid mood swings"
"Excess religiosity"

The survey results indicate that the DSM-III criteria are not applied at all consistently in the diagnosis of schizophrenia and that many psychiatrists still use subjective criteria. A hopeful note was the finding that younger psychiatrists tended to use diagnostic criteria that were closer to those of DSM-III.

TYPES OF SCHIZOPHRENIA

DSM-III recognizes five types of schizophrenic disorders: disorganized, catatonic, paranoid, undifferentiated, and residual. Clinicians have generally had trouble using earlier diagnostic schemes to distinguish among these types (Garfield 1974). However, the authors of DSM-III have attempted to provide additional criteria and to specify them more precisely. The reliability and validity of these newer criteria have yet to be fully tested.

Disorganized schizophrenia

Disorganized schizophrenia is characterized by severe disintegration and regressive behaviors beginning at an early age. The diagnostic criteria include frequent incoherence of speech, the absence of systematized delusions (delusions are fragmented or disorganized instead), and inappropriate affect (DSM-III). Individuals with this disorder act in an absurd, incoherent, or very odd manner that conforms to the stereotype of ''crazy'' behavior. Their emotional responses to real-life situations are typically flat, but a silly smile and childish giggle may be exhibited at inappropriate times. The hallucinations and delusions of disorganized schizophrenics tend to shift from theme to theme rather than remaining centered on a single idea, such as persecution or sin. Because of the severity of the disorder, many affected individuals are unable to care for themselves and are institutionalized.

Disorganized schizophrenics usually exhibit extremely bizarre and seemingly childish behaviors, such as masturbating in public or fantasizing out loud. An example appears in the following excerpt from a clinical interview with a young adult female.

> DOCTOR: Do you know why your mother brought you to this clinic?
> PATIENT: Well, Mom started yelling at me. She gets too excited about things. People are so excited nowadays. You know what I mean?
> DOCTOR: What did she yell at you about?
> PATIENT: Just because I smeared some shit on a painting I was doing for school (silly giggle). See, the teacher in art class wanted us to do some finger painting at home. She said that we should be creative. I ran out of paint so I thought

Untitled (pencil and crayon), Johann Knopf (pseudonym, Knüpfer)

> I would use some of my shit. After all, it is natural (giggle) and it feels like paint.

Catatonic schizophrenia

Disturbance in motor activity—either extreme excitement or extreme withdrawal—is the prime characteristic of **catatonic schizophrenia.** This disorder is quite rare nowadays.

Excited catatonics exhibit great agitation and hyperactivity. Individuals with this form of the disorder may talk and shout constantly, while at the same time moving or running until they drop from exhaustion. They sleep little and are continually ''on the go.'' Their behavior can become dangerous, however, and acts of violence are not uncommon. *Withdrawn catatonics* exhibit extreme unresponsiveness with respect to motor activity. Such individuals show prolonged periods of stupor and mutism, despite their awareness of all that is going on around them. Some adopt and maintain

Untitled (pencil on cardboard), Berthold L. (or L. Berthold)

strange postures and refuse to move or change position. Others exhibit a *waxy flexibility,* allowing themselves to be "arranged" in almost any position and then remaining in that position for long periods of time. During periods of extreme withdrawal, catatonic schizophrenics may fail to eat or pay attention to bladder or bowel control.

Catatonics may alternate between excited motor activity and withdrawal, as is illustrated in the following case:

A 43-year-old man was admitted to a hospital after his wife became alarmed over his complete inactivity. He had been unemployed for the last 2 months but had become progressively more uncommunicative over a period of some 8 months. A few days before, he had stoped talk-

ing altogether, and he now sat in his chair all day with his eyes closed. His wife thought that he might be sick, but a physical examination failed to reveal any disease or physical difficulties. While he was in the hospital, he did open his eyes and talk for brief periods of time, although it was difficult to understand what he was trying to say. After about a week in the hospital, a nurse reported that the patient had gotten out of bed and was standing in the hospital's recreation room, giving what appeared to be a lecture to other patients. The ward psychiatrist immediately asked the nurse to bring the patient to his office, where the following conversation took place.

PATIENT: You wanted to see me, Doctor?

DOCTOR: Yes. You know you hardly said anything for the past week and now the nurse indicates that you are interacting with other patients.

PATIENT: This past week, Doctor, I've been thinking and meditating.

DOCTOR: About what?

PATIENT: You see, Doctor, the patient next door always has his television set on. I've been carefully listening to the kinds of programs on television—the walls in the hospital are thin. I am appalled at the continual outpouring of filth, decadence, sin, immorality, sex, violence. My God! People are so numbed by the stuff that they don't realize the kind of brainwashing that goes on. No wonder we are a sick society. I have decided to counter this trend by informing others of the filth, but it is almost impossible for them to comprehend. If the hospital staff and patients fail to understand, I may start Phase Two of my efforts by breaking the television sets in this hospital!

A few days later the patient attempted to smash the television set in the next room but was restrained by several ward attendants.

Paranoid schizophrenia

One of the most common forms of schizophrenia is the paranoid type. **Paranoid schizophrenia** is characterized by persistent and *systematized* delusions that are illogical or contradictory. Delusions of persecution are the most common. The deluded individuals

Capgras's Syndrome

A rather rare delusion that has most often been reported in individuals diagnosed as paranoid schizophrenics is *Capgras's syndrome,* named after the person who first reported it. This is a belief in the existence of identical "doubles," who may coexist with or replace significant others or the patients themselves. Individuals with this delusion generally accuse close friends or relatives of being doubles; however, in the case reported by Capgras (a 53-year-old woman), the delusion also involved a whole range of other persons in the community. One individual even claimed that his dog had been replaced by a double.

A patient treated by Berson (1983) believed that her relatives had been killed and replaced. She also claimed to have two doubles of herself—one who was being groomed for the presidency and another who was engaged in sadistic sexual acts. Later she asserted that Berson himself was a double.

believe that others are plotting against them, are talking about them, or are out to harm them in some way. They are constantly suspicious, and their interpretations of the behavior and motives of others are distorted: A friendly, smiling bus driver is seen as someone who is laughing at them derisively; a busy clerk who fails to offer help is part of a plot to mistreat them; a telephone call that was a wrong number is an act of harassment or an attempt to monitor their comings and goings.

Another common delusion among paranoid schizophrenics involves exaggerated grandiosity and self-importance. Individuals with such delusions of grandeur may assume the identities of famous people, living or dead, and genuinely believe in their own great power or fame (see Figure 15.1, p. 440). A less common delusion is described in Focus 15.3.

The diagnostic category *paranoid schizophrenia* is subject to controversy because of uncertainty about which group or groups of delusional patients should be included in it (Torrey 1981). This problem is acknowledged in DSM-III: "The boundaries of this group of disorders [the paranoid disorders] and their differentiation from such other disorders as severe Paranoid Personality Disorder and Schizophrenia, Paranoid Type are unclear"

(p. 195). (The **paranoid disorders** are psychoses that are characterized by delusions of persecution or delusional jealousy.) Individuals with these three types of disorders share several characteristics, including suspiciousness, hypersensitivity, and argumentativeness. They have little or no sense of humor, and their interpersonal relationships tend to be formal and stilted. Table 15.1 (p. 441) lists other major characteristics of these disorders.

It is possible that the three disorders with paranoid features are related to one another, so that a person with paranoid personality disorder may be predisposed to develop the other, more severe, paranoid disorders. But there are some differences among the three. Delusions and hallucinations are not present in paranoid personality disorder. And the paranoid disorders are distinguished from paranoid schizophrenia by the absence of consequential hallucinations, incoherence, loosening of associations, and deterioration of functioning. These differences may not, however, be sufficient for differential diagnosis. In fact, it has been suggested that paranoid schizophrenia be considered a subtype of the paranoid disorders rather than the schizophrenic disorders (Magaro 1981). It will be possible to assess the effectiveness of the DSM-III

Figure 15.1   "Please Come Thursday"

A letter from a schizophrenic college student who has delusions of grandeur.

Dear Pete:

Remember how I reluctantly entered the hospital in order to prove to the World that I am sane and have superior intellect? I just wanted to report to you that I do have the shrinks baffled. Last night I took psychological tests and, needless to say, I was astounding. Superior intellect, increased sensitivity, total awareness, extreme creativity — like a god suspended above the masses. Poor souls, poor creatures below.

Be sure to come visit me soon. I'll show you how to hustle girls. Wow, have I turned on the nurses here. In fact, Thursday I'm scheduled to have an interview with this social worker (I wouldn't be interested unless she was good looking, of course). If you can come Thursday at 11, I'll tell her that I would like you to sit in on the interview. For your benefit, I'll start turning her on. Yesterday, when I talked with her briefly, I almost had her fondling me! Last week, when I entered the hospital, I noticed that the nurses here would eye me. One in particular even walked past me with her uniform partly unbuttoned! They all act formal but I get different vibes. They want it from me. Man, what a life.

There's this one old hag of a nurse who just sits in the nurses station looking at patients. She thinks she has everyone psyched out. Remember how I can outstare everyone? I just started looking back at her for about 10 minutes. She had to turn away and then pretended to read papers. If she hadn't, I could have used my mind control and made her sweat. I tell you they can't deal with me. Things here are easier than I thought. I haven't even used .001% of my mental powers.

Please come Thursday. In fact, I insist upon it.

Best, Ralph

Table 15.1 *Comparison of Disorders with Paranoid Features*

Paranoid Personality Disorder	Schizophrenia, Paranoid Type	Paranoid Disorders
A. Pervasive, unwarranted suspiciousness and mistrust	A. At least one of the following: hallucinations, delusions, incoherence, loosening of associations	A. Persistent persecutory delusions or delusional jealousy
B. Easily slighted and ready to counterattack	B. Deterioration from a previous level of functioning	B. Emotions and behavior appropriate to the context of the delusional system
C. Restricted affectivity (cold, humorless)	C. Duration of at least 6 months	C. Duration of at least 1 week
D. No hallucinations or delusions	D. Onset before the age of 45	D. No bizarre delusions, incoherence, or loosening of associations
E. Not due to another mental disorder	E. Not due to an affective disorder or an organic mental disorder	E. No prominent hallucinations
		F. Not due to an affective disorder or an organic mental disorder

SOURCE: DSM-III diagnostic criteria. Used by permission of the American Psychiatric Association.

diagnostic criteria only after they have been used for some time.

Undifferentiated and residual schizophrenia

Undifferentiated schizophrenia is diagnosed when the symptoms are obviously schizophrenic but are mixed or undifferentiated, so that they do not clearly fit into the disorganized, catatonic, or paranoid category. These symptoms may include thought disturbance, delusions, hallucinations, incoherence, and severely impaired behavior. Sometimes the undifferentiated disorder turns out to be an early stage of one of the more specific subtypes.

The diagnosis of **residual schizophrenia** is reserved for individuals who have experienced at least one episode of schizophrenia in the past but are presently exhibiting no *prominent* signs of the disorders (which may be in remission). These individuals may show some schizophrenic symptoms, but the symptoms are neither strong enough nor prominent enough to warrant classification as one of the other types of schizophrenia.

Other psychotic disorders similar to schizophrenia

DSM-III lists two other serious disorders with symptoms similar to those found in schizophrenia. The essential features of *schizophreniform disorders* are similar to those of schizophrenia; however, the duration of the disorder is between two weeks and six months. Recovery to earlier, higher levels of functioning is more likely in this disorder than in schizophrenia. In *brief reactive psychosis,* the psychotic disturbances last at least a few hours but no longer than two weeks, with eventual return to premorbid levels of functioning. The disorder is always caused by an overwhelming stressor. Some differences between these two disorders and schizophrenia are indicated in Table 15.2 (p. 442).

THE COURSE OF SCHIZOPHRENIA

It is popularly believed that overwhelming stress can cause a well-adjusted and relatively normal person to experience a schizophrenic breakdown. There are, in fact, recorded

Table 15.2 *Comparison of Brief Reactive Psychosis, Schizophreniform Disorders, and Schizophrenia*

	Brief Reactive Psychosis	Schizophreniform Disorders	Schizophrenia
Duration	Less than 2 weeks	Less than 6 months but more than 2 weeks	6 months or more
Psychosocial stressor	Always present	Usually present	May or may not be present
Symptoms	Emotional turmoil, psychotic symptoms	Emotional turmoil, vivid hallucinations	Emotional reactions variable; psychotic symptoms
Outcome	Return to premorbid level of functioning	Likely to return to earlier, higher level of functioning	Return to earlier, higher level of functioning is rare
Family members	No information	No increased prevalence of schizophrenia among family members	Higher prevalence of schizophrenia among family members

instances of the sudden onset of schizophrenic behaviors in previously well-functioning persons. However, in most cases the individual's *premorbid personality* (the personality prior to the onset of major symptoms) shows some degree of impairment. Similarly, most schizophrenics exhibit gradual, rather than sudden, recovery. The typical course of schizophrenia consists of three phases: prodromal, active, and residual.

The *prodromal phase* includes the onset and build-up of schizophrenic symptoms. Social withdrawal and isolation, peculiar behaviors, inappropriate affect, poor communication patterns, and neglect of personal grooming may become evident during this phase. Friends and relatives often consider the afflicted individual odd or peculiar.

Often, psychosocial stressors or excessive demands on a person who is in the prodromal phase result in the onset of prominent psychotic symptoms, or the *active phase* of schizophrenia. The person now exhibits the full-blown symptoms of schizophrenia—including severe disturbances in thinking, deterioration in social relationships, and flat or markedly inappropriate affect.

At some later time, the individual may enter the *residual phase,* in which the symptoms are no longer prominent. The severity of the symptoms declines, and the individual may show the milder impairment found in the prodromal phase. (At this point, the diagnosis would be residual schizophrenia.) Complete recovery is rare, although long-term studies show that many schizophrenics can lead relatively productive lives. The subjects in such studies were diagnosed according to criteria that preceded those of DSM-III, so the results should be interpreted carefully. Nonetheless, they do present an optimistic outlook.

For example, Ciompi (1980) conducted a 37-year follow-up of 289 schizophrenic patients and found that the long-term prognosis was favorable in 50 percent of the cases. Only about half had been hospitalized more than once in their lives. Ciompi found that, with advanced age (the average age of the subjects was 75), there was a "pronounced general tendency toward improvement and recovery." In fact, 62 percent of all individual symptoms disappeared with age, and an additional 11 percent showed obvious improvement. More than half the subjects were in good physical condition and were employed either full- or part-time. Although the majority still showed evidence of problems with social relationships or independence, most indicated that they felt peaceful and free of conflicts. The findings prompted Ciompi to conclude that "Quite contrary to the original—and today still popular—concepts of the nature of schizophrenia, a good majority of definitely 'genuine' schizophrenias (from initial diagnoses) may develop favorably in the long run" (p. 611).

Similar results were obtained in a 22-year follow-up of 502 schizophrenic patients (Huber et al. 1980). Of this group, 22 percent had experienced complete remission, 43 percent showed only residual symptoms, and 35 percent remained unimproved; 87 percent lived in their own homes. An interesting finding was that the long-term prognosis is unrelated to the original duration of the disorder and that it is more favorable for women than for men. The increasing number of studies indicating positive long-term outcome for schizophrenia has prompted the comment that there is a "new optimism about this disorder" (Zubin and Ludwig 1983). Unfortunately, this optimism has yet to spread to the general public, as you can see in Focus 15.4.

FOCUS 15.4

Discrimination Against the Mentally Ill

Mental illnesses, especially psychoses such as schizophrenia, are still feared and misunderstood by the public. The discrimination that may result is illustrated by the experiences of a former schizophrenic patient. After he was released from a hospital psychiatric ward, he told his employer about his illness. This marked the beginning of a series of encounters with the general prejudice against former mental patients.

> I was at work only a few days when I was fired but "assured" that I would receive good references. The fact that I had been there for nearly 4 years and [was] a good worker did not matter. (Anonymous 1981, p. 736)

In applying for a new job, he faced additional problems.

> I also noticed that many job applications would inquire about medical and psychological stability. . . . I learned that honesty is not always the best policy. . . . I am considering graduate school, and there too, questions about past and present psychiatric treatment confront me. . . . The admission forms often request a biographical sketch describing how the student became interested in the field and any personal experiences with psychiatry. This, too, obviously is a Catch-22 position. To admit my personal experiences is to court possible and realistic rejection. (I have spoken off the record with an instructor in a well-known school of social work about the situation, and his advice was: "I do not think discussing your hospital experiences would be a plus." [But if] I do not discuss it, I would in a way be compromising my principles. (pp. 736–737)

The former patient blames the media in part.

> Hardly a month goes by that we do not read a lurid news story of "man goes berserk and kills neighbor" or "former mental patient kills wife." . . . The evidence is overwhelming that the majority of mental patients are, as a class, less dangerous than the "average citizen." . . . Psychotherapy and psychotropic drugs have helped thousands of people to continue to go about their daily lives . . . but at times, I am sure they painfully wonder, for what? (p. 737)

Dance (pencil, pen, and watercolor), Gustav Sievers (top) and *Air Apparition* (pencil), August Neter (bottom)

SUMMARY

1. Schizophrenia is a group of psychotic disorders characterized by impaired thinking. It is manifested in thought disturbances, including lack of insight, delusions, and loosening of associations; attention problems; perceptual distortion in the form of hallucinations; extremes of motor behavior; and inappropriate affect.

2. The criteria that differentiate schizophrenia, its subtypes, and other psychotic disorders are specified more precisely in DSM-III than they have been in the past. However, the criteria must be applied consistently if they are to be effective.

3. DSM-III distinguishes five types of schizophrenia. Disorganized schizophrenia is characterized by inappropriate affect and frequent incoherence. Extreme social impairment and severe regressive behaviors are often seen. Paranoid schizophrenia is characterized by systematized delusions that are illogical and contradictory. Delusions of persecution or grandeur are common. The major feature of catatonic schizophrenia is disturbance of motor activity. Patients show excessive excitement, agitation and hyperactivity, or withdrawn behavior patterns. The undifferentiated type includes schizophrenic behavior that cannot be classified as one of the other types. And residual schizophrenia is a category for persons who have had at least one episode of schizophrenia but are not now showing prominent symptoms. In addition, other severe disorders may include schizophrenia-like symptoms.

4. The typical course of schizophrenia consists of three phases. In the prodromal phase the symptoms first begin and build. In the active phase they become quite prominent. And in the residual phase they gradually decline in severity. Although complete recovery from schizophrenia is rare, the majority of schizophrenics recover enough to lead relatively productive lives.

KEY TERMS

catatonic schizophrenia A schizophrenic disorder characterized by extreme agitation and excitement or by extreme withdrawal and lack of responsiveness

cognition The processes of thinking, perceiving, judging, and recognizing

delusion A false belief that is firmly and consistently held despite disconfirming evidence or logic

disorganized schizophrenia A schizophrenic disorder characterized by severe disintegration and absurd and incoherent behaviors beginning at at early age

hallucinations Sensory perceptions that are not directly attributable to environmental stimuli

paranoid schizophrenia A schizophrenic disorder characterized by persistent and systematized delusions

residual schizophrenia A category of schizophrenic disorder reserved for individuals who have experienced at least one schizophrenic episode but do not now exhibit prominent signs of the disorder

schizophrenia A group of disorders characterized by severe impairment of cognitive processes, personality disintegration, and social withdrawal

undifferentiated schizophrenia A schizophrenic disorder characterized by mixed or undifferentiated symptoms that do not clearly fit any of the other types of schizophrenia

16

Schizophrenia: Etiology and Treatment

*T*he thirteen-year-old boy was having behavioral and academic problems in school and was taking part in a series of family therapy sessions. Near the end of one session, he suddenly broke down and cried out, "I don't want to be like her." He was referring to his mother, who had been receiving treatment for schizophrenia and was taking antipsychotic medication. He had often been frightened by her bizarre behaviors, and he was concerned that his friends would "find out" about her condition. But his greatest fear was that he would inherit the disorder. Sobbing, he turned to the therapist and asked, "Am I going to be crazy too?"

Researchers generally agree that the boy's chances of developing schizophrenia are greater than those of the average individual. But there is much less agreement on *why* he is more likely to become schizophrenic. Etiological theories emphasizing genetic, physiological, psychological, and environmental factors have been put forth, but none is universally accepted and all are incomplete. As you will see in this chapter, methodological flaws and the limitations of research design—especially with human subjects—have limited the conclusions that can be drawn about schizophrenia. Yet an incomplete understanding of the causes of these disorders has not kept clinicians from developing reasonably successful and promising treatments.

HEREDITY AND SCHIZOPHRENIA

A prominent research scientist posed the following challenge to his colleagues:

> You [are] required to write down a procedure for selecting an individual from the population who would be diagnosed as schizophrenic by a psychiatric staff; you have to wager $1,000 on being

right. You may not include in your selection procedure any behavioral fact, such as a symptom or trait, manifested by the individual. (Meehl 1962, p. 827)

What procedure would give you the highest probability of selecting a schizophrenic from the general population when you *cannot* consider the person's symptoms or traits?

According to Meehl, you should look for an individual whose identical twin has already been diagnosed as schizophrenic. This solution reflects the belief that heredity is an important factor in the etiology of schizophrenia—a belief that has been supported by past and present research (Kendler 1983). However, the degree of influence is still open to very active controversy. In this section we shall discuss several kinds of research that link heredity to the schizophrenic disorders and, with each type of research, the major sources of controversy.

Studies involving blood relatives

Close blood relatives have greater genetic similarity than more distant blood relatives. For example, 50 percent of the genes of two siblings are expected to be the same, whereas a much lower proportion of the genes of two second cousins, say, would be expected to be the same. If schizophrenia has a genetic basis, one should find higher rates of schizophrenia among close relatives of diagnosed schizophrenics than among more distant relatives.

Table 16.1 seems to indicate that this is indeed the case. The data in the table are summarized from several major studies of the incidence of schizophrenia (Zerbin-Rudin 1972). They show that closer blood relatives of diagnosed schizophrenics run a greater risk of developing the disorders. Thus the boy described at the start of this chapter has a 9 to 16 percent chance of being diagnosed as schizophrenic, but his mother's nieces or nephews have only a 1 to 4 percent chance. (Note that

Table 16.1   *Risk of Schizophrenia among Blood Relatives of Schizophrenics*

Relationship to the Schizophrenic Person	Morbidity Risk, percent
Parents	5–10
Children	9–16
Siblings	8–14
Children of two affected parents	40–68
Half-siblings	1–7
Step-siblings	1–8
Grandchildren	2–8
Cousins	2–6
Nieces and nephews	1–4
Uncles and aunts	2–7
Grandparents	1–2
No relationship	1

SOURCE: From Zerbin-Rudin (1972).

the risk for the general population is 1 percent.)

Unfortunately (or perhaps fortunately), the association between relatedness and risk is not so clear-cut as Table 16.1 seems to make it. Other studies have yielded different results, showing morbidity risks of 1.6 to 3.2 percent for first-degree relatives—that is, parents and children—of schizophrenics (Abrams and Taylor 1983; Guze et al. 1983; Tsuang, Winokur, and Crowe 1980). In fact, in one study no increased risk at all was found among first-degree relatives (Pope, Jonas, and Cohen 1982).

What might account for the discrepancies among the various study results? According to one pair of researchers, the differing results are the products of methodological differences (Abrams and Taylor 1983). They make the following suggestions for conducting genetic studies of schizophrenia.

1. The use of well-defined and restricted criteria for schizophrenia. Many studies, especially those performed before 1972, made use of very broad definitions that encompassed patients with affective disorders—and the affective disorders do have a strong genetic component (Pope and Lipinski

1978). This obviously had a confounding effect on conclusions regarding the heritability of schizophrenia. The more precise criteria of DSM-III should be of help in this regard.

2. Rediagnosis of the *probands* (individuals with the trait that is under investigation—in this case, schizophrenia) planned as part of future studies. This would indicate the reliability and validity of their original diagnoses and, thus, of the studies themselves.

3. The use of the same standardized interview for both at-risk and control relatives. This would improve confidence in results showing differences between these two groups.

4. The blind and independent diagnosis of probands, controls, and their relatives to avoid bias. A rater who knows that he or she is interviewing relatives of a schizophrenic, for example, might be more likely to find pathology. There is some evidence that studies that do not utilize blind ratings tend to report higher rates of morbidity than those that do (Gottesman and Shields 1982).

Because previous studies have not incorporated all these precautions, they must be interpreted very carefully (Abrams and Taylor 1983).

However, even if well-designed studies indicated that there is a relationship between degree of relatedness and schizophrenia, they would not be able to demonstrate clearly the role of heredity. Why? Simply because closer blood relatives are more likely to share the same environmental factors or stressors, as well as the same genes. To confirm a genetic basis for schizophrenia, it is necessary to separate genetic influences from environmental influences.

Twin studies

We have already described the use of twin studies in attempts to differentiate between

Identical and fraternal twins are studied to determine the relative importance of genetic factors in schizophrenia and other disorders. Identical twins share exactly the same genes. Thus differences between identical twins can be attributed to differences in their environment rather than in their genetic makeup. Fraternal twins share some of the genes, but no more so than any other pair of siblings.

the effects of heredity and those of environment. The concept, in somewhat more detail, is this: Identical, or monozygotic (MZ), twins are genetically identical; hence, differences between two MZ twins can presumably be attributed to differences in their environments. If they are reared together, MZ twins share the same general environment as well as the same hereditary makeup. On the other hand, fraternal, or dizygotic (DZ) twins, though they were born at approximately the same time, are not more genetically similar than any other two siblings. If DZ twins are reared together, they share the same general environment, but their genetic makeup is, on the average, only 50 percent identical.

In a twin study, concordance rates for a particular disorder are measured among groups of MZ and DZ twins. (Recall that a **concordance rate** is the likelihood that both of a pair of subjects exhibit the feature that is being studied.) If environmental factors are of major importance in the disorder, there should be little difference between the concordance rate for MZ twins and that for DZ twins. If genetic factors are of prime importance, however, MZ twins should show a higher concordance rate than DZ twins.

In general, concordance rates for schizophrenia among MZ twins have been found to be two or four times higher than among DZ twins. This seems to point to a strong genetic basis for the disorders. However, in one study of sixteen pairs of MZ twins, the concordance rate was found to be zero; not one MZ twin of a schizophrenic individual was found to have the disorder (Tienari 1963). In fact, concordance rates among MZ twins have been found to vary from 0 to 86 percent (Weiner 1975). How is it possible for some twin studies to show little or no genetic influence while other studies indicate a strong genetic component in schizophrenia?

Again, methodological differences seem to be involved. To see this, consider Table 16.2,

which lists the results of several twin studies performed in Scandinavian countries. Two percentages are given for most of the entries in the concordance-rate columns. The first (not in parentheses) is the rate measured according to a strict, narrow definition of schizophrenia. The second (in parentheses) is the rate measured according to a broadened definition, the "schizophrenia spectrum," which would include latent or borderline schizophrenia, acute schizophrenic reactions, and schizoid and inadequate personality (Kety et al. 1968). Note that the Tienari (1963) MZ concordance rate of zero would be increased to 19 percent if three twins who exhibited "borderline" psychotic features were counted. This is true, to varying degrees, of the other studies as well.

The broader definition of schizophrenia is the one that was utilized in most studies that indicate high concordance rates. Unfortunately, this decreases the diagnostic reliability and validity of twin studies as a whole. In one blind and independent study, for example, 25 percent of a normal comparison control group received one of the spectrum schizophrenia diagnoses (Haier, Rosenthal, and Wendler 1978). (Problems of diagnosis and diagnostic criteria also arise with regard to the deinstitutionalization of mental patients, which is discussed in Focus 16.1.)

Other problems involve the details of sampling and of measuring concordance. But even

Table 16.2 *Concordance Rates Found in Twin Studies in the Nordic Countries*

Study	Country	MZ Pairs		DZ Pairs	
		Number of Pairs	Concordance Rate, percent	Number of Pairs	Concordance Rate, percent
Tienari (1963)	Finland	16	0 (19)*	21	5 (14)
Kringlin (1967)	Norway	55	25 (38)	90	10 (19)
Essen-Moller (1970)	Sweden	7	29 (75)	–	– –
Fischer (1973)	Denmark	21	24 (56)	41	10 (19)
Tienari (1975)	Finland	20	15 –	42	7.5 –

* The percentages that are not in parentheses are those measured according to a narrow definition of schizophrenia. The percentages in parentheses are concordance rates for the wider "schizophrenia spectrum"; for example, if one twin has schizophrenia and the other twin has a "borderline" diagnosis, the pair is considered concordant according to this latter definition.
SOURCE: From Kringlen (1980).

The Deinstitutionalization of Mental Patients

Deinstitutionalization is the shifting of responsibility for the care of mental patients from large central institutions to agencies within local communities. For several reasons, an increasing number of patients have been deinstitutionalized over the past two decades. First, there has been (and still is) a feeling that large hospitals provide mainly custodial care, which produces little benefit for the patient and may even retard improvement. Such symptoms as flat affect and nonresponsiveness, which were generally thought to be clinical signs of schizophrenia, may actually result from hospitalization. Moreover, institutionalization appears to lower self-sufficiency in patients: The longer patients are hospitalized, the more likely they are to want to remain hospitalized, even if they have improved (Wing 1980).

Second, the issue of patients' rights has received increased attention. Legislative decisions supporting those rights require that patients live in the "least restrictive environment possible."

Third, a nationwide lack of funding for state hospitals has almost forced these institutions to release some patients back into their communities.

What has been the impact of deinstitutionalization on patients? The data are mixed, and results depend on factors such as the availability of family and community support systems, the existence of community treatment facilities, and the severity of the individual disorder. There are alarming indications that deinstitutionalization has been responsible for placing on the streets up to one million former patients and individuals who would have been committed to institutions in the past. The majority are severely disabled and have difficulty coping with the demands of daily living (Cordes 1984a).

There also seems to have been some "criminalization" of the mentally ill. Lamb and Grant (1982, 1983) studied male and female county jail inmates who were referred for psychiatric evaluation. They found that over 85 percent had a history of psychiatric hospitalizations and that over 50 percent met the current criteria for involuntary hospitalization (either dangerous to oneself or others, or "gravely disabled"). Over one-third were living on the streets or in missions, and fewer than 12 percent were employed. On the basis of their findings, Lamb and Grant have supported the position that involuntary hospitalization should be available to these individuals. But at least one other study has resulted in only modest evidence of such criminalization (Teplin 1983). Nonetheless, it is becoming apparent that many individuals who are mentally ill are not receiving treatment. The solution is probably not a return to institutionalization (although this may be necessary in some cases), but rather the provision of more and better community-based treatment facilities.

For patients who are involved in alternative community programs, the picture appears to be somewhat more positive. After reviewing reports of experimental studies on alternative treatment, a group of researchers concluded that such patients fared at least as well as those in institutions. And where differences were found, they favored the alternative programs (Braun et al. 1981). However, it is also clear that such studies are few in number and that much remains to be done if deinstitutionalized patients are to be provided with the best supportive treatment.

though the high concordance rates reported in many earlier studies have been inflated by use of the broad definition of schizophrenia, we can conclude that there is some genetic influence—primarily because the majority of studies indicate a greater risk for MZ twins than for DZ twins. This is so whether a strict definition is employed or the schizophrenia spectrum is included. Moreover, it appears that the spectrum disorders are more likely to be found in "at-risk" groups: those whose families include diagnosed schizophrenics.

Adoption studies

Even with twin studies, it is difficult to separate the effects of heredity from the effects of environment, because twins are usually raised together. Thus, when the child of a schizophrenic parent develops schizophrenia, three explanations are possible: The schizophrenic mother or father may have genetically transmitted schizophrenia to the child; the parent, being disturbed, may have provided a stressful environment for the child; or the child's schizophrenia may have resulted from a combination of genetic factors and a stressful environment.

In an attempt to separate completely the effects of heredity from the effects of environment, the incidence of schizophrenia and other disorders was determined for a group of individuals who were born to schizophrenic mothers but who had no contact with their mothers and had left the maternity hospital within three days of birth (Heston 1966; Heston and Denny 1968). This condition eliminated the possibility that contact with the mother increased the chance of developing the disorder. The lives of these individuals were traced through the records of child-care institutions; all had been adopted by families where both parents were present. A control group, consisting of individuals who were born to normal mothers and were adopted through the same child-care institutions, was selected and matched. Information regarding both the at-risk and control groups was obtained from a variety of sources (including school records, court records, and interviews), and the individuals themselves were interviewed and given a battery of psychological tests. The major results are in Table 16.3. Note that five of the children in the at-risk group were later diagnosed as schizophrenic, compared to none in the control group. These results are highly significant and support a genetic explanation for schizophrenia. The greater incidence of the other disorders among the at-risk group is difficult to explain because they are not part of the schizophrenia spectrum.

The study appears to have been well designed. Its only weaknesses might involve the diagnostic criteria, which were described as being based on "generally accepted standards" for schizophrenia, and the fact that the schizophrenic mothers "as a group were biased in the direction of severe, chronic disease" [It has been found that, the more severe a disorder is rated, the more evidence there is for hereditary influences in the disorder (Gottesman and Shields 1972).]

Two additional criticisms have been raised, however. First, the schizophrenic mothers received antipsychotic medication during pregnancy, and such drugs are acknowledged to be a potential risk to the fetus (PDR 1982). Second, most of the families who adopted the child of a schizophrenic mother were aware of the mother's disorder. This knowledge could have influenced the adoptive parents' attitude toward the child (Rosenthal 1973).

Of special interest is the finding that nearly half the at-risk group were "notably successful adults."

The 21 experimental subjects who exhibited no significant psycho-social impairment were not only successful adults but in comparison to the control group were more spontaneous when interviewed and had more colorful life histories. They held the more creative jobs: musician, teacher, home-designer; and followed the more imaginative hobbies: oil painting, music, antique aircraft. Within the experimental group there

Table 16.3   *Comparison of Disorders in Individuals Separated from Schizophrenic and from Normal Mothers Early in Life*

Characteristic	At-Risk Children	Control
Number of individuals	47	50
Males	30	33
Mean age	35.8	36.3
Ratings of mental health/sickness*	65.2	80.1
Number diagnosed as schizophrenic	5	0
Number with mental deficiency (IQ less than 70)	4	0
Number with sociopathic personality	9	2
Number with neurotic personality	13	7
Number spending more than 1 year in a penal or psychiatric institution	11	2

*A lower score indicates greater severity.
SOURCE: From Heston (1966).

was much more variability of personality and behaviour in all social dimensions. (Heston 1966, p. 825)

Being "at risk" does not necessarily (or even usually) lead to a negative outcome.

In another study designed to separate hereditary and environmental influences, investigators identified adult schizophrenics who had been adopted in infancy. They then located both the adoptive parents (the families that had raised the children who became schizophrenic) and the biological parents, who had had minimal contact with the children. If environmental factors play the major role in schizophrenia, the adoptive families should be more disturbed than the biological parents. On the other hand, if heredity is the more important factor, the biological families should show more disturbance than the adoptive families. Interviews with both sets of families indicated a greater incidence of the schizophrenia spectrum in the biological family (Kety et al. 1975).

Another group of researchers studied children who had normal biological parents but were adopted and raised by a parent who later was diagnosed as schizophrenic. If environmental factors are of primary importance, these children should be more likely than others to develop schizophrenia, but no difference was found (Wender et al. 1977). Thus the

various adoption studies do indicate that heredity has a role in the transmission of schizophrenia.

High-risk studies

Perhaps the most comprehensive means of studying the etiology of schizophrenia is to monitor a large group of children over a long period of time in order to observe the differences between those who eventually develop schizophrenia and those who do not. This sort of **developmental study** has the advantage of allowing the investigator actually to see how the disorders develop, beginning well before onset. But because the incidence of schizophrenia in the general population is only 1 percent, a prohibitively large group would have to be monitored if a random sample of children were chosen. Instead, investigators have chosen subjects from "high-risk" populations; this increases the probability that a smaller group of subjects will include some who develop schizophrenia.

The best-known developmental studies are those of Mednick (1970) and Mednick and Schulsinger (1968), who are still in the process of studying approximately 200 children with schizophrenic mothers (the high-risk group) and approximately 100 children with nonschizophrenic mothers (the low-risk control group). The investigators intend to study these groups for a total of 25 years. However, on the basis of existing data, they have predicted the eventual outcome for both high-risk and low-risk subjects. Their prediction is displayed in Figure 16.1; about half the high-risk group is expected eventually to display some form of psychopathology, including but not limited to schizophrenia.

By the time of the first follow-up, twenty members of the high-risk group had already displayed psychological problems ranging from theft to psychotic symptoms (Mednick 1970). Thirteen of these individuals had been admitted to psychiatric hospitals. Mednick felt that the subjects in this "sick group" were the most likely to have or to develop schizophrenia. But a later follow-up revealed that, of fifteen individuals who had been diagnosed as schizophrenic, only four came from the sick group (Schulsinger 1976). The high-risk sub-

jects who became schizophrenic were compared with those who did not, and it was found that those who became schizophrenic were more likely to:

☐ Have mothers who displayed more severe symptoms
☐ Have been separated from their parents and placed in children's homes early in their lives
☐ Have had more serious pregnancy or birth complications
☐ Have been characterized by their teachers as extremely aggressive and disruptive
☐ Have a slower autonomic recovery rate

This is a promising line of research, and its value should become more evident when the study is completed. However, some methodological problems have already been pointed out. First, it may not be possible to generalize results that are obtained in a study whose sub-

Figure 16.1 *Mednick and Schulsinger's Predictions about the Development of Deviance and Schizophrenia in High-Risk and Control Children.*

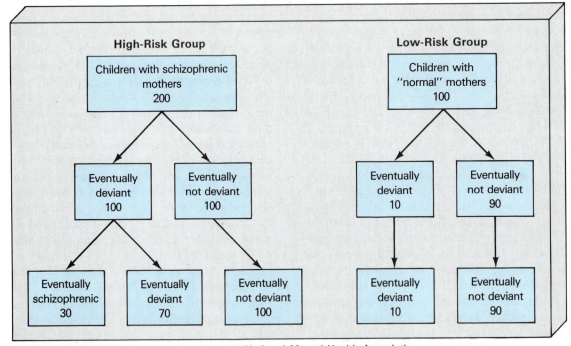

SOURCE: Mednick (1970). *Mental Hygiene, 54,* National Mental Health Association.

jects are the offspring of schizophrenic parents. About 85 to 90 percent of diagnosed schizophrenics *do not* have a schizophrenic parent (Zerbin-Rudin 1972). And differences have been found between patients with familial schizophrenia (those with a schizophrenic first-degree relative) and those patients whose family histories do not include schizophrenia (Kendler and Hays 1982). Second, the study does not include control groups with other forms of psychopathology; thus it is difficult to determine whether the characteristics that are found are specific to schizophrenia. For example, of the characteristics listed above, pregnancy and birth complications, separation from parents, and problems in school are also reported for other disorders. Third, there is uncertainty about whether the most relevant variables are being measured. Mednick believes that autonomic reactivity is an important factor in schizophrenia and has assessed this variable carefully. But parent–child interaction was not assessed because the investigators consider it less important.

PHYSIOLOGICAL FACTORS IN SCHIZOPHRENIA

Two important areas of research into the etiology of schizophrenia involve the chemistry of the brain and brain pathology. Logically, it would seem that either of these could serve as a vehicle for the genetic transmission of schizophrenia, but no substantive evidence to that effect has yet been found. Nonetheless, research in these areas has implications for treatment as well as etiology.

Biochemistry: The dopamine hypothesis

Biochemical explanations of schizophrenia have a long history. A century ago, for example, Emil Kraepelin suggested that these disorders result from a chemical imbalance that develops due to abnormal secretion by the sex glands. Since then, a number of studies have been undertaken to demonstrate that body chemistry is involved in schizophrenia. Most have led only to dead ends.

What generally happens is that a researcher finds a particular chemical substance in schizophrenic subjects and does not find it in "normal" controls, but other researchers cannot replicate those findings. This was the case with a substance called *taraxein,* which was isolated from the blood serum of schizophrenics (Heath 1960; Heath, Guschwan, and Coffey 1970). The problem generally arises because schizophrenic patients differ from normals in lifestyle and in food and medication intake, all of which affect body chemistry and tend to confound research results.

One promising line of biochemical research has focused on one of the neurotransmitters, *dopamine,* and its involvement in schizophrenia (Carlsson 1978; Snyder 1974; Bowers 1981). According to the *dopamine hypothesis,* which was discussed briefly in Chapter 2, schizophrenia may result from an excess of dopamine activity at certain synaptic sites. This high level of activity is due either to the release of excess dopamine by presynaptic neurons or to the oversensitivity of dopamine receptors (Neale and Oltmanns 1980).

Support for the dopamine hypothesis has come from research with three types of drugs. The first is the *phenothiazines,* which are antipsychotic drugs that decrease the severity of thought disorders, alleviate withdrawal and hallucinations, and improve the mood of schizophrenics. Their effectiveness is not due to a generalized sedating effect (phenobarbital, a depressant with sedative properties, is not nearly so effective against schizophrenic symptoms). Rather, there is increasing evidence that the phenothiazines reduce dopamine activity in the brain by blocking dopamine receptor sites in postsynaptic neurons.

Another drug, *L-Dopa,* is generally used to treat such symptoms of Parkinson's disease as muscle and limb rigidity and tremors. The body converts L-Dopa to dopamine, and the drug sometimes produces schizophrenic-like symptoms. (By contrast, the phenothiazines, which reduce dopamine activity, can produce side effects that are similar to the symptoms of Parkinson's disease.)

Finally, there is research on the effects of the *amphetamines,* stimulants that increase the availability of dopamine and norepinephrine (another neurotransmitter) in the brain (Snyder 1976). When nonschizophrenic subjects are given continual doses of amphetamines, they exhibit symptoms very much like those found in acute paranoid schizophrenia. Continual low dosages of these drugs also produce psychotic-like symptoms in monkeys (Nielsen, Lyon, and Ellison 1983). And very small doses may increase the severity of symptoms in diagnosed schizophrenics. Other stimulants, such as caffeine, do not produce these effects.

Thus a drug that is believed to block dopamine reception has the effect of reducing the severity of schizophrenic symptoms, whereas two drugs that increase dopamine availability either produce or worsen these symptoms. Such evidence supports the idea that excess dopamine may cause schizophrenic symptoms (Carlsson 1978).

The evidence is not all positive, however. For example, on the basis of the dopamine hypothesis, one would expect that the treatment of schizophrenia with phenothiazines would be effective in the vast majority of cases. Yet approximately one-fourth of schizophrenic patients were found to be minimally responsive or unresponsive to antipsychotic medication (Davis et al. 1980). In fact, in one study of 65 schizophrenics who were treated with antipsychotic medications, 25 percent reported that the medication had *negative* effects on them (Van Putten, May, and Marder 1984). In addition, of a group of schizophrenics who were given amphetamines, one-third did not experience a worsening of their symptoms (Angrist, Rontrosen, and Gershon 1980). Such results point to the involvement of something other than excess dopamine.

As we noted in Chapter 15, schizophrenia may very well be a group of disorders with differing etiologies; such an explanation could account for the variable course of the disorders and the unevenness of schizophrenics' responses to the phenothiazines. Moreover, researchers may be looking for too simple an explanation by focusing on dopamine alone, without considering the interactive functioning of the brain and the biochemical system as a whole (Csernansky, Holman, and Hollister 1983). Or perhaps dopamine blockers can influence the symptoms of schizophrenia but not the course of the illness. Obviously, much more remains to be discovered.

Neurological findings

From 20 to 35 percent of schizophrenics exhibit some form of brain impairment (Seidman 1983). By using computerized axial tomography (CAT) scans, which produce very reliable cross-sectional representations of the brain, researchers have shown that schizophrenics are more likely than controls to exhibit ventricular enlargement, cerebellar atrophy, cortical atrophy, and reversed cerebral asymmetry. The first two conditions appear to be correlated with the more severe and chronic forms of schizophrenia. In fact, the existing data indicate that there may be two or three subgroups of schizophrenia, each involving a different area of the brain. Such data "argue against a unitary disease concept of schizophrenia" (Seidman 1983).

Ventricles are fluid-filled cavities in the brain. Luchins (1982) has found that the incidence of enlarged ventricles in schizophrenics, as reported in different studies, ranges from 0 to 60 percent. He feels that this variation reflects differences in measurement techniques and patient populations and that a more reasonable prevalence is about 20 percent. He also notes that support for findings of cortical atrophy or reversed symmetry of the brain seems to be lacking. Luchins's estimate of the prevalence of ventricular enlargement seems

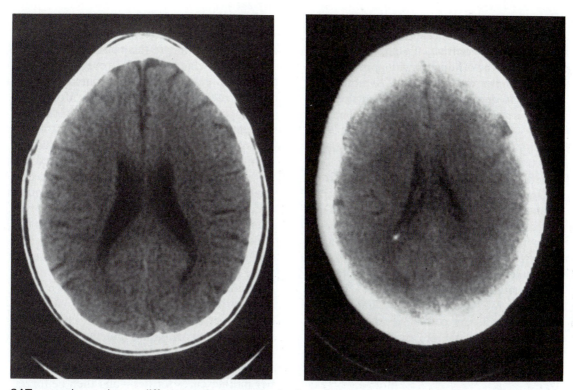

CAT scans have shown differences between the brains of normal and schizophrenic individuals. The photograph on the left shows the brain of a schizophrenic individual; the dark areas in the center are enlarged ventricles. The photograph on the right shows the brain of a normal individual.

to be supported by a recent study in which CAT scans were performed on thirty-five patients with schizophreniform disorder, seventeen with chronic schizophrenia, twenty-three with affective disorders, twenty-seven with other serious psychiatric disorders, and twenty-six controls (Weinberger et al. 1982). Significantly larger cerebral ventricles were found in 20 percent of those with schizophreniform disorder and 24 percent of those with schizophrenia. The researchers feel that enlarged ventricles may be a "marker" for a distinct subtype of schizophrenia.

Such findings are intriguing, and continuing advances in neuropsychology may lead to solid information regarding the etiology of schizophrenia. However, it is important to remember that the majority of schizophrenics do not show evidence of organic brain problems.

ENVIRONMENTAL FACTORS IN SCHIZOPHRENIA

Genetic and biological research has obviously not yet clarified the etiology of the various schizophrenic disorders. If for no other reason, then, psychologists must look to environmental factors as causes. Here we shall examine available information and theories concerning the role of family dynamics, social class, and cultural differences in the development of these disorders.

We should first note, however, that environmental factors become involved in psychopathology by acting as stressors. A logical question, then, is "Can stress produce schizophrenia?" Attempts to find an answer have been less than successful, primarily because most rely on retrospective reports from individuals who have sought treatment. Such individuals do not comprise the entire population of schizophrenics, and their memories of past events may be inaccurate.

In spite of these limitations, it appears that a substantial minority of patients do experience a greater frequency of stressful events prior to diagnosis than comparison groups. There is also a correlation between the number of stressful events and the probability of relapse after treatment (Dohrenwend and Egri 1981). In addition, a large minority report a single precipitating factor: In a study of 502 schizophrenic individuals, 25 percent reported the death of a spouse or close relative as a precipitating event, 9 percent reported an illness or surgery, and 5 percent had gone through childbirth before diagnosis; the remaining 61 percent reported no precipitating factor (Huber et al. 1980). We do not know whether such stressful events are combined with the types of environmental factors that are discussed next.

Family influences

Theoretical constructs Theorists have suggested two means by which family interaction can contribute to the development of schizophrenia. The first was proposed by psychodynamic theorists who believed that certain behavioral patterns of parents could inhibit appropriate ego development in the child. This, in turn, would make the child vulnerable to the severe regression that is characteristic of schizophrenia. Attention was focused mainly on the mother, who usually has a great deal of contact with the child; the **schizophrenogenic** (or schizophrenia-producing) mother was characterized as being simultaneously or alternately cold and overprotecting, rejecting and dominating.

The second theory involving family interaction is the communication **double-bind theory** mentioned in Chapter 3 (Bateson et al. 1956). Proponents suggest that the preschizophrenic child has repeated experiences with one or more family members (usually the mother and/or father) in which he or she receives two contradictory messages. The child is unable either to discriminate the parent's meaning or to escape the situation. This eventually leads to difficulty in interpreting communications that are received from others and in accurately and appropriately conveying the child's own thoughts and feelings.

Assume, for example, that a mother harbors hostile feelings toward her daughter and yet wishes to be a good and loving mother. She might send her child to bed, saying, "You're tired and sleep will do you good." The overt message conveys the mother's concern for her child's health. Her tone of voice, however, is such that the child senses anger and the desire to be alone. The child then can interpret the contradictory messages in one of two ways (Bateson 1956): She may correctly interpret her mother's hostility, in which case she is faced with the awful fact that she is not loved or wanted by her mother. Or she may accept the overt message—that she is tired and that her mother cares for her—and then be forced to deny her real understanding of the message. The child is punished whether she discriminates the message correctly or incorrectly (the double bind).

If the child were able to comment on the contradictory message to the effect that "You seem to care for me because you want me to protect my health, but you sound very angry and hostile toward me," she could break away from the double bind. But the child is too dependent on the parent to risk the disapproval that such a statement would evoke; the mother would feel threatened by this statement and would insist that there was no hostility. Instead, to survive, the child must resort to self-deception, falsely interpreting her own thoughts as well as those communicated by others. A false concept of reality, an inability to communicate effectively, withdrawal, and other symptoms of schizophrenia may result.

Problems with earlier research Most studies conducted before the mid-1970s supported the view that clarity and accuracy of communication were lower in families with a schizophrenic member than in normal families (Jacob 1975). However, methodological shortcomings prevented researchers from generalizing these results to a relationship between schizophrenia and family dynamics. The most common flaws were (1) the fact that a family's interactions were studied only after one of its members had been diagnosed as schizophrenic and (2) the lack of control groups. Thus, even if a correlation was found between difficulties in family interaction and schizophrenia, researchers could not tell which was

the cause and which the effect or whether the correlation was unique to schizophrenia (Some effects of severe mental illness on a family, especially after deinstitutionalization, are suggested in Focus 16.2.)

Perhaps in reaction to such methodological impedimenta, a procedure that would permit the discovery *and support* of a causal relationship has been proposed:

First, the hypothesized variables must be clearly defined by reliable and objective methods. Second, the causal role of the variable must be as-

FOCUS 16.2

Another View of Deinstitutionalization

What follows was written by Mary Jean Willis, founder and president of Families and Friends of the Adult Mentally Ill and the mother of a schizophrenic son.

Now we have deinstitutionalization, release of the mentally ill from hospitals as soon as they are stabilized (and sometimes even sooner).

We think that our son was prematurely discharged from hospitals at least twice. At one time he was sent home on a weekend pass from a state hospital. When the family, including our oldest son, daughter-in-law, and their infant daughter, was gathered around to celebrate his homecoming, he suddenly disappeared into his room where he proceeded to smash a glass and slash at his throat. Another time, when he was hospitalized in San Francisco after throwing himself in front of a car, he refused medication and demanded to be released. The hospital would not keep him against his will, so he was discharged after a few days, whereupon he jumped in front of a truck and was severely injured.

Deinstitutionalization has meant not only early discharge, but also inaccessibility of hospitals. Because our son is suicidal, we have not had any great difficulty getting him into a hospital. However, I know of a mother

who has not been able to gain hospital admission for her son, even though he is violent and a danger to society when he is in his manic phase. . . .

Another common problem for family members is the feeling of being tied down and not able to live one's own life. Families of a chronic mentally ill person find it difficult to travel or to maintain much of a social life. Our own social life has become practically nonexistent, not necessarily because our friends have deserted us due to the stigma of mental illness, but because of the unpredictability of our son's illness, and because, after coping with the many problems it causes, we have little energy left over for entertaining.

The financial burden of mental illness is another big problem which families must face. When insurance (if there is any) runs out as it eventually does in most cases, not even well-to-do families can handle the frequent hospitalizations at exorbitant rates. . . .

When all of the above problems are considered, it can be seen that deinstitutionalization has in some ways made life for the families of the chronic mentally ill more difficult than it was for my mother-in-law back in the days when lifelong hospitalization was the fate of most of the mentally ill. (Willis 1982, pp. 617–619)

Recent research indicates that family dynamics may play a role in the development of schizophrenia. The relationship between the mother and child, communication deviances combined with criticism, hostility, and overinvolvement, and presence or absence of the father may be involved in the development of schizophrenia.

sessed by demonstrating that it (1) is specifically linked with schizophrenia as opposed to other conditions and states, (2) has an impact on the individual before the onset of schizophrenia, and (3) is not confounded with a covarying or concomitant variable that is the ''true'' etiological variable. (Reiss 1976), p. 181)

More recent studies   Later studies seem to be more carefully controlled. In one, researchers collected data on forty-five patients who had received a diagnosis of schizophrenia during military service in the 1940s and 1950s; these subjects were part of a larger group that had

been followed since their first contacts with child-guidance clinics (Roff and Knight 1981). Information on family dynamics was available in clinic files, and family interaction patterns were obtained by scoring case-history material. Two distinct patterns were discovered in the families of these schizophrenics: The first was characterized by an overprotective and intrusive mother who was low on nurturance, generally with a father who was weak and uninvolved. The second pattern involved maternal irresponsibility or indifference, with resulting family disorganization.

The relationship between parental communication styles and the development of ''schizophrenic-like'' disorders was examined in another *longitudinal,* or continuing, study (Doane et al. 1981). First, measurements of communication patterns were obtained in sixty-five families involving thirty-eight male and twenty-seven female adolescents seen at the UCLA Psychology Outpatient Clinic. None of the adolescents had either a history of, or current symptoms of, psychoses. Of the initial sample, fifty-two subjects were located and re-evaluated five years later, at which time it was found that:

☐ 35 of the subjects were either normal or had mild to marked character neuroses.
☐ 4 had antisocial personalities.
☐ 1 had schizoid personality.
☐ 5 had possible ''borderline'' schizophrenia.
☐ 3 had definite ''borderline'' schizophrenia.
☐ 3 had ''probable'' schizophrenia.
☐ 1 had definite schizophrenia.

The researchers did not find a unique relationship between deviant parental communication and borderline or schizophrenic offspring. But the combination of communication deviances (such as unclear messages, lack of commitment to ideas, language anomalies, and disruptive speech) and a pattern of criticism, hostility, and overinvolvement was found to be related to offspring having the schizophrenia spectrum disorders.

There is also some evidence that the father

has a positive effect on high-risk children (the offspring of schizophrenic mothers). A group of high-risk males who developed schizophrenia was compared with a group of high-risk males with identical characteristics who did not develop the disorder (Walker et al. 1981). The major difference found by the researchers was a greater likelihood that the fathers of the schizophrenic group were absent from the home. It seems that, when the mother is disturbed, the father can function as a stabilizing force. Identification with the father may serve as a buffer against the influence of a sick mother.

All three studies seem to support the belief that family dynamics plays a part in the development of schizophrenia. However, although their methodology is much more sound than that of previous studies, these studies still do not meet Reiss's requirements for supporting a causal relationship. Because they begin with disturbed samples, they are subject to many of the same criticisms as earlier studies.

Effect of social class

Schizophrenia is most prevalent at the lower socioeconomic levels, regardless of whether prevalence is measured relative to patient populations or general populations (Dohrenwend and Dohrenwend 1969; Hollingshead and Redlich 1958; Srole et al. 1962). According to the Research Task Force of the National Institute of Mental Health (1975), one of the most consistent findings in schizophrenia research is that the disorder is disproportionately concentrated among individuals in the poorest areas of large cities and in the occupations with the lowest status.

There are two possible explanations for this correlation between social class and schizophrenia: (1) Low socioeconomic status is itself stressful. Physical and psychological stressors associated with poverty, a lack of education, menial employment, and the like increase the chance that schizophrenia will develop. (2) Schizophrenic and preschizophrenic individu-

als tend to drift to the poorest urban areas and the lowest socioeconomic levels because they cannot function effectively elsewhere in society. This explanation is called the *downward drift theory*.

One way to test downward drift is to determine whether schizophrenics actually move downward in occupational status. However, the results of such studies have been inconclusive. Some have found evidence of downward mobility (Turner and Wagonfeld 1967), but others have found none (Clausen and Kohn 1959).

Another research strategy is to compare the occupations of schizophrenics with those of their fathers. If the schizophrenics generally had lower-status jobs than their fathers, a downward drift interpretation would be supported. In one such comparison, schizophrenics were found to have lower-status occupations than their fathers (Goldberg and Morrison 1963). However, other studies have yielded mixed results. Overall, the evidence seems to suggest that both interpretations apply. For some individuals, the stressors and limitations associated with membership in the lowest socioeconomic class facilitate the development of schizophrenia; for others, low socioeconomic status is a result of the disorders.

Cross-cultural comparisons

In the *International Pilot Study of Schizophrenia* cited in Focus 15.1, no significant differences were found in the incidence of the disorders in the nine countries that were studied (WHO 1973, 1981). However, various differences in symptomology have emerged from a number of studies, and these may be the result of environmental influences.

In a comparison of the symptoms of hospitalized schizophrenic Americans of Irish and of Italian descent, it was found that Irish–Americans tended to show less hostility and acting out, but more fixed delusions, than Italian–Americans. These differences have been attributed to cultural–familial backgrounds: In Irish families, mothers played a very dominant role, were quite strict, and prohibited strong emotional displays; in Italian families, mothers showed the opposite pattern (Opler 1967). Similarly, Japanese who are hospitalized for schizophrenia are often described as rigid, compulsive, withdrawn, and passive—symptoms that reflect the Japanese cultural value of conformity within the community and reserve within the family (Kitano 1969).

The content of delusions appears to be influenced by cultural and societal factors. Since the Chinese "Liberation," with its attendant social and political changes, a number of new delusions have been observed among Chinese schizophrenic patients (Yu-Fen and Neng 1981). These include the delusion of leadership lineage, in which patients insist that their parents are individuals in authority; the delusion of being tested, in which patients feel that their superiors are assessing them to determine whether they are suitable for promotion; the delusion of impending arrest, in which the patient assumes that he is about to be arrested by authorities; and the delusion of being married, in which a female patient insists she has a husband even though she is unmarried. Each of these is associated with some facet of the new Chinese society.

Racial differences have been observed as well. In a study of 273 schizophrenic patients admitted to hospitals and mental health centers in Missouri over a $3\frac{1}{2}$-year period, researchers found that black patients exhibited more severe symptoms than white patients. This increased severity took the form of angry outbursts, impulsivity, and more strongly antisocial behavior. Blacks also exhibited greater disorientation and confusion and more severe hallucinatory behaviors than whites (Abebimpe et al. 1982). These research findings may be interpreted as real differences in symptomology that may have environmental explanations, but, according to Abebimpe (1981), they may also be the product of diagnostic errors. He notes that blacks are less likely than whites

to be given a diagnosis of affective disorder and more likely to receive a diagnosis of schizophrenia, even when the two racial groups exhibit similar sets of symptoms. Also, cultural differences between patient and clinician tend to result in diagnostic errors—the greater the difference, the greater the likelihood of error. Finally, misdiagnosis can result from racial stereotyping or bias or from the application of diagnostic systems based on white middle-class norms to other racial groups.

INTERACTIONAL THEORIES OF SCHIZOPHRENIA

The lack of evidence pointing to a single etiology for the schizophrenic disorders has led Bleuler (1984) to conclude that

> Today, it is certain that in their formation, unfavorable hereditary predispositions interact with unfavorable experiences in life.
>
> Neither a single, inherited predisposition specific only to schizophrenia nor a specific damaging experience in the life course has ever been found.
>
> Instead, there are multitudes of physical and mental, inherited and acquired dispositions that form predispositions for schizophrenia. (p. 8)

In this vein, researchers have developed a general model that emphasizes the interaction between genetics and environmental stressors in schizophrenia (Rosenthal 1970; Zubin and Spring 1977; Zubin and Ludwig 1983). This **vulnerability/stress model** involves a vulnerability to the disorder, which may be inherited or acquired, combined with the impact of stressors. Schizophrenia develops when a vulnerable individual encounters stress and does not have access to the resources or social-support systems that are needed to cope with it.

According to this model, a psychotic episode ends if the stress is eliminated. The affected individual then returns to his or her earlier, higher ("premorbid") level of functioning.

If this level of functioning is an adequate one, the person is considered to be recovered. However, if the individual was only marginally adjusted before the episode, he or she is still considered ill after returning to the premorbid level of functioning. Episodes of psychosis are considered to be limited in duration; the only enduring aspect of schizophrenia is the individual's vulnerability to future stress (Zubin and Ludwig 1983).

A particularly elaborate version of the vulnerability/stress model has been developed by Neuchterlein and Dawson (1984). As is shown in Figure 16.2, its creators feel that schizophrenics suffer from several "enduring vulnerability characteristics." These are (1) a predisposition toward poor processing of information and difficulty in sustaining attention, brought on by various thought impairments; (2) overreaction to even mildly aversive stimuli; and (3) lack of adequate social competence and coping skills.

The vulnerable individual may not experience psychotic episodes if he or she is raised

Figure 16.2 *The Vulnerability/Stress Model of Neuchterlein and Dawson*

The vulnerable individual overreacts to environmental stressors that are not buffered by his or her social-support system. The feedback loop has the effect of "transforming" such overreaction into added stressors that eventually build up sufficiently to cause a schizophrenic episode.

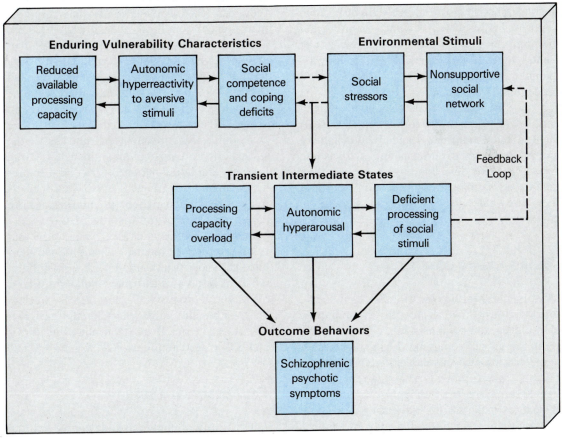

SOURCE: Neuchterlein and Dawson (1984).

in a supportive family and encounters only minor stressors. However, in a family that is not sufficiently supportive, perhaps through the absence of a parent, stressors are not buffered and the individual's reactions to stressors are more severe. When they become severe enough to overload the processing capability of the individual, a feedback loop is created that has the effect of continually compounding the stress. The eventual outcome is the development of schizophrenic symptoms.

THE TREATMENT OF SCHIZOPHRENIA

Through the years, schizophrenia has been "treated" by a variety of means ranging from the "warehousing" of severely disturbed patients in overcrowded asylums to prefrontal lobotomy, a surgical procedure in which the frontal lobes are disconnected from the remainder of the patient's brain. Such radical procedures were generally abandoned in the 1950s, when the beneficial effects of antipsychotic drugs were discovered. Today the treatment of schizophrenia typically consists of antipsychotic medication along with some type of psychosocial therapy. More severely disordered patients are still hospitalized until they are able to function adequately in society.

Antipsychotic medication

Most mental health professionals consider the introduction of *Thorazine,* the first antipsychotic drug, the beginning of a new era in the treatment of schizophrenia. For the first time, a medication was available that sufficiently relaxed even violent schizophrenics and helped organize their thoughts to the point that strait jackets were no longer needed to contain them. Three decades later, the phenothiazines, which are variations of Thorazine,

are still viewed as the most effective drug treatment for schizophrenia (Donaldson, Gelenberg, and Baldessarini 1983).

The antipsychotic medications (also called *major tranquilizers*) are, however, far from perfect. They appear to be quite effective in reducing the severity of the so-called "positive" symptoms of schizophrenia, such as hallucinations, delusions, bizarre speech, and thought disorders. But they offer little in terms of treatment for such "negative" symptoms as social withdrawal, apathy, and impaired personal hygiene (Wahba, Donlon, and Meadow 1981). And some schizophrenics do not derive any benefit at all from antipsychotic medication.

The antipsychotic drugs can produce a number of extremely unwelcome side effects; they are sometimes called *neuroleptics* because they can produce symptoms that resemble neurological conditions (see Focus 16.3, pp. 466–467). It has been suggested that a patient should not be considered a candidate for drug therapy if he or she becomes depressed and exhibits excessive side effects after one dose of an antipsychotic (Buckley 1982). There are several other ways to combat side effects. One is to determine, through trial and error, the lowest effective dose of an antipsychotic drug for each individual patient. A second is to prescribe major tranquilizers only when there is evidence that the patient is entering a more advanced stage of the disorder. But the best solution is to find some other type of drug that is also effective against schizophrenia. Perhaps the most promising new drug is lithium, which is used to treat the bipolar disorders. However, it too produces side effects, particularly within the cardiovascular and gastrointestinal systems (Brewerton and Reus 1983; Delva and Letemendia 1982).

Psychosocial therapy

The majority of clinicians today agree that the most beneficial treatment for schizophrenia is

Supportive counseling or other forms of psychotherapy can supplement drug therapy for schizophrenic patients. Once a patient's psychotic symptoms are under control, a therapist can try to help the patient improve his or her social and coping skills.

some combination of antipsychotic medication and therapy (Feinsilver and Yates 1984; Falloon and Liberman 1983). This is a fairly new attitude, and one that was resisted for many years by strict advocates of a medical approach. But even as scientists continued to introduce drugs that effectively reduced or eliminated many symptoms of schizophrenia, it became clear that one vital fact was being ignored: Medicated and adequately functioning schizophrenics who were discharged from the protective environment of hospitals were being returned to stressful home or occupational situations (Mosher and Keith 1980; Donaldson et al. 1983). The typical result was repeated rehospitalization; medication alone was insufficient to help schizophrenics function in their natural environment (Caton 1982; Brown 1982).

Clinicians soon realized that antipsychotic medication had to be supplemented with outpatient therapy. But which therapeutic strategy would yield the best results? This question was eventually answered in two ways—with supportive counseling and with behavior therapy.

Supportive counseling For a schizophrenic patient, supportive counseling typically involves weekly sessions that focus on the patient's current problems in living. Once these problems are clearly identified, the patient and therapist together explore possible solutions. Suppose, for example, that a male schizophrenic patient reports to his therapist that he is feeling low but is not sure why. A supportive therapist would gently examine the various possible reasons for the client's depression.

Together, they might eventually discover that the patient is unhappy with himself because he is unemployed. The therapist would then help the client generate potential solutions to this problem, such as calling previous employers, reading the classified ads, or submitting applications to local establishments. The patient's attitude toward looking for a job and his fears about returning to work might also be covered in his supportive counseling sessions.

Supportive counseling and other forms of "traditional" psychotherapy have frequently been criticized as inappropriate for schizophrenics (Mosher and Keith 1979). However, recent evidence suggests that they enhance the treatment effects of antipsychotic medication, particularly by improving the schizophrenic's functioning at work and in social situations (Stanton et al. 1984).

Behavior therapy In behavior therapy, the therapist concentrates on teaching the patient specific skills that he or she lacks. Whereas supportive counseling is a "talking" therapy, behavior therapy is a "doing" therapy.

Because schizophrenics are typically deficient in social skills, a social-skills training program is almost always included as part of behavior therapy (Curran and Monti 1982). In many cases, it is the major part of the therapy. Communication skills in general are emphasized, as is assertiveness training (Bellack,

FOCUS 16.3

Side Effects and Patients' Rights

"There is no known effective treatment for tardive dyskinesia." This warning, contained in the *Physician's Desk Reference* (1984), represents a major source of concern for patients receiving antipsychotic medications. Perhaps even more alarming is the fact that neuroleptics are being prescribed to treat anxiety, hyperactivity in children, aggression, and mood disorders.

Tardive dyskinesia is characterized by involuntary and rhythmic movements of the protruding tongue; chewing, lip smacking, and other facial movements; and jerking movements of the limbs. At risk are elderly patients, women, and those on long-term neuroleptic treatment. However, this syndrome is becoming increasingly prevalent in younger patients and nonpsychotic patients. A review of thirty-six studies indicates symptoms of tardive dyskinesia in about 26 percent of chronically ill patients treated with neuroleptics (Jesti and

Wyatt 1981). In the majority of cases, the symptoms of tardive dyskinesia persist and cannot be eliminated.

Neuroleptics can produce such Parkinson-like symptoms as loss of facial expression, immobility, shuffling gait, tremors of the hand, rigidity of the body, and poor postural stability. However, these symptoms are usually reversible (Granacher 1981). *Akathisia* (motor restlessness) and *dystonia* (slow and continued contrasting movements of the limbs and tongue), which are also controllable, may appear as well. Other side effects include drowsiness, skin rashes, blurred vision, dry mouth, nausea, and tachycardia.

Should schizophrenics have the right to refuse antipsychotic medications that produce potentially hazardous side effects? Patients in most state hospitals do not have this right. Groups that support the concept of patients' rights argue that forced admin-

Hersen, and Turner 1976). The patient is repeatedly placed in social situations that he or she tends to avoid. Experience with such situations eventually decreases the patient's anxiety concerning them to the point where he or she will seek out, rather than avoid, these situations. This is a critically important contribution of social-skills training, because social withdrawal is a major schizophrenic symptom that is untouched by antipsychotic medication (Wallace et al. 1980).

Suppose our same male schizophrenic patient, who is concerned about being unemployed, began to attend a social-skills training program. The weekly group meeting would focus on getting him (and other similar participants) to observe the behavior of others, identifying new behaviors that he would like to try himself, and practicing these new behaviors. He would be taught how to accept and benefit from positive and negative comments (feedback) made by patients and staff in regard to his performance. Frequently, this performance would take the form of role playing, in which he would "act" the part of himself or some other person during a short scene created by the therapist.

For instance, the unemployed schizophrenic might be invited to play the role of the interviewee at a job interview. A second patient would play the part of the employer. They would hold a mock interview lasting

istration of drugs is a violation of a person's basic freedoms. On the other hand, hospital staff members fear that violent patients may be a danger to themselves, other patients, and staff if they are not medicated. One resident-care aide stated that "Those who refuse drugs may be those who need them most because they are dangerous. We don't have enough staff on the units to deal with that" (*Ann Arbor News,* 1984, p. 4). As the funding of state mental institutions has decreased, the use of medication has increased. According to the Director of the Michigan Department of Mental Health, 98 percent of patients in state hospitals are on psychotropic drugs.

The movement for patients' rights seems to be increasing in strength. In 1982, relatives of a woman who developed tardive dyskinesia successfully sued the State of Michigan for $1 million. Since that time, a bill has been proposed in the Michigan legislature to grant the following rights to patients in state hospitals:

☐ The approximately 15 percent of all patients who are voluntarily hospitalized should have the right to refuse drugs.

☐ The remaining 85 percent, who are involuntary patients, should have a limited right to refuse drugs. Such a patient could refuse medication, but then a three-member panel from the hospital would review the case and decide whether it was necessary. The patient could be represented by advocates or an attorney at the review.

Many patients'-rights advocates feel that *all* patients should be able to refuse drugs. They expect that increased awareness of the potential harmfulness of neuroleptics will force more careful monitoring of their use and encourage the development of alternative forms of treatment for the psychoses.

perhaps five minutes, which might include the following exchange:

> PATIENT APPLICANT: I understand that you are looking for someone to do some simple computer programming.
> EMPLOYER: Yes, I am. Do you have any experience in that area?
> PATIENT APPLICANT: Well, I've had a few jobs in programming, but they were quite a while ago. I'm not sure that I'm up on the latest technology.
> EMPLOYER: You've had a *few* jobs? Did you have trouble holding down a job?
> PATIENT APPLICANT: Well, you see, I've had some psychological problems that have kept me out of the work force. I'm on medication now, but occasionally I need to be rehospitalized.

At the conclusion of the interview, each participant would explain how it felt to be in his or her particular role. The observers—patients and staff members—would comment on the strengths and weaknesses of each patient's performance. Advice would be offered about the types of statements that should be made to a potential employer and those that should not. The interview would then be repeated so that the patient could incorporate the feedback into his performance.

> PATIENT APPLICANT: I understand you are looking for someone to do some computer programming. I believe I am qualified for the position.
> EMPLOYER: Are you? What kind of background do you have in the area of programming?
> PATIENT APPLICANT: Well, I'm familiar with a number of different computer languages, including BASIC, FORTRAN, and COBAL. I've worked on projects that have tested new ways to teach these languages to high school students. My boss was very pleased with my work.
> EMPLOYER: I see from your application that you've been out of work for over a year. What have you been doing?
> PATIENT APPLICANT: I was going through a very stressful period, so I took some time off from work. But I'm feeling fine now, and I'm really eager to get back into programming again.

Social-skills programs are generally accepted as effective for teaching basic interpersonal skills to schizophrenics. Their major shortcoming is the problem of transferring what is learned and perfected in therapeutic sessions to real-life situations outside the clinic (Wallace et al. 1980). This problem is often addressed through "homework" assignments, in which the patient practices his or her new skills in an actual situation. Thus, when the unemployed schizophrenic had achieved a certain level of competence in mock interviews, he would be asked to go on a real job interview. In the next session he would report his experience to the group and then be given the opportunity to role-play the situation again.

The combination of medication and therapy has provided hope for many schizophrenic patients; continuing research points to an even more promising future. This optimism is reflected in the words of a young pharmacy student who is also a schizophrenic:

> And even now in 1980, in a professional pharmacy school, it would probably shock many people to know that a schizophrenic was in their class, was going to be a pharmacist, and could do a good job. And knowledge of it could cause the loss of many friends and acquaintances. So even now I must write this article anonymously. But I want people to know that I have schizophrenia, that I need medicine and psychotherapy, and at times I have required hospitalization. . . . When you think about schizophrenia next time, try to remember me; there are more people like me out there trying to overcome a poorly understood disease. . . . And some of them are making it. (Anonymous 1983)

SUMMARY

1. Much research and theorizing has focused on the etiology of schizophrenia. Using such research strategies as the analysis of family trees, twin studies, and adoption studies, investigators have shown that heredity does

have an influence on this group of disorders. The degree of influence is open to question, however; when methodological problems are taken into account, it appears to be less than has been reported. It is obvious, though, that heredity alone is not sufficient to cause schizophrenia; environmental factors are also involved.

2. The process by which genetic influences are transmitted has not been explained. Attempts to find specific biochemical or neurological differences between schizophrenics and nonschizophrenics have not yielded many positive findings. The most promising area of research involves the relationship between brain dopamine (a neurotransmitter) and schizophrenia.

3. The search for an environmental basis for schizophrenia has met with no more success than the search for genetic influences. Certain negative family patterns, involving parental characteristics or intrafamilial communication processes, seem to be correlated with schizophrenia. These disorders have been found to be most prevalent among individuals in low-status occupations who live in the poorest areas of large cities, and differences in symptomology seem to be loosely related to cultural variables. But again, the effects of such sociocultural variables are still open to speculation.

4. The research on the etiology of schizophrenia thus suggests an interaction between genetic and environmental factors. The theoretical vulnerability/stress model of schizophrenia includes a personal vulnerability that may be caused by hereditary, biological, or psychological factors. When the vulnerable person is exposed to strong environmental stressors but does not have the resources to cope with them, a schizophrenic episode may result.

5. Schizophrenia seems to involve both biological and psychological factors, and treatment programs that combine drugs with psychotherapy seem to hold the most promise. Drug therapy usually involves the phenothiazines, or antipsychotics, and the accompanying psychosocial therapy consists of either supportive counseling or behavior therapy, with an emphasis on social-skills training.

KEY TERMS

concordance rate The likelihood that both of a pair of subjects exhibit the feature that is being studied

deinstitutionalization The shifting of responsibility for the care of mental patients from large central institutions to agencies within local communities

developmental study A long-term study of a group of individuals, beginning before the onset of a disorder, that allows investigators to see how the disorder develops

dopamine hypothesis The suggestion that schizophrenia results from an excess of dopamine activity at certain brain synapses

double-bind theory The suggestion that schizophrenia develops in an individual as a result of the continual reception of contradictory messages from parents during the individual's upbringing

schizophrenogenic Causing or producing schizophrenia; generally used to describe a parent who is simultaneously or alternately cold and overprotecting, rejecting and dominating

vulnerability/stress model A theoretical model postulating that innate vulnerability and the effect of environmental stressors combine in the production of schizophrenic episodes

PART 5

Organic and Developmental Problems

17
Organic Brain Disorders

In the ring, Muhammad Ali was able to "float like a butterfly, sting like a bee" as he won, lost, and twice regained the world heavyweight boxing championship. Outside the ring he was known for his ego, his wit and rapidfire speech, and his never-ending rhyming. But it was a different Muhammad Ali who, at age 42 and retired from boxing, entered a New York City hospital for neurological testing. His speech was slurred and sometimes unintelligible, and he tended to shuffle when he walked; he often seemed remote and expressionless, constantly felt tired, and suffered occasional lapses of memory.

Ali's symptoms are very much like those of Parkinson's disease, a brain disorder. But are they due to that disorder or to the poundings he must have taken in more than twenty years of boxing? His doctors reported that he did not have Parkinson's disease nor is he "punch-drunk." His disorder was diagnosed as Parkinson's syndrome, meaning that he has many of the symptoms of Parkinson's disease although he does not have the disorder.

Anti-Parkinson's medication has reduced the severity of some of Ali's symptoms, but the prognosis is vague. The former champion has been able to make a few public appearances, but he is far from the old Ali. Five months after his disorder was diagnosed, he was an honored guest at the sixtieth annual Boxing Writers Association dinner:

> At times, Ali disappeared within himself, as if in a trance. A boxing annual from 1965—the cover headlined "Can Ali Beat Liston a Second Time?"—was deposited in front of him [by a fan]. Ali opened it to a picture of himself and Sonji, his first wife.
>
> "He kept staring at that page," said Schulian [who was sitting next to Ali]. "He put the magazine down in his shrimp and avocado salad and kept staring at it. Finally, Jose Torres lifted the magazine gently and asked him if he wanted his salad."

473

Later, while somebody gave an award-acceptance speech, Ali allowed his eyelids to fall, and he slept for 10 minutes. Only then did a faintly quizzical expression replace his usually benign and bemused countenance. (Marantz 1985, p. 63)

Muhammad Ali's symptoms have not been tied specifically to the head blows he received as a boxer. However, elimination of Parkinson's disease as the cause would seem to indicate that they are due to brain trauma.

As you will see in this chapter, it is often difficult to discern the exact causes of **organic mental disorders,** which are behavioral disturbances that result from organic brain pathology—damage to the brain. Possible causes include aging, trauma, infection, loss of blood supply, and various biochemical imbalances. These may result in cognitive, emotional, and behavioral symptoms that can resemble the symptoms of the *functional* disorders that we have discussed in preceding chapters. (The **functional disorders** are those mental disorders for which no physical basis can be found and that are assumed to be due primarily to psychological factors.) In fact, even highly experienced diagnosticians often have trouble determining whether some mental disorders are organic or functional.

This problem stems in part from the fact that the behavioral disturbance that results from brain pathology is influenced by social and psychological factors as well as by the specific pathology. In other words, individuals with similar types of brain damage may behave quite differently, depending on their premorbid personalities, their coping skills, and the availability of such resources as family support systems. Furthermore, those with organic brain dysfunctions often encounter insensitivity in others and, as a result, experience a great deal of stress. This may add to or modify the symptoms exhibited as a result of the organic disorder.

Physical, social, and psychological factors thus interact in a complicated fashion to produce the behaviors seen in individuals with organic brain disturbances. Treatment, too, often entails some combination of physical, medicinal, and psychological therapy, behavior modification, and skills training. For some patients who have experienced severe and irreversible brain damage, rehabilitation, modified skills training, and the creation of a supportive environment may be the only available options.

THE HUMAN BRAIN

The brain is an organ that weighs approximately 3 pounds and is composed of more than 10 billion cells. As we have noted in earlier chapters, *neurons* (or nerve cells) transfer information within the brain. This information travels along a neuron in the form of electrical impulses; the transfer of electrical impulses from neuron to neuron is aided by chemical transmitters that are called *neurotransmitters* or *neuroregulators*.

As viewed from above, the brain is separated into a left and a right cerebral hemisphere by the longitudinal fissure (see Figure 17.1). Disturbance of these hemispheres (such as by a tumor or by electrical stimulation with electrodes) may produce specific sensory or motor effects. It is known that each hemisphere controls the opposite side of the body. Thus, for example, paralysis on the left side of the body indicates a dysfunction in the right hemisphere. In addition, the right hemisphere is associated with visual–spatial abilities and emotional behavior. The left hemisphere controls the language functions for nearly all right-handed individuals and for the majority of left-handed individuals (Golden and Vincente 1983).

Viewed in cross section, the brain can be considered to be comprised of three sections: the forebrain, the midbrain, and the hindbrain. Although each of these sections is vital for functioning and survival, the forebrain is prob-

Figure 17.1 The Gross Structure of the Human Brain

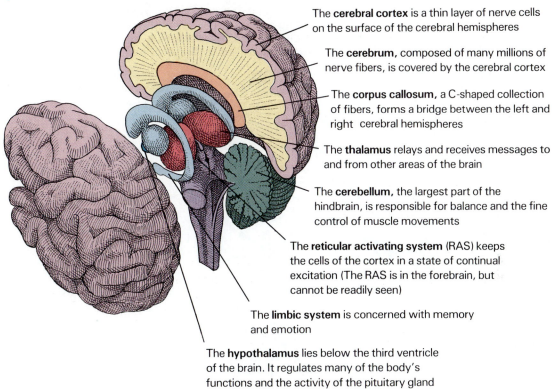

The **cerebral cortex** is a thin layer of nerve cells on the surface of the cerebral hemispheres

The **cerebrum,** composed of many millions of nerve fibers, is covered by the cerebral cortex

The **corpus callosum,** a C-shaped collection of fibers, forms a bridge between the left and right cerebral hemispheres

The **thalamus** relays and receives messages to and from other areas of the brain

The **cerebellum,** the largest part of the hindbrain, is responsible for balance and the fine control of muscle movements

The **reticular activating system** (RAS) keeps the cells of the cortex in a state of continual excitation (The RAS is in the forebrain, but cannot be readily seen)

The **limbic system** is concerned with memory and emotion

The **hypothalamus** lies below the third ventricle of the brain. It regulates many of the body's functions and the activity of the pituitary gland

SOURCE: Adapted from The Rand McNally atlas of the body and mind (p. 75). (1976). London: Mitchell Beazley. © Mitchell Beazley Publishers Limited.

ably the most relevant to a discussion of abnormal behavior. Within the forebrain are the thalamus, hypothalamus, reticular activating system, limbic system, and cerebrum. The specific functions of these structures are still being debated, but we can discuss their more general functions with some degree of confidence. The *thalamus,* for example, seems to serve as a "relay station," transmitting nerve impulses to other parts of the brain. The *hypothalamus* regulates bodily drives (such as hunger, thirst, and sex) and body conditions such as temperature and hormone balance. The *reticular activating system* is a bundle of nerve fibers that controls bodily states such as sleep, alertness, and attention. The *limbic system* seems to be involved in the experi-

ence and expression of emotions and motivation—pleasure, fear, aggressiveness, sexual arousal, and pain.

The largest structure in the brain is the *cerebrum,* whose outermost layer of grey matter is called the *cerebral cortex.* The cerebrum is the seat of human consciousness and of all learning, speech, thought, and memory. It processes sensory information, controls motor activity, and produces and controls language. The two cerebral hemispheres are connected by a collection of nerve fibers called the *corpus callosum.*

The brain and the spinal cord together comprise the **central nervous system**. The spinal cord links the brain to the rest of the body by transmitting sensory and motor information to

Figure 17.2 *The Autonomic Nervous System*

The autonomic nervous system (ANS) helps to regulate internal bodily processes. The sympathetic division prepares the body for action by increasing heart rate, constricting blood vessels, and decreasing intestinal secretions. The parasympathetic division conserves energy by decreasing heart rate and promoting digestive processes. Important organs controlled by the ANS are shown below.

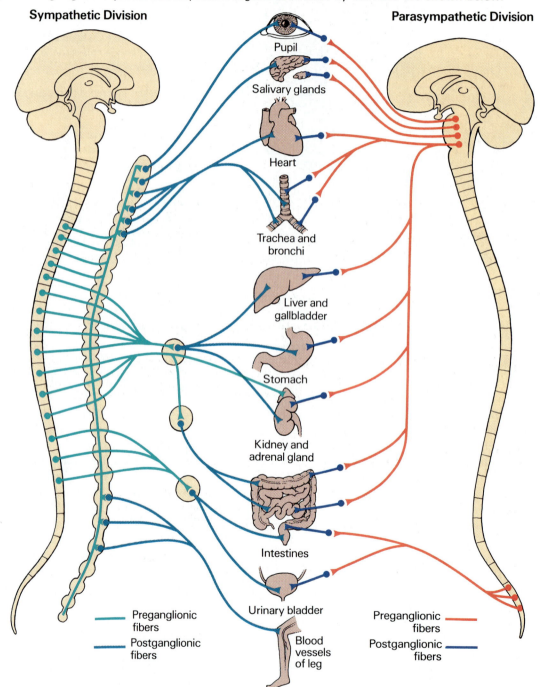

Sympathetic Division

Parasympathetic Division

Pupil

Salivary glands

Heart

Trachea and bronchi

Liver and gallbladder

Stomach

Kidney and adrenal gland

Intestines

Urinary bladder

Blood vessels of leg

Preganglionic fibers
Postganglionic fibers

Preganglionic fibers
Postganglionic fibers

and from the brain. The spinal cord has some primitive reflex capabilities, but complex behaviors that depend on memory and learning experiences are controlled by the brain. Beyond the central nervous system is the **autonomic nervous system** (see Figure 17.2, p. 476), which links the spinal cord with the smooth muscles of various vital organs and with the different glands. (We discussed the autonomic nervous system in Chapter 6 on the anxiety disorders.)

THE ASSESSMENT OF BRAIN DAMAGE

The techniques used in assessing brain damage were discussed in Chapter 4. Recall that these are of two types: neuropsychological tests that require patient responses and that assess such functions as memory and manual dexterity, and neurological tests that allow one to "look into" the brain. The neurological tests include the electroencephalograph (EEG) and computerized axial tomography (CAT) scanning.

Two newer techniques involve the monitoring of a radioactive substance as it moves through the brain (Boller et al. 1984). In *cerebral blood flow measurement,* the patient inhales a radioactive gas, which flows through the brain with the blood. The gas—and thus the flow of blood—is monitored with a gamma ray camera. In *positron emitting tomography* (PET), the patient is injected with a radioactive glucose substance. By monitoring the radioactivity, one can study the metabolism of glucose in the patient's brain, which provides a very accurate means of assessing brain function.

These techniques will no doubt increase diagnostic accuracy in cases of brain damage. But of equal importance is an assessment of the patient's general cognitive functioning, personality characteristics, and coping skills, as well as his or her behaviors and emotional reactions—particularly when they differ from

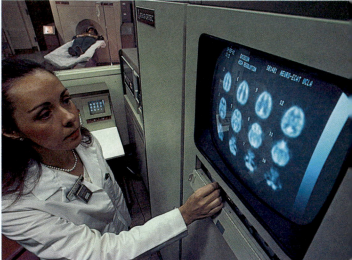

Computerized axial tomography (CAT) scanning (top) uses X-rays to make a three-dimensional representation of the brain. A neurologist can study these computer-enhanced X-rays and locate abnormal tissues within the brain (bottom).

reported premorbid functioning. Such an assessment can provide crucial information about brain dysfunction, and it is of utmost importance in the planning of treatment and rehabilitation.

Localization of brain damage

Neurological techniques such as CAT and PET scans are used to determine the location and extent of brain damage. But can the location of a damaged or disrupted area of the brain be determined from the loss of function exhibited by the patient? Neuropsychologists have debated this question for a number of years, and there have been many attempts to relate functions to specific areas of the brain.

In one study, researchers used computerized tomography to examine eighty-seven patients, each of whom had a brain lesion (organic brain damage) that was localized within one of eight areas of the brain (Golden et al. 1981). Each area was then matched with the particular functions that were affected. The brain areas (four in each hemisphere) are shown in Figure 17.3; the functions that they seemed to control are listed in Table 17.1.

Figure 17.3 *The Left Hemisphere of the Brain*

The four major areas in each hemisphere, as shown, were matched with losses of functioning to obtain Table 17.1.

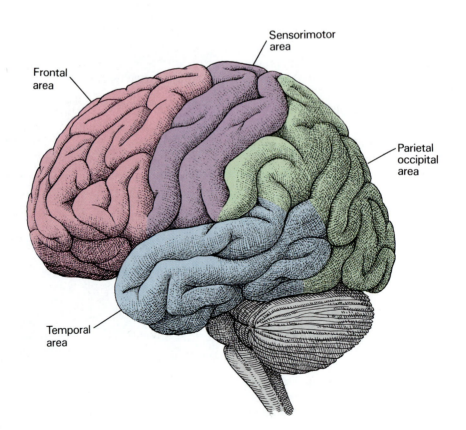

Table 17.1 *Brain Areas and the Functions They Control*

Left Frontal Area	Right Frontal Area
Expression via speech	Motor
Mathematics	Rhythm
Reception of speech	Mathematics
Left Sensorimotor Area	Right Sensorimotor Area
Expression via speech	Motor
Mathematics	Tactile
Left Parietal–Occipital Area	Right Parietal–Occipital Area
Mathematics	Tactile
Expression via speech	Motor
Writing	
Reading	
Left Temporal Lobe	Right Temporal Lobe
Reception of speech	Rhythm
Expression via speech	Motor
Memory	Tactile
Intelligence	

SOURCE: Golden, C.J., et al. Difference in brain densities between chronic alcoholic and normal control patients. *Science, 211,* 508–510, Table 30, January 1981. Copyright © 1981 by the American Association for the Advancement of Science. Used by permission.

Note the extensive overlapping of functions, which complicates the assessment of brain damage by determining functional losses. Moreover, "No two human brains are identical in appearance or in distribution of the functional organization of psychological skills. Although there are close approximations in most cases, it is not possible to find one-to-one correspondences for specific physical areas related to specific psychological functions from brain to brain" (Golden et al. 1981, p. 504).

Two processes that may occur within the brain can further complicate the matching of function (or loss of function) with specific brain areas. The first, which has been documented by numerous experimental and clinical studies, is *diaschisis,* in which a lesion in a specific area of the brain disrupts other anatomically intact areas, sometimes even in the opposite hemisphere (Smith 1982). A possible mechanism for diaschisis is the vast network of neurological pathways connecting the different areas and systems within the brain.

These pathways, by which a "message" may be rerouted if it is blocked at a damaged area, may also explain the second process—the recovery of function after an area of the brain has been damaged. Other explanations stress *redundancy,* in which an "unused" portion of the brain takes up the function of the damaged area, or *plasticity,* in which a portion of the brain that has not yet become fully specialized substitutes for the damaged portion. The plasticity explanation would account for the development of language in young children with left-hemisphere damage. For example, a five-year-old boy whose left hemisphere was removed to eliminate seizures was found, in a later examination, to have developed superior language and intellectual abilities. Because the right hemisphere had not yet become fully specialized, it was able to develop the structure necessary to support language and intellectual ability (Smith and Sugar 1975).

There is, however, some evidence that such a shift of function from one hemisphere to the other may decrease the functional space that is available for the development of other skills: One individual who had left-hemisphere damage at birth did develop normal language ability, but his visual–spatial memory was impaired. The development of language may have required functional space that would normally be devoted to visual–spatial ability (Bullard-Bates and Satz 1983).

The dimensions of brain damage

Organic brain damage can be evaluated along a continuum of degree, from mild to moderate to severe. In addition, clinicians often distinguish between causes that are endogenous and exogenous, between damage that is diffuse and specific, and between conditions that are acute and chronic.

Endogenous brain damage is damage that has been caused by something within the person. Examples of internal causes are the loss of blood flow to the brain and congenital disorders such as epilepsy that was acquired at birth. *Exogenous* brain damage is caused by some external factor, such as a severe blow to the head or poisoning.

The diffuse–specific distinction is used to indicate the extent of the brain damage. *Diffuse* damage is rather generalized destruction; it typically involves widespread impairment of functioning, including disorientation, poor memory and judgment, and emotional instability. *Specific* brain damage is fairly localized tissue destruction that usually causes impairment or behavioral consequences that correspond only to the psychological or physiological function of the injured area.

An *acute* brain disorder is one that is not accompanied by significant and permanent damage to brain tissue. A high fever or a severe episode of alcoholic intoxication can result in acute organic changes that are reversible and thus temporary. (We should note, however, that the ability of the central nervous system to repair itself when damaged is extremely limited.) A *chronic* disorder involves permanent and irreversible brain damage—for example, as a result of severe lead poisoning in children. Symptoms that may signal an acute organic condition include:

1. *Impairment of consciousness*. This is usually the most obvious change in an acute disorder, and it can range from a barely perceptible loss of consciousness to coma. The individual may have difficulty in judging time, focusing attention, or thinking coherently.
2. *Changes in psychomotor behavior*. The level of activity may decrease, and movements may become automatic, slow, and hesitant.
3. *Changes in thinking processes*. Reasoning and comprehension may be impaired, and the individual may tend to place greater significance on subjective experiences and thoughts.
4. *Emotional lability*. At first the individual may exhibit depression, anxiety, and irritability. As time passes, these may be replaced by apathy, indifference, and emotional withdrawal (Lishman 1978).

Individuals with chronic organic disorders may display similar symptoms, but an impaired memory is usually the first noticeable sign of a chronic condition. Over time, the affected individual may learn to compensate for many of the other symptoms.

A syndrome that appears quite often in chronic organic disorders but only occasionally in acute organic brain dysfunctions is dementia (see Focus 17.1). **Dementia** is characterized by the deterioration of intellectual ability and by impaired judgment, of sufficient severity to interfere with social and occupational functioning. The most prominent feature appears to be the impairment of memory. Individuals with dementia may forget to finish tasks that have been begun, forget the names of significant others, and have difficulty recalling past events. In addition, their ability to think abstractly may be impaired. Some individuals exhibiting this syndrome also display impulse problems. They may, for example, disrobe in public or make sexual advances to strangers (DSM-III).

FOCUS 17.1

Dementia

Although dementia is most often encountered in the elderly, only a small proportion actually develop this syndrome. Only 5 percent of older individuals are severely demented, and 10 percent are mildly or moderately demented (NIH 1981).

Dementia is, in fact, associated with a range of disorders. Wells (1978) analyzed the records of 222 patients who displayed dementia as the primary manifestation, rather than secondarily to a diagnosed disorder. The dementia was later attributed to the following causes:

Atrophy of uncertain cause (probably Alzheimer's disease), 51%
Vascular disease, 8%

Normal pressure hydrocephalus, 6%
Dementia in alcoholics, 6%
Intracranial masses, 5%
Huntington's chorea, 5%
Depression, 4%
Drug toxicity, 3%
Dementia uncertain, 3%
Others, 9%
(Wells 1978, p. 2)

These findings have important diagnostic implications because such problems as depression, drug toxicity, normal pressure hydrocephalus, and benign intracranial masses are correctable. The identification of noncorrectable causes of dementia is also important, because some may require specific therapeutic intervention.

Diagnostic problems

The two major problems in diagnosing brain damage arise because of similarities between the symptoms of organic and functional disorders. Thus individuals who have not suffered brain damage may be diagnosed as having an organic disorder. Deeply depressed individuals often show characteristics that are similar to those of brain-damaged individuals; in particular, the neuropsychological tests that are used to assess a wide range of functions (including language, cognition, motor functions, and visual–motor functions) were found to be subject to the effects of depression (Sweet 1983). It is also difficult to distinguish brain-damaged from schizophrenic patients through the use of neuropsychological tests (Portnoff et al. 1983).

The elderly are particularly vulnerable to inaccurate diagnosis as being brain-damaged. An aged adult may perform poorly during assessment testing because of reduced sensory acuity, performance anxiety, fatigue, or a lack of understanding of test instructions. For this reason, tests that differentiate between normal and brain-damaged young adults cannot be assumed to apply to older individuals. In a study of fifty retired teachers, many scored in the brain-damaged range on the Halstead–Reitan Neuropsychological Test Battery, even though they scored in the superior range on the WAIS and maintained a high level of functioning in their daily lives (Price et al. 1980).

To ensure that a particular set of symptoms stems from an organic brain disorder, clinicians usually try to determine whether the central nervous system has been damaged or whether a causal agent (such as a poison) is responsible for the symptoms. In some cases, support for a diagnosis of organic brain disorder can come from a patient's positive response to a treatment that is known to be effective against a particular disorder. For

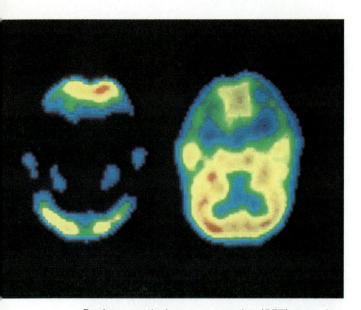

Positron emission tomography (PET) scanning uses a radioactive glucose substance to assess brain activity, which is represented in the photo by different color intensities. Red indicates areas of greatest brain activity. Yellow, blue, and green indicate decreasing levels of brain activity, with black representing the least. The photo on the left is of an Alzheimer's diseased brain, while the photo on the right is of a normal brain.

example, a diagnosis of Parkinson's disease is supported by the patient's response to treatment with L-Dopa.

The second major diagnostic problem is opposite in effect: Individuals who have suffered brain damage may be diagnosed as having a psychological disorder.

Larry D., age thirty-eight, was an energetic community college teacher and athletic coach and the happily married father of four children. During a particularly busy period, he suffered an apparent seizure while attending a professional conference. Just prior to the seizure, he reported smelling an unusual odor; he then temporarily lost consciousness. Medical evaluations following the episode revealed no obvious cause for Larry's loss of consciousness, and it was assumed to be due to a lack of sleep and general fatigue.

Although he did not pass out again, Larry began to exhibit such symptoms as loss of appetite, difficulty in sleeping, fatigue, and some mental confusion. He became increasingly withdrawn both from his family and from his professional activities, and he mentioned suicide several times. His family and colleagues became extremely concerned about his behavior. A mental health professional was consulted, and psychiatric hospitalization was recommended. But Larry's condition continued to deteriorate.

At this point Larry's wife sought a second opinion from the neuropsychology clinic at a local university. The results of neuropsychological testing suggested organic difficulties originating in the right temporal lobe of the brain. A CAT scan was performed and a brain tumor was located.

In Larry's case, joint neuropsychological and medical assessment was able to pinpoint the cause of the disorder. Naturally, the course of treatment changed significantly once the brain tumor was discovered. In many cases, as here, the initial neuropsychological assessment or even the initial use of techniques such as CAT scanning may not yield information that clearly points to an organic impairment. For this reason, follow-up testing at regular intervals is often recommended. This also allows the monitoring of the patient's performance on succeeding neuropsychological tests, to detect significant patterns of deterioration.

CAUSES OF BRAIN DAMAGE

The sources of organic brain damage that are discussed here are brain trauma, aging, disease and infection, tumors, and epilepsy. In addition, toxic substances, drugs, alcohol, malnutrition, and even brain surgery may produce organic brain syndromes.

Brain trauma

A **brain trauma** is a physical wound or injury to the brain. The severity, duration, and symptoms may differ widely, depending on the premorbid personality of the individual and on the extent and location of the neural damage. Generally, the greater the amount of tissue damage, the greater the impairment of functioning. In some cases, however, interactions among various parts of the brain, coupled with brain redundancy, may compensate for some loss of tissue.

Head injuries are usually classifed as either concussions, contusions, or lacerations. A **concussion** is a mild brain injury that is typically caused by a blow to the head. Blood vessels in the brain are often ruptured, and circulatory and other brain functions may be disrupted temporarily. The individual may become dazed or even lose consciousness and, upon regaining consciousness, may experience postconcussion headaches, disorientation, confusion, and memory loss. The symptoms are usually temporary, lasting no longer than a few weeks.

In a **contusion,** the brain is forced to shift slightly and press against the side of the skull. The cortex of the brain may be bruised (that is, blood vessels may rupture) on impact with the skull. As in concussion, the person may lose consciousness for a few hours or even for days. Postcontusion symptoms often include headaches, nausea, an inability to concentrate, and irritability. Although the symptoms are similar to those of concussion, they are generally more severe and last longer.

> Thirteen-year-old Ron G. was the catcher for his school baseball team. During a game, one of the players from the other school's team accidentally lost his grip on the bat as he swung at a pitch. The bat hit Ron on the forehead. Although his catcher's mask absorbed some of the blow, the blow knocked Ron out. An hour elapsed before he regained consciousness at a nearby hospital, where he was diagnosed as having a cerebral contusion. Headaches, muscle weakness, and nausea continued for two weeks.

Lacerations are brain traumas in which brain tissue is torn, pierced, or ruptured, usually by an object that has penetrated the skull. When an object also penetrates the brain, death may result. If the person survives and regains consciousness, a variety of temporary or permanent effects may be observed. Symptoms may be quite serious, depending on the extent of damage to the brain tissue and on the amount of hemorrhaging. Cognitive processes are frequently impaired, and personality changes may be exhibited.

More than 8 million Americans suffer head injuries each year, and about 20 percent of these result in serious brain trauma. The majority of affected individuals show deficits in attention and poor concentration, are easily fatigued, and tend to be irritable (Webster and Scott 1983). Emotional reactions are also displayed: In one study, the subjects were 23 patients with severe traumatic brain injuries (17 closed-head injuries, 3 penetrating missile wounds, 2 cerebral contusions, and 1 brain-stem contusion) who had spent an average of 20 days in a coma. Every one of them displayed a distress syndrome characterized by depression, anxiety, tension, and nervousness—yet they all denied having these feelings (Sbordone and Jennison 1983). It is, in fact, common for patients with severe traumatic injuries to deny emotional reactions and physical dysfunctions until they begin to recover from their injuries.

Closed-head injuries are the most common form of brain trauma and the most common reason for the referral of individuals under forty to neurologists (Golden et al. 1983). They usually result from a blow that causes damage at the site of the impact and at the opposite side of the head. If the victim's head was in motion before the impact (as is generally the case in automobile accidents), the blow produces a forward-and-back movement of the brain, accompanied by tearing and hemorrhaging of brain tissue. Epilepsy develops in about 5 percent of closed-head injuries and in over 30 percent of open-head injuries in which the brain tissue is penetrated. Damage to brain tissues in the left hemisphere most often results in psychiatric and intellectual disorders,

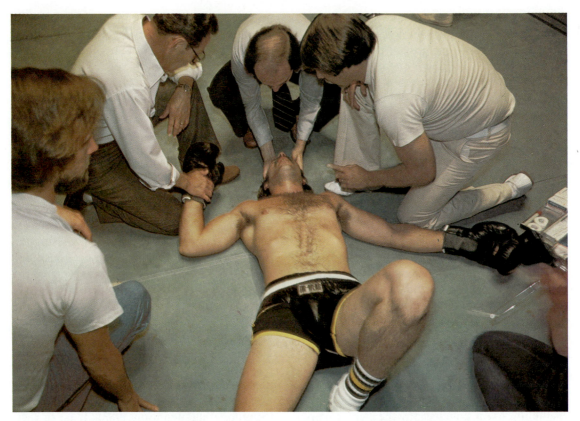

Boxing has recently come under the intense scrutiny and censure of physicians because of the sport's potential for producing brain damage. Blows to the head can cause contusions and concussions. Doctors fear that repeatedly sustained brain trauma can lead to long-term negative consequences.

whereas affective disorders more frequently result from damage to brain tissues in the right hemisphere (Lishman 1978).

Severe brain trauma has long-term negative consequences for the affected individual. Young adults who are comatose for at least 24 hours later experience residual cognitive deficits that interfere with employment and psychosocial adjustment. Recovery from the trauma often does not ensure a return to the victim's premorbid level of functioning. Along with any physical or mental disabilities that may be produced by the brain damage, motivational and emotional disturbances result from the frustration of coping with these physical or mental deficits. As a consequence, only one-third of patients with severe closed-head

injuries are able to return to gainful employment after traditional rehabilitative therapy (Prigatano et al. 1984).

Newer treatment techniques appear to be more promising. In one approach, intensive cognitive retraining is combined with psychotherapeutic intervention. This new program provides patients with increased awareness and acceptance of their injuries and residual deficits, cognitive retraining to counter selected residual deficits, a repertoire of compensatory skills, and understanding of their emotional and motivational disturbance. When patients in this program were compared with patients in a traditional program, the former showed better neuropsychological functioning, greater improvement in personality traits, and greater success at work (Prigatano et al. 1984).

Disorders associated with aging

The organic disorders that occur most commonly among the elderly are stroke and Alzheimer's disease. Although these conditions are correlated with aging, they can also occur among younger individuals.

Strokes Although the brain represents only 2 percent of the body weight, it requires 15 percent of the blood flow and 20 percent of the oxygen used by the body (Oliver et al. 1982). A **stroke** or **cerebrovascular accident** is a sudden stoppage of blood flow to a portion of the brain, which leads to a loss of brain function.

Strokes are the third major cause of death in the United States, afflicting more than 400,000 individuals annually. Only about 50 to 60 percent of stroke victims survive, and they generally require long-term care while suffering from a variety of mental and sensory–motor disabilities (Oliver et al. 1982). (See Focus 17.2, p. 486.) Stroke victims are often frustrated and depressed by their handicaps, and they exhibit greater depression and interpersonal sensitivity than other groups of patients. Moreover, their depression seems to deepen with time (Magni and Schifano 1984). Anxiety regarding their disabilities occasionally leads to further disability.

The bursting of blood vessels (and the attendant intercranial hemorrhaging) causes 25 percent of all strokes and often occurs during exertion. Victims report feeling that something is wrong within the head, along with headaches and nausea. Confusion, paralysis, and loss of consciousness follow rapidly. Mortality rates for this type of stroke are extremely high.

Strokes may also be caused by the narrowing of blood vessels due to a build-up of fatty material on interior walls (**atherosclerosis**) or by the blockage of blood vessels. In either case, the result is *infarction,* the death of brain tissue due to a decrease in the supply of blood. These strokes often occur during sleep, with the individual being paralyzed when he or she awakens. Approximately 20 percent die, 20 percent exhibit full to nearly full recovery, and 60 percent of the stroke victims suffer residual disabilities (Lishman 1978).

The residual loss of function after a stroke usually involves only one side of the body, most often the left. Interestingly, one of the residual symptoms of stroke is a "lack of acknowledgment" of one particular side of various stimuli. For example, a patient who is asked to copy a pattern may draw half the pattern and may ignore, say, the left side of his or her body (Golden et al. 1983).

Some functional reorganization of the brain may occur after a stroke to compensate for the loss of function. Three months after suffering a stroke due to cerebral infarction, one patient exhibited significantly reduced cerebral blood flow in the left angular gyrus area. An examination performed one year later revealed no residual abnormalities. However, the observed pattern of blood flow suggested increased activation in brain areas surrounding the left angular gyrus area. It is possible that the patient's clinical improvement was due to a reorganization of the brain in which the function of the destroyed area was taken over by other areas.

A series of infarctions may lead to a syndrome known as **multi-infarct dementia,** which is characterized by the uneven deterioration of intellectual abilities (although some mental functions may remain intact). The specific symptoms of this disruption depend on the area and extent of the brain damage. Both physical and intellectual functioning are usually impaired. The patient may show gradual improvement in intellectual functioning, but repeated episodes of infarction can occur and produce additional disability.

Alzheimer's disease The disorder that is perhaps most often associated with aging is **Alz-**

Aphasia

Aphasia is the loss of motor or sensory functions that are associated with language. Aphasic persons with motor disturbances may have trouble expressing themselves via verbal language *(speech aphasia)*, be unable to recall the names of familiar objects *(nominal aphasia)*, or have problems in writing words *(manual aphasia)*. Sensory aphasias include the inability to understand spoken words *(auditory aphasia)* and the inability to understand written words *(visual aphasia* or *alexia)*. Aphasic problems may be extremely specific. For example, persons with visual aphasia lose the ability to understand written words, although they have no difficulty in reading the words aloud or in understanding spoken words.

Two primary problems in aphasia are the loss of access to words and their meanings and the inability to retain words and their meanings (Schuell 1974). Persons with aphasia may become quite emotional and frustrated over their deficits, and this, in turn, can impede efforts at rehabilitation.

The following dialogue illustrates some of the problems involved in aphasia. Albert Harris is a 67-year-old man who suffered a stroke. In addition to physical therapy for his partially paralyzed right side, an effort was made to rehabilitate his speech. Mr. Harris was unable to fully communicate and expressed himself almost exclusively with the words "Mrs. Harris," his wife's name.

PSYCHOLOGIST: Hello, Mr. Harris.
MR. HARRIS: (responding to psychologist): Hello, Mrs. Harris. Hello, Mrs. Harris.
PSYCHOLOGIST: You look pretty cheerful today.
MR. HARRIS: Yes, Mrs. Harris. Ah . . . Ah . . . Ah (apparently trying to elaborate on his response) Yes, Mrs. Harris. Ah . . . Ah (looking disappointed and frustrated).
PSYCHOLOGIST: I know it's hard to say what you want to say.
MR. HARRIS: Yes, Mrs. Harris, yes. Things will get better, Mrs. Harris.
PSYCHOLOGIST: You've already shown improvement, don't you think?
MR. HARRIS: Mrs. Harris a little bit better, yes. Slow but sure, Mrs. Harris.

Speech and skills training are frequently used to treat aphasia. Although many patients recover from the problem, the reasons for recovery are not well understood. It is possible that other areas of the brain can be trained to compensate for the damaged areas. A relatively new field, called *neurolinguistics,* is concerned with the relationship between language development and brain functioning and with the interrelationship among brain function, speech and language skills, cognitive capacities, and behavior (Blumstein 1981).

heimer's disease, which involves the atrophy of cortical tissue within the brain and leads to marked deterioration of intellectual and emotional functioning. Irritability, cognitive impairment, and memory loss are early symptoms that gradually become worse. Social withdrawal, depression, delusions, impulsive behaviors, neglect of personal hygiene, and other symptoms may eventually appear as well. Death usually occurs within five years of the onset of the disorder.

Autopsies that have been performed on the brains of Alzheimer's disease victims reveal *neurofibrillary tangles* (abnormal fibers that appear to be tangles of brain-tissue filaments) and *senile plaques* (patches of degenerated nerve endings). Both of these conditions are believed to disrupt the transmission of impulses among brain cells, thereby producing the symptoms of the disorder.

Alzheimer's disease is generally considered a disease of the elderly, and its incidence does increase with increasing age. However, it also can attack individuals in their forties or fifties. It occurs most frequently in women.

> Elizabeth R., a 46-year-old woman diagnosed as suffering from Alzheimer's disease, is trying to cope with her increasing problems with memory. She writes notes to herself and tries to compensate for her difficulties by rehearsing conversations with herself, anticipating what might be said. However, she is gradually losing the battle and has had to retire from her job. She quickly forgets what she has just read, and she loses the meaning of an article after reading only a few sentences. She sometimes has to ask where the bathroom is in her own house and is depressed by the realization that she is a burden to her family. (Clark, Gosnell, and Witherspoon et al. 1984, p. 60)

The deterioration of memory seems to be the most poignant and disturbing symptom of Alzheimer's disease. An affected individual may at first forget appointments, phone numbers, and addresses. As the disorder progresses, the individual may become unaware of the time of day, have trouble remembering recent and past events, and forget who he or she is (Reisberg et al. 1982). But even when memory is almost gone, contact with loved ones is still important.

> I believe the emotional memory of relationships is the last to go. You can see daughters or sons come to visit, for example, and the mother will respond. She doesn't know who they are, but you can tell by her expression that she knows they're persons to whom she is devoted. (Materka 1984, p. 13)

Dorothy Coons, who spoke the lines quoted above, works at the University of Michigan Institute of Gerontology. She notes that Alzheimer's disease is the fourth leading cause of

The increasing deterioration of intellectual and emotional functioning is perhaps the most debilitating aspect of Alzheimer's disease. Support groups try to help patients maintain their independence, sense of self-worth, and dignity by encouraging them to make personal decisions for themselves and to maintain social contacts.

death in the United States, and she predicts that by the year 2000 as many as 4 million people may be suffering this disorder (Materka 1984). Yet even then, only about 2 to 3 percent of those in their sixties and seventies, and fewer than 15 percent of those in their nineties, are expected to be victims of Alzheimer's disease (Butler 1984). Most will be living happy and enjoyable lives, as is indicated in Focus 17.3 (p. 488).

The problem of memory loss in the elderly As we have noted, memory loss is one of the most

FOCUS 17.3

Is Mental Deterioration the Fate of the Elderly?

The loss of cognitive and mental capabilities is the symptom that is most feared among the elderly. One 82-year-old man noted that

> It's not the physical decline I fear so much. It's becoming a mental vegetable inside of a healthy body. It is a shame that we can rehabilitate or treat so much of the physical ills, but when your mind goes, there's nothing you can do. (Gatz et al. 1980, p. 12)

The intellectual decline that accompanies aging has, in fact, been overstated. Although tests of intellectual functioning indicate that performance abilities generally start to decline in one's late sixties or early seventies, verbal fluency and cognitive skills are usually quite stable over time (Gallagher et al. 1980). Approximately 75 percent of older individuals retain sharp mental functioning, and an additional 10 to 15 percent experience only mild to moderate memory loss (Butler 1984).

The vast majority of noninstitutionalized individuals aged 60 or more have the ability to live independently within the community. A statewide sample of 2146 Virginians, aged 60 to over 85 and living in their own communities (rather than in institutions) was studied to determine the prevalence of mental disorders in the elderly population (Romaniuk et al. 1983). Information from questionnaires, self-ratings, and interviews indicated that rates of psychopathology are relatively low. Only 6.3 percent displayed mild cognitive impairment, and 2.1 percent showed moderate to severe cognitive impairment. Only 15 percent displayed any signs of mental illness.

Most of the subjects seemed satisfied with their health: 13 percent rated their health as excellent, 46 percent as good, 31 percent as fair, and only 9 percent as poor. Approximately 90 percent of the sample displayed "common sense," "mental alertness," and "coping ability."

Over 75 percent said they enjoyed their life.

obvious symptoms of Alzheimer's disease. It is also a major symptom of **senile dementia,** which is a severe loss of intellectual functioning produced by the deterioration of brain cells as a consequence of aging—usually after the age of seventy-five. Loss of memory may also be exhibited by elderly individuals suffering multi-infarct dementia. And finally, occasional loss of memory is part of the normal aging process, the gradual wearing down of the brain and other body organs.

Because memory loss characterizes many disorders as well as normal aging, it is of concern to the elderly and yet difficult for clinicians to assess. Consider, for example, the following letter:

Dear Dr. Smyer:

I have toyed with the idea of writing you ever since I heard you speak at the Presbyterian Church a couple of years ago. The occasion was one of the series of brown-bag lunches sponsored, I think, by the Area Agency on Aging. You may remember me, since I'm sure you were embarrassed when I substituted one word for another in trying to ask a question about the part inheritance plays in senility. My question made no sense, and you tactfully said, "I don't believe I understand your question," and I repeated it, correctly, saying, "You can see I'm senile already." (I was trying to be funny, but I was not amused.)

The question I asked is one that has haunted me all my adult life (I've just turned 78), and I think I have always known the answer. My father's father, my father, and the three sisters who lived long enough were all senile. I am obviously following in their footsteps, and have discussed the matter with Dr. Klein, who became my physician last year. I have told him that I have never taken much medication and have been opposed to "pain-killers," tranquilizers, etc., but that the day may come when I will accept medical help as the lesser of two evils. He assures me that there are new drugs that may help.

My question, Dr. Smyer, is this: Since I'm sure there must be ongoing research into the problem of senility, would it be of any value to such research if I volunteered as a test subject? At this point, my memory is failing so rapidly, and I suffer such frequent agonies of confusion, that I am at the point of calling on Dr. Klein for the help he has promised. But I don't want to do so yet if my experience can be of value to someone else, and particularly to the nine daughters of my sisters, ranging in age from 58 to 70, and to my own daughter, 42, who must be wondering if they too are doomed.

Is there any merit to this proposal? I will be most grateful for any advice you can give me. (Smyer 1984, p. 20)*

From her clear, lucid writing and her recall of events that took place several years ago, it is obvious that the writer is not suffering from senility. Yet her occasional lapses of memory are causing her to become worried. Smyer points out that complaints of memory loss have to be examined in light of the individual's perception of the event, concurrent factors such as depression or anxiety that might contribute to memory problems, and actual memory behavior. If the Halstead–Reitan Neuropsychological Battery was employed, Gallagher et al. (1980) believe that the majority of normal elderly subjects would be incorrectly identified as brain-damaged. This is because there are no normative standards established for their age group.

One of the most common reasons for memory loss and confusion in older patients is therapeutic drug intoxication, which may occur in individuals who are taking several medications that can interact with one another to produce negative side effects (Butler 1984). Medication often has a stronger effect on older people and takes longer to be cleared from the body, yet dosages are often determined by testing on younger adults only. In addition, cardiac, metabolic, and endocrine disorders and nutritional deficiencies can produce symptoms resembling dementias.

Coping techniques Like normal aging, the disorders associated with aging are generally irreversible. Nonetheless, there are a variety of means by which individuals with these disorders may be helped to live comfortably and with dignity while making use of those abilities that remain. The following interventions have been proposed by Butler (1984).*

1. To preserve the patient's sense of independence and control over his or her life, the environment must be modified to make it safer. Rails can be installed to allow the patient to move freely in the house. A chair that is easy to get into and out of, a remote-control device for the television set, and guard rails for the bathtub will help the patient do things for himself or herself. The patient should be encouraged to make as many personal decisions as possible—to choose which clothing to wear and which activities to take part in—even if the choices are not always perfect.
2. Continued social contacts are important, but visits by friends and relatives should be kept short so that the patient does not feel pressured to continue the social interaction. Visits should not involve large groups of individuals, which could tend to overwhelm the patient.

3. Diversions, such as going out for a walk, are important. It is better to stroll through a calm and peaceful area than to visit a crowded shopping mall, where the environment tends to be unpredictable.

4. Tasks should be assigned to the patient to increase his or her sense of self-worth. These tasks may not be completed to perfection, but they will provide a very important sense of having contributed. In addition, the elderly can be taught the use of memory aids and other strategies to facilitate remembering.

Diseases and infections of the brain

Parkinson's disease **Parkinson's disease** is a progressively worsening disorder that is characterized by muscle tremors, a stiff, shuffling gait, a lack of facial expression, and social withdrawal. It is usually first diagnosed in individuals between the ages of fifty and sixty. In some cases the disorder stems from such causes as infections of the brain, cerebrovascular disorders, brain trauma, and poisoning with carbon monoxide; in other cases a specific origin cannot be determined. Death generally follows within ten years of the onset of Parkinson's disease, although some patients have survived for twenty years or longer.

Parkinson's disease seems to be associated with lesions in the motor area of the brain stem and with a diminished level of dopamine in the brain. Treatment with L-Dopa, which increases dopamine levels, has been found to be useful in relieving most of its symptoms (Lishman 1978). Muhammad Ali's Parkinson-like syndrome is being treated with Sinemet and Symmetrel, which have the same effect.

Neurosyphilis (general paresis) Syphilis is caused by the spirochete *Treponema pallidum,* which enters the body through contact with an infected person. The spirochete is most commonly transmitted from infected to uninfected individuals through intercourse or oral–genital contact. In addition, a pregnant woman can transmit the disease to the fetus, and the spirochete can enter the body through direct contact with mucous membranes or breaks in the skin. Within a few weeks, the exposed individual develops a chancre, a small sore at the point of infection. If it is undetected or untreated, the infection spreads throughout the body. There may be no noticeable symptoms for ten to fifteen years after the initial infection, but eventually the body's organs are permanently damaged. In about 10 percent of untreated cases of syphilis, the spirochete directly damages the brain or nervous system, causing **general paresis.**

The most commonly described form of paresis, which includes about 18 percent of all cases, has grandiose characteristics: Individuals display expansive and euphoric symptoms along with delusions of power or wealth. A depressive form has also been described, in which the affected individual displays all the classic symptoms of depression.

The most frequent course for the illness begins with simple dementia, including memory impairment and early loss of insight. If the disorder remains untreated, the dementia increases, the occasional delusions fade away, and the patient becomes quiet, apathetic, and incoherent. Paralysis, epileptic seizures, and death usually occur within five years of the onset of symptoms.

If general paresis is treated early, however, clinical remission occurs and the patient is often able to return to work. After five years of treatment, more than half the patients with disorientation, convulsions, tremors, and euphoria generally experience a resolution of symptoms (Golden et al. 1983).

Encephalitis **Encephalitis,** or sleeping sickness, is an inflammation of the brain that is caused by a viral infection. It is not known whether the virus enters the central nervous system directly or the brain is hypersensitive to a viral infection at some other site in the body. One form, *epidemic encephalitis,* was widespread during World War I, but the disease is now very rare in the United States. It is still a problem, however, in certain areas of Africa and Asia.

Most cases follow a rapidly developing course that begins with headache, prostration, and diminished consciousness. Epileptic seizures are common in children with encephalitis, and they may be the most obvious feature of the disease. Acute symptoms include lethargy, fever, delirium, and long periods of sleep and stupor. When wakeful the victim may manifest markedly different symptoms: hyperactivity, irritability, agitation, and seizures. In contrast to past behaviors, a child may become restless, irritable, cruel, and antisocial. A coma, if there is one, may end abruptly. Usually a long period of physical and mental recuperation is necessary, and the prognosis can vary from no residual effects to profound brain damage (Golden et al. 1983).

Meningitis Meningitis is an inflammation of the *meninges,* the membrane that surrounds the brain and spinal cord. Research on meningitis is complicated by the fact that there are three major forms of the disorder. In the United States there are about 400,000 cases of *bacterial meningitis* annually (Wasserman and Gromisch 1981). This bacterial form of meningitis generally begins with a localized infection that spreads, via the blood stream, first to the meninges and subsequently into the cerebrospinal fluid. *Viral meningitis,* which involves symptoms that are much less serious than those of the bacterial type, is associated with a variety of diseases, including mumps, herpes simplex, toxoplasmosis, syphilis, and rubella. *Fungal meningitis* usually occurs in children with such immunological deficiencies as leukemia.

The symptoms of meningitis vary with the age of the patient. In neonates and young infants the symptoms are nonspecific (fever, lethargy, poor eating, and irritability), which makes diagnosis difficult (McCracken 1976).

In patients beyond one year of age, symptoms may include stiffness of the neck, headache, and cognitive and sensory impairment. All three forms can produce cerebral infarction and seizures, but their incidence is much greater in the bacterial form than in the others (Edwards and Baker 1981; Stovring et al. 1981). The outcome is most serious when meningitis is contracted during the neonatal period.

Residual effects of the disorder may include partial or complete hearing loss as a result of cerebral infarction (Berlow et al. 1981), mental retardation, and seizures (Snyder et al. 1981). Meningitis also appears to affect the abstract thinking ability of some of its victims (Wright 1978).

Huntington's chorea Huntington's chorea is a rare, genetically transmitted disorder that is characterized by involuntary twitching movements and eventual dementia. Because it is transmitted from parent to child through an abnormal gene, approximately 50 percent of the offspring of an affected individual develop this disorder. Huntington's chorea cannot be treated, so the genetic counseling of afflicted individuals is extremely important in preventing its transmission.

The first symptoms usually occur as behavioral disturbances when the individual is between the ages of twenty-five and fifty. The first physical symptoms are generally twitches in the fingers or facial grimaces. As the disorder progresses, these symptoms become more widespread and abrupt, now involving jerky, rapid, and repetitive movements. Changes in personality and emotional stability also occur. The individual may, for example, become moody and quarrelsome (Golden et al. 1983).

Woody Guthrie, a well-known folk singer and the father of Arlo Guthrie, was a victim of Huntington's chorea. His first symptoms were increased moodiness and depression. Later he developed a peculiar manner of walking, and he found it difficult to speak normally. His

are given in one-third to two-thirds of the cases; schizophrenia is the most common of these (Lishman 1978).

Cerebral tumors

A **cerebral tumor** is a mass of abnormal tissue growing within the brain. The symptoms of a cerebral tumor depend on which particular area is affected by the tumor and on the degree to which it increases the intracranial pressure. Fast-growing tumors generally produce severe mental symptoms, whereas slow growth may result in few symptoms. Unfortunately, in the latter case, the tumor is often not discovered until death occurs in a psychiatric hospital (Lishman 1978). With regard to location, tumors affecting the temporal area produce the highest frequency of psychological symptoms (Golden et al. 1983).

The most common symptoms of cerebral tumors are disturbances of consciousness, which can range from diminished attention and drowsiness to coma. Individuals with tumors may also show mild dementia and other problems involving thinking processes. Affective changes may also occur, as a result of either the direct physical impact of the tumor or the reaction of the patient to his or her problem. The removal of a cerebral tumor can produce dramatic results.

Woody Guthrie (1912–1967), a popular folk-singer during the 1940s and 1950s, suffered from Huntington's Chorea. There is a 50 percent chance that his son Arlo Guthrie, also a successful folk singer, has the disease.

inability to control his movements was often blamed on alcoholism. On one occasion, his apparent disorientation, his walking problems, and his disheveled appearance prompted police to arrest him. When his wife sought his release, she was met by a staff psychiatrist who said, "Your husband is a very disturbed man . . . with many hallucinations. He says that he has written a thousand songs." His wife responded by saying, "It is true." The psychiatrist went on: "He also says he has written a book." Guthrie's wife responded, "That is also true." Then the psychiatrist delivered the *coup de grâce:* "He says that a record company has put out nine records of his songs!" The doctor's voice dripped disbelief. "That is also the truth," she replied (Yurchenco 1970, pp. 147–148).

Huntington's chorea always ends in death, on average from thirteen to sixteen years after the onset of symptoms. Early misdiagnoses

The woman was admitted to a mental hospital, exhibiting dementia and confusion. She responded little to questioning by staff, or to attempts at therapy, even after 12 years of hospitalization. She would simply sit blindly, with her tongue protruding to the right, making repetitive movements of her right arm and leg. She also showed partial paralysis of the left side of her face.

This "left-side, right-side" pattern of symptoms suggested that her condition might be due to a physical problem. Surgery was performed, and a massive brain tumor was discovered and removed. After the operation, the patient improved remarkably. She regained her speech and sight and was able to recognize and converse with her relatives for the first time in 12 years. (Hunter et al. 1968)

Epilepsy

Epilepsy is a general term that refers to a set of symptoms rather than to a specific etiology. In particular, **epilepsy** is any disorder that is characterized by intermittent and brief periods of altered consciousness, often accompanied by seizures, and excessive electrical discharge from brain cells. It is the most common of the neurological disorders; 1 to 2 percent of the population has epileptic seizures at some time during their lives. It also seems to be one of the earliest recognized organic brain syndromes: Julius Caesar, Napoleon, Dostoevsky, and Van Gogh are among those who are presumed to have been afflicted by epilepsy.

Epilepsy is most frequently diagnosed during the first year of life. It can be symptomatic of some primary disorder of the brain without apparent etiology, or it can arise from such causes as brain tumors, injury, degenerative diseases, and drugs (Lishman 1978). Epileptic seizures and unconsciousness may last anywhere from a few seconds to several hours; they may occur only a few times during the patient's entire life or many times in one day. And they may involve only a momentary disturbance of consciousness or a complete loss of consciousness—in which case they can be accompanied by violent convulsions and a coma lasting for hours. Alcohol, lack of sleep, fever, a low blood sugar level, hyperventilation, a brain lesion or injury, or general fatigue can induce an epileptic seizure. Particular musical notes, flickering lights, and emotionally charged situations have also been known to bring about these attacks in epileptics. Even day-to-day stress can precipitate a seizure (Laidlaw and Rickens 1976).

Epilepsy can often be controlled but it cannot be cured. Although epileptics usually behave and function quite normally between attacks, theirs is a chronic long-term illness that is still regarded with suspicion and repugnance by much of society. An attack can be frightening to the afflicted person and observers alike. Epileptics face fear and anxiety resulting from the unpredictable nature of their seizures. They are embarrassed by their seeming lack of control over their illness, and must deal with society's negative stereotypes concerning epilepsy (University of Minnesota 1977). Perhaps as a result, approximately 30 to 50 percent of epileptics have accompanying psychological problems (Golden et al. 1983). We shall discuss the four types of epilepsy. Each type is associated with a different type of seizure—petit mal, Jacksonian, psychomotor, and grand mal (see also Focus 17.4, pp. 494–495).

Petit mal seizures **Petit mal** ("little illness") **seizures** involve a momentary dimming or loss of consciousness, sometimes with convulsive movements. During an attack, which usually lasts a few seconds, the epileptic displays a blank stare. There may be a fluttering of the eyelids or slight jerking movements, but in general there is little overall movement. After an attack the epileptic individual may continue with whatever he or she was doing earlier, unaware that a seizure has occurred and that there was a momentary loss of consciousness.

Petit mal seizures are usually seen in children and adolescents; they rarely persist into adulthood. The following description highlights a common problem among petit mal epileptics.

> Jack D. is a sixteen-year-old student who was admitted to the outpatient psychiatric service of a large hospital to receive treatment for petit mal epilepsy. Jack and his parents explained that the seizures lasted only a few seconds each but occurred twenty to thirty times a day. His parents were especially concerned because Jack was very eager to get a driver's license; driving a car would be quite dangerous if he were subject to momentary losses of consciousness. Jack was interviewed at a case conference where a group

of mental health professionals, medical students, and paraprofessionals discussed his symptoms, the etiology of the disorder, the prognosis, and treatment.

During the fifteen-minute interview, Jack experienced two petit mal seizures. The first occurred while he was answering a question. A psychiatrist had asked Jack whether his seizures significantly handicapped him in school. Jack replied, "It really hasn't been that bad. Sometimes I lose track of what the teacher is . . ." At that point, Jack paused. He had a blank stare on his face, and his mouth was slightly opened.

After about four seconds, he resumed speaking and said, "Uh, writing on the blackboard." A psychologist then asked Jack if he had noticed that he had paused in midsentence. Jack answered that he was not aware of the pause or the brief seizure. Interestingly, several of those present at the case conference later admitted that they too were unaware that a seizure had occurred at that time. They thought Jack's pause was due to an attempt to find the right words.

Later Jack had another seizure that went unnoticed by most of the interviewers. While the resident psychiatrist was elaborating on a ques-

FOCUS 17.4

Recognizing Epilepsy

The following table has been compiled from *Epilepsy: Recognition and First Aid*, published by the Epilepsy Foundation of America.

Seizure Type	What It Looks Like	What It Is Often Mistaken for
Convulsive		
Grand mal	Sudden cry, fall, rigidity, followed by muscle jerks, frothy saliva on lips, shallow breathing, or temporarily suspended breathing; bluish skin, possible loss of bladder or bowel control. Usually lasts 2–5 minutes; normal breathing then starts again. There may be some confusion and/or fatigue, followed by return to full consciousness.	Heart attack Stroke Unknown but life-threatening emergency
Nonconvulsive		
Petit mal	A blank stare, lasting only a few seconds, most common in children. May be accompanied by rapid blinking, some chewing movements of the mouth. The child having the seizure is unaware of what is going on during the seizure, but quickly returns to full awareness once it has stopped. May result in learning difficulties if not recognized and treated.	Daydreaming Lack of attention Deliberate ignoring of adult instructions

tion, Jack appeared to be listening. But when the psychiatrist finished, Jack had a puzzled look on his face. He said, ''It [a seizure] happened again. I was listening to what you were saying and suddenly you were all finished. I must have blanked out. Could you repeat the question?''

As you can see, such brief interruptions of consciousness may go unnoticed by people interacting with petit mal epileptics—and sometimes by the epileptics themselves. Fortunately the prognosis for Jack was good. Petit mal seizures usually disappear with age and

can be controlled with proper medication and treatment.

Jacksonian seizures **Jacksonian seizures** typically begin in one part of the body and then spread to other parts. For example, the hands or feet may first begin to twitch, then the whole arm or leg, and then other parts of the body. Usually the individual does not completely lose consciousness unless the seizure spreads to the entire body. At this point, the convulsions resemble those of grand mal epi-

Seizure Type	What It Looks Like	What It Is Often Mistaken for
Nonconvulsive (continued)		
Jacksonian	Jerking begins in fingers or toes; can't be stopped by patient, but patient stays awake and aware. Jerking may proceed to involve hand, then arm, and sometimes spreads to whole body and becomes a convulsive seizure.	Acting out, bizarre behavior
Psychomotor	Usually starts with blank stare, followed by chewing, followed by random activity. Person appears unaware of surroundings, may seem dazed and mumble. Unresponsive. Actions clumsy, not directed. May pick at clothing, pick up objects, try to take clothes off. May run, appear afraid. May struggle or flail at restraint. Once a pattern is established, the same set of actions usually occurs with each seizure. Lasts a few minutes, but post-seizure confusion can last substantially longer. No memory of what happened during seizure period.	Drunkenness Intoxication on drugs Mental illness Indecent exposure Disorderly conduct Shoplifting

SOURCE: Adapted from *Epilepsy: Recognition and First Aid,* Revised Edition (Epilepsy Foundation of America 1983).

lepsy. Jacksonian seizures are frequently due to a localized and specific brain lesion: Surgical removal of the affected area can bring about recovery.

Psychomotor seizures About 25 percent of epileptic seizures are of this type (Horwitz 1970). **Psychomotor seizures** are characterized by a loss of consciousness during which the individual engages in well-organized and normal-appearing behavioral sequences. For example, one psychomotor epileptic had an attack and lost consciousness while he was mowing his lawn. During the next hour, he went into his house, changed into swim trunks, and proceeded to take a swim in his pool. An hour later, when he came out of the "trance," he did not recall how he had gotten into the pool. His last memory was of mowing the lawn.

The disturbance in consciousness typically lasts for a brief period of time, usually just a few minutes; occasionally, however, it may affect an individual for days. It was originally felt that many individuals were prone to violence during such seizures. This association can be seen in the following report concerning a 29-year-old female psychomotor epileptic.

> There was a dramatic change in her affect following the onset of spells. The patient developed deepening emotions and reported a marked tendency to become angry about trivial events. Over the past two years sounds of even normal volume had led to angry outbursts in which she had smashed furniture or struck her cat. During a recent examination, this highly intelligent woman had become tearful and anxious while attempting rapid serial seven subtraction. She then turned to the examiner and said in a menacing voice, "You're lucky I didn't punch you in the face for making me do that." (Devinsky and Bear 1984, p. 651)

Some investigators have suggested that there is a relationship between psychomotor epilepsy and psychotic or schizophrenic behaviors (Glaser, Newman, and Schafer 1963; Stevens et al. 1969). The artist Van Gogh is supposed to have cut off his ear during a psy-

chomotor attack. And the defense attorneys for Jack Ruby, the killer of Lee Harvey Oswald (the alleged assassin of President John F. Kennedy), argued that Ruby had epileptic seizures and consequently was not responsible for his actions. But such accounts provide a misleading view of epilepsy. In only a very few cases have acts of violence and epileptic seizures been related (Gunn and Fenton 1971; Turner and Merlis 1962).

Grand mal seizures The most common and dramatic type of epileptic seizure is the **grand mal** ("great illness") **seizure.** Although this type usually lasts no longer than a few minutes, it typically consists of four distinct phases. A majority of grand mal epileptics report that they experience an *aura* prior to the loss of consciousness. The aura lasts only a few seconds and signals the onset of a seizure. During this first phase, the individual has physical or sensory sensations such as headaches, hallucinations, mood changes, dizziness, or feelings of unreality. During the *tonic* phase, the individual becomes unconscious and falls to the ground. The muscles become rigid and the eyes remain open. During the third or *clonic* phase, jerking movements result from the rapid contraction and relaxation of body muscles. These movements may be so violent that epileptics bruise their heads on the ground, bite their tongues, or vomit. Fourth and finally, the muscles relax and a *coma* ensues, lasting from a few minutes to several hours. When the epileptic awakens, he or she may feel exhausted, confused, and sore. Some individuals report that they awaken relieved and refreshed.

Grand mal attacks may occur daily or be limited to only once to twice during an entire lifetime. In rare cases, grand mal attacks may occur in rapid succession (a condition known as *status epilepticus*), and result in death if untreated.

Etiological factors As we have noted, the epilepsies have been attributed to a wide range of factors. Somehow, these result in excessive neuronal discharge within the gray matter of the brain. Sometimes the discharge appears to be quite localized and to result in focal seizures or twitching in isolated parts of the body. Generalized seizures are presumably caused by general cortical discharge, and the effects involve the whole body.

Some researchers have investigated the hypothesis that genetic or personality factors predispose persons to epilepsy. There is evidence that the concordance rate for epilepsy is greater among identical than among fraternal twins, and that seizures are much more frequent among family members of an epileptic than among unrelated persons (DeJong and Sugar 1972; Jasper, Ward, and Pope 1969; Lennox and Lennox 1960). However, heredity may not be a necessary or sufficient condition for the onset of epilepsy. With respect to personality factors, no single type of personality has been associated with epilepsy (Tizard 1962). Although personality disturbances have been found to be correlated with some epileptics, it is unclear whether personality factors predispose individuals to epilepsy or whether epilepsy influences personality development. Another possibility is that epileptics are under great stress because of their condition and because of the stigma attached to the disorder. This stress, rather than either the disorder or its causes, may affect the personalities of epileptics.

TREATMENT CONSIDERATIONS

Because organic brain disorders can be caused by a number of different factors, a wide variety of treatment approaches have been used. The major approaches include surgery, medication, skills training, cognitive preparation, psychotherapy, and environmental intervention. Surgical procedures may be used to remove cerebral tumors, relieve the pressure caused by tumors, or restore ruptured blood vessels. Drugs can be used to control or reduce the symptoms of brain disorders. Psy-

chotherapy may be helpful in dealing with the emotional aspects of these disorders. And some patients who have lost motor skills can be retrained to compensate for their deficiencies or can be retaught these skills. Often, complete hospital care is required for patients with organic brain disorders.

The *cognitive* therapeutic approaches appear to be particularly promising. As an example, researchers have hypothesized that the impaired attention and concentration shown by head-injured individuals result from the disruption of *private speech,* which regulates behavior and thought processes (Luria 1982). A therapeutic program that is based on this hypothesis involves self-instructional training to enhance the self-regulation of speech and behavior (Webster and Scott 1983). The program was used to treat a 24-year-old construction worker who had been in a coma for 4 days as a result of a car accident. Tests showed him to have poor recall, poor concentration, and attentional difficulties; he was unable to concentrate on any task for an extended period of time. He also complained that intrusive nonsexual thoughts kept him from maintaining an erection during intercourse.

To begin his training, the patient was told to repeat the following self-instructions aloud before performing any task.

> 1. "To really concentrate, I must look at the person speaking to me."
> 2. "I also must focus on what is being said, not on other thoughts which want to intrude."
> 3. "I must concentrate on what I am hearing at any moment by repeating each word in my head as the person speaks."
> 4. "Although it is not horrible if I lose track of conversation, I must tell the person to repeat the information if I have not attended to it." (Webster and Scott 1983, p. 71)

After he had learned to use these vocalized instructions (actually, he rephrased them in his own words), he was taught to repeat them subvocally before each task. The patient soon demonstrated great improvement in concentration and attention and was able to return to his former job. He was also successful in eliminating intrusive thoughts during sexual intercourse by focusing on his partner.

A similar program was developed to eliminate the anger response that is sometimes displayed by brain-injured individuals, either as a result of the brain damage or in reaction to their deficits. One 22-year-old patient had suffered a severe head trauma in a motorcycle accident at the age of sixteen. After 2 months of intensive medical treatment, he had returned home to live with his parents. There he displayed outbursts of anger toward people and objects, a low frustration level, and impulsivity. These, in turn, had led to numerous failures in a vocational rehabilitation program. Medication was of no help in controlling his outbursts.

A stress-innoculation training program was developed for this patient. It involved twelve 30-minute sessions spread over three weeks and was composed of the following elements:

1. *Cognitive preparation*. The function and appropriateness of anger were explained, as were alternatives to being destructive. The situations that produced anger were identified and appropriate responses were demonstrated.
2. *Skills acquisition*. The patient was taught to stop himself from becoming angry, to re-evaluate anger-evoking situations, and to use self-verbalizations that were incompatible with the expression of anger.
3. *Application training*. A hierarchy of situations evoking anger was developed. The patient role-played and practiced the use of cognitive and behavioral skills to cope with progressively greater anger-evoking stimuli. He also employed these techniques in the hospital setting and received feedback about his performance.

Before treatment the patient had averaged about three outbursts each week. No outbursts at all were recorded immediately after treatment, and a follow-up five months later indicated that the gain had been maintained. The patient was able to obtain part-time employment as a clerk and was living independently.

Medication is of most benefit in controlling the symptoms of organic disorders. For example, approximately 50 percent of all epileptics can control their seizures with medication; in another 30 percent, medication reduces the frequency of seizures. Only 20 percent of epileptics find that current medications are not helpful (Epilepsy Foundation of America 1982).

An interesting seizure-prevention program utilizing classical conditioning was reported by Efron (1956, 1957). It is best described through an example—the case of a woman, suffering from grand mal seizures, who could prevent the occurrence of the tonic and clonic phases by sniffing an unpleasant odor during the initial stage of an attack. The odor was first presented to the woman while she stared at a bracelet. After the smell was paired with the bracelet over a period of several days, the bracelet alone was sufficient to elicit thoughts of the unpleasant odor. At that point the patient was able to stop a seizure by staring at her bracelet when she felt the attack starting. Eventually she could cut an attack short by just thinking about the bracelet. Other behavior modification and biofeedback techniques have also been helpful in reducing seizure activity (Mostofsky and Balaschak 1979).

SUMMARY

1. The left hemisphere of the brain is generally associated with language functions, whereas the right hemisphere is associated with visual–spatial functions. Although there appears to be some specialization within each hemisphere, there is also evidence that lost functions can be regained—especially in a young brain that has not yet become fully specialized.

2. The effects of organic brain damage can vary greatly, but the symptoms most often manifested include the impairment of consciousness and memory, the impairment of judgment, orientation difficulties, and personality changes. The effects can be acute (often temporary) or chronic (long-term); the causes can be endogenous (internal) or exogenous (external); and the tissue damage can be diffuse or specific (localized). The assessment of brain damage is complicated by the fact that its symptoms are often similar to those of functional disorders.

3. Many different agents can cause organic brain syndromes; among these are physical wounds or injuries to the brain, aging, diseases that destroy brain tissue (such as neurosyphilis and encephalitis), and brain tumors. Epilepsy, which is an organic brain syndrome, is characterized by intermittent and brief periods of altered consciousness, frequently accompanied by seizures, and excessive electrical discharge by neurons.

4. Treatment strategies include corrective surgery, cognitive training, behavior modification, and psychotherapy. Medication is often used, either alone or with other therapies, to decrease or control the symptoms of the various organic brain disorders.

KEY TERMS

Alzheimer's disease An organic brain disorder that involves the atrophy of brain tissue and leads to marked deterioration of intellectual and emotional functioning

brain trauma A physical wound or injury to the brain

cerebrovascular accident A sudden stoppage of blood flow to a portion of the brain, leading to a loss of brain function; also called stroke

dementia A syndrome that is characterized by the deterioration of intellectual ability and by impaired judgment, of sufficient severity to interfere with social and occupational functioning

epilepsy Any disorder that is characterized by intermittent and brief periods of altered consciousness, often accompanied by seizures, and excessive electrical discharge from brain cells

functional disorder A mental disorder for which no physical basis can be found and that is assumed to be due primarily to psychological factors

multi-infarct dementia An organic brain syndrome characterized by uneven deterioration of intellectual abilities and resulting from a number of cerebral infarctions

organic mental disorder A behavioral disturbance that results from organic brain pathology—that is, damage to the brain

Parkinson's disease A progressively worsening organic brain disorder that is characterized by muscle tremors, a stiff, shuffling gait, a lack of facial expression, and social withdrawal

18
Disorders of Childhood and Adolescence

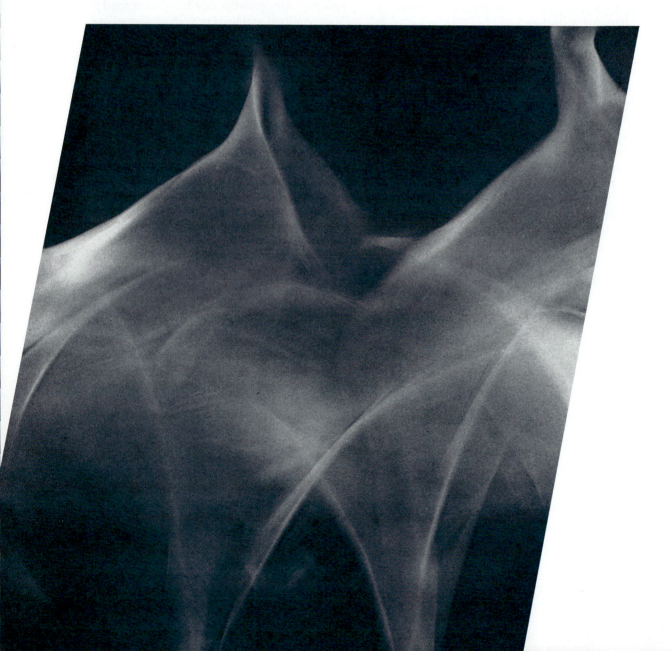

At the age of four, Jerry was diagnosed as suffering from the "Kanner syndrome" (infantile autism), a severe and pervasive developmental disorder.

As a child Jerry B. showed little responsiveness to mothering, refused new foods, cried out at loud noises, and showed exaggerated negative responses to certain odors. His speech development was slow and unusual, and his speech did not appear to be aimed at communicating. At a very early age, Jerry exhibited a fondness for classical music. And, although he did not seem to understand the meanings of words, he memorized an amazing number of song lyrics.

Jerry was fascinated with spinning things. He would spend hours spinning various objects or watching records spin on his parents' phonograph. When his mother took him to nursery school each day, he would not acknowledge her leaving but would spend his entire time there spinning objects. Alterations in his routine and the moving of things in his room would precipitate strong emotional outbursts. In the third grade Jerry became very interested in mathematics, and he would spend hours writing multiplication tables.

Now a 31-year-old adult, Jerry describes his childhood as having been filled with confusion and terror. He felt that he was "living in a frightening world that was unpredictable and painful. Noises were unbearably loud and sounds were overpowering. Nothing seemed to be constant." Dogs seemed especially frightening because he believed they were somehow humanoid and yet not really human. Children also frightened him, because he could never understand or predict their behavior.

Jerry's growing recognition that he was different from others made his adolescence extremely painful. He wanted social contact but was unable to behave appropriately; as a result he was usually rejected or ignored by others. His feelings of isolation are reflected in his responses on the Thematic Apperception Test. For example, when he was shown a picture of a boy staring at a violin, Jerry responded, "He will have to spend the rest of his life alone in agony."

Jerry has a job completing fiscal efficiency reports. He functions well only if he is given explicit instructions, and he cannot be relied on to use "common sense." A poem that he wrote when he was fifteen reflects the sense of isolation and confusion that he still feels today at age thirty-one:

I prayed to the Lord
That he show me a path
I waited for his work
He guided me to the subject of math.

The people envy me now and then
As the Lord guided me thru this thunderous
    world
I like numbers, decimal points and fractions.
Many equations, I learned to create
With multiplications, additions and subtractions
I see mathematics will be my fate. (Bemporad
    1979)

The disorders of childhood and adolescence encompass a wide variety of behavioral problems, ranging from psychoses to the less severe *developmental* disturbances—those that are typically associated with the process of "growing up." Children and adolescents are, in fact, subject to many of the "adult" disorders that we have discussed in previous chapters. Here, however, we shall discuss only those problems that arise primarily during the earlier stages of life. We begin with two severe disturbances that were formerly known as childhood psychoses; then we examine several of the less disabling disorders of childhood and adolescence.

PERVASIVE DEVELOPMENTAL DISORDERS

In the past, severe disturbances that led to bizarre behaviors in children were given such labels as "childhood schizophrenia" and "childhood psychosis." However, there are distinct differences between these childhood disorders and the psychotic conditions ob-

served in adolescents and adults. For example, the childhood disorders do not include such symptoms as hallucinations, delusions, the loosening of associations, and incoherence. (A child who exhibited these symptoms would most likely be diagnosed as schizophrenic.)

In an attempt to distinguish the severe childhood disorders from the adult psychoses, the former were given the name *pervasive developmental disorders*. This name is also more descriptive of the problems suffered by affected children. The **pervasive developmental disorders** are severe disorders of childhood that affect psychological functioning in such areas as language, social relationships, attention, perception, and affect. They include both infantile autism and childhood onset pervasive developmental disorder. These impairments are not simply delays in development but rather are distortions that would not be normal at any stage of the developmental process. They are fairly rare, with a prevalence of approximately 4 or 5 cases in every 10,000 children (Wing and Gould 1979; Gilberg 1984). There is some controversy about whether they are or are not early manifestations of the adult psychoses.

Infantile autism

In 1943 Leo Kanner, a child psychiatrist, described a group of children who shared certain symptoms with other psychotic children but who also displayed some unique behaviors. Kanner termed the syndrome **infantile autism,** from the Greek *autos* (meaning "self"), to reflect the profound aloneness and detachment of these children. A highly unusual symptom of autistic children is their extreme lack of responsiveness to adults: "The child is aware of people . . . but considers them not differently from the way he (or she) considers the desk, bookshelf, or filing cabinet" (Kanner and Lesser 1958, p. 659).

Along with extreme social isolation and lack

of responsiveness to others, a distinct and particularly puzzling characteristic of autism is language and speech deficits. In fact, infantile autism is usually defined in terms of those two characteristics. Approximately 50 percent of autistic children fail to develop speech. Those who do speak generally exhibit such oddities as *echolalia* (echoing what has previously been said) and the constant repeating of phrases. One autistic child continually repeated the slogan "How do you spell relief?" without any apparent reason. Such speech does not appear to have communication as its purpose.

Autistic children also display various social deficits. In particular, they do not seem to need contact with their parents or others, and a lack of bonding, or attachment to people, is often noted. Other characteristics of autism, whose onset occurs before the age of $2\frac{1}{2}$, are indicated in the following composite picture of its development (Ornitz and Ritvo 1968; Maltz 1982; Rutter 1983).

Children suffering from autism are profoundly alone. Their unresponsiveness to adults, lack of bonding to parents and others, and language and speech deficits keep them locked in a socially isolated world.

☐ *First six months:* Lack of crying in infancy; no unhappiness at being left alone; failure to notice the coming and going of the mother; lack or delay of the smiling response; lack of anticipatory response to being picked up; lack of attachment behavior; failure to vocalize; overreactivity to certain stimuli; lack of appropriate eye contact

☐ *Second six months:* Limp or stiff when picked up; no imitation of sounds or words; lack of emotional expression; failure to play "peek-a-boo," "patty-cake"; unaffectionate; may appear deaf

☐ *Two to three years:* Intense interest in self-induced sounds; staring at hands and fingers; bizarre food preferences; lack of attentiveness to meaningful stimuli; unusual repetitive habits, mannerisms, and gestures; may stare into space, spin objects, whirl themselves, flutter or flap their arms, hands, and fingers; walking or running exclusively on toes; deviant eye contact

☐ *Four to five years:* Underdeveloped speech or muteness; echolalia; pronoun reversals using "you" for "I" and "I" for "me"; atonal, arrhythmic, and hollow voice; decreased overreactivity; most symptoms of earlier years

During middle childhood and adolescence, autistic children display a lack of cooperative play, a failure to form friendships, and a lack of empathy. Those who do develop speech often display good language skills, but they may have an unusual atonal speech quality and an inability to respond appropriately to others during conversations. Early repetitive habits may develop into more complex compulsions involving numbers or the study of maps (Schopler, Rutter, and Chess 1979).

Jerry B, the autistic adult described at the beginning of this chapter, showed many of these characteristics. During adolescence, for example, he was able to perceive that he was different from others, but he lacked the ability to understand the viewpoint of others. Once, during a trip to Mexico with his parents, Jerry "took off" by himself for most of a day without saying he was going. When he returned, he simply could not understand the frantic search that his parents had conducted.

As a 31-year-old adult, Jerry still lacks social awareness. When he is with his parents (his only social contacts), he spends his time silently watching television in their presence. He has no ability whatsoever to make "small talk." Jerry's need for sameness also remains, though it has shifted to accommodate adult activities. Taking a shower requires about two hours, because Jerry must first ensure that every item in the bathroom is in its "proper" place, and he has to wash himself in a certain prescribed pattern. Jerry reports having no daydreams, and he does not engage in leisure activities.

Bemporad (1979), who has described Jerry's behaviors in detail, concluded that "He remains an isolated, mechanical being, unable to intuit the social nuances of behavior and therefore forced to retreat from a world that is persistently surprising and lacking in regularity" (p. 195). This lack of social empathy is evident in another autistic adult, who complained that he could not "mind-read." He felt that most people had this capacity because they seemed to know how others would respond. He, on the other hand, could never predict how others would react until they actually responded (Rutter 1983).

Up to three-fourths of autistic children have IQs below 70. Only about 20 percent have average to above-average intelligence (Maltz 1982). In the past, some researchers believed that these children were unusually bright, primarily because of two features often found in autism: First, autistic children do not show uniform performance on IQ subtests. Rather, they exhibit specific *splinter skills*—often doing well with drawings, puzzle construction, and rote memory but poorly with verbal tasks and those requiring language skills and symbolic thinking. Second, they often display unusual abilities, such as Jerry's memorization of an "amazing" number of song lyrics at the age of three.

Autistic children with unusual abilities have been described as "autistic savants" (Rimland 1978). In a survey of over 5400 autistic children, 10 percent were found to have such special talents. One child who had a talent for arithmetic was asked for the product of 6427 and 4234. According to Rimland (1978),

> Arthur turned his head in my direction and said, slowly but without hesitation, "27,211,918." His voice was stilted but precise. His eyes never lost their blank stare, and now he returned to gazing into space, without seeing anything, a handsome, impassive eight-year-old. (p. 69)

Another child could tell the day of the week on which any specific date—past or future—would fall. The special abilities most frequently found in autistic children involved music (such as playing a large number of songs), rote memory, drawings, and mathematics.

Perhaps 1 child in 3000 is autistic. The disorder occurs 3 or 4 times more frequently in boys than in girls (Wing and Gould 1979; Gilberg 1984).

Diagnosis Autism would seem to be relatively easy to diagnose, given its two relatively unique characteristics. Yet, as Focus 18.1 indicates, the opposite is true. The diagnosis of autism remains a major problem, primarily because it shares a number of characteristics

What's Wrong with My Child?

In response to a survey conducted by the Michigan Society for Autistic Citizens (1979), forty-eight parents of autistic children described the difficulties they had had in obtaining accurate diagnoses. Their experiences were surprisingly similar.

1. The parents (usually the mother) were the first to notice that something was wrong with their child. The problems that were most frequently reported involved communication: The child "never talked" or "acted as if deaf." Some parents also noticed that their children continually performed rocking movements.
2. The parents were frequently told by their pediatricians that the children would "grow out of it" or that they, the parents, were "overly concerned." Mental health professionals and physicians seemed generally unable to diagnose the condition.
3. The parents (again, most often the mothers) typically concluded that something must be wrong but became less sure of their beliefs when they were contra-

dicted by professionals and, often, by relatives. They tended to feel that the problem might have been caused by poor parenting techniques. (This guilt is often reinforced when a diagnosis of autism is made. Nearly one-fourth of the parents were told by professionals that the condition is caused by the inability of parents to respond in a loving way to their child.)

4. Diagnoses were difficult to obtain, inaccurate, and conflicting. Of the sixty-two first diagnoses given the children by various professionals, only two indicated autism. The most frequent diagnoses were mental retardation, hearing impairment, brain damage, and emotional disturbances. In 12 percent of the cases, a correct diagnosis was not given until the child was at least eight years old.

As is obvious from these results, the mental health professions have yet to solve the problems involved in the early identification of autism. In addition, there is a need to expunge the myth that autism is caused by parental rejection.

with other disorders. In addition, symptoms can vary widely among autistic children, especially with regard to developmental age and level of functioning (Maltz 1982).

Because the majority of autistic children are mentally retarded, they are often diagnosed as such. However, there are ways to distinguish autistic from mentally retarded children. For example, the former exhibit splinter skills much more often than the latter. And mentally retarded children are more likely to relate to others and to be socially aware than are autistic children.

Developmental aphasia, a disorder in which meaningful speech is affected, is sometimes confused with autism. Aphasic children also exhibit echolalia and have difficulty in understanding language. However, unlike autistic children, they do relate to their parents, they communicate through gestures, and they engage in appropriate play with toys.

Etiology　What causes the bizarre and puzzling behavioral abnormalities that are seen in autistic children? Why do they occur so early in life? The search for answers to these questions

Even though autistic children often display unusual abilities their IQs tend to be below average. Their performance on IQ tests is not uniform. Although they might do well on subtests that require drawing, puzzle construction, or rote memory, they tend to do poorly on subtests that require verbal skills, language skills, and symbolic thinking.

has given rise to a number of theories concerning the etiology of infantile autism.

Genetic influences Virtually no correlation has been found between autism in a child and the presence of psychiatric disorders in his or her blood relatives. Of a group of 100 autistic children, only 1 had a parent who exhibited ''severe mental illness''; furthermore, of 973 relatives of these children (parents, siblings, aunts, uncles, and grandparents), only 1 percent were psychotic (Kanner 1949). There is some evidence, however, that innate factors do play a role in autism. In a study of 11 sets of identical twins, all were concordant for autism; but once again, in all cases the parents and relatives of these identical twins were free of psychoses and other serious mental disorders (Rimland 1964).

In another twin study, there was no concordance for autism among ten pairs of dizygotic twins (Folstein and Rutter 1977). However, four of eleven pairs of monozygotic twins were concordant for the disorder, and the seven nonconcordant twins showed some form of language impairment. The researchers concluded that some type of inherited cognitive impairment is associated with autism. Supporting this view is the finding that 15 percent of the siblings of autistic children have some form of language disorder, learning disability, or mental retardation (August et al. 1981).

Central nervous system impairment Cognitive and language deficits constitute a major characteristic of autism. This lifelong problem may indicate that the central nervous system has been damaged—in particular, in the left hemisphere, which is associated with the cognitive and language functions (Prior 1984). Some researchers feel that damage that occurs during the prenatal, perinatal, and postnatal periods can produce the symptoms of autism (Eshkevari 1979; Gilberg and Forsell 1984).

Neurological problems were indeed found in approximately 50 percent of one group of autistic children (Garreau et al. 1984). In addition, abnormal EEG readings have been found in autistic children (DeMyer 1975); and approximately 20 percent of autistic children can be expected to develop seizures (Deykin and MacMahon 1979). Evidence of left-hemisphere involvement was uncovered with a series of neuropsychological tests that were administered to autistic individuals, retarded individuals who were matched with them in IQ, and patients with diffuse brain damage. Unlike the other two groups, the autistic subjects showed a pattern that suggests a signficantly greater degree of left-hemisphere dysfunction (Dawson 1983).

But other researchers have found little evidence of either birth complications or abnormal EEGs among autistic children, compared

Similar to many normal children, autistic children are more likely to respond to an attentive adult than to an unattentive adult. Even when they do respond, however, their eye contact tends to be unrelated to the social context.

with other groups of severely disturbed children (Kanner 1943; Lotter 1966; Treffert 1970). Such conflicting data are difficult to interpret. It is possible that autism stems from at least two separate etiologies and that the conflicting evidence was obtained from different subgroups of the population of autistic children. If that is so, the autistic syndrome shown by children with no detectable neurological disorder is "remarkably similar" to that shown by children with definite neurological impairment (Garreau et al. 1984).

Physiological overarousal Can such behaviors as the avoidance of eye contact and with-drawal from social relationships reflect a homeostatic response of autistic children that helps them to avoid overstimulation? Compared to normal and mentally retarded controls, autistic children have shown greater physiological reaction to novel stimuli and slower habituation to those stimuli (Zentall and Zentall 1983). Many of the bizarre symptoms of autism may be indicative of attempts to block incoming stimulation.

Hutt and Ounsted (1966) have hypothesized that autistic children are in a state of high physiological arousal. Eye contact is physiologically arousing and is therefore unpleasant for already chronically aroused autistic children. It is for this reason, they contend, that these children avoid eye contact. To test their hypothesis, Hutt and Ounsted exposed autistic and normal children to five pictures mounted on standards: a happy face, a sad face, a blank human face, a monkey face, and a dog face. From behind a one-way mirror, observers recorded the length of time during which each child fixated on each picture. The normal children showed the least interest in the blank face and displayed approximately equal visual contact with the other faces. By contrast, the autistic children tended to spend most of their time looking at environmental stimuli, such as the light switches, water taps, and a window. They preferred the animal faces and the blank face to the happy human face (see Figure 18.1).

To determine which aspect of the human face is aversive to autistic children, the investigators blotted out different features, such as the mouth or eyes, one at a time. The eyes elicited the fewest approach responses, in support of Hutt and Ounsted's concept. Their arousal hypothesis is still conjectural, and has found little other experimental support.

For example, no significant differences in visual responding to strange adults was found between fourteen autistic and schizophrenic children and matched normal controls (Churchill and Bryson 1972). All the children responded more to an attentive adult than to a preoccupied adult. These results are surprising because lack of eye contact and social withdrawal are considered major symptoms of autism. However, it may not be the lack of eye contact itself that is abnormal but rather the fact that it is unrelated to social context (Schopler, Rutter, and Chess 1979). Lack of appropriate eye contact has been observed in autistic children as they manipulated objects or toys. Moreover, eye-contact behavior changes with age. Such contact occurs more frequently as the autistic child grows older, but the eyes appear vacant and without expression (Maltz 1982).

If autistic children are hypersensitive to external stimuli, it seems logical that they would seek an environment that provides minimal stimulation. Thus their withdrawal could be an attempt to maintain a low level of external stimulation. In one test of this hypothesis, groups of autistic, schizophrenic, and normal children were exposed to auditory stimulation. Their preferences for level of sound volume were compared by allowing them to adjust the volume of tape-recorded sounds coming from a loudspeaker. In contradiction of the hypersensitivity hypothesis, the autistic children selected higher volume settings than both the schizophrenic and the normal children (Metz 1967). Such contradictory results tend only to add to the complicated puzzle of autism, especially when they are contrasted with observations of auditory and visual acuity in autistic children.

Perceptual handicaps   The lack of responsiveness of autistic children, who often appear to be deaf or blind, has been attributed to *overselective attention* (Lovaas, Koegel, and Schreibman 1979). For example, during imitation training an autistic child may be exposed to both auditory and visual cues. The therapist may ask the child to say "ah" by making this sound and by moving the mouth and lips. Lovaas found that autistic children would attend to only one kind of cue—for example, visual cues but not auditory cues. Although a child might reliably learn to say "ah" after watching the therapist say this word, the child would not repeat this sound if it was presented with the therapist's mouth hidden or if the child was looking away.

In a previous study, investigators had presented a stimulus that contained auditory, visual, and tactile cues to three groups of children: autistic, retarded, and normal (Lovaas et al. 1971). The three dimensions of the stimulus were presented separately to determine which cue (or cues) controlled the children's behavior. The autistic children responded primarily to one stimulus, the retarded children to two; the normal children showed no preference among the cues, responding to all three.

Figure 18.1 *Comparison of Time Spent Attending to Five Faces and to Incidental Environmental Stimuli*

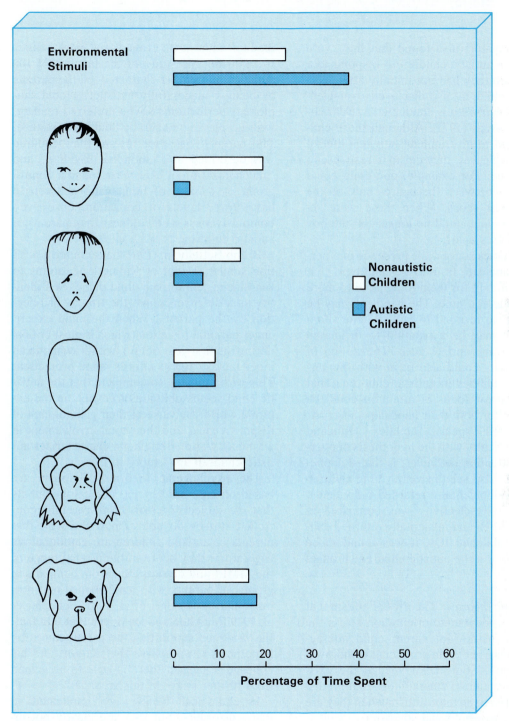

SOURCE: Hutt, C., and Ounsted, C. (1966). The biological significance of gaze aversion with particular reference to the syndrome of infantile autism. Reprinted from *Behavioral Science, 11,* 5, 349 by permission of James Grier Miller, M.D., Ph.D., editor.

(The investigators also found that they were able to train autistic children to respond to a cue to which they had not initially attended.)

Autistic children also displayed overselective attention in a study conducted by Schreibman and Lovaas (1973). Although these children learned to discriminate between lifelike boy and girl figures, they did so in response to only one cue. For example, one child could discriminate between the figures only on the basis of their shoes. When these were removed, the child could no longer tell the boy and girl figures apart.

These studies suggest the presence of a perceptual handicap in autistic children that makes it difficult for them to respond to more than one cue at a time. The handicap may be an inability to respond to multiple-cue situations, or it may be a reaction to incidental rather than appropriate cues. The notion of overselectivity could also fit in with findings of unusual abilities in autistic children. That is, their narrow focus of attention could be responsible for both their handicaps and their often-reported special abilities (Rimland 1964). A difficulty with the hypothesis of overselective attention, however, is that this phenomenon is also seen in very young children and in developmentally retarded individuals. Yet when overselectivity was compared in autistic children and in mentally retarded children with matched IQs, it was found to be more evident in the autistic children (Frankel et al. 1984).

Psychogenic theories Theories of autism that have a psychodynamic orientation stress the importance of deviant parent–child interactions as causal agents in producing withdrawal and rejection. Some acknowledge the existence of congenital vulnerabilities that predispose children to develop autism when they are exposed to psychological stressors.

Kanner (1943) concluded that cold and unresponsive parenting, especially on the part of the mother, is responsible for the development of autism. He hypothesized that a lack of warmth and attention to the child results in a gradual withdrawal from social interactions. In reporting his study of the families of 100 autistic children, he characterized the parents as being "successfully autistic," "cold, humorless perfectionists who preferred reading, writing, playing music, or thinking" (p. 663). The parents' behavior toward their children was described as "emotional frigidity" and "mechanization of care." He found a control group of parents of nonautistic children to have lower levels of education, obsessive–compulsiveness, and coldness than parents of autistic children.

Bruno Bettelheim (1967) has adopted a position similar to that of Kanner. According to Bettelheim, an autistic child denies self-identity as a defense against the trauma of rejection by the parents. When the child experiences parental rejection (which is most critical during the first year of life), withdrawal into an inner fantasy world affords some protection. This withdrawal is so complete that the autistic child seems oblivious to events in the external world. Because of their general lack of responsiveness and their total involvement in a fantasy world, Bettelheim characterizes autistic children as "empty fortresses."

The psychogenic theories of autism are based on case studies and clinical judgments that are subject to error. More carefully controlled studies do not support the view that parents of autistic children are emotional refrigerators; they score in the normal range of the MMPI and do not differ from comparison groups of parents with handicapped and normal children (Koegel et al. 1983; Schopler et al. 1979; McAdoo and DeMeyer 1978). In fact, the evidence supporting the parent-causation hypothesis is so sparse that Koegel and his colleagues suggest there is little to be gained from further study in this area.

Psychological factors are implicated in many disorders, but they are clearly not involved in autism. Unfortunately, as is evident in Focus 18.1, many mental health professionals continue to inflict a sense of guilt on parents who already have the burden of contending with an autistic child. In light of current research findings, there is no justification for allowing parents to think that they are responsible for infantile autism.

Childhood-onset pervasive developmental disorder

Childhood onset-pervasive developmental disorder (COPDD) is a new diagnostic category. The disorder is characterized by severe disturbances in social relations and "multiple oddities of behavior" that are manifested between the ages of thirty months and twelve years. As we have noted, children with the pervasive developmental disorders do not exhibit such schizophrenic symptoms as delusions and hallucinations. COPDD does, however, share some symptoms with autism, including an insistence on sameness, a lack of responsiveness to others, and occasional oversensitivity or undersensitivity to stimuli and self-injurious behavior. The major differences between the two are the age of onset and the language disturbances that are typical of autism but not of COPDD. Other differences are listed in Table 18.1.

Little is known about COPDD, and no information is currently available on predisposing factors or family patterns (DSM-III). The disorder is evidently very rare, occurring in 2 of every 10,000 children. More than 75 percent of the afflicted children have IQs under 70 (Gilberg 1984).

Prognosis for pervasive developmental disorders

The prognosis for children with pervasive developmental disorders is uniformly poor. In a follow-up study of twenty patients who had been given diagnoses of autism or childhood psychosis, researchers found that their symptomology had not changed. The behaviors of these patients—now adults—resembled those of mild schizophrenics, with the exception that none of them displayed hallucinations or delusions (Howells and Guirguis 1984).

Two other studies have resulted in similarly gloomy findings: In a sample of ninety-six individuals who had been diagnosed as autistic, only 10 percent were employable or had no obvious behavior problems as adults. The only positive prognostic signs were the acquisition of speech before the age of five and the

Table 18.1 *Diagnostic Criteria for Autism and Childhood Onset Disorder*

1. Early onset before $2\frac{1}{2}$ years of age	1. Onset after $2\frac{1}{2}$ years and before 12 years of age
2. Extreme lack of responsiveness to others	2. Pervasive impairment of social relationships (asociality, lack of empathy)
3. Gross speech deficits (muteness)	3. Three of the following:

4. If speech is present, it has unusual qualities (echolalia, pronoun reversal)	*a.* Sudden and excessive anxiety
	   b. Inappropriate emotional response
	   c. Resistance to changes in the environment

5. Bizarre reactions to the environment, such as resistance to change	*d.* Oddities of motor movements (peculiar walking or movement of the hands)
	   e. Speech with question-like melody
	   f. Self-mutilation
	   g. Lack of sensitivity or oversensitivity to stimuli

SOURCE: DSM-III. Used by permission of the American Psychiatric Association.

capability of residing outside an institution (Kanner, Rodriguez, and Ashendeau 1972). A 5- to 15-year follow-up of autistic children showed that approximately 60 percent had improved, but the impairment of social skills and social relationships was still evident. Again, learning to speak before the age of five was a positive sign (Rutter, Greenfeld, and Lockyer 1967).

The emotional costs for parents who raise their autistic children to adulthood are great. In Focus 18.2 a sensitive mother describes an autistic child who has attained adulthood. She is particularly concerned about the future of her son because she and her husband are in their late fifties. She presents a clear case for sheltered living arrangements to provide for the special emotional and physical needs of autistic adults.

Treatment of pervasive developmental disorders

Because of the symptomatic lack of communication and/or social unresponsiveness, autism and COPDD are very difficult to treat. Therapy with the parents, family therapy, drug

FOCUS 18.2

Our Son Sam

Sam, our son, is an exceptionally handsome 6-foot 2-inch, 190-pound young man. At first glance he can "pass for normal," and part of learning to enjoy living with such a child is to be able to respond with compassionate humor to the baffled responses that he evokes, as well as to be understanding and helpful when people are frightened of him.

Sam can follow simple directions. As long as the request or suggestion fits into his expectations, he responds appropriately. But his confusion and his attempts to do something when instructions are not the usual ones suggest the degree of distress he must feel in a verbal world that he cannot share. . . . His self-help skills are fair to good. He dresses himself completely and with an innate color sense. He is still learning to brush his teeth well enough to suit his dentist; shaving is new and difficult to master.

Today, even in the body of a man, Sam, the emotional child, is a lovely fey person, one who knows how to enjoy simple plea-sures, who has a kind of unself-consciousness and delight that is infectious and lovable. . . . His expressions of distress are equally unrestrained. Suddenly, without apparent antecedents he will be found weeping silently, inconsolably, or he may beat his head and bite his hands in what appears to be deep frustration or inturned anger. Although Sam uses self-destructive rather than outwardly aggressive behaviors to express his distress, the spectacle of an almost 200-pound man so unrestrained is frightening to the uninitiated. . . . Lost one day and searching for help, Sam looked into the windows of a stranger's house. He was reported as a "peeping Tom" and came close to being brutalized by the police. . . . *Sam is a child, in the body of man, and I wonder if it is not better that the world he contacts knows this as soon as possible.*

SOURCE: Stokes, K. S. (1977) Planning for the future of a severely handicapped autistic child. *Journal of Autism and Child Schizophrenia,* 7, 290–291. Used by permission of Plenum Publishing Corporation.

therapy, and behavior modification techniques are all currently being used to treat autism (there is little in the psychological literature on the treatment of COPDD as such). Although they may improve social adjustment somewhat, their overall success has been limited (Bender 1973; Ornitz and Ritvo 1976). Intensive behavior modification programs seem to be the most promising form of treatment (Maltz 1982).

Psychodynamic therapy As we have noted, Bruno Bettelheim considers autism to be the result of a rejecting home environment. His therapeutic program, which is based on this hypothesis, begins with the placement of autistic children in a residential treatment school, where their other emotional needs can be satisfied. To correct their sense of rejection and distrust of the external environment, the staff gives these children total and completely loving acceptance. Once the children learn that they can influence their environment, autonomous and independent growth becomes possible.

Bettelheim reports a remarkably high rate of success with his psychodynamic treatment. In terms of adjustment, 42 percent of treated children were rated as ''good,'' 37 percent as ''fair,'' and only 8 percent as ''poor'' (Bettelheim 1967). But because Bettelheim evaluated the progress of the children himself, it is possible that the assessment was biased (this is a fairly common phenomenon). Moreover, most of the children had exhibited functional speech by age five, which indicates a better-than-average prognosis. Finally, there was no control group with which to compare results.

Bettelheim's reports of positive outcomes contrast with other reports of less successful psychoanalytically oriented therapy for autistic children (Clarizio and McCoy 1976).

Behavior modification Behavior modification procedures have been used effectively to eliminate such inappropriate behaviors as echolalia, self-mutilative activities, and self-stimula-

tion. They also have been effective in increasing attending behaviors, verbalizations, and social play (Churchill 1969; Lovaas 1974; Margolies 1977; Phillips and Ray 1980; Schreibman and Koegel 1975; Tramontana and Stimbert 1970). A three-year follow-up study of twenty autistic children who had been treated by Lovaas and his colleagues indicated that most had improved on intellectual test scores, social adjustment, and the use of language (Lovaas et al. 1973). In an extensive review of the behavioral approaches, however, Margolies (1977) concluded that, even though these techniques have produced beneficial changes, ''these children are not made normal. Speech and classroom behavior . . . only grossly approximate that of a normal child.''

Four of the children in the Lovaas study (Ricky, Pam, Billy, and Chuck) are well known to many college students and professors through their appearance in a film demonstrating behavior modification procedures. All four showed remarkable progress during the treatment, but they all regressed when returned to a local state institution that provided mainly custodial care. Without the use of contingency reinforcement procedures, appropriate speech and play decreased and self-stimulation increased. After spending three years in the institution, the children were again treated at Lovaas' facility. He found that a brief period of behavior modification therapy (fourteen hours for Rick and three weeks for Pam) promptly reestablished the earlier gains. However, because Lovaas's program was experimental, the children again re-entered the state hospital. As of 1973, Pam and Rick were still hospitalized. Pam showed little effect of the behavioral treatment that she had undergone, but Rick retained some gains in verbalization and the display of positive affect. Billy and Chuck were able to retain most of their gains but also showed an increase in inappropriate behaviors.

The behavior modification treatment was much more successful with children who were

Behavior modification procedures have been effective in increasing attending behaviors and verbalizations in autistic children. A favorite food or drink is used to reinforce the desired behaviors. The autistic child in this photo must give the proper sign before he can get his drink.

either treated at home or released to their parents. Progress was greatest when the parents had been trained in the use of behavioral techniques. The most successful parents seemed willing to use aversive stimuli, such as spanking or removing food, and to commit a large part of their lives to working with their child. Permissive parents encountered more difficulty than parents who were stricter.

Lovaas's study indicates the necessity of long-term, if not lifelong, contingency management programs in treating autistic children. However, two colleagues of Lovaas reported an astonishingly high success rate in using behavior modification techniques to treat sixteen autistic children. (Six were completely mute, and the other ten exhibited little verbal behavior; the majority demonstrated self-stimulative and destructive behaviors.) In an intensive training program, both teachers and parents helped the children develop verbalization and social skills (Schreibman and Koegel 1975).

Within 18 months, ten of the sixteen children were discharged from the program and went on to regular or special-education classes in the public schools. The remaining children also showed progress, but at a slower rate. According to the researchers, the effectiveness of the program stemmed from the training of both teachers and parents in the use of behavioral techniques. The apparent gains lead them to conclude that autism can be overcome. However, additional studies will be required to determine whether these gains are permanent.

NONPSYCHOTIC CHILDHOOD DISORDERS

The less severe childhood and adolescent disturbances include attention deficits, anxiety disorders, conduct disturbances, and stereotyped-movement disorders. Guidelines as to the behaviors that constitute such a disturbance are often vague, and diagnosis may depend on arbitrary interpretations of the extent to which a given child deviates from some "acceptable" norm.

Kanner has observed that the definition of a childhood disorder is frequently dependent on the tolerance of the referring agent for that particular behavior. He points out that many of the childhood problems are transient and situational and that, in fact, "a multitude of early breathholders, nose-pickers, and casual masturbators" develop into normal adults. If, however, the child is referred to a mental health clinic, it is likely that the difficulties will be interpreted as being "far out of proportion to their role as everyday problems of the everyday child" (Kanner 1960, p. 19).

Kanner's observations emphasize the absence of distinct, mutually exclusive categories for the specific childhood disorders that are described in this section. As we noted in the introductory chapter, normality and abnormality lie along a continuum of behaviors; where the line between "normal" and "abnormal" is drawn depends a great deal on the reactions of others. Nowhere is this more evident than in the area of child behavior (see Focus 18.3, p. 516).

In the past, when little was known about childhood disorders, any bothersome behavior exhibited by a child could be interpreted by clinicians as a pathological sign. For example, in 1908 nail biting was described as a "stigmata of degeneration"; in 1932 it was "an exquisite psychopathic symptom" and "sign of an unresolved Oedipal complex" (Kanner 1960). However, it has been estimated that two-thirds of all school children have engaged in this behavior and, as Kanner points out, it is "hardly realistic to assume that two-thirds of our youth are degenerate, exquisitely psychopathic, or walking around with an unresolved Oedipal complex" (p. 19). Interestingly, a classification proposed by the Group for the Advancement of Psychiatry listed whispering and loud or incessant talking as symptoms of childhood disorders (GAP 1966)! Certainly, something seems to be missing, at least with regard to whether the behavior is symptomatic of a more serious problem.

Can the behaviors of normal children be differentiated in terms of severity or frequency from the behaviors of those with childhood disorders? A number of studies indicate that this is difficult at best. For example, of one group of seven-year-olds, researchers found that 30 percent were identified by parents and/or teachers as having a high incidence of behavioral problems (McGee et al. 1984). The boys were more likely to be identified as exhibiting antisocial behaviors, but girls and boys were equally likely to be rated as having "neurotic" or anxiety problems. Twelve percent of the children were rated as "certainly" displaying poor concentration and 46 percent were rated as showing "somewhat" poor concentration.

A number of problems were also noted in a group of three-year-old children (Jenkins et al. 1984). Eight percent were "frequently difficult to manage," and up to 46 percent displayed tantrum behaviors. However, in the majority of the children, the majority of the problems were short-lived and were contingent on such variables as parent–child interaction and environmental stressors. The child's temperament also depended on these variables (Barons and Earls 1984).

Comparisons between children seen at clinics and children used as normal controls have revealed few qualitative differences between the two groups (Conners 1970). However, the percentage of children exhibiting specific symptoms are somewhat (but not dramatically) higher in clinic samples as is the severity of the symptoms. Table 18.2 (p. 517) lists the incidences of various behaviors as obtained from parents' ratings of 316 psychiatric outpatient children and 365 normal control–group children. Connors points out that the ratings for the clinic children may be inflated, because parents who refer their children for treatment (or who have them referred) may overestimate the number and severity of their symptoms. Considering the large number of symptoms present in the control group of children, one wonders whether those children would be diagnosed as suffering from a childhood disorder if their parents or teachers were to refer them for psychiatric treatment.

Childhood Disorders: Developmental Problems or Psychiatric Disorders?

There are almost twice as many categories for childhood and adolescent disorders in DSM-III as there were in DSM-II. This expansion is likely to result in a greater tendency to label as mental disorders those troublesome but transient behaviors that are sometimes described as "problems in living." The American Psychological Association has indicated some concern about the trend, reflected in DSM-III, to "extend the definition of mental illness into areas not previously claimed by psychiatry" (Foltz 1980). Some of the new diagnostic categories in DSM-III include

☐ *Developmental arithmetic disorder:* Significant impairment in the development of arithmetic skills not accounted for by chronological age, mental age, or inadequate schooling.
☐ *Adjustment disorder with work (or academic inhibition):* Current problems with work or academic performance in a child whose past performance was adequate. The child may be anxious or depressed about taking examinations or may be unable to study or work.
☐ *Oppositional disorder:* "A pattern, for at least six months, of disobedient, negativistic, and provocative opposition to authority figures." The behavior of such children is characterized by excessive argumentativeness, emotional outbursts, and stubbornness.
☐ *Identity disorder:* Severe anxiety over the inability to develop a psychological

sense of self-identity. The disturbance is manifested by an inability to establish goals or choose a career and uncertainty about friendship patterns, values, and loyalties. Frequently, this uncertainty is expressed in the question 'Who am I?'

The purpose of the expansion was to increase diagnostic accuracy, but new difficulties are created by labeling developmental problems of children and adolescents as mental disorders. Under the new guidelines, nearly all children and adolescents can, at some point in their lives, be found to be suffering from a "psychiatric condition." The deleterious effects of labeling are well known. One study indicated that normal children who were given a "deviant" label were rated by observers as significantly more disturbed than the exact same children when they were given a "normal" label (Critchley 1979). The researcher argued for "decreased reliance on psychiatric labels and greater emphasis on precise descriptive behavioral observations."

Although DSM-III is an improvement over DSM-II in many areas, it appears to have taken a step backward with regard to child and adolescent disorders, because now any bothersome behavior can be interpreted as symptomatic of a psychiatric disorder. Fears of low reliability may be justified, at least for the subcategories of childhood disorders, according to Werry et al. (1983); they found that these subcategories "have serious problems."

Table 18.2 *Percentage of Children Displaying Behavior Problems (as reported by their parents)*

Behavior Problem	Clinic Children (%)	Control Group (%)
Bed-wetting	29	15
Nightmares	31	24
Undereating	35	48
Overeating	19	11
Restlessness	80	65
Stuttering	13	11
Twitching, jerking	35	17
Thumb sucking	15	7
Biting, sucking, or chewing objects	39	20
Biting nails	55	43

SOURCE: Conners, C. K. (1970). Symptom patterns in hyperkinetic, neurotic, and normal children. *Child Development, 41,* 667–682. Copyright © The Society for Research in Child Development, Inc.

Attention-deficit disorder

Ron, an only child, was "always on the go" as a toddler and preschooler. He had many accidents as a result of his continual climbing and risk-taking. Temper outbursts were frequent.

In kindergarten Ron was reported to have a great deal of difficulty in staying seated for group work and in completing projects. The quality of his work was poor. In the first grade Ron was referred to the school psychologist for evaluation. Although his high activity level and lack of concentration were not so pronounced in this one-on-one situation, his impulsive approach to tasks and short attention span were evident throughout the interview. Ron was referred to a local pediatrician who specializes in attention deficit disorders. The pediatrician prescribed Ritalin, which helped reduce Ron's activity level.

Attention-deficit disorder (ADD) is characterized by a short attention span, impulsivity, constant activity, and a lack of self-control. This disorder may be diagnosed either with or without hyperactivity, depending on whether the signs listed in item 3 of Table 18.3 are present or absent. Both are relatively common

(but much more so in males than in females); their combined incidence is estimated to be as high as 10 percent of all elementary school children (Feighner and Feighner 1974). Primarily for that reason, ADD is the disturbance that is most fequently seen at child guidance clinics in the United States (Barkley 1981). However, diagnosis is made difficult by the fact that many "normal" children show some of its characteristics.

Etiology Early researchers felt that ADD could be an organic disorder. For example, it was suggested that all hyperactive children suffered from a brain injury that produced an incapacity to ignore irrelevant stimuli (Strauss and Lehtinen 1947). Symptoms of this defect were restlessness, distractibility, and short attention span. However, this theoretical position was criticized by clinicians who noted

Table 18.3 *Diagnostic Criteria for Attention-Deficit Disorders*

1. Inattention (at least three of the following):
   a. Often does not complete tasks.
   b. Often does not seem to listen.
   c. Is easily distracted.
   d. Exhibits problems in concentrating on schoolwork or other tasks.
   e. Has problems with sticking to a specific play activity.

2. Impulsivity (at least three of the following):
   a. Often acts before thinking.
   b. Moves excessively from one activity to another.
   c. Has problems in organizing work.
   d. Needs to be closely supervised.
   e. Often calls out in class.
   f. Has difficulty waiting for turns in games or group situations.

3. Hyperactivity (at least two of the following):
   a. Excessive running or climbing.
   b. Has difficulty sitting still or fidgits excessively.
   c. Has difficulty in staying seated.
   d. Moves excessively during sleep.
   e. Is always on the go.

4. Onset before the age of seven.

5. Duration of six months or more.

SOURCE: DSM-III. Used by permission of the American Psychiatric Association.

Some estimates indicate that as many as 10 percent of all elementary school children suffer from attention deficit disorder. These children may show a variety of symptoms such as a short attention span, impulsivity, constant activity, and a lack of self-control.

that many children labeled "hyperactive" were able to concentrate while engaging in an activity they enjoyed, such as watching a movie or television (Zentall 1975).

In some early studies, signs of mild brain damage (such as abnormal EEGs or poor coordination) were found in hyperactive children (Burks 1960; Clements and Peters 1962). But subsequent research has produced equivocal or negative findings (Langhorne et al. 1976). Moreover, the organic hypothesis has been seriously questioned because normal children may exhibit EEG abnormalities, most brain-damaged children do not display the same symptoms as hyperactive children, and most hyperactive children have normal EEGs and show no abnormal neurological symptoms (Satterfield et al. 1974). Finally, the selective nature of the behavior problems exhibited by many hyperactive children does not support an organic etiology; disruptive behaviors may occur only in certain situations (in class or at home) and not in others (Kenny et al. 1971).

It is also possible that ADD with hyperactivity is not a single syndrome. An elaborate analysis of its symptoms as presented by psychiatrists, teachers, and parents of ninety-four boys treated at a child-psychiatry clinic indicated that very few symptoms and ratings were related to one another; the researchers concluded that ADD refers to a variety of syndromes (Langhorne et al. 1976). And participants at a Consensus Development Panel on ADD came to the conclusion that

> The cluster of symptoms does not represent a single disease, nor is it likely that the etiology is singular; rather, the syndrome may be secondary to (1) organic factors such as trauma, infection, lead intoxication, and significant perinatal hypoxia; (2) predisposing genetic (familial) factors; or (3) psychological factors such as anxiety, inadequate parenting, and environmental stresses. In most cases the etiology is unknown and may be the result of the synergism of several of the predisposing factors listed above. (Consensus Development Panel 1982, p. 627)

Family variables also seem to be related to ADD, although it is not clear whether genetic factors, environmental factors, or a combination of the two are involved. Two patterns were found: Those ADD children with conduct (antisocial) disorders were more likely than comparison groups to have parents displaying personality disorders, alcoholism, or drug abuse. Parents of ADD children without conduct disorders were free from psychopathology but tended to have problems related to cognitive and intellectual deficits (August and Stewart 1982, 1983).

Prognosis The prognosis for this disorder is mixed. When 110 adolescent boys with ADD were compared with 88 normal boys, researchers found that the delinquency rates for the ADD boys ranged from 36 to 58 percent and were 19 times higher than those for the comparison group. However, relatively few of the ADD boys became chronic offenders during their adult years, although most still exhibited such symptoms as impulsivity, low educational achievement, poor social skills, and low self-esteem. Only a small percentage continued to have significant antisocial or psychiatric problems as adults (Hechtman and Weiss 1983).

The prognosis also seems to be dependent on the presence or absence of antisocial

FOCUS 18.4

Diet and Hyperactivity

Does eating certain food or food additives produce physiological changes in the body or brain that result in hyperactive behaviors? Dr. Ben Feingold, a pediatrician, thought the answer was yes—based on his clinical observations of hyperactive children who went on restricted diets. Feingold believed that the salicylates in certain foods (almonds, cucumbers, tomatoes, berries, apples, and oranges) and artificial additives were responsible for hyperactive behavior.

Many parents tried Feingold's recommended diet on their children and supported his claims. However, as we noted in Chapter 5, uncontrolled observations and information based on case studies are subject to a number of errors. Biased observers who look specifically for certain changes very often find them. And children who are placed on diets are given increased attention, which might produce a reduction of their problem behaviors. To determine whether certain chemicals are implicated in hyperactivity, carefully controlled double-blind studies are necessary. Reviews of such studies indicate that elimination of food additives or certain chemicals from the diets of hyperactive children has little effect on their behavior (Divorky 1978; Consensus Development Panel 1982).

behavior. A four-year follow-up study demonstrated that ADD children without conduct disorders later showed few aggressive and antisocial behaviors but still had attention problems. But ADD boys with conduct disorders were still exhibiting antisocial behaviors, drug use, and aggression.

Treatment The majority of children with ADD have been treated through drug therapy. Stimulants in particular have been found to increase the attention span without affecting academic performance to any degree (Ottenbacher and Cooper 1983). But drugs seem to treat the symptoms of ADD rather than the causes, so that drug therapy does not have long-term benefits (Aman 1984; Satterfield et al. 1982, 1980). This lack of long-term effects has led to the following observation:

> An important question for physicians to consider is whether stimulant medication alone results in more harm than benefit to the child and his family, since it may convince the parents that the child is receiving adequate treatment [but its effect may be to] direct attention from the need for treatment aimed at other associated disabilities such as poor peer relationships, poor self-image, anti-social behavior, and learning disabilities. (Satterfield et al. 1982, pp. 797–798)

In other words, drug therapy may tend to conceal a need for other types of therapies. Other clinicians have suggested that therapists pay more attention to family dynamics and child-management problems (Prior et al. 1983).

Psychological treatments for ADD have met with some success. Self-control training was found to produce better results than medication, and a combination of medication and individualized psychological intervention provided both academic gains and better psychological adjustment (Hinshaw et al. 1984). Self-instructional procedures, modeling, role-playing, and self-evaluation have been useful in dealing with the problems involved in ADD (Kendall 1984).

One approach to the teaching of self-control skills is based on the finding that overactive children are deficient in verbal control over their behavior (Meichenbaum and Goodman 1971). In this approach, hyperactive children are trained to talk to themselves in a manner that facilitates self-control. Here is an example of the kind of self-statements that a child learns to make, first overtly and then covertly.

> Okay, what is it I have to do? You want me to copy the picture with the different lines. I have to go slowly and carefully. Okay, draw the line down, down, good; then to the right; that's it; now down some more and to the left. Good, I'm doing fine so far. Remember, go slowly. Now back up again. No, I was supposed to go down. That's okay. Just erase the line carefully. . . . Good. Even if I make an error I can go on slowly and carefully. Okay, I have to go down now. Finished, I did it! (Meichenbaum 1974, p. 266)

Other researchers have also found that hyperactive preschool children can develop self-control through the use of verbalizations (Karoly and Dirks 1977).

Anxiety disorders

Children and adolescents suffer from a variety of problems involving chronic anxiety—fears, nightmares, school phobia, shyness, timidity, and lack of self-confidence. Children with these disturbances display exaggerated autonomic responses and are apprehensive in new situations, preferring to stay at home or in other familiar environments. The childhood disorders in which anxiety plays a prominent role include separation anxiety disorders, avoidant disorder of childhood and adolescence, and overanxious disorder.

Separation-anxiety disorder Children who suffer from a **separation-anxiety disorder** show excessive anxiety when they are separated from their parents or from their home. They constantly seek the company of their parents and may worry excessively about losing them. Separation may produce such physical symptoms as vomiting, diarrhea, and headaches in these children (DSM-III). This behavior must last at least two weeks to be diagnosed as a disorder.

One type of separation anxiety disorder that has been studied extensively is *school phobia*. The physical symptoms may occur merely at the prospect of having to go to school. It is estimated that approximately 17 out of each 1000 children per year display this disorder, which is more common in girls than in boys (Kennedy 1965; Ross 1982). The aversion to school usually develops over a period of a year or more and may be triggered by a specific event, such as failing a test or being ridiculed by schoolmates. Once the fear develops, the child often lies about her or his reasons for not wanting to attend school (Clarizio and McCoy 1976).

Psychoanalytic explanations of school phobia stress the overdependence of the child on the mother. The reluctance to attend school is not seen as a fear of school but as anxiety over separation from the mother (Eisenberg 1958). However, if separation anxiety is the primary etiological factor in this disorder, it should occur in the early school history of the child. But many cases of school phobia do not develop until the third or fourth grade. Also, these children often do not display "separation anxiety" in other situations that require separation from their mothers.

School phobia has also been explained in terms of learning principles (Yates 1970). Parents are strong reinforcing stimuli during a child's preschool period. Going to school necessitates the development of new skills and encounters with uncertain and anxiety-arousing situations. If the mother reinforces these fears (for example, by continually warning the child not to get lost), the child may seek refuge away from school, where he or she can obtain the reinforcement received earlier in life.

For young children who are treated with most forms of psychotherapy, the prognosis for separation-anxiety disorder is very good. But separation anxiety that develops during adolescence may be more resistant to change. In a study of 125 adolescents with school phobia who were treated in a psychiatric inpatient unit, two-thirds showed "appreciable" or "complete" improvement, but the remainder showed little change. School attendance problems remained in about 50 percent of the cases. The researchers feel that "severe school phobia in early adolescence resembled adult affective disorders (six of the children had already developed agoraphobic difficulties) in some clinical features and in outcome" (Berg, Butler, and Hall 1976, p. 80).

Avoidant disorder of childhood or adolescence

This disorder is similar to social phobias in adults (see Chapter 6). Children or adolescents with **avoidant disorder** feel severe anxiety in situations that involve contact with peers or strangers. The typical response to this anxiety is withdrawal, which interferes with the establishment of friendships. Avoidant disorder is thus characterized by low rates of interaction with peers, low sociometric choice, deficits in social skills, anxiety, and unhappiness. Children with the disorder are hypersensitive to rejection or criticism (Wanlass and Prinz 1982).

Avoidant disorder may occur in children as young as 2½ years of age (DSM-III), but social anxiety is also common among adolescents. Such adolescents experience difficulty when meeting new people, feel depressed or lonely, lack assertiveness, and are excessively self-conscious (Zimbardo 1977). In its milder forms, the problem dissipates with time and generally does not require treatment. More severe cases may persist because social anxiety hampers the development of the necessary social and interactional skills. Social-skills training and desensitization procedures are effective in treating avoidant disorder

Children as young as 2½ years of age can experience severe anxiety in situations that involve contact with peers or strangers. These children may be overly sensitive to rejection and interact very little with peers or strangers.

(Curran 1977; Zimbardo 1977; Conger and Keane 1981).

Overanxious disorder **Overanxious disorder** is similar to obsessive disorder or generalized anxiety disorder in adults (see Chapter 6). It is characterized by excessive worry about future or past events, overconcern about performance, and a constant need for reassurance.

Physical complaints may also be expressed. The disorder is common and is more prevalent in males than in females (DSM-III). About 12 percent of the children seen at the Institute of Juvenile Research were classified as suffering from an overanxious reaction (Jenkins 1968). Most cases do not require treatment, and the disorder usually disappears as the child grows older (Robins 1971).

Conduct disorders

Charles F. was well known to school officials for his numerous fights with peers. After a stabbing incident at school, he was placed on probation and then transferred to another junior high school. Two months later, at age fourteen, Charles was charged with armed robbery and placed in a juvenile detention facility. He had few positive peer contacts at the juvenile facility and seemed unwilling or unable to form close relationships. Some progress was achieved with a behavioral contract program that involved positive reinforcement from adults and praise for refraining from aggression in handling conflicts. Unfortunately, his transfer to a maximum-security juvenile facility became necessary when Charles seriously injured two of his peers whose teasing had angered him. Charles completed a vocational training program in this second facility, but he was unable to hold a regular job. He was sent to prison following a conviction for armed robbery. Diagnosis: conduct disorder, unsocialized aggressive type.

Peter D. was a high-achieving student during his elementary school years. However, in the seventh grade he began to exhibit a pattern of truancy, declining school performance, and frequent lying. Peter had a number of friends, most of whom also skipped school. They spent most of their time taking drugs, playing video games, or "cruising" in an older friend's car. School officials eventually contacted the juvenile court because of Peter's chronic truancy and drug use. When Peter was found to have cocaine in his possession, he was placed in a juvenile detention facility by the court. Diagnosis: conduct disorder, socialized nonaggressive type.

Table 18.4 *The Four Types of Conduct Disorders*

1. *Unsocialized, Aggressive Type*
  a. Repetitive and persistent pattern of aggression that violates the rights of others
  b. Failure to establish normal social ties or bonds with others
  c. Pattern of aggressive behavior for six months or more
	2. *Unsocialized, Nonaggressive Type*
	  a. Repetitive and persistent pattern of nonaggressive rule-breaking behaviors (running away from home, substance abuse, truancy)
	  b. Failure to establish social ties or bonds with others
	  c. Duration of six months or more

3. *Socialized, Aggressive Type*
  a. Repetitive and persistent pattern of aggression (physical confrontation) that violates the rights of others
  b. Evidence of social ties and bonds
  c. Duration of six months
	4. *Socialized, Nonaggressive Type*
	  a. Repetitive and persistent pattern of nonaggressive rule-breaking behaviors
	  b. Evidence of social ties and bonds
	  c. Duration of six months or more

SOURCE: DSM-III. Used by permission of the American Psychiatric Association.

Childhood **conduct disorders** involve a persistent pattern of antisocial behaviors that violate the rights of others. Many children may display isolated instances of antisocial behavior, but this diagnosis is given only when the behavior is repetitive and persistent.

Four subtypes of conduct disorders are recognized in DSM-III. Two of these are illustrated by the individuals described at the start of this section; all four are summarized in Table 18.4.

☐ The *undersocialized, aggressive* type exhibits a failure to establish affectionate relationships and a lack of concern for others. Aggression is displayed against property or against other individuals.

☐ The *socialized, aggressive* type exhibits normal socialization processes. The individual establishes attachment to significant others and friends but displays physical violence against those who are not in these two groups.

☐ The *socialized, nonaggressive* type exhibits attachment for certain individuals or groups and is not physically violent. Instead the individual breaks rules, may be truant, or may engage in other nonviolent actions.

☐ The *undersocialized, nonaggressive* type exhibits few bonds with others. Violations involve rule-breaking that is not directly aggressive toward others.

All four types are more common in males than in females. Their typical features include conflicts in the home, school, and community; low self-esteem; the early use of drugs, alcohol, and tobacco; poor academic performance; and attentional difficulties (DSM-III).

Etiology *Congenital variables* A small subgroup of delinquents who are generally labeled *antisocial personalities* are characterized as impulsive, unable to delay gratification, and unable to profit from punishment or experience. Several hypotheses that have been advanced suggest that congenital factors predispose these individuals to antisocial behaviors. Some theorists, for example, believe that an innate tendency for underarousal causes them to seek stimulation through antisocial behaviors (Zentall and Zentall 1983). As a test of this hypothesis, a group of normal boys, a group of boys diagnosed as having chronic anxiety, and a group of boys displaying antisocial characteristics were exposed to slides and allowed to control the rate at which the slides were changed. The antisocial group of children spent the least amount of viewing time on each slide (DeMeyer-Gaspin and Scott 1976). These results seem to support the hypothesis that antisocial individuals are understimulated. It is possible, however, that the results indicate only how willing different groups of boys are to respond freely in such a situation. In any case, the results apply only to the small percentage of conduct-disordered children who are antisocial personalities.

Psychodynamic explanations   Psychoanalysts interpret antisocial and delinquent behaviors in children as symptoms of an underlying anxiety conflict in the child. This conflict is a result of an inadequate relationship with the parents; the problem behaviors can be produced by either emotional deprivation of overindulgence (Levy 1951). In the first case, the parents offer the child little affection or concern, so childhood conflicts are not resolved and the superego does not develop adequately. The lack of a strong conscience increases the likelihood of aggressive and antisocial behaviors. The child becomes unable to form close personal relationships with others.

If the child is overindulged during early childhood, the same pattern may develop. Overindulgence allows the child to display aggression freely, and normal internal controls over aggressive behaviors are never fully developed.

Social learning perspectives   According to the social learning view, aggressive behaviors are learned through reinforcement and modeling; antisocial acts can themselves often provide the individual with possessions and other forms of reinforcement. For example, aggressive children in a nursery school were found to be rewarded by both the victims (through capitulation to the aggressor) and the teacher (through attention to the aggressor) (Patterson, Littman, and Bircher 1967).

Although aggression is an effective means of obtaining material and social needs, it also can cause the aggressive child to become an aversive stimulus. Then, when other children avoid the child exhibiting this behavior, their avoidance may increase the child's aggression, because he or she is not given the opportunity to learn cooperative forms of behavior by interacting with others.

Exposure to aggressive models, live or symbolic, may also produce aggression. Bandura and Walters (1963) found an association between the use of physical punishment by parents and aggression in their children: The more punitive parents had the more aggressive children. Bandura and Walters concluded that the parents served as models for the children's behavior outside the home environment.

Symbolic modeling of aggressive figures on television or in movies has also been found to increase the frequency of aggression. Children who were exposed to television programs that portrayed violence and other antisocial acts exhibited more aggressive behaviors than those who watched a neutral program (Murray 1973). How much aggression is produced by exposure to aggressive models (live or symbolic) is still open to controversy. The impact of modeling probably varies with other environmental factors.

The lack of appropriate interpersonal and academic skills is also strongly correlated with conduct disorders (Dishion et al. 1984). Difficulty in relating to others or in performing schoolwork can have a long-term impact on adjustment. However, the improvement of social skills has not been found to produce obviously lower rates of delinquency (Spense and Marzillier 1981).

Family influences   The family has been implicated in the development of conduct disorders in still another way. A comprehensive survey of studies on delinquency has indicated that *parental management techniques* (such as means of supervision and discipline) are the

When children fight the attention they get from the teacher can reinforce their aggressive behavior. Furthermore, the victim who gives in to the aggressor reinforces the aggressive behavior by capitulating.

variable that best predicts the occurrence of delinquency. Another strong predictor is criminality or antisocial behavior among family members (Loeber and Dishion 1983).

Prognosis and treatment Unlike many other childhood disturbances, the conduct disorders show a clear connection with adult problems. Children and adolescents with the unsocialized types of conduct disorders in particular are likely to continue experiencing conflicts with society during adulthood. As we noted in Part 3, nearly all adult offenders have a history of repeated episodes of antisocial behavior as

children. The inability to form social ties may be a major influence in this poor prognosis.

The outlook for the socialized types of conduct disorders is much brighter. Many with these disorders later form appropriate social relationships. Generally speaking, the prognosis is also better for

☐ Boys who have not been involved in group delinquent behavior (Achenbach 1974)
☐ Girls, generally (Mellsop 1972; Roff and Wirt 1984)
☐ Children who have the nonaggressive types of conduct disorders

Conduct disorders and group delinquency have resisted traditional forms of psychotherapy, although new behavior-oriented programs are promising. In these programs, therapists attempt to train adolescents to engage in prosocial (constructive, cooperative, or helpful) behaviors and to extinguish antisocial behaviors. Some make use of positive reinforcement to increase prosocial behavior; others rely on punishment. As we have noted, however, punishment may not be effective in eliminating antisocial behaviors. Even when punishment does suppress a certain behavior in a particular situation, the extinction may be brief, and antisocial acts may reappear. There is also the possibility that the attention provided to antisocial behaviors through punishment will increase the frequency of these behaviors.

Stereotyped-movement disorders

Children with **stereotyped-movement disorders** display unusual and repetitive movements. Psychologists do not yet know whether these disorders are related to each other or are separate entities with distinct etiologies.

Transient and chronic tic disorders Tics are stereotyped and repetitive twitchings or spasms of the voluntary muscles. The most common tics are eye blinking and jerking movements of the face and head, although in some cases the extremities and larger body-muscle groups may be involved. In tic disorders, the movements, which are normally under voluntary control, occur automatically and involuntarily. Examples of tics reported in the literature include eye blinking, facial grimacing, throat clearing, head jerking, hiccoughing, foot tapping, flaring of the nostrils, flexing of the elbows and fingers, and contractions of the shoulders or abdominal muscles.

Tics are fairly common in young children; their occurrence seems to reach a peak at age six for girls and at age seven for boys (MacFarlane, Allen, and Honzik 1954). From 12 to 35 percent of the children referred for problem behaviors, and 17 percent of normal children, exhibit unusual repetitive movements and tics (Lapouse and Monk 1968; Conners 1970). The majority of tics in children are *transient* and disappear without treatment. If a tic lasts longer than one year, it is diagnosed as a *chronic* tic disorder. Chronic disorders may persist into and through adulthood.

Anxiety and stress seem to be primary factors in the production, maintenance, and exacerbation of tic disorders. In the psychodynamic view, tics represent the expression of underlying aggressive or sexual conflicts. For example, eye blinking may be related to attempts to block out thoughts of the "primal scene" (intercourse between the child's parents) or other anxiety-evoking stimuli (Fenichel 1945). Although tics do appear early in life, when the fixation of sexual or aggressive impulses is most likely to occur, little empirical support has been found for this psychodynamic explanation.

According to the learning theorists, tics are conditioned avoidance responses that are initially evoked by stress; these responses become habit through reinforcement when they result in the reduction of anxiety (Yates 1958). The therapeutic technique of *negative practice* or *massed practice* is based on this viewpoint. The technique requires that the individual perform the tic intentionally, over and over again. This forced practice of the behavior produces fatigue, which inhibits the response. The tic gradually acquires aversive properties, and *not performing the tic* becomes reinforcing. The procedure has had mixed results (Walen, Hauserman, and Lavin 1977).

Tourette's syndrome Gilles de la Tourette's **syndrome** usually begins in childhood, between the ages of 2 and 13. This puzzling disorder is characterized by facial and body tics, which increase in frequency and intensity as the individual grows older, and by grunting and barking sounds that generally develop into explosive *coprolalia,* the compulsion to shout obscenities. Stress may increase the severity of these symptoms (Bornstein et al. 1983). Estimates of the number of individuals with this disorder range from a few thousand up to 3.5 million (Bauer and Shea 1984; Friel 1973). It occurs three to six times more frequently in males than in females (Fernando 1967; Corbett 1971).

Researchers have not yet determined whether Tourette's syndrome is different from the tic disorders. However, studies of patients seem to indicate that the two are quite similar. For example, data on groups of children and adults suffering from single or multiple tics, from tics with vocalizations, and from tics with coprolalia (Tourette's syndrome) were studied by Corbett (1971). These three groups displayed no significant differences in IQ, psychiatric symptoms, or EEG readings. The prognosis was found to be more favorable for those with single or multiple tics (94 percent improved) than for those with Tourette's syndrome (approximately 60 percent improved). Corbett concluded that the different tic disorders may be different stages of the same syndrome. This view was supported by the finding that both multiple tics and Tourette's syndrome appear to be transmitted in families and that "having a parent affected with [multiple tics] is associated with an increased risk for [Tourette's syndrome] in the siblings of probands" (Pauls et al. 1981, p. 1093). This relationship may be due to either genetic or environmental factors—or perhaps to both.

The psychodynamic and behavioral explanations for Tourette's syndrome are similar to those for the tic disorders. In addition, several investigators feel that Tourette's syndrome may stem from an organic impairment of the central nervous system (Bauer and Shea 1984). Reported therapeutic success with the drug *haloperidol* has supported this view

(Friel 1973). However, there have also been reports that drug treatment has had unfavorable results (Bauer and Shea 1984).

Behavioral treatment—primarily massed practice—seems to be successful in some cases but not in others. One patient exhibited head and arm jerks and uncontrollable utterances of obscene words (loud enough to disturb others in clinic rooms 30 yards away) that made his life intolerable. Because of his vocal tic, he was unable to use public transportation, make or keep friends, or visit retail shops. His therapist required him to repeat his current obscenity as often and as loud as possible until he could no longer repeat it even once each minute. Four years later, the patient was still free of symptoms (Clark 1966).

On the other hand, only minimal success was reported by researchers who used massed practice and relaxation training to treat three individuals with Tourette's syndrome (Turpin and Powell 1984). The patients were required to reproduce their tics as frequently as possible for five minutes; were also taught to relax on cue. The massed practice failed to reduce tic frequency at all, and the cue-controlled relaxation resulted in only a moderate decrease in one tic in one patient.

SUMMARY

1. Infantile autism is characterized by an extreme lack of responsiveness and by language and speech deficits. It appears early in life and does not seem to be an inherited condition. Autistic children may suffer from perceptual handicaps, paying attention to only a small number of cues at any time. Psychological theories of autism have emphasized the nature of the parent–child relationship. Physiological overarousal and underarousal have also been proposed as explanations. These theories are all highly speculative, and evidence on them is lacking or contradictory.

2. Childhood-onset pervasive developmental disorder is characterized by self-injurious behaviors, either very little or very great emotional reactions, and grossly impaired social relationships. This reaction occurs between thirty months and twelve years of age. Genetic factors, congenital defects, and disrupted familial communication patterns have all been proposed as explanations, but no single hypothesis is sufficient to explain the disorder. The prognosis for both COPDD and autism is poor. Behavior modification procedures have yielded promising results, but evidence suggests that long-term (if not lifelong) treatment is needed.

3. Developmental problems are reported in both "normal" children and children who are clinic patients. Attention-deficit disorder (characterized by overactivity, restlessness, distractibility, short attention span, and impulsivity) is a relatively common problem. Although this disorder may be produced by organic problems, many children diagnosed as "hyperactive" do not show pathological neurological signs. Drugs have been used extensively to treat this disorder, but the use of behavior modification and self-control methods is increasing.

4. Children may also suffer from a variety of problems related to anxiety. Separation-anxiety disorder involves physical symptoms that appear when the child is separated from parents and home; avoidant disorder involves social situations; and overanxious disorder is similar to generalized anxiety disorder in adults. Children's anxiety reactions are usually transitory and disappear with age.

5. Antisocial behaviors (conduct disorders) constitute one of the few childhood conditions that show a clear continuity with adult problems. The behaviors that are exhibited may be socialized or unsocialized and aggressive or nonaggressive. Unfortunately, their prognosis is poor. Explanations include understimulation; inadequate superego development; the learning, reinforcement, and modeling of aggression; and the influence of the family.

6. Tics and other stereotyped movements often occur in children and adolescents. In most cases the disorder is a transient one that disappears with or without treatment. Cases that last longer than a year are diagnosed as chronic tic disorders. A more severe problem is Tourette's syndrome, which may involve organic problems, and which may last into adulthood. Drugs and behavior therapy have been only partially successful in treating the movement disorders.

KEY TERMS

attention-deficit disorder A disorder of childhood and adolescence characterized by short attention span, impulsivity, constant activity, and lack of self-control

avoidant disorder A disorder of childhood and adolescence that involves severe anxiety in situations that demand contact with peers or strangers

childhood-onset pervasive developmental disorder Profound disturbances in social relations and multiple oddities of behavior manifested between the ages of $2\frac{1}{2}$ and 12 years

conduct disorders Disorders of childhood and adolescence that involve a persistent pattern of antisocial behaviors that violate the rights of others

infantile autism A severe childhood disorder that is characterized by onset before the age of thirty months, an extreme lack of interest in interpersonal relationships, and muteness or unusual language development

overanxious disorder A childhood disorder that is characterized by excessive worry and a constant need for reassurance

pervasive developmental disorders Severe disorders of childhood that affect language, social relationships, attention, perception, and affect; include infantile autism and childhood-onset pervasive developmental disorder

separation-anxiety disorder A childhood disorder characterized by excessive anxiety concerning separation from parents and home

stereotyped-movement disorders Disorders with onset in childhood and characterized by unusual and repetitive movements; include tics and Tourette's syndrome

tics Stereotyped and repetitive but involuntary twitchings or spasms of the voluntary muscles

Tourette's syndrome A stereotyped movement disorder characterized by multiple motor and verbal tics (coprolalia)

19
Mental Retardation

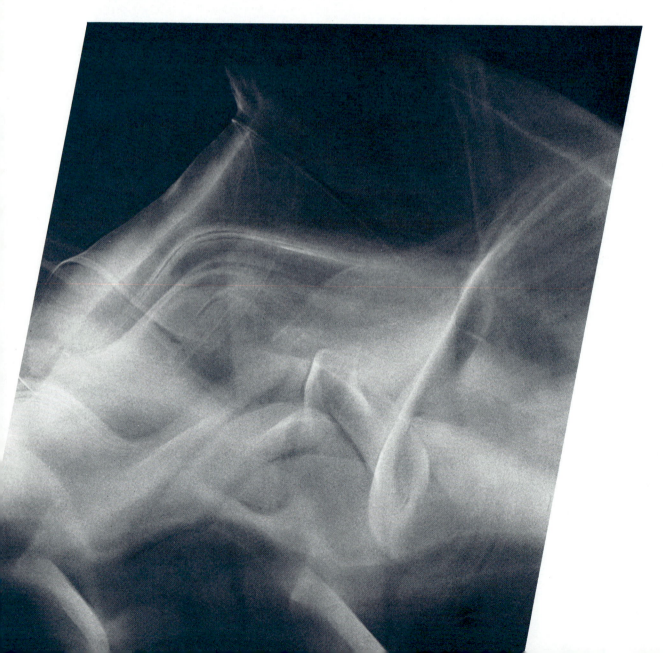

The following "insider's" view of mental retardation comes from a 26-year-old man who has a tested IQ of 49.

I kind of knew that I was different—I knew that I had a problem, but when you're young you don't think of it as a problem. A lot of people are like I was. The problem is getting labeled as being something. After that you're not really a person. . . . Like that teacher and the way she looked at me. In the fifth grade my classmates thought I was different. . . . Her negative picture of me stood out like a sore thumb. . . .

Right before they sent me and my sister to the State School, they had six psychologists examine us to determine how intelligent we were. I think that was a waste of time. They asked me things like, "What comes to mind when I say dawn?"—so you say, "Light." Things like that. What was tough was putting the puzzles together and the mechanical stuff. They start off very simple and then they build it up and it gets harder and harder. . . .

I never thought of myself as a retarded individual but who would want to. You're not knowledgeable about what they are saying behind your back. You get a feeling from people around you; they try to hide it but their intentions don't work. . . . You get the feeling that they love you but that they are looking down at you. You always have that sense of barrier between you and the ones who love you. . . .

What is retardation? It's hard to say. I guess it's having problems thinking. Some people think that you can tell if a person is retarded by looking at them. If you think that way you don't give people the benefit of the doubt. You judge a person by how they talk or what the tests show, but you can never really tell what is inside the person.

Take a couple of friends of mine, Tommy McCan and P. J. Tommy was a guy who was really nice to be with. You could sit down with him and have a nice conversation and enjoy yourself. He was a mongoloid. The trouble was people couldn't see beyond that. If he didn't look that way it would have been different, but there he was locked into what the other people

531

thought he was. Now P. J. was really something else. I've watched that guy and I can see in his eyes that he is aware. He knows what's going on. He can only crawl and doesn't talk, but you don't know what's inside. When I was with him and I touched him, I know that he knows.

I don't know. Maybe I used to be retarded. That's what they said anyway. I wish they could see me now. I wonder what they'd say if they could see me holding down a regular job and doing all kinds of things. I bet they wouldn't believe it. (Bogdan and Taylor 1976, pp. 48–51)

Although this man was placed in a state institution for the retarded at the age of 15, he now lives in a boarding house with 4 other former residents of institutions—and works as a janitor in a large nursing home. His comments challenge most of the beliefs that people hold about retarded individuals; they reflect a degree of perceptiveness and sensitivity that we simply do not associate with the retarded. The investigators who reported his case have observed that, "To be labeled retarded is to have a wide range of imperfections imputed to you. One imperfection is the inability to analyze your life and current situation" (Bogdan and Taylor 1976, p. 47).

Unlike other disorders of childhood or adolescence, mental retardation is primarily an *intellectual* disturbance. **Mental retardation** is characterized by substandard intellectual functioning (an IQ of 70 or less), deficiencies in adaptive behavior, and onset before the age of eighteen. (Subnormal intellectual functioning manifested after age eighteen would be categorized as *dementia*. If it were exhibited before the age of eighteen by an individual of previously normal intelligence, the diagnosis would include both mental retardation and dementia.) Twice as many males as females are diagnosed as mentally retarded. And such childhood disorders as autism, hyperactivity, and stereotyped-movement disorders are more prevalent among the retarded than among the general population (DSM-III).

In this chapter we discuss what mental retardation is (and what it is not), the means for

assessing it, its etiology, and some programs that have been developed to help the mentally retarded lead independent and fruitful lives—at least to the extent that their condition permits. In doing so, we shall examine a number of controversies that surround the subject of mental retardation. Among these are questions regarding the appropriateness of the tools used to diagnose retardation, the institutionalization of the retarded, and the extremely delicate issue of whether mentally retarded individuals should have and raise children.

MENTAL RETARDATION AND THE MENTALLY RETARDED

Misconceptions about the retarded

More than 6 million people in the United States are estimated to be mentally retarded according to our definition (an IQ of 70 or less). The only pathologies that are more prevalent are mental illness, cardiac disease, arthritis, and cancer (Carpenter 1975). If "dull normal" individuals or "slow learners" (with IQs between 71 and 85) were included, the total would rise to over 41 million people. Only about 200,000 of the most seriously retarded live in state institutions.

It would seem, then, that a great many people have had either direct or indirect experience with retarded individuals—so that misconceptions about the retarded would be short-lived. However, attitudes toward retarded people are slow to change, and unfavorable stereotypes remain. The label "retarded" seems to function as a barrier to communication between retarded and nonretarded individuals.

The very strong influence of this label was evident in the results of an experiment in which nonretarded subjects rated an individual either favorably (a success) or unfavorably (a failure) according to transcripts of a bogus interview. This hypothetical female individual was either labeled "retarded" by the researchers or given no label at all. The subjects were found to be less likely to express blame for failure, and less likely to give credit for success, when the individual was labeled retarded. She was simply not expected to be able to do much. Even when this individual was successful, her success was seen not as an indication of ability but rather as good luck. The nonretarded subjects did not believe that a "retarded" individual had much control over her life, no matter how hard she tried. Obviously, such an attitude can become a self-fulfilling prophecy and reduce motivation. It leads to retarded individuals' not being given the feedback required to reinforce appropriate responses.

Negative reactions to the retarded result from other common misconceptions. Many people believe that mentally retarded individuals are dangerous. The news media tend to play up possible associations between mental retardation and criminal acts. However, researchers have concluded that there is only a slight positive correlation between retardation and criminality and that social factors are much more important than low intelligence in predicting criminality (Biklen 1977; MacEachron 1979).

Another misconception, touched on in the passage that opens this chapter, is that mentally retarded individuals cannot meaningfully assess their own situation and capabilities. Responses to a questionnaire by a sample of mildly retarded adults indicate that they do have accurate and realistic information about retardation (see Table 19.1, pp. 534–535).

Still another misconception is that retarded individuals are generally all alike—that "retarded is retarded." In fact, as is implied by our definition, there are various degrees of retardation ranging from very mild to extremely serious. Furthermore, there appear to be two broad categories of mental retardation: cultural–familial and organic. Some researchers

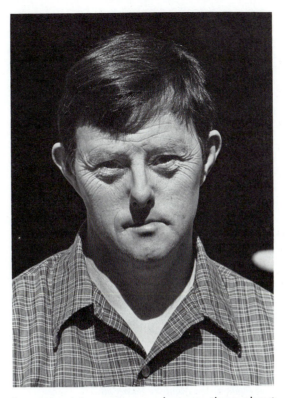

In contrast to common misconceptions about mental retardation, most research shows that retarded individuals can successfully perform many tasks necessary for daily living. They can be in control of their own lives and can have a remarkably clear picture of their own situation and capabilities.

feel that this distinction, which is primarily etiological, should be carried over to the treatment and prevention of mental retardation as well (Zigler 1966). We shall briefly describe the two categories here and discuss them more fully later in the chapter.

The two-group distinction

The names of the two categories of mental retardation are pretty much self-explanatory. **Cultural–familial retardation** is thought to be produced by normal genetic processes, by

Table 19.1 *Responses of Mildly Mentally Retarded Adults to a Mental Retardation Questionnaire*
The majority responses to the questions are exceptionally accurate.

Questionnaire Item	Responses (in percentages*)				
	I agree	I think I agree	I'm not sure	I think I disagree	I disagree
Knowledge of Mental Retardation					
1. There are many forms of mental retardation.	82	3	6		9
2. You cannot tell if a person is retarded by his or her looks.	88	3	3		6
3. If a person is retarded, his or her children will be retarded.	15	3	21		61
Attitude toward Mental Retardation					
4. There is no reason to fear mentally retarded people.	82			6	12
5. The worth of a human being should not be measured by how smart he or she is.	67	12	18		3
6. Other people do not make fun of the mentally retarded.	18		12	6	64
General Ability of the Mentally Retarded					
7. The mentally retarded cannot get around town on public transportation.	18	3			79
8. The mentally retarded do not always need someone around to help them make up their minds.	85		3		12
9. Mentally retarded people cannot live alone and take care of themselves.	21		3		76
Job Skills of the Mentally Retarded					
10. Most mentally retarded can hold some kind of job that they can be paid for.	97			3	
11. On the job, a mentally retarded person cannot follow simple directions from the boss like other people can.	30		3	12	54
12. Most mentally retarded people do things more slowly than people who are not retarded.	73	6	3		18

*Based on responses from 33 completed questionnaires out of 50. Seventeen were filled out incorrectly or returned blank.

environmental factors (such as poor living conditions), or by a combination of the two. No known organic or physiological condition that is associated with mental retardation is found in this type of retardation. It has been suggested that the normal range of intelligence lies between the IQ scores of 50 and 150 and that cultural–familial retardation represents the lower end of this normal range (Zigler 1967). In any case, it accounts for the majority of individuals classified as mildly retarded who have normal health, appearance, and physical abilities, and it is disproportionately overrepresented in the lower socioeconomic classes.

Organic retardation, which accounts for about 25 percent of all cases of mental deficiency, is the consequence of a physiological or anatomical defect. Individuals with this type of retardation generally have more severe intellectual impairment than is characteristic of cultural–familial retardation, though a small number are only mildly retarded. Many of these individuals appear "different" from others in both physical appearance and displayed behaviors. The differences can be attributed

Table 19.1 *(continued)*

Questionnaire Item	Responses (in percentages*)				
	I agree	*I think I agree*	*I'm not sure*	*I think I disagree*	*I disagree*
Integration of the Mentally Retarded					
13. Mentally retarded people should be able to get along with people who are not retarded.	91	3			6
14. I would not mind if a mentally retarded person moved into my neighborhood.	94	3	3		
15. It is fine for other children to play with mentally retarded children.	100				
Rights of the Mentally Retarded					
16. The mentally retarded should be allowed to vote.	94	6			
17. The mentally retarded should have children if they want to.	61		18	12	9
18. The mentally retarded should not be allowed to have credit or take out loans.	9		15	6	70
Special Needs of the Mentally Retarded					
19. Special marriage and family counseling should be available for the mentally retarded.	61	9	19	3	9
20. Mentally retarded people do not need other people to help them with everything they do.	73	3	3		21
Personality of the Mentally Retarded					
21. Mentally retarded people know that they are retarded.	45	3	39		12
22. The mentally retarded do not know right from wrong.	6		27	6	61
23. Mentally retarded people can control their feelings.	67	18	3	6	6

SOURCE: Gan, S., Tymchuk, A. J., and Nishihara, A. (1977). Mentally retarded adults: Their attitudes toward retardation, *Mental Retardation, 15,* 5–9. Reprinted with permission of the American Association on Mental Deficiency.

to the organic disorders associated with their impaired intellectual functioning.

Figure 19.1(a) (p. 536) shows the distribution of IQ scores expected if these scores followed the theoretical normal distribution. Figure 19.1(b) shows that the actual distribution follows the theoretical distribution quite closely except at the low end of the scale; that is, there are more people with IQs below 50 than would be expected. Figure 19.1(c) illustrates one explanation for this phenomenon— that the organic retarded form a distinct group whose physiological defects set them apart

from other low-IQ individuals. When this group is separated from the actual distribution of intelligence, that distribution approaches the theoretical through the entire range of IQs.

Levels of retardation

The American Association on Mental Deficiency (AAMD) specifies four different levels of retardation, which are based only on IQ scores. The IQ ranges used in the following discussion are those attained on the revised

Figure 19.1   *Distribution of Intelligence as Measured by IQ Scores*

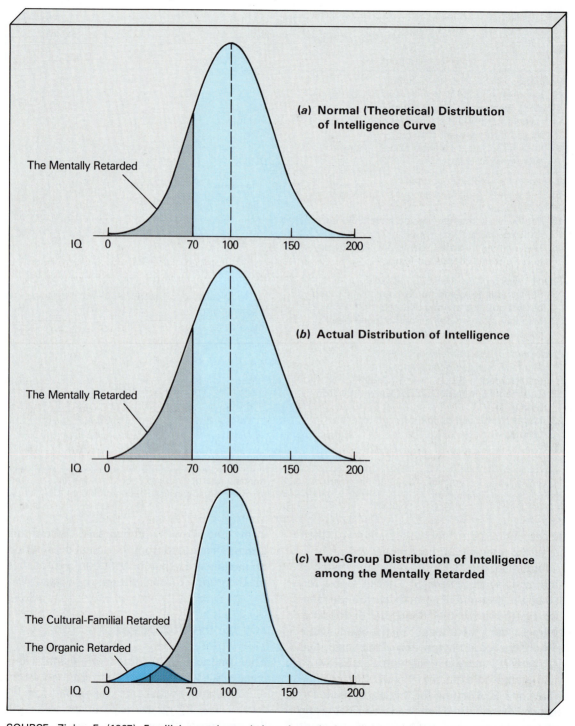

SOURCE: Zigler, E. (1967). Familial mental retardation: A continuing dilemma. *Science, 155,* 292–298, Fig. 20. Copyright © 1967 by the American Association for the Advancement of Science.

Table 19.2 *Estimated Number of Mentally Retarded Persons by Level*

Level	Range Wechsler IQ	Percentage of All Mentally Retarded	Number
Mild	50–70	80	5,025,200
Moderate	35–49	12	753,780
Severe	20–34	7	439,705
Profound	0–19	1	62,815

SOURCE: Estimates based on percentages from the President's Committee on Mental Retardation (1969) and a United States population of 210 million.

Wechsler scales (WISC-R and WAIS-R). The general characterizations of individuals at each of the levels are based on the work of Cruikshank and Johnson (1975) and Robinson and Robinson (1976). However, social and vocational skills and degree of adaptability may vary greatly for individuals within each category. Table 19.2 contains estimates of the number of people within each level in the United States.

Mild (IQ 50 to 70) It is evident from Table 19.2 that the majority (80 percent) of retarded individuals (often referred to as "educable") suffer from only mild intellectual impairment, although it seems that a disproportionate amount of attention has been devoted to those with more severe deficits. The majority of these *mildly retarded* individuals suffer from cultural–familial retardation, but some organically retarded individuals with minimal intellectual deficits also score in this range. In some cases their retardation is not identified until they begin to acquire academic skills; as adults, they may function quite adequately in the community. Many shed the label "retarded" when they enter the work force, though they tend to be employed in unskilled jobs. Many marry and maintain families.

In a study of forty-five mildly retarded adults with a mean IQ of 59, researchers found that seven were currently married and that three had been divorced: twenty-three were unemployed; eleven were living independently. Approximately 60 percent of the subjects perceived themselves as having impaired

intellectual functioning and used such labels as "slow" or "handicapped" to describe their abilities and disabilities. The others denied being mentally retarded, but many participated in programs for the retarded, such as the Special Olympics or sheltered workshops. The majority acknowledged problems with math, reading, writing, self-maintenance, or occupation. The parents of most of these people were aware that their children were "handicapped" even before they entered school.

Moderate (IQ 35 to 49) Approximately 12 percent of mentally retarded persons are *moderately retarded*. Children in this group are considered "trainable"; they develop intellectually at about one-fourth to one-half the rate of normal children. When other children are beginning school at the age of six, moderately retarded children may be functioning at a mental age between eighteen months and three years; at adulthood their intellectual development may peak at a mental age of between six and eight years. Most develop self-care skills and can be employed either in sheltered workshops or at unskilled occupations. The moderately retarded are generally identified as such during their preschool years. They have little opportunity for heterosexual contacts, and few marry. Brain damage or some other organic pathology is often evident in these individuals.

Severe (IQ 20 to 34) About 7 percent of the mentally retarded are *severely retarded*. Most individuals in this group can be toilet trained and can learn personal-care skills related to cleanliness, eating, and dressing. However, their rate of learning is very slow, and constant care and supervision are usually required. Most severely retarded individuals can be identified by their physical appearance and evident sensorimotor problems, and the majority suffer organic retardation.

Profound (IQ 0 to 19)   Only about 1 percent of the retarded are *profoundly retarded,* but these individuals are so intellectually deficient that constant and total care and supervision are necessary. Many are confined to a bed or wheelchair by the congenital defects that produced the retardation. Their mortality rate during childhood is extremely high.

IQ and adaptive measures in diagnosing retardation

The use of IQ scores to define and diagnose mental retardation is strongly contested by spokespersons for minority groups, who contend that, because IQ tests were standardized on a white middle-class population, they may not be valid for use with other populations. Blacks score approximately 1 standard deviation, or 15 points, below whites on IQ tests; this means that ''mental retardation,'' defined as an IQ below 70, is diagnosed 7 times as often among blacks as among whites (Jensen 1969, 1973). This discrepancy has been blamed on the extrapolation of data from white populations to minority groups whose living conditions, educational opportunities, and social environment do not provide the same opportunities for intellectual development (Dobzhansky 1973).

It has also been argued that IQ tests measure not intelligence but familiarity with mainstream middle-class culture. Nor do IQ tests measure the positive coping characteristics of the disadvantaged, which they surely need in order to adapt to their environment (Ginsburgh 1972).

Such objections seem to be supported by research. In one study, researchers obtained individual Wechsler IQ scores and teachers' ratings of social competence, social GPA (grades from school records on social attitudes, work habits, and the like), and academic GPA for 430 white, 201 black, and 430 Mexican–American children attending public elementary school in Riverside, California. IQ score was found to be a good instrument for predicting scholastic achievement for white children, but it was nearly useless for minority-group children (Goldman and Hartig 1976).

The American Association on Mental Deficiency acknowledged the danger of depending only on IQ test scores in defining mental retardation when they set forth a definition that refers to subaverage intellectual functioning ''existing concurrently with deficits in adaptive behavior and manifested during the developmental period'' (AAMD 1973a, p. 11). According to this definition, an individual must show deficits on IQ tests *and* in the area of adaptive behavior to be classified as retarded. An individual who receives a low score on an IQ test but who functions well socially and in the classroom would not be considered mentally retarded. (See Focus 19.1.)

If IQ measures are inadequate for diagnosing mental retardation among members of minority groups, how useful are measures of social competence, or adaptive ability? One widely used instrument is the Vineland Social Maturity Scale (VSMS), developed by Doll (1953) and revised in 1984. Items on this adaptive measure are arranged in order of increasing difficulty and are age-graded from zero to twenty-five years. The areas that are assessed are self-help, self-direction, locomotion, occupation, communication, and social relations. Information for the assessment is obtained during interviews with the parents of the child who is being tested.

To compare the effectiveness of IQ tests and adaptive behavior measures (also known as social quotients), researchers examined the records of fifty black children and fifty-nine white children between the ages of four and

FOCUS 19.1

The Declassification Controversy

The number of mildly retarded students in special-education programs has decreased by 13 percent since 1976. To some extent, this reduction has resulted from legal challenges of diagnostic methods and the development of new means of assessing intelligence (Polloway and Smith 1983). In two court cases (*Diana* vs. *State Board of Education*, concerning Mexican–American children, and *Larry P.* vs. *Riles*, concerning black children), plaintiffs argued that intelligence tests are culturally biased and that the overrepresentation of minorities in special-education programs is a result of discriminatory practices. Decisions for the plaintiffs have resulted in decreases of 11,000 to 14,000 in the educable mentally retarded (EMR) population in California to date.

A reduction of the number of EMR children is also credited to the development of the *System of Multicultural Pluralistic Assessment* (SOMPA) by Jane Mercer (1973). This comprehensive package incorporates into the assessment process information about the child's medical history, perceptual and motor skills, adaptive behavior within the home and the community, and sociocultural background. Separate norms are provided for black, Hispanic, and white children. A child who scores in the retarded range on an IQ measure may not be assessed as retarded when these other variables are considered. According to Mercer and Lewis (1977), it is "a more serious error to underestimate the child's potential than to overestimate it."

Some educators have found fault with both the court decisions and the use of SOMPA. They note that intelligence tests have received extensive validation and that IQ is measured *after* a child has been referred for evaluation because of academic or behavioral problems. Intellectual measures, they say, are needed to determine whether a child requires special services (Lambert 1981). Critics of SOMPA note that its focus on adaptive behavior outside of the school setting "downplays the real difficulties experienced within the school" (Polloway and Smith 1983, p. 151).

Removing the classification of mentally retarded may not always be in the best interest of the child, according to some observers. Many children who were declassified from EMR programs were no longer eligible for alternative special-education services, even though they continued to exhibit intellectual limitations and learning problems (Reschly 1981).

The controversy is obviously not yet over.

seventeen who had been classified as mentally retarded. IQ measures indicated that the blacks had greater intellectual impairment than the whites, but the adaptive measures indicated that the two groups were similar. These results show not only that there are differences between measured intelligence and adaptive behavior scores but also that the relative weights given these measures for classifi-

cation purposes are very important. The researchers concluded, "The decision of how much emphasis to place upon measured intelligence as compared to adaptive behavior in the classification of mentally retarded children is of relatively greater importance in dealing with [black] children" (Adams, McIntosh, and Weade 1973, p. 2). No doubt their conclusion applies to other minority-group children as well. Current recommended practice is to give equal weight to the two measures, but most practitioners seem to continue to place the most emphasis on IQ scores (Adams 1973).

THE ETIOLOGY OF ORGANIC MENTAL RETARDATION

Genetic syndromes

As we noted earlier, cultural–familial retardation may be caused by the *normal* interaction of genes. Here we are concerned only with mental defects that are caused by genetic anomalies. These conditions are rare and generally result in the more severe forms of mental retardation. Individuals with these genetic syndromes often exhibit unusual physical characteristics as well.

Chromosomal anomalies   The genetic makeup of the human being includes twenty-two pairs of **autosomes** (nonsex chromosomes) and one pair of **sex chromosomes** (XX in the female and XY in the male). Two categories of chromosomal aberrations are associated with mental retardation—those due to abnormalities of the autosomes and those due to abnormalities of the sex chromosomes.

Autosomal abnormalities   **Down's syndrome,** which is due to an autosomal abnormality, is one of the most common clinically defined forms of mental retardation; it may occur as often as twice per 1000 live births. Approximately 10 percent of children with severe or moderate retardation exhibit this genetic anomaly. The condition was first described in 1866 by John Langdon Down, an English physician, who labeled the syndrome "mongolism" in the mistaken belief that children with the disorder were manifesting genetic throwbacks to the Mongoloid race (Achenbach 1974). The relationship between Down's syn-

drome and chromosomal aberration was not discovered until 1956.

The well-known physical characteristics of Down's syndrome are short in-curving fingers, short broad hands, slanted eyes, furrowed protruding tongue, flat and broad face, harsh voice, and incomplete or delayed sexual development. Cosmetic surgery (consisting primarily of a modification of tongue size) is being used with some Down's syndrome children in an effort to make their physical appearance more nearly normal, and to allow them to speak more clearly and to demonstrate more normal eating habits (*APA Monitor* 1984). The procedure, which has been used extensively in Germany, is intended to allow Down's syndrome individuals to fit in as much as possible with their peers in order to enhance their social interactions and communication abilities.

Males with this condition may be sterile; there is no known instance of a Down's syndrome male fathering a child. There are some reports of women with Down's syndrome having offspring. Approximately half the children of these women were normal and half had Down's syndrome (Heber 1970). This proportion is just as expected for a chromosomal disorder.

The average height of individuals with Down's syndrome is 5 feet for males and 4 feet 7 inches for women. Individuals with Down's syndrome who live past the age of 40 are at high risk for developing Alzheimer's disease (Miniszek 1983). Congenital heart abnormalities are also common in individuals with Down's syndrome, causing a high mortality rate. Recent surgical procedures have improved the probability of surviving these heart defects but have given rise to legal and ethical issues (see Focus 19.2).

Much has been written about the personality characteristics of children with Down's syndrome. Terms such as *good-natured, happy, affectionate,* and *socially well adjusted* have frequently been used (Moore 1973; Brink and Grundlingh 1976). Down's syndrome chil-

Rights of Down's Syndrome Children and Their Parents

Phillip is a Down's syndrome child who has a life-threatening hole in his heart. His parents denied him an operation that would have repaired the defect, and the California courts supported their decision. Later, however, against the wishes of his parents, guardianship of Phillip was awarded to volunteer workers at the institution where he has lived since birth. Warren and Patricia Becker, Phillip's natural parents, responded that they love their son, took good care of him, and feel that their rights as parents have been violated: "You can lose your loved one solely because you do not meet a level of involvement expected of you by a court of law" (Becker and Becker 1983, p. 17).

In another case, the parents of an infant with Down's syndrome denied him correc-tive surgery that would have allowed food to reach his stomach. This decision was upheld by the Indiana Supreme Court, and the infant was allowed to die. Columnist George Will, who has a teen-age son with Down's syndrome, argued that the parents and the court acted as they did solely because the infant was retarded. He characterized their decision as "the right to kill inconvenient life." However, opponents of this viewpoint feel that there is no absolutely right or wrong position and that the quality of life for both the child and the parents must be taken into consideration.

Controversies concerning the rights of the child, the parents, and society in such cases will probably become more heated as advances in medical technology increase survival rates for infants with birth defects.

dren are more likely than other noninstitutionalized retarded children to be called "clownish," "sociable," and "affectionate," regardless of their race or sex (Gibbs and Thorpe 1983).

Down's syndrome is caused by the presence of one more than the normal complement of forty-six chromosomes (twenty-three from the mother and twenty-three from the father). During *meiosis* each parent's twenty-three pairs of chromosomes should separate so that the egg and sperm contain only twenty-three chromosomes each. The extra chromosome results from the failure of one parent's number-21 chromosome to separate. When fertilization occurs, the result is a set of three number-21 chromosomes instead of the normal two. This anomaly is called **trisomy 21** (see Figure 19.2, p. 542).

The incidence of this disorder increases with the age at which the mother gives birth, from 1 in 15,000 live births for mothers under the age of 30 to 1 in 65 births for mothers over 45 (Mikkelsen and Stene 1970). One-third of all Down's syndrome children are born to mothers over the age of 38. Although much is made of the fact that older women are more likely than younger women to conceive children with Down's syndrome, it must also be remembered that approximately two-thirds of all children with this disorder are born to women under 37.

The prenatal detection of Down's syndrome is possible through **amniocentesis,** which is performed during the fourteenth or fifteenth week of pregnancy. In this procedure a hollow needle is inserted through the abdominal wall into the amniotic fluid sac. Some of the fluid is withdrawn, and the fetal cells are cultivated. Within three weeks, these cells can be tested to determine whether Down's syndrome is present. This procedure involves some risk for

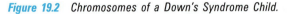

Figure 19.2 *Chromosomes of a Down's Syndrome Child.*
The anomaly that causes Down's syndrome is the third number-21 chromosome.

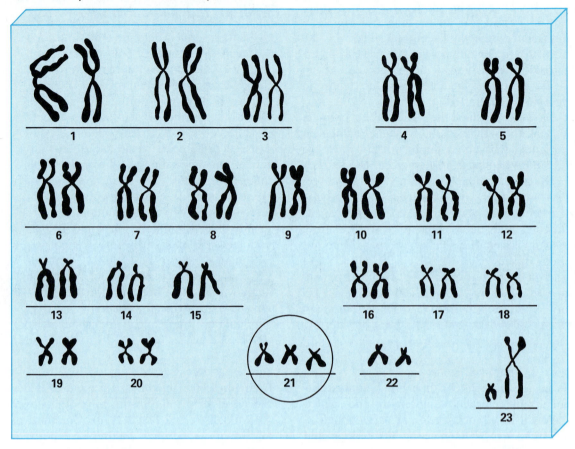

both mother and fetus, so it is employed only when the chance of finding Down's syndrome is high—as, for example, with women over 35.

Anomalies of the sex chromosomes The normal sex-chromosome configuration is XY in males and XX in females. **Turner's syndrome,** or *gonadal dygenesis,* is caused by the lack of one X chromosome in a female (X0). This condition is rare, occurring in approximately 1 of every 3,000 female births (Crome and Stern 1972). The facial appearance remains normal, but some webbing of the neck and retarded growth are typical. Secondary sex characteristics usually fail to appear during puberty.

Most individuals with Turner's syndrome are not mentally retarded or display only mild retardation, but they generally exhibit severe deficits in space–form perception; this finding has prompted an investigation into the relationship between X chromosomes and visual–spatial abilities (Bock and Kolakowski 1973). Women with Turner's syndrome can be treated with female hormones for their lack of sexual development, but they remain sterile.

Klinefelter's syndrome is a disorder in males that is caused by an excessive number of X chromosomes (XXY or XXXY instead of XY). This condition occurs approximately 1.7 times per 1000 live male births. Mental retardation is found in fewer than half the cases; generally, a greater number of X chromosomes is associated with more severe retardation (Forssman 1970). No specific cognitive deficits are involved, but there is a delay in the development of secondary sex characteristics, which can be treated with testosterone.

Recessive-gene disorders These genetic disorders are caused by the pairing of two recessive genes, which produces a disturbance or abnormality in the metabolic processes. These disturbances, in turn, produce a variety of physical defects and differing levels of mental retardation. The most common recessive-gene disorders are phenylketonuria (PKU), Tay-Sachs disease, and cretinism.

Phenylketonuria (PKU) is a metabolic disorder that is transmitted by a recessive gene that prevents the conversion of *phenylalanine,* one of the amino acids present in many foods, into *tyrosine.* The phenylalanine is instead retained or converted into abnormal substances. It is hypothesized that excessive amounts of these substances result in central nervous system degeneration and brain damage (Carter 1975). The level of mental retardation in untreated individuals is generally severe to profound; few achieve an IQ above 40 (Heber 1970). One-third of these individuals cannot walk or control excretion, and two-thirds cannot talk. They are described as hyperactive and irritable (Robinson and Robinson 1976). PKU occurs at a rate of approximately 1 per 15,000 births in the United States (Carter 1975).

Infants with PKU appear normal at birth, but their mental retardation becomes apparent within a year. The accumulation of phenylalanine and the consequent absence of tyrosine also cause a decrease in pigmentation; thus individuals with this condition are often fair-haired and light-skinned.

Early diagnosis of PKU is essential for the reduction or prevention of mental retardation; mass screening for the disorder is routinely performed in most hospitals. The treatment,

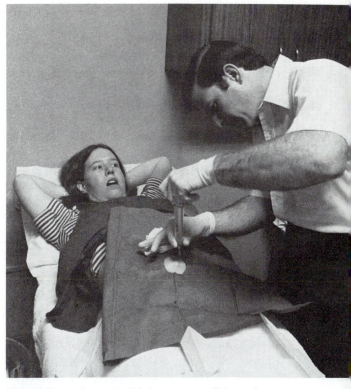

Through amniocentesis it is now possible to detect Down's syndrome during the fourteenth or fifteenth week of pregnancy. Fetal cells are collected from amniotic fluid, are cultured, and are then tested for the presence of an extra chromosome in pair number twenty-one.

which consists of eliminating foods high in phenylalanine from the diet, is usually started during the first six months of life and continued until the age of four to six years; after that, it can be discontinued without harm (Tredgold and Soddy 1970). The diet must be administered very carefully, because many of the restricted foods contain nutrients necessary for life.

The successful treatment of children with PKU has produced an unfortunate side effect. In the past, very few PKU women became pregnant because they were severely retarded and were usually institutionalized. Now, many successfully treated and hence intellectually normal women with PKU bear children who suffer birth defects because of their exposure to high levels of phenylalanine in the fetal environment. Dietary treatment during pregnancy has been unsuccessful, and the probability of a treated PKU woman having a child who is retarded and a victim of other defects is very high. Genetic counseling is usually recommended (Carter 1975).

Tay-Sachs disease is a recessive-gene metabolic disorder in which fatty substances accumulate in the brain and other tissues of the body. More than 50 new cases are reported each year, primarily among Jews. It is estimated that approximately 1 in 33 American Jews of European ancestry are carriers of this gene (Carter 1975), compared to 1 in 300 in other groups (Robinson and Robinson 1976). Through the use of amniocentesis, scientists have discovered that 25 percent of the fetuses of two carrier parents have this recessive disorder.

Children with this disease appear normal at birth but soon display progressive muscle weakness (such as an inability to roll over or raise the chest and head), loss of the ability to initiate movements, lack of appetite, and loss of sight and hearing. Death occurs between two and four years of age. There is no known treatment for the disorder. However, detection is possible via blood tests, and mass screening programs are available in many hospitals.

Cretinism, or **hypothyroidism,** can result either from a genetically produced metabolic disorder that prevents the proper synthesis of a hormone of the thyroid gland or from iodine deficiency in the mother during pregnancy. Cretinism due to the latter cause has been reduced greatly in the United States via the addition of iodine to table salt.

Some diagnostic signs of this condition appear within the first few weeks of life. The heart rate, respiratory rate, body temperature, and blood temperature are typically low. Other characteristics include poor appetite, a large and protruding tongue, and dry and thick skin. If the problem remains untreated, the child becomes mentally retarded. As adults, cretins are characterized by short stature, listlessness, coarse facial features (puffy eyelids and thick ears and lips), obesity, and a protruding abdomen (Carter 1975). Very early treatment with iodine can prevent the appearance of these symptoms. Once irreversible damage occurs, however, this thyroid therapy loses most of its effect.

Until recently it was difficult to diagnose cretinism in an infant prior to three months of age. Fortunately, a new test for hypothyroidism in the newborn allows routine screening at birth, ensuring prompt treatment.

Nongenetic organic factors

Mental retardation may be caused by a variety of environmental mishaps that can occur during the prenatal period (from conception to birth), the perinatal period (during the birth process), and the postnatal period (after birth). During the prenatal period, the developing organism is susceptible to viruses, infections, drugs, radiation, poor nutrition, and other nongenetic influences. During the perinatal period, mental retardation can result from birth trauma, prematurity, or asphyxiation. After birth, head injuries, infections, tumors, malnutrition, and the ingestion of toxic substances such as lead can cause brain damage and consequent mental retardation.

Prenatal factors A number of viral and bacterial infections can be transmitted to the fetus through the placenta. Many of these can produce inflammation of the fetal brain and subsequent degeneration of brain tissue. It is known, for example, that mental retardation can follow a case of *rubella,* or German measles. In the mother the infection is mild, usually causing a low temperature and a slight rash. The danger to the fetus is greatest during the first trimester, when about 50 percent of infected mothers transmit the disease to the fetus (Cooper and Krugman 1966). Then birth defects such as sensory handicaps, congenital heart lesions, and mental retardation may result, depending on the severity and location of the damage to the fetal brain (Carter 1975).

Increasing attention is being focused on the problem of mental deficits related to alcohol consumption during pregnancy. Some children born to alcoholic mothers have been found to exhibit, to varying degrees, a constellation of congenital physical and mental defects known as **fetal alcohol syndrome** (FAS). Children with this syndrome tend to be small in size and to suffer from **microcephaly,** an anomoly whose most distinguishing feature is an unusually small brain. They are generally mildly retarded, but neither moderate retardation nor average intelligence is uncommon in these children (Streissguth et al. 1980). However, those with normal intelligence seem to have significant academic and attentional difficulties, as well as a history of hyperactivity and behavioral deficits (Shaywitz, Cohen, and Shaywitz 1980).

Other common neurological and physical symptoms of FAS include coordination difficulties, shortened eyeslits, impaired development of midfacial tissue, inner epicanthal folds, abnormal creases in the palm of the hand, and cardiac abnormalities (Hanson, Jones, and Smith 1976). Generally, the more pronounced physical abnormalities are associated with greater retardation of intellectual development (Streissguth, Herman, and Smith 1978). Yet some FAS children exhibit the mental and behavioral deficits associated with the syndrome but none of the physical abnormalities (Streissguth et al. 1980).

Estimates of the incidence of FAS in the children of alcoholic women range from 26 to 76 percent, depending on the criteria used to diagnose FAS and on the severity of the alcoholism (Streissguth et al. 1980). Smoking and poor nutrition may increase the likelihood that an alcoholic mother will have FAS offspring. Presently available information suggests that 1 case of FAS occurs in each 750 live births, which places alcohol among the most common

Alcohol is one of the most common causes of retardation. Researchers do not know how much or how little alcohol is necessary to produce fetal alcohol syndrome. Abstention from drinking during pregnancy may be the only way to prevent this disorder that causes retardation.

causes of retardation for which an etiology can be determined (Streissguth et al. 1980).

The alcohol that is consumed by a pregnant woman crosses the placental barrier and reaches the fetus in almost full concentration. Researchers assume that the greatest harm to the fetus occurs in the first trimester, but they do not yet know what amount of alcohol, if any, is "safe" for the fetus. Efforts to prevent

FAS are presently directed toward the encouragement of abstention from alcohol by pregnant women.

Perinatal factors   Prolonged birth, pressures to the head during the birth process, physical trauma, and compression of the umbilical cord can produce hemorrhages or other damage to the brain. Compared with prenatal factors, however, these hazards account for only a small proportion of organically caused mental retardation. The most common birth condition associated with mental retardation is low birth weight, which has been found in the medical histories of retarded children whose condition cannot be linked to any other cause. In a study of over 53,000 women in the United States and their children, researchers found that low birth weight was generally associated with low IQ scores. The average IQ of children who had birth weights between 26 ounces and 52.5 ounces was 86, whereas those with birth weights between 122 ounces and 140 ounces had an average IQ of 105 (Broman, Nichols, and Kennedy 1975).

The once widespread practice of bathing newborn infants with hexachlorophene has also been indicted as a cause of brain damage (Robinson and Robinson 1976). It is now strictly regulated.

Postnatal factors   Relatively few cases of mental impairment are due to damage to the central nervous system after birth. But mental retardation *can* result from asphyxiation, brain tumors, head injury, severe malnutrition, or infectious diseases such as meningitis and encephalitis. The last are particularly virulent when they occur during the first years of life, while the brain is still in a period of rapid development.

Although most types of mental retardation now have decreasing prevalence rates, postnatal mental retardation is on the increase. The cause is direct trauma to the head, producing hemorrhaging and tearing of the brain tissue, often as the result of an injury sustained in an automobile accident or from *child abuse*. One conservative estimate (based on self-admitted acts of parents) indicates that, in the United States each year, between 1.5 and 2 million children are subjected to violent abuse that could cause serious injury (Starr 1979). The authors of a British study of child abuse go so far as to argue that violence-induced handicaps should be recognized as a major cause of retardation: "Children rendered mentally handicapped as a result of abuse may account for more cases than PKU. The consequences are frequently more severe than those of Down's syndrome" (Buchanan and Oliver 1977, p. 465).

Another postnatal cause of retardation is *lead poisoning,* a result of the ingestion of lead-based paints by infants who chew on cribs or window sills or who eat paint that has flaked off a wall or ceiling. (The public has been alerted to these hazards, and some towns have banned lead-based paint. But if a home has not been painted in the past few years, one should assume the old paint contains lead.)

THE ETIOLOGY OF CULTURAL–FAMILIAL RETARDATION

As we noted earlier, cultural–familial retardation is generally mild intellectual impairment that does not have an identifiable organic cause. This category of retardation has produced a great number of controversies concerning etiology and the cognitive processes. Braginsky and Braginsky (1973) suggest that the "retarded" label should be abandoned entirely because cultural–familial retarded persons are within the normal range of intelligence. From their observations of individuals in institutions, they conclude that cultural–familial retarded persons are "adept, rational, resourceful human beings, capable of protecting their own interests by using complex, subtle interpersonal tactics" (p. 24). The backgrounds of most of these individuals indicate that they were unwanted and unloved by their families; Braginsky and Braginsky feel that society deals with this problem by labeling them "mentally retarded." This point is well taken. But in fact there is indeed a class of children and adults who display considerable difficulty in learning academic skills. We need to find out why, rather than to discard the category of cultural–familial retardation.

The "defect/development" controversy

An extensive review of research on the cognitive processes of the retarded has provided the following findings (Robinson and Robinson 1976): Retarded individuals seem to miss the cues utilized by normal individuals in problem-solving situations and to have difficulty in determining what is relevant in discrimination learning tasks. They are less likely to employ active strategies, such as mnemonic (memory-improving) tactics, and they cannot easily be trained to spontaneously transfer learned skills and techniques. Laboratory tests often show that retarded individuals perform at a lower level than nonretarded persons of an equivalent mental age.

Mental retardation as defect Although most researchers agree that retarded and non-retarded individuals display differences in performance, a controversy exists over the interpretation of these differences as applied to cultural–familial retardation. Those who adhere to the "defect" or "difference" viewpoint support the notion that *all* retarded individuals—not only the organically retarded—suffer from specific cognitive or physiological defects. They further believe that these defects result in qualitatively different intellectual functioning from that of individuals with average intelligence (Milgram 1969). Some hypotheses that are consistent with this "defect" orientation suggest that

1. Retarded persons have greater rigidity of boundaries between cognitive regions,

which accounts for their inability to generalize (Kounin 1941; Lewin 1951).
2. An impeded flow of neural processes reduces the ability of the retarded to form new memory traces or patterns (Spitz 1963).
3. Mentally retarded persons have an impaired central nervous system and a lessened capacity for cognitive functioning (Benoit 1957).

Although no physiological etiology can be found in the majority of mildly retarded individuals, the "defect" theorists point to the inferior cognitive performance of this group to support their position.

Mental retardation as developmental lag In opposition to the "defect" view, the "developmental" theorists claim that only a slower rate of cognitive development with a more limited potential distinguishes cultural–familial retarded persons from nonretarded persons and that both groups proceed through the same stages of cognitive development. One implication of this view is that retarded and nonretarded individuals of equivalent mental age should perform similarly on cognitive tasks. Findings that retarded individuals perform more poorly even when matched in mental age with those of normal intelligence are attributed by developmental theorists to confounding variables. For example, many studies involving cultural–familial retardation do not control for emotional and motivational differences between retarded and nonretarded persons, in spite of the fact that retarded individuals are more likely to have been exposed to failure and to the deleterious effects of institutionalization and to be members of a lower socioeconomic class or minority group (Zigler 1969).

Much of the research of developmental theorists has been directed toward discovering the motivational and emotional variables that can account for differences in performance between retarded and nonretarded persons who are matched in mental age. For example, the retarded are more likely to show a history of repeated failure and frustration, which might lead to a low expectancy of success and a low expectancy of reinforcement. If this is so, it is also possible that lower-socioeconomic-class individuals of normal intelligence have experienced some of the problems faced by retarded individuals. To test this hypothesis, Gruen and Zigler (1968) compared the performance of middle-class and lower-class normal children and of lower-class noninstitutionalized retarded children, all matched with regard to mental age. The results were consistent with the expectancy-of-success hypothesis. Both the retarded and the lower-class normal children displayed a low expectancy of success.

Other studies have also shown that motivational and emotional factors influence the performance of the retarded. The "rigidity" (continued responding during nonreinforcement) characteristic of retarded persons has been attributed to the partial reinforcement schedule of the retarded, which results in slower extinction. That is, retarded individuals may persevere in a task even when it is not rewarded—not because of a cognitive defect but because their behavior is reinforced so infrequently (Viney, Clarke, and Lord 1973).

Several researchers hypothesize that the general learning difficulties exhibited by mentally retarded individuals are similar to those exhibited by nonretarded individuals who are in a state of learned helplessness (a condition of passive acceptance produced when an organism is exposed to uncontrollable events). Under these conditions, the individual feels that responding is hopeless and ineffective. Hence institutionalization or the behavior of overly protective parents may produce passivity and deficient problem-solving ability in retarded individuals (De Vellis 1977; DeVellis and McCauley 1979). Adults may foster learned helplessness in mentally retarded children by indicating to them that their poor performance is due to an unchangeable condition (low intelligence) and by not encouraging persistence on difficult tasks (Weisz 1981).

Retarded children also tend to blame themselves for their slowness and to perceive even the interruption of a task as personal failure, whereas nonretarded children do not (MacMillan and Keogh 1971). Nonretarded children explained their inability to complete tasks with such statements as "You stopped me," "Time ran out," or "You didn't give me enough time." Retarded children displayed a sense of personal failure with statements such as "I went too slow" or "I didn't do good."

Emotional and motivational variables do seem to play a role in the performance of retarded children. However, the most crucial factor in testing the defect hypothesis against the developmental hypothesis may be the inclusion or exclusion of organically impaired subjects (Weisz and Yeates 1981). Studies that included the organically impaired tended to yield findings consistent with the defect hypothesis; those that excluded them supported the developmental hypothesis. At this point, the available data seem to support the view that cultural–familial retardation stems from a developmental lag rather than a fundamental abnormality.

Heredity or environment?

Certain features of the environment may contribute to retardation. Among these are the absence of stimulating factors or situations, a lack of attention and reinforcement from parents or significant others, and chronic stress and frustration (Clarizio and McCoy 1976). One of the conditions associated with cultural–familial retardation is illiteracy. In families with incomes under $3000 per year, the illiteracy rate is three times higher than the national average (Robinson and Robinson 1976). A lower socioeconomic status generally implies a lower mean group intelligence score.

The number of children in a family also influences IQ scores: The children in larger families tend to score lower. The reason for this inverse relationship is not known, although one hypothesis suggests that each succeeding child reduces the intellectual environment provided by the parents (Zajonc 1975).

Poor nutrition, inadequate housing, and substandard school environments also tend to decrease IQ scores. In one study, higher scores were obtained by children from a family of low socioeconomic status after they were placed in an adequate environment (Scarr and Weinberg 1976). The investigators predicted that, if the children were reared by their natural parents, their mean IQ would be 90. However, these children scored above the national average of 100 on standard IQ tests. This study seems to point up the importance of environmental factors in the full development of intellectual capabilities. But one can also argue that the IQ scores of these children reflect exposure to middle-class values and skills rather than increases in native intellectual ability.

Heredity is also a factor in cultural–familial retardation. One researcher found that the mental retardation associated with slums is not randomly distributed among families with a poor living environment, but rather is concentrated within individual families that can be identified on the basis of maternal IQ. The data indicated that mothers with IQs below 80 accounted for almost 80 percent of the children with IQs below 80. And the lower the maternal IQ, the greater was the probability that an offspring would score low on an intelligence test (Heber 1970). This finding can be used to support the belief that innate factors cause cultural–familial retardation, but it is also possible that retarded mothers create a less stimulating social environment than that created by a mother of normal intelligence. And so we still cannot tell whether genetic or environmental factors are more important.

Results of early intervention

Programs such as Head Start have not produced dramatic increases in intellectual ability among "at risk" children (those from low-income families). But long-term follow-up stud-

Both hereditary and environmental factors contribute to mental retardation. Research shows that poor nutrition, inadequate housing, and substandard school and living environments tend to decrease IQ scores.

ies have found that they do produce positive results (Royce, Lazar, and Darlington 1983; Zigler and Berman 1983). Children who participated in early intervention programs were found to be performing better in school than nonparticipants, and the difference between the two groups continued to widen up to the twelfth grade. In addition, a greater proportion of the participants finished high school, which no doubt will help them to obtain and hold better jobs.

The families of participants were also positively affected by the programs. They rated the programs as personally helpful, spent more time working with their children on school tasks, and perceived their children as becoming happier and healthier. There is continuing optimism about the efficacy of such programs, even though two well-known studies that reported large increases in IQ [the studies of Heber, Garber, and Falender (1973) and Skeels (1966)] were found to have severe methodological flaws (Longstreth 1981; Page 1972).

Recently attention has focused on the work of Israeli psychologist Reuven Feuerstein, who refuses to believe that intelligence cannot be changed (*APA Monitor* 1984). Feuerstein is not satisfied with simply preparing low-IQ individuals to function as well as possible, given their particular level of development. Instead, he strongly believes that an "active-modification approach" should be used, to allow the individual to move toward increasingly higher levels of functioning (Harth 1982). Feuerstein has developed a specialized curriculum for remediating cognitive deficits; his approach involves the regulation of behaviors, the improvement of deficient cognitive functions, an enrichment of the individual's repertoire of problem-solving strategies, and an increase in the child's understanding of basic concepts.

Feuerstein does not rely on standardized tests to assess intelligence. Rather, he uses an approach that involves testing a child on a task, teaching a series of problem-solving strategies, and then retesting to see how the child's problem-solving ability has been modified by the instruction. This approach focuses on the *process* of learning rather than on the product—that is, the child's answer or solution. Feuerstein's approach appears to include a number of promising techniques that may be employed with the mentally retarded, and it is

a refreshing departure from the more standard "static" view of intellectual abilities. However, it has yet to be rigorously and fully validated.

As you can see in Focus 19.3, there is cause for both optimism and pessimism regarding retardation.

PROGRAMS FOR THE MENTALLY RETARDED

Most public schools now have special programs for "educable" and "trainable" children. This policy contradicts the view, held in the past, that the retarded are not capable of learning academic skills or holding a job. The effectiveness of special-education classes for the "educable" retarded can be summarized as follows:

☐ Approximately 80 percent of the graduates of these programs become self-supporting.
☐ About 80 percent marry and maintain a family.
☐ Most are employed in jobs of a service nature, but a number have semiskilled jobs or occupations.
☐ Although the crime rate among retarded individuals is higher than among those of normal intellect, the crimes are of a minor nature (Clarizio and McCoy 1976).

One researcher investigated the ability of thirty-two married retarded couples to maintain themselves independently in the community. Both partners in each marriage had been designated subnormal in intelligence, and most had IQs in the 50s and 60s. The majority (more than 78 percent) of the marriages were described as affectionate and supportive by both husband and wife. The partners accepted their low intelligence level, and the marriage provided a complementary base in which the skills of each helped to compensate for the other's weaknesses. One wife, for example,

Optimism and Pessimism about the Prevention of Mental Retardation

The President's Committee on Mental Retardation presented a very optimistic view about the prevention of mental retardation in 1972. "Using present knowledge and techniques from the biomedical and behavioral sciences, it is possible to reduce the occurrence of mental retardation by 50 percent before the end of the century" (p. 31). To assess possible progress in achieving this goal, Clarke and Clarke (1977) analyzed epidemiological studies on different degrees of mental retardation. Their analysis revealed that the incidence of the more severe forms of mental retardation had dropped by about one-third from the early 1900s to the 1960s. Advances in immunization against the diseases associated with neurological damage and better prenatal and postnatal care have contributed to this reduction. Amniocentesis and the development of other early-detection procedures can further reduce the incidence of severe retardation.

Clarke and Clarke are more pessimistic, however, about substantial reductions in the incidence of milder forms of mental retardation, particularly of the cultural–familial type. Environmental factors such as malnutrition, poor living conditions, and "poverty of culture" are difficult to eradicate, and early and comprehensive intervention would be difficult to apply nationwide. Unless more resources are directed to relieving the conditions that produce cultural–familial retardation, the prospect of reducing its incidence by 50 percent is bleak.

said her husband did all the reading for the family and she did all the writing. Resentment toward the spouse was noted in four marriages in which one partner was heavily dependent on the other. However, only three of the marriages were predominantly unsatisfactory relationships (Mattison 1973).

In a study of fifteen mildly retarded persons whose mean IQ and mean age were both 62, researchers identified such common stressors as poverty, illness, loss of a job or spouse, and lack of social support. Even with these problems they all appeared to be hopeful, confident, and independent. One woman, who maintained her positive self-esteem in spite of her joblessness, remarked, "Where can I get a job when those knuckleheads there in Washington cut all the plants and everything?" (Edgerton, Bollinger, and Herr 1984, p. 347).

The issue of child rearing by mentally impaired couples involves a host of difficult ethical and practical questions. In a study relating the intelligence of children to the intelligence of their parents, researchers found that 89 children with two retarded parents had a mean IQ of 74; 654 children with only one retarded parent had a mean IQ of 90; and children whose parents both were of normal intelligence had a mean IQ of 107 (Higgins, Reed, and Reed 1962). Although mentally retarded parents love their children, many of them are unable to provide adequate care, even with the assistance of social-service agencies (Green and Paul 1974).

Just as genetic counseling can provide normal parents with the information they need as they decide whether to give birth to a child who will be handicapped, counseling can also

Special-education classes for the educable retarded are helping these individuals to learn academic, job-related, living, and social skills. Most graduates of special-education programs become self-supporting, marry and maintain a family, and hold service jobs or even semiskilled occupations.

help to give retarded couples a realistic picture of the responsibilities and economic and psychological burdens of parenthood. However, such counseling must acknowledge the fact that a retarded husband and wife have the right to make their own decision about whether to have children.

The trainable retarded are often placed in special classes that provide instruction and training in practical self-help skills, such as the recognition of traffic signs and rudimentary reading and counting. Programs for moderately retarded school children also include play activities, such as riding bicycles or working with blocks. After leaving school, many of them enter sheltered workshops where they can accomplish useful work. Although some are able to live with their families or in group-care homes in the community, others who do not have this opportunity must be institutionalized.

Unfortunately, institutions for the mentally retarded are often substandard and overcrowded, with unfavorable staff-to-resident ratios (Hubbard 1969). In many of these institutions, mentally retarded individuals are still considered incompetent and incapable of responsible interaction or useful work. The mistreatment and "warehousing" of mentally retarded individuals have been well-documented (Murdock 1973). About 25 percent of the states prohibit marriage between mentally retarded individuals, and 50 percent of them allow involuntary sterilization to be performed on this population. Recently enacted federal legislation (Public Law 94-142) mandates that special education be provided for all handicapped individuals between the ages of three and twenty-one. This legislation applies even to the most profoundly retarded individuals; it is certainly a step in the right direction.

Recently there has been an increase in the deinstitutionalization of the mentally retarded—that is, the placement of these individuals in group homes or in situations where they can live independently or semi-independently within the community. The idea is to provide the "least restrictive environment" that is consistent with their condition and can give them the opportunity to develop more fully. The implication seems to be that institutions are bad places, but the fact is that they do not have uniformly negative effects. Nor are group homes uniformly positive in their effects on residents. What seems to be most important are the goals; programs that promote social interaction and the development of competence have positive effects on the residents of either institutions or group homes (Tjosvold and Tjosvold 1983).

Nontraditional group arrangements, in which a small number of individuals live together in a home, sharing meals and chores, do provide more opportunity for social interactions. These "normalized" living arrangements were found to produce such benefits as increased adaptive functioning, improved language development, and improved socialization (MacEachron 1983; Kleinberg and Galligan 1983). However, many of these positive behaviors were already part of the residents' repertoires; what they need are systematic programs that will teach them additional living skills (Kleinberg and Galligan 1983). Merely moving the retarded from one environment to another does not alone provide such programs. Nonetheless, properly planned and supported deinstitutionalization does provide the opportunity to experience a more "normal" life (but see also Focus 19.4).

Behavioral therapeutic approaches have been used to help retarded individuals develop

FOCUS 19.4

Another View of Institutions

Although there is an increasing movement toward deinstitutionalization, the institutions continue to perform a useful function for many retarded children and their parents. The need for mental institutions is evident in this article by Fern Kupfer.

I watched Phil Donahue recently. He had on mothers of handicapped children who talked about the pain and blessing of having a "special" child. As the mother of a severely handicapped six-year-old boy who cannot sit, who cannot walk, who will be in diapers all of his days, I understand the pain. The blessing part continues to elude me—notwithstanding the kind and caring people we've met through this tragedy. . . .

Our child Zachariah has not lived at home for almost four years. I knew when we placed him, sorry as I was, that this was the right decision, for his care precluded any semblance of normal family life for the rest of us. I do not think that we "gave him up," although he is cared for daily by nurses, caseworkers, teachers and therapists, rather than by his mother and father. When we come to visit him at his "residential facility," a place housing 50 severely physically and mentally handicapped youngsters, we usually see him being held and rocked by a foster grandma who has spent the better part of the afternoon singing him nursery rhymes. I do not feel that we have "put him away." Perhaps it is just a question of language. I told another mother who was going through the difficult decision regarding placement for her retarded child, "Think of it as going to boarding school rather than institutionalization." Maybe euphemisms help ease the pain a little bit. But I've also seen enough to know that institution need not be a dirty word. . . .

This anti-institutional trend has some very frightening ramifications. We force mental patients out into the real world of cheap welfare hotels and call it "community placement." We parole youthful offenders because "jails are such dangerous places to be," making our city streets dangerous places for the law-abiding. We heap enormous guilt on the families that need, for their own survival, to put their no-longer-competent elderly in that dreaded last stop: the nursing home. . . .

Most retarded people do not belong in institutions any more than most people over 65 belong in nursing homes. What we need are options and alternatives for a heterogeneous population. We need group homes and halfway houses and government subsidies to families who choose to care for dependent members at home. We need accessible housing for independent handicapped people; we need to pay enough to foster-care families to show that a good home is worth paying for. We need institutions. And it shouldn't have to be a dirty word.

basic skills, from bathing and brushing their teeth to the ability to live independently (Spiegler 1983). At Mimosa Cottage, for example, girls aged eight to twenty-one with IQs ranging from 25 to 55 are given training for independent living. Ellen, a graduate of the Mimosa program, works as a nurse's aide, prepares and serves meals for her family, and babysits for her younger brother. When she first entered the program at the age of fifteen, Ellen could not tell time or count money, and she would get lost on the way from her dormitory room to the dining hall.

The goal of the program is to teach the participants to behave as much like nonretarded members of the community as possible. Material and social reinforcers are used to help develop appropriate personal appearance, occupational skills, social behaviors, and academic skills. With regard to personal appearance, for example, the girls learn to match clothing, to groom themselves, and to sit and walk appropriately. (Many retarded individuals walk with the head down and at an inappropriate rate of speed.) This very effective use of behavioral principles suggests that other therapeutic approaches may also be helpful in providing retarded persons with the opportunity for independent living (Lent 1968).

SUMMARY

1. Myths and misconceptions about mental retardation still abound, even though 80 percent of the retarded suffer only mild intellectual impairment. Two kinds of retardation are recognized: cultural–familial retardation (produced by normal genetic processes, environmental factors, or a combination of the two) and organic retardation (severe intellectual impairment that is a consequence of physiological or anatomical defect). The American Association on Mental Deficiency identifies four different levels of retardation, which are based only on IQ scores: mild or "educable" (IQ 50 to 70), moderate or "trainable" (IQ 35 to 49), severe (IQ 20 to 34), and profound (IQ 0 to 19). Research indicates that IQ tests have differential validity for whites and blacks. As a result, adaptive measures—which include assessments of self-help, self-direction, communication, and social skills—are now being used in conjunction with IQ scores to assess intellectual ability.

2. A minority of cases of mental retardation stem from organic factors. These factors include chromosomal anomalies (Down's syndrome), disturbances of metabolic processes (PKU, cretinism), prenatal problems (infections and bacteria entering the fetus from the mother), perinatal difficulties (birth trauma), and postnatal influences (severe malnutrition, ingestion of lead, brain trauma).

3. Cultural–familial retardation does not have an identifiable organic cause and is associated with only mild intellectual impairment. Certain features of the environment may contribute to retardation: absence of stimulating materials, lack of attention and reinforcement from parents, chronic stress and frustration, poor nutrition, and substandard school environments. A controversy of major proportions exists between "defect" theorists, who believe that all retarded individuals suffer from a specific cognitive defect, and "developmental" theorists, who argue that the cognitive processes of cultural–familial retarded persons are the same as those of people of normal intelligence. Studies have found that there are a variety of motivational and emotional differences between retarded and nonretarded persons, but these results are not conclusive.

4. Most public schools now have special programs for "educable" and "trainable" children, in which the retarded are given instruction and training in practical self-help skills. Some communities also provide group-care homes. Those who are more severely retarded may be institutionalized. Various approaches—behavioral therapy in particular—

are being used successfully to help retarded individuals acquire needed ''living'' skills.

KEY TERMS

cultural–familial retardation   Generally mild mental retardation that is thought to be produced by normal genetic processes, environmental factors, or both

Down's syndrome   A condition produced by the presence of an extra chromosome (trisomy 21) and resulting in mental retardation and distinctive physical characteristics

fetal alcohol syndrome   A group of symptoms, including mental retardation and physical defects, that are produced in the infant by the ingestion of alcohol by a pregnant woman

mental retardation   Substandard intellectual functioning accompanied by deficiencies in adaptive behavior, with onset before the age of eighteen

organic retardation   Generally more severe mental retardation that is a consequence of a physiological or anatomical defect

trisomy 21   The existence of an extra chromosome in pair number 21; the anomaly responsible for Down's syndrome

PART 6

Individual, Group, and Community Intervention

20
Individual and Group Therapy

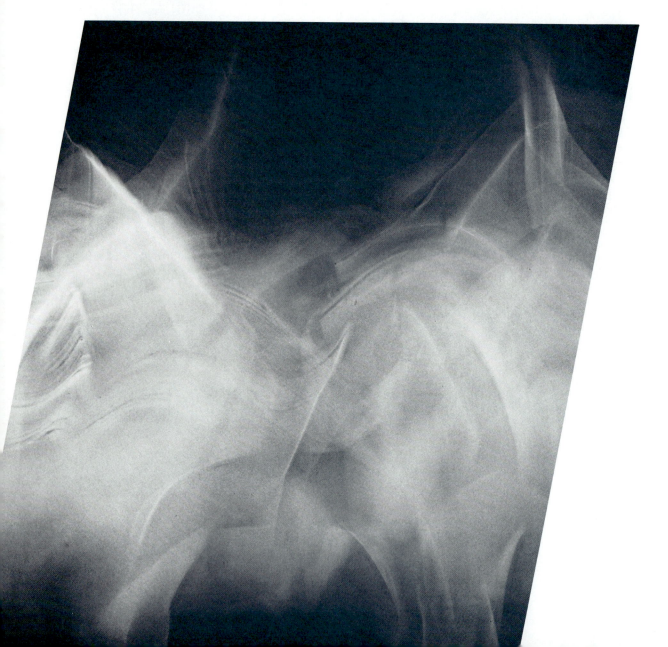

*N*early everyone, at some point in his or her life, has experienced a problem that led to emotional distress but that seemed almost to evaporate after it was discussed with some significant other person who was able to provide reassurance and advice. People have always tended to rely on friends, relatives, members of the clergy, teachers, and even strangers for advice, emotional and social support, approval, and validation. In the recent past, however, this function has been increasingly taken over by professionals who practice psychotherapy (Zilbergeld 1983). In fact, some psychologists have referred to therapists as the new "secular priests" of our society (London 1964).

In preceding chapters we have examined a wide variety of disorders ranging from personality disturbances to schizophrenia. We have also touched on the treatment approaches that seem to be most helpful to people suffering from these disorders. In this chapter we provide a more rounded view of the various techniques used to treat psychopathology: biological, insight-oriented, behavioral, and group and family therapies. Then, to close the chapter, we examine one possible eclectic (or combined) approach to the treatment of Steven V., whose psychological history was described and discussed in Part 1.

BIOLOGICALLY BASED TREATMENT TECHNIQUES

Biological or somatic treatment techniques make use of physical means to alter the physiological state and hence the psychological state of the patient. Four biologically based techniques are examined here: electroconvulsive therapy, psychosurgery, electrical brain stimulation, and chemotherapy.

Electroconvulsive therapy

Many people consider the delivery of a physical shock to the patient's body an abhorrent form of treatment. But the fact remains that such treatment can be used to successfully treat certain mental disorders.

The first therapeutic use of shock was *insulin shock treatment,* introduced in the 1930s by psychiatrist Manfred Sakel. Insulin is injected into the patient's body; this drastically reduces the blood sugar level, whereupon the patient goes into convulsions and then coma. The behavior of some schizophrenic patients is improved after they awaken from this shock treatment.

Also in the 1930s, another psychiatrist, Ladislas Meduna, hypothesized that schizophrenia and epileptic seizures are antagonistic and that, by inducing convulsions in schizophrenics he could eliminate their bizarre behaviors. Meduna injected patients with the drug *metrazol* to induce the seizures. However, neither insulin nor metrazol shock treatment was very effective, and their use declined with the advent of electroconvulsive therapy.

Two Italian psychiatrists, Ugo Cerletti and Lucio Bini, introduced **electroconvulsive therapy** (ECT), or electroshock treatment, in 1938. In ECT, the patient lies on a padded bed or couch and is first injected with a muscle relaxant to minimize the chance of self-injury during the later convulsions. Then 65 to 140 volts of electricity are applied to the temporal region of the patient's skull, through electrodes, for a period of from 0.1 to 0.5 seconds. The treatment induces convulsions of the tonic clonic type, followed by coma. Upon regaining consciousness, the patient is often confused and suffers a memory loss for events immediately before and after the ECT.

ECT is much more useful in the treatment of depression than in that of schizophrenia, against which it provides at most temporary relief (Berkwitz 1974). But *how* ECT acts to relieve depression is still unclear (Alexander

and Selesnick 1966). Some investigators have suggested that ECT is so aversive that some patients get better simply to avoid treatment. Alternatively, the shocks may stimulate the amines in the brain, leading to increased activity and improved mood. Another possibility is that depressed patients feel better after experiencing ECT because they see the shocks as punishment for perceived sins. Whatever the mechanism, though, ECT does appear to be effective against severe depression.

For several reasons, the use of ECT declined in the 1960s and 1970s, despite its success. First, there is concern that ECT might cause permanent damage to important parts of the brain. Second, a tiny percentage of patients experience bone fractures or dislocations during treatment. Although modern application techniques have reduced the pain and the frequency of side effects (to the point where the convulsions are almost unnoticeable), many patients anticipate a very unpleasant experience. Third, the abuses and side effects of ECT have been dramatized—often sensationally—in the mass media. In the movie *One Flew Over the Cuckoo's Nest,* for instance, ECT was administered repeatedly to the central character because he failed to conform to regulations while in a mental hospital (this use of ECT is now illegal and probably nonexistent). Fourth and most important, recent advances in drug therapy have led to a diminished need for ECT, except with profoundly depressed patients for whom drugs are too slow-acting.

The 1980s have seen a slight increase in the use of ECT for carefully selected patients. Severe depression in old age and the depressed stages of bipolar disorders are most responsive to shock therapy.

Psychosurgery

As we noted in Chapter 17, damage to brain tissue can dramatically alter one's emotional characteristics and intellectual functioning. In

Electroconvulsive therapy has been a successful treatment for depression, but has also been used abusively. The movie *One Flew Over the Cuckoo's Nest* depicts one such abuse when it shows the central character being treated with electroconvulsive therapy largely because he would not conform to a mental hospital's rules and regulations.

the 1930s the Portuguese neurologist Egas Moniz theorized that destroying certain connections in the brain, particularly those in the frontal lobes, could disrupt psychotic thought patterns and behaviors. During the 1940s and 1950s, this **psychosurgery** became increasingly popular. The treatment was applied most often to schizophrenic and severely depressed patients, though many patients with personality disorders and neuroses also underwent psychosurgery.

Several procedures or techniques may be used. *Prefrontal lobotomy* involves drilling holes in the skull, through which a scalpel is inserted to sever nerve fibers between the frontal lobes and the thalamus or hypothala-

mus. In *transorbital lobotomy* the scalpel is inserted through the eye socket; this eliminates the need to drill holes in the skull. In a *lobectomy,* some or all of the frontal lobe is removed (to treat such disorders as brain tumors). Parts of the brain may also be subjected to electrical *cauterization* (searing or burning), which destroys selected brain tissue.

Psychosurgical techniques have been refined to the point where it is possible to operate on extremely small and contained areas of the brain. However, both scientific and ethical objections to these procedures have been raised. Initial reports of results were enthusiastic, but later evaluations seemed to indicate that lobotomies have little therapeutic effect

(Becker and McFarland 1955). Whether patients improved or failed to improve was independent of psychosurgical treatment. In addition, serious negative and irreversible side effects were frequently observed. Although postlobotomy patients often became quite manageable, calm, and less anxious, many emerged from surgery with impaired cognitive and intellectual functioning, listless, even vegetative, or exhibited uninhibitable impulsive behavior (Barahal 1958; Landis and Ehrlick 1950; Sykes and Tredgold 1964). Some patients were described as "robots" or "zombies." In rare cases psychosurgery resulted in death. Finally, because permanent brain damage is always involved, some critics called for a halt to this form of treatment on humanitarian grounds (Gaylin, Meister, and Neville 1975).

Although surgery is widely accepted in the treatment of some organic brain disorders such as tumors, it has now been almost totally abandoned as a treatment for functional mental disorders. Along with the problems we have cited, an increased reliance on chemotherapy has contributed to its demise. Nowadays, psychosurgery is considered only as a last resort, in the most intractable cases of dangerous pathological behavior. On the whole, this severe restriction and regulation of its use seems wise.

Electrical brain stimulation

Experiments with animals have shown that it is possible to implant electrodes in the brain either to record electrical activity or to stimulate the brain electrically. Depending on the intensity and site of such **electrical brain stimulation,** human subjects have reported a variety of vivid experiences involving resurgent memories, involuntary body movements or the cessation of movements, and pleasant sensations that are difficult to describe.

As a form of treatment, brain implants may eventually be used to detect impending epileptic seizures or agitated and violent behaviors and to provide either a warning or electrical stimulation that would control the problem. Such techniques have not yet been perfected. A few patients with intractable pain have received electrical implants on an experimental basis, and their pain seems to be made more "tolerable" by electrical stimulation.

Chemotherapy

As we have said, **chemotherapy,** or drug treatment, has generally replaced shock treatment and psychosurgery for treating serious behavior disorders. Since the 1950s it has been a major factor in allowing the early discharge of hospitalized mental patients and permitting them to function in the community. Drug treatment is now widely used throughout the United States: More mental patients receive medication than receive all other forms of therapy combined (Kovel 1976).

Three major categories of drugs, which have been mentioned in previous chapters, are discussed in this section. These are the **minor tranquilizers** (or antianxiety drugs), the **major tranquilizers** (or antipsychotic drugs), and the **antidepressant drugs** (which relieve depression by elevating one's mood). Table 20.1 lists the generic and brand names of the drugs most frequently prescribed to treat psychological disorders.

Minor tranquilizers   Prior to the 1950s barbiturates were often prescribed to relieve anxiety. *Barbiturates* are sedatives that have a calming effect, but they are also addictive. Many persons who take barbiturates develop a physical tolerance to these drugs and require increasing doses to obtain the same effects. An overdose can result in death, and discontinuation of the drug can produce agonizing withdrawal symptoms. Moreover, physical and mental disturbances such as muscular incoordination and mental confusion can result from even normal dosages. For these reasons the barbiturates were replaced with antianxiety drugs almost as soon as the latter became available.

During the 1940s and 1950s, researchers first developed *meprobamate* (the generic name of Miltown), for use as a muscle relaxant and anxiety reducer. Within a few short years it was being prescribed for patients who exhibited neurotic symptoms, who complained of anxiety and nervousness, or who showed psychosomatic problems. Soon other antianxiety drugs, including Librium and Valium, were marketed. The latter has become the most often prescribed drug in all of medicine.

The antianxiety drugs can produce addiction and the impairment of psychomotor skills, and discontinuation of the drugs after prolonged usage at high doses can result in withdrawal symptoms. But they are considered safer than barbiturates, and there is little doubt that they are effective in reducing anxiety and the behavioral symptoms of anxiety disorder (Rickels 1966).

The major problem associated with the minor tranquilizers is the great potential for overuse and overreliance. Almost everyone experiences anxiety at one time or another, and the antianxiety drugs are effective, readily available, low in cost, and easy to administer. They are, in other words, a quick and easy alternative to the development of personal

The advent during the 1950s of successful drug treatments for severe psychological problems has radically changed the prognosis and course of many mental disorders. A major result has been the early release of mental patients who were once thought to be chronic and incurable.

Table 20.1 *The Drugs Most Commonly Used in Chemotherapy*

Category	Generic Name	Brand Name
Minor Tranquilizers	Meprobamate Chlordiazepoxide Diazepam	Miltown, Equanil Librium Valium
Major Tranquilizers (phenothiazines)	Chlorpromazine Triflouperazine Thioxanthene	Thorazine Stelazine Haldol Prolixin
Antidepressants	Phenelzine Isocarboxazid Tranylcypromine Imipramine Doxepin Amitriptyline	Nardil Marplan Parnate Tofranil Sinequan Elavil

coping skills. As a result, people tend to choose the short-term relief offered by these drugs over the long-term but slower gains that accrue from the ability to manage stress and solve one's own problems.

Major tranquilizers In 1950 a synthetic sedative was developed in France. This drug, *chlorpromazine* (the generic name of Thorazine), was observed to have an unexpected tranquilizing effect, which decreased patients' interest in the events taking place around them. Chlorpromazine also seemed to reduce psychotic symptoms. From this beginning, a number of other major tranquilizers were developed for administration mainly to patients suffering from schizophrenia.

Many schizophrenic patients who use these drugs become calm and manageable, show a reduction in inappropriate behaviors and disturbed associations, exhibit fewer delusional and hallucinatory symptoms, and are more amenable to other forms of treatment, such as psychotherapy. Several experimental studies have demonstrated the efficacy of antipsychotic drugs in the treatment of schizophrenia. A review of numerous large-scale controlled studies indicated that the beneficial effects of Thorazine, Stelazine, Prolixin, and other antipsychotic drugs have been responsible for the release of thousands of chronic "incurable" mental patients throughout the country (Wender and Klein 1981). When hospitalized schizophrenics were given *phenothiazines* (a class of major tranquilizers), they exhibited more social interaction with others, better self-management, and less agitation and excitement than when they were given **placebos** (chemically inert or inactive substances). The placebos were used to rule out the possibility that indicated gains might be due to patients' expectations of improvement or to the attention given patients by the staff in administering the drugs (Cole 1964).

Outcome research on drug treatment (and, for that matter, on psychotherapy) must be designed to ensure that *placebo effects* are controlled: These are positive responses to a drug that result from the patient's understanding of the drug's action, from faith in the doctor, or from other psychological factors unrelated to the specific physiological action of the drug (Korchin 1976). Similarly, in the evaluation of any form of treatment or psychotherapy, the patient's expectancy of improvement and the attention received from the doctor may influence improvement rates. A particular treatment is usually considered effective if it results in greater improvement than a placebo, as in the Cole (1964) research.

May (1968) assessed the relative effectiveness of phenothiazine treatment, individual psychotherapy, phenothiazine treatment in combination with individual psychotherapy, ECT, and milieu therapy (in which a hospital is organized to provide a total *therapeutic community*). The use of phenothiazine alone was *as effective as* phenothiazine plus individual psychotherapy. And both forms of treatment were *superior to* individual psychotherapy alone, ECT, and milieu therapy on measures of improvement that included staff ratings of patients and discharge rates from the hospital. All patients in the experimental groups were given some sort of therapy, so placebo effects were assumed to have no bearing on the results.

Despite their recognized effectiveness, antipsychotic drugs do not always reduce anxiety, and they can produce certain side effects. Patients may exhibit psychomotor symptoms resembling those of Parkinson's disease, sensitivity to light, dryness of the mouth, drowsiness, or liver disease. After at least six months of continuous treatment with antipsychotic drugs, some patients (they are usually over forty years of age) develop tardive dyskinesia, a side effect that is discussed in Focus 16.3.

Patients who are discharged from hospitals typically show only marginal adjustment to community life, and psychotic symptoms usually return when the medication is discontinued. As a result the rehospitalization rate for discharged patients is high. Nevertheless, chemotherapy is of major importance in the treatment of schizophrenia, and nearly all psychiatric institutions use it. Antipsychotic drugs have dramatically increased the proportion of schizophrenic patients who can return and function in the community, even though such patients may show residual symptoms (Lehmann 1974).

Antidepressants As in the case of the antipsychotic drugs, the development of antidepressants was aided by a fortunate coincidence. During the 1950s, it was noticed that patients who were treated with the antituberculosis drug *iproniazid* became happier and more optimistic. When the drug was tested on depressed patients, it was found to be effective as an antidepressant. Unfortunately, liver damage and fatalities due to the drug were relatively high. Other drugs, such as *phenelzine,* were soon found to have similar antidepressant effects and to be less dangerous. In another development during the late 1950s, the drug *imipramine,* which was used in treating schizophrenics because of its chemical similarity to phenothiazine, was also found to be valuable in relieving the symptoms of depression.

Psychopharmacological considerations Deciding which drug to use with which kind of patient under what circumstances is a major issue in **psychopharmacology**—the study of the effects of drugs on the mind and on behavior. For example, imipramine is more effective with endogenous than with exogenous depressives and is particularly indicated for persons over the age of forty and for those with psychomotor retardation or psychotic symptoms (Research Task Force 1975). But antidepressants often do not begin to benefit patients until two to three weeks after treatment. Hence ECT is often the preferred treatment for severely depressed or suicidal patients when rapid improvement is necessary.

The use of antidepressants, minor tranquilizers, and major tranquilizers has resulted in great changes in therapy. Patients who take them report that they feel better, that symptoms are reduced, and that overall functioning is enhanced. Prolonged hospitalization is no longer needed in most cases, and patients are more amenable to other forms of treatment, such as psychotherapy. Remember, however, that drugs do not cure mental disorders. Medication does not help the patient improve his or her living skills. Many patients discharged from hospitals require medication on a continuing basis in order to function even minimally in the community. Unfortunately, many do not continue taking their medication once they leave the regimented environment of the mental hospital.

PSYCHOTHERAPY

In most cases, biological modes of treatment like chemotherapy are used as an adjunct to psychotherapy. But beyond general agreement that psychotherapy is an internal approach to the treatment of psychopathology, involving interaction between one or more clients and a therapist, there is little consensus on exactly what it is. Psychotherapy has been termed ''a conversation with a therapeutic purpose'' (Korchin 1976); somewhat facetiously, it has been called ''the talking cure'' or the ''purchase of friendship'' (Schofield 1964). One observer suggests that psychotherapy can best be defined by its goals, by its procedures and methods, by its practitioners, or by the relationship formed between the therapist and client (Reisman 1971).

For our purposes, **psychotherapy** may be defined as the systematic application of techniques derived from psychological principles by a trained and experienced professional therapist, for the purpose of aiding psychologically troubled individuals. We cannot be more succinct or precise without becoming involved in the specific types of therapy. Depending on their perspective and theoretical orientation, therapists may attempt to modify attitudes,

The practice of therapy is both a science and an art. A trained professional must select the appropriate therapy techniques that will be beneficial to a particular client. Moreover, the therapist must establish a rapport with the client in order for the therapeutic process to be successful.

thoughts, feelings, or behaviors; to facilitate self-insight and the rational control of the client's own life; to cure mental illness; to enhance mental health and self-actualization; to make clients somehow "feel better"; to remove a causal agent; to change a self-concept; or to facilitate adaptation. Psychotherapy is practiced by many different kinds of individuals in many different ways—a fact that seems to preclude the establishment of a single set of standard therapeutic procedures. And despite our emphasis on the scientific basis of therapy, in practice it is often more art than science.

We can, however, identify four characteristics of this thing called psychotherapy—whether we can define it or not and whether it is art or science or a combination of the two

(Korchin 1976). First, psychotherapy is an opportunity for *relearning* on the part of the client. Many persons seen by psychotherapists say, "I know I shouldn't feel or act this way, but I just can't help it." In essence, psychotherapy provides the opportunity to unlearn, relearn, develop, or change certain behaviors or levels of functioning.

Second, psychotherapy generates the development of new, emotionally important experiences. An individual questioning the value of psychotherapy may ask, "If I talk about my problems, how will that cause me to change, even though I may understand myself better? I do this now with friends." Psychotherapy is not merely a "talking cure." It involves the experiencing of emotions that clients may have avoided because of the painful and helpless feelings fostered by these emotions. This *experiencing* allows relearning as well as emotional and intellectual insight into problems and conflicts.

Third, there is *a therapeutic relationship.* Therapists have been trained to listen, show sympathetic concern, be objective, value the client's integrity, communicate understanding, and use their professional knowledge and skills. Therapists may provide reassurance, interpretations, self-disclosures, reflections of the client's feelings, or information, each at the appropriate times. As a team, therapist and client are better prepared to venture into frightening areas that the client would not have faced alone.

Finally, clients in psychotherapy have certain *motivations and expectations.* Most persons enter therapy with both anxiety and hope. They are frightened by their emotional difficulties and by treatment, but they expect or hope that therapy will be helpful.

The goals and general characteristics of psychotherapy seem highly admirable, and most individuals consider them so. However, psychotherapy has been criticized as being biased and inappropriate to the lifestyles of clients who are members of minority groups. A few of its more specific characteristics, and their potential effects on culturally different clients, are outlined in Focus 20.1 (pp. 568–569).

We shall first discuss individual psychotherapy, in which one therapist treats one client at any one time, and then group therapy and family therapy. In addition, we shall distinguish between insight-oriented and action-oriented approaches to individual therapy. This distinction has been used to separate approaches that stress awareness, understanding, and consciousness of one's own motivations (that is, insight) from those that stress such actions as changing one's behavior patterns or cognitions (London 1964). The former include the psychoanalytic and humanistic–existential viewpoints, whereas the latter encompass mainly the behavioral perspectives. Despite this variety of approaches, many therapists display similarities in their treatment strategies (Weiner 1976). And, as we noted in Chapter 1, many therapists choose relevant techniques from all of the various "pure" approaches in order to develop the most effective *eclectic* approach for each particular client.

INSIGHT-ORIENTED APPROACHES TO INDIVIDUAL PSYCHOTHERAPY

The theoretical bases of the major insight-oriented psychotherapies were discussed in Chapter 2. Here we shall briefly review these theoretical perspectives on psychotherapy and then discuss their most commonly used treatment techniques.

Psychoanalysis

According to the theory of personality devised by Sigmund Freud, individuals are born with certain instinctual drives that constantly seek discharge or expression. As the personality structure develops, conflicts occur between the id, ego, and superego. If conflicts remain unresolved the problem will resurface during adulthood. The relative importance of such unresolved conflict depends on the psychosexual stage (oral, anal, phallic, latency, or genital) in which it occurs: The earlier the stage in which an unresolved conflict arises, the greater its effect on subsequent behaviors. The repression of unacceptable thoughts and impulses (within the unconscious) is the primary mechanism of defense against their occurrence.

Psychoanalytic therapy, or **psychoanalysis,** is an attempt to induce ego-weakness so that repressed material can be uncovered, the client can achieve insight into his or her inner motivations and desires, and unresolved childhood conflicts can be controlled. Psychoanalysis requires many sessions of therapy over a long period of time. It may not be appropriate for certain types of individuals, such as non-verbal adults, young children who cannot be verbally articulate or reasonable, schizoid persons, those with urgent problems requiring immediate reduction of symptoms, and the feeble-minded (Fenichel 1945).

Psychoanalysts traditionally use four methods to achieve their therapeutic goals: free association, analysis of resistance, transference, and interpretation.

Free association In **free association** the patient just talks, saying whatever comes to mind, regardless of how illogical or embarrassing it may seem. Psychoanalysts believe the material that surfaces in this process is determined by the patient's psychic makeup and that it can provide some understanding of the patient's conflicts, unconscious processes, and personality dynamics. Simply asking the patient to talk about his or her conflicts is fruitless, because the really important material is

FOCUS 20.1

Psychotherapy and Cultural Bias

Psychotherapy has frequently been criticized by racial and ethnic minorities as being a "handmaiden of the status quo," a "transmitter of society's values," and an "instrument of oppression." Rather than helping people to attain their full potential, critics say, it has often been used to subjugate the very individuals it was meant to free. The meaning of such statements is clear. The process and goals of psychotherapy are culture-bound and thus culturally biased against people whose values differ from those of mainstream America. Certain "generic characteristics of therapy," which seem to be common to most schools of thought, often come in conflict with the cultural values held by clients (Sue 1981).

☐ *Focus on the individual*. Most forms of counseling and psychotherapy stress the importance and uniqueness of the individual, as reflected in the I–thou relationship, the one-to-one encounter, and the belief that the client must take responsibility for himself or herself. In many cultural groups, however, the basic psychosocial unit is not the individual but the family, the group, or the col-

lective society. For example, many Asian–Americans and Hispanics define their identities within the family constellation. Whatever one does reflects not only on oneself, but on also one's entire family. Important decisions are thus made by the entire family rather than by the individual.

Therapists who work with individuals from such cultures may see their clients as "dependent," "lacking in maturity," or "avoiding responsiblity." These negative labels do much harm to the self-esteem of minority-group members, especially when they become part of a diagnosis.

☐ *Verbal expression of emotions*. The psychotherapeutic process works best for clients who are verbal, articulate, and able to express their feelings and be assertive. The major medium of communication is the spoken word (in standard English). Those who tend to be less verbal, who speak with an accent, or who do not use standard English are placed at a disadvantage. In addition, many cultural groups (including Asians and American Indians) are brought up to conceal

repressed from the patient's consciousness. Instead, reports of dreams, feelings, thoughts, and fantasies are what reflect the patient's psychodynamics; the therapist's task is to facilitate continuous free association of thoughts and to interpret the results.

Analysis of resistance Throughout the course of psychoanalytic therapy, the patient's unconscious may attempt to impede the process—to prevent the exposure of repressed material.

In free association, for example, the patient may suddenly change the subject, lose the train of thought, go blank, or become silent. As we noted in Chapter 2, such **resistance** may also be manifested in a patient's late arrival or failure to keep an appointment. A trained analyst is alert to these telltale signs of resistance, because they indicate that a sensitive area is being approached. The therapist can make therapeutic use of properly interpreted instances of resistance, to show the patient that

rather than verbalize their feelings; therapists often perceive them as "inhibited," "lacking in spontaneity," or "repressed." Thus the therapeutic process, by valuing expressiveness, may not only force minority clients to violate their cultural norms but also label them as having negative personality traits.

□ *Openness and intimacy.* Self-disclosure and discussion of the most intimate and personal aspects of one's life are hallmarks of therapy. However, cultural and sociopolitical factors may make some clients unwilling or unable to engage in such self-disclosure. For example, in Focus 1.1 we discussed the "cultural paranoia" that many black Americans have developed as a defense against discrimination and oppression—a healthy distrust that would make them reluctant to disclose their innermost thoughts and feelings to a white therapist. Unfortunately, therapists who encountered this reluctance might perceive their clients as suspicious, guarded, and paranoid. Likewise, many therapists do not understand the cultural implications of disclosure among Asians, who discuss intimate

matters only with close acquaintances, and not with strangers (which therapists may well be).

□ *Insight.* Most closely associated with the psychodynamic approach but valued in many theoretical orientations, **insight** is the ability to understand the basis of one's motivations, perceptions, and behavior. But many cultural groups do not value insight. In China, for example, when a person becomes depressed or anxious, he or she may be advised to avoid the thoughts that are causing the distress. This contrasts abruptly with the Western belief that insight is always helpful in therapy.

The solution to this "culture gap" is obvious: Therapists need to (1) become aware of their own cultural values, biases, and assumptions; (2) learn and understand the cultural values of other groups; and (3) develop more appropriate culture-specific intervention strategies for use with minority-group clients (Sue 1981).

SOURCE: From Sue, D. W. *Counseling the culturally different.* Copyright © 1981 by D. W. Sue. Reprinted by permission of John Wiley & Sons, Inc.

repressed material is coming close to the surface and to suggest means of uncovering it.

Transference   When a patient begins to perceive, or behave toward, the therapist as though the therapist were an important person in his or her past, the process of transference is occurring. In **transference** the patient reenacts early conflicts by carrying over and applying to the therapist feelings and attitudes that the patient had toward significant others—primarily parents—in the past. These feelings and attitudes then become accessible to understanding. They may be positive, involving feelings of love for the analyst, or negative, involving feelings of anger and hostility.

Part of the psychoanalyst's strategy is to remain ''unknown'' or ambiguous, so that the client can freely develop whatever kind of transference is required. The patient is allowed, even encouraged, to develop unrealistic expectations and attitudes regarding the therapist. These expectations and attitudes are used as a basis for helping the patient deal realistically with painful early experiences. In essence, a miniature neurosis is re-created; its resolution is crucial to the therapy.

At the same time, the therapist must be careful to recognize and control any instances of *countertransference*. This is a process in which the therapist—who is also a human being with feelings and fears—transfers those feelings to the patient.

Interpretation   Through **interpretation,** or the explanation of a patient's free associations, reports of dreams, and the like, a sensitive analyst can help the patient gain insight (both intellectual and emotional) into his or her repressed conflicts. By pointing out the symbolic attributes of a transference relationship or by noting the peculiar timing of symptoms, the therapist can direct the patient toward conscious control of unconscious conflicts.

Here is an example that illustrates the timely interpretation of an important instance of transference.

SANDY (the patient): John [her ex-husband] was just like my father. Always condemning me, always making me feel like an idiot! Strange, the two of them . . . the most important men in my life . . . they did the most to screw me up. When I would have fun with my friends and come home at night, he would be sitting there . . . waiting . . . to disapprove.
MALE THERAPIST: Who would be waiting for you?
SANDY: Huh . . . ?
THERAPIST: Who's the ''he'' that would be waiting?
SANDY: John . . . I mean my father . . . you're confusing me now. . . . My father would sit there . . . smoking his pipe. I knew what he was thinking, though . . . he didn't have to say it . . . he was thinking I was a slut! Someone . . . who, who was a slut! So what if I stayed up late and had some fun? What business was it of his? He never took any interest in any of us (begins to weep). . . . It was my mother . . . rest her soul . . . who loved us, not our father. . . . He worked her to death . . . Lord, I miss her (weeps uncontrollably). . . . I must sound angry at my father. . . . Don't you think I have a right to be angry?
THERAPIST: Do you think you have a right to be angry?
SANDY: Of course, I do! Why are you questioning me? You don't believe me, do you?
THERAPIST: You want me to believe you.
SANDY: I don't care whether you believe me or not. As far as I'm concerned, you're just a wall that I'm talking to . . . I don't know why I pay for this rotten therapy. . . . Don't you have any thoughts or feelings at all? I know what you're thinking . . . you think I'm crazy . . . you must be laughing at me . . . I'll probably be a case in your next book! You're just sitting there . . . smirking . . . making me feel like a bad person . . . thinking I'm wrong for being mad, that I have no right to be mad.
THERAPIST: Just like your father.
SANDY: Yes, you're just like my father. . . . Oh my God! Just now . . . I . . . I . . . thought I was talking to him.
THERAPIST: You mean your father.
SANDY: Yes . . . I'm really scared now . . . how could I have . . . can this really be happening to me?

THERAPIST: I know it must be awfully scary to realize what just happened . . . but don't run away now, Sandy. Could it be that your relationship with your father has affected many of the relationships you've had with other men? It seems that your reaction to me just now, and your tendency to sometimes refer to your ex-husband as your father . . .

SANDY: God! . . . I don't know . . . what should I do about it? . . . Is it real?

An interesting tool that is often used in psychoanalysis is discussed in Focus 20.2.

The effectiveness of psychoanalysis The theoretical validity of psychoanalysis has come under attack, as have its lack of research support and its methods. The impossibility of providing operational definitions for such constructs as the *unconscious* and the *libido*

FOCUS 20.2

Hypnotherapy

Some critics of hypnosis do not believe in the existence of a so-called hypnotic state, though they think the phenomenon should be investigated (Spanos and Barber 1974). Probably the most outspoken critic of hypnosis as a separate state is Theodore Barber (1969), who has been able to demonstrate that nonhypnotized subjects who are strongly motivated can be induced, by simple urging or role-playing, to exhibit many of the behaviors observed in hypnotized subjects. Although the controversy continues, the weight of research evidence strongly supports the belief (which we share) that hypnosis can be helpful in treating a wide variety of disorders.

The use of hypnosis as an adjunct to psychotherapy is called **hypnotherapy.** It has been used to help patients seeking relief from such hysterical behaviors as paralysis or blindness as well as to treat problems of insomnia, overeating, and alcoholism. Simply suggesting to patients during hypnosis that their symptoms will disappear when they come out of the hypnotic state has not proved effective, however. Most psychologists now recognize that, to facilitate the treatment of abnormal behavior, hypnosis needs to be part of a broader therapeutic program.

Hypnotherapists use complex variations of hypnosis. An example is hypnotic *age regression,* in which hypnotized patients are told that they are reliving their childhood at a specific age and that their thoughts, speech, and actions will reflect this age. Regressing to the time of traumatic events and reliving them in their entirety often desensitizes patients to these events, helping them to gain insight into unconscious dynamics and to achieve greater control over their own lives.

Although controversy surrounds the phenomenon of hypnotic age regression, many cases have been put forth as convincing proof of its authenticity and effectiveness. For example, one 24-year-old man had suffered convulsive seizures for 6 years, beginning at age 18. During this time, irregular brain wave patterns that are usually observed in epileptics were recorded in his electroencephalograms. When he regressed under hypnosis to age 12, his brain waves appeared to be normal; they did not become abnormal until he advanced again to age 18 (Kupper 1945).

Hypnosis has been defined as an altered state of consciousness that involves tuning

(Focus 20.2 continued on p. 572)

makes it extremely difficult to confirm the various aspects of the theory. For example, psychoanalytic theory suggests that neurotic symptoms are caused by underlying emotional conflicts. When these symptoms are eliminated without removing the conflict, the individual merely expresses the neurosis in other ways and exhibits other symptoms, a phenomenon that is known as **symptom substitution.** Many reseachers, particularly behavior therapists, assert that it *is* possible to eliminate neu-

rotic symptoms without symptom substitution occurring (Rachman 1971). Furthermore, they contend that, when the symptoms are eliminated, the neurosis is cured.

In a classic study, the effectiveness of various treatment approaches was examined, and the possible occurrence of symptom substitution was assessed in a follow-up that was performed two years later (Paul 1967): Students with strong fears of public speaking were assigned to one of four treatment groups: a sys-

FOCUS 20.2 *(continued)*

out irrelevant stimuli and tuning in to the hypnotist's subtle suggestions. The following is a typical induction sequence employed by one of the authors. We shall use it to analyze what is happening and to illustrate the conditions that facilitate the hypnotic trance. (Key words are italicized.)

[The hypnotherapist asks for a *volunteer* and instructs him or her to sit in a chair next to the hypnotherapist.] "I want you to get into a very *comfortable* and *relaxed* position. I want you to stare closely at that spot on the wall. That's right, stare closely at that spot on the wall. *Very good, you're doing just fine. Focus* all your attention on that spot. *Concentrate* on that spot. After a few seconds, you will notice how *tired* and *heavy* your eyelids are becoming. So tired and heavy. Very tired and heavy. . . . The longer you stare, the more tired you will become. Soon you will find yourself *blinking* more and more often. [The volunteer's eyelids are closing.] *Very good.* . . . It'll *feel so good* just to *allow* them to close completely. [Eyelids are now fluttering.] Your eyelids are so *heavy* that they will soon close completely and stick together so tightly that you'll think they're *glued* together. You feel yourself drifting deeper and deeper into a *trance.* . . . So deep. [Eyes finally close.] Very good."

First, it is important to elicit the subject's *cooperation* (asking for a volunteer facili-

tates this part of the induction sequence) and relaxation. Second, *monotony* in the tone of voice and *repetition* reduce the subject's defenses. Third, *narrowing* and *focusing* of attention are accomplished by having the subject stare (eye fixation) or tune in to a particular stimulus (a spot on the wall, the hypnotherapist's voice, or the like). Fourth, the hypnotist implants in the subject's mind the *suggestion* of fatigue and heavy eyelids. This suggestion is usually *in anticipation of normal bodily responses.* For example, eye fixation causes eyelid strain and the consequent desire to blink or close the eyes. However, the subject attributes these sensations to the hypnotist and is therefore convinced that he or she is going into a trance. Fifth, the hypnotist generously dispenses *reinforcement* and *reassurances* through positive feedback ("You're doing fine," "Very good"). Sixth, the manner in which the hypnotist *verbalizes* suggestions is very important. To illustrate this, let's return to the induction sequence (at this point the subject has closed his or her eyes).

"Good, very good. . . . Completely relax, and notice how good you feel. . . . You're going deeper and deeper, deeper and deeper. . . . In a few minutes I am going to tell you to *try* to open your eyes. In a moment I'm going to tell

tematic desensitization group with which a behavior modification approach involving relaxation was used (this technique is discussed later in this chapter); an attention–placebo group that was given placebo pills and told that the pills would reduce anxiety; an insight therapy group conducted by experienced psychotherapists to help the subjects gain insight into their anxieties; and a control group that received no treatment. Anxiety was measured in several ways, both before and after the treatments, which were conducted over a five-week period. As Table 20.2 (p. 574) shows, the systematic desensitization treatment was the most effective approach, though insight therapy and attention–placebo treatment also reduced more anxiety than no treatment. These results persisted over two years; symptom substitution did not occur.

Proponents of psychoanalysis might argue, however, that treatment over a five-week period is too brief to provide full benefit and that

you to try to open your eyes. But you will find yourself *unable* to do so. In just a minute I'm going to tell you to try to open your eyes but you will not be able to do so. In fact, you *feel so good and so relaxed* that you will *not even want to try*. You won't even want to try to open your eyes. . . . In fact, the *harder* you try, the *deeper* you'll go. The harder you try, the deeper you'll go. All right, now open your eyes! Open them!''

At these commands the subject may respond by making obvious but unsuccessful attempts to open the eyes; by making no attempt to do so; by struggling but going into a deeper trance (shown by slumping over in the chair, for example); or by opening the eyes and breaking the trance. All but the last response are highly correlated with the hypnotist's suggestions. First, the subject has been told that he or she will *try* to open the eyes. The word *try* suggests the subject's failure to do so, and the challenge to try is directly counteracted by the statement that the subject will be *unable* to do so. Second, striking to the heart of the subject's desire and motivation to open the eyes, the hypnotist states that the subject is so comfortable and relaxed that he or she will make no attempt to open the eyes. Third, the subject is placed in a double bind—the greater the effort to open the eyes, the deeper the trance.

Hypnotic induction is largely based on what has been termed the "foot in the door" technique (Freedman and Fraser 1966). If a subject tries hard to open the eyes, the hypnotist's first suggestion has been accepted, and awakening is inconsistent with that suggestion. The principle is that getting someone to comply with a small request ("Your eyelids are getting heavy," "You are trying to open your eyes") increases the probability of obtaining compliance to a more demanding request. As the subject complies with increasingly difficult requests, the trance state becomes correspondingly deeper.

Approximately 15 percent of the general population is not susceptible enough to suggestion for effective hypnosis (Cohen 1970). Children tend to be more susceptible than adults; susceptibility increases from the age of five or six to a peak at age nine to fourteen. From that point it levels off and eventually declines (London 1964). The sex of the subject or hypnotist and previous experience with hypnosis do not appear to be critical variables. The general pattern is that the "good" subject has rich ideational rather than athletic interests, welcomes new experience, follows his or her own impulses, and is unafraid to withdraw from reality for a time.

Table 20.2   *Results of Three Treatments for Public Speaking Anxiety*

	Results Found at 2-Year Followup		
Treatment	Significantly Improved (%)	No Change (%)	Significantly Worse
Desensitization	85	15	—
Attention-Placebo	50	50	—
Insight	50	50	—
Control	22	78	—

SOURCE: Adapted from Paul, G. L. (1967). Insight versus Desensitization in Psychotherapy Two Years after Termination. *Journal of Consulting Psychology, 31,* 333–348. Copyright © 1967 by American Psychological Association. Reprinted with permission.

the student subjects did not have the kinds of problems that are typically seen in treatment. Furthermore, in clinical practice it is often evident that *the symptom is not the disorder.* For example, a child who exhibits antisocial behavior and aggression may really be suffering from neglect. If the symptoms are removed but the neglect remains, symptom substitution may occur. Some behavior therapists acknowledge this potential problem (O'Leary and Wilson 1975); meanwhile, psychoanalysis continues to have many strong supporters (Silverman 1976).

Humanistic–existential therapies

By contrast to the psychic determinism implicit in psychoanalysis, the humanistic–existential therapies stress the importance of self-actualization, self-concept, free will, and responsibility. The focus is on qualities of "humanness"; human beings cannot be understood without reference to their personal uniqueness and wholeness. Among the several humanistic–existential therapies are person-centered therapy, existential analysis, and gestalt therapy.

Person-centered therapy Rogerian (or humanistic) therapists believe that clients can develop better self-concepts and move toward self-actualization if the therapist provides certain therapeutic conditions. These are the conditions in which clients utilize their own innate tendencies to grow, to actively negotiate with their environment, and to realize their potential. Thus therapists must be accepting of clients as persons, empathic and respectful, and unconditionally positive in their regard for clients. A therapist should not control, inhibit, threaten, or interpret a client's behaviors. These actions are manipulative, and they undermine the client's ability to find his or her own direction.

Person-centered therapy thus emphasizes the *kind of person* the therapist should be in the therapeutic relationship rather than the precise techniques to use in therapy. Particular details were discussed in Chapter 2.

Existential analysis Existential analysis adheres to no single theory or group of therapeutic techniques; it is instead concerned with the person's experience and involvement in the world as a being with consciousness and self-consciousness. Existential therapists believe that the inability to accept death or nonbeing as a reality restricts self-actualization. In contemporary society many individuals feel lonely and alienated; they lose a sense of the meaning of life, of self-responsibllity, and of free will. This state is popularly termed "existential crisis." The task of the therapist is to engage clients in an encounter in which they can experience their own existence as being real. The encounter should be a genuine sharing between partners, in which the therapist, too, may grow and be influenced. (The *encounter group,* described in Focus 20.4, owes much to Rogerian and existential analysis.) When clients are able to experience their existence and nonexistence, then responsibility, choice, and meaning re-emerge. (Again, see Chapter 2 for additional details.)

Existential approaches to therapy are strongly philosophical in nature. They have not received any research scrutiny because many existential concepts and methods are difficult to define operationally for research purposes. Furthermore, existential therapists point out that therapist and client are engaged in a complex encounter that cannot be broken down into components for empirical observation, so research studies are incapable of assessing the impact of therapy. Although there are impressive case histories indicating its effectiveness, little empirical support exists.

Gestalt therapy The German word *gestalt* means "whole." As conceptualized by Fritz Perls in 1969, **gestalt therapy** emphasizes the importance of an individual's *totality* of experience, which should not be fragmented or separated. Perls felt that, when affective and cognitive experiences are isolated, people lose a full awareness of their total experience.

In gestalt therapy, clients are required to discuss the totality of the here-and-now. Only experiences, feelings, and behaviors that are occurring in the present situation are stressed. Past experiences or anticipated future experiences are brought up only in relation to current feelings. Dreams too are interpreted in relation to the here-and-now. As a means of opening clients to their experiences, they are encouraged to

1. Make personalized and unqualified statements that help them "act out" their emotions. For example, instead of hedging by saying, "It is sometimes upsetting when *your* boss yells at *you,*" a client is encour-

Fritz Perls (1893–1970) developed gestalt therapy to help troubled clients become aware of themselves as a whole. He believed this awareness to be therapeutic in and of itself. Experiencing, feeling, and being in the here-and-now were the goals of his therapy.

aged to say "*I* get scared when *my* boss yells at me."
2. Exaggerate the feelings associated with behaviors in order to gain greater awareness of their experiences and to eliminate intellectual explanations.
3. Role-play situations and then focus on what was experienced during the role-playing.

As in the case of existential analysis, gestalt therapy has generated little research. Thus it is difficult to evaluate its effectiveness. Proponents of gestalt therapy are convinced that clients are helped, but sufficient empirical support has never emerged. (You might, however, be interested in reading Perls's remarkable *Gestalt Therapy Verbatim* for a fuller explanation of this approach.)

ACTION-ORIENTED APPROACHES TO INDIVIDUAL PSYCHOTHERAPY

The principles underlying the action-oriented or behaviorist approaches to abnormal behavior were discussed in Chapter 3. Treatment based on classical conditioning, operant conditioning, observational learning, and cognitive–behavioral processes has gained widespread popularity, and behavior therapists typically make use of a variety of techniques (Kazdin and Wilson 1978). Many of these techniques have been examined in preceding chapters; this section presents selected key behavioral techniques.

Classical conditioning techniques

Systematic desensitization   As noted in Chapter 3, the treatment technique referred to as **systematic desensitization** was developed by Joseph Wolpe (1973) as a treatment for anxiety. Its objective is to reduce anxiety that is a response to a stimulus situation by eliciting, in the given situation, a response that is incompatible with anxiety. For example, if a woman is fearful of flying in a jet plane, her anxiety response could be reduced by training her to relax while in airplanes.

Systematic desensitization typically includes training in relaxation, the construction of a fear hierarchy, and the combination of relaxation and imagined scenes from the fear hierarchy. We can use the example of the person who wants to overcome her fear of flying to illustrate the process. The therapist would first train her to relax, probably employing a progressive relaxation method in which the muscles are alternately tensed and relaxed (Jacobson 1964). To develop a fear hierarchy, the client would be asked to list situations involved in flying that elicit anxiety and to order them from least upsetting to most anxiety-producing. For example, making airline reservations might create a little anxiety; taking a taxi

to the airport could result in more anxiety; entering the plane, fastening the seatbelt, taking off, flying 35,000 feet above sea level, and so on would probably involve progressively increased anxiety levels.

In the systematic desensitization procedure, the client is asked to *imagine* she is in each of these situations. It is obviously more convenient to imagine situations than actually to go through them, and most clients do experience anxiety when they imagine situations in the hierarchy. (*In vivo* approaches, in which clients are actually present in the fear-provoking situations, have also been used.)

Once the person is able to relax and to imagine the scenes in the hierarchy, the therapist asks the client first to imagine a low-anxiety scene (such as making flight reservations) and to relax at the same time. The client is then asked to proceed up the fear hierarchy, imagining each situation in order. If a particular situation elicits too much anxiety, the client is told to return to a less anxiety-provoking one. This procedure is repeated until the client can imagine the entire hierarchy without anxiety.

Behavior therapists believe that systematic desensitization is more effective than psychotherapy; it certainly requires fewer sessions to achieve desired results (Paul 1967; Wolpe 1973). Systematic desensitization has stimulated a great deal of research, and its efficacy in reducing fears has been well documented (Rachman and Hodgeson 1980). Some researchers have questioned the need for certain procedural aspects of the treatment approach. For example, the rather rigid format for desensitization advocated by Wolpe may be unnecessary, and alternatives to relaxation may be used in the process (Nathan and Jackson 1976; Sue 1972).

Implosive therapy   Another technique that is used to reduce anxiety and that has certain features of classical conditioning is **implosive therapy** (Stampfl and Levis 1967). In implosive therapy, great anxiety is aroused in patients by having them imagine anxiety-producing scenes. Escape from the anxiety is made impossible so that they cannot develop avoidant behaviors; instead, their anxiety can be reduced only through the extinction of irrational fears. In applying implosive therapy, a therapist might, for example, ask the client with a fear of flying to close her eyes and imagine the following:

> You are flying in a jet plane. Suddenly the plane hits an air pocket and begins to shake violently from side to side. Meal trays fly around, and passengers who do not have their seat belts fastened are thrown from their seats. People start to scream. As you look out the window, the plane's wing is flying by. The pilot's frantic voice over the loudspeaker is shouting: "Prepare to crash, prepare to crash!" Your seat belt breaks and you must hang on for dear life, while the plane is spinning around and careening. You can tell that the plane is falling rapidly. The ground is coming up toward you. The situation is hopeless—all will die.

Undoubtedly the client would experience intense anxiety, after which she would be told to "wake up." Repeated exposure to such a "flood" of anxiety would eventually cause the stimulus to lose its power to elicit anxiety and would lead to extinction.

The developers of implosive therapy believe that it can be effective, though some clients find the procedure too traumatic and discontinue treatment. In general, the method has not been scrutinized as carefully as systematic desensitization, but it has been used successfully with some clients (Barrett 1969; Baum 1970).

Aversive conditioning In **aversive conditioning,** a widely used classical conditioning technique, the undesirable behavior is paired with a noxious stimulus. For example, it was used in an attempt to modify the smoking behaviors of heavy smokers (Franks, Fried, and Ashem 1966). The smokers were asked to sit in front of an apparatus that delivers smoke or fresh air to one's face. They were told to smoke

their favorite cigarettes; as long as they continued puffing, smoke was blown into their faces. When the smoke became unbearable, they could put out their cigarettes and have fresh air delivered. The program showed limited positive results: Of twenty-three volunteer smokers, fourteen did not complete the four-week program because of low motivation, dislike of the method, or unavailability. Of the remaining nine who completed the project, four discontinued smoking, one smoked less, one changed to a pipe, and two exhibited no change.

Aversive conditioning has also been applied to alcoholics, drug addicts, and persons with sexual disorders, again with varying degrees of success. The noxious stimuli have included electric shock, drugs, odors, verbal censure, and reprimands. Some aversive conditioning programs also provide positive reinforcement for alternative behaviors that are deemed appropriate.

Several problems have been encountered in the use of aversive conditioning: First, because noxious stimuli are used, many individuals in treatment discontinue therapy, as in the smoking-reduction program just described. Second, aversive methods often suppress the undesirable behavior only temporarily, especially when punishment for those behaviors is applied solely in a laboratory situation that bears little resemblance to real life. Third, anxiety or hostility may develop in the client as a result of being placed in an aversive situation. And some critics argue that, because a form of punishment is involved, the technique is unethical or has potential for misuse and abuse (Silverstein 1972).

Operant conditioning techniques

Behavior modification using operant methods has flourished, and many ingenious programs have been developed. As in the case of classical conditioning, only a few key examples are presented here.

Token economies have been successful treatments for juvenile delinquents, school children, retarded persons, and patients in residential communities. Patients receive tokens as rewards for appropriate behaviors and can exchange them for reinforcers such as special food, cigarettes, television viewing, or weekend passes.

Token economies Treatment programs that reward patients with tokens for appropriate behaviors are known as **token economies** (Kazdin 1980). The tokens may be exchanged for hospital privileges, food, or weekend passes. The goal is to modify patient behaviors using a secondary reinforcer (the tokens). Money operates as a secondary reinforcer in much the same way for individuals who work.

Three ingredients are necessary to a token economy: (1) the designation by hospital staff of certain patient behaviors as desirable and reinforceable; (2) a medium of exchange, such as coinlike tokens, Green Stamps, or tallies on a piece of paper; and (3) goods, services, or privileges that the tokens or stamps can buy. It is up to the hospital staff to dispense the tokens for desirable patient behaviors (Ullman and Krasner 1975). In one such program that was operated in a psychiatric hospital ward, tokens could be exchanged for hospital passes, cigarettes, food, television viewing,

and the selection of one's dining room tablemates. Patients were given tokens for good grooming and neat physical appearance, for washing dishes, and for performing other chores. The program resulted in marked improvement in the behavior of schizophrenic patients, and when tokens were no longer given, patient involvement in the previously reinforced activities was found to decrease (Ayllon and Azrin 1965). This finding supported the conclusion that tokens were responsible for the success. Other studies have also indicated that token-economy systems are effective with chronic hospitalized patients who are considered resistant to treatment (Paul 1982). Token economies also tend to increase the morale of staff members (Ullman and Krasner 1975).

Token-economy programs are used in a variety of settings, with such different types of individuals as juvenile delinquents, school children, retarded persons, and patients in residential community homes. Although they have been extremely successful in modifying behaviors in institutional settings, problems remain. Some patients do not respond to token economies; complex behaviors, such as those involving language, are difficult to modify with this technique; and desirable patient behaviors that are exhibited in a hospital may not be continued outside the hospital setting.

Punishment When less drastic methods are ineffective, **punishment** is sometimes used in the treatment of autistic and schizophrenic children (Lovaas 1977; Lovaas, Schaeffer, and Simmons 1965). In an early study, Lovaas and his colleagues attempted to modify the behaviors of two 5-year-old identical twins who were diagnosed as schizophrenics. The children had shown no response to conventional treatment and were largely unresponsive in everyday interpersonal situations. They showed no reaction to speech and did not themselves speak; they did not recognize adults or each other; and they exhibited temper tantrums, self-destructive behaviors, and inappropriate handling of objects. The experimenters decided to use electric shock as a punishment for the purpose of modifying the children's behaviors. A floor gridded with metal tape was constructed so that a painful but not physically damaging shock could be administered to their bare feet. By turning the shock on and off, the experimenters found it possible to condition approach (social) behaviors in the children. Affectionate responses (kissing and hugging) were developed and tantrum behaviors were eliminated—all via the use of shock as an aversive stimulus.

Lovaas's work has shown that operant conditioning is a powerful technique for changing the behavior of autistic children who have failed to respond to other forms of treatment. For many years researchers have stressed that autism and childhood schizophrenia are learned disorders and that autistic behaviors can be modified with behavioral techniques (Ferster 1961). However, because of the ethical issues raised by the use of electric shocks, use of the punishment technique has declined in recent years (Harris and Ersner-Hershfield 1978; Russo, Carr, and Lovaas 1980).

Observational learning techniques

As we saw in Chapter 3, **observational learning** is the acquisition of new behaviors by watching them. The process of observing and imitating these behaviors is called **modeling.** Modeling has been shown to be effective in helping individuals acquire more appropriate behaviors. In one experiment, young adults who exhibited an intense fear of snakes were assigned to four groups.

1. The *live modeling with participation* group watched a live model who initiated progressively more fearful activities with the snake. Subjects were then guided to imitate the model and encouraged to touch the snake first with a gloved hand and then with a bare hand.

2. The *symbolic modeling* group underwent relaxation training and then viewed a film in which children and adults were seen handling snakes in progressively more fearful circumstances.
3. The *systematic desensitization* group received systematic desensitization treatment for snake phobias.
4. The *control* group received no treatment.

Before treatment, the approach responses of all the subjects toward snakes were equally low. After treatment, the ability to approach and touch snakes had increased for all treated subjects (the first three groups), who performed better than the no-treatment group. The *live modeling with participation* group showed the greatest change: Nearly all of the subjects voluntarily touched the snake (Bandura, Blanchard, and Ritter 1969).

In a different kind of application, modeling was used to effect changes in institutionalized delinquent boys. The boys were asked to observe the behavior of a model and then to imitate that behavior. The model demonstrated how to behave appropriately in situations that the boys were likely to encounter: job situations, school settings, interactions with parents and authority figures, and such. The results were encouraging. The boys behaved more maturely than an untreated control group and, in a follow-up study, were found less likely to be institutionalized (Sarason and Ganzer 1973).

Recently the modeling of behaviors shown in films has been successfully used in medical and dental practices to reduce fears of medical procedures (Wilson and O'Leary 1980).

Self-control therapy

In **self-control therapy** it is assumed that individuals can actively modify their own behaviors by managing behavioral contingencies. For example, people who are trying to decrease their smoking could patronize only restaurants that have nonsmoking areas and avoid situations that are associated with smoking, such as cocktail parties. One may manage one's own behaviors through the self-presentation of positive consequences, the removal of negative consequences, the self-presentation of negative consequences, or the removal of positive consequences. As an example of the first of these strategies, a person with an obesity problem may save the money not spent on snacks and use it to buy new clothes in a smaller size.

Self-control therapy is based on the motivation and commitment of individuals to change. However, few studies have examined the effectiveness of this approach in severely disturbed individuals. More research is obviously needed to determine its usefulness.

Cognitive–behavioral therapy

Cognitive approaches to therapy are directed toward helping clients develop perceptual skills with which to interpret environmental inputs and internal stimulation. Clients are shown that thoughts and images play an important role in adjustment and that skills training will increase their effectiveness in dealing with external and internal environments.

Cognitive–behavioral therapy is particularly appealing to psychologists who see the importance of skills training, reinforcement, and learning principles but who also acknowledge the central role of cognitive processes in human behavior and emotions (Mahoney and Arnkoff 1978; Mahoney and Kazdin 1978). This approach includes such techniques as cognitive restructuring, coping-skills training, and problem solving. **Cognitive restructuring** is a form of therapy in which the client's cognitions are changed from irrational, self-defeating, and distorted thoughts and attitudes to more rational, positive, and appropriate ones (Beck 1976; Ellis 1973; Meichenbaum 1977). **Coping skills training** is aimed at helping clients learn to manage or overcome stress.

Problem-solving therapy provides clients with strategies for dealing with specific problems encountered in life.

As indicated in Chapter 3, there is an increasing trend toward integration of the cognitive and behavioral approaches in psychology and therapy.

> Despite their long history of often bitter rivalry, behaviorists and cognitive psychologists appear to be cautiously easing into the same theoretical bed. This rather startling flirtation is not, of course, without its detractors. . . . By and large, however, a substantial percentage of each group appear to favor the increased permeability between cognitive and behavioral perspectives. (Mahoney 1977, p. 5)

Biofeedback therapy

Biofeedback therapy is a combination of physiological and behavioral approaches in which a patient receives information, or feedback, regarding particular autonomic functions such as heart rate, blood pressure, and brain wave activity and is rewarded for influencing those functions. The information is provided by monitoring devices; the rewards vary, depending on the patient and the situation.

In an exploratory study, researchers attempted to help patients with essential hypertension (elevated blood pressure) to lower their systolic pressure. They used an operant-conditioning feedback system in which patients saw a flash of light and heard a tone whenever their systolic blood pressure decreased. They were told that the light and tone were desirable and were given rewards—slides of pleasant scenes and money—for achieving a certain number of light flashes and tones. The patients did gradually reduce their blood pressure at succeeding biofeedback sessions. However, when they reached the point where they were unable to reduce their pressure further for five consecutive sessions, the experiment was discontinued (Benson et al. 1971).

In another experiment, subjects were trained to identify their own alpha brain wave activity through feedback of EEG readings and to control it to the point where they could either produce or eliminate alpha activity (Kamiya 1962; Nowlis and Kamiya 1970). Alpha brain waves are associated with pleasant, relaxed, meditative, and happy feelings. The potential benefits of such control—and of the control of heart rate, blood pressure, and muscle tension—are numerous, provided that control can be extended beyond the laboratory to real-life situations. This question and the applicability of biofeedback therapy to the treatment of behavioral disorders are still being investigated.

EVALUATING INDIVIDUAL PSYCHOTHERAPY

We have discussed only some of the more traditional, or generally practiced, modes of individual psychotherapy. (There are, in addition, numerous less widely used systems of treatment, the so-called ''extra-establishment'' systems; a few of these are described in Focus 20.3, pp. 582–583). Both the insight-oriented and the action-oriented approaches have attracted devout proponents and vocal critics. Proponents of the behavioral therapies, for example, believe that this approach has solid theoretical support and empirical justification; that it provides a rapid means of changing behaviors; and that (unlike the insight-oriented approaches) it includes specific goals, procedures, and means of assessing its effectiveness. Critics argue that behavioral therapy is dehumanizing, mechanical, and manipulative; that its relationship to learning theory is more apparent than real; and that it is applicable only to a narrow range of problems.

Whether one argues for or against either insight-oriented or action-oriented therapies depends largely on whether one believes that human behavior is determined primarily by

Two nontraditional therapies that have not been evaluated through research are primal scream therapy (top) and rolfing (bottom). In primal scream therapy a patient is encouraged to express emotions through violent thrashing, primal screams, and convulsions. In rolfing the muscles are stretched and manipulated to correct chronic postural imbalances.

internal or external factors. But there are also psychologists who argue against psychotherapy of every sort.

Nearly three decades ago, Eysenck (1952) concluded that there was *no evidence that psychotherapy facilitates recovery* from what were then classified as neurotic disorders. Since that time, others have claimed that its success has been oversold and that much time, money, and effort are being wasted by practitioners and clients in psychotherapy (Scriven 1975; Tannov 1977). Opponents feel

so strongly about its uselessness that they advocate "truth in packaging" for psychotherapy: Prospective clients should be warned that "Psychotherapy will probably not help you very much." To understand the basis for this claim, we need to examine Eysenck's procedure, findings, and conclusions.

Eysenck surveyed recovery rates for patients who received psychotherapy and for those who received no psychotherapy. There were two no-psychotherapy groups; one was composed of individuals discharged from New

FOCUS 20.3

Extra-Establishment Systems of Therapy

Extra-establishment systems of therapy have been founded on philosophical or religious considerations, have not been well researched, or have been based on faith rather than scientific findings. Depending on one's perspective, these treatment approaches can be viewed as innovative and potentially helpful or as unproven and even potentially harmful. Interestingly, some widely used and well-accepted forms of treatment such as behavior modification were once considered by many to be dangerous and ineffective. At the same time, once-popular modes of therapy such as psychosurgery are now declining. Here are some short descriptions of less-well-established systems of therapy, for which more research attention is required in order to evaluate their usefulness.

☐ *Primal therapy* is intended to help patients re-experience early psychological and physical hurts in their original form. To facilitate contact with dissociated experiences, patients are encouraged to express emotions through violent thrashing, primal screams, and convulsions.

Intense individual therapy is rendered for about three weeks, and then group meetings are arranged once or twice a week. Proponents believe that primal therapy relieves neurotic symptoms and results in the reduction of tension. However, little research has been conducted.

☐ *Transcendental meditation* is a variant of relaxation training adopted from Far Eastern philosophies. Some techniques of meditation have been westernized and have gained popularity in this country. They do not require special postures, lengthy training, or specific religious beliefs. Individuals are given a particular phrase or *mantra* to repeat over and over, while sitting comfortably, for about twenty minutes twice a day. Individuals engaging in meditation report deriving feelings of freedom from tension and good health from the experience.

☐ *Rolfing therapy* assumes that psychological and emotional factors may produce chronic postural imbalance because of muscular tension and changes in the supporting connective tissues. Treatment consists of stretching and manipulating

York State hospitals without receiving formal psychotherapy (though custodial care was provided) and the other of individuals who had collected disability insurance for their disorders but had received care only from general practitioners (using sedatives, reassurance, and suggestion) and not from psychotherapists. Eysenck's findings indicated that about 70 percent of the neurotics who received no psychotherapy in hospitals were discharged each year as recovered or improved. And 72 percent of the patients who received disability

insurance benefits were considered to be recovered after two years. (Recovery was measured by return to work, absence of major problems, and successful social adjustment.) Thus, in the two groups of untreated patients, the recovery rate (the rate of spontaneous remission) was about 70 percent.

Eysenck argued that, if psychotherapy is indeed effective, the recovery rate for psychotherapy-treated patients should exceed 70 percent. What he found was a recovery rate of 44 percent for patients treated via psychoanalysis

the muscles to make them more elastic. The treatment is painful and often stimulates recall of old emotions and trauma. Proponents postulate, however, that emotional and psychological changes occur because of body manipulation rather than through recall of emotions and traumas.

☐ *Provocative psychotherapy* is characterized by confrontation and the use of humor with the intention of getting to the heart of the problem quickly. The client is provoked by the therapist to affirm his or her self-worth (often in defense against the therapist's attacks), to assert himself or herself, to defend himself or herself, to test reality in terms of the therapist's challenges, and to take chances in the real world. For example, the therapist might tell a client that "You talk like a slut; you dress like a slut; you walk like a slut and you look like a slut" or that "I am going to teach you how to be joyfully sadistic" (Corsini 1984). It is assumed that the client will move in a direction opposite to the therapist's definition of him or her. When a client is urged humorously to continue a self-de-

feating behavior, the client is expected to engage in constructive behaviors instead.

☐ *Z-Process attachment therapy* was developed by Robert W. Zaslow (1970, 1981), who makes the point that autistic children and schizophrenic adults do not respond well to traditional forms of therapy. They avoid people, ignore them, and are poorly oriented to reality. Neither loving and affectionate approaches nor hostile and aggressive approaches work effectively with this population. Zaslow's therapy is an attempt to combine the two—to elicit love or concern and rage from clients who have avoided both. For example, a schizophrenic patient may be held down by five individuals (who do care for him or her) and tickled. The constraint and the tickling may induce rage in the patient, and, in the course of that rage, the patient may finally look the therapist in the eye, seething with anger. *This is contact!* And once contact is made, a relationship (attachment) may begin and the normal process of therapy can proceed.

and a rate of 64 percent for those treated via eclectic psychotherapy. Thus, according to the criteria used by Eysenck, patients receiving no formal psychotherapy recovered at least as well as those who were treated!

Several objections have been raised by critics of the Eysenck study (Bergin 1971; DeCharms, Levy, and Wertheimer 1954; Luborsky et al. 1971; Rosenzweig 1954; Strupp 1963). First, it is unclear whether the groups of treated and untreated patients were comparable. Patients who enter state hospitals may not be the same kind of individuals as those seen by psychotherapists. Similarly, patients collecting disability insurance are probably less severely disturbed than patients seen in psychoanalysis for presumably chronic problems. We also do not know whether the treated and the untreated patients were comparable in demographic variables such as age, socioeconomic class, and race—factors that are known to be associated with prognosis. Second, the improvement criteria that were applied to the untreated patients (discharge rate, return to work, lack of complaints) are not the same as those used by many psychotherapists, who aim for far more substantial personality changes. Furthermore, Eysenck's calculation of a 44 percent improvement rate for patients in psychoanalysis is open to question. He placed patients who improved slightly, who died, or who left treatment in the did-not-improve category, thus underestimating the improvement rate. In fact, one critic has demonstrated how it is possible to come up with an improvement rate of over 80 percent for psychoanalysis using Eysenck's data (Bergin 1971). Finally, was the untreated group really untreated? We know that disturbed individuals often seek help from relatives, friends, or members of the clergy during times of stress. A form of psychotherapy may have been rendered by these other sources.

Reviews of outcome research indicate that psychotherapy *is* effective and that individuals who are treated exhibit desirable changes to a greater degree than those who do not receive formal psychotherapy (Bergin 1971; Meltzoff and Kornreich 1970; Smith and Glass 1977). In one such review, hundreds of studies on the outcome of psychoanalysis and behavior therapy were examined. The adequacy of the design of these studies, the outcome measures, and therapist and client factors were all considered, and the investigators systematically weighed and compared variables. They concluded that treated patients show far more improvement than untreated individuals (Smith and Glass 1977). It seems that, in general, the better the quality of the research into effectiveness, the more the results support psychotherapy.

Controversy over the effectiveness of the various approaches to psychotherapy—and of psychotherapy itself—is likely to continue. We believe that psychotherapy *is* valuable and that the unreserved acceptance or rejection of a whole group of treatments, either behavioral or insight-oriented, is unproductive. A more meaningful issue that must be addressed is how best to match therapist, client, and situational variables.

GROUP AND FAMILY THERAPY

GROUP MEMBER 1: What you just said really makes me angry, Frank. You're blaming me for something you should be responsible for.

FRANK: I was just pointing out that you never contribute to the decision-making process. I wasn't blaming you! What's your problem anyway?

GROUP MEMBER 1: There you go again! I don't have a problem with the group exercises. When they go wrong, I try to see what happened and why. If it's my fault, I'll try to correct it . . . okay?

FRANK: If the shoe fits, wear it!

GROUP MEMBER 1: Damn! It's useless talking to you . . . why do you always blame others?

FRANK (angrily): Piss on you! It seems like

you're the only one who thinks that way. I totally reject your accusations!

GROUP MEMBER 2 (somewhat hesitantly): Frank, you do blame others a lot . . .

FRANK: Shit! Do I have to put up with another conspirator?

GROUP MEMBER 3: I don't think he's the only one in the group who sees you in that way. For the past few times I've been angry at you too. You make me and the others feel incompetent and anxious. Last week you made fun of me when I talked about my problems with Janice.

FRANK (somewhat bewildered): I wasn't making fun of you. Why are you so defensive?

THERAPIST: Frank, it seems that we have at least three members in this group who are giving you feedback about your behavior and how it affects them. Maybe you should check out how the others feel and think about your behavior.

FRANK: Well . . . I don't want to waste our time . . . there are more important things . . .

THERAPIST: It's important for us to give and ask for feedback from one another. I know it's hard sometimes, but that's one part of learning about ourselves. . . . If it's okay with you I'd like to start . . .

FRANK (quietly): It's okay.

The classic form of psychotherapy involves a one-to-one relationship between one therapist and one client. In **group therapy,** the therapeutic experience always involves more than one client and may involve more than one therapist. The increasing popularity of group therapy stems from certain economic and therapeutic advantages: Because the therapist sees several clients at each session, he or she is able to dispense a much greater amount of mental health service to the community. And, because several clients participate in the sessions, the cost to each is noticeably reduced. Saving time and money is important, but the increasing use of group therapy seems to be related to the fact that many psychological difficulties are basically interpersonal in nature; that is, they involve relationships with others. These problems are best treated within a group rather than individually.

Group therapy is a technique well-suited for treating psychological difficulties that are basically interpersonal in nature. One of the most powerful mechanisms of group therapy is that groups provide an environment in which an individual can develop new communication skills, social skills, and insights.

Most of the techniques of individual psychotherapy are utilized in group therapy. Rather than repeat them here, we shall first discuss some general features of group therapy and then focus on a particularly important group—the family.

Group therapy

There are now a great variety of group therapies, reflecting the many dimensions along which a therapeutic group may be characterized. (Focus 20.4, pp. 586–587 presents several examples.) One obvious dimension is the type of people who comprise the group. In marital and family therapy, they are related; in most other groups, they are initially strangers. Group members may share various characteristics. Groups may be formed to treat elderly clients, unemployed workers, or pregnant women; to treat clients with similar psychological disturbances; or to treat individuals with similar therapeutic goals.

Therapeutic groups also differ with regard to psychological orientation and treatment techniques, size, the frequency with which they meet and the duration of each meeting, and the role of the therapist or group leader. Some groups work together without a leader. Others have leaders who play active or passive roles within the group. Moreover, the focus of the group may be on interrelationships and the dynamics of interaction or the focus may be on the individual members. And groups may be organized to *prevent* problems as well as to solve them: Group therapy has been suggested for divorced individuals who

FOCUS 20.4

Some Types of Therapy Groups

1. *Sensitivity Training Groups (T-Groups)*. The goal of sensitivity training is to help individuals increase their sensitivity to others and improve their human relations skills so that they can be more efficient and responsive in their relationships with others—particularly in schools or business organizations. The group leader focuses on group processes (such as how members are relating to one another and what is happening in the group) and encourages members to be open, honest, and flexible. Rather than dominating the sessions, the leader helps members develop their own ideas (Korchin 1976).

2. *Encounter Groups*. Drawing on certain principles of sensitivity training, Carl Rogers conceived of encounter groups to facilitate human growth and development (greater effectiveness, openness, spontaneity, and flexibility) through encounter experiences. Freedom of expression and the reduction of defensiveness are encouraged. The group leader acts as a facilitator, refusing to direct the group authoritatively or to manipulate group activities. By merely providing a climate of respect and freedom, the group helps members develop trust and become less defensive and allows greater freedom to grow and utilize positive experiences. Although Rogers observed that group members are initially frustrated and anxious over the lack of group structure and direction, they later begin to feel freedom and trust.

3. *Transactional Analysis*. Transactional Analysis (TA) is a technique of group therapy that is based on the assumption that people play certain "games" that hinder the development of genuine and deep interpersonal relationships. These games are used as means of achieving disguised ends, which are usually related to the need for recognition. The game of "one-up" is an example: Individual A may approach individual B as a supplicant with a problem. B sincerely attempts to help A by offering advice and sympathy, taking on the role of therapist. A rejects the advice and points out its flaws. B offers alternative advice, only to have it rejected again. B then feels helpless and perhaps guilty for letting A down. A has gained "one-up" over B, who has been "put down" and has become apol-

are likely to encounter stress (Bloom, Asher, and White 1978).

Commonalities of group therapy

Despite the wide diversity of groups and group approaches, the successful ones share several features that promote therapeutic change in clients (Yalom 1970).

First, the group experience allows each client to become involved in a social situation and to see how his or her behavior affects others. In the group dialog that begins this section, Frank is slowly and painfully being asked to examine the impact of his behavior on others. He may easily dismiss unpleasant feedback about his behavior from one member as inaccurate, but it is much more difficult to do so when others reinforce the feedback (agreeing that Frank externalizes his problems and avoids responsibility for his own behavior). Once the group member can view his or her interpersonal relationships realistically, problems can be identified and subsequently resolved.

ogetic. A transactional role reversal has been accomplished by Individual A.

Underlying TA is the idea that people adopt certain roles (*Child, Adult,* and *Parent*) that reflect their ego states (Berne 1972). "Spoiled brat" behavior or excessive dependency is indicative of the Child role; the Adult role is characterized by mature and rational behaviors; the Parent role is a controlling one, in which others are treated as children. Often in marriages, one spouse acts as Parent (dominating, commanding) while the other adopts the role of Child (incapable, immature). Berne felt that such interpersonal transactions hinder the development of authentic relationships. The purpose of TA therapy is first to make the client aware of the games he or she is playing and then to eliminate them and allow more authentic means of expression, more meaningful relationships with others, and better life adjustment. Transactional analysis may be used for families or for unrelated persons in group therapy.

4. *Assertiveness Training Groups.* Assertiveness training groups use behavior therapy techniques to help individuals who want to be better able to assert or express themselves. Many persons feel unable to express hostility, criticism, or warmth. In assertiveness training, individuals are constantly reminded of the negative consequences of nonassertive behaviors and are encouraged to act out and practice assertive skills (both in the group sessions and outside of the sessions).

Assertiveness training has been unfairly characterized as a breeding ground for the development of overly critical and hostile persons. The actual intent is to train persons to express themselves appropriately.

5. *Psychodrama.* Jacob Moreno (1946) was among the first to use the term *group therapy* in his writings. He developed psychodrama, a form of group therapy in which patients and other persons role-play situations. When clients act out current or anticipated situations, they gain an awareness of their feelings, and they are able to rehearse techniques for working out their problems. Others may play supporting roles, so that the client can fully act out the situation and interact with them. At times the client and another person may exchange roles, so that the client can understand the motives and behaviors of others with whom he or she interacts.

Second, in group therapy the therapist can see how clients respond in a real-life social and interpersonal context. In individual therapy the therapist must either rely on what clients say about their social relationships or assess those relationships on the basis of client–therapist interactions. But data gathered in these ways are often unrepresentative or inaccurate. In the group context, response patterns are *observed* rather than communicated or inferred. For example, Frank's therapist could see and hear him try to blame his fellow group members with such statements as

□ What's your problem anyway?
□ I totally reject your accusations!
□ Why are you so defensive?

Third, group members can develop new communication skills, social skills, and insights. (This is one of the most powerful mechanisms of group therapy.) The group provides an environment for imitative learning and practice. Frank's group members can show him that his statements and behaviors are indicative of defensiveness and that they affect others negatively. He may then be able to correct the flaws in his interpersonal behavior by imitating others in the group and practicing better social and communication skills with them.

Fourth, groups often help their members to feel less isolated and fearful about their problems. Many clients enter therapy because they believe that their problems are unique: No one else could possibly be burdened with such awful impulses, evil or frightening thoughts, and unacceptable ways. The fear of having others find out how "sick" they are may be as problematic to clients as their actual disorders. But when they suddenly realize that their problems are common ones, that others experience them, and that others have similar fears, the sense of isolation is eased. This allows group members to be more open about their thoughts and feelings.

Finally, groups can provide their members with strong social and emotional support. The feelings of intimacy, belonging, protection, and trust (which members may not be able to experience outside the group) can be a powerful motivation to confront one's problems and actively seek to overcome them. The group represents a safe environment in which to share one's innermost thoughts and to try new adaptive behaviors without fear of ridicule or rejection.

Evaluating group therapy   Clients are sometimes treated in group and individual psychotherapy simultaneously. There are no simple rules for determining when one or the other, or both, should be employed. The decision is usually based on the therapist's judgment, the client's wishes, and the availability (or unavailability) of one treatment or the other. Of course, individuals who are likely to be disruptive are generally excluded from group therapy.

As desirable as it would be to base decisions regarding treatment techniques on the observed effectiveness of group therapy, there has been little substantial research on that topic. The problems encountered in evaluating the success of group therapy include all those involved in assessing individual therapy, compounded by group variables and the behaviors of group members.

Some disadvantages of group therapy have been pointed out. For example, groups cannot give intensive and sustained attention to the problems of individual clients (Korchin 1976). Moreover, clients may not want to share some of their problems with a large group, and the sense of intimacy with one's therapist is often lost in a group. Group pressures may prove too strong for some members, or the group may adopt values or behaviors that are themselves deviant. And, in leaderless groups, the group members may not recognize or be able to treat psychotic or potentially suicidal persons.

Family therapy

Johnny B. is a 7-year-old boy, attractive and energetic, who came to the attention of the school psychologist midway through his third year in grade school. He had been a good student in the first and second grades, but his schoolwork and attention span deteriorated dramatically at the beginning of the third year. Among the symptoms noticed by his teacher were multiple fears, tardiness, and failure to complete school assignments.

Johnny's mother, Mrs. B., was contacted by his teacher several times in the three months before Johnny was referred to the psychologist. Mrs. B. reported that her son had become school-phobic only this year, and that she had tried unsuccessfully to reassure Johnny that there was nothing to fear. Nevertheless, getting Johnny to school was a daily struggle; he would oversleep, eat breakfast at a snail's pace, and take what seemed like hours to wash and get dressed. When she dropped him off at school, he would cry and beg to be taken back home. Mr. B. noted that Johnny was younger than his classmates and wondered whether his son was simply finding the work too demanding.

Both parents were obviously concerned about their son. They were subsequently referred to a reputable child psychologist, who saw the family together several times. After their third session, both parents reported a marked improvement in Johnny's behavior. The therapist suggested that Johnny be seen individually for a period of time but also recommended marital counseling for the parents. Mr. B. vigorously objected to that suggestion and stated that there was nothing wrong with their marriage; the problem was helping Johnny overcome his school phobia and helping him cope with the pressures of school. At the urging of the wife, however, they did seek marital counseling, attending four sessions before Mr. B. abruptly terminated treatment. His reason was that the counseling was not helping with the family relationships and that, in fact, he and his wife had begun to argue and express anger at one another. In addition, shortly after Mr. and Mrs. B. had sought marital counseling, Johnny had reverted to his earlier fears and behaviors. The husband felt that the marital therapy had diverted their attention from the real problem—Johnny.

Family therapy may be broadly defined as an attempt to modify relationships within a family in such a way as to achieve harmony (Foley 1984). We shall consider this definition to encompass all forms of therapy that involve more than one family member in joint sessions, including marital therapy and parent–child therapy. The important point is that the focus is not on an individual, but rather on the family as a whole. Family therapy is based on three assumptions: (1) it is logical and economical to treat together all those who exist and operate within a system of relationships (here, the primary nuclear family); (2) the problems of the "identified patient" are only symptoms, and the family itself is the client; and (3) the task of the therapist is to modify the relationships within the family system.

These basic tenets have arisen from the repeated observations of therapists who have worked with individuals and families. They are illustrated nicely by the case of Johnny B. It appears that both parents saw their son as the "identified patient" and the problem. Even the teacher and school psychologist saw the problem as one of adjustment for Johnny. Attempts to treat Johnny individually had to fail, because the problem was in the family system. For example, marital therapy revealed basic antagonisms and conflicts between Mr. and Mrs. B., but as long as Johnny was the identified patient, the parental problems could be covered up. When Johnny improved with therapy, and the focus shifted to the marital relationship, many of the husband–wife problems were uncovered. To maintain the family's stability, Johnny, who sensed the worsening relationship, became phobic again.

Johnny's return to a phobic state is typical of family dynamics, and it actually serves several functions for the entire family. First, Johnny again becomes the center of attention and helps ward off a possible divorce. Second,

In family therapy the focus is on the family as a whole, which is considered the client. If one family member has been identified as the patient, family therapy considers his or her problems as symptoms of a deeper problem in the family itself.

the husband and wife can avoid examining their own relationship and its problems. Third, the status quo of the system is maintained.

Obviously, as long as the family members are treated as individuals, little progress will be made. The family is a social system that needs to be treated as a whole. It appears that Mr. and Mrs. B. would benefit from both marital therapy and therapy involving the entire family.

Two general classes of family therapy have been identified: the *communications approach* and the *systems approach* (Foley 1984). Let us look briefly at each of them.

The communications approach   The communications approach to family therapy is based on

the assumption that family difficulties are difficulties in communication. We have already noted, in Chapters 3 and 16, how the double bind may arise from faulty communication and then work to create and maintain pathological relationships within the family. Many family communication problems are much more subtle and complex. Family therapists may have to concentrate on the improvement not only of faulty communications, but also of interactions and relationships among family members (Satir 1967). The way in which rules, agreements, and perceptions are communicated from one person to another may also be important (Haley 1963).

The role of the therapist in repairing faulty family communications is an active but not a dominating one. He or she must attempt to show family members how they are presently communicating with one another; prod them into revealing what they feel and think about themselves and other family members and what they want from the family relationship; and convince them to practice new ways of responding. The following excerpt from a family session illustrates how a therapist might try to clarify and alter a family's communication patterns.

THERAPIST: Betty [the wife], I wonder if the last two sessions have been helpful to you in saying more openly what you think and feel.
HUSBAND: Well, I think she's feeling better about the sessions, but there's been no big change in how she relates to the kids.
THERAPIST: Is that right, Betty?
HUSBAND: Of course it is. She's always been afraid of . . .
THERAPIST (interrupting): I'd like to hear from Betty.
WIFE: Well . . . Leonard [the husband] . . . he's not exactly right . . . I have . . .
HUSBAND: She tried, but nothing's happened.
THERAPIST (to Leonard): Do you realize that several times now you've spoken for your wife and cut her off when I've directed questions to her? I wonder if this is something that frequently happens with you and your wife?
HUSBAND: I wasn't doing that. I was just trying to help my wife clarify her thoughts and feelings.
WIFE: But . . . you don't . . . you only make me feel worse.
HUSBAND: Betty does need a lot of . . .
THERAPIST: What did your wife just say to you?
HUSBAND: Huh! Uh . . . she said something about . . . about not feeling well . . . I think . . . isn't that right?
WIFE: I said you make me feel like a child who can't think or feel for myself.
THERAPIST (after a long silence): What do you think your wife is saying to you? Can you paraphrase it?
HUSBAND: She's saying that I make her feel incompetent . . . or dumb.

THERAPIST: I wonder, Betty, if you could turn to Leonard now, and tell him exactly how you feel. . . . Did he hear what you said?
WIFE: You do make me feel stupid and incompetent, when . . . when you always speak for me. Don't you realize that I'm my own person with my own feelings and thoughts!
HUSBAND (to therapist): I didn't realize . . . that my wife or that . . . I was doing that . . . I'm sorry if . . . if . . .
THERAPIST: Don't tell me, tell your wife.
HUSBAND (to wife): I'm sorry . . . for . . . for . . . I didn't know that's what I was doing.

The systems approach Those who favor the systems approach to family therapy also consider communication important, but they especially emphasize the interlocking roles of family members (Minuchin 1974). Their basic assumption is that the family system itself contributes to pathological behavior in the family. As in the case of Johnny B., a family member becomes "sick" because the family system requires a sick member. Treating that individual outside the system may result in transitory improvement, but once the client returns to the family system, he or she will be forced into the "sick role" again. Thus, family systems therapy is directed toward the organization of the family. It stresses accurate assessment of family roles and dynamics, and intervention strategies to create more flexible or changed family roles that foster positive interrelationships.

SYSTEMATIC ECLECTICISM

The therapies discussed in this chapter share the common goal of relieving human suffering. Yet, as we have seen, they differ considerably in their basic conception of psychopathology and in the methods used to treat mental disorders. In many cases, various theories and techniques seem almost diametrically opposed to one another. For example, early criticisms of psychoanalysis concentrated on the mystical and unscientific nature of its explanation and treatment of behavioral pathology. Most of these criticisms came from behaviorists, who were likewise attacked by psychoanalysts as being superficial and concerned with "symptom removal" rather than the cure of "deeper conflicts in the psyche." Recently there have been attempts at rapprochement between psychoanalysis and behavior therapy (Marmor and Woods 1980; Wachtel 1982; Davis 1983; Murray 1983). But even these sophisticated attempts have come under fire as being empirically and theoretically inconsistent (Yates 1983).

As we mentioned in Chapter 1, the majority of practicing clinicians consider themselves eclectics. Therapeutic *eclecticism* has been defined as the "process of selecting concepts, methods, and strategies from a variety of current theories which work" (Brammer and Shostrom 1982, p. 35). An example is the early "technical eclecticism" of Lazarus (1967). This approach has now been refined into a theoretical model called *multimodal behavior therapy* (Lazarus 1976, 1984). Though behavioral in basis, it embraces numerous cognitive and affective concepts as well.

Although the eclectic model calls for openness and flexibility, it can also encourage the indiscriminate, haphazard, and inconsistent use of therapeutic techniques and concepts. As a result, therapists who call themselves eclectic have been severely criticized as confused, inconsistent, contradictory, lazy, and unsystematic (Patterson 1980). The resulting negative impact of the term *eclecticism* has led to other terminology (including *creative synthesis, masterful integration,* and *systematic eclecticism*) that is more positively associated with attempts to integrate, to be consistent, to validate, and to create a unique and personalized theoretical position.

There is, of course, no single eclectic "theory" or "position." Rather, eclecticism implies a recognition that no one theory or approach is sufficient to explain and treat the complex human organism. All the therapies that we have discussed have both strengths and weaknesses; no one of them can claim to tell "the whole truth." The integration of those therapies that work best with specific clients exhibiting specific problems under specific conditions is the goal of the eclectic approach. Thus, in one sense, all therapists are eclectics; each has his or her own personal and unique approach to therapy.

In the remainder of this chapter, we present one systematic eclectic approach to the treatment of Steven V. Before you read it, we encourage you to review the discussion of Steve's case in Chapters 1, 2, and 3, to reacquaint yourself with his background and history. And, as you read, remember that what follows is representative of *one therapist's* integrative attempt to work with Steve as a feeling, thinking, behaving, social, and biological being.

A SYSTEMATIC ECLECTIC APPROACH TO THE CASE OF STEVEN V.

I am the therapist who has worked with Steve throughout his academic career. I have been asked to comment on our sessions and to provide you with insights into Steve's progress, but before I do so, it is important that I explain my therapeutic approach and goals.

I believe strongly that therapy should

involve a blend of techniques aimed at recognizing that each client is a whole human being. Many of the current schools of thought on psychotherapy are one-dimensional; they concentrate only on feelings, or only on cognitions, or only on behaviors. It is important to realize that each of us is comprised of all these and more. I also believe that no single theory or approach to therapy is appropriate for *all* populations and *all* problems. People are similar in many respects, but each is also different and unique. To recognize this difference means to use different strategies and techniques for each individual.

I have tried to organize my comments topically. This may give you the impression that I worked with isolated parts of Steve's makeup, but that would be a wrong impression. I try always to work in an integrated fashion and to deal with all aspects of the client's cognitive, affective, and behavioral makeup.

Meeting Steve: The initial session
Steven V. first came to my attention during the early part of his junior year. A very "unstable" relationship with Linda, his woman friend, had just ended, and he seemed quite disturbed by it. As I found out later, his own private therapist was on vacation, and he could not relate to the therapist who was on call. As a result, he contacted the University Psychological Services Center and was assigned to me.

During our initial contact, Steve appeared extremely suspicious, withdrawn, and reluctant to disclose his thoughts or feelings. I can recall the long periods of silence following my questions and his short but sarcastic responses. It was almost as though he were testing me to see what kind of therapist I was, to see whether he could trust me. Usually I try to be less active at first

and to encourage the client to tell his or her own story. I employ almost a person-centered approach, listening and mirroring the client's thoughts, feelings, and perceptions. It was obvious, however, that this was not having the desired effect with Steve. It seemed to be alienating him and to be compounding a relationship problem.

Here is a portion of our initial conversation.

> THERAPIST: My name is Dr. S., Steve. . . . I wonder if we could begin by having you tell me what brought you here.
> (Long silence; Steve looks down, looks up at the therapist, looks down again, crosses his arms in front of his chest, and turns away.)
> THERAPIST: It's hard for you to tell me what's on your mind.
> STEVE: Yeah (sarcastic tone, but does not change body posture). I'm not sure you can help me. . . . My therapist is on vacation, otherwise I would be seeing him. He's a *psychiatrist,* you know.
> THERAPIST: It must be hard to begin a new therapy relationship again . . . to start all over.
> STEVE: Great, that's real perceptive.
> THERAPIST: You sound angry right now. . . . Where is it coming from?
> (Silence)

This type of interaction—or lack of interaction—was characteristic of nearly the entire first half of our first session. Attempts to get Steve to open up and to trust me did not seem to work. It was at this point that I felt a change in approach was necessary. I took on an active and directive manner characteristic of the behavioral therapies.

> THERAPIST: We don't seem to be connecting, Steve; something is blocking us from working together.
> STEVE: You're the therapist, so you tell me what it is!

THERAPIST: You want me to tell you what the answer is.

STEVE: I don't need a damned *parrot* for a therapist!

THERAPIST (raising voice): Look, Steve! If you want to waste this session in a tug-of-war, let's just end it now. I'm not going to sit here and be insulted by you. You respect me, and I'll respect you! . . . I know it must be difficult to trust a stranger. You'd rather be seeing your own therapist, but the fact is he's not available. You're hurting enough to come for help. If you want to waste it playing games, go ahead!

STEVE (looking up and obviously surprised): I didn't mean to be disrespectful . . . I was only . . . only . . .

THERAPIST: Testing me . . . to see if you could trust me, to see where I'm coming from . . . to see if you could manipulate me.

STEVE: Yeah, it was nothing personal.

THERAPIST: I know. Now suppose we start over again. . . . What brings you here, Steve?

As I look back, I believe this brief but heated exchange represented the beginning of our relationship. I think Steve realized that I was an authentic person who could get angry but would not let the anger become destructive. Clients like Steve often test the therapist with attempts at manipulation. They are ambivalent about this ploy because they want it to succeed (so they can "win"), but they also want it to fail (which means the therapist is perceptive and competent enough to see through their manipulations and thus to give them the help they need). In any event, this tactic changed the entire tone of our session. Steve became much more cooperative and open, and he lost the conscious antagonism and resistance he exhibited during the early part of our meeting. For me, it became much easier to employ a nondirective approach.

Gathering information   The gathering of biographical information is very important to my understanding of clients, and I do much of it during the actual therapy sessions. I needed to know Steven V. Who is he? How does he see things? What are the critical events and relationships of his past and present? What type of medical history does he have? Are there any biological conditions that have significant impact on his psychological or social life? What type of therapy has Steve had in the past, and how successful was it? The more information I have about a client, the better I can identify his or her problems and formulate treatment strategies.

In some of our early sessions, Steve briefly mentioned how much he had hated physical education classes in high school. When I asked why, he indirectly referred to the "jocks" who were always exhibiting themselves in the shower rooms.

STEVE: They strut around like Greek gods, showing off their bodies. . . . They don't seem to have any shame at all.

THERAPIST: Shame of what?

STEVE: I mean, I don't exactly mean shame. . . . yes—they're trying to make the others feel ashamed of their own . . . well you know.

THERAPIST: Tell me what you mean.

STEVE: Just because they have bigger genitals, they're trying to show off and make the others feel bad.

THERAPIST: When they did that, how did it make you feel?

STEVE: I didn't pay any attention to them. They're not worth it. . . . Let them strut around, I got *bigger* grades than all of them.

THERAPIST: But how did that make you feel?

STEVE: I know what you're trying to imply. (Raising voice) You're trying to get me to say I felt inadequate!

(Silence)

STEVE: The size of a penis is no measure of a man! Those dumb pricks—most of them barely made it out of high school. . . . I could outthink all of them.

THERAPIST: You sound very angry at them. What exactly did they do?

STEVE: When I had to take a shower, they . . . they made fun of me.

THERAPIST: How did they make fun of you?

STEVE: Nothing in particular . . . but I knew what they were thinking.

THERAPIST: What were they thinking?

STEVE: I don't want to talk about it.

THERAPIST: I know it's difficult to talk about these things, Steve. . . . Maybe when you feel ready.

STEVE: You'd laugh at me.

THERAPIST: Is that what you really think?

STEVE (after a silence): I had this operation when I was young; they removed my left . . . I mean, I've only got one. And those bastards never let me forget it. They wanted to humiliate me.

When Steve was six years old, his left testicle was surgically removed because of a malignant growth. Apparently this incident and Steve's self-consciousness about it had haunted him throughout his life. I am not particularly psychoanalytic in orientation, but I believe that Steve did relate his sexual potency and his own masculinity to the absence of a testicle. His feelings of inferiority, low self-esteem, and periodic impotence may have evolved from his interpretation of this erroneous relationship. In this discussion Steve also made what might be labeled a Freudian slip (or a slip of the tongue) in describing his grades as *bigger* (unconscious equation of penis size?) when he probably meant *better*. (Steve's Rorschach responses also led the therapist who originally administered the test to infer a severe castration anxiety related to his surgery.)

Our discussions also revealed some potential areas for treatment. For example, cognitive strategies might be used to directly attack Steve's implicit equating of the size and intactness of his genitals with the idea of masculinity. Perhaps strategies aimed at helping Steve get in touch with his feelings would be helpful; he continually avoided "feeling" statements in our conversations.

Using tests and formal assessment To gather information about my clients, I sometimes resort to more structured, formal assessment means. I may use homework assignments (asking the client to keep a diary of significant events or to write an autobiography) or actual psychological tests. I rarely use projective testing but rely more on objective personality measures. (The use of tests is consistent with the behavioral, the cognitive, and even the psychoanalytic approaches. It is inconsistent, however, with the humanistic–existential school.) When I do use tests, I consider them mainly as a source of corroborating data. I try to demystify testing for the client by explaining what testing is, what its limitations are, and how we will use the results.

The computer interpretation of Steve's MMPI responses, for example, seems to reinforce what I have learned during our interviews. The interpretation suggests that Steve is moderately to severely disturbed. It indicates that he is defensive, is hostile, and has a tendency to blame others. (I saw many of these tendencies in our first interview.) The MMPI suggests that a more confrontive, direct approach might work best with Steve. Other problems that are noted, like Steve's poor perception of his social impact on others, difficulty in getting close to people, confusion of aggression with sexuality and depression, and suicidal tendencies, seem right on target. The MMPI interpretation does note, however, that patients with Steve's profile are typically poor academic achievers. But we know that Steve has consistently performed well in school, despite his emotional problems.

Steve keeps a diary, so I asked him to write a brief autobiography, emphasizing such critical parts of his life as important childhood experiences, relationships with peers, relationships with his parents, current struggles, and future goals and aspirations. My intent was first to help Steve actively sort out his life experiences, away from our therapy sessions, and second to help me understand his subjective world. Here is a portion that reveals his reactions to our first therapy session; I believe Steve copied it out of his diary.

> My first time with Dr. S. was very confusing. I thought I was in complete control. I'm still not sure what really happened. I know I was angry and resentful the moment I saw him. He was sitting there sipping a cup of coffee without offering me one. When I called the Center, they told me I could only come in for an 8 A.M. appointment. I'm not even alive at that time of the morning. Usually Dr. Jones, the psychiatrist I've been seeing, sees me in the afternoons. I guess I was angry at Dr. Jones for going on vacation and for making me see another therapist who isn't even a psychiatrist.
>
> I really wanted to talk to somebody about Linda. I guess I was pretty bad with Dr. S. I wasn't sure I could trust him, and I took out my anger on him. I tried to put him down and make him uncomfortable. I tried to make him feel defensive by saying he was *only* a psychologist and not a *psychiatrist.* It scared the shit out of me when he got *angry* back at me. I never had a therapist do that to me. It was like he knew

what I was doing. He thinks I do it with other people too. Maybe he's right. He seems to be able to see through me, and I don't like that. I'm afraid to have someone really know what's going on inside. What is going on inside? I don't know! Why should I be afraid? Strange, I really don't like Dr. S. Or do I? Why am I seeing him now instead of my therapist? Mom and Dad are angry at me because I won't go back to Dr. Jones.

There are some very revealing elements in this passage. First, it supports my previous impression that Steve finds it difficult to trust people and behaves so as to push others away. Second, he is beginning to gain some insight into his behaviors—how he attributes his feelings to others and blames them for his troubles. Third, he has a long way to go. There is something within that he is afraid to reveal to himself and others. When he expresses the fear that I can "see through" him, his writing becomes disjointed and fragmented. Obviously, this "dark secret" is deeply frightening to him. It affects not only his emotional state but his cognitive state as well.

What was encouraging was that, despite his discomfort with me, Steve decided to continue in therapy—and with me rather than with his previous therapist. A part of him didn't want to look at himself, but another part seemed to know that this was the only way he could ever get better.

Overall objectives in therapy   As I got to know Steve better and better, I was able to identify some treatment objectives that would benefit him. Again, let me emphasize that I saw Steve as I see each of my clients—as a complex individual who feels, thinks, experiences emotions, behaves, and is a social being. I had to deal with each of these aspects during the two years I worked with him. Here, though, I shall discuss only a few facets of Steve's self to illustrate my therapeutic approaches.

Dealing with Steve's feelings   One of the themes that persisted throughout my work with Steve was his inability to get in touch with his feelings. He found it difficult to experience feelings or to make "feeling" statements. The autobiographical passage suggests that there is something he was afraid to acknowledge. He was ambivalent about therapy because it was forcing him to face frightening parts of his existence; he could no longer be safe and avoid taking risks.

It would have been a mistake to directly reassure Steve that he could trust me and that things would turn out well. Such reassurance would have been transitory at best, unless Steve ventured out on his own to take the risk and to confront his own fears. I saw myself as a guide who would use various strategies to help Steve confront himself. In this respect I relied on existential psychology, which places choice and responsibility clearly in the hands of the client. Here is an example, from one of our sessions.

> STEVE: My parents are upset with me for terminating with Dr. Jones. They think I should continue because he's a psychiatrist, and I've been with him for years. . . . I like him . . . and he really understands me. I feel comfortable with him.
> THERAPIST: What made you decide to continue seeing me instead of Dr. Jones?
> STEVE: I don't know, I mean . . . I'm not sure I even like you. Maybe it's just so much more convenient to go to a campus shrink than to travel across town.
> THERAPIST: I don't believe that's the reason. You're hiding from yourself again! When are you finally going to start facing yourself?

> STEVE (angrily): That's what I mean. I don't know if I like you . . . you're always picking on me. . . . Shit!
> THERAPIST: Say it again.
> STEVE: Shit! (Pounds the table)
> THERAPIST: Again and louder!
> STEVE: Shit! Shit!
> THERAPIST: What are you feeling?
> STEVE: I'm pissed off at you!
> THERAPIST: That's not a feeling!
> STEVE: I'm angry! (Yells at the top of his lungs) Are you satisfied now?
> THERAPIST (after a silence): That was real.
> STEVE: Yeah. (Exhales) Funny how I felt like an overcooked artichoke crumbling just then.
> THERAPIST: I want you to close your eyes and become that artichoke. What are you feeling now?
> STEVE: I want to keep all the leaves from falling away so that no one will see my artichoke heart. I want to strike out at whoever tries to peel the leaves off.
> THERAPIST: Imagine the leaves being peeled away . . .
> STEVE: No, I can't do it!
> THERAPIST: You *don't want* to do it. . . . What are you afraid of?
> STEVE: I'm afraid you'll see me . . . what's really wrong with me.
> THERAPIST: Become that fear and tell me what's going on now.
> STEVE: I've got to hide. . . . All the artichoke leaves help me hide, so others won't see.
> THERAPIST: Can you peel off just a few of the leaves?
> STEVE: Yes, but it doesn't feel good.
> THERAPIST: For each leaf you peel off, say what it is.
> STEVE: I'm peeling off my phony self . . . I'm peeling off my mask . . . I'm peeling off my rationalizations . . . I'm peeling off my anger.
> THERAPIST: Okay, open your eyes. What's happening now?
> STEVE: I feel naked, I feel everyone can see how inadequate I really am. I don't like myself either. . . . I feel scared . . . scared you won't like me anymore. I feel ashamed

because you saw a part of me that no one else did.

THERAPIST: I know. It's scary to let others see the real you. . . . But look at you. Before we began this session you were very uptight and defensive. Your fists were clenched; you were sitting bolt upright on the edge of your chair; you had a strained expression on your face; your voice was tight. Now your body looks more relaxed. . . . Can you feel it?

STEVE: Yeah . . .

THERAPIST: Get into your body. . . . What is it telling you?

STEVE: It's funny . . . I don't like what I see in myself, but . . . but . . . I hate myself but I feel relieved. I don't have to always hide from you.

THERAPIST: You mean you don't have to always hide from yourself.

STEVE: Yeah.

Dealing with irrational thoughts I had to discover how Steve's feelings and many of his self-defeating behaviors were related to his cognitions. I had enough evidence to indicate that Steve created his own miseries through the thoughts and beliefs he held. My work with him in this vein tended to parallel cognitive behavior modification and rational–emotive therapy: In some way, Steve was feeding himself irrational and unrealistic assumptions. My task was to identify these irrational beliefs, show Steve that he was constantly reindoctrinating himself with these messages, and teach him how to challenge or dispute them.

Some of Steve's irrational beliefs are evident in these words of his, taken from another session:

I just feel like I'm a miserable failure. I've disappointed my parents. I know Dad wanted someone who was more athletic. I tried, but I'm not a jock. I did well in school and Mom is proud of that . . . but . . . I

thought when I went to college and could do well at the university, Dad would come around. So far I have a 3.75 GPA, but I should have a 4. In several classes I missed an A by just a few points. When I told him [Steve's father] my grade point average last night, he told me Jeff, my cousin, has a 3.9 GPA. I guess I let him down again. What a "downer" I had last night . . . I couldn't sleep . . . maybe it's not worth going on. Life just isn't worth it. Why should I keep trying? Maybe I should just take courses I know I'll do well in.

Several themes in this paragraph appear to form the basis for Steve's feelings of worthlessness and his low self-esteem. These absolutist themes are often punctuated with *must, should,* and *ought.*

1. I *must* do what is necessary to please my parents, especially Dad. I *must* get my parents' approval, love, and recognition. If I fail to do this, I will never be able to value myself or feel I have succeeded. If they don't love me, I can't love myself. And life would not be worth living without their love and approval.

2. I *must* be at the top of my class. I *must* live up to the expectations of my professors, peers, and parents. I *must* be perfect. If I fail to attain straight A's, it means I've failed again and am basically stupid.

3. I *must* be thoroughly competent in everything I do. If I can't, I'll avoid trying anything new. I *cannot* make mistakes because they will prove how deficient I really am.

After identifying these themes with Steve, I proceeded to show him how these thoughts and self-indoctrinations are at the root of many of his problems. For example, he thinks that his parents' lack of approval has caused him to feel unloved and unappreciated. I attempted to show Steve that it is *his belief* about a *real or imagined* situation, rather than an actual situation, that is causing his difficulties. In therapy sessions I confronted his belief system by having him respond to these questions:

☐ Who is telling you that you are worthless unless your parents approve of you?
☐ Do you need to be loved and liked by everyone?
☐ Do you want to spend the rest of your life in a futile attempt to win over your father?

This line of questioning was helpful in getting Steve to think, to challenge himself, and to decide—for himself—how he would live.

Learning new behaviors One of the things that I have discovered is that a client's insight into or understanding of a problem does not necessarily lead to a behavior change. The understanding that he feared rejection by members of the opposite sex because he equated rejection with his "worthlessness" would not have made it easier for Steve to interact with women. And from my work with Steve, it had become clear that he suffered from immense interpersonal anxiety, especially with women. Not only did he not know how to interact with others or to "make small talk," but he also engaged in inappropriate behaviors that put people off. When Steve was with his friend Linda, he had constantly attempted to make her prove she "cared for him." He had accused her of not being faithful to him, of not caring for him, and of not including him in her extracurricular school activities. This contin-

ual "prove you love me" testing of their relationship never ended, because no amount of reassurance seemed to be enough. In fact, it had the effect of pushing Linda away from him.

This mode of interaction was characteristic of nearly all Steve's relationships. While he worked to combat this irrational belief ("I am worthless; therefore no one can like me"), I felt it was important to help Steve become more comfortable in interpersonal and heterosexual relationships. I attempted to help Steve remove anxiety from his interpersonal encounters by using a behavioral technique: assertiveness training.

Here is Steve talking to me again:

> The truth is I'm always afraid. I panic when I think about being in a group of people and having to talk to them. What am I going to say? Even if I could say something, who would listen? Last month I went to a party with Linda—it was thrown by her friends. . . . When she introduced me all I could way was "hi." I stuttered when I said anything else. It was like in class . . . I really felt inadequate. And one of the guys was trying to hustle Linda. He knew Linda came with me, but he ignored me completely. He asked her to dance, and I spent the whole evening sitting in the corner. I was really angry at him and Linda too, but I couldn't do anything about it. Then he came over and asked if I would mind if he took her home. . . . I could only say "Sure, go ahead." What I really wanted to say was "Go to hell." I feel like I'm a doormat for the world.

Obviously we had to work on Steve's assertive behaviors. What I intended to do was, briefly, the following:

1. Identify Steve's unassertive behaviors that were linked to specific situations (for example, withdrawing and sitting

in a corner by himself and not being able to say "no").

2. Determine the specific skills he needed for assertion (saying "no," introducing himself to strangers, asking Linda to dance, and so on). Then try to grade these skills from least to most assertive.

3. Recreate the problematic situations, as vividly as possible, in the consultation room. Engage Steve in role-playing and behavioral rehearsal with me or volunteers.

4. Get Steve to practice the assertive behaviors in actual situations, under my guidance and monitoring.

Our first use of the procedure will illustrate how we implemented it. Steve and I identified an upcoming event that was causing him considerable apprehension—a class assignment. He was to give an oral critical analysis of an assigned novel in his English class and then lead a discussion of the novel.

Steve needed to practice the assertive skills related to the oral presentation. First, to desensitize him, I had him practice very low-level assertive skills in front of groups. For example, he practiced *raising his hand* in class in situations where he was sure he would not be called on—for example, when many other students raised their hands or while he was out of sight of the professor. To Steve this act was an assertive one. After he attained a degree of comfort with that, I asked him to *raise his hand* and *ask a simple question* (a safe assertive skill), such as "Could you repeat that last point?" After his anxiety regarding this act was conquered, he proceeded to *paraphrasing* what the instructor had said and finally to *stating an opinion.* Each succeeding act represented an increase in assertiveness.

While he was practicing these classroom acts, Steve was finishing his book report. I then asked him to do an oral presentation of his report for me. Next I asked another counselor and the two clerical staff members to be present while he repeated the report. After a second repetition, we simulated a question-and-answer session and then repeated that several times.

This systematic training helped Steve greatly when he finally presented his report to his English class. Although he was anxious throughout the presentation, he felt that he had the anxiety under control.

A similar program, which I developed for his heterosexual anxiety, proved to be only moderately successful.

Steve's threat against Linda "She doesn't deserve to live . . . I swear, I'm going to kill her." Given the context in which it occurred, Steve's threat to kill Linda placed me in a dilemma. My conflicting feelings and apprehension were, no doubt, similar to those experienced by any therapist whose client threatens to kill someone or to commit suicide. Today more than ever, we as therapists must recognize that our work does not occur in a social vacuum. What we do or don't do in therapy has not only clinical implications but ethical, moral, and legal ramifications as well.

In that particular session Steve was becoming increasingly agitated about his breakup with Linda; his expressions of anger were stronger and stronger. He was quite depressed at the time, and it was my therapeutic judgment that the venting of his feelings was healthy. I had been working on that with him when he blurted out his threat. The first thoughts that came to my mind were questions: "Does he really mean what he's saying?"

"How likely is he to carry out the threat?" "Is this just an empty threat characteristic of his anger and hostility?" "What should I do?" "Should I inform the proper authorities, breaking confidentiality, and risk losing Steve's trust?"

I chose to go along with my clinical judgment: to let Steve continue to express his feelings without cutting him off, while constantly assessing the strength of his anger and the likelihood of his acting impulsively. I made that decision for several reasons. First, in the time I had known Steve, he had made several suicide threats. In each case, when he was allowed to express his feelings, the suicidal ideation and threats diminished. I felt that his threat to kill Linda would follow a similar course. Second, despite his often bizarre thoughts and behaviors, I had never considered Steve to be a danger to others. He was more a danger to himself than to anyone else. Third, I felt that some other perspective was needed. There was still time to consult with colleagues about the case and to get their input. And last, I was prepared to cancel other appointments and extend our session if that became necessary. I felt that I could monitor Steve closely, and I even made an appointment for him to return the following day. In other words, after pondering all the issues, including the need to protect myself by informing the proper authorities or even Linda, I decided that the likelihood of his carrying out the threat was very low. Luckily this did prove to be the case.

The dilemma for me as a therapist was not whether I should inform a potential victim or the appropriate authorities about a homicide that I deemed likely. I have no doubt that I would have taken that action if it were necessary. What disturbed me was lacking the ability to precisely assess dangerousness and—even more—being unable to inform a client about the legal limits of confidentiality without adversely affecting our therapist–client relationship.

An epilog to the case Several years have passed since my sessions with Steve came to an end. He graduated from the university with a degree in English literature and went to a graduate school in the east. I did get the chance to see some changes in Steve that are definitely for the better. He relates reasonably well to people now, though I still consider him a loner. His bizarre behavior and ideation have eased off, but he still suffers from periodic bouts of depression. Whereas most clients need only brief periodic therapy to help them cope with life's problems, Steve is one of those individuals, I'm afraid, who will need some form of therapy for the rest of his life. He has chosen to work toward a doctorate degree and to become a teacher, doing research and writing. I think this is as good a vocational choice as any. Not only does it play to his strengths (writing, reading, and research), but the college environment seems to be one of the few in which Steve has done well and has felt sufficiently secure. Perhaps this is a statement about academic life as well as about Steve. Some people perceive it as a protected environment that is quite structured and, in some ways, rather undemanding.

I do not know what has happened to Steve since he left this university. I am aware that he signed a release of information form so that his case records could be transferred to the university he now attends. I can only assume that he has chosen to continue therapy, and I wish him well.

SUMMARY

1. A variety of psychotherapeutic or treatment procedures are used to change behaviors, modify attitudes, and facilitate self-insight. Biological (or somatic) treatments use physical means to alter the bodily and psychological states of patients. Electroconvulsive therapy (ECT), popularly known as "shock treatment," has diminished in use but is still the preferred treatment for some severely depressed patients. Because it results in the permanent destruction of brain tissue, psychosurgery too is now rarely used and strictly regulated. One reason for the decline in the use of ECT and psychosurgery is an increasing reliance on chemotherapy, or drug treatment. Minor tranquilizers reduce anxiety, major tranquilizers help to control or eliminate psychotic symptoms, and antidepressants are effective in reducing depression. Chemotherapy has, to a great extent, enabled patients to function in the community and to be more amenable to other forms of treatment, particularly insight-oriented and behavioral therapy.

2. The insight-oriented therapeutic approaches include psychoanalysis, person-centered therapy, existential analysis, and gestalt therapy. These approaches provide the patient with an opportunity to develop better levels of functioning, to undergo new and emotionally important experiences, to develop a therapeutic relationship with a professional, and to relate personal and private thoughts and feelings.

3. Action-oriented or behavior therapies (based on classical conditioning, operant conditioning, modeling, and cognitive restructuring) have been applied to a variety of disorders. Behavioral assessment, procedures, goals, and outcome measures are more clearly defined and more easily subjected to empirical investigation than is the case with insight-oriented approaches.

4. Although critics have argued that behavior therapy is dehumanizing, limited to a narrow range of human problems, and mechanical, those in favor of it consider behavior modification an effective and efficient treatment modality. Some critics have claimed that the effectiveness of psychotherapy—of whatever orientation—has not been demonstrated. Others have refuted that claim. The real issue, however, may be one of finding the best combination of therapies and situational variables for each client.

5. Group therapy involves the simultaneous treatment of more than one person. There is a strong belief that many psychological difficulties are interpersonal in nature, and the group format allows the therapist and clients to work in an interpersonal context. One form of group therapy, family therapy, sees psychological problems as residing within the family rather than in one individual. The communications approach to family therapy concentrates on improving family communications, whereas the systems approach stresses the understanding and restructuring of family roles and dynamics.

6. Most practicing therapists are eclectic in perspective. They try to select therapeutic methods, concepts, and strategies from a variety of current theories that work. Eclecticism is sometimes viewed as haphazard and inconsistent, but every therapist who fits the therapy to the client is, in a sense, practicing eclecticism.

KEY TERMS

biofeedback therapy A therapeutic approach in which a patient receives information regarding particular autonomic functions and is rewarded for influencing those functions in a desired direction

chemotherapy The treatment of mental disorders with drugs

electroconvulsive therapy The application of an electric voltage to the brain to induce convulsions and reduce depression

existential analysis A therapeutic approach that is concerned mainly with the person's experience and involvement in the world and that involves a complex encounter between client and therapist

family therapy Group therapy characterized by the attempt to modify relationships within the family so as to achieve harmony

gestalt therapy A humanistic–existential approach to therapy that emphasizes the client's awareness of the ''here and now'' and his or her totality of experience with the present

group therapy A form of therapy that involves the simultaneous treatment of two or more clients

person-centered therapy A humanistic therapy that emphasizes the kind of person the therapist should be in the therapeutic process, rather than the techniques that should be used

psychosurgery Brain surgery performed for the purpose of correcting a severe mental disorder

psychotherapy The systematic application, by a trained therapist, of techniques derived from psychological principles, for the purpose of helping psychologically troubled individuals; includes both insight-oriented and action-oriented therapies

21
Community Psychology

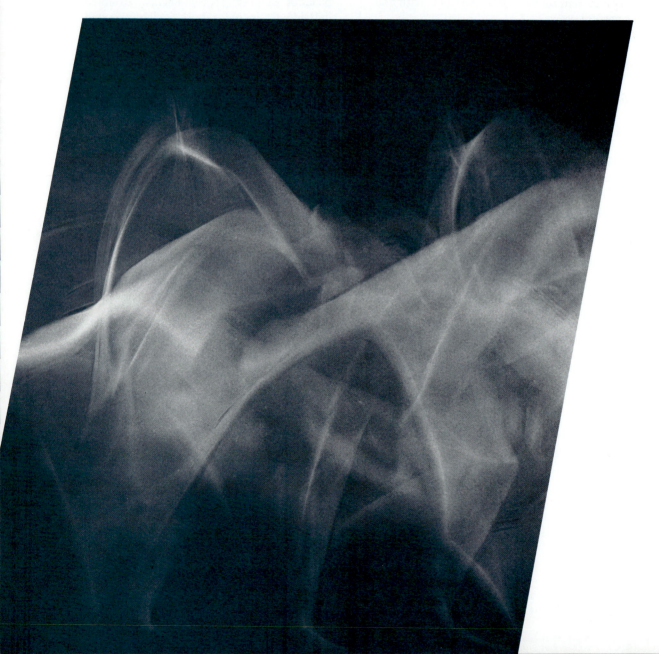

*T*he writer of the following lines is disturbed by realizing that individual, or one-to-one, treatment (in which one therapist treats one client) cannot possibly address the needs of the mentally disturbed—which he puts at 15 percent of the total population.

> The number and distribution of persons with serious emotional problems in our society were far beyond what our resources, in terms of both personnel and institutions, could deal with on a one-to-one basis. The gap was so wide as to be impossible even to bridge. This reality forced me to look for alternatives to the "early treatment." . . . I became convinced of the logic of the public health dictum that holds that no mass disorder afflicting humankind is ever eliminated or brought under control by attempting to treat affected individuals, or by attempting to train individual practitioners in large numbers. . . . Every assessment of the distribution of disturbance in the society arrives at an estimate of approximately 15 percent of the population. In addition to this number of "hard-core cases," each year there is a much larger number of people experiencing intense life crisis. And when we realize that in any given year only about 7 million separate persons are seen throughout the entire mental health system, both public and private, we can appreciate the hopelessness of our present efforts. (Albee 1983, p. xi)

The situation may be worse than he suggests: According to a recent large-scale survey, about 19 percent of adult Americans (more than 29 million people) suffer from a mental disorder or have suffered from one in the previous six months (Myers et al. 1984). The fact that only a small proportion of these individuals actually seek treatment within the mental health system has caused great concern among many mental health professionals. Other afflicted persons may utilize such sources of assistance as ministers, teachers, physicians, friends, relatives, and folk healers, but Albee's major concern is that the entire concept—that of treating mental disturbances after they have appeared—may not be a sufficiently potent one. This has caused many psychologists to look for alternatives to treatment; one such alternative is the community psychology approach.

In this chapter we examine some of the factors that led to this approach, as well as the various activities of community psychologists. For the sake of completeness, we discuss a fairly wide range of activities, some of which not everyone considers to be within the domain of community psychology.

WHY COMMUNITY PSYCHOLOGY?

Community psychology is an approach to mental health that takes into account the influence of environmental factors and stresses the use of community resources and agencies to eliminate conditions that produce psychological problems. To many it represents a sharp departure from the practices of clinical psychology. This difference is especially apparent in three major areas of concentration.

☐ *Ecological focus.* Whereas clinical psychology has been concerned with diagnosing and treating individuals, community psychology is interested in human ecology— the interaction between human beings and their environments. Thus, whereas clinical psychology has attempted to alter the behaviors and personality of clients, community psychologists attempt to modify the social settings, institutions, and ecological systems in their environments.

☐ *Emphasis on psychological strengths and competencies.* Clinical psychology has traditionally focused on deviance and disorders among human beings. By contrast, community psychology often attempts to foster competencies and to enhance the potential of persons who may or may not exhibit mental disorders.

☐ *Prevention activities.* Rather than attending to the treatment of individuals with disorders, community psychology advocates programs to prevent the occurrence of emotional and behavioral problems (Heller et al. 1984).

Community psychology has evolved primarily in reaction to a growing dissatisfaction with traditional approaches to mental health (Goodstein and Sandler 1978). A major source of this dissatisfaction is the perceived inability of the one-to-one treatment approach to provide for the mental health needs of the nation. Another is the emphasis of traditional approaches—primarily the biogenic model but others as well—on the concept that mental problems are *illnesses* that result from *individual dynamics.* Interest in community psychology grew in part because psychologists became more concerned with the role of environmental forces than with the dynamics of the individual's psyche. Klein (1968) suggests that an individual's adjustment depends on the nature and extent of environmental stressors, on the person's competencies and skills, and on the kinds of resources available in the community to help individuals deal with stress. According to this view, the healthiest individuals would come from communities in which stressors were minimized and resources were readily available. Klein's notion reflects the focus of community psychologists on promoting prevention programs (to reduce stress) and on increasing the availability of mental health resources.

Here are some other problems that have led to the search for new approaches and to the growth of community psychology.

The ineffectiveness of mental institutions

The system of psychiatric hospitals has been another source of dissatisfaction. As early as the eighteenth century, many hospitals freed psychiatric patients from chains and encouraged the human rights of patients, but hospitalization appeared to be an increasingly unsatisfactory means for treating more and more patients. First, it is financially costly. Second, psychiatric hospitals are frequently understaffed and lack the resources to provide more than custodial care. Third, state mental hospitals tend to be located away from populated areas, making them somewhat inaccessible. Fourth, and most important, hospitalization often prevents development of the coping behaviors necessary for life in the community. When institutionalized mental patients are dehumanized and degraded, they learn to adjust to a role that is inconsistent with community demands for responsibility and competence (Goffman 1961).

Hospitalized mental patients are sometimes treated as powerless, irresponsible individuals. Many patients receive minimal care and attention from hospital staff, so that hospital treatment has little value (Rosenhan 1973).

An opposing view suggests that patients in mental hospitals often manipulate the image that others have of them in such a way as to control their own fate (Braginsky, Grosse, and Ring 1966). In so doing, these patients may regard the hospital as a resort and may see themselves as free of responsibilities and worries. But again, the problem is that these patients may not learn the skills needed to survive in the community.

In one experiment, hospitalized patients were found to fall into two groups. One group of patients tended to have low discharge rates and presumably wanted to stay hospitalized; the other group was composed of individuals who tended to be discharged rather early and presumably were motivated to leave the hospital. Patients of both types were given a short version of the Minnesota Multiphasic Personality Inventory (MMPI). Half the patients in each group were told that high scores would increase the likelihood of long hospitalization; the other half were told that high scores would probably mean short hospitalization. Despite

Psychiatric hospitals are often overcrowded, understaffed, and costly. Consequently, patients may receive only minimal care and attention, and sometimes are even treated as powerless, irresponsible individuals. Hospital treatment may have little value in some cases.

the fact that all patients received the same tests, their performances on the test varied according to the group into which the patient had been placed and the type of instructions given. Among patients motivated to remain hospitalized, higher scores were obtained from those who were told that high scores indicated long hospitalization. Among patients motivated to leave as soon as possible, the reverse was found: Lower scores were obtained from those who were told that high scores meant long hospitalization. On the basis of these and other findings, the investigators concluded that patients can manage and control their status in hospitals (Braginsky, Grosse, and Ring 1966).

The important issue is whether there is a better way to facilitate the patient's early return to, and functioning in, the community. In the early 1900s, psychiatrist Adolph Meyers suggested that the mental patient's recovery was enhanced when hospital treatment could be integrated with the patient's family and community. Involving the family and community would help smooth the transition between the hospital setting and community life. Along the same lines, Maxwell Jones (1953) conceived of a **therapeutic community** in which all the hospital activities would be structured to be therapeutic. The environment, or "milieu," would be crucial to the therapy. Patients would be free to interact with staff, who would relinquish much of their traditional authority. Patients would be encouraged to make constructive criticisms during "gripe" sessions and to become more involved in decisions about their own treatment. Patients would receive training in social, recreational, and job skills and would participate in role-playing activities to facilitate the formation of adaptive behaviors. Patient alumni clubs, halfway houses, and day treatment would also be available as a bridge to community life.

One group of investigators carried the idea of patient autonomy a step further. Noting that adjustment to hospital life often hinders adjustment to community life, they developed an innovative program through which chronic mental patients could be placed in patient "lodges." These lodges, located in the community, were set up so that patients could gain a sense of autonomy, manage their own lives, and develop a small business (janitorial services). At the same time, patients could also be learning the skills necessary to function in the community. Comparing the patients in the lodge program with a matched group of discharged patients who received traditional outpatient mental health care, the investigators found that lodge patients were better able to remain in the community and to work productively. On other measures of adjustment, however, the two groups showed few differences (Fairweather et al. 1969).

Reviews of such programs, in which patients are given autonomy and an alternative to hospitalization, have been favorable. Alternative programs result in less cost and in lower rates of rehospitalization than treatment

in mental institutions (Kiesler 1982). Given such findings, it is unfortunate that alternative programs have not gained a stronger foothold in the mental health field. Three reasons have been cited for this slow growth: First, the public is often resistant to the idea of housing mental patients in the community rather than in the hospital. Fears of having mental patients in one's neighborhood have caused the public to frown on alternative treatment programs. Second, hospitalization for mental disorders is strongly affected by public and private insurance plans. It is the only treatment for which insurance programs provide full payment, and treatment in alternative programs may not qualify for any payment at all. Third, the mental health staff may oppose alternative programs. Accustomed to the roles, procedures, and responsibilities of the hospital system, staff members may be interested in maintaining that system (Kiesler 1982).

Rising costs and the potential negative side effects of hospitalization have given added impetus to the current trend toward deinstitutionalization. Admissions to hospitals are discouraged, and hospital stays are briefer. The hope has been that community resources (such as halfway houses and outpatient clinics) can be used as alternatives to hospitalization. As we have noted, deinstitutionalization has reduced the dominance of mental hospitals in long-term mental health care, but some former patients are now living only marginally in communities because alternative resources are not available.

Inequities in the delivery of services

Another important factor in stimulating the community psychology movement was the highly discriminatory and unresponsive quality of mental health services available to members of minority groups and the poor. For example, it was found that psychiatric patients from lower socioeconomic classes were more likely to receive less "preferred" and more mechanical therapies (such as drugs and shock treatment) than upper-class patients, who received more expensive "talking" therapies (Hollingshead and Redlich 1958). An analysis of the community mental health system based on nearly 14,000 patients showed that minority-group patients tend to drop out of therapy after one session at almost twice the rate for white patients (Sue 1977). A number of studies have indicated the difficulties in establishing trust, rapport, and a working relationship between patients and therapists who differ in race, socioeconomic class, and lifestyle (Jones and Korchin 1982; Lorion 1973; Luborsky et al. 1971; White 1984). Therapists who differ from patients in these characteristics may be insensitive to their clients' needs or may fail to adequately consider the influence of the social environment in which their clients live. As a result, minority or lower-class patients often prematurely terminate therapy at mental health facilities.

In addition, therapists themselves have been found to select patients on the basis of characteristics that place persons from low socioeconomic levels at a severe disadvantage. One critic argued that many therapists often prefer patients who are young, attractive, verbal, intelligent, and successful—the "YAVIS" syndrome in patient selection (Schofield 1964). This led others to urge that greater attention be given to "HOUND" patients—those who are homely, old, unattractive, nonverbal, and dumb (Goldstein and Simonson 1971). The problem is twofold: Minority and poor patients find therapists unresponsive, and therapists prefer not to work with lower-class or less articulate patients.

The search for alternative approaches to mental health care has thus been stimulated by the lack of sufficient professional personnel to meet needs on a one-to-one basis, by dissatisfaction with the present approach, by the high cost and ineffectiveness of psychiatric hospitalization, and by inequities in the delivery of mental health services. Many mental health professionals have turned to a model in which psychologists draw on community resources to deliver mental health care. Programs based in the community are quite diverse. Several features are, however, particularly characteristic of the community approach to psychology. These include the establishment of the community mental health center system, an emphasis on prevention, the training of paraprofessionals, the expanding role of psychologists in consultation, new attempts at social and political activism, and the increased use of social supports.

COMMUNITY MENTAL HEALTH CENTERS

The community mental health center system, established by Congress in 1963, was created in recognition of the following facts: Psychiatric hospitals were overcrowded, short-term treatment appeared to be effective, medication could be used to control grossly bizarre behaviors, and the social stigma attached to the mental patient was declining (Levenson 1972). The goal of the program was to make psychological services more accessible to the community. **Community mental health centers** were planned to be centrally located and physically harmonious with communities of 75,000 to 200,000 individuals and to provide short-term inpatient care, outpatient care, partial hospitalization, emergency services, and community consultation and education (Smith and Hobbs 1966).

From the inception of the program, many centers had difficulty fulfilling their goals. First, the number of centers that were opened remained low; only about one-third of the originally planned 2000 centers received funding (Bellack and Hersen 1980). More important, community mental health centers were criticized for being unresponsive to their communities and for lacking community participation. Critics charged that many centers were structured in a rigid, authoritarian manner and that decisions were made by administrators who took little account of the attitudes and opinions of staff members and consumers. Critics also expressed concern about the system's continued adherence to the biogenic model, which stresses intrapsychic therapy rather than environmental intervention and prevention (Chu and Trotter 1974; Goldenberg 1973). Because patients become the passive recipients of treatment, this model discourages the active participation of consumers and of the community.

These criticisms have some validity. The community mental health center system has, in some cases, failed to form strong enough roots in the communities that it serves. And funding problems have indeed limited its development (Bloom 1977). Of necessity, most professional personnel in these centers were those who had been trained traditionally, with emphasis on the biogenic model. But the current growth of training programs in community psychology should help to alleviate this problem (Heller et al. 1984).

PREVENTION PROGRAMS

The prevention of psychopathology is one of the most innovative features of community psychology. Prevention programs are attempts to maintain health rather than to treat sickness. The main emphasis is on reducing the number of new cases of mental disorders, the duration of disorders among afflicted individuals, and the disabling effects of disorders. These three areas of prevention have been called *primary, secondary,* and *tertiary* prevention (Cowen 1983).

Primary prevention

Primary prevention is an effort to lower the incidence of new cases of behavioral disorders by strengthening or adding to resources that promote mental health and by eliminating agents or features of a community that threaten mental health. As an example of the former, Project Headstart was initiated in 1964 with the goal of setting up a new and massive preschool program that would help neglected or deprived children develop social, emotional, and intellectual skills. Examples of the latter are efforts to eliminate discrimination against members of minority groups in order to help them fulfill their potential. Both techniques—introducing new resources and eliminating causal factors—can be directed toward specific groups of individuals or toward the community as a whole.

In one primary-prevention program, researchers demonstrated that mothers can be trained to facilitate the development of interpersonal cognitive problem-solving skills in their children. Children of trained mothers demonstrated greater ability to think of alternative solutions to interpersonal problems and to exhibit less impulsive or inhibited behaviors than a control group of children (Shure and Spivack 1979). The same researchers also examined the feasibility of having teachers implement an interpersonal, problem-solving, skills-training program with young children. When the children learned coping and problem-solving skills, they exhibited fewer behavioral disturbances and fewer other problems than a control group of untrained children (Shure and Spivack 1982).

Marital separation or divorce is a major stressor that is likely to produce emotional distress. One group of investigators reasoned that, by providing emotional support and by enhancing the competencies of separated persons, they could reduce the likelihood of disturbance. Newly separated individuals were found through media advertisements and by reference from agencies and practitioners, and they were divided into an experimental group and a control group. Both groups were given intensive interviews and were reassessed six months later. In addition, the experimental group participated in a prevention program that consisted of individual consultation with a representative who provided emotional support and served as the link between the individual and the program. Those in the experimental group were also given the opportunity to participate in study groups that focused on such skills and tasks as job hunting and career planning; legal, financial, and child custody issues; and child-rearing and single-parenting problems; housing and homemaking issues; and socialization and self-esteem building. Results indicated that, after participating in the program, the experimental group (1) favorably evaluated the program, (2) exhibited significantly fewer problems and better adjustment than the control group, and (3) showed a decrease in adjustment problems on a questionnaire of psychological distress and a symptom checklist (Bloom, Hodges, and Caldwell 1982).

A community-wide project to prevent depression was initiated by Munoz and co-workers (1982). During a two-week period, nine 4-minute programs intended to prevent depression were televised in San Francisco. They showed viewers how to think positively, engage in rewarding activities, deal with depression, and so on. Telephone interviews were conducted with 294 San Francisco residents. Some respondents were interviewed one week before the showing of the television segments; others were interviewed one week after the segments were aired; and still others were interviewed before and after the segments. Information about respondents' depression levels was collected during the interviews (for those who were interviewed before and after the segments, the depression measure was administered twice). Respondents interviewed after the televised segments were also asked to indicate whether they had watched any of the segments. Results indicated that those who saw the segments exhibited a significantly lower level of depression than nonviewers. However, the results held only for respondents who had some depressive symptoms to begin with. Watching the television programs did not change the depression levels of those who initially (before the segments) reported little depression.

The results indicate that a community-wide prevention program can be beneficial. A large

As a primary prevention program, Head Start was designed to help deprived children develop social, emotional, and intellectual skills. By fostering these competencies in children, the program hoped to prevent possible future mental health problems.

proportion (about one-third) of the viewers had some depressive symptoms, and it was this group that demonstrated a reduction of symptoms. Obviously the long-term effects of the programs were not assessed. Another problem in the study was that those who benefited from the television programs exhibited some initial symptoms. If they were clinically diagnosable as being depressed, intervention might be considered secondary rather than primary prevention. Nevertheless, the San Francisco study demonstrates the effects of large-scale interventions that may result in the prevention of disorders.

The range of primary-prevention programs is immense. They include the use of behavioral approaches in schools (Jason 1980); the prevention of child maltreatment (Garbarino

1980); the enhancement of competence in older adults (Gatz et al. 1982); and the reduction of domestic violence (Carlson and Davis 1980). And such programs can have an enormous impact. Consider, for example, the following parallel from the field of public health: The development of the polio vaccines cost less than $40 million. Since they were first used, these vaccines have prevented 2000 deaths and 2500 permanently crippling cases of polio and have saved over $1 billion *each year* in hospital costs and lost income (Jason et al. 1983). The primary prevention of mental disorders can yield similar benefits.

Although interest in primary prevention continues to grow, resistance to prevention is also strong (see Focus 21.1). Problems have been noted by a number of researchers (Cowen 1983; Felner, Moritsugu, and Farber 1983; Glidewell 1983). First, primary prevention is future-oriented in that the benefits of the effort are not immediately apparent. Second, it competes with traditional programs aimed at treating persons who already exhibit emotional disturbances. Third, prevention may require social and environmental changes so that stressors can be reduced or resources can be enhanced. Most mental health workers are either unable or unwilling to initiate such changes; many others doubt that we have the ability to modify social structures. Fourth, the funding for mental health programs has traditionally been earmarked for treatment. Prevention efforts constitute a new demand on the funding system. And fifth, primary prevention requires a great deal of planning, work, and long-term evaluation. This alone discourages many from becoming involved.

Secondary prevention

Secondary prevention is an attempt to shorten the duration of mental disorders and reduce their impact. If the presence of a disorder can be detected early and an effective treatment found, it is possible to minimize the impact of the disorder or to prevent its developing into a more serious and debilitating form. For example, classroom teachers can play an important role in secondary prevention by identifying children who are not adjusting to the school environment. Once identified, these children can be helped by teachers, parents, or school counselors.

In practice, secondary prevention has encountered a number of problems. First, traditional diagnostic methods are often unreliable and imply little with regard to treatment procedures. It has been suggested that more specialized diagnostic techniques be used, perhaps focusing on certain behaviors or on demographic characteristics that may be related to psychopathology (Zax and Spector 1974). Second, once a disorder is detected, it is often difficult to decide what form of treatment will be most effective with a particular patient. Third, prompt treatment is frequently unavailable because of the shortage of mental health personnel and the inaccessibility of services. Indeed, many mental health facilities have long lists of would-be patients who must wait months before receiving treatment. "Walk-in" clinics, crisis intervention facilities, and emergency telephone lines have been established in an attempt to provide immediate treatment.

One of the most elaborate secondary-prevention programs focused on first-grade public-school children in Rochester, New York, in an attempt to answer the following questions:

1. Is it possible to identify "high-risk" first-grade children—those who are likely to become emotionally disturbed later on?
2. Can special efforts be made to help high-risk children adjust and to prevent later emotional disturbance?

In the first, or early-detection, phase of the study, the investigators used interviews with mothers, teachers' ratings, and psychological tests to determine which children had (or could potentially have) emotional problems;

Prevention versus Psychotherapy: Who's Wasting the Public's Time and Money?

With all the lip service paid to prevention these days, it might not sound like it wants for support. But when the bureaucracy doesn't want to do something [prevention programs], including something urgently recommended by the White House, it stalls. . . . Resistance is coming from the mental health industry, from psychotherapists, and from the organicists–geneticists who disparage social causation. . . . Prevention is bad for business. . . . [Mental health] Centers simply can't spare staff for activities that are not reimbursable, and the immediate problems of the mentally distressed leave little time free for prevention efforts that might show results only after many years. (Albee 1979a, p. 2)

Prevention has remained largely an unrealized hope rather than a technological reality for most health conditions. . . . Albee's assertion . . . that greedy psychotherapists, in collusion with other profit-oriented groups, have conspired to prevent prevention because it is bad for business is a falsehood. (Wiggins 1979, p. 2)

I hereby request a debate with Jack Wiggins at a time and place to be chosen by him and his seconds. . . . Anyone with the most elementary knowledge of health care in the Western world knows that practically every significant advance in health maintenance has resulted from primary prevention efforts. (Albee 1979b, p. 31)

This exchange of pro-prevention and pro-psychotherapy views in the *APA Monitor*

set the stage for a debate on the controversy at a meeting of the Division of Psychotherapy of the American Psychological Association at its 1980 convention in San Diego, California.

The prevention advocates acknowledged the importance of psychotherapy in mental health efforts but emphasized the potential benefits of primary prevention. They argued that substantial opposition to primary prevention was based on (1) mental health professionals' lack of training in prevention, (2) the personal satisfaction and economic benefits of conducting psychotherapy, (3) the ''newness'' of systematic prevention efforts in the mental health field, (4) numerous misconceptions about the concept of primary prevention, and (5) a reluctance to initiate the social reforms that are needed to reduce stress.

The psychotherapy advocates acknowledged the value of prevention but denied that therapists resist prevention because of their own economic interests. They felt that, whereas psychotherapy has demonstrated its value, the field of prevention suffers from disunity and a lack of consensus regarding priorities, goals, and procedures.

Although agreement on the value of both prevention *and* psychotherapy was reached, important questions about what types of prevention efforts are needed and how mental health resources should be distributed between prevention and psychotherapy remained unresolved.

these children were given a "red tag." The remaining children—about 70 percent of the total—were designated "non-red-tag" children. All the students in this school, whether red-tagged or not, were compared with control students from two demographically comparable schools.

The second, or prevention, phase was initiated in the experimental school but not in the control schools. It consisted of special meetings during and after school for teachers, parents, and mental health specialists. These meetings were designed to help teachers understand child development and focus on the needs of individual children. During the prevention phase, teachers gave special after-school attention to particular children who needed it.

In the final, or assessment, phase of the study, the investigators used academic scores and peer and teacher ratings to measure the children's adjustment.

In answer to question 1, results showed that children given a red tag in the first grade were more likely to exhibit problems in the third and seventh grades than non-red-tag children. Findings about the effectiveness of prevention efforts (question 2), however, were less consistent. After third grade, children in the experimental group did not do consistently better than control-group children on the various adjustment measures. Furthermore, by the seventh grade it was no longer possible to demonstrate positive effects of the prevention program. One benefit of the program, however, was the finding that it resulted in a more positive attitude toward mental health personnel on the part of parents and teachers (Cowen et al. 1963; Zax and Cowen 1972; Zax and Spector 1974).

In the prevention phase of the Rochester experiment, teachers were both the evaluators and the helping agents for the children. In such a situation, the teachers' ratings of the children may have been biased by their participation as helping agents (Levine and Graziano 1972). Furthermore, control-school children were not divided into red tag and non-

red-tag categories, so it was not possible to compare high-risk children who received the prevention efforts with high-risk children who did not participate in the prevention program.

Cowen and his colleagues have continued to modify the program and to increase the number of children in the project. Over 2000 children have been studied so far. A summary of the overall results argues that, despite methodological problems (such as the lack of more varied outcome measures and of more comparable, nontreated control groups), the findings are quite consistent across a large population (Weissberg et al. 1983). The series of studies showed that intervention reduced problems involving shyness, learning difficulties, and (to some extent) acting-out and aggressive behaviors. In addition, adaptive assertiveness, peer sociability, and frustration tolerance were improved.

Secondary-prevention programs have also been initiated in suicide control. It has been estimated that well over 20,000 self-inflicted deaths occur per year and that there are eight suicide attempts for every suicidal death (Shneidman 1972). These alarming statistics have required major efforts to prevent suicide (Farberow and Shneidman 1961). Hundreds of suicide-prevention centers, functioning autonomously or within mental health centers or hospitals, have been organized. These centers try to identify potentially suicidal individuals and to prevent the occurrence of suicides. Once a person is identified as a high-risk individual, attempts can be made to intervene directly.

Suicide-prevention centers vary a great deal in complexity, from simple round-the-clock telephone "hot lines" to comprehensive therapeutic services (Roen 1971). Many have publicized their availability or have established working relationships with police, hospitals, churches, and other organizations in order to more quickly identify, reach, and serve potentially suicidal persons. Crisis-intervention services are also available for alcoholics, compulsive gamblers, and drug addicts. Some communities have also initiated services to help rape victims handle the emotional trauma and stress of their experience.

Tertiary prevention

The goal of **tertiary prevention** is to facilitate the readjustment of the individual to community life after hospital treatment for a mental disorder. Tertiary prevention focuses on reversing the effects of institutionalization and providing a smooth transition to a productive life in the community. Several programs have been developed to accomplish this goal. One involves the use of ''passes,'' whereby hospitalized patients are encouraged to leave the hospital for short periods of time. By spending gradually increasing periods of time in the community (and then returning each time to the hospital), the patient can slowly readjust to life away from the hospital while still benefiting from therapy.

Psychologists can also ease readjustment to the community by educating the public about mental disorders. Public attitudes toward mental patients are often based on fears and stereotypes. Factual information can help to modify these attitudes so that patients will be more graciously accepted. This is especially important for the family, friends, and business associates of patients, who must interact frequently with them.

A more difficult problem to deal with is the growing backlash against the discharge of former mental patients into nursing homes or rooming houses in the community. Many community members feel threatened when such patients live in their neighborhoods. Again, education programs may help to dispel the fears and stereotypes held by such members of the community.

Halfway-house programs can provide patients with a support system while they learn or redevelop skills they will need if they are to function in the community. In *outpatient* and *night hospital* programs, patients can receive therapy and still hold down a job or spend time with their families. Such programs help

This suicide hotline (top), installed on a bridge noted for a history of suicides, was designed to prevent suicides and suicide attempts by providing a source of accessible psychological assistance. The support group (bottom) for developmentally disabled, retarded, or multiply-handicapped young adults was designed to shorten the duration or reduce the impact of psychological problems the members might experience.

smooth the transition from the hospital to the community environment by offering exposure to both settings.

Evaluating prevention

The concept of prevention has obvious appeal. It adds an active component to community psychology. That is, rather than waiting for individuals to exhibit disorders before treating them, community psychologists actively seek to eliminate the causes of the antecedents of disorders and use community resources to prevent disorders. But the goals of prevention—to reduce the incidence and severity of mental disorders and to foster mental health—are difficult to attain for several reasons. We have noted some of them; others also should be mentioned. First, attempts to identify individuals at high risk of exhibiting juvenile delinquency or behavioral disorders have come under attack for fear that certain members of political or minority groups may be falsely identified and unwillingly assigned to a prevention program. Second, doubts still remain about whether community psychologists have enough knowledge and control to implement effective programs. Third, prevention programs often require massive funding, and results are difficult to obtain in a short period of time. Because intensive evaluations of program effectiveness are generally rare, there is a reluctance to invest in prevention (Bloom 1972). And fourth, some fear that prevention efforts constitute an invasion of personal privacy. Continuing efforts are needed to reorganize priorities and to educate reluctant persons about the benefits of prevention.

TRAINING PARAPROFESSIONALS

If you had a serious marital problem or a personal-adjustment difficulty, where would you seek help? Obviously many factors enter into such a choice. In an analysis of help-seeking behavior, it was found that disturbed individuals turn first to relatives, friends, and co-workers for assistance. Others within their social networks, such as ministers or teachers, are also used. Relief agencies and professional mental health services are often utilized as a last resort (Gourash 1978).

Clearly, then, people who are not mental health professionals help a substantial proportion of disturbed individuals (Gottlieb 1981). In an attempt to expand the availability of mental health services and at the same time take advantage of resources outside the mental health profession, community psychologists are training paraprofessional therapists and becoming more involved in consultation.

Paraprofessional therapists are persons who provide some mental health services but do not have formal mental health training. The training of more paraprofessionals would help solve the personnel shortage. In addition, many paraprofessionals have intimate knowledge of and experience in the community, which can help them understand patients and their environment. And paraprofessionals do not typically trigger the reluctance of many patients to enter therapy, a reluctance stemming from distrust or suspicion of mental health professionals.

The role of paraprofessionals in caring for others is not new. For many years Alcoholics Anonymous has used alcoholics who are no longer drinking as therapeutic agents for other alcoholics who are trying to stop drinking. The central issue is whether paraprofessionals are as effective as professionals, and there appears to be ample evidence that they *are* effective (Durlak 1979; Guerney 1969; Karlsruher 1974).

One interesting experiment concerning the effectiveness of paraprofessionals had controversial results (Poser 1966). The study was designed to test the effectiveness of psychotherapy with male chronic schizophrenics. The schizophrenics were divided into three groups. The first group was treated by fifteen professional therapists (psychiatrists, social workers, and occupational therapists); the second group was treated by thirteen nonprofessionals (two patients and eleven undergraduate students with no training or background in psychology or mental health); and the control group of patients received no treatment. Each professional therapist and each nonprofessional was assigned to a group of patients and asked to conduct group therapy in any manner for one hour, five days a week, for five months. The three groups of patients were matched in age, severity of illness, length of hospitalization, and test performance prior to therapy.

The results, based on test performance after treatment, indicated that patients in the treatment groups showed significantly greater improvement on some tests than untreated patients. Even more interesting, however, was the discovery that patients working with nonprofessionals performed *better* on several measures than those working with professionals! A three-year follow-up of some of the patients treated by the untrained therapists indicated that their improvement was not a transitory phenomenon. These patients were still performing better three years after treatment than they did prior to treatment. The experimenter speculated that the "naive enthusiasm" and the lack of a "professional stance" gave the untrained therapists more freedom in responding to patients. Unfortunately, he did not analyze what went on in the various sessions, which might have been responsible for the greater improvement among patients of untrained therapists. The outcome measures used in the study have been criticized, and it has been noted that the discharge rates for treated and untreated clients were similar (Cartwright 1968). In any event, the study did demonstrate that untrained therapists could be a potential resource for community mental health.

In general, the nature and extent of training of paraprofessionals has varied considerably from program to program. Some programs have selected paraprofessionals on the basis of personality test results (Holzberg, Knapp, and Turner 1967), others on the basis of per-

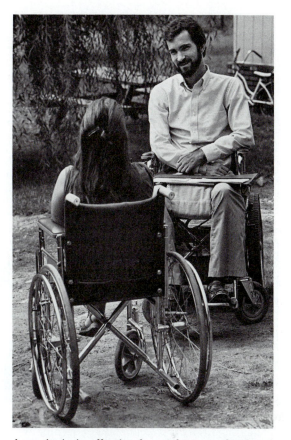

A particularly effective form of paraprofessional assistance might be to pair therapists and clients with similar backgrounds, problems, or disabilities. Such paraprofessional therapists can be a valuable community mental health resource with great potential.

formance in small-group interaction (Goodman 1972). Different types of individuals have also been used as paraprofessionals, including unscreened ghetto youths, many of whom were high-school dropouts (Klein 1967), college students (Gruver 1971; Mitchell 1983), mothers (Shah 1969), teachers (Harris, Wolf, and Baer 1964), grandparents (Johnston 1967), foster parents (Cobb, Leitenberg, and Burchard 1982), and minority-group members (Sue 1973). Non-mental-health professionals who frequently offer aid in the course of their work have also been studied; hairdressers, divorce lawyers, industrial foremen, and bartenders

Figure 21.1   *Community Psychology: The Education and Training Pyramid for Mental Health Workers*

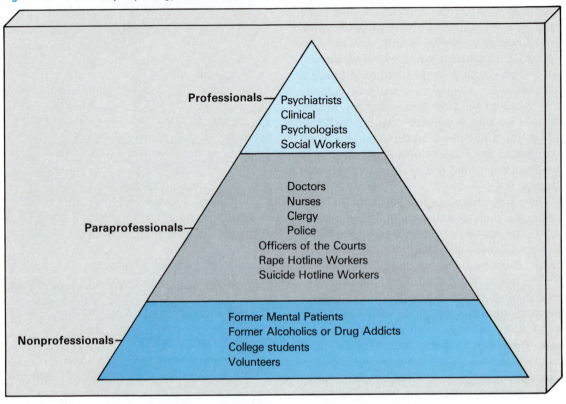

often render assistance to others (Cowen 1982). Furthermore, paraprofessionals have acted as therapists (Rioch 1967), companions (Goodman 1972), and foster grandparents (Johnston 1967) and have used a wide variety of therapeutic orientations, including person-centered therapy, behavior modification, and filial therapy (Guerney 1969). One review of forty-two studies of paraprofessional helpers led to the conclusion that paraprofessionals are effective as therapeutic agents (Durlak 1979). Again, however, there was little information about the reason for this effectiveness.

The roles of professionals, paraprofessionals, and nonprofessionals have been conceptualized as a "mental health pyramid," as shown in Figure 21.1 (Seidman and Rappaport 1974). At the narrow top of the pyramid are experienced mental health professionals who

serve as teachers, consultants, and supervisors. As one moves down toward the base of the pyramid, one finds more people with less intensive mental health training. For example, in a university setting, psychology faculty (at the pyramid's top) might train graduate students (in the middle of the pyramid), who, in turn, would train undergraduates (near the pyramid's base) to act as therapeutic agents. The influence of this training expands progressively, because a small number of professionals can train a larger number of paraprofessionals, who can train an even larger number of nonprofessionals.

The wide range of programs for training paraprofessionals is indicative of the growing involvement of lay workers in the mental health field. The community psychology approach gives nonprofessional mental health workers significant responsibility in taking care of others—a role that was formerly thought to belong exclusively to professionals.

CONSULTATION

Another feature of community mental health programs is consultation between psychologists and individuals or institutions within the community. For example, a police department may ask a psychologist to act as a resource person for police officers who must often intercede in family disputes, or an industrial firm may need a mental health consultant to help in raising employee morale and improving communication. Psychologists have an important impact on the community as consultants to schools, law-enforcement agencies, the clergy, courts, welfare offices, juvenile and family services, and others.

Consultation is conceived of in many different ways, but perhaps the most popular is that of Gerald Caplan (1964). He distinguished four types of consultation:

1. In *person-centered case consultation,* the consultant's efforts are directed at helping the consultee deal more effectively with a particular client. For example, a consultant may help a teacher deal with an aggressive student.
2. In *consultee-centered case consultation,* the consultant helps the consultee develop general mental health skills. For example, a consultant may help a teacher increase his or her general counseling skills.
3. In *program-centered administrative consultation,* the consultant increases the effectiveness of an administrative program. For example, a consultant may help a school principal handle a morale problem among teachers.
4. In *consultee-centered administrative consultation,* the consultant helps the consultee develop better administrative skills.

In this case, a consultant may focus on helping a school principal improve his or her administrative skills.

Consultation expands the sphere of influence (and usefulness) of community psychologists. Rather than waiting for patients in a hospital, clinic, or private setting, the consulting psychologist seeks out opportunities to use psychological principles to help others within the community. The eventual recipients of this aid may be disturbed individuals, or they may be other professionals, administrators, or lay persons who need help to function more effectively. They may also be agencies or organizations, and they need not be directly involved in mental health care. University libraries, for example, are often plagued with the problems of other service organizations: a need for more effective communication among the staff; conflicts between professionals and paraprofessionals over roles, responsibilities, or status; value conflicts among staff members; and poor relations with users and other university programs. One pair of investigators initiated a three-month program to help a library staff develop better communication skills, improved means of resolving conflicts, and cooperative team-building strategies. The self-reports of the staff were highly favorable toward the program, and presumably the overall functioning of the library was made more effective (Haas and Weatherly 1981).

SOCIAL AND POLITICAL ACTION

The development of community psychology has led to a deeper appreciation of the massive influence of environmental forces and resources on mental health. This appreciation, however, has led to a serious conflict among psychologists about the wisdom of political activism: Should psychologists become active in the social–political arena, or should they remain within their traditional professional roles? Advocates of social and political activism argue that, if psychologists are to effect major improvements in mental health, they must be able to influence political decisions and policies regarding environmental resources; that mental health services are already politicized; and that separating one's professional role from one's social and political concerns is to abnegate responsibility for the future of society (Altrocchi 1972). In other words, mental health professionals should implement their knowledge of human behavior. Supporters of the opposing position contend that, when psychologists become social activists, they renounce their professional role. They fear that politically active psychologists may start imposing their own community-action programs and social policies. (See also Focus 21.2.)

Actually, psychologists within the American Psychological Association have long been addressing policy issues of four kinds. The first are Association housekeeping issues, such as devising its own criteria for the accreditation of psychology programs. The second issues deal with professional interests (for example, seeing that congressional appropriations are sufficient for psychological research and training). The third involve public-interest issues, such as effective programs for children, the elderly, and minority groups. The fourth involve moral and ethical stances concerning such issues as gun control, abortion, and a nuclear freeze (Kelly 1984). It is the last two kinds of issues that have created the greatest controversy among psychologists.

Is it possible for community psychologists to facilitate social action without directly imposing their own values on others? The answer is "yes and no." Rappaport (1981) has advocated an empowerment model whereby community psychologists enhance the ability of people to control their own lives. Rappaport's belief is that resources already exist in communities, people already know what is best for their communities, and no single solution is applicable to all communities. The task of psychologists is to help others find better

means to use already existing competencies and to solve their own problems.

Rappaport's model is not without value. Advocating the empowerment of the people as a preferred model for social action is itself a value decision, and choosing which community groups to empower may also have political implications. However, the model represents a shift from the position that mental health professionals are the sole experts, the group that must decide what is best for mental health. It reflects a view that recognizes, appreciates and makes use of existing competencies in laypersons.

IMPROVING SOCIAL SUPPORTS

As we have noted, individuals often turn to others for assistance and guidance during emotional stress. They seek support from family members, friends, co-workers, or ministers, and then perhaps from mental health professionals. By **social supports** we mean the availability and quality of these interpersonal resources. Social supports can provide guidance, feedback, material aid, behavioral assistance, intimate relationships, and positive social interactions (Barrera and Ainlay 1983). Community psychologists are particularly interested in social supports as resources that already exist and are available within communities (Rappaport 1981). Of particular interest is their potential for preventing emotional problems.

Individuals with effective support networks tend to have fewer symptoms of both physical and mental disorders in the face of stress than those without such support (Heller et al 1984). The relationship between social supports, stressors, and psychiatric symptoms was examined in a study in which social supports were measured in terms of interactions and involvement with, as well as feelings toward, friends, neighbors, community organizations, and the like (Lin et al. 1979). Measures of life-event stressors and self-reported psychiatric

Mental Health Professionals and Social Action

Mental health professionals show little consensus on the issue of whether they should become involved in social or political activism, especially when the action involves confrontation or agitation. Professionals trained as social workers, however, have long been at the forefront of activist—even militant—community organizations.

In his *Rules for Radicals* (1972), social reformer Saul Alinksy advocated the use of confrontation and conflict tactics by disadvantaged groups. Here, for example, he describes the action planned by a grassroots ghetto organization in Chicago when City Hall failed to live up to its commitments to the organization.

O'Hare Airport is the world's busiest airport. Think for a moment of the common experience of jet travelers. . . . As the airplane starts its landing approach, you decide to wait . . . and use the [lavatory] facilities in the terminal. This is obvious to anyone who watches the unloading of passengers at various gates in any airport—many of the passengers are making a beeline for the men's or the ladies' room.

With this in mind, the tactic becomes obvious—we tie up the lavatories. In the restrooms you drop a dime, enter, push the lock on the door—and you can stay there all day. Therefore the occupation of the sit-down toilets present no problem. It would take just a relatively few people to walk into these cubicles, armed with books and newspapers, lock the doors, and tie up all the facilities. What

are the police going to do? Break in and demand evidence of legitimate occupancy? Therefore, the ladies' restrooms could be occupied completely; the only problem in the men's lavatories would be the stand-up urinals. This, too, could be taken care of, having groups busy themselves around the airport and then move in on the stand-up urinals to line up four or five deep whenever a flight arrived.

The consequences of this kind of action would be catastrophic in many ways. People would be desperate for a place to relieve themselves. . . . O'Hare would soon become a shambles. The whole scene would become unbelievable and the laughter and ridicule would be nationwide. It would be a source of great mortification and embarrassment to the city administration.

The threat of this tactic was leaked (a Freudian slip here?) back to the administration, and within 48 hours the Woodlawn Organization found itself in conference with [city hall officials] who said that they were certainly going to live up to their commitments and they could never understand where anyone got the idea that a promise made by Chicago's City Hall would not be observed. At no point, then or since, has there ever been any open mention of the threat of the O'Hare tactic. Very few of the members of the Woodlawn Organization knew how close they were to writing history.

SOURCE: Alinsky, S. D. (1971). *Rules for radicals*. New York: Random House. Copyright © 1971 by S. D. Alinsky. Reprinted by permission of Random House, Inc.

symptoms were also obtained. The results indicated that more severe stressors were related to increased numbers and severity of symptoms, but stronger social supports reduced the number of symptoms. The researchers speculate that social supports mediate the relationship between stress and emotional dis-

turbance. That is, social supports may help to decrease the impact of stress on mental health. Others have also recognized the possibility that social supports cushion the impact of stress (Cassel 1974; Cobb 1976).

If social supports *are* important in mental health, then, by improving the number, range, and quality of these supports, we may enable more individuals to cope better with stress. Many of the studies cited earlier have shown that this is in fact so—that increasing interpersonal resources can reduce or prevent emotional distress. This is especially important because it would be impossible to eliminate all the stressors that human beings may face.

Although a great deal of research has recently been done on social support, much is still unknown (Gottlieb 1983). Precisely how do social supports enable one to cope? What aspects of social supports are beneficial? What kinds of persons, with what kinds of support, exposed to what kinds of stressors, are able to adjust and adapt? What are the most effective means for enhancing social supports? These and many more questions have yet to be addressed.

RACISM AND SEXISM: TWO PROBLEMS FOR COMMUNITY PSYCHOLOGISTS

Because of its ecological perspective, community psychology must be involved in the modification or alteration of social–environmental conditions that give rise to and maintain stress. Such conditions can have a tremendous impact on the mental well-being of large groups of individuals. One of the most invidious is the personal and institutional practice of prejudice, discrimination, and stereotyping—which has been directed against ethnic and religious minorities, individuals with physical handicaps, homosexuals, elderly adults, and women. Here we shall examine the psychological consequences of racism and sexism.

Racism

Blacks, Hispanics, native Americans, and Asian–Americans share many of the experiences of oppression that are manifested through **racism,** discrimination, and prejudice

that are aimed at a specific group because its members are supposedly inferior in some way. The standard of living of many minority-group members is much below that enjoyed by whites.

Discrimination has a long history in the areas of housing, employment, income, and education. The results are high unemployment rates, less desirable jobs, and a much lower income for minorities than for whites, as well as higher suicide and juvenile delinquency rates and poorer health. An analysis of census figures reveals that the median income of black families is 57 percent of that of white familes, and black males have an unemployment rate nearly two and one-half times that of whites (Moore 1982). Historically, blacks have suffered from segregated and inferior education—inferior in terms of class size, teacher qualifications, physical facilities, and allocation of funds for extracurricular activities.

Beyond such deprivation, extreme acts of racism can come close to wiping out an entire minority group (Wrightsman 1972). Native Americans have experienced a succession of massacres of genocidal proportions. Time after time, their leadership has been decimated. The native American population has dropped from 3 million to 600,000, and the native American's life expectancy is 44 years, compared to 71 for white Americans!

Effects on self-esteem   The psychological costs of racism for members of minority groups are immense (Sue 1978; Ruiz and Padilla 1977; Jones and Korchin 1982). Constantly bombarded on all sides by reinforcement for the beliefs that whites and their way of life are superior and that, conversely, all other life-styles are inferior, many minority-group members begin to wonder whether they themselves are not to blame for being different and whether subordination and segregation are not justified. A sense of confused self-identity among black children, to which racism may contribute, was first brought to the attention of social scientists by Clark and Clark (1947). In a study of racial awareness and preference among black and white children, they found that black children preferred to play with a white doll rather than a black one; that the black doll was perceived as being somehow "bad"; and that approximately one-third of the black children, when asked to pick the doll that looked like them, picked the white one.

In the *Autobiography of Malcolm X* (Haley 1966), Malcolm relates how, as a young man, he tried desperately to appear as white as possible. He went to painful lengths to straighten and dye his hair so that he would look more like white males.

The development of a negative self-image and the fostering of racial self-hatred are not unique to blacks. Many minority groups come to accept white standards for physical attractiveness, personality characteristics, and social relationships (Kardiner and Ovesey 1962). That such an orientation may lead to racial self-hatred is evident in the following clinical description of Janet T., a Chinese–American girl:

Janet T. a 21-year-old senior majoring in sociology, was born and raised in Portland, Oregon, where she had limited contact with members of her own race. Her father, a second-generation Chinese–American, is a doctor. Her mother is a homemaker. Janet is the middle sibling; she has an older brother in medical school and a younger brother, age 17.

Janet entered therapy suffering from a severe depressive reaction manifested by feelings of worthlessness, by suicidal ideation, and by an inability to concentrate. She was unable to recognize the cause of her depression throughout the initial interviews. However, much light was shed on the problem when the therapist, also a Chinese–American, noticed an inordinate amount of hostility; it became apparent that Janet really resented being seen by a psychologist of her own race. She suspected that she had been deliberately assigned a Chinese–American therapist. When asked about this, Janet openly expressed scorn for "anything that reminds me of Chinese." She expressed hostility towards Chinese customs and especially the Chinese male, whom she described as introverted, passive, and sexually unattractive.

Racism not only affects housing, employment, income, education, and health care for minority group members, but also affects their self-esteem and self-image. Prejudice and discriminatory behavior may induce negative self-images and even racial self-hatred.

Further exploration revealed that all through school she had associated only with Caucasians. When she was in high school, Janet would frequently bring home white boyfriends, greatly upsetting her parents. It was as though she blamed her parents for having been born Chinese and used this method to hurt them.

During her college years, Janet became involved in two love affairs with Caucasians, both ending unsatisfactorily and abruptly. The last breakup had occurred four months earlier, when the boy's parents had threatened to cut off financial support for their son unless he ended the relationship. Apparently, objections had arisen because of Janet's race.

Although not completely conscious of it, Janet was having increasing difficulty denying her racial heritage. The breakup of her last love affair brought home to her the fact that she was a member of a group that was not fully accepted by all segments of society. At first she vehemently and bitterly denounced the Chinese for her present dilemma. Later, much of her hostility was turned inward against herself. Feeling alienated from her own subculture and not fully accepted by American society, she experienced an identity crisis. This resulted in feelings of worthlessness and depression. It was at this point that Janet had come for therapy. (Sue and Sue 1971, p. 41)

Researchers have suggested that racial consciousness develops through five successive stages (Atkinson et al. 1979).

☐ *The conformity stage.* A person in the conformity stage accepts and conforms to white standards and values. Personal worth is dictated by conformance to these standards, which translates into an active rejection and devaluation of the minority individual's cultural and racial heritage. People in this stage believe that there is no race problem, that the problem resides within the members of minority groups, and that minority groups have to work harder to get ahead. Unfortunately, the constant denial of one's internal needs in favor of external standards leads to increased frustrations, as in the case of Janet T. These frustrations often lead to the next stage.

☐ *The dissonance stage.* Cultural confusion and conflict characterize the dissonance stage. The minority person encounters information or experiences that are inconsistent with previously held beliefs and values. Admonitions to be proud of one's cultural

and racial heritage may lead to a questioning of the dominant views acquired in the conformity stage. The cultural values of the minority group may begin to have appeal, causing ambivalent feelings of shame and pride in the self. In this stage, the individual's psychic energies are aimed at resolving the conflict between positive and negative attitudes toward the self and the minority group.

☐ *The resistance and immersion stage.* During this stage the person is committing his or her personal energies to rejecting white standards, white activities, white relationships, and the mainstream culture. If the focus stays on rejection, strong antiwhite values and goals may develop. Anger and hostility toward whites are strong. The overthrow of white power structures and the destruction of white people become the person's goals. The emphasis is on rejection rather than positive growth. This may be seen as an extreme reaction to racism. If, however, the need for identification and development of minority goals and values becomes stronger than this hatred, a rechanneling of personal energy must occur.

☐ *The introspection stage.* At this stage the person begins to experience feelings of discontent and discomfort with group views that the person rigidly endorsed in the previous stage. Attention is now focused on greater individual autonomy. Conflicts may occur between allegiance to the minority group and notions of personal autonomy. The individual begins to recognize the utility of many elements of the dominant culture yet is confused about whether to synthesize them with his or her minority culture.

☐ *The synergetic articulation and awareness stage.* Minority individuals in this stage experience self-fulfillment with regard to cultural identity. Conflicts from the earlier stages are resolved, allowing for greater individual control and autonomy. The person is able to examine objectively and accept those aspects of the mainstream culture and other minority cultures that are desirable, while resisting those that are harmful (such as racism and sexism). An openness to the constructive elements of the dominant culture becomes possible, as does a bicultural identification.

The notion that blacks exhibit low self-esteem or tend to pass through stages involving conformity or resistance has been challenged by Banks (1982) and Powell (1983). They note that many current studies fail to support the contention that low self-esteem or conformity to white standards is exhibited at any "stage."

This can be explained in a number of ways. First, as Banks and Powell claim, many studies of self-esteem contain methodological or conceptual flaws. This may be particularly true of early research studies that were relatively unsophisticated. Second, *some* blacks may exhibit racial self-hatred, and focusing on these individuals may result in overgeneralizations concerning all blacks. Third, being socialized in this country, blacks may adopt some white patterns and standards but not others. Undue emphasis on the former may lead to a misconception that blacks have low self-esteem. (It should also be noted that the adoption of behavioral patterns and standards is a two-way process. For example, many nonblack athletes have adopted handshakes, gestures, mannerisms, and expressions that were initiated by black athletes.) Fourth, times have changed. During the 1960s and 1970s we witnessed a movement to redefine the minority group's existence by raising consciousness of, and pride in, racial and cultural heritage. Positive aspects of ethnic cultures were emphasized, and many ethnic-group individuals (blacks, Hispanics, native Americans, Asian–Americans, and others) joined in the fight against racism. This may have had the effect of obscuring some of the developmental stages.

Racism and mental health We indicated earlier that oppression, racism, prejudice, and dis-

During the 1960s and 1970s positive aspects of ethnic cultures were emphasized to combat racism and its ill effects. Raising consciousness and fostering pride in racial and cultural heritage were used to change prejudicial attitudes and racial stereotypes.

crimination have deleterious effects. If racism is viewed as a stressor, it would seem reasonable to assume that rates of mental disorders would be greater among oppressed groups. Indeed, the authors of one report on the distribution of mental disorders go so far as to state that "Racist practices undoubtedly are key factors—perhaps the most important ones—

in producing mental disorders in blacks and other underprivileged groups'' (Kramer, Rosen, and Willis 1973, p. 355). But is there any evidence to indicate that blacks, for example, experience higher rates of psychopathology than whites?

Two methods are used to assess the incidence of mental disorders (Dohrenwend and Dohrenwend 1973). In the first, the rate of disorders in a population is estimated by noting how many persons from that population are *treated* for psychological disorders in mental institutions and clinics and by practitioners. (The assumption is that the greater the number of treated cases, the greater the psychological disturbance in that group or population.) In the second method, the rate of disorders is obtained for a *sample* of the population through interviews, testing, or the like; the rate for the sample is then used to estimate the rate for the population.

The results of such assessments have so far been conflicting. Most studies of treated cases support the notion that blacks have higher rates of mental disorders than whites. That is, most studies have found that higher relative proportions of blacks than whites are admitted to mental institutions (Fischer 1969). A few investigators have found no difference or have found lower rates among blacks (Thomas and Sillen 1972). These contradictory results may be due to the following conceptual and methodological problems.

1. Treatment rates may not be an accurate indicator of disorder rates, especially in cross-cultural comparisons.
2. Many studies comparing black and white treatment patterns have failed to control for variables such as age, socioeconomic status, or marital status that may confound the effects of race.
3. Because of difficulties in diagnosing individuals who differ culturally, many blacks may be misdiagnosed by white therapists.
4. Stress may result in increased maladjustment or in adjustment, depending on coping skills, resources, and the ability to learn

from negative life experiences (Myers and King 1983).

The second method of assessing disorder rates—sampling the population—has not been used to any great degree in comparing blacks and whites. This may be due to a lack of adequate data and valid measures of psychopathology for use in comparing ethnic groups. In any case, the question of whether blacks and whites have different rates of psychopathology cannot be fully answered on the basis of the currently available data (Dohrenwend and Dohrenwend 1974).

In a survey of psychological distress among 1000 blacks and whites, blacks were found to be more likely than whites to report the presence of psychological symptoms (Neff 1984). However, after the effects of age and social class were removed, the racial differences were largely negligible. This finding suggests that blacks may not have higher rates of mental disorder. Because blacks are overrepresented among the lower socioeconomic classes (which do have higher rates for certain disorders), race and social class effects may often be confounded. Above and beyond social class, the stress experienced by blacks and other ethnic minority groups may result in problems involving alienation, autonomy, and achievement rather than mental disorders.

Reducing racism In 1968 the National Advisory Committee on Civil Disorders noted that

> Of the basic causes [of urban riots of the 1960s], the most fundamental is the racial attitude and behavior of white Americans toward black Americans. Race prejudice has shaped our history decisively; it now threatens our future. White racism is essentially responsible for the explosive mixture that has been accumulating in our cities. (p. 10)

The commission recognized that the history of the United States is intertwined with racial prejudice, and that racism represents a ''sickness'' in our society.

Much has been written about the elimination of racism through legislative, judicial, economic, political, and social changes of one kind or another. Various communitywide or nationwide strategies include

1. The widespread use of educational programs and the mass media to correct racial stereotypes and to provide accurate information on minority groups
2. Increasing the quality of interpersonal and interracial contacts
3. Changing the way people view violence
4. Rewarding nonaggressive responses
5. Legal remedies (Katz 1976)

Psychological approaches to the reduction of prejudice have included self-insight and psychotherapy, socialization practices that are helpful in rearing unbiased children, and role modeling (Allport 1954; Collins 1970).

The primary goal is to change prejudicial attitudes and eliminate discriminatory behaviors. It is possible to change attitudes and behaviors, but the main problem has been to demonstrate that such changes are long-lasting, meaningful rather than superficial, and comprehensive.

Sexism

Sexism is prejudice and discrimination that are directed against either sex. On the basis of employment, income, and education statistics, women qualify as an oppressed group in our society (Grefe 1980). (See also Focus 21.3.) In the field of mental health, studies indicate that a significant number of mental health professionals have allowed sex-role biases, stereotypes, and a double standard of mental health to influence their practice with women clients (APA 1975). Understanding these biases may be the first step toward eliminating them.

The historical view In the sixth century B.C., Pythagoras, the respected Greek philosopher, mathematician, and religious reformer, stated that "There is a good principle which created order, light, and man, and an evil principle which created chaos, darkness, and women" (Morgan 1970, pp. 31–32). This eloquently phrased but nonetheless extremely sexist attitude has prevailed throughout history, with rare exceptions.

The persecution and degradation of women took a bizarre turn during the Inquisition.

FOCUS 21.3

The Status of Women

1. In 1981, more than half of all adult women in the United States were in the labor force. In 1940, that proportion was only about one-sixth.
2. Even among working couples without children, women spend twice as many hours on household chores as do men.
3. The wages of women working at permanent full-time jobs averaged only about 59 percent of the wages paid to men. Women with four or more years of college education received about the same salaries as men with one to three years of high school.
4. In 1982, approximately one in six families was maintained by a woman (41 percent of black families, 23 percent of Hispanic families, and 13 percent of white families were headed by a female). The proportion of poor families headed by women was 47 percent in 1981.

SOURCE: Russo and Denmark (1984).

Malleus Maleficarum (The Witches' Hammer), published in 1487, was a manual written to prove the existence of witchcraft and to specify procedures for the examination and legal sentencing of suspected witches. The book clearly reflects a misogynous orientation:

> All wickedness is but little to the wickedness of a woman . . . they have slippery tongues, and are unable to conceal from their fellow women those things which by evil arts they know . . . since they are feebler both in mind and body it is not surprising that they should come under the spell of witchcraft . . . formed from a rib, which is bent as it were in a contrary direction to a man. . . . Nearly all the kingdoms of the world have been overthrown by women . . . she is a liar by nature . . . a wheedling and secret enemy. (Kraemer and Sprenger 1928, p. 24)

The tract goes on to accuse women of causing male impotence, crop failures, and other types of disasters. Many people were executed as witches during this period, but the ratio of women to men executed was at least six to one in England. It was fifty to one on the continent (Anderson 1972).

The creators of the Inquisition were not the last to persecute and degrade women. Later, in the Age of Enlightenment, Napoleon Bonaparte announced that "Nature intended women to be our slaves . . . they are our property; we are not theirs. . . . What a mad idea to demand equality for women. . . . Women are nothing but machines for producing children" (Morgan 1970, p. 34).

Sex-role stereotyping The values of our society have traditionally affirmed male supremacy. In an industrial, highly technological society such as ours, great value is placed on a person's role in the labor force. Although there has been a great increase in the number of women in the labor force, especially in the last two decades, this increase has mainly affected the jobs that are customarily held by women—secretarial, retail sales, and elementary school teaching. Some feel that inborn

differences in competencies between men and women justify differential sex roles. Yet there is substantial evidence that sex differences in cognitive abilities are actually quite small (Deaux 1984). In the Soviet Union, one-third of the engineers and three-fourths of the physicians are women.

Children are usually reared in accordance with sex-role stereotypes from birth. A sex-role preference can be observed by age three and is well established by age five (Williams 1977). Boys are taught to be aggressive, competitive, and independent; girls are encouraged to be passive and dependent. There is even more explicit sex-role training as children grow older. By the ninth grade, 25 percent of boys but only 3 percent of girls are considering careers in science or engineering (Bem and Bem 1970). Sex-role standards usually stress that a female should feel needed and desired by a man; standards for males emphasize independence and the ability to dominate others.

The effectiveness of such socialization practices was illustrated in a national survey in which eight personality characteristics had to be attributed to either males or females. Eighty percent of the respondents said that four of the traits (aggressiveness, independence, objectivity, and mathematical reasoning) were typically male while the remaining traits (nurturance, empathy, monogamy, and emotionality) were typically female (Tavris 1972). In another study, aging men were seen as becoming more *mature,* distinguished, and respected. Older women, however, were seen as becoming sexually undesirable, unattractive, powerless, and *old* (Nutt 1979).

Men are thought to be more influential than women, and women more easily influenced. In one experiment, subjects were given written scenarios describing two employees (male and female), one of whom was trying to persuade the other on a policy issue. Subjects rated the female as more likely than the male to be influenced by the attempt to persuade. They also inferred that the man in the scenario had a higher-status job than the woman, although no information was provided about job statuses. However, when job titles (a high-status and a low-status title) were assigned to the hypothetical employees, subjects felt that the low-status person would be more compliant than the high-status person, regardless of sex (Eagly 1983). This finding emphasizes the importance of status and implies an effect on behavior: The stereotypes that convey a low-status image for women also create expectations about how women should perform. Men and women then may perform in accordance with these expectations. However, such expectations are more likely to affect performance on interactive and interpersonal tasks than on less social and more individualistic tasks (Deaux 1984).

Like many others, mental health professionals have been found to engage in sex-role stereotyping. However, that practice appears to be moderating (Hare-Mustin 1983). It seems to be due, at least in part, to a lack of knowledge or misinformation that therapists have about women's problems. If this is indeed the case, more accurate information, along with education and training, may eventually eliminate it altogether. Meanwhile, as we are about to see, sex-role stereotyping in the mental health professions does have implications for the mental health of women.

Sexism and mental health   Many studies have shown that most patients in therapy are women (Chesler 1976; Gove and Tudor 1973; Kulka 1982). The role of patient is highly consistent with a female sex role that is characterized by weakness, dependency, irrationality, and acceptance of care (Williams 1977).

Relative to the incidence of physical and medical illnesses among women and men, women are the more likely to seek medical and psychiatric help (Chesler 1971). This again might be explained in terms of socialization; a woman's sex role permits her to seek help, whereas males may consider it ''unmasculine'' to do so. As a group, women are not more prone to mental disorders than men, except for some specific disorders such as depression. They are also less prone to some disorders, including antisocial personality (Myers et al. 1984).

Especially critical to an understanding of the mental health of women is recognizing the value that society (including mental health professionals) places on the different behaviors that are approved for the sexes. An early study suggests that many clinicians view their patients in a very traditional manner (Broverman and Broverman 1970). Therapists were asked to complete a questionnaire on sex-role stereotypes in which a healthy male, a healthy female, and a healthy adult were rated in terms of 122 antonymous (opposite) pairs of traits. There was high agreement among the clinicians on their ratings, and there were no major differences between male and female clinicians. The results indicated that there is a double standard of mental health for males and females. A healthy male was described and rated in the same terms as a healthy adult. The healthy female was described differently from both, with such terms as *submissive, emotional, easily influenced, sensitive to hurt, excitable, conceited about appearance, dependent, less competitive, unaggressive,* and *unobjective*. This study has powerful implications. When the traits that are said to characterize a healthy woman are considered socially undesirable for a healthy adult, it is not the least bit surprising that women are more likely to seek therapy!

The DSM-III diagnostic system has been criticized as being biased in that females may be diagnosed as being disturbed for acting ''out of line''—that is, for not acting like women (Kaplan 1983). On the other hand, DSM-III has been defended by others as being unbiased (Williams and Spitzer 1983). At this point there is no evidence that DSM-III should be considered a sex-biased system. However, this does not mean that every category within the diagnostic system is unbiased and accurate. The value of criticism is to encourage continuing research into the validity of all the DSM-III categories and critieria as they apply to both men and women.

Reducing sexism As is true for racism, the elimination of sexism requires ambitious psychological, educational, and legal efforts—in this case aimed at correcting sex biases, sexual stereotypes, and inequities. To change the image of women that is conveyed through the mass media alone is a massive undertaking, fortunately already underway. Making the educational system more responsive to the concerns and needs of women is another primary goal. For victims of sexual harassment, legal redress is possible; many employers have now developed guidelines for determining and eliminating harassment (Livingston 1982). In the mental health field, counselors and therapists have available a publication of the American Psychological Association outlining "Principles Concerning the Counseling and Therapy of Women" (Ad Hoc Committee on Women 1979). It includes specific recommendations to help therapists confront their own sexism in a way that will enhance their ability to help women clients.

SUMMARY

1. Community psychology is concerned with the influence of community and environmental forces on human behavior and with the use of these forces as resources to alleviate human problems. Community psychology grew out of dissatisfaction with the inability of the treatment approach to care for the large number of disturbed persons, with the biogenic or disease model of psychopathology, with the ineffectiveness of psychiatric hospitals, and with inequities in the delivery of mental health services.

2. As a result of this dissatisfaction, community mental health centers were initiated in the 1960s. These centers are located in many communities and are accessible to the surrounding population. They offer a wide range of services including outpatient and short-term inpatient care, consultation, emergency services, and partial hospitalization. Despite the lack of adequate financial support and of more community involvement in some centers, they are a major mental health resource.

3. One of the goals of community psychology is the prevention of mental disorders. This prevention takes three forms. Primary prevention (reducing the incidence of new cases) is an attempt to introduce new resources and reduce stressors. Secondary prevention is an attempt to reduce the duration or severity of a disorder through early detection and prompt treatment. Tertiary prevention is an attempt to reduce the disabling effects of a disorder by facilitating the adjustment and early return to the community of those who have experienced mental disorders.

4. To alleviate the shortage of professional mental health personnel, psychologists have begun to train paraprofessionals or laypersons to act as therapeutic agents. In this way psychologists can take advantage of the knowledge and experience of community members and can combat the reluctance of some persons to enter therapy with unfamiliar mental health professionals.

5. Community psychologists have expanded their influence on the commmunity by becoming more involved in consultation and education. In their role as consultants, psychologists can help community agencies, businesses, schools, courts, or individuals to be more informed about and responsive to mental health needs and more effective in encouraging mental health.

6. Some believe that the prevention of mental disorders in the community requires that environmental forces and resources be controlled or modified. This approach, however, raises the controversial question of whether mental health professionals should become active in the social or political arena in order to effect major changes in mental health.

7. Social supports, too, have been explored as a tool for fostering adjustment and for preventing disorders. They may act as a buffer against stress.

8. Racism and sexism are community problems that have an effect on mental health. Racism is manifested in a lower standard of living for racial minorities (Asian–Americans, blacks, Hispanics, and native Americans). It can cause some people to believe that they are inferior and to feel racial self-hatred. The development of feelings of racial pride and identity is necessary to reverse this negative attitude. Women, like members of racial minorities, represent an oppressed group in our society. Historically, women have been subordinated and controlled through sex-role stereotyping. Studies reveal that some therapists allow sex-role biases, stereotypes, and a double standard of mental health to influence their practice with women clients. The elimination of racism and sexism will not be an easy task. Proposed strategies include using educational programs to correct stereotyping, increasing the quality of interracial contacts, changing perceptual processes, using the mass media for change, using rewards, and instituting legal remedies.

In this book we have explored research, theory, and clinical case examples in an attempt to help you understand the symptoms, nature, possible causes, and treatment of behavioral disorders. Although tremendous advances have been made in our understanding of abnormal behavior and the means that can be used to relieve human distress, we still have far to go. Mental health professionals are in a key position to add to this body of knowledge and to improve on methods of therapy. They are also very dependent on the support of individuals in the community, who can help them overcome popular misconceptions about mental health and reach those who need their services.

KEY TERMS

community mental health centers Centrally located mental health facilities that provide a number of services to individuals within medium-sized communities; more comprehensive alternative to hospitalization

community psychology An approach to mental health that takes into account the influence of environmental factors and stresses the use of community resources to eliminate various conditions that produce psychological problems

paraprofessional therapists Persons who are taught by professionals to provide some mental health services but who do not have formal mental health training

primary prevention An effort to lower the incidence of new cases of behavioral disorders by strengthening resources that promote mental health and eliminating features that threaten mental health

secondary prevention An attempt to shorten the duration of mental disorders and to reduce their impact

social supports The availability and quality of interpersonal resources that individuals can call on during emotional distress

tertiary prevention Efforts to facilitate readjustment of the individual to community life after hospital treatment for a mental disturbance

therapeutic community A hospital environment in which all activities are structured to have a therapeutic function and in which patients participate to the degree that is possible

Glossary

abnormal behavior Behavior that departs from some norm and is detrimental to the affected individual or to others

abnormal psychology The scientific study whose objectives are to describe, explain, predict, and control behaviors that are considered strange or unusual

action-oriented therapy Therapies that base treatment on classical conditioning, operant conditioning, observational learning, and cognitive-behavioral processes

adjustment disorders Reactive disorders resulting from the common stressors of everyday life, such as illness and marital conflicts

adjustment disorder with work (academic inhibition) Current problems with work or academic performance in a person whose past performance was adequate

affect Emotion or mood

affective disorders Severe disturbances of mood in which depression is almost always the primary event

age regression The hypnotic process in which patients are told that they are reliving their childhood at a specific age and that their thoughts, speech, and actions will reflect this age

agoraphobia An intense fear of open spaces or of being alone where help may not be available; in extreme cases, a fear of leaving one's home

alcohol amnestic disorder A syndrome sometimes found in chronic alcoholics in which the individual displays a loss of memory of recent events and fills in memory gaps with false or fanciful accounts

alcohol hallucinosis Auditory hallucinations that occur in some alcoholics when they abruptly cease alcohol consumption; similar to delirium tremens

alcohol idiosyncratic intoxication A condition in which an acute behavior change takes place after the ingestion of a small amount of alcohol

alcoholism Substance dependence in which the substance used is alcohol

alexia Inability to understand written words; visual aphasia

altruistic suicide Suicide that is motivated by the need to further group goals or to achieve some greater good

Alzheimer's disease An organic brain disorder that involves the atrophy of brain tissue and leads to marked deterioration of intellectual and emotional functioning

amnesia The partial or total loss of memory due to either organic or psychological causes

amniocentesis A procedure in which a hollow needle is inserted through the abdominal wall and into the amniotic sac to draw out fluid containing fetal cells

amphetamines Drugs that speed up central nervous system activity and produce increased alertness, energy, and euphoria; also known as "uppers"

anal retentive personality In Freudian theory, a stubborn, stingy, and constantly procrastinating character, caused by childhood conflict with parents over toilet training

anal sadistic phase In Freudian theory, a childhood revolt against authority characterized by the expulsion of feces or gas from the bowels at inappropriate times; fixation at this phase may produce an *obsessive-compulsive* adult

anal stage In Freudian theory, the stage during the second year of life in which the anal region becomes the focus of pleasurable sensations

anomic suicide Suicide that results from a maladaptive relation to society

anorexia nervosa An eating disorder in which the affected individual is intensely fearful of becoming obese and engages in self-starvation

antabuse Drug that produces an aversion to alcohol

anterograde amnesia Loss of memory for very recent or immediately preceding events

antidepressant drugs Drugs that relieve depression by elevating mood; include iproniazid, phenelzine, and imipramine

antisocial personality A type of delinquency characterized by impulsivity, inability to delay gratifi-

632

cation, inability to profit from punishment or experience, and lack of guilt

antisocial personality disorder A personality disorder characterized by failure to conform to social and legal norms, superficial relationships with others, and lack of guilt feelings for wrongdoing

anxiety Feelings of fear and apprehension

anxiety disorders Disorders (panic disorder, generalized anxiety disorders, phobias, and obsessive-compulsive disorders) whose major characteristics are irrational feelings of fear and apprehension

aphasia Loss of motor or sensory functions that are associated with language

aphonia Loss of speech

arrythmia Irregular heartbeat

assertiveness training Therapy that uses behavioral techniques to help individuals become better able to assert or express themselves

assessment With regard to psychopathology, the process of gathering information and drawing conclusions about the traits, skills, abilities, emotional functioning, and psychological problems of an individual

asthma A respiratory disorder characterized by attacks in which breathing becomes extremely difficult because of constriction of the airways in the lungs

atherosclerosis Narrowing of the blood vessels due to a buildup of fatty material on their interior walls

attention deficit disorder A disorder of childhood and adolescence characterized by short attention span, impulsivity, constant activity, and lack of self-control

autistic savant Autistic child having unusual abilities or special talents

autonomic nervous system The part of the nervous system that controls involuntary functions and bodily changes during emotional states; composed of the sympathetic and parasympathetic systems

autonomic response specificity The concept that each individual has a unique physiological reaction to all types of stressful situations

autosome Nonsex chromosome

aversive behavior rehearsal (ABR) An aversive conditioning treatment for exhibitionism that uses shame or humiliation as the aversive stimulus

aversive conditioning A classical conditioning technique in which an undesirable behavior is paired with a noxious stimulus in order to suppress the undesirable behavior

aversion therapy A conditioning procedure in which the attractiveness of a stimulus is decreased by pairing it with an aversive stimulus

avoidant personality disorder A personality disorder characterized by a fear of rejection and humiliation, and a resultant reluctance to enter into social relationships

barbiturates Addictive drugs that depress central nervous system activity and are used to induce relaxation and sleep; downers

baseline In behavior therapy, the initial level of responses emitted by the individual

being An existential concept referring to the awareness that human beings have of their own existence; this awareness makes people responsible for choosing their own direction in life

being-in-the-world An existential concept referring to the awareness that human beings exist in the context of a ''world'' of meaningful relationships with other human beings and with nature

behavioral medicine An interdisciplinary field concerned with the integration of behavioral and biomedical science, knowledge, and techniques relevant to health and illness

behavioral models Theories of psychopathology that are concerned with the role of learning in abnormal behavior

behavioral repertoire The range of responses an individual has learned to make in each given situation

Bender-Gestalt Visual-Motor Test A test used to assess visual-motor integration skills; can detect neurological impairment

biofeedback therapy A therapeutic approach in which a patient receives information about particular autonomic functions and is rewarded for influencing those functions in a desired direction

biofeedback training A therapeutic technique in which the individual is taught to voluntarily control a particular physiological function, such as heart rate or blood pressure

biogenic model The theory or expectation that every mental disorder has an organic basis and cure

biogenic view The belief or theory that mental disorders have a physical or physiological basis

biological stressors Physical conditions, such as infections, trauma, malnutrition, and fatigue, that can produce stress

bipolar disorder An affective disorder in which both depression and mania are exhibited, or one in which only mania has been exhibited

borderline personality disorder A personality disorder characterized by intense fluctuations in mood, self-image, and interpersonal relationships

bradycardia Slowing-down of the heartrate

brain pathology Dysfunction or disease of the brain

brain trauma Physical wound or injury to the brain

brief reactive psychosis A psychotic disorder due to a stressor that lasts from only a few hours to two weeks

bulimia An eating disorder characterized by the rapid consumption of large quantities of food, usually followed by self-induced vomiting

caffeine Stimulant found in coffee, tea, and cola drinks

case study Intensive study of one individual that relies on observation, psychological tests, and historical and biographical data

castration anxiety In Freudian theory, the fear in males that they will be punished for their forbidden oedipal desires by suffering the loss of their penis

catatonic schizophrenia A schizophrenic disorder characterized by extreme agitation and excitement or extreme withdrawal and lack of responsiveness

catecholamines Neurotransmitter substances that are implicated in states of arousal and mood states

cathartic method The therapeutic use of verbal expression to release pent-up unconscious conflicts

central nervous system The brain and the spinal cord

cerebral blood flow measurement A technique for assessing brain damage in which the patient inhales a radioactive gas and the movement of the substance is followed throughout the brain

cerebral cortex The outermost layer of the cerebrum, which is involved in higher mental processes

cerebral tumor A mass of abnormal tissue growing within the brain

cerebrovascular accident A sudden stoppage of blood flow to a portion of the brain, leading to loss of brain function; stroke

cerebrum The largest structure in the brain; the seat of human consciousness and of all learning, speech, thought, and memory

chemotherapy A drug treatment for mental disorder

child abuse Physical or psychological mistreatment of a child, carried out by parents, adult relatives, or other adult caretakers and resulting in physical or psychological trauma that can produce a variety of disorders, among them mental retardation

childhood-onset pervasive developmental disorder Profound disturbances in social relations and multiple oddities of behavior manifested between the ages of 2½ and 12 years

chromosomal anomaly Abnormality or irregularity that produces inherited defects or vunerabilities such as Down's syndrome or PKU

classical conditioning An associative learning process through which neutral stimuli become able to evoke involuntary responses

classification system With regard to psychopathology, a system of mutually exclusive categories, indicators, and nomenclature for distinct patterns of behavior, thought processes, and emotional reactions

clinical psychology The professional field concerned with the study, assessment, treatment, and prevention of abnormal behavior in disturbed individuals

cocaine Drug which induces feelings of euphoria and self-confidence in users; usually inhaled into the nasal cavity

cognition The process of thinking, perceiving, judging, and recognizing

cognitive behavioral therapy A therapy approach directed toward helping clients to restructure their thoughts and to reinterpret environmental inputs and internal stimulation

cognitive behaviorism A learning theory that mental processes mediate, or modify, an individual's behavior in response to a stimulus

cognitive restructuring A form of therapy in which the client's cognitions are changed from irrational, self-defeating, and distorted thoughts and attitudes to more rational, positive, and appropriate ones

cognitive slippage The continual shifting of thoughts from topic to topic without any apparent logical or meaningful connection among topics (see also *loosening of associations*)

collective unconscious A term devised by Jung that refers to ancient, primordial memories common to all humanity

combat neurosis Mental problems in soldiers produced by prolonged exposure to combat

community mental health centers Centrally located mental health facilities that provide a number of psychological services to individuals within medium-sized communities; a more comprehensive alternative to hospitalization

community psychology An approach to mental health that takes into account the influence of environmental factors and stresses the use of community resources to eliminate conditions that produce psychological problems

competence to stand trial The legal requirement that a defendent must be able to understand the charges brought against him and the relevant facts and legal issues before he can stand trial

compulsion An involuntary impulse to perform a particular act repeatedly

compulsive personality disorder A personality disorder characterized by perfectionism, indecision, devotion to details, and lack of personal warmth

computerized axial tomography (CAT) scanning Neurological test for the assessment of brain damage

concordance rate The likelihood that both of a pair of subjects exhibit the feature that is being studied

conduct disorders Disorders of childhood and adolescence that involve a persistent pattern of antisocial behaviors that violate the rights of others

concussion A mild brain injury often involving the rupture of blood vessels, typically caused by a blow to the head

conditioned response (CR) In classical conditioning, a response similar to an unconditioned response that is elicited by a conditioned stimulus

conditioned stimulus (CS) In classical conditioning, a formerly neutral stimulus that acquires some of the properties of an unconditioned stimulus through a temporal association with it

confabulation Filling memory gaps with false or fanciful accounts that the individual believes are true

congenital Present from birth but not inherited

conjoint family therapy A type of family therapy in which family members are taught message-sending and message-receiving skills

conscience In Freudian theory, the component of the *superego* that inculcates guilt feelings about engaging in immoral or unethical behavior

consultation Working with and through community institutions such as police, schools, the courts, or corporations to help individuals in the community

contingency Relationship, usually causal, between two events in which one is usually followed by the other

control group A group exposed to the same conditions as the experimental group with the exception of the independent variable

controlled drinking A treatment for alcoholism whose goal is to teach alcoholics to control their intake and become social drinkers, rather than to abstain entirely

contusion A brain injury in which the brain shifts slightly and presses against the skull

conversion disorder A somatoform disorder in which there is significant impairment of organic function without an underlying physical cause (also known as *conversion reaction*)

coping skills training A form of cognitive behavioral therapy aimed at helping clients learn to manage or overcome stress

coping strategies Cognitive and behavioral skills used in stressful situations to reduce the stress

coprolalia A compulsion to shout obscenities; a symptom of Tourette's syndrome

coronary heart disease A cardiovascular disease in which the flow of blood and oxygen to the heart is restricted by a narrowing of the arteries in or near the heart

corpus callosum A collection of nerve fibers that connect the two hemispheres of the cerebrum

correlation The degree to which two variables covary or are associated with each other

counseling psychology A professional field similar to *clinical psychology*, but usually more concerned with the study of life problems in relatively normal people

counterconditioning A therapeutic means of eliminating anxiety by gradually pairing the fear-producing stimulus with an antagonistic response, such as relaxation

countertransference A process during psychotherapy in which feelings that the *therapist* had toward significant others (primarily parents) in the past are transferred to the patient; therapist must recognize and control this process

covert sensitization An aversive conditioning procedure in which patients are asked to imagine unpleasant consequences occuring after engaging in undesirable but tempting behavior

cretinism (hypothyroidism) A genetically produced metabolic disorder that can cause mental retardation; also caused by iodine deficiency in the mother during pregnancy

criminal insanity A legal term referring either to a criminal's unawareness that he had committed a crime or incomprehension that it was wrong to do so because of a mental disturbance

cultural-familial retardation Generally mild mental retardation thought to be produced through normal genetic processes, by environmental factors, or by both

cyclothymic disorders Mild affective disorders characterized by extreme mood swings of non-psychotic intensity

death instincts In Freudian theory, the drive for the biological death of the organism, used to explain phenomena such as war and suicide; Thanatos

decompensation Loss of the ability to deal successfully with stress

defense mechanism In Freudian theory, the unconscious and automatic means by which the ego is protected from anxiety-provoking conflicts

deinstitutionalization The shifting of responsibility for the care of mental patients from large central institutions to agencies within local communities

delusion A false belief that is firmly and consistently held despite disconfirming evidence or logic

delusion system An internally coherent, systematized pattern of delusions

dementia A syndrome characterized by the deterioration of intellectual ability and impaired judgment of sufficient severity to interfere with social and occupational functioning

demonology The belief, commonly held by ancient peoples, that both mental and physical disorders are caused by the influence of supernatural forces

dependent personality disorder A personality disorder characterized by extreme reliance on others and unwillingness to assume responsibility

dependent variable In a experiment, the variable that changes with the introduction of the independent variable

depersonalization disorder A dissociative disorder in which there are feelings of unreality or distortion concerning the self or the environment

depression An emotional state characterized by intense sadness, feelings of futility and worthlessness, and withdrawal from others

detoxification A treatment aimed at removing all alcohol (or other substance) from a user's body and insuring that none is ingested

developmental aphasia A childhood speech disorder; children may exhibit *echolalia* or be completely mute

developmental arithmetic disorder A significant impairment in the development of arithmetic skills not accounted for by chronological age or inadequate schooling

developmental study A long-term study beginning before the onset of a disorder that allows investigators to see how the disorder develops

diaschisis A condition in which a lesion in one specific area of the brain disrupts other anatomically intact areas

diathesis–stress theory The theory that a predisposition to develop mental illness is inherited or acquired, and that this predisposition may or may not be activated by environmental factors

diminished mental responsibility See *criminal insanity*

disaster syndrome A hypothesized series of phases an individual goes through when exposed to disaster

discriminative stimulus A stimulus that, through its presence or absence, indicates the likelihood of reinforcement

diseases of adaptation Diseases, such as ulcers or hypertension, that result from long-term stress (according to the general adaptation syndrome model)

disorganized schizophrenia A schizophrenic disorder (beginning at an early age) characterized by severe distintegration and absurd and incoherent behaviors

disorientation A state of confusion with regard to identity, place, or time

displacement A defense mechanism in which an individual's negative emotions are expressed toward a substitute target

dissociative disorders Mental disorders characterized by alteration or disruption of the individual's identity or consciousness; include psychogenic amnesia, psychogenic fugue, depersonalization disorder, and multiple personality disorder

dizygotic (DZ) twins (fraternal) Twins from two separate eggs; such twins share about 50 percent of the same genes

dopamine A catecholamine neurotransmitter substance

dopamine hypothesis The theory that schizophrenia results from an excess of dopamine at certain brain synapses

double-bind theory The suggestion that schizophrenia develops in an individual as a result of the continual reception of contradictory messages from parents during the individual's upbringing

Down's syndrome (mongolism) A condition produced by the presence of an extra chromosome (*trisomy 21*), resulting in mental retardation and distinctive physical characteristics

DSM I, II, III The diagnostic and statistical manuals of mental disorders published by the American Psychiatric Association; contain the diagnostic categories and criteria for differential diagnosis of abnormal behavior

dyspareunia Painful coitus in males or females

dysthymic disorder A mild affective disorder characterized by extended periods of nonpsychotic depression

echolalia Echoing what has previously been said; a symptom of autism and other disorders

eclectic approach An openness to all models of abnormal behavior, along with a willingness to borrow and integrate techniques from all approaches and to use them selectively with clients

eclecticism In treatment and diagnosis, selection of concepts, methods, and strategies from a variety of current theories in a systematic fashion

ego In Freudian theory, the part of the personality that mediates between instinctual urges and the environment

ego-dystonic Unacceptable to the ego

ego-dystonic homosexuality Homosexuality that is unacceptable to the ego and is thus a source of distress

ego ideal In Freudian theory, the part of the superego that rewards altruistic or moral behavior with feelings of pride

egoistic sucide Suicide that results from an inability to integrate oneself with society

ego psychologists Followers of Anna Freud and Erik Erikson who accept Freud's three-part division of the personality, but believe the ego is independent of the sexual and aggressive drives

ego weakness In Freudian theory, a state during sleep or times of excessive fatigue when the ego's guard over repressed desires is relaxed and unconscious impulses often seep out

ejaculation In males, the expulsion of semen during orgasm

Electra complex In Freudian theory, a daughter's feelings of possessive love for the father that occur during the phallic stage

electrical brain stimulation Stimulating specific areas of the brain with an electric current through electrodes implanted directly in the brain; a possible treatment for epilepsy

electroconvulsive therapy The application of an electrical voltage to the brain to induce convulsions and thereby reduce depression

electroencephalograph (EEG) A neurological test for the assessment of brain damage

encephalitis Inflammation of the brain caused by viral infection that produces symptoms of lethargy, fever, and long periods of stupor and sleep; sleeping sickness

encounter groups Group therapy designed to facilitate human growth and development by encouraging freedom of expression and reduction of defensiveness

endogenous Internal; within the body

endogenous depression A depression that is caused largely by internal, chemical imbalances

enuresis Bed-wetting

epilepsy Any disorder characterized by intermittent and brief periods of altered consciousness, often accompanied by seizures, and excessive electrical discharge from brain cells

erectile dysfunction Inability of a male to attain or maintain a penile erection sufficient for sexual intercourse

essential hypertension High blood pressure with no known organic cause

etiology The causes or origins of a disorder

eustress Any kind of stress that is good for people; a concept developed by Hans Selye

exhibitionism A disorder in which sexual gratification is obtained through the exposure of the genitals to strangers

existential analysis A therapeutic approach that is concerned with the person's experience and involvement in the world

existential approach The belief that contemporary society has a dehumanizing affect, that mental disorders result from a conflict between the essential human nature and the demands made on people by themselves and others

existential crisis A state in which individuals feel lonely and alienated and lose a sense of the meaning of life, of self-responsibility, and of free will

exogenous External; outside the body

exogenous depression A depression that is due largely to environmental or external causes

exorcism The procedures, such as prayers or flogging, that were used to cast evil sprits out of the body of an afflicted individual

experiencing The facet of psychotherapy in which the client experiences emotions that he or she may have avoided because of the painful or helpless feelings they fostered

experiment A technique of scientific inquiry in which an independent variable is manipulated, the changes in a dependent variable are measured, and extraneous variables are controlled

experimental group In an experiment, a group that is exposed to the independent variable

exposure A therapeutic technique in which a client is gradually introduced to an increasingly fear-arousing situation

external validity The degree to which the results of an experiment may be generalized

extinction In classical and operant conditioning, the process by which a respose is gradually eliminated by not being reinforced

extraneous variable A variable not being tested or controlled that influences the outcome of a study; a source of error in an experiment

factitious disorders Deliberately self-induced or simulated physical or mental condition

family counseling A professional field of psychology focusing on relationships within the family

family dynamics Everyday patterns of operation in a family system, including communication among its members

family system model A theory of psychopathology which emphasizes the influence of the family on individual behavior

family therapy A group therapy characterized by the attempt to modify relationships within the family so as to achieve harmony

fetal alcohol syndrome A group of symptoms, including mental retardation and physical defects, that are produced in the infant by the ingestion of alcohol (by the mother) during pregnancy

fetishism A disorder characterized by an extremely strong sexual attraction for a particular nongenital part of the anatomy or for an inanimate object

field study An investigative technique in which behaviors are observed and recorded in the natural environment

fixation In Freudian theory, the arresting of emotional development at a particular psychosexual stage due to either overgratification or insufficient gratification at that developmental level

flagellantism A form of mass madness involving self-inflicted whipping

flat affect Abnormal lack of emotional response

flooding A therapeutic technique that involves continued *in vivo* or imagined exposure to a fear-arousing stituation

folie à deux A condition in which delusional beliefs are shared by two or more individuals

forcible rape An act of sexual intercourse that is accomplished through force or the threat of force

free association A psychoanalytic method during which the patient says whatever comes to mind, regardless of how illogical or embarrassing it may seem; the material is thought to represent the contents of the patient's unconscious

free-floating anxiety Pervasive anxiety without an identifiable external source

functional disorder A mental disorder for which no physical basis can be found and which is assumed to be due primarily to psychological factors

gender identity disorder A psychological disorder characterized by conflict between an individual's anatomical sex and his or her sexual identity

general adaptation syndrome (GAS) A model for understanding the body's physical and psychological reaction to biological stressors

general paresis Damage to the brain as a result of untreated syphilis

generalization The phenomenon of responding to stimuli that are similar to a conditioned stimulus

generalized anxiety disorders Disorders characterized by persistent high levels of anxiety in situations where no real danger is present

genital stage In Freudian theory, the psychosexual stage beginning at puberty during which true heterosexual rather than narcissistic love can develop

genotype The genetic component of a trait or characteristic

gestalt A German word that means whole

gestalt therapy A humanistic-existential approach to therapy developed by Fritz Perls that emphasizes the client's awareness of the "here and now" and his or her totality of experience with the present

grand mal seizure The most severe and dramatic form of epilepsy; involves violent contractions, relaxation of body muscles, and loss of consciousness

group therapy A form of therapy that involves the simultaneous treatment of two or more clients

half-way house A program that provides deinstitutionalized patients with a support system while they learn or redevelop skills they will need if they are to function in the community

hallucinations Sensory perceptions not directly attributable to environmental stimuli

hallucinogens Drugs that produce hallucinations, more vivid sensory awareness, or increased insight

Halstead-Reitan Neuropsychological Test Battery A series of tests used to differentiate brain-damaged from non-brain-damaged patients, and to locate areas of damage

hardiness factor A concept developed by Kobasa and Maddi that refers to an individual's ability to deal well with stress

historical research The systematic and objective reconstruction of some aspect of the past by use of the evidence available in historical documents

histrionic personality disorder A personality disorder characterized by self-dramatization, the exaggerated expression of emotion, and attention-seeking behaviors

homeostasis A state of physiological, psychological, or emotional equilibrium produced by a balance of functions and chemical composition within the individual

homeostatic Maintaining conditions to insure a constant level of physiological functioning

homosexuality Sexual preference for members of one's own sex

humanism An emphasis on human welfare and on the worth and uniqueness of the individual

humanistic-existential therapy A therapy that stresses the importance of self-growth, self-concept, free will, and responsibility; includes person-centered therapy, existential analysis, and gestalt therapy

humanistic perspective The optimistic viewpoint that people are born with the ability to fulfill their potential, and that abnormal behavior results from disharmony between the person's potential and self-concept

Huntington's chorea A genetically transmitted degenerative disease involving personality changes, depression, delusion, and a loss of control over bodily functions

hyperactive Restless, distractable, and having a short attention span (with reference to a childhood syndrome; sometimes accompanied by attention deficit disorder)

hypnotherapy The use of hypnosis as an adjunct to psychotherapy to help patients seeking relief from psychological problems and wishing to change

hypnotism An induced state of narrowed perception in which the individual becomes highly suggestible

hypochondriasis A somatoform disorder characterized by persistent and strong preoccupation with one's health and physical condition

hypomania Mild form of manic reaction in which affected individuals seem to be high-spirited and are overactive in their behaviors

hypotension Low blood pressure

hypothalamus Part of the brain in the subcortex concerned with the regulation of bodily activities such as hunger, sex, temperature, and hormone balance

hypothesis A conjectural statement that describes a relationship between variables

hysteria The appearance of physical symptoms that seem to have no organic basis

id In Freudian theory, the part of the personality that is subjective, impulsive, selfish, and pleasure-seeking

identification In Freudian theory, resolution of the Oedipal conflict through adoption of the values or mannerisms of the same-sex parent

identity disorder Severe anxiety over the inability to develop a psychological sense of self-identity; an inability to establish goals or choose a career; uncertainty about friendship patterns, values, and loyalties

idiographic orientation An approach that stresses the in-depth study of individuals in order to discover the unique factors that account for individual differences

implosive therapy A treatment in which great anxiety is aroused in patients by having them imagine anxiety-producing scenes, while escape from the anxiety is made impossible

incest Sexual relations between close relatives

independent variable In an experiment, the factor that is manipulated so as to observe its effect on the dependent variable

individual psychology An approach to psychoanalysis developed by Alfred Alder that deemphasizes biological drives in favor of social drives

infantile autism A severe childhood disorder characterized by an extreme lack of interest in interpersonal relationships, muteness or unusual language development, and onset before the age of 30 months

infarction Death of brain tissue due to a decrease in the blood supply

inhibited orgasm A sexual dysfunction in which the individual is unable to achieve orgasm during coitus with adequate stimulation after entering the excitement phase of the sexual response cycle

inhibited sexual desire A sexual dysfunction involving a lack of sexual interest as reflected in low levels of sexual activity and fantasizing

inhibited sexual excitement A sexual dysfunction characterized by erectile dysfunction in males or by an inability to attain or sustain arousal in females

insight The ability to understand the basis of one's motivations, perceptions, and behavior

instinct An unlearned behavior pattern

insulin shock treatment An early treatment for schizophrenia in which insulin was injected into the patient, causing convulsions and a coma

intelligence quotient (IQ) A number used to express a person's relative intelligence as assessed by a standardized test, such as the Stanford-Binet or Wechsler scales

internal validity In an experiment, the extent to which changes in the dependent variable are actually brought about by the independent variable rather than by extraneous variables

interpretation An explanation of the patient's free associations, reports of dreams, etc.; used to help the patient gain insight into his or her repressed conflicts

introjection In Freudian theory, the process by which a depressed person identifies with the faults of the loved one he or she has lost

introversion–extroversion A personality dimension; introverts are inhibited, less sociable, and quick to learn; extroverts are more sociable, impulsive, and slow to learn

in vivo Taking place in actuality, rather than in the imagination

involuntary commitment The hospitalization of persons judged to be mentally disturbed and dangerous or incapacitated, without their consent

Jacksonian seizures A form of epileptic seizure in which a twitch develops in one part of the body and spreads; loss of consciousness does not usually occur

Klinefelter syndrome A disorder in males caused by an excessive number of X chromosomes, somtimes causing mental retardation

Korsakoff's disease See *alcohol amnestic disorder*

lacerations Brain traumas in which brain tissue is torn, pierced, or ruptured, usually by an object that has penetrated the skull

latency stage In Freudian theory, the psychosexual stage that occurs between six and twelve years of age and is generally devoid of sexual motivation

lead poisoning A postnatal cause of retardation produced by an infant's ingestion of lead-based or lead-containing substances

libido In Freudian theory, the energy of the id, often associated with the sexual drive

life-change model A model for understanding the cumulative effects of changes in an individual's life, which act as stressors on the individual

life instincts In Freudian theory, the drives associated with sex and self-preservation; Eros

limbic system The part of the brain involved with experiencing and expressing emotions

lobotomy Severing of the fibers between the frontal lobes and the thalamus or hypothalamus

longitudinal fissure Separation between the left and right hemispheres of the brain

loosening of associations Continual shifting of thoughts from topic to topic without any apparent logical or meaningful connection among topics (see also *cognitive slippage*)

Luria-Nebraska Neuropsychological Battery An inexpensive standardized test used in screening for brain damage and in pinpointing damaged areas

lycanthropy A form of hysteria that historically occurred in rural areas, in which individuals believed themselves to be wolves

lysergic acid diethylamide (LSD) A strong hallucinogen

major depression A major affective disorder in which only depression and not mania has been exhibited (see also *unipolar disorders*)

major tranquilizers Antipsychotic drugs, such as the phenothiazines

malingering Faking an illness to obtain a goal

mania An emotional state characterized by great elation, seemingly boundless energy, and irritability

manic-depressive The term formerly used for *bipolar disorder*

marijuana The mildest and most commonly used hallucinogen; pot

marital schism An antagonistic marital relationship characterized by threats of separation and divorce, mutual distrust, and attempts to coerce the children into siding with one parent or the other

marital skew A marriage in which the serious pathology of one parent dominates the home

marriage counseling A professional field of psychology concerned with improving interaction and communication between husband and wife

masochism A sexual disorder in which erotic or sexual gratification is obtained by receiving pain or punishment

mass madness Hysterical reactions in which groups of people are collectively afflicted with a similar disorder

medical model A model of psychopathology that conceptualizes abnormal behavior in the same way as physical disorder

meiosis The process by which the 23 pairs of chromosomes in each parent separate so that the egg and sperm contain only 23 chromosomes each

melancholia Biologically caused depression characterized by loss of pleasure in all activities, weight loss, and guilt

meningitis Inflammation of the membrane surrounding the brain and spinal cord; can produce cerebral infarction and seizures

mental disorder (or mental disturbance) Any of a range of recognizable patterns of abnormal behavior

mentally disturbed Displaying some form of abnormal behavior

mental retardation Substandard intellectual functioning accompanied by deficiencies in adaptive behavior, with onset before age 18

mesmerism A treatment developed by Anton Mesmer that induced a sleeplike state; considered to be the forerunner of modern hypnotism

methadone A drug prescribed during heroin detoxification to decrease the intensity of withdrawal symptoms

microcephaly An anomaly characterized by an unusually small brain; found in children with fetal alcohol syndrome

migraine headache A severe headache resulting from constriction and then dilation of the cerebral blood vessels

mildly retarded (educable) Suffering from mild intellectual impaiment caused mainly by cultural-familial retardation

milieu therapy A type of therapy in which a hospital is organized to provide a total therapeutic community

Minnesota Multiphasic Personality Inventory (MMPI) An objective personality inventory used widely in clinical settings to assess psychological disturbances

minor tranquilizers Drugs prescribed to relieve anxiety, such as barbiturates, meprobamate (Miltown), Librium, and Valium

modeling A form of learning in which an individual imitates an observed behavior

modeling therapy A therapeutic approach to phobias in which the phobic individual observes a fearless model coping with the fear-producing situation

moderately retarded Intellectually developed to about one-half to one-fourth the degree of normal children; considered trainable; intellectual development may peak at a mental age of 6-8 years; the cause is often some organic pathology

modern psychoanalysis An adaptation of psychoanalytic treatment that relies less heavily on the patient's ability to be emotionally or intellectually capable of understanding interpretations

monozygotic (MZ) twins (identical) Genetically identical twins who developed from one fertilized egg

moral treatment movement A shift to more humane treatment of the mentally disturbed, generally attributed to Philippe Pinel

moralistic anxiety In Freudian theory, anxiety produced when an individual does not live up to his or her own moral standards

multi-infarct dementia An organic brain syndrome characterized by uneven deterioration of intellectual abilities and resulting from a number of cerebral infarctions

multimodal behavior therapy A model of psychotherapy that advocates using a variety of concepts, methods, and strategies from behavioral as well as cognitive and affective theories

multiple-baseline design A type of single-subject experiment that involves recording multiple behaviors, serially applying the same modification to each behavior, and measuring any changes that occur

multiple personality A disorder in which two or more relatively distinct personalities exist in one individual

narcissistic personality disorder A personality disorder characterized by an exaggerated sense of self-importance

narcotics Opium and its derivatives, which depress the central nervous system, provide relief from pain and anxiety, and are addictive

negative/mass practice A treatment for tics in which the individual performs the tic intentionally over and over again so that fatigue sets in and the tic acquires aversive properties

negative reinforcer In operant conditioning, an aversive event whose removal increases the frequency of a behavior

Neo-Freudians Psychologists whose ideas are strongly influenced by Freud's psychoanalytic model, but who have modified that model in various ways

neologisms New words typically formed by combining words in common usage; often invented by schizophrenics

neurasthenia A disorder characterized by complaints of extreme mental and physical weariness

neuroleptics Antipsychotic drugs that produce symptoms resembling neurological conditions

neuron Nerve cell

neurosis Formerly a category of mental disorders including the present anxiety, dissociative, and somatoform disorders; now generally a less severe mental disorder; no longer listed as a DSM category

neurotic anxiety In Freudian theory, anxiety produced when the ego loses control over the id's wild impulses

neuroticism A personality dimension of autonomic instability or emotionality

neurotransmitters Substances that contribute to the transmission of nerve impulses from one neuron to another

nicotine A stimulant found in tobacco

night hospital program A program that allows patients to carry on their normal activities during the day while remaining institutionalized at night

nomothetic orientation The scientific approach taken by experimenters who study large groups of individuals to find common laws and principles

nonbeing An existential concept referring to the awareness that human beings have of their impending death; this awareness is the source of *existential anxiety*

norepinephrine A catecholamine neurotransmitter substance

objective personality test An inventory of personality attributes in which the test-taker either agrees or disagrees with specific self-descriptive statements

observational learning Acquisition of new behaviors by watching someone perform them

observational learning theory A theory of learning which holds that individuals can learn new behaviors by observing those behaviors and then imitating them

obsession An intrusive, uncontrollable, and persistent thought

obsessive-compulsive disorders Anxiety disorders characterized by intrusive and uncontrollable thoughts, or the need to perform specific acts repeatedly, or both

Oedipus complex In Freudian theory, a process during which a male child desires sexual possession of his mother and wants to eliminate his father; eventually resolved by identification with the father

operant behavior A voluntary and controllable behavior that effects a change in the individual's environment

operant conditioning A theory of learning which holds that certain behaviors are controlled by the consequences that follow them, and that new behaviors are learned through reinforcement

operational definition In an experiment, a method of defining inherently vague terms, such as aggression or frustration, in terms of the operations used to measure them

oppositional disorder A behavioral pattern lasting at least six months and characterized by disobedient, negativistic, and provocative opposition to authority figures

oral stage In Freudian theory, the stage during the first year of life in which the primary source of pleasure involves the mouth and lips

organicity Damage to the central nervous system

organic mental disorder A behavioral disturbance that results from organic brain pathology, that is, damage to the brain

organic retardation Relatively severe mental retardation that is a consequence of a physiological or anatomical defect

orgasm The pleasurable culmination of sexual arousal that is usually accompanied by ejaculation in males and vaginal contractions in females

orgasmic reconditioning A behavioral technique aimed at increasing appropriate heterosexual arousal

outpatient program A program that allows patients to return to their homes in the community while still receiving therapeutic services from the hospital

overanxious disorder A childhood disorder that is characterized by excessive worry and constant need for reassurance

overselective attention The tendency of an autistic child to focus on only one kind of stimulus or cue, such as either auditory or visual cues but not both

panic disorders Anxiety disorders characterized by severe and frightening episodes of apprehension and feelings of impending doom

paranoid disorders Severe mental disorders characterized by delusions of persecution or delusional jealousy

paranoid personality disorder A personality disorder characterized by unwarranted suspiciousness, hypersensitivity, lack of emotion, and preoccupation with unfounded beliefs

paranoid pseudocommunity The delusional fantasy world of a paranoid, constructed from subjective interpretations

paranoid schizophrenia A schizophrenic disorder characterized by persistent and systematized delusion

paraphilias Sexual disorders in which unusual or bizarre acts, images, or objects are required for sexual arousal

paraprofessional therapists Persons who are taught by a professional to provide some mental health services but who do not have formal mental health training

parascientific Untestable and outside the realm of scientific inquiry

parasympathetic nervous system The division of the nervous system that controls metabolic function and conserves energy when the organism is at rest

parental management techniques Ways in which a parent can relate to a child, such as a means of supervision or discipline

Parkinson's disease A progressively worsening organic brain disorder characterized by muscle tremors, a stiff, shuffling gait, lack of facial expression, and social withdrawal

passive-aggressive personality disorder A personality disorder characterized by the passive expression of aggression through stubbornness, inefficiency, procrastination, and resistance to reasonable demands

pedophilia A disorder in which an adult obtains erotic gratification through sexual contact with children

penis envy In Freudian theory, a condition in which females desire to possess a penis or demonstrate masculine characteristics

peptic ulcer An open sore within the digestive system

personality disorder A maladaptive behavior pattern that stems from an immature or distorted personality structure

person-centered therapy A form of humanistic therapy emphasizing the importance of the person's subjective world; the therapist adopts a reflective and nonjudgmental stance

pervasive developmental disorders Severe disorders of childhood that affect language, social relationships, attention, perception, and affect; include infantile autism and childhood onset pervasive developmental disorder

petit mal seizure A mild form of epileptic seizure in which there is a momentary dimming or loss of consciousness, sometimes with convulsive movements

phallic stage In Freudian theory, the third stage of life, during which the genital region becomes the focus of pleasurable sensations

phencyclidine (PCP) Hallucinogen that produces perceptual distortions, euphoria, nausea, confusion, delusions, and violent psychotic behavior; also known as angel dust

phenothiazines Drugs used to control thought disorders, affect, and hallucinations in schizophrenics

phenotype The observable results of the interaction

of the genotype and the environment

phenylketonuria (PKU) A metabolic disorder, transmitted by a recessive gene, that causes abnormal substances to build up; results in central nervous system degeneration and brain damage

phobia A strong, persistent, and unwarranted fear of a specific object or situation

placebo A chemically inert or inactive substance, administered to a patient who believes it is an active medication

placebo effects Positive responses to a drug that result from the patient's understanding of the drug's action, faith in the doctor, or other psychological factors unrelated to the specific physiological action of the drug

pleasure principle In Freudian theory, the demand for the immediate gratification of instinctual needs

positive reinforcer In operant conditioning, anything that increases the frequency of the response it follows

positron emitting tomography (PET) scanning A technique for assessing brain damage in which the patient is injected with radioactive glucose and the metabolism of the glucose is monitored

posttraumatic stress disorders Reactive disorders resulting from extraordinary stressors that are severe and are outside the range of common experience; symptoms may occur months or years after the traumatic incident

predisposition An inherited characteristic which favors the development of a certain condition, especially a disease

premature ejaculation Ejaculation before penile entry into the vagina, or so soon after entry that an unsatisfactory sexual experience results

premorbid Existing prior to the onset of mental disorder

preparedness A theory that humans are physiologically predisposed to fears that were necessary for the survival of pretechnological man

primal therapy A therapy intended to help patients reexperience early psychological and physical hurts in their original form by encouraging them to express their emotions through violent thrashing, screams, and convulsions

primary prevention An effort to lower the incidence of new cases of behavioral disorders by strengthening resources that promote mental health and eliminating features that threaten mental health

proband In genetic study, an individual with the trait that is under investigation

problem-solving therapy A form of cognitive-behavioral therapy aimed at providing clients with strategies for dealing with specific problems encountered in life

profoundly retarded Intellectually deficient to the extent that constant and total care and supervision are necessary; the defects that cause the retardation are congenital

prognosis A prediction of the future course of an untreated disorder

projection A defense mechanism in which unacceptable impulses are handled by attributing them to others

projective personality test A personality assessment technique in which the test-taker is presented with ambiguous stimuli and is asked to respond to them in some way

provocative psychotherapy A therapy characterized by confrontation and the use of humor with the intention of getting to the heart of the problem quickly

psychiatric epidemiology The study of relationships between immediate environmental stressors and psychopathological reactions

psychiatric social worker A social worker trained to work with clients who have mental disorders and with their families

psychiatry A medical specialty dealing with the prevention, diagnosis, treatment, and cure of mental disorders

psychoanalysis The therapy based on the Freudian view that unconscious conflicts must be aired and understood by the patient if abnormal behavior is to be eliminated

psychoanalytic model The viewpoint that adult disorders arise from the unconscious operation of repressed anxieties originally experienced during childhood

psychodiagnosis A description of an individual's psychological condition

psychodrama A group therapy in which patients and other persons role-play situations

psychogenic amnesia A dissociative disorder characterized by the inability to recall information of personal significance, usually after a traumatic event

psychogenic fugue A dissociative disorder in which psychogenic amnesia is accompanied by flight from familiar surroundings (also called *fugue state*)

psychogenic pain disorder A somatoform disorder

characterized by severe pain that has a psychological rather than physical basis; psychalgia

psychogenic view The belief or theory that mental disorders are caused by psychological and emotional factors

psychological autopsy A systematic examination of existing information in order to understand and explain the behavior exhibited by an individual prior to his or her death

psychological factors affecting physical condition A new classification category in DSM-III that acknowledges both physical and psychological factors in all physical disorders

psychological test Any test-type instrument used to assess maladaptive behavior, social skills development, intellectual abilities, vocational interest, or brain damage

psychometrics Mental measurement, including its study and techniques

psychomotor retardation Slowing of bodily movements, expressive gestures, and spontaneous responses

psychomotor seizures A form of epilepsy characterized by loss of contact with the environment during which the individual may engage in well-organized and normal-appearing behavioral sequences

psychopath An individual with an antisocial personality

psychopathology Abnormal behavior

psychopharmacology The study of the effects of drugs on the mind and on behavior

psychophysiological disorder A physical disorder that has a strong psychological basis or component

psychosexual dysfunction A disruption of any part of the normal sexual response cycle, in a male or female

psychosexual stages In Freudian theory, the developmental sequence through which all people move; experiences during these stages are responsible for adult personality

psychosis A severe mental disorder in which there is a loss of contact with reality or a significant distortion of reality

psychosomatic disorder An outdated term for *psychophysiological disorder;* implies that only certain illnesses are susceptible to emotional variables

psychosurgery Brain surgery performed for the purpose of correcting severe mental disorder; varieties include prefrontal lobotomy, transorbital lobotomy, and cauterization

psychotherapy The systematic application of techniques derived from psychological principles by a trained therapist, for the purpose of aiding psychologically troubled individuals; includes both insight-oriented and action-oriented therapies

psychotomimetic drugs Drugs whose effects mimic acute psychotic reactions

punishment In operant conditioning, either the removal of a positive reinforcer or the presentation of an aversive stimulus to reduce the frequency or probability of a response

racism Discrimination and prejudice that are aimed at a specific group because they are considered inferior in some way

rational-emotive therapy (RET) A therapy developed by Albert Ellis, who believes anxiety, depression, and other maladaptive responses are produced by irrational beliefs; the therapy involves the identification and elimination of these beliefs

rationalization A defense mechanism in which individuals justify their behavior through explanation

reaction formation A defense mechanism in which a dangerous impulse is repressed and converted to its direct opposite

reactive disorders Unusual or bizarre behaviors exhibited under stress-producing conditions

realistic anxiety In Freudian theory, anxiety that occurs when there is a potential danger from the external environment

reality principle In Freudian theory, awareness of the demands of the environment and adjustment of behavior to meet these demands; acts to modify the *pleasure principle* and is part of the ego structure

recessive gene A gene that produces a physical effect only when it is paired with an identical gene

recessive-gene disorder Genetic disorder caused by the pairing of two recessive genes, producing a disturbance or abnormality in the metabolic processes which, in turn, may produce a physical defect or mental retardation

regression A defense mechanism involving a retreat to an earlier developmental level in the face of stress

reinforcer In operant conditioning, a consequence that increases the frequency or magnitude of the behavior it follows

relaxation training A therapeutic technique in which the individual acquires the ability to relax the muscles of the body in almost any circumstances

relearning A characteristic of psychotherapy that refers to the client's opportunity to unlearn, develop, or change certain behaviors or levels of functioning

reliability The degree to which a procedure or test will yield the same result repeatedly, under the same circumstances

replication Repetition of an experiment to ensure that the results obtained in the original experiment are valid

repression A defense mechanism that prevents unacceptable desires from reaching consciousness and expels painful experiences from consciousness

residual schizophrenia A category of schizophrenic disorder reserved for individuals who have experienced at least one schizophrenic episode but do not now exhibit prominent signs of schizophrenia

resistance The process during psychoanalysis in which the patient's unconscious attempts to impede the psychoanalysis by preventing the exposure of repressed material; tactics include silence, late arrival, or failure to keep an appointment

reticular activating system Bundle of nerve fibers connected to the higher brain centers; controls sleep, attention, and memory

reuptake The process by which a neurotransmitter is reabsorbed by the nerve cells

rights of mental patients The legal and moral issue of what constitutes adequate treatment for mental patients

rolfing A deep massage therapy based on the assumption that psychological and emotional factors may produce chronic postural imbalance because of muscular tension and changes in the connective tissues

Rorschach technique A projective technique employing symmetrical inkblots

rubella German measles; when contracted by a woman during the first trimester of pregnancy, can result in mental retardation and birth defects in the fetus

sadism A sexual disorder in which erotic gratification is obtained by inflicting pain or punishment on others

schema A pattern of thinking or a cognitive set that determines (or colors) an individual's reactions and responses

schizoid personality disorder A personality disorder characterized by social isolation

schizophrenia A group of disorders characterized by severe impairment of cognitive processes, personality disintegration, and social withdrawal

schizophreniform disorders Disorders similar to the schizophrenic disorders but shorter in duration, from two weeks to six months

schizophrenogenic Causing or producing schizophrenia; generally used to describe a parent who is simultaneously or alternately cold and overprotecting, rejecting and dominating

schizotypal personality disorder A personality disorder characterized by oddities of thinking and behavior such as recurrent illusions, belief in the possession of magical powers, and digression or vagueness of speech

school phobia A type of separation anxiety whose symptoms may occur merely at the prospect of having to go to school

scientific method A method of inquiry that provides for the systematic collection of data through controlled observation, and the testing of hypotheses based on those data

secondary gain Indirect benefits from neurotic or other symptoms

secondary prevention An attempt to shorten the duration of mental disorders and reduce their impact

self The individual's sense of personal identity

self-actualization An inherent tendency in people to strive towards the realization of their full potential

self-concept An individual's assessment of his or her own value and worth

self-control therapy A therapy approach that assumes people can actively modify their own behaviors by managing behavioral contingencies

senile dementia A severe loss of intellectual functioning that is produced by a deterioration of brain cells

sensitivity training groups (T-groups) A group therapy designed to help individuals increase their sensitivity to others and improve their human relations skills

separation anxiety Excessive anxiety over separating from parents or significant others

serotonin A catecholamine neurotransmitter substance

severely retarded Individuals whose rate of learning is very slow, who usually require constant care and supervision, and who can be identified by their physical appearance and evident sensorimotor problems; major cause is organic

sex chromosomes Determinants of the sex of an individual; an XX pair of chromosomes produces a female; an XY combination produces a male

sexism Prejudice and discrimination directed against either sex

shaping A procedure for developing a new or complex behavior by reinforcing successive behaviors that increasingly approximate the desired final behavior

simple phobia An extreme fear of a specific object or situation; a phobia not classed as either agoraphobia or a social phobia

simulation An investigative technique in which a real-life situation is recreated under controlled conditions

single-subject experiment An experiment performed on a single individual in which some aspect of that individual's own behavior is used as the control

socialized, aggressive conduct disorder A type of conduct disorder characterized by attachments to significant others and friends, and displays of physical violence against people who are not in these two groups

socialized, nonaggressive conduct disorder A type of conduct disorder in which the person is not physically violent and exhibits attachment for certain people or groups, but breaks rules, is truant, or engages in other nonviolent actions

social phobia An irrational and strong fear of social situations

social supports The availability and quality of interpersonal resources that individuals may call on during emotional distress

somatization disorder A somatoform disorder in which the individual chronically complains of a number of symptoms for which no physiological basis can be found; also called Briquet's syndrome

somatoform disorders Mental disorders involving complaints of physical symptoms that closely mimic authentic medical conditions but have no physical basis; include somatization disorder, conversion disorder, psychogenic pain disorder, and hypochondriasis

somnambulism Sleepwalking

splinter skills A characteristic of some autistic children that refers to their facility with drawing, puzzle construction, and rote memory but their lack of ability with verbal tasks, language skills, and symbolic thinking

Stanford-Binet Intelligence Scale An individual intelligence test used to assess cognitive development and functioning

statutory rape The seduction of a girl who has not yet reached the legal age of consent

stereotyped movement disorders Disorders that begin in childhood and are characterized by unusual and repetitive movements; include tics and Tourette's syndrome

stimulus control In classical and operant conditioning, the situation in which the occurrence or nonoccurrence of a particular behavior is influenced by a preceding stimulus

stimulus discrimination In classical conditioning, the ability to detect differences in stimuli and not respond to a stimulus different from the conditioned stimulus

stress An individual's internal reaction to a physical or psychological demand placed on the individual by the environment

stress-intolerance syndrome A condition characterized by lowered tolerance to stress

stressor A physical or psychological demand placed on an individual by some external event or situation

stroke See *cerebrovascular accident*

structural family therapy A treatment in which the therapist helps clients to restructure the roles and relationships within a pathogenic family system

substance abuse A pathological pattern of excessive use of a substance, resulting in physical harm or impairing social and occupational functioning

substance dependence A pathological pattern of excessive use of a substance, resulting in either tolerance or withdrawal symptoms or both

substance use disorder Maladaptive behavior associated with the pathological use of a substance over a period of at least one month

suicide The taking of one's own life

superego In Freudian theory, the purely moral facet of the personality, whose goals are idealistic rather than realistic

sympathetic nervous system A division of the nervous system that prepares the body for emergency action

symptom substitution The concept that if neurotic symptoms are eliminated without resolving or removing the underlying conflict, then the individual will merely express the neurosis in other ways and exhibit other symptoms

synapse Location where one neuron communicates with another

syncope Loss of consciousness

syndrome A cluster of symptoms that tend to occur together and are believed to be indicative of a particular disorder

systematic desensitization A therapy in which relaxation is used to eliminate the anxiety associated with phobias and other fear-evoking situations

tachycardia Rapid heart rate; may exceed 100 beats per minute

tarantism A hysterical reaction, common in the thirteenth century and attributed to the sting of the tarantula, in which people raved, danced, and had convulsions

taraxein A substance found in the blood of schizophrenics; believed by some to be responsible for schizophrenia

tardive dyskinesia A syndrome characterized by involuntary and rhythmic movements of the protruding tongue, chewing, lip smacking, other facial movements, and sidewise jaw movements; a possible side effect of antipsychotic drugs

Tay-Sachs disease A recessive-gene metabolic disorder resulting in death in which fatty substances accumulate in the brain and other tissues of the body

tension headache A headache produced by prolonged contraction of the scalp and neck muscles

tertiary prevention Efforts to facilitate the readjustment of the individual to community life after hospital treatment for a mental disturbance

thalamus The part of the brain stem that serves as a relay station, transmitting nerve impulses to other regions of the brain

Thematic Apperception Test (TAT) A projective test involving a series of pictures most portraying scenes of two or more people; subjects make up a story about the pictures

theory A group of principles and hypotheses that together explain some aspect of a particular area of inquiry

therapeutic community A hospital environment in which all activities are structured to have a therapeutic function and in which patients participate to the degree that is possible

therapeutic relationship The interaction between

therapist and client in which the therapist may provide reassurance, interpretations, self-disclosures, reflections of the client's feelings, or information, each at the appropriate time

therapy A program of systematic intervention whose purpose is to modify a client's behavioral, affective, or cognitive state

tics Stereotyped and repetitive but involuntary twitching or spasms of the voluntary muscles

token economy A treatment program, based on principles of operant conditioning, that rewards patients for appropriate behaviors with tokens, which can then be exchanged for hospital passes, special privileges, or food

tolerance A condition in which the body requires increasing doses of a substance in order to achieve the desired effect

Tourette's syndrome A stereotyped movement disorder characterized by multiple motor and verbal tics (coprolalia)

transactional analysis (TA) A technique of group therapy based on the assumption that people play certain games that hinder the development of genuine and deep interpersonal relationships

transaction model A stress model in which stress is considered to be a transaction between the person and the stressful situation; the person's internal processes and makeup intervene between the stressor and the development of stress

transcendental meditation A variant of relaxation training adapted from Far Eastern philosophies

transference A process during psychotherapy in which the patient reenacts early conflicts by carrying over and applying to the therapist feelings and attitudes that the patient had toward significant others (primarily parents) in the past

transsexualism The self-identification of an individual with the opposite sex

transvestism A disorder in which sexual gratification is obtained by wearing the attire that is appropriate to the opposite sex

trephining A treatment for abnormal behavior used during the Stone Age in which a circular hole was chipped in the skull in order to allow an evil sprit to leave the body

trisomy 21 The existence of an extra chromosome in pair number 21; responsible for Down's syndrome

Turner's syndrome A rare condition caused by the lack of one X chromosome in a female, resulting in severe space-form perceptual deficits

unconditional positive regard A humanistic concept referring to love and acceptance of an individual, regardless of his or her behavior

unconditioned response (UCR) An innate, unlearned response to an unconditioned stimulus, such as salivation to food in the mouth

unconditioned stimulus (UCS) A stimulus that automatically elicits an unconditioned response without prior conditioning

unconscious In Freudian theory, an area of unawareness into which repressed desires and memories are forced

undersocialized, aggressive conduct disorder A type of conduct disorder characterized by failure to establish affectionate relationships, lack of concern for others, and aggression toward property or against others

undersocialized, nonaggressive conduct disorder A type of conduct disorder characterized by few bonds with others; violations involve rule-breaking that is not directly aggressive toward others

undifferentiated schizophrenia A schizophrenic disorder characterized by mixed or undifferentiated symptoms that do not clearly fit the other types of schizophrenia

undoing A defense mechanism involving ritualistic and repetitive behaviors performed in an attempt to atone for misdeeds

unipolar disorders Major affective disorders in which no mania has been exhibited, only depression (see also *major depression*)

vaginismus Involuntary contraction of the outer part of the vagina, so as to restrict or prevent penile insertion

validity The degree to which a procedure or test actually performs the function that it was designed to perform

vicarious conditioning The development of an emotional response by observing reactions in others

voyeurism A disorder in which sexual gratification is obtained through the surreptitious observation of disrobing individuals or couples engaged in coitus

vulnerability/stress model A theoretical model that combines an innate vulnerability and the effect of environmental stressors in the production of mental disorders

Wechsler Adult Intelligence Scale The most widely used individual intelligence test

withdrawal symptoms Physical or emotional symptoms such as shaking or irritability that appear when the intake of a regularly used substance is reduced or halted

Z-process attachment therapy A therapy that attempts to elicit love, concern, or rage in clients so that contact can be made, a relationship may begin, and the normal process of therapy can proceed

References

Abebimpe, V. R. (1981). Overview: White norms and psychiatric diagnosis of black patients. *American Journal of Psychiatry, 138,* 279–285.

Abebimpe, V. R., Chu, C. C., Klein, H. E., & Lange, M. H. (1982). Racial and geographic differences in the psychopathology of schizophrenia. *American Journal of Psychiatry, 139,* 888–891.

Abel, G. G., Barlow, D. H., Blanchard, E. B., & Guild, D. (1977). The components of rapists' sexual arousal. *Archives of General Psychiatry, 34,* 895–903.

Abel, G. G., Levis, D. J., & Clancy, J. (1970). Aversion therapy applied to taped sequences of deviant behavior in exhibitionism and other sexual deviations: A preliminary report. *Journal of Behavior Therapy and Experimental Psychiatry, 1,* 59–66.

Abels, G. (1975). *The double bind: Paradox in relationships.* Unpublished doctoral dissertation, Boston University.

Abels, G. (1976). Researching the unresearchable: Experimentation on the double bind. In C. E. Sluzki & D. C. Ransom (Eds.), *Double bind: The foundation of the communication approach to the family.* New York: Grune & Stratton.

Abraham, K. (1948). Notes on psychoanalytic investigation and treatment of manic-depressive insanity and allied conditions. In D. Bryan & A. Strachey (Eds. and Trans.), *Selected papers of Karl Abraham, M.D.* London: Hogarth Press. (Original work published 1911)

Abrams, R., & Taylor, M. A. (1983). The genetics of schizophrenia: A reassessment using modern criteria. *American Journal of Psychiatry, 140,* 171–175.

Abramson, L. Y., Seligman, M. E. P., & Teasdale, J. D. (1978). Learned helplessness in humans: Critique and reformulation. *Journal of Abnormal Psychology, 87,* 49–74.

Achenbach, T. M. (1974). *Developmental psychopathology.* New York: Ronald Press.

Ad Hoc Committee on Women. (1979). Principles concerning the counseling and therapy of women. *The Counseling Psychologist, 8,* 21.

Adams, J. (1973). Adaptive behavior and measured intelligence in the classification of mental retardation. *American Journal of Mental Deficiency, 78,* 77–81.

Adams, J., McIntosh, E., & Weade, B. L. (1973). Ethnic background, measured intelligence, and adaptive behavior scores in mentally retarded children. *American Journal of Mental Deficiency, 78,* 1–6.

Adams, P. L. (1972). Family characteristics of obsessive children. *American Journal of Psychiatry, 128,* 1414–1417.

Adams, P. R., & Adams, G. R. (1984). Mount St. Helen's Ashfall: Evidence for a disaster stress reaction. *American Psychologist, 39,* 252–260.

Adler, J., & Gosnell, M. (1979, December 31). A question of fraudulent fever. *Newsweek,* p. 65.

Adler, J., Hager, M., Zabarsky, M., Jackson, T., Friendly, D. T., & Abramson, P. (1984, April 23). The fight to conquer fear. *Newsweek,* pp. 66–72.

Albee, G. W. (1979a). Preventing prevention. *APA Monitor, 10,* 2.

Albee, G. W. (1979b). Anytime, anyplace. *APA Monitor, 10,* 31.

Albee, G. W. (1983). Foreword. In R. D. Felner, L. A. Jason, J. N. Moritsugu, & S. S. Farber (Eds.), *Preventive psychology: Theory, research and practice.* New York: Pergamon.

Alexander, F. (1950). *Psychosomatic medicine.* New York: Norton.

Alexander, F. G., & Selesnick, S. T. (1966). *The history of psychiatry.* New York: Harper & Row.

Alford, G. S. (1980). Alcoholics Anonymous: An empirical outcome study. *Addictive Behaviors, 5,* 359–370.

Alinsky, S. D. (1972). *Rules for radicals.* New York: Vintage Books.

Allport, G. W. (1937). *Personality: A psychological interpretation.* New York: Holt, Rinehart & Winston.

Allport, G. W. (1954). *The nature of prejudice.* Reading, MA: Addison-Wesley.

Allyon, T., & Michael, J. (1959). The psychiatric nurse as a behavioral engineer. *Journal of the Experimental Analysis of Behavior, 2,* 323–334.

Altman, K., & Krupsaw, R. (1983). Suppressing aggressive-destructive behavior by delayed overcorrection. *Journal of Behavior Therapy and Experimental Psychiatry, 14,* 359–362.

Altrocchi, J. (1972). Mental health consultation. In S. E. Golann & C. Eisdorfer (Eds.), *Handbook of community mental health.* New York: Appleton-Century-Crofts.

Aman, M. G. (1984). Hyperactivity: Nature of the syndrome and its natural history. *Journal of Autism and Developmental Disorders, 14,* 39–56.

American Association on Mental Deficiency. (1973a). *Manual on terminology and classification in mental retardation* (rev. ed.). H. J. Grossman (Ed.), Special Publication Series No. 2. Washington, DC: American Association on Mental Deficiency.

American Association on Mental Deficiency. (1973b). Rights of the mentally retarded. *Mental Retardation, 11,* 59–62.

American Psychiatric Association. (1952). *Diagnostic and statistical manual of mental disorders* (1st ed.). Washington, DC: American Psychiatric Association.

American Psychiatric Association. (1968). *Diagnostic and statistical manual of mental disorders* (2nd ed.). Washington, DC: American Psychiatric Association.

American Psychiatric Association. (1980). *Diagnostic and statistical manual of mental disorders* (3rd ed.). Washington, DC: American Psychiatric Association.

American Psychological Association. (1978). *Ethical standards of psychologists*. Washington, DC: American Psychological Association.

American Psychological Association. (1981). *Ethical principles of psychologists. American Psychologist, 36,* 633–638.

American Psychological Association Task Force on Sex Bias and Sex Role Stereotyping in Psychotherapeutic Practice. (1975). *American Psychologist, 30,* 1169–1175.

Amir, M. (1971). *Patterns of forcible rape*. Chicago: University of Chicago Press.

Ananth, J. (1976). Treatment of obsessive-compulsive neurosis: Pharmacological approach. *Psychosomatics, 17,* 180–184.

Anastasi, A. (1982). *Psychological testing*. New York: Macmillan.

Anderson, A., Hedblom, J., & Hubbard, F. (1983). A multidisciplinary team treatment for patients with anorexia nervosa and their families. *International Journal of Eating Disorders, 2,* 181–192.

Anderson, B. L. (1983). Primary orgasmic dysfunction: Diagnostic considerations and review of treatment. *Psychological Bulletin, 93,* 105–136.

Anderson, R. D. (1972). Witchcraft and sex. *Sexual Behavior, 2,* 8–14.

Andrasik, F., Holroyd, K. A., & Abell, T. (1979). Prevalence of headache within a college student population: A preliminary analysis. *Headache, 20,* 384–387.

Angrist, B., Rotrosen, J., & Gershon, S. (1980). Responses to apomorphine and amphetamine, and neuroleptics in schizophrenia subjects. *Psychopharmacology, 67,* 31–38.

Annesley, P. (1969). Nardil response in a chronic obsessive compulsive. *British Journal of Psychiatry, 115,* 748.

Annon, J. (1971). *The extension of learning principles to the analysis and treatment of sexual problems*. Unpublished doctoral dissertation. University of Hawaii, Hilo.

Anonymous. (1981). First person account: The quiet discrimination. *Schizophrenia Bulletin, 7,* 739.

Anonymous. (1983). First person account: Schizophrenia—a pharmacy student's view. *Schizophrenia Bulletin, 9,* 152–155.

Antonovsky, A. (1979). *Health, stress, and coping*. San Francisco: Jossey-Bass.

Archibald, N. C., & Tuddenham, R. D. (1965). Persistent stress reaction after combat. *Archives of General Psychiatry, 12,* 475–481.

Arkonac, O., & Guze, S. (1963). A family study of hysteria. *New England Journal of Medicine, 268,* 239–242.

Ash, P. (1949). The reliability of psychiatric diagnosis. *Journal of Abnormal and Social Psychology, 44,* 272–276.

Atkinson, D. R., Morten, G., & Sue, D. W. (1979). *Counseling American minorities: A cross-cultural perspective*. Dubuque, IA: Brown.

August, G. J., & Stewart, M. A. (1982). Is there a syndrome of pure hyperactivity? *British Journal of Psychiatry, 140,* 305–311.

August, G. J., Stewart, M. A., & Holmes, C. S. (1983). A four-year follow-up of hyperactive boys with and without conduct disorders. *British Journal of Psychiatry, 143,* 192–198.

August, G. J., Stewart, M. A., & Tsai, L. (1981). The incidence of cognitive disabilities in the siblings of autistic children. *British Journal of Psychiatry, 138,* 416–422.

Ausubel, D. P. (1961). Causes and types of narcotic addiction: A psychosocial view. *Psychiatric Quarterly, 35,* 523–531.

Ayllon, T., & Azrin, N. (1965). The measurement and reinforcement of behavior of psychotics. *Journal of the Experimental Analysis of Behavior, 8,* 323–334.

Bakal, D. A. (1975). Headache: A biopsychological perspective. *Psychological Bulletin, 82,* 369–382.

Baker, R. K., & Ball, S. J. (1969). *Mass media and violence* (Vol. 9). Washington, DC: U.S. Government Printing Office.

Bandura, A. (1969). *Principles of behavior modification*. New York: Holt, Rinehart & Winston.

Bandura, A., Blanchard, E., & Ritter, B. (1969). Relative efficacy of desensitization and modeling approaches for inducing behavioral, affective, and attitudinal changes. *Journal of Personality and Social Psychology, 13,* 173–199.

Bandura, A., & Rosenthal, T. L. (1966). Vicarious classical conditioning as a function of arousal level. *Journal of Personality and Social Psychology, 3,* 54–62.

Bandura, A., & Walters, R. H. (1963). *Social learning and personality development*. New York: Holt, Rinehart & Winston.

Banks, W. C. (1982). Deconstructive falsification: Foundations of a critical method in black psychology. In E. E. Jones & S. J. Korchin (Eds.), *Minority mental health*. New York: Praeger.

Barahal, H. S. (1958). 100 prefrontal lobotomies: Five-to-ten-year follow-up study. *Psychiatric Quarterly, 32,* 653–678.

Barbaree, H. E., Marshall, W. L., & Lanthier, R. D. (1979). Deviant sexual arousal in rapists. *Behaviour Research and Therapy, 17,* 215–222.

Barber, T. X. (1969). *Hypnosis: A scientific approach*. New York: Van Nostrand Reinhold.

Barber, T. X. (1984). Hypnosis, deep relaxation, and active relaxation: Data, theory, and clinical applications. In R. Woolfolk & P. Lehrer (Eds.), *Principles and practice of stress management*. New York: Guilford Press.

Barchas, J., Berger, P., Ciaranello, R., & Elliott, G. (1977). *Psychopharmacology: From theory to practice*. New York: Oxford University Press.

Barkley, R. A. (1981). Hyperactivity. In E. Mash & L. Terdal (Eds.), *Behavioral assessment of childhood disorders*. New York: Guilford Press.

Barlow, D. H. (1974). The treatment of sexual deviation: Towards a comprehensive behavioral approach. In K. Calhoun, H. Adams, and K. Mitchell (Eds.), *Innovative treatment methods in psychopathology*. New York: Wiley.

Barlow, D. H., Abel, G., & Blanchard, E. (1979). Gender identity change in transsexuals. *Archives of General Psychiatry, 36,* 1001–1007.

Barlow, D. H., Cohen, A., Waddell, M., Vermilyea, B., Klosko, J., Blanchard, E., & DiNardo, P. (1984). Panic and generalized anxiety disorders: Nature and treatment. *Behavior Therapy, 15,* 431–449.

Barlow, D. H., O'Brien, G., & Last, C. (1984). Couples treatment of agoraphobia. *Behavior Therapy, 15,* 41–58.

Barons, A. P., & Earls, F. (1984). The relation of temperament and social factors to behavior problems in three-year-old children. *Journal of Child Psychology and Psychiatry, 25,* 23–33.

Barrera, M., & Ainlay, S. L. (1983). The structure of social support: A conceptual and empirical analysis. *Journal of Community Psychology, 11,* 133–143.

Barrett, C. L. (1969). Systematic desensitization versus implosive therapy. *Journal of Abnormal Psychology, 74,* 587–592.

Barron, F. (1963). *Creativity and psychological health.* Princeton, NJ: Van Nostrand.

Bartemeier, L. H., Kubie, L. S., Menninger, K. A., Romano, J., & Whitehorn, J. C. (1946). Combat exhaustion. *Journal of Nervous and Mental Diseases, 104,* 384–389.

Bartlett, K. (1984, August 26). Bulimia: The secret that becomes a compulsion. *Ann Arbor News,* p. F1.

Bass, B. A. (1974). Sexual arousal as an anxiety inhibitor. *Journal of Behaviour Therapy and Experimental Psychiatry, 5,* 151–152.

Bates, J. E., Bentler, P. N., & Thompson, S. K. (1979). Gender-deviant boys compared with normal and clinical control boys. *Journal of Abnormal Child Psychology, 7,* 243–259.

Bateson, G. (1978). The birth of a matrix or double-bind and epistemology. In M. M. Berger (Ed.), *Beyond the double bind.* New York: Brunner/Mazel.

Bateson, G., Jackson, D., Haley, J., & Weakland, J. (1956). Toward a theory of schizophrenia. *Behavioral Science, 1,* 251–264.

Bauer, A. M., & Shea, T. M. (1984). Tourette syndrome: A review and educational implications. *Journal of Autism and Developmental Disorders, 14,* 69–80.

Baum, M. (1970). Extinction of avoidance responding through response prevention (flooding). *Psychological Bulletin, 74,* 276–284.

Baum, S. K., & Boxley, R. L. (1983). Depression and old age identification. *Journal of Clinical Psychology, 39,* 584–590.

Beal, E. (1978). Use of the extended family in the treatment of multiple personality. *American Journal of Psychiatry, 135,* 539–543.

Beck, A., Rush, A., Shaw, B., & Emery, G. (1979). *Cognitive therapy of depression.* New York: Guilford Press.

Beck, A. T. (1962). Reliability of psychiatric diagnosis: A critique of systematic studies. *American Journal of Psychiatry, 119,* 210–216.

Beck, A. T. (1970). Cognitive therapy: Nature and relationship to behavior therapy. *Behavior Therapy, 1,* 184–200.

Beck, A. T. (1974). The development of depression: A cognitive model. In R. J. Friedman & M. M. Katz (Eds.), *The psychology of depression: Contemporary theory and research.* New York: Wiley.

Beck, A. T. (1976). *Cognitive therapy and emotional disorders.* New York: International Universities Press.

Beck, A. T. (1982). Cognitive therapy of depression: New perspectives. In P. Clayton & J. Barrett (Eds.), *Treatment of depression: Old controversies and new approaches.* New York: Raven.

Beck, A. T., Laude, R., & Bohnert, M. (1974). Ideational components of anxiety neurosis. *Archives of General Psychiatry, 31,* 319–325.

Beck, J. G., Barlow, D. H., & Sakheim, D. K. (1984). The effects of attentional focus and partner arousal on sexual responding in functional and dysfunctional men. *Behaviour Research and Therapy, 21,* 1–8.

Beck, S. J. (1953). The science of personality: Nomothetic or idiographic? *Psychological Review, 60,* 353–359.

Becker, J. (1974). *Depression: Theory and research.* Washington, D.C.: Winston-Wiley.

Becker, W. C., & McFarland, R. (1955). A lobotomy prognosis scale. *Journal of Consulting Psychology, 19,* 157–162.

Becker, W. M., & Becker, P. (1983, May 30). Mourning the loss of a son. *Newsweek,* p. 17.

Beers, C. W. (1908). *A mind that found itself.* New York: Longmans.

Bell, A. P., & Weinberg, M. S. (1978). *Homosexualities: A study of diversity among men and women.* New York: Simon & Schuster.

Bell, A. P., Weinberg, M. S., & Hammersmith, S. K. (1981). *Sexual preference: Its development in men and women.* Bloomington: Indiana University Press.

Beiman, I., Israel, E., & Johnson, S. (1978). Error during training and posttraining effects of live and taped extended progressive relaxation, self-relaxation, and electromyogram biofeedback. *Journal of Consulting and Clinical Psychology, 46,* 314–321.

Bellack, A. S., & Hersen, M. (1980). *Introduction to clinical psychology.* New York: Oxford University Press.

Bem, S. L., & Bem, D. J. (1970). We're all nonconscious sexists. *Psychology Today, 4,* 22–28.

Bemporad, J. R. (1979). Adult recollections of a formerly autistic child. *Journal of Autism and Developmental Disorders, 9,* 179–197.

Bender, L. (1938). A visual-motor Gestalt test and its clinical use. *Research Monographs of the American Orthopsychiatric Association, 3.*

Bender, L. (1973). The life course of children with schizophrenia. *American Journal of Psychiatry, 130,* 783–786.

Bender, L. (1983). A visual-motor Gestalt test and its clinical use. *Research Monographs of the American Orthopsychiatric Association, No. 3.*

Benjamin, H. (1967). Transvestism and transsexualism in the male and female. *Journal of Sex Research, 3,* 107–127.

Benoit, E. P. (1957). Relevance of Hebb's theory of the organization of behavior to educational research in the mentally retarded. *American Journal of Mental Deficiency, 61,* 497–507.

Benson, H., Shapiro, D., Tursky, B., & Schwartz, G. (1971). Decreased systolic blood pressure through operant conditioning techniques in patients with essential hypertension. *Science, 173,* 740–742.

Bentler, P. M., & Prince, C. (1969). Personality characteristics of male transvestites. *Journal of Abnormal Psychology, 74,* 140–143.

Berg, I., Butler, A., & Hall, G. (1976). The outcome of adolescent school phobia. *British Journal of Psychiatry, 128,* 80–85.

Berger, D. M. (1973). The return of neurasthenia. *Comprehensive Psychiatry, 14,* 557–562.

Berger, S. M. (1962). Conditioning through vicarious instigation. *Psychological Review, 69,* 450–466.

Bergin, A. E. (1971). The evaluation of therapeutic outcomes. In A. E. Bergin & S. L. Garfield (Eds.), *Handbook of psychotherapy and behavior change: An empirical analysis.* New York: Wiley.

Bergin, A. E. (1980). Psychotherapy and religious values. *Journal of Consulting and Clinical Psychology, 48,* 95–105.

Berkman, L. F., & Syme, S. L. (1979). Social networks, host resistance, and mortality: A nine-year follow-up study of

Alameda County residents. *American Journal of Epidemiology, 109,* 186–204.

Berkowitz, L. (1962). *Aggression: A social-psychological analysis.* New York: McGraw-Hill.

Berkowitz, L., & LePage, A. (1967). Weapons as aggression-eliciting stimuli. *Journal of Personality and Social Psychology, 7,* 202–207.

Berkwitz, N. J. (1974). Up-to-date review of theories of shock therapies. *Diseases of the Nervous System, 35,* 523–527.

Berlin, F. S., & Meinecke, C. F. (1981). Treatment of sex offenders with antiandrogenetic medication: Conceptualization, review of treatment modalities, and preliminary findings. *American Journal of Psychiatry, 138,* 601–607.

Berlow, S. J., Caldarelli, D. D., Matz, G. J., Meyer, D. H., & Harsch, G. G. (1981). Bacterial meningitis and SHL. *Laryngoscope, 4,* 1445–1452.

Bernard, J. (1976). Homosociality and female depression. *Journal of Social Issues, 32,* 213–238.

Berne, E. (1972). *What do you say after you say hello?* New York: Grove Press.

Bernstein, S. M., Steiner, B. W., Glaisler, J. T. D., & Muir, C. F. (1981). Changes in patients with gender identity—problems after parental death. *American Journal of Psychiatry, 138,* 41–45.

Bersoff, D. N. (1981). Testing and the law. *American Psychologist, 36,* 1047–1056.

Berson, R. J. (1983). Capgras syndrome. *American Journal of Psychiatry, 140,* 969–978.

Bettelheim, B. (1967). *The empty fortress.* New York: Free Press.

Bianchi, G. N. (1973). Patterns of hypochondriasis: A principle components analysis. *British Journal of Psychiatry, 122,* 541–548.

Biken, D. (1977). Myths, mistreatment, and pitfalls: Mental retardation and criminal justice. *Journal of Mental Retardation, 15,* 51–57.

Bild, R., & Adams, H. E. (1980). Modification of migraine headaches by cephalic blood volume pulse and EMG biofeedback. *Journal of Consulting and Clinical Psychology, 48,* 51–57.

Biran, M., & Wilson, G. T. (1981). Treatment of phobic disorders using cognitive and exposure methods: A self-efficacy analysis. *Journal of Consulting and Clinical Psychology, 49,* 886–899.

Bishop, E. R., & Torch, E. M. (1979). Dividing ''hysteria'': A preliminary investigation of conversion disorder and psychalgia. *Journal of Nervous and Mental Diseases, 167,* 348–356.

Blair, C. D., & Lanyon, R. I. (1981). Exhibitionism: Etiology and treatment. *Psychological Bulletin, 89,* 439–463.

Blanchard, E., & Epstein, L. (1977). The clinical usefulness of biofeedback. In M. Hersen, R. Eisler, & P. Miller (Eds.), *Progress in behavior modification* (Vol. 4). New York: Academic Press.

Blanchard, E. B., & Andrasik, F. (1982). Psychological assessment and treatment of headache: Recent developments and emerging issues. *Journal of Consulting and Clinical Psychology, 50,* 859–879.

Blank, R. J. (1981). The partial transsexual. *American Journal of Psychiatry, 35,* 107–112.

Bleecker, E. R., & Engel, B. T., (1973). Application of operant conditioning techniques to the control of cardiac arrhyth-mias. In P. Obrist, A. Black, J. Brener, & L. DiCara (Eds.), *Contemporary trends in cardiovascular psychophysiology.* Chicago: Aldine-Atherton.

Bleuler, M. (1984). What is schizophrenia? *Schizophrenia Bulletin, 10,* 8–10.

Bliss, E. L. (1980). Multiple personalities: A report of 14 cases with implications for schizophrenia and hysteria. *Archives of General Psychiatry, 39,* 823–825.

Bliss, E. L. (1984). Hysteria and hypnosis. *The Journal of Nervous and Mental Disease, 172,* 203–208.

Bliss, E., Clark, L., & West, C. (1959), Studies in sleep deprivation-relationship to schizophrenia. *Archives of Neurology and Psychiatry, 81,* 348–359.

Bloch, H. S. (1969). Army clinical psychiatry in the combat zone. *American Journal of Psychiatry, 126,* 289–298.

Bloom, B. L. (1972). Mental health program evaluation. In S. E. Golann & C. Eisdorfer (Eds.), *Handbook of community mental health.* New York: Appleton-Century-Crofts.

Bloom, B. L. (1977). *Community mental health: A general introduction.* Monterey, CA: Brooks/Cole.

Bloom, B. L., Asher, S. J., & White, S. W. (1978). Marital disruption as a stressor: A review and analysis. *Psychological Bulletin, 85,* 867–894.

Bloom, B. L., Hodges, W. F., & Caldwell, R. A. (1982). A preventive program for the newly separated: Initial evaluation. *American Journal of Community Psychology, 10,* 251–264.

Blumstein, S. (1981). Neurolinguistic disorders: Language-brain relationships. In S. Filskov and T. Boll (Eds.), *Handbook of clinical neuropsychology.* New York: John Wiley.

Bock, R. D., & Kolakowski, D. (1973). Further evidence of sex-linked major-gene influence on human spatial visualizing ability. *American Journal of Genetics, 25,* 1–14.

Boersma, K., Den Hengst, S., Dekker, J., & Emmelkamp, P. M. G. (1976). Exposure and response prevention in the natural environment: A comparison with obsessive-compulsive patients. *Behaviour Research and Therapy, 14,* 12–24.

Bogdan, R., & Taylor, S. (1976). The judged, not the judges: An insider's view of mental retardation. *American Psychologist, 31,* 47–52.

Bohman, M., Cloninger, R., von Knorring, A., & Sigvardsson, S. (1984). An adoption study of somatoform disorders. *Archives of General Psychiatry, 41,* 872–878.

Boll, T. J. (1983). Neuropsychological Assessment. In I. B. Weiner (Ed.), *Clinical methods in psychology.* New York: John Wiley.

Boller, F., Kim, Y., & Detre, T. (1984). Assessment of temporal lobe disorder. In P. E. Logue & J. M. Schear (Eds.), *Clinical neuropsychology,* Springfield, IL: Charles C. Thomas.

Bond, I. K., & Hutchison, H. C. (1965). Application of reciprocal inhibition therapy to exhibitionism. In L. Krasner & L. F. Ullmann (Eds.), *Case studies in behavior modification.* New York: Holt, Rinehart & Winston.

Bonn, J., Readhead, C., & Timmons, B. (1984, September). Enhanced adaptive behavioural response in agoraphobic patients pretreated with breathing retraining. *The Lancet,* pp. 665–669.

Bornstein, R. A., King, G., & Carroll, A. (1983). Neuropsychological abnormalities in Gilles de la Tourette's syndrome. *Journal of Nervous and Mental Disorders, 171,* 497–502.

Bowers, M. B. (1981). Biochemical processes in schizophrenia: An update. In S. J. Keith & L. R. Mosher (Eds.), *Special report: Schizophrenia 1981* (pp. 27–37). Washington, DC: U.S. Government Printing Office.

Bowman, J. A. (1967). Recent experiences in combat psychiatry in Vietnam. *Proceedings of Social and Preventive Psychiatry Short Course*. Washington, DC: Walter Reed Army Medical Center.

Bozzuto, J. C. (1975). Cinematic neurosis following *The Exorcist*. *Journal of Nervous and Mental Disease, 161,* 43–48.

Brady, R. J. (1975). *Emergency psychiatric care: Management of mental health crises*. Bowie, MD: Charles Press.

Braginsky, B. M., & Braginsky, D. D. (1973). The mentally retarded: Society's Hansels and Gretels. *Psychology Today, 7,* 18–20.

Braginsky, B. M., Grosse, M., & Ring, K. (1966). Controlling outcomes through impression management: An experiential study of the manipulative tactics of mental patients. *Journal of Consulting Psychology, 30,* 295–300.

Brammer, L. M., & Shostrom, E. (1984). *Therapeutic psychology*. Englewood Cliffs, NJ: Prentice-Hall.

Brammer, L. M., & Shostrom, E. L. (1982). *Therapeutic psychology*. Englewood Cliffs, NJ: Prentice-Hall.

Brandsma, J. (1979). *Outpatient treatment of alcoholism*. Baltimore: University Park Press.

Bratter, T. (1973). Treating alienated, unmotivated, drug-abusing adolescents. *American Journal of Psychotherapy,* 585–599.

Braucht, G. (1982). Problem drinking among adolescents: A review and analysis of psychosocial research. In National Institute on Alcohol Abuse and Alcoholism, *Alcohol Monograph 4: Special Population Issues*. Washington, DC: U.S. Government Printing Office.

Braucht, G., Follingstad, D., Brakarsh, D., & Berry, K. (1973). A review of goals, approaches, and effectiveness, and a paradigm for evaluation. *Quarterly Journal on the Study of Alcoholism, 34,* 1279–1292.

Braun, P., Kochonsky, G., Shapiro, R., Greenberg, S., Gudeman, J. E., Johnson, S., & Shore, M. F. (1981). Overview: Deinstitutionalization of psychiatric patients: A critical review of outcome studies. *American Journal of Psychiatry, 138,* 736–749.

Bregman, E. D. (1934). An attempt to modify the emotional attitudes of infants by the conditioned response technique. *Journal of Genetic Psychology, 45,* 169–198.

Breier, A., & Strauss, J. S. (1983). Self-control in psychotic disorders. *Archives of General Psychiatry, 40,* 1141–1145.

Brenner, M. H. (1969). Patterns of psychiatric hospitalization among different socioeconomic groups in response to economic stress. *Journal of Nervous and Mental Disease, 148,* 31–38.

Brenner, M. H. (1973). *Mental illness and the economy*. Cambridge, MA: Harvard University Press.

Breuer, J., & Freud, S. (1957). *Studies in hysteria*. New York: Basic Books.

Brewerton, T., & Reus, V. (1983). Lithium carbonate and L-tryptophan in the treatment of bipolar and schizoaffective disorders. *American Journal of Psychiatry, 140,* 757–760.

Brink, M., & Grundlingh, E. M. (1976). Performance of persons with Down's syndrome on two projective techniques. *American Journal of Mental Deficiency, 81,* 265–270.

Broman, S. H., Nichols, P. L., & Kennedy, W. A. (1975). *Preschool IQ: Prenatal and early developmental correlates*. Hillsdale, NJ: Lawrence Erlbaum.

Brotman, A. W., & Stern, T. A. (1983). Case study of cardiovascular abnormalities in anorexia nervosa. *American Journal of Psychiatry, 140,* 1227–1228.

Broverman, I. K., & Broverman, D. (1970). Sex role stereotypes and clinical judgments of mental health. *Journal of Consulting and Clinical Psychology, 34,* 1–7.

Brown, D. G. (1961). Transvestism and sex-role inversion. In A. Ellis & A. Arbanel (Eds.), *The encyclopedia of sexual behavior*. New York: Hawthorn Books.

Brown, G. W. (1974). Meaning, measurement, and stress of life events. In B. S. Dohrenwend & B. P. Dohrenwend (Eds.), *Stressful life events*. New York: Wiley.

Brown, M. (1982). Maintenance and generalization issues in skills training with chronic schizophrenics. In J. Curran & P. Monti (Eds.), *Social skills training*. New York: Guilford Press.

Brownell, K., & Barlow, D. (1980). The behavioral treatment of sexual deviation. In A. Goldstein & E. Foa (Eds.), *Handbook of behavioral interventions*. New York: John Wiley. Copyright © 1980 by John Wiley & Sons, Inc. Used by permission.

Bruch, H. (1978). Obesity and anorexia nervosa. *Psychosomatics, 19,* 208–221.

Bruch, H. (1982). Anorexia nervosa: Therapy and theory. *American Journal of Psychiatry, 139,* 1531–1538.

Bryan, J. H., & Schwartz, T. (1971). Effects of film material upon children's behavior. *Psychological Bulletin, 75,* 50–59.

Buchanan, A., & Oliver, J. E. (1977). Abuse and neglect as a cause of mental retardation. *British Journal of Psychiatry, 131,* 458–467.

Buckley, P. (1982). Identifying schizophrenic patients who should not receive medication. *Schizophrenia Bulletin, 8,* 429–432.

Buckner, H. T. (1970). The transvestic career path. *Psychiatry, 33,* 381–389.

Buhrich, N. (1981). Psychological adjustment in transvestism and transsexualism. *Behaviour Research and Therapy, 19,* 407–411.

Bullard-Bates, P. C., & Satz, P. (1983). A case of pathological left-handedness. *Clinical Neuropsychology, 5,* 128–135.

Bunney, W. E., Pert, A., Rosenblatt, J., Pert, C. B., & Gallaper, D. (1979). Mode of action of lithium: Some biological considerations. *Archives of General Psychiatry, 36,* 898–901.

Burgess, A. W., Groth, A. N. McCausland, M. P. (1981). *American Journal of Orthopsychiatry, 51,* 110–119.

Burgess, A. W., Hartman, C. R., McCausland, M. P., Powers, P. (1984). Response pattern in children and adolescents exploited through sex rings and pornography. *American Journal of Psychiatry, 141,* 656–662.

Burgess, A. W., & Holmstrom, L. L. (1979a). Rape: Sex disruption and recovery. *American Journal of Orthopsychiatry, 49,* 648–657.

Burgess, A. W., & Holmstrom, L. L. (1979b). Adaptive strategies and recovery. *American Journal of Orthopsychiatry, 136,* 1278–1282.

Burks, H. (1960). The hyperactive child. *Exceptional Children, 27,* 18–26.

Buss, A. H. (1966). *Psychopathology*. New York: Wiley.

Butler, G., Cullington, A., Munby, M., Amies, P., & Gelder, M. (1984). Exposure and anxiety management in the treatment of social phobia. *Journal of Consulting and Clinical Psychology, 52,* 642–650.

Butler, G., & Mathews, A. (1983). Cognitive processes in anxiety. *Advances in Behavior Research and Therapy, 5,* 51–62.

Butler, R. N. (1984). Senile dementia: Reversible and irreversible. *The Counseling Psychologist, 12,* 75–79.

Cadoret, R. J., & Cain, C. (1981). Environmental and genetic factors in predicting adolescent antisocial behavior in adoptees. *The Psychiatric Journal of the University of Ottawa, 6,* 220–225.

Calhoun, K. S., & Atkeson, B. M., Resick, P. A. (1982). A longitudinal examination of fear reactions in victims of rape. *Journal of Counseling Psychology, 29,* 655–661.

Cameron, N. A. (1959). Paranoid conditions and paranoia. In S. Arieti (Ed)., *American handbook of psychiatry.* New York: Basic Books.

Campbell, D., Sanderson, R. E., & Laverty, S. G. (1964). Characteristics of a conditioned response in human subjects during extinction trials following a single traumatic conditioning trial. *Journal of Abnormal and Social Psychology, 68,* 627–639.

Campbell, R. J. (1981). *Psychiatric dictionary* (5th ed.). New York: Oxford University Press.

Camus, A. (1946). *The stranger.* New York: Random House.

Caplan, G. (1964). *Principles of preventive psychiatry.* New York: Basic Books.

Cappell, H., & Pliner, P. (1973). Volitional control of marijuana intoxication: A study of the ability to "come down" on command. *Journal of Abnormal Psychology, 82,* 428–434.

Carlson, B. E., & Davis, L. V. (1980). Prevention of domestic violence. In R. H. Price, R. F. Ketterer, B. C. Bader, & J. Monahan (Eds.), *Prevention in mental health: Research, policy, and practice.* Beverly Hills, CA: Sage.

Carlsson, A. (1978). Antipsychotic drugs, neurotransmitters, and schizophrenia. *American Journal of Psychiatry, 135,* 164–173.

Carpenter, D. C. (1975). Some statistics in mental retardation. In C. H. Carter (Ed.), *Handbook of mental retardation syndromes.* Springfield, IL: Charles C. Thomas.

Carpenter, L. W., Straus, J. S., & Mulch, S. (1973). Are there parthognomic symptoms in schizophrenia? *Archives of General Psychiatry, 28,* 847–852.

Carr, A. T. (1974). Compulsive neurosis: A review of the literature. *Psychological Bulletin, 81,* 311–318.

Carr, E. G. (1977). The motivation of self-injurious behavior: A review of some hypotheses. *Psychological Bulletin, 84,* 800–816.

Carter, C. H. (Ed.). (1975). *Handbook of mental retardation syndromes.* Springfield, IL: Charles C. Thomas.

Cartwright, R. D. (1968). Psychotherapeutic processes. *Annual Review of Psychology, 19,* 387–416.

Casper, R. C., Eckert, E. D., Halmi, K. A., Goldberg, S. C., & Davis, J. M. (1980). Bulimia: Its incidence and clinical importance in patients with anorexia nervosa. *Archives of General Psychiatry, 37,* 1030–1035.

Cassel, J. (1974). Psychosocial processes and "stress": Theoretical formulations. *International Journal of Health Services, 4,* 471–482.

Caton, C. (1982). Effect of length of inpatient treatment for chronic schizophrenia. *American Journal of Psychiatry, 139,* 856–861.

Cautela, J. R. (1966). Treatment of compulsive behavior by covert sensitization. *Psychological Record, 16,* 33–41.

Caviness, V. O., & O'Brien, P. (1980). Current concepts: Headache. *New England Journal of Medicine, 302,* 446.

Center for Disease Control. (1981). *Morbidity and Mortality Weekly Report, 30,* 582.

Chambless, D., & Goldstein, A. (1980). The treatment of agoraphobia. In A. Goldstein and E. Foa (Eds.), *Handbook of behavioral interventions.* New York: John Wiley.

Chapman, L. J., & Chapman, J. P. (1967). Genesis of popular but erroneous psychodiagnostic observations. *Journal of Abnormal Psychology, 72,* 193–204.

Chesler, P. (1971). Men drive women crazy. *Psychology Today, 5,* 22–28.

Chesler, P. (1976). Patient and patriarch: Women in the psychotherapeutic relationship. In S. Cox (Ed.), *Female psychology: The emerging self.* Chicago: Science Research Associates.

Chess, S., Thomas, A., & Birch, H. G. (1965). *Your child is a person.* New York: Viking.

Christenson, R. M., Walker, J., Ross, D., & Maltrie, A. (1981). Reactivation of traumatic conflicts. *American Journal of Psychiatry, 138,* 984–989.

Chu, F. D., & Trotter, S. (1974). *The madness establishment.* New York: Grossman.

Churchill, D. W. (1969). Psychotic children and behavior modification. *American Journal of Psychiatry, 125,* 1585–1590.

Churchill, D. W., & Bryson, N. (1972). Looking and approach behavior of psychotic and normal children as a function of adult attention and preoccupation. *Comprehensive Psychiatry, 13,* 171–177.

Cinciripini, P., Kornblith, S., Turner, S., & Hersen, M. (1983). A behavioral program for the management of anorexia and bulimia. *The Journal of Nervous and Mental Disease, 171,* 186–189.

Ciompi, L. (1980). Long-term study on the course of life and aging of schizophrenics. *Schizophrenia Bulletin, 6,* 606–618.

Clarizio, H. F., & McCoy, G. F. (1976). *Behavior disorders in children* (2nd ed.). New York: Crowell.

Clark, D. F. (1966). Behaviour therapy of Gilles de la Tourette's syndrome. *British Journal of Psychiatry, 122,* 771–778.

Clark, D., Salkovskis, P., & Chalkley, A. (in press). Respiratory control as a treatment for panic attacks. *Journal of Behavior Therapy and Experimental Psychiatry.*

Clark, K. B., & Clark, M. K. (1947). Racial identification and preference in Negro children. In T. M. Newcomb & E. L. Hartley (Eds.), *Readings in social psychology.* New York: Holt, Rinehart & Winston.

Clark, M., Gosnell, M., Witherspoon, Huck, J., Hager, M., Junkin, D., King, P., Wallace, A., & Robinson, T. (1984, December 3). A slow death of the mind. *Newsweek,* pp. 56–62.

Clarke, A. D. B., & Clarke, A. M. (1977). Prospects for prevention and amelioration of mental retardation: A quest editorial. *American Journal of Mental Deficiency, 81,* 523–533.

Clausen, J. A., & Kohn, M. L. (1959). Relation of schizophrenia to the social structure of a small city. In B. Pasamanick (Ed.), *Epidemiology of mental disorder.* Washington, DC: American Association for the Advancement of Science.

Cleckley, H. (1964). *The mask of sanity* (4th ed.). St. Louis: Mosby.

Clements, S. D., & Peters, S. (1962). Minimal brain dysfunction in the school-age child. *Archives of General Psychiatry, 6,* 185–197.

Coates, J. (1980, March 26). Pot more perilous than we thought. *Chicago Tribune,* pp. 1, 14.

Cobb, E. J., Leitenberg, H., & Burchard, J. D. (1982). Foster parents teaching foster parents: Communication and conflict resolution skills training. *Journal of Community Psychology, 10,* 240–249.

Cobb, S. (1976). Support as a moderator of life stress. *Psychosomatic Medicine, 38,* 300–314.

Cochrane, R. (1973). Hostility and neuroticism among unselected essential hypertensives. *Journal of Psychosomatic Research, 17,* 215–218.

Coelho, G. V., Hamburg, D. A., & Murphy, E. G. (1963). Coping strategies in a new learning environment: A study of American college freshman. *Archives of General Psychiatry, 9,* 433–443.

Cohen, J. (1969). *Personality dynamics.* Chicago: Rand McNally.

Cohen, J. (1970). *Secondary motivation I: A survey of experience, interest, and opinion.* Chicago: Rand McNally.

Cohen, M., Seghorn, T., & Calmas, W. (1969). Sociometric study of sex offenders. *Journal of Abnormal Psychology, 74,* 249–255.

Cohen, M. J., Rickles, W. H., & McArthur, D. L. (1978). Evidence for physiological response stereotypy in migraine headaches. *Psychosomatic Medicine, 40,* 344–354.

Cohen, S., Montero, W., & Marks, I. M. (1984). Imipramine and brief therapist-aided exposure in agoraphobics having self-exposure homework. *Archives of General Psychiatry, 40,* 153–162.

Colby, J. M. (1977). Appraisal of four psychological theories of paranoid phenomena. *Journal of Abnormal Psychology, 86,* 54–59.

Cole, J. O. (1964). Phenothiazine treatment in acute schizophrenia: Effectiveness. *Archives of General Psychiatry, 10,* 246–261.

Collins, B. E. (1970). *Social psychology.* Reading, MA: Addison-Wesley.

Collins, J. K., McCabe, M., Jupp, J. J., & Sutton, J. J. (1983). Body percept change in obese females after weight reduction therapy. *Journal of Clinical Psychology, 39,* 507–511.

Commission on Obscenity and Pornography. (1970). *The report of the commission on obscenity and pornography.* New York: Bantam.

Conger, J. C., & Keane, S. P. (1981). Social skills intervention in the treatment of isolated or withdrawn children. *Psychological Bulletin, 90,* 478–495.

Conger, J. J. (1951). The effects of alcohol on conflict behavior in the albino rat. *Quarterly Journal of Studies on Alcohol, 12,* 1–30.

Conners, C. K. (1970). Symptom patterns in hyperkinetic, neurotic and normal children. *Child Development, 41,* 667–682.

Consensus Development Panel. (1982). Defined diets and childhood hyperactivity. *Clinical Pediatrics, 21,* 627–630.

Coons, P. M., Milstein, V., & Marley, C. (1982). EEG studies of two multiple personalities and a control. *Archives of General Psychiatry, 39,* 823–825.

Cooper, A. (1963). A case of fetishism and impotence treated by behavior therapy. *British Journal of Psychiatry, 109,* 649–652.

Cooper, A. J. (1969). A clinical study of coital anxiety in male potency disorders. *Journal of Psychosomatic Research, 13,* 143–147.

Cooper, L. Z., & Krugman, S. (1966). Diagnosis and management: Congenital rubella. *Pediatrics, 37,* 335.

Corbett, J. A. (1971). The nature of tics and Gilles de la Tourette's syndrome. *Journal of Psychosomatic Research, 15,* 32.

Cordes, C. (1984a). The plight of the homeless mentally ill. *APA Monitor, 15,* 1, 13.

Cordes, C. (1984b). Reuven Feuerstein makes every child count. *APA Monitor, 15,* 18, 20.

Corey, G., Corey, M., & Callahan, P. (1984). *Issues and ethics in the helping professions.* Monterey, CA: Brooks/Cole.

Corsini, R. J. (1984). *Current psychotherapies.* Itasca, IL: F. E. Peacock.

Cosand, B. J., Bourque, L. B., & Kraus, J. F. (1982). Suicide among adolescents in Sacramento County, California 1950–1979. *Adolescence, 17,* 917–930.

Costello, C. G. (1982). Fears and phobias in women: A community study. *Journal of Abnormal Psychology, 91,* 280–286.

Cowen, E. L. (1982). Help is where you find it: Four informal helping groups. *American Psychologist, 37,* 385–395.

Cowen, E. L. (1983). Primary prevention in mental health: Past, present, and future. In R. D. Felner, L. A. Jason, J. N. Moritsugu, & S. S. Farber (Eds.), *Preventive psychology: Theory, research and practice.* New York: Pergamon.

Cowen, E. L., Izzo, L. D., Miles, H. C., Teleschow, E. F., Trost, M. A., & Zax, M. (1963). A preventive mental health program in the school setting: Description and evaluation. *Journal of Psychology, 56,* 307–356.

Cox, D. J., & McMahon, B. (1978). Incidence of male exhibitionism in the United States as reported by victimized college students. *International Journal of Law and Psychiatry, 1,* 453–457.

Coyne, J. C. (1976). Depression and the response of others. *Journal of Abnormal Psychology, 85,* 186–193.

Creer, T. L. (1982). Asthma. *Journal of Consulting and Clinical Psychology, 50,* 912–921.

Critchley, D. L. (1979). The adverse influence of psychiatric diagnostic labels on the observation of child behavior. *American Journal of Orthopsychiatry, 49,* 157–160.

Crome, L., & Stern, J. (1972). *Pathology of mental retardation.* Edinburgh, Scotland: Churchill Livingstone.

Cruikshank, W. M., & Johnson, G. O. (Eds.). (1975). *Education of exceptional children and youth.* Englewood Cliffs, NJ: Prentice-Hall.

Csernansky, J. G., Holman, C. A., & Hollister, L. E. (1983). Variability and the dopamine hypothesis of schizophrenia. *Schizophrenia Bulletin, 9,* 325–328.

Cummings, N. A. (1984). The future of clinical psychology in the United States. *The Clinical Psychologist, 37,* 19–20.

Curran, J., & Monti, P. (1982). *Social skills training: A practical handbook for assessment and treatment.* New York: Guilford Press.

Curran, J. P. (1977). Skills training as an approach to the treatment of heterosexual-social skills: A review. *Psychological Bulletin, 84,* 140–157.

Curtis, G. C. (1981). Sensory experiences during treatment of phobias by *in vivo* exposure. *American Journal of Psychiatry, 138,* 1095–1097.

Curtis, J. D., & Detert, R. A. (1981). *How to relax: A holistic approach to stress management.* Palo Alto, CA: Mayfield.

Dahlstrom, W. G., & Welch, G. S. (1965). *An MMPI handbook*. Minneapolis: University of Minnesota Press.

Danto, B. L. (1971, Fall). Assessment of the suicidal person in the telephone interview. *Bulletin of Suicidology,* pp. 48–56.

Darrach, D. (1976, March 8). Poetry and poison. *Time*.

Darwin, C. (1859). *On the origin of the species by means of natural selection*. London: John Murray.

Davis, J. D. (1983). Slaying the psychoanalytic dragon: An integrationist's commentary on Yates. *British Journal of Clinical Psychology, 22,* 133–134.

Davis, J. M., Schaffer, C. B., Killian, G. A., Kinard, C., & Chan, C. (1980). Important issues in the drug treatment of schizophrenia. In S. J. Keith and L. R. Mosher (Eds.), *Special report: Schizophrenia 1981.* (pp. 109–126). Washington, DC: U.S. Government Printing Office.

Davison, G. (1968). Elimination of a sadistic fantasy by a client-controlled counterconditioning technique: A case study. *Journal of Abnormal Psychology, 73,* 84–90.

Davison, G. (1974). *Homosexuality: The ethical challenge*. Presidential address at the meeting of the Association for the Advancement of Behavior Therapy, Chicago.

Dawson, G. (1983). Lateralized brain dysfunction in autism: Evidence from the Halstead-Reitan neuropsychological battery. *Journal of Autism and Developmental Disorders, 13,* 269–286.

de Gobineau, A. (1915). *The inequality of human races*. New York: Putnam.

Deaux, K. (1984). From individual differences to social categories: Analysis of a decade's research on gender. *American Psychologist, 39,* 105–116.

DeCharms, R., Levy, J., & Wertheimer, M. (1954). A note on attempted evaluations of psychotherapy. *Journal of Clinical Psychology, 21,* 233–235.

Declaration of general and special rights of the mentally retarded. (1969). *Mental Retardation, 4,* 7.

DeGood, D. (1983). Reducing medical patients' reluctance to participate in psychological therapies: The initial session. *Professional Psychology: Research and Practice, 14,* 570–579.

DeJong, R. N., & Sugar, O. (1972). *The yearbook of neurology and neurosurgery*. Chicago: Year Book Medical Publishers.

Delva, N., & Letemendia, F. (1982). Lithium treatment in schizophrenia and schizo-affective disorders. *British Journal of Psychiatry, 141,* 387–400.

DeMyer, M. K. (1975). Research in infantile autism: A strategy and its results. *Biological Psychiatry, 10,* 433–450.

Department of Health, Education and Welfare. (1979). *Mental health and the elderly: Report of the President's Commission on Mental Health*. Washington, DC: U.S. Government Printing Office.

Derogatis, L. R., Meyer, J. K., & Gallant, B. W. (1977). Distinctions between male and female partners in sexual disorders. *American Journal of Psychiatry, 134,* 384–390.

DeVellis, R. F. (1977). Learned helplessness in institutions. *Mental Retardation, 15,* 10–13.

DeVellis, R. F., & McCauley, C. (1979). Perception of contingency and mental retardation. *Journal of Autism and Developmental Disorders, 9,* 261–270.

Devinsky, O., & Bear, D. (1984). Varieties of aggressive behavior in temporal lobe epilepsy. *American Journal of Psychiatry, 141,* 651–656.

Deykin, E. Y., & MacMahon, B. (1979). The incidence of seizures among children with autistic symptoms. *American Journal of Psychiatry, 136,* 1310–1312.

Dishion, T. J., Loeber, R., Stouthamer-Loeber, M., & Patterson, G. R. (1984). Skill deficits and male adolescent delinquency. *Journal of Abnormal Child Psychology, 12,* 37–54.

Divorky, D. (1978, December). Behavior and food coloring: Lessons of a diet fad. *Psychology Today,* pp. 145–148.

Doane, J. A., West, M. J., Goldstein, M. J., & Rodnick, E. H. (1981). Parental communication deviance and affective style: Predictions of subsequent schizophrenia spectrum disorders in vulnerable adolescents. *Archives of General Psychiatry, 38,* 679–685.

Dobzhansky, T. (1973). Differences are not deficits. *Psychology Today, 7,* 96–101.

Dohrenwend, B. P., & Dohrenwend, B. S. (1969). *Social status and psychological disorder: A causal inquiry*. New York: Wiley.

Dohrenwend, B. P., & Dohrenwend, B. S. (1974). Social and cultural influences on psychopathology. *Annual Review of Psychology, 25,* 417–452.

Dohrenwend, B. P., & Dohrenwend, B. S. (1982). Perspectives on the past and future of psychiatric epidemiology: The 1981 Rema Lapouse Lecture. *American Journal of Public Health, 72,* 1271–1279.

Dohrenwend, B. P., Dohrenwend, B. S., Gould, M. S., Link, B., Neugebauer, R., & Wunsch-Hitzig, R. (1980). *Mental illness in the United States: Epidemiological estimates*. New York: Praeger.

Dohrenwend, B. P., & Egri, G. (1981). Recent stressful life events and episodes of schizophrenia. *Schizophrenia Bulletin, 7,* 12–23.

Dohrenwend, B. S., & Dohrenwend, B. P. (1973). An approach to the problem of valid comparison of psychiatric disorders in contrasting class and ethnic groups from the general population. In M. Hammer, K. Salzinger, & S. Sutton (Eds.), *Psychopathology: Contributions from social, behavioral, and biological sciences*. New York: Wiley.

Doll, E. A. (1953). *Measurement of social competence: A manual for the Vineland Social Maturity Scale*. Circle Pines, MN: American Guidance Service.

Donaldson, S., Gelenberg, A., & Baldessarini, R. (1983). The pharmacologic treatment of schizophrenia: A progress report. *Schizophrenia Bulletin, 9,* 504–527.

Donnerstein, E., & Berkowitz, L. (1981). Victim reactions in aggressive-erotic films as a factor in violence against women. *Journal of Personality and Social Psychology, 41,* 710–724.

Dorfman, D. D. (1978). The Cyril Burt Question: New findings. *Science, 201,* 1177–1186.

Dragstedt, L. R. (1956). A concept of the etiology of gastric duodenal ulcer. *American Journal of Roentgenology, 75,* 219–229.

Dublin, L. I. (1963). *Suicide: A sociological and statistical study*. New York: Ronald Press.

Dubos, R. (1965). *Man adapting*. New Haven: Yale University Press.

Dubos, R. (1971, February). Man overadapting. *Psychology Today,* pp. 50–53.

Dubovsky, S., Franks, R., Lifschitz, M., & Coen, R. (1982). Effectiveness of verapamil in the treatment of a manic patient. *American Journal of Psychiatry, 139,* 502–504.

Durkheim, E. (1951). *Suicide*. New York: Free Press.

Durlak, J. A. (1979). Comparative effectiveness of paraprofessional and professional helpers. *Psychological Bulletin, 86*, 80–92.

Eagly, A. H. (1983). Gender and social influence: A social psychological analysis. *American Psychologist, 38*, 971–981.

Edgerton, R. B., Bollinger, M., & Herr, B. (1984). The cloak of competence: After two decades. *American Journal of Mental Deficiency, 88*, 345–351.

Edwards, M. S., & Baker, C. J. (1981). Meningitis infections in children. *Journal of Pediatrics, 99*, 540–545.

The effects of bombing on health and medical care in Germany. (1945). In *U.S. Strategic Bombing Survey*. Washington, DC: U.S. Government Printing Office.

Efron, R. (1956). The effect of olfactory stimuli in arresting uncinate fits. *Brain, 79*, 267–281.

Efron, R. (1957). The conditioned inhibitions of uncinate fits. *Brain, 80*, 251–262.

Egbert, L., Battit, G., Welch, C., & Bartlett, M. (1964). Reduction of postoperative pain. *New England Journal of Medicine, 270*, 835–837.

Ehrhardt, A. A., Grisanti, G., & McCauley, E. A. (1979). Female-to-male transsexuals compared to lesbians: Behavioral patterns of childhood and adolescent development. *Archives of Sexual Behavior, 8*, 481–490.

Eisenberg, L. (1958). School phobia: A study in the communication of anxieties. *American Journal of Psychiatry, 114*, 712–718.

Eisenberg, M. M. (1978). *Ulcers*. New York: Random House. Copyright ©1978 by Michael M. Eisenberg, M.D. Reprinted by permission of Random House, Inc.

Ellenberger, H. F. (1972). The Story of "Anna O.": A critical review with new data. *Journal of the History of the Behavior Sciences, 8*, 267–279.

Ellingson, R. (1954). Incidence of EEG abnormality among patients with mental disorders of apparently nonorganic origin: A critical review. *American Journal of Psychiatry, 111*, 363–375.

Ellis, A. (1957). Outcome of employing three techniques of psychotherapy. *Journal of Clinical Psychology, 13*, 344–350.

Ellis, A. (1962). *Reason and emotion in psychotherapy*. New York: Lyle-Stuart.

Ellis, A. (1971). *Growth through reason*. Palo Alto, CA: Science and Behavior Books.

Ellis, A. (1973). Are cognitive behavior therapy and rational therapy synonymous? *Rational Living, 8*, 8–11.

Emslie, G. J., & Rosenfeld, A. (1983). Incest reported by children and adolescents hospitalized for severe psychiatric problems. *American Journal of Psychiatry, 140*, 108–111.

Endler, N. S. (1982). *Holiday of darkness*. New York: Wiley. Copyright © 1982 by John Wiley & Sons, Inc., Used by permission.

Engel, G. (1971). Sudden and rapid death during psychological stress. *Annals of Internal Medicine, 74*, 771.

English, H. B. (1929). Three cases of the conditioned fear response. *Journal of Abnormal and Social Psychology, 24*, 221–225.

Epilepsy Foundation of America. (1983). *Questions and answers about epilepsy*. Landover, MD: Epilepsy Foundation of America.

Epstein, S. (1962). The measurement of drive and conflict in humans: Theory and experiment. In M. R. Jones (Ed.), *Nebraska symposium on motivation*. Lincoln: University of Nebraska Press.

Epstein, S. (1972). The nature of anxiety with emphasis upon its relationship to expectancy. In C. D. Spielberger (Ed.), *Anxiety: Current trends in theory and research* (Vol. 2). New York: Academic Press.

Erikson, E. (1962). *Young man Luther*. New York: Norton.

Erikson, E. H. (1968). *Identity: Youth and crisis*. New York: Norton.

Eron, L. D. (1963). Relationship of television viewing habits and aggressive behavior in children. *Journal of Abnormal and Social Psychology, 76*, 193–196.

Eron, L. D. (1980). Prescription for reduction of aggression. *American Psychologist, 35*, 244–252.

Eron, L. D. (1982). Parent-child interaction, television violence, and aggression of children. *American Psychologist, 37*, 197–211.

Eron, L. D., Lefkowitz, M. M., Huesmann, L. R., Walder, L. O. (1972). Does television violence cause aggression? *American Psychologist, 27*, 253–263.

Eshkevari, H. S. (1979). Early infantile autism in monozygotic twins. *Journal of Autism and Developmental Disorders, 9*, 105–109.

Evans, D. R. (1968). Masturbatory fantasy and sexual deviations. *Behaviour Research and Therapy, 6*, 17–19.

Exner, J. E. (1983). Rorschach assessment. In I. B. Weiner (Ed.), *Clinical methods in psychology*. New York: John Wiley.

Eysenck, H. J. (1952). The effects of psychotherapy: An evaluation. *Journal of Consulting Psychology, 16*, 319–324.

Eysenck, H. J. (1954). The science of personality: Nomothetic vs. idiographic. *Psychological Review, 61*, 339–342.

Eysenck, H. J. (1957). *Dynamics of anxiety and hysteria*. London: Routledge & Kegan Paul.

Eysenck, H. J., & Rachman, S. (1965). *The causes and cures of neurosis*. San Diego: Knapp.

Fagan, J., & McMahon, P. P. (1984). Incipient multiple personality in children: Four cases. *Journal of Nervous and Mental Disease, 172*, 26–36.

Fairburn, C., & Cooper, P. (1983). The epidemiology of bulimia nervosa. *International Journal of Eating Disorders, 2*, 61–67.

Fairweather, G. W., Sanders, D. H., Cressler, D. L., & Maynard, H. (1969). *Community life for the mentally ill: An alternative to institutional care*. Chicago: Aldine.

Falloon, I., & Liberman, R. (1983). Interactions between drug and psychosocial therapy in schizophrenia. *Schizophrenia Bulletin, 9*, 555–562.

Farberow, N. L. (1970). Ten years of suicide prevention—past and future. *Bulletin of Suicidology, 6*, 5–11.

Farberow, N. L., & Shneidman, E. S. (Eds.). (1961). *The cry for help*. New York: McGraw-Hill.

Feighner, A. C., & Feighner, J. P. (1974). Multimodality treatment of the hyperactive child. *American Journal of Psychiatry, 13*, 459–463.

Feinsilver, D., & Yates, B. (1984). Combined use of psychotherapy and drugs in chronic, treatment-resistant schizophrenic patients. *The Journal of Nervous and Mental Disease, 172*, 133–139.

Feldman, M., & MacCulloch, M. (1965). The application of anticipatory avoidance learning to the treatment of homosexuality: 1. Theory, technique, and preliminary results. *Behaviour Research and Therapy, 2,* 165–183.

Feldman, M. P., MacCulloch, M. H., & MacCulloch, M. L. (1968). The aversion therapy treatment of a heterogeneous group of five cases of sexual deviation. *Acta Psychiatrica Scandinavica, 44,* 581–585.

Feldman-Summers, S., Gordon, P. E., & Meagher, J. R. (1979). The impact of rape on sexual satisfaction. *Journal of Abnormal Psychology, 88,* 101–105.

Felner, R. D., Jason, L. A., Moritsugu, J., & Farber, S. S. (1983). Preventive psychology: Evolution and current status. In R. D. Felner & L. A. Jason (Eds.), *Preventive psychology: Theory, research and practice.* New York: Pergamon.

Fenichel, O. (1945). *The psychoanalytic theory of neuroses.* New York: Norton.

Fenton, W. S., Mosher, L. R., & Mathews, S. M. (1981). Diagnosis of schizophrenia: A critical review of current diagnostic systems. *Schizophrenia Bulletin, 7,* 452–475.

Fernando, S. J. M. (1967). Gilles de la Tourette's syndrome. *British Journal of Psychiatry, 113,* 607–617.

Ferster, C. B. (1961). Positive reinforcement and behavior deficits of autistic children. *Child Development, 32,* 437–456.

Ferster, C. B. (1965). Classification of behavior pathology. In L. Krasner & L. P. Ullmann (Eds.), *Research in behavior modification.* New York: Holt, Rinehart & Winston.

Feshbach, S., & Singer, R. D. (1971). *Television and aggression.* San Francisco: Jossey-Bass.

Festinger, L., Riecken, H. W., & Schachter, S. (1957). *When prophecy fails.* Minneapolis: University of Minnesota Press.

Fichter, M. M., Wallace, C. J., Liberman, R. P., & Davis, J. R. (1976). Improving social interaction in a chronic psychotic using discriminated avoidance (''nagging''): Experimental analysis and discrimination. *Journal of Applied Behavioral Analysis, 9,* 377–386.

Fieve, R., Dunner, D., Kumbaraci, et al. (1976). Lithium carbonate prophylaxis in three subtypes of primary affective disorder. *Pharmakopsychiatri Neuropsychopharmakol, 9,* 100–107.

Fink, M. (1979). *Convulsive therapy: Theory and practice.* New York: Raven Press.

Finkelhor, D. (1980). Sex among siblings: A survey on prevalence, variety, and effects. *Archives of Sexual Behavior, 9,* 171–194.

Fiore, N. (1984). *The road back to health: Coping with the emotional side of cancer.* New York: Bantam.

Fischer, J. (1969). Negroes, whites and rates of mental illness: Reconsideration of a myth. *Psychiatry, 32,* 438–446.

Fisher, S. (1973). *The female orgasm.* New York: Basic Books.

Fishman, A. (1982). *Arteriosclerosis 1981.* Washington, DC: U.S. Department of Health and Human Services.

Fleming, M. Z., MacGowan, B. R., Robinson, L., Spitz, J., & Salt, P. (1982). The body image of the post-operative female-to-male transsexual. *Journal of Consulting and Clinical Psychology, 50,* 461–462.

Foa, E. B., Steketee, G., & Ascher, M. (1980). Systematic desensitization. In A. Goldstein & E. Foa (Eds.), *Handbook of behavioral interventions.* New York: John Wiley.

Foa, E. B., Steketee, G., & Milby, J. B. (1980). Differential effects of exposure and response prevention in obsessive-compulsive washers. *Journal of Consulting and Clinical Psychology, 48,* 71–79.

Foa, E., Steketee, G., Turner, R., & Fischer, S. (1980). Effects of imaginal exposure to feared disasters in obsessive compulsive checkers. *Behaviour Research and Therapy, 18,* 449–455.

Foa, E., & Tillmanns, A. (1980). The treatment of obsessive-compulsive neurosis. In A. Goldstein & E. Foa (Eds.), *Handbook of behavioral interventions.* New York: John Wiley.

Foley, V. D. (1984). Family therapy. In R. Coisine, *Current psychotherapies.* Itasca, IL: F. E. Peacock.

Folstein, S., & Rutler, M. (1977). Infantile autism: A genetic study of 21 twin pairs. *Journal of Child Psychology, 18,* 297–321.

Foltz, D. (1980). Judgment withheld on DSM-III, new child classification pushed. *APA Monitor, 11,* 33.

Footlick, J. K., & Lowell, J. (1978, December 18). The ten faces of Billy. *Newsweek,* p. 106.

Ford, M., Stroebel, C., Strong, P., & Szarek, B. (1982). Quieting response training: Treatment of psychophysiological disorders in psychiatric inpatients. *Biofeedback and Self-Regulation, 7,* 331–339.

Fordyce, W. E. (1976). *Behavioral methods for chronic pain and illness.* St. Louis: C. V. Mosby.

Fordyce, W. E. (1982). A behavioral perspective on chronic pain. *British Journal of Clinical Psychiatry, 21,* 313–320.

Forgac, G. E., Cassel, C. A., & Michaels, E. J. (1984). Chronicity of criminal behavior and psychopathology in male exhibitionists. *Journal of Clinical Psychology, 40,* 827–832.

Forgac, G. E., & Michaels, E. J. (1982). Personality characteristics of two types of male exhibitionism. *Journal of Abnormal Psychology, 91,* 287–293.

Forssman, H. (1970). Klinefelter's syndrome. *British Journal of Psychiatry, 117,* 35–37.

Foxx, R., & Brown, R. (1979). Nicotine fading and self-monitoring for cigarette abstinence or controlled smoking. *Journal of Applied Behavior Analysis, 12,* 111–125.

Framo, J. (1982). *Family interaction: A dialogue between family therapists and family researchers.* New York: Springer.

Frank, E., Anderson, C., & Rubenstein, D. (1978). Frequency of sexual dysfunction in ''normal'' couples. *New England Journal of Medicine, 299,* 111–115.

Franks, C., Fried, R., & Ashem, B. (1966). An improved apparatus for the aversive conditioning of cigarette smokers. *Behaviour Research and Therapy, 4,* 301–308.

Freedman, B. J., & Chapman, L. J. (1973). Early subjective experience in schizophrenic episodes. *Journal of Abnormal Psychology, 82,* 46–54.

Freedman, J. L., & Fraser, S. C. (1966). Compliance without pressure: The foot-in-the-door techniques. *Journal of Personality and Social Psychology, 4,* 195–202.

Frerichs, R. R., Aneshensel, C. S., & Clark, V. A. (1981). Prevalence of depression in Los Angeles County. *American Journal of Epidemiology, 113,* 691–699.

Freud, S. (1905). Psychical (or mental) treatment. In J. Strachey (Ed. and Trans.), *The complete psychological works* (Vol. 7). New York: Norton.

Freud, S. (1924). Mourning and melancholia. In J. Riviere (Trans.), *Collected papers* (Vol. 4). London: Hogarth Press. (Original work published 1917)

Freud, S. (1938). The psychopathology of everyday life. In

A. B. Brill (Ed.), *The basic writings of Sigmund Freud*. New York: Modern Library.

Freud, S. (1949). *An outline of psychoanalysis*. New York: Norton.

Freud, S. (1959). *Beyond the pleasure principle*. New York: Bantam.

Freud, S., & Breuer, J. (1895). *Studies in hysteria*. Vienna: G. S.

Friedman, A. P. (1979). Characteristics of tension headache: Profile of 1,420 cases. *Psychosomatics, 20*, 451–461.

Friedman, H. S., Harris, M. J., & Hall, J. A. (1984). Nonverbal expression of emotion: Healthy charisma or coronary-prone behavior. In C. Van Dyke, L. Temoshok, & L. S. Zegan (Eds.), *Emotion in health and illness: Application to clinical practice*. New York: Grune & Stratton.

Friedman, M., & Rosenman, R. H. (1959). Association of specific overt behavior pattern with blood and cardiovascular findings. *Journal of the American Medical Association, 169*, 1286–1296.

Friedman, M., & Rosenman, R. H. (1974). *Type A Behavior*. New York: Knopf.

Friedman, P., & Linn, L. (1957). Some psychiatric notes on the *Andrea Doria* disaster. *American Journal of Psychiatry, 114*, 426.

Friedrich, J. (1985, January 7). Seven who have succeeded. *Time*, pp. 41–45.

Friel, P. B. (1973). Familial incidence of Gilles de la Tourette's disease with observations on etiology and treatment. *British Journal of Psychiatry, 122*, 655–658.

Fromm, E. (1941). *Escape from freedom*. New York: Holt, Rinehart & Winston.

Frontline. (1984). *The mind of a murderer, Part 1 and 2*. WGBH Education Foundation.

Fuchs, K. (1975). Vaginismus: The hypno-therapeutic approach. *The Journal of Sex Research, 11*, 39–45.

Gallahorn, G. E. (1981). Borderline personality disorders. In J. R. Lion (Ed.), *Personality disorders: Diagnosis and management*. Baltimore: Williams & Wilkins.

Galton, F. (1869). *Hereditary genius: An inquiry into its laws and consequences*. London: Macmillan.

Gamble, E., & Elder, S. (1983). Multimodal biofeedback in the treatment of migraine. *Biofeedback and Self-Regulation, 8*, 383–392.

Gan, S., Tymchuk, A. J., & Nishihara, A. (1977). Mentally retarded adults: Their attitudes toward retardation. *Mental Retardation, 15*, 5–9.

Gangadhar, B., Kapur, R., & Kalyanasundaram, S. (1982). Comparison of electroconvulsive therapy with imipramine in endogenous depression: A double blind study. *British Journal of Psychiatry, 141*, 367–371.

Garakani, H., Zitrin, C. M., & Klein, D. F. (1984). Treatment of panic disorder with imipramine alone. *American Journal of Psychiatry, 141*, 446–448.

Garbarino, J. (1980). Preventing child maltreatment. In R. H. Price, R. F. Ketterer, B. C. Bader, & J. Monahan (Eds.), *Prevention in mental health: Research, policy, and practice*. Beverly Hills, CA: Sage.

Garcia, J. (1981). The logic and limits of mental aptitude testing. *American Psychologist, 36*, 1172–1180.

Garfield, S. L. (1974). *Clinical psychology: The study of personality and behavior*. Chicago: Aldine.

Garfield, S. L., & Kurtz, R. (1976). Clinical psychologists in the 1970s. *American Psychologist, 31*, 1–9.

Garfield, S. L., & Kurtz, R. (1977). A study of eclectic views. *Journal of Consulting and Clinical Psychology, 45*, 78–83.

Garfinkel, B., Froese, M., & Hood, J. (1982). Suicide attempts in children and adolescents. *American Journal of Psychiatry, 139*, 1257–1261.

Garfinkel, P. E., Moldofsky, H., & Garner, D. M. (1980). The heterogeneity of anorexia nervosa. *Archives of General Psychiatry, 37*, 1036–1040.

Garmezy, N. (1978). Never mind the psychologist: Is it good for the children? *The Clinical Psychologist, 31*, 1, 4–6.

Garreau, B., Barthelemy, C., Sauvage, D., Leddet, I., & Lelord, G. (1984). A comparison of autistic syndromes with and without neurological problems. *Journal of Autism and Developmental Disorders, 14*, 105–111.

Gatz, M., Barbarin, O. A., Tyler, F. B., Mitchell, R. E., Moran, J. A., Wirzbicki, P. J., Crawford, J., & Engelman, A. (1982). Enhancement of individual and community competence: The older adult as community worker. *American Journal of Community Psychology, 10*, 291–304.

Gatz, M., Smyer, M. A., Lawton, M. P. (1980). The mental health system and the older adult. In L. W. Poon (Ed.), *Aging in the 1980s*. Washington, DC: American Psychological Association.

Gaylin, W., Meister, J., & Neville, R. (Eds.). (1975). *Operating on the mind: The psychosurgery conflict*. New York: Basic Books.

Gebhard, P. H. (1966). Factors in marital orgasm. *Journal of Social Issues, 22*, 88–95.

Gebhard, P. H., Gagnon, J. H., Pomeroy, W. B., & Christerson, C. V. (1965). *Sex offenders*. New York: Harper & Row.

Gelder, M. G., & Marks, I. M. (1969). Aversion treatment in transvestism and transsexualism. In R. Green & J. Money (Eds.), *Transsexualism and sex reassignment*. Baltimore: Johns Hopkins University Press.

Gelhorn, E. (1967). *Principles of autonomic-somatic integrations*. Minneapolis: University of Minnesota Press.

Gentry, W. D. (Ed.). (1984). *Handbook of behavioral medicine*. New York: Guilford Press.

Gentry, W. D., Chesney, A. P., Gary, H., Hall, R. P., & Harburg, E. (1982). Habitual anger-coping styles: I. Effect on male/female blood pressure and hypertensive status. *Psychosomatic Medicine, 44*, 195–202.

Gershman, H. (1978). A psychoanalyst's evaluation of the sexual revolution. *American Journal of Psychoanalysis, 38*, 143–154.

Gershman, L. (1970). Case conference: A transvestite fantasy treated by thought-stopping, covert sensitization and aversive shock. *Journal of Behavior Therapy and Experimental Psychiatry, 4*, 159–162.

Gibbs, J. P., & Martin, W. T. (1964). *Status integration and suicide*. Eugene: University of Oregon Press.

Gibbs, M. V., & Thorpe, J. G. (1983). Personality stereotype of non-institutionalized Down's syndrome children. *American Journal of Mental Deficiency, 87*, 601–605.

Gilberg, C. (1984). Infantile autism and other childhood psychoses in a Swedish urban region: Epidemiological aspects. *Journal of Child Psychology and Psychiatry, 25*, 35–43.

Gilberg, C., & Forsell, C. (1984). Childhood psychosis and neurofibromatosis—more than a coincidence? *Journal of Autism and Developmental Disorders, 14,* 1–8.

Gillie, D. (1977). The Cyril Burt affair. *Phi Delta Kappan, 58,* 469.

Ginsburg, H. (1972). *The myth of the deprived child.* Englewood Cliffs, NJ: Prentice-Hall.

Girard, F. (1984, August 5). State crime data called flawed, late. *Detroit News,* pp. 1, 12.

Glaser, G. H., Newman, R. J., & Schafer, R. (1963). Interictal psychosis in psychomotor-temporal lobe epilepsy: An EEG psychological study. In G. H. Glaser (Ed.), *EEG and behavior.* New York: Basic Books.

Glasgow, M., Gaarder, K., & Engel, B. (1982). Behavioral treatment of high blood pressure 11. Acute and sustained effects of relaxation and systolic blood pressure biofeedback. *Psychosomatic Medicine, 44,* 155–170.

Glass, D. C. (1976). Stress, competition and heart attacks. *Psychology Today, 10,* 56–59.

Glass, D. C., & Singer, J. E. (1972). *Urban stress: Experiments on noise and social stressors.* New York: Academic Press.

Glidewell, J. C. (1983). Prevention: The threat and the promise. In R. D. Felner, L. A. Jason, J. Moritsugu, & S. S. Farber (Eds.), *Preventive psychology: Theory, research, and practice.* New York: Pergamon.

Goffman, E. (1961). *Asylums.* Garden City, NY: Doubleday.

Goldberg, E. M., & Morrison, S. L. (1963). Schizophrenia and social class. *British Journal of Psychiatry, 109,* 785–802.

Golden, C. J. (1981). A standardized version of Luria's neuropsychological tests: A quantitative and qualitative approach to neuropsychological evaluation. In S. Filskov & T. J. Boll (Eds.), *Handbook of clinical neuropsychology.* New York: Wiley.

Golden, C. J., Grabber, B., Blose, I., Berg, R., Coffman, J., & Bloch, S. (1981). Differences in brain densities between chronic alcoholic and normal control patients. *Science, 211,* 508–510.

Golden, C. J., Moses, J. A., Coffman, J. A., Miller, W. R., Strider, F. D. (1983). *Clinical neuropsychology.* New York: Grune & Stratton.

Golden, C. J., Moses, J. A., Fishburne, F. J., Engum, E., Lewis, G. P., Wisniewski, A. M., Conley, F. K., Berg, R. A., & Graber, B. (1981). Cross-validation of the Luria-Nebraska Neuropsychological Battery for the presence, lateralization, and location of brain damage. *Journal of Consulting and Clinical Psychology, 49,* 491–507.

Golden, C. J., & Vincente, P. J. (Eds.). (1983). *Foundation of clinical neuropsychology.* New York: Plenum Press.

Goldenberg, H. (1973). *Contemporary clinical psychology.* Monterey, CA: Brooks/Cole.

Goldfried, M. R., & Davison, G. C. (1976). *Clinical behavior therapy.* San Francisco: Holt, Rinehart & Winston.

Goldman, R. D., & Hartig, L. K. (1976). The WISC may not be a valid predictor of school performance for primary grade minority children. *American Journal of Mental Deficiency, 80,* 583–587.

Goldstein, A., & Chambless, D. (1978). A reanalysis of agoraphobia. *Behavior Therapy, 9,* 47–59.

Goldstein, A. P., & Simonson, N. (1971). Social psychological approaches to psychotherapy research. In A. Bergin & S.

Garfield (Eds.), *Psychotherapy and behavior change.* New York: Wiley.

Goldstein, J. G. (1973). Exposure to erotic stimuli and sexual deviance. *Journal of Social Issues, 29,* 197–219.

Goleman, D. (1976). Why your temples pound. *Psychology Today, 10,* 41–47.

Goodman, G. (1972). Systematic selection of psychotherapeutic talent: Group assessment of interpersonal traits. In S. E. Golann & C. Eisdorfer (Eds.), *Handbook of community mental health.* New York: Appleton-Century-Crofts.

Goodstein, L. D., & Sandler, I. (1978). Using psychology to promote human welfare: A conceptual analysis of the role of community psychology. *American Psychologist, 33,* 882–892.

Goodstein, R. K. (1981). Inextricable interaction: Social, psychologic and biologic stresses facing the elderly. *American Journal of Orthopsychiatry, 51,* 219–229.

Goodwin, D. W. (1979). Alcoholism and heredity. *Archives of General Psychiatry, 36,* 57–61.

Goodwin, D. W., & Guze, S. B. (1984). *Psychiatric diagnosis* (3rd ed.). New York: Oxford University Press.

Goodwin, D. W., Guze, S. B., & Robins, E. (1969). Follow-up studies in obsessional neurosis. *Archives of General Psychiatry, 10,* 182–187.

Goodwin, D. W., Schulsinger, F., Hermansen, L., Guze, S. B., & Winokur, G. (1973). Alcohol problems in adoptees raised apart from alcoholic biological parents. *Archives of General Psychiatry, 28,* 238–243.

Goodwin, D. W., Schulsinger, F., Knop, J., Mednick, S., & Guze, S. B. (1977). Alcoholism and depression in adopted-out daughters of alcoholics. *Archives of General Psychiatry, 34,* 751–754.

Goodwin, F. (1974). On the biology of depression. In R. J. Friedman & M. M. Katz (Eds.), *The psychology of depression: Contemporary theory and research.* New York: Wiley.

Goodwin, F. K. (1977). Diagnosis of affective disorders. In M. Jarvik (Ed.), *Psychopharmacology in the practice of medicine.* New York: Appleton-Century-Crofts.

Goranson, R. E. (1969). The catharsis effect: Two opposing views. In R. K. Baker & J. J. Ball (Eds.), *Mass media and violence.* Washington, DC: U.S. Government Printing Office.

Goranson, R. E. (1970). Media violence and aggressive behavior: A review of experimental research. In L. Berkowitz (Ed.), *Advances in experimental social psychology.* New York: Academic Press.

Gossett, T. F. (1963). *The history of an idea in America.* Dallas: Southern Methodist University Press.

Gottesman, I. I., & Shields, J. (1966). Contributions of twin studies to perspectives on schizophrenia. In B. A. Maher (Ed.), *Progress in experimental personality research* (Vol. 3). New York: Academic Press.

Gottesman, I. I., & Shields, J. (1972). *Schizophrenia and genetics: A twin study vantage point.* New York: Academic Press.

Gottesman, I. I., & Shields, J. (1982). *Schizophrenia: The epigenetic puzzle.* New York: Cambridge University Press.

Gottlieb, B. H. (Ed.). (1981). *Social networks and social support.* Beverly Hills, CA: Sage.

Gottlieb, B. H. (1983). Social support as a focus for integrative research in psychology. *American Psychologist, 38,* 278–287.

Gourash, N. (1978). Help-seeking: A review of the literature. *American Journal of Community Psychology, 6,* 413–424.

Gove, W. R., & Tudor, J. F. (1973). Adult sex roles and mental illness. *American Journal of Sociology, 78,* 812–835.

Grace, W., & Graham, D. T. (1952). Relationship of specific attitudes and emotions to certain bodily diseases. *Psychosomatic Medicine, 14,* 243–251.

Graham, D. T., Kabler, J. D., & Graham, F. K. (1962). Physiological response to the suggestion of attitudes specific for hives and hypertension. *Psychosomatic Medicine, 24,* 159–169.

Graham, D. T., Stern, J. A., & Winokur, G. (1958). Experimental investigation of the specificity of attitude hypothesis in psychosomatic disease. *Psychosomatic Medicine, 20,* 446–457.

Granacher, R. P. (1981). Differential diagnosis of tardive dyskinesia: An overview. *American Journal of Psychiatry, 138,* 1288–1297.

Gray, S. H. (1977). Social aspects of body image: Perception of normalcy of weight and affect on college undergraduates. *Perceptual and Motor Skills, 45,* 1035–1040.

Greaves, G. B. (1980). Multiple personality: 165 years after Mary Reynolds. *Journal of Nervous Mental Disease, 168,* 577–596.

Green, B., & Paul, R. (1974). Parenthood and the mentally retarded. *University of Toronto Law Journal, 24,* 117–125.

Green, L. E., Green, A. M., & Walters, E. D. (1970). *Self-regulation of internal stress in progress of cybernetics: Proceedings of the International Congress of Cybernetics.* London: Gordon & Breech.

Green, R. (1968). Childhood cross-gender identification. *Journal of Nervous and Mental Disease, 147,* 500–509.

Green, R. (1974). A profile of boyhood femininity. *Psychology Today, 7,* 51–54.

Green, R. (1978). Sexual identity of 37 children raised by homosexual or transsexual parents. *American Journal of Psychiatry, 135,* 692–697.

Greenberg, J. S. (1983). *Comprehensive stress management.* Dubuque, IA: Wm. C. Brown.

Grefe, M. A. (1980, March/April). Equity—a cause for every woman. *Graduate Woman,* pp. 11–17.

Greist, H., Klein, H. H., & Erdman, H. P. (1976). Routine on-line psychiatric diagnosis by computer. *American Journal of Psychiatry, 133,* 1405–1408.

Grier, W. H., & Cobbs, P. M. (1968). *Black rage.* New York: Basic Books.

Grinker, R. R., & Robbins, F. P. (1954). *Psychosomatic case book.* New York: Blakiston.

Grinker, R. R., & Spiegel, J. P. (1945). *War neuroses.* Philadelphia: Blakiston.

Groth, A. N., Burgess, A. W., & Holstrom, L. (1977). Rape: Power, anger, and sexuality. *American Journal of Psychiatry, 134,* 1239–1243.

Group for the Advancement of Psychiatry. (1966). *Psychopathological disorders in childhood: Theoretical considerations and a proposed classification* (p. 62). GAP Report.

Gruen, G., & Zigler, E. (1968). Expectancy of success and the probability learning of middle-class, lower-class, and retarded children. *Journal of Abnormal Psychology, 73,* 343–352.

Gruver, G. G. (1971). College students as therapeutic agents. *Psychological Bulletin, 76,* 111–127.

Guerney, B. G. (Ed.) (1969). *Psychotherapeutic agents: New roles for nonprofessionals, parents, and teachers.* New York: Holt, Rinehart & Winston.

Gunn, J., & Fenton, G. (1971, June 5). Epilepsy, automatism, and crime. *The Lancet,* pp. 1173–1176.

Guze, S. B., Cloninger, C. R., Martin, R. L., & Clayton, P. J. (1983). A follow-up and family study of schizophrenia. *Archives of General Psychiatry, 40,* 1273–1276.

Haas, L. J., & Weatherly, D. (1981). Community psychology in the library: Potentials for consultation. *American Journal of Community Psychology, 9,* 109–122.

Hackett, T. P. (1975). Encounters by women or children with exhibitionists. *Medical Aspects of Human Sexuality, 9,* 139–140.

Hafner, R. J. (1983). Behaviour therapy for agoraphobic men. *Behaviour Research and Therapy, 21,* 51–56.

Haier, R. J., Rosenthal, D., & Wendler, P. H. (1978). MMPI assessment of psychopathology in the adopted-away offspring of schizophrenics. *Archives of General Psychiatry, 35,* 171–175.

Haley, A. (1966). *The autobiography of Malcolm X.* New York: Grove.

Haley, J. (1963). *Strategies of psychotherapy.* New York: Grune & Stratton.

Haley, J. (1980). *Leaving home.* New York: McGraw-Hill.

Hall, C. S., & Lindsey, G. (1970). *Theories of personality.* New York: Wiley.

Hall, G. S. (1904). *Adolescence: Its psychology and its relation to physiology, anthropology, sociology, sex, crime, religion and education.* New York: Appleton.

Hall, J. E., & Hare-Mustin, R. T. (1983). Sanctions and the diversity of ethical complaints against psychologists. *American Psychologists, 39,* 714–729.

Hallam, R. S. (1978). Agoraphobia: A critical review of the concept. *British Journal of Psychiatry, 133,* 314–319.

Halmi, K., Falk, J., & Schwartz, E. (1981). Binge eating and vomiting: A survey of a college population. *Psychosomatic Medicine, 11,* 697–706.

Hammen, C., & Peters, S. (1978). Interpersonal consequences of depression: Responses to men and women enacting a depressed role. *Journal of Abnormal Psychology, 87,* 322–332.

Hammen, C. L. (1985). Predicting depression: A cognitive-behavioral perspective. In P. Kendall (Ed.), *Advances in cognitive-behavioral research and therapy* (Vol. 4). New York: Academic Press.

Hampe, E., Noble, H., Miller, L. C., & Barrett, C. L. (1973). Phobic children: One and two years' posttreatment. *Journal of Abnormal Psychology, 82,* 446–453.

Hanback, J. W., & Revelle, W. (1978). Arousal and perceptual sensitivity in hypochondriacs. *Journal of Abnormal Psychology, 87,* 523–530.

Hanson, C. L., Henggeler, S. W., Haefele, W. F., & Rodick, J. D. (1984). Demographic individual, and family relationship correlates of serious and repeated crime among adolescents and their siblings. *Journal of Consulting and Clinical Psychology, 52,* 528–538.

Harburg, E., Blackelock, E. H., & Roeper, P. J. (1979). Resentful and reflective coping with arbitrary authority and blood pressure: Detroit. *Psychosomatics, 41,* 189–202.

Hare, R. D. (1968). Psychopathy, autonomic functioning and

the orienting response. *Journal of Abnormal Psychology, 73,* 1–24.

Hare, R. D. (1970). *Psychopathy: Theory and research.* New York: Wiley.

Hare, R. D. (1975). Anxiety, stress, and psychopathy. In I. Saranson & C. Spielberger (Eds.), *Stress and anxiety* (Vol. 2). Washington, DC: Hemisphere Publishing.

Hare, R. D. (1981). Psychopathy and violence. In J. Hays, T. Roberts, & K. Solway (Eds.), *Violence and the violent individual.* New York: SP Books.

Hare-Mustin, R. T. (1983). An appraisal of the relationship between women and psychotherapy: 80 years after the case of Dora. *American Psychologist, 38,* 593–601.

Harris, B. (1979). Whatever happened to little Albert? *American Psychologist, 34,* 151–160.

Harris, E. L., Noyes, R., Crowe, R. R., & Chaudhry, D. R. (1983). Family study of agoraphobia. *Archives of General Psychiatry, 40,* 1061–1064.

Harris, R. R., Wolf, M. M., & Baer, D. M. (1964). Effects of adult social reinforcement of child behavior. *Young Children, 20,* 8–17.

Harris, S. L., & Ersner-Hershfield, R. (1978). Behavioral suppression of seriously disruptive behavior in psychotic and retarded patients: A review of punishment and its alternatives. *Psychological Bulletin, 85,* 1352–1375.

Harrow, M., Grossman, L. S., Silverstein, M. L., & Meltzer, H. Y. (1982). Thought pathology in manic and schizophrenic patients. *Archives of General Psychiatry, 39,* 665–671.

Harth, R. (1982). The Feuerstein perspective on the modification of cognitive performance. *Focus on Exceptional Children, 15,* 1–12.

Hathaway, S. R., & McKinley, J. C. (1943). *Manual for the Minnesota Multiphasic Personality Inventory.* New York: Psychological Corp.

Hayes, B., & Marshall, W. (1984). Generalization of treatment effects in training public speakers. *Behaviour Research and Therapy, 22,* 519–533.

Hayes, S. C., Brownell, K. D., Barlow, D. H. (1983). Heterosexual skills training and covert sensitization: Effects on social skills and sexual arousal in sexual deviants. *Behaviour Research and Therapy, 21,* 383–392.

Hayes, S. C., & Zettle, R. D. (1979). The mythology of behavioral training. *Behavior Therapist, 2,* 5–6.

Heath, R. G. (1960). A biochemical hypothesis on the etiology of schizophrenia. In D. D. Jackson (Ed.), *The etiology of schizophrenia.* New York: Basic Books.

Heath, R. G., Guschwan, A. F., & Coffey, J. W. (1970). Relation of taraxein to schizophrenia. *Diseases of the Nervous System, 31,* 391–395.

Heber, R. (1970). *Epidemiology of mental retardation.* Springfield, IL: Charles C. Thomas.

Heber, R., Garber, H., & Falender, C. (1973). *The Milwaukee project: An experiment in the prevention of cultural-familial retardation.* Unpublished manuscript.

Hechtman, L., & Weiss, G. (1983). Long-term outcome of hyperactive children. *American Journal of Orthopsychiatry, 53,* 532–541.

Heiby, E. M. (1983). Depression as a function of the interaction of self- and environmentally controlled reinforcement. *Behavior Therapy, 14,* 430–433.

Heilig, S. M. (1970). Training in suicide prevention. *Bulletin of Suicidology, 6,* 41–44.

Heim, N. (1981). Sexual behavior of castrated sex offenders. *Archives of Sexual Behavior, 10,* 11–19.

Hekmat, H., Lubitz, R., & Deal, R. (1984). Semantic desensitization: A paradigmatic intervention approach to anxiety disorders. *Journal of Clinical Psychology, 40,* 463–466.

Heller, K., Price, R. H., Reinharz, S., Riger, S., & Wandersman, A. (1984). *Psychology and community change: Challenge of the future.* Homewood, IL: Dorsey.

Hendin, H., Pollenger, A., Singer, P., & Ulman, R. (1981). Meanings of combat and the development of posttraumatic stress disorder. *American Journal of Psychiatry, 131,* 1490–1493.

Henryk-Gutt, R., & Rees, L. W. (1973). Psychological aspects of migraine. *Journal of Psychosomatic Research, 17,* 141–153.

Herman, J., & Hirschman, L. (1981). Families at risk for father-daughter incest. *American Journal of Psychiatry, 38,* 967–970.

Herrnstein, R. (1982). IQ. *Atlantic Monthly,* pp. 43–64.

Herschkowitz, S., & Dickes, R. (1978). Suicide attempts in a female-to-male transsexual. *American Journal of Psychiatry, 135,* 368–369.

Hersen, M., Bellack, A., & Himmelhoch, J. (1980). Treatment for unipolar depression with social skills training. *Behavior Modification, 4,* 547–556.

Hertzog, D. B. (1982). Anorexia nervosa: A treatment challenge. *Drug Therapy, 7,* 3.

Heston, L. L. (1966). Psychiatric disorders in foster-home-reared children of schizophrenic mothers. *British Journal of Psychiatry, 122,* 819–825.

Heston, L. L., & Denny, D. (1968). Interactions between early life experience and biological factors in schizophrenia. In D. Rosenthal & S. Kety (Eds.), *The transmission of schizophrenia.* New York: Pergamon Press.

Hetherington, E., & Martin, B. (1979). Family interaction. In H. C. Quay & J. S. Werry (Eds.), *Psychopathological disorders of childhood.* New York: John Wiley.

Hibbert, G. (1984). Ideational components of anxiety: Their origin and content. *British Journal of Psychiatry, 144,* 618–624.

Higgins, J. V., Reed, E. W., & Reed, S. C. (1962). Intelligence and family size: A paradox resolved. *Eugenics Quarterly, 9,* 84–90.

Hill, D., & Watterson, D. (1942). Electroencephalographic studies of the psychopathic personality. *Journal of Neurology and Psychiatry, 5,* 47–64.

Hillyer, J. (1964). Reluctantly told. In B. Kaplan (Ed.), *The inner world of mental illness.* New York: Harper & Row.

Hingtgen, J. N., & Trost, F. C. (1966). Shaping cooperative responses in early childhood schizophrenics: Reinforcement of mutual physical contact and vocal responses. In R. Ulrich, T. Stachnik, & J. Mabry (Eds.), *Control of human behavior.* Glenview, IL: Scott, Foresman.

Hinshaw, S., Henker, B., & Whalen, C. K. (1984). Self-control in hyperactive boys in anger-inducing situations: Effects of cognitive-behavioral training and methyl-phenidate. *Journal of Abnormal Child Psychology, 12,* 55–77.

Hiroto, D. S. (1974). Locus of control and learned helplessness. *Journal of Experimental Psychology, 102,* 187–193.

Hite, S. (1976). *The Hite report.* Chicago: Dell Publishing.

Hoch, Z., Safir, M. P., Peres, Y., & Stepler, J. (1981). An evaluation of sexual performance—comparison between sexually dysfunctional and functional couples. *Journal of Sex and Marital Therapy, 7,* 195–206.

Hodgson, R. J., & Rachman, S. (1972). The effects of contamination and washing in obsessional patients. *Behaviour Research and Therapy, 10,* 111–117.

Hoffman, L. (1981). *Foundations of family therapy.* New York: Basic Books.

Hole, J. W. (1983). *Essentials of human anatomy and physiology.* Dubuque, IA: Wm. C. Brown, pp. 236–237.

Hollender, M. H. (1980). The case of Anna O.: A reformulation. *American Journal of Psychiatry, 137,* 797–800.

Hollingshead, A. B., & Redlich, F. C. (1958). *Social class and mental illness: A community study.* New York: Wiley.

Holmes, T. H., Goodell, H., Wolff, S., & Wolff, H. G. (1950). *The nose: An experimental study of reactions within the nose in human subjects during varying life experiences.* Springfield, IL: Charles C. Thomas.

Holmes, T. H., & Masuda, M. (1974). Life change and illness susceptibility. In B. S. Dohrenwend & B. P. Dohrenwend (Eds.), *Stressful life events.* New York: Wiley.

Holmes, T. H., & Rahe, R. H. (1967). The social readjustment rating scale. *Journal of Psychosomatic Research, 11,* 213–218.

Holt, L. R. (1978). Psychoanalytic principles in sex therapy. *American Journal of Psychoanalysis, 38,* 49–56.

Holt, R. R. (1962). The logic of the romantic point of view in personology. *Journal of Psychoanalysis, 38,* 377–402.

Holt, R., & LeCann, A. (1984). Use of an integrative interview to manage somatization. *Psychosomatics, 25,* 663.

Holzberg, J. D., Knapp, R. H., & Turner, J. L. (1967). College students as companions to the mentally ill. In E. L. Cowen, E. A. Gardner, & M. Zax (Eds.), *Emergent approaches to mental health problems.* New York: Appleton-Century-Crofts.

Horowitz, J. J., & Solomon, G. F. (1975). A prediction of delayed stress response syndromes in Vietnam veterans. *Journal of Social Issues, 31,* 67–80.

Horowitz, M. J. (1970). *Psychosocial function in epilepsy.* Springfield, IL: Charles C. Thomas.

Howells, J. G., & Guirgis, W. R. (1984). Childhood schizophrenia 20 years later. *Archives of General Psychiatry, 41,* 123–128.

Hoyt, M. F. (1979). Primal-scene experiences: Quantitative assessment of an interview study. *Archives of Sexual Behavior, 8,* 225–245.

Hsu, L. (1980). Outcome of anorexia nervosa: A review of the literature (1954–1978). *Archives of General Psychiatry, 37,* 1041–1046.

Hubbard, J. E. (1969). *Results of team evaluations in 134 state residential institutions in the U.S.* Final project report to the Division of Mental Retardation.

Huber, G., Gross, G., Schuttler, R., & Linz, M. (1980). Longitudinal studies of schizophrenic patients. *Schizophrenia Bulletin, 6,* 592–605.

Hudgens, A. (1979). Family-oriented treatment of chronic pain. *Journal of Marital and Family Therapy, 5,* 67–78.

Hudgens, R. W. (1974). Personal catastrophe and depression: A consideration of the subject with respect to medically ill adolescents and a requiem for retrospective life-event studies. In B. S. Dohrenwend & B. P. Dohrenwend (Eds.), *Stressful life events.* New York: Wiley.

Hugdahl, K., Fredrickson, M., & Ohman, A. (1977). Prepar-

edness and arousability determinants of electrodermal conditioning. *Behaviour Research and Therapy, 15,* 345–353.

Hunt, M. M. (1974). *Sexual behavior in the 1970s.* Chicago: Playboy Press.

Hunter, R., Blackwood, W., & Bull, J. (1968). Three cases of frontal meningiomas presenting psychiatrically. *British Medical Journal, 3,* 9–16.

Hunter, R., & Macalpine, I. (1963). *Three hundred years of psychiatry, 1535–1860.* London: Oxford University Press.

Hutchings, B., & Mednick, S. A. (1977). Criminality in adoptees and their adoptive and biological parents: A pilot study. In S. A. Mednick & K. L. Christianson (Eds.), *Biosocial bases of criminal behavior.* New York: Garden Press.

Hutt, C., & Ounsted, C. (1966). The biological significance of gaze aversion with particular reference to the syndrome of infantile autism. *Behavioral Science, 11,* 346–361.

Hyler, S. E., & Spitzer, R. L. (1978). Hysteria split asunder. *American Journal of Psychiatry, 135,* 1500–1504.

Isaac, S., & Michael, W. B. (1977). *Handbook in research and evaluation.* San Diego: Edits.

Jackson, B. A case of voyeurism treated by counterconditioning. *Behavioral Research and Therapy, 7,* 133–134.

Jackson, H. J., & King, N. J. (1981). The emotive imagery treatment of a child's trauma-induced phobia. *Journal of Behavior Therapy and Experimental Psychiatry, 14,* 343–347.

Jacob, T. (1975). Family interaction in disturbed and normal families: A methodological and substantive review. *Psychological Bulletin, 18,* 35–65.

Jacobson, E. (1938). *Progressive relaxation.* Chicago: University of Chicago Press.

Jacobson, E. (1964). *Self-operations control.* New York: Lippincott.

Jacobson, E. (1967). *Tension in medicine.* Springfield, IL: Charles C. Thomas.

Jacobson, N. S., & Anderson, E. A. (1982). Interpersonal skill and depression in college students: An analysis of the timing of self-disclosures. *Behavior Therapy, 13,* 271–282.

Jahoda, M. (1958). *Current concepts of positive mental health.* New York: Basic Books.

Janis, I. (1971). *Stress and frustration.* New York: Harcourt, Brace, & World.

Jason, C. A. (1980). Prevention in the schools: Behavioral approaches. In R. H. Price, R. F. Ketterer, B. C. Bader, & J. Monahan (Eds.), *Prevention in mental health: Research, policy, and practice.* Beverly Hills, CA: Sage.

Jason, L. A., Felner, R. D., Moritsugu, J., & Farber, S. S. (1983). Future directions for preventive psychology. In R. D. Felner, L. A. Jason, J. Moritsugu, & S. S. Farber (Eds.), *Preventive psychology: Theory, research, and practice.* New York: Pergamon.

Jasper, H. H., Ward, A., & Pope, A. (Eds.). (1969). *Basic mechanisms of the epilepsies.* Boston: Little, Brown.

Jeans, R. F. (1976). An independently validated case of multiple personality. *Journal of Abnormal Psychology, 81,* 249–255. *Behavior, 4,* 337–345.

Jellinek, E. M. (1971). Phases of alcohol addiction. In G. Shean (Ed.), *Studies in abnormal behavior.* Chicago: Rand McNally.

Jenike, M., Surman, O., Cassem, N., Zusky, P., & Anderson, W. (1983). Monoamine oxidase inhibitors in obsessive-compulsive disorder. *Journal of Clinical Psychiatry, 44,* 131–132.

Jenkins, R. L. (1968). The varieties of children's behavior problems and family dynamics. *American Journal of Psychiatry, 124,* 1440–1445.

Jenkins, S., Owen, C., Bax, M., & Hart, H. (1984). Continuities of common behavior problems in preschool children. *Journal of Child Psychology and Psychiatry, 25,* 75–89.

Jenner, F. A., Gjessing, L. R., Cox, J. R., Davies-Jones, A., Hullin, R. R., & Hanna, S. M. (1967). A manic-depressive psychotic with a persistent forty-eight-hour cycle. *British Journal of Psychiatry, 113,* 895–910.

Jensen, A. (1969). How much can we boost IQ and school achievement? *Harvard Educational Review, 39,* 1–123.

Jensen, A. (1973). The differences are real. *Psychology Today, 7,* 79–86.

Jersild, A. T., Markey, F. V., & Jersild, C. L. (1960). Children's fears, dreams, wishes, daydreams, likes, dislikes, pleasant and unpleasant memories. In A. T. Jersild (Ed.), *Child psychology.* Englewood Cliffs, NJ: Prentice-Hall.

Jessor, R., & Jessor, S. L. (1977). *Problem behavior and psycho-social development: A longitudinal study of youth.* New York: Academic Press.

Jesti, D. V., & Wyatt, R. J. (1981). Changing epidemiology of tardive dyskinesia: An overview. *American Journal of Psychiatry, 138,* 297–309.

Johnson, A. W. (1969). Combat psychiatry, historical view. *Medical Bulletin of the U.S. Army, Europe, 26,* 305–308.

Johnson, C., & Berndt, D. J. (1983). Preliminary investigation of bulimia and life adjustment. *American Journal of Psychiatry, 140,* 774–777.

Johnson, C., Connors, M., & Stuckey, M. (1983). Short-term group treatment of bulimia. *International Journal of Eating Disorders, 2,* 199–208.

Johnson, R. N. (1972). *Aggression in man and animals.* Philadelphia: Saunders.

Johnston, R. (1967). Some casework aspects of using foster grandparents for emotionally disturbed children. *Children, 14,* 46–52.

Jones, E. E., & Korchin, S. J. (Eds.). (1982). *Minority mental health.* New York: Praeger.

Jones, F. D., & Johnson, A. W. (1975). Medical and psychiatric treatment policy and practice in Vietnam. *Journal of Social Issues, 31,* 39–65.

Jones, K. L., Shainberg, L. W., & Byer, C. O. (1977). *Sex and people.* New York: Harper & Row.

Jones, M. (1953). *The therapeutic community: A new treatment method in psychiatry.* New York: Basic Books.

Jones, M. C. (1924). A laboratory study of fear: The case of Peter. *Pedagogical Seminary, 31,* 308–315.

Jones, M. C. (1968). Personality correlates and antecedents of drinking patterns in adult males. *Journal of Consulting and Clinical Psychology, 32,* 2–12.

Jones, M. C. (1971). Personality antecedents and correlates of drinking patterns in women. *Journal of Consulting and Clinical Psychology, 36,* 61–69.

Jones, N. F., Kahn, N. W., & Langsley, D. G. (1965). Prediction of admission to a psychiatric hospital. *Archives of General Psychiatry, 12,* 607–610.

Jost, H., & Sontag, L. W. (1944). The genetic factor in autonomic nervous system function. *Psychosomatic Medicine, 6,* 308–310.

Judd, L. L. (1965). Obsessive-compulsive neurosis in children. *Archives of General Psychiatry, 12,* 136–143.

Kaats, G. R., & Davis, D. E. (1975). The dynamics of sexual behavior of college students. In J. R. DeLora & J. S. DeLora (Eds.), *Intimate life styles* (2nd ed.). Pacific Palisades, CA: Goodyear Publishing.

Kagan, D. M., & Squires, R. L. (1984). Eating disorders among adolescents: Patterns and prevalence. *Adolescence, 19,* 15–29.

Kahn, A. U., Staerk, M., & Bonk, C. (1977). Role of counterconditioning in the treatment of asthma. *Journal of Psychosomatic Research, 18,* 88–92.

Kallman, W. M., Hersen, M., & O'Toole, D. H. (1975). The use of social reinforcement in a case of conversion reaction. *Behavior Therapy, 6,* 411–413.

Kamin, L. (1974). *The Science and Politics of I.Q.* Hillsdale, NJ: Erlbaum.

Kamiya, J. (1962, April). *Conditioning discrimination of the EEG alpha rhythm in humans.* Paper presented at the meeting of the Western Psychological Association.

Kanfer, F. H., & Phillips, J. S. (1969). A survey of current behavior therapies and a proposal for classification. In C. M. Franks (Ed.), *Behavior therapy: Appraisal and status.* New York: Wiley.

Kanin, E. J. (1969). Selected dyadic aspects of male sex aggression. *Journal of Sex Research, 5,* 12–28.

Kanin, E. J., & Parcell, S. R. (1977). Sexual aggression: A second look at the offended female. *Archives of Sexual Behavior, 6,* 67–76.

Kanner, L. (1943). Autistic disturbances of affective content. *Nervous Child, 2,* 217–240.

Kanner, L. (1960). Do behavior symptoms always indicate psychopathology? *Journal of Child Psychological Psychiatry, 1,* 17–25.

Kanner, L., Rodriguez, A., & Ashendeau, B. (1972). How far can autistic children go into matters of social adaptation? *Journal of Autism and Childhood Schizophrenia, 2,* 9–33.

Kaplan, H. I., & Sadock, B. J. (1981). *Modern synopsis of comprehensive textbook of psychiatry* (3rd ed.). Baltimore: Williams & Wilkins.

Kaplan, H. S. (1974). No nonsense therapy for six sexual malfunctions. *Psychology Today, 8,* 76–80, 83, 86.

Kaplan, H. S. (1983). *The evaluation of sexual disorders.* New York: Brunner/Mazel.

Kaplan, M. (1983). A woman's view of DSM-III. *American Psychologist, 38,* 786–792.

Kardiner, A., & Ovesey, L. (1962). *The mark of oppression.* New York: Norton.

Karlsruher, A. E. (1974). The nonprofessional as a psychotherapeutic agent. *American Journal of Community Psychology, 2,* 61–78.

Karpman, B. (1941). On the need of separating psychopathy into two distinct clinical types: The symptomatic and the idiopathic. *Journal of Criminal Psychopathology, 3,* 112–137.

Kashiwagi, T., McClure, J. N., & Wetzel, R. D. (1972). Headache and psychiatric disorders. *Diseases of the Nervous System, 33,* 659–663.

Katchadourian, H. A., & Lunde, D. T. (1975). *Fundamentals*

of human sexuality (2nd ed.). New York: Holt, Rinehart & Winston.

Katz, J. L., Kuperberg, A., Pollack, C. P., Walsh, B. T., Zumoff, B., & Weiner, H. (1984). Is there a relationship between eating disorder and affective disorder? New evidence from sleep recordings. *American Journal of Psychiatry, 141,* 753–759.

Katz, P. A. (Ed.). (1976). *Toward the elimination of racism.* New York: Pergamon.

Kaufman, A. S., & Kaufman, N. L. (1983). *Kaufman assessment battery for children.* Circle Pines, MN: American Guidance Services.

Kaufmann, H. (1970). *Aggression and altruism.* New York: Holt, Rinehart & Winston.

Kay, D., & Roth, M. (1961). Environmental and hereditary factors in schizophrenics of old age and their bearing on the general problems of causation in schizophrenia. *Journal of Mental Science, 107,* 649–686.

Kazdin, A. E. (1980). *Behavior modification in applied settings* (2d ed.). Homewood, IL: Dorsey.

Kazdin, A. E., & Wilson, G. T. (1978). *Evaluation of behavior therapy: Issues, evidence and research strategies.* Cambridge, MA: Ballinger.

Keane, T. M., Martin, J. E., Berler, E. S., Wooten, L. S., Fleece, E. L., & Williams, J. G. (1982). Are hypertensives less assertive? A controlled evaluation. *Journal of Consulting and Clinical Psychology, 50,* 499–508.

Kellner, R. (1982). Psychotherapeutic strategies in hypochondriasis: A clinical study. *American Journal of Psychotherapy, 36,* 146–157.

Kelly, D. H., & Walters, C. J. S. (1968). The relationship between chemical diagnosis and anxiety, assessed by forearm blood flow and other measurements. *British Journal of Psychiatry, 112,* 789–798.

Kelly, H. H., Condry, J. C., Dahlke, A. E., & Hill, A. H. (1965). Collective behavior in a simulated panic situation. *Journal of Experimental and Social Psychology, 1,* 20–54.

Kendall, P. C. (1984). Cognitive-behavioral self-control therapy for children. *Journal of Child Psychology and Psychiatry, 25,* 173–179.

Kendell, R. (1970), Relationship between aggression and depression. *Archives of General Psychiatry, 22,* 308–318.

Kendler, K. S. (1983). A current perspective on twin studies of schizophrenia. *American Journal of Psychiatry, 140,* 1413–1425.

Kendler, K. S., Glaser, W. M., & Morgenstern, H. (1983). Dimensions of delusional experience. *American Journal of Psychiatry, 140,* 466–469.

Kendler, K. S., & Hays, P. (1982). Familial and sporadic schizophrenia: A symptomatic, prognostic, and EEG comparison. *American Journal of Psychiatry, 139,* 1557–1562.

Kennedy, E. C. (Ed.) (1975). *Human rights and psychological research.* New York: Crowell.

Kenny, T. J., Clemens, R. D., Hudson, B. W., Lentz, G. A., Cicci, R., & Nair, P. (1971). Characteristics of children referred because of hyperactivity. *Journal of Pediatrics, 79,* 618–622.

Kerlinger, F. N. (1971). *Foundations of behavioral research.* New York: Holt, Rinehart & Winston.

Kernberg, O. F. (1975). *Borderline conditions and pathological narcissism.* New York: Jason Aronson.

Kety, S., Rosenthal, D., Wender, P. H., & Schulsinger, F. (1968). The types and prevalence of mental illness in the biologic and adoptive families of adopted schizophrenics. In D. Rosenthal & S. Kety (Eds.), *The transmission of schizophrenia.* New York: Pergamon.

Kety, S. S. (1979). Disorders of the human brain. *Scientific American, 241,* 202–214.

Kety, S. S., Rosenthal, D., Wendler, P. H., Schulsinger, F., & Jacobsen, B. (1975). Mental illness in the biological and adoptive families of adopted individuals who have become schizophrenic: A preliminary report based on psychiatric interviews. In R. R. Fieve, D. Rosenthal, & H. Brill (Eds.), *Genetic research in psychiatry.* Baltimore: Johns Hopkins University Press.

Kiersch, T. A. (1962). Amnesia: A clinical study of ninety-eight cases. *American Journal of Psychiatry, 119,* 57–60.

Kiesler, C. A. (1982). Mental hospitals and alternative care: Noninstitutionalization as potential public policy for mental patients. *American Psychologist, 37,* 349–360.

Kilbourne, B., & Richardson, J. T. (1984). Psychotherapy and new religions in a pluralistic society. *American Psychologist, 39,* 237–251.

Kilmann, P., Sabalis, R., Gearing, M., Bukstel, L., & Scovern, A. (1982). The treatment of sexual paraphilias: A review of the outcome research. *The Journal of Sex Research, 18,* 193–252.

Kilmann, P. R., & Auerbach, R. (1979). Treatments of premature ejaculation and psychogenic impotence: A critical review of the literature. *Archives of Sexual Behavior, 8,* 81–100.

Kilpatrick, D. G., Veronen, L. J., & Resick, P. A. (1979). The aftermath of rape: Recent empircal findings. *American Journal of Orthopsychiatry, 49,* 658–669.

Kinsey, A. C., Pomeroy, W. G., & Martin, C. E. (1948). *Sexual behavior in the human male.* Philadelphia: Saunders.

Kinsey, A. C., Pomeroy, W. B., Martin, C. E., & Gebhard, P. H. (1953). *Sexual behavior in the human female.* Philadelphia: Saunders.

Kirkpatrick, D. R. (1984). Age, gender and patterns of common intense fears among adults. *Behavior Research and Therapy, 22,* 141–150.

Kirkpatrick, J. S. (1975). Guidelines for counseling young people with sexual concerns. *Personnel and Guidance Journal, 54,* 145–148.

Kirkpatrick, M., Smith, D., & Roy, R. (1981). Lesbian mothers and their children: A comparative survey. *American Journal of Orthopsychiatry, 5,* 545–551.

Kitano, H. H. (1969). Japanese-American mental illness. In S. C. Plog & R. B. Edgerton (Eds.), *Changing perspectives in mental illness.* New York: Holt, Rinehart & Winston.

Klagsbrun, F. (1976). Too young to die: Youth and suicide. Boston: Houghton Mifflin.

Klein, D., Gittelman, R., & Quitkin, F., et al. (1980). *Diagnosis and drug treatment of psychiatric disorders: Adults and children.* Baltimore: Williams & Wilkins, pp. 268–404.

Klein, D. C. (1968). *Community dynamics and mental health.* New York: Wiley.

Klein, W. L. (1967). The training of human service aides. In E. L. Cowen, E. A. Gardner, & M. Zax (Eds.), *Emergent approaches to mental health problems.* New York: Appleton-Century-Crofts.

Kleinberg, J., & Galligan, B. (1983). Effects of deinstitutionalization on adaptive behavior of mentally retarded adults. *American Journal of Mental Deficiency, 88,* 21–27.

Kleinmuntz, B. (1982). *Personality and psychological assessment* (p. 195). New York: St. Martin's Press.

Klerman, G. L. (1982). Practical issues in the treatment of depression and mania. In E. S. Paykel (Ed.), *Handbook of affective disorders*. New York: Guilford Press.

Klopfer, B., & Davidson, H. (1962). *The Rorschach technique*. New York: Harcourt, Brace, & World.

Kluft, R. P. (1983). Hypnotherapeutic crisis intervention in multiple personality. *American Journal of Clinical Hypnosis, 26*, 73–83.

Knott, J., Platt, E., Ashley, M., & Gottlieb, J. (1953). A familial evaluation of the electroencephalogram of patients with primary behavior disorder and psychopathic personality. *EEG and Clinical Neurophysiology, 5*, 363–370.

Kobasa, S. C., Hilker, R. J., & Maddi, S. R. (1979). Psychological hardiness. *Journal of Occupational Medicine, 21*, 595–598.

Koegel, R. L., Schreibman, L., O'Neill, R. E., & Burke, J. C. (1983). The personality and family-interaction characteristics of parents of autistic children. *Journal of Consulting and Clinical Psychology, 51*, 683–692.

Kohlenberg, R. J. (1973). Behavioristic approach to multiple personality: A case study. *Behavior Therapy, 4*, 137–140.

Kohlenberg, R. J. (1974a). Directed masturbation and the treatment of primary orgasmic dysfunction. *Archives of Sexual Behavior, 3*, 349–356.

Kohn, P. M., Barnes, G. E., & Hoffman, F. M. (1979). Drug use history and experience seeking among adult male correctional inmates. *Journal of Consulting and Clinical Psychology, 47*, 708–715.

Kollias, K., & Tucker, J. (1974). Interview: Women and rape. *Medical Aspects of Human Sexuality, 5*, 183–197.

Korchin, S. J. (1976). *Modern clinical psychology*. New York: Basic Books.

Korchin, S. J., & Ruff, G. E. (1964). Personality characteristics of the Mercury astronauts. In G. H. Grosser, H. Wechsler, & M. Greenblatt (Eds.), *The threat of impending disaster*. Cambridge, MA: M.I.T. Press.

Kosky, R. (1983). Childhood suicidal behavior. *Journal of Child Psychology and Psychiatry, 24*, 3, 457–468.

Kounin, J. (1941). Experimental studies of rigidity. *Character and Personality, 9*, 251–82.

Kovacs, M. (1980). The efficacy of cognitive and behavior therapies for depression. *The American Journal of Psychiatry, 137*, 1495–1501.

Kovacs, M., Rush, A., Beck, A., & Hollon, S. (1981). Depressed outpatients treated with cognitive therapy or pharmacotherapy. *Archives of General Psychiatry, 38*, 33–39.

Kovel, J. (1976). *A complete guide to therapy*. New York: Crown.

Kraemer, G. W., & McKinney, W. T. (1979). Interactions of pharmacological agents which alter biogenic amine metabolism and depression. *Journal of Affective Disorders, 1*, 33–54.

Kraemer, H., & Sprenger, J. (1928). *Malleus malificarum* (M. Summers, Trans.). London: John Rodker.

Kraepelin, E. (1923). *Textbook of psychiatry* (8th ed.). New York: Macmillan. (Original work published 1883).

Kramer, Barry. (1983, November 16). Mass hysteria: An age-old illness still crops up in modern times. *The Wall Street Journal*, p. 36b.

Kramer, M., Rosen, B. M., & Willis, E. M. (1973). Definitions and distributions of mental disorders in a racist society. In C. V. Willie, B. M. Kramer, & B. S. Brown (Eds.), *Racism and mental health*. Pittsburgh: University of Pittsburgh Press.

Kressel, K., & Deutch, M. (1977). Divorce therapy: An in-depth survey of therapists' views. *Family Process, 16*, 413–443.

Kringlen, E. (1964). *Schizophrenia in male MZ twins*. Copenhagen: Scandinavia University Books.

Kringlen, E. (1980). Schizophrenia: Research in Nordic countries. *Schizophrenia Bulletin, 6*, 566–578.

Kroll, P., Chamberlain, K. R., & Halpern, J. (1979). The diagnosis of Briquet's syndrome in a male population: The Veteran's Administration revisited. *Journal of Nervous and Mental Disorders, 167*, 171–174.

Krystal, H. (Ed.). (1968). *Massive psychic trauma*. New York: International Universities Press.

Kulka, R. A. (1982). Monitoring social change via survey replication: Prospects and pitfalls from a replication survey of social roles and mental health. *Journal of Social Issues, 38*, 17–38.

Kupfer, F. (1982, December 13). My turn. *Newsweek*, p. 17.

Kupper, H. I. (1945). Psychic concomitants in wartime injuries. *Psychosomatic Medicine, 7*, 15–21.

Kushner, M. (1965). The reduction of a long-standing fetish by means of aversive conditioning. In L. P. Ullmann & L. Krasner (Eds.), *Case studies in behavior modification*. New York: Holt, Rinehart & Winston.

Kutchinsky, B. (1973). The effect of easy availability of pornography on the incidence of sex crimes: The Danish experience. *Journal of Social Issues, 29*, 163–181.

Lacey, J. I., Bateman, D. E., & Van Lehn, R. (1953). Autonomic response specificity. *Psychosomatic Medicine, 15*, 8–21.

Lacoursiere, R. B., Godfrey, K. E., & Ruby, L. M. (1980). Traumatic neurosis in the etiology of alcoholism: Viet Nam combat and other trauma. *American Journal of Psychiatry, 137*, 966–968.

Lader, M. H. (1967). Palmar skin conductance measures in anxiety and phobic states. *Journal of Psychosomatic Research, 11*, 271–281.

Lader, M. H., & Wing, L. (1964). Habituation of the psychogalvanic reflex in patients with anxiety states and in normal subjects. *Journal of Neurology, Neurosurgery, and Psychiatry, 27*, 210–218.

Lader, M. H., & Wing, L. (1966). *Physiological measures, sedative drugs, and morbid anxiety*. London: Oxford University Press.

Laidlaw, J., & Rickens, A. (Eds.). (1976). *A textbook of epilepsy*. Edinburgh, Scotland: Churchill & Livingston.

Laing, R. D. (1965). Mystification, confusion and conflict. In I. Boszormenyi-Nagy & J. Framo (Eds.), *Intensive family therapy*. New York: Harper & Row.

Lake, C. R., Sternberg, D. E., Van Kammen, D. P., Ballenger, J. C., Ziegler, M. G., Post, R. M., Kopin, I. J., & Bunney, W. E. (1980). Elevated cerebrospinal fluid norepinephrine. *Science, 207*, 331–333.

Lam, T. (1984, June 6). Mental patients may get right to refuse psychotropic drugs. *Ann Arbor News*, pp. 1–4.

Lamb, H. R., & Grant, R. W. (1982). The mentally ill in an urban county jail. *Archives of General Psychiatry, 39*, 17–22.

Lamb, H. R., & Grant, R. W. (1983). Mentally ill women in a county jail. *Archives of General Psychiatry, 40,* 363–368.

Lambert, N. (1981). Psychological evidence in Larry P. vs. Wilson Riles: An evaluation by a witness for the defense. *American Psychologist, 36,* 937–952.

Lambley, P. (1974). Treatment of transvestism and subsequent coital problems. *Journal of Behavior Therapy and Experimental Psychiatry, 5,* 101–102.

Landis, C., & Ehrlick, D. (1950). Analysis of Porteus maze as affected by psychosurgery. *American Journal of Psychology, 63,* 557.

Lang, P., & Lazovik, A. (1963). Experimental desensitization of a phobia. *Journal of Abnormal and Social Psychology, 66,* 519–525.

Langer, D. H., Brown, G. L., & Docherty, J. P. (1981). Dopamine receptor supersensitivity and schizophrenia: A review. *Schizophrenia Bulletin, 7,* 209–224.

Langer, W. C. (1973). *The mind of Adolf Hitler.* New York: Basic Books.

Langevin, R., Paitich, D., Ramsay, G., Anderson, C., Kamrad, J., Pope, S., Geller, G., Pearl, L., & Newman, S. (1979). Experimental studies of exhibitionism. *Archives of Sexual Behavior, 8,* 307–331.

Langhorne, J. E., Loney, J., Paternite, C. E., & Bechtoldt, H. P. (1976). Childhood hyperkinesis: A return to the source. *Journal of Abnormal Psychology, 85,* 201–209.

Larkin, A. R. (1979). The form and content of schizophrenic hallucinations. *American Journal of Psychiatry, 136,* 940–943.

Laughlin, H. P. (1967). *The neuroses.* Washington, DC: Butterworth.

Lazarus, A. A. (1967). In support of technical eclecticism. *Psychological Reports, 21,* 415–416.

Lazarus, A. A. (1968). Learning theory and the treatment of depression. *Behavior Research and Therapy, 6,* 83–90.

Lazarus, A. A. (Ed.). (1976). *Multimodel behavior therapy.* New York: Springer.

Lazarus, A. A. (1977). Has behavior therapy outlived its usefulness? *American Psychologist, 32,* 550–554.

Lazarus, A. A. (1984). Multimodel therapy. In R. J. Corsini (Ed.), *Current psychotherapies.* Itasca, IL: F. E. Peacock.

Lazarus, R. S. (1966). *Patterns of adjustment and human effectiveness.* New York: McGraw-Hill.

Lazarus, R. S. (1969). *Psychological stress and the coping process.* New York: McGraw-Hill.

Lazarus, R. S. (1979, November). Positive denial: The case for not facing reality. *Psychology Today,* pp. 44–60.

Lazarus, R. S. (1983). *Psychological stress.* New York: McGraw-Hill.

Lazarus, R. S., & Launier, R. (1979). Stress-related transactions between person and environment. In L. A. Pervin and M. Lewis (Eds.), *Internal and external determinants.* New York: Plenum.

Leff, M. J., Roach, J. F., & Bunney, W. E. (1970). Environmental factors preceding the onset of severe depressions. *Psychiatry, 33,* 298–311.

Lehmann, H. E. (1974). Physical therapies of schizophrenia. In S. Arieti (Ed.), *American handbook of psychiatry* (2nd ed., Vol. 2). New York: Basic Books.

Leitenberg, H., Agras, S., Edwards, J., Thomson, L., & Wince, J. (1970). Practice as a psychotherapeutic variable: An experimental analysis within single cases. *Journal of Psychiatric Research, 7,* 215–225.

Leitenberg, H., Gross, J., Peterson, J., & Rosen, J. (1984). Analysis of an anxiety model and the process of change during exposure plus response prevention treatment of bulimia nervosa. *Behavior Therapy, 15,* 3–20.

Lennox, W. J., & Lennox, M. A. (1960). *Epilepsy and related disorders.* Boston: Little, Brown.

Lent, J. R. (1968). Mimosa cottage: Experiment in hope. *Psychology Today, 2,* 51–58.

Leonard, S. R., & Hayes, S. C. (1983). Sexual fantasy alternation. *Journal of Behavior Therapy and Experimental Psychiatry, 14,* 241–249.

Levenkron, J. C., Cohen, J. D., Mueller, H. S., & Fisher, E. B. (1983). Modifying the type A coronary-prone behavior pattern. *Journal of Consulting and Clinical Psychology, 51,* 192–204.

Levenson, A. I. (1972). The community mental health centers program. In S. E. Golann & C. Eisdorfer (Eds.), *Handbook of community mental health.* New York: Appleton-Century-Crofts.

Levine, D. S., & Willner, S. G. (1976, February). *The cost of mental illness, 1974.* Mental Health Statistical Note No. 125, pp. 1–7. Washington, DC: National Institute of Mental Health.

Levine, M., & Graziano, A. M. (1972). Intervention programs in elementary schools. In S. E. Golann & C. Eisdorfer (Eds.), *Handbook of community mental health.* New York: Appleton-Century-Crofts.

Levine, S. V. (1984). *Radical departures: Desperate detours to growing up.* New York: Harcourt, Brace, Jovanovich.

Levy, D. M. (1951). The deprived and indulged forms of psychopathic personality. *American Journal of Orthopsychiatry, 21,* 250–254.

Lewin, K. (1951). *Field theory in social science: Selected theoretical papers.* New York: Harper & Row.

Lewinsohn, P. M. (1974a). Clinical and theoretical aspects of depression. In K. S. Calhoun, H. C. Adams, & K. M. Mitchell (Eds.), *Innovative treatment methods of psychopathology.* New York: Wiley.

Lewinsohn, P. M. (1974b). A behavioral approach to depression. In R. J. Friedman & M. M. Katz (Eds.), *The psychology of depression: Contemporary theory and research.* New York: Wiley.

Lewinsohn, P. M. (1977). The behavioral study and treatment of depression. In M. Hersen, R. M. Eisler, & P. M. Miller (Eds.), *Progress in behavior modification.* New York: Academic Press.

Lewinsohn, P. M., & Graf, M. (1973). Pleasant activities and depression. *Journal of Consulting and Clinical Psychology, 41,* 261–268.

Lewinsohn, P. M., & Libet, J. (1972). Pleasant events, activity schedules, and depression. *Journal of Abnormal Psychology, 79,* 291–295.

Lewinsohn, P. M., Weinstein, M. S., & Alper, T. (1970). A behavioral approach to the group treatment of depressed persons: A methodological contribution. *Journal of Chemical Psychology, 26,* 525–532.

Lewis, N. D. C., & Engle, B. (Eds.). (1954). *Wartime psychiatry.* New York: Oxford Book.

Lichtenstein, E. (1982). The smoking problem: A behavioral perspective. *Journal of Consulting and Clinical Psychology, 50,* 804–819.

Lichtenstein, E., & Danaher, B. (1976). Modification of smoking behavior: A critical analysis of theory, research, and practice. In M. Hersen, R. Eisler, & P. Miller (Eds.), *Progress in behavior modification: 3*, New York: Academic Press.

Lichtenstein, E., & Glasgow, R. (1977). Rapid smoking: Side effects and safeguards. *Journal of Consulting and Clinical Psychology, 45*, 815–821.

Lichtenstein, E., & Rodrigues, M. (1977). Long-term effects of rapid smoking treatment for dependent cigarette smokers. *Addictive Behaviors, 2*, 109–112.

Lidz, T., Cornelison, A., Fleck, S., & Terry, D. (1957). The intrafamilial environment of schizophrenic patients: II. Marital schism and marital skew. *American Journal of Psychiatry, 114*, 241–248.

Liebert, R. M. (1972). Television and social learning: Some relationships between viewing violence and behaving aggressively. In J. P. Murray, E. A. Rubinstein, & G. A. Comstock (Eds.), *Television and social behavior*. Washington, DC: U.S. Government Printing Office.

Liebert, R. M., & Baron, R. A. (1972). Some immediate effects of television violence on children's behavior. *Developmental Psychology, 6*, 469–475.

Lifton, R. J. (1970). *History and human survival*. New York: Random House.

Lin, N., Simeone, R. S., Ensel, W. M., & Kuo, W. (1979). Social support, stressful life events, and illness: A model and an empirical test. *Journal of Health and Social Behavior, 20*, 108–119.

Lindemann, E. (1960). Psychosocial factors as stressor agents. In I. H. Tanner (Ed.), *Stress and psychiatric disorder*. Oxford, England: Basil, Blockwell & Mott.

Linden, W. (1980). Multi-component behavior theory in a case of compulsive binge-eating followed by vomiting. *Journal of Behavior Therapy and Experimental Psychiatry, 11*, 297–300.

Lipkowitz, M. H., & Indupuganti, S. (1983). Diagnosing schizophrenia in 1980: A survey of U.S. psychiatrists. *American Journal of Psychiatry, 140*, 52–55.

Lipsitt, D. R. (1974). Psychodynamic considerations of hypochondriasis. *Psychosomatic Medicine, 23*, 132–141.

Lishman, W. A. (1978). *The psychological consequences of cerebral disorder*. Oxford, England: Blackwell.

Livingston, J. A. (1982). Responses to sexual harassment on the job: Legal, organizational, and individual actions. *Journal of Social Issues, 38*, 5–22.

Loeber, R., & Dishion, T. (1983). Early predictors of male delinquency: A review. *Psychological Bulletin, 94*, 68–99.

London, P. (1964a). *The modes and morals of psychotherapy*. New York: Holt, Rinehart & Winston.

London, P. (1964b). Subject characteristics in hypnosis research: Part 1. A survey of experience, interest, and opinion. *International Journal of Experimental Hypnosis, 9*, 151–161.

Longstretch, L. E. (1981). Revisiting Skeels's final study: A critique. *Developmental Psychology, 17*, 620–625.

LoPiccolo, J., & Lobitz, C. (1971). *The role of masturbation in the treatment of orgasmic dysfunction*. Paper presented at the meeting of the Western Psychological Association, Portland, OR.

LoPiccolo, L. (1980). Low sexual desire. In S. R. Leiblum & L. A. Pervin (Eds.), *Principles and practice of sex therapy*. New York: Guilford Press.

Lord, W. (1955). *A night to remember*. New York: Holt, Rinehart & Winston.

Lorion, R. P. (1973). Socioeconomic status and traditional treatment approaches reconsidered. *Psychological Bulletin, 79*, 262–270.

Lothstein, L. (1977). Psychotherapy with patients with gender dysphoria syndromes. *Bulletin of Menninger Clinic, 41*, 563–582.

Lothstein, L. M. (1982). Sex reassignment surgery: Historical, bioethical, and theoretical issues. *American Journal of Psychiatry, 139*, 417–426.

Lotter, V. (1966). Epidemiology of autistic conditions in young children: I. Prevalence. *Social Psychiatry, 1*, 124–137.

Lovaas, I. (1975). After you hit a child, you can't just get up and leave him; you are hooked to that kid. *Psychology Today, 7*, 76–84.

Lovaas, O. I. (1977). *The autistic child: Language development through behavior modification*. New York: Halsted Press.

Lovaas, O. I., Koegel, R., Simmons, J. Q., & Long, J. S. (1973). Some generalization and follow-up measures on autistic children in behavior therapy. *Journal of Applied Behavior Analysis, 6*, 131–166.

Lovaas, O. I., Schaeffer, B., & Simmons, J. Q. (1965). Building social behavior in autistic children by use of electric shock. *Journal of Experimental Research in Personality, 1*, 99–109.

Lovaas, O. I., Schreibman, L., Koegel, R., & Rehm, R. (1971). Selective responding by autistic children to multiple sensory input. *Journal of Abnormal Psychology, 77*, 211–222.

Lown, G., DeSilva, R. A., Reich, P., & Murawski, B. J. (1980). Psychophysiologic factors in sudden cardiac death. *American Journal of Psychiatry, 137*, 1325–1335.

Luborsky, L., Chandler, M., Averbach, A. H., Cohen, J., & Bachrach, H. (1971). Factors influencing the outcome of psychotherapy: A review of quantitative research. *Psychological Bulletin, 75*, 145–185.

Luchins, D. J. (1982). Computed tomography in schizophrenia. *Archives of General Psychiatry, 39*, 859–860.

Ludwig, A. M., Brandsma, J. M., Wilbur, C. B., Bendfeldt, F., & Jameson, D. H. (1972). The objective study of multiple personality. *Archives of General Psychiatry, 26*, 298–310.

Luiselli, J. K., & Slocumb, P. R. (1983). Management of multiple aggression behaviors by differential reinforcement. *Journal of Behavior Therapy and Experimental Psychiatry, 14*, 343–347.

Luparello, T., Lyons, H. A., Bleecker, E. R., & McFadden, E. R. (1968). Influences of suggestion on airway reactivity in asthmatic subjects. *Psychosomatic Medicine, 30*, 819–825.

Luria, A. R. (1982). *Language and cognition*. New York: Oxford University Press.

Lykken, D. F. (1957). A study of anxiety in the sociopathic personality. *Journal of Abnormal and Social Psychology, 55*, 6–10.

MacEachron, A. E. (1979). Mentally retarded offenders: Prevalence and characteristics. *American Journal of Mental Deficiency, 84*, 165–176.

MacEachron, A. E. (1983). Institutional reform and adaptive functioning of mentally retarded persons: A field experiment. *American Journal of Mental Deficiency, 88*, 2–12.

Machover, K. (1949). *Personality projection in the drawing of the human figure: A method of personality investigation*.

Springfield, IL: Charles C. Thomas.

MacMillan, D. L., & Keogh, B. K. (1971). Normal and retarded children's expectancy for failure. *Developmental Psychology, 4,* 343–348.

Maddi, S. R. (1972). *Personality theories.* Homewood, IL: Dorsey.

Madsen, C. H., Becker, W. C., Thomas, D. R., Koser, L., & Plager, E. (1970). An analysis of the reinforcing function of "sit-down" commands. In R. K. Parker (Ed.), *Readings in educational psychology.* Boston: Allyn & Bacon.

Magaro, P. A. (1981). The paranoid and the schizophrenic: The case for distinct cognitive styles. *Schizophrenia Bulletin, 7,* 632–661.

Magni, G., & Schifano, F. (1984). Psychological distress after stroke. *Journal of Neurology, Neurosurgery and Psychiatry, 47,* 567–568.

Maher, B. A. (1966). *Principles of psychopathology.* New York: McGraw-Hill.

Mahoney, M. J. (1977). Reflections on the cognitive-learning trend in psychotherapy. *American Psychologist, 32,* 5–13.

Mahoney, M. J., & Arnkoff, D. B. (1978). Cognitive and self-control therapies. In S. L. Garfield & A. E. Bergin (Eds.), *Handbook of psychotherapy and behavior change.* New York: Wiley.

Mahoney, M. J., & Kazdin, A. E. (1978). Cognitive behavior modification: Misconception and premature evaluation in psychology. *Psychological Records, 28,* 157–160.

Mailer, Norman. (1981). *Marilyn.* New York: Grossett & Dunlap.

Malamuth, N. M. (1981). Rape fantasies as a function of exposure to violent sexual stimuli. *Archives of Sexual Behavior, 10,* 33–47.

Malatesta, V. J., Pollack, R. H., Wilbanks, W. A., & Adams, H. E. (1979). Alcohol effects on the orgasmic-ejaculatory response in human males. *Journal of Sex Research, 15,* 101–107.

Malinow, K. L. (1981). Passive-aggressive personality. In J. R. Lion (Ed.), *Personality disorders: Diagnosis and management.* Baltimore: Williams & Wilkins.

Maltz, A. (1982). *Autism: Diagnostic and placement consideration.* Michigan State Planning Council for Developmental Disabilities.

Marantz, S. (1985, May 12). In the eyes of his public Ali is still the greatest. *Boston Globe,* p. 63.

Margolies, P. J. (1977). Behavioral approaches to the treatment of early infantile autism: A review. *Psychological Bulletin, 84,* 359–365.

Marks, I. M. (1976). The current status of behavioral psychotherapy: Theory and practice. *American Journal of Psychiatry, 133,* 253–261.

Marks, I. M. (1983). Are there anticompulsive or antiphobic drugs? Review of the evidence. *British Journal of Psychiatry, 143,* 338–347.

Marks, I. M., & Gelder, M. G. (1966). Different onset ages in varieties of phobia. *American Journal of Psychiatry, 123,* 218–221.

Marlatt, G. A. (1975). Alcohol, stress, and cognitive control. In I. Sarason & C. Spielberger (Eds.), *Stress and anxiety* (Vol. 2). Washington, DC: Hemisphere.

Marlatt, G. A. (1978). Craving for alcohol, loss of control and relapse: A cognitive-behavioral analysis. In P. E. Nathan & G. A. Marlatt (Eds.), *Experimental and behavioral approaches to alcoholism.* New York: Plenum.

Marlatt, G. A. (1983). The controlled-drinking controversy: A commentary. *American Psychologist, 38,* 1097–1110.

Marlatt, G. A., Demming, B., & Reid, J. (1973). Loss of control in drinking alcoholics: An experimental analogue. *Journal of Abnormal Psychology, 81,* 233–241.

Marmor, J., & Woods, S. M. (1980). *The interface between the psychodynamic and behavioral therapies.* New York: Plenum Medical.

Marmot, M. G., & Syme, S. L. (1976). Acculturation and coronary heart disease in Japanese-Americans. *American Journal of Epidemiology, 104,* 225–247.

Marquis, J. (1970). Orgasmic reconditioning: Changing sexual object choice through controlling masturbation fantasies. *Journal of Behavior Therapy and Experimental Psychiatry, 1,* 263–271.

Martin, B. (1971). *Anxiety and neurotic disorders.* New York: Wiley.

Martin, C. E. (1981). Factors affecting sexual functioning in 60–79-year-old married males. *Archives of Sexual Behavior, 10,* 399–420.

Marussen, R. M., & Wolff, H. G. (1949). A formulation of the dynamics of the migraine attack. *Psychosomatic Medicine, 1,* 251–256.

Maslach, C., & Jackson, S. E. (1979). Burned-out cops and their families. *Psychology Today, 12,* 59–62.

Maslach, C., & Pines, A. (1977). The burnout syndrome in the day care setting. *Child Care Quarterly, 6,* 100–113.

Maslow, A. H. (1954). *Motivation and personality.* New York: Harper & Row.

Masserman, J., Yum, K., Nicholson, J., & Lee, S. (1944). Neurosis and alcohol: An experimental study. *American Journal of Psychiatry, 101,* 389–395.

Masters, W. H., & Johnson, V. E. (1970). *Human sexual inadequacy.* London: Churchill.

Masters, W. H., & Johnson, V. E. (1979). *Homosexuality in perspective.* Boston: Little, Brown.

Masterson, J. F. (1981). *The narcissistic and borderline disorders: An integrated developmental approach.* New York: Brunner/Mazel.

Masuda, M., & Holmes, T. H. (1976). The social readjustment rating scale: A cross-cultural study of Japanese and Americans. *Journal of Psychosomatic Research, 11,* 227–237.

Matarazzo, J. D. (1980). Behavioral health and behavioral medicine. *American Psychologist, 35,* 807–817.

Materka, P. R. (1984). Families caring, coping with Alzheimer's disease. *Michigan Today, 16,* 13–14.

Mathe, A. A., & Knapp, P. H. (1977). Emotional and adrenal reactors to stress in bronchial asthma. *Psychosomatic Medicine, 33,* 323–327.

Mathews, A., & Shaw, P. (1977). Case histories and shorter communications. *Behaviour Research and Therapy, 15,* 503–505.

Mathis, J., & Collins, M. (1970). Mandatory group therapy for exhibitionists. *American Journal of Psychiatry, 126,* 1162–1167.

Mattison, J. (1973). Marriage and mental handicap. In F. F. De la Crux & G. D. Laveck (Eds.), *Human sexuality and the mentally retarded.* New York: Brunner/Mazel.

Mavissakalian, M., Michelson, L., & Dealy, R. S. (1983). Pharmacological treatment of agoraphobia: Imipramine with programmed practice. *British Journal of Psychiatry, 143,*

348–355.

May, P. R. (1968). *Treatment of schizophrenia: A comparative study of five treatment methods.* New York: Science House.

May, R. (1958). Existence: A new dimension in psychiatry and psychology. New York: Basic Books.

May, R. (Ed.). (1961). *Existential psychology.* New York: Random House.

May, R. (1967). *Psychology and the human dilemma.* New York: Van Nostrand.

May, R., Angel, E., & Ellenberger, H. F. (Eds.). (1958). *Existence.* New York: Basic Books.

McAdoo, W. G., & DeMeyer, M. K. (1978). Personality characteristics of parents. In M. Rutter & E. Schopler (Eds.), *Autism: A reappraisal of concepts and treatment.* New York: Plenum Press.

McCary, J. L. (1973). *Human sexuality.* New York: Van Nostrand.

McCauley, E., & Ehrhardt, A. A. (1984). Follow-up of females with gender identity disorders. *Journal of Nervous and Mental Disease, 172,* 353–358.

McClelland, D., Davis, W., Kalin, R., & Wanner, E. (1972). *The drinking man.* New York: Free Press.

McConaghy, N. (1983). Agoraphobia, compulsive behaviours, and behaviour completion mechanisms. *Australian and New England Journal of Psychiatry, 17,* 170–179.

McCord, W., & McCord, J. (1964). *The psychopath: An essay on the criminal mind.* Princeton, NJ: Van Nostrand.

McCord, W., McCord, J., & Gudeman, J. (1960). *Origins of alcoholism.* Stanford: Stanford University Press.

McCracken, G. H. (1976). Neonatal septicemia and meningitis. *Hospital Practice, 11,* 89–97.

McCranie, E. J. (1979). Hypochondriacal neurosis. *Psychosomatics, 20,* 11–15.

McCranie, E. J. (1980). Neurasthenic neurosis: Psychogenic weakness and fatigue. *Psychosomatics, 21,* 19–24.

McEwan, K. L., & Devins, G. M. (1983). Is increased arousal in social anxiety noticed by others? *Journal of Abnormal Psychology, 92,* 417–421.

McGee, R., Silva, P. A., & Williams, S. (1984). Behaviour problems in a population of seven-year-old children: Prevalence, stability and types of disorder—a research project. *Journal of Child Psychology and Psychiatry, 25,* 251–259.

McGeer, P. L., & McGeer, E. G. (1980). Chemistry of mood and emotions. *Annual Review of Psychology, 31,* 273–307.

McGlashan, T. H. (1982). DSM III schizophrenia and individual psychotherapy. *Journal of Nervous and Mental Disease, 170,* 752–757.

McGuire, L., & Wagner, N. (1978). Sexual dysfunction in women who were molested as children. *Journal of Sex and Marital Therapy, 4,* 11–15.

McGuire, R. J., Carlisle, J. M., & Young, B. G. (1965). Sexual deviations as conditioned behavior: A hypothesis. *Behaviour Research and Therapy, 2,* 185–190.

McIntosh, J. L., & Santos, J. F. (1981). Suicide among Native Americans: A compilation of findings. *Omega: Journal of Death and Dying, 11,* 303–316.

McNamee, H. B., Mello, N. K., & Mendelson, J. H. (1968). Experimental analysis of drinking patterns of alcoholics: Concurrent psychiatric observations. *American Journal of Psychiatry, 124,* 1063–1069.

McNeil, E. B. (1974). *The psychology of being human.* San Francisco: Canfield Press.

Mechanic, D. (1974). Discussion of research programs on relations between stressful life events and episodes of physical illness. In B. S. Dohrenwend & B. P. Dohrenwend (Eds.), *Stressful life events.* New York: Wiley.

Mechanic, D. (Coordinator). (1978). Report of the task panel on the nature and scope of the problems. In *President's Commission on Mental Health* (Vol. 2, pp. 1–138). Washington, DC: U.S. Government Printing Office.

Mednick, S., & Christiansen, K. O. (Eds.). (1977). *Biosocial basis of criminal behavior.* New York: Gardner Press.

Mednick, S. A. (1970). Breakdown in individuals at high risk for schizophrenia: Possible predispositional perinatal factors. *Mental Hygiene, 54,* 50–63.

Mednick, S. A., & Schulsinger, F. (1968). Some premorbid characteristics related to breakdown in children with schizophrenic mothers. In D. Rosenthal & S. Kety (Eds.), *The transmission of schizophrenia.* New York: Pergamon Press.

Meehl, P. E. (1962). Schizotaxia, schizotypia, schizophrenia. *American Psychologist, 17,* 827–838.

Megargee, E., & Bohn, M. (1977). Empirically determined characteristics of the ten types. *Criminal Justice and Behavior, 4,* 149–210.

Megargee, E., & Bohn, M. (1979). *Classifying criminal offenders.* Beverly Hills, CA: Sage.

Mehlman, B. (1952). The reliability of psychiatric diagnosis. *Journal of Abnormal and Social Psychology, 47,* 477–578.

Meichenbaum, D. (1974). The clinical potential of modifying what clients say to themselves. In M. J. Mahoney & C. E. Thoresen (Eds.), *Self-Control: Power to the person.* Monterey, CA: Brooks/Cole.

Meichenbaum, D., & Goodman, J. (1971). Training impulsive children to talk to themselves: A means for developing self-control. *Journal of Abnormal Psychology, 77,* 115–126.

Meichenbaum, D. H. (1966). Sequential strategies in two cases of hysteria. *Behaviour Research and Therapy, 4,* 89–94.

Meichenbaum, D. H. (1972). Cognitive modification of test-anxious college students. *Journal of Consulting and Clinical Psychology, 39,* 370–380.

Meichenbaum, D. H. (1976). Cognitive behavior modification. In J. T. Spence, R. C. Carson, & J. W. Thibaut (Eds.), *Behavioral approaches to therapy.* Morristown, NJ: General Learning Press.

Meichenbaum, D. H. (1977). *Cognitive-behavior modification: An integrative approach.* New York: Plenum.

Meichenbaum, D. H., Gilmore, J., & Fedoravicius, A. (1971). Group insight versus group desensitization in treating speech anxiety. *Journal of Consulting and Clinical Psychology, 36,* 410–421.

Melges, F., & Bowlby, J. (1969). Types of hopelessness in psychopathological process. *Archives of General Psychiatry, 20,* 690–699.

Mellsop, G. W. (1972). Psychiatric patients seen as children and adults: Childhood predictors of adult illness. *Journal of Child Psychology and Psychiatry, 13,* 91–101.

Meltzoff, J., & Kornreich, M. (1970). *Research in psychotherapy.* New York: Atherton.

Mendels, J. (1970). *Concepts of depression* (p. 6). New York: Wiley.

Menninger, W. C. (1948). *Psychiatry in a troubled world.* New York: Macmillan.

Mental health statistics. (1984). [Special issue]. *Archives of General Psychiatry, 132.*

Mercer, J. R. (1973). *Labeling the mentally retarded.* Berkeley: University of California Press.

Mercer, J. R. (1979). *System of Multicultural Pluralistic Assessment (SOMPA): Technical manual.* New York: Psychological Corp.

Mercer, J. R., & Lewis, J. F. (1977). *SOMPA: For the meaningful assessment of culturally different children.* New York: Psychological Corp.

Merton, R. K. (1968). *Social theory and social structure.* New York: Free Press.

Metcalfe, M. (1956). Demonstration of a psychosomatic relationship. *British Journal of Medicinal Psychology, 29,* 63–66.

Meyer, J., & Peter, D. (1979). Sex reassignment: Follow-up. *Archives of General Psychiatry, 36,* 1010–1015.

Meyer, R. G., & Osborne, Y. V. H. (1982). *Case studies in abnormal behavior.* Boston: Allyn & Bacon.

Meyer, V., Levey, R., & Schnurer, A. (1974). The behavioral treatment of obsessive compulsive disorders. In H. Beech (Ed.), *Obsessional states.* London: Methuen.

Michigan Society for Autistic Citizens. (1979). *Autism: Parent survey of early identification and interaction services.* William P. Walsh, M.S.W.

Mikkelsen, M., & Stene, J. (1970). Genetic counseling in Down's syndrome. *Human Heredity, 20,* 457–464.

Milgram, N. A. (1969). The rational and irrational in Zigler's motivational approach to mental retardation. *American Journal of Mental Deficiency, 73,* 527–532.

Miller, N. (1983). Behavioral medicine: Symbiosis between laboratory and clinic. *Annual Review of Psychology, 34,* 1–31.

Miller, N. E. (1974). Applications of learning and biofeedback to psychiatry and medicine. In A. M. Freedman, H. I. Kaplan, & B. J. Sadock (Eds.), *Comprehensive textbook of psychiatry* (2nd ed.). Baltimore: Williams & Wilkins.

Millon, T. (1973). *Theories of psychopathology and personality.* Philadelphia: Saunders.

Millon, T. (1975). Reflections on Rosenhan's "On being sane in insane places." *Journal of Abnormal Psychology, 84,* 456–461.

Millon, T. (1981). The avoidant personality. In J. R. Lion (Ed.), *Personality disorders: Diagnosis and management.* Baltimore: Williams & Wilkins.

Millon, T. (1983). The DSM-III: An insider's perspective. *American Psychologist, 38,* 804–814.

Millon, T., & Diesenhaus, H. I. (1972). *Research methods in psychopathology.* New York: Wiley.

Mills, C. J., & Noyes, H. L. (1984). Patterns and correlates of initial and subsequent drug use among adolescents. *Journal of Consulting and Clinical Psychology, 52,* 231–243.

Miniszek, N. A. (1983). Development of Alzheimer's disease in Down syndrome individuals. *American Journal of Mental Deficiency, 87,* 377–385.

Mintz, A. (1951). Nonadaptive group behavior. *Journal of Abnormal and Social Psychology, 46,* 150–159.

Mintz, I. (1983). Psychoanalytic description: The clinical picture of anorexia nervosa and bulimia. In C. Wilson (Ed.), *Fear of being fat.* New York: Jason Aronson.

Minuchin, S. (1974). *Families and family therapy.* Cambridge, MA: Harvard University Press.

Minuchin, S., & Fishman, H. (1981). *Family therapy techniques.* Cambridge, MA: Harvard University Press.

Minuchin, S., Rosman, B., & Baker, L. (1978). *Psychosomatic families: Anorexia nervosa in context.* Cambridge, MA: Harvard University Press.

Mitchell, C. M. (1983). The dissemination of a social intervention: Process and effectiveness of two types of paraprofessional change agents. *American Journal of Community Psychology, 11,* 723–740.

Mitchell, J. E., Pyle, R. L., & Eckert, E. D. (1981). Frequency and duration of binge-eating episodes in patients with bulimia. *American Journal of Psychiatry, 138,* 835–836.

Mohr, J. W., Turner, R. E., & Jury, M. B. (1964). *Pedophilia and exhibitionism.* Toronto: University of Toronto Press.

Money, J., & Brennan, J. G. (1968). Sexual dimorphism in the psychology of female transsexuals. *Journal of Nervous and Mental Diseases, 247,* 487–499.

Money, J., & Ehrhardt, A. (1972). *Man and woman, boy and girl.* Baltimore: Johns Hopkins University Press.

Money, J., Hampson, J. G., & Hampson, J. L. (1957). Imprinting and establishing gender role. *Archives of Neurological Psychiatry, 77,* 333–336.

Money, J., & Primrose, C. (1968). Sexual dimorphism and dissociation in the psychology of male transsexuals. *Journal of Nervous and Mental Diseases, 147,* 472–486.

Moore, B. C. (1973). Some characteristics of institutionalized mongoloids. *Journal of Mental Deficiency Research, 17,* 46–54.

Moore, H. E. (1958). Some emotional concomitants of disaster. *Mental Hygiene, 42,* 45.

Moore, T. (1982). Blacks: Rethinking service. In L. R. Snowden (Ed.), *Reaching the underserved: Mental health needs of neglected populations.* Beverly Hills, CA: Sage.

Moos, R. H., & Finney, J. W. (1983). The expanding scope of alcoholism treatment evaluation. *American Psychologist, 38,* 1036–1044.

Moreland, J., & Schwebel, A. (1981). A gender role transcendent perspective on fathering. *Counseling Psychologist, 9*(4), 45–54.

Moreno, J. L. (1946). *Psychodrama.* New York: Beacon.

Moreno, J. L. (1959). Psychodrama. In S. Arieti (Ed.), *American handbook of psychiatry* (Vol. 2). New York: Basic Books.

Morey, L. C., & Blashfield, R. K. (1981). A symptom analysis of the DSM III definition of schizophrenia. *Schizophrenia Bulletin, 7,* 258–268.

Morgan, R. (1970). *Sisterhood is powerful.* New York: Vintage Books.

Mosher, L. R., & Keith, S. J. (1979). Research on the psychosocial treatment of schizophrenia: A summary report. *The American Journal of Psychiatry, 136,* 623–631.

Mosher, L. R., & Keith, S. J. (1980). Psychosocial treatment—individual, group, family, and community support approaches. *Schizophrenia Bulletin, 6,* 10–41.

Mostofsky, D. I., & Balaschak, B. A. (1979). Psychological control of seizures. *Psychological Bulletin, 84,* 723–750.

Mowrer, O. H., & Mowrer, W. M. (1938). Enuresis—a method for its study and treatment. *American Journal of Orthopsychiatry, 8,* 436–459.

Mucha, T. F., & Reinhardt, R. F. (1970). Conversion reactions in student aviators. *American Journal of Psychiatry, 127,* 493–496.

Mulford, H. A. (1982). The epidemiology of alcoholism and its implications. In M. Pattison & E. Kaufman (Eds.), *Encyclopedia handbook of alcoholism*. New York: Gardner Press.

Munford, P. R., & Pally, R. (1979). Outpatient contingency management of operant vomiting. *Journal of Behavior Therapy and Experimental Psychiatry, 10,* 135–137.

Munoz, R. F., Glish, M., Soo-Hoo, T., & Robertson, J. (1982). The San Francisco mood survey project: Preliminary work toward the prevention of depression. *American Journal of Community Psychology, 10,* 317–330.

Murdock, C. W. (1973). Civil rights of the mentally retarded—some critical issues. *Family Law Quarterly, 7,* 1–74.

Murphree, O. D., & Dykman, R. A. (1965). Litter patterns in the offspring of nervous and stable dogs: I. Behavioral tests. *Journal of Nervous and Mental Disorders, 141,* 321–332.

Murphy, C. E. (1973). Suicide and the right to die. *American Journal of Psychiatry, 130,* 472–473.

Murray, E. J. (1983). Beyond behavioral and dynamic therapy. *British Journal of Clinical Psychology, 22,* 127–128.

Murray, H. A., & Morgan, H. (1938). *Explorations in personality*. New York: Oxford University Press.

Murray, J. P. (1973). Television and violence: Implications of the surgeon general's research program. *American Psychologist, 28,* 72–78.

Myers, H. F., & King, L. M. (1983). Mental health issues in the development of the black American child. In G. J. Powell (Ed.), *The psychosocial development of minority group children*. New York: Brunner/Mazel.

Myers, J. K., Weissman, M. M., Tischler, G. L., Holzer, C. E., Leaf, P. J., Orvaschel, H., Anthony, J. C., Boyd, J. H., Burke, J. D., Kramer, M., & Stoltzman, R. (1984). Six-month prevalence of psychiatric disorders in three communities. *Archives of General Psychiatry, 41,* 959–967.

Nathan, P., & Jackson, A. (1976). Behavior modification. In I. Weiner (Ed.), *Clinical methods in psychology*. New York: Wiley.

Nathan, P. E. (1976). Alcoholism. In H. Leitenberg (Ed.), *Handbook of behavior modification and behavior therapy*. Englewood Cliffs, NJ: Prentice-Hall.

Nathan, P. E., & Wiens, A. N. (1983). Alcoholism: Introduction and overview. *American Psychologist, 38,* 1035.

National Academy of Sciences. (1982). *Marijuana and health*. Washington, DC: National Academy Press.

National Center for Health Statistics. (1980). *The nation's use of health resources 1980*. Hyattsville, MD: National Center for Health Statistics.

National Commission on the Causes and Prevention of Violence. (1969). *To establish justice, to insure domestic tranquility*. New York: Award Books.

National Institute of Mental Health. (1970). U.S. Department of Health, Education, and Welfare. Mental Health Publication No. 5027. Washington, DC: U.S. Government Printing Office.

National Institute of Mental Health (1975). *Report of research task force: Research in the service of mental health*. (DHEW Pub. 75–236). Rockville, MD.

National Institute on Alcohol Abuse and Alcoholism. (1981). Patterns of alcohol consumption. *Alcohol Health and Research World, 5,* 2–6.

National Institutes of Health. (1981). *The dementias: Hope through research*. Bethesda, MD: National Institutes of Health.

Neale, J. M., & Oltmanns, T. F. (1980). *Schizophrenia*. New York: Wiley.

Neff, J. A. (1984). Race differences in psychological distress: The effects of SES, urbanicity, and measurement strategy. *American Journal of Community Psychology, 12,* 337–352.

Nettlebladt, P., & Uddenberg, N. (1979). Sexual dysfunction and sexual satisfaction in 58 married Swedish men. *Journal of Psychosomatic Research, 23,* 141–148.

Neugebauer, R. (1979). Medieval and early modern theories of mental illness. *Archives of General Psychiatry, 36,* 477–483.

Newman, L. E., & Stoller, R. J. (1974). Nontranssexual men who seek sex reassignment. *American Journal of Psychiatry, 131,* 437–441.

Nichols, M. (1984). *Family therapy*. New York: Gardner Press.

Nielsen, E. B., Lyon, M., & Ellison, G. (1983). Apparent hallucinations in monkeys during the around-the-clock amphetamine for seven to fourteen days. *Journal of Nervous and Mental Disease, 171,* 222–233.

Nowlis, D., & Kamiya, J. (1970). The control of EEG algorithm through auditory feedback and the associated mental activity. *Psychophysiology, 6,* 476–484.

Nuechterlein, K. H., & Dawson, M. E. (1984). A heuristic vulnerability/stress model of schizophrenic episodes. *Schizophrenic Bulletin, 10,* 300–311.

Nutt, R. L. (1979). Review and preview of attitudes and values of counselors of women. *The Counseling Psychologist, 8,* 18–20.

Office of Technical Assessment. (1983). *The effectiveness of costs of alcoholism treatment*. Washington, DC: U.S. Congress.

Ohman, A., Ericksson, A., & Olofsson, C. (1975). One-trial learning and superior resistance to extinction of autonomic responses conditioned to potentially phobic stimuli. *Journal of Comparative Physiological Psychology, 88,* 619–627.

Ohman, A., Frederickson, M., Hugdahl, K., & Rimmo, P. A. (1976). The premise of equipotentiality in human classical conditioning: Conditioned electrode responses to potentially phobic stimuli. *Journal of Experimental Psychology: General, 105,* 313–337.

O'Leary, K. D., & Wilson, G. T. (1975). *Behavior therapy: Application and outcome*. Englewood Cliffs, NJ: Prentice-Hall.

Oliver, J., Shaller, C. A., Majovski, L. V., & Jacques, S. (1982). Stroke mechanisms: Neuropsychological implications. *Clinical Neuropsychology, 4,* 81–84.

Oltmanns, T. F., Ohayon, J., & Neale, S. M. (1978). The effect of antipsychotic medication and diagnostic criteria on distractibility in schizophrenia. In L. C. Wynne, R. L. Cromwell, & S. Matthysse (Eds.), *The nature of schizophrenia: New approaches to research and treatment* (pp. 283–286). New York: John Wiley.

Opler, M. K. (1967). *Culture and social psychiatry*. New York: Atherton Press.

Ornitz, E. M., & Ritvo, E. R. (1976). The syndrome of autism: A critical review. *American Journal of Psychiatry, 133,* 609–621.

Osgood, C. E., Luria, Z., & Smith, S. W. (1976). A blind analysis of another case of multiple personality using the semantic differential technique. *Journal of Abnormal Psychology, 85,* 256–270.

Ost, L. G., & Hugdahl, K. (1981). Acquisition of phobias and anxiety response patterns in clinical patients. *Behaviour Research and Therapy, 19,* 439–447.

Ost, L. G., Jerremalm, A., & Jansson, L. (1984). Individual response patterns and the effects of different behavioral methods in the treatment of agoraphobia. *Behaviour Research and Therapy, 22,* 697–707.

Ost, L. G., Sterner, U., & Lindahl, I. L. (1984). Physiological responses in blood phobics. *Behaviour Research and Therapy, 22,* 109–117.

Ottenbacher, K. H., & Cooper, H. M. (1983). Drug treatment of hyperactivity in children. *Developmental Medicine in Child Neurology, 25,* 358–366.

Ottenberg, P., Stein, M., Lewis, J., & Hamilton, C. (1958). Learned asthma in the guinea pig. *Psychosomatic Medicine, 20,* 395–400.

Overmier, J. B., & Seligman, M. E. P. (1967). Effects of inescapable shock upon subsequent escape and avoidance learning. *Journal of Comparative and Physiological Psychology, 63,* 23–33.

Page, E. B. (1972). Miracle in Milwaukee: Raising the IQ. *Educational Researcher, 1,* 3–16.

Pardine, P., & Napoli, A. (1983). Physiological reactivity and recent life-stress experience. *Journal of Consulting and Clinical Psychology, 51,* 467–469.

Patterson, C. H. (1980). *Theories of counseling and psychotherapy.* New York: Harper & Row.

Patterson, G. R., Littman, R. A., & Bircher, W. (1967). Assertive behavior in children: A step toward a theory of aggression. *Monographs of the Society for Research in Child Development, 32,* 113.

Paul, G. L. (1966). *Insight vs. desensitization in psychotherapy.* Stanford: Stanford University Press.

Paul, G. L. (1967). Insight versus desensitization in psychotherapy two years after termination. *Journal of Consulting Psychology, 31,* 333–348.

Paul, G. L. (1982). *The development of a "transportable" system of behavioral assessment for chronic patients.* Address at University of Minnesota, Minneapolis.

Pauls, D. L., Cohen, D. J., Heimbuch, R., Dettor, J., Kidd, K. K. (1981). Familial pattern and transmission of Gilles de la Tourette syndrome and multiple tics. *Archives of General Psychiatry, 38,* 1091–1093.

Pauly, I. B. (1968). The current status of the change of sex operation. *Journal of Nervous and Mental Diseases, 147,* 460–471.

Paykel, E. S. (1974). Life stress and psychiatric disorder. In B. S. Dohrenwend & B. P. Dohrenwend (Eds.), *Stressful life events.* New York: Wiley.

Pearl, D., Bouthilet, L., & Lazar, J. (Eds.). (1982). *Television and behavior: Ten years of scientific progress and implications for the eighties* (Vols. 1 & 2). Washington, DC: U.S. Government Printing Office.

Pendery, M. L., Maltzman, I. M., & West, L. J. (1982). Controlled drinking by alcoholics? New findings and a reevaluation of a major affirmative study. *Science, 217,* 169–175.

Penk, W. E., Fridge, J. W., & Robinowitz, R. (1979). Personality characteristics of compulsive heroin, amphetamine, and barbiturate users. *Journal of Consulting and Clinical Psychology, 47,* 583–585.

Perris, C. (1966). A study of bipolar (manic-depressive) and unipolar recurrent depressive psychosis. *Acta Psychiatrica Scandinavica* (Suppl. 194).

Perry, S. E. (1956). *The child and his family in disaster: A study of the 1953 Vicksburg tornado* (Disaster Study No. 5). Washington, DC: National Academy of Science, National Research Council.

Pfeffer, C. R. (1981). Suicide behavior of children: A review with implications for research and practice. *American Journal of Psychiatry, 138,* 154–159.

Phares, E. J. (1984). *Clinical psychology: Concepts, methods, and professions.* Homewood, IL: Dorsey.

Phillips, J. S., & Ray, R. S. (1980). Behavioral approaches to childhood disorders. *Behavior Modification, 4,* 3–34.

Phobias are becoming "distressingly common." (1984, July 6). *Independent Journal,* p. C-3.

Physician's Desk Reference. (1982). Oradell, NJ: Medical Economics Company.

Physician's Desk Reference. (1984). Oradell, NJ: Medical Economics Company.

Pickering, P. G., Harshfield, G. A., Kleinert, H. D., Blank, S., & Laragh, J. L. (1982). Blood pressure during normal daily activities, sleep, and exercise: Comparison of values in normal and hypertensive subjects. *Journal of the American Medical Association, 247,* 992–996.

Pilisuk, M. (1975). The legacy of the Vietnam veteran. *Journal of Social Issues, 31*(4), 3–12.

Pines, M. (1983, October). *Science,* p. 55–58.

Platt, J. J. (1975). "Addiction proneness" and personality in heroin addicts. *Journal of Abnormal Psychology, 84,* 303–306.

A plea from Chinese students in U.S. (1976, June 16). *East–West.*

Pohl, R., Rainey, J., & Gershon, S. (1984). Changes in the drug treatment of anxiety disorders. *Psychopathology, 17,* 6–14.

Polivy, J., Schueneman, A. L., & Carlson, K. (1976). Alcohol and tension reduction: Cognitive and physiological effects. *Journal of Abnormal Psychology, 85,* 595–600.

Pollin, W., Allen, M. G., Hoffer, A., Stabenau, J. R., & Hrubec, Z. (1969). Psychopathology in 15,909 pairs of veteran twins. *American Journal of Psychiatry, 126,* 597–609.

Pollitt, J. D. (1960). Natural history studies in mental illness: A discussion based on a pilot study of obsessional states. *Journal of Mental Science, 106,* 93–113.

Polloway, E. A., & Smith, J. D. (1983). Changes in mild mental retardation: Population, programs, and perspectives. *Exceptional Children, 50,* 149–159.

Pope, H. G., Hudson, J. I., Jonas, J., & Yurgelun-Todd, D. (1983). Bulimia treated with imipramine: A placebo-controlled, double-blind study. *American Journal of Psychiatry, 140,* 554–558.

Pope, H. G., Hudson, J. I., & Yurgelun-Todd, D. (1984). Anorexia nervosa and bulimia among 300 suburban women shoppers. *American Journal of Psychiatry, 141,* 292–294.

Pope, H. G., Jonas, J. M., Cohen, B. M. (1982). Failure to find evidence of schizophrenic probands. *American Journal of Psychiatry, 139,* 826–828.

Pope, H. G., & Lipinski, J. F. (1978). Diagnosis in schizophrenia and manic-depression illness: A reassessment of the specificity of "schizophrenic" symptoms in light of current research. *Archives of General Psychiatry, 35,* 811–828.

Portnoff, L. A., Golden, C. J., Wood, R. E., & Gustavson,

J. L. (1983). Discrimination between schizophrenic and parietal lesion patients with neurological tests of parietal involvement. *Clinical Neuropsychology, 5,* 175–178.

Portwood, D. (1978, January). A right to suicide. *Psychology Today,* pp. 66–74.

Poser, E. G. (1966). The effect of therapist's training upon group therapeutic outcome. *Journal of Consulting Psychology, 30,* 283–289.

Powell, C. J. (1982, August). *Adolescence and the right to die: Issues of autonomy, competence, and paternalism.* Paper presented at the meeting of the American Psychological Association, Washington, DC.

Powell, G. J. (1983). Coping with adversity: The psychosocial development of Afro-American children. In G. J. Powell (Ed.), *The psychosocial development of minority group children.* New York: Brunner/Mazel.

President's Commission on Mental Health. (1978). *Report to the President.* Washington, DC: U.S. Government Printing Office.

President's Committee on Mental Retardation. (1969). *MR 69: Toward progress: The story of a decade.* Washington, DC: U.S. Government Printing Office.

President's Committee on Mental Retardation. (1972). *Entering the era of human ecology.* Washington, DC: U.S. Government Printing Office.

Press, A., Abramson, P., & Newhall, E. F. (1979, September 3). Who speaks for the child? *Newsweek,* p. 49.

Price, L. J., Fein, G., & Feinberg, I. Neurological assessment of cognitive function in the elderly. In L. W. Poon (Ed.), *Aging in the 1980's.* Washington, DC: American Psychological Association.

Prichard, J. C. (1835). *A treatise on insanity.* Philadelphia, PA: Barrington & Hassurd.

Prigatano, G. P., Fordyce, D. J., Zeiner, H. K., Roueche, J. R., Pepping, M., & Wood, B. C. (1984). Neuropsychological rehabilitation after closed head injury in young adults. *Journal of Neurology and Neuropsychology, 47,* 505–513.

Prince, M. (1906). *The dissociation of personality.* New York: Longman.

Prior, M. (1984). Developing concepts of childhood autism: The influence of experimental cognitive research. *Journal of Consulting and Clinical Psychology, 52,* 4–16.

Prior, M., Leonard, A., & Wood, G. (1983). A comparison study of preschool children diagnosed as hyperactive. *Journal of Pediatric Psychology, 8,* 191–207.

Quay, H. C. (1965). Psychopathic personality as pathological stimulation seeking. *American Journal of Psychiatry, 122,* 180–183.

Rabkin, J. G. (1979). The epidemiology of forcible rape. *American Journal of Orthopsychiatry, 49,* 634–647.

Rachman, S. (1966). Sexual fetishism: An experimental analogue. *Psychological Record, 16,* 293–296.

Rachman, S. (1971). *The effects of psychotherapy.* New York: Pergamon.

Rachman, S. (1974). *The meaning of fear.* Middlesex, England: Penguin Books.

Rachman, S. (1984). Agoraphobia—A safety-signal perspective. *Behaviour Research and Therapy, 22,* 59–70.

Rachman, S., & Hodgson, R. (1980). *Obsessions and compulsions.* Englewood Cliffs, NJ: Prentice-Hall.

Rachman, S., Marks, I. M., & Hodgson, R. (1973). The treatment of obsessive-compulsive neurotics by modelling and flooding in vivo. *Behaviour Research and Therapy, 13,* 271–279.

Radloff, L. S., & Rae, D. S. (1981). The components of the sex difference in depression. In R. G. Simmons (Ed.), *Research in community and mental health* (Vol. 2). Greenwood, CT: JAI Press.

Rahe, R. H. (1968). Life change measurement as a predictor of illness. *Proceedings of the Royal Society of Medicine, 61,* 1124–1126.

Raher, J. W., Wallace, A. F. C., & Raymer, J. F. (1956). *Emergency medical care in disasters* (Disaster Study No. 6). Washington, DC: National Academy of Science, National Research Council.

Raines, G. N., & Rohrer, J. H. (1955). The operational matrix of psychiatric practice: 1. Consistency and variability in interview impressions of different psychiatrists. *American Journal of Psychiatry, 110,* 721–733.

Rapaport, K., & Burkhart, B. R. (1984). Personality and attitudinal characteristics of sexually coercive college males. *Journal of Abnormal Psychology, 93,* 216–221.

Rappaport, J. (1977). *Community psychology: Values, research, and action.* New York: Holt, Rinehart, & Winston.

Rappaport, J. (1981). In praise of paradox: A social policy of empowerment over prevention. *American Journal of Community Psychology, 9,* 1–26.

Rappaport, J., & Cleary, C. P. (1980). Labeling theory and the social psychology of experts and helpers. In M. S. Gibbs, J. R. Lachenmyer, & J. Sigal (Eds.), *Community psychology: Theoretical and empirical approaches.* New York: Gardner Press.

Raps, C. S., Peterson, C., Reinhard, K. E., Abramson, L. Y., & Seligman, M. E. P. (1982). Attributional styles among depressed patients. *Journal of Abnormal Psychology, 91,* 102–108.

Raskin, M., Pecke, H. V. S., Dickman, W., Pinsker, H. (1982). Panic and generalized anxiety disorders. *Archives of General Psychiatry, 39,* 687–689.

Rasmussen, S. (1984). Lithium and tryptophan augmentation in clomipramine-resistant obsessive-compulsive disorder. *American Journal of Psychiatry, 141,* 1283–1285.

Reading, C., & Mohr, P. (1976). Biofeedback control of migraine: A pilot study. *British Journal of Social and Clinical Psychology, 15,* 429–433.

Redestam, K. E. (1977). Physical and psychological response to suicide in the family. *Journal of Consulting and Clinical Psychology, 45,* 162–170.

Redlich, R. C., & Freedman, D. X. (1966). *The theory and practice of psychiatry.* New York: Basic Books.

Rees, L. (1964). The importance of psychological, allergic, and infective factors in childhood asthma. *Journal of Psychosomatic Research, 7,* 253–262.

Rees, L. (1983). The development of psychosomatic medicine during the past 25 years. *Journal of Psychosomatic Research, 27,* 157–164.

Regier, D. A., Goldberg, I. O., & Taube, C. A. (1978). The de facto U.S. mental health services systems: A public health perspective. *Archives of General Psychiatry, 35,* 685–693.

Reid, W. H. (1981). The antisocial personality and related symptoms. In J. R. Lion (Ed.), *Personality disorders: Diagnosis and management.* Baltimore: Williams & Wilkins.

Reilly, D. (1984). Family therapy with adolescent drug abusers and their families: Defying gravity and achieving escape velocity. *Journal of Drug Issues, 14,* 381–389.

Reisberg, B., Ferris, S. H., Crook, T. (1982). Signs, symptoms, and course of age-associated cognitive decline. In S. Corkin, K. L. Davis, J. H. Growdon, E. Usdin, & R. J. Wurtman (Eds.), *Alzheimer's disease: A report of progress.* New York: Raven Press.

Reisman, J. (1971). *Toward the integration of psychotherapy.* New York: Wiley.

Reiss, D. (1976). The family and schizophrenia. *American Journal of Psychiatry, 133,* 181–185.

Rekers, G. A., & Lovaas, O. I. (1974). Behavioral treatment of deviant sex-role behaviors in a male child. *Journal of Applied Behavior Analysis, 7,* 173–190.

Rekers, G. A., & Varni, J. W. (1977a). Self-monitoring and self-reinforcement processes in a pre-transsexual boy. *Behaviour Research and Therapy, 15,* 177–180.

Rekers, G. A., & Varni, J. W. (1977b). Self-regulation of gender-role behaviors: A case study. *Journal of Behavior Therapy and Experimental Psychiatry, 8,* 427–432.

Rekers, G. A., & Yates, C. E. (1976). Sex-typed play in feminoid boys versus normal boys and girls. *Journal of Abnormal Child Psychology, 4,* 1–8.

Reschly, D. (1981). Psychological testing in educational classification and placement. *American Psychologist, 36,* 1094–1102.

Research Task Force of the National Institute of Mental Health. (1975). *Research in the service of mental health* (DHEW Publication No. ADM 75–236). Washington, DC: U.S. Government Printing Office.

Resick, P. A. (1983). The rape reaction: Research findings and implications for intervention. *Behavior Therapist, 6,* 129–132.

Rhoads, J. M., & Borjes, E. P. (1981). Incidence of exhibitionism in Guatemala and the United States. *British Journal of Psychiatry, 139,* 242–244.

Richter, C. P. (1957). On the phenomenon of sudden death in animals and man. *Psychosomatic Medicine, 19,* 191–198.

Rickels, K. (1966). Drugs in the treatment of neurotic anxiety. In P. Solomon (Ed.), *Psychiatric drugs.* New York: Grune & Stratton.

Rimland, B. (1964). *Infantile autism.* New York: Appleton-Century-Crofts.

Rimland, B. (1978). Inside the mind of the autistic savant. *Psychology Today, 12,* 69–80.

Rimm, D. C., Janda, L. H., Lancaster, D. W., Nahl, M., & Dittmar, K. (1977). An exploratory investigation of the origin and maintenance of phobias. *Behaviour Research and Therapy, 15,* 231–238.

Rimm, D. C., & Litvak, S. B. (1969). Self-verbalization and emotional arousal. *Journal of Abnormal Psychology, 74,* 181–187.

Rimm, D. C., & Masters, J. C. (1979). *Behavior therapy: Techniques and empirical findings* (2nd ed.). New York: Academic Press.

Rioch, M. J. (1967). Pilot projects in training mental health counselors. In E. L. Cowen, E. A. Gardner, & M. Zax (Eds.), *Emergent approaches to mental health problems.* New York: Appleton-Century-Crofts.

Risley, T. R., & Baer, D. M. (1970). Operant conditioning: "Develop" is a transitive verb. In B. Caldwell & H. Ricciuti (Eds.), *Review of child development research: Vol. 3. Social influences and social action.* Chicago: University of Chicago Press.

Rist, K. (1979). Incest: Theoretical and clinical views. *American Journal of Orthopsychiatry, 49,* 680–691.

Robbins, P. R., Tanck, R. H., & Meyersburg, H. A. (1972). A study of three psychosomatic hypotheses. *Journal of Psychosomatic Research, 16,* 93–98.

Roberto, L. (1983). Issues in diagnosis and treatment of transsexualism. *Archives of Sexual Behavior, 12,* 445–473.

Robertson, J., Wendiggensen, P., & Kaplan, I. (1983). Toward a comprehensive treatment for obsessional thoughts. *Behaviour Research and Therapy, 21,* 347–356.

Robins, L. N. (1966). *Deviant children grown up: A sociological and psychiatric study of sociopathic personality.* Baltimore: Williams & Wilkins.

Robins, L. N. (1971). Follow-up studies involving childhood disorders. In E. H. Hare & J. K. Wing (Eds.), *Psychiatric Epidemiology.* London: Oxford University Press.

Robinson, L. R. (1975). Basic concepts in family therapy: A differential comparison with individual treatment. *American Journal of Psychiatry, 132*(10), 1045–1048.

Robinson, N. M., & Robinson, H. B. (1976). *The mentally retarded child.* New York: McGraw-Hill.

Roen, S. R. (1971). Evaluative research and community mental health. In A. E. Bergin & S. L. Garfield (Eds.), *Handbook of psychotherapy and behavior change.* New York: Wiley.

Roff, J. D., & Knight, R. (1981). Family characteristics, childhood symptoms, and adult outcome in schizophrenia. *Journal of Abnormal Psychology, 90,* 510–520.

Roff, J. D., & Wirt, R. D. (1984). Childhood aggression and social adjustment as antecedents of delinquency. *Journal of Abnormal Child Psychology, 12,* 111–126.

Rogers, C. R. (1951). *Client-centered therapy.* Boston: Houghton Mifflin.

Rogers, C. R. (1959). A theory of therapy, personality, and interpersonal relationships, as developed in client-centered framework. In S. Koch (Ed.), *Psychology: A study of science* (Vol. 3). New York: McGraw-Hill.

Rogers, C. R. (1961). *On becoming a person.* Boston: Houghton Mifflin.

Rohs, R. G., & Noyes, R. (1978). Agoraphobia: Newer treatment approaches. *Journal of Nervous and Mental Disease, 166,* 701–708.

Romaniuk, M., McAuley, W. J., & Arling, G. (1983). An examination of the prevalence of mental disorders among the elderly in the community. *Journal of Abnormal Psychology, 92,* 458–467.

Rooth, G. (1973). Exhibitionism, sexual violence and paedophilia. *British Journal of Psychiatry, 122,* 705–710.

Roper, G., & Rachman, S. (1976). Obsessive-compulsive checking: Experimental replication and development. *Behaviour Research and Therapy, 14,* 25–32.

Roper, G., Rachman, S., & Monks, I. M. (1975). Passive and participant treatment of obsessive-compulsive neurotics. *Behaviour Research and Therapy, 13,* 271–279.

Rosen, A. C., & Rehm, L. P. (1977). Long-term follow-up in two cases of transvestism treated with aversion therapy. *Journal of Behavior Therapy and Experimental Psychiatry, 8,* 295–300.

Rosen, J., & Leitenberg, H. (1982). Bulimia nervosa: Treatment with exposure and response prevention. *Behavior Therapy, 13,* 117–124.

Rosen, M. (1975). A dual model of obsessional neurosis. *Journal of Consulting and Clinical Psychology, 43,* 453–459.

Rosenbaum, M., & Weaver, G. M. (1980). Dissociated state: Status of a case after 38 years. *Journal of Nervous and Mental Disease, 168,* 597–603.

Rosenhan, D. L. (1973). On being sane in insane places. *Science, 179,* 250–258.

Rosenthal, D. (1970). *Genetic theory and abnormal behavior.* New York: McGraw-Hill.

Rosenthal, D. (1971). *Genetics of psychopathology.* New York: McGraw-Hill.

Rosenthal, J., & Jacobson, L. (1968). *Pygmalion in the classroom.* New York: Holt, Rinehart & Winston.

Rosenthal, P., & Rosenthal, S. (1984). Suicidal behavior by preschool children. *American Journal of Psychiatry, 141,* 520–525.

Rosenzweig, S. (1954). A transvaluation of psychotherapy—a reply to Hans Eysenck. *Journal of Abnormal and Social Psychology, 49,* 298–304.

Roth, D., Bielski, R., Jones, M., Parker, W., & Osborn, G. (1982). A comparison of self-control therapy and combined self-control therapy and antidepressant medication in the treatment of depression. *Behavior Therapy, 13,* 133–144.

Rotter, J. B., & Rafferty, J. E. (1950). *Manual for the Rotter Incomplete Sentences Blank, college form.* New York: Psychological Corp.

Royce, J. M., Lazar, I., & Darlington, R. B. (1983). Minority families, early education, and later life changes. *American Journal of Orthopsychiatry, 53,* 706–720.

Rubinstein, E. A. (1983). Television and behavior. *American Psychologist, 38,* 7.

Ruch, F. L., & Zimbardo, P. G. (1971). *Psychology and life.* Glenview, IL: Scott, Foresman.

Rueger, D., & Liberman, R. (1984). Behavioral family therapy for delinquent and substance-abusing adolescents. *Journal of Drug Issues, 14,* 403–417.

Ruff, G. E., & Korchin, S. J. (1964). Psychological responses of Mercury astronauts to stress. In G. H. Grosser, H. Wechsler, & M. Greenblatt (Eds.), *The threat of impending disaster.* Cambridge, MA: M.I.T. Press.

Ruiz, R. A., & Padilla, A. M. (1977). Counseling Latinos. *Personnel and Guidance Journal, 55,* 401–408.

Russo, N. F., & Denmark, F. L. (1984). Women, psychology, and public policy: Selected issues. *American Psychologist, 39,* 1161–1165.

Rutter, M. (1983). Cognitive deficits in the parthogenesis of autism. *Journal of Child Psychology and Psychiatry, 24,* 513–531.

Rutter, M., Greenfeld, D., & Lockyer, L. (1967). A five- to fifteen-year follow-up on infantile psychosis: 2. Social and behavioral outcome. *British Journal of Psychiatry, 113,* 1183–1199.

Sabalis, R. F., Frances, A., Appenzeller, S. N., & Moseley, W. B. (1974). The three sisters: Transsexual male siblings. *American Journal of Psychiatry, 131,* 907–909.

Sabalis, R. F., Staton, M. A., & Appenzeller, S. N. (1977). Transsexualism: Alternative diagnostic etiological considerations. *American Journal of Psychoanalysis, 37,* 223–228.

Sackeim, H. A., Nordlie, J. W., & Gur, R. C. (1979). A model of hysterical and hypnotic blindness: Cognition, motivation, and awareness. *Journal of Abnormal Psychology, 88,* 474–489.

Sackeim, H. A., & Vingiano, W. (1984). Dissociative disorders. In S. Turner & M. Hersen (Eds.), *Adult psychopathology and diagnosis.* New York: John Wiley.

Sacks, M., Carpenter, W., & Strauss, J. (1974). Recovery from delusions. *Archives of General Psychiatry, 30,* 117–120.

Sahakian, W. S. (1979). *Psychopathology today.* Itasca, IL: F. E. Peacock.

Sakheim, D. K., Barlow, D. H., Beck, J. G., & Abrahamson, D. J. (1984). The effects of an increased awareness of erectile cues on sexual arousal. *Behaviour Research and Therapy, 22,* 151–158.

Salkovskis, P., Jones, D., & Clark, D. (in press). Respiratory control in the treatment of panic attacks: Replication and extension with concurrent measurement of behaviour and pCO2.

Sarason, I. G. (1958). The effects of anxiety, reassurance, and meaningfulness of material to be learned on verbal learning. *Journal of Experimental Psychology, 45,* 162–170.

Sarason, I. G., & Ganzer, V. (1973). Modeling and group discussion in the rehabilitation of delinquents. *Journal of Counseling Psychology, 20,* 442–449.

Sarason, I. G., Johnson, J. H., & Siegel, J. M. (1978). Assessing the impact of life changes: Development of the Life Experiences Survey. *Journal of Consulting and Clinical Psychology, 46,* 932–946.

Sarason, S. B. (1984). If it can be studied or developed, should it be? *American Psychologist, 39,* 477–485.

Sarbin, P. R., & Cole, W. C. (1979). Hypnosis and psychopathology: Replacing old myths with fresh metaphors. *Journal of Abnormal Psychology, 88,* 506–526.

Satir, V. (1967). A family of angels. In J. Haley & L. Hoffman (Eds.), *Techniques of family therapy.* New York: Basic Books.

Satow, R. (1979). Where has all the hysteria gone? *The Psychoanalytic Review, 66,* 463–477.

Satterfield, J. H., Cantwell, D. P., Saul, R. E., Yustin, A. (1974). Intelligence, academic achievement, and EEG abnormalities in hyperactive children. *American Journal of Psychiatry, 131,* 391–395.

Satterfield, J. H., Hoppe, C. M., & Schell, A. M. (1982). A prospective study of delinquency in 110 adolescent boys with attention deficit disorder and 88 normal adolescent boys. *American Journal of Psychiatry, 139,* 795–798.

Satterfield, J. H., Satterfield, B. T., & Cantwell, D. P. (1980). Multimodality treatment: A two-year evaluation of 61 hyperactive boys. *Archives of General Psychiatry, 37,* 915–919.

Savicki, V., & Cooley, E. J. (1982). Implications of burnout research and theory for counselor educators. *Personnel and Guidance Journal, 60,* 415–419.

Sbordone, R. J., & Jennison, J. H. (1983). A comparison of the OBD-168 and MMPI to assess the emotional adjustment of traumatic brain-injured inpatients to their cognitive deficits. *Clinical Neuropsychology, 5,* 87–88.

Scarr, S., & Weinberg, R. A. (1976). IQ test performance of black children adopted by white families. *American Psychologist, 31,* 726–739.

Schacht, R., & Nathan, P. E. (1977). But is it good for the psychologists? Appraisal and status of DSM-III. *American Psychologist, 32,* 1017–1025.

Schachter, S. (1959). *The psychology of affiliation*. Stanford: Stanford University Press.

Schachter, S. (1977). Nicotine regulation in heavy and light smokers. *Journal of Experimental Psychology* [General], *106*, 5–12.

Schachter, S., & Latane, B. (1964). Crime, cognition, and the autonomic nervous system. *Nebraska Symposium on Motivation*, *12*, 221–274.

Schaefer, H. H. (1970). Self-injurious behavior: Shaping "head banging" in monkeys. *Journal of Applied Behavior Analysis*, *3*, 111–116.

Schaefer, H. H., & Martin, P. L. (1969). *Behavioral therapy*. New York: McGraw-Hill.

Scheppele, K. L., & Bart, P. B. (1983). Through women's eyes: Defining danger in the wake of sexual assault. *Journal of Social Issues*, *39*, 63–80.

Schildkraut, J. J. (1965). The catecholamine hypothesis of affective disorders: A review of supporting evidence. *American Journal of Psychiatry*, *122*, 509–522.

Schmauk, F. J. (1970). Punishment, arousal, and avoidance learning. *Journal of Abnormal Psychology*, *76*, 325–335.

Schmidt, J. A. (1974). Research techniques for counselors: The multiple baseline. *Personnel and Guidance Journal*, *53*, 200–206.

Schmidt, H. O., & Fonda, C. P. (1956). The reliability of psychiatric diagnosis: A new look. *Journal of Abnormal and Social Psychology*, *52*, 262–267.

Schneidman, B., & McGuire, L. (1976). Group therapy for nonorgasmic women: Two age levels. *Archives of Sexual Behavior*, *5*, 239–247.

Schofield, W. (1964). *Psychotherapy: The purchase of friendship*. Englewood Cliffs, NJ: Prentice-Hall.

Schopler, E., Rutter, M., & Chess, S. (1979). Editorial: Change of journal scope and title. *Journal of Autism and Developmental Disorders*, *9*, 1–10.

Schover, L. R., Friedman, J. M., Weiler, S. J., Heiman, J. R., & LoPiccolo, J. (1982). Multiaxial problem-oriented system for sexual dysfunctions. *Archives of General Psychiatry*, *39*, 614–619.

Schramm, W., Lyle, J., & Parker, E. B. (1961). *Television in the lives of our children*. Stanford: Stanford University Press.

Schreiber, F. R. (1973). *Sybil*. Chicago: Regnery.

Schreibman, L., & Koegel, R. L. (1975). Autism: A defeatable horror. *Psychology Today*, *8*, 61–67.

Schroth, M. L., & Sue, D. W. (1975). *Introductory psychology*. Homewood, IL: Dorsey.

Schuell, H. (1974). *Aphasia theory and therapy: Selected lectures and papers of Hildred Schuell*. Baltimore: University Park Press.

Schulsinger, F. (1972). Psychopathy: Heredity and environment. *International Journal of Mental Health*, *1*, 190–206.

Schulsinger, F. (1976). A ten-year follow-up of children of schizophrenic mothers: Clinical assessment. *Acta Psychiatrica Scandinavica*, *53*, 371.

Schultz, B. (1982). *Legal liability and psychotherapy*. San Francisco: Jossey-Bass.

Schwab, J. J., Fennell, E. B., & Warheit, G. J. (1974). The epidemiology of psychosomatic disorders. *Psychosomatics*, *15*, 88–93.

Schwartz, D. M., & Thompson, M. G. (1981). Do anorectics get well? Future research and current needs. *American Journal of Psychiatry*, *138*, 319–323.

Schwebel, A. I., Moreland, J., Steinkohl, R., Lentz, S., & Stewart, J. (1982). Research-based interventions with divorced families. *The Personnel and Guidance Journal*, *60*, 523–528.

Scriven, M. (1975). First, the roses . . . *APA Monitor*, *6*, 2–3.

The secret world of Howard Hughes. (1976, April 19). *Newsweek*, pp. 24–31.

Seiden, R. H. (1966). Campus tragedy: A study of student suicide. *Journal of Abnormal and Social Psychology*, *71*, 389–399.

Seidman, E., & Rappaport, J. (1974). The educational pyramid: A paradigm for research, training, and manpower utilization in community psychology. *American Journal of Community Psychology*, *2*, 119–130.

Seidman, L. J. (1983). Schizophrenia and brain dysfunction: An integration of recent neurodiagnostic findings. *Psychological Bulletin*, *94*, 195–238.

Seligman, J., Huck, J., Joseph, N., Namuth, T., Prout, L. R., Robinson, T. L., & McDaniel, A. L. (1984, April 9). The date who rapes. *Newsweek*, pp. 91–92.

Seligman, M. E. P. (1971). Phobias and preparedness. *Behavior Therapy*, *2*, 307–320.

Seligman, M. E. P. (1974, May). Submissive death: Giving up on life. *Psychology Today*, 80–85.

Seligman, M. E. P. (1975). *Helplessness*. San Francisco: Freeman.

Seligman, M. E. P., & Maier, S. F. (1967). Failure to escape traumatic shock. *Journal of Experimental Psychology*, *74*, 1–9.

Seligmann, J., Zabarsky, M., Witherspoon, D., Rotenberk, L., & Schmidt, M. (1983, March 7). A deadly feast and famine. *Newsweek*, pp. 59–60.

Selkin, J. (1975). Rape. *Psychology Today*, *8*, 70–74.

Selye, H. (1956). *The stress of life*. New York: McGraw-Hill.

Selye, H. (1982). Stress: Eustress, distress, and human perspectives. In S. B. Day (Ed.), *Life stress* (pp. 3–13). New York: Van Nostrand Reinhold Co.

Semans, J. H. (1956). Premature ejaculation: A new approach. *Southern Medical Journal*, *49*, 353–357.

Serber, M. (1970). Shame aversion therapy. *Journal of Behavior Therapy and Experimental Psychiatry*, *1*, 213–215.

Shah, S. (1969). Training and utilizing a mother as a therapist for her child. In B. G. Guerney (Ed.), *Psychotherapeutic agents: New roles for nonprofessionals, parents, and teachers*. New York: Holt, Rinehart & Winston.

Shahar, A., & Marks, I. (1980). Habituation during exposure treatment of compulsive rituals. *Behavior Therapy*, *11*, 397–401.

Shapiro, D., & Goldstein, I. B. (1982). Biobehavioral perspectives on hypertension. *Journal of Consulting and Clinical Psychology*, *50*, 841–858.

Shave, D. (1976). Transsexualism as a manifestation of orality. *American Journal of Psychoanalysis*, *36*, 57–66.

Shine, K. I. (1984). Anxiety in patients with heart disease. *Psychosomatics*, *25*, 27–31.

Shneidman, E. S. (Ed.). (1957). The logic of suicide. In *Clues to suicide*. New York: McGraw-Hill.

Shneidman, E. S. (1961). Psycho-logic: A personality approach to patterns of thinking. In Kagan, J., & Lesser, K. (Eds.), *Contemporary issues in thematic apperceptive methods*. Springfield, IL: Charles C. Thomas.

Shneidman, E. S. (1968). *Classifications of suicide phenom-*

ena: Bulletin of suicidology. The National Institute of Mental Health, Alcohol, Drug Abuse, and Mental Retardation, U.S. Department of Health, Education, and Welfare. Washington, DC: U.S. Government Printing Office.

Shneidman, E. S. (1972). Prevention of suicide: A challenge for community service. In S. E. Golann & C. Eisdorfer (Eds.), *Handbook of community mental health*. New York: Appleton-Century-Crofts.

Shneidman, E. S. (1976). Introduction: Contemporary overview of suicide. In *Suicidology: Contemporary developments*. New York: Grune & Stratton.

Shneidman, E. S., Farberow, N. L., & Litman, R. E. (Eds.). (1970). *The psychology of suicide*. New York: Jason Aronson.

Shockley, W. (1972). *Journal of Criminal Law and Criminology, 7*, 530–543.

Shore, E. (1984). The former transsexual: A case study. *Archives of Sexual Behavior, 13*, 277–281.

Shuey, A. (1966). *The testing of Negro intelligence*. New York: Social Science.

Shure, M. B., & Spivack, G. (1979). Interpersonal problem-solving thinking and adjustment in the mother-child dyad. In M. W. Kent & J. E. Rolf (Eds.), *Primary prevention of psychopathology* (Vol. 3). Hanover, NH: University Press of New England.

Shure, M. B., & Spivack, G. (1982). Interpersonal problem-solving in young children: A cognitive approach to prevention. *American Journal of Community Psychology, 10*, 341–356.

Sibler, E., Hamburg, D. A., Coelho, G. V., Murphy, E. B., Rosenberg, M., & Perle, L. I. (1961). Adaptive behavior in competent adolescents. *Archives of General Psychiatry, 5*, 354–365.

Siegel, A. E. (1970). Violence in the mass media. In D. D. Daniels, M. F. Gilula, & F. M. Ochberg (Eds.), *Violence and the struggle for existence*. Boston: Little, Brown.

Siegel, R. A. (1978). Probability of punishment and suppression of behavior in psychopathic and nonpsychopathic offenders. *Journal of Abnormal Psychology, 87*, 514–522.

Siegelman, M. (1972). Adjustment of homosexual and heterosexual women. *American Journal of Psychiatry, 120*, 477–481.

Siever, L. J. (1981). Schizoid and schizotypal personality disorders. In J. R. Lion (Ed.), *Personality disorders: Diagnosis and management*. Baltimore: Williams & Wilkins.

Silverman, L. H. (1976). Psychoanalytic theory: "The reports of my death are greatly exaggerated." *American Psychologist, 31*, 621–637.

Silverstein, C. (1972). *Behavior modification and the gay community*. Paper presented at the annual convention of the Association for Advancement of Behavior Therapy, New York.

Singer, J. L., & Singer, D. G. (1983). Psychologists look at television: Cognitive developmental, personality, and social policy implications. *American Psychologist, 38*, 826–834.

Sizemore, C. C., & Pittillo, E. S. (1977). *I'm Eve*. Garden City, NY: Doubleday.

Skeels, H. M. (1966). Adult status of children with contrasting early life experiences. *Monographs of the Society for Research in Child Development, 31*.

Skinner, B. F. (1948). "Superstition" in the pigeon. *Journal of Experimental Psychology, 38*, 168–172.

Slater, E. (1975). The diagnosis of "hysteria." *British Medical Journal, 1*, 1395–1399.

Slater, E., & Cowie, V. (1971). *The genetics of mental disorders*. London: Oxford University Press.

Slater, E., & Shields, J. (1969). Genetic aspects of anxiety. In M. H. Lader (Ed.), *Studies of anxiety*. Ashford, Kent, England: Headley Brothers.

Sloane, R. B., Staples, F. R., Cristol, A. H., Yorkston, N. J., & Whipple, K. (1975). *Psychotherapy versus behavior therapy*. Cambridge, MA: Harvard University Press.

Smart, D. E., Beaumont, P. J., & George, G. C. (1976). Some personality characteristics of patients with anorexia nervosa. *British Journal of Psychiatry, 128*, 57–60.

Smith, A., & Sugar, O. (1975). Development of above normal language and intelligence 21 years after left hemispherectomy. *Neurology, 25*, 813–818.

Smith, D. (1982). Trends in counseling and psychotherapy. *American Psychologist, 37*, 802–809.

Smith, D., & Kraft, W. A. (1983). DSM-III: Do psychologists really want an alternative? *American Psychologist, 38*, 777–785.

Smith, E. K. (1972). *The effect of double-bind communications upon the state of anxiety of normals*. Unpublished doctoral dissertation, University of New Mexico, Albuquerque.

Smith, M. B. (1949). Combat motivations among ground troops. In S. A. Stouffer (Ed.), *The American soldier*. Princeton, NJ: Princeton University Press.

Smith, M. B. (1950). The phenomenological approach in personality theory: Some critical remarks. *Journal of Abnormal and Social Psychology, 45*, 516–522.

Smith, M. B. (1976). Some perspectives in ethical/political issues on social science research. *Personality and Social Psychology Bulletin, 2*, 445–453.

Smith, M. B., & Hobbs, N. (1966). The community and the community mental health center. *American Psychologist, 21*, 299–309.

Smith, M. L., & Glass, G. V. (1977). Meta-analysis of psychotherapy outcome studies. *American Psychologist, 32*, 752–760.

Smyer, M. A. (1984). Life transitions and aging: Implications for counseling older adults. *The Counseling Psychologist, 12*, 17–28.

Snyder, R. D., Stovring, J., Cushing, A. H., Davis, L. E., & Hardy, T. L. (1981). Cerebral infarction in childhood bacterial meningitis. *Journal of Neurology, Neurosurgery, and Psychiatry, 44*, 581–585.

Snyder, S. H. (1974). *Madness and the brain*. New York: McGraw-Hill.

Snyder, S. H. (1976). The dopamine hypothesis of schizophrenia. *American Journal of Psychiatry, 133*, 197–202.

Snyder, S. H., Baneyee, S. P., Yamamura, H. I., & Greenberg, D. (1974). Drugs, neurotransmitters and schizophrenia. *Science, 184*, 1243–1253.

Sobell, M. B., & Sobell, L. C. (1978). *Behavioral treatment of alcohol problems*. New York: Plenum.

Solomon, R. L. (1977). An opponent-process theory of motivation: The affective dynamics of drug addiction. In J. D. Maser & M. E. Seligman (Eds.), *Psychopathology: Experimental models*. San Francisco: Freeman.

Solomon, R. L. (1980). The opponent-process theory of acquired motivation: The costs of pleasure and the benefits of pain. *American Psychologist, 35*, 691–712.

Sotile, W. M., & Kilmann, P. R. (1977). Treatment of psychogenic female dysfunctions. *Psychological Bulletin, 84,* 619–633.

Southern, S., & Gayle, R. (1982). A cognitive behavioral model of hypoactive sexual desire. *Behavioral Counselor, 2,* 31–48.

Spanos, N. P., & Barber, T. X. (1974). Toward a convergence in hypnosis research. *American Psychologist, 29,* 500–511.

Speer, D. C. (1971). Rate of caller re-use of a telephone crisis service. *Crisis Intervention, 3,* 83–86.

Speer, D. C. (1972). *An evaluation of a telephone crisis service.* Paper presented at the meeting of the Midwestern Psychological Association, Cleveland, OH.

Speltz, M. L., & Bernstein, D. A. The use of participant modeling for claustrophobia. (1979). *Journal of Behavior Therapy and Experimental Psychology, 10,* 251–255.

Spence, S. H., & Marzillier, J. S. (1981). Social skills training with adolescent male offenders: Short-term, long-term, and generalized effects. *Behaviour Research and Therapy, 19,* 349–368.

Spiegler, M. D. (1983). *Contemporary behavioral therapy.* Palo Alto, CA: Mayfield Publishing.

Spiess, W. F., Geer, J. H., & O'Donohue, W. T. (1984). Premature ejaculation: Investigation of factors in ejaculatory latency. *Journal of Abnormal Psychology, 93,* 242–245.

Spitz, H. H. (1963). Field theory in mental deficiency. In N. R. Ellis (Ed.), *Handbook of mental deficiency.* New York: McGraw-Hill.

Spitzer, R., & Forman, J. B. (1979). DSM-III field trials: 2. Initial experience with the multiaxial system. *American Journal of Psychiatry, 136,* 818–820.

Spitzer, R., Skodol, A. E., Gibbon, M., & Williams, J. B. W. (1981). *DSM-III casebook.* Washington, DC: American Psychiatric Association.

Spitzer, R. L. (1975). On pseudoscience in science, logic in remission, and psychiatric diagnosis: A critique of Rosenhan's ''On being sane in insane places.'' *Journal of Abnormal Psychology, 84,* 442–452.

Spitzer, R. L. (1981). The diagnostic status of homosexuality in DSM III: A reformation of the issues. *American Journal of Psychiatry, 138,* 210–215.

Spitzer, R. L., Endicott, J., Mesnikoff, A., & Cohen, G. (1967–1968). *Psychiatric evaluation form: Diagnostic version.* New York: Biometric Research, New York State Psychiatric Institute.

Spitzer, R. L., Forman, J. B., & Nee, J. (1979). DSM-III field trials: 1. Initial interrater diagnostic reliability. *American Journal of Psychiatry, 136,* 815–817.

Spitzer, R. L., Williams, J. B. W., & Skodol, A. E. (1980). DSM-III: The major achievements and an overview. *American Journal of Psychiatry, 137,* 151–164.

Spotnitz, H. (1963). The toxoid response. *The Psychoanalytic Review, 50*(4), 81–94.

Spotnitz, H. (1968). *Modern psychoanalysis and the schizophrenic patient.* New York: Grune & Stratton.

Spotnitz, H. (1976). *Psychotherapy of preoedipal conditions.* New York: Jason Aronson.

Srole, L., & Fischer, A. K. (1980). The midtown Manhattan longitudinal study vs. ''the mental paradise lost'' doctrine: A controversy joined. *Archives of General Psychiatry, 37*(2), 209–221.

Srole, L., Langer, T. S., Michael, S. T., Opler, M. K., & Rennie, T. A. (1962). *Mental health in the metropolis: The midtown Manhattan study.* New York: McGraw-Hill.

Stampfl, T., & Levis, D. (1967). Essentials of implosive therapy: A learning-theory-based psychodynamic behavioral therapy. *Journal of Abnormal Psychology, 72,* 496–503.

Stanton, A., Gunderson, J., Knapp, P., Frank, A., Vannicelli, M., Schnitzer, R., & Rosenthal, R. (1984). Effects of psychotherapy in schizophrenia: Design and implementation of a controlled study. *Schizophrenia Bulletin, 10,* 520–551.

Stark, E. (1984). The unspeakable family secret. *Psychology Today, 18,* 38–46.

Starr, R. H., Jr. (1979). Child abuse. *American Psychologist, 34,* 872–878.

Stefanis, C., Markidis, M., & Christodoulou, G. (1976). Observations on the evolution of the hysterical symptomatology. *British Journal of Psychiatry, 128,* 269–275.

Steffen, J. J., Nathan, P. E., & Taylor, H. A. (1974). Tension-reducing effects of alcohol: Further evidence and methodological considerations. *Journal of Abnormal Psychology, 83,* 542–547.

Stern, R. S., & Cobb, J. P. (1978). Phenomenology of obsessive-compulsive neuroses. *British Journal of Psychiatry, 182,* 233–239.

Stevens, E. V., & Salisbury, J. D. (1984). Group therapy for bulimic adults. *Archives of Orthopsychiatry, 54,* 156–161.

Stevens, J., Mark, B., Erwin, F., Pacheco, P., & Suematsu, K. (1969). Deep temporal stimulation in man. *Archives of Neurology, 21,* 157–169.

Stevens, J. H., Turner, C. W., Rhodewalt, F., & Talbot, S. (1984). The type A behavior pattern and carotid artery atherosclerosis. *Psychosomatic Medicine, 46,* 105–113.

Stokes, K. S. (1977). Planning for the future of a severely handicapped autistic child. *Journal of Autism and Child Schizophrenia, 7,* 288–298.

Stoller, R. J. (1969). Parental influences on male transsexualism. In R. Green & J. Money (Eds.), *Transsexualism and sex reassignment.* Baltimore: Johns Hopkins University Press.

Stoller, R. J., Marmon, J., Bieber, I., Gold, R., Socarides, C. W., Green, R., & Spitzer, R. I. (1973). A symposium: Should homosexuality be in the APA nomenclature? *American Journal of Psychiatry, 130,* 1207–1216.

Stoudenmire, J. (1973). Behavioral treatment of voyeurism and possible symptom substitution. *Psychotherapy: Theory, Research, and Practice, 10,* 328–330.

Straker, N., & Tamerin, J. (1974). Aggression and childhood asthma: A study in a natural setting. *Journal of Psychosomatic Research, 18,* 131–135.

Strange, R. E., & Brown, D. E., Jr. (1970). Home from the wars. *American Journal of Psychiatry, 127,* 488–492.

Strassberg, D. S., Roback, H., Cunningham, J., McKee, E., & Larson, P. (1979). Psychopathology in self-identified female-to-male transsexuals, homosexuals, and heterosexuals. *Archives of Sexual Behavior, 8,* 491–496.

Strauss, A., & Lehtinen, L. (1947). *Psychopathology and the education of the brain-injured child* (Vol. 1). New York: Grune & Stratton.

Strayer, R., & Ellenhorn, L. (1975). Vietnam veterans: A study exploring adjustment patterns and attitudes. *Journal of Social Issues, 31,* 81–93.

Streissguth, A. P., Herman, C. S., & Smith, D. W. (1978). Intelligence, behavior and dysmorphogenesis in the fetal alcohol syndrome: A report on 20 patients. *Journal of Pediat-*

rics, 92, 363–368.

Streissguth, A. P., Landesman-Dwyer, S., Martin, J. C., & Smith, D. W. (1980). Teratogenic effects of alcohol in humans and laboratory animals. *Science, 209,* 353–361.

Strupp, H. H. (1963). The outcome problem in psychotherapy revisited. *Psychotherapy: Theory, Research, and Practice, 1,* 1–13.

Strupp, H. H., & Hadley, S. W. (1977). A tripartite model of mental health and therapeutic outcomes. *American Psychologist, 32,* 187–196.

Sue, D. (1972). The role of relaxation in systematic desensitization. *Behaviour Research and Therapy, 10,* 153–158.

Sue, D. (1978). The use of masturbation in the in vivo treatment of impotence. *Journal of Behavior Therapy and Experimental Psychiatry, 9,* 75–76.

Sue, D. (1979). Erotic fantasies of college students during coitus. *Journal of Sex Research, 15,* 299–305.

Sue, D. W. (1975). Asian-Americans: Social-psychological forces affecting their lifestyles. In J. S. Picon & R. E. Campbell (Eds.), *Career behavior of special groups.* Columbus, OH: Charles E. Merrill.

Sue, D. W. (1978). Eliminating cultural oppression in counseling: Toward a general theory. *Journal of Counseling Psychology, 25,* 419–428.

Sue, D. W. (1981). *Counseling the culturally different: Theory and practice.* New York: Wiley.

Sue, S. (1973). The training of third world students to function as counselors. *Journal of Counseling Psychology, 20,* 73–78.

Sue, S. (1977). Community mental health services to minority groups: Some optimism, some pessimism. *American Psychologist, 32,* 616–624.

Sue, S., & Nakamura, C. Y. (1984). An integrative model of physiological and social/psychological factors in alcohol consumption among Chinese and Japanese Americans. *Journal of Drug Issues, 14,* 349–364.

Sue, S., and Sue, D. W. (1971). Chinese-American personality and mental health. *Amerasia Journal, 1,* 36–49.

Suinn, R. (1977). Anxiety management training for general anxiety. In R. Suinn & R. Weigel (Eds.), *The innovative psychological therapies: Critical and creative contributions.* San Francisco: Harper & Row.

Suinn, R. M. (1977). Type A behavior pattern. In K. B. Williams & W. D. Gentry (Eds.), *Behavioral approaches to medical treatment.* Cambridge, MA: Ballinger.

Suinn, R. M. (1982). Intervention with type A behavior. *Journal of Consulting and Clinical Psychology, 50,* 933–949.

Sullivan, H. S. (1953). *The interpersonal theory of psychiatry.* H. S. Perry & M. L. Gawel (Eds.). New York: Norton.

Sulser, F. (1979). Pharmacology: New cellular mechanisms of antidepressant drugs. In S. Fielding & R. C. Effland (Eds.), *New frontiers in psychotropic drug research.* Mount Kisco, NY: Futura.

Sundberg, N. D., Taplin, J. R., & Tyler, L. E. (1983). *Introduction to clinical psychology.* Englewood Cliffs, NJ: Prentice-Hall.

Surwit, R. S., Williams, R. B., Shapiro, D. (Eds.). (1982). *Behavioral approaches to cardiovascular disease.* New York: Academic Press.

Sutherland, E. H., & Cressey, D. R. (1966). *Principles of criminology* (7th ed.). Philadelphia: Lippincott.

Swanson, B. W., Bohnert, T. J., & Smith, J. A. (1970). *The paranoid.* Boston: Little, Brown.

Sweet, J. J. (1983). Confounding effects of depression on neuropsychological testing: Five illustrative cases. *Clinical Neuropsychology, 5,* 103–108.

Sykes, K., & Tredgold, R. (1964). Restricted orbital undercutting, a study of its effects on 350 patients over the ten years 1951–1960. *American Journal of Psychiatry, 110,* 609.

Szasz, T. S. (1977). *Psychiatric slavery.* New York: Free Press.

Tal, A., & Miklich, D. R. (1976). Emotionally induced decreases in pulmonary flow rates in asthmatic children. *Psychosomatic Medicine, 38,* 190–200.

Tasto, D. L., & Huebner, L. (1976). The effects of muscle relaxation and stress on the blood pressure levels of normotensives. *Behaviour Research and Therapy, 14,* 89–91.

Tavris, C. (1972, March). Woman and man. *Psychology Today,* pp. 57–64.

Taylor, J. A. (1953). A personality scale of manifest anxiety. *Journal of Abnormal and Social Psychology, 48,* 285–290.

Taylor, S. E. (1983). Adjustments to threatening events: A theory of cognitive adaptation. *American Psychologist, 38,* 1161–1173.

Tearnan, B. H., Telch, M. J., & Keefe, P. (1984). Etiology and onset of agoraphobia: A critical review. *Comprehensive Psychiatry, 25,* 51–62.

Telch, M. J., Tearnan, B. H., & Taylor, C. B. (1983). Antidepressant medication in the treatment of agoraphobia: A critical review. *Behaviour Research and Therapy, 21,* 505–517.

Teplin, L. A. (1983). The criminalization of the mentally ill: Speculation in search of data. *Psychological Bulletin, 94,* 54–67.

Terman, L. M. (1916). *The measurement of intelligence.* Boston: Houghton Mifflin.

Terman, L. M., & Merrill, M. A. (1960). *Measuring intelligence.* Boston: Houghton Mifflin.

Thienes-Hontos, P., Watson, C. G., & Kucala, T. (1982). Stress disorder symptoms in Vietnam and Korean war veterans. *Journal of Consulting and Clinical Psychology, 50,* 4, 558–561.

Thigpen, C. H., & Cleckley, H. (1957). *The three faces of Eve.* Kingsport, TN: Kingsport Press.

Thomas, A., Chess, S., & Birch, H. G. (1968). *Temperament and behavior disorders in children.* New York: New York University Press.

Thomas, A., & Sillen, S. (1972). *Racism and psychiatry.* New York: Brunner/Mazel.

Thompkins, V. H. (1959). *Stress in aviation.* In J. Hambling (Ed.), *The nature of stress disorder.* Springfield, IL: Charles C. Thomas.

Thompson, N. L., McCandless, B. R., & Strickland, B. R. (1971). Personal adjustment of male and female homosexuals and heterosexuals. *Journal of Abnormal Psychology, 78,* 237–240.

Thorpe, G., & Burns, L. (1983). *The agoraphobic syndrome.* Chichester, England: Wiley.

Thyer, B. A. (1981). Prolonged in vivo exposure therapy with a 70-year-old woman. *Journal of Behavior Therapy and Experimental Psychiatry, 12,* 69–71.

Tienari, P. (1963). Psychiatric illness in identical twins. *Acta Psychiatrica Scandinavica, 39*(Suppl. 171).

Tippin, J., & Henn, F. (1982). Modified leukotomy in the treatment of intractable obsessional neurosis. *American Journal of Psychiatry, 139,* 1601–1603.

Tizard, B. (1962). The personality of epileptics: A discussion of the evidence. *Psychological Bulletin, 59,* 1906–2010.

Tjosvold, D., & Tjosvold, M. M. (1983). Social psychological analysis of residences for mentally retarded persons. *American Journal of Mental Deficiency, 88,* 28–40.

Tobin, J. J., & Friedman, J. (1983). Spirits, shamans, and nightmare death: Survivor stress in a Hmong refugee. *American Journal of Orthopsychiatry, 53,* 439–448.

Toffler, A. (1970). *Future shock.* New York: Random House.

Torrey, E. F. (1981). The epidemiology of paranoid schizophrenia. *Schizophrenia Bulletin, 7,* 588–593.

Tramontana, J., & Stimbert, V. E. (1970). Some techniques of behavior modification with autistic children. *Psychological Reports, 27,* 498.

Treffert, D. A. (1970). Epidemiology of infantile autism. *Archives of General Psychiatry, 22,* 431–438.

Tregold, R. F., & Soddy, K. (1970). *Tregold's mental retardation.* Baltimore: Williams & Wilkins.

Trotzer, J. (1982). Engaging families in therapy: A pilot study. *International Journal of Family Therapy, 4,* 4–19.

Tsuang, M. T., Winokur, G., & Crowe, R. (1980). Morbidity risks of schizophrenia and affective disorders among first degree relatives of patients with schizophrenia, mania, depression, and surgical conditions. *British Journal of Psychiatry, 137,* 497–504.

Tuckman, J., Kleiner, R., & Lavell, M. (1959). Emotional content of suicide notes. *American Journal of Psychiatry, 16,* 59–63.

Tuohy, W. (1967, March 2). Battlefield psychiatrist sees task as two-fold. *Los Angeles Times.*

Turner, R. J., & Wagonfeld, M. O. (1967). Occupational mobility and schizophrenia. *American Sociological Review, 32,* 104–113.

Turner, W. J., & Merlis, A. (1962). Clinical correlations between electroencephalography and antisocial behavior. *Medical Times, 90,* 505–511.

Tyrer, P., Lee, I., & Alexander, J. (1980). Awareness of cardiac function in anxious, phobic, and hypochondriacal patients. *Psychological Medicine, 10,* 171–174.

Ullmann, L. P., & Krasner, L. (1965). Introduction. In L. P. Ullmann & L. Krasner (Eds.), *Case studies in behavior modification.* New York: Holt, Rinehart & Winston.

Ullmann, L. P., & Krasner, L. (1975). *A psychological approach to abnormal behavior.* Englewood Cliffs, NJ: Prentice-Hall.

Unemployment and mental health: The human equation. *APA Monitor, 14,* 1.

Uniform Crime Reports. (1983). Federal Bureau of Investigation, U.S. Department of Justice. Washington, DC: U.S. Government Printing Office.

U.S. Department of Health, Education and Welfare. (1971). National health survey. *Roche Report, 1*(9), 2.

University of Minnesota. (1977). *Epilepsy and the school age child.* Minneapolis, MN: State of Minnesota.

Vaillant, G. E. (1975). Sociopathy as a human process: A viewpoint. *Archives of General Psychiatry, 32,* 178–183.

Vaillant, G. E., & Milofsky, E. S. (1982). The etiology of alcoholism. *American Psychologist, 37,* 494–503.

Van Evra, J. P. (1983). *Psychological disorders of children and adolescents.* Boston: Little, Brown.

Van Putten, T., Philip, R. A., May, M. D., & Marder, S. R. (1984). Response to antipsychotic medication: The doctor's and the consumer's view. *American Journal of Psychiatry, 141,* 16–19.

Varni, J. W., Russo, D. C., & Cataldo, M. F. (1978). Assessment in modification of delusional speech in an 11-year-old child: A comparative analysis of behavior therapy and stimulant drug effect. *Journal of Behavior Therapy and Experimental Psychiatry, 9,* 377–380.

Velten, E. (1968). A laboratory task for induction of mood states. *Behaviour Research and Therapy, 6,* 473–482.

Viney, L. L., Clarke, A. M., & Lord, J. (1973). Resistance to extinction and frustration in retarded and nonretarded children. *American Journal of Mental Deficiency, 78,* 308–315.

Vogel, G., Vogel, F., McAbee, R., & Thurmond, A. (1980). Improvement of depression by REM sleep deprivation. *Archives of General Psychiatry, 37,* 247–253.

Vogler, R. E., & Bartz, W. R. (1983). *The better way to drink.* New York: Simon & Schuster.

von Baeyer, W. (1972). Preface to the reprint of 1968. In H. Prinzhorn (Ed.), *Artistry of the mentally ill: A contribution to the psychology and psychopathology of configuration.* New York: Springer-Verlag.

Wachtel, P. L. (1977). *Psychoanalysis and behavior therapy.* New York: Basic Books.

Wachtel, P. L. (1982). Vicious circles: The self and the rhetoric of emerging and unfolding. *Contemporary Psychoanalysis, 18,* 280–282.

Wahba, M., Donlon, P. T., & Mendow, A. (1981). Cognitive changes in acute schizophrenia with brief neuroleptic treatment. *American Journal of Psychiatry, 138,* 1307–1310.

Walen, S., Hauserman, N. M., & Lavin, P. J. (1977). *Clinical guide to behavior therapy.* Baltimore: Williams & Wilkins.

Walker, E., Hoppes, E., Emory, E., Mednick, S., & Schulsinger, F. (1981). Environmental factors related to schizophrenia in psychophysiologically labile high-risk males. *Journal of Abnormal Psychology, 90,* 313–320.

Walker, V., & Beech, R. H. (1969). Mood state and ritualistic behavior in obsessional patients. *British Journal of Psychiatry, 115,* 1261–1263.

Wallace, A. F. C. (1956). *Tornado in Worcester.* Washington, DC: National Academy of Sciences, National Research Council.

Wallace, C., Nelson, C., Liberman, R., Aitchison, R., Lukoff, D., Elder, J., & Ferris, C. (1980). A review and critique of social skills training with schizophrenic patients. *Schizophrenia Bulletin, 6,* 42–64.

Wallerstein, J., & Kelly, J. B. (1980). *Surviving the breakup: How children actually cope with divorce.* New York: Basic Books.

Walters, R., Thomas, E. L., & Acker, C. W. (1962). Enhancement of punitive behavior by audiovisual displays. *Science, 136,* 872–873.

Wanlass, R. L., & Prinz, R. J. (1981). Methodological issues in conceptualizing and treating childhood social isolation. *Psychological Bulletin, 92,* 39–55.

Ward, C. H., Beck, A. T., Mendelson, M., Mock, J. E., & Erbaught, J. K. (1962). The psychiatric nomenclature: Reasons for diagnostic disagreement. *Archives of General Psychiatry, 7,* 198–205.

Ward, M. J. (1946). *The snake pit.* New York: Knopf.

Wasserman, E., & Gromisch, D. (1981). *Survey of clinical pediatrics.* New York: McGraw-Hill.

Watson, C. G., & Buranen, C. (1979). The frequencies of conversion reaction symptoms. *Journal of Abnormal Psychology, 88,* 209–211.

Watson, J. B. (1913). Psychology as a behaviorist views it. *Psychological Review, 20,* 158–177.

Watson, J. B., & Rayner, R. (1920). Conditioned emotional responses. *Journal of Experimental Psychology, 3,* 1–14.

Weakland, J. H. (1960). The "double-bind" hypothesis of schizophrenia and three-party interaction. In D. D. Jackson (Ed.), *The etiology of schizophrenia.* New York: Basic Books.

Webster, J. S., & Scott, R. P. (1983). The effects of self-instruction training in attention deficit following head injury. *Clinical Neuropsychology, 5,* 69–74.

Wechsler, D. (1981a). *Manual for the Wechsler Adult Intelligence Scale—Revised (WAIS-R).* New York: Psychological Corp.

Wechsler, D. (1981b). *Wechsler Adult Intelligence Scale.* New York: Harcourt, Brace, Jovanovich.

Weddington, W. W. (1979). Single case study: Conversion reaction in an 82-year-old man. *Journal of Nervous and Mental Diseases, 167,* 368–369.

Weile, E. F. (1960). On social psychological questions in suicidal personalities. *Psychological Research, 11,* 37–44.

Weinberger, D. R., DeLisi, L. E., Perman, G. P., Targum, S., Wyatt, R. J. (1982). Computed tomography in schizophreniform disorder and other acute psychiatric disorders. *Archives of General Psychiatry, 39,* 778–783.

Weiner, B. (1975). On being sane in insane places: A process (attributional) analysis and critique. *Journal of Abnormal Psychology, 84,* 433–441.

Weiner, H., Thaler, M., Reisner, M. F., & Mirsky, I. A. (1957). Etiology of duodenal ulcer: 1. Relation of specific psychological characteristics to rate of gastric secretion. *Psychosomatic Medicine, 19,* 1–10.

Weiner, I. B. (Ed.). (1976). Individual psychotherapy. *Clinical Methods in Psychology.* New York: Wiley.

Weiner, J. W. (1969). The effectiveness of suicide prevention programs. *Mental Hygiene, 53,* 357–363.

Weintraub, W. (1981). Compulsive and paranoid personalities. In J. R. Lion (Ed.), *Personality disorders: Diagnosis and management.* Baltimore: Williams & Wilkins.

Weiss, J. M., Glazer, H. I., & Pohorecky, L. A. (1975). Coping behavior and neurochemical changes: Alternative explanation for the original "learned helplessness" experiments. In G. Serban & A. Ling (Eds.), *Relevance of the animal model to the human.* New York: Plenum.

Weissberg, R. P., Cowen, E. L., Lotyczewski, B. S., & Gesten, E. L. (1983). The primary mental health project: Seven consecutive years of program outcome research. *Journal of Consulting and Clinical Psychology, 51,* 100–107.

Weissman, M. M., & Klerman, G. L. (1977). Sex differences and the epidemiology of depression. *Archives of General Psychiatry, 34,* 98–111.

Weisz, J. R. (1981). Effects of the "mentally retarded" label on adult judgments about child failure. *Journal of Abnormal Psychology, 90,* 371–374.

Weisz, J. R., & Yeates, K. O. (1981). Cognitive development in retarded and nonretarded persons: Piagetian tests of the similar structure hypothesis. *Psychological Bulletin, 90,* 153–178.

Weitz, S. (1977). *Sex roles: Biological, psychological, and social foundations.* New York: Oxford University Press.

Welgan, P. R. (1974). Learned control of gastric acid secretions in ulcer patients. *Psychosomatic Medicine, 36,* 411–419.

Wells, C. E. (1978). Role of stroke in dementia. *Stroke, 9,* 1–3.

Wender, P. H., & Klein, D. F. (1981, February). The promise of biological psychiatry. *Psychology Today,* pp. 25–41.

Wender, P. H., Rosenthal, D., Rainer, J. D., Greenbill, L., & Sarlan, M. B. (1977). Schizophrenics' adopting parents. *Archives of General Psychiatry, 34,* 777–784.

Werner, A. (1975). Sexual dysfunction in college men and women. *American Journal of Psychiatry, 132,* 164–168.

Werry, J. S., Methven, R. J., Fitzpatrick, J. (1983). The interrater reliability of DSM-III in children. *Journal of Abnormal Child Psychology, 11,* 341–354.

Wexler, L., Weissman, M. M., & Kasl, S. V. (1978). Suicide attempts 1970–1975: Updating a United States study and comparison with international trends. *British Journal of Psychiatry, 132,* 180–185.

Wheat, W. D. (1960). Motivational aspects of suicide in patients during and after psychiatric treatment. *Southern Medical Journal, 53,* 273.

White, J. L. (1984). *The psychology of blacks.* Englewood Cliffs, NJ: Prentice-Hall.

White, M. (1983). Anorexia nervosa: A transgenerational system perspective. *Family Process, 22,* 255–273.

Whitehead, W. E., Winget, C., Fedoravicius, A. S., Wooley, S., & Blackwell, B. (1982). Learned illness behavior in patients with irritable bowel syndrome and peptic ulcer. *Digestive Diseases and Sciences, 27,* 202–208.

Whitehill, M., DeMeyer-Gapin, S., & Scott, T. J. (1976). Stimulus seeking in antisocial preadolescent children. *Journal of Abnormal Psychology, 85,* 101–104.

Wickramasekera, I. (1976). Aversive behavior rehearsal for sexual exhibitionism. *Behavior Therapy, 7,* 167–176.

Widom, C. S. (1976). Interpersonal and personal construct systems in psychopaths. *Journal of Consulting and Clinical Psychology, 44,* 614–623.

Widom, C. S. (1977). A methodology for studying noninstitutionalized psychopaths. *Journal of Consulting and Clinical Psychology, 45,* 674–683.

Wiens, A. N. (1983). The assessment interview. In I. B. Weiner (Ed.), *Clinical methods in psychology.* New York: John Wiley.

Wiggins, J. (1979). Attractive notion. *APA Monitor, 10,* 2.

Wiggins, J. S., Wiggins, N., & Conger, J. C. (1968). Correlates of heterosexual somatic preference. *Journal of Personality and Social Psychology, 10,* 82–90.

Wild, C. (1965). Creativity and adaptive regression. *Journal of Personality and Social Psychology, 2,* 161–169.

Wilding, T. (1984). Is stress making you sick? *America's Health, 6*(1), 2–5.

Wilkinson, C. B. (1983). Aftermath of a disaster: The collapse of the Hyatt Regency Hotel skywalks. *American Journal of Psychiatry, 140,* 1134–1139.

Williams, J. B., & Spitzer, R. L. (1983). The issue of sex bias in DSM-III: A critique of a woman's view of DSM-III. *American Psychologist, 38,* 793–798.

Williams, J. H. (1977). *Psychology of women: Behavior in a biosocial context.* New York: Norton.

Williams, J. M. (1984a). *The psychological treatment of depression: A guide to the theory and practice of cognitive-behaviour therapy.* London: Croom Helm.

Williams, J. M. (1984b). Cognitive-behaviour therapy for depression: Problems and perspectives. *British Journal of Psychiatry, 145,* 254–262.

Williams, R. (1974). The problem of match and mismatch. In L. Miller (Ed.), *The testing of black children.* Englewood Cliffs, NJ: Prentice-Hall.

Willis, M. J. (1982). The impact of schizophrenia on families: One mother's point of view. *Schizophrenia Bulletin, 8,* 617–619.

Wilson, G. T., & O'Leary, K. D. (1980). *Principles of behavior therapy.* Englewood Cliffs, NJ: Prentice-Hall.

Wilson, M. S., & Meyer, E. (1962). Diagnostic consistency in a psychiatric liaison service. *American Journal of Psychiatry, 19,* 207–209.

Wilson, P. (1982). Combined pharmacological and behavioural treatment of depression. *Behaviour Research and Therapy, 20,* 173–184.

Wincze, J. P., Hoon, E. F., & Hoon, P. W. (1978). Multiple measure analysis of women experiencing low sexual arousal. *Behaviour Research and Therapy, 16,* 43–49.

Wing, J. K. (1980). Social psychiatry in the United Kingdom: The approach to schizophrenia. *Schizophrenia Bulletin, 6,* 557–565.

Wing, L., & Gould, J. (1979). Severe impairment of social interaction and associated abnormalities in children: Epidemiology and classification. *Journal of Autism and Developmental Disorders, 9,* 11–29.

Winokur, G. (1974). Depression: The clinical perspective. *Practical Psychiatry, 2,* 1–4.

Winokur, G., Clayton, P. J., & Reich, T. (1969). *Manic depressive illness.* St. Louis: Mosby.

Winokur, G., Reich, T., Rimmer, J., & Pitts, F. (1970). Alcoholism III: Diagnosis and familial psychiatric illness in 259 alcoholic probands. *Archives of General Psychiatry, 23,* 104–111.

Winters, K. C., Weintraub, S., & Neale, J. M. (1981). Validity of MMPI code types in identifying DSM III schizophrenics, unipolars, and bipolars. *Journal of Consulting and Clinical Psychology, 49,* 486–487.

Wolf, L. E. M., & Crowther, J. H. (1983). Personality and eating habit variables as predictors of severity of binge eating and weight. *Addictive Behavior, 8,* 335–344.

Wolff, H. G. (1950). Stress and cardiovascular disorders. *Circulation, 1,* 187–203.

Wolpe, J. (1958). *Psychotherapy by reciprocal inhibition.* Stanford: Stanford University Press.

Wolpe, J. (1973). *The practice of behavior therapy.* New York: Pergamon.

Wolpe, J., & Lang, P. J. (1964). A fear survey schedule for use in behavior therapy. *Behaviour Research and Therapy, 2,* 27.

World Health Organization. (1973a). *Manual of the international statistical classification of diseases, injuries and causes of death* (Vol. 1). Geneva: World Health Organization.

World Health Organization. (1973b). *Report on the international pilot study of schizophrenia* (Vol. 1). Geneva: World Health Organization. Used by permission of the World Health Organization, Geneva.

World Health Organization. (1981). *Current state of diagnosis and classification in the mental health field.* Geneva: World Health Organization. Used by permission of the World Health Organization, Geneva.

Wright, L. (1978). A method for predicting sequelae to meningitis. *American Psychologist, 33,* 1037–1039.

Wrightsman, L. S. (1972). *Social psychology in the seventies.* Monterey, CA: Brooks/Cole.

Wyler, A. R., Masuda, M., & Holmes, T. H. (1971). Magnitude of the life events and seriousness of illness. *Journal of Psychosomatic Medicine, 33,* 115–122.

Yalom, I. D. (1970). *The theory and practice of group psychotherapy.* New York: Basic Books.

Yarnold, P. R., & Grimm, L. G. (1982). Time urgency among coronary-prone individuals. *Journal of Abnormal Psychology, 91,* 175–177.

Yates, A. (1983). Behavior therapy and psychodynamic psychotherapy: Basic conflict or reconciliation and integration? *British Journal of Clinical Psychology, 22,* 107–125.

Yates, A. J. (1958). The application of learning theory to the treatment of tics. *Journal of Abnormal and Social Psychology, 56,* 175–182.

Youngren, M., & Lewinsohn, P. M. (1978). *The functional relationship between depression and problematic interpersonal behavior.* Manuscript submitted for publication.

Yu-Fen, H., & Neng, T. (1981). Transcultural investigation of recent symptomatology of schizophrenia in China. *American Journal of Psychiatry, 138,* 1484–1486.

Yurchenco, H. (1970). *A mighty hard road: The Woody Guthrie story.* New York: McGraw-Hill.

Zajonc, R. B. (1975). Birth order and intelligence: Dumber by the dozen. *Psychology Today, 8,* 37–43.

Zaslow, R. W. (1970). *Resistances to growth and attachment.* San Jose, CA: San Jose State University Press.

Zaslow, R. W. (1981). Z-process attachment therapy. In R. J. Corsini (Ed.), *Handbook of innovative psychotherapies.* New York: Wiley.

Zax, M., & Cowen, E. L. (1972). *Abnormal psychology.* New York: Holt, Rinehart & Winston.

Zax, M., & Spector, G. A. (1974). *An introduction to community psychology.* New York: Wiley.

Zeiss, A. M., Rosen, G. M., & Zeiss, R. A. (1977). Orgasm during intercourse: A treatment strategy for women. *Journal of Consulting and Clinical Psychology, 45,* 891–895.

Zeiss, R. A. (1977). Self-directed treatment for premature ejaculation: Preliminary case reports. *Journal of Behavior Therapy and Experimental Psychiatry, 8,* 87–91.

Zelt, D. (1981). First person account: The messiah quest. *Schizophrenia Bulletin, 7,* 527–531.

Zentall, S. (1975). Optimal stimulation as the theoretical basis of hyperactivity. *American Journal of Orthopsychiatry, 45,* 549–563.

Zentall, S. S., & Zentall, T. R. (1983). Optimal stimulation: A model of disordered activity and performance in normal and deviant children. *Psychological Bulletin, 94,* 446–471.

Zerbin-Rudin, E. (1972). Genetic research and the theory of

schizophrenia. *International Journal of Mental Health, 1,* 42–62.

Zigler, E. (1966). Mental retardation: Current issues and approaches. In M. L. Hoffman & L. W. Hoffman (Eds.), *Review of child development research*. New York: Russell Sage Foundation.

Zigler, E. (1967). Familial mental retardation: A continuing dilemma. *Science, 155,* 292–298.

Zigler, E. (1969). Developmental versus difference theories of mental retardation and the problem of motivation. *American Journal of Mental Deficiency, 73,* 536–555.

Zigler, E., & Bergman, W. (1983). Discerning the future of early childhood intervention. *American Psychologist, 38,* 893–905.

Zigler, E., & Phillips, L. (1969). Psychiatric diagnosis and symptomatology. *Journal of Abnormal and Social Psychology, 63,* 69–75.

Zilbergeld, B. (1983). *The shrinking of America*. Boston: Little, Brown.

Zilboorg, G., & Henry, G. W. (1941). *A history of medical psychology*. New York: Norton.

Zimbardo, P. (1977). *Shyness: What is it, what to do about it.* Reading, MA: Addison-Wesley.

Zubin, J. (1978). But is it good for science? *The Clinical Psychologist, 31,* 1, 5–7.

Zubin, J., & Ludwig, A. M. (1983). What is schizophrenia? *Schizophrenia Bulletin, 9,* 331–334.

Zubin, J., & Spring, B. (1977). Vulnerability—a new view of schizophrenia. *Journal of Abnormal Psychology, 86,* 103–126.

Zuger, B. (1984). Early effeminate behavior in boys: Outcome and significance for homosexuality. *Journal of Nervous and Mental Disease, 172,* 90–97.

Zussman, L., & Zussman, S. (1976). Continuous time-limited treatment of sexual disorders. In J. K. Meyer (Ed.), *Clinical management of sexual disorder*. Baltimore: Williams & Wilkins.

Name Index

Subject Index

Mark/Archive. *Page 611:* © Charles Harbutt/Archive. *Page 615 top:* © Mark Antman/The Image Works. *Page 615 bottom:* © Michael Weisbrot and Family. *Page 617:* © Judy Canty/Stock, Boston. *Page 623:* © Laurie Cameron/Stock, Boston. *Page 625:* © Robert V. Eckert Jr./Stock, Boston.

Text Credits

Page 151: Isaac, S., & Michael, W. B. (1977). *Handbook in research and evaluation.* San Diego: Edits. Reproduced by permission. *Pages 154–156:* American Psychological Association. (1981). Ethical principles of psychologists. *American Psychologist, 36,* 633–630. Copyright 1981 by the American Psychological Association. Reprinted by permission of the publisher and author. *Pages 204–205:* Lipsitt, D. R. (1974). Psychodynamic considerations of hypochondriasis. *Psychosomatic Medicine, 23,* 134–136. Copyright © 1974 by the American Psychosomatic Society, Inc. Reprinted by permission of Elsevier Science Publishing Co., Inc. *Page 206:* Kallman, W. M., Hersen, M., & O'Toole, D. H. (1975). The use of social reinforcement in a case of conversion reaction. *Behavior Therapy, 6,* 411–413. Used by permission of Academic Press and Michel Hersen. *Page 249:* Tobin, J. J., & Friedman, J. (1983). Spirits, shamans, and nightmare death: Survivor stress in a Hmong refugee. *American Journal of Orthopsychiatry, 53,* 439–448. Copyright © 1983 by the American Orthopsychiatric Association, Inc. Reproduced by permission. *Pages 275, 329–330:* Spitzer, R., Skodol, A. E., Gibbon, M., & Williams, J. B. W. (1981). *DSM-III casebook.* Washington, DC: American Psychiatric Association. Used by permission of the American Psychiatric Association. *Pages 357–358:* Brownell, K., & Barlow, D. (1980). The behavioral treatment of sexual deviation. In A. Goldstein & E. Foa (Eds.), *Handbook of behavioral*

interventions. New York: John Wiley. Copyright 1980 by John Wiley & Sons, Inc. Used by permission. *Page 380:* Mendels, J. (1970). *Concepts of depression* (p. 6). New York: John Wiley. Copyright © 1970 by John Wiley & Sons, Inc. Used by permission. *Page 397:* From Beck, A. T., Rush, A. J., Shaw, B. F., and Emery, G. D. (1979). *Cognitive therapy of depression.* New York: Guilford Press. Used by permission of A. T. Beck. *Pages 398–399:* Endler, N. S. (1982). *Holiday of darkness.* New York: John Wiley. Copyright © 1982 by John Wiley & Sons, Inc. Used by permission. *Page 428:* World Health Organization. (1973). *Report on the international pilot study of schizophrenia* (Vol. 1). World Health Organization (1981). *Current state of diagnosis and classification in the mental health field.* Geneva: World Health Organization. Used by permission of the World Health Organization, Geneva. *Page 481:* Wells, C. E. (1978). Role of stroke in dementia. *Stroke, 9,* 1–3. Reprinted by permission of the American Heart Association, Inc. *Page 502, 504:* Bemporad, J. R. (1979). Adult recollections of a formerly autistic child. *Journal of Autism and Developmental Disorders, 9,* 179–197. Used by permission of Plenum Publishing Corporation. *Page 624:* Sue, S., & Sue, D. W. (1971). Chinese-American personality and mental health. *Amerasia Journal, 1,* 36–49. Grateful acknowledgment is made to: *Amerasia Journal,* Asia American Studies Center, University of California, Los Angeles, for permission to reprint excerpts from this article. Copyright © by The Regents of the University of California.

Illustration Credits

Pages 475, 476, and 478: Illustrations by Maggie Siner/J. Hurd Studio.

STUDENT EVALUATION OF **UNDERSTANDING ABNORMAL BEHAVIOR,** SECOND EDITION, BY SUE, SUE, AND SUE

Your comments on this book will help us in developing other new textbooks and future editions of this book. Please answer the following questions and mail this page to:

College Marketing Services
Houghton Mifflin Company
One Beacon Street
Boston, MA 02108

1. What was your overall impression of the text? _____
   _____

2. Did you find the book easy to read and understand? ☐ Yes ☐ No

   If not, what problems did you have? _____
   _____

3. Did the tables, graphs, and figures clarify the text in a useful way?
   _____

4. How would you rate the following features of the text?

	Excellent	Very good	Good	Fair	Poor
Interest level	☐	☐	☐	☐	☐
Definitions of terms	☐	☐	☐	☐	☐
Explanations of psychological concepts	☐	☐	☐	☐	☐
Descriptions of theories and research	☐	☐	☐	☐	☐
Discussion of symptoms of disorders	☐	☐	☐	☐	☐
Descriptions of the etiology of abnormal behavior	☐	☐	☐	☐	☐
Descriptions of the treatment of abnormal behavior	☐	☐	☐	☐	☐
Clinical cases	☐	☐	☐	☐	☐
Extended Steven V. case	☐	☐	☐	☐	☐
Focus boxes	☐	☐	☐	☐	☐

   Feel free to comment on any of the above items. _____
   _____

5. Which chapters were required reading for your class? _____
   _____

6. Did you read any chapters on your own that were not required reading?

_____

7. Did your instructor assign any additional books for this course?   □ Yes   □ No

   If so, what were they? _____

8. Did you find the key terms and glossary useful? _____

_____

9. Do you have any suggestions that might help make this a better textbook?

_____

Name of your school: _____

Course title: _____

Number of students in the class: _____

Your age: _____

Your major: _____

Thank You!